DaguerreotypeS
8th Edition

DaguerreotypeS
8th Edition

Editor/Daguerreotypes
CRAIG CARTER

Cover Design
MIKE BRUNER

President-Chief Operating Officer
THOMAS G. OSENTON

Book Publisher
GREGORY WILEY

Editorial Director of Books and Periodicals
RON SMITH

Published in the United States by THE SPORTING NEWS
Publishing Co., 1212 North Lindbergh Boulevard,
St. Louis, Missouri 63132.

Library of Congress Catalog Card Number: 89-63683

ISBN: 0-89204-351-2

10 9 8 7 6 5 4 3 2 1

Introduction

In 1839, the year that baseball was founded in Upstate New York (or so the legend goes), Frenchman Louis Daguerre invented the first practical process of photography.

Daguerre's discovery proved timely in terms of baseball's ability to chronicle its formative years. Indeed, the game's early goings-on were captured in part on "daguerreotypes," photographs which were made on plates of chemically treated glass or metal.

The art of playing baseball and the art of taking photographs both have come a long way over the years. And while the game is now recorded for historical safekeeping by highly sophisticated photographic and video equipment, baseball's storied past also lives on in DAGUERREOTYPES, The Sporting News' book that creates its own vivid images of yesteryear by presenting lifetime records of baseball's retired greats.

DAGUERREOTYPES, first published by The Sporting News in 1934, contains the records of 397 former notables of the game (players, managers, umpires and executives), with Hall of Fame members making up only a little more than half of the entries.

Among the records and personality sketches in this book are those of 69 Hall of Famers who would not have been eligible for inclusion were it not for their membership in the Cooperstown shrine, including 11 former black baseball greats added to the Hall.

Names of those appearing in DAGUERREOTYPES are listed in the back of the book. Alongside each name are the categories in which the entrant qualified.

Every player in DAGUERREOTYPES meets at least one of the following criteria:

BATTING—A lifetime average of .300, with a minimum of 10 years and 4,000 at-bats in the majors; 2,500 major league games, 2,500 hits; 250 home runs.

PITCHING—200 victories; 4,000 innings; 2,000 strikeouts.

In addition, all Hall of Famers and all players appearing in 20 or more big-league seasons are included in this book.

Major league records of all players in DAGUERREOTYPES are based on performance in the following leagues:

NATIONAL LEAGUE—1876 through 1989.

AMERICAN ASSOCIATION—1882 through 1891.

UNION ASSOCIATION—1884.

PLAYERS LEAGUE—1890.

AMERICAN LEAGUE—1901 through 1989.

(Federal League records of 1914 and 1915, while carried in the players' year-by-year performances, are not included in the players' major league career totals. This league was not recognized as a major league by The Sporting News, the National League and the American League.)

★ Indicates led the league.

● Indicates tied for the league lead.

Most photographs in this book came from The Sporting News' baseball archives. Other sources: John Thorn, president of Baseball Ink (James McCormick, page 198); the Baseball Hall of Fame (Thomas P. Burns, page 41; Rube Foster, page 93; Deacon McGuire, page 203; Jack O'Connor, page 221, and Jimmy Ryan, page 254).

HENRY LOUIS (HANK) AARON

Born February 5, 1934, at Mobile, Ala.

Height, 6.00. Weight, 190.

Threw and batted righthanded.

Brother of Tommie Aaron, former major league infielder-outfielder.

Holds major league records for most years, 100 or more runs (15); most home runs, lifetime (755); most years, 30 or more home runs (15); most years and most consecutive years, 20 or more home runs (20); most total bases, lifetime (6,856); most years leading league, total bases (8); most years, 300 or more total bases (15); most long hits, lifetime (1,477); most extra bases on long hits, lifetime (3,085); most years and most consecutive years, 100 or more extra bases on long hits (19); most runs batted in, lifetime (2,297).

Shares major league record for most consecutive years, 100 or more runs (13).

Holds National League records for most years, 40 or more home runs (8); most years, 100 or more runs batted in (11).

Shares National League record for most years leading league in runs batted in (4).

Shares modern National League record for most bases on balls, game (5), July 11, 1972 (15 innings).

Hit three home runs in a game, June 21, 1959.

Led National League outfielders in double plays with 6 in 1960, 5 in 1964 and 5 in 1966.

Led National League in slugging percentage with .636 in 1959, .586 in 1963, .573 in 1971 and .669 in 1971; led in total bases with 340 in 1956; 369 in 1957; 400 in 1959; 334 in 1960; 358 in 1961; 370 in 1963; 344 in 1967; 332 in 1969.

Named outfielder on THE SPORTING NEWS All-Star Major League Teams, 1956-58-59.

Named outfielder on THE SPORTING NEWS National League All-Star Teams, 1963-65-67-69-70-71.

Most Valuable Player in National League, 1957.

Named National League Player of the Year by THE SPORTING NEWS, 1956 and 1963.

Named outfielder on THE SPORTING NEWS National League All-Star fielding team, 1958-59-60.

Vice-President, director of player development, Atlanta Braves, 1977 to date.

Named to Hall of Fame, 1982.

Year	Club	League	Pos.	G.	AB.	R.	H.	2B.	3B.	HR.	RBI.	B.A.	PO.	A.	E.	F.A.
1952—Eau Claire		North.	SS	87	345	79	116	19	4	9	61	.336	137	265	35	.920
1953—Jacksonville		Sally	2B	137	574	*115	*208	*36	14	22	*125	*.362	*330	*310	*36	.947
1954—Milwaukee		Nat.	OF	122	468	58	131	27	6	13	69	.280	223	5	7	.970
1955—Milwaukee		Nat.	OF-2B	153	602	105	189	●37	9	27	106	.314	340	93	15	.967
1956—Milwaukee		Nat.	OF	153	609	106	*200	*34	14	26	92	*.328	316	17	●13	.962
1957—Milwaukee		Nat.	OF	151	615	*118	198	27	6	*44	*132	.322	346	9	6	.983
1958—Milwaukee		Nat.	OF	153	601	109	196	34	4	30	95	.326	305	12	5	.984
1959—Milwaukee		Nat.	OF-3B	154	629	116	*223	46	7	39	123	*.355	263	22	5	.983
1960—Milwaukee		Nat.	OF-2B	153	590	102	172	20	11	40	*126	.292	321	13	6	.982
1961—Milwaukee		Nat.	OF-3B	*155	603	115	197	*39	10	34	120	.327	379	15	7	.983
1962—Milwaukee		Nat.	OF-1B	156	592	127	191	28	6	45	128	.323	341	11	7	.981
1963—Milwaukee		Nat.	OF	161	631	*121	201	29	4	●44	*130	.319	267	10	6	.979
1964—Milwaukee		Nat.	OF-2B	145	570	103	187	30	2	24	95	.328	284	28	6	.981
1965—Milwaukee		Nat.	OF	150	570	109	181	*40	1	32	89	.318	298	9	4	.987
1966—Atlanta		Nat.	OF-2B	158	603	117	168	23	1	*44	*127	.279	315	12	4	.988
1967—Atlanta		Nat.	OF-2B	155	600	●113	184	37	3	*39	109	.307	322	12	7	.979
1968—Atlanta		Nat.	OF-1B	160	606	84	174	33	4	29	86	.287	418	20	5	.989
1969—Atlanta		Nat.	OF-1B	147	547	100	164	30	3	44	97	.300	299	13	5	.984
1970—Atlanta		Nat.	OF-1B	150	516	103	154	26	1	38	118	.298	319	10	7	.979
1971—Atlanta		Nat.	1B-OF	139	495	95	162	22	3	47	118	.327	733	40	5	.994
1972—Atlanta		Nat.	1B-OF	129	449	75	119	10	0	34	77	.265	996	70	17	.984
1973—Atlanta		Nat.	OF	120	392	84	118	12	1	40	96	.301	206	5	5	.977
1974—Atlanta (a)		Nat.	OF	112	340	47	91	16	0	20	69	.268	142	3	2	.986
1975—Milwaukee		Amer.	DH-OF	137	465	45	109	16	2	12	60	.234	2	0	0	1.000
1976—Milwaukee		Amer.	DH-OF	85	271	22	62	8	0	10	35	.229	1	0	0	1.000
American League Totals—2 Years				222	736	67	171	24	2	22	95	.232	3	0	0	1.000
National League Totals—21 Years				3076	11628	2107	3600	600	96	733	2202	.310	7433	429	144	.982
Major League Totals—23 Years				3298	12364	2174	3771	624	98	755	2297	.305	7436	429	144	.982

aTraded to Milwaukee Brewers for Outfielder Dave May and minor league Pitcher Roger Alexander, November 2, 1974.

CHAMPIONSHIP SERIES RECORD

Year	Club	League	Pos.	G.	AB.	R.	H.	2B.	3B.	HR.	RBI.	B.A.	PO.	A.	E.	F.A.
1969—Atlanta		Nat.	OF	3	14	3	5	2	0	3	7	.357	4	1	1	.833

WORLD SERIES RECORD

Year	Club	League	Pos.	G.	AB.	R.	H.	2B.	3B.	HR.	RBI.	B.A.	PO.	A.	E.	F.A.
1957—Milwaukee		Nat.	OF	7	28	5	11	0	1	3	7	.393	11	0	0	1.000
1958—Milwaukee		Nat.	OF	7	27	3	9	2	0	0	2	.333	14	0	0	1.000
World Series Totals—2 Years				14	55	8	20	2	1	3	9	.364	25	0	0	1.000

JOSEPH WILBUR (JOE) ADCOCK

Born October 30, 1927, at Coushatta, La.
Height, 6.04. Weight, 231.
Threw and batted righthanded.

Hit four home runs in a game, July 31, 1954.
Holds major league records for most total bases (18) and extra bases on long hits (13), game, July 31, 1954.
Shares major league records for most home runs (4) and long hits (5), game, July 31, 1954; most home runs (5), total bases (25), long hits (7) and extra bases on long hits (17), two consecutive games, July 30, 31, 1954.
Manager, Cleveland Indians, 1967; Seattle, Pacific Coast League, 1968.

Year Club	League	Pos.	G.	AB.	R.	H.	2B.	3B.	HR.	RBI.	B.A.	PO.	A.	E.	F.A.
1947—Columbia	Sally	1B	73	280	35	74	11	5	7	43	.264	731	37	8	.990
1948—Columbia	Sally	1B	117	434	58	121	25	2	6	64	.279	1100	★89	14	★.988
1949—Tulsa	Tex.	1B	149	598	95	178	41	7	19	116	.298	1332	77	7	★.995
1950—Cincinnati	Nat.	OF-1B	102	372	46	109	16	1	8	55	.293	346	17	8	.978
1951—Cincinnati	Nat.	OF	113	395	40	96	16	4	10	47	.243	221	8	4	.983
1952—Cincinnati(a)(b)...	Nat.	OF-1B	117	378	43	105	22	4	13	52	.278	306	8	3	.991
1953—Milwaukee............	Nat.	1B	157	590	71	168	33	6	18	80	.285	1389	96	13	.991
1954—Milwaukee............	Nat.	1B	133	500	73	154	27	5	23	87	.308	1229	67	6	.995
1955—Milwaukee............	Nat.	1B	84	288	40	76	14	0	15	45	.264	725	44	8	.990
1956—Milwaukee............	Nat.	1B	137	454	76	132	23	1	38	103	.291	1086	75	6	★.995
1957—Milwaukee............	Nat.	1B	65	209	31	60	13	2	12	38	.287	477	30	2	.996
1958—Milwaukee............	Nat.	1B-OF	105	320	40	88	15	1	19	54	.275	564	37	7	.988
1959—Milwaukee............	Nat.	1B-OF	115	404	53	118	19	2	25	76	.292	807	81	7	.992
1960—Milwaukee............	Nat.	1B	138	514	55	153	21	4	25	91	.298	★1229	104	9	●.993
1961—Milwaukee............	Nat.	1B	152	562	77	160	20	0	35	108	.285	★1471	102	11	.993
1962—Milwaukee(c).......	Nat.	1B	121	391	48	97	12	1	29	78	.248	907	57	3	★.997
1963—Cleveland(d)........	Amer.	1B	97	283	28	71	7	1	13	49	.251	608	36	3	.995
1964—Los Angeles	Amer.	1B	118	366	39	98	13	0	21	64	.268	959	54	7	.993
1965—California..............	Amer.	1B	122	349	30	84	14	0	14	47	.241	789	45	3	.996
1966—California..............	Amer.	1B	83	231	33	63	10	3	18	48	.273	565	39	2	.997
American League Totals—4 Years			420	1229	130	316	44	4	66	208	.256	2921	174	15	.995
National League Totals—13 Years			1539	5377	693	1516	251	31	270	914	.282	10757	726	87	.992
Major League Totals—17 Years...............			1959	6606	823	1832	295	35	336	1122	.277	13678	900	102	.993

aTransferred to Boston Braves as part of four-club deal; trade started with Boston Braves sending First Baseman Earl Torgeson to the Philadelphia Phillies for Pitcher Russ Meyer and cash. The Braves then traded Meyer to the Brooklyn Dodgers for Infielders Rocky Bridges and Jim Pendleton; Bridges and cash were sent to the Cincinnati Reds for Adcock, February 16, 1953.
bBoston franchise transferred to Milwaukee, March 18, 1953.
cTraded to Cleveland Indians with Pitcher Jack Curtis for Pitcher Frank Funk, Outfielder Don Dillard and player to be named later, November 27, 1962; Outfielder Ty Cline assigned to Braves March 18, 1963, to complete deal.
dTraded to Los Angeles Angels with Pitcher Barry Latman for Outfielder Leon Wagner. Latman and Wagner changed clubs December 2, and Adcock completed deal on December 6, 1963.

WORLD SERIES RECORD

Year Club	League	Pos.	G.	AB.	R.	H.	2B.	3B.	HR.	RBI.	B.A.	PO.	A.	E.	F.A.
1957—Milwaukee............	Nat.	1B-PH	5	15	1	3	0	0	0	2	.200	38	2	1	.976
1958—Milwaukee............	Nat.	1B-PH	4	13	1	4	0	0	0	0	.308	23	2	0	1.000
World Series Totals—2 Years			9	28	2	7	0	0	0	2	.250	61	4	1	.985

GROVER CLEVELAND ALEXANDER
(Pete)

Born February 26, 1887, at St. Paul, Neb.
Died November 4, 1950, at St. Paul, Neb.
Height, 6.01. Weight, 185.
Threw and batted righthanded.

Shares major league records for most games won, lifetime (373); most shutouts, season (16), 1916; most one-hit games, season (4), 1915.

Holds National League record for most shutouts, lifetime (90).
Holds modern National League record for most complete games, lifetime (436).
Led National League in complete games, 1911-14-15-16-17-20; shutouts, 1911-13-15-16-17-19, and tied in 1921.
Named to Hall of Fame, 1938.

Year	Club	League	G.	IP.	W.	L.	Pct.	H.	R.	ER.	SO.	BB.	ERA.
1909—Galesburg	Ill.-Mo.	24	219	15	8	.652	124	49	....	198	42	......
1910—Syracuse	N.Y. State	★43	245	★29	14	.674	215	....	....	204	67	......
1911—Philadelphia	Nat.	48	★366	★28	13	.683	285	133	....	227	129	......
1912—Philadelphia	Nat.	46	●310	19	17	.528	289	133	97	★195	105	2.81
1913—Philadelphia	Nat.	47	306	22	8	.733	288	106	96	159	75	2.82
1914—Philadelphia	Nat.	46	★355	●27	15	.643	★327	133	94	★214	76	2.38
1915—Philadelphia	Nat.	49	★376	★31	10	★.756	253	86	51	★241	64	★1.22
1916—Philadelphia	Nat.	48	★390	★33	12	.733	★323	90	67	★167	50	★1.55
1917—Philadelphia(a)	Nat.	45	★387	★30	13	.698	★336	107	79	★200	56	★1.83
1918—Chicago	Nat.	3	26	2	1	.667	19	7	5	15	3	1.73
1919—Chicago	Nat.	30	235	16	11	.593	180	51	45	121	38	★1.72
1920—Chicago	Nat.	46	★363	★27	14	.659	★335	96	77	★173	69	★1.91
1921—Chicago	Nat.	31	252	15	13	.536	286	110	95	77	33	3.39
1922—Chicago	Nat.	33	246	16	13	.552	283	111	99	48	34	3.62
1923—Chicago	Nat.	39	305	22	12	.647	308	128	108	72	30	3.19
1924—Chicago	Nat.	21	169	12	5	.706	183	82	57	33	25	3.03
1925—Chicago	Nat.	32	236	15	11	.577	270	106	89	63	29	3.39
1926—Chicago(b)-St. Louis	Nat.	30	200	12	10	.545	191	83	68	47	31	3.06
1927—St. Louis	Nat.	37	268	21	10	.677	261	94	75	48	38	2.52
1928—St. Louis	Nat.	34	244	16	9	.640	262	106	91	59	37	3.36
1929—St. Louis(c)	Nat.	22	132	9	8	.529	149	65	57	33	23	3.89
1930—Philadelphia	Nat.	9	22	0	3	.000	40	24	22	6	6	9.00
1930—Dallas	Texas	5	24	1	2	.333	35	23	22	4	11	8.25
Major League Totals—20 Years		696	5188	373	208	.642	4868	1851	†1372	2198	951	†2.56

†Does not include 1911 season when earned runs were not compiled.

aTraded with Catcher William Killefer to Chicago Cubs for Pitcher Mike Prendergast, catcher Pickles Dillhoefer and cash, December 11, 1917.

bWaived to St. Louis Cardinals, June 22, 1926.

cTraded to Philadelphia Phillies with Catcher Harry McCurdy for Outfielder Homer Peel and Pitcher Bob McGraw, December 11, 1929.

WORLD SERIES RECORD

Year	Club	League	G.	IP.	W.	L.	Pct.	H.	R.	ER.	SO.	BB.	ERA.
1915—Philadelphia	National	2	17⅔	1	1	.500	14	3	3	10	4	1.53
1926—St. Louis	National	3	20⅓	2	0	1.000	12	4	3	17	4	1.33
1928—St. Louis	National	2	5	0	1	.000	10	11	11	2	4	19.80
World Series Totals—3 Years		7	43	3	2	.600	36	18	17	29	12	3.56

ETHAN NATHAN ALLEN

Born January 1, 1904, at Cincinnati, O.

Height, 6.01. Weight, 180.

Threw and batted righthanded.

Year	Club	League	Pos.	G.	AB.	R.	H.	2B.	3B.	HR.	RBI.	B.A.	PO.	A.	E.	F.A.
1926—Cincinnati	Nat.	OF	18	13	3	4	1	0	0	0	.308	9	0	0	.000
1927—Cincinnati	Nat.	OF	111	359	54	106	26	4	2	20	.295	250	6	3	.988
1928—Cincinnati	Nat.	OF	129	485	55	148	30	7	1	62	.305	348	12	7	.981
1929—Cincinnati	Nat.	OF	143	538	69	157	27	11	6	64	.292	393	12	5	★.988
1930—Cinn.(a)-N. Y.	Nat.	OF	97	284	58	83	10	2	10	38	.292	153	6	3	.981
1931—New York	Nat.	OF	94	298	58	98	18	2	5	43	.329	151	2	4	.975
1932—New York(b)	Nat.	OF	54	103	13	18	6	2	1	7	.175	44	1	2	.957
1933—St. Louis(c)	Nat.	OF	91	261	25	63	7	3	0	36	.241	179	8	3	●.984
1934—Philadelphia	Nat.	OF	145	581	87	192	●42	4	10	85	.330	337	19	8	.978
1935—Philadelphia	Nat.	OF	●156	645	90	198	46	1	8	60	.307	412	★26	9	★.980
1936—Phil.(d)-Chi.(e)	Nat.	OF	121	498	68	141	27	7	4	48	.295	273	3	8	.972
1937—St. Louis	Amer.	OF	103	320	39	101	18	1	0	31	.316	186	8	4	.980
1938—St. Louis	Amer.	OF	19	33	4	10	3	1	0	4	.303	11	0	0	1.000
National League Totals—11 Years			1159	4065	580	1214	234	43	47	466	.299	2549	95	52	.981
American League Totals—2 Years			122	353	43	111	21	2	0	35	.314	197	8	4	.981
Major League Totals—13 Years			1281	4418	623	1325	255	45	47	501	.300	2746	103	56	.981

aTraded with Pitcher Peter Donohue to New York Giants for Infielder Clifford Crawford, May 27, 1930.

bTraded with Pitchers Bill Walker and Jim Mooney and Catcher Bob O'Farrell to St. Louis Cardinals for Catcher

Gus Mancuso and Pitcher Ray Starr, October 10, 1932.

cSold to Philadelphia Phillies, January, 1934.

dTraded with Pitcher Curt Davis to Chicago Cubs for Outfielder Chuck Klein and Pitcher Fabian Kowalik, May 21, 1936.

eSold to St. Louis Browns, December 2, 1936.

RICHARD ANTHONY (DICK) ALLEN

Born March 8, 1942, at Wampum, Pa.

Height, 5.11. Weight, 187.

Threw and batted righthanded.

Brother of Hank Allen, former major league utilityman, and Ron Allen, former major league first baseman.

Shares major league record for most games, rookie season (162), 1964.

Holds National League record for most total bases, rookie season (352), 1964.

Shares modern National League record for most bases on balls, game (5), August 16, 1968.

Hit three home runs in a game, September 29, 1968.

Led National League in total bases with 352 in 1964; led third basemen in double plays with 29 in 1965; led in slugging percentage with .632 in 1966.

Led American League in slugging percentage with .603 in 1972 and .563 in 1974.

Named American League Most Valuable Player in 1972.

Named National League Rookie of the Year, 1964, by Baseball Writers' Association and National League Rookie Player of the Year by THE SPORTING NEWS, 1964.

Named first baseman on THE SPORTING NEWS American League All-Star Team, 1972 and 1974.

Named THE SPORTING NEWS American League Player of the Year, 1972.

Year	Club	League	Pos.	G.	AB.	R.	H.	2B.	3B.	HR.	RBI.	B.A.	PO.	A.	E.	F.A.
1960—Elmira	NYP	SS	88	320	56	90	19	10	8	42	.281	141	173	★48	.867
1961—Magic Valley	Pion.	2B	117	460	101	146	17	8	21	94	.317	★258	★298	★27	.953
1962—Williamsport	East.	OF-2B	132	511	97	168	★32	10	20	109	.329	255	59	17	.949
1963—Arkansas	Int.	OF	145	544	93	157	19	★12	★33	★97	.289	246	8	★11	.958
1963—Philadelphia	Nat.	OF-3B	10	24	6	7	2	1	0	2	.292	10	0	2	.833
1964—Philadelphia	Nat.	3B	162	632	★125	201	38	●13	29	91	.318	154	325	★41	.921
1965—Philadelphia	Nat.	3B-SS	161	619	93	187	31	14	20	85	.302	130	305	26	.944
1966—Philadelphia	Nat.	3B-OF	141	524	112	166	25	10	40	110	.317	146	182	14	.959
1967—Philadelphia	Nat.	★3B-2B-SS	122	463	89	142	31	10	23	77	.307	95	249	★35	.908
1968—Philadelphia	Nat.	OF-3B	152	521	87	137	17	9	33	90	.263	215	20	12	.951
1969—Philadelphia (a)	Nat.	1B	118	438	79	126	23	3	32	89	.288	1024	54	16	.985
1970—St. Louis (b)	Nat.	1B-3B-OF	122	459	88	128	17	5	34	101	.279	708	109	18	.978
1971—Los Angeles (c)	Nat.	3B-OF-1B	155	549	82	162	24	1	23	90	.295	382	151	21	.962
1972—Chicago	Amer.	1B-3B	148	506	90	156	28	5	★37	★113	.308	1235	69	7	.995
1973—Chicago	Amer.	1B-2B	72	250	39	79	20	3	16	41	.316	601	46	4	.994
1974—Chicago (d-e)	Amer.	★1B-2B	128	462	84	139	23	1	★32	88	.301	998	50	★16	.985
1975—Philadelphia (f)	Nat.	1B	119	416	54	97	21	3	12	62	.233	900	70	★18	.982
1976—Philadelphia (f)	Nat.	1B	85	298	52	80	16	1	15	49	.268	671	44	8	.989
1977—Oakland	Amer.	1B	54	171	19	41	4	0	5	31	.240	389	37	7	.984
American League Totals—4 Years			402	1389	232	415	75	9	90	273	.299	3223	202	34	.990
National League Totals—11 Years			1347	4943	867	1433	245	70	261	846	.290	4435	1509	211	.966
Major League Totals—15 Years			1749	6332	1099	1848	320	79	351	1119	.292	7658	1711	245	.975

aTraded with Infielder Cookie Rojas and Pitcher Jerry Johnson for Catcher Tim McCarver, Pitcher Joe Hoerner, Outfielder Curt Flood and Outfielder Byron Browne to St. Louis Cardinals, October 7, 1969. Flood refused to report and the Cardinals sent First Baseman Willie Montanez and a player to be named later to Philadelphia to complete the deal, April 8, 1970. Pitcher Jim Browning was sent "as the player to be named later" from the Cardinals to Philadelphia, August 30, 1970.

bTraded to Los Angeles Dodgers for Infielder Ted Sizemore and Catcher Bob Stinson, October 5, 1970.

cTraded to Chicago White Sox for Pitcher Tommy John and Infielder Steve Huntz, December 2, 1971.

dTraded to Atlanta Braves for $5,000 and a player to be named later, December 3, 1974; Braves sent Catcher Jim Essian to White Sox, May 15, 1975, to complete deal.

eTraded with Catcher Johnny Oates by Atlanta Braves to Philadelphia Phillies for Catcher Jim Essian, Outfielder Barry Bonnell, a player to be named later and an estimated $150,000, May 7, 1975; deal was completed with a cash payment.

fSigned as free agent with Oakland A's, March 16, 1977.

CHAMPIONSHIP SERIES RECORD

Year	Club	League	Pos.	G.	AB.	R.	H.	2B.	3B.	HR.	RBI.	B.A.	PO.	A.	E.	F.A.
1976—Philadelphia	Nat.	1B	3	9	1	2	0	0	0	0	.222	28	0	1	.966

WILLIAM ROBERT (BOB) ALLISON

Born July 11, 1934, at Raytown, Mo.

Height, 6.04. Weight, 212.

Threw and batted righthanded.

Shares major league records for most doubles, inning (2), July 1, 1964, fourth inning; most strikeouts, nine-inning game (5), September 2, 1965.

Hit three home runs in a game, May 17, 1963.

Named American League Rookie Player of the Year by THE SPORTING NEWS, 1959 and American League Rookie of the Year by Baseball Writers' Association, 1959.

Year Club	League	Pos.	G.	AB.	R.	H.	2B.	3B.	HR.	RBI.	B.A.	PO.	A.	E.	F.A.
1955—Hagerstown	Pied.	OF	122	446	55	114	15	2	5	49	.256	★289	★24	12	.963
1956—Charlotte	Sally	OF	122	344	47	80	10	6	12	55	.233	240	20	11	.959
1957—Chattanooga	South.	OF	125	395	56	97	14	●11	2	38	.246	239	8	7	.972
1958—Chattanooga	South.	OF	150	525	84	161	28	9	9	93	.307	372	13	★18	.955
1958—Washington	Amer.	OF	11	35	1	7	1	0	0	0	.200	24	0	0	1.000
1959—Washington	Amer.	OF	150	570	83	149	18	★9	30	85	.261	333	8	9	.974
1960—Washington	Amer.	OF-1B	144	501	79	126	30	3	15	69	.251	311	13	11	.967
1961—Minnesota	Amer.	OF-1B	159	556	83	136	21	3	29	105	.245	417	18	10	.978
1962—Minnesota	Amer.	OF	149	519	102	138	24	8	29	102	.266	287	10	7	.977
1963—Minnesota	Amer.	OF	148	527	★99	143	25	4	35	91	.271	326	11	10	.971
1964—Minnesota	Amer.	1B-OF	149	492	90	141	27	4	32	86	.287	829	58	12	.987
1965—Minnesota	Amer.	OF-1B	135	438	71	102	14	5	23	78	.233	247	12	7	.974
1966—Minnesota	Amer.	OF	70	168	34	37	6	1	8	19	.220	86	3	3	.967
1967—Minnesota	Amer.	OF	153	496	73	128	21	6	24	75	.258	220	6	5	.978
1968—Minnesota	Amer.	OF-1B	145	469	63	116	16	8	22	52	.247	316	16	8	.976
1969—Minnesota	Amer.	OF-1B	81	189	18	43	8	2	8	27	.228	96	3	0	1.000
1970—Minnesota	Amer.	OF-1B	47	72	15	15	5	0	1	7	.208	54	4	2	.967
Major League Totals—13 Years			1541	5032	811	1281	216	53	256	796	.255	3546	162	84	.978

CHAMPIONSHIP SERIES RECORD

Year Club	League	Pos.	G.	AB.	R.	H.	2B.	3B.	HR.	RBI.	B.A.	PO.	A.	E.	F.A.
1969—Minnesota	Amer.	OF	2	8	0	0	0	0	0	1	.000	6	0	0	1.000
1970—Minnesota	Amer.	PH	3	2	0	0	0	0	0	0	.000	0	0	0	.000
Championship Series Totals—2 Years			5	10	0	0	0	0	0	1	.000	6	0	0	1.000

WORLD SERIES RECORD

Year Club	League	Pos.	G.	AB.	R.	H.	2B.	3B.	HR.	RBI.	B.A.	PO.	A.	E.	F.A.
1965—Minnesota	Amer.	OF	5	16	3	2	1	0	1	2	.125	11	0	0	1.000

MATEO ROJAS (MATTY) ALOU

Born December 22, 1938, at Haina, Dominican Republic.

Height, 5.09. Weight, 160.

Threw and batted lefthanded.

Brother of Felipe and Jesus Alou, former major league outfielders.

Named outfielder on THE SPORTING NEWS National League All-Star Team, 1969.

Year Club	League	Pos.	G.	AB.	R.	H.	2B.	3B.	HR.	RBI.	B.A.	PO.	A.	E.	F.A.
1957—Michigan City	Midwest	OF	124	481	79	119	15	1	6	46	.247	271	20	10	.967
1958—St. Cloud	North.	OF	121	448	92	144	13	5	4	52	.321	261	11	10	.965
1959—Springfield	East.	OF	121	489	93	141	30	7	11	57	.288	319	★23	13	.963
1960—Tacoma	P.C.	OF	150	★627	97	192	39	8	14	73	.306	★408	●20	●13	.971
1960—San Francisco	Nat.	OF	4	3	1	1	0	0	0	0	.333	1	0	0	1.000
1961—San Francisco	Nat.	OF	81	200	38	62	7	2	6	24	.310	85	2	2	.978
1962—San Francisco	Nat.	OF	78	195	28	57	8	1	3	14	.292	80	3	2	.976
1963—San Francisco	Nat.	OF	63	76	4	11	1	0	0	2	.145	19	1	1	.952
1963—Tacoma	P.C.	OF	25	83	6	26	2	1	2	10	.313	48	0	1	.980
1964—San Francisco	Nat.	OF	110	250	28	66	4	2	1	14	.264	120	2	3	.976

Year—Club	League	Pos.	G.	AB.	R.	H.	2B.	3B.	HR.	RBI.	B.A.	PO.	A.	E.	F.A.
1965—San Fran.(a)	Nat.	OF-P	117	324	37	75	12	2	2	18	.231	139	6	2	.986
1966—Pittsburgh	Nat.	OF	141	535	86	183	18	9	2	27	★.342	264	11	8	.972
1967—Pittsburgh	Nat.	OF-1B	139	550	87	186	21	7	2	28	.338	252	9	3	.989
1968—Pittsburgh	Nat.	OF	146	558	59	185	28	4	0	52	.332	298	8	5	.984
1969—Pittsburgh	Nat.	OF	162	★698	105	★231	★41	6	1	48	.331	327	10	8	.977
1970—Pittsburgh (b)	Nat.	OF	155	★677	97	201	21	8	1	47	.297	297	15	8	.975
1971—St. Louis	Nat.	OF-1B	149	609	85	192	28	6	7	74	.315	710	35	9	.988
1972—St. Louis (c)	Nat.	1B-OF	108	404	46	127	17	2	3	31	.314	587	44	7	.989
1972—Oakland (d)	Amer.	OF-1B	32	121	11	34	5	0	1	16	.281	57	3	0	1.000
1973—New York (e)	Amer.	OF-1B	123	497	59	147	22	1	2	28	.296	522	26	12	.979
1973—St. Louis (f)	Nat.	1B-OF	11	11	1	3	0	0	0	1	.273	3	1	0	1.000
1974—San Diego	Nat.	OF-1B	48	81	8	16	3	0	0	3	.198	33	0	1	.971
National League Totals—15 Years			1512	5171	710	1596	209	49	28	383	.309	3215	147	59	.983
American League Totals—2 Years			155	618	70	181	27	1	3	44	.293	579	29	12	.981
Major League Totals—15 Years			1667	5789	780	1777	236	50	31	427	.307	3794	176	71	.982

aTraded to Pittsburgh Pirates for Pitcher Joe Gibbon and Infielder Ossie Virgil, December 1, 1965.

bTraded with Pitcher George Brunet to St. Louis Cardinals for Pitcher Nelson Briles and Outfielder Vic Davalillo, January 29, 1971.

cTraded to Oakland A's for Outfielder Bill Voss and Pitcher Steve Easton, August 27, 1972.

dTraded to New York Yankees for Pitcher Rob Gardner and minor league Third Baseman Rich McKinney, November 24, 1972.

eTraded to St. Louis Cardinals, September 6, 1973.

fSold to San Diego Padres, October 25, 1973.

CHAMPIONSHIP SERIES RECORD

Year—Club	League	Pos.	G.	AB.	R.	H.	2B.	3B.	HR.	RBI.	B.A.	PO.	A.	E.	F.A.
1970—Pittsburgh	Nat.	OF	3	12	1	3	1	0	0	0	.250	6	0	0	1.000
1972—Oakland	Amer.	OF	5	21	2	8	4	0	0	2	.381	8	0	0	1.000
Championship Series Totals—2 Years			8	33	3	11	5	0	0	2	.333	14	0	0	1.000

WORLD SERIES RECORD

Year—Club	League	Pos.	G.	AB.	R.	H.	2B.	3B.	HR.	RBI.	B.A.	PO.	A.	E.	F.A.
1962—San Francisco	Nat.	OF	6	12	2	4	1	0	0	1	.333	3	0	0	1.000
1972—Oakland	Amer.	OF	7	24	0	1	0	0	0	0	.042	11	1	1	.923
World Series Totals—2 Years			13	36	2	5	1	0	0	1	.139	14	1	1	.938

PITCHING RECORD

Year—Club	League	G.	IP.	W.	L.	Pct.	H.	R.	ER.	SO.	BB.	ERA.
1965—San Francisco	National	1	2	0	0	.000	3	0	0	3	1	0.00

WALTER EMMONS (WALT) ALSTON
(Smokey)

Born December 1, 1911, at Butler County, O.

Died October 1, 1984, at Oxford, O.

Height, 6.02. Weight, 210.

Threw and batted righthanded.

Player-manager, Portsmouth, Middle Atlantic League, 1940; Springfield, Middle Atlantic League, 1941-42; Trenton, Interstate League, 1944-45; Nashua, New England League, 1946; Pueblo, Western League, 1947; manager, St. Paul, American Association, 1948-49; Montreal, International League, 1950 through 1953; Brooklyn Dodgers, 1954 through 1957; Los Angeles Dodgers, 1958 through 1976.

Named to Hall of Fame in 1983 for service apart from playing the game.

Year—Club	League	Pos.	G.	AB.	R.	H.	2B.	3B.	HR.	RBI.	B.A.	PO.	A.	E.	F.A.
1935—Greenwood	E. Dixie	3B	82	319	46	104	25	11	1	46	.326	94	172	27	.908
1936—Huntington	Mid. Atl.	1B-OF-2B	120	482	89	157	16	8	★35	114	.326	900	91	22	.978
1936—St. Louis	Nat.	1B	1	1	0	0	0	0	0	0	.000	1	0	1	.500
1937—Rochester	Int.	1B	66	203	20	50	6	3	6	36	.246	472	43	6	.988
1937—Houston	Texas	1B	65	208	20	44	9	1	0	16	.212	592	46	1	.998
1938—Portsmouth	Mid. Atl.	1B	122	444	76	138	22	3	28	106	.311	1084	56	9	●.992
1939—Portsmouth	Mid. Atl.	1B	2	6	1	2	0	0	0	0	.333	21	0	1	.955
1939—Columbus	Sally	1B	105	399	69	129	26	8	11	82	.323	982	51	6	★.994
1940—Portsmouth	Mid. Atl.	1B	127	446	79	122	18	3	★28	112	.274	1015	77	14	.987
1941—Springfield	Mid. Atl.	★1B-P	125	456	★88	131	26	4	★25	★102	.287	1135	★86	13	★.989
1942—Springfield	Mid. Atl.	★●1B-P	129	462	54	143	16	3	★12	★90	.310	★1117	★106	12	●.990
1943—Rochester	Int.	1B-3B	115	313	37	75	12	2	5	40	.240	551	75	13	.980
1944—Rochester	Int.	1B-2B	13	19	2	3	0	0	2	2	.158	29	2	1	.969
1944—Trenton	Int.-St.	1B-P	52	180	46	63	10	2	9	48	.350	428	37	8	.983
1945—Trenton	Int.-St.	★1B-P	126	447	91	140	30	4	14	93	.313	947	★74	12	★.988
1946—Nashua	N. Eng.	1B	50	165	21	43	5	6	2	30	.261	327	26	3	.992
1947—Pueblo	West.	PH	2	1	0	0	0	0	0	0	.000	0	0	0	.000
Major League Totals—1 Year			1	1	0	0	0	0	0	0	.000	1	2	1	.500

Year	Club	League	G.	IP.	W.	L.	Pct.	H.	R.	ER.	SO.	BB.	ERA.
1941—Springfield	Mid. Atl.	3	9	0	0	.000	....	....	....	....	....	......
1942—Springfield	Mid. Atl.	7	21	1	0	1.000	....	....	....	....	....	......
1944—Trenton	Int.-St.	1	2	0	0	.000	....	....	....	....	....	......
1945—Trenton	Int.-St.	1	2	0	0	.000	....	....	....	....	....	......

RECORD AS MAJOR LEAGUE MANAGER

Year	Club	League	Position	W.	L.	Year	Club	League	Position	W.	L.
1954—Brooklyn	Nat.	Second	92	62	1966—Los Angeles	Nat.	First	95	67
1955—Brooklyn	Nat.	First	98	55	1967—Los Angeles	Nat.	Eighth	73	89
1956—Brooklyn	Nat.	First	93	61	1968—Los Angeles	Nat.	§Seventh	76	86
1957—Brooklyn	Nat.	Third	84	70	1969—Los Angeles	Nat.	Fourth(W)	85	77
1958—Los Angeles	Nat.	Seventh	71	83	1970—Los Angeles	Nat.	Second(W)	87	74
1959—Los Angeles	Nat.	†First	88	68	1971—Los Angeles	Nat.	Second(W)	89	73
1960—Los Angeles	Nat.	Fourth	82	72	1972—Los Angeles	Nat.	Third(W)	85	70
1961—Los Angeles	Nat.	Second	89	65	1973—Los Angeles	Nat.	Second(W)	95	66
1962—Los Angeles	Nat.	‡Second	102	63	1974—Los Angeles	Nat.	First(W)	102	60
1963—Los Angeles	Nat.	First	99	63	1975—Los Angeles	Nat.	Second(W)	88	74
1964—Los Angeles	Nat.	§Sixth	80	82	1976—Los Angeles	Nat.	Second(W)	90	68
1965—Los Angeles	Nat.	First	97	65	Major League Totals—23 Years				2040	1613

†Defeated Milwaukee Braves, two games to none in playoff for championship.
‡Lost to San Francisco Giants, two games to one in playoff for championship.
§Tied for position.

CHAMPIONSHIP SERIES RECORD

Year	Club	League	W.	L.
1974—Los Angeles	National	3	1

WORLD SERIES RECORD

Year	Club	League	W.	L.	Year	Club	League	W.	L.
1955—Brooklyn	National	4	3	1965—Los Angeles	National	4	3
1956—Brooklyn	National	3	4	1966—Los Angeles	National	0	4
1959—Los Angeles	National	4	2	1974—Los Angeles	National	1	4
1963—Los Angeles	National	4	0				

ADRIAN CONSTANTINE (CAP) ANSON
(Pop)

Born April 17, 1852, at Marshalltown, Ia.

Died April 14, 1922, at Chicago, Ill.

Height, 6.01. Weight, 220.

Threw and batted righthanded.

Holds National League record for most years batting .300 or over, 50 or more games (18).
Shares National League record for most years with one club (22).
Manager, Chicago Nationals, 1879-1897; New York Giants, 1898.
Named to Hall of Fame, 1939.

Year	Club	League	Pos.	G.	AB.	R.	H.	2B.	3B.	HR.	S.B.	B.A.	PO.	A.	E.	F.A.
1870—Marshalltown	Ind.			......	....	....	....	....	....	....	......	......	......	......	......
1871—Rockford	N.As'n	C-2-3	25	122	30	43	....	....	....		.352	56	67	....	......
1872—Ath. of Phila	N.As'n	3B	45	231	60	88	....	....	....		.381	86	82	33	.836
1873—Ath. of Phila	N.As'n	C-I-O	51	....	52	103	....	....	....		......	440	28	....	......
1874—Ath. of Phila	N.As'n	I-OF	55	267	51	98	....	....	....		.367	285	95	....	......
1875—Ath. of Phila	N.As'n	1-C-3-O	69	330	83	105	....	....	....		.318	273	14	32	.900
1876—Chicago	Nat.	3B	66	321	63	110	13	6	2		.343	137	147	50	.850
1877—Chicago	Nat.	3B-C	47	200	36	67	★20	1	0		.335	137	93	35	.871
1878—Chicago	Nat.	2B-OF	59	256	54	86	12	2	0		.336	80	31	21	.841
1879—Chicago	Nat.	1B	49	221	41	90	22	1	0		★.407	602	8	16	.974
1880—Chicago	Nat.	INF	84	346	52	117	22	1	1		.338	811	15	19	.978
1881—Chicago	Nat.	1-C-SS	84	343	66	★137	25	7	1		★.399	892	43	24	.973
1882—Chicago	Nat.	1B-C	82	348	69	126	30	8	1		.362	810	27	45	.949
1883—Chicago	Nat.	1-C-P	98	413	69	127	33	6	0		.308	1031	41	40	.964
1884—Chicago	Nat.	1-C-S-P	111	471	108	★159	32	5	19		.338	1203	39	58	.900
1885—Chicago	Nat.	1B-C	112	464	100	144	★35	6	7		.310	★1253	39	★57	.958
1886—Chicago	Nat.	1B	125	504	117	★187	34	11	10	29	.371	1188	★66	★48	.963
1887—Chicago†	Nat.	1B	122	532	107	224	33	13	7	27	★.421	1232	★70	36	.973
1888—Chicago	Nat.	1B	134	515	101	177	17	13	10	28	★.344	1314	65	20	★.986
1889—Chicago	Nat.	1B	134	518	99	177	30	6	7	27	.342	★1409	★79	27	★.982
1890—Chicago	Nat.	1B	★139	504	102	157	17	4	6	29	.312	1345	★49	31	.978
1891—Chicago	Nat.	1B	136	537	82	158	25	9	8	21	.294	1406	77	28	.981

Year	Club	League	Pos.	G.	AB.	R.	H.	2B.	3B.	HR.	SB.	B.A.	PO.	A.	E.	F.A.
1892—Chicago	Nat.		1B	147	561	62	154	23	9	1	15	.275	1491	61	∗46	.971
1893—Chicago	Nat.		1B	101	381	70	123	25	3	0	13	.323	998	42	20	.981
1894—Chicago	Nat.		1B	83	347	87	137	26	6	5	17	.395	748	45	9	.989
1895—Chicago	Nat.		1B	122	476	88	161	23	6	2	16	.338	1172	67	14	.989
1896—Chicago	Nat.		1B	106	403	72	135	17	3	2	28	.335	886	53	17	.982
1897—Chicago	Nat.		1B	112	423	66	128	16	3	3	16	.303	940	23	13	.987
National League Totals—22 Years				2253	9084	1712	3081	530	129	92	266	.339	21085	1180	674	.971

†Bases on balls counted as hits in 1887.

LUIS ERNESTO APARICIO

Born April 29, 1934, at Maracaibo, Venezuela.

Height, 5.08. Weight, 155.

Threw and batted righthanded.

Holds major league records for most consecutive years leading league in stolen bases (9); most games (2,581), assists (8,016), chances accepted (12,564) and double plays (1,553), shortstop, lifetime.

Shares major league records for most consecutive years leading league in fielding average (8), assists (7) and chances accepted (7), shortstop.

Holds American League records for most years leading league in games played, shortstop (5); most putouts, shortstop, lifetime (4,548).

Led American League in stolen bases with 21 in 1956, 28 in 1957, 29 in 1958, 56 in 1959, 51 in 1960, 53 in 1961, 31 in 1962, 40 in 1963 and 57 in 1964.

Led American League shortstops in double plays, 1960, 1968 (tie).

Named American League Rookie of the Year by the Baseball Writers' Association and THE SPORTING NEWS, 1956.

Named shortstop on THE SPORTING NEWS American League All-Star Team, 1963-66-68-70-72.

Named shortstop on THE SPORTING NEWS American League All-Star fielding team, 1958-59-60-61-62-64-66-68-70.

Named to Hall of Fame, 1984.

Year	Club	League	Pos.	G.	AB.	R.	H.	2B.	3B.	HR.	RBI.	B.A.	PO.	A.	E.	F.A.
1954—Waterloo	I.I.I.		SS	94	390	85	110	18	4	4	47	.282	220	275	31	.941
1955—Memphis	South.		SS	150	564	92	154	24	3	6	51	.273	∗314	∗433	●44	.944
1956—Chicago	Amer.		SS	152	533	69	142	19	6	3	56	.266	∗250	∗474	∗35	.954
1957—Chicago	Amer.		SS	143	575	82	148	22	6	3	41	.257	246	∗449	20	.972
1958—Chicago	Amer.		SS	145	557	76	148	20	9	2	40	.266	∗289	∗ 463	21	.973
1959—Chicago	Amer.		SS	152	612	98	157	18	5	6	51	.257	∗282	∗ 460	23	∗.970
1960—Chicago	Amer.		SS	153	600	86	166	20	7	2	61	.277	305	∗551	18	∗.979
1961—Chicago	Amer.		SS	156	625	90	170	24	4	6	45	.272	264	∗487	30	∗.962
1962—Chicago (a)	Amer.		SS	153	581	72	140	23	5	7	40	.241	280	452	20	∗.973
1963—Baltimore	Amer.		SS	146	601	73	150	18	8	5	45	.250	275	403	12	∗.983
1964—Baltimore	Amer.		SS	146	578	93	154	20	3	10	37	.266	260	437	15	∗.979
1965—Baltimore	Amer.		SS	144	564	67	127	20	10	8	40	.225	238	439	20	∗.971
1966—Baltimore	Amer.		SS	151	∗659	97	182	25	8	6	41	.276	∗303	441	17	∗.978
1967—Baltimore (b)	Amer.		SS	134	546	55	127	22	5	4	31	.233	221	333	25	.957
1968—Chicago	Amer.		SS	155	622	55	164	24	4	4	36	.264	269	∗535	19	.977
1969—Chicago	Amer.		SS	156	599	77	168	24	5	5	51	.280	248	563	20	.976
1970—Chicago (c)	Amer.		SS	146	552	86	173	29	3	5	43	.313	251	483	18	.976
1971—Boston	Amer.		SS	125	491	56	114	23	0	4	45	.232	194	338	16	.971
1972—Boston	Amer.		SS	110	436	47	112	26	3	3	39	.257	183	304	16	.968
1973—Boston	Amer.		SS	132	499	56	135	17	1	0	49	.271	190	404	21	.966
Major League Totals—18 Years				2599	10230	1335	2677	394	92	83	791	.262	4548	8016	366	.971

aTraded to Baltimore Orioles with Outfielder-Third Baseman Al Smith for Pitcher Hoyt Wilhelm, Third Baseman Pete Ward, Shortstop Ron Hansen and Outfielder Dave Nicholson, January 14, 1963.

bTraded to Chicago White Sox with Outfielder Russ Snyder and Outfielder-First Baseman John Matias for Infielder Don Buford and Pitchers Bruce Howard and Roger Nelson, November 29, 1967.

cTraded to Boston Red Sox for Second Baseman Mike Andrews and Shortstop Luis Alvarado, December 1, 1970.

WORLD SERIES RECORD

Year	Club	League	Pos.	G.	AB.	R.	H.	2B.	3B.	HR.	RBI.	B.A.	PO.	A.	E.	F.A.
1959—Chicago	Amer.		SS	6	26	1	8	1	0	0	0	.308	10	16	2	.929
1966—Baltimore	Amer.		SS	4	16	0	4	1	0	0	2	.250	9	8	0	1.000
World Series Totals—2 Years				10	42	1	12	2	0	0	2	.286	19	24	2	.956

—DID YOU KNOW—

That Luke Appling is the only White Sox player ever to win an American League batting title? Appling won batting crowns in 1936 (.388) and 1943 (.328).

LUCIUS BENJAMIN (LUKE) APPLING

Born April 2, 1907, at High Point, N. C.

Height, 5.11. Weight, 200.

Threw and batted righthanded.

Holds American League record for highest batting average by shortstop, season (.388), 1936.
Led American League shortstops in double plays, 1936-37-46.
Named as shortstop on THE SPORTING NEWS' All-Star Major League Teams, 1936-40-43.
Manager, Memphis, Southern Association, 1951-52-53; Richmond, International League, 1955; Memphis, Southern Association, 1959; coach, Detroit Tigers, 1960 until August 8, when he traded jobs with Jo Jo White of Cleveland Indians; coach, Cleveland Indians, through 1961; manager, Indianapolis, American Association, 1962; coach, Baltimore Orioles, 1963; Kansas City Athletics, 1964 to 1967; manager, Kansas City Athletics, 1967; scout, Oakland Athletics, 1968-69; coach, Chicago White Sox, 1970-71.
Named to Hall of Fame, 1964.

Year Club League	Pos.	G.	AB.	R.	H.	2B.	3B.	HR.	RBI.	B.A.	PO.	A.	E.	F.A.
1930—Atlanta .... South.	SS	104	374	63	122	19	17	5	75	.326	224	302	⋆42	.926
1930—Chicago .... Amer.	SS	6	26	2	8	2	0	0	2	.308	12	17	4	.879
1931—Chicago .... Amer.	SS-2B	96	297	36	69	13	4	1	28	.232	151	233	43	.899
1932—Chicago .... Amer.	INF	139	489	66	134	20	10	3	63	.274	270	419	49	.934
1933—Chicago .... Amer.	SS	151	612	90	197	36	10	6	85	.322	314	⋆534	⋆55	.939
1934—Chicago .... Amer.	SS-2B	118	452	75	137	28	6	2	61	.303	264	357	35	.947
1935—Chicago .... Amer.	SS	153	525	94	161	28	6	1	71	.307	⋆335	⋆556	⋆39	.958
1936—Chicago .... Amer.	SS	138	526	111	204	31	7	6	128	⋆.388	320	471	41	.951
1937—Chicago .... Amer.	SS	154	574	98	182	42	8	4	77	.317	280	⋆541	⋆49	.944
1938—Chicago(a)............. Amer.	SS	81	294	41	89	14	0	0	44	.303	149	258	20	.953
1939—Chicago .... Amer.	SS	148	516	82	162	16	6	0	56	.314	289	⋆461	⋆39	.951
1940—Chicago .... Amer.	SS	150	566	96	197	27	13	0	79	.348	307	436	37	.953
1941—Chicago .... Amer.	SS	154	592	93	186	26	8	1	57	.314	294	⋆473	42	.948
1942—Chicago .... Amer.	SS	142	543	78	142	26	4	3	53	.262	269	418	38	.948
1943—Chicago .... Amer.	SS	●155	585	63	192	33	2	3	80	⋆.328	300	⋆500	36	.957
1944—								(In Military Service)						
1945—Chicago(b)............. Amer.	SS	18	57	12	21	2	2	1	10	.368	37	56	7	.930
1946—Chicago .... Amer.	SS	149	582	59	180	27	5	1	55	.309	252	⋆505	⋆39	.951
1947—Chicago .... Amer.	SS-3B	139	503	67	154	29	0	8	49	.306	233	423	35	.949
1948—Chicago .... Amer.	3B-SS	139	497	63	156	16	2	0	47	.314	217	373	35	.944
1949—Chicago .... Amer.	SS	142	492	82	148	21	5	5	58	.301	253	450	26	.964
1950—Chicago .... Amer.	INF	50	128	11	30	3	4	0	13	.234	128	62	3	.984
Major League Totals—20 Years...............		2422	8856	1319	2749	440	102	45	1116	.310	4674	7543	672	.948

aFractured leg sliding into base in exhibition game against Chicago Cubs, March 27, 1938.
bIn Military Service part of season.

DON RICHARD (RICHIE) ASHBURN

Born March 19, 1927, at Tilden, Neb.

Height, 5.10. Weight, 175.

Threw right and batted lefthanded.

Holds major league records for most years with 400 or more putouts (9) and 500 or more putouts (4).
Shares major league record for most years leading league in putouts, outfielder (9).
Shares National League record for most years leading league in singles (4).
Led National League in stolen bases with 32 in 1948.
Named by THE SPORTING NEWS as Rookie of the Year, 1948.

Year Club League	Pos.	G.	AB.	R.	H.	2B.	3B.	HR.	RBI.	B.A.	PO.	A.	E.	F.A.
1945—Utica .... East.	OF-C	106	356	63	111	17	6	1	42	.312	189	19	7	.967
1946—Utica .... East.						(In Military Service)								
1947—Utica .... East.	OF	137	536	⋆128	⋆194	21	12	3	52	.362	242	14	6	.977
1948—Philadelphia .... Nat.	OF	117	463	78	154	17	4	2	40	.333	344	14	7	.981
1949—Philadelphia .... Nat.	OF	154	⋆662	84	188	18	11	1	37	.284	⋆514	13	11	.980
1950—Philadelphia .... Nat.	OF	151	594	84	180	25	⋆14	2	41	.303	⋆405	8	5	.988

Year	Club	League	Pos.	G.	AB.	R.	H.	2B.	3B.	HR.	RBI.	B.A.	PO.	A.	E.	F.A.
1951—Philadelphia	Nat.		OF	154	643	92	*221	31	5	4	63	.344	*538	15	7	.988
1952—Philadelphia	Nat.		OF	*154	613	93	173	31	6	1	42	.282	*428	*23	9	.980
1953—Philadelphia	Nat.		OF	156	622	110	*205	25	9	2	57	.330	*496	*18	5	.990
1954—Philadelphia	Nat.		OF	153	559	111	175	16	8	1	41	.313	*483	12	8	.984
1955—Philadelphia	Nat.		OF	140	533	91	180	32	9	3	42	*.338	387	10	7	.983
1956—Philadelphia	Nat.		OF	154	628	94	190	26	8	3	50	.303	*503	11	9	.983
1957—Philadelphia	Nat.		OF	•156	626	93	186	26	8	0	33	.297	*502	*18	7	.987
1958—Philadelphia	Nat.		OF	152	615	98	*215	24	*13	2	33	*.350	*495	8	8	.984
1959—Philadelphia(a)	Nat.		OF	153	564	86	150	16	2	1	20	.266	359	4	11	.971
1960—Chicago	Nat.		OF	151	547	99	159	16	5	0	40	.291	317	11	8	.976
1961—Chicago(b)	Nat.		OF	109	307	49	79	7	4	0	19	.257	131	4	3	.978
1962—New York	Nat.		OF	135	389	60	119	7	3	7	28	.306	187	9	5	.975
Major League Totals—15 Years				2189	8365	1322	2574	317	109	29	586	.308	6089	178	110	.983

aTraded to Chicago Cubs for Pitcher John Buzhardt, Infielder Al Dark and Third Baseman Jim Woods, January 11, 1960.

bSold to New York Mets, December 8, 1961.

WORLD SERIES RECORD

Year	Club	League	Pos.	G.	AB.	R.	H.	2B.	3B.	HR.	RBI.	B.A.	PO.	A.	E.	F.A.
1950—Philadelphia	Nat.		OF	4	17	0	3	1	0	0	1	.176	9	0	0	1.000

HOWARD EARL AVERILL
(Known by middle name.)

Born May 21, 1902, Snohomish, Wash.

Died August 15, 1983, at Everett, Wash.

Height, 5.09½. Weight, 172.

Threw right and batted lefthanded.

Father of Earl Douglas Averill, former major league catcher-outfielder.

Shares major league record by hitting home run in first at-bat, April 16, 1929.

Shares American League records for most home runs (4) and runs batted in (11), doubleheader, September 17, 1930.

Selected by Baseball Writers' Association of America as outfielder on THE SPORTING NEWS All-Star Major League Teams, 1931-32-34-36.

Named to Hall of Fame, 1975.

Year	Club	League	Pos.	G.	AB.	R.	H.	2B.	3B.	HR.	RBI.	B.A.	PO.	A.	E.	F.A.
1926—San Francisco	P. C.		OF	188	679	131	236	49	6	23	119	.348	364	17	14	.965
1927—San Francisco	P. C.		OF	183	754	134	244	47	6	20	116	.324	451	*45	19	.963
1928—San Francisco	P. C.		OF	189	763	*178	270	53	11	36	173	.354	462	25	18	.964
1929—Cleveland(a)	Amer.		OF	152	596	110	198	43	13	18	96	.332	*383	14	14	.966
1930—Cleveland	Amer.		OF	139	534	102	181	33	8	19	119	.339	345	11	*19	.949
1931—Cleveland	Amer.		OF	155	*627	140	209	36	10	32	143	.333	398	9	10	.976
1932—Cleveland	Amer.		OF	153	631	116	198	37	14	32	124	.314	412	12	16	.964
1933—Cleveland	Amer.		OF	151	599	83	180	39	16	11	92	.301	390	8	12	.971
1934—Cleveland	Amer.		OF	•154	598	128	187	48	6	31	113	.313	*410	12	13	.970
1935—Cleveland	Amer.		OF	140	563	109	162	34	13	19	79	.288	371	6	7	.982
1936—Cleveland	Amer.		OF	152	614	136	*232	39	•15	28	126	.378	369	11	12	.969
1937—Cleveland	Amer.		OF	156	609	121	182	33	11	21	92	.299	362	11	9	.976
1938—Cleveland	Amer.		OF	134	482	101	159	27	15	14	93	.330	331	14	9	.975
1939—Clev.(b)-Detroit	Amer.		OF	111	364	66	96	28	6	11	65	.264	169	3	4	.977
1940—Detroit	Amer.		OF	64	118	10	33	4	1	2	20	.280	23	2	1	.962
1941—Boston	Nat.		OF	8	17	2	2	0	0	0	2	.118	5	2	0	1.000
1941—Seattle	P. C.		OF	78	223	24	55	9	0	1	17	.247	147	10	3	.981
American League Totals—12 Years				1661	6335	1222	2017	401	128	238	1162	.318	3963	113	126	.970
National League Totals—1 Year				8	17	2	2	0	0	0	2	.118	5	2	0	1.000
Major League Totals—13 Years				1669	6352	1224	2019	401	128	238	1164	.318	3968	115	126	.970

aPurchased for reported price of $50,000.

bTraded to Detroit Tigers for Pitcher Harry Eisenstat and cash, June 14, 1939.

WORLD SERIES RECORD

Year	Club	League	Pos.	G.	AB.	R.	H.	2B.	3B.	HR.	RBI.	B.A.	PO.	A.	E.	F.A.
1940—Detroit	Amer.		PH	3	3	0	0	0	0	0	0	.000	0	0	0	.000

—DID YOU KNOW—

That Cleveland's Earl Averill collected the first pinch-hit in All-Star Game history when he singled for the American League in the sixth inning of the 1933 midsummer classic?

JOHN FRANKLIN (HOME RUN) BAKER
(Frank)

Born March 13, 1886, at Trappe, Md.

Died June 28, 1963, at Trappe, Md.

Height, 5.11. Weight, 173.

Threw right and batted lefthanded.

Manager, Easton, Eastern Shore League, 1924-25; president of Easton club in 1941.
Named to Hall of Fame, 1955.

Year	Club	League	Pos.	G.	AB.	R.	H.	2B.	3B.	HR.	RBI.	B.A.	PO.	A.	E.	F.A.
1907—Baltimore		East.	3B	5	15	0	2	0	0	0	....	.133	9	5	2	.875
1908—Reading		Tri-State	3B	119	451	65	135	11	12	6	....	.299	★174	246	27	.940
1908—Philadelphia		Amer.	3B	9	30	5	9	3	0	0	4	.300	12	18	0	1.000
1909—Philadelphia		Amer.	3B	148	541	73	165	27	★19	4	89	.305	★209	★277	★42	.920
1910—Philadelphia		Amer.	3B	146	561	83	159	25	15	2	73	.283	★207	313	45	.920
1911—Philadelphia		Amer.	3B	148	592	96	198	40	14	★11	115	.334	217	274	30	★.942
1912—Philadelphia		Amer.	3B	149	577	116	200	40	21	●10	★133	.347	217	321	34	.941
1913—Philadelphia		Amer.	3B	149	564	116	190	34	9	★12	★126	.337	★233	279	★45	.919
1914—Philadelphia		Amer.	3B	150	570	84	182	23	10	★9	97	.319	★221	292	24	.955
1915—Philadelphia (a)		Amer.							(Refused to report; played with Upland, Pa.)							
1916—New York		Amer.	3B	100	360	46	97	23	2	10	52	.269	133	210	22	.940
1917—New York		Amer.	3B	146	553	57	156	24	2	6	70	.282	★202	★317	28	★.949
1918—New York		Amer.	3B	126	504	65	154	24	5	6	68	.306	★175	282	13	★.972
1919—New York		Amer.	3B	●141	567	70	166	22	1	10	78	.293	★176	286	22	.955
1920—New York		Amer.							(Voluntarily retired; played with Upland, Pa.)							
1921—New York		Amer.	3B	94	330	46	97	16	2	9	71	.294	84	173	11	.959
1922—New York		Amer.	3B	69	234	30	65	12	3	7	36	.278	68	108	7	.962
1924—Easton		Ea. Shore	3B	43	92	14	27	1	1	5	....	.293	25	43	4	.944
Major League Totals—13 Years				1575	5983	887	1838	313	103	96	1012	.307	2154	3150	323	.942

aSold to New York Yankees for $35,000, February 15, 1916.

WORLD SERIES RECORD

Year	Club	League	Pos.	G.	AB.	R.	H.	2B.	3B.	HR.	RBI.	B.A.	PO.	A.	E.	F.A.
1910—Philadelphia		Amer.	3B	5	22	6	9	3	0	0	4	.409	9	11	3	.869
1911—Philadelphia		Amer.	3B	6	24	7	9	2	0	2	5	.375	10	10	2	.909
1913—Philadelphia		Amer.	3B	5	20	2	9	0	0	1	7	.450	6	6	1	.923
1914—Philadelphia		Amer.	3B	4	16	0	4	2	0	0	2	.250	10	15	0	1.000
1921—New York		Amer.	3B-PH	4	8	0	2	0	0	0	0	.250	2	3	0	1.000
1922—New York		Amer.	PH	1	1	0	0	0	0	0	0	.000	0	0	0	.000
World Series Totals—6 Years				25	91	15	33	7	0	3	18	.363	37	45	6	.932

DAVID JAMES (DAVE) BANCROFT
(Beauty)

Born April 20, 1892, at Sioux City, Ia.

Died October 9, 1972, at Superior, Wis.

Height, 5.09½. Weight, 160.

Threw right and batted left and righthanded.

Led National League shortstops in double plays, 1922.
Manager, Boston Braves, 1924 through 1927; coach, New York Giants, 1930-31-32; manager, Minneapolis, American
Association, 1933; Sioux City, Western League, 1936; St. Cloud, Northern League, 1947.
Named to Hall of Fame, 1971.

Year	Club	League	Pos.	G.	AB.	R.	H.	2B.	3B.	HR.	RBI.	B.A.	PO.	A.	E.	F.A.
1909—Duluth-Sup		Wis.-Min.	SS	111	367	43	77	4	1	1	....	.210	★230	★359	54	.916
1910—Superior		Wis.-Min.	SS	●127	438	55	117	16	1	1	....	.267	★323	350	59	.919
1911—Superior		Wis.-Min.	SS	122	524	73	143	....	....	....	....	.273	....	....	....	....
1912—Portland		P. C.	SS-2B	166	565	68	120	29	8	0	....	.213	390	512	52	.945
1913—Portland		N. W.	SS-2B	133	483	79	118	19	9	2	....	.244	325	418	46	.942
1914—Portland		P. C.	SS-2B	177	668	99	185	35	14	2	....	.277	★453	585	59	.946
1915—Philadelphia		Nat.	SS	153	563	85	143	18	2	7	33	.254	336	492	64	.928

Year Club	League	Pos.	G.	AB.	R.	H.	2B.	3B.	HR.	RBI.	B.A.	PO.	A.	E.	F.A.
1916—Philadelphia .... Nat.		SS	142	477	53	101	10	0	3	27	.212	326	510	★60	.933
1917—Philadelphia .... Nat.		SS	127	478	56	116	22	5	4	38	.243	274	439	49	.936
1918—Philadelphia .... Nat.		SS	125	499	69	132	19	4	0	18	.265	★371	457	★64	.928
1919—Philadelphia .... Nat.		SS	92	335	45	91	13	7	0	29	.272	242	306	28	.951
1920—Phila. (a)-N.Y. ...... Nat.		SS	150	613	102	183	36	9	0	36	.299	★362	★598	45	★.955
1921—New York .... Nat.		SS	153	606	121	193	26	15	6	67	.318	★396	★546	39	.960
1922—New York .... Nat.		SS	●156	651	117	209	41	5	4	60	.321	★405	★579	★62	.941
1923—New York (b) .... Nat.		SS-3B	107	444	80	135	33	3	1	31	.304	246	381	43	.936
1924—Boston.................. Nat.		SS	79	319	49	89	11	1	2	21	.279	186	259	18	.961
1925—Boston.................. Nat.		SS	128	479	75	153	29	8	2	49	.319	300	459	44	★.945
1926—Boston.................. Nat.		SS	127	453	70	141	18	6	1	44	.311	317	398	33	.956
1927—Boston (c) .... Nat.		SS	111	375	44	91	13	4	1	31	.243	275	329	39	.939
1928—Brooklyn .... Nat.		SS	149	515	47	127	19	5	0	51	.247	350	484	46	.948
1929—Brooklyn (d) .... Nat.		SS	104	358	35	99	11	3	1	44	.277	224	309	25	.955
1930—New York .... Nat.		SS-PH	10	17	0	1	1	0	0	0	.059	13	15	1	.966
1936—Sioux City .... West.		SS	1	4	1	1	0	0	0	0	.250	1	1	0	1.000
Major League Totals—16 Years..............			1913	7182	1048	2004	320	77	32	579	.279	4623	6561	660	.944

aTraded to New York Giants for Shortstop Art Fletcher and Pitcher Wilbur Hubbell, June 8, 1920.
bTraded with Outfielders Casey Stengel and Bill Cunningham to Boston Braves for Pitcher Joe Oeschger and Outfielder Billy Southworth, November, 1923.
cUnconditionally released, October 17, 1927; signed with Brooklyn Dodgers.
dReleased following 1929 season and signed by New York Giants as player-coach.

WORLD SERIES RECORD

Year Club	League	Pos.	G.	AB.	R.	H.	2B.	3B.	HR.	RBI.	B.A.	PO.	A.	E.	F.A.
1915—Philadelphia .... Nat.		SS	5	17	2	5	0	0	0	1	.294	13	10	1	.958
1921—New York .... Nat.		SS	8	33	3	5	1	0	0	3	.152	16	17	1	.971
1922—New York .... Nat.		SS	5	19	4	4	0	0	0	2	.211	9	17	1	.963
1923—New York .... Nat.		SS	6	24	1	2	0	0	0	1	.083	11	24	0	1.000
World Series Totals—4 Years			24	93	10	16	1	0	0	7	.172	49	68	3	.975

ERNEST (ERNIE) BANKS

Born January 31, 1931, at Dallas, Tex.

Height, 6.01. Weight, 186.

Threw and batted righthanded.

Holds major league records for most consecutive games played from start of career (424), September 17, 1953 through August 10, 1957; most home runs by shortstop, season (47), 1958.

Shares major league records for most games by first baseman, season (162), 1965; most sacrifice flies, game (3), June 2, 1961; most putouts by first baseman, nine-inning game (22), May 9, 1963.

Shares modern major league record for most triples, game (3), June 11, 1966.

Holds National League record for most grand slams, season (5), 1955.

Shares National League record for most years leading league in games (6).

Hit three home runs in a game, August 4, 1955; September 14, 1957; May 29, 1962, and June 9, 1963.

Named Outstanding National League Player by THE SPORTING NEWS, 1958-59.

Named Most Valuable Player, National League, 1958-59.

Named shortstop on THE SPORTING NEWS All-Star Major League Teams, 1955-58-59-60.

Named shortstop on THE SPORTING NEWS National League All-Star fielding team, 1960.

Player-coach, Chicago Cubs, 1967 through 1969; coach, Chicago Cubs, 1972-73; Cub organization instructor, batting and infield, 1974 through 1976.

Named to Hall of Fame, 1977.

Year Club	League	Pos.	G.	AB.	R.	H.	2B.	3B.	HR.	RBI.	B.A.	PO.	A.	E.	F.A.
1953—Chicago .... Nat.		SS	10	35	3	11	1	1	2	6	.314	19	33	1	.981
1954—Chicago .... Nat.		SS	●154	593	70	163	19	7	19	79	.275	312	475	34	.959
1955—Chicago .... Nat.		SS	●154	596	98	176	29	9	44	117	.295	290	482	22	★.972
1956—Chicago .... Nat.		SS	139	538	82	160	25	8	28	85	.297	279	357	25	.962
1957—Chicago .... Nat.		SS-3B	●156	594	113	169	34	6	43	102	.285	241	348	14	.977
1958—Chicago .... Nat.		SS	★154	★617	119	193	23	11	★47	★129	.313	292	468	●32	.960
1959—Chicago .... Nat.		SS	●155	589	97	179	25	6	45	★143	.304	271	★519	12	★.985
1960—Chicago .... Nat.		SS	★156	597	94	162	32	7	★41	117	.271	★283	★488	18	★.977
1961—Chicago .... Nat.		SS-OF-1B	138	511	75	142	22	4	29	80	.278	273	370	21	.968
1962—Chicago .... Nat.		★1B-3B	154	610	87	164	20	6	37	104	.269	★1462	★107	11	.993
1963—Chicago .... Nat.		1B	130	432	41	98	20	1	18	64	.227	1178	78	9	.993
1964—Chicago .... Nat.		1B	157	591	67	156	29	6	23	95	.264	★1565	★132	10	.994
1965—Chicago .... Nat.		1B	163	612	79	162	25	3	28	106	.265	★1682	93	15	.992
1966—Chicago .... Nat.		1B-3B	141	511	52	139	23	7	15	75	.272	1183	92	13	.990
1967—Chicago .... Nat.		1B	151	573	68	158	26	4	23	95	.276	★1383	★91	10	.993
1968—Chicago .... Nat.		1B	150	552	71	136	27	0	32	83	.246	1379	88	6	.996

Year Club	League	Pos.	G.	AB.	R.	H.	2B.	3B.	HR.	RBI.	B.A.	PO.	A.	E.	F.A.
1969—Chicago	Nat.	1B	155	565	60	143	19	2	23	106	.253	*1419	87	4	*.997
1970—Chicago	Nat.	1B	72	222	25	56	6	2	12	44	.252	528	35	4	.993
1971—Chicago	Nat.	1B	39	83	4	16	2	0	3	6	.193	167	12	0	1.000
Major League Totals—19 Years			2528	9421	1305	2583	407	90	512	1636	.274	14206	4355	261	.986

ALBERT J. (AL) BARLICK

Born April 2, 1915, at Springfield, Ill.

Height, 5.10½. Weight, 195.

Al Barlick was one of the loudest, most colorful and highly respected umpires in major league history—and he can probably thank a coal miner's strike for that.

Born on a farm in Springfield, Ill., on April 2, 1915, Barlick worked as a coal miner until a strike closed down the mines, forcing Barlick family members to seek odd jobs to make ends meet. Al found work umpiring sandlot baseball games—for $1 a game—in 1935 at Springfield.

He was impressive enough to earn a job in organized ball the following year. Barlick umpired in the Northeast Arkansas League in 1936, followed by two years in the Piedmont League and a year in the Eastern League. After beginning the 1940 season in the International League, Barlick was promoted to the National League in September to replace Bill Klem, who had taken ill.

Upon his promotion, the 25-year-old Barlick, one of the youngest umpires ever called up to the major leagues, accompanied his prospective partner, Lee Ballanfant, on a visit to Klem's hotel room. After being introduced to his replacement, Klem roared, "What did you say your name was?"

"Al Barlick," the youngster replied.

"Where did you come from?", Klem asked.

"The International League, sir," Barlick said.

"I never heard of you," bellowed Klem.

"I don't doubt that, Mr. Klem," Barlick answered.

But it didn't take long for Klem—or the rest of the baseball world—to find out about Al Barlick. Soon Klem was boasting that the youngster would become the second greatest umpire in history (behind him, of course).

"As soon as I talked to this boy, I knew we had something," Klem said.

Everyone in the park knew when Barlick was calling the balls and strikes. His booming voice quickly became his trademark. He umpired the first major league game he had ever witnessed. The contest provided one of the most embarrassing moments of his life.

"It was Ladies' Day and a good crowd was watching," Barlick recalled. "Right in the first inning I bent down to call a play, and I could hear my pants split from here to there. What a spot to be in. To make matters worse, I had hurried so to get there that I had brought along only this one suit.

"I didn't know what to do, but I called time and walked over to Lee Ballanfant, another umpire, and told him about it. Lee laughed so hard for five minutes I thought the same thing was going to happen to him. But he told me to go into the dressing room and get one of his. I've never been so embarrassed in my life."

Barlick began his first full season in the National League in 1941 and stayed there through the 1971 season, losing two years to Coast Guard duty during World War II and two more when he was sidelined by a heart ailment in the 1950s.

Following his retirement, Barlick became a National League umpire supervisor. He was named to the Hall of Fame in 1989.

EDWARD GRANT (ED) BARROW

Born May 10, 1868, near Springfield, Ill.

Died December 15, 1953, at Port Chester, N. Y.

The name of Ed Barrow was synonymous with the success of the New York Yankees for a quarter of a century. During his tenure as front-office boss, the Bombers became the scourge of both leagues, winning 14 American League pennants and ten World Series, five of them without the loss of a game.

An acquaintanceship he made in Pittsburgh with Harry Stevens, the caterer and scorecard man, helped Barrow get into baseball. The two formed a partnership and had the scoreboard and pop concessions at the Pirates' old Exposition Park, among other places. In 1894 Barrow took his first fling in baseball when he and Stevens backed the Wheeling (W. Va.) club of the Interstate League. Ed was manager as well as business manager.

When the Atlantic League was organized in December, 1895, Barrow acquired the Paterson (N. J.) franchise. One of the players he signed for his club was Honus Wagner, whom he later sold to Louisville (N.L.). Barrow was elected president of the Atlantic League in 1897 and headed the circuit three years.

In 1900 he bought a quarter interest in the Toronto club and became manager. After leading the team to a pennant in '02, he moved up to Detroit as pilot the next year. He also managed the Tigers part of '04 before resigning following a dispute with Frank J. Navin, then business manager and minority stockholder.

Barrow piloted Indianapolis and Montreal in 1905 and Toronto again in '06. Out of the game the next three years, he returned in December, 1910, as president of the Eastern League, which he subsequently renamed the International. He retained that position until 1918, when he became manager of the Boston Red Sox. Ed immediately led the club to another pennant. That same season he began the conversion of Babe Ruth, then an ace Red Sox pitcher, into an outfielder. In January, 1920, Red Sox Owner Harry Frazee sold Ruth to the Yankees for $125,000, and at the close of the '20 season Barrow left Boston to become business manager of the Yankees, succeeding Harry Sparrow, who had died.

In 1921, Barrow's first year with the club, the Yankees won their initial pennant, repeating in 1922-23. Later with the help of a farm system built by Barrow and his assistant, George Weiss, the Yankees developed into the most consistent pennant-winning organization in major league history. During Barrow's long reign as front-office chief, the Yankees had only three managers—Miller Huggins, Bob Shawkey for one year, 1930, and Joe McCarthy.

When Col. Jake Ruppert, owner of the club, died in 1939, Barrow became president. He continued in this position until January, 1945, when the Ruppert estate sold the club to Larry MacPhail, Dan Topping and Del Webb. Barrow then became chairman of the board, but relinquished the title two years later.

Barrow was named to the Hall of Fame as a manager-executive by the Committee on Veterans on September 28, 1953, less than three months before his death.

DONALD EDWARD (DON) BAYLOR

Born June 28, 1949, at Austin, Tex.

Height, 6.01. Weight, 210.

Threw and batted righthanded.

Holds major league record for most times hit by pitch, lifetime (267).

Shares major league records for most consecutive home runs (4), July 1, 2, 1975; most long hits, opening game of season (4), April 6, 1973; most times caught stealing, inning (2), June 15, 1974, ninth inning.

Shares modern major league record for most at-bats, nine-inning game (7), August 25, 1979.

Holds American League record for most times hit by pitcher, season (35), 1986.

Hit three home runs in a game, July 2, 1975.

Led American League in game-winning RBIs with 21 in 1982.

Led American League in sacrifice flies with 12 in 1978.

Led American League in being hit by pitch with 13 in 1973, 20 in 1976, 18 in 1978, 23 in 1984, 24 in 1985, 35 in 1986, 28 in 1987 and tied for lead with 13 in 1975.

Led International League in being hit by pitch with 19 in 1970 and 16 in 1971.

Led International League in total bases with 296 in 1970.

Led Texas League in being hit by pitch with 13 in 1969.

Led Appalachian League in stolen bases with 26, total bases with 135 and tied for lead in caught stealing with 6 in 1967.

Named American League Most Valuable Player by Baseball Writers' Association of America, 1979.

Named American League Player of the Year by THE SPORTING NEWS, 1979.

Named designated hitter on THE SPORTING NEWS American League All-Star Team, 1979, 1985 and 1986.

Named designated hitter on THE SPORTING NEWS American League Silver Slugger team, 1983, 1985 and 1986.

Named Appalachian League Player of the Year, 1967.

Named Minor League Player of the Year by THE SPORTING NEWS, 1970.

Year	Club	League	Pos.	G.	AB.	R.	H.	2B.	3B.	HR.	RBI.	B.A.	PO.	A.	E.	F.A.
1967—Bluefield	Appal.	OF	•67	246	50	*85	10	*8	8	47	*.346	106	5	5	.957
1968—Stockton	Calif.	OF	68	244	52	90	6	3	7	40	.369	135	3	7	.952
1968—Elmira	East.	OF	6	24	4	8	1	1	1	3	.333	10	1	0	1.000
1968—Rochester	Int.	OF	15	46	4	10	2	0	0	4	.217	29	1	4	.882
1969—Miami	Fla. St.	OF	17	56	19	21	5	4	3	24	.375	30	2	3	.914
1969—Dal.-Ft. Worth	Texas	OF	109	406	71	122	17	•10	11	57	.300	241	7	*13	.950
1970—Rochester	Int.	OF	•140	508	*127	166	*34	*15	22	107	.327	286	5	7	.977
1970—Baltimore	Amer.	OF	8	17	4	4	0	0	0	4	.235	15	0	0	1.000
1971—Rochester	Int.	OF	136	492	104	154	•31	10	20	95	.313	210	4	9	.960
1971—Baltimore	Amer.	OF	1	2	0	0	0	0	0	1	.000	4	0	0	1.000
1972—Baltimore	Amer.	OF-1B	102	320	33	81	13	3	11	38	.253	206	4	5	.977
1973—Baltimore	Amer.	OF-1B	118	405	64	116	20	4	11	51	.286	228	10	6	.975
1974—Baltimore	Amer.	OF-1B	137	489	66	133	22	1	10	59	.272	260	2	5	.981
1975—Baltimore†	Amer.	OF-1B	145	524	79	148	21	6	25	76	.282	286	8	5	.983
1976—Oakland‡	Amer.	OF-1B	157	595	85	147	25	1	15	68	.247	781	45	12	.986
1977—California	Amer.	OF-1B	154	561	87	141	27	0	25	75	.251	280	16	7	.977
1978—California	Amer.	OF-1B	158	591	103	151	26	0	34	99	.255	194	9	6	.971
1979—California	Amer.	OF-1B	•162	628	*120	186	33	3	36	*139	.296	203	3	5	.976
1980—California	Amer.	OF	90	340	39	85	12	2	5	51	.250	119	4	4	.969
1981—California	Amer.	1B-OF	103	377	52	90	18	1	17	66	.239	38	3	0	1.000
1982—California§	Amer.	DH	157	608	80	160	24	1	24	93	.263	0	0	0	.000
1983—New York	Amer.	OF-1B	144	534	82	162	33	3	21	85	.303	23	2	1	.962
1984—New York	Amer.	OF	134	493	84	129	29	1	27	89	.262	8	0	1	.889

Year Club League	Pos.	G.	AB.	R.	H.	2B.	3B.	HR.	RBI.	B.A.	PO.	A.	E.	F.A.
1985—New York x .... Amer.	DH	142	477	70	110	24	1	23	91	.231	0	0	0	.000
1986—Boston.................. Amer.	1B-OF	160	585	93	139	23	1	31	94	.238	71	4	1	.987
1987—Bos.y-Minn.z.......... Amer.	DH	128	388	67	95	9	0	16	63	.245	0	0	0	.000
1988—Oakland a .... Amer.	DH	92	264	28	58	7	0	7	34	.220	0	0	0	.000
Major League Totals—19 Years		2292	8198	1236	2135	366	28	338	1276	.260	2716	110	58	.980

Selected by Baltimore Orioles' organization in 2nd round of free-agent draft, June 6, 1967.

†Traded with Pitchers Mike Torrez and Paul Mitchell to Oakland Athletics for Outfielder Reggie Jackson and Pitchers Ken Holtzman and Bill Van Bommel, April 2, 1976.

‡Played out option year and granted free agency, November 1, 1976; signed as free agent by California Angels, November 16, 1976.

§Granted free agency, November 10, 1982; signed by New York Yankees, December 1, 1982.

xTraded to Boston Red Sox for Designated Hitter Mike Easler, March 28, 1986.

yTraded to Minnesota Twins for a player to be named later, August 31, 1987; Boston Red Sox acquired Pitcher Enrique Rios to complete deal, December 18, 1987.

zReleased, December 21, 1987; signed by Oakland Athletics, February 9, 1988.

aGranted free agency, November 4, 1988.

CHAMPIONSHIP SERIES RECORD

Holds major league record for most runs batted in, series (10), 1982.

Shares major league records for most grand slams, game (1) and runs batted in, inning (4), October 9, 1982, eighth inning; most times hit by pitch, series (2), 1986.

Holds American League record for longest batting streak, lifetime (12 games), October 8, 1982 through October 11, 1987.

Shares American League record for most times hit by pitch, lifetime (3).

Holds record for most runs batted in, series (10), 1982.

Shares records for most grand slams, game (1), October 9, 1982; most runs batted in, inning (4), October 9, 1982, eight inning.

Holds record for longest consecutive-game hitting streak (12 games), October 8, 1982 through October 11, 1987.

Shares American League record for most runs batted in, game (5), October 5, 1982.

Year Club League	Pos.	G.	AB.	R.	H.	2B.	3B.	HR.	RBI.	B.A.	PO.	A.	E.	F.A.
1973—Baltimore .... Amer.	OF-PH	4	11	3	3	0	0	0	1	.273	7	0	0	1.000
1974—Baltimore .... Amer.	OF	4	15	0	4	0	0	0	0	.267	9	0	0	1.000
1979—California .... Amer.	DH-OF	4	16	2	3	0	0	1	2	.188	4	0	0	1.000
1982—California .... Amer.	DH	5	17	2	5	1	1	1	10	.294	0	0	0	.000
1986—Boston .... Amer.	DH	7	26	6	9	3	0	1	2	.346	0	0	0	.000
1987—Minnesota .... Amer.	PH-DH	2	5	0	2	0	0	0	1	.400	0	0	0	.000
1988—Oakland................. Amer.	DH	2	6	0	0	0	0	0	1	.000	0	0	0	.000
Championship Series Totals—7 Years.....		28	96	13	26	4	1	3	17	.271	20	0	0	1.000

WORLD SERIES RECORD

Shares record for most at-bats, inning (2), October 17, 1987, fourth inning.

Year Club League	Pos.	G.	AB.	R.	H.	2B.	3B.	HR.	RBI.	B.A.	PO.	A.	E.	F.A.
1986—Boston..................... Amer.	DH-PH	4	11	1	2	1	0	0	1	.182	0	0	0	.000
1987—Minnesota .... Amer.	DH-PH	5	13	3	5	0	0	1	3	.385	0	0	0	.000
1988—Oakland................. Amer.	PH	1	1	0	0	0	0	0	0	.000	0	0	0	.000
World Series Totals—3 Years		10	25	4	7	1	0	1	4	.280	0	0	0	.000

CLARENCE HOWETH (GINGER) BEAUMONT

Born July 23, 1876, at Rochester, Wis.

Died April 10, 1956, at Burlington, Wis.

Height, 5.08. Weight, 190.

Threw right and batted lefthanded.

Year Club League	Pos.	G.	AB.	R.	H.	2B.	3B.	HR.	SB.	B.A.	PO.	A.	E.	F.A.
1898—Milwaukee............... West.	OF	24	96	24	34	....	....	....	11	.354	43	3	6	.885
1899—Pittsburgh.............. Nat.	OF	104	425	87	149	15	7	3	32	.351	227	24	20	.926
1900—Pittsburgh.............. Nat.	OF	138	566	107	160	14	9	5	19	.283	270	9	15	.949
1901—Pittsburgh.............. Nat.	OF	132	555	118	182	14	6	8	32	.328	289	7	19	.939
1902—Pittsburgh.............. Nat.	OF	131	544	101	*194	21	6	0	33	*.357	260	15	8	.972
1903—Pittsburgh.............. Nat.	OF	•141	*613	*137	*209	30	6	7	23	.341	258	15	15	.948
1904—Pittsburgh.............. Nat.	OF	153	*615	97	*185	12	12	3	28	.301	287	14	10	.968
1905—Pittsburgh.............. Nat.	OF	97	384	60	126	12	8	3	21	.328	200	12	6	.972
1906—Pittsburgh(a)........ Nat.	OF	78	310	48	82	9	3	2	1	.265	148	6	9	.944
1907—Boston..................... Nat.	OF	149	580	67	*187	19	14	4	25	.322	296	30	13	.962
1908—Boston..................... Nat.	OF	121	476	66	127	20	6	2	13	.267	259	17	10	.965
1909—Boston(b)................ Nat.	OF	111	407	35	107	11	4	0	12	.263	234	15	8	.969
1910—Chicago.................. Nat.	OF	56	172	30	46	5	1	2	4	.267	107	5	5	.957
1911—St. Paul.................. A. A.	OF	74	233	35	58	5	5	2	8	.249	117	10	5	.962
Major League Totals—12 Years...............		1411	5647	953	1754	182	82	39	243	.311	2835	169	138	.956

aTraded with second baseman Claude Ritchey to Boston Braves for infielder Ed Abbaticchio, December, 1906.
bTraded to Chicago Cubs for pitcher Fred Liese, February, 1910.

WORLD SERIES RECORD

Year Club	League	Pos.	G.	AB.	R.	H.	2B.	3B.	HR.	SB.	B.A.	PO.	A.	E.	F.A.
1903—Pittsburgh............	Nat.	OF	8	34	6	9	0	1	0	2	.265	22	0	0	1.000
1910—Chicago.................	Nat.	PH	3	2	1	0	0	0	0	0	.000	0	0	0	.000
World Series Totals—2 Years			11	36	7	9	0	1	0	2	.250	22	0	0	1.000

JACOB PETER (JAKE) BECKLEY

Born August 4, 1867, at Hannibal, Mo.

Died June 25, 1918, at Kansas City, Mo.

Height, 6.01. Weight, 180.

Threw and batted lefthanded.

Holds major league records for most games (2,368), putouts (23,696) and chances accepted (25,000) by first baseman, lifetime.

Shares major league records for most years leading league in putouts (6) and chances accepted (6).

Hit three home runs in a game, September 26, 1897, first game.

Manager, Kansas City, American Association, 1908-09; Bartlesville, Western Association, 1910; umpire, Federal League, 1913.

Named to Hall of Fame, 1971.

Year Club	League	Pos.	G.	AB.	R.	H.	2B.	3B.	HR.	SB.	B.A.	PO.	A.	E.	F.A.
1886—Leavenworth........	West.	1B	....	305	65	104	....	....	....	....	.341	147	171	54	.855
1887—Leav.-Lincoln........	West.	1B	....	526	....	211	....	....	....	....	.401	957	29	47	.955
1888—St. Louis.................	W. A.	1B	34	145	23	41	....	....	....	17	.283	342	6	7	.980
1888—Pittsburgh.............	Nat.	1B	71	283	35	97	16	3	1	20	.343	744	19	16	.979
1889—Pittsburgh.............	Nat.	1B	123	522	92	157	22	10	9	11	.301	1236	53	24	●.982
1890—Pittsburgh.............	Play	1B	121	517	109	168	●41	20	9	19	.325	1258	55	27	.980
1891—Pittsburgh.............	Nat.	1B	129	535	91	156	20	★20	4	17	.292	1220	84	23	.983
1892—Pittsburgh.............	Nat.	1B	152	603	102	151	21	19	10	40	.250	★1524	★127	32	.981
1893—Pittsburgh.............	Nat.	1B	131	497	108	161	23	19	5	24	.324	1360	★96	22	.985
1894—Pittsburgh.............	Nat.	1B	132	534	122	184	32	19	7	20	.345	★1236	★82	31	.977
1895—Pittsburgh.............	Nat.	1B	131	536	105	174	30	20	5	19	.325	★1375	57	31	.979
1896—Pitts.-N.Y.............	Nat.	1B	99	395	79	106	15	10	9	19	.268	941	51	16	.984
1897—N.Y.-Cinn.	Nat.	1B	114	437	84	142	19	11	8	22	.325	994	58	23	.979
1898—Cincinnati.............	Nat.	1B	116	458	86	137	17	13	3	7	.299	1172	54	18	★.986
1899—Cincinnati.............	Nat.	1B	135	519	87	173	23	18	3	18	.333	1294	71	18	★.987
1900—Cincinnati.............	Nat.	1B	138	559	99	192	26	9	2	22	.343	★1388	92	31	.979
1901—Cincinnati.............	Nat.	P-1B	140	590	80	177	●39	13	3	6	.300	1353	69	★32	.978
1902—Cincinnati.............	Nat.	1B	129	532	82	176	21	7	5	16	.331	★1275	69	★23	.983
1903—Cincinnati.............	Nat.	1B	119	459	85	150	29	10	2	23	.327	1127	78	30	.976
1904—St. Louis...............	Nat.	1B	142	551	72	179	22	9	1	17	.325	★1526	64	20	.988
1905—St. Louis...............	Nat.	1B	134	514	48	147	20	10	1	12	.286	1442	69	28	.982
1906—St. Louis...............	Nat.	1B	85	320	29	79	16	6	0	3	.247	928	43	13	.987
1907—St. Louis...............	Nat.	1B	32	115	6	24	3	0	0	0	.209	303	13	4	.988
1907—Kansas City..........	A. A.	1B	100	378	65	138	10	4	1	12	.365	1118	52	18	.985
1908—Kansas City..........	A. A.	1B	136	496	66	134	19	5	1	13	.270	1432	87	15	.990
1909—Kansas City..........	A. A.	1B	113	428	41	120	16	3	1	12	.280	1186	57	21	.983
1910—Bartlesville...........	W. A.	1B	70	249	21	64	15	0	0	13	.257	561	26	3	.995
1910—Topeka.................	West.	1B	63	233	19	60	11	0	1	1	.258	565	35	13	.979
1911—Hannibal...............	C. A.	1B	98	355	50	100	7	4	0	22	.282	917	45	10	.990
National League Totals—19 Years.........			2252	8959	1492	2762	414	226	78	316	.308	22438	1249	435	.982
Players League Totals—1 Year...............			121	517	109	168	41	20	9	19	.325	1258	55	27	.980
Major League Totals—20 Years.............			2373	9476	1601	2930	455	246	87	335	.309	23696	1304	462	.982

DAVID GUS (BUDDY) BELL

Born August 27, 1951, at Pittsburgh, Pa.

Height, 6.03. Weight, 200.

Threw and batted righthanded.

Son of Gus Bell, former major league outfielder.

Led American League in sacrifice flies with 10 in 1981.
Led American League third basemen in total chances with 495 in 1978, 361 in 1981, 540 in 1982 and 523 in 1983.
Led American League third basemen in assists with 364 in 1979 and 281 in 1981.
Led American League third basemen in putouts with 144 and double plays with 44 in 1973.
Tied for American League lead in game-winning RBIs with 16 in 1979.
Tied for American League lead in double plays by third basemen with 30 in 1978.
Led Gulf Coast League second basemen in double plays with 26 in 1969.
Named third baseman on THE SPORTING NEWS American League All-Star Team, 1981 and 1984.
Named third baseman on THE SPORTING NEWS American League All-Star fielding team, 1979 through 1984.
Named third baseman on THE SPORTING NEWS American League Silver Slugger team, 1984.

Year	Club	League	Pos.	G.	AB.	R.	H.	2B.	3B.	HR.	RBI.	B.A.	PO.	A.	E.	F.A.
1969—Sarasota Indians	...Gulf C.		2B	51	170	18	39	4	●3	3	24	.229	119	108	7	★.970
1970—Sumter	W. Car.		3B-2B-SS	121	442	81	117	19	3	12	75	.265	116	189	27	.919
1971—Wichita	A. A.		★3-2-S-O	129	470	65	136	23	1	11	59	.289	★139	203	16	.955
1972—Cleveland	Amer.		OF-3B	132	466	49	119	21	1	9	36	.255	284	23	3	.990
1973—Cleveland	Amer.		3B-OF	156	631	86	169	23	7	14	59	.268	146	363	22	.959
1974—Cleveland	Amer.		3B	116	423	51	111	15	1	7	46	.262	112	274	15	.963
1975—Cleveland	Amer.		3B	153	553	66	150	20	4	10	59	.271	★146	330	25	.950
1976—Cleveland	Amer.		3B-1B	159	604	75	170	26	2	7	60	.281	109	331	20	.957
1977—Cleveland	Amer.		3B-OF	129	479	64	140	23	4	11	64	.292	134	253	16	.960
1978—Cleveland†	Amer.		3B	142	556	71	157	27	8	6	62	.282	125	★355	15	.970
1979—Texas	Amer.		3B-SS	●162	★670	89	200	42	3	18	101	.299	147	429	17	.971
1980—Texas	Amer.		★3B-SS	129	490	76	161	24	4	17	83	.329	125	282	8	★.981
1981—Texas	Amer.		3B-SS	97	360	44	106	16	1	10	64	.294	67	284	14	.962
1982—Texas	Amer.		★3B-SS	148	537	62	159	27	2	13	67	.296	★131	397	13	★.976
1983—Texas	Amer.		3B	156	618	75	171	35	3	14	66	.277	123	★383	17	.967
1984—Texas	Amer.		3B	148	553	88	174	36	5	11	83	.315	129	323	●20	.958
1985—Texas‡	Amer.		3B	84	313	33	74	13	3	4	32	.236	70	192	16	.942
1985—Cincinnati	Nat.		3B	67	247	28	54	15	2	6	36	.219	54	105	9	.946
1986—Cincinnati	Nat.		3B-2B	155	568	89	158	29	3	20	75	.278	105	291	10	.975
1987—Cincinnati	Nat.		3B	143	522	74	148	19	2	17	70	.284	93	241	7	★.979
1988—Cinc.§-Hou.x	Nat.		3B-1B	95	323	27	78	10	1	7	40	.241	88	140	15	.938
1989—Texas y	Amer.		3B-1B	34	82	4	15	4	0	0	3	.183	10	13	0	1.000
American League Totals—15 Years				1945	7335	933	2076	352	48	151	885	.283	1853	4231	221	.965
National League Totals—4 Years				460	1660	218	438	73	8	50	221	.264	340	777	41	.965
Major League Totals—18 Years				2405	8995	1151	2514	425	56	201	1106	.279	2193	5008	262	.965

Selected by Cleveland Indians' organization in 16th round of free-agent draft, June 5, 1969.

†Traded to Texas Rangers for Third Baseman Toby Harrah, December 8, 1978.

‡Traded to Cincinnati Reds for Outfielder Duane Walker and a player to be named later, July 19, 1985; Texas Rangers' organization acquired Pitcher Jeff Russell to complete deal, July 23, 1985.

§Traded to Houston Astros for a player to be named later, June 19, 1988; Cincinnati Reds' organization acquired Pitcher Carl Grovom to complete deal, October 20, 1988.

xReleased, December 21, 1988; signed by Texas Rangers, January 9, 1989.

yOn voluntarily retired list, June 24, 1989; signed by Cleveland Indians to work in minor league development.

JAMES THOMAS (COOL PAPA) BELL

Born May 17, 1903, at Starkville, Miss.

Height, 6.00. Weight, 143.

Threw left and batted right and lefthanded.

Cool Papa Bell is rated by most observers of both the white and Negro major leagues as the fastest base runner ever to wear a professional baseball uniform. He was such a student of pitching and on-base moves that situations became patent to him. A prime, documented example occurred when he played, at 45 years of age, in an exhibition game in California against major leaguers on an all-star type club, common in those days of post-season and winter barnstorming. The date: October 24, 1948, at Los Angeles, Calif.

To set the stage, Bell had been managing a second Kansas City Monarchs team, on which the Monarchs placed their young talent for Bell to develop. His pitcher for a while was Satchel Paige, who was nursing an ailing arm after chilling it in a cool breeze while playing Caribbean ball. After the season was over, Paige, who then had joined Cleveland, told Bell he'd help him make some money, on a percentage basis, from the sale of young players. But Paige was going out to the West Coast to pick up some fresh money by barnstorming and he asked Bell to come along, bring some of his best young players and play center field whenever he (Satch) pitched.

Bell begged off, protesting that he was out of playing condition, 45 years old, and working out only while he was coaching the kids and playing occasional league and World Series ball when needed by the Monarchs. That meant nothing to Satch, so Bell reluctantly agreed.

Paige headed westward first to line up some games and firm up the ones he already had scheduled. On meeting teammate Bob Lemon, Cleveland's pitching star, Satch told him, "I've got an old man, older than I am, I'm going to bring out to play against you and he's going to make a damn fool out of you." Lemon vowed no one would do that to him.

Bell, three years older than Paige, arrived in Los Angeles before the game. He had no throwing warmup at all. Cool Papa had to go into the outfield to scamper around and loosen up his aching bones. He told Satch to bat him low in the lineup because he was going to leave the game the minute Satch did. Bell batted eighth.

Facing Lemon the first time, Bell punched a low strike into right center for two bases following two brushback pitches. But the second time he faced Lemon, Bell lined out a single. With Paige up and Bell on first, they worked a sacrifice.

Paige dropped the ball down perfectly and the third baseman, pitcher, first baseman and catcher all converged plateward. Bell had watched Lemon on television and at Sportsman's Park in St. Louis many times and concentrated on his man-on-base motion, as all good base stealers do. He noticed that Lemon, once he had checked the base runner with a hard look, never looked back again. On the bunt, Bell saw the look and, when Lemon turned plateward, he took off for second which he made without a throw on him. But his trained eye noticed that third base was uncovered because the third baseman had failed to retreat after the bunt, and he kept on running.

Roy Partee, Red Sox and Browns catcher, was handling Lemon. He saw Bell heading for third unmolested and ran toward the bag trying to head him off. Bell peeked at Partee waving the ball and saw past him to the plate, which also was uncovered. So Bell coolly rounded third, eluded Partee easily and flew across home plate without a play being made on him the whole trip around the bases. Partee also had tried to call time out as Bell passed him and headed for home, but the umpire said there was no way he could do it with the ball in play.

Lemon was fit to be tied, but old Cool Papa had done it, aching muscles and all.

This incident bears out the mark of a true professional—one who has all his wits about him while in the heat of competition. This is the residue of years of practice, study and performance. When blessed with blinding speed, a consistently high batting average in Negro competition and a trigger-quick brain, all the elements for stardom were present. Then when you add the high level of morality he maintained and his constant care of his body by a sensible intake of food and abstinence from drinking, you can understand better how James (Cool Papa) Bell remained the scourge of catchers, pitchers and infielders throughout most of his 29 years as a professional player.

Bell is most proud of the fact his center field-expertise was recognized by the former master of the middle garden, Oscar Charleston. Oscar, playing center field for the Indianapolis ABCs at the time, saw the handwriting on the wall one day while both were out in center field in practice. Bell was pitching for San Juan at the time and played little in the outfield. Charleston had fungoes hit out there. Whoever got the ball first would catch it. Bell was there, catching it and in the act of throwing the ball back to the infield by the time Oscar arrived at the spot. This was the first time Bell had a chance to show he also could rank with the best center fielders of the time.

Cool Papa was born in Mississippi and played sandlot and semi-pro ball there, always competing with and against adults, never against youngsters his own age. He was a pitcher then, primarily, with a good curve and a devilish knuckler. Only his sister could hold his knuckler. He also played in the outfield and was rated a top versatile athlete. Four of his brothers had gone to St. Louis and played on the Compton Hills, a strong local semi-pro club, and they urged James to join them. At age 15, Bell went to St. Louis and then there were five Bells in action. The catchers refused to call for his knuckler because they were getting split fingers trying to corral it. Bell could make the knuckler break three ways, but they liked it two ways.

On May 3, 1922, Bell, two weeks shy of his 19th birthday, signed his first professional contract with the St. Louis Stars of the National League's Western Division. He signed at the urging of his older brother Lewis. James didn't have any wish to play professional ball, but his brother wanted him to sign so that he could say proudly he had a brother who played major league professional baseball.

Bell starred for the St. Louis club for 10 seasons, the first two of which were spent as a part-time pitcher. That first season, 1922, on a trip to Chicago to play the Giants, Bell discovered his reputation for speed had preceded him. When the Stars arrived, Rube Foster, organizer of the Negro professional leagues when "league" ball was revived in 1920 and owner-manager of the Chicago Giants, challenged Bell to race the fastest man in the league up to that time, his own Jimmy Lyons. Bell won handily and Foster purchased for Bell the best pair of spikes made then, a $21.50 (Spalding) kangaroo beauty.

In his first season of pro ball, Bell picked up the nickname of Cool Papa. "I had become 17 just 14 days after signing my contract and the players said I looked cool out there, so they called me Cool. The manager, Bob Gatewood, said that was not enough and added Papa. That's how I became Cool Papa."

It should be noted here that Cool Papa had a brother, Fred, two years older, who was an outstanding pitcher. He played about seven years and had the most fabulous throwing arm anyone ever saw. He could, in the opinion of Cool Papa, who is more straight-laced honest than a flock of angels, pitch faster than Satchel Paige at his best. Fred, six foot and rangy, pitched for Oscar Charleston on the Harrisburg (Pa.) Giants.

As the Depression dried up Negro league cash sources, the Pittsburgh Crawfords persuaded Bell to play for them in the Negro Eastern League, the other division. Cool Papa starred for them and then joined the Pittsburgh Homestead Grays, where he saw the younger Josh Gibson and Buck Leonard grow in stature.

As Leonard said, "Cool Papa was a veteran by that time, 1933, but he still could fly, still could run those bases like no one else and catch balls all over the outfield. He had a touch of arthritis by then and would get all tuckered out after a doubleheader, but he would recover fast and fly some more."

Then Leonard added, "Cool Papa also was our resident doctor—with all sorts of remedies for aches, pains, coughs and colds and even injuries. He was so doggoned talented, he even could shave while the bus was moving."

Bell was rated a solid .350 hitter and even gave away some of his percentage points to assure younger blacks the chance to be batting champions and thus rate a better shot at the white major leagues. That also included Bell giving up some batting championships of his own.

Cool Papa did some scouting after his playing and managing days were over, but his total reward (for Ernie Banks) was a basket of fruit. He became an employee of the City of St. Louis, working in City Hall until his retirement.

He still looks sharp—tall, lean, proud and vibrant. His proudest possession is his Hall of Fame ring.

"We just felt it wasn't the right time when we played," Cool Papa said on his visit to THE SPORTING NEWS, in 1979. "They said they'd sign a colored player when they found one good enough, and we kept on beating them regularly, out-hitting them and out-stealing them, but they signed nobody. That's why we knew it wasn't the right time yet. We knew it was coming, but we didn't know when. It was too late for me, but thank God I've lived for the day when I made the Hall of Fame. And that's a pure gift from white big league baseball and I appreciate it. And I thank Ted Williams for starting it all with his kind words the day he, too, entered the Hall of Fame."

Named to Hall of Fame, 1974.

—DID YOU KNOW—

That Johnny Bench, Cincinnati's Hall of Fame catcher, is the only player in baseball history to belt three home runs in All-Star Game, League Championship Series and World Series competition?

JOHNNY LEE BENCH

Born December 7, 1947, at Oklahoma City, Okla.
Height, 6.01. Weight, 210.
Threw and batted righthanded.

Holds major league records for most games by catcher, rookie season (154), 1968; most home runs by catcher, lifetime (327).

Shares major league records for most consecutive seasons leading league in sacrifice flies (2); fewest passed balls, season, 100 or more games (0), 1975; most bases on balls, game (5), July 22, 1979; most consecutive years by catcher, with 100 or more games (13).

Holds National League record for most years by catcher, with 100 or more games (13).

National League records for most home runs, five consecutive games (7), May 30 through June 3, 1972; most home runs through July 31 (36), 1970; most seasons leading league in sacrifice flies (3); most doubles by catcher, season (40), 1968.

Hit three home runs in a game, July 26, 1970, May 9, 1973 and May 29, 1980.

Led National League in total bases with 315 in 1974.

Led National League in sacrifice flies with 11 in 1970, 12 in 1972 and tied for lead with 10 in 1973.

Led National League in intentional bases on balls received with 23 in 1972.

Led National League catchers in putouts with 651, total chances with 713 and fielding percentage with .997 in 1976.

Led National League catchers in double plays with 16 in 1974.

Led National League in passed balls with 18 in 1968.

Led International League catchers in assists with 70 in 1967.

Named Major League Player of the Year by THE SPORTING NEWS, 1970.

Named National League Player of the Year by THE SPORTING NEWS, 1970.

Named National League Most Valuable Player by Baseball Writers' Association of America, 1970 and 1972.

Named catcher on THE SPORTING NEWS National League All-Star Team, 1968, 1969, 1970, 1972, 1973, 1974 and 1975.

Named catcher on THE SPORTING NEWS National League All-Star fielding team, 1968 through 1977.

Named National League Rookie Player of the Year by THE SPORTING NEWS, 1968.

Named National League Rookie of the Year by Baseball Writers' Association of America, 1968.

Named Minor League Player of the Year by THE SPORTING NEWS, 1967.

Named Carolina League Player of the Year, 1966.

Named to Hall of Fame, 1989.

Year	Club	League	Pos.	G.	AB.	R.	H.	2B.	3B.	HR.	RBI.	B.A.	PO.	A.	E.	F.A.
1965—Tampa	Fla. St.	C-OF	68	214	29	53	13	1	2	35	.248	415	40	6	.987
1966—Peninsula	Carol.	C	98	350	59	103	16	0	22	68	.294	692	●87	⋆17	.979
1966—Buffalo	Int.	C	1	0	0	0	0	0	0	0	.000	2	0	0	1.000
1967—Buffalo	Int.	C-3-O-1	98	344	39	89	17	2	23	68	.259	577	82	13	.981
1967—Cincinnati	Nat.	C	26	86	7	14	3	1	1	6	.163	175	16	1	.995
1968—Cincinnati	Nat.	C	154	564	67	155	40	2	15	82	.275	⋆942	⋆102	9	.991
1969—Cincinnati	Nat.	C	148	532	83	156	23	1	26	90	.293	793	76	7	.992
1970—Cincinnati	Nat.	C-O-1-3	158	605	97	177	35	4	⋆45	⋆148	.293	854	78	15	.984
1971—Cincinnati	Nat.	C-O-1-3	149	562	80	134	19	2	27	61	.238	735	67	10	.988
1972—Cincinnati	Nat.	C-O-1-3	147	538	87	145	22	2	⋆40	⋆125	.270	791	63	10	.988
1973—Cincinnati	Nat.	C-O-1-3	152	557	83	141	17	3	25	104	.253	757	63	6	.993
1974—Cincinnati	Nat.	C-3B-1B	160	621	108	174	38	2	33	⋆129	.280	794	123	9	.990
1975—Cincinnati	Nat.	C-OF-1B	142	530	83	150	39	1	28	110	.283	646	52	8	.989
1976—Cincinnati	Nat.	C-OF-1B	135	465	62	109	24	1	16	74	.234	655	60	4	.994
1977—Cincinnati	Nat.	C-O-1-3	142	494	67	136	34	2	31	109	.275	735	69	11	.987
1978—Cincinnati	Nat.	C-1B-OF	120	393	52	102	17	1	23	73	.260	680	53	9	.988
1979—Cincinnati	Nat.	C-1B	130	464	73	128	19	0	22	80	.276	632	69	10	.986
1980—Cincinnati	Nat.	C	114	360	52	90	12	0	24	68	.250	505	39	5	.991
1981—Cincinnati	Nat.	1B-C	52	178	14	55	8	0	8	25	.309	375	28	7	.983
1982—Cincinnati†	Nat.	3B-1B-C	119	399	44	103	16	0	13	38	.258	108	159	19	.934
1983—Cincinnati†	Nat.	3-1-C-O	110	310	32	79	15	2	12	54	.255	292	74	10	.973
Major League Totals—17 Years			2158	7658	1091	2048	381	24	389	1376	.267	10469	1191	150	.987

Selected by Cincinnati Reds' organization in 2nd round of free-agent draft, June 21, 1965.

†On voluntarily retired list, October 19, 1983.

CHAMPIONSHIP SERIES RECORD

Year	Club	League	Pos.	G.	AB.	R.	H.	2B.	3B.	HR.	RBI.	B.A.	PO.	A.	E.	F.A.
1970—Cincinnati	Nat.	C	3	9	2	2	0	0	1	1	.222	20	3	0	1.000
1972—Cincinnati	Nat.	C	5	18	3	6	1	1	1	2	.333	28	3	1	.969
1973—Cincinnati	Nat.	C	5	19	1	5	2	0	1	1	.263	31	2	0	1.000
1975—Cincinnati	Nat.	C	3	13	1	1	0	0	0	0	.077	18	4	0	1.000
1976—Cincinnati	Nat.	C	3	12	3	4	1	0	1	1	.333	11	4	0	1.000
1979—Cincinnati	Nat.	C	3	12	1	3	0	1	1	1	.250	17	2	0	1.000
Championship Series Totals—6 Years			22	83	11	21	4	2	5	6	.253	125	18	1	.993

Year	Club	League	Pos.	G.	AB.	R.	H.	2B.	3B.	HR.	RBI.	B.A.	PO.	A.	E.	F.A.
1970—Cincinnati		Nat.	C	5	19	3	4	0	0	1	3	.211	36	3	0	1.000
1972—Cincinnati		Nat.	C	7	23	4	6	1	0	1	1	.261	41	7	1	.980
1975—Cincinnati		Nat.	C	7	29	5	6	2	0	1	4	.207	44	6	0	1.000
1976—Cincinnati		Nat.	C	4	15	4	8	1	1	2	6	.533	18	2	0	1.000
World Series Totals—4 Years				23	86	16	24	4	1	5	14	.279	139	18	1	.994

CHARLES ALBERT (CHIEF) BENDER

Born May 5, 1884, at Brainerd, Minn.

Died May 22, 1954, at Philadelphia, Pa.

Height, 6.02. Weight, 185.

Threw and batted righthanded.

Pitched 4-0 no-hit victory against Cleveland May 12, 1910, at Philadelphia; pitched 3-0 no-hit victory against Bridgeport, August 19, 1920.

Manager, Richmond, Virginia League, 1919; New Haven, Eastern League, 1920-21; Reading, International League, 1922; coach, Chicago White Sox, 1925-26; manager, Johnstown, Middle Atlantic League, 1927; coached at U.S. Naval Academy, 1928; coach, New York Giants, 1931; manager, Wilmington, Inter-State League, 1940; Newport News, Virginia League, 1941; scout, Philadelphia Athletics, 1945; manager, Savannah, Sally League, 1946; scout, Philadelphia Athletics, 1947 through 1950; coach, Philadelphia Athletics, 1951-53.

Named to Hall of Fame, 1953.

Year	Club	League	G.	IP.	W.	L.	Pct.	H.	R.	ER.	SO.	BB.	ERA.
1903—Philadelphia		Amer.	36	270	17	15	.531	233	116	....	122	67	......
1904—Philadelphia		Amer.	29	205	10	11	.476	174	66	....	148	59	......
1905—Philadelphia		Amer.	35	230	18	11	.621	199	105	....	142	83	......
1906—Philadelphia		Amer.	36	240	15	10	.600	211	96	....	159	48	......
1907—Philadelphia		Amer.	33	222	16	8	.667	183	72	....	125	31	......
1908—Philadelphia		Amer.	18	139	8	9	.471	121	48	....	85	21	......
1909—Philadephia		Amer.	34	250	18	8	.692	196	68	....	162	45	......
1910—Philadelphia		Amer.	30	250	23	5	★.821	182	63	....	155	47	......
1911—Philadelphia		Amer.	31	216	17	5	★.773	198	66	....	114	58	......
1912—Philadelphia		Amer.	27	171	13	8	.619	169	63	....	90	33	......
1913—Philadelphia		Amer.	48	238	21	10	.667	208	78	58	135	59	2.19
1914—Philadelphia		Amer.	28	179	17	3	★.850	159	49	45	107	55	2.26
1915—Baltimore		Federal	26	179	4	16	.200	198	101	85	90	38	4.27
1916—Philadelphia		Nat.	27	123	7	7	.500	137	71	51	43	34	3.73
1917—Philadelphia		Nat.	20	113	8	2	.800	84	24	21	43	26	1.67
1918—		(Voluntarily retired—worked in shipyards)											
1919—Richmond		Va.	34	★280	★29	2	★.935	209	53	....	★195	22	......
1920—New Haven		East.	★47	★324	★25	12	.676	256	104	70	252	71	1.94
1921—New Haven		East.	36	196	13	7	.650	168	70	42	131	59	1.93
1922—Reading		Inter.	30	183	8	13	.381	172	76	49	88	33	2.42
1923—Baltimore		Inter.	18	93	6	3	.667	109	65	52	44	30	5.03
1924—New Haven		East.	12	91	6	4	.600	94	38	31	55	18	3.07
1925—Chicago		Amer.	1	1	0	0	.000	1	2	2	0	1	18.00
1927—Johnstown		Mid. Atlantic	18	108	7	3	.700	74	18	16	39	13	1.33
American League Totals—13 Years			386	2611	193	103	.652	2234	982	....	1544	607	......
National League Totals—2 Years			47	236	15	9	.625	221	95	72	86	60	2.75
Major League Totals—15 Years			433	2847	208	112	.650	2455	987	....	1630	667	......

WORLD SERIES RECORDS

Year	Club	League	G.	IP.	W.	L.	Pct.	H.	R.	ER.	SO.	BB.	ERA.
1905—Philadelphia		Amer.	2	17	1	1	.500	9	2	2	13	6	1.06
1910—Philadelphia		Amer.	2	18⅔	1	1	.500	12	5	4	14	4	1.93
1911—Philadelphia		Amer.	3	26	2	1	.667	16	6	3	20	8	1.04
1913—Philadelphia		Amer.	2	18	2	0	1.000	19	9	8	9	1	4.00
1914—Philadelphia		Amer.	1	5⅓	0	1	.000	8	6	6	3	2	10.13
World Series Totals—5 Years			10	85	6	4	.600	64	28	23	59	21	2.44

—DID YOU KNOW—

That former New York Yankees catcher Yogi Berra hit the first pinch-hit home run in World Series history? Berra belted a seventh-inning solo shot against the Brooklyn Dodgers in Game 3 of the 1947 classic.

WALTER ANTONE (WALLY) BERGER

Born October 10, 1905, at Chicago, Ill.
Died November 30, 1988, at Redondo Beach, Calif.
Height, 6.03. Weight, 205.
Threw and batted righthanded.

Shares National League record for most home runs by rookie, season (38), 1930.
Named as outfielder on THE SPORTING NEWS All-Star Major League Team, 1933.
Manager, Manchester, New England League, 1949.

Year Club	League	Pos.	G.	AB.	R.	H.	2B.	3B.	HR.	RBI.	B.A.	PO.	A.	E.	F.A.
1927—Pocatello	Ut.-Ida.	OF	92	361	73	139	21	8	24	.....	●.385	★223	16	7	.972
1927—Los Angeles	Pac. C'st	OF	14	63	12	23	5	0	3	15	.365	21	3	1	.960
1928—Los Angeles	Pac. C'st	OF	138	535	94	175	34	7	20	94	.327	310	12	12	.964
1929—Los Angeles	Pac. C'st	OF	199	744	170	249	41	5	40	166	.335	449	16	13	.973
1930—Boston	Nat.	OF	151	555	98	172	27	14	38	119	.310	307	10	11	.966
1931—Boston	Nat.	OF	●156	617	94	199	44	8	19	84	.323	457	16	11	.977
1932—Boston	Nat.	1B-OF	145	602	90	185	34	6	17	73	.307	498	14	3	★.994
1933—Boston	Nat.	OF	137	528	84	165	37	8	27	106	.313	382	6	9	.977
1934—Boston	Nat.	OF	150	615	92	183	35	8	34	121	.298	385	9	9	.978
1935—Boston	Nat.	OF	150	589	91	174	39	4	★34	★130	.295	★458	8	★17	.965
1936—Boston	Nat.	OF	138	534	88	154	23	3	25	91	.288	384	10	14	.966
1937—Boston(a)-N.Y.	Nat.	OF	89	312	54	89	20	3	17	65	.285	158	5	4	.976
1938—N.Y.(b)-Cin.	Nat.	OF	115	439	79	131	23	4	16	60	.298	221	7	7	.970
1939—Cincinnati	Nat.	OF	97	329	36	85	15	1	14	44	.258	158	6	5	.970
1940—Cin.(c)-Phila.	Nat.	OF	22	43	3	13	2	0	1	5	.302	18	0	1	.947
1940—Indianapolis	A. Assn.	PH	41	155	27	38	8	1	5	19	.245	104	1	3	.972
1941—Los Angeles	P. C.	1B-OF	59	141	19	34	7	0	8	18	.241	68	4	4	.947
Major League Totals—11 Years			1350	5163	809	1550	299	59	242	898	.300	3426	91	91	.975

aTraded to New York Giants for Pitcher Frank Gabler and $35,000, June 15, 1937.
bTraded to Cincinnati Reds for Second Baseman Alex Kampouris, June 6, 1938.
cReleased, 1940; signed with Philadelphia Phillies.

WORLD SERIES RECORD

Year Club	League	Pos.	G.	AB.	R.	H.	2B.	3B.	HR.	RBI.	B.A.	PO.	A.	E.	F.A.
1937—New York	Nat.	OF	3	3	0	0	0	0	0	0	.000	0	0	0	.000
1939—Cincinnati	Nat.	OF	4	15	0	0	0	0	0	1	.000	8	0	0	1.000
World Series Totals—2 Years			7	18	0	0	0	0	0	1	.000	8	0	0	1.000

LAWRENCE PETER (YOGI) BERRA

Born May 12, 1925, at St. Louis, Mo.
Height, 5.08. Weight, 191.
Threw right and batted lefthanded.

Holds major league records for most years leading league in games by catcher (8); most consecutive chances accepted without an error by catcher (950), July 28, 1957, second game to May 10, 1959, second game.
Shares major league records for most years leading league in chances accepted by catcher (8); most unassisted double plays by catcher, lifetime (2).
Led American League catchers in double plays, 1949-50-51-52-54-56.
Named American League Most Valuable Player, 1951-54-55.
Named as catcher on THE SPORTING NEWS All-Star Major League Teams, 1950-52-54-56.
Manager, New York Yankees, 1964; player-coach, New York Mets, 1965; coach, Mets, 1966 through 1971; manager, Mets, 1972 to 1975; coach, New York Yankees, 1976 through 1983; manager, Yankees, 1984 to 1985 (part); coach, Houston Astros, 1986 through 1989.
Named to Hall of Fame, 1972.

Year Club	League	Pos.	G.	AB.	R.	H.	2B.	3B.	HR.	RBI.	B.A.	PO.	A.	E.	F.A.
1943—Norfolk	Pied.	C	111	376	52	95	17	8	7	56	.253	★480	75	★16	.972
1944-45—Kansas City	A. A.						(In Military Service)								
1946—Newark	Int.	C-OF	77	277	41	87	14	1	15	59	.314	344	45	11	.973

Year Club	League	Pos.	G.	AB.	R.	H.	2B.	3B.	HR.	RBI.	B.A.	PO.	A.	E.	F.A.
1946—New York............	Amer.	C	7	22	3	8	1	0	2	4	.364	28	6	0	1.000
1947—New York............	Amer.	C-OF	83	293	41	82	15	3	11	54	.280	307	18	9	.973
1948—New York............	Amer.	C-OF	125	469	70	143	24	10	14	98	.305	390	40	9	.979
1949—New York............	Amer.	C	116	415	59	115	20	2	20	91	.277	544	60	7	.989
1950—New York............	Amer.	C	151	597	116	192	30	6	28	124	.322	★777	●64	13	.985
1951—New York............	Amer.	C	141	547	92	161	19	4	27	88	.294	★693	★82	●13	.984
1952—New York............	Amer.	C	142	534	97	146	17	1	30	98	.273	★700	★73	6	.992
1953—New York............	Amer.	C	137	503	80	149	23	5	27	108	.296	566	64	9	.986
1954—New York............	Amer.	★C-3B	151	584	88	179	28	6	22	125	.307	★718	64	8	.990
1955—New York............	Amer.	C	147	541	84	147	20	3	27	108	.272	★721	54	★13	.984
1956—New York............	Amer.	★C-OF	140	521	93	155	29	2	30	105	.298	★733	57	★11	.986
1957—New York............	Amer.	★C-OF	134	482	74	121	14	2	24	82	.251	★707	61	4	★.995
1958—New York............	Amer.	★C-OF-1B	122	433	60	115	17	3	22	90	.266	558	44	2	.997
1959—New York............	Amer.	★C-OF	131	472	64	134	25	1	19	69	.284	★706	62	4	★.995
1960—New York............	Amer.	C-OF	120	359	46	99	14	1	15	62	.276	312	24	5	.985
1961—New York............	Amer.	OF-C	119	395	62	107	11	0	22	61	.271	237	15	2	.992
1962—New York............	Amer.	C-OF	86	232	25	52	8	0	10	35	.224	238	17	6	.977
1963—New York............	Amer.	C	64	147	20	43	6	0	8	28	.293	244	13	3	.988
1964—New York(a)........	Amer.		(Did not play—served as manager.)												
1965—New York............	Nat.	C	4	9	1	2	0	0	0	0	.222	15	1	1	.941
American League Totals—18 Years.......			2116	7546	1174	2148	321	49	358	1430	.285	9179	818	124	.988
National League Totals—1 Year.............			4	9	1	2	0	0	0	0	.222	15	1	1	.941
Major League Totals—19 Years..............			2120	7555	1175	2150	321	49	358	1430	.285	9194	819	125	.988

aReleased by New York Yankees, October 16, 1964.

WORLD SERIES RECORD

Holds records for most series played (14), games (75), years on winning club (10), at-bats (259), hits (71), singles (49), series by catcher (12), games by catcher (63), putouts by catcher (421), chances accepted by catcher (457), lifetime.

Shares records for most runs batted in, inning (4), October 5, 1956, second inning; most doubles, lifetime (10).

Year Club	League	Pos.	G.	AB.	R.	H.	2B.	3B.	HR.	RBI.	B.A.	PO.	A.	E.	F.A.
1947—New York............	Amer.	C-OF	6	19	2	3	0	0	1	2	.158	21	2	2	.920
1949—New York............	Amer.	C	4	16	2	1	0	0	0	1	.063	37	3	0	1.000
1950—New York............	Amer.	C	4	15	2	3	0	0	1	2	.200	30	1	0	1.000
1951—New York............	Amer.	C	6	23	4	6	1	0	0	0	.261	27	3	1	.968
1952—New York............	Amer.	C	7	28	2	6	1	0	2	3	.214	59	7	1	.985
1953—New York............	Amer.	C	6	21	3	9	1	0	1	4	.429	36	3	0	1.000
1955—New York............	Amer.	C	7	24	5	10	1	0	1	2	.417	40	4	0	1.000
1956—New York............	Amer.	C	7	25	5	9	2	0	3	10	.360	50	3	0	1.000
1957—New York............	Amer.	C	7	25	5	8	1	0	1	2	.320	44	2	1	.979
1958—New York............	Amer.	C	7	27	3	6	3	0	0	2	.222	60	6	0	1.000
1960—New York............	Amer.	C-OF-PH	7	22	6	7	0	0	1	8	.318	18	1	0	1.000
1961—New York............	Amer.	OF	4	11	2	3	0	0	1	3	.273	11	0	1	.917
1962—New York............	Amer.	C	2	2	0	0	0	0	0	0	.000	6	1	0	1.000
1963—New York............	Amer.	PH	1	1	0	0	0	0	0	0	.000	0	0	0	.000
World Series Totals—14 Years			75	259	41	71	10	0	12	39	.274	439	36	6	.988

VIDA ROCHELLE BLUE JR.

Born July 28, 1949, at Mansfield, La.

Height, 6.00. Weight, 200.

Threw left and batted left and righthanded.

Pitched 6-0 no-hit victory against Minnesota Twins, September 21, 1970.
Pitched seven-inning, 4-0 no-hit victory against Appleton, June 19, 1968.
Led American League in shutouts with 8 in 1971.
Named National League Pitcher of the Year by THE SPORTING NEWS, 1978.
Named American League Pitcher of the Year by THE SPORTING NEWS, 1971.
Named American League Most Valuable Player by Baseball Writers' Association of America, 1971.
Won American League Cy Young Memorial Award, 1971.
Named lefthanded pitcher on THE SPORTING NEWS National League All-Star Team, 1978.
Named lefthanded pitcher on THE SPORTING NEWS American League All-Star Team, 1971.

Year Club	League	G.	IP.	W.	L.	Pct.	H.	R.	ER.	SO.	BB.	ERA.
1968—Burlington	Midwest	24	152	8	●11	.421	102	67	42	★231	80	2.49
1969—Birmingham	Southern	15	104	10	3	.769	80	40	37	112	52	3.20
1969—Oakland..........................	American	12	42	1	1	.500	49	34	31	24	18	6.64
1970—Iowa	Am. Assoc.	17	133	12	3	★.800	88	40	32	★165	55	2.17
1970—Oakland..........................	American	6	39	2	0	1.000	20	12	9	35	12	2.08

Year	Club	League	G.	IP.	W.	L.	Pct.	H.	R.	ER.	SO.	BB.	ERA.
1971—Oakland	American	39	312	24	8	.750	209	73	63	301	88	★1.82
1972—Oakland	American	25	151	6	10	.375	117	55	47	111	48	2.80
1973—Oakland	American	37	264	20	9	.690	214	108	96	158	105	3.27
1974—Oakland	American	40	282	17	15	.531	246	118	102	174	98	3.26
1975—Oakland	American	39	278	22	11	.667	243	103	93	189	99	3.01
1976—Oakland	American	37	298	18	13	.581	268	90	78	166	63	2.36
1977—Oakland†	American	38	280	14	●19	.424	●284	138	●119	157	86	3.83
1978—San Francisco	National	35	258	18	10	.643	233	87	80	171	70	2.79
1979—San Francisco	National	34	237	14	14	.500	246	143	★132	138	111	5.01
1980—San Francisco	National	31	224	14	10	.583	202	79	74	129	61	2.97
1981—San Francisco ‡	National	18	125	8	6	.571	97	40	34	63	54	2.45
1982—Kansas City	American	31	181	13	12	.520	163	80	76	103	80	3.78
1983—Kansas City §	American	19	85⅓	0	5	.000	96	62	57	53	35	6.01
1984—						(Out of Organized Baseball)						
1985—San Francisco x	National	33	131	8	8	.500	115	70	65	103	80	4.47
1986—San Francisco y	National	28	156⅔	10	10	.500	137	65	57	100	77	3.27
National League Totals—6 Years		179	1131⅔	72	58	.554	1030	484	442	704	453	3.52
American League Totals—11 Years		323	2212⅓	137	103	.571	1909	873	771	1471	732	3.14
Major League Totals—17 Years		502	3344	209	161	.565	2939	1357	1213	2175	1185	3.26

Selected by Kansas City A's organization in 2nd round of free-agent draft, June 6, 1967.

†Traded to San Francisco Giants for Outfielder Gary Thomasson, Catcher Gary Alexander, Pitchers Dave Heaverlo, Alan Wirth, John Johnson and Phillip Huffman, a player to be named later and cash estimated at $390,000, March 15, 1978; Oakland acquired Shortstop Mario Guerrero to complete deal, April 7, 1978.

‡Traded with Pitcher Bob Tufts to Kansas City Royals for Pitchers Atlee Hammaker, Craig Chamberlain and Renie Martin and a player to be named later, March 30, 1982; San Francisco Giants' organization acquired Second Baseman Brad Wellman to complete deal, April 19, 1982.

§Released, August 5, 1983; signed by San Francisco Giants, April 6, 1985.

xGranted free agency, November 12, 1985; re-signed by Giants, December 17, 1985.

yGranted free agency, November 12, 1986.

CHAMPIONSHIP SERIES RECORD

Shares major league record for fewest hits allowed, game (2), October 8, 1974.

Year	Club	League	G.	IP.	W.	L.	Pct.	H.	R.	ER.	SO.	BB.	ERA.
1971—Oakland	American	1	7	0	1	.000	7	5	5	8	2	6.43
1972—Oakland	American	4	5⅓	0	0	.000	4	0	0	5	1	0.00
1973—Oakland	American	2	7	0	1	.000	8	8	8	3	5	10.29
1974—Oakland	American	1	9	1	0	1.000	2	0	0	7	0	0.00
1975—Oakland	American	1	3	0	0	.000	6	3	3	2	0	9.00
Championship Series Totals—5 Years		9	31⅓	1	2	.333	27	16	16	25	8	4.60

WORLD SERIES RECORD

Year	Club	League	G.	IP.	W.	L.	Pct.	H.	R.	ER.	SO.	BB.	ERA.
1972—Oakland	American	4	8⅔	0	1	.000	8	4	4	5	5	4.15
1973—Oakland	American	2	11	0	1	.000	10	6	6	8	3	4.91
1974—Oakland	American	2	13⅔	0	1	.000	10	5	5	9	7	3.29
World Series Totals—3 Years		8	33⅓	0	3	.000	28	15	15	22	15	4.05

BOBBY LEE BONDS

Born March 15, 1946, at Riverside, Calif.

Height, 6.01. Weight, 190.

Threw and batted righthanded.

Father of Barry Bonds, major league outfielder.

Holds major league records for most home runs as leadoff batter, season (11), 1973; most strikeouts, season (189), 1970.

Shares major league records by hitting grand slam, first major league game, June 25, 1968, 6th inning; most unassisted double plays by outfielder, game (1), May 31, 1972.

Holds National League record for most home runs as leadoff batter, lifetime (30).

Led National League in total bases with 341 in 1973.

Led National League outfielders in double plays with 7 in 1970.

Led National League batters in strikeouts with 187 in 1969, 189 in 1970 and 148 in 1973.

Led California League batters in strikeouts with 146 in 1966.

Led American League in caught stealing with 23 in 1979.

Tied for National League lead in double plays by outfielders with 5 in 1973.

Named by The Sporting News as National League Player of the Year, 1973.

Named as outfielder on The Sporting News National League All-Star Team, 1973.

Named as outfielder on The Sporting News American League All-Star Team, 1977.

Named as outfielder on The Sporting News National League All-Star fielding teams, 1971, 1973 and 1974.

Year	Club	League	Pos.	G.	AB.	R.	H.	2B.	3B.	HR.	RBI.	B.A.	PO.	A.	E.	F.A.
1965—Lexington	W. Car.	OF	112	418	*103	135	12	11	25	86	.323	200	14	12	.947
1965—Fresno	Calif.	OF	7	32	6	7	0	0	1	2	.219	16	0	1	.941
1966—Fresno	Calif.	OF	117	455	93	119	12	6	26	91	.262	181	15	10	.951
1967—Waterbury	East.	*OF-1B	137	476	65	124	19	8	15	68	.261	229	13	*11	.957
1968—Phoenix	P.C.	OF	60	219	47	81	16	7	8	47	.370	156	7	2	.988
1968—San Francisco	Nat.	OF	81	307	55	78	10	5	9	35	.254	169	6	4	.978
1969—San Francisco	Nat.	OF	158	622	●120	161	25	6	32	90	.259	339	9	8	.978
1970—San Francisco	Nat.	OF	157	663	134	200	36	10	26	78	.302	326	14	11	.969
1971—San Francisco	Nat.	OF	155	619	110	178	32	4	33	102	.288	329	10	2	*.994
1972—San Francisco	Nat.	OF	153	626	118	162	29	5	26	80	.259	345	8	8	.978
1973—San Francisco	Nat.	OF	160	643	*131	182	34	4	39	96	.283	346	12	11	.970
1974—San Francisco†	Nat.	OF	150	567	97	145	22	8	21	71	.256	305	11	11	.966
1975—New York‡	Amer.	OF	145	529	93	143	26	3	32	85	.270	287	12	4	.987
1976—California	Amer.	OF	99	378	48	100	10	3	10	54	.265	199	9	5	.977
1977—California §	Amer.	OF	158	592	103	156	23	9	37	115	.264	272	5	4	.986
1978—Chi.x-Tex.y	Amer.	OF	156	565	93	151	19	4	31	90	.267	253	16	9	.968
1979—Cleveland z	Amer.	OF	146	538	93	148	24	1	25	85	.275	267	9	6	.979
1980—St. Louis a	Nat.	OF	86	231	37	47	5	3	5	24	.203	114	5	4	.967
1981—Wichita b	A.A.	OF	35	127	18	31	5	0	6	25	.244	27	2	1	.967
1981—Chicago c	Nat.	OF	45	163	26	35	7	1	6	19	.215	108	2	2	.982
1982—Columbus d	Int.	OF	28	84	10	15	6	0	2	7	.179	34	0	3	.919
American League Totals—5 Years			704	2602	430	698	102	20	135	429	.268	1278	51	28	.979
National League Totals—9 Years			1145	4441	828	1188	200	46	197	595	.268	2381	77	61	.976
Major League Totals—14 Years			1849	7043	1258	1886	302	66	332	1024	.268	3659	128	89	.977

Signed as free agent by San Francisco Giants' organization, August 4, 1964.

†Traded to New York Yankees for Outfielder Bobby Murcer, October 21, 1974.

‡Traded to California Angels for Outfielder Mickey Rivers and Pitcher Ed Figueroa, December 11, 1975.

§Traded with Outfielder Thad Bosley and Pitcher Dick Dotson to Chicago White Sox for Pitcher Chris Knapp and Dave Frost and Catcher Brian Downing, December 5, 1977.

xTraded to Texas Rangers for Outfielders Claudell Washington and Rusty Torres and cash, May 16, 1978.

yTraded with Pitcher Len Barker to Cleveland Indians for Infielder Larvell Blanks and Pitcher Jim Kern, October 3, 1978.

zTraded to St. Louis Cardinals for Pitcher John Denny and Outfielder Jerry Mumphrey, December 7, 1979.

aReleased, December 22, 1980; signed by Texas Rangers' organization, April 17, 1981.

bSold to Chicago Cubs, June 4, 1981.

cReleased, October 13, 1981; signed by Columbus (New York Yankees' organization), May 18, 1982.

dReleased, June 21, 1982.

CHAMPIONSHIP SERIES RECORD

Year	Club	League	Pos.	G.	AB.	R.	H.	2B.	3B.	HR.	RBI.	B.A.	PO.	A.	E.	F.A.
1971—San Francisco	Nat.	OF	3	8	0	2	0	0	0	0	.250	3	0	1	.750

JAMES LEROY (JIM) BOTTOMLEY
(Sunny Jim)

Born April 23, 1900, at Oglesby, Ill.

Died December 11, 1959, at St. Louis, Mo.

Height, 6.00. Weight, 175.

Threw and batted lefthanded.

Holds major league record for most runs batted in, game (12), September 16, 1924.

Led National League first basemen in double plays, 1925, 1927.

Named National League Most Valuable Player, 1928.

Named as first baseman on THE SPORTING NEWS All-Star Major League Team, 1925.

Manager, St. Louis Browns, 1937; Syracuse, International League, 1938; scout, Chicago Cubs, 1957, until named manager, Pulaski, Appalachian League, 1957.

Named to Hall of Fame, 1974.

Year	Club	League	Pos.	G.	AB.	R.	H.	2B.	3B.	HR.	RBI.	B.A.	PO.	A.	E.	F.A.
1920—Sioux City	West.	1B	6	14	0	1	0	0	0	0	.071	35	1	0	1.000
1920—Mitchell	S. Dak.	1B	●97	378	69	118	...	...	7	...	.312	*1110	37	15	*.987
1921—Houston	Tex.	1B-2B	130	459	50	104	16	5	4	62	.227	1114	59	●27	.978
1922—Syracuse	Int.	1B	119	460	78	160	29	15	14	94	.348	1245	61	10	.992
1922—St. Louis	Nat.	1B	37	151	29	49	8	5	5	35	.325	346	12	5	.986
1923—St. Louis	Nat.	1B	134	523	79	194	34	14	8	94	.371	1264	43	18	.986
1924—St. Louis	Nat.	1B	137	528	87	167	31	12	14	111	.316	1297	48	*24	.982
1925—St. Louis	Nat.	1B	●153	619	92	*227	*44	12	21	128	.367	*1466	74	*21	.987
1926—St. Louis	Nat.	1B	154	603	98	180	*40	14	19	*120	.299	1607	54	*19	.989
1927—St. Louis	Nat.	1B	152	574	95	174	31	15	19	124	.303	*1656	70	20	.989
1928—St. Louis	Nat.	1B	149	576	123	187	42	*20	●31	*136	.325	1454	52	●20	.987
1929—St. Louis	Nat.	1B	146	560	108	176	31	12	29	137	.314	1347	75	13	.991
1930—St. Louis	Nat.	1B	131	487	92	148	33	7	15	97	.304	1164	41	12	.990
1931—St. Louis	Nat.	1B	108	382	73	133	34	5	9	75	.348	897	43	12	.987

Year Club League	Pos.	G.	AB.	R.	H.	2B.	3B.	HR.	RBI.	B.A.	PO.	A.	E.	F.A.
1932—St. Louis (a).......... Nat.	1B	91	311	45	92	16	3	11	48	.296	662	41	10	.986
1933—Cincinnati............. Nat.	1B	145	549	57	137	23	9	13	83	.250	1511	72	15	.991
1934—Cincinnati............. Nat.	1B	142	556	72	158	31	11	11	78	.284	1303	77	15	.989
1935—Cincinnati (b)....... Nat.	1B	107	399	44	103	21	1	1	49	.258	934	53	8	.992
1936—St. Louis................. Amer.	1B	140	544	72	162	39	11	12	95	.298	1250	47	10	.992
1937—St. Louis (c).......... Amer.	1B	65	109	11	26	7	0	1	12	.239	179	12	1	.995
1938—Syracuse................ Int.	1B	7	14	0	1	0	0	0	0	.071	31	0	1	.969
American League Totals—2 Years		205	653	83	188	46	11	13	107	.288	1429	59	11	.993
National League Totals—14 Years..........		1786	6818	1094	2125	419	140	206	1315	.312	16908	755	212	.988
Major League Totals—16 Years...............		1991	7471	1177	2313	465	151	219	1422	.310	18337	814	223	.988

aTraded to Cincinnati Reds for pitcher Owen Carroll and outfielder Estel Crabtree, December 17, 1932.
bTraded to St. Louis Browns for infielder John Burnett, March 21, 1936.
cUnconditionally released by St. Louis Browns, November 19, 1937.

WORLD SERIES RECORD

Year Club League	Pos.	G.	AB.	R.	H.	2B.	3B.	HR.	RBI.	B.A.	PO.	A.	E.	F.A.
1926—St. Louis................. National	1B	7	29	4	10	3	0	0	5	.345	79	1	0	1.000
1928—St. Louis................. National	1B	4	14	1	3	0	1	1	3	.214	36	2	0	1.000
1930—St. Louis................. National	1B	6	22	1	1	1	0	0	0	.045	58	2	0	1.000
1931—St. Louis................. National	1B	7	25	2	4	1	0	0	2	.160	61	2	1	.984
World Series Totals—4 Years		24	90	8	18	5	1	1	10	.200	234	7	1	.996

LOUIS (LOU) BOUDREAU

Born July 17, 1917, at Harvey, Ill.

Height, 5:11. Weight, 193.

Threw and batted righthanded.

Shares major league records for most doubles, game (4), July 14, 1946; most years leading league in fielding average by shortstop, 100 or more games (8); most years leading league in putouts by shortstop (4).
Led American League shortstops in double plays, 1940-43-44-47-48.
Named American League Most Valuable Player, 1948.
Named Major League Player of the Year by THE SPORTING NEWS, 1948.
Named as shortstop on THE SPORTING NEWS All-Star Major League Teams, 1947-48.
Manager, Cleveland Indians, 1942 through 1950; Boston Red Sox, 1952 through 1954; Kansas City Athletics, 1955 through 1957; Chicago Cubs, 1960.
Named to Hall of Fame, 1970.

Year Club League	Pos.	G.	AB.	R.	H.	2B.	3B.	HR.	RBI.	B.A.	PO.	A.	E.	F.A.
1938—Cedar Rapids........ I.I.I.	3B	60	231	56	67	13	4	3	29	.290	74	128	14	.935
1938—Cleveland.............. Amer.	3B	1	1	0	0	0	0	0	0	.000	0	0	0	.000
1939—Buffalo................... Int.	SS	115	481	88	159	32	7	17	57	.331	234	371	38	.941
1939—Cleveland.............. Amer.	SS	53	225	42	58	15	4	0	19	.258	103	184	14	.953
1940—Cleveland.............. Amer.	SS	155	627	97	185	46	10	9	101	.295	277	★454	24	★.968
1941—Cleveland.............. Amer.	SS	148	579	95	149	★45	8	10	56	.257	★296	444	26	★.966
1942—Cleveland.............. Amer.	SS	147	506	57	143	18	10	2	58	.283	281	426	26	★.965
1943—Cleveland.............. Amer.	★SS-C	152	539	69	154	32	7	3	67	.286	★331	489	25	★.970
1944—Cleveland.............. Amer.	★SS-C	150	584	91	191	★45	5	3	67	★.327	★340	★517	19	★.978
1945—Cleveland.............. Amer.	SS	97	345	50	106	24	1	3	48	.307	217	289	9	.983
1946—Cleveland.............. Amer.	SS	140	515	51	151	30	6	6	62	.293	★315	405	22	★.970
1947—Cleveland.............. Amer.	SS	150	538	79	165	★45	3	4	67	.307	305	475	14	★.982
1948—Cleveland.............. Amer.	★SS-C	152	560	116	199	34	6	18	106	.355	297	483	20	★.975
1949—Cleveland.............. Amer.	INF	134	475	53	135	20	3	4	60	.284	253	353	12	.981
1950—Cleveland(a)........ Amer.	INF	81	260	23	70	13	2	1	29	.269	156	176	4	.988
1951—Boston................... Amer.	INF	82	273	37	73	18	1	5	47	.267	94	181	15	.948
1952—Boston................... Amer.	SS-3B	4	2	1	0	0	0	0	2	.000	0	1	0	1.000
Major League Totals—15 Years...............		1646	6029	861	1779	385	66	68	789	.295	3265	4877	230	.973

aReleased, November 22, 1950; signed with Boston Red Sox, November 27, 1950.

WORLD SERIES RECORD

Year Club League	Pos.	G.	AB.	R.	H.	2B.	3B.	HR.	RBI.	B.A.	PO.	A.	E.	F.A.
1948—Cleveland.............. Amer.	SS	6	22	1	6	4	0	0	0	.273	11	14	0	1.000

—DID YOU KNOW—

That Cleveland's Lou Boudreau was the last player-manager to lead his team to a pennant (1948)?

KENTON LLOYD (KEN) BOYER

Born May 20, 1931, at Liberty, Mo.

Died September 7, 1982, at St. Louis, Mo.

Height, 6.02. Weight, 208.

Threw and batted righthanded.

Brother of Clete Boyer, former major league infielder; Cloyd Boyer, former major league pitcher; Len and Ron Boyer, former minor league infielders.

Named as third baseman on THE SPORTING NEWS All-Star Major League Team, 1956, and on THE SPORTING NEWS National League All-Star Team, 1961-62-63-64.

Named Major League Player of the Year by THE SPORTING NEWS, 1964.

Named Most Valuable Player in National League, 1964.

Named third baseman on THE SPORTING NEWS National League All-Star Fielding Team, 1958-59-60-61-63.

Signed as minor league instructor, St. Louis Cardinals, in November of 1969, but later signed to manage St. Louis farm team, Arkansas, Texas League, 1970; coach, St. Louis Cardinals, 1971-72; retained as minor league instructor, then became non-playing manager, Sarasota, Gulf Coast League, 1973; manager, Tulsa, American Association, 1974-76; Rochester, International League, 1977; St. Louis Cardinals, 1978 to 1980.

Year	Club	League	Pos.	G.	AB.	R.	H.	2B.	3B.	HR.	RBI.	B.A.	PO.	A.	E.	F.A.
1949—Lebanon	N. Atl.		P	16	33	10	15	1	1	3	9	.455	4	10	5	.737
1950—Hamilton	Pony		3-P-O	80	240	41	82	17	6	9	61	.342	55	89	10	.935
1951—Omaha	West.		3B	151	565	87	173	28	7	14	90	.306	★154	231	●33	.921
1952-53—Houston	Tex.							(In Military Service)								
1954—Houston	Tex.		3B	159	634	116	202	42	7	21	116	.319	145	333	★39	.925
1955—St. Louis	Nat.		3B-SS	147	530	78	140	27	2	18	62	.264	155	295	21	.955
1956—St. Louis	Nat.		3B	150	595	91	182	30	2	26	98	.306	130	★309	18	.961
1957—St. Louis	Nat.		★OF-3B	142	544	79	144	18	3	19	62	.265	316	95	14	★.966
1958—St. Louis	Nat.		★3-OF-S	150	570	101	175	21	9	23	90	.307	448	350	20	.963
1959—St. Louis	Nat.		3B-SS	149	563	86	174	18	5	28	94	.309	143	310	22	.954
1960—St. Louis	Nat.		3B	151	552	95	168	26	10	32	97	.304	140	300	19	.959
1961—St. Louis	Nat.		3B	153	589	109	194	26	11	24	95	.329	117	★346	24	.951
1962—St. Louis	Nat.		3B	160	611	92	178	27	5	24	98	.291	158	318	22	.956
1963—St. Louis	Nat.		3B	159	617	86	176	28	2	24	111	.285	129	293	★34	.925
1964—St. Louis	Nat.		3B	162	628	100	185	30	10	24	★119	.295	131	337	24	.951
1965—St. Louis (a)	Nat.		3B	144	535	71	139	18	2	13	75	.260	113	250	12	★.968
1966—New York	Nat.		3B-1B	136	496	62	132	28	2	14	61	.266	125	294	21	.952
1967—New York (b)	Nat.		3B-1B	56	166	17	39	7	2	3	13	.235	79	87	6	.965
1967—Chicago	Amer.		3B-1B	57	180	17	47	5	1	4	21	.261	154	79	5	.979
1968—Chicago (c)	Amer.		3B-1B	10	24	0	3	0	0	0	0	.125	12	8	1	.952
1968—Los Angeles	Nat.		3B-1B	83	221	20	60	7	2	6	41	.271	279	64	10	.972
1969—Los Angeles	Nat.		1B	25	34	0	7	2	0	0	4	.206	31	2	1	.971
National League Totals—15 Years				1967	7251	1087	2093	313	67	278	1120	.289	2214	3650	268	.956
American League Totals—2 Years				67	204	17	50	5	1	4	21	.245	166	87	6	.977
Major League Totals—15 Years				2034	7455	1104	2143	318	68	282	1141	.287	2380	3737	274	.957

aTraded to New York Mets for third baseman Charlie Smith and pitcher Al Jackson, October 20, 1965.

bTraded to Chicago White Sox for cash and infielder Billy Southworth (transferred from Evansville to Williamsport), July 22. As part of deal White Sox obtained infielder Santos Alomar from New York Mets, August 15, 1967, and White Sox sent catcher J. C. Martin to Mets, November 27, 1967.

cReleased by Chicago White Sox, May 2, 1968; signed by Los Angeles Dodgers, May 10, 1968.

WORLD SERIES RECORD

Year	Club	League	Pos.	G.	AB.	R.	H.	2B.	3B.	HR.	RBI.	B.A.	PO.	A.	E.	F.A.
1964—St. Louis	National		3B	7	27	5	6	1	0	2	6	.222	9	16	1	.962

PITCHING RECORD

Year	Club	League	G.	IP.	W.	L.	Pct.	H.	R.	ER.	SO.	BB.	ERA.
1949—Lebanon	N. Atl.		12	71	5	1	.833	57	35	27	32	34	3.42
1950—Hamilton	Pony		21	121	6	8	.429	117	76	59	43	71	4.39

ROGER PHILLIP BRESNAHAN
(Duke)

Born June 11, 1879, at Toledo, O.

Died December 4, 1944, at Toledo, O.

Height, 5.08. Weight, 180.

Threw and batted righthanded.

Manager, St. Louis Cardinals, 1909 through 1912; Chicago Cubs, 1915; manager and owner, Toledo, American Association, 1916 through 1923; coach, New York Giants, 1925 through 1928; coach, Detroit Tigers, 1930-31. Named to Hall of Fame, 1945.

Year Club	League	Pos.	G.	AB.	R.	H.	2B.	3B.	HR.	SB.	B.A.	PO.	A.	E.	F.A.
1897—Washington	Nat.	P	7	18	2	6	0	0	0	0	.333	2	8	0	1.000
1898—Toledo	Int.-State	P	4	12	0	5	3	0	0	0	.417	1	3	1	.800
1899—Minneapolis	West.	P-C	3	1	0	1	0	1	0	0	1.000	1	5	1	.857
1900—Chicago	Nat.	C	1	2	0	0	0	0	0	0	.000	0	0	0	.000
1901—Baltimore(a)	Amer.	P-C	86	293	40	77	9	9	1	10	.263	193	69	20	.929
1902—Baltimore(b)	Amer.	C-3-O	66	234	31	64	9	6	4	11	.274	141	72	20	.914
1902—New York	Nat.	C-INF	50	178	16	52	13	3	1	6	.292	113	25	8	.945
1903—New York	Nat.	OF	111	406	87	142	30	8	4	34	.350	150	14	6	.965
1904—New York	Nat.	OF	107	402	81	114	21	8	5	13	.284	151	14	8	.954
1905—New York	Nat.	C	95	331	58	100	18	3	0	11	.302	492	114	19	.970
1906—New York	Nat.	C-OF	124	405	69	114	22	4	0	25	.281	478	131	17	.973
1907—New York	Nat.	C	104	328	57	83	9	7	4	15	.253	483	94	8	.986
1908—New York(c)	Nat.	C	139	449	70	127	25	3	1	14	.283	⋆657	140	12	.985
1909—St. Louis	Nat.	C	69	234	27	57	4	1	0	11	.244	211	78	12	.960
1910—St. Louis	Nat.	C	78	234	35	65	15	3	0	13	.278	295	100	16	.961
1911—St. Louis	Nat.	C	78	227	22	63	17	8	3	4	.278	325	102	14	.968
1912—St. Louis	Nat.	C	48	108	8	36	7	2	1	4	.333	138	49	5	.974
1913—Chicago(d)	Nat.	C	69	162	20	37	5	2	1	7	.228	194	67	10	.963
1914—Chicago	Nat.	C	101	248	42	69	10	4	0	14	.278	365	113	11	.978
1915—Chicago	Nat.	C	77	221	19	45	8	1	1	19	.204	345	95	8	.982
1916—Toledo	A. A.	C	44	120	19	29	6	1	2	4	.242	95	13	0	1.000
1917—Toledo	A. A.	C	40	80	10	22	5	0	0	1	.275	67	20	3	.967
1918—Toledo	A. A.	C	19	52	4	12	2	0	1	0	.231	24	1	1	.962
National League Totals—16 Years			1258	3953	613	1110	204	57	21	190	.281	4399	1144	154	.973
American League Totals—2 Years			152	527	71	141	18	15	5	21	.268	334	141	40	.922
Major League Totals—17 Years			1410	4480	684	1251	222	72	26	211	.279	4733	1285	194	.969

aJumped to American League.

bJumped with John McGraw, catcher Frank Bowerman and pitchers Joe McGinnity and John Cronin to New York Giants, July 6, 1902.

cTraded to St. Louis Cardinals for pitcher Bugs Raymond, outfielder John Murray and catcher George Schlei, December, 1908, Cardinals getting Schlei from Cincinnati for pitchers Art Fromme and Eddie Karger.

dPurchased by Chicago Cubs, June 8, 1913, after prolonged contract squabble with St. Louis club, which had attempted to release him in October, 1912, without asking waivers.

PITCHING RECORD

Year Club	League	G.	W.	L.	Pct.	SO.	BB.	H.
1897—Washington	National	7	4	0	1.000	12	8	52
1898—Toledo	Inter-State	4	2	2	.500	11	8	40
1899—Minneapolis	Western	3	0	2	.000	5	8	....
1901—Baltimore	American	1	0	0	.000	4	0	10
1910—St. Louis	National	1	0	0	.000	0	1	6
American League Totals—1 Year		1	0	0	.000	4	0	10
National League Totals—2 Years		8	4	0	1.000	12	8	58
Major League Totals—3 Years		9	4	0	1.000	16	8	68

WORLD SERIES RECORD

Year Club	League	Pos.	G.	AB.	R.	H.	2B.	3B.	HR.	SB.	B.A.	PO.	A.	E.	F.A.
1905—New York	Nat.	C	5	16	3	5	2	0	0	1	.313	27	7	0	1.000

LOUIS CLARK (LOU) BROCK

Born June 18, 1939, at El Dorado, Ark.

Height, 5.11½. Weight, 172.

Threw and batted lefthanded.

Holds major league records for most stolen bases, lifetime (938); most years and most consecutive years, 50 or more stolen bases (12); most times caught stealing, lifetime (307).

Holds modern National League record for most stolen bases, season (118), 1974.

Shares National League record for fewest times grounded into double play, season, 150 or more games (2), 1965 and 1969.

Led National League outfielders in double plays with 7 in 1963.

Led National League in stolen bases with 74 in 1966, 52 in 1967, 62 in 1968, 53 in 1969, 64 in 1971, 63 in 1972, 70 in 1973 and 118 in 1974.

Named National League and Major League Player of the Year by THE SPORTING NEWS, 1974.

Named as outfielder on THE SPORTING NEWS National League All-Star Team, 1974.

Named National League Comeback Player of the Year by THE SPORTING NEWS, 1979.

Named to Hall of Fame, 1985.

Year Club League	Pos.	G.	AB.	R.	H.	2B.	3B.	HR.	RBI.	B.A.	PO.	A.	E.	F.A.
1961—St. Cloud .... North.	OF	●128	501	★117	★181	★33	6	14	82	★.361	★277	14	14	.954
1961—Chicago .... Nat.	OF	4	11	1	1	0	0	0	0	.091	6	0	2	.750
1962—Chicago .... Nat.	OF	123	434	73	114	24	7	9	35	.263	243	7	9	.965
1963—Chicago .... Nat.	OF	148	547	79	141	19	11	9	37	.258	269	17	8	.973
1964—Chi.(a)-St. Louis.... Nat.	OF	155	634	111	200	30	11	14	58	.315	266	15	★14	.953
1965—St. Louis.................. Nat.	OF	155	631	107	182	35	8	16	69	.288	272	11	★12	.959
1966—St. Louis.................. Nat.	OF	156	643	94	183	24	12	15	46	.285	269	9	★19	.936
1967—St. Louis.................. Nat.	OF	159	★689	●113	206	32	12	21	76	.299	272	12	★13	.956
1968—St. Louis.................. Nat.	OF	159	660	92	184	★46	★14	6	51	.279	269	9	●14	.952
1969—St. Louis.................. Nat.	OF	157	655	97	195	33	10	12	47	.298	255	7	14	.949
1970—St. Louis.................. Nat.	OF	155	664	114	202	29	5	13	57	.304	247	9	10	.962
1971—St. Louis.................. Nat.	OF	157	640	★126	200	7	7	7	61	.313	262	7	14	.951
1972—St. Louis.................. Nat.	OF	153	621	81	193	26	8	3	42	.311	253	6	★13	.952
1973—St. Louis.................. Nat.	OF	160	650	110	193	29	8	7	63	.297	310	3	●12	.963
1974—St. Louis.................. Nat.	OF	153	635	105	194	25	7	3	48	.306	283	8	10	.967
1975—St. Louis.................. Nat.	OF	136	528	78	163	27	6	3	47	.309	247	5	9	.966
1976—St. Louis.................. Nat.	OF	133	498	73	150	24	5	4	67	.301	221	6	4	.983
1977—St. Louis.................. Nat.	OF	141	489	69	133	22	6	2	46	.272	184	2	9	.954
1978—St. Louis.................. Nat.	OF	92	298	31	66	9	0	0	12	.221	114	2	3	.975
1979—St. Louis.................. Nat.	OF	120	405	56	123	15	4	5	38	.304	152	7	7	.958
Major League Totals—19 Years		2616	10332	1610	3023	486	141	149	900	.293	4394	142	196	.959

aTraded to St. Louis Cardinals with Pitchers Jack Spring and Paul Toth for Pitchers Ernie Broglio and Bobby Shantz and Outfielder Doug Clemens, June 15, 1964.

WORLD SERIES RECORD

Holds records for highest batting average, lifetime, 20 or more games (.391); most stolen bases, series (7), 1967 and 1968.

Shares records for most hits, series (13), 1968; most stolen bases, lifetime (14); most stolen bases, game (3), October 12, 1967 and October 5, 1968; most stolen bases, inning (2), October 12, 1967, fifth inning.

Year Club League	Pos.	G.	AB.	R.	H.	2B.	3B.	HR.	RBI.	B.A.	PO.	A.	E.	F.A.
1964—St. Louis.................. Nat.	OF	7	30	2	9	2	0	1	5	.300	8	1	1	.900
1967—St. Louis.................. Nat.	OF	7	29	8	12	2	1	1	3	.414	13	0	0	1.000
1968—St. Louis.................. Nat.	OF	7	28	6	13	3	1	2	5	.464	13	0	1	.929
World Series Totals—3 Years		21	87	16	34	7	2	4	13	.391	34	1	2	.946

WALTER SCOTT (STEVE) BRODIE

Born September 11, 1868, at Warrenton, Va.

Died October 29, 1933, at Baltimore, Md.

Threw righthanded and batted lefthanded.

Year Club League	Pos.	G.	AB.	R.	H.	2B.	3B.	HR.	SB.	B.A.	PO.	A.	E.	F.A.
1888—Wheeling .... Tri-St.	OF	.....	.....			....	....	....						
1889—Hamilton................ Int.	OF	111	487	87	141	....	....	....	50	.302	200	26	19	.922
1890—Boston.................... Nat.	OF	132	514	78	152	18	9	0	29	.295	225	19	12	.953
1891—Boston.................... Nat.	OF	134	519	83	138	17	6	2	23	.266	259	22	15	.943
1892—St. Louis.................. Nat.	2B-OF	154	600	86	154	9	8	3	28	.256	290	22	17	.948
1893—St. L.-Balt. .... Nat.	OF	132	549	89	188	20	11	2	52	.342	275	26	16	.950
1894—Baltimore .... Nat.	OF	129	574	132	212	22	12	2	50	.369	311	11	19	.944
1895—Baltimore .... Nat.	OF	130	528	84	193	26	11	2	36	.365	301	20	11	.961
1896—Baltimore .... Nat.	OF	132	516	90	152	19	10	2	30	.294	★321	20	10	.972
1897—Pittsburgh.............. Nat.	OF	100	372	47	111	10	11	2	17	.298	216	11	4	★.983
1898—Pitts.-Baltimore .. Nat.	OF	65	255	28	71	10	2	0	4	.278	164	9	7	.961
1899—Baltimore .... Nat.	OF	138	533	80	165	29	1	3	20	.309	309	18	7	★.979
1900—Chicago .... Amer.	OF	64	229	41	60	6	3	0	8	.262	117	8	11	.919
1901—Baltimore .... Amer.	OF	84	309	41	96	5	6	2	10	.311	182	4	9	.954
1902—New York .... Nat.	OF	109	417	35	117	8	2	3	12	.281	222	20	11	.957
1903—Balt.-Montreal ...... East.	OF	103	389	34	97	12	1	0	15	.255	230	12	14	.945
1904—Binghamton .... N.Y.	OF	50	177	21	20	....	....	....	12	.163	77	7	5	.943
1905—Providence............ East.	OF	134	500	45	135	12	3	0	18	.270	236	18	13	.951
1906—Prov.-Newark ...... East.	OF	112	387	41	110	14	4	0	10	.284	220	16	11	.955
1907—Birmingham .... South.	OF	5	17	2	2	0	0	0	0	.117	11	2	0	1.000
1907—Roanoke .... Va.	OF	72	238	26	74	....	....	....	20	.311	130	8	1	.993
1908—Ports.-Norfolk....... N. Y.	OF	51	177	18	40	....	....	....	6	.226	101	7	1	.991
1909—Wilmington .... E. Car.	OF	80	262	31	67	....	....	....	....	.255	190	8	2	.990
1910—Newark .... East.	OF	11	28	2	6	0	0	0	0	.214	......	.....	.....	....
American League Totals—1 Year		84	309	41	96	5	6	2	10	.311	182	4	9	.954
National League Totals—11 Years		1355	5377	832	1653	188	83	21	301	.307	2893	198	129	.960
Major League Totals—12 Years		1439	5686	873	1749	193	89	23	311	.308	3075	202	138	.960

DENNIS (DAN) BROUTHERS

Born May 8, 1858, at Sylvan Lake, N. Y.
Died August 3, 1932, at East Orange, N. J.
Height, 6.02. Weight, 200.
Threw and batted lefthanded.

Scout, New York Giants, 1907.
Named to Hall of Fame, 1945.

Year Club	League	Pos.	G.	AB.	R.	H.	2B.	3B.	HR.	SB.	B.A.	PO.	A.	E.	F.A.
1879—Troy	Nat.	P-1B	39	168	17	46	13	1	4	.....	.274	406	6	33	.926
1880—Troy	Nat.	1B	3	13	0	2	0	0	0	.....	.154	25	0	3	.893
1881—Buffalo	Nat.	1B-OF	65	270	60	86	15	7	⋆8	.....	.319	377	18	33	.923
1882—Buffalo	Nat.	1B	84	351	71	⋆129	25	11	6	.....	⋆.368	882	19	24	.974
1883—Buffalo	Nat.	P-1-3	97	420	83	⋆156	39	⋆17	2	.....	⋆.371	1030	34	44	.960
1884—Buffalo	Nat.	1B-3B	90	381	80	124	22	16	14	.....	.325	908	29	35	.964
1885—Buffalo(a)	Nat.	1B	98	407	87	146	27	13	7	.....	.359	996	25	26	.975
1886—Detroit	Nat.	1B	121	489	139	181	⋆41	16	10	21	.370	1256	27	42	.968
1887—Detroit†	Nat.	1B	122	570	⋆153	⋆239	⋆35	20	13	34	.419	1189	35	38	.970
1888—Detroit(b)	Nat.	1B	129	522	⋆118	160	35	13	10	34	.306	1345	48	⋆42	.970
1889—Boston(c)	Nat.	1B	126	485	105	181	25	8	6	22	⋆.373	1243	58	35	.974
1890—Boston(d)	Players	1B	123	464	116	160	32	9	1	26	.345	1193	66	⋆52	.960
1891—Boston	A. A.	1B	123	458	111	⋆160	26	20	5	33	⋆.349	1239	33	24	.981
1892—Brooklyn	Nat.	1B	152	588	121	⋆197	●33	⋆20	3	36	●.335	1485	99	37	.977
1893—Brooklyn(e)	Nat.	1B	75	267	53	93	21	11	2	8	.348	729	42	14	.982
1894—Baltimore	Nat.	1B	123	528	137	182	33	25	9	40	.345	1180	65	31	.976
1895—Balt.(f)-L'ville	Nat.	1B	29	121	15	35	9	2	2	1	.289	255	14	10	.964
1896—Philadelphia	Nat.	1B	57	218	41	72	15	3	1	8	.330	570	23	10	.983
1896—Springfield	East.	1B	51	205	42	82	....	....	....	9	.400	513	13	12	.977
1897—Springfield	East.	1B	126	501	112	⋆208	44	13	14	21	⋆.415	1239	44	22	.983
1898—Spring.-Toronto	East.	1B	50	189	42	63	10	2	4	2	.333	511	19	13	.976
1899—Spring.-Roch.	East.	1B	45	170	27	40	5	4	3	2	.235	421	26	13	.972
1904—New York	Nat.	1B	2	5	0	0	0	0	0	0	.000	6	0	0	1.000
1904—Poughkeepsie	Hudson River	1B	.....	424	.....	158	....	....	....	.....	⋆.373	1129	31	31	.974
1905—Poughkeepsie	Hudson River	1B	.....	308	.....	91	....	....	....	.....	.295	810	29	31	.967
American Assn. Totals—1 Year			123	458	111	160	26	20	5	33	.349	1239	33	24	.981
National League Totals—17 Years			1412	5803	1280	2029	388	183	97	204	.350	13882	542	457	.969
Players League Totals—1 Year			123	464	116	160	32	9	1	26	.345	1193	66	52	.960
Major League Totals—19 Years			1658	6725	1507	2349	446	212	103	263	.349	16314	641	533	.970

†Bases on balls counted as hits in 1887.
aSold to Detroit with utilityman Hardie Richardson, third baseman Jim White and shortstop Charlie Rowe for 1886 season.
bDisbanding of Detroit team caused players to be distributed throughout circuit. Brouthers awarded to Boston, 1888.
cJumped to Players League (Brotherhood), 1890.
dSigned with Boston (A. A.) after disbanding of Brotherhood.
eTraded to Baltimore with outfielder Willie Keeler for third baseman Billy Shindle and outfielder George Treadway, January, 1894.
fSold to Louisville, May 9, 1895.

MORDECAI PETER CENTENNIAL BROWN
(Three Finger and Miner)

Born October 19, 1876, at Nyesville, Ind.
Died February 14, 1948, at Terre Haute, Ind.
Height, 5.10. Weight, 175.
Threw right and batted left and righthanded.

Manager, St. Louis, Federal League, 1914; Terre Haute, Three-I League, 1919; Indianapolis, American Association, September, 1919; Terre Haute, 1920.
Named to Hall of Fame, 1949.

Year Club	League	G.	IP.	W.	L.	Pct.	H.	R.	ER.	SO.	BB.	ERA.
1901—Terre Haute	I.I.I.	31	....	*23	8	*.742	198	....	....	138	41	......
1902—Omaha	Western	●43	352	27	15	.643	309	....	....	140	82	......
1903—St. Louis (a)	National	26	201	9	13	.409	231	105	....	83	59	......
1904—Chicago	National	26	212	15	10	.600	155	74	....	81	50	......
1905—Chicago	National	30	249	18	12	.600	219	89	....	89	44	......
1906—Chicago	National	36	278	26	6	.813	198	56	....	143	61	......
1907—Chicago	National	34	233	20	6	.769	180	51	....	107	40	......
1908—Chicago	National	44	312	29	9	.763	214	64	....	123	49	......
1909—Chicago	National	*50	*343	*27	9	.750	246	78	....	172	53	......
1910—Chicago	National	46	295	25	14	.641	256	95	....	143	64	......
1911—Chicago	National	*53	270	21	11	.656	267	110	....	129	55	......
1912—Chicago (b)	National	15	89	5	6	.455	92	35	26	34	20	2.63
1913—Cincinnati (c)	National	39	167	11	12	.478	174	79	56	41	44	3.02
1914—St.L. (d)-Brooklyn	Federal	35	233	14	11	.560	233	106	80	118	61	3.09
1915—Chicago (e)	Federal	35	238	17	8	.680	190	75	56	97	65	2.12
1916—Chicago	National	12	48	2	3	.400	52	27	21	21	9	3.94
1917—Columbus	Am. Assoc.	30	185	10	12	.455	167	70	57	61	51	2.77
1918—Columbus	Am. Assoc.	12	50	3	2	.600	49	18	15	13	9	2.70
1919—Terre Haute	I.I.I.	33	175	16	6	.727	161	69	56	72	20	2.88
1919—Indianapolis	Am. Assoc.	6	34	0	3	.000	39	....	....	9	11	......
1920—Terre Haute	I.I.I.	13	80	4	6	.400	74	31	23	42	13	2.59
Federal League Totals—2 Years		70	471	31	19	.620	423	181	136	215	126	2.60
National League Totals—12 Years		411	2697	208	111	.652	2284	863	....	1166	548	......
Major League Totals—12 Years		411	2697	208	111	.652	2284	863	....	1166	548	......

aTraded to Chicago with catcher Jack O'Neill for pitcher Jack Taylor.
bReleased to Louisville, October, 1912, and traded to Cincinnati for pitcher Grover Lowdermilk, January, 1913.
cReleased by Cincinnati, January, 1914, and signed as manager of St. Louis Feds.
dReleased as St. Louis Feds manager, July, 1914, but remained as player until released to Brooklyn in August, 1914.
eAssigned to Chicago Cubs in peace agreement, January, 1916.

WORLD SERIES RECORD

Year Club	League	G.	IP.	W.	L.	Pct.	H.	R.	ER.	SO.	BB.	ERA.
1906—Chicago	National	3	19⅔	1	2	.333	14	9	7	12	4	3.20
1907—Chicago	National	1	9	1	0	1.000	7	0	0	4	1	0.00
1908—Chicago	National	2	11	2	0	1.000	6	1	0	5	1	0.00
1910—Chicago	National	3	18	1	2	.333	23	16	11	14	7	5.50
World Series Totals—4 Years		9	57⅔	5	4	.556	50	26	18	35	13	2.81

LOUIS RODGERS (PETE) BROWNING

Born July 17, 1861, at Louisville, Ky.

Died September 10, 1905, at Louisville, Ky.

Height, 6.02. Weight, 200.

Threw and batted righthanded.

Year Club	League	Pos.	G.	AB.	R.	H.	2B.	3B.	HR.	SB.	B.A.	PO.	A.	E.	F.A.
1882—Louisville	A.A.	INF	69	288	64	110	*19	3	5	....	*.382	192	185	68	.847
1883—Louisville	A.A.	INF	84	360	95	121	14	11	4	....	.336	134	96	50	.821
1884—Louisville	A.A.	P-1B-3B	105	454	101	155	34	8	4	....	.341	382	86	51	.902
1885—Louisville	A.A.	OF	113	479	98	*176	32	10	9	....	*.367	214	21	28	.894
1886—Louisville	A.A.	OF	112	469	88	159	29	7	3	32	.339	153	14	37	.819
1887—Louisville	A.A.	OF	134	596	133	281	36	18	4	121	.471	291	22	43	.879
1888—Louisville	A.A.	OF	99	384	59	120	23	8	3	39	.313	169	17	20	.903
1889—Louisville	A.A.	OF	83	324	39	82	18	4	2	23	.253	157	14	18	.903
1890—Cleveland	Players	OF	118	488	114	191	●41	7	5	33	*.391	245	18	27	.907
1891—Pitts.-Cin.	Nat.	OF	101	398	62	129	22	5	3	15	.324	206	12	19	.920
1892—Louis.-Cin.	Nat.	OF	102	387	58	113	15	5	3	8	.292	197	15	20	.914
1893—Louisville	Nat.	OF	57	214	37	79	9	3	1	10	.369	114	4	15	.887
1894—St. Louis-Brook.	Nat.	OF	3	9	2	3	0	0	0	0	.333	3	0	0	1.000
American Assn. Totals—8 Years			799	3354	677	1204	205	69	34	....	.359	1692	455	315	.872
National League Totals—4 Years			263	1008	159	324	46	13	7	33	.321	520	31	54	.911
Players League Totals—1 Year			118	488	114	191	41	7	5	33	.391	245	18	27	.907
Major League Totals—13 Years			1180	4850	950	1719	292	89	46	....	.354	2457	504	396	.882

Bases on balls counted as hits in 1887.

CHARLES G. (CHARLIE) BUFFINTON

Born June 14, 1861, at Fall River, Mass.
Died September 23, 1907, at Fall River, Mass.
Threw and batted righthanded.

Year Club	League	G.	W.	L.	Pct.	H.	R.	CG.	ShO.
1882—Boston	National	5	2	3	.400	55	34	4	1
1883—Boston	National	43	25	14	.641	310	169	34	4
1884—Boston	National	67	48	16	.750	496	228	63	8
1885—Boston	National	51	22	27	.449	423	237	49	6
1886—Boston	National	18	7	10	.412	196	132	16	0
1887—Philadelphia	National	39	21	17	.553	471	233	34	1
1888—Philadelphia	National	45	28	17	.622	321	134	45	6
1889—Philadelphia	National	43	26	17	.605	393	200	39	2
1890—Philadelphia	Players	36	19	15	.559	340	219	28	0
1891—Boston	American Assn.	48	29	9	*.763	266	140	33	2
1892—Baltimore	National	13	4	8	.333	130	....	9	0
National League Totals—9 Years		324	183	129	.587	2795	1367	293	28
Players League Totals—1 Year		36	19	15	.559	340	219	28	0
American Association Totals—1 Year		48	29	9	.763	266	140	33	2
Major League Totals—11 Years		408	231	153	.602	3401	1726	354	30

MORGAN G. BULKELEY

Born December 26, 1837, at East Haddam, Conn.
Died November 6, 1922, at Hartford, Conn.

In the first year of its organization, the National League needed a man of prominence and firmness to handle the executive affairs of the circuit, and its members prevailed upon Morgan Bulkeley to accept the office, although he announced at that time his probable inability to continue as head of the organization after one year of service.

Bulkeley's father was the first president of the Aetna Life Insurance Co. In 1872, Bulkeley organized the United States Bank of Hartford, serving as its president until 1879. That year he was chosen as the head of the Aetna Life Insurance Co. and, subsequently, as the head of its two affiliated concerns. He became a director of other Hartford institutions. Bulkeley served on the Hartford City Council in 1875, on the Board of Aldermen in 1876, and was mayor from 1880 to 1888. While mayor he gave his salary to the city's poor fund.

Bulkeley was chosen Governor of the state of Connecticut in 1888 and served in that office until 1893. He was elected United States Senator in 1905 for the six-year term. He was a delegate to the Republican National Convention, 1888 to 1896. During the drive for the sale of Liberty Bonds, Bulkeley was instrumental in obtaining more than 30 percent of Hartford's quota. Yale University conferred upon him the degree of Master of Arts in 1889, and in 1917 Trinity College honored him with the LLD degree. He was a member of the G.A.R., being former department commander; Massachusetts Commandery of the Loyal Legion, Society of the Cincinnati Sons of the American Revolution, Society of Mayflower Descendants, Society of Colonial Wars and Society of the War of 1812. Bulkeley was former president of the Sons of the American Revolution and former marshal of the Baronial Order of Runnymede. For more than 30 years, he was a member of the National Trotting Association, and his fondness for horses lasted all his life.

He was named to Hall of Fame in 1937 for service to baseball apart from playing the game.

—DID YOU KNOW—

That Mordecai (Three Finger) Brown pitched his last major league game on September 4, 1916, facing off against the great Christy Mathewson, who also was pitching his last big-league game? Mathewson, pitching for the Cincinnati Reds, beat Brown and the Chicago Cubs, 10-8, in the second game of a doubleheader.

JAMES PAUL DAVID (JIM) BUNNING

Born October 23, 1931, at Southgate, Ky.
Height, 6.03. Weight, 203.
Threw and batted righthanded.

Shares major league record by striking out three batters on nine pitched balls, August 2, 1959, ninth inning.
Pitched 6-0 perfect-game victory against New York Mets, June 21, 1964, and 3-0 no-hit victory against Boston Red Sox, July 20, 1958.
Named as pitcher on THE SPORTING NEWS All-Star Major League Team, 1957; named as pitcher on the National League All-Star Team by THE SPORTING NEWS, 1964.
Manager, Reading, Eastern League, 1972; Eugene, Pacific Coast League, 1973; minor league instructor and manager, Philadelphia Phillies system, 1974-75; manager, Oklahoma City (American Association), 1976.

Year	Club	League	G.	IP.	W.	L.	Pct.	H.	R.	ER.	SO.	BB.	ERA.
1950—Richmond	Ohio-Ind.	17	123	7	8	.467	120	69	44	83	68	3.22
1951—Davenport	I.I.I.	22	150	8	10	.444	110	61	48	103	105	2.88
1952—Williamsport	Eastern	20	129	5	9	.357	113	62	50	85	63	3.49
1953—Buffalo	International	3	5	0	0	.000	6	1	1	4	0	1.80
1953—Little Rock	Southern	34	158	5	12	.294	151	98	80	124	66	4.56
1954—Little Rock	Southern	35	193	13	11	.542	182	107	92	140	91	4.29
1955—Buffalo	International	20	129	8	5	.615	106	59	54	105	81	3.77
1955—Detroit	American	15	51	3	5	.375	59	38	36	37	32	6.35
1956—Charleston	Amer. Assoc.	22	163	9	11	.450	142	70	64	144	56	3.53
1956—Detroit	American	15	53	5	1	.833	55	24	22	34	28	3.74
1957—Detroit	American	45	★267	●20	8	.714	214	91	80	182	72	2.70
1958—Detroit	American	35	220	14	12	.538	188	96	86	177	79	3.52
1959—Detroit	American	40	250	17	13	.567	220	111	108	★201	75	3.89
1960—Detroit	American	36	252	11	14	.440	217	92	78	★201	64	2.79
1961—Detroit	American	38	268	17	11	.607	232	113	95	194	71	3.19
1962—Detroit	American	41	258	19	10	.655	★262	112	103	184	74	3.59
1963—Detroit (a)	American	39	248	12	13	.480	245	●119	107	196	69	3.88
1964—Philadelphia	National	41	284	19	8	.704	248	99	83	219	46	2.63
1965—Philadelphia	National	39	291	19	9	.679	253	92	84	268	62	2.60
1966—Philadelphia	National	43	314	19	14	.576	260	91	84	252	55	2.41
1967—Philadelphia (b)	National	40	★302	17	15	.531	241	94	77	★253	73	2.29
1968—Pittsburgh	National	27	160	4	14	.222	168	75	69	95	48	3.88
1969—Pitts.(c)-Los Angeles (d)	National	34	212	13	10	.565	212	97	87	157	59	3.69
1970—Philadelphia	National	34	219	10	15	.400	233	111	100	147	56	4.11
1971—Philadelphia	National	29	110	5	12	.294	126	72	67	58	37	5.48
American League Totals—9 Years		304	1867	118	87	.576	1692	796	715	1406	564	3.45
National League Totals—8 Years		287	1892	106	97	.522	1741	731	651	1449	436	3.10
Major League Totals—17 Years		591	3759	224	184	.549	3433	1527	1366	2855	1000	3.27

aTraded to Philadelphia Phillies with Catcher Gus Triandos for Pitcher Jack Hamilton and Outfielder Don Demeter, December 4, 1963.

bTraded to Pittsburgh Pirates for Infielder Don Money and Pitchers Woodie Fryman, Harold Clem and Bill Laxton, December 15, 1967.

cTraded for cash and Outfielder Ron Mitchell and Infielder Chuck Goggin, to Los Angeles Dodgers, August 16, 1969.

dSigned as free agent by Philadelphia Phillies, October 29, 1969.

SELVA LEWIS (LEW) BURDETTE JR.

Born November 22, 1926, at Nitro, W. Va.
Height, 6.02. Weight, 201.
Threw and batted righthanded.

Pitched 1-0 no-hit victory against Philadelphia Phillies, August 18, 1960.
Led National League in shutouts with 6 in 1956 and tied for lead with 4 in 1959.
Tied for National League lead in complete games with 18 in 1960.
Scout, southeastern area, Central Scouting Bureau, 1968; coach, Atlanta Braves, 1972-73.

Year Club	League	G.	IP.	W.	L.	Pct.	H.	R.	ER.	SO.	BB.	ERA.
1947—Norfolk	Pied.	6	27	1	1	.500	23	18	13	10	20	4.33
1947—Amsterdam	Can.-Am.	24	150	9	10	.474	125	66	47	79	80	2.82
1948—Quincy	I. I. I.	31	214	●16	11	.593	164	73	48	185	72	2.02
1949—Kansas City	A. A.	36	118	6	7	.462	147	76	69	51	47	5.26
1950—Kansas City	A. A.	27	139	7	7	.500	150	79	74	77	52	4.79
1950—New York	American	2	1	0	0	.000	3	1	1	0	0	9.00
1951—San Francisco(a)	P. C.	30	210	14	12	.538	202	88	75	118	78	3.21
1951—Boston	National	3	4	0	0	.000	6	4	3	1	5	6.75
1952—Boston	National	45	137	6	11	.353	138	58	55	47	47	3.61
1953—Milwaukee	National	46	175	15	5	.750	177	73	63	58	56	3.24
1954—Milwaukee	National	38	238	15	14	.517	224	87	73	79	62	2.76
1955—Milwaukee	National	42	230	13	8	.619	253	114	103	70	73	4.03
1956—Milwaukee	National	39	256	19	10	.655	234	92	77	110	52	★2.71
1957—Milwaukee	National	37	257	17	9	.654	260	117	106	78	59	3.71
1958—Milwaukee	National	40	275	20	10	●.667	279	102	★89	113	50	2.91
1959—Milwaukee	National	41	290	●21	15	.583	★312	★141	★131	105	38	4.07
1960—Milwaukee	National	45	276	19	13	.594	●277	116	103	83	35	3.36
1961—Milwaukee	National	40	★272	18	11	.621	★295	★131	★121	92	33	4.00
1962—Milwaukee	National	37	144	10	9	.526	172	85	78	59	23	4.88
1963—Milwaukee(b)-St. L.	National	36	183	9	13	.409	177	90	75	73	40	3.69
1964—St. Louis(c)-Chicago	National	36	141	10	9	.526	162	77	73	43	22	4.66
1965—Chicago(d)-Phila.(e)	National	26	91	3	5	.375	121	67	55	28	21	5.44
1966—California	American	54	80	7	2	.778	80	32	30	27	12	3.38
1967—California	American	19	18	1	0	1.000	16	10	10	8	0	5.00
1967—Seattle	P. C.	13	19	0	1	.000	18	12	9	8	4	4.26
National League Totals—15 Years		551	2969	195	142	.579	3087	1357	1205	1039	616	3.65
American League Totals—3 Years		75	99	8	2	.800	99	43	41	35	12	3.73
Major League Totals—18 Years		626	3068	203	144	.585	3186	1400	1246	1074	628	3.66

aRecalled by New York Yankees and sent to Boston Braves with $50,000 for Pitcher Johnny Sain, August 29, 1951.
bTraded to St. Louis Cardinals for Pitcher Bob Sadowski and Catcher-Outfielder Gene Oliver, June 15, 1963.
cTraded to Chicago Cubs for Pitcher Glen Hobbie, June 2, 1964.
dSold to Philadelphia Phillies May 30, 1965.
eReleased by Philadelphia Phillies, October 13, 1965, and signed by California Angels, December 15, 1965.

WORLD SERIES RECORD

Shares records for most games won, series (3), 1957; most home runs allowed, series (5), 1958.

Year Club	League	G.	IP.	W.	L.	Pct.	H.	R.	ER.	SO.	BB.	ERA.
1957—Milwaukee	Nat.	3	27	3	0	1.000	21	2	2	13	4	0.67
1958—Milwaukee	Nat.	3	22⅓	1	2	.333	22	17	14	12	4	5.64
World Series Totals—2 Years		6	49⅓	4	2	.667	43	19	16	25	8	2.92

JESSE CAIL BURKETT
(The Crab)

Born February 12, 1870, at Wheeling, W. Va.
Died May 27, 1953, at Worcester, Mass.
Height, 5.08. Weight, 155.
Threw and batted lefthanded.

Shares major league record for most years hitting .400 or over (2).
Owner and manager, Worcester, New England League, 1906 to 1913; manager, Lawrence and Hartford, Eastern League, 1916; scout, New York Giants and coach, Holy Cross College, 1920; coach, New York Giants, 1921; manager, Worcester, Eastern League, 1923-24; Lewiston, New England League, 1928; Lewiston, Northeastern League, 1929; Lowell, New England League, 1933; coach, Assumption College, 1931-32.
Named to Hall of Fame, 1946.

Year Club	League	Pos.	G.	AB.	R.	H.	2B.	3B.	HR.	SB.	B.A.	PO.	A.	E.	F.A.
1888—Scranton	Cent.	2B	35	115	25	26	2	1	0	.....	.226	29	229	13	.952
1889—Worcester	Atl. A.	2B	49	175	31	49	8	1	3	16	.280	16	200	17	.927
1890—New York(a)	Nat.	OF-P	101	401	67	124	22	12	4	14	.309	108	23	28	.824
1891—Lincoln	W. A.	OF	93	395	78	138	15	11	3	.....	.349	165	16	28	.866
1891—Cleveland	Nat.	OF	40	166	30	45	7	4	0	2	.271	50	3	5	.914
1892—Cleveland	Nat.	OF	145	605	117	168	15	14	3	36	.278	282	18	28	.915
1893—Cleveland	Nat.	OF	124	480	144	179	23	15	6	39	.373	240	18	★42	.860
1894—Cleveland	Nat.	OF-P	124	518	134	185	25	15	8	32	.357	242	18	24	.915
1895—Cleveland	Nat.	OF	132	555	149	★235	21	15	5	47	★.423	274	18	35	.893
1896—Cleveland	Nat.	OF	●133	★585	★159	★240	26	16	6	32	★.410	271	15	23	.926
1897—Cleveland	Nat.	OF	128	519	128	199	28	8	2	27	.383	220	14	14	.944
1898—Cleveland(b)	Nat.	OF	148	624	115	★215	18	9	0	20	.345	266	18	10	.966
1899—St. Louis	Nat.	OF	138	567	115	228	17	10	7	22	.402	300	20	25	.928
1900—St. Louis	Nat	OF	●142	560	88	202	14	12	7	31	.361	★345	16	23	.940

Year Club	League	Pos.	G.	AB.	R.	H.	2B.	3B.	HR.	SB.	B.A.	PO.	A.	E.	F.A.
1901—St. Louis	Nat.	OF	●142	★597	★139	★228	21	17	10	27	★.382	305	17	21	.939
1902—St. Louis(c)	Amer.	SS-3-O	137	549	99	168	29	9	5	22	.306	296	17	★26	.923
1903—St. Louis	Amer.	OF-P	133	514	74	152	20	7	3	16	.296	231	10	15	.941
1904—St. Louis(d)	Amer.	OF	147	576	72	157	15	9	2	12	.273	258	26	15	.950
1905—Boston	Amer.	OF	149	573	78	147	13	13	4	13	.257	276	11	★22	.929
1906—Worcester	N. Eng.	OF	98	363	59	125	21	7	1	.....	★.344	137	6	6	.960
1907—Worcester	N. Eng.	OF	52	195	23	66	8	1	1	9	.338	80	7	7	.926
1908—Worcester	N. Eng.	OF	97	375	49	110	11	5	1	8	.293	165	9	16	.916
1909—Worcester	N. Eng.	OF	75	218	30	71	10	1	1	6	.326	99	4	9	.920
1910—Worcester	N. Eng.	OF	38	72	3	24	3	0	0	1	.333	15	1	2	.889
1911—Worcester	N. Eng.	OF	76	243	42	83	8	1	1	1	.342	80	10	11	.891
1912—Worcester	N. Eng.	OF	28	60	6	21	4	0	0	1	.350	17	0	0	1.000
1913—Worcester	N. Eng.	OF	19	42	4	10	3	0	0	0	.238	18	1	4	.826
1916—Low.-Law.-Hart.	East.	OF	24	38	5	8	....	....	....	0	.211	8	0	1	.889
American League Totals—4 Years			566	2212	323	624	77	38	14	63	.282	1061	64	78	.935
National League Totals—12 Years			1497	6177	1385	2248	237	147	58	329	.364	2903	198	278	.918
Major League Totals—16 Years			2063	8389	1708	2872	314	185	72	392	.342	3964	262	356	.922

aSold to Cleveland in 1891 and farmed to Lincoln until mid-August.
bTransferred with pick of Cleveland players to St. Louis by Frank De Hass Robison, owner of both clubs, 1899.
cJumped to American League.
dTraded to Boston Red Sox for Outfielder George Stone, January 1905.

PITCHING RECORD

Year Club	League	G.	CG.	IP.	W.	L.	Pct.	ShO.	H.	SO.	BB.
1890—New York	National	21	6	116	1	11	.083	0	130	81	91
1894—Cleveland	National	1	0	4	0	0	.000	0	6	0	1
1902—St. Louis	American	1	0	1	0	1	.000	0	4	2	1
National League Totals—2 Years		22	6	120	1	11	.083	0	136	81	92
American League Totals—1 Year		1	0	1	0	1	.000	0	4	2	1
Major League Totals—3 Years		23	6	121	1	12	.077	0	140	83	93

GEORGE HENRY BURNS

Born January 31, 1893, at Niles, O.

Died January 7, 1978, at Kirkland, Wash.

Height, 6.01. Weight, 185.

Threw and batted righthanded.

Made unassisted triple play against Cleveland Indians, September 14, 1923.
Named Most Valuable Player in American League, 1926.
Manager, Seattle, Pacific Coast League, 1932-33-34; Portland, Pacific Coast League, 1934-35.

Year Club	League	Pos.	G.	AB.	R.	H.	2B.	3B.	HR.	RBI.	B.A.	PO.	A.	E.	F.A.
1913—Burl.-Ottumwa	C.A.	1B	37	142	26	48	....	....	....	.....	.338	405	17	9	.979
1913—Sioux City	West.	1B	92	355	54	107	20	6	12	.....	.301	854	61	23	.975
1914—Detroit	Amer.	1B	137	478	55	139	22	5	5	57	.291	★1576	79	★30	.982
1915—Detroit	Amer.	1B	105	392	49	99	18	3	5	56	.253	1155	57	17	.986
1916—Detroit	Amer.	1B	135	479	60	137	22	6	4	73	.286	1355	54	22	.985
1917—Detroit(a)	Amer.	1B	119	407	42	92	14	10	1	42	.226	1127	57	12	.990
1918—Philadelphia	Amer.	1B	●130	505	61	★178	22	9	6	●74	.352	★1384	★104	★26	.983
1919—Philadelphia	Amer.	1B	126	470	63	139	29	9	8	53	.296	971	75	24	.978
1920—Phila.(b)-Cleve.	Amer.	1B	66	116	8	29	7	1	1	20	.250	97	11	4	.964
1921—Cleveland(c)	Amer.	1B	84	244	52	88	21	4	0	48	.361	534	41	6	.990
1922—Boston	Amer.	1B	147	558	71	171	32	5	12	73	.306	1412	94	★20	.987
1923—Boston(d)	Amer.	1B	146	551	91	181	47	5	7	82	.328	1485	92	★16	.990
1924—Cleveland	Amer.	1B	129	462	64	143	37	5	4	68	.310	1227	110	18	.987
1925—Cleveland	Amer.	1B	127	488	69	164	41	4	6	79	.336	1195	82	14	.989
1926—Cleveland	Amer.	1B	151	603	97	●216	★64	3	4	114	.358	1499	99	19	.988
1927—Cleveland	Amer.	1B	140	549	84	175	51	2	3	78	.319	1362	102	15	.990
1928—Cleve.(e)-N.Y.	Amer.	1B	86	213	30	54	12	1	5	30	.254	477	38	8	.985
1929—N.Y.(f)-Phila.	Amer.	1B	38	58	5	13	5	0	1	11	.224	99	5	0	1.000
1930—Missions	P.C.	1B	200	767	106	268	58	4	22	131	.349	★1896	★154	24	.988
1931—Missions-L.A.	P.C.	1B	178	696	131	226	52	4	18	129	.325	1575	★120	16	★.991
1932—Seattle	P.C.	1B	172	687	125	243	53	7	11	★140	.354	1629	117	22	.988
1933—Seattle	P.C.	1B	169	643	116	217	32	5	27	128	.337	1515	85	16	.990
1934—Seat.-Portland	P.C.	1B	118	394	45	115	10	1	2	54	.292	914	57	16	.984
Major League Totals—16 Years			1866	6573	901	2018	444	72	72	958	.307	16955	1100	251	.986

aTraded to Philadelphia Athletics for Outfielder Ping Bodie, March 8, 1918.
bSold to Cleveland Indians, May 29, 1920.

cTraded to Boston Red Sox with Outfielders Elmer Smith and Joe Harris for First Baseman Stuffy McInnis, December 24, 1921.

dTraded to Cleveland Indians with Catcher Roxy Walters and Infielder Chick Fewster for Pitcher Danny Boone, Catcher Steve O'Neill, Outfielder Joe Donnelly and Infielder Bill Wambsganss, January 7, 1924.

eReleased, September, 1928; subsequently signed with New York Yankees.

fReleased, June, 1929; signed by Philadelphia Athletics in same month.

WORLD SERIES RECORD

Year Club League	Pos.	G.	AB.	R.	H.	2B.	3B.	HR.	RBI.	B.A.	PO.	A.	E.	F.A.
1920—Cleveland.............. Amer.	1B	5	10	1	3	1	0	0	3	.300	38	1	1	.975
1929—Philadelphia .... Amer.	PH	1	2	0	0	0	0	0	0	.000	0	0	0	.000
World Series Totals—2 Years		6	12	1	3	1	0	0	3	.250	38	1	1	.975

THOMAS P. (OYSTER) BURNS

Born September 6, 1862, at Philadelphia, Pa.

Died November 16, 1928, at Brooklyn, N.Y.

Height, 5.09. Weight, 187.

Threw and batted righthanded.

Manager, Hartford, Atlantic League, 1897.

Year Club League	Pos.	G.	AB.	R.	H.	2B.	3B.	HR.	SB.	B.A.	PO.	A.	E.	F.A.
1883—Harrisburg .... Int.-St.	OF-IF-P	....	....	....	....	...	...	...	....	.220	.....	....	...	......
1884—Wilmington .... East.	SS-P	55	249	....	84	...	...	...	....	.337	44	175	35	.862
1884—Wilmington .... Union Assn.	SS	2	7	0	1	0	1	0	0	.143	1	6	2	.778
1884—Baltimore .... A.A.	IF-OF-P	36	135	35	41	2	6	6	....	.304	.....	....	...	......
1885—Baltimore .... A.A.	OF-IF-P	76	319	49	73	11	6	5	....	.229	.....	....	....	......
1885—Newark .... East.	3B-P	12	45	2	8	0	0	0	....	.178	(13 PO-A)		1	.929
1886—Newark .... East.	3B	82	262	74	79	25	4	9	20	.302	93	106	17	*.921
1887—Baltimore .... A.A.	SS-3B	140	611	120	245	33	20	10	57	.401	.....	....	...	......
1888—Balt.-Brooklyn ...... A.A.	SS-OF	129	528	95	158	27	13	6	48	.299	.....	....	...	......
1889—Brooklyn .... A.A.	OF	132	499	104	157	19	11	5	37	.315	134	23	16	.908
1890—Brooklyn .... Nat.	OF	119	472	102	134	22	13	●13	21	.284	137	23	10	.941
1891—Brooklyn .... Nat.	OF	122	465	75	131	23	14	4	23	.282	177	16	23	.894
1892—Brooklyn .... Nat.	OF	139	545	94	168	25	18	4	35	.308	155	14	10	.944
1893—Brooklyn .... Nat.	OF	107	397	67	111	31	10	6	21	.280	155	19	14	.926
1894—Brooklyn .... Nat.	OF	126	513	107	184	30	14	5	29	.359	212	16	14	.942
1895—Brook.-N.Y. .... Nat.	OF	50	187	28	48	5	5	1	5	.257	85	8	9	.912
1896—Newark .... Atl.	OF-1B-P	111	426	118	168	39	15	12	51	.394	300	28	17	.951
1897—Hartford .... Atl.	OF	128	478	82	159	35	8	1	32	.333	168	12	15	.923
American Assn. Totals—5 Years		513	2092	403	674	92	56	32	142	.322	.....	....	....	......
National League Totals—6 Years.........		663	2579	473	776	136	74	33	134	.301	921	96	80	.927
Union Association Totals—1 Year........		2	7	0	1	0	1	0	0	.143	1	6	2	.778
Major League Totals—11 Years............		1178	4678	876	1451	228	131	65	276	.310	....	.....	....	......

Pitching record shows no wins, no losses in 1884 with Baltimore; seven wins, four losses in 1885. With Harrisburg in 1883, record was 8-3—.727.

ROY CAMPANELLA
(Campy)

Born November 19, 1921, at Philadelphia, Pa.

Height, 5.09½. Weight, 205.

Threw and batted righthanded.

Holds major league record for most home runs by catcher, season (40), 1953.

Hit three home runs in a game, August 26, 1950.

Led National League catchers in double plays with 12 in 1948 and tied for lead with 12 in 1951.

Named Outstanding Player in the National League by THE SPORTING NEWS, 1953.

Named Most Valuable Player, National League, 1951-53-55.

Named as catcher on THE SPORTING NEWS All-Star Major League Teams, 1949-51-53-55.

Named to Hall of Fame, 1969.

Year Club	League	Pos.	G.	AB.	R.	H.	2B.	3B.	HR.	RBI.	B.A.	PO.	A.	E.	F.A.
1946—Nashua	New Eng.	C	113	396	75	115	19	8	13	96	.290	★687	★64	★15	.980
1947—Montreal	Int.	C	135	440	64	120	25	3	13	75	.273	★642	★83	9	★.988
1948—St. Paul	A.A.	C-OF	35	123	31	40	5	2	13	39	.325	147	19	6	.965
1948—Brooklyn	Nat.	C	83	279	32	72	11	3	9	45	.258	413	45	9	.981
1949—Brooklyn	Nat.	C	130	436	65	125	22	2	22	82	.287	★684	55	11	★.985
1950—Brooklyn	Nat.	C	126	437	70	123	19	3	31	89	.281	★683	54	11	.985
1951—Brooklyn	Nat.	C	143	505	90	164	33	1	33	108	.325	★722	★72	★11	.986
1952—Brooklyn	Nat.	C	128	468	73	126	18	1	22	97	.269	662	55	4	★.994
1953—Brooklyn	Nat.	C	144	519	103	162	26	3	41	★142	.312	★807	57	10	★.989
1954—Brooklyn	Nat.	C	111	397	43	82	14	3	19	51	.207	600	58	7	.989
1955—Brooklyn	Nat.	C	123	446	81	142	20	1	32	107	.318	★672	54	6	.992
1956—Brooklyn	Nat.	C	124	388	39	85	6	1	20	73	.219	★659	49	11	.985
1957—Brooklyn (a)	Nat	C	103	330	31	80	9	0	13	62	.242	618	51	5	★.993
Major League Totals—10 Years..............			1215	4205	627	1161	178	18	242	856	.276	6520	550	85	.988

aIncurred injuries in automobile accident, January 28, 1958, which ended his playing career.

WORLD SERIES RECORD

Year Club	League	Pos.	G.	AB.	R.	H.	2B.	3B.	HR.	RBI.	B.A.	PO.	A.	E.	F.A.
1949—Brooklyn	Nat.	C	5	15	2	4	1	0	1	2	.267	32	2	0	1.000
1952—Brooklyn	Nat.	C	7	28	0	6	0	0	1	1	.214	39	5	0	1.000
1953—Brooklyn	Nat.	C	6	22	6	6	0	0	1	2	.273	47	9	0	1.000
1955—Brooklyn	Nat	C	7	27	4	7	3	0	2	4	.259	42	3	1	.978
1956—Brooklyn	Nat.	C	7	22	2	4	1	0	0	3	.182	49	3	0	1.000
World Series Totals—5 Years			32	114	14	27	5	0	4	12	.237	209	22	1	.996

RODNEY CLINE (ROD) CAREW

Born October 1, 1945, at Gatun, Panama.
Height, 6.00. Weight, 182.
Threw right and batted lefthanded.

Shares major league records for most times stealing home, season (7), 1969; most stolen bases, inning (3), May 18, 1969, third inning.

Shares American League records for most double plays by first baseman, game (6), August 29, 1977, first game (10 innings); most putouts by first baseman, game (32), April 13, 1982 (20 innings); most chances accepted by first baseman, game (34), April 13, 1982 (20 innings); most seasons leading league in intentional bases on balls (3).

Led American League in intentional bases on balls received with 18 in 1975, 15 in 1977 and 19 in 1978.

Led American League first basemen in double plays with 149 in 1976 and 161 in 1977.

Led American League first basemen in assists with 121 in 1977.

Led American League first basemen in total chances with 1,590 in 1977.

Named Major League Player of the Year by THE SPORTING NEWS, 1977.

Named American League Player of the Year by THE SPORTING NEWS, 1977.

Named American League Most Valuable Player by Baseball Writers' Association of America, 1977.

Named American League Rookie Player of the Year by THE SPORTING NEWS, 1967.

Named American League Rookie of the Year by Baseball Writers' Association of America, 1967.

Named first baseman on THE SPORTING NEWS American League All-Star Team, 1977 and 1978.

Named second baseman on THE SPORTING NEWS American League All-Star Team, 1967 through 1969 and 1972 through 1975.

Year Club	League	Pos.	G.	AB.	R.	H.	2B.	3B.	HR.	RBI.	B.A.	PO.	A.	E.	F.A.
1964—Melbourne Twins	Coc. Rk.	2B	37	123	17	40	5	●3	0	21	.325	86	48	7	.950
1965—Orlando	Fla. St.	2B	125	439	57	133	20	8	1	52	.303	290	328	●28	.957
1966—Wilson	Carol.	2B	112	383	64	112	19	3	1	30	.292	248	275	21	.961
1967—Minnesota	Amer.	2B	137	514	66	150	22	7	8	51	.292	289	314	15	.976
1968—Minnesota	Amer.	●2B-SS	127	461	46	126	27	2	1	42	.273	266	285	●18	.968
1969—Minnesota	Amer.	2B	123	458	79	152	30	4	8	56	★.332	244	302	17	.970
1970—Minnesota	Amer.	2B-1B	51	191	27	70	12	3	4	28	.366	79	122	8	.962
1971—Minnesota	Amer.	2B-3B	147	577	88	177	16	10	2	48	.307	324	331	16	.976
1972—Minnesota	Amer.	2B	142	535	61	170	21	6	0	51	★.318	331	378	16	.978
1973—Minnesota	Amer.	2B	149	580	98	★203	30	●11	6	62	★.350	383	413	13	.984
1974—Minnesota	Amer.	2B	153	599	86	★218	30	5	3	55	★.364	375	416	★33	.960
1975—Minnesota	Amer.	2B-1B	143	535	89	192	24	4	14	80	★.359	408	377	21	.974
1976—Minnesota	Amer.	1B-2B	156	605	97	200	29	12	9	90	.331	1398	150	12	.990
1977—Minnesota	Amer.	1B-2B	155	616	★128	★239	38	★16	14	100	★.388	1463	124	10	.994
1978—Minnesota†	Amer.	1B-2B-OF	152	564	85	188	26	10	5	70	★.333	1363	105	16	.989
1979—California	Amer.	1B	110	409	78	130	15	3	3	44	.318	804	55	10	.988
1980—California	Amer.	1B	144	540	74	179	34	7	3	59	.331	897	57	6	.994
1981—California	Amer.	1B	93	364	57	111	17	1	2	21	.305	877	60	5	.995
1982—California	Amer.	1B	138	523	88	167	25	5	3	44	.319	1339	94	12	.992

Year	Club	League	Pos.	G.	AB.	R.	H.	2B.	3B.	HR.	RBI.	B.A.	PO.	A.	E.	F.A.
1983—California‡	Amer.		1B-2B	129	472	66	160	24	2	2	44	.339	891	42	6	.994
1984—California	Amer.		1B	93	329	42	97	8	1	3	31	.295	724	59	●15	.981
1985—California§	Amer.		1B	127	443	69	124	17	3	2	39	.280	1055	65	7	.994
Major League Totals—19 Years				2469	9315	1424	3053	445	112	92	1015	.328	13510	3709	260	.985

Signed as free agent by Minnesota Twins' organization, June 25, 1964.

†Traded to California Angels for Outfielder Ken Landreaux, Pitchers Paul Hartzell and Brad Havens and Third Baseman Dave Engle, February 3, 1979.

‡Granted free agency, November 7, 1983; re-signed by Angels, November 22, 1983.

§Granted free agency, November 12, 1985.

CHAMPIONSHIP SERIES RECORD

Year	Club	League	Pos.	G.	AB.	R.	H.	2B.	3B.	HR.	RBI.	B.A.	PO.	A.	E.	F.A.
1969—Minnesota	Amer.		2B	3	14	0	1	0	0	0	0	.071	6	3	1	.900
1970—Minnesota	Amer.		PH	2	2	0	0	0	0	0	0	.000	0	0	0	.000
1979—California	Amer.		1B	4	17	4	7	3	0	0	1	.412	34	1	0	1.000
1982—California	Amer.		1B	5	17	2	3	1	0	0	0	.176	43	4	0	1.000
Championship Series Totals—4 Years				14	50	6	11	4	0	0	1	.220	83	8	1	.989

MAX GEORGE CAREY
(Scoops)

Born January 11, 1890, at Terre Haute, Ind.
Died May 30, 1976, at Miami Beach, Fla.
Height, 5.11½. Weight, 170.
Threw right and batted left and righthanded.

Holds major league record for most years leading league in stolen bases (10).
Shares major league records for most times with two hits in inning, game (2), June 22, 1925, first and eighth innings; most years leading league in putouts (9) and assists (9), by outfielder.
Holds National League record for most double plays by outfielder, lifetime (86).
Holds modern National League record for most assists by outfielder, lifetime (339).
Selected as outfielder on THE SPORTING NEWS All-Star Major League Team, 1925.
Coach, Pittsburgh Pirates, 1930; manager, Brooklyn Dodgers, 1932-33; Miami, Florida East Coast League, 1940; scout, Baltimore Orioles, 1955; manager, Cordele, Georgia-Florida League, 1955; Louisville, American Association, 1956.
Named to Hall of Fame, 1961.

Year	Club	League	Pos.	G.	AB.	R.	H.	2B.	3B.	HR.	RBI.	B.A.	PO.	A.	E.	F.A.
1909—South Bend	Cent.		OF-SS	48	158	5	25	2	0	0	.....	.158	129	92	24	.902
1910—South Bend	Cent.		OF	96	327	39	96	15	8	2	.....	.293	192	56	15	.943
1910—Pittsburgh	Nat.		OF	2	6	2	3	0	1	0	2	.500	10	1	0	1.000
1911—Pittsburgh	Nat.		OF	122	427	77	110	15	10	5	41	.258	304	11	8	.975
1912—Pittsburgh	Nat.		OF	150	587	114	177	23	8	5	61	.302	★369	19	13	●.968
1913—Pittsburgh	Nat.		OF	154	★620	●99	172	23	10	5	53	.277	★363	★28	16	.961
1914—Pittsburgh	Nat.		OF	●156	★593	76	144	25	★17	1	32	.243	318	23	12	.966
1915—Pittsburgh	Nat.		OF	140	564	76	143	26	5	3	28	.254	307	21	6	.982
1916—Pittsburgh	Nat.		OF	154	599	90	158	23	11	7	42	.264	★419	★32	8	.983
1917—Pittsburgh	Nat.		OF	155	588	82	174	21	12	1	53	.296	★440	28	10	.979
1918—Pittsburgh	Nat.		OF	126	468	70	128	14	6	3	44	.274	★359	★25	★17	.958
1919—Pittsburgh	Nat.		OF	66	244	41	75	10	2	0	9	.307	173	5	10	.947
1920—Pittsburgh	Nat.		OF	130	485	74	140	18	4	1	35	.289	345	10	12	.967
1921—Pittsburgh	Nat.		OF	140	521	85	161	34	4	7	56	.309	★431	15	★20	.957
1922—Pittsburgh	Nat.		OF	155	629	140	207	28	12	10	70	.329	★449	22	15	.969
1923—Pittsburgh	Nat.		OF	153	610	120	188	32	●19	6	63	.308	★450	★28	19	.962
1924—Pittsburgh	Nat.		OF	149	599	113	178	30	9	7	55	.297	★428	16	●16	.965
1925—Pittsburgh	Nat.		OF	133	542	109	186	39	13	5	44	.343	363	20	★20	.950
1926—Pitts.(a)-Brook.	Nat.		OF	113	424	64	98	17	6	0	35	.231	295	8	19	.941
1927—Brooklyn	Nat.		OF	144	538	70	143	30	10	1	54	.266	331	19	11	.970
1928—Brooklyn	Nat.		OF	108	296	41	73	11	0	2	19	.247	202	8	3	.986
1929—Brooklyn	Nat.		OF	19	23	2	7	0	0	0	1	.304	7	0	0	1.000
Major League Totals—20 Years				2469	9363	1545	2665	419	159	69	797	.285	6363	339	235	.966

aReleased to Brooklyn Dodgers on waivers, July, 1926.

WORLD SERIES RECORD

Year	Club	League	Pos.	G.	AB.	R.	H.	2B.	3B.	HR.	RBI.	B.A.	PO.	A.	E.	F.A.
1925—Pittsburgh	Nat.		OF	7	24	6	11	4	0	0	2	.458	14	0	1	.933

—DID YOU KNOW—

That Rod Carew won the 1972 American League batting title with a .318 mark—10 points below his final career average of .328?

STEVEN NORMAN (STEVE) CARLTON

Born December 22, 1944, at Miami, Fla.
Height, 6.05. Weight, 210.
Threw and batted lefthanded.

Holds major league records for most consecutive starting assignments, lifetime (544); most strikeouts by lefthanded pitcher, game (19), September 15, 1969.

Holds National League records for most years and most consecutive years pitched (22); most games started, lifetime (677); most consecutive starting assignments, lifetime (534); most years, 100 or more strikeouts (18); most consecutive years, 100 or more strikeouts (18); most strikeouts, lifetime (4,000); most bases on balls issued, lifetime (1,717); most balks, season (11), 1979.

Shares National League record for most strikeouts, game (19), September 15, 1969.

Shares modern National League record for most games won, season, by lefthander (27), 1972.

Led National League pitchers in games started with 41 in 1972, 38 in 1982 and tied for lead with 40 in 1973 and 38 in 1980.

Led National League in shutouts with 6 in 1982.

Led National League in complete games with 30 in 1972, 19 in 1982 and tied for lead with 18 in 1973.

Led National League in balks with 7 in 1977, 11 in 1979, 7 in 1980 and 9 in 1982 and 1983 and tied for lead with 7 in 1975, 1978 and 1984.

Led National League in wild pitches with 17 in 1980.

Led National League in home runs allowed with 30 in 1978.

Won National League Cy Young Memorial Award, 1972, 1977, 1980 and 1982.

Named National League Pitcher of the Year by THE SPORTING NEWS, 1972, 1977, 1980 and 1982.

Named lefthanded pitcher on THE SPORTING NEWS National League All-Star Team, 1969, 1971, 1972, 1977, 1979, 1980 and 1982.

Named pitcher on THE SPORTING NEWS National League All-Star fielding team, 1981.

Year Club	League	G.	IP.	W.	L.	Pct.	H.	R.	ER.	SO.	BB.	ERA.
1964—Rock Hill	W. Carol.	11	79	10	1	.909	39	17	9	91	36	1.03
1964—Winnipeg	Northern	12	75	4	4	.500	63	40	28	79	48	3.36
1964—Tulsa	Texas	4	24	1	1	.500	16	13	7	21	18	2.63
1965—St. Louis	National	15	25	0	0	.000	27	7	7	21	8	2.52
1966—Tulsa	P. Coast	19	128	9	5	.643	110	65	51	108	54	3.59
1966—St. Louis	National	9	52	3	3	.500	56	22	18	25	18	3.12
1967—St. Louis	National	30	193	14	9	.609	173	71	64	168	62	2.98
1968—St. Louis	National	34	232	13	11	.542	214	87	77	162	61	2.99
1969—St. Louis	National	31	236	17	11	.607	185	66	57	210	93	2.17
1970—St. Louis	National	34	254	10	★19	.345	239	123	105	193	109	3.72
1971—St. Louis†	National	37	273	20	9	.690	275	120	108	172	98	3.56
1972—Philadelphia	National	41	★346	★27	10	.730	★257	84	76	★310	87	★1.98
1973—Philadelphia	National	40	●293	13	★20	.394	★293	★146	★127	223	113	3.90
1974—Philadelphia	National	39	291	16	13	.552	249	118	104	★240	★136	3.22
1975—Philadelphia	National	37	255	15	14	.517	217	116	101	192	104	3.56
1976—Philadelphia	National	35	253	20	7	★.741	224	94	88	195	72	3.13
1977—Philadelphia	National	36	283	★23	10	.697	229	99	83	198	89	2.64
1978—Philadelphia	National	34	247	16	13	.552	228	91	78	161	63	2.84
1979—Philadelphia	National	35	251	18	11	.621	202	112	101	213	89	3.62
1980—Philadelphia	National	38	★304	★24	9	.727	243	87	79	★286	90	2.34
1981—Philadelphia	National	24	190	13	4	.765	152	59	51	179	62	2.42
1982—Philadelphia	National	38	★295⅓	★23	11	.676	★253	114	102	★286	86	3.10
1983—Philadelphia	National	37	★283⅔	15	16	.484	★277	117	98	★275	84	3.11
1984—Philadelphia	National	33	229	13	7	.650	214	104	91	163	79	3.58
1985—Philadelphia	National	16	92	1	8	.111	84	43	34	48	53	3.33
1986—Phila.‡-San Francisco§	National	22	113	5	11	.313	138	90	74	80	61	5.89
1986—Chicago x	American	10	63⅓	4	3	.571	58	30	26	40	25	3.69
1987—Cleveland y-Minnesota z	American	32	152	6	14	.300	165	111	97	91	86	5.74
1988—Minnesota a	American	4	9⅔	0	1	.000	20	19	18	5	5	16.76
National League Totals—22 Years		695	4991⅓	319	226	.585	4429	1970	1723	4000	1717	3.11
American League Totals—3 Years		46	225	10	18	.357	243	160	141	136	116	5.64
Major League Totals—24 Years		741	5216⅓	329	244	.574	4672	2130	1864	4136	1833	3.22

Signed as free agent by St. Louis Cardinals' organization, October 8, 1963.

†Traded to Philadelphia Phillies for Pitcher Rick Wise, February 25, 1972.

‡Released, June 24, 1986; signed by San Francisco Giants, July 4, 1986.

§Released, August 7, 1986; signed by Chicago White Sox, August 12, 1986.

xGranted free agency, November 12, 1986; signed by Cleveland Indians, April 4, 1987.

yTraded to Minnesota Twins for a player to be named later, July 31, 1987; Cleveland Indians' organization acquired Pitcher Jeff Perry to complete deal, August 18, 1987.

zReleased, December 21, 1987; re-signed by Twins, January 29, 1988.

aReleased, April 28, 1988.

CHAMPIONSHIP SERIES RECORD

Holds major league record for most bases on balls, lifetime (28).

Shares major league record for most games won, lifetime (4).

Holds National League records for most games started (8), innings pitched (53⅔), hits allowed (53), earned runs allowed (21) and strikeouts (39), lifetime.

Year Club	League	G.	IP.	W.	L.	Pct.	H.	R.	ER.	SO.	BB.	ERA.
1976—Philadelphia	National	1	7	0	1	.000	8	5	4	6	5	5.14
1977—Philadelphia	National	2	11⅔	0	1	.000	13	9	9	6	8	6.94
1978—Philadelphia	National	1	9	1	0	1.000	8	4	4	8	2	4.00
1980—Philadelphia	National	2	12⅓	1	0	1.000	11	3	3	6	8	2.19
1983—Philadelphia	National	2	13⅔	2	0	1.000	13	1	1	13	5	0.66
Championship Series Totals—5 Years		8	53⅔	4	2	.667	53	22	21	39	28	3.52

WORLD SERIES RECORD

Year Club	League	G.	IP.	W.	L.	Pct.	H.	R.	ER.	SO.	BB.	ERA.
1967—St. Louis	National	1	6	0	1	.000	3	1	0	5	2	0.00
1968—St. Louis	National	2	4	0	0	.000	7	3	3	3	1	6.75
1980—Philadelphia	National	2	15	2	0	1.000	14	5	4	17	9	2.40
1983—Philadelphia	National	1	6⅔	0	1	.000	5	3	2	7	3	2.70
World Series Totals—4 Years		6	31⅔	2	2	.500	29	12	9	32	15	2.56

ALEXANDER JOY CARTWRIGHT

Born April 17, 1820, at New York, N. Y.

Died July 12, 1892, at Honolulu, T. H.

Height, 6.02. Weight, 210.

Organized first baseball club, the Knickerbocker Ball Club of New York, 1845. Served as Secretary and vice-president. Umpired first match game of baseball ever played. New York vs. Knickerbockers, June 19, 1846. Also played infield, outfield and catcher (then called "behind"). Four years after he organized the Knickerbockers, Cartwright left New York and set out on horseback and later foot for California. He taught the game to frontiersmen and Indians along the way. After reaching California, he and his brother, Alfred, whom he met there, intended to sail back to New York—by way of China—but Alexander took sick near the Sandwich Islands (Hawaii) and was put ashore. He prospered there and set up baseball leagues while he made a financial bonanza out of the Islands.

Named to Hall of Fame in 1938 for service apart from playing the game.

Year Club	G.	†O.	R.
1845—Knickerbockers of New York City	10	19	30
1846—Knickerbockers of New York City	40	137	161
1847—Knickerbockers of New York City	45	131	161
1848—Knickerbockers of New York City	26	67	96
Totals	121	354	448

†Outs means number of times put out.

ROBERT LEE (BOB) CARUTHERS
(Parisian Bob)

Born January 5, 1864, at Memphis, Tenn.

Died August 5, 1911, at Peoria, Ill.

Height, 5.10. Weight, 150.

Threw right and batted lefthanded.

Umpire, Western League, 1905-06; Three-I League, 1910-11.

Year Club	League	G.	IP.	W.	L.	Pct.	H.	R.	BB.	SO.	ShO.	CG.
1883—Grand Rapids	Northwestern					(Played outfield)						
1884—Minneapolis	Northwestern	35	....	15	16	.484	....	....	....	....	....	27
1884—St. Louis	Amer. Assn.	12	76	7	2	.778	78	51	15	47	0	6
1885—St. Louis	Amer. Assn.	53	482	⋆40	13	⋆.755	416	196	79	195	6	53
1886—St. Louis	Amer. Assn.	44	390	30	14	.682	323	163	81	173	2	43
1887—St. Louis†	Amer. Assn.	39	399	29	9	⋆.763	392	182	62	50	2	39
1888—Brooklyn	Amer. Assn.	44	393	29	15	.659	341	180	80	110	4	44
1889—Brooklyn	Amer. Assn.	55	442	⋆40	12	⋆.769	326	206	104	109	⋆7	45
1890—Brooklyn	National	37	304	23	11	.676	294	159	89	62	2	30

Year Club	League	G.	IP.	W.	L.	Pct.	H.	R.	BB.	SO.	ShO.	CG.
1891—Brooklyn	National	41	311	17	17	.500	336	201	101	69	2	29
1892—St. Louis	National	16	102	2	8	.200	125	77	32	23	0	10
1893—Chicago	National	1	....	....	....	....	....	....	....	....	....	....
1894—Grand Rapids	Western					(No pitching record)						
1895—Jackson	West. Assn.					(No pitching record)						
1896—Burlington	West. Assn.					(No pitching record)						
American Association Totals—6 Years		247	2122	175	65	.729	1972	961	356	701	21	230
National League Totals—4 Years		95	717	42	36	.538	755	437	235	162	4	69
Major League Totals—10 Years		342	2839	217	101	.682	2727	1398	591	863	25	299

BATTING RECORD

Year Club	League	Pos.	G.	AB.	R.	H.	2B.	3B.	HR.	SB.	B.A.
1883—Grand Rapids	Northwestern	OF-P	50	227	51	63	...	...	...	....	.288
1884—Minneapolis	Northwestern	OF-P	....	....	....	....	...	...	...	....	....
1884—St. Louis	Amer. Assn.	OF-P	23	84	15	22	2	0	2	....	.262
1885—St. Louis	Amer. Assn.	OF-P	60	217	38	45	9	2	1	....	.207
1886—St. Louis	Amer. Assn.	OF-P	86	313	91	107	22	12	3	24	.342
1887—St. Louis†	Amer. Assn.	OF-P	98	425	94	195	23	9	7	59	.459
1888—Brooklyn	Amer. Assn.	OF-P	94	335	59	77	11	4	4	33	.230
1889—Brooklyn	Amer. Assn.	OF-P	57	171	45	46	8	3	2	15	.269
1890—Brooklyn	National	OF-P	71	238	46	63	6	3	1	13	.265
1891—Brooklyn	National	OF-P	47	165	25	48	5	3	2	5	.291
1892—St. Louis	National	OF-P	142	508	75	141	16	7	3	21	.277
1893—Chicago-Cincinnati	National	OF	14	52	15	14	2	0	1	3	.269
1894—Grand Rapids	Western	OF	132	544	166	181	...	...	...	....	.333
1895—Jackson	West. Assn.	OF	92	371	100	119	...	...	...	....	.319
1896—Burlington	West. Assn.	OF	52	....	45	....	...	...	...	23	.291
American Association Totals—6 Years			418	1545	342	492	75	30	19	131	.318
National League Totals—4 Years			274	963	161	266	29	13	7	42	.276
Major League Totals—10 Years			692	2508	503	758	104	43	26	173	.302

†Bases on balls counted as hits in 1887.

NORMAN DALTON (NORM) CASH

Born November 10, 1934, at Justiceburg, Tex.

Died October 12, 1986, at Beaver Island, Mich.

Height, 5.11½. Weight, 190.

Threw and batted lefthanded.

Shares major league record by having no putouts or chances at first base, June 27, 1963.
Named first baseman on THE SPORTING NEWS American League All-Star Team, 1961 and 1971.
Named American League Comeback Player of the Year by THE SPORTING NEWS, 1965 and 1971.

Year Club	League	Pos.	G.	AB.	R.	H.	2B.	3B.	HR.	RBI.	B.A.	PO.	A.	E.	F.A.
1955—Waterloo	I.I.I.	OF	92	315	54	100	13	5	17	64	.290	173	6	7	.962
1956—Waterloo	I.I.I.	OF	115	419	81	140	20	3	23	96	.334	201	6	6	.972
1957—Chicago	Amer.								(In Military Service)						
1958—Chicago	Amer.	OF	13	8	2	2	0	0	0	0	.250	2	0	0	1.000
1958—Indianapolis	A.A.	OF-1B	29	81	10	20	6	0	1	10	.247	40	3	2	.956
1959—Chicago (a-b)	Amer.	1B	58	104	16	25	0	1	4	16	.240	231	14	4	.984
1960—Detroit	Amer.	1B-OF	121	353	64	101	16	3	18	63	.286	743	59	7	.991
1961—Detroit	Amer.	1B	159	535	119	*193	22	8	41	132	*.361	*1231	127	11	.992
1962—Detroit	Amer.	1B-OF	148	507	94	123	16	2	39	89	.243	1091	116	10	.992
1963—Detroit	Amer.	1B	147	493	67	133	19	1	26	79	.270	1161	99	7	.994
1964—Detroit	Amer.	1B	144	479	63	123	15	5	23	83	.257	1105	92	4	*.997
1965—Detroit	Amer.	1B	142	467	79	124	23	1	30	82	.266	1091	●97	9	.992
1966—Detroit	Amer.	1B	160	603	98	168	18	3	32	93	.279	1271	*114	*17	.988
1967—Detroit	Amer.	1B	152	488	64	118	16	5	22	72	.242	1135	*112	6	*.995
1968—Detroit	Amer.	1B	127	411	50	108	15	1	25	63	.263	924	88	8	.992
1969—Detroit	Amer.	1B	142	483	81	135	15	4	22	74	.280	1016	96	7	.994
1970—Detroit	Amer.	1B	130	370	58	96	18	2	15	53	.259	868	70	10	.989
1971—Detroit	Amer.	1B	135	452	72	128	10	3	32	91	.283	1020	75	9	.992
1972—Detroit	Amer.	1B	137	440	51	114	16	0	22	61	.259	1060	70	8	.993
1973—Detroit	Amer.	1B	121	363	51	95	19	0	19	40	.262	856	64	8	.991
1974—Detroit	Amer.	1B	53	137	17	34	3	2	7	12	.228	368	24	6	.985
Major League Totals—17 Years			2089	6705	1046	1820	241	41	377	1103	.271	15173	1317	131	.992

aTraded to Cleveland Indians with Catcher John Romano and Third Baseman-Outfielder Bubba Phillips for Pitchers Don Ferrarese and Jake Striker, Catcher Dick Brown and Outfielder Minnie Minoso, December 6, 1959.
bTraded to Detroit Tigers for Third Baseman Steve Demeter, April 12, 1960.

CHAMPIONSHIP SERIES RECORD

Year Club League	Pos.	G.	AB.	R.	H.	2B.	3B.	HR.	RBI.	B.A.	PO.	A.	E.	F.A.
1972—Detroit .... Amer.	OF-PH	5	15	1	4	0	0	1	2	.267	39	3	0	1.000

WORLD SERIES RECORD

Shares records for most at-bats (2) and hits (2), inning, October 9, 1968, third inning.

Year Club League	Pos.	G.	AB.	R.	H.	2B.	3B.	HR.	RBI.	B.A.	PO.	A.	E.	F.A.
1959—Chicago .... Amer.	PH	4	4	0	0	0	0	0	0	.000	0	0	0	.000
1968—Detroit .... Amer.	1B	7	26	5	10	0	0	1	5	.385	58	7	2	.970
World Series Totals—2 Years		11	30	5	10	0	0	1	5	.333	58	7	2	.970

PHILIP JOSEPH (PHIL) CAVARRETTA

Born July 19, 1916, at Chicago, Ill.

Height, 5.11½. Weight, 175.

Threw and batted lefthanded.

Led National League first basemen in double plays, 1935.

Named National League Most Valuable Player by Baseball Writers' Association, 1945.

Named as first baseman for THE SPORTING NEWS' All-Star Major League Team, 1945.

Manager, Chicago Cubs, 1951-52-53; Buffalo, International League, 1956-57-58; Lancaster, Eastern League, 1960; coach, Detroit Tigers, 1961-62-63; scout, Detroit Tigers, 1964; manager, Salinas, California League, 1965; Reno, California League, 1966-67; Waterbury, Eastern League, 1968; Birmingham, Southern League, 1970-72; minor league batting instructor, New York Mets, 1973 to 1980.

Year Club League	Pos.	G.	AB.	R.	H.	2B.	3B.	HR.	RBI.	B.A.	PO.	A.	E.	F.A.
1934—Peoria .... Central	1B	23	98	22	31	7	3	3	.....	.316	149	10	2	.988
1934—Reading .... N.Y.P.	1B	85	341	65	105	33	5	4	49	.308	727	52	18	.977
1934—Chicago .... Nat.	1B	7	21	5	8	0	1	1	6	.381	53	5	0	1.000
1935—Chicago .... Nat.	1B	146	589	85	162	28	12	8	82	.275	1347	98	●20	.986
1936—Chicago .... Nat.	1B-OF	124	458	55	125	18	1	9	56	.273	980	71	14	.987
1937—Chicago .... Nat.	1B-OF	106	329	43	94	18	7	5	56	.286	454	40	10	.980
1938—Chicago .... Nat.	1B	92	268	29	64	11	4	1	28	.239	277	21	4	.987
1939—Chicago .... Nat.	1B	22	55	4	15	3	1	0	0	.273	106	6	1	.991
1940—Chicago .... Nat.	1B-OF	65	193	34	54	11	4	2	22	.280	524	30	5	.991
1941—Chicago .... Nat.	1B-OF	107	346	46	99	18	4	6	40	.286	463	15	5	.990
1942—Chicago .... Nat.	1B-OF	136	482	59	130	28	4	3	54	.270	744	49	7	.991
1943—Chicago .... Nat.	1B-OF	143	530	93	154	27	9	8	73	.291	1305	67	★18	★.987
1944—Chicago .... Nat.	1B-OF	152	614	106	●197	35	15	5	82	.321	1363	78	13	.991
1945—Chicago .... Nat.	1B-OF	132	498	94	177	34	10	6	97	★.355	1172	78	9	.993
1946—Chicago .... Nat.	1B-OF	139	510	89	150	28	10	8	78	.294	646	47	11	.984
1947—Chicago .... Nat.	1B-OF	127	459	56	144	22	5	2	63	.314	420	24	8	.982
1948—Chicago .... Nat.	1B-OF	111	334	41	93	16	5	3	40	.278	446	32	3	.994
1949—Chicago .... Nat.	1B-OF	105	360	46	106	22	4	8	49	.294	712	67	5	.994
1950—Chicago .... Nat.	1B-OF	82	256	49	70	11	1	10	31	.273	609	47	9	.986
1951—Chicago .... Nat.	1B-OF	89	206	24	64	7	1	6	28	.311	444	42	3	.994
1952—Chicago .... Nat.	1B	41	63	7	15	1	1	1	8	.238	98	10	1	.991
1953—Chicago .... Nat.	PH	27	21	3	6	3	0	0	3	.286	0	0	0	.000
1954—Chicago .... Am.	1-O-PH	71	158	21	50	6	0	3	24	.316	269	17	3	.990
1955—Chicago .... Am.	1B-PH	6	4	1	0	0	0	0	0	.000	3	0	0	1.000
1956—Buffalo .... Int.	1B	57	69	10	18	2	0	1	10	.261	58	4	0	1.000
American League Totals—2 Years		77	162	22	50	6	0	3	24	.309	272	17	3	.990
National League Totals—20 Years		1953	6592	968	1927	341	99	92	896	.292	12163	827	146	.989
Major League Totals—22 Years		2030	6754	990	1977	347	99	95	920	.293	12435	844	149	.989

WORLD SERIES RECORD

Year Club League	Pos.	G.	AB.	R.	H.	2B.	3B.	HR.	RBI.	B.A.	PO.	A.	E.	F.A.
1935—Chicago .... Nat.	1B	6	24	1	3	0	0	0	0	.125	58	3	1	.984
1938—Chicago .... Nat.	OF	4	13	1	6	1	0	0	0	.462	4	1	0	1.000
1945—Chicago .... Nat.	1B	1	26	7	11	2	0	1	5	.423	71	3	0	1.000
World Series Totals—3 Years		17	63	9	20	3	0	1	5	.317	133	7	1	.993

—DID YOU KNOW—

That Detroit slugger Norm Cash reached the .300 mark only once in his major league career—but won the batting title that season (1961) when he hit .361?

ORLANDO MANUEL CEPEDA
(The Baby Bull)

Born September 17, 1937, at Ponce, Puerto Rico.
Height, 6.02. Weight, 215.
Threw and batted righthanded.

Tied major league record for most doubles, game (4), August 8, 1973.
Hit three home runs in a game, July 26, 1970, first game.
Named National League Rookie Player of the Year by THE SPORTING NEWS, 1958 and National League Rookie of the Year by Baseball Writers' Association, 1958.
Named First Baseman on THE SPORTING NEWS All-Star Major League Team, 1959.
Named First Baseman on THE SPORTING NEWS National League All-Star Team, 1961-62-67.
Named National League Most Valuable Player, 1967.
Named National League Player of the Year by THE SPORTING NEWS, 1967.
Scout, Chicago White Sox organization, 1980.

Year	Club	League	Pos.	G.	AB.	R.	H.	2B.	3B.	HR.	RBI.	B.A.	PO.	A.	E.	F.A.
1955—Salem		Appal.	3B	26	93	12	23	6	1	1	16	.247	33	49	16	.837
1955—Kokomo		M.-O.V.	3B	92	374	83	147	23	2	21	91	★.393	93	158	27	.903
1956—St. Cloud		North.	1B-3B	●125	499	100	★177	33	9	★26	★112	.355	.958	106	26	.976
1957—Minneapolis		A.A.	1B-3B-OF	151	563	91	174	31	3	25	108	.309	1162	103	18	.986
1958—San Francisco		Nat.	1B	148	603	88	188	★38	4	25	96	.312	★1322	97	●16	.989
1959—San Francisco		Nat.	1B-OF-3B	151	605	92	192	35	4	27	105	.317	995	74	22	.980
1960—San Francisco		Nat.	OF-1B	151	569	81	169	36	3	24	96	.297	681	37	13	.982
1961—San Francisco		Nat.	1B-OF	152	585	105	182	28	4	★46	★142	.311	774	51	5	.994
1962—San Francisco		Nat.	1B-OF	162	625	105	191	26	1	35	114	.306	1356	88	14	.990
1963—San Francisco		Nat.	★1B-OF	156	579	100	183	33	4	34	97	.316	1262	83	★21	.985
1964—San Francisco		Nat.	★1B-OF	142	529	75	161	27	2	31	97	.304	1211	80	★18	.986
1965—San Francisco		Nat.	1B-OF	33	34	1	6	1	0	1	5	.176	28	2	0	1.000
1966—S.F.(a)-St. Louis		Nat.	1B-OF	142	501	70	151	26	0	20	73	.301	1171	63	15	.988
1967—St. Louis		Nat.	1B	151	563	91	183	37	0	25	★111	.325	1304	90	10	.993
1968—St. Louis (b)		Nat.	1B	157	600	71	149	26	2	16	73	.248	1362	90	17	.988
1969—Atlanta		Nat.	1B	154	573	74	147	28	2	22	88	.257	1318	101	9	.994
1970—Atlanta		Nat.	1B	148	567	87	173	33	0	34	111	.305	1288	112	12	.992
1971—Atlanta		Nat.	1B	71	250	31	69	10	1	14	44	.276	586	49	5	.992
1972—Atlanta (c)		Nat.	1B	28	84	6	25	3	0	4	9	.298	171	13	0	1.000
1972—Oakland (d)		Amer.	PH	3	3	0	0	0	0	0	0	.000	0	0	0	.000
1973—Boston (e)		Amer.	DH	142	550	51	159	25	0	20	86	.289	0	0	0	.000
1974—Yucatan (f)		Mex.	1B	28	80	7	17	1	0	4	17	.213	19	1	0	1.000
1974—Kansas City		Amer.	DH	33	107	3	23	5	0	1	18	.215	0	0	0	.000
National League Totals—15 Years				1946	7267	1077	2169	387	27	358	1261	.298	14829	1030	177	.989
American League Totals—3 Years				178	660	54	182	30	0	21	104	.276	0	0	0	.000
Major League Totals—17 Years				2124	7927	1131	2351	417	27	379	1365	.297	14829	1030	177	.989

aTraded to St. Louis Cardinals for Pitcher Ray Sadecki, May 8, 1966.
bTraded to Atlanta Braves for Catcher-First Baseman Joe Torre, March 17, 1969.
cTraded for cash and Pitcher Denny McLain to Oakland A's, June 29, 1972.
dSigned by Boston Red Sox as free agent, January 19, 1973.
eSigned as free agent by Yucatan (Mexican League), June 15, 1974.
fSigned as free agent by Kansas City Royals, August 6, 1974.

CHAMPIONSHIP SERIES RECORD

Year	Club	League	Pos.	G.	AB.	R.	H.	2B.	3B.	HR.	RBI.	B.A.	PO.	A.	E.	F.A.
1969—Atlanta		Nat.	1B	3	11	2	5	2	0	1	3	.455	29	1	2	.938

WORLD SERIES RECORD

Year	Club	League	Pos.	G.	AB.	R.	H.	2B.	3B.	HR.	RBI.	B.A.	PO.	A.	E.	F.A.
1962—San Francisco		Nat.	1B	5	19	1	3	1	0	0	2	.158	39	4	0	1.000
1967—St. Louis		Nat.	1B	7	29	1	3	2	0	0	1	.103	52	4	0	1.000
1968—St. Louis		Nat.	1B	7	28	2	7	0	0	2	6	.250	47	4	0	1.000
World Series Totals—3 Years				19	76	4	13	3	0	2	9	.171	138	12	0	1.000

—DID YOU KNOW—

That Orlando Cepeda was the first player to win the National League Most Valuable Player award unanimously? The St. Louis Cardinals first baseman batted .325, hit 25 home runs, led the league with 111 runs batted in and collected the maximum 280 MVP votes in 1967.

RONALD CHARLES (RON) CEY
(The Penguin)

Born February 15, 1948, at Tacoma, Wash.
Height, 5.09. Weight, 185.
Threw and batted righthanded.

Led National League third basemen in double plays with 39 in 1973.
Led Pacific Coast League in bases on balls received with 117 in 1972.
Led Northwest League in sacrifice flies with 7 in 1968.
Led Pacific Coast League third baseman in putouts with 106, assists with 274 and tied for lead in double plays with 24 in 1972.
Led California League third basemen in double plays with 22 in 1969.
Tied for Pacific Coast League lead in being hit by pitch with 9 in 1971.

Year	Club	League	Pos.	G.	AB.	R.	H.	2B.	3B.	HR.	RBI.	B.A.	PO.	A.	E.	F.A.
1968—Tri-City		N'west	3B	74	254	50	76	11	4	9	*62	.299	46	*175	10	*.957
1969—Albuquerque		Texas	3B	13	32	8	5	1	0	0	2	.156	13	19	1	.970
1969—Bakersfield		Calif.	3B	98	353	68	117	16	1	22	56	.331	82	197	22	.927
1970—Albuquerque		Texas	3B	71	239	31	79	22	1	4	56	.331	44	132	10	.946
1971—Spokane		P. C.	3B	137	500	85	164	26	4	32	*123	.328	95	283	24	*.940
1971—Los Angeles		Nat.	PH	2	2	0	0	0	0	0	0	.000	0	0	0	.000
1972—Albuquerque		P. C.	3B-2B	142	496	99	163	25	7	23	103	.329	108	279	21	.949
1972—Los Angeles		Nat.	3B	11	37	3	10	1	0	1	3	.270	7	20	3	.900
1973—Los Angeles		Nat.	3B	152	507	60	124	18	4	15	80	.245	111	*328	18	.961
1974—Los Angeles		Nat.	3B	159	577	88	151	20	2	18	97	.262	155	365	22	.959
1975—Los Angeles		Nat.	3B	158	566	72	160	29	2	25	101	.283	144	309	19	.960
1976—Los Angeles		Nat.	3B	145	502	69	139	18	3	23	80	.277	111	334	16	.965
1977—Los Angeles		Nat.	3B	153	564	77	136	22	3	30	110	.241	138	346	18	.964
1978—Los Angeles		Nat.	3B	159	555	84	150	32	0	23	84	.270	116	336	16	.966
1979—Los Angeles		Nat.	3B	150	487	77	137	20	1	28	81	.281	123	265	9	*.977
1980—Los Angeles		Nat.	3B	157	551	81	140	25	0	28	77	.254	*127	317	13	.972
1981—Los Angeles		Nat.	3B	85	312	42	90	15	2	13	50	.288	71	184	16	.941
1982—Los Angeles†		Nat.	3B	150	556	62	141	23	1	24	79	.254	93	320	16	.963
1983—Chicago		Nat.	3B	159	581	73	160	33	1	24	90	.275	90	270	17	.955
1984—Chicago		Nat.	3B	146	505	71	121	27	0	25	97	.240	97	230	11	*.967
1985—Chicago		Nat.	3B	145	500	64	116	18	2	22	63	.232	75	273	*21	.943
1986—Chicago‡		Nat.	3B	97	256	42	70	21	0	13	36	.273	41	118	8	.952
1987—Oakland x		Amer.	1B-3B	45	104	12	23	6	0	4	11	.221	56	4	1	.984
National League Totals—16 Years				2028	7058	965	1845	322	21	312	1128	.261	1499	4015	223	.961
American League Totals—1 Year				45	104	12	23	6	0	4	11	.221	56	4	1	.984
Major League Totals—17 Years				2073	7162	977	1868	328	21	316	1139	.261	1555	4019	224	.961

Selected by New York Mets' organization in 24th round of free-agent draft, June 6, 1966.
Selected by Los Angeles Dodgers' organization in 3rd round of free-agent draft, June 7, 1968.
†Traded to Chicago Cubs for Outfielder Dan Cataline and Pitcher Vance Lovelace, January 19, 1983.
‡Traded to Oakland A's for Shortstop Luis Quinones, January 30, 1987.
xReleased, July 15, 1987.

CHAMPIONSHIP SERIES RECORD

Shares major league records for most doubles, lifetime (7); most grand slams, game (1), October 4, 1977; most runs batted in, inning (4), October 4, 1977, seventh inning.
Shares National League record for most hits, game (4), October 6, 1974.

Year	Club	League	Pos.	G.	AB.	R.	H.	2B.	3B.	HR.	RBI.	B.A.	PO.	A.	E.	F.A.
1974—Los Angeles		Nat.	3B	4	16	2	5	3	0	1	1	.313	2	4	2	.750
1977—Los Angeles		Nat.	3B	4	13	4	4	1	0	1	4	.308	7	14	1	.955
1978—Los Angeles		Nat.	3B	4	16	4	5	1	0	1	3	.313	2	13	0	1.000
1981—Los Angeles		Nat.	3B	5	18	1	5	1	0	0	3	.278	5	16	1	.955
1984—Chicago		Nat.	3B	5	19	3	3	1	0	1	3	.158	1	6	0	1.000
Championship Series Totals—5 Years				22	82	14	22	7	0	4	14	.268	17	53	4	.946

WORLD SERIES RECORD

Year	Club	League	Pos.	G.	AB.	R.	H.	2B.	3B.	HR.	RBI.	B.A.	PO.	A.	E.	F.A.
1974—Los Angeles		Nat.	3B	5	17	1	3	0	0	0	0	.176	5	9	1	.933
1977—Los Angeles		Nat.	3B	6	21	2	4	1	0	1	3	.190	5	7	0	1.000
1978—Los Angeles		Nat.	3B	6	21	2	6	0	0	1	4	.286	2	12	0	1.000
1981—Los Angeles		Nat.	3B	6	20	3	7	0	0	1	6	.350	4	11	0	1.000
World Series Totals—4 Years				23	79	8	20	1	0	3	13	.253	16	39	1	.982

HENRY CHADWICK

Born October 5, 1824, at Exeter, England.
Died April 29, 1908, at Brooklyn, N.Y.

Henry Chadwick, "Father of Baseball," was born on October 5, 1824, in Jessamine Cottage, St. Thomas, Exeter, England. He died on April 20, 1908, in Brooklyn, N. Y. He was the son of James Chadwick, editor of the Western Times, Exeter, and a brother of Sir Edwin Chadwick.

The "Dean of Baseball Writers," as he subsequently became known, came to the United States when a boy of 13. Six years later, he did his first newspaper work, contributing to the Long Island Star, and when he was 32, he became a reporter on the New York Times. In 1858, when he was 34 years old, he joined the editorial staff of the New York Clipper, a famous amusement-sports weekly of the time, and remained with that publication until 1888. He did his first baseball writing in 1858. In 1864, he wrote baseball for the old New York Herald, remaining a contributor to that paper for several years, and then transferred to the New York Sun.

As early as 1860, Chadwick's name is found in Beadle's "Dime Baseball Player." He also was editor of Haney's Baseball Book of Reference, 1866 to 1870; DeWitt's Baseball Guide, 1869 to 1880; Our Boys' Baseball Guide, 1877 to 1878; "The Art of Batting and Base Running," which was printed in the early eighties; "The American Boy's Book of Sports," and books on how to play cricket, handball, football, chess and many other sports and other works, mostly on baseball. Chadwick was a member of the editorial staff of the Brooklyn Eagle more than 45 years chiefly as a baseball writer and also occasionally covering other sports events. He contributed to Outing Magazine and for years articles from his pen appeared in THE SPORTING NEWS and Sporting Life. Chadwick became editor of the Spalding Official Baseball Guide in 1881 and held the position until his death. He frequently wrote for the New York World, the New York Evening Telegram and other eastern dailies, contributing specialized articles for which he had a reputation from coast to coast, especially for those which had to do largely with statistical and itemized detail. He was editor of the first weekly newspaper devoted exclusively to baseball, the "Ball Players' Chronicle," published from June, 1867 to July, 1869. He also edited the first fans' paper, a weekly known as "The Metropolitan, a Journal of the Polo Grounders," published from 1882 to 1884.

Chadwick became connected with the National Baseball Association in 1858, and up to the last year of its existence—1870—he was conspicuous as chairman of its committee on rules and author of many changes in the rules from which developed the game of today.

He was named to Hall of Fame in 1938 for service to baseball apart from playing the game.

FRANK LEROY CHANCE
(Husk and The Peerless Leader)

Born September 9, 1877, at Fresno, Calif.
Died September 15, 1924, at Los Angeles, Calif.
Height, 6.00. Weight, 190.
Threw and batted righthanded.

Player-manager, Chicago Cubs, 1905; manager, New York Americans, 1913-14; owner and manager, Los Angeles, Pacific Coast League, 1916-17; manager, Boston Red Sox, 1923.
Named to Hall of Fame, 1946.

Year Club	League	Pos.	G.	AB.	R.	H.	2B.	3B.	HR.	SB.	B.A.	PO.	A.	E.	F.A.
1898—Chicago	Nat.	C-OF	42	146	32	42	2	3	1	5	.288	85	20	8	.929
1899—Chicago	Nat.	C	57	190	36	55	6	2	1	11	.289	165	66	12	.951
1900—Chicago	Nat.	C	48	151	26	46	8	4	0	9	.305	160	64	17	.929
1901—Chicago	Nat.	C	63	228	37	66	11	4	0	30	.289	63	7	5	.933
1902—Chicago	Nat.	C-1B-O	67	236	40	67	8	4	1	28	.284	503	45	15	.978
1903—Chicago	Nat.	1B	123	441	83	144	24	10	2	★67	.327	1204	68	★36	.972
1904—Chicago	Nat.	1B	124	451	89	140	16	10	6	42	.310	1205	106	13	●.990
1905—Chicago	Nat.	1B	115	392	92	124	16	12	2	38	.316	1165	75	13	.990
1906—Chicago	Nat.	1B	136	474	●103	151	24	10	3	★57	.319	1376	82	16	.989
1907—Chicago	Nat.	1B	109	382	58	112	19	2	1	35	.293	1129	80	10	★.992
1908—Chicago	Nat.	1B	126	452	65	123	27	4	2	27	.272	1291	86	15	.989
1909—Chicago	Nat.	1B	92	324	53	88	16	4	0	29	.272	901	40	6	.994
1910—Chicago	Nat.	1B	87	295	54	88	12	8	0	16	.298	773	38	3	.996
1911—Chicago	Nat.	1B	29	88	23	21	6	3	1	9	.239	289	11	3	.990
1912—Chicago(a)	Nat.	1B	2	5	2	1	0	0	0	1	.200	22	0	0	1.000
1913—New York	Amer.	1B	11	24	3	5	0	0	0	1	.208	88	4	0	1.000

Year	Club	League	Pos.	G.	AB.	R.	H.	2B.	3B.	HR.	SB.	B.A.	PO.	A.	E.	F.A.
1914—New York		Amer.	1B	1	0	0	0	0	0	0	0	.000	1	0	0	1.000
1916—Los Angeles		P.C.	1B	11	7	0	2	1	0	0	0	.286	0	0	0	.000
American League Totals—2 Years				12	24	3	5	0	0	0	1	.208	89	4	0	1.000
National League Totals—15 Years				1220	4255	793	1268	195	80	20	404	.298	10331	788	172	.985
Major League Totals—17 Years				1232	4279	796	1273	195	80	20	405	.297	10420	792	172	.985

aReleased, September 28, 1912, and signed by New York Americans, January 8, 1918.

WORLD SERIES RECORD

Year	Club	League	Pos.	G.	AB.	R.	H.	2B.	3B.	HR.	SB.	B.A.	PO.	A.	E.	F.A.
1906—Chicago		Nat.	1B	6	21	3	5	1	0	0	2	.238	60	2	0	1.000
1907—Chicago		Nat.	1B	4	14	3	3	1	0	0	3	.214	44	1	0	1.000
1908—Chicago		Nat.	1B	5	19	4	8	0	0	0	5	.421	66	0	3	.957
1910—Chicago		Nat.	1B	5	17	1	6	1	1	0	0	.353	51	4	0	1.000
World Series Totals—4 Years				20	71	11	22	3	1	0	10	.310	221	7	3	.987

ALBERT BENJAMIN (HAPPY) CHANDLER

Born July 14, 1898, at Corydon, Ky.

When major league club owners started to vote for a successor to deceased Commissioner K.M. Landis on April 24, 1945, the name of a United States senator from Kentucky led from the first ballot.

The owners, meeting in Cleveland, reduced the list of candidates to three, then to two—the senator and Bob Hannegan, chairman of the Democratic National Committee. In the runoff, the Kentuckian was ahead, 12 votes to 4, when the executives—in a move for unity—decided to make the vote unanimous.

Albert B. (Happy) Chandler inspired ringing accolades from the owners.

"He'll give us a good administration," said American League President Will Harridge.

"He's the best choice we possibly could have made," added Senators Owner Clark Griffith.

Jack Zeller, representing the Tigers, chortled, "I think we've made a wise decision."

Yet within six years of the auspicious start, Chandler was on his way back to the Bluegrass State to resume his political career. On December 11, 1950, at a meeting in St. Petersburg, Fla., the owners voted down a new contract for Chandler.

"It was the only election I ever lost where I got the majority of votes," Chandler said after receiving nine of the 12 votes required for reelection.

Between the starting gate and the finish line, Chandler ran a stormy race. Few, if any, decisions were universally endorsed. Political campaigns were cakewalks compared with the commissionership.

Chandler made his first major decision less than a year after taking office. From his desk in Cincinnati, he announced that all players jumping to the Mexican League would be suspended automatically from Organized Baseball for five years. Three years later, all jumpers were granted amnesty.

When Branch Rickey, majordomo of the Brooklyn Dodgers, sought to introduce Jackie Robinson to the all-white major leagues in 1947 and owners voted 15-1 against the move, Chandler gave the blessings of his office. The commissioner's stand against discrimination opened a new and profitable era to the game.

While Happy won the admiration of the players by supporting their efforts for a pension plan, he angered executives with other actions. Del Webb, co-owner of the Yankees, and Fred Saigh, owner of the Cardinals, were openly hostile to the commissioner. Both were investigated for possible conduct detrimental to baseball. In addition, Saigh was irked when Chandler ordered him to cancel a scheduled Sunday night game.

Early in his reign, Chandler suspended Leo Durocher for an entire season for slugging a fan under the stands after a night game in Brooklyn and for associating with known gamblers.

"I had to suspend him before he killed somebody," Chandler explained years later. In the same decision, Chandler suspended Dodgers coach Charley Dressen for 30 days and fined the Yankees and Dodgers undisclosed amounts for airing a dispute publicly.

In 1949, after Durocher had become manager of the Giants, the New York club was fined $2,000 and the Lip and coach Fred Fitzsimmons were penalized $500 each as a result of a tampering case involving Fitzsimmons while he was employed by the Boston Braves. The same year, Leo was suspended briefly while Happy investigated allegations that he had struck another fan. Durocher was restored to good standing when the probe found Leo blameless.

The New York press, almost to a man, launched a full-scale attack on Chandler. "They even found fault when I said I love baseball," Happy quipped.

When Leslie O'Connor, general manager of the White Sox, signed a high school player, he was fined $500. His refusal to pay led to O'Connor's suspension and some heated words before the matter was settled. The episode helped turn the Sox against Happy.

After leaving office in 1951, Chandler returned to Kentucky where he was born (Corydon) and where he went to college (Centre). A life-long Democrat, he won two terms as governor and was instrumental in the construction of the University of Kentucky medical center that bears his name.

After terminating his years of public service, Chandler returned to his Versailles, Ky., home. He became a familiar figure on the local golf courses and handled legal cases on a limited scale.

With Bowie Kuhn as commissioner, Chandler made annual guest appearances at the All-Star Game. When introduced, Happy drew standing ovations as an old but newly appreciated friend of baseball.

Chandler was elected to the Hall of Fame by the Veterans Committee in 1982, joining Earle Combs as the only Kentuckians in the shrine.

Chandler was at home when word came of his enshrinement. He was soon inundated with congratulatory messages. Among the callers was Indians President Gabe Paul, who as a Reds official in 1950 had notified the press that Happy's contract as commissioner would not be renewed.

"You were too progressive for your time," said Gabe. "If baseball had had your foresight, it would have avoided many of the problems it has today."

WILLIAM BENJAMIN (BEN) CHAPMAN

Born December 25, 1908, at Nashville, Tenn.

Height, 6.00. Weight, 190.

Threw and batted righthanded.

Shares modern major league record for most triples, game (3), July 3, 1939.
Led South Atlantic League in stolen bases with 30 in 1928.
Led American League in stolen bases with 61 in 1931, 38 in 1932, 27 in 1933 and 35 in 1937 (tied).
Hit three home runs in a game, July 9, 1932, second game.
Led modern major league record for most triples, game (3), July 3, 1939.
Led South Atlantic League in stolen bases with 30 in 1928.
Led American League in stolen bases with 61 in 1931, 38 in 1932, 27 in 1933; 35 (tied) in 1937.
Led American League outfielders in double plays, 1935, 1938.
Manager, Richmond, Piedmont League, 1942 and 1944; Philadelphia Phillies, 1946 through 1948; Gadsden, Southeastern League, 1949; Danville, Carolina League, 1950; Tampa, Florida-International League, 1951; coach, Cincinnati Reds, 1952; manager, Tampa, Florida-International League, 1953; Toronto, International League, 1953.

Year Club League	Pos.	G.	AB.	R.	H.	2B.	3B.	HR.	RBI.	B.A.	PO.	A.	E.	F.A.
1928—Asheville............ Sally	SS	147	545	105	183	32	17	7	98	.336	*316	*508	*67	.925
1929—St. Paul.............. A. A.	3B	168	660	*162	222	43	17	31	137	.336	163	307	*43	.916
1930—New York............ Amer.	2-*3B	138	513	74	162	31	10	10	81	.316	232	295	*42	.926
1931—New York............ Amer.	2-OF	149	600	120	189	28	11	17	122	.315	325	47	14	.964
1932—New York............ Amer.	OF	151	581	101	174	41	15	10	107	.299	303	13	17	.949
1933—New York............ Amer.	OF	147	565	112	176	36	4	9	98	.312	288	*24	8	.975
1934—New York............ Amer.	OF	149	588	82	181	21	*13	5	86	.308	368	12	13	.967
1935—New York............ Amer.	OF	140	553	118	160	38	8	8	74	.289	372	*25	15	.964
1936—N.Y.(a)-Wash....... Amer.	OF	133	540	110	170	50	10	5	81	.315	377	13	16	.961
1937—Wash.(b)-Boston.. Amer.	OF	148	553	99	164	30	12	7	69	.297	349	10	8	.978
1938—Boston(c)............. Amer.	OF-3	127	480	92	163	40	8	6	80	.340	267	16	10	.966
1939—Cleveland............... Amer.	OF	149	545	101	158	31	9	6	82	.290	356	12	11	.971
1940—Cleveland(d)........ Amer.	OF	143	548	82	157	40	6	4	50	.286	307	10	12	.964
1941—Wash.(e)-Chi. .... Amer.	OF	85	200	35	71	15	1	3	29	.237	176	9	1	.995
1942—Richmond(f)......... Pied.	IF-O-P	118	373	48	121	27	4	3	69	.324	137	161	29	.911
1943—Richmond............. Pied.										(Ineligible)				
1944—Richmond(g)........ Pied.	P-3B	57	165	31	50	10	2	2	38	.303	34	62	8	.923
1944—Brooklyn.............. Nat.	P-PH	20	38	11	14	4	0	0	11	.368	3	6	1	.900
1945—Brook.(h)-Phil ...... Nat.	PH-O-3	37	73	6	19	2	0	0	7	.260	17	21	4	.905
1946—Philadelphia .... Nat.	P	1	1	1	0	0	0	0	0	.000	0	0	0	.000
1949—Gadsden................ So'east	P-PH	11	12	1	3	1	0	0	2	.250	....	....	....	....
American League Totals—12 Years		1659	6366	1126	1925	401	107	90	959	.302	3720	486	167	.962
National League Totals—3 Years............		58	112	18	33	6	0	0	18	.295	20	27	5	.900
Major League Totals—15 Years..............		1717	6478	1144	1958	407	107	90	977	.302	3740	513	172	.961

aTraded to Washington Senators for outfielder Alvin (Jake) Powell, June 14, 1936.
bTraded to Boston Red Sox with pitcher Louis (Bobo) Newsom for outfielder Mel Almada, catcher Rick Ferrell and pitcher Wesley Ferrell, June 10, 1937.
cTraded to Cleveland Indians for pitcher Dennis Galehouse and infielder Tom Irwin, December 15, 1938.
dTraded to Washington Senators for pitcher Joe Krakauskas, December 24, 1940.
eUnconditionally released by Washington Senators, May 26, 1941, and signed by Chicago White Sox, May 29, 1941.
fSuspended one year for assault on umpire I. H. Case, September 16, 1942.
gSold to Brooklyn Dodgers, August 1, 1944.
hTraded to Philadelphia Phillies for catcher John Peacock, September 16, 1945.

WORLD SERIES RECORD

Year Club League	Pos.	G.	AB.	R.	H.	2B.	3B.	HR.	RBI.	B.A.	PO.	A.	E.	F.A.
1932—New York............. Amer.	OF	4	17	1	5	2	0	0	6	.294	6	1	0	1.000

PITCHING RECORD

Year Club League	G.	IP.	W.	L.	Pct.	H.	R.	ER.	SO.	BB.	ERA.
1942—Richmond...............Pied.	16	95	6	3	.667	77	24	18	56	34	1.71
1943—Richmond...............Pied.					(Ineligible)						
1944—Richmond...............Pied.	21	163	13	6	.684	127	46	40	147	63	2.21
1944—Brooklyn................ Nat.	11	79	5	3	.625	75	36	30	37	33	3.42

Year Club	League	G.	IP.	W.	L.	Pct.	H.	R.	ER.	SO.	BB.	ERA.
1945—Brooklyn-Philadelphia	Nat.	13	61	3	3	.500	71	41	39	27	38	5.75
1946—Philadelphia	Nat.	1	1	0	0	.000	1	0	0	1	0	.000
1949—Gadsden	So'east	9	22	0	1	.000	22	17	....	19	14	......
Major League Totals—3 Years		25	141	8	6	.571	147	77	69	65	71	4.40

OSCAR CHARLESTON

Born October 14, 1896, at Indianapolis, Ind.

Died October 5, 1954, at Philadelphia, Pa.

Height, 5:11½. Weight, 190

Threw and batted lefthanded.

Oscar Charleston is credited in Negro circles with writing the book on how to play center field and he was the model for base runners who find themselves blocked from a base by a fielder who's holding the ball. He was a fielding stylist and a "mean" base runner, but Charleston also was a tremendous hitter, and for distance, too.

Called the "Hoosier Comet" by his fans, Oscar became a student of the inside game and later was a manager. But he was a poor manager because, like most stars, he demanded his players all play as well as he did. A player playing as best he could did not satisfy Oscar.

He was a record-setting speedster as a youngster and blossomed into one of the Negro League's most popular players. He drew kids around him like Babe Ruth did. He was lauded, in particular, for his great sense in locating a ball while on the dead run, always coming under it in position to catch it and throw.

After a tour of duty in the army (he was stationed in the Philippines), Charleston joined the Indianapolis ABCs in 1915. By the time he left them to seek greener pastures, he was the game's highest-paid player and the unquestioned "big man" of Negro baseball. He became the No. 1 power of the league when it came to a combination of perfect defense and awesome offense. Called a gazelle in center in his prime, he eventually slowed up so much that first base became his base of operations, both as a player and a manager. A powerful man physically, his body was heavily muscled on top in the power areas but slim ankles supported his frame. His legs weakened, but his bat never lost its destructive power, to the day he quit.

But he never lost his fire as a base runner, either, and never lost his trace of meanness. As Buck Leonard recalled, "I remember in 1934, on July 4, the Homestead Grays were playing a game at Greenlee Field in Pittsburgh. Charleston came home and 'undressed' our Grays' catcher, Tex Burnett. Tex was out of action for a long time as a result. Charleston said later that all he was trying to do was get home safe. He was 39 years old at the time, but just as mean as ever."

An insight into the "mean" part of the game was given by Cool Papa Bell. "Charleston would run over men he knew he could whip. We had other strong players in the league, but they didn't fight each other. They just picked on men they thought they could take easily.

"I remember," Bell said, "back in 1933, Charleston grabbed Josh Gibson to 'test him out.' Gibson was young, but big and strong, and he stretched Charleston's neck around but good, Charleston said, 'I.give up. Turn me loose.' And he never bothered Gibson again. But Gibson, always a fun-loving man, never seemed to have that kind of a mean streak in him. I guess with his talent, too, he didn't have to prove anything to anyone."

As a stylist in center field, Charleston also had his light moments. Sometimes, while playing the small parks that dotted the East and Central U.S. at the time, Oscar would put on a show for the fans with his center field antics. He had absolute knowledge of the position of a fly ball, whether over his head or either side of him. When a good straight fly would come out to him, he'd turn a flip and catch the ball or sometimes just walk after the ball and catch it. To give the fans a special treat, he'd even make tumbling catches. A master at the art of clowning—and a good clown is only a good professional who wants to clown—he never gave a batter a free ride. Everyone was an out—period.

Note what 84-year-old Dave Malarcher, one of the Negro leagues' greatest third basemen and smartest managers, had to say about Charleston as a center fielder:

"I was young and had just joined the Indianapolis ABCs. I was a third basemen, but they put me at second base because Bingo DeMoss had left the club. But he returned and they put me out in right field, with Oscar in center.

"Some people asked me, 'Why are you playing so close to the right field foul line?' What they didn't know was Charleston played ALL THREE fields and I made sure of the balls down the line and all foul ones, too.

"Oh, that man could play the outfield! There was no one like him for all-round greatness. He and John Henry Lloyd," said Gentleman Dave, "were the two greatest ballplayers I ever saw, black or white."

The line on Charleston as a hitter runs like this:

If there was no one on base, the pitcher would throw every bit of junk he had in his repertoire and hope for better results. Oscar always was itching to hit, and slow stuff was a pitcher's only way to get an even break against him. With men on base and fast balls necessary to keep the runners honest, Charleston would power the ball every time he connected. It didn't do any good to throw curves at him; he'd murder them. He hit long, hard and often. In his later years as a manager and pinch-hitter, he often would pass up at-bat opportunities when no one was on base. He said he could get aroused only when there were runners to be driven home.

The test of his greatness is that Charleston's name is one of the first mentioned when you think in terms of an all-time Negro league team—just Charleston, not by position, just Charleston.

Because Oscar was a great hitter and fielder, had a fine arm and was a clutch batter to boot, he is ranked as one of Negro baseball's premier players of any era. Also tabbed the Greyhound of the Garden, Charleston was often compared with Tris Speaker in center field skills . . . both could field, hit, throw and run in levels far above the ordinary major leaguer.

In Negro ball, there were only two center fielders mentioned at any time—Charleston and later Bell. All others couldn't draw a vote on their own clubs.

Oscar also played with the Harrisburg Giants, the Pittsburgh Crawfords and Homestead Grays in the Smoky City area and the Hillsdales of Philadelphia, among others. He turned into the game's resident slugger when the chips were down and the elder statesman in player and club councils.

A credit to all of baseball, Charleston was selected to take his place in the Hall of Fame in 1976 when the Special Committee on Negro Leagues named him to join his fellow Black players in that other world of major league professional baseball.

JOHN DWIGHT (JACK) CHESBRO

Born June 5, 1874, at North Adams, Mass.
Died November 6, 1931, at Conway, Mass.
Height, 5.09. Weight, 180.
Threw and batted righthanded.

Holds American League record for most victories, season (41), 1904.
Named to Hall of Fame, 1946.

Year Club	League	G.	IP.	W.	L.	Pct.	ShO.	H.	R.	SO.	BB.
1895—Albany-Johnstown	N.Y.L.	19	156	7	10	.412	....	206	....	85	56
1895—Springfield	Eastern	7	33	3	0	1.000	....	34	....	8	23
1896—Roanoke	Virginia	20	156	7	11	.389	....	162	....	56	62
1897—Richmond	Atlantic	38	283	16	18	.471	....	281	....	89	58
1898—Richmond	Atlantic	40	351	23	15	.605	....	296	....	135	80
1899—Richmond	Atlantic	21	192	17	4	.810	....	165	....	67	51
1899—Pittsburgh	National	19	141	6	10	.375	0	158	98	27	61
1900—Pittsburgh	National	32	213	14	12	.538	3	213	125	58	75
1901—Pittsburgh	National	36	289	21	9	★.700	●6	245	101	123	49
1902—Pittsburgh(a)	National	35	286	★28	6	★.824	●8	240	81	137	64
1903—New York	American	40	325	21	15	.583	1	289	137	147	65
1904—New York	American	★55	★454	★41	13	★.759	6	337	128	240	87
1905—New York	American	41	302	19	13	.594	3	265	121	172	72
1906—New York	American	★49	326	24	16	.600	4	313	142	150	67
1907—New York	American	30	206	10	10	.500	1	194	85	78	52
1908—New York	American	45	289	14	20	.412	3	271	133	124	67
1909—New York(b)-Boston	American	10	55	0	4	.000	0	77	51	20	15
American League Totals—7 Years		270	1957	129	91	.586	18	1746	797	931	425
National League Totals—4 Years		122	929	69	37	.651	17	856	405	345	249
Major League Totals—11 Years		392	2886	198	128	.607	35	2602	1202	1276	674

aJumped to New York A.L. for 1903 season.
bReleased to Boston, August, 1909.

CLARENCE ALGERNON (CUPID) CHILDS

Born August 14, 1868, at Calvert County, Md.
Died November 8, 1912, at Baltimore, Md.
Height, 5.08. Weight, 186.
Threw right and batted lefthanded.

Year Club	League	Pos.	G.	AB.	R.	H.	2B.	3B.	HR.	SB.	B.A.	PO.	A.	E.	F.A.
1886—Petersburg	Virginia	2B					(No averages available)								
1887—Shamokin	Cen. Pa.	2B					(No averages available)								
1888—Philadelphia	Nat.	2B	2	4	0	0	0	0	0	0	.000	2	4	1	.857
1888—Kalamazoo	Tri-St.	2B	53	216	....	61	....	....	....	19	.283	....	....	....	.904
1889—Syracuse	Int.	2B	105	425	79	145	....	....	....	53	.341	322	356	47	.935
1890—Syracuse	A.A.	2B	136	494	109	170	32	14	2	59	.344	374	360	61	.923
1891—Cleveland	Nat.	2B	141	549	119	162	20	11	2	41	.295	373	456	★74	.918
1892—Cleveland	Nat.	2B	144	552	★135	185	15	12	3	31	●.335	358	440	46	★.946
1893—Cleveland	Nat.	2B	122	481	143	160	16	12	3	27	.332	342	425	60	.916
1894—Cleveland	Nat.	2B	117	476	144	174	19	11	3	20	.365	308	380	56	.924
1895—Cleveland	Nat.	2B	120	461	97	144	15	4	4	26	.312	335	394	55	.930
1896—Cleveland	Nat.	2B	132	502	109	175	22	10	1	21	.348	★369	★496	●57	.938
1897—Cleveland	Nat.	2B	114	443	105	149	15	10	1	25	.336	322	386	42	.944
1898—Cleveland	Nat.	2B	109	422	91	122	12	2	1	5	.289	271	375	49	.915
1899—St. Louis	Nat.	2B	125	465	73	124	12	10	1	9	.266	324	348	46	.936

Year Club League	Pos.	G.	AB.	R.	H.	2B.	3B.	HR.	SB.	B.A.	PO.	A.	E.	F.A.
1900—Chicago .... Nat.	2B	138	538	70	131	13	6	0	18	.243	*334	*425	*49	.939
1901—Chicago .... Nat.	2B	63	237	23	61	9	0	0	3	.257	151	192	20	.945
1901—Toledo .... W.A.	2B	71	287	....	71	17	0	0	14	.247	163	224	26	.937
1902—Jersey City .... East.	2B	33	138	29	40	....	....	....	....	.290	88	103	16	.923
1902—Syracuse .... N.Y.	2B	74	285	59	102	....	....	....	14	.357	231	225	27	.944
1903—Montgomery .... South.	2B	108	331	12	38	....	....	....	5	.314	279	313	*47	.925
1904—Scranton .... N.Y.	2B	41	155	12	38	....	....	....	1	.245	50	122	26	.874
American Association Totals—1 Year .		136	494	109	170	32	14	2	59	.344	374	360	61	.923
National League Totals—12 Years		1327	5130	1109	1587	168	88	19	226	.309	3489	4321	555	.934
Major League Totals—13 Years		1463	5624	1218	1757	200	102	21	285	.312	3863	4681	616	.933

EDWARD V. (ED) CICOTTE

Born June 19, 1884, at Detroit, Mich.

Died May 5, 1969, at Detroit, Mich.

Height, 5.07. Weight, 160.

Threw and batted righthanded.

Pitched 11-0, no-hit victory against St. Louis, April 14, 1917.

Year Club League	G.	IP.	W.	L.	Pct.	H.	R.	ER.	SO.	BB.	ERA.
1905—Augusta ....South Atlantic	32	....	15	9	.625	153	65	....	182	71	......
1905—Detroit...American	3	19	1	1	.500	25	8	....	2	5	......
1906—Indianapolis ....Amer. Assn.	10	72	1	4	.200	65	40	....	33	17	......
1906—Des Moines ....Western	27	....	18	9	.667	....	....	....	....	....	......
1907—Lincoln ....Western	39	....	23	10	.697	....	....	....	....	....	......
1908—Boston..American	38	208	11	12	.478	193	73	....	93	57	......
1909—Boston..American	27	160	13	5	.722	117	58	....	82	56	......
1910—Boston..American	36	250	15	11	.577	213	94	....	104	86	......
1911—Boston..American	35	220	11	15	.423	236	118	....	106	73	......
1912—Boston (a)-Chicago ....American	29	197	10	10	.500	217	97	....	90	52	......
1913—Chicago ....American	42	267	18	12	.600	222	77	48	119	68	1.62
1914—Chicago ....American	45	269	13	16	.448	220	96	61	122	72	2.04
1915—Chicago ....American	39	223	13	12	.520	216	89	75	106	48	3.03
1916—Chicago ....American	44	187	15	7	*.682	138	56	37	91	70	1.78
1917—Chicago ....American	49	*345	*28	12	.700	246	76	59	150	70	*1.54
1918—Chicago ....American	38	265	12	●19	.387	275	98	78	104	40	2.65
1919—Chicago ....American	40	*307	*29	7	*.806	256	77	62	110	49	1.82
1920—Chicago ....American	37	303	21	10	.677	316	128	110	87	74	3.27
Major League Totals—14 Years...............................	502	3220	210	149	.585	2890	1145	....	1366	820	......

aSold to Chicago White Sox, July 10, 1912.

WORLD SERIES RECORD

Year Club League	G.	IP.	W.	L.	Pct.	H.	R.	ER.	SO.	BB.	ERA.
1917—Chicago .... American	3	23	1	1	.500	23	6	5	13	2	1.96
1919—Chicago .... American	3	21⅔	1	2	.333	19	9	7	7	5	2.91
World Series Totals—2 Years	6	44⅔	2	3	.400	42	15	12	20	7	2.42

FRED CLIFFORD CLARKE

Born October 3, 1872 in Madison County (Winterset), Ia.

Died August 14, 1960, at Winfield, Kan.

Height, 5.10. Weight, 165.

Threw right and batted lefthanded.

Shares major league record for most hits, first major league game (5), June 30, 1894.

Manager, Louisville, N. L., 1897 through 1899; Pittsburgh Pirates, 1900 through 1915; coach, 1925; vice-president and assistant manager, 1926.

Named to Hall of Fame, 1945.

Year	Club	League	Pos.	G.	AB.	R.	H.	2B.	3B.	HR.	SB.	B.A.	PO.	A.	E.	F.A.
1892—Hastings	Neb. St.	OF														
					(No Records Available)											
1893—St. Joseph	W. Ass'n	OF														
					(No Records Available)											
1893—Montgomery	South.	OF	32	120	21	35	5	5	0	1	.292	72	9	5	.942
1894—Savannah	South.	OF	54	219	60	68	11	2	2	20	.311	100	14	9	.927
1894—Louisville	Nat.	OF	76	316	55	87	10	5	7	24	.275	166	14	23	.887
1895—Louisville	Nat.	OF	132	556	94	197	23	4	3	36	.354	338	25	★41	.899
1896—Louisville	Nat.	OF	131	517	93	169	13	18	9	32	.327	276	17	★31	.904
1897—Louisville	Nat.	OF	129	525	122	213	28	15	6	60	.406	283	23	24	.927
1898—Louisville	Nat.	OF	147	598	115	190	24	11	2	★66	.318	346	22	14	.963
1899—Louisville(a)	Nat.	OF	147	601	124	209	21	11	5	47	.348	324	21	13	.964
1900—Pittsburgh	Nat.	OF	103	398	85	112	14	12	3	18	.281	263	9	16	.944
1901—Pittsburgh	Nat.	OF	128	525	118	166	26	14	6	22	.316	283	14	10	.967
1902—Pittsburgh	Nat.	OF	114	461	104	148	27	14	2	34	.321	217	12	9	.962
1903—Pittsburgh	Nat.	OF	102	427	88	150	●32	15	5	21	.351	168	10	7	.962
1904—Pittsburgh	Nat.	OF	70	278	51	85	7	11	0	11	.306	135	4	3	.979
1905—Pittsburgh	Nat.	OF	137	525	95	157	18	15	2	24	.299	270	16	7	.976
1906—Pittsburgh	Nat.	OF	110	417	69	129	14	●13	1	18	.309	209	15	6	.974
1907—Pittsburgh	Nat.	OF	144	501	97	145	18	13	2	37	.289	298	15	4	★.987
1908—Pittsburgh	Nat.	OF	151	551	83	146	18	15	2	24	.265	★346	15	10	.973
1909—Pittsburgh	Nat.	OF	152	550	97	158	16	11	3	31	.287	★362	17	5	★.987
1910—Pittsburgh	Nat.	OF	118	429	57	113	23	9	2	12	.263	284	10	10	.967
1911—Pittsburgh	Nat.	OF	101	392	73	127	25	13	5	10	.324	216	8	7	.970
1913—Pittsburgh	Nat.	OF	9	13	0	1	1	0	0	0	.077	2	0	0	1.000
1914—Pittsburgh	Nat.	PH	2	2	0	0	0	0	0	0	.000	0	0	0	.000
1915—Pittsburgh	Nat.	OF	1	2	0	1	0	0	0	0	.500	0	0	0	.000
Major League Totals—21 Years				2204	8584	1620	2703	358	219	65	527	.315	4786	267	240	.955

aTransferred with 14 other players to Pittsburgh when Louisville dropped out of the National League.

WORLD SERIES RECORD

Year	Club	League	Pos.	G.	AB.	R.	H.	2B.	3B.	HR.	SB.	B.A.	PO.	A.	E.	F.A.
1903—Pittsburgh	Nat.	OF	8	34	3	9	2	1	0	1	.265	17	0	1	.944
1909—Pittsburgh	Nat.	OF	7	19	7	4	0	0	2	3	.211	20	0	1	.952
World Series Totals—2 Years				15	53	10	13	2	1	2	4	.245	37	0	2	.949

JOHN GIBSON CLARKSON

Born July 1, 1861, at Cambridge, Mass.

Died February 4, 1909, at Cambridge, Mass.

Height, 5.10. Weight, 160.

Threw and batted righthanded.

Pitched 4-0 no-hit victory against Providence, July 27, 1885.
Named to Hall of Fame, 1963.

Year	Club	League	G.	IP.	W.	L.	Pct.	SO.	BB.	H.	CG.	ShO.
1882—Worcester	National	3	24	1	2	.333	4	2	51	2	0
1883—Saginaw(a)	Northwestern	23	....	....	....	....	....	....	....	....	....
1884—Saginaw	Northwestern	42	357	31	8	.795	399	45	329	46	10
1884—Chicago	National	14	109	10	3	.769	101	30	96	12	0
1885—Chicago	National	★70	★622	★53	16	.768	★318	99	502	★68	★10
1886—Chicago	National	53	469	35	17	.673	340	86	400	51	3
1887—Chicago(b)	National	★60	★496	★38	21	.644	★233	87	620	★55	2
1888—Boston	National	53	★485	33	20	.623	228	119	436	★53	3
1889—Boston	National	★72	★629	★49	19	★.721	292	204	572	★69	★8
1890—Boston	National	44	383	26	18	.591	132	141	369	44	2
1891—Boston	National	55	465	33	19	.635	135	155	444	47	3
1892—Boston(c)-Cleveland	National	45	386	25	16	.610	136	125	354	42	5
1893—Cleveland	National	36	296	16	17	.485	61	100	359	31	0
1894—Cleveland	National	22	150	8	8	.500	33	44	181	13	1
Major League Totals—12 Years		527	4514	327	176	.650	2013	1192	4384	487	37

aPlayed 30 games in the outfield and had 84 hits, batting .295, in 1883. He participated in 14 games in the outfield in 1884, batting an overall .302, with 14 doubles, seven triples and four home runs. Seven times he struck out 15 or more batters in a game. Over five successive games, June 30, July 4, p.m. game, July 8, July 10 and July 14, he fanned 19, 16, 8, 16 and 14 batters. The Saginaw club was suspended after Clarkson's victory of August 13 and he was called up immediately by Chicago.

bSold to Boston for $10,000 in winter of 1887-88.

cReleased by Boston in midseason of 1892, due to arm trouble and signed with Cleveland.

ROBERTO WALKER CLEMENTE

Born August 18, 1934, at Carolina, Puerto Rico.
Died December 31, 1972, at San Juan, Puerto Rico.
Height, 5.11. Weight, 185.
Threw and batted righthanded.

Holds National League record for most years leading league, assists, outfielder (5).
Shares National League record for most triples, game (3), September 8, 1958.
Hit three home runs in game, May 15, 1967, and August 13, 1969.
Named outfielder on THE SPORTING NEWS National League All-Star Teams, 1961-64-66-67-72.
Named outfielder on THE SPORTING NEWS National League All-Star fielding teams, 1961-62-63-64-65-66-67-68-69-70-71-72.
Named National League Most Valuable Player, 1966.
Named National League Player of the Year by THE SPORTING NEWS, 1966.
Named to Hall of Fame, 1973.

Year Club League	Pos.	G.	AB.	R.	H.	2B.	3B.	HR.	RBI.	B.A.	PO.	A.	E.	F.A.
1954—Montreal (a) .... Int.	OF-3B	87	148	27	38	5	3	2	12	.257	81	1	1	.988
1955—Pittsburgh............. Nat.	OF	124	474	48	121	23	11	5	47	.255	253	18	6	.978
1956—Pittsburgh............. Nat.	●OF-2B-3B	147	543	66	169	30	7	7	60	.311	275	20	●15	.952
1957—Pittsburgh............. Nat.	OF	111	451	42	114	17	7	4	30	.253	272	9	6	.979
1958—Pittsburgh............. Nat.	OF	140	519	69	150	24	10	6	50	.289	312	★22	6	.982
1959—Pittsburgh............. Nat.	OF	105	432	60	128	17	7	4	50	.296	229	10	★13	.948
1960—Pittsburgh............. Nat.	OF	144	570	89	179	22	6	16	94	.314	246	★19	8	.971
1961—Pittsburgh............. Nat.	OF	146	572	100	201	30	10	23	89	★.351	256	★27	9	.969
1962—Pittsburgh............. Nat.	OF	144	538	95	168	28	9	10	74	.312	269	19	8	.973
1963—Pittsburgh............. Nat.	OF	152	600	77	192	23	8	17	76	.320	239	11	11	.958
1964—Pittsburgh............. Nat.	OF	155	622	95	●211	40	7	12	87	★.339	289	13	10	.968
1965—Pittsburgh............. Nat.	OF	152	589	91	194	21	14	10	65	★.329	288	16	10	.968
1966—Pittsburgh............. Nat.	OF	154	638	105	202	31	11	29	119	.317	318	★17	12	.965
1967—Pittsburgh............. Nat.	OF	147	585	103	★209	26	10	23	110	★.357	273	★17	9	.970
1968—Pittsburgh............. Nat.	OF	132	502	74	146	18	12	18	57	.291	297	9	5	.984
1969—Pittsburgh............. Nat.	OF	138	507	87	175	20	★12	19	91	.345	226	14	5	.980
1970—Pittsburgh............. Nat.	OF	108	412	65	145	22	10	14	60	.352	189	12	7	.966
1971—Pittsburgh............. Nat.	OF	132	522	82	178	29	8	13	86	.341	267	11	2	.993
1972—Pittsburgh............. Nat.	OF	102	378	68	118	19	7	10	60	.312	199	5	0	1.000
Major League Totals—18 Years..............		2433	9454	1416	3000	440	166	240	1305	.317	4697	269	142	.972

aDrafted by Pittsburgh Pirates from Brooklyn Dodgers' organization, November 22, 1954.

CHAMPIONSHIP SERIES RECORD

Year Club League	Pos.	G.	AB.	R.	H.	2B.	3B.	HR.	RBI.	B.A.	PO.	A.	E.	F.A.
1970—Pittsburgh............. Nat.	OF	3	14	1	3	0	0	0	1	.214	7	0	0	1.000
1971—Pittsburgh............. Nat.	OF	4	18	2	6	0	0	0	4	.333	12	0	0	1.000
1972—Pittsburgh............. Nat.	OF	5	17	1	4	1	0	1	2	.235	10	0	0	1.000
Championship Series Totals—3 Years.....		12	49	4	13	1	0	1	7	.265	29	0	0	1.000

WORLD SERIES RECORD

Year Club League	Pos.	G.	AB.	R.	H.	2B.	3B.	HR.	RBI.	B.A.	PO.	A.	E.	F.A.
1960—Pittsburgh............. Nat.	OF	7	29	1	9	0	0	0	3	.310	19	0	0	1.000
1971—Pittsburgh............. Nat.	OF	7	29	3	12	2	1	2	4	.414	15	0	0	1.000
World Series Totals—2 Years		14	58	4	21	2	1	2	7	.362	34	0	0	1.000

TYRUS RAYMOND (TY) COBB
(The Georgia Peach)

Born December 18, 1886, at Narrows, Banks County, Ga.
Died July 17, 1961, at Atlanta, Ga.
Height, 6.01. Weight, 175.
Threw right and batted lefthanded.

Holds major league records for highest lifetime batting average, 15 or more years (.367), most years leading league in batting average (12) and hits (8); most runs, lifetime (2,245); most times, five or more hits in game, lifetime (14).

Shares major league records for most consecutive years leading league in hits (3); most times five or more hits in a game, season (4), 1922.

Holds American League records for most hits (4,191), singles (3,052), triples (298) and stolen bases (892), lifetime; most years with 200 or more hits (9).

Hit three home runs in a game, May 5, 1925.

Tied for American League lead in double plays by outfielder with 8 in 1924.

Named Most Valuable Player, American League (Chalmers Award), 1911.

Player-manager, Detroit Tigers, 1921 through 1926.

Named to Hall of Fame, 1936.

Year	Club	League	Pos.	G.	AB.	R.	H.	2B.	3B.	HR.	RBI.	B.A.	PO.	A.	E.	F.A.
1904—Augusta		Sally	OF	37	135	14	32	6	0	1	....	.237	62	9	4	.946
1904—Ann.-Shef.(a)		Tn.-Ala.	OF-P	37	149	23	45	5	9	0	....	.302	46	2	5	.906
1905—Augusta		Sally	OF	103	411	60	134	13	4	1	....	★.326	149	15	13	.927
1905—Detroit		Amer.	OF	41	150	19	36	6	0	1	12	.240	85	6	4	.958
1906—Detroit		Amer.	OF	98	350	45	112	13	7	1	41	.320	209	14	9	.961
1907—Detroit		Amer.	OF	150	605	97	★212	29	15	5	★116	★.350	238	30	11	.961
1908—Detroit		Amer.	OF	150	581	88	★188	★36	★20	4	★101	.324	212	★23	14	.944
1909—Detroit		Amer.	OF	156	573	★116	★216	33	10	★9	★115	★.377	222	24	14	.946
1910—Detroit		Amer.	OF	140	509	★106	196	36	13	8	88	★.385	300	18	14	.958
1911—Detroit		Amer.	OF	146	591	★147	★248	★47	★24	8	★144	★.420	★376	24	18	.957
1912—Detroit		Amer.	OF	140	553	119	★227	30	23	7	90	★.410	324	21	22	.940
1913—Detroit		Amer.	OF	122	428	70	167	18	16	4	65	★.390	262	22	16	.947
1914—Detroit		Amer.	OF	97	345	69	127	22	11	2	57	★.368	177	8	10	.949
1915—Detroit		Amer.	OF	156	563	★144	★208	31	13	3	95	★.369	328	22	18	.951
1916—Detroit		Amer.	OF-1B	145	542	★113	201	31	10	5	67	.371	335	18	17	.954
1917—Detroit		Amer.	OF	152	★588	107	★225	★44	★24	6	108	★.383	373	27	11	.973
1918—Detroit		Amer.	OF-INF-P	111	421	83	161	19	★14	3	64	★.382	359	26	9	.977
1919—Detroit		Amer.	OF	124	497	92	●191	36	13	1	69	★.384	272	19	8	.973
1920—Detroit		Amer.	OF	112	428	86	143	28	8	2	63	.334	246	8	9	.966
1921—Detroit		Amer.	OF	128	507	124	197	37	16	12	101	.389	301	27	10	.970
1922—Detroit		Amer.	OF	137	526	99	211	42	16	4	99	.401	330	14	7	.980
1923—Detroit		Amer.	OF	145	556	103	189	40	7	6	88	.340	362	14	12	.969
1924—Detroit		Amer.	OF	●155	625	115	211	38	10	4	74	.338	417	12	6	●.986
1925—Detroit		Amer.	OF-P	121	415	97	157	31	12	12	102	.378	267	10	15	.949
1926—Detroit(b)		Amer.	OF	79	233	48	79	18	5	4	62	.339	109	4	6	.950
1927—Philadelphia		Amer.	OF	133	490	104	175	32	7	5	94	.357	243	9	8	.969
1928—Philadelphia		Amer.	OF	95	353	54	114	27	4	1	40	.323	154	7	6	.964
Major League Totals—24 Years				3033	11429	2245	4191	724	298	117	1960	.367	6501	407	274	.962

aLeague not in Organized Ball.

bReleased, November 2, 1926; signed with Philadelphia Athletics, February, 1927.

WORLD SERIES RECORD

Year	Club	League	Pos.	G.	AB.	R.	H.	2B.	3B.	HR.	RBI.	B.A.	PO.	A.	E.	F.A.
1907—Detroit		Amer.	OF	5	20	1	4	0	1	0	....	.200	9	0	0	1.000
1908—Detroit		Amer.	OF	5	19	3	7	1	0	0	4	.368	3	0	2	.600
1909—Detroit		Amer.	OF	7	26	3	6	3	0	0	6	.231	8	0	1	.889
World Series Totals—3 Years				17	65	7	17	4	1	0	10	.262	20	0	3	.870

GORDON STANLEY (MICKEY) COCHRANE

Born April 6, 1903, at Bridgewater, Mass.

Died June 28, 1962, at Lake Forest, Ill.

Height, 5.10½. Weight, 180.

Threw right and batted lefthanded.

Led American League catchers in double plays, 1930, 1932.

Hit three home runs in a game, May 21, 1925.

Manager, Detroit Tigers, 1934 to 1938; coach and later general manager, Philadelphia Athletics, 1950; scout, New York Yankees, 1955; Detroit Tigers, 1960 until named vice-president of club, 1961-62.

Named American League Most Valuable Player, 1928, 1934.

Named to Hall of Fame, 1947.

Year	Club	League	Pos.	G.	AB.	R.	H.	2B.	3B.	HR.	RBI.	B.A.	PO.	A.	E.	F.A.
1923—Dover(a)		East. Sh.	C	65	245	56	79	12	6	5	.....	.322	222	70	★13	.957
1924—Portland		P. C.	C	99	300	43	100	8	5	7	56	.333	278	49	14	.959
1925—Philadelphia		Amer.	C	134	420	69	139	21	5	6	55	.331	419	79	8	★.984
1926—Philadelphia		Amer.	C	120	370	50	101	8	9	8	47	.273	★502	90	★15	.975
1927—Philadelphia		Amer.	C	126	432	80	146	20	6	12	80	.338	★559	85	9	.986
1928—Philadelphia		Amer.	C	131	468	92	137	26	12	10	57	.293	★645	71	★25	.966
1929—Philadelphia		Amer.	C	135	514	113	170	37	8	7	95	.331	★659	77	13	★.983
1930—Philadelphia		Amer.	C	130	487	110	174	42	5	10	85	.357	★654	★69	5	★.993
1931—Philadelphia		Amer.	C	122	459	87	160	31	6	17	89	.349	560	63	9	.986

Year Club League	Pos.	G.	AB.	R.	H.	2B.	3B.	HR.	RBI.	B.A.	PO.	A.	E.	F.A.
1932—Philadelphia .... Amer.	C	139	518	118	152	35	4	23	112	.293	*652	*94	5	*.993
1933—Philadelphia(b).... Amer.	C	130	429	104	138	30	4	15	60	.322	476	67	6	.989
1934—Detroit.................. Amer.	C	129	437	74	140	32	1	2	76	.320	517	69	7	.988
1935—Detroit.................. Amer.	C	115	411	93	131	33	3	5	47	.319	504	50	6	.989
1936—Detroit.................. Amer.	C	44	126	24	34	8	0	2	17	.270	159	13	3	.983
1937—Detroit(c) .... Amer.	C	27	98	27	30	10	1	2	12	.306	103	13	0	1.000
Major League Totals—13 Years		1482	5169	1041	1652	333	64	119	832	.320	6409	840	111	.985

aPlayed under name of Frank King.

bSold to Detroit Tigers for $100,000 and catcher John Pasek, December, 1933.

cSuffered fractured skull when hit by pitched ball by pitcher Irving (Bump) Hadley of New York, May 25, 1937, ending career as active player.

WORLD SERIES RECORD

Year Club League	Pos.	G.	AB.	R.	H.	2B.	3B.	HR.	RBI.	B.A.	PO.	A.	E.	F.A.
1929—Philadelphia .... Amer.	C	5	15	5	6	1	0	0	0	.400	59	2	0	1.000
1930—Philadelphia .... Amer.	C	6	18	5	4	1	0	2	4	.222	39	1	1	.976
1931—Philadelphia .... Amer.	C	7	25	2	4	0	0	1	1	.160	40	4	1	.978
1934—Detroit.................. Amer.	C	7	28	2	6	1	0	0	1	.214	36	5	0	1.000
1935—Detroit.................. Amer.	C	6	24	3	7	1	0	0	1	.292	32	3	1	.972
World Series Totals—5 Years		31	110	17	27	4	0	2	7	.245	206	15	3	.987

ROCCO DOMENICO (ROCKY) COLAVITO

Born August 10, 1933, at New York, N. Y.

Height, 6.03. Weight, 198.

Threw and batted righthanded.

Holds major league record for most consecutive errorless games, season (162), 1965.

Shares major league records for most home runs and consecutive home runs, game (4), June 10, 1959; most total bases, game (16), June 10, 1959; most home runs, doubleheader (4), August 27, 1961; highest fielding percentage by outfielder, season, 150 or more games (1.000), 1965.

Holds American League record for most years leading league in games played by outfielder (5).

Hit three home runs in a game, August 27, 1961, second game, and July 5, 1962.

Named as outfielder on THE SPORTING NEWS American League All-Star Team, 1961.

Scout, New York Yankees, 1969; coach, Cleveland Indians, 1973 and 1975 through 1978; Kansas City Royals, 1982-83.

Year Club League	Pos.	G.	AB.	R.	H.	2B.	3B.	HR.	RBI.	B.A.	PO.	A.	E.	F.A.
1951—Daytona Beach .... Fl. St.	OF-P	•140	506	98	139	35	3	•23	111	.275	*303	19	•20	.942
1952—Cedar Rapids....... I. I. I.	OF	32	94	14	16	1	1	8	21	.170	49	4	1	.981
1952—Spartanburg .... Tri.-St.	OF	66	226	42	57	14	1	11	55	.252	100	4	1	.990
1953—Reading................. East.	OF	146	528	89	143	21	6	*28	*121	.271	263	12	5	.982
1954—Indianapolis .... A. A.	OF	149	528	94	143	30	3	*38	116	.271	271	16	7	.976
1955—Indianapolis .... A. A.	OF	150	555	92	149	30	3	30	104	.268	314	*23	10	.971
1955—Cleveland.............. Amer.	OF	5	9	3	4	2	0	0	0	.444	7	1	0	1.000
1956—San Diego .... P. C.	OF	35	133	31	49	10	1	12	32	.368	50	3	3	.946
1956—Cleveland.............. Amer.	OF	101	322	55	89	11	4	21	65	.276	177	6	6	.968
1957—Cleveland.............. Amer.	OF	134	461	66	116	26	0	25	84	.252	268	12	•11	.962
1958—Cleveland.............. Amer.	O-1B-P	143	489	80	148	26	3	41	113	.303	327	15	9	.974
1959—Cleveland(a)........ Amer.	OF	154	588	90	151	24	0	•42	111	.257	319	7	5	.985
1960—Detroit.................. Amer.	OF	145	555	67	138	18	1	35	87	.249	271	11	7	.976
1961—Detroit.................. Amer.	OF	•163	583	129	169	30	2	45	140	.290	329	*16	9	.976
1962—Detroit.................. Amer.	OF	161	601	90	164	30	2	37	112	.273	359	10	3	.992
1963—Detroit(b) .... Amer.	OF	160	597	91	162	29	2	22	91	.271	319	10	4	.988
1964—Kansas City(c) ..... Amer.	OF	160	588	89	161	31	2	34	102	.274	275	10	8	.973
1965—Cleveland.............. Amer.	OF	•162	592	92	170	25	2	26	*108	.287	265	9	0	*1.000
1966—Cleveland.............. Amer.	OF	151	533	68	127	13	0	30	72	.238	261	10	5	.982
1967—Clev.(d)-Chi.(e)..... Amer.	OF	123	381	30	88	13	1	8	50	.231	158	4	5	.970
1968—Los Angeles(f)...... Nat.	OF	40	113	8	23	3	0	3	11	.204	45	2	0	1.000
1968—New York............. Amer.	OF-P	39	91	13	20	2	2	5	13	.220	27	1	2	.933
American League Totals—14 Years		1801	6390	963	1707	280	21	371	1148	.267	3362	122	74	.979
National League Totals—1 Year		40	113	8	23	3	0	3	11	.204	45	2	0	1.000
Major League Totals—14 Years		1841	6503	971	1730	283	21	374	1159	.266	3407	124	74	.979

aTraded to Detroit Tigers for Outfielder Harvey Kuenn, April 17, 1960.

bTraded to Kansas City Athletics with Pitcher Bob Anderson and cash for Pitchers Ed Rakow and Dave Wickersham and Second Baseman Jerry Lumpe, November 18, 1963.

cTraded to Chicago White Sox for Outfielders Jim Landis and Mike Hershberger and a pitcher to be named later, January 20, 1965, as part of three-way deal which saw White Sox immediately send Colavito and Catcher Camilo Carreon to Cleveland Indians for Pitcher Tommy John, Catcher John Romano and Outfielder Tommie Agee; White Sox assigned Pitcher Fred Talbot to Athletics, February 10, 1965, to complete deal.

dTraded to Chicago White Sox for Outfielder Jim King and player to be named later, July 29, 1967. Infielder Marv Staehle assigned to Portland to complete deal, July 29, 1967.

eSold to Los Angeles Dodgers, March 26, 1968.

fReleased by Los Angeles Dodgers, July 11, 1968; signed by New York Yankees, July 15, 1968.

PITCHING RECORD

Year	Club	League	G.	IP.	W.	L.	Pct.	H.	R.	ER.	SO.	BB.	ERA.
1951—Daytona Beach		Fla. St.	1	4	0	0	.000	1	1	1	3	3	2.52
1958—Cleveland		Amer.	1	3	0	0	.000	0	0	0	1	3	0.00
1968—New York		Amer.	1	3	1	0	1.000	1	0	0	1	2	0.00
Major League Totals—2 Years			2	6	1	0	1.000	1	0	0	2	5	0.00

EDWARD TROWBRIDGE (EDDIE) COLLINS

Born May 2, 1887, at Millerton, N. Y.

Died March 25, 1951, at Boston, Mass.

Height, 5.09. Weight, 175.

Threw right and batted lefthanded.

Holds major league records for most years leading league in fielding percentage (9); most games (2,651), putouts (6,526), assists (7,630), chances accepted (14,156) and errors (435) by second baseman, lifetime.

Holds American League records for most years (25); most stolen bases, game (6), September 11, 1912 and September 22, 1912, first game.

Shares American League record for most years leading league in double plays (5).

Led American League in stolen bases with 81 in 1910, 33 in 1919, 49 in 1923 and 42 in 1924.

Named Most Valuable Player in American League, 1914.

Manager, Chicago White Sox, 1925-26; coach, Philadelphia Athletics, 1931-32; vice-president and general manager, Boston Red Sox, 1933 to 1947; vice-president, Red Sox, 1947 to time of death.

Named to Hall of Fame, 1939.

Year	Club	League	Pos.	G.	AB.	R.	H.	2B.	3B.	HR.	RBI.	B.A.	PO.	A.	E.	F.A.
1906—Philadelphia(a)		Amer.	3B	6	17	1	4	0	0	0	0	.235	8	12	2	.909
1907—Philadelphia		Amer.	SS	14	20	0	5	0	0	0	3	.250	11	10	3	.875
1907—Newark		East.	2B-SS	4	16	6	7	0	0	0		.438	5	12	4	.810
1908—Philadelphia		Amer.	2B-SS	102	330	39	90	18	7	1	37	.273	190	189	24	.940
1909—Philadelphia		Amer.	2B	153	571	104	198	30	10	3	69	.346	★373	★406	27	★.967
1910—Philadelphia		Amer.	2B	153	581	81	188	16	15	3	80	.322	★402	★451	25	★.972
1911—Philadelphia		Amer.	2B	132	493	92	180	22	13	3	71	.365	★348	349	24	.967
1912—Philadelphia		Amer.	2B	153	543	★137	189	25	11	0	66	.348	★	426	38	.955
1913—Philadelphia		Amer.	2B	148	534	★125	184	23	13	3	75	.345	314	★449	28	.965
1914—Philadelphia(b)		Amer.	2B	152	526	★122	181	23	14	2	81	.344	354	387	23	★.970
1915—Chicago		Amer.	2B	155	521	118	173	22	10	4	78	.332	344	★487	22	★.974
1916—Chicago		Amer.	2B	155	545	87	168	14	17	0	56	.308	346	415	19	★.976
1917—Chicago		Amer.	2B	156	564	91	163	18	12	0	67	.289	★353	388	24	.969
1918—Chicago(c)		Amer.	2B	97	330	51	91	8	2	2	32	.276	231	285	14	.974
1919—Chicago		Amer.	2B	140	518	87	165	19	7	4	73	.319	★347	401	20	.974
1920—Chicago		Amer.	2B	153	600	113	220	37	13	3	75	.369	★449	471	23	★.976
1921—Chicago		Amer.	2B	139	526	79	177	20	10	2	58	.337	376	458	28	★.968
1922—Chicago		Amer.	2B	154	598	92	194	20	12	1	69	.324	406	451	21	★.976
1923—Chicago		Amer.	2B	145	505	89	182	22	5	5	67	.360	347	430	20	.975
1924—Chicago		Amer.	2B	152	556	108	194	27	7	6	86	.349	396	446	20	★.977
1925—Chicago		Amer.	2B	118	425	80	147	26	3	3	80	.346	290	346	20	.970
1926—Chicago(d)		Amer.	2B	106	375	66	129	32	4	1	62	.344	228	307	15	.973
1927—Philadelphia		Amer.	2B	95	226	50	76	12	1	1	15	.338	124	150	10	.965
1928—Philadelphia		Amer.	SS	36	33	3	10	3	0	0	7	.303	0	1	0	1.000
1929—Philadelphia		Amer.	PH	9	7	0	0	0	0	0	0	.000	0	0	0	.000
1930—Philadelphia		Amer.	PH	3	2	1	1	0	0	0	0	.500	0	0	0	.000
Major League Totals—25 Years				2826	9946	1816	3309	437	186	47	1307	.333	6624	7715	450	.970

aPlayed under name of Edward Sullivan.

bSold to Chicago White Sox for $50,000, December 8, 1914.

cIn Military Service most of season.

dReleased by Chicago White Sox, November 11, 1926; signed with Philadelphia Athletics, December 23, 1926.

WORLD SERIES RECORD

Shares record for most stolen bases, lifetime (14).

Year	Club	League	Pos.	G.	AB.	R.	H.	2B.	3B.	HR.	RBI.	B.A.	PO.	A.	E.	F.A.
1910—Philadelphia		Amer.	2B	5	21	5	9	4	0	0	3	.429	17	17	1	.971
1911—Philadelphia		Amer.	2B	6	21	4	6	1	0	0	0	.286	12	22	4	.895
1913—Philadelphia		Amer.	2B	5	19	5	8	0	2	0	3	.421	16	18	1	.971
1914—Philadelphia		Amer.	2B	4	14	0	3	0	0	0	1	.214	9	12	0	1.000
1917—Chicago		Amer.	2B	6	22	4	9	1	0	0	2	.409	11	22	0	1.000
1919—Chicago		Amer.	2B	8	31	2	7	1	0	0	1	.226	21	31	2	.963
World Series Totals—6 Years				34	128	20	42	7	2	0	10	.328	86	122	8	.963

JAMES JOSEPH (JIMMY) COLLINS

Born January 16, 1873, at Niagara Falls, N. Y.
Died March 6, 1943, at Buffalo, N. Y.
Height, 5.07½. Weight, 160.
Threw and batted righthanded.

Holds National League record for most chances accepted by third baseman, season (601), 1899.
Manager, Boston Red Sox, 1901 to 1906; Minneapolis, American Association, 1909; Providence, Eastern League, 1910-11.
Named to Hall of Fame, 1945.

Year	Club	League	Pos.	G.	AB.	R.	H.	2B.	3B.	HR.	SB.	B.A.	PO.	A.	E.	F.A.
1893—Buffalo	East.	SS-OF	76	297	49	85	13	2	2	10	.286	131	249	65	.854
1894—Buffalo	East.	OF	125	562	126	∗98	51	13	8	18	.352	299	∗34	21	.940
1895—Bos.(a)-L'ville	Nat.	3B	104	410	75	114	15	8	7	14	.278	128	185	30	.913
1896—Boston	Nat.	3B	83	303	52	91	7	6	1	10	.300	135	208	32	.915
1897—Boston	Nat.	3B	133	529	102	183	25	11	6	16	.346	∗213	∗303	38	.931
1898—Boston	Nat.	3B	152	600	106	202	34	4	∗14	10	.337	∗246	333	40	.935
1899—Boston	Nat.	3B	151	597	98	164	26	13	4	16	.275	225	376	30	.952
1900—Boston	Nat.	3B	●142	∗585	104	175	20	6	6	20	.299	∗252	∗323	47	.924
1901—Boston(b)	Amer.	3B	138	563	109	185	42	16	5	18	.329	210	●323	50	.914
1902—Boston	Amer.	3B	105	425	71	138	21	10	6	11	.325	138	247	20	∗.951
1903—Boston	Amer.	3B	130	541	87	160	34	17	5	22	.296	172	258	26	.943
1904—Boston	Amer.	3B	156	633	85	168	32	13	3	19	.265	∗191	320	30	.945
1905—Boston	Amer.	3B	131	508	66	140	25	5	4	18	.276	164	268	36	.923
1906—Boston	Amer.	3B	37	142	17	39	9	4	1	1	.275	43	70	11	.911
1907—Bos.(c)-Phila.	Amer.	3B	141	523	51	146	29	1	0	8	.279	143	257	47	.895
1908—Philadelphia	Amer.	3B	115	433	34	94	14	3	0	5	.217	117	216	26	.928
1909—Minneapolis	A. A.	3B	153	556	61	152	21	3	2	13	.273	170	342	45	.919
1910—Providence	East.	3B	121	438	35	98	11	4	1	12	.224	148	255	30	.931
1911—Providence	East.	3B	8	23	3	4	0	0	0	0	.174	6	15	2	.913
American League Totals—8 Years			953	3768	520	1070	206	69	24	102	.284	1178	1959	246	.927
National League Totals—6 Years			765	3024	537	929	127	48	38	86	.307	1199	1728	217	.931
Major League Totals—14 Years			1718	6792	1057	1999	333	117	62	188	.294	2377	3687	463	.929

aLoaned to Louisville, subject to recall, May 17, 1895.
bJumped to American League.
cTraded to Philadelphia for infielder Jack Knight, June 7, 1907.

WORLD SERIES RECORD

Year	Club	League	Pos.	G.	AB.	R.	H.	2B.	3B.	HR.	SB.	B.A.	PO.	A.	E.	F.A.
1903—Boston	Amer.	3B	8	36	5	9	1	2	0	3	.250	7	23	2	.938

EARLE BRYAN COMBS

Born May 14, 1899, at Pebworth, Ky.
Died July 21, 1976, at Richmond, Ky.
Height, 6.00. Weight, 185.
Threw right and batted lefthanded.

Shares American League record for most triples, game (3), September 22, 1927.
Coach, New York Yankees, 1935 through 1944; St. Louis Browns, 1947; Boston Red Sox, 1948 through 1952; Philadelphia Phillies, 1954.
Named to Hall of Fame, 1970.

Year	Club	League	Pos.	G.	AB.	R.	H.	2B.	3B.	HR.	RBI.	B.A.	PO.	A.	E.	F.A.
1922—Louisville	A.A.	OF	130	485	86	167	21	●18	4	55	.344	282	12	17	.945
1923—Louisville	A.A.	OF	166	634	127	∗241	46	15	14	145	.380	373	13	18	.955
1924—New York	Amer.	OF	24	35	10	14	5	0	0	2	.400	12	0	0	1.000
1925—New York	Amer.	OF	150	593	117	203	36	13	3	61	.342	370	12	9	.977
1926—New York	Amer.	OF	145	606	113	181	31	12	8	56	.299	375	8	12	.970
1927—New York	Amer.	OF	152	∗648	137	∗231	36	∗23	6	64	.356	∗411	6	14	.968
1928—New York	Amer.	OF	149	626	118	194	33	∗21	7	56	.310	∗424	11	9	.980
1929—New York	Amer.	OF	142	586	119	202	33	15	3	65	.345	358	10	13	.966

Year Club League	Pos.	G.	AB.	R.	H.	2B.	3B.	HR.	RBI.	B.A.	PO.	A.	E.	F.A.
1930—New York............ Amer.	OF	137	532	129	183	30	★22	7	82	.344	275	5	9	.969
1931—New York............ Amer.	OF	138	563	120	179	31	13	5	58	.318	335	5	9	.974
1932—New York............ Amer.	OF	144	591	143	190	32	10	9	65	.321	343	6	12	.967
1933—New York............ Amer.	OF	122	417	86	125	22	16	5	60	.300	227	3	6	.975
1934—New York............ Amer.	OF	63	251	47	80	13	5	2	25	.319	145	1	1	.993
1935—New York............ Amer.	OF	89	298	47	84	7	4	3	35	.282	143	2	1	.993
Major League Totals—12 Years...............		1455	5746	1186	1866	309	154	58	629	.325	3418	69	95	.973

WORLD SERIES RECORD

Shares record for most runs, game (4), October 2, 1932.

Year Club League	Pos.	G.	AB.	R.	H.	2B.	3B.	HR.	RBI.	B.A.	PO.	A.	E.	F.A.
1926—New York............ Amer.	OF	7	28	3	10	2	0	0	2	.357	17	0	0	1.000
1927—New York............ Amer.	OF	4	16	6	5	0	0	0	2	.313	16	0	0	1.000
1928—New York............ Amer.	OF	1	0	0	0	0	0	0	1	.000	0	0	0	.000
1932—New York............ Amer.	OF	4	16	8	6	1	0	1	4	.375	10	0	0	1.000
World Series Totals—4 Years		16	60	17	21	3	0	1	9	.350	43	0	0	1.000

CHARLES ALBERT (CHARLIE) COMISKEY
(Old Roman)

Born August 15, 1859, at Chicago, Ill.

Died October 26, 1931, at Eagle River, Wis.

Height, 6.00. Weight, 180.

Threw and batted righthanded.

Manager, St. Louis Browns, American Association, 1883, 1885 to 1889; Chicago, Players League, 1890; St. Louis Browns, 1891; Cincinnati, 1892-93-94; owner-manager, St. Paul, Western League, 1895 to 1899; owner and manager, Chicago White Sox, 1900; president, Chicago White Sox, 1901 to time of death.

Named to Hall of Fame in 1939 for exceptional ability among players whose active careers ended prior to 1900, and also as a builder of baseball.

Year Club League	Pos.	G.	AB.	R.	H.	2B.	3B.	HR.	SB.	B.A.	PO.	A.	E.	F.A.
1877—Elgin .... Ind.		....	....	....	....	....	....	....	....	....	....	....	....	......
1878—Dubuque................ Ind.	P-1B	21	....	....	....	....	....	....	....	.282	....	....	....	.883
1879—Dubuque................ N.W.	P-1B	45	....	....	....	....	....	....	....	.235	....	....	....	.824
1880—Dubuque................ Ind.		....	....	....	....	....	....	....	....	....	....	....	....	......
1881—Dubuque................ Ind.		....	....	....	....	....	....	....	....	....	....	....	....	......
1882—St. Louis................. A.A.	P-1B	78	327	58	80	9	7	1	....	.245	859	18	29	.968
1883—St. Louis................. A.A.	1B-OF	96	404	76	120	17	9	2	....	.297	(1088 PO-A)	43		.962
1884—St. Louis................. A.A.	1B	108	461	86	111	17	6	2	....	.241	(1205 PO-A)	36		.971
1885—St. Louis................. A.A.	1B	83	342	66	89	13	7	2	....	.260	(973 PO-A)	27		.973
1886—St. Louis................. A.A.	1B	131	577	94	150	17	8	3	47	.260	1152	44	29	.976
1887—St. Louis................. A.A.	1B	125	563	136	207	22	6	4	122	.368	1137	49	29	.976
1888—St. Louis................. A.A.	1B	137	576	101	156	20	5	5	77	.271	1279	44	42	.969
1889—St. Louis (a).......... A.A.	1B	137	586	105	169	24	10	3	71	.288	1223	39	35	.973
1890—Chicago .... Players	1B	88	375	53	93	11	3	0	35	.248	883	45	32	.967
1891—St. Louis (b).......... A.A.	1B	130	532	82	141	16	2	3	39	.265	1431	60	27	.982
1892—Cincinnati .... Nat.	1B	140	554	60	124	14	5	4	28	.224	1460	71	25	.984
1893—Cincinnati .... Nat.	1B	62	253	38	58	11	1	0	12	.229	671	21	14	.980
1894—Cincinnati .... Nat.	1B	59	230	26	61	8	0	0	9	.265	558	26	16	.973
1895—St. Paul .... West.	1B	17	67	15	23	....	....	....	3	.343	134	5	4	.972
American Assn. Totals—9 Years		1025	4368	804	1223	155	60	25	356	.280	(10601 PO-A)	297		.973
National League Totals—3 Years..........		261	1037	124	243	33	6	4	49	.234	2689	118	55	.981
Players League Totals—1 Year.............		88	375	53	93	11	3	0	35	.248	883	45	32	.967
Major League Totals—13 Years.............		1374	5780	981	1559	199	69	29	440	.270	(14336 PO-A)	884		.974

aJumped to Players League.

bSigned with Cincinnati after consolidation of National League and American Association.

JOHN BERTRAND (JOCKO) CONLAN

Born December 6, 1899, at Chicago, Ill.

Died April 1, 1989, at Scottsdale, Ariz.

Height, 5.07½. Weight, 160.

Threw and batted lefthanded.

Jocko Conlan was a fiesty son of the sod who took no extra lip from anyone. He took the brunt of legitimate beefs but one cuss word and the offender was gone. He was a master psychologist in the charged-up world of the baseball diamond, knowing when to cajole, when to rebuff and when to ignore. He knew the rules as well as any umpire but he also used the feel of the rules as they applied to plays and players. He was a vocal defender of the umpires' integrity and he lived that integrity to the hilt all the years of his career. Doubtless his years as a player gave him an insight that few others could match, but it never affected the correctness or proper application of the rules and decisions therefrom.

Umpire, New York-Pennsylvania League, 1936-37; American Association, 1938-39-40; National League, 1941-64.
World Series umpire, 1945-50-54-57-61.
All-Star Game umpire, 1943-47-50-53-58-62 (second game).
Named to Hall of Fame, 1974.

RECORD AS PLAYER

Year	Club	League	Pos.	G.	AB.	R.	H.	2B.	3B.	HR.	RBI.	B.A.	PO.	A.	E.	F.A.
1920—Wichita		West.	OF	117	430	50	106	15	5	4	....	.247	209	14	19	.921
1921—							(Out of game)									
1922—Wichita		West.	OF	10	40	5	11	1	1	1	....	.275	22	1	0	1.000
1923—Wichita		West.	OF	167	656	135	204	37	7	18	....	.311	*465	28	16	.969
1924—Rochester		Int.	OF	165	*666	135	*214	44	15	12	64	.321	*420	●24	13	.972
1925—Rochester		Int.	OF	143	544	95	168	36	10	6	69	.309	328	*25	15	.959
1926—Rochester		Int.	OF	123	497	98	142	29	8	3	49	.286	277	19	●17	.946
1927—Newark		Int.	OF	157	626	119	201	33	11	4	75	.321	373	15	10	.975
1928—Newark		Int.	OF	154	609	104	183	27	9	7	58	.300	382	23	12	.971
1929—Newark		Int.	OF	160	613	116	186	34	13	10	62	.303	287	13	10	.968
1930—Toledo		A.A.	OF	69	279	46	81	13	2	2	....	.290	141	9	7	.955
1931—Montreal		Int.	OF	149	594	77	178	28	6	2	43	.300	257	12	9	.968
1932—Montreal		Int.	OF	112	353	50	100	22	5	2	31	.283	149	14	4	.976
1933—							(Out of game)									
1934—Chicago		Amer.	OF	63	225	35	56	11	3	0	16	.249	122	5	6	.955
1935—Chicago		Amer.	OF	65	140	20	40	7	1	0	15	.286	71	3	3	.961
Major League Totals—2 Years				128	365	55	96	18	4	0	31	.263	193	8	9	.957

THOMAS HENRY (TOMMY) CONNOLLY

Born December 31, 1870, at Manchester, England.
Died April 28, 1961, at Natick, Mass.
Height, 5.07. Weight, 170.

A pioneer member of the American League umpire staff, Tommy Connolly spent 60 years in Organized Ball's umpiring profession. He served the A. L. for 53 seasons, the last 23 as chief of staff, before retiring on January 14, 1954 at the age of 83.

Born in England, he came to the United States with his family at the age of 13. He mastered the baseball rules as a youth and turned to umpiring. While working school and sandlot games around Natick, Mass., he was spotted by Tim Hurst, National League arbiter, who recommended him to the New England League in 1894. Four years later, Connolly advanced to the National League. He called them in that loop from 1898 through 1900.

In 1901, President Ban Johnson expanded the American League to major status and hired Connolly as an umpire on the recommendation of Connie Mack, manager of the new Philadelphia club. Tommy fitted perfectly into Johnson's policy that the arbiters were boss of the game and should be respected as representatives of the league.

Connolly had the distinction of umpiring the first game in the A. L.'s initial season as a major. On opening day, April 24, 1901, he called the Cleveland-Chicago game at the old White Sox park. The three other games scheduled for that day were rained out. Tommy handled the game alone and continued to call 'em by himself until 1907. He also umpired the first games played at the old New York Highlander's field, Comiskey Park in Chicago, Shibe Park (now Connie Mack Stadium) in Philadelphia, Fenway Park in Boston and Yankee Stadium in New York. He and Hank O'Day of the National League were the umpires in charge of the first modern World Series in 1903. Tommy was on duty in eight World Series.

Connolly quit the active ranks in June, 1931, and became chief of staff for the American League. He retained this job until his retirement in January, 1954. For many years he was a member of O. B.'s Rules Committee and in this capacity was responsible for numerous changes in the playing code. On May 27, 1953, he was awarded a gold lifetime pass—a memento usually reserved for players with 20 years of service—by both majors.

He and Bill Klem were named to the Hall of Fame in September, 1953, by the Committee on Veterans as the first umpires to be so recognized.

—DID YOU KNOW—

That as a first baseman for the St. Louis Browns in the American Association in the 1880s, Charlie Comiskey revolutionized first-base play by stationing himself away from the bag?

ROGER CONNOR

Born July 1, 1857, at Waterbury, Conn.
Died January 4, 1931, at Waterbury, Conn.
Height, 6.02. Weight, 210.
Threw and batted lefthanded.

Hit three home runs in a game, May 9, 1888.
Manager, St. Louis, National League, 1896; manager and owner, Springfield, Connecticut League, 1902.
Named to Hall of Fame, 1976.

Year	Club	League	Pos.	G.	AB.	R.	H.	2B.	3B.	HR.	SB.	B.A.	PO.	A.	E.	F.A.
1880—Troy		Nat.	3B	83	340	53	113	17	10	3	....	.332	116	159	60	.821
1881—Troy		Nat.	1B	84	361	54	104	17	6	2	....	.288	826	40	44	.952
1882—Troy		Nat.	1-3B-O	79	339	63	111	22	★17	4	....	.327	474	24	34	.936
1883—New York		Nat.	1B	96	401	80	145	28	14	1	....	.362	941	39	44	.957
1884—New York		Nat.	2-3B-O	112	462	93	146	27	4	4	....	.316	284	212	82	.858
1885—New York		Nat.	1B	110	455	102	★169	23	●15	1	....	★.371	1178	42	31	.975
1886—New York		Nat.	1B	118	485	105	172	30	★19	7	17	.355	1164	65	34	.973
1887—New York		Nat.	1B	127	546	113	209	26	22	17	43	.383	1325	44	30	.979
1888—New York		Nat.	1B	134	481	98	140	15	●17	14	27	.291	1337	43	26	.982
1889—New York		Nat.	1B	131	496	117	157	32	●17	13	21	.317	1265	32	30	.977
1890—New York		Players	1B	123	484	134	180	25	15	●14	23	.372	1332	80	18	.987
1891—New York		Nat.	1B	129	477	110	140	27	12	7	32	.293	1380	52	27	.981
1892—Philadelphia		Nat.	1B	153	558	122	159	31	11	11	20	.285	1461	60	23	★.985
1893—New York		Nat.	1B	●135	490	111	158	25	8	11	29	.322	★1419	81	★40	.974
1894—N.Y.-St. Louis		Nat.	1B-OF	121	462	93	145	34	26	8	15	.313	1084	81	28	.977
1895—St. Louis		Nat.	1B	104	402	78	131	28	7	6	8	.326	957	63	17	.984
1896—St. Louis		Nat.	1B	126	485	68	137	19	6	8	14	.282	1223	★86	17	★.987
1897—St. Louis		Nat.	1B	22	83	13	19	3	1	1	3	.229	237	11	4	.984
1987—Fall River		N. Eng.	1B	47	171	32	49	....	....	....	9	.287	473	31	9	.982
1898—Waterbury		Conn.	1B	95	....	....	....	....	....	....	....	.319	★890	....	....	★.980
1899—Waterbury		Conn.	1B	92	347	79	136	28	2	5	18	★.392	....	....	....	★.982
1900—Waterbury		Conn.	1B	83	286	54	82	9	3	2	20	.287	851	32	15	.983
1901—Water.-N. Hav.		Conn.	1B	107	411	58	123	....	....	....	....	.299	....	....	....	......
1902—Springfield		Conn.	1B	62	224	25	58	7	1	1	15	.259	642	27	15	.978
1903—Springfield		Conn.	1B	75	279	28	76	12	3	0	12	.272	789	28	21	.975
National League Totals—17 Years				1864	7323	1473	2355	404	212	118	229	.322	16671	1134	571	.969
Players League Totals—1 Year				123	484	134	180	25	15	14	23	.372	1332	80	18	.987
Major League Totals—18 Years				1987	7807	1607	2535	429	227	132	252	.325	18003	1214	589	.970

JOHN WALTER (JOHNNY) COONEY

Born March 18, 1901, at Cranston, R.I.
Died July 8, 1986, at Sarasota, Fla.
Height, 5.10. Weight, 165.
Threw left and batted righthanded.
Son of James J. Cooney and brother of James E. Cooney, former major league shortstops.

Player-coach, Boston Braves, 1940 through 1942; coach, Boston Braves, 1946 through 1952; Milwaukee Braves, 1953 through 1955; Chicago White Sox, 1957 through 1964.

Year	Club	League	Pos.	G.	AB.	R.	H.	2B.	3B.	HR.	RBI.	B.A.	PO.	A.	E.	F.A.
1921—Boston		Nat.	P	8	5	0	1	0	0	0	0	.200	2	5	0	1.000
1922—New Haven		East.	P-OF	45	123	21	29	2	3	2	....	.236	29	36	2	.970
1922—Boston		Nat.	P	4	8	0	0	0	0	0	0	.000	1	6	0	1.000
1923—Boston		Nat.	P-OF-1B	42	66	7	25	1	0	0	3	.379	34	17	0	1.000
1924—Boston		Nat.	P-OF-1B	55	130	10	33	2	1	0	4	.254	68	33	5	.953
1925—Boston		Nat.	P-1B-OF	54	103	17	33	7	0	0	13	.320	32	61	5	.949
1926—Boston		Nat.	P-1B	64	126	17	38	3	2	0	18	.302	248	45	3	.990
1927—Boston		Nat.	PH	10	1	3	0	0	0	0	0	.000	0	0	0	.000
1928—Boston		Nat.	P	33	41	2	7	0	0	0	2	.171	11	32	0	1.000
1929—Boston		Nat.	1B-OF-P	41	72	10	23	4	1	0	6	.319	45	16	1	.964
1930—Boston		Nat.	P	4	3	0	0	0	0	0	0	.000	0	4	0	1.000
1930—Jer. City-New'k		Int.	OF-1B-P	61	145	19	39	4	3	1	10	.269	210	8	1	.993

Year	Club	League	Pos.	G.	AB.	R.	H.	2B.	3B.	HR.	RBI.	B.A.	PO.	A.	E.	F.A.
1931—Toledo	A. A.		OF-1B-P	117	342	46	99	19	2	3	29	.286	305	87	4	.990
1932—Indianapolis	A. A.		P-1B	78	175	29	51	9	0	0	21	.291	176	62	4	.983
1933—Indianapolis	A. A.		●OF-P	138	519	91	171	35	12	3	73	.329	377	14	4	●.990
1934—Indianapolis	A. A.		OF	109	461	79	142	26	10	0	38	.308	261	5	5	.982
1935—Indianapolis	A. A.		OF	142	603	111	*224	37	7	3	92	*.371	361	13	7	.982
1935—Brooklyn	Nat.		OF	10	29	3	9	0	1	0	0	.310	23	0	0	1.000
1936—Brooklyn	Nat.		OF	130	507	71	143	17	5	0	30	.282	336	11	2	*.994
1937—Brooklyn†	Nat.		OF-1B	120	430	61	126	18	5	0	37	.293	279	9	7	.976
1938—Boston‡	Nat.		1B-OF	120	432	45	117	25	5	0	17	.271	296	10	4	.987
1939—Boston	Nat.		OF-1B	118	368	39	101	8	1	2	27	.274	236	10	2	.992
1940—Boston	Nat.		OF-1B	108	365	40	116	14	3	0	21	.318	294	9	2	.993
1941—Boston	Nat.		*OF-1B	123	442	52	141	25	2	0	29	.319	315	11	1	*.997
1942—Boston§	Nat.		OF-1B	74	198	23	41	6	0	0	7	.207	254	12	2	.993
1943—Brooklyn	Nat.		OF-1B	37	34	7	7	0	0	0	2	.206	20	0	0	1.000
1944—Brooklyn	Nat.		PH-OF	7	4	0	3	0	0	0	1	.750	3	0	0	1.000
1944—New York	Am.		PH-OF	10	8	1	1	0	0	0	1	.125	3	0	0	1.000
1944—Toronto	Int.		OF	34	121	12	33	2	0	0	9	.273	76	0	1	.987
1945—Kansas City	A. A.		OF	27	108	20	37	2	1	0	9	.343	58	2	1	.984
National League Totals—20 Years.........				1162	3364	407	964	130	26	2	217	.286	2497	291	34	.988
American League Totals—1 Year				10	8	1	1	0	0	0	1	.125	3	0	0	1.000
Major League Totals—20 Years..............				1172	3372	408	965	130	26	2	218	.286	2500	291	34	.988

†Traded with Infielder James Bucher, Third Baseman Joe Stripp and Pitcher Roy Henshaw to St. Louis Cardinals for Shortstop Leo Durocher, October 4, 1937.
‡Released April 18, 1938; signed by Boston Braves, April 19, 1938.
§Released January 10, 1943; signed by Brooklyn Dodgers, January 21, 1943.

PITCHING RECORD

Year	Club	League	G.	IP.	W.	L.	Pct.	H.	R.	ER.	SO.	BB.	ERA.
1921—Boston................................	Nat.	8	12	0	1	.000	19	12	9	9	10	3.86
1922—New Haven	East.	23	195	19	3	.864	157	54	42	99	37	1.94
1922—Boston................................	Nat.	4	25	1	2	.333	19	10	6	7	6	2.16
1923—Boston................................	Nat.	23	98	3	5	.375	92	43	36	23	22	3.31
1924—Boston................................	Nat.	34	181	8	9	.471	176	79	64	67	50	3.18
1925—Boston................................	Nat.	31	246	14	14	.500	267	123	95	65	50	3.48
1926—Boston................................	Nat.	19	83	3	3	.500	106	52	37	23	29	4.01
1928—Boston................................	Nat.	24	90	3	8	.300	106	47	43	18	31	4.30
1929—Boston................................	Nat.	14	45	2	2	.400	57	29	25	11	22	5.00
1930—Boston................................	Nat.	2	7	0	0	.000	16	14	14	1	3	18.00
1930—Newark	Int.	8	12	0	1	.000	12	5	5	2	2	3.75
1931—Toledo	A. A.	25	166	10	7	.588	172	66	46	55	36	*2.49
1932—Indianapolis	A. A.	37	174	10	6	.625	205	88	...	71	40	......
1933—Indianapolis	A. A.	6	20	2	1	.667	26	13	12	12	11	5.40
Major League Totals—9 Years............................		159	796	34	44	.436	858	409	329	224	223	3.72

ARLIE WILBUR COOPER

(Known by middle name.)

Born February 24, 1892, at Bearsville, W. Va.

Died August 7, 1973, at Van Nuys, Calif.

Height, 5.11½. Weight, 165.

Threw left and batted righthanded.

Led National League in complete games 1919 and 1922.
Manager, McKeesport, Penn State Association, 1935; Jeannette, Evangeline League, 1936; Greensburg, Penn State Association, 1937.

Year	Club	League	G.	IP.	W.	L.	Pct.	H.	R.	ER.	SO.	BB.	ERA.
1911—Marion......................................	Ohio State	34	....	17	11	.607	....	....	....	....	....	......
1912—Columbus	Amer. Assn.	31	219	16	9	.640	184	95	....	117	107	......
1912—Pittsburgh..............................	National	6	38	3	0	1.000	32	7	7	30	15	1.67
1913—Pittsburgh..............................	National	30	93	5	5	.625	98	52	34	39	45	3.29
1914—Pittsburgh..............................	National	40	267	16	15	.516	246	99	63	102	79	2.12
1915—Pittsburgh..............................	National	38	186	5	16	.238	180	92	68	71	52	3.29
1916—Pittsburgh..............................	National	42	246	12	11	.522	189	72	51	111	74	1.87
1917—Pittsburgh..............................	National	40	298	17	11	.607	276	96	78	99	54	2.36
1918—Pittsburgh..............................	National	38	273	19	14	.576	219	86	64	117	65	2.11
1919—Pittsburgh..............................	National	35	287	19	13	.594	229	97	*85	106	74	2.66
1920—Pittsburgh..............................	National	44	327	24	15	.615	307	113	87	114	52	2.39
1921—Pittsburgh..............................	National	38	*327	●22	14	.611	*341	145	*118	134	80	3.25
1922—Pittsburgh..............................	National	41	295	23	14	.622	330	130	104	129	61	3.18
1923—Pittsburgh..............................	National	39	295	17	*19	.472	331	136	117	77	71	3.57
1924—Pittsburgh(a)..........................	National	38	269	20	14	.588	296	116	98	62	40	3.28

Year Club	League	G.	IP.	W.	L.	Pct.	H.	R.	ER.	SO.	BB.	ERA.
1925—Chicago	National	32	212	12	14	.462	249	115	101	41	61	4.29
1926—Chicago(b)	National	8	55	2	1	.667	65	32	27	18	21	4.42
1926—Detroit	American	8	14	0	4	.000	27	18	17	2	9	10.93
1926—Toledo	Amer. Assn	9	55	2	5	.286	75	38	26	25	9	4.45
1927—Oakland	Pac. Coast	36	231	15	12	.556	238	99	86	65	51	3.35
1928—Oakland	Pac. Coast	27	212	10	16	.385	261	113	82	45	45	3.48
1929—Shreveport	Texas	30	232	17	9	.654	260	131	110	55	56	4.23
1930—Shreve.-San Ant.	Texas	24	104	3	11	.214	133	86	73	38	44	6.30
American League Totals—1 Year		8	14	0	4	.000	27	18	17	2	9	10.93
National League Totals—15 Years		509	3468	216	174	.554	3388	1388	1102	1250	844	2.86
Major League Totals—15 Years		517	3482	216	178	.548	3415	1406	1119	1252	853	2.89

aTraded with First Baseman Charley Grimm and Infielder Rabbit Maranville to Chicago Cubs for First Baseman Al Niehaus, Infielder George Grantham and Pitcher Vic Aldridge, October, 1924.
bSold to Detroit Tigers, May, 1926.

STANLEY (STAN) COVELESKI

Born July 13, 1890, at Shamokin, Pa.
Died March 20, 1984, at South Bend, Ind.
Height, 5.09½. Weight, 178.
Threw and batted righthanded.

Brother of Frank Coveleski, former pitcher with outlaw Union League (1907);
John Coveleski, former minor league third baseman-outfielder,
and Harry Coveleski, former major league pitcher.

Led American League in shutouts with 9 in 1917 and 5 in 1923.
Named to Hall of Fame, 1969.

Year Club	League	G.	IP.	W.	L.	Pct.	H.	R.	ER.	SO.	BB.	ERA.
1908—Shamokin	Atlantic	12	....	6	2	.750	....	....	....	....	....	......
1909—Lancaster	Tri-State	43	272	★23	11	.676	225	84	....	78	68	......
1910—Lancaster	Tri-State	30	....	15	8	.652	....	....	....	....	....	......
1911—Lancaster	Tri-State	36	272	15	●19	.441	288	120	....	154	65	......
1912—Atlantic City	Tri-State	39	....	20	13	.606	....	....	....	....	....	......
1912—Philadelphia	Amer.	5	21	2	1	.667	18	9	....	9	4	......
1913—Spokane	N. W.	48	316	17	★20	.459	300	140	....	197	95	......
1914—Spokane	N. W.	43	314	20	15	.571	269	109	....	★214	99	......
1915—Portland	P. C.	●64	293	17	17	.500	279	123	87	171	82	2.67
1916—Cleveland	Amer.	45	232	15	12	.556	247	100	88	76	58	3.41
1917—Cleveland	Amer.	45	297	19	14	.576	202	78	60	133	94	1.81
1918—Cleveland	Amer.	38	311	22	13	.629	261	90	63	87	76	1.82
1919—Cleveland	Amer.	43	286	24	12	.667	★286	99	83	118	60	2.52
1920—Cleveland	Amer.	41	315	24	14	.632	284	110	87	★133	65	2.49
1921—Cleveland	Amer.	43	316	23	13	.639	341	137	118	99	84	3.36
1922—Cleveland	Amer.	35	277	17	14	.548	292	120	102	98	64	3.31
1923—Cleveland	Amer.	33	228	13	14	.481	251	98	70	54	42	★2.76
1924—Cleveland (a)	Amer.	37	240	15	16	.484	286	140	108	58	73	4.05
1925—Washington	Amer.	32	241	20	5	★.800	230	86	76	58	73	★2.84
1926—Washington (b)	Amer.	36	245	14	11	.560	272	122	85	50	81	3.12
1927—Washington	Amer.	5	14	2	1	.667	13	7	5	3	8	3.21
1928—New York	Amer.	12	58	5	1	.833	72	41	37	5	20	5.74
Major League Totals—14 Years		450	3081	215	141	.604	3055	1237	982	981	802	2.88

aTraded to Washington for pitcher Byron Speece and outfielder Carr Smith, December 12, 1924.
bReleased, June 12, 1927; signed by New York Yankees, December, 1927.

WORLD SERIES RECORD

Year Club	League	G.	IP.	W.	L.	Pct.	H.	R.	ER.	SO.	BB.	ERA.
1920—Cleveland	Amer.	3	27	3	0	1.000	15	2	2	8	2	0.67
1925—Washington	Amer.	2	14⅓	0	2	.000	16	7	6	3	5	3.77
World Series Totals—2 Years		5	41⅓	3	2	.600	31	9	8	11	7	1.74

—DID YOU KNOW—

That Sam Crawford is the only player to win home run titles in both the National and American leagues?

ROGER MAXWELL (DOC) CRAMER
(Flint)

Born July 22, 1906, at Beach Haven, N. J.
Height, 6.02. Weight, 185.
Threw right and batted lefthanded.

Holds major league record for most years leading league in at-bats (7).
Led American League outfielders in double plays, 1936 (tie).
Named as outfielder on THE SPORTING NEWS All-Star Major League Team in 1935.
Coach, Detroit Tigers, 1948; Seattle, Pacific Coast League, 1950; Chicago White Sox, 1951 through 1953.

Year Club League	Pos.	G.	AB.	R.	H.	2B.	3B.	HR.	RBI.	B.A.	PO.	A.	E.	F.A.
1929—Martinsburg .... B. R.	IN-P	104	366	75	148	31	13	5	.....	*.404	153	126	17	.943
1929—Philadelphia .... Amer.	OF	2	6	0	0	0	0	0	0	.000	6	0	0	1.000
1930—Philadelphia .... Amer.	OF	30	82	12	19	1	1	0	6	.232	37	1	3	.927
1930—Portland............... P. C.	OF	74	300	53	104	24	3	5	46	.347	141	11	3	.961
1931—Philadelphia .... Amer.	OF	65	223	37	58	8	2	2	20	.260	133	5	3	.979
1932—Philadelphia .... Amer.	OF	92	384	73	129	27	6	3	46	.336	233	7	6	.976
1933—Philadelphia .... Amer.	OF	152	*661	109	195	27	8	8	75	.295	387	13	12	.971
1934—Philadelphia .... Amer.	OF	153	*649	99	202	29	9	6	46	.311	385	12	6	.985
1935—Philadelphia (a)... Amer.	OF	149	*644	96	214	37	4	3	70	.332	429	6	11	.975
1936—Boston.................. Amer.	OF	154	643	99	188	31	7	0	41	.292	*443	20	12	.975
1937—Boston.................. Amer.	OF	133	560	90	171	22	11	0	51	.305	365	12	12	.969
1938—Boston.................. Amer.	OF-P	148	*658	116	198	36	8	0	71	.301	*417	15	6	.986
1939—Boston.................. Amer.	OF	137	589	110	183	30	6	0	56	.311	356	12	6	.984
1940—Boston (b)............. Amer.	OF	150	*661	94	●200	27	12	1	51	.303	333	11	11	.969
1941—Washington (c).... Amer.	OF	154	*660	93	180	25	6	2	66	.273	369	9	6	.984
1942—Detroit.................. Amer.	OF	151	*630	71	166	26	4	0	43	.263	352	15	7	.981
1943—Detroit.................. Amer.	OF	140	606	79	182	18	4	1	43	.300	346	9	4	.989
1944—Detroit.................. Amer.	OF	143	578	69	169	20	9	2	42	.292	337	13	7	.980
1945—Detroit.................. Amer.	OF	141	541	62	149	22	8	6	58	.275	314	7	3	*.991
1946—Detroit.................. Amer.	OF	68	204	26	60	8	2	1	26	.294	89	2	0	1.000
1947—Detroit.................. Amer.	OF	73	157	21	42	2	2	2	30	.268	79	3	3	.965
1948—Detroit (d)............ Amer.	OF	4	4	1	0	0	0	0	1	.000	2	0	0	1.000
1949—Buffalo................ Int.	OF	65	135	22	37	7	0	3	27	.274	44	2	2	.958
1950—Seattle.................. P. C.	PH	2	2	0	0	0	0	0	0	.000	0	0	0	.000
Major League Totals—20 Years..............		2239	9140	1357	2705	396	109	37	842	.296	5412	172	118	.979

WORLD SERIES RECORD

Shares records for most at-bats, nine-inning game (6), October 8, 1945; most at-bats, inning (2), October 7, 1945, sixth inning.

Year Club League	Pos.	G.	AB.	R.	H.	2B.	3B.	HR.	RBI.	B.A.	PO.	A.	E.	F.A.
1931—Philadelphia .... Amer.	PH	2	2	0	1	0	0	0	2	.500	0	0	0	.000
1945—Detroit.................. Amer.	OF	7	29	7	11	0	0	0	4	.379	21	0	0	1.000
World Series Totals—2 Years		9	31	7	12	0	0	0	6	.387	21	0	0	1.000

aTraded to Boston Red Sox with Infielder Donald McNair for Pitcher Henry Johnson, Infielder Al Niemiec and cash, January 4, 1936.

bTraded to Washington Senators for Outfielder Gee Walker, December 12, 1940.

cTraded to Detroit Tigers with Infielder Jimmy Bloodworth for Outfielder Bruce Campbell and Shortstop Frank Croucher, December 12, 1941.

dReleased, November 11, 1948.

PITCHING RECORD

Year Club League	G.	IP.	W.	L.	Pct.	H.	R.	ER.	SO.	BB.	ERA.
1929—Martinsburg................................. B. Ridge	11	44	2	2	.500	43	27	....	35	23	......
1938—Boston... Amer.	1	4	0	0	.000	3	2	2	1	3	4.50

SAMUEL EARL (SAM) CRAWFORD
(Wahoo Sam)

Born April 18, 1880, at Wahoo, Neb.
Died June 15, 1968, at Hollywood, Calif.
Height, 6.00. Weight, 190.
Threw and batted lefthanded.

Holds major league record for most triples, lifetime (312); most years leading league in triples (6).
Shares American league records for most triples, season (26); most consecutive years leading league in triples (3).
Umpire, Pacific Coast League, 1935 through 1938.
Named to Hall of Fame, 1957.

Year Club	League	Pos.	G.	AB.	R.	H.	2B.	3B.	HR.	SB.	B.A.	PO.	A.	E.	F.A.
1899—Chatham	Canadian	OF	43	173	34	64	...	...	0	7	.370	(110 PO-A)		13	.894
1899—Col.-Gr. Rapids.....	Western	OF	60	261	46	87	...	...	5	3	.333	112	9	8	.938
1899—Cincinnati	Nat.	OF	31	127	25	39	2	8	0	3	.307	60	9	3	.958
1900—Cincinnati	Nat.	OF	96	385	67	104	14	15	6	15	.270	230	16	12	.953
1901—Cincinnati	Nat.	OF	124	523	89	175	22	16	*16	12	.335	.208	20	20	.919
1902—Cincinnati (a)	Nat.	OF	●140	555	94	185	16	*23	3	15	.333	204	●25	18	.927
1903—Detroit	Amer.	OF	137	545	93	181	23	*25	4	23	.332	225	16	9	.964
1904—Detroit	Amer.	OF	150	571	46	141	21	17	2	20	.247	230	17	8	.969
1905—Detroit	Amer.	1B-OF	154	575	73	171	40	10	6	22	.297	630	59	13	*.981
1906—Detroit	Amer.	1B-OF	145	563	65	166	23	16	2	24	.295	458	36	5	.990
1907—Detroit	Amer.	OF	144	582	*102	188	34	17	4	18	.323	311	22	12	.965
1908—Detroit	Amer.	1B-OF	152	*591	102	184	33	16	*7	15	.311	428	22	14	.970
1909—Detroit	Amer.	1B-OF	156	589	83	185	*35	14	6	30	.314	486	17	17	.967
1910—Detroit	Amer.	OF	154	588	83	170	26	*19	5	20	.289	223	10	9	.963
1911—Detroit	Amer.	OF	146	574	109	217	36	14	7	37	.378	181	16	5	.975
1912—Detroit	Amer.	OF	149	581	81	189	30	21	4	41	.325	169	16	3	.984
1913—Detroit	Amer.	OF	153	*610	78	193	32	*23	9	13	.316	357	21	14	.964
1914—Detroit	Amer.	1B-OF	157	582	74	183	22	*26	8	25	.314	193	18	5	.977
1915—Detroit	Amer.	OF	156	612	81	183	31	*19	4	24	.299	219	8	6	.974
1916—Detroit	Amer.	OF	100	322	41	92	11	13	0	10	.286	85	6	2	.978
1917—Detroit	Amer.	OF	61	104	6	18	4	0	2	0	.173	158	2	2	.988
1918—Los Angeles	P.C.	1B-OF	96	356	38	104	14	7	1	8	.292	....	....	....	......
1919—Los Angeles	P.C.	OF	173	664	103	*239	41	18	14	14	.360	289	14	4	.987
1920—Los Angeles	P.C.	OF	187	719	99	239	46	*21	12	3	.332	284	30	7	.978
1921—Los Angeles	P.C.	OF	175	626	92	199	40	10	9	10	.318	323	21	8	.977
American League Totals—15 Years			2114	7989	1117	2461	401	250	70	322	.308	4353	286	124	.974
National League Totals—4 Years..........			391	1590	275	503	54	62	25	45	.316	702	70	53	.936
Major League Totals—19 Years.............			2505	9579	1392	2964	455	312	95	367	.309	5055	356	177	.968

aJumped from Cincinnati to Detroit.

WORLD SERIES RECORD

Year Club	League	Pos.	G.	AB.	R.	H.	2B.	3B.	HR.	SB.	B.A.	PO.	A.	E.	F.A.
1907—Detroit	Amer.	OF	5	21	1	5	1	0	0	0	.238	7	2	0	1.000
1908—Detroit	Amer.	OF	5	21	2	5	1	0	0	0	.238	16	0	0	1.000
1909—Detroit	Amer.	OF	7	28	4	7	3	0	1	1	.250	17	1	2	.900
World Series Totals—3 Years			17	70	7	17	5	0	1	1	.243	40	3	2	.956

JOSEPH EDWARD (JOE) CRONIN

Born October 12, 1906, at San Francisco, Calif.

Died September 7, 1984, at Osterville, Mass.

Height, 6.00. Weight, 187.

Threw and batted righthanded.

Holds American League record for most home runs by pinch-hitter, season (5), 1943.
Selected Most Valuable Player, American League, 1930.
Named by Baseball Writers' Association of America as shortstop for THE SPORTING NEWS All-Star Major League Teams, 1930-31-32-33-34-38 and 1939.
Manager, Washington Senators, 1933-34; Boston Red Sox, 1935 through 1947; vice-president, treasurer and general manager, Red Sox, 1948 to 1959; president of American League, 1959 to 1973.
Named to Hall of Fame, 1956.

Year Club	League	Pos.	G.	AB.	R.	H.	2B.	3B.	HR.	RBI.	B.A.	PO.	A.	E.	F.A.
1925—Johnstown	Mid.-Atl.	2B-SS	99	352	64	110	18	11	3	....	.313	....	....	....	......
1926—Pittsburgh	Nat.	2B-SS	38	83	9	22	2	2	0	11	.265	55	82	3	.979
1926—New Haven	East.	SS	66	244	61	78	11	8	2		.320	136	222	27	.930
1927—Pittsburgh	Nat.	SS	12	22	2	5	1	0	0	3	.227	12	10	4	.846
1928—Kansas City	A.A.	SS	74	241	34	59	10	6	2	32	.245	87	146	14	.943
1928—Washington	Amer.	SS	63	227	23	55	10	4	0	25	.242	133	190	16	.953
1929—Washington	Amer.	SS	145	494	72	139	29	8	8	60	.281	285	●459	*62	.923
1930—Washington	Amer.	SS	●154	587	127	203	42	9	13	126	.346	*336	*509	35	.960
1931—Washington	Amer.	SS	*156	611	103	187	44	13	12	126	.306	*323	488	43	.950
1932—Washington	Amer.	SS	143	557	95	177	43	*18	6	116	.318	*306	*448	32	*.959
1933—Washington	Amer.	SS	152	602	89	186	*45	11	5	118	.309	297	528	34	*.960

Year Club League	Pos.	G.	AB.	R.	H.	2B.	3B.	HR.	RBI.	B.A.	PO.	A.	E.	F.A.
1934—Washington (a) .... Amer.	SS	127	504	68	143	30	9	7	101	.284	246	486	38	.951
1935—Boston.................. Amer.	1B-SS	144	556	70	164	37	14	9	95	.295	277	435	37	.951
1936—Boston.................. Amer.	SS-3B	81	295	36	83	22	4	2	43	.281	133	229	26	.933
1937—Boston.................. Amer.	SS	148	570	102	175	40	4	18	110	.307	300	414	31	.958
1938—Boston.................. Amer.	SS	143	530	98	172	★51	5	17	94	.325	304	449	36	.954
1939—Boston.................. Amer.	SS	143	520	97	160	33	3	19	107	.308	306	437	32	.959
1940—Boston.................. Amer.	SS-3B	149	548	104	156	35	6	24	111	.285	253	445	★38	.948
1941—Boston.................. Amer.	1-SS-3-OF	143	518	98	161	38	8	6	95	.311	247	362	★27	.958
1942—Boston.................. Amer.	1B-SS-3B	45	79	7	24	3	0	4	24	.304	47	28	6	.926
1943—Boston.................. Amer.	3B	59	77	8	24	4	0	5	29	.312	12	18	1	.968
1944—Boston.................. Amer.	1B	76	191	24	46	7	0	5	28	.241	428	27	9	.981
1945—Boston (b)............. Amer.	3B	3	8	1	3	0	0	0	1	.375	2	8	0	1.000
American League Totals—18 Years		2074	7474	1222	2258	513	116	170	1409	.302	4235	5960	503	.953
National League Totals—2 Years...........		50	105	11	27	3	2	0	14	.257	67	92	7	.958
Major League Totals—20 Years..............		2124	7579	1233	2285	516	118	170	1423	.301	4302	6052	510	.953

aTraded to Boston Red Sox for shortstop Lyn Lary and $250,000, October, 1934.
bSuffered fractured right leg, April 19, 1945, and out of action remainder of season.

WORLD SERIES RECORD

Year Club League	Pos.	G.	AB.	R.	H.	2B.	3B.	HR.	RBI.	B.A.	PO.	A.	E.	F.A.
1933—Washington .... Amer.	SS	5	22	1	7	0	0	0	2	.318	7	15	1	.957

LAFAYETTE NAPOLEON (LAVE) CROSS

Born May 12, 1867, at Milwaukee, Wis.

Died September 6, 1927, at Philadelphia, Pa.

Height, 5.08½. Weight, 165.

Threw and batted righthanded.

Year Club League	Pos.	G.	AB.	R.	H.	2B.	3B.	HR.	SB.	B.A.	PO.	A.	E.	F.A.
1887—Louisville .... A. A.	C	54	214	27	70	9	3	0	15	.327	(PO-A 307)		24	.927
1888—Louisville .... A. A.	C	47	183	21	39	4	0	0	9	.213	(PO-A 271)		21	.928
1889—Philadelphia .... A. A.	C	55	199	25	45	7	2	0	10	.226	278	102	19	.952
1890—Philadelphia .... Players	C	60	244	42	73	9	8	3	5	.299	184	68	24	.913
1891—Philadelphia .... A. A.	3-OF-C	106	387	64	115	19	13	4	14	.297	287	102	22	.946
1892—Philadelphia .... Nat.	C-O-3B	134	530	85	139	14	10	4	17	.262	292	180	26	.948
1893—Philadelphia .... Nat.	C-3B	94	414	85	125	16	6	4	15	.302	190	151	18	.950
1894—Philadelphia .... Nat.	3B	120	543	128	211	32	12	5	28	.389	177	240	40	.912
1895—Philadelphia .... Nat.	3B	124	535	95	148	24	8	2	19	.277	184	297	36	.930
1896—Philadelphia .... Nat.	3B-SS	106	409	62	107	22	4	0	10	.262	173	266	27	.942
1897—Philadelphia .... Nat.	2B-3B	88	345	37	90	17	4	3	11	.261	136	212	26	.930
1898—St. Louis................ Nat.	2B	151	601	71	192	26	7	3	14	.319	213	349	33	.945
1899—St. Louis-Cleve..... Nat.	3B	141	561	77	164	19	5	5	16	.292	222	364	26	.958
1900—St. Louis-Brook..... Nat.	3B	133	519	79	152	15	6	4	21	.293	184	317	31	.941
1901—Philadelphia .... Amer.	3B	100	420	82	139	31	11	2	21	.331	144	239	32	.923
1902—Philadelphia .... Amer.	3B	137	558	90	189	37	8	0	26	.339	★197	309	28	★.947
1903—Philadelphia .... Amer.	3B	137	554	61	162	23	5	2	13	.292	157	216	18	.954
1904—Philadelphia .... Amer.	3B	155	611	80	177	29	9	2	13	.290	173	246	31	.931
1905—Philadelphia .... Amer.	3B	146	583	68	155	26	5	0	8	.266	161	249	32	.928
1906—Washington .... Amer.	3B	130	494	55	130	14	6	1	19	.263	157	242	20	★.952
1907—Washington .... Amer.	3B	41	161	13	32	8	0	0	3	.199	38	98	3	.978
1907—New Orleans........ South.	3B	86	337	40	90	....	....	....	11	.267	99	178	3	.989
1908—New Orleans........ South.	3B	15	55	4	14	....	....	....	1	.254	24	27	3	.944
1909—Charlotte.............. Car. Assn.	2B	50	187	20	59	....	....	....	....	.315	111	142	5	.981
1910—Charlotte.............. Car. Assn.	3B	109	396	43	117	....	....	....	....	.295	139	225	18	.953
1911—Charlotte.............. Car. Assn.	3B	79	295	32	95	....	....	....	....	.322	147	219	25	.936
1912—Haverhill............... New Eng.	3B	126	452	53	132	20	1	1	14	.292	113	220	14	.960
American Assn. Totals—4 Years		262	983	137	269	39	18	4	48	.274	565	204	86	.940
Players League Totals—1 Year...............		60	244	42	73	9	8	3	5	.299	184	68	24	.913
American League Totals—7 Years		846	3381	449	984	168	44	7	103	.291	1027	1599	164	.941
National League Totals—9 Years............		1091	4457	719	1328	185	62	30	151	.298	1771	2376	263	.940
Major League Totals—21 Years............		2259	9065	1347	2654	401	132	44	307	.293	3547	4247	537	.936

WORLD SERIES RECORD

Year Club League	Pos.	G.	AB.	R.	H.	2B.	3B.	HR.	RBI.	B.A.	PO.	A.	E.	F.A.
1905—Philadelphia .... Amer.	3B	5	19	0	2	0	0	0	0	.105	6	7	2	.867

WILLIAM ARTHUR (CANDY) CUMMINGS

Born October 17, 1848, at Ware, Mass.
Died May 17, 1924, at Toledo, O.
Height, 5.09. Weight, 120.
Threw and batted righthanded.

President of first minor league, International Association, 1877.
Named to Hall of Fame, 1939.

Year Club	League	G.	W.	L.	Pct.	ERA.	Sh.O.
1866—Hercules of Fulton, N. Y.	Ind.	....	....	....	....	....	....
1866—Excelsior Jrs. of Brooklyn	Ind.	6	....	....	....	....	....
1867—Excelsior Jrs. of Brooklyn	Ind.	15	....	....	....	....	....
1868—Star of Brooklyn	Ind.	11	....	....	....	....	....
1869—Star of Brooklyn	Ind.	22	....	....	....	....	....
1870—Star of Brooklyn	Ind.	26	....	....	....	....	....
1871—Star of Brooklyn	Ind.		....	....	....	....	....
1872—Mutuals of New York	Nat. Assn.	53	34	19	.642	....	3
1873—Baltimore	Nat. Assn.	43	29	14	.674	....	1
1874—Philadelphia	Nat. Assn.	54	28	26	.519	....	3
1875—Hartford	Nat. Assn.	52	34	11	.756	1.73	6
1876—Hartford	Nat.	24	16	8	.667	1.66	5
1877—Live Oaks of Lynn	I. Assn.	8	1	7	.125	....	1
1877—Cincinnati	Nat.	19	5	14	.263	....	0
1878—Forest City of Cleveland	Ind.		(No record available)				
1878—Hartford	I. Assn.	4	0	4	.000	....	0
Major League Totals—2 Years		43	21	22	.488	....	5

HAZEN SHIRLEY (KIKI) CUYLER

Born August 30, 1899, at Harrisville, Mich.
Died February 11, 1950, at Ann Arbor, Mich.
Height, 5.11. Weight, 185.
Threw and batted righthanded.

Shares National League record for most consecutive hits (10), September 18 to 21, 1925.
Led National League in stolen bases with 35 in 1926, 37 in 1928, 43 in 1929 and 37 in 1930.
Named by Baseball Writers' Association of America for THE SPORTING NEWS All-Star Major League Team, 1925.
Manager, Chattanooga, Southern Association, 1939 to 1941; Atlanta, Southern Association, 1945 through 1948; coach, Chicago Cubs, 1941 through 1943; Boston Red Sox, 1949.
Named to Hall of Fame, 1968.

Year Club	League	Pos.	G.	AB.	R.	H.	2B.	3B.	HR.	RBI.	B.A.	PO.	A.	E.	F.A.
1920—Bay City	Mich.-Ont.	OF	69	240	24	62	8	3	1	26	.258	108	10	7	.944
1921—Bay City	Mich.-Ont.	OF	116	417	79	132	18	16	8	82	.317	★271	20	13	.957
1921—Pittsburgh	Nat.	OF	1	3	0	0	0	0	0	0	.000	1	0	0	1.000
1922—Charleston	Sally	OF	131	489	84	151	29	15	12	46	.309	274	13	12	.960
1922—Pittsburgh	Nat.	PR	1	0	0	0	0	0	0	0	.000	0	0	0	.000
1923—Nashville	Southern	OF	149	574	114	195	39	17	9	108	.340	★383	★35	●12	.972
1923—Pittsburgh	Nat.	OF	11	40	4	10	1	1	0	2	.250	26	1	2	.931
1924—Pittsburgh	Nat.	OF	117	466	94	165	27	16	9	85	.354	246	19	●16	.943
1925—Pittsburgh	Nat.	OF	●153	617	★144	220	43	★26	18	102	.357	362	21	13	.967
1926—Pittsburgh	Nat.	OF	★157	614	★113	197	31	15	8	92	.321	405	19	14	.968
1927—Pittsburgh(a)	Nat.	OF	85	285	60	88	13	7	3	31	.309	195	6	4	.980
1928—Chicago	Nat.	OF	133	499	92	142	25	9	17	79	.285	257	18	5	.982
1929—Chicago	Nat.	OF	139	509	111	183	29	7	15	102	.360	288	15	8	.974
1930—Chicago	Nat.	OF	●156	642	155	228	50	17	13	134	.355	377	21	8	.980
1931—Chicago	Nat.	OF	154	613	110	202	37	12	9	88	.330	347	11	11	.970
1932—Chicago	Nat.	OF	110	446	58	130	19	9	10	77	.291	239	7	8	.969
1933—Chicago	Nat.	OF	70	262	37	83	13	3	5	35	.317	130	2	3	.978
1934—Chicago	Nat.	OF	142	559	80	189	●42	8	6	69	.338	319	15	10	.971
1935—Chi.(b)-Cinc.	Nat.	OF	107	380	58	98	13	4	6	40	.258	221	10	4	.983
1936—Cincinnati	Nat.	OF	144	567	96	185	29	11	7	74	.326	322	9	9	.974

Year Club League	Pos.	G.	AB.	R.	H.	2B.	3B.	HR.	RBI.	B.A.	PO.	A.	E.	F.A.
1937—Cincinnati(c) .... Nat.	OF	117	406	48	110	12	4	0	32	.271	174	8	5	.973
1938—Brooklyn .... Nat.	OF	82	253	45	69	10	8	2	23	.273	125	9	1	.993
1939—Chattanooga .... Southern	OF	58	159	19	43	7	3	0	18	.270	105	5	2	.982
1940—Chattanooga .... Southern	PH	1	1	1	1	0	0	0	0	1.000	0	0	0	.000
Major League Totals—18 Years		1879	7161	1305	2299	394	157	128	1065	.321	4034	191	121	.972

aTraded to Chicago Cubs for infielder Earl Adams and outfielder Floyd Scott, November 28, 1927.
bReleased by Chicago Cubs, July 3, 1935, and signed by Cincinnati, July 5, 1935.
cUnconditionally released by Cincinnati, October, 1937, and signed with Brooklyn, February, 1938.

WORLD SERIES RECORD

Year Club League	Pos.	G.	AB.	R.	H.	2B.	3B.	HR.	RBI.	B.A.	PO.	A.	E.	F.A.
1925—Pittsburgh.............. Nat.	OF	7	26	3	7	3	0	1	6	.269	12	0	1	.923
1929—Chicago .... Nat.	OF	5	20	4	6	1	0	0	4	.300	8	0	1	.889
1932—Chicago .... Nat.	OF	4	18	2	5	1	1	1	2	.278	5	0	0	1.000
World Series Totals—3 Years		16	64	9	18	5	1	2	12	.281	25	0	2	.926

WILLIAM FREDERICK (BILL) DAHLEN
(Bad Bill)

Born January 5, 1871, at Fort Plain, N. Y.

Died December 5, 1950, at Brooklyn, N. Y.

Height, 5.08. Weight, 170.

Threw and batted righthanded.

Holds National League record for most assists, shortstop, lifetime (7,414).
Manager, Brooklyn Dodgers, 1910 through 1913.

Year Club League	Pos.	G.	AB.	R.	H.	2B.	3B.	HR.	SB.	B.A.	PO.	A.	E.	F.A.
1890—Cobleskill .... N.Y. St.	2B	85	400	88	137	....	....	....	20	.343	353	284	58	.917
1891—Chicago .... Nat.	INF-OF	135	551	113	145	20	13	9	29	.263	212	258	63	.882
1892—Chicago .... Nat.	SS-3B	143	587	116	173	23	19	5	60	.295	295	430	58	.926
1893—Chicago .... Nat.	SS-OF	115	463	113	144	28	16	5	33	.311	256	303	66	.894
1894—Chicago .... Nat.	SS-3B	121	508	150	184	30	14	15	49	.362	286	384	75	.899
1895—Chicago .... Nat.	SS	131	509	107	139	19	9	6	44	.273	290	★533	★84	.907
1896—Chicago .... Nat.	SS	125	476	137	172	24	18	9	60	.361	315	463	75	.912
1897—Chicago .... Nat.	SS	75	277	67	82	17	8	6	16	.296	215	297	39	.929
1898—Chicago .... Nat.	SS	141	524	96	152	34	9	1	25	.290	369	410	78	.909
1899—Brooklyn .... Nat.	SS	122	428	88	118	20	9	4	29	.276	257	373	42	.938
1900—Brooklyn .... Nat.	SS	134	485	87	126	15	12	1	31	.260	317	★515	51	●.942
1901—Brooklyn .... Nat.	SS	130	513	69	134	17	10	4	23	.261	306	446	51	.936
1902—Brooklyn .... Nat.	SS	136	520	68	139	26	7	2	29	.267	271	438	67	.914
1903—Brooklyn .... Nat.	SS	138	474	71	124	17	9	1	34	.262	296	★477	42	★.948
1904—New York .... Nat.	SS	145	523	70	140	26	2	2	47	.268	316	★494	61	.930
1905—New York .... Nat.	SS	148	520	67	126	20	4	7	37	.242	313	501	45	.948
1906—New York .... Nat.	SS	143	471	63	113	18	3	1	16	.240	287	454	49	.938
1907—New York .... Nat.	SS	143	464	40	96	20	1	0	11	.207	292	426	45	.941
1908—Boston .... Nat.	SS	144	524	50	125	23	2	3	10	.239	291	553	43	.952
1909—Boston .... Nat.	SS	57	197	22	46	6	1	2	4	.234	101	184	29	.908
1910—Brooklyn .... Nat.	PH	3	2	0	0	0	0	0	0	.000	0	0	0	.000
1911—Brooklyn .... Nat.	SS	1	3	0	0	0	0	0	0	.000	2	5	0	1.000
1913—Brooklyn .... Nat.	3B	1	0	0	0	0	0	0	0	.000	0	0	0	.000
Major League Totals—21 Years		2431	9019	1594	2478	403	166	83	587	.275	5287	7944	1063	.926

WORLD SERIES RECORD

Year Club League	Pos.	G.	AB.	R.	H.	2B.	3B.	HR.	SB.	B.A.	PO.	A.	E.	F.A.
1905—New York .... Nat.	SS	5	15	1	0	0	0	0	2	.000	10	19	0	1.000

RAY DANDRIDGE

Born August 31, 1913, at Richmond, Va.

Height, 5.07. Weight, 175.

Threw and batted righthanded.

In 1951, a 20-year-old outfielder for the Minneapolis Millers was launching one of the greatest careers in baseball history. Just 35 games into his second professional season, the youngster was ripping the Triple-A league's pitching for a .477 average.

Batting behind the young sensation was the 37-year-old third baseman, steadily on his way to another .300-plus season. The year before, he was voted the American Association's Most Valuable Player and the Millers' most popular player.

But when the New York Giants called their farm club early in that '51 season, their only interest was the rising star, Willie Mays.

Mays played in 2,992 major league games, became a legend and entered the Hall of Fame in 1979. His old teammate never did get that call to the majors. But 36 years after they parted company as teammates, Raymond Emmett Dandridge joins his one-time roommate in the Cooperstown shrine.

Dandridge, a bandy-legged infielder who was born in Richmond, Va., on August 31, 1913, starred year-round in the Negro leagues, Mexico, Cuba, Puerto Rico, Venezuela and the minors during his career of more than 20 years.

"I played with Billy Cox and I saw Brooks Robinson and a lot of other good third basemen," Roy Campanella said. "Believe me, Dandridge could match them all. . . . He belongs."

Dandridge's bowlegs bent like a croquet wicket, making him an inviting target to the naive, big-swinging pull hitters who eyed the third-base line. After one at-bat, they looked elsewhere.

Quick as lightning, "Dannie" could spear the fiercest drives with a flick of his glove and scoop up the crazy-hopping bouncers with the surest of hands. Lest the opponents think of tapping bunts and dying grounders down the line, Dandridge would undo their strategy with a dazzling bit of showmanship. Showcasing his powerful arm, he would charge in from third, snatch the ball bare-handed and unleash a bullet to first without looking up.

"You almost couldn't hit a ball past him," said Monte Irvin, his teammate on the Newark Eagles in the Negro National League. "He made very few errors and he was flashy. People would come just to see him play third."

"People used to ask me, 'Ray, why do you throw that ball without looking up?'" Dandridge said. "And I would say, 'That ball is too hot for me to handle. I always get rid of it fast—overhand, underhand, sideways, whatever.'"

Cum Posey, an outfielder, officer and club owner in the Negro leagues, rated Dandridge as one of the all-time greats. "There simply never was a smoother-functioning master at third base than Dandridge," he said in 1944. "And he can hit that apple, too."

The 5-foot-7, 175-pound Dandridge, a righthanded batter, was equally adept at second base and shortstop. As a young man with the Richmond All-Stars, Dandridge played in the outfield.

He began his career in the Negro leagues in 1933 and, as a member of the Detroit Stars, learned to drive the ball to all fields. He went on to star for the Newark Eagles (originally the Dodgers), the New York Cubans and countless teams in Mexico and Cuba. He batted above .350 almost every year in Mexico and attracted the attention of New York Giants scouts in 1948, when he won the Mexican League batting crown with an average over .370.

Dandridge signed with the Giants the following year—"I was 35, but I told them I was 30"—and batted .362 in his first season with the Millers. He led the league's third basemen in fielding with a .981 average and had a .987 mark in 16 games at second.

"I guess I had my most fun in Mexico," Dandridge said that season, "but playing in the (American) Association is great. I think we batted against harder throwers, maybe, in the colored league, but these boys have got more types of deliveries. They're cute."

Dandridge so enjoyed watching them pitch that he batted .311 in 1950 and became the first black to win the league's MVP award. He hit .324 in 1951 and .291 in '52, his final year at Minneapolis. He moved on to Sacramento and Oakland in the Pacific Coast League in 1953, batting .268 in his final minor league season. After retiring as a player, Dandridge was briefly a scout with the San Francisco Giants.

Longtime Newark first baseman Lenny Pearson remembered Dandridge as a demanding manager in Cuba and Mexico. "He wanted perfection," Pearson said. "Complete perfection. That's the way he played baseball."

Dandridge thought that reputation was finally going to get him to the majors after Mays had been called up. "All the boys on the Giants wanted (Manager Leo) Durocher to bring me up," he said. "And I felt good then, saying, 'Boy, I'm up now.'

"I just wanted to put that right foot in a major league ball park."

Dandridge was named to the Hall of Fame in 1987.

JACOB ELLSWORTH (JAKE) DAUBERT

Born May 14, 1885, at Lewellyn, Pa.

Died October 9, 1924, at Cincinnati, O.

Height, 5.10. Weight, 160.

Threw and batted lefthanded.

Brother of Harry Daubert, former major league pinch-hitter.

Named Most Valuable Player, National League, 1913 (Chalmers Award).
Led National League first basemen in double plays, 1922.

Year	Club	League	Pos.	G.	AB.	R.	H.	2B.	3B.	HR.	RBI.	B.A.	PO.	A.	E.	F.A.
1907—Kane		Int.St.	1B	42	157	18	47	....	....	....	....	.299	433	26	7	.985
1907—Marion		O.-P.	1B	71	265	26	75	....	....	....	....	.283	709	40	8	.989
1908—Nashville		South.	1B	138	473	49	124	12	11	6	....	.262	1331	17	15	.989
1909—Toledo		A. A.	1B	35	129	16	24	6	0	0	....	.186	371	23	7	.983
1909—Memphis		South.	1B	81	283	35	89	11	2	0	....	.314	806	58	4	.995
1910—Brooklyn		Nat.	1B	144	552	67	146	15	15	8	52	.264	1418	72	16	.989
1911—Brooklyn		Nat.	1B	149	573	89	176	17	8	5	46	.307	1485	88	18	.989
1912—Brooklyn		Nat.	1B	145	559	81	172	19	16	3	73	.308	1373	76	10	*.993
1913—Brooklyn		Nat.	1B	139	508	76	178	17	7	2	46	*.350	1279	80	13	.991
1914—Brooklyn		Nat.	1B	126	474	89	156	17	7	6	44	*.329	1097	48	8	.993

Year Club League	Pos.	G.	AB.	R.	H.	2B.	3B.	HR.	RBI.	B.A.	PO.	A.	E.	F.A.
1915—Brooklyn .... Nat.	1B	150	544	62	164	21	8	2	42	.301	1441	*102	11	.993
1916—Brooklyn .... Nat.	1B	127	478	75	151	16	7	3	35	.316	1195	66	9	*.993
1917—Brooklyn .... Nat.	1B	125	468	59	122	4	4	2	30	.261	1188	82	12	.991
1918—Brooklyn(a) .... Nat.	1B	108	396	50	122	12	*15	2	47	.308	1069	63	10	.991
1919—Cincinnati .... Nat.	1B	●140	537	79	148	10	12	2	42	.276	1437	80	17	.989
1920—Cincinnati .... Nat.	1B	142	553	97	168	28	13	4	48	.304	1358	63	15	.990
1921—Cincinnati .... Nat.	1B	136	516	69	158	18	12	2	64	.306	1290	78	10	.993
1922—Cincinnati .... Nat.	1B	●156	610	114	205	15	*22	12	66	.336	*1652	79	11	●.994
1923—Cincinnati .... Nat.	1B	125	500	63	146	27	10	2	54	.292	1224	77	9	.993
1924—Cincinnati .... Nat.	1B	102	405	47	114	14	9	1	31	.281	1128	74	12	.990
Major League Totals—15 Years		2014	7673	1117	2326	250	165	56	720	.303	19634	1128	181	.991

aTraded to Cincinnati Reds for Outfielder Tommy Griffith, March, 1919.

WORLD SERIES RECORD

Year Club League	Pos.	G.	AB.	R.	H.	2B.	3B.	HR.	RBI.	B.A.	PO.	A.	E.	F.A.
1916—Brooklyn .... Nat.	1B	4	17	1	3	0	1	0	0	.176	40	3	0	1.000
1919—Cincinnati .... Nat.	1B	8	29	4	7	0	1	0	1	.241	81	5	2	.977
World Series Totals—2 Years		12	46	5	10	0	2	0	1	.217	121	8	2	.985

GEORGE AUGUST (HOOKS) DAUSS

Born September 22, 1889, at Indianapolis, Ind.

Died July 27, 1963, at St. Louis, Mo.

Height, 5.10. Weight, 160.

Threw and batted righthanded.

Year Club League	G.	IP.	W.	L.	Pct.	H.	R.	ER.	SO.	BB.	ERA.
1909—Duluth....................Minn.-Wis.	33	....	19	10	.655	....	....	....	....	....	......
1910—Duluth....................Minn.-Wis.	18	....	7	7	.500	....	....	....	....	....	......
1911—St. Paul..................Amer. Assn.	3	....	1	1	.500	....	....	6	....	6	3	......
1912—St. Paul..................Amer. Assn.	●51	271	12	19	.387	277	154	....	156	120	......
1912—Detroit....................American	2	17	1	1	.500	11	7	....	7	9	......
1913—Detroit....................American	31	226	13	12	.520	186	101	67	107	82	2.67
1914—Detroit....................American	45	302	18	15	.545	286	126	*96	150	87	2.86
1915—Detroit....................American	46	310	24	13	.649	261	115	86	132	115	2.50
1916—Detroit....................American	39	239	19	12	.613	220	102	85	95	90	3.20
1917—Detroit....................American	38	270	17	14	.548	243	105	73	102	87	2.43
1918—Detroit....................American	33	250	12	16	.429	243	105	●83	73	58	2.99
1919—Detroit....................American	34	256	21	9	.700	262	*125	101	73	63	3.55
1920—Detroit....................American	38	270	13	21	.382	308	*158	107	82	84	3.57
1921—Detroit....................American	32	233	10	15	.400	275	141	112	68	81	4.33
1922—Detroit....................American	39	219	13	13	.500	251	123	102	78	59	4.19
1923—Detroit....................American	50	316	21	13	.618	331	140	127	105	78	3.62
1924—Detroit....................American	40	131	12	11	.522	155	78	67	44	40	4.60
1925—Detroit....................American	35	228	16	11	.593	238	110	80	58	85	3.16
1926—Detroit....................American	34	124	12	6	.667	135	63	58	27	49	4.21
Major League Totals—15 Years..................................	536	3391	222	182	.550	3405	1599	1244	1201	1067	3.32

GEORGE STACEY DAVIS

Born August 23, 1870, at Cohoes, N.Y.

Died October 17, 1940, at Philadelphia, Pa.

Height, 5.09. Weight, 180.

Threw right and batted right and lefthanded.

Manager, New York Giants, 1895 and 1900-01; Des Moines, Western League, 1910; scout, New York Yankees, 1915; St. Louis Browns, 1917.

Year	Club	League	Pos.	G.	AB.	R.	H.	2B.	3B.	HR.	SB.	B.A.	PO.	A.	E.	F.A.
1889—Albany, N.Y.							(Independent club—no records available)									
1890—Cleveland..............	Nat.		OF	134	526	98	139	22	12	6	22	.264	282	*35	18	.946
1891—Cleveland..............	Nat.		OF-3B-P	136	571	115	167	34	11	3	43	.292	292	71	30	.924
1892—Cleveland..............	Nat.		INF-OF	143	595	96	151	22	14	4	36	.254	192	226	36	.921
1893—New York (a).......	Nat.		3B	133	533	112	199	23	26	10	54	.373	191	307	58	.896
1894—New York..............	Nat.		3B	124	492	124	170	28	20	9	37	.346	154	251	40	.910
1895—New York..............	Nat.		3B	110	433	106	143	32	11	5	45	.330	121	162	33	.896
1896—New York..............	Nat.		3B-SS	124	495	98	155	22	10	3	49	.313	224	312	41	.929
1897—New York..............	Nat.		SS	131	525	114	188	34	11	9	64	.358	*346	436	57	.932
1898—New York..............	Nat.		SS	121	484	80	148	21	5	1	22	.306	351	420	57	.931
1899—New York..............	Nat.		SS	111	413	69	144	25	4	1	38	.349	313	421	39	*.950
1900—New York..............	Nat.		SS	113	425	70	138	20	4	3	32	.325	276	455	45	.942
1901—New York..............	Nat.		SS-3B	130	495	69	153	21	6	7	26	.309	325	442	44	.946
1902—Chicago	Amer.		SS	132	480	77	143	27	7	3	33	.298	289	421	40	.947
1903—New York (b).......	Nat.		SS	4	15	2	4	0	0	0	0	.267	11	10	3	.875
1904—Chicago	Amer.		SS	152	558	74	143	25	14	1	32	.256	351	*518	59	.936
1905—Chicago	Amer.		SS	151	550	74	153	28	3	1	31	.278	330	501	46	*.948
1906—Chicago	Amer.		SS	133	484	63	134	25	6	0	27	.277	236	475	42	.944
1907—Chicago	Amer.		SS	132	466	59	111	18	2	1	15	.238	223	485	38	.949
1908—Chicago	Amer.		2B-SS	128	419	41	91	14	1	0	22	.217	242	379	32	.951
1909—Chicago	Amer.		1B	28	68	5	9	1	0	0	4	.132	189	15	3	.986
1910—Des Moines	West		2B-SS	32	99	14	19	0	0	0	4	.192	64	60	10	.925
American League Totals—7 Years				856	3025	393	784	138	33	6	164	.259	1860	2794	260	.947
National League Totals—13 Years........				1514	6002	1153	1899	304	134	61	468	.316	3078	3548	501	.930
Major League Totals—20 Years.............				2370	9027	1546	2683	442	167	67	632	.297	4938	6342	761	.937

aTraded to New York for catcher Buck Ewing, March, 1893.

bJumped Chicago American League club and played in game for New York Nationals against Pittsburgh, June 26, 1903, in defiance of peace treaty between American and National leagues; President Charles Comiskey of Chicago secured an injunction in New York courts to prevent Davis from playing with the New Yorkers on July 3, 1903, and on July 15, the courts issued an injunction against Davis playing with any club but Chicago; Davis played his last game for the New York club on July 1 and reported to Chicago for the 1904 season.

Pitching Record: Saw brief service as pitcher in 1891, no wins or losses.

WORLD SERIES RECORD

Year	Club	League	Pos.	G.	AB.	R.	H.	2B.	3B.	HR.	SB.	B.A.	PO.	A.	E.	F.A.
1906—Chicago	Amer.		SS	3	13	4	4	3	0	0	1	.308	7	14	2	.913

HARRY H DAVIS
(Jasper)

Born July 18, 1873, at Philadelphia, Pa.

Died August 11, 1947, at Philadelphia, Pa.

Height, 5.10. Weight, 180.

Threw and batted righthanded.

Manager, Cleveland, 1912 (part); player-coach, Philadelphia Athletics, 1913 through 1917; scout, Athletics, 1918 through 1927.

Year	Club	League	Pos.	G.	AB.	R.	H.	2B.	3B.	HR.	SB.	B.A.	PO.	A.	E.	F.A.
1895—Pawtucket.............	New Eng.		1B	104	495	118	200	49	10	17	..	*.404	..	..	..	.967
1895—Metropolitans......	Atl.		1B	2	5	1	1	0	0	0	..	.200	1	0	1	.500
1895—New York..............	Nat.		1B	7	24	1	8	0	1	0	1	.333	64	4	1	.986
1896—N.Y.(a)-Pitts.	Nat.		1B-OF	107	401	68	94	17	16	2	33	.234	553	27	19	.965
1897—Pittsburgh..............	Nat.		1B-3B-OF	107	427	69	132	9	25	2	23	.309	619	86	38	.949
1898—Pitts.(b)-Lou.	Nat.		1B-OF-2B	94	358	40	97	14	14	2	12	.271	901	44	24	.975
1899—Washington...........	Nat.		1B	18	64	3	12	2	3	0	9	.188	162	4	2	.988
1899—Providence...........	Eastern		1B	110	445	88	151	..	..	..	29	.339	1037	63	30	.973
1900—Providence...........	Eastern		1B	135	549	108	182	..	..	..	70	.332	303	15	16	.952
1901—Philadelphia	Amer.		1B	117	498	92	153	30	8	8	26	.307	1273	81	33	.976
1902—Philadelphia	Amer.		1B-OF	132	555	87	171	*43	7	6	31	.308	1238	83	23	.983
1903—Philadelphia	Amer.		1B-OF	101	403	74	120	28	7	6	24	.298	972	58	30	.972
1904—Philadelphia	Amer.		1B	102	403	54	124	22	12	*10	15	.308	1006	58	18	.983
1905—Philadelphia	Amer.		1B	149	602	*92	171	*47	6	*8	36	.284	1621	91	24	.986
1906—Philadelphia	Amer.		1B	145	551	94	161	40	8	*12	33	.292	1352	91	*37	.975
1907—Philadelphia	Amer.		1B	149	582	84	155	*37	8	*8	20	.266	1478	103	*38	.977
1908—Philadelphia	Amer.		1B	147	513	65	127	23	9	5	20	.248	1410	86	22	.986
1909—Philadelphia	Amer.		1B	149	530	73	142	22	11	4	20	.268	1432	74	19	.988
1910—Philadelphia	Amer.		1B	139	492	61	122	19	4	1	17	.248	1353	64	20	.986
1911—Philadelphia	Amer.		1B	57	183	27	36	9	1	1	2	.197	427	36	11	.977
1912—Cleveland..............	Amer.		1B	2	5	0	0	0	0	0	0	.000	14	2	1	.941
1913—Philadelphia	Amer.		1B	7	17	2	6	2	0	0	0	.353	33	3	0	1.000
1914—Philadelphia	Amer.		1B	5	7	0	3	0	0	0	0	.429	12	0	0	1.000

Year Club League	Pos.	G.	AB.	R.	H.	2B.	3B.	HR.	SB.	B.A.	PO.	A.	E.	F.A.
1915—Philadelphia .... Amer.	1B	5	3	0	1	0	0	0	0	.333	0	0	0	.000
1916—Philadelphia .... Amer.	OF	4	6	0	1	0	0	0	0	.167	1	1	0	1.000
1917—Philadelphia .... Amer.	PH	1	1	0	0	0	0	0	0	.000	0	0	0	.000
National League Totals—5 Years..........		333	1274	181	343	42	59	6	78	.269	2299	165	84	.967
American League Totals—17 Years		1411	5351	805	1493	322	81	69	244	.279	13622	831	276	.981
Major League Totals—22 Years.............		1744	6625	986	1836	364	140	75	322	.277	15921	996	360	.979

aTraded to Pittsburgh for First Baseman Jake Beckley, July 30, 1896.
bReleased and signed with Louisville, July, 1898.

WORLD SERIES RECORD

Year Club League	Pos.	G.	AB.	R.	H.	2B.	3B.	HR.	SB.	B.A.	PO.	A.	E.	F.A.
1905—Philadelphia .... Amer.	1B	5	20	0	4	1	0	0	0	.200	50	1	0	1.000
1910—Philadelphia .... Amer.	1B	5	17	5	6	3	0	0	0	.353	43	1	3	.936
1911—Philadelphia .... Amer.	1B	6	24	3	5	1	0	0	0	.208	54	3	0	1.000
World Series Totals—3 Years		16	61	8	15	5	0	0	0	.246	147	5	3	.981

VIRGIL LAWRENCE DAVIS
(Spud)

Born December 20, 1904, at Birmingham, Ala.

Died August 14, 1984, at Birmingham, Ala.

Height, 6.01. Weight, 220.

Threw and batted righthanded.

Led National League catchers in double plays, 1932.
Coach, Pittsburgh Pirates, 1941-42-43-46; scout, Pirates, 1947-48-49; coach, Chicago Cubs, 1950 through 1953.

Year Club League	Pos.	G.	AB.	R.	H.	2B.	3B.	HR.	RBI.	B.A.	PO.	A.	E.	F.A.
1926—Gulfport .... Ct. St.	C-PH	27	90	10	32	8	5	2	.....	.356	26	6	3	.914
1927—Reading................ Int.	C-PH	137	383	50	118	17	3	11	70	.308	271	86	12	.967
1928—St.L. (a)-Phila. ...... Nat.	C	69	168	17	47	2	0	3	19	.280	155	46	6	.971
1929—Philadelphia .... Nat.	C	98	263	31	90	18	0	7	48	.342	198	47	10	.961
1930—Philadelphia .... Nat.	C	106	329	41	103	16	1	14	65	.313	307	50	5	.986
1931—Philadelphia .... Nat.	C	120	393	30	128	32	1	4	51	.326	420	*78	3	.994
1932—Philadelphia .... Nat.	C	125	402	44	135	23	5	14	70	.336	408	54	6	.987
1933—Philadelphia (b)... Nat.	C	141	495	51	173	28	3	9	65	.349	395	69	8	.983
1934—St. Louis................ Nat.	C	107	347	45	104	22	4	9	65	.300	459	42	6	.988
1935—St. Louis................ Nat.	C-1B	102	315	28	100	24	2	1	60	.317	335	34	3	.992
1936—St. Louis (c).......... Nat.	C-3B	112	363	24	99	26	2	4	59	.273	390	59	7	.985
1937—Cincinnati............. Nat.	C	76	209	19	56	10	1	3	33	.268	300	40	7	.980
1938—Cin. (d)-Phila. ...... Nat.	C	82	251	14	59	8	0	2	24	.235	260	34	7	.977
1939—Philadelphia (e)... Nat.	C	87	202	10	62	8	1	0	23	.307	260	40	0	1.000
1940—Pittsburgh............. Nat.	C	99	285	23	93	14	1	5	39	.326	288	61	12	.967
1941—Pittsburgh (f)....... Nat.	C	57	107	3	27	4	1	0	6	.252	97	16	0	1.000
1944—Pittsburgh............. Nat.	C	54	93	6	28	7	0	2	14	.301	76	10	3	.966
1945—Pittsburgh............. Nat.	C	23	33	2	8	2	0	0	6	.242	26	4	1	.968
Major League Totals—16 Years...............		1458	4255	388	1312	244	22	77	647	.308	4374	684	84	.984

aTraded with Outfielder Homer Peel to Philadelphia Phillies for Catcher Jimmy Wilson, May 11, 1928.
bTraded with Infielder Eddie Delker to St. Louis Cardinals for Catcher Jimmy Wilson, November 15, 1933.
cSold to Cincinnati, December 2, 1936.
dTraded with Pitcher Al Hollingsworth and $55,000 to Philadelphia Phillies for Pitcher Bucky Walters, June 13, 1938.
eSold to Pittsburgh, October 27, 1939.
fReleased as active player, October 2, 1941; restored to active list, April, 1944.

WORLD SERIES RECORD

Year Club League	Pos.	G.	AB.	R.	H.	2B.	3B.	HR.	RBI.	B.A.	PO.	A.	E.	F.A.
1934—St. Louis................ Nat.	PH	2	2	0	2	0	0	0	1	1.000	0	0	0	.000

—DID YOU KNOW—

That Willie Davis, Vince DiMaggio and Tim McCarver are the only players to compile lifetime batting averages of 1.000 in All-Star Game competition (based on three or more at-bats)?

WILLIAM HENRY (WILLIE) DAVIS

Born April 15, 1940, at Mineral Springs, Ark.
Height, 6.02½. Weight, 185.
Threw and batted lefthanded.

Shares National League record for most singles, game (6), May 24, 1973 (19 innings).
Led Carolina League in total bases with 304 in 1959.
Led Pacific Coast League in total bases with 347 and stolen bases with 30 in 1960.
Named outfielder on THE SPORTING NEWS National League All-Star Team, 1971.
Named outfielder on THE SPORTING NEWS National League All-Star fielding team, 1971, 1972 and 1973.
Named Minor League Player of the Year by THE SPORTING NEWS, 1960.
Named Pacific Coast League Most Valuable Player, 1960.
Player-manager, Aguila, Mexican League, 1980.

Year—Club	League	Pos.	G.	AB.	R.	H.	2B.	3B.	HR.	RBI.	B.A.	PO.	A.	E.	F.A.
1959—Green Bay	I.I.I.	OF	7	30	5	4	0	0	0	1	.133	12	2	0	1.000
1959—Reno	Calif.	OF	117	513	*135	*187	*40	*16	15	90	*.365	*302	10	11	.966
1960—Spokane	P.C.	OF	147	624	*126	*216	43	*26	12	75	*.346	384	6	●13	.968
1960—Los Angeles	Nat.	OF	22	88	12	28	6	1	2	10	.318	52	1	1	.981
1961—Los Angeles	Nat.	OF	128	339	56	86	19	6	12	45	.254	224	4	4	.983
1962—Los Angeles	Nat.	OF	157	600	103	171	18	●10	21	85	.285	379	13	*15	.963
1963—Los Angeles	Nat.	OF	156	515	60	126	19	8	9	60	.245	337	16	8	.978
1964—Los Angeles‡	Nat.	OF	157	613	91	180	23	7	12	77	.294	*400	16	7	.983
1965—Los Angeles	Nat.	OF	142	558	52	133	24	3	10	57	.238	318	6	11	.967
1966—Los Angeles	Nat.	OF	153	624	74	177	31	6	11	61	.284	347	9	11	.970
1967—Los Angeles	Nat.	OF	143	569	65	146	27	9	6	41	.257	300	6	9	.971
1968—Los Angeles	Nat.	OF	160	643	86	161	24	10	7	31	.250	345	9	10	.973
1969—Los Angeles	Nat.	OF	129	498	66	155	23	8	11	59	.311	271	8	6	.979
1970—Los Angeles	Nat.	OF	146	593	92	181	23	*16	8	93	.305	342	12	3	.992
1971—Los Angeles	Nat.	OF	158	641	84	198	33	10	10	74	.309	*404	7	8	.981
1972—Los Angeles	Nat.	OF	149	615	81	178	22	7	19	79	.289	373	10	5	.987
1973—Los Angeles†	Nat.	OF	152	599	82	171	29	9	16	77	.285	344	6	7	.980
1974—Montreal‡	Nat.	OF	153	611	86	180	27	9	12	89	.295	369	8	●12	.969
1975—Texas§	Amer.	OF	42	169	16	42	8	2	5	17	.249	100	1	1	.990
1975—St. Louis x	Nat.	OF	98	350	41	102	19	6	6	50	.291	187	5	6	.970
1976—San Diego y	Nat.	OF	141	493	61	132	18	10	5	46	.268	349	6	3	.992
1977—Chunichi z	Cent.	OF	72	288	47	88	13	2	25	63	.306	131	2	4	.971
1978—Crown Lighter a	Pac.	OF-1B	127	509	67	149	21	4	18	69	.293	317	6	8	.976
1979—California b	Amer.	OF	43	56	9	14	2	1	0	2	.250	8	0	0	1.000
1980—Aguila	Mex.	OF	91	326	55	98	21	6	6	37	.301	129	2	2	.985
National League Totals—17 Years			2344	8949	1192	2505	385	135	177	1034	.280	5341	142	126	.978
American League Totals—2 Years			85	225	25	56	10	3	5	19	.249	108	1	1	.991
Major League Totals—18 Years			2429	9174	1217	2561	395	138	182	1053	.279	5449	143	127	.978

Signed as free agent by Los Angeles Dodgers' organization, June 20, 1958.
†Traded to Montreal Expos for Pitcher Mike Marshall, December 5, 1973.
‡Traded to Texas Rangers for Pitcher Don Stanhouse and Infielder Pete Mackanin, December 5, 1974.
§Traded to St. Louis Cardinals for Shortstop Ed Brinkman and Pitcher Tommy Moore, June 4, 1975.
xTraded to San Diego Padres for Outfielder Dick Sharon, October 20, 1975.
yReleased, January 20, 1977; played professional baseball in Japan for Chunichi Dragons and Crown Lighter Lions.
zTraded to Crown Lighter Lions.
aSigned as free agent by California Angels, March 27, 1979.
bReleased to Salt Lake City, Pacific Coast League, Novemer 26, 1979; released and signed with Aguila Mexican League, March 6, 1980.

CHAMPIONSHIP SERIES RECORD

Year—Club	League	Pos.	G.	AB.	R.	H.	2B.	3B.	HR.	RBI.	B.A.	PO.	A.	E.	F.A.
1979—California	Amer.	PH	2	2	1	1	0	0	0	0	.500	0	0	0	.000

WORLD SERIES RECORD

Shares record for most stolen bases, game (3), October 11, 1965.

Year—Club	League	Pos.	G.	AB.	R.	H.	2B.	3B.	HR.	RBI.	B.A.	PO.	A.	E.	F.A.
1963—Los Angeles	Nat.	OF	4	12	2	2	2	0	0	3	.167	6	0	0	1.000
1965—Los Angeles	Nat.	OF	7	26	3	6	0	0	0	0	.231	11	0	0	1.000
1966—Los Angeles	Nat.	OF	4	16	0	1	0	0	0	0	.063	6	0	3	.667
World Series Totals—3 Years			15	54	5	9	2	0	0	3	.167	23	0	3	.885

JAY HANNA (DIZZY) DEAN

Born January 16, 1911, at Lucas, Ark.

Died July 17, 1974, at Reno, Nev.

Height, 6.03. Weight, 202.

Threw and batted righthanded.

Brother of Paul Dean, former major league pitcher.

Named to Hall of Fame, 1953.

Year Club	League	G.	IP.	W.	L.	Pct.	H.	R.	ER.	SO.	BB.	ERA.
1930—St. Joseph	Western	32	217	17	8	.680	204	118	89	134	77	3.69
1930—Houston	Texas	14	85	8	2	.800	62	31	27	95	49	2.86
1930—St. Louis	National	1	9	1	0	1.000	3	1	1	5	3	1.00
1931—Houston	Texas	41	304	∗26	10	.722	210	71	52	∗303	90	∗1.57
1932—St. Louis	National	46	∗286	18	15	.545	280	122	105	∗191	102	3.30
1933—St. Louis	National	∗48	293	20	18	.526	279	113	99	∗199	64	3.04
1934—St. Louis	National	50	312	∗30	7	∗.811	288	110	92	∗195	75	2.65
1935—St. Louis	National	50	∗324	∗28	12	.700	∗326	128	112	∗182	82	3.11
1936—St. Louis	National	●51	∗315	24	13	.649	310	128	111	195	53	3.17
1937—St. Louis (a)	National	27	197	13	10	.565	200	76	59	120	33	2.70
1938—Chicago	National	13	75	7	1	.875	63	20	15	22	8	1.80
1939—Chicago	National	19	96	6	4	.600	98	40	36	27	17	3.38
1940—Chicago	National	10	54	3	3	.500	68	35	31	18	20	5.17
1940—Tulsa	Texas	21	142	8	8	.500	149	69	50	51	19	3.17
1941—Chicago (b)	National	1	1	0	0	.000	3	3	2	1	0	18.00
1947—St. Louis (c) (d)	American	1	4	0	0	.000	3	0	0	0	1	0.00
American League Totals—1 Year		1	4	0	0	.000	3	0	0	0	1	0.00
National League Totals—11 Years		316	1962	150	83	.644	1918	776	663	1155	457	3.04
Major League Totals—12 Years		317	1966	150	83	.644	1921	776	663	1155	458	3.04

aTraded to Chicago Cubs for Pitchers Curt Davis and Clyde Shoun, Outfielder Tuck Stainback and cash, April 16, 1938.

bReleased as player and signed as coach with Chicago Cubs, May 14, 1941; retired as coach to accept baseball broadcasting job in St. Louis, July 12, 1941.

cSigned by St. Louis Browns to pitch final game as gate attraction.

dMade promotional appearances with Sioux Falls and Denver in Western League and Fargo-Moorhead in Northern in 1941; with Clovis in West Texas-New Mexico in 1949.

WORLD SERIES RECORD

Year Club	League	G.	IP.	W.	L.	Pct.	H.	R.	ER.	SO.	BB.	ERA.
1934—St. Louis	National	3	26	2	1	.667	20	6	5	17	5	1.73
1938—Chicago	National	2	8⅓	0	1	.000	8	6	6	2	1	6.48
World Series Totals—2 Years		5	34⅓	2	2	.500	28	12	11	19	6	2.88

EDWARD JAMES (ED) DELAHANTY
(Big Ed)

Born October 31, 1867, at Cleveland, O.

Died July 2, 1903, at Fort Erie, Ont.

Height, 5.10. Weight, 170.

Threw and batted righthanded.

Brother of former outfielder Frank Delahanty, infielder Tom Delahanty and infielder-outfielders Jim and Joe Delahanty.

Shares major league records for most doubles, game (4), May 3, 1899; most home runs, game (4), July 13, 1896.

Shares National League record for most consecutive hits (10), July 13, first game, to July 14, 1897.

Named to Hall of Fame, 1945.

Year Club	League	Pos.	G.	AB.	R.	H.	2B.	3B.	HR.	SB.	B.A.	PO.	A.	E.	F.A.
1887—Mansfield	Ohio St.	2-1B	73	366	90	130	20	7	5	.....	.355	212	184	47	.894
1888—Wheeling	Tri. St.	2-1B	21	98	20	40	9	4	5	15	.408	64	59	18	.872
1888—Philadelphia	Nat.	2B	74	290	40	66	11	1	1	38	.228	157	173	47	.875
1889—Philadelphia(a)	Nat.	2B-OF	54	246	37	72	13	3	0	19	.293	116	61	17	.912
1890—Cleveland(b)	Play.	2-S-O	115	513	106	152	24	15	3	24	.296	244	300	92	.855
1891—Philadelphia	Nat.	1B-OF	128	545	92	136	19	9	5	27	.250	463	34	34	.936
1892—Philadelphia	Nat.	OF	120	470	78	147	∗33	19	6	35	.313	254	29	23	.925
1893—Philadelphia	Nat.	OF	132	∗588	145	218	31	20	∗19	36	.371	312	32	19	.948

Year	Club	League	Pos.	G.	AB.	R.	H.	2B.	3B.	HR.	SB.	B.A.	PO.	A.	E.	F.A.
1894—Philadelphia	Nat.	OF	114	497	149	199	36	16	4	29	.400	224	21	16	.939
1895—Philadelphia	Nat.	OF	116	481	148	192	*47	8	11	46	.399	230	29	15	.915
1896—Philadelphia	Nat.	1B-OF	122	505	131	199	*42	14	●13	37	.394	482	27	23	.957
1897—Philadelphia	Nat.	OF	129	530	110	200	37	15	4	28	.377	262	22	10	.966
1898—Philadelphia	Nat.	OF	142	547	114	183	37	11	3	62	.335	300	20	12	.964
1899—Philadelphia	Nat.	OF	145	573	133	*234	*56	9	9	38	*.408	285	20	9	.971
1900—Philadelphia(c)	Nat.	1B	130	542	82	173	32	10	1	14	.319	1293	69	25	.982
1901—Philadelphia	Nat.	1B-OF	138	538	106	192	38	16	8	28	.357	723	24	21	.973
1902—Washington	Amer.	1B-OF	123	474	103	178	41	15	10	14	*.376	251	12	9	.967
1903—Washington	Amer.	OF	43	154	22	52	11	1	1	3	.338	74	6	3	.964
American League Totals—2 Years			166	628	125	230	52	16	11	17	.366	325	18	12	.966
National League Totals—13 Years			1544	6352	1365	2211	432	151	84	437	.348	5101	561	271	.954
Players League Totals—1 Year			115	513	106	152	24	15	3	24	.296	244	300	92	.855
Major League Totals—16 Years			1825	7493	1596	2593	508	182	98	478	.346	5670	879	375	.946

aJumped to Players League (Brotherhood), 1890.
bReturned to Philadelphia N. L. after disbanding of Brotherhood in 1890.
cJumped to American League, 1902.

PAUL M. DERRINGER

Born October 17, 1907, at Springfield, Ky.

Died November 17, 1987, at Sarasota, Fla.

Height, 6.04. Weight, 217.

Threw and batted righthanded.

Led National League in complete games, 1938.
Named by Baseball Writers' Association of America for THE SPORTING NEWS All-Star Major League Team, 1940.

Year	Club	League	G.	IP.	W.	L.	Pct.	H.	R.	ER.	SO.	BB.	ERA.
1927—Danville	I.I.I.	26	172	10	8	.556	160	84	64	46	75	3.35
1928—Danville	I.I.I.	33	243	15	11	.577	248	109	99	92	80	3.67
1929—Rochester	Int.	41	244	17	12	.586	259	120	106	94	96	3.91
1930—Rochester	Int.	44	*289	*23	11	.676	*310	147	125	164	72	3.89
1931—St. Louis	Nat.	35	212	18	8	*.692	225	88	79	134	65	3.35
1932—St. Louis	Nat.	39	233	11	14	.440	296	*133	105	78	60	4.06
1933—St. Louis(a)-Cincinnati	Nat.	36	248	7	*27	.206	264	117	91	89	60	3.30
1934—Cincinnati	Nat.	47	261	15	21	.417	297	129	104	122	59	3.59
1935—Cincinnati	Nat.	45	277	22	13	.629	295	132	108	120	49	3.51
1936—Cincinnati	Nat.	●51	282	19	19	.500	*331	*147	*126	121	42	4.02
1937—Cincinnati	Nat.	43	223	10	14	.417	240	112	100	94	55	4.04
1938—Cincinnati	Nat.	41	*307	21	14	.600	*315	110	100	132	49	2.93
1939—Cincinnati	Nat.	38	301	25	7	*.781	*321	115	98	128	35	2.93
1940—Cincinnati	Nat.	37	297	20	12	.625	280	110	101	115	48	3.06
1941—Cincinnati	Nat.	29	228	12	14	.462	233	91	84	76	54	3.32
1942—Cincinnati(b)	Nat.	29	209	10	11	.476	203	83	71	68	49	3.06
1943—Chicago	Nat.	32	174	10	14	.417	184	90	69	75	39	3.57
1944—Chicago	Nat.	42	180	7	13	.350	205	96	83	69	39	4.15
1945—Chicago	Nat.	35	214	16	11	.593	223	99	82	86	51	3.45
1946—Indianapolis	A.A.	32	180	9	11	.450	185	74	53	84	55	2.65
Major League Totals—15 Years		579	3646	223	212	.513	3912	1652	1401	1507	761	3.46

aTraded to Cincinnati Reds with Infielder Earl Adams and Pitcher Allen Stout for Shortstop Leo Durocher and Pitchers Frank Henry and John Ogden, May 7, 1933.
bSold to Chicago Cubs, January 7, 1943.

WORLD SERIES RECORD

Year	Club	League	G.	IP.	W.	L.	Pct.	H.	R.	ER.	SO.	BB.	ERA.
1931—St. Louis	Nat.	3	12⅔	0	2	.000	14	10	6	14	7	4.26
1939—Cincinnati	Nat.	2	15⅓	0	1	.000	9	4	4	9	3	2.35
1940—Cincinnati	Nat.	3	19⅓	2	1	.667	17	8	6	6	10	2.79
1945—Chicago	Nat.	3	5⅓	0	0	.000	5	4	4	1	7	6.75
World Series Totals—4 Years		11	52⅔	2	4	.333	45	26	20	30	27	3.42

—DID YOU KNOW—

That Paul Derringer started and won the first night game in major league history? Derringer pitched the Reds to a 2-1 victory over the Philadelphia Phillies on May 24, 1935, at Cincinnati's Crosley Field.

WILLIAM MALCOLM (BILL) DICKEY

Born June 6, 1907, at Bastrop, La.
Height, 6.01½. Weight, 185.
Threw right and batted lefthanded.

Shares major league record for most grand slams, two consecutive games (2), August 3, second game, and August 4, 1937; most consecutive years with 100 or more games by catcher (13); most assists by catcher, inning (3), May 13, 1929, sixth inning; fewest passed balls, season, 100 or more games (0), 1931.

Named by Baseball Writers' Association of America for THE SPORTING NEWS All-Star Major League Teams, 1932-33-36-38-39 and 1941.

Manager, New York Yankees, 1946 (part); Little Rock, Southern Association, 1947; coach, Yankees, 1949 through 1957; scout, Yankees, 1959; coach, Yankees, 1960 (part).

Named to Hall of Fame, 1954.

Year Club League	Pos.	G.	AB.	R.	H.	2B.	3B.	HR.	RBI.	B.A.	PO.	A.	E.	F.A.
1925—Little Rock .... South.	C	3	10	1	3	0	0	0	.....	.300	8	2	0	1.000
1926—Muskogee .... W.A.	C	61	212	27	60	6	2	7	.....	.283	300	58	13	.965
1926—Little Rock .... South.	C	21	46	6	18	1	5	0	8	.391	36	4	2	.952
1927—Jackson .... Cot. St.	C	101	364	46	108	31	3	3	.....	.297	★457	★84	9	★.984
1928—Little Rock .... South.	C	60	203	22	61	12	6	4	32	.300	151	52	8	.962
1928—Buffalo .... Int.	C	3	8	0	1	0	1	0	0	.125	12	4	2	.889
1928—New York .... Amer.	C	10	15	1	3	1	1	0	2	.200	6	2	0	1.000
1929—New York .... Amer.	C	130	447	60	145	30	6	10	65	.324	476	★95	12	.979
1930—New York .... Amer.	C	109	366	55	124	25	7	5	65	.339	418	51	★11	.977
1931—New York .... Amer.	C	130	477	65	156	17	10	6	78	.327	★670	78	3	★.996
1932—New York .... Amer.	C	108	423	66	131	20	4	15	84	.310	639	53	9	.987
1933—New York .... Amer.	C	130	478	58	152	24	8	14	97	.318	★721	82	6	.993
1934—New York .... Amer.	C	104	395	56	127	24	4	12	72	.322	527	49	8	.986
1935—New York .... Amer.	C	120	448	54	125	26	6	14	81	.279	★536	62	3	★.995
1936—New York .... Amer.	C	112	423	99	153	26	8	22	107	.362	499	61	14	.976
1937—New York .... Amer.	C	140	530	87	176	35	2	29	133	.332	★692	80	7	★.991
1938—New York .... Amer.	C	132	454	84	142	27	4	27	115	.313	★518	★74	8	.987
1939—New York .... Amer.	C	128	480	98	145	23	3	24	105	.302	★571	57	7	★.989
1940—New York .... Amer.	C	106	372	45	92	11	1	9	54	.247	425	55	3	.994
1941—New York .... Amer.	C	109	348	35	99	15	5	7	71	.284	422	45	3	★.994
1942—New York .... Amer.	C	82	268	28	79	13	1	2	37	.295	322	44	9	.976
1943—New York .... Amer.	C	85	242	29	85	18	2	4	33	.351	322	37	2	.994
1944-45—New York .... Amer.	C					(In Military Service)								
1946—New York .... Amer.	C	54	134	10	35	8	0	2	10	.261	201	29	3	.987
1947—Little Rock .... South.	C	8	12	2	4	2	0	1	2	.333	13	2	0	1.000
Major League Totals—17 Years		1789	6300	930	1969	343	72	202	1209	.313	7965	954	108	.988

WORLD SERIES RECORD

Shares record for most at-bats, game (6), October 2, 1932; most at-bats, inning (2), October 2, 1932, seventh inning and October 6, 1936, ninth inning.

Year Club League	Pos.	G.	AB.	R.	H.	2B.	3B.	HR.	RBI.	B.A.	PO.	A.	E.	F.A.
1932—New York .... Amer.	C	4	16	2	7	0	0	0	4	.438	25	1	0	1.000
1936—New York .... Amer.	C	6	25	5	3	0	0	1	5	.120	38	4	1	.977
1937—New York .... Amer.	C	5	19	3	4	0	0	1	3	.211	26	1	0	1.000
1938—New York .... Amer.	C	4	15	2	6	0	0	1	2	.400	31	5	0	1.000
1939—New York .... Amer.	C	4	15	2	4	0	0	2	5	.267	27	2	0	1.000
1941—New York .... Amer.	C	5	18	3	3	1	0	0	1	.167	24	2	0	1.000
1942—New York .... Amer.	C	5	19	1	5	0	0	0	0	.263	25	1	1	.963
1943—New York .... Amer.	C	5	18	1	5	0	0	1	4	.278	28	3	0	1.000
World Series Totals—8 Years		38	145	19	37	1	1	5	24	.255	224	19	2	.992

MARTIN DIHIGO

Born May 24, 1905, at Matanzas, Cuba.
Died May 20, 1971, at Cienfuegos, Cuba.
Height, 6.03. Weight, 225.
Threw and batted righthanded.

Possessor of one of the finest arms in baseball, Martin Dihigo was unquestionably the best all-round baseball performer in the history of the Negro leagues. He was a top pitcher, with a blazing fastball, and a standout at every position on the diamond.

He is the first Cuban to enter the Hall of Fame and was the first to pitch a no-hitter in the history of the Mexican League. He's also the first to be a member of the Cuban, Mexican and American Halls of Fame. Noted for his warm, friendly attitude, he was among the best-liked players by his teammates and rivals.

As Buck Leonard said, "Dihigo was the best all-round baseball player I have ever seen. He could run, hit, throw, think, pitch and manage. He both knew the game and could play it. I was in the game for 23 years and I never saw anyone better than he was. And that includes not only the United States but also Puerto Rico, Venezuela, Colombia, Cuba and Mexico. When I heard of Dihigo's passing, I was really saddened for I had lost a dear friend."

Dihigo was the hero of the islands, and was a player-manager in the winter leagues. He brought Leonard down there to play for his Marianao team. Buck told of one special time when Dihigo invited him to his home on an off-day. He lived in Matanzas, Cuba, not far from Havana. In Leonard's honor, Martin cooked a big pig.

"They dug a hole in the ground and heated rocks on the bottom with a wood fire. They put a spit through the pig, put a cover over it and then shoveled dirt over the whole thing. They left it in the ground a long while, until it was time to eat. Then they dug up the pig and you never tasted anything so delicious. Martin was a supreme host. I guess you couldn't match him at that, either."

As a Cuban teenager, Dihigo played against the winter travelers from the American Negro leagues. Two in particular, Oscar Charleston and John Henry Lloyd, took Martin under their wings and taught him the tricks of the trade. Both Oscar and John Henry were amazed at Dihigo's versatility and they encouraged him to follow his talents. At 18, then a Cuban phenom, Dihigo headed for the States and a pro career.

He joined the New York Cubans and later starred for the Philadelphia Hilldales and the Derby (Pa.) Daisies. He spent two years with the Homestead Grays as an outfielder almost exclusively. A big player, 6-3 and 225 pounds, he could belt the long ball consistently and was a smart player. He was fast on the bases and had one of the greatest arms of any player. It was good enough to be an outstanding pitcher, a fast-baller, but he was sufficiently maneuverable to be capable of playing any infield or outfield position.

As Cool Papa Bell put it, "Dihigo was the greatest all-round player we ever had. Now, a super star at his position, say an Oscar Charleston in center field or a Judy Johnson at third or a Buck Leonard at first or a John Henry Lloyd at short, no one was their equal and neither was Dihigo, but no one else could play so many positions and as well as he could. He was a great player at all of them; therefore, he was a great addition to your ball club. His disposition was even-tempered and he never caused any trouble. He was a manager when he played back home, and he made no enemies there, either."

So respected was Dihigo and so admired both as a player and as a man, he became the favorite of President Batista of Cuba, who continually praised Dihigo for his all-round excellence and the contribution he made to Cuban sports. The people of Mexico also adopted him as their native hero because of his fan-pleasing play, his popular switching of positions in a game to demonstrate the multiplicity of his talents, and his personal warmth and regard for the fans. His charm and persuasive ability lured many of the stars of the Negro professional leagues to the islands to play for the teams he managed. For the most part, aside from occasional government problems, tours to the Caribbean area on a Dihigo junket were pure fun for the players.

Dihigo was a hero to Minnie Minoso, Cuba's contribution to the American League as a longtime star of the Chicago White Sox. As Minoso, also from Matanzas, said:

"Dihigo used to let me carry his shoes and glove and that's how I got into the ball park down there when I was a kid. He was a big man, all muscle with not an ounce of fat on him. He helped me by teaching me how to play properly. When I played a few years in the Negro leagues, with the New York Cubans, Dihigo was past his prime and just a manager then, so I never really competed against him as a player. But it is difficult to explain what a great hero he was in Cuba. Everywhere he went, he was recognized and mobbed for autographs. I'd have to say he was most responsible for me getting to the major leagues. He was a big man, but he was big in all ways, as a player, as a manager, as a teacher, as a man."

Leonard said that Dihigo could hit "a long ball, a real long one." He added, "He had a picture swing, effortless and smooth, and he had a great batting eye. He was fast for so big a man and they all had to play him honest. What a lineup we had when he was pitching down there in the Caribbean. We had nine hitters in the lineup and he used to bat anywhere from second spot to fifth. That little old ball took one hell of a beating that day. And he was such a great fellow to have around the club, never a dull moment. As I said, he could do anything."

Minoso disagreed on this. He said he never heard Dihigo sing.

In his declining years (Dihigo died four days short of his 66th birthday), he spent much time working with youth teams and encouraging the young to play baseball. At the time of his death, the Cuban government was utilizing his talents as the nation's Minister of Sports.

U.S. sports representatives who visited Cuba during the 1977 lifting of travel barriers saw baseball diamonds all over the island, excellent lighted stadiums with good seating capacities, games in progress at all hours and the whole nation seemingly involved. And the visitors estimated there was an immense lode of untapped talent.

The hand of Martin Dihigo fashioned a great deal of this program. It would be fitting that more Cubans make the major leagues, a tribute from him to the United States he loved next to his native land, and a nation which gave him the highest honor a ballplayer can attain—the Hall of Fame.

Dihigo was named to the Hall of Fame in 1977.

JOSEPH PAUL (JOE) DiMAGGIO
(Joltin' Joe and The Yankee Clipper)

Born November 25, 1914, at Martinez, Calif.

Height, 6.02. Weight, 193.

Threw and batted righthanded.

Brother of Dom and Vince DiMaggio, former major league outfielders.

Holds major league record for longest consecutive-game hitting streak, season (56 games), 1941.
Shares major league record for most home runs, inning (2), June 24, 1936, fifth inning.
Shares modern major league record for most triples, game (3), August 27, 1938, first game.
Led American League outfielders in double plays, 1941 (tie).
Named Most Valuable Player, American League, 1939, 1941 and 1947.
Named by Baseball Writers' Association of America for THE SPORTING NEWS All-Star Major League Team, 1937-38-39-40-41-42-47-48.
Named by THE SPORTING NEWS as the No. 1 Major League Player of the Year, 1939.
Executive vice-president-coach, Oakland Athletics, 1968 through 1969.
Named to Hall of Fame, 1955.

Year	Club	League	Pos.	G.	AB.	R.	H.	2B.	3B.	HR.	RBI.	B.A.	PO.	A.	E.	F.A.
1932—San Francisco	P. C.		OF	3	9	2	2	1	1	0	2	.222	4	7	1	.917
1933—San Francisco	P. C.		OF	187	762	129	259	45	13	28	★169	.340	407	★32	17	.963
1934—San Francisco	P. C.		OF	101	375	58	128	18	6	12	69	.341	236	11	8	.969
1935—San Francisco	P. C.		OF	172	679	★173	270	48	★18	34	★154	.398	430	★32	21	.957
1936—New York	Amer.		OF	138	637	132	206	44	●15	29	125	.323	339	★22	8	.978
1937—New York	Amer.		OF	151	621	★151	215	35	15	★46	167	.346	★413	21	★17	.962
1938—New York	Amer.		OF	145	599	129	194	32	13	32	140	.324	366	20	15	.963
1939—New York	Amer.		OF	120	462	108	176	32	6	30	126	★.381	328	13	5	.986
1940—New York	Amer.		OF	132	508	93	179	28	9	31	133	★.352	359	5	8	.978
1941—New York	Amer.		OF	139	541	122	193	43	11	30	★125	.357	385	16	9	.978
1942—New York	Amer.		OF	154	610	123	186	29	13	21	114	.305	409	10	8	.981
1943-44-45—New York										(In Military Service)						
1946—New York	Amer.		OF	132	503	81	146	20	8	25	95	.290	314	15	6	.982
1947—New York	Amer.		OF	141	534	97	168	31	10	20	97	.315	316	2	1	★.997
1948—New York	Amer.		OF	153	594	110	190	26	11	★39	★155	.320	441	8	13	.972
1949—New York	Amer.		OF	76	272	58	94	14	6	14	67	.346	195	1	3	.985
1950—New York	Amer.		OF	139	525	114	158	33	10	32	122	.301	376	9	9	.977
1951—New York	Amer.		OF	116	415	72	109	22	4	12	71	.263	288	11	3	.990
Major League Totals—13 Years				1736	6821	1390	2214	389	131	361	1537	.325	4529	153	105	.978

WORLD SERIES RECORD

Shares records for most at-bats, game (6), October 6, 1936; most at-bats, inning (2), October 6, 1936, ninth inning and October 6, 1937, sixth inning; most hits, inning (2), October 6, 1936, ninth inning.

Year	Club	League	Pos.	G.	AB.	R.	H.	2B.	3B.	HR.	RBI.	B.A.	PO.	A.	E.	F.A.
1936—New York	Amer.		OF	6	26	3	9	3	0	0	3	.346	18	0	1	.947
1937—New York	Amer.		OF	5	22	2	6	0	0	1	4	.273	18	0	0	1.000
1938—New York	Amer.		OF	4	15	4	4	0	0	1	2	.267	10	0	0	1.000
1939—New York	Amer.		OF	4	16	3	5	0	0	1	3	.313	11	0	0	1.000
1941—New York	Amer.		OF	5	19	1	5	0	0	0	1	.263	19	0	0	1.000
1942—New York	Amer.		OF	5	21	3	7	0	0	0	3	.333	20	0	0	1.000
1947—New York	Amer.		OF	7	26	4	6	0	0	2	5	.231	22	0	0	1.000
1949—New York	Amer.		OF	5	18	2	2	0	0	1	2	.111	7	0	0	1.000
1950—New York	Amer.		OF	4	13	2	4	1	0	1	2	.308	8	0	0	1.000
1951—New York	Amer.		OF	6	23	3	6	2	0	1	5	.261	17	0	0	1.000
World Series Totals—10 Years				51	199	27	54	6	0	8	30	.271	150	0	1	.993

LAWRENCE EUGENE (LARRY) DOBY

Born December 13, 1924, at Camden, S. C.

Height, 6.01. Weight, 180.

Threw right and batted lefthanded.

Hit three home runs in a game, August 2, 1950.
Named by Baseball Writers' Association of America as center fielder on THE SPORTING NEWS All-Star Major League Team, 1950.
Scout, Montreal Expos, 1969; Montreal minor league instructor, 1970; coach, Expos, 1971-73; Cleveland Indians, 1974; Montreal, 1976; Chicago White Sox, 1977 to 1978; manager, White Sox, 1978; batting instructor, White Sox, 1979.

Year	Club	League	Pos.	G.	AB.	R.	H.	2B.	3B.	HR.	RBI.	B.A.	PO.	A.	E.	F.A.
1947—Cleveland	Amer.		INF	29	32	3	5	1	0	0	2	.156	11	4	0	1.000
1948—Cleveland	Amer.		OF	121	439	83	132	23	9	14	66	.301	287	12	★14	.955
1949—Cleveland	Amer.		OF	147	547	106	153	25	3	24	85	.280	355	7	9	.976
1950—Cleveland	Amer.		OF	142	503	110	164	25	5	25	102	.326	367	2	5	.987
1951—Cleveland	Amer.		OF	134	447	84	132	27	5	20	69	.295	321	12	8	.977
1952—Cleveland	Amer.		OF	140	519	★104	143	26	8	★32	104	.276	398	11	6	.986
1953—Cleveland	Amer.		OF	149	513	92	135	18	5	29	102	.263	354	10	6	.984
1954—Cleveland	Amer.		OF	153	577	94	157	18	4	★32	★126	.272	411	14	2	.995
1955—Cleveland(a)	Amer.		OF	131	491	91	143	17	5	26	75	.291	313	6	2	.994
1956—Chicago	Amer.		OF	140	504	89	135	22	3	24	102	.268	371	4	5	.987
1957—Chicago (b) (c)	Amer.		OF	119	416	57	120	27	2	14	79	.288	255	3	4	.985

Year Club League	Pos.	G.	AB.	R.	H.	2B.	3B.	HR.	RBI.	B.A.	PO.	A.	E.	F.A.
1958—Cleveland(d) .... Amer.	OF	89	247	41	70	10	1	13	45	.283	141	5	0	1.000
1959—Det.(e)-Chicago.... Amer.	OF	39	113	6	26	4	2	0	13	.230	43	2	2	.957
1960—San Diego .... PCL	OF	9	27	2	6	0	1	0	3	.222	7	0	0	1.000
Major League Totals—13 Years		1533	5348	960	1515	243	52	253	970	.283	3627	92	63	.983

aTraded to Chicago White Sox for Shortstop Chico Carrasquel and Outfielder Jim Busby, October 25, 1955.

bTraded to Baltimore Orioles with Pitcher Jack Harshman and First Baseman Jim Marshall for Pitcher Ray Moore, First Baseman-Outfielder Tito Francona and Infielder-Outfielder Billy Goodman, December 3, 1957.

cTraded to Cleveland Indians with Pitcher Don Ferrarese for Pitcher Bud Daley and Outfielders Dick Williams and Gene Woodling, April 1, 1958.

dTraded to Detroit Tigers for Outfielder Tito Francona, March 3, 1959.

eReleased to Chicago White Sox, May 13, 1959.

WORLD SERIES RECORD

Year Club League	Pos.	G.	AB.	R.	H.	2B.	3B.	HR.	RBI.	B.A.	PO.	A.	E.	F.A.
1948—Cleveland............... Amer.	OF	6	22	1	7	1	0	1	2	.318	11	0	1	.917
1954—Cleveland............... Amer.	OF	4	16	0	2	0	0	0	0	.125	7	0	0	1.000
World Series Totals—2 Years		10	38	1	9	1	0	1	2	.237	18	0	1	.947

ROBERT PERSHING (BOBBY) DOERR

Born April 7, 1918, at Los Angeles, Calif.

Height, 5.11. Weight, 185.

Threw and batted righthanded.

Led American League second basemen in double plays, 1938-40-43-46-47.

Named Most Valuable Player, American League, by THE SPORTING NEWS, 1944.

Named as second baseman for THE SPORTING NEWS All-Star Major League Team, 1944.

Scout, Boston Red Sox, 1957 through 66; coach, Red Sox, 1967 through 1969; Toronto Blue Jays, 1977 through 1981; minor league instructor for Toronto, 1982 to 1984.

Named to Hall of Fame, 1986.

Year Club League	Pos.	G.	AB.	R.	H.	2B.	3B.	HR.	RBI.	B.A.	PO.	A.	E.	F.A.
1934—Hollywood .... P. C.	2B	67	201	12	52	6	0	0	11	.259	135	164	14	.955
1935—Hollywood .... P. C.	2B	172	647	87	205	22	8	4	74	.317	444	466	38	.960
1936—San Diego .... P. C.	2B	175	695	100	★238	37	12	2	77	.342	399	★504	33	.965
1937—Boston.................... Amer.	2B	55	147	22	33	5	1	2	14	.224	94	124	6	.973
1938—Boston.................... Amer.	2B	145	509	70	147	26	7	5	80	.289	372	420	26	.968
1939—Boston.................... Amer.	2B	127	525	75	167	28	2	12	73	.318	336	431	19	.976
1940—Boston.................... Amer.	2B	151	595	87	173	37	10	22	105	.291	★401	480	21	●.977
1941—Boston.................... Amer.	2B	132	500	74	141	28	4	16	93	.282	290	389	20	.971
1942—Boston.................... Amer.	2B	144	545	71	158	35	5	15	102	.290	376	453	21	★.975
1943—Boston.................... Amer.	2B	●155	604	78	163	32	3	16	75	.270	★415	●490	9	★.990
1944—Boston.................... Amer.	2B	125	468	95	152	30	10	15	81	.325	341	363	17	.976
1945—Boston.................... Amer.		(In Military Service)												
1946—Boston.................... Amer.	2B	151	583	95	158	34	9	18	116	.271	★420	★483	13	★.986
1947—Boston.................... Amer.	2B	146	561	79	145	23	10	17	95	.258	376	●466	16	.981
1948—Boston.................... Amer.	2B	140	527	94	150	23	6	27	111	.285	366	430	6	●.993
1949—Boston.................... Amer.	2B	139	541	91	167	30	9	18	109	.309	395	439	17	.980
1950—Boston.................... Amer.	2B	149	586	103	172	29	●11	27	120	.294	★443	431	11	★.988
1951—Boston.................... Amer.	2B	106	402	60	116	21	2	13	73	.289	303	311	12	.981
Major League Totals—14 Years		1865	7093	1094	2042	381	89	223	1247	.288	4928	5710	214	.980

WORLD SERIES RECORD

Year Club League	Pos.	G.	AB.	R.	H.	2B.	3B.	HR.	RBI.	B.A.	PO.	A.	E.	F.A.
1946—Boston.................... Amer.	2B	6	22	1	9	1	0	1	3	.409	18	31	0	1.000

PATRICK JOSEPH (PATSY) DONOVAN

Born March 16, 1865, at Lawrence, Mass.

Died December 25, 1953, at Lawrence, Mass.

Height, 5.11½. Weight, 175.

Threw and batted lefthanded.

Manager, Pittsburgh, National League, 1897-99; St. Louis Cardinals, 1901-02-03; Washington Senators, 1904; Brooklyn Dodgers, 1906-07-08; Boston Red Sox, 1910-11; Buffalo, International, 1915-16-17; Syracuse, International, 1918; Newark, International, 1919; Jersey City, International, 1921; Springfield, Eastern, 1923; Jersey City, International, 1924-25-26; Providence, Eastern, 1927; Attleboro, New England, 1928.

Year	Club	League	Pos.	G.	AB.	R.	H.	2B.	3B.	HR.	SB.	B.A.	PO.	A.	E.	F.A.
1886—Lawrence		N. Eng.	OF	66	281	45	82	8	1	0	....	.292	101	9	14	.887
1887—Lawrence-Salem..		N. Eng.	OF	88	....	120	....	....	....	....	54	*.398	....	....	....	.821
1888—London		Int.	OF	103	460	115	165	25	10	1	80	*.359	224	15	28	.895
1889—London		Int.	OF	53	224	45	60	8	1	1	27	.268	120	21	12	.922
1890—Boston-Brooklyn..		Nat.	OF	58	244	34	62	6	1	0	19	.254	110	9	8	.937
1891—Louisv'le-Wash.		A.A.	OF	115	475	79	143	9	3	2	31	.301	199	17	19	.919
1892—Wash'gton-Pitts....		Nat.	OF	128	543	108	159	18	7	4	59	.293	171	28	29	.873
1893—Pittsburgh		Nat.	OF	110	465	110	154	6	7	2	49	.331	173	14	14	.930
1894—Pittsburgh		Nat.	OF	133	575	146	176	21	9	4	31	.306	267	24	21	.933
1895—Pittsburgh		Nat.	OF	126	522	124	165	18	6	1	36	.316	189	13	10	.953
1896—Pittsburgh		Nat.	OF	129	569	110	180	21	5	3	50	.316	222	*30	14	.947
1897—Pittsburgh		Nat.	OF	120	475	83	155	17	6	0	39	.326	185	16	11	.948
1898—Pittsburgh		Nat.	OF	147	610	112	184	17	8	0	43	.302	239	21	16	.942
1899—Pittsburgh		Nat.	OF	123	537	82	159	10	6	1	24	.296	187	12	11	.948
1900—St. Louis		Nat.	OF	127	509	78	165	12	1	0	44	.324	181	12	8	.960
1901—St. Louis		Nat.	OF	129	524	91	154	23	6	1	24	.294	216	17	5	.979
1902—St. Louis		Nat.	OF	126	502	68	155	12	4	0	41	.309	178	22	8	.962
1903—St. Louis		Nat.	OF	105	410	63	134	15	3	0	25	.327	142	16	8	.952
1904—Washington		Amer.	OF	125	434	32	104	6	0	0	16	.240	215	15	9	.962
1905—							(Out of Organized Ball)									
1906—Brooklyn		Nat.	OF	7	21	1	5	0	0	0	0	.238	9	0	0	1.000
1907—Brooklyn		Nat.	OF	1	1	0	0	0	0	0	0	.000	4	0	0	1.000
American League Totals—1 Year				125	434	32	104	6	0	0	16	.240	215	15	9	.962
American Assn. Totals—1 Year				115	475	79	143	9	3	2	31	.301	199	17	19	.919
National League Totals—15 Years				1569	6507	1210	2007	196	69	16	484	.308	2473	234	163	.943
Major League Totals—17 Years				1809	7416	1321	2254	211	72	18	531	.304	2887	266	191	.943

JOHN JOSEPH (JACK) DOYLE

Born October 25, 1869, at Killorglin, Co. Kerry, Ireland.

Died December 31, 1958, at Holyoke, Mass.

Height, 5.09. Weight, 174.

Threw and batted righthanded.

Manager, Milwaukee, American Association, 1907; umpire, Eastern League, 1910; National League, 1911; New England League, 1911; scout, Cleveland Indians, 1913; umpire, American Association, 1915; Pacific Coast League, 1916; Three-I League, 1919; scout, Chicago Cubs, 1920-1958.

Year	Club	League	Pos.	G.	AB.	R.	H.	2B.	3B.	HR.	SB.	B.A.	PO.	A.	E.	F.A.
1888—Lynn		N. Eng.	C	12	48	12	16	4	0	1	8	.333	78	27	21	.838
1889—Canton		Tri-St.	C	80	368	89	103	....	....	....	81	.280	327	81	26	.940
1889—Columbus		A. A.	C	11	31	6	11	1	1	0	2	.355	33	17	5	.909
1890—Columbus		A. A.	C-SS	76	290	48	79	16	8	2	29	.272	201	140	36	.905
1891—Cleveland		Nat.	C-3-OF	64	247	43	65	13	4	0	23	.263	167	77	37	.868
1892—Cleve.-N.Y.		Nat.	C-3-OF	108	449	97	133	24	3	5	70	.296	247	129	49	.885
1893—New York		Nat.	C-OF	80	307	55	100	17	6	1	49	.326	242	68	16	.951
1894—New York		Nat.	1B	105	425	94	157	29	8	3	48	.369	987	60	*33	.969
1895—New York		Nat.	1B	78	316	52	100	20	3	1	33	.316	591	34	21	.967
1896—Baltimore		Nat.	1B	118	487	115	168	27	4	1	71	.345	1157	43	*33	.973
1897—Baltimore		Nat.	1B	114	463	93	165	27	3	1	62	.356	1102	75	25	.979
1898—Wash.-N.Y.		Nat.	1B-OF	121	472	68	138	19	4	3	20	.292	590	35	20	.969
1899—New York		Nat.	1B	117	454	57	140	14	7	3	41	.308	1129	69	31	.975
1900—New York		Nat.	1B	130	504	69	138	23	1	1	45	.274	1281	*95	*43	.970
1901—Chicago		Nat.	1B	73	278	19	67	10	2	0	11	.241	687	62	17	.978
1902—Washington		Amer.	2B	78	315	50	75	15	2	1	7	.238	194	193	25	.931
1902—New York		Nat.	1B	50	190	25	57	12	2	0	10	.300	506	39	9	.984
1903—Brooklyn		Nat.	1B	139	524	84	164	27	6	0	34	.313	*1418	83	29	.981
1904—Brook.-Phila.		Nat.	1B	72	258	22	57	11	3	1	5	.221	667	59	15	.980
1905—New York		Amer.	1B	3	3	0	0	0	0	0	0	.000	10	0	2	.833
American Assn. Totals—2 Years				87	321	54	90	17	9	2	31	.280	234	157	41	.905
American League Totals—2 Years				79	318	50	75	15	2	1	7	.236	154	193	27	.928
National League Totals—14 Years				1369	5374	893	1649	273	56	20	522	.307	10771	928	378	.969
Major League Totals—17 Years				1535	6013	997	1814	305	67	23	560	.302	11159	1278	446	.965

DONALD SCOTT (DON) DRYSDALE

Born July 23, 1936, at Van Nuys, Calif.

Height, 6.06. Weight, 208.

Threw and batted righthanded.

Holds major league record for most consecutive shutout games won (6), May 14 through June 4, 1968.
Shares National League records for most home runs by pitcher, season (7), 1958 and 1965; most shutout games won, month (5), May, 1968.
Received Cy Young Award as outstanding major league pitcher, 1962.
Named Major League Pitcher of the Year by THE SPORTING NEWS, 1962.
Named as pitcher on THE SPORTING NEWS National League All-Star Team, 1962.
Named to Hall of Fame, 1984.

Year—Club	League	G.	IP.	W.	L.	Pct.	H.	R.	ER.	SO.	BB.	ERA.
1954—Bakersfield	Calif.	15	112	8	5	.615	97	54	43	73	58	3.45
1955—Montreal	Int.	28	173	11	11	.500	163	78	64	80	68	3.33
1956—Brooklyn	Nat.	25	99	5	5	.500	95	35	29	55	31	2.64
1957—Brooklyn	Nat.	34	221	17	9	.654	197	76	66	148	61	2.69
1958—Los Angeles	Nat.	44	212	12	13	.480	214	107	98	131	72	4.16
1959—Los Angeles	Nat.	44	271	17	13	.567	237	113	104	★242	93	3.45
1960—Los Angeles	Nat.	41	269	15	14	.517	214	93	85	★246	72	2.84
1961—Los Angeles	Nat.	40	244	13	10	.565	236	111	100	182	83	3.69
1962—Los Angeles	Nat.	43	★314	★25	9	.735	272	122	99	★232	78	2.84
1963—Los Angeles	Nat.	42	315	19	17	.528	★287	114	92	251	57	2.63
1964—Los Angeles	Nat.	40	★321	18	16	.529	242	91	78	237	68	2.19
1965—Los Angeles	Nat.	44	308	23	12	.657	★270	113	95	210	66	2.78
1966—Los Angeles	Nat.	40	274	13	16	.448	279	114	104	177	45	3.42
1967—Los Angeles	Nat.	38	282	13	16	.448	269	101	86	196	60	2.74
1968—Los Angeles	Nat.	31	239	14	12	.538	201	68	57	155	56	2.15
1969—Los Angeles	Nat.	12	63	5	4	.556	71	34	31	24	13	4.43
Major League Totals—14 Years		518	3432	209	166	.557	3084	1292	1124	2486	855	2.95

WORLD SERIES RECORD

Year—Club	League	G.	IP.	W.	L.	Pct.	H.	R.	ER.	SO.	BB.	ERA.
1956—Brooklyn	Nat.	1	2	0	0	.000	2	2	2	1	1	9.00
1959—Los Angeles	Nat.	1	7	1	0	1.000	11	1	1	5	4	1.29
1963—Los Angeles	Nat.	1	9	1	0	1.000	3	0	0	9	1	0.00
1965—Los Angeles	Nat.	2	11⅔	1	1	.500	12	9	5	15	3	3.86
1966—Los Angeles	Nat.	2	10	0	2	.000	8	5	5	6	3	4.50
World Series Totals—5 Years		7	39⅔	3	3	.500	36	17	13	36	12	2.95

HUGH DUFFY

Born November 26, 1866, at River Point, R. I.

Died October 19, 1954, at Allston, Mass.

Height, 5.07. Weight, 168.

Threw and batted righthanded.

Holds major league record for highest batting average, season, 100 or more games (.438), 1894.
Manager, Milwaukee Brewers, 1901; Milwaukee, Western League, 1902-03; Philadelphia Phillies, 1904-05-06; owner and manager, Providence, Eastern League, 1907-08-09; manager, Chicago White Sox, 1910-11; Milwaukee, American Association, 1912; president-manager, Portland, New England League, 1913 through 1916; scout, Boston Braves, 1917-18-19; manager, Toronto, International League, 1920; Boston Red Sox, 1921-22; scout, Red Sox, 1924 to date of death.
Named to Hall of Fame, 1945.

Year—Club	League	Pos.	G.	AB.	R.	H.	2B.	3B.	HR.	SB.	B.A.	PO.	A.	E.	F.A.
1886—Hartford	East.	OF	7	18	3	5	1	0	0	1	.278	16	16	3	.914
1887—Springfield	East.	OF	17	80	20	28	4	2	1	17	.350	......	......	....	......
1887—Salem-Lowell	N. Eng.	OF	78	325	103	139	24	8	16	16	.428	......	......	....	.831
1888—Chicago	Nat.	OF	71	298	60	84	11	4	7	13	.282	103	19	12	.910
1889—Chicago (a)	Nat.	OF	●136	★584	144	182	21	7	12	52	.312	184	19	24	.894

Year Club League	Pos.	G.	AB.	R.	H.	2B.	3B.	HR.	SB.	B.A.	PO.	A.	E.	F.A.
1890—Chicago (b) .... Play.	OF	137	591	*161	194	33	14	7	79	.328	261	33	22	.930
1891—Boston (c)............. A. A.	OF	121	511	124	174	23	10	10	83	.341	154	23	13	.932
1892—Boston.................... Nat.	OF	146	609	125	184	25	13	5	61	.302	259	21	23	.924
1893—Boston.................... Nat.	OF	131	537	●149	203	23	7	6	50	*.378	313	13	14	*.959
1894—Boston.................... Nat.	OF	124	539	160	*236	*50	13	●18	49	*.438	313	23	28	.923
1895—Boston.................... Nat.	OF	131	540	113	190	25	6	8	42	.352	327	21	20	.946
1896—Boston.................... Nat.	OF	131	533	93	161	17	8	5	45	.302	250	17	12	.957
1897—Boston.................... Nat.	OF	134	554	131	189	23	10	8	45	.341	263	12	12	.958
1898—Boston.................... Nat.	OF	151	561	97	179	12	3	8	32	.319	328	14	19	.947
1899—Boston.................... Nat.	OF	147	588	102	164	25	8	5	18	.279	343	9	13	.964
1900—Boston.................... Nat.	OF	50	181	28	54	5	4	2	12	.298	107	5	6	.949
1901—Milwaukee............ Amer.	OF	78	286	41	88	14	8	2	13	.308	143	5	4	.974
1902—Milwaukee.......... West.	OF	140	505	79	147	25	6	2	37	.291	302	12	11	.966
1903—Milwaukee.......... West.	OF	71	257	45	77	8	1	0	30	.300	157	6	13	.926
1904—Philadelphia .... Nat.	OF	18	46	10	13	1	1	0	3	.283	16	0	3	.842
1905—Philadelphia .... Nat.	OF	15	40	7	12	2	1	0	0	.300	17	1	2	.900
1906—Philadelphia .... Nat.	PH	1	1	0	0	0	0	0	0	.000	0	0	0	.000
1907—Providence........... East.	OF	35	73	9	22	1	0	0	5	.301	38	1	0	1.000
1908—Providence........... East.	OF	37	57	10	19	5	2	1	5	.333	18	0	0	1.000
American Assn. Totals—1 Year		121	511	124	174	23	10	10	83	.340	154	23	13	.931
American League Totals—1 Year		78	286	41	88	14	8	2	13	.308	143	5	4	.947
National League Totals—14 Years		1386	5611	1219	1851	240	85	84	422	.330	2823	174	188	.941
Players League Totals—1 Year		137	591	161	194	33	14	7	79	.328	261	33	22	.930
Major League Totals—17 Years		1722	6999	1545	2307	310	117	103	597	.330	3381	235	227	.941

aJumped to Players League (Brotherhood), 1890.
bSigned with Boston A. A. after disbanding of Brotherhood, 1891.
cAwarded to Boston N. L. following consolidation of National League and American Association, 1892.

JAMES JOSEPH (JIMMIE) DYKES

Born November 10, 1896, at Philadelphia, Pa.

Died June 15, 1976, at Philadelphia, Pa.

Height, 5.09. Weight, 192.

Threw and batted righthanded.

Shares American League record for most chances accepted by second baseman, nine-inning game, (17), August 28, 1921.

Manager, Chicago White Sox, 1934 to 1946; Hollywood, Pacific Coast League, 1946 to 1948; coach, Philadelphia Athletics, 1949 to 1950; manager, Athletics, 1951-52-53; Baltimore Orioles, 1954; coach, Cincinnati Reds, 1955 until named manager, 1958; coach, Pittsburgh Pirates, 1959 until named manager, Detroit Tigers, 1959; swapped managerial jobs with Joe Gordon, shifting to manager of Cleveland Indians, 1960-61; coach, Milwaukee Braves, 1962; Kansas City Athletics, 1963-64.

Year Club League	Pos.	G.	AB.	R.	H.	2B.	3B.	HR.	RBI.	B.A.	PO.	A.	E.	F.A.
1917—Gettysburg .... B. R.	2B	79	286	52	62	11	2	4	.....	.217	189	173	17	.955
1918—Philadelphia (a)... Amer.	2B	59	186	13	35	3	3	0	18	.188	139	189	21	.940
1919—Philadelphia .... Amer.	2B	17	49	4	9	1	0	0	0	.184	28	58	5	.945
1919—Atlanta .... South.	2B	110	390	58	96	28	5	2	.....	.246	337	264	30	.952
1920—Philadelphia .... Amer.	2-3B	142	546	81	140	25	4	8	35	.256	353	458	45	.947
1921—Philadelphia .... Amer.	2B	155	613	88	168	32	13	16	77	.274	*434	*522	*46	.954
1922—Philadelphia .... Amer.	3B	145	501	66	138	23	7	12	68	.275	*186	*295	*28	.945
1923—Philadelphia .... Amer.	2B-SS	124	416	50	105	28	1	4	43	.252	283	363	25	.963
1924—Philadelphia .... Amer.	2B-3B	110	410	68	128	26	6	3	50	.312	249	318	26	.956
1925—Philadelphia .... Amer.	2B-3B	122	465	93	150	32	11	5	55	.323	225	302	21	.962
1926—Philadelphia .... Amer.	2B-3B	124	429	54	123	32	5	1	44	.287	195	324	20	.963
1927—Philadelphia .... Amer.	1B-3B	121	417	61	135	33	6	3	60	.324	839	101	14	.985
1928—Philadelphia .... Amer.	2-3B-SS	85	242	39	67	11	0	5	30	.277	130	164	8	.974
1929—Philadelphia .... Amer.	2-3B-SS	119	401	76	131	34	6	13	79	.327	203	273	33	.935
1930—Philadelphia .... Amer.	3B	125	435	69	131	28	4	6	73	.301	124	191	13	.960
1931—Philadelphia .... Amer.	SS-3B	101	355	48	97	28	2	3	46	.273	136	188	15	.956
1932—Philadelphia (b)... Amer.	*3-2B-SS	153	558	71	148	29	5	7	90	.265	158	282	11	*.976
1933—Chicago .... Amer.	3B	151	554	49	144	22	6	1	68	.260	132	*296	21	.953
1934—Chicago .... Amer.	1-2B-3B	127	456	52	122	17	4	7	82	.268	383	252	27	.959
1935—Chicago .... Amer.	1B-3B	117	403	45	116	24	2	4	61	.288	290	185	15	.969
1936—Chicago .... Amer.	3B	127	435	62	116	16	3	7	60	.267	108	140	18	.951
1937—Chicago .... Amer.	1-3B	30	85	10	26	5	0	1	23	.306	152	27	1	.994
1938—Chicago .... Amer.	2-3B-SS	26	89	9	27	4	2	2	13	.303	75	72	9	.942
1939—Chicago .... Amer.	3B	2	1	0	0	0	0	0	0	.000	2	0	1	.667
Major League Totals—22 Years..............		2282	8046	1108	2256	453	90	108	1075	.280	4824	5100	423	.959

aIn Military Service after close of 1918 season.
bSold with Outfielders Al Simmons and George (Mule) Haas to Chicago White Sox for $150,000, September 28, 1932.

Shares records for most at-bats and hits, inning (2), October 12, 1929, seventh inning.

Year Club League	Pos.	G.	AB.	R.	H.	2B.	3B.	HR.	RBI.	B.A.	PO.	A.	E.	F.A.
1929—Philadelphia .... Amer.	3B	5	19	2	8	1	0	0	4	.421	3	5	2	.800
1930—Philadelphia .... Amer.	3B	6	18	2	4	3	0	1	5	.222	8	6	1	.933
1931—Philadelphia .... Amer.	3B	7	22	2	5	0	0	0	2	.227	4	12	0	1.000
World Series Totals—3 Years		18	59	6	17	4	0	1	11	.288	15	23	3	.927

DELMER (DEL) ENNIS

Born June 8, 1925, at Philadelphia, Pa.

Height, 6.00. Weight, 200.

Threw and batted righthanded.

Hit three home runs in a game, July 23, 1955.

Named Rookie of the Year by THE SPORTING NEWS, 1946.

Year Club League	Pos.	G.	AB.	R.	H.	2B.	3B.	HR.	RBI.	B.A.	PO.	A.	E.	F.A.
1943—Trenton .... Int.-St.	OF	●140	570	104	197	37	16	18	93	.346	201	★24	10	.957
1944-45—Philadelphia... Nat.					(In Military Service)									
1946—Philadelphia .... Nat.	OF	141	540	70	169	30	6	17	73	.313	332	16	9	.975
1947—Philadelphia .... Nat.	OF	139	541	71	149	25	6	12	81	.275	320	12	7	.979
1948—Philadelphia .... Nat.	OF	152	589	86	171	40	4	30	95	.290	297	15	★14	.957
1949—Philadelphia .... Nat.	OF	154	610	92	184	39	11	25	110	.302	359	10	★13	.966
1950—Philadelphia .... Nat.	OF	153	595	92	185	34	8	31	★126	.311	279	10	9	.970
1951—Philadelphia .... Nat.	OF	144	332	76	142	20	5	15	73	.267	268	14	9	.969
1952—Philadelphia .... Nat.	OF	151	592	90	171	30	10	20	107	.289	277	11	9	.970
1953—Philadelphia .... Nat.	OF	152	578	79	165	22	3	29	125	.285	184	14	6	.980
1954—Philadelphia .... Nat.	★OF-1B	145	556	73	145	23	2	25	119	.261	311	9	★15	.955
1955—Philadelphia .... Nat.	OF	146	564	82	167	24	7	29	120	.296	298	9	4	.987
1956—Philadelphia(a).... Nat.	OF	153	630	80	164	23	3	26	95	.260	269	8	11	.962
1957—St. Louis................. Nat.	OF	136	490	61	140	24	3	24	105	.286	180	3	11	.943
1958—St. Louis(b).......... Nat.	OF	106	329	22	86	18	1	3	47	.261	122	11	1	.993
1959—Cincinnati(c) .... Nat.	OF	5	12	1	4	0	0	0	1	.333	5	0	0	1.000
1959—Chicago .... Amer.	OF	26	96	10	21	6	0	2	7	.219	23	2	3	.909
American League Totals—1 Year..........		26	96	10	21	6	0	2	7	.219	23	2	3	.909
National League Totals—14 Years.........	1877	7158	975	2042	352	69	286	1277	.285	3601	148	118	.969	
Major League Totals—14 Years..............	1903	7254	985	2063	358	69	288	1284	.284	3624	150	121	.969	

aTraded to St. Louis Cardinals for Infielder Bobby Morgan and Outfielder Rip Repulski, November 19, 1956.

bTraded to Cincinnati Reds with Pitcher Bobby Mabe and Shortstop Eddie Kasko for Pitcher Alex Kellner, First Baseman George Crowe and Shortstop Alex Grammas, October 3, 1958.

cTraded to Chicago White Sox for Pitcher Don Rudolph and Outfielder Lou Skizas, May 2, 1959.

Year Club League	Pos.	G.	AB.	R.	H.	2B.	3B.	HR.	RBI.	B.A.	PO.	A.	E.	F.A.
1950—Philadelphia .... Nat.	OF	4	14	1	2	1	0	0	0	.143	9	0	0	1.000

WILLIAM GEORGE (BILLY) EVANS

Born February 10, 1884, at Chicago, Ill.

Died January 23, 1956, at Miami, Fla.

Height, 5.11½. Weight, 205.

Attended Cornell University three years (1903). Reporter, Youngstown (O.) Vindicator (1904). Umpire, Ohio-Penn-sylvania League, 1905; umpire, American League, 1906-27.

Vice-president/general manager, Cleveland Indians, 1928-35; supervisor, farm clubs, Boston Red Sox, 1936-41; general manager, Cleveland Rams football team, 1941-42; president of Southern League, 1942-46; general manager, Detroit Tigers, 1946-51.

Evans wrote classic books on umpiring, models today on their advice on position, decorum and rules interpretations. He was a master of the rule book and began a series of interpretations of tricky plays for THE SPORTING NEWS which evolved into the book, "KNOTTY PROBLEMS," an unquestioned leader in the field of rules applications on tricky plays and odd situations on the field. Billy was a fearless man when he knew he was right, having taken on Ty Cobb in a fight that lasted anywhere from a "brief encounter" to an hour-long, no-holds-barred, back-alley type of fight. Each version agrees on the outcome—a bloody draw, and deep, respected friends thereafter.

Evans, Bill Klem and Bill McGowan are considered the three greatest ball-and-strike umpires in the history of the game.

Evans was named to the Hall of Fame in 1973.

JOHN JOSEPH (JOHNNY) EVERS
(The Crab and The Trojan)

Born July 21, 1881, at Troy, N. Y.

Died March 28, 1947, at Albany, N. Y.

Height, 5.09. Weight, 140.

Threw right and batted lefthanded.

Manager, Chicago Cubs, 1913; coach, New York Giants, 1920; manager, Chicago Cubs, 1921; coach, Chicago White Sox, 1922-23; manager, White Sox, 1924; assistant manager, Boston Braves, 1929 through 1932; scout, Braves, 1933-34; manager, Albany, International League, 1935; vice-president and general manager, Albany, Eastern League, 1939.

Named Most Valuable Player in National League, 1914.

Named to Hall of Fame, 1946.

Year	Club	League	Pos.	G.	AB.	R.	H.	2B.	3B.	HR.	RBI.	B.A.	PO.	A.	E.	F.A.
1902—Troy		N.Y.S.	SS-2B	84	333	50	95	7	6	10	.....	.285	238	285	65	.889
1902—Chicago		Nat.	SS-2B	25	89	7	20	0	0	0	.....	.225	38	58	1	.990
1903—Chicago		Nat.	2B	123	464	70	136	27	7	0	.....	.293	245	306	37	.937
1904—Chicago		Nat.	2B	152	532	49	141	14	7	0	.....	.265	★381	★518	★54	.943
1905—Chicago		Nat.	2B	99	340	44	94	11	2	1	.....	.276	249	290	36	.937
1906—Chicago		Nat.	2B	154	533	65	136	17	6	1	.....	.255	★344	441	●44	.947
1907—Chicago		Nat.	2B	151	508	66	127	18	4	2	55	.250	346	★500	32	.964
1908—Chicago		Nat.	2B	123	416	83	125	19	6	0	35	.300	237	361	25	.960
1909—Chicago		Nat.	2B	126	463	88	122	19	6	1	20	.263	262	354	38	.942
1910—Chicago		Nat.	2B	125	433	87	114	11	7	0	25	.263	282	347	33	.950
1911—Chicago		Nat.	2B	44	155	29	35	4	3	0	9	.226	66	90	4	.975
1912—Chicago		Nat.	2B	143	478	73	163	23	11	1	56	.341	319	439	32	.959
1913—Chicago(a)		Nat.	2B	136	446	81	127	20	5	3	48	.285	303	426	30	.960
1914—Boston		Nat.	2B	139	491	81	137	20	3	1	33	.279	301	397	17	★.976
1915—Boston		Nat.	2B	83	278	38	73	4	1	1	23	.263	170	209	16	.959
1916—Boston		Nat.	2B	71	241	33	52	4	1	0	15	.216	98	175	14	.951
1917—Bos.(b)-Phila.		Nat.	2B	80	266	25	57	5	1	1	11	.214	114	210	9	.973
1922—Chicago		Amer.	2B	1	3	0	0	0	0	0	1	.000	3	3	0	1.000
1929—Boston		Nat.	2B	1	0	0	0	0	0	0	0	.000	0	0	1	.000
Major League Totals—18 Years				1776	6136	919	1659	216	70	12	....	.270	3758	5124	423	.955

aReleased by Chicago Cubs, December 12, 1913, and signed by Boston Braves, February, 1914.

bReleased to Philadelphia Phillies, July 12, 1917.

WORLD SERIES RECORD

Year	Club	League	Pos.	G.	AB.	R.	H.	2B.	3B.	HR.	RBI.	B.A.	PO.	A.	E.	F.A.
1906—Chicago		Nat.	2B	6	20	2	3	1	0	0	1	.150	12	20	1	.970
1907—Chicago		Nat.	2B	5	20	2	7	2	0	0	1	.350	9	12	3	.875
1908—Chicago		Nat.	2B	5	20	5	7	1	0	0	2	.350	5	21	1	.963
1914—Boston		Nat.	2B	4	16	2	7	0	0	0	2	.438	8	16	1	.960
World Series Totals—4 Years				20	76	11	24	4	0	0	6	.316	34	69	6	.946

WILLIAM BUCKINGHAM (BUCK) EWING

Born October 27, 1859, at Cincinnati, O.

Died October 20, 1906, at Cincinnati, O.

Height, 5.10. Weight, 188.

Threw and batted righthanded.

Manager, New York, Players League, 1890; Cincinnati, 1895 through 1899; New York Giants, 1900.

Named to Hall of Fame, 1939.

Year Club League	Pos.	G.	AB.	R.	H.	2B.	3B.	HR.	SB.	B.A.	PO.	A.	E.	F.A.
1878—Mohawk Browns.. Ind.		.....												
1879—Mohawk Browns.. Ind.		.....	.....	.....	.....	....	....	....	.....	......	......	....	....	......
1880—Cin. Buckeyes...... Ind.		.....												
1880—Rochester............ N. Assn.	C-OF	13	.....	.....	.....	....	....	....	.....	.148	......	....	....	.931
1880—Troy .... Nat.	C-OF	13	46	1	8	1	0	0	.....	.174	45	5	13	.794
1881—Troy .... Nat	C-3-S-O	65	267	38	65	13	6	0	.....	.243	211	89	28	.915
1882—Troy(a).................. Nat.	C-3-1-2-O	72	318	65	87	16	11	2	.....	.274	69	108	22	.889
1883—New York........... Nat.	C-2-3-OF	85	369	88	113	9	13	*10	.....	.306	262	92	31	.919
1884—New York........... Nat.	C-SS-OF	88	374	87	104	13	*18	3	.....	.278	431	125	41	.931
1885—New York........... Nat.	C-1-3-S-O	81	342	81	104	14	11	6	.....	.304	354	*106	41	.918
1886—New York........... Nat.	C-OF	70	275	59	85	10	8	4	18	.309	297	95	33	.922
1887—New York........... Nat.	2B-3B	76	348	81	127	17	13	6	36	.365	115	159	46	.856
1888—New York(b)........ Nat.	C-3B	103	415	83	127	17	15	5	53	.306	480	143	35	.947
1889—New York............ Nat.	C	96	407	91	133	23	14	3	34	.327	*524	*149	45	.937
1890—New York............ Play.	C	83	349	99	122	20	15	7	39	.350	372	123	23	.956
1891—New York............ Nat.	C-2B	14	49	8	17	1	1	0	3	.347	30	33	10	.863
1892—New York(c)........ Nat.	C-1B	97	394	58	126	12	15	8	53	.320	855	96	30	.969
1893—Cleveland............ Nat.	OF	114	477	116	177	27	17	6	53	.371	197	10	18	.920
1894—Cleveland(d)........ Nat.	OF	53	212	32	54	12	4	2	19	.255	91	7	8	.925
1895—Cincinnati............ Nat.	1B	103	439	90	139	23	13	3	34	.317	948	83	24	.977
1896—Cincinnati............ Nat.	1B	67	266	41	75	9	5	1	47	.282	669	49	14	.981
1897—Cincinnati............ Nat.	1B	1	1	0	0	0	0	0	0	.000	3	0	1	.750
National League Totals—17 Years		1198	4999	1019	1541	217	164	59	.....	.308	5581	1349	440	.940
Players League Totals—1 Year		83	349	99	122	20	15	7	39	.350	372	123	23	.956
Major League Totals—18 Years		1281	5348	1118	1663	237	179	66	.....	.311	5953	1472	463	.941

aTroy disbanded.
bJumped to Players League.
cTraded to Cleveland for shortstop George Davis, March, 1893.
dReleased by Cleveland and signed to manage Cincinnati, December, 1894.

URBAN CLARENCE (RED) FABER

Born September 6, 1888, at Cascade, Ia.

Died September 25, 1976, at Chicago, Ill.

Height, 6.01. Weight, 195.

Threw right and batted left and righthanded.

Pitched perfect game against Davenport, August 18, 1910.
Coach, Chicago White Sox, 1946 through 1948.
Named to Hall of Fame, 1964.

Year Club	League	G.	IP.	W.	L.	Pct.	H.	R.	ER.	SO.	BB.	ERA.
1909—Dubuque............................	I.I.I.	15	114	7	6	.538	93	58	....	92	50	......
1910—Dubuque............................	I.I.I.	44	334	18	19	.486	239	119	....	200	98	......
1911—Minneapolis	Amer. Assn.	2	6	0	0	.000	10	....	....	1	1	......
1911—Pueblo	Western	29	180	12	8	.600	191	....	....	99	39	......
1912—Des Moines	Western	43	304	21	14	.600	293	142	....	190	69	......
1913—Des Moines	Western	50	*373	20	17	.541	*328	157	103	*265	103	2.49
1914—Chicago..............................	American	40	181	10	9	.526	154	77	54	88	64	2.69
1915—Chicago..............................	American	•50	300	24	14	.632	264	118	85	182	99	2.55
1916—Chicago..............................	American	35	205	17	9	.654	167	67	46	87	61	2.02
1917—Chicago..............................	American	41	248	16	13	.552	222	92	53	84	85	1.92
1918—Chicago..............................	American	11	81	4	1	.800	70	23	11	26	23	1.22
1919—Chicago..............................	American	25	162	11	9	.550	185	92	69	45	45	3.83
1920—Chicago..............................	American	40	319	23	13	.639	332	136	106	108	88	2.99
1921—Chicago..............................	American	43	331	25	15	.625	293	107	91	124	87	*2.47
1922—Chicago..............................	American	43	*353	21	17	.553	334	128	110	148	83	*2.80
1923—Chicago..............................	American	32	234	14	11	.560	233	114	88	91	62	3.41
1924—Chicago..............................	American	21	161	9	11	.450	173	78	69	47	58	3.86
1925—Chicago..............................	American	34	238	12	11	.522	266	117	100	71	59	3.78
1926—Chicago..............................	American	27	185	15	8	.652	203	84	73	65	57	3.55
1927—Chicago..............................	American	18	111	4	7	.364	131	64	56	39	41	4.54
1928—Chicago..............................	American	27	201	13	9	.591	223	98	84	43	68	3.76
1929—Chicago..............................	American	31	234	13	13	.500	241	119	101	68	61	3.88
1930—Chicago..............................	American	29	169	8	13	.381	188	101	79	62	49	4.21
1931—Chicago..............................	American	44	184	10	14	.417	210	96	78	49	57	3.82
1932—Chicago..............................	American	42	106	2	11	.154	123	61	44	26	38	3.74
1933—Chicago..............................	American	36	86	3	4	.429	92	41	33	18	28	3.45
Major League Totals—20 Years		669	4089	254	212	.545	4104	1813	1430	1471	1213	3.15

WORLD SERIES RECORD

Year Club	League	G.	IP.	W.	L.	Pct.	H.	R.	ER.	SO.	BB.	ERA.
1917—Chicago	American	4	27	3	1	.750	21	7	7	9	3	2.33

RONALD RAY (RON) FAIRLY

Born July 12, 1938, at Macon, Ga.
Height, 5.10. Weight, 178.
Threw and batted lefthanded.

Year Club	League	Pos.	G.	AB.	R.	H.	2B.	3B.	HR.	RBI.	B.A.	PO.	A.	E.	F.A.
1958—Des Moines	West.	OF	51	172	32	51	7	0	13	41	.297	128	7	3	.978
1958—St. Paul	A.A.	OF	18	57	8	17	2	1	1	8	.298	57	1	1	.983
1958—Los Angeles	Nat.	OF	15	53	6	15	1	0	2	8	.283	33	0	1	.971
1959—Los Angeles	Nat.	OF	118	244	27	58	12	1	4	23	.238	97	8	4	.963
1960—Los Angeles	Nat.	OF	14	37	6	4	0	3	1	3	.108	15	1	0	1.000
1960—Spokane	P.C.	OF	147	505	98	153	34	4	27	100	.303	299	•20	8	.976
1961—Los Angeles	Nat.	OF-1B	111	245	42	79	15	2	10	48	.322	242	18	3	.989
1962—Los Angeles	Nat.	1B-OF	147	460	80	128	15	7	14	71	.278	1007	45	11	.990
1963—Los Angeles	Nat.	*1B-OF	152	490	62	133	21	0	12	77	.271	946	48	7	*.993
1964—Los Angeles	Nat.	1B	150	454	62	116	19	5	10	74	.256	1081	82	15	.987
1965—Los Angeles	Nat.	OF-1B	158	555	73	152	28	1	9	70	.274	361	13	6	.984
1966—Los Angeles	Nat.	OF-1B	117	351	53	101	20	0	14	61	.288	264	14	4	.986
1967—Los Angeles	Nat.	OF-1B	153	486	45	107	19	0	10	55	.220	727	55	11	.986
1968—Los Angeles	Nat.	OF-1B	141	441	32	103	15	1	4	43	.234	406	26	3	.993
1969—L.A.(a)-Montreal	Nat.	1B-OF	100	317	38	87	16	6	12	47	.274	543	46	7	.988
1970—Montreal	Nat.	1B-OF	119	385	54	111	19	0	15	61	.288	945	90	5	.995
1971—Montreal	Nat.	1B-OF	146	447	58	115	23	0	13	71	.257	1116	104	10	.992
1972—Montreal	Nat.	OF-1B	140	446	51	124	15	1	17	68	.278	646	46	6	.991
1973—Montreal	Nat.	OF-1B	142	413	70	123	13	1	17	49	.298	202	5	5	.976
1974—Montreal (b)	Nat.	1B-OF	101	282	35	69	9	1	12	43	.245	603	43	7	.989
1975—St. Louis	Nat.	1B-OF	107	229	32	69	13	2	7	37	.301	383	33	8	.981
1976—St. Louis (c)	Nat.	1B	73	110	13	29	4	0	0	21	.264	174	21	1	.995
1976—Oakland (d)	Amer.	1B	15	46	9	11	1	0	3	10	.239	121	10	0	1.000
1977—Toronto (e)	Amer.	1B-OF	132	458	60	128	24	2	19	64	.279	375	34	7	.983
1978—California	Amer.	1B-DH	91	235	23	51	5	0	10	40	.217	482	31	1	.998
National League Totals—19 Years			2204	6445	839	1723	277	31	183	930	.267	9791	698	114	.989
American League Totals—3 Years			238	739	92	190	30	2	32	114	.257	978	75	8	.992
Major League Totals—21 Years			2442	7184	931	1913	307	33	215	1044	.266	10769	773	122	.989

aTraded with Infielder Paul Popovich to Montreal Expos for Infielder Maury Wills and Outfielder Manny Mota, June 11, 1969.

bTraded to St. Louis Cardinals for Second Baseman Rudy Kinard and Outfielder-First Baseman Ed Kurpiel, December 6, 1974.

cSold to Oakland A's, September 14, 1976.

dTraded to Toronto Blue Jays for Infielder Mike Weathers and cash, February 24, 1977.

eTraded to California Angels for Catcher Pat Kelly and First Baseman Butch Alberts, December 8, 1977.

WORLD SERIES RECORD

Year Club	League	Pos.	G.	AB.	R.	H.	2B.	3B.	HR.	RBI.	B.A.	PO.	A.	E.	F.A.
1959—Los Angeles	Nat.	OF	6	3	0	0	0	0	0	0	.000	0	0	0	.000
1963—Los Angeles	Nat.	OF	4	1	0	0	0	0	0	0	.000	3	0	0	1.000
1965—Los Angeles	Nat.	OF	7	29	7	11	3	0	2	6	.379	8	0	0	1.000
1966—Los Angeles	Nat.	OF-1B	3	7	0	1	0	0	0	0	.143	5	0	1	.833
World Series Totals—4 Years			20	40	7	12	3	0	2	6	.300	16	0	1	.941

BIBB AUGUST FALK

Born January 27, 1899, at Austin, Tex,.
Died June 8, 1989, at Austin, Tex.
Height, 6.00. Weight, 180.
Threw and batted lefthanded.
Brother of Chet Falk, former major league pitcher.

Manager, Toledo, American Association, 1932; coach, Cleveland Indians, 1933; Boston Red Sox, 1934 through 1939.

Year Club	League	Pos.	G.	AB.	R.	H.	2B.	3B.	HR.	RBI.	B.A.	PO.	A.	E.	F.A.
1920—Chicago	Amer.	OF	7	17	1	5	1	1	0	2	.294	5	0	0	1.000
1921—Chicago	Amer.	OF	152	585	62	167	31	11	5	82	.285	288	9	13	.958
1922—Chicago	Amer.	OF	131	483	58	144	27	1	12	79	.298	253	10	10	.963
1923—Chicago	Amer.	OF	87	274	44	84	18	6	5	38	.307	148	6	8	.951
1924—Chicago	Amer.	OF	138	526	77	185	37	8	6	99	.352	292	26	10	.970
1925—Chicago	Amer.	OF	154	602	80	181	35	9	4	99	.301	306	18	14	.959
1926—Chicago	Amer.	OF	155	566	86	195	43	4	8	108	.345	338	16	3	★.992
1927—Chicago	Amer.	OF	145	535	76	175	35	6	9	83	.327	372	22	9	.978
1928—Chicago (a)	Amer.	OF	98	286	42	83	18	4	1	37	.290	164	9	5	.972
1929—Cleveland	Amer.	OF	126	430	66	133	30	7	13	94	.309	219	15	14	.944
1930—Cleveland	Amer.	OF	82	191	34	62	12	1	4	36	.325	84	4	3	.967
1931—Cleveland	Amer.	OF	79	161	30	49	13	1	2	28	.304	55	1	3	.949
1932—Toledo	A.A.	OF	79	246	42	79	11	5	5	46	.321	140	4	6	.960
Major League Totals—12 Years			1354	4656	656	1463	300	59	69	785	.314	2524	136	92	.967

aTraded to Cleveland Indians for Catcher Martin Autry, February 28, 1929.

ROBERT WILLIAM ANDREW (BOB) FELLER
(Rapid Robert)

Born November 3, 1918, at Van Meter, Ia.

Height, 6.00. Weight, 185.

Threw and batted righthanded.

Pitched 1-0 no-hit victory against Chicago White Sox, April 16, 1940; pitched 1-0 no-hit victory against New York Yankees, April 30, 1946; pitched 2-1 no-hit victory against Detroit Tigers, July 1, 1951.

Holds American League record for most bases on balls, season (208), 1938.

Scout, Cleveland Indians, 1958.

Named by Baseball Writers' Association of America for THE SPORTING NEWS All-Star Major League Teams, 1939-40-41-46-47.

Named by THE SPORTING NEWS as the No. 1 Major League Player of the Year, 1940.

Named by THE SPORTING NEWS as Top Pitcher in the American League, 1951.

Named to Hall of Fame, 1962.

Year Club	League	G.	IP.	W.	L.	Pct.	H.	R.	ER.	SO.	BB.	ERA.
1936—Cleveland	American	14	62	5	3	.625	52	29	23	76	47	3.34
1937—Cleveland	American	26	149	9	7	.563	116	68	56	150	106	3.38
1938—Cleveland	American	39	278	17	11	.607	225	136	126	★240	★208	4.08
1939—Cleveland	American	39	★297	★24	9	.727	227	105	94	★246	★142	2.85
1940—Cleveland	American	★43	★320	★27	11	.711	245	102	93	★261	118	★2.62
1941—Cleveland	American	★44	★343	★25	13	.658	★284	129	120	★260	★194	3.15
1942-43-44—Cleveland	American				(In Military Service)							
1945—Cleveland	American	9	72	5	3	.625	50	21	20	59	35	2.50
1946—Cleveland	American	★48	★371	●26	15	.634	★277	101	90	★348	★153	2.18
1947—Cleveland	American	42	★299	★20	11	.645	230	97	89	★196	127	2.68
1948—Cleveland	American	44	280	19	15	.559	★255	123	111	★164	116	3.57
1949—Cleveland	American	36	211	15	14	.517	198	104	88	108	84	3.75
1950—Cleveland	American	35	247	16	11	.593	230	105	94	119	103	3.43
1951—Cleveland	American	33	250	★22	8	★.733	239	105	97	111	95	3.49
1952—Cleveland	American	30	192	9	13	.409	219	●124	101	81	83	4.73
1953—Cleveland	American	25	176	10	7	.588	168	78	70	60	60	3.58
1954—Cleveland	American	19	140	13	3	.813	127	53	48	59	39	3.09
1955—Cleveland	American	25	83	4	4	.500	71	43	32	25	31	3.47
1956—Cleveland	American	19	58	0	4	.000	63	34	32	18	23	4.97
Major League Totals—18 Years		570	3828	266	162	.621	3271	1557	1384	2581	1764	3.25

WORLD SERIES RECORD

Year Club	League	G.	IP.	W.	L.	Pct.	H.	R.	ER.	SO.	BB.	ERA.
1948—Cleveland	American	2	14⅓	0	2	.000	10	8	8	7	5	5.02

—DID YOU KNOW—

That when Wes Ferrell pitched a no-hitter against the Browns in 1931, the only questionable call came on a ball hit by his brother? In the eighth inning, Rick Ferrell hit a hard grounder to the shortstop, who fielded the ball, but threw wide to first. The play was ruled an error, keeping the no-hitter intact.

RICHARD BENJAMIN (RICK) FERRELL

Born October 12, 1906, at Durham, N. C.
Height, 5.11. Weight, 170.
Threw and batted righthanded.
Brother of Wes Ferrell, former major league pitcher.

Coach, Washington Senators, 1946 through 1949; Detroit Tigers, 1950 through 1953; scout, Tigers, 1954 through 1958; general manager, Tigers, 1959-60; vice-president, Tigers, 1962 through 1975; consultant, Tigers, 1976 to date.
Named to Hall of Fame, 1984.

Year Club	League	Pos.	G.	AB.	R.	H.	2B.	3B.	HR.	RBI.	B.A.	PO.	A.	E.	F.A.
1926—Kinston	Virginia	C	64	192	24	51	6	0	2	20	.266	208	38	9	.965
1926—Columbus	A. A.	C	5	14	2	4	1	0	0	....	.286	9	4	0	1.000
1927—Columbus	A. A.	C	104	345	42	86	14	4	2	44	.249	274	92	●15	.961
1928—Columbus*	A. A.	C	126	339	51	113	31	5	2	65	.333	251	106	8	.978
1929—St. Louis	Amer.	C	64	144	21	33	6	1	0	20	.229	140	35	7	.962
1930—St. Louis	Amer.	C	101	314	43	84	18	4	1	41	.268	336	66	7	.983
1931—St. Louis	Amer.	C	117	386	47	118	30	4	3	57	.306	412	★86	★14	.973
1932—St. Louis	Amer.	C	126	438	67	138	30	5	2	65	.315	486	78	8	.986
1933—St. L.†-Boston	Amer.	C	140	493	58	143	21	4	4	77	.290	591	★92	★7	.990
1934—Boston	Amer.	C	132	437	50	130	29	4	1	48	.297	★531	72	6	★.990
1935—Boston	Amer.	C	133	458	54	138	34	4	3	61	.301	520	79	●13	.979
1936—Boston	Amer.	C	121	410	59	128	27	5	8	55	.312	★556	55	8	★.987
1937—Boston‡-Wash.	Amer.	C	104	344	39	84	8	0	2	36	.244	434	52	6	.988
1938—Washington	Amer.	C	135	411	55	120	24	5	1	58	.292	512	69	★11	.981
1939—Washington	Amer.	C	87	274	32	77	13	1	0	31	.281	327	46	9	.976
1940—Washington	Amer.	C	103	326	35	89	18	2	0	28	.273	427	67	10	.980
1941—Wash.§-St. L.	Amer.	C	121	387	38	99	19	3	2	36	.256	425	64	4	.992
1942—St. Louis	Amer.	C	99	273	20	61	6	1	0	26	.223	356	57	6	.986
1943—St. Louis x	Amer.	C	74	209	12	50	7	0	0	20	.239	327	52	5	.987
1944—Washington	Amer.	C	99	339	14	94	11	1	0	25	.277	403	71	9	.981
1945—Washington	Amer.	C	91	286	33	76	12	1	1	38	.266	331	64	4	.990
1947—Washington	Amer.	C	37	99	10	30	11	0	0	12	.303	134	22	1	.994
Major League Totals—18 Years			1884	6028	687	1692	324	45	28	734	.281	7248	1127	135	.984

*Made free agent by Commissioner Landis, March, 1929, and signed by St. Louis Browns for bonus of $25,000.
†Traded with Pitcher Lloyd Brown to Boston Red Sox for Catcher Merv Shea and cash, May 9, 1933.
‡Traded with Outfielder Melo Almada and Pitcher Wes Ferrell to Washington for Outfielder Ben Chapman and Pitcher Buck Newsom, June 10, 1937.
§Traded to St. Louis Browns for Pitcher Vern Kennedy, May 15, 1941.
xTraded to Washington Senators for Catcher Angelo Giuliani and cash, March 1, 1944; Browns returned Giuliani when he announced retirement and received Outfielder Gene Moore to complete deal, March 28, 1944.

FREDERICK LANDIS (FRED) FITZSIMMONS

Born July 28, 1901, at Mishawaka, Ind.
Died November 18, 1979, at Yucca Valley, Calif.
Height, 5.11. Weight, 205.
Threw and batted righthanded.

Coach, Brooklyn Dodgers, 1942; manager, Philadelphia Phillies, 1943 through 1945; coach, Boston Braves, 1948; New York Giants, 1949 through 1955, although assigned as manager of a Giants' farm club for part of 1953 season; manager, Binghamton, Eastern, 1956; coach, Chicago Cubs, 1957 through 1959; Kansas City Athletics, 1960; Salt Lake City, Pacific Coast, 1961; Chicago Cubs, 1966.

Year Club	League	G.	IP.	W.	L.	Pct.	H.	R.	ER.	SO.	BB.	ERA.
1920—Muskegon	Central	12	100	3	9	.250	114	59	....	38	30	......
1921—Muskegon	Central	34	251	14	13	.519	244	118	89	126	81	3.19
1922—Muskegon	Central	36	245	16	11	.593	250	110	91	138	74	3.34
1922—Indianapolis	Am. Assoc.	7	48	3	4	.429	48	21	17	16	20	3.19
1923—Indianapolis	Am. Assoc.	33	173	9	4	.692	185	104	87	58	49	4.53
1924—Indianapolis	Am. Assoc.	39	279	14	17	.452	313	170	141	100	74	4.55
1925—Indianapolis	Am. Assoc.	27	184	14	6	.700	189	91	77	55	50	3.77

Year	Club	League	G.	IP.	W.	L.	Pct.	H.	R.	ER.	SO.	BB.	ERA.
1925—New York	National	10	75	6	3	.667	70	25	22	17	18	2.64
1926—New York	National	37	219	14	10	.583	224	90	70	48	58	2.88
1927—New York	National	42	245	17	10	.630	260	127	101	78	67	3.71
1928—New York	National	40	261	20	9	.690	264	119	107	67	65	3.69
1929—New York	National	37	222	15	11	.577	242	122	101	55	66	4.09
1930—New York	National	41	224	19	7	★731	230	125	106	76	59	4.26
1931—New York	National	35	254	18	11	.621	242	111	86	78	62	3.05
1932—New York	National	35	238	11	11	.500	287	132	★117	65	83	4.42
1933—New York	National	36	252	16	11	.593	243	106	81	65	72	2.89
1934—New York	National	38	263	18	14	.563	266	114	89	73	51	3.05
1935—New York	National	18	94	4	8	.333	104	43	42	23	22	4.02
1936—New York	National	28	141	10	7	.588	147	58	52	35	39	3.32
1937—N.Y.(a)-Brooklyn	National	19	118	6	10	.375	119	61	57	42	40	4.35
1938—Brooklyn	National	27	203	11	8	.579	205	83	68	38	43	3.01
1939—Brooklyn	National	27	151	7	9	.438	178	79	65	44	28	3.87
1940—Brooklyn	National	20	134	16	2	★889	120	43	42	35	25	2.82
1941—Brooklyn	National	13	83	6	1	.857	78	33	19	19	26	2.06
1942—Brooklyn	National	1	3	0	0	.000	6	5	5	0	1	15.00
1943—Brooklyn(b)	National	9	45	3	4	.429	50	29	27	12	21	5.40
Major League Totals—19 Years		513	3225	217	146	.598	3335	1505	1257	870	846	3.51

aTraded to Brooklyn for pitcher Thomas Baker, June 11, 1937.
bReleased, July 28, 1943, to become manager of Philadelphia Phillies.

WORLD SERIES RECORD

Year	Club	League	G.	IP.	W.	L.	Pct.	H.	R.	ER.	SO.	BB.	ERA.
1933—New York	National	1	7	0	1	.000	9	4	4	2	0	5.14
1936—New York	National	2	11⅔	0	2	.000	13	7	7	6	2	5.40
1941—Brooklyn	National	1	7	0	0	.000	4	0	0	1	3	0.00
World Series Totals—3 Years		4	25⅔	0	3	.000	26	11	11	9	5	3.86

ELMER HARRISON FLICK

Born January 11, 1876, at Bedford, O.
Died January 9, 1971, at Bedford, O.
Height, 5.08½. Weight, 160.
Threw right and batted lefthanded.

Shares major league record for most consecutive years leading league in triples (3).
Named to Hall of Fame, 1963.

Year	Club	League	Pos.	G.	AB.	R.	H.	2B.	3B.	HR.	SB.	B.A.	PO.	A.	E.	F.A.
1896—Youngstown	Int. St.	OF	31	130	34	57	....	....	....	....	.438	....	....	....	.826
1897—Dayton	Int. St.	OF	126	474	135	183	....	....	....	....	.386	197	25	19	.921
1898—Philadelphia	Nat.	OF	133	447	84	142	16	14	7	29	.318	242	25	13	.954
1899—Philadelphia	Nat.	OF	125	486	101	167	21	14	2	31	.344	234	21	14	.948
1900—Philadelphia	Nat.	OF	138	547	106	207	33	16	11	37	.378	237	19	23	.918
1901—Philadelphia	Nat.	OF	138	542	111	182	31	17	8	26	.336	275	22	12	.961
1902—Phil.(a)-Cleve		OF	121	464	83	137	22	12	2	24	.295	171	16	13	.935
1903—Cleveland	Amer.	OF	★142	529	84	158	22	16	2	27	.299	216	14	11	.954
1904—Cleveland	Amer.	OF	149	575	95	174	31	18	5	●42	.303	231	18	10	.961
1905—Cleveland	Amer.	OF	131	500	72	154	29	★19	4	35	★308	177	18	13	.938
1906—Cleveland	Amer.	OF	★157	★624	●98	194	33	★22	1	●39	.311	248	13	5	.981
1907—Cleveland	Amer.	OF	147	549	80	166	17	★18	3	41	.302	219	22	11	.956
1908—Cleveland	Amer.	OF	9	35	4	8	1	1	0	0	.229	10	1	0	1.000
1909—Cleveland	Amer.	OF	66	235	28	60	10	2	0	9	.255	87	4	4	.958
1910—Cleveland	Amer.	OF	24	68	5	18	2	1	1	1	.265	21	0	1	.955
1911—Toledo	A. A.	OF	84	313	63	102	13	7	3	10	.326	165	10	9	.951
1912—Toledo	A. A.	OF	115	382	60	100	16	5	2	28	.262	177	9	13	.935
American League Totals—9 Years			946	3579	549	1069	167	109	18	218	.299	1380	106	68	.956
National League Totals—4 Years			534	2022	402	698	101	61	28	123	.345	988	87	62	.945
Major League Totals—13 Years			1480	5601	951	1767	268	170	46	341	.315	2368	193	130	.952

aSold to Cleveland Indians, May 16, 1902.

—DID YOU KNOW—

That although Elmer Flick batted over .310 five times in his big-league career, he won his only batting title with a .308 mark in 1905?

EDWARD CHARLES (WHITEY) FORD

Born October 21, 1928, at New York, N. Y.
Height, 5.10. Weight, 181.
Threw and batted lefthanded.

Shares major league record for most consecutive one-hit games (2), September 2 and 7, 1955.
Named as Pitcher on THE SPORTING NEWS All-Star Major League Teams, 1955-56.
Named as Pitcher on THE SPORTING NEWS American League All-Star Teams, 1961-63.
Named American League Pitcher of the Year by THE SPORTING NEWS, 1955-61-63.
Won Cy Young Memorial Award, 1961.
Scout and minor league pitching coach, New York Yankees, 1967; coach, Yankees, 1968.
Named to Hall of Fame, 1974.

Year Club	League	G.	IP.	W.	L.	Pct.	H.	R.	ER.	SO.	BB.	ERA.
1947—Butler	Mid. Atl.	24	157	13	4	.765	151	86	67	114	58	3.84
1948—Norfolk	Pied.	30	216	16	8	.667	182	83	62	171	113	2.58
1949—Binghamton	East.	26	168	16	5	.762	118	38	30	151	54	★1.61
1950—Kansas City	A. A.	12	95	6	3	.667	81	39	34	80	48	3.22
1950—New York	Amer.	20	112	9	1	.900	87	39	35	59	52	2.81
1951-52—New York	Amer.					(In Military Service)						
1953—New York	Amer.	32	207	18	6	.750	187	77	69	110	110	3.00
1954—New York	Amer.	34	211	16	8	.667	170	72	66	125	101	2.82
1955—New York	Amer.	39	254	●18	7	.720	188	83	74	137	113	2.62
1956—New York	Amer.	31	226	19	6	★.760	187	70	62	141	84	★2.47
1957—New York	Amer.	24	129	11	5	.688	114	46	37	84	53	2.58
1958—New York	Amer.	30	219	14	7	.667	174	62	49	145	62	★2.01
1959—New York	Amer.	35	204	16	10	.615	194	82	69	114	89	3.04
1960—New York	Amer.	33	193	12	9	.571	168	76	66	85	65	3.08
1961—New York	Amer.	39	★283	★25	4	★.862	242	108	101	209	92	3.21
1962—New York	Amer.	38	258	17	8	.680	243	90	83	160	69	2.90
1963—New York	Amer.	38	★269	★24	7	★.774	240	94	82	189	56	2.74
1964—New York	Amer.	39	245	17	6	.739	212	67	58	172	57	2.13
1965—New York	Amer.	37	244	16	13	.552	241	97	88	162	50	3.25
1966—New York	Amer.	22	73	2	5	.286	79	33	20	43	24	2.47
1967—New York	Amer.	7	44	2	4	.333	40	11	8	21	9	1.64
Major League Totals—16 Years		498	3171	236	106	.690	2766	1107	967	1956	1086	2.74

WORLD SERIES RECORD

Holds records for most series by pitcher (11); most games by pitcher (22), games started (22), games won (10), games lost (8), innings pitched (146), bases on balls (34), strikeouts (94) and consecutive scoreless innings (33), total series.

Year Club	League	G.	IP.	W.	L.	Pct.	H.	R.	ER.	SO.	BB.	ERA.
1950—New York	Amer.	1	8⅔	1	0	1.000	7	2	0	7	1	0.00
1953—New York	Amer.	2	8	0	1	.000	9	4	4	7	2	4.50
1955—New York	Amer.	2	17	2	0	1.000	13	6	4	10	8	2.12
1956—New York	Amer.	2	12	1	1	.500	14	8	7	8	2	5.25
1957—New York	Amer.	2	16	1	1	.500	11	2	2	7	5	1.13
1958—New York	Amer.	3	15⅓	0	1	.000	19	8	7	16	5	4.11
1960—New York	Amer.	2	18	2	0	1.000	11	0	0	8	2	0.00
1961—New York	Amer.	2	14	2	0	1.000	6	0	0	7	1	0.00
1962—New York	Amer.	3	19⅔	1	1	.500	24	9	9	12	4	4.12
1963—New York	Amer.	2	12	0	2	.000	10	7	6	8	3	4.50
1964—New York	Amer.	1	5⅓	0	1	.000	8	5	5	4	1	8.44
World Series Totals—11 Years		22	146	10	8	.556	132	51	44	94	34	2.71

ANDREW (RUBE) FOSTER

Born September 17, 1879, at Calvert, Tex.
Died December 9, 1930, at Kankakee, Ill.
Height, 6:04. Weight, 240.

Rube Foster was more than the father and savior of Negro baseball. He was the dominating factor.

As a pitcher, he was a crafty tactician. It has been said that the only "good" balls he ever threw were the fresh ones handed him by the umpire—after that first pitch, batter beware. His craftiness carried over into his managing career, where he set the style most others copied.

Dave Malarcher, the premier third baseman of his day and later a multi-pennant producer as manager in the Negro leagues, was one who learned by Foster's example.

"Foster, without a doubt, was an absolute genius in handling men, in devising strategies of defense and attack," said Malarcher. "He called every play and expected everyone to do his job . . . when it HAD to be done. His philosophy of the 'big inning' paralleled the later American League gospel—the winning team will score more runs in one inning than the losing team will score in the whole game.

"I'm proud to say he was my idol as a baseball man."

It was Foster who, having spent decades as a player in the unorganized days of independent teams representing scattered cities, devised the plan of organizing the solitary clubs into regular-schedule leagues.

His personal force and finances were the key to the better parks, better attendance and bigger income for the once-wandering teams. Contracts came into play as a rule rather than an exception and the Negro leagues became a factor in providing young black players a place to hone their talents. From this fountain came the black players who populated the major league teams after Jackie Robinson opened the door in 1947.

Foster had a varied career as player, manager, league president and founder of the Negro American and Negro National leagues. His club, the American Giants, based in Chicago, was the model from which all other Negro clubs were built.

Foster played with the Chicago Union Giants, the Cuban X Giants, the Philadelphia Giants, the Chicago Leland Giants (all independent clubs) and then the famed Chicago American Giants.

As a pitcher, Foster faced many of the top hurlers of the major leagues during exhibition play. He supposedly picked up his nickname from Rube Waddell, after recording a victory over the A's star. Foster was a colorful figure along the barnstorming trail that extended from coast to coast.

He had an eye for talent. Three of his signings attest to his genius. Catcher Bruce Petway once threw out the legendary Ty Cobb three times in one exhibition game in Cuba. John Henry Lloyd, who made the Cooperstown Hall of Fame as a shortstop, rivaled the wizardry of Honus Wagner, who personally called Lloyd his equal as a shortstop. And Malarcher, the first Negro League player to graduate from college, was a third base super star and a successful manager.

After the leagues proved successful, and after normalcy had returned to league play and the All-Star Game had become a money-maker, Foster's mind snapped.

He was committed to a mental institution in Kankakee, Ill., in 1926 and died four years later.

Thus passed a giant, a genius, a powerful pitcher, a brilliant strategist, a visionary figure who saved the Negro teams from extinction. He was a man of morality and total abstinence and the best money-maker in the history of Negro baseball.

Foster was named to the Hall of Fame in 1981. He was the 10th Negro League player to be so enshrined, but none of the previous nine would have argued if he had been the first.

GEORGE ARTHUR FOSTER

Born December 1, 1948, at Tuscaloosa, Ala.

Height, 6.01. Weight, 198.

Threw and batted righthanded.

Shares major league record for most consecutive seasons leading league in runs batted in (3).
Shares National League record for grand slams, month (2), August, 1983.
Hit three home runs in a game, July 14, 1977.
Led National League in total bases with 388 and slugging percentage with .631 in 1977.
Led California League outfielders in total chances with 285 in 1969.
Led Northwest League outfielders in double plays with 4 in 1968.
Named National League Player of the Year by THE SPORTING NEWS, 1976 and 1977.
Named National League Most Valuable Player by Baseball Writers' Association of America, 1977.
Named outfielder on THE SPORTING NEWS National League All-Star Team, 1976 through 1978 and 1981.
Named outfielder on THE SPORTING NEWS National League Silver Slugger team, 1981.

Year Club	League	Pos.	G.	AB.	R.	H.	2B.	3B.	HR.	RBI.	B.A.	PO.	A.	E.	F.A.
1968—Medford	N'west	OF	72	253	47	70	9	5	3	30	.277	★142	6	5	.967
1969—Fresno	Calif.	OF	121	449	68	144	5	8	14	85	.321	★267	14	4	★.986
1969—San Francisco	Nat.	OF	9	5	1	2	0	0	0	1	.400	3	0	0	1.000
1970—Phoenix	P. C.	OF	114	403	54	124	18	6	8	66	.308	202	5	9	.958
1970—San Francisco	Nat.	OF	9	19	2	6	1	1	1	4	.316	10	0	0	1.000
1971—S.F.†-Cin.	Nat.	OF	140	473	50	114	23	4	13	58	.241	315	9	5	.985
1972—Cincinnati	Nat.	OF	59	145	15	29	4	1	2	12	.200	71	1	2	.973
1973—Indianapolis	A. A.	OF	134	496	77	130	26	1	15	60	.262	★332	7	10	.971
1973—Cincinnati	Nat.	OF	17	39	6	11	3	0	4	9	.282	19	1	0	1.000
1974—Cincinnati	Nat.	OF	106	276	31	73	18	0	7	41	.264	172	2	2	.989
1975—Cincinnati	Nat.	OF-1B	134	463	71	139	24	4	23	78	.300	299	11	3	.990
1976—Cincinnati	Nat.	★OF-1B	144	562	86	172	21	9	29	★121	.306	322	9	2	★.994
1977—Cincinnati	Nat.	OF	158	615	★124	197	31	2	★52	★149	.320	352	12	3	.992
1978—Cincinnati	Nat.	OF	158	604	97	170	26	7	★40	★120	.281	319	10	10	.971
1979—Cincinnati	Nat.	OF	121	440	68	133	18	3	30	98	.302	214	7	4	.982

Year	Club	League	Pos.	G.	AB.	R.	H.	2B.	3B.	HR.	RBI.	B.A.	PO.	A.	E.	F.A.
1980—Cincinnati	Nat.		OF	144	528	79	144	21	5	25	93	.273	295	6	1	.997
1981—Cincinnati‡	Nat.		OF	108	414	64	122	23	2	22	90	.295	224	8	2	.991
1982—New York	Nat.		OF	151	550	64	136	23	2	13	70	.247	289	12	8	.974
1983—New York	Nat.		OF	157	601	74	145	19	2	28	90	.241	314	12	4	.988
1984—New York	Nat.		OF	146	553	67	149	22	1	24	86	.269	278	6	7	.976
1985—New York	Nat.		OF	129	452	57	119	24	1	21	77	.263	198	7	5	.976
1986—New York§	Nat.		OF	72	233	28	53	6	1	13	38	.227	96	4	4	.962
1986—Chicago x	Amer.		OF	15	51	2	11	0	2	1	4	.216	19	2	0	1.000
National League Totals—18 Years				1962	6972	984	1914	307	45	347	1235	.275	3790	117	62	.984
American League Totals—1 Year				15	51	2	11	0	2	1	4	.216	19	2	0	1.000
Major League Totals—18 Years				1977	7023	986	1925	307	47	348	1239	.274	3809	119	62	.984

Selected by San Francisco Giants' organization in 3rd round of free-agent draft, January 27, 1968.
†Traded to Cincinnati Reds for Shortstop Frank Duffy and Pitcher Vern Geishert, May 29, 1971.
‡Traded to New York Mets for Catcher Alex Trevino and Pitchers Jim Kern and Greg Harris, February 10, 1982.
§Released, August 7, 1986; signed by Chicago White Sox, August 15, 1986.
xReleased, September 7, 1986.

CHAMPIONSHIP SERIES RECORD

Year	Club	League	Pos.	G.	AB.	R.	H.	2B.	3B.	HR.	RBI.	B.A.	PO.	A.	E.	F.A.
1972—Cincinnati	Nat.		PR	1	0	1	0	0	0	0	0	.000	0	0	0	.000
1975—Cincinnati	Nat.		OF	3	11	3	4	0	0	0	0	.364	7	0	0	1.000
1976—Cincinnati	Nat.		OF	3	12	2	2	0	0	2	4	.167	7	0	0	1.000
1979—Cincinnati	Nat.		OF	3	10	1	2	0	0	1	2	.200	6	2	0	1.000
Championships Series Totals—4 Years				10	33	7	8	0	0	3	6	.242	20	2	0	1.000

WORLD SERIES RECORD

Year	Club	League	Pos.	G.	AB.	R.	H.	2B.	3B.	HR.	RBI.	B.A.	PO.	A.	E.	F.A.
1972—Cincinnati	Nat.		PR-OF	2	0	0	0	0	0	0	0	.000	0	0	0	.000
1975—Cincinnati	Nat.		OF	7	29	1	8	1	0	0	2	.276	13	1	0	1.000
1976—Cincinnati	Nat.		OF	4	14	3	6	1	0	0	4	.429	14	0	0	1.000
World Series Totals—3 Years				13	43	4	14	2	0	0	6	.326	27	1	0	1.000

JACQUES FRANK (JACK) FOURNIER

Born September 28, 1892, at Au Sable, Mich.
Died September 5, 1973, at Tacoma, Wash.
Height, 6.00. Weight, 190.
Threw right and batted lefthanded.

Hit three consecutive home runs, July 3, 1926.
Manager, Johnstown, Middle Atlantic League, 1937; Toledo, American Association, 1943; coach, University of California at Los Angeles, 1934-35; scout, St. Louis Browns, 1938 through 1942, 1944 through 1947; Chicago Cubs, 1950 through 1957; Detroit Tigers, 1960; Cincinnati Reds, 1961-62.

Year	Club	League	Pos.	G.	AB.	R.	H.	2B.	3B.	HR.	SB.	B.A.	PO.	A.	E.	F.A.
1908—Aberdeen-Seat.	N.W.		1B	34	114	5	26	4	1	1	5	.228	166	44	9	.951
1909—Portland	P.C.		1B	17	28	2	7	2	1	0	2	.250	33	9	3	.933
1909—Portland	N.W.		1B	101	345	39	73	7	4	3	17	.212	374	78	28	.942
1910—Sacramento	P.C.		1B	14	27	4	7	4	0	0	2	.259	53	10	4	.940
1911—Moose Jaw	W. Can.		1B	109	395	★106	★149	★28	★19	5	33	.377	261	121	40	.906
1912—Chicago	Amer.		1B	35	73	5	14	5	2	0	1	.192	154	16	2	.988
1912—Montreal	Int.		1B	60	217	39	67	12	8	3	13	.309	551	18	12	.979
1913—Chicago	Amer.		1B-OF	68	171	20	40	8	5	1	9	.234	306	23	5	.985
1914—Chicago	Amer.		1B	109	379	44	118	14	9	6	10	.311	1025	78	25	.978
1915—Chicago	Amer.		1B-OF	126	422	86	136	20	18	5	21	.322	784	51	17	.980
1916—Chicago	Amer.		1B	105	313	36	75	13	9	3	19	.240	855	49	20	.978
1917—Chicago	Amer.		PH	1	1	0	0	0	0	0	0	.000	0	0	0	.000
1917—Los Angeles	P.C.		1B	144	512	76	156	29	6	7	38	.305	1431	88	17	.989
1918—Los Angeles	P.C.		1B	★104	400	52	130	●26	★13	4	37	.325	....	....	...	.....
1918—New York	Amer.		1B	27	100	9	35	6	1	0	7	.350	274	13	7	.976
1919—Los Angeles	P.C.		1B	169	638	108	209	36	★19	11	44	.328	1731	114	10	★.995
1920—St. Louis	Nat		1B	141	530	77	162	33	14	3	26	.306	1373	88	★25	.983
1921—St. Louis	Nat.		1B	149	574	103	197	27	9	16	20	.343	1416	73	19	.987
1922—St. Louis (a)	Nat		1B	128	404	64	119	23	9	10	6	.295	902	60	18	.982
1923—Brooklyn	Nat.		1B	133	515	91	181	30	13	22	11	.351	1281	82	★21	.985
1924—Brooklyn	Nat.		1B	★154	563	93	188	25	4	★27	7	.334	1388	★99	22	.985
1925—Brooklyn	Nat.		1B	145	545	99	191	21	16	22	4	.350	1317	82	15	.989
1926—Brooklyn (b)	Nat.		1B	87	243	39	69	9	2	11	0	.284	548	28	8	.986

Year	Club	League	Pos.	G.	AB.	R.	H.	2B.	3B.	HR.	SB.	B.A.	PO.	A.	E.	F.A.
1927—Boston		Nat.	1B	122	374	55	106	18	2	10	4	.283	901	63	11	.989
1928—Newark		Int.	1B	148	504	87	145	26	8	22	16	.288	1177	79	17	.987
American League Totals—7 Years				471	1459	200	418	66	44	15	67	.286	3398	230	76	.979
National League Totals—8 Years				1059	3748	621	1213	186	69	121	78	.324	9126	575	139	.986
Major League Totals—15 Years				1530	5207	821	1631	252	113	136	145	.313	12524	805	215	.984

aTraded to Brooklyn Dodgers for Outfielder Hi Myers and First Baseman Ray Schmandt, February 15, 1923.
bSold to Boston Braves, November 5, 1926.

JACOB NELSON (NELLIE) FOX

Born December 25, 1927, at St. Thomas, Pa.

Died December 1, 1975, at Baltimore, Md.

Height, 5.09. Weight, 160.

Threw right and batted lefthanded.

Holds major league records for most years (8) and most consecutive years (7) leading league in singles; most years leading league in fewest strikeouts (11); most consecutive games played by second baseman (798); most years leading league in games played (8), putouts (10) and chances accepted (9) by second baseman.

Holds American League record for most years and most consecutive years with 600 or more at-bats (12); most double plays by second baseman, lifetime (1,568).

Shares American League record for most years leading league in double plays (5).

Named Most Valuable Player, American League, 1959.

Named Outstanding American League Player by THE SPORTING NEWS, 1959.

Named as second baseman on THE SPORTING NEWS All-Star Major League Teams, 1955-56-58-59.

Received Rawlings Gold Glove award as outstanding major league fielding second baseman, 1957; named for Gold Glove award as outstanding American League fielding second baseman, 1958-59-60.

Player-coach, Houston Astros, 1965; coach, 1966 through 1967; Washington Senators, 1968 through 1971; Texas Rangers, 1972.

Year	Club	League	Pos.	G.	AB.	R.	H.	2B.	3B.	HR.	RBI.	B.A.	PO.	A.	E.	F.A.
1944—Lancaster		Int.St.	1-OF	24	77	11	25	6	0	0	12	.325	123	10	6	.957
1944—Jamestown		Pony	OF	56	230	40	70	11	0	0	18	.304	114	5	3	.975
1945—Lancaster		Int.-St.	2B	●140	★573	★128	★180	19	★19	1	68	.314	★426	★400	24	★.972
1946—Philadelphia		Amer.						(In Military Service)								
1947—Lancaster		Int.-St.	2B	55	228	42	64	8	4	1	22	.281	178	165	9	.974
1947—Philadelphia		Amer.	2B	7	3	2	0	0	0	0	0	.000	1	0	0	1.000
1948—Lincoln		West.	2B	136	★576	97	★179	28	14	5	60	.311	★354	★361	28	.962
1948—Philadelphia		Amer.	2B	3	13	0	2	0	0	0	0	.154	13	6	1	.950
1949—Philadelphia(a)		Amer.	2B	88	247	42	63	6	2	0	21	.255	191	196	7	.982
1950—Chicago		Amer.	2B	130	457	45	113	12	7	0	30	.247	340	344	18	.974
1951—Chicago		Amer.	2B	147	604	93	189	32	12	4	55	.313	413	449	17	.981
1952—Chicago		Amer.	2B	152	★648	76	★192	25	10	0	39	.296	★406	★433	13	★.985
1953—Chicago		Amer.	2B	154	624	92	178	31	8	3	72	.285	★451	426	15	.983
1954—Chicago		Amer.	2B	●155	631	111	●201	24	8	2	47	.319	★400	392	9	★.989
1955—Chicago		Amer.	2B	●154	★636	100	198	28	7	6	59	.311	★399	★483	★24	.974
1956—Chicago		Amer.	2B	154	★649	109	192	20	10	4	52	.296	★478	★396	12	★.986
1957—Chicago		Amer.	2B	★155	619	110	★196	27	8	6	61	.317	★453	★453	13	.986
1958—Chicago		Amer.	2B	●155	623	82	★187	21	6	0	49	.300	★444	399	13	●.985
1959—Chicago		Amer.	2B	★156	★624	84	191	34	6	2	70	.306	★364	★453	10	★.988
1960—Chicago		Amer.	2B	150	★605	85	175	24	★10	2	59	.289	★412	★447	13	.985
1961—Chicago		Amer.	2B	159	606	67	152	11	5	2	51	.251	●413	407	15	.982
1962—Chicago		Amer.	2B	157	621	79	166	27	7	2	54	.267	376	428	★8	★.990
1963—Chicago(b)		Amer.	2B	137	539	54	140	19	0	2	42	.260	305	342	8	●.928
1964—Houston(c)		Nat.	2B	133	442	45	117	12	6	0	28	.265	231	317	13	.977
1965—Houston		Nat.	3-1-OF	21	41	3	11	2	0	0	1	.268	12	14	0	1.000
American League Totals—17 Years				2213	8749	1231	2535	341	106	35	761	.290	5859	6054	196	.984
National League Totals—2 Years				154	483	48	128	14	6	0	29	.265	243	331	13	.978
Major League Totals—19 Years				2367	9232	1279	2663	355	112	35	790	.288	6102	6385	209	.984

aTraded to Chicago White Sox for Catcher Joe Tipton, October 19, 1949.
bTraded to Houston Colt .45's for Pitcher Jim Golden, Outfielder Danny Murphy and cash, December 10, 1963.
cReleased as player and signed as coach by Houston Colts, October 9, 1964; reactivated as player, May 13, 1965.

WORLD SERIES RECORD

Year	Club	League	Pos.	G.	AB.	R.	H.	2B.	3B.	HR.	RBI.	B.A.	PO.	A.	E.	F.A.
1959—Chicago		Amer.	2B	6	24	4	9	3	0	0	0	.375	14	23	0	1.000

JAMES EMORY (JIMMIE) FOXX
(Double X and The Beast)

Born October 22, 1907, at Sudlersville, Md.
Died July 21, 1967, at Miami, Fla.
Height, 5.11½. Weight, 190.
Threw and batted righthanded.

Holds major league record for most consecutive years with 30 or more home runs (12).
Shares major league records for most consecutive home runs (4), June 7, 8, 1933; most grand slams, two consecutive games (2), May 20, 21, 1940.
Shares American League record for most home runs, doubleheader (4), July 2, 1933.
Led American League in bases on balls, 1934 and 1938 (tied).
Hit three home runs in a game, July 10, 1932 (18 innings) and June 8, 1933.
Named Most Valuable Player in American League, 1932-33-38.
Manager, Portsmouth, Piedmont League, 1944 (part); St. Petersburg, Florida International League, 1947; Bridgeport, Colonial League, 1949 (part); coach, Minneapolis, American Association, 1958.
Named to Hall of Fame, 1951.

Year Club	League	Pos.	G.	AB.	R.	H.	2B.	3B.	HR.	RBI.	B.A.	PO.	A.	E.	F.A.
1924—Easton	East.Sh.	C	76	260	33	77	11	2	10	....	.296	379	★73	●16	.966
1925—Philadelphia	Amer.	C	10	9	2	6	1	0	0	0	.667	0	0	0	.000
1925—Providence...........	Int.	C	41	101	12	33	6	3	1	15	.327	75	9	4	.955
1926—Philadelphia	Amer.	C	26	32	8	10	2	1	0	5	.313	19	5	0	1.000
1927—Philadelphia	Amer.	1B	61	130	23	42	6	5	3	20	.323	263	15	7	.975
1928—Philadelphia	Amer.	1B-3B-C	118	400	85	131	29	10	13	79	.328	416	155	17	.971
1929—Philadelphia	Amer.	1B	149	517	123	183	23	9	33	117	.354	1226	74	6	.995
1930—Philadelphia	Amer.	1B	153	562	127	188	33	13	37	156	.335	★1362	79	14	.990
1931—Philadelphia	Amer.	1B-3B	139	515	93	150	32	10	30	120	.291	988	104	15	★.986
1932—Philadelphia	Amer.	1B-3B	154	585	★151	213	33	9	★58	★169	.364	1338	97	11	★.992
1933—Philadelphia	Amer.	1B	149	573	125	204	37	9	★48	★163	★.356	1402	★93	15	.990
1934—Philadelphia	Amer.	1B	150	539	120	180	28	6	44	130	.334	1378	85	10	.993
1935—Philadelphia(a).....	Amer.	1B-3B-C	147	535	118	185	33	7	●36	115	.346	1226	93	4	★.997
1936—Boston....................	Amer.	1B-OF	●155	585	130	198	32	8	41	143	.338	1253	76	13	.990
1937—Boston....................	Amer.	1B	150	569	111	162	24	6	36	127	.285	1287	★106	8	★.994
1938—Boston....................	Amer.	1B	149	565	139	197	33	9	50	★175	★.349	1282	116	★19	.987
1939—Boston....................	Amer.	1B	124	467	130	168	31	10	★35	105	.360	1101	91	10	.992
1940—Boston....................	Amer.	1B-3B-C	144	515	106	153	30	4	36	119	.297	1023	100	10	.991
1941—Boston....................	Amer.	1B-3B-C	135	487	87	146	27	8	19	105	.300	1162	★118	14	★.989
1942—Boston(b)............	Amer.	1B	30	100	18	27	4	0	5	14	.270	231	34	1	.996
1942—Chicago................	Nat.	1B-C	70	205	25	42	8	0	3	19	.205	491	24	9	.983
1943—Chicago..................Nat.						(Did not play)									
1944—Chicago(c)............	Nat.	C-3B	15	20	0	1	1	0	0	2	.050	9	6	0	1.000
1944—Portsmouth(d)	Pied.	PH-1B	5	2	0	0	0	0	0	0	.000	0	1	0	1.000
1945—Philadelphia	Nat.	1B-3B	89	224	30	60	11	1	7	38	.268	304	54	8	.978
1946—						(Out of Organized Ball)									
1947—St. Petersburg.......	Fla. Int.	PH	6	6	0	1	....	....	....	....	.167	......	....	....	......
American League Totals—18 Years			2143	7685	1696	2543	438	124	524	1862	.331	16957	1441	173	.991
National League Totals—3 Years............			174	449	55	103	20	1	10	59	.229	804	84	17	.981
Major League Totals—20 Years..............			2317	8134	1751	2646	458	125	534	1921	.325	17761	1525	190	.990

aTraded with Pitcher John Marcum to Boston Red Sox for Pitcher Gordon Rhodes, Catcher George Savino and $150,000, December 10, 1935.
bReleased on waivers to Chicago Cubs, June 1, 1942.
cReleased as player and signed as coach, July 6, 1944; released to Portsmouth as manager, August 25, 1944.
dReleased, December, 1944; signed by Philadelphia Phillies, February 10, 1945.

PITCHING RECORD

Year Club	League	G.	IP.	W.	L.	Pct.	H.	R.	ER.	SO.	BB.	ERA.
1939—Boston...............................	Amer.	1	1	0	0	.000	0	0	0	0	0	0.00
1945—Philadelphia	Nat.	9	23	1	0	1.000	13	4	4	10	14	1.57
Major League Totals—2 Years............................		10	24	1	0	1.000	13	4	4	10	14	1.50

WORLD SERIES RECORD

Year Club	League	Pos.	G.	AB.	R.	H.	2B.	3B.	HR.	RBI.	B.A.	PO.	A.	E.	F.A.
1929—Philadelphia	Amer.	1B	5	20	5	7	1	0	2	5	.350	38	1	0	1.000
1930—Philadelphia	Amer.	1B	6	21	3	7	2	1	1	3	.333	53	3	0	1.000
1931—Philadelphia	Amer.	1B	7	23	3	8	0	0	1	3	.348	69	2	1	.986
World Series Totals—3 Years			18	64	11	22	3	1	4	11	.344	160	6	1	.994

FORD FRICK

Born December 19, 1894, at Wawaka, Ind.
Died April 8, 1978, at Bronxville, N.Y.

Born on a small farm outside Wawaka, Ind., Ford Frick retained his quiet, reserved Hoosier background his entire life. After graduating from his home state's De Pauw University in 1915, he traveled to Walsenburg, Colo., where he played first base for a semi-pro team. He remained to teach English in the high school there. From that position, he moved to an assistant professorship at Colorado College in Colorado Springs. While there, he did some sports writing for the local Gazette. By the end of the 1917 school term, he quit teaching to become a full-time reporter for the Gazette. In World War I, he did rehabilitation work with the War Department in Colorado, New Mexico and Wyoming.

Later returning to newspaper work, he did a masterful job in covering the disastrous Pueblo flood, which inundated the city and swept away hundreds of lives and millions of dollars in property. Frick found a pilot with a two-seater plane and covered the flood on-scene from the low-flying craft. He also took graphic pictures of the devastation which earned him national recognition. Arthur Brisbane, editor of the New York American, saw Frick's work and offered him a post on the sports staff, which Ford accepted.

Frick preferred the simple life and quickly settled in Bronxville, N. Y., a suburb in Westchester County, where he lived all through his active career. He covered spring training of the New York teams and even ghosted for Babe Ruth, writing a syndicated column and also a work entitled "Babe Ruth's Own Book of Baseball." Frick was an oddity in the press box, using all his fingers when he typed, whereas most of the writers used the one-, two- and three-fingered pick and peck method.

In the summer of 1934, Frick surprised his sportswriter friends by leaving the newspaper beat to become director of the National League Service Bureau, the league's publicity outlet. He didn't have to wait long for a promotion. In October of the same year, John Heydler, president of the National League, retired and a month later, Frick became N. L. president.

His chief problem as National League head was the advent of the Negro into major league ball. Jackie Robinson, the first of the modern Negroes in the majors, entered midst a storm of protest caused by racist sympathizers who feared the demise of their white refuge. Frick warned the rabble-rousers that if they persisted they would be barred from baseball . . . "even if there are so many of them that it would mean the dissolution of the National League."

After Commissioner Happy Chandler resigned under fire early in 1951, Frick became the popular choice to succeed. He was elected on September 20, 1951, and took office on October 8. He served through December 14, 1965, when he himself retired.

During his 15-year span, franchises were shifted and new ones created. The game expanded from coast-to-coast, TV became a dominant financial force in the game's policies and outcome on the field, according to the size of the market in which a club played, and the never-ending battle with Congress and the courts continued. Frick above all was a solid administrator and the financial status of the National League and the majors during his reign attest to his acumen. He felt his role was to tie in the wishes of one owner with the wishes of another, so that both could work together for the common purpose and, in a larger sense, channel all the drives of all the owners into one direction—the betterment of the game.

Named to Hall of Fame, 1970.

FRANK FRANCIS (FRANKIE) FRISCH
(The Fordham Flash)

Born September 9, 1898, at New York, N. Y.
Died March 12, 1973, at Wilmington, Del.
Height, 5.10. Weight, 185.
Threw right and batted right and lefthanded.

Holds major league records for most assists (641) and chances accepted (1,037) by second baseman, season, 1927.
Led National League in stolen bases with 49 in 1921, 48 in 1927 and 28 in 1931.
Led National League second basemen in double plays with 104 in 1927.
Manager, St. Louis Cardinals, 1933 to 1938; Pittsburgh, 1940 through 1946; Chicago Cubs, 1949 to 1951.
Named Most Valuable Player in National League, 1931.
Named to Hall of Fame, 1947.

Year	Club	League	Pos.	G.	AB.	R.	H.	2B.	3B.	HR.	RBI.	B.A.	PO.	A.	E.	F.A.
1919—New York		Nat.	2B-3B	54	190	21	43	3	2	2	22	.226	100	130	6	.975
1920—New York		Nat.	3B	110	440	57	123	10	10	4	77	.280	104	251	12	.967
1921—New York		Nat.	2B-3B	153	618	121	211	31	17	8	100	.341	226	418	33	.951
1922—New York		Nat.	2B-3B	132	514	101	168	16	13	5	51	.327	228	405	22	.966
1923—New York		Nat.	★2B-3B	151	641	116	★223	32	10	12	111	.348	327	493	22	★.974

Year	Club	League	Pos.	G.	AB.	R.	H.	2B.	3B.	HR.	RBI.	B.A.	PO.	A.	E.	F.A.
1924—New York............	Nat.		2B	145	603	•121	198	33	15	7	69	.328	★391	537	27	.972
1925—New York............	Nat.		2B-3B-SS	120	502	89	166	26	6	11	48	.331	215	393	37	.943
1926—New York (a)......	Nat.		2B	135	535	75	171	29	4	5	44	.314	261	471	19	.975
1927—St. Louis.................	Nat.		2B	153	617	112	208	31	11	10	78	.337	396	★641	22	★.979
1928—St. Louis.................	Nat.		2B	141	547	107	164	29	9	10	86	.300	383	474	21	•.976
1929—St. Louis.................	Nat.		2B-3B	138	527	93	176	40	12	5	74	.334	304	407	22	.970
1930—St. Louis.................	Nat.		2B-3B	133	540	121	187	46	9	10	114	.346	315	493	27	.968
1931—St. Louis.................	Nat.		2B	131	518	96	161	24	4	4	82	.311	290	424	19	.974
1932—St. Louis.................	Nat.		2B-3B	115	486	59	142	26	2	3	60	.292	252	309	14	.976
1933—St. Louis.................	Nat.		•2B-SS	147	585	74	177	32	6	4	66	.303	395	413	18	•.978
1934—St. Louis.................	Nat.		2B-3B	140	550	74	168	30	6	3	75	.305	325	388	20	.973
1935—St. Louis.................	Nat.		2B	103	354	52	104	16	2	1	55	.294	193	252	8	.982
1936—St. Louis.................	Nat.		2B-3B	93	303	40	83	10	0	1	26	.274	159	192	14	.962
1937—St. Louis.................	Nat.		2B	17	32	3	7	2	0	0	4	.219	12	14	0	1.000
Major League Totals—19 Years...............				2311	9112	1532	2880	466	138	105	1242	.316	4876	7105	363	.971

aTraded with Pitcher Jimmy Ring to St. Louis Cardinals for Second Baseman Rogers Hornsby, December 20, 1926.

WORLD SERIES RECORD

Year	Club	League	Pos.	G.	AB.	R.	H.	2B.	3B.	HR.	RBI.	B.A.	PO.	A.	E.	F.A.
1921—New York............	Nat.		3B	8	30	5	9	0	1	0	1	.300	13	24	2	.949
1922—New York............	Nat.		2B	5	17	3	8	1	0	0	2	.471	10	20	1	.968
1923—New York............	Nat.		3B	6	25	2	10	0	1	0	1	.400	17	18	1	.972
1924—New York............	Nat.		2B-3B	7	30	1	10	4	1	0	0	.333	17	25	0	1.000
1928—St. Louis.................	Nat.		2B	4	13	1	3	0	0	0	1	.231	8	13	0	1.000
1930—St. Louis.................	Nat.		2B	6	24	0	5	2	0	0	0	.208	13	14	3	.900
1931—St. Louis.................	Nat.		2B	7	27	2	7	2	0	0	1	.259	23	19	0	1.000
1934—St. Louis.................	Nat.		2B	7	31	2	6	1	0	0	4	.194	16	26	2	.955
World Series Totals—8 Years				50	197	16	58	10	3	0	10	.294	117	159	9	.968

JAMES F. (PUD) GALVIN

Born December 25, 1856, at St. Louis, Mo.

Died March 7, 1902, at Pittsburgh, Pa.

Height, 5.08. Weight, 190.

Threw and batted righthanded.

Pitched no-hit games against Worcester, August 20, 1880, and Detroit, August 4, 1884, his previous game against Detroit being a one-hitter. On an independent team pitching for St. Louis, Galvin hurled no-hitters against Philadelphia, July 4, 1876, and Detroit, August 17, 1876, and also for N. L. Buffalo in an exhibition against Philadelphia, October 11, 1881.

Named to Hall of Fame, 1965.

Year	Club	League	G.	IP.	W.	L.	Pct.	H.	R.	SO.	BB.	CG.	ShO.
1875—St. Louis..........................	National Assn.	9	....		4	2	.667			....		....	....
1876—St. Louis Red Stockings						(Independent ball)						
1877—Allegheny	Int. Assn.	19	....	....	....	....	....	....	....	....	....	4
1878—Buffalo............................	Int. Assn.	43	380	28	10	.737	268	....	....	....	....	7
1879—Buffalo............................	National	66	592	37	27	.578	573	299	129	28	65	6
1880—Buffalo............................	National	58	462	20	37	.351	534	276	123	32	46	5
1881—Buffalo............................	National	56	470	29	24	.547	531	248	127	47	48	5
1882—Buffalo............................	National	52	437	28	22	.560	472	256	153	40	48	3
1883—Buffalo............................	National	76	★656	46	29	.613	644	363	293	48	72	★5
1884—Buffalo............................	National	72	636	46	22	.676	525	254	373	55	71	★12
1885—Buffalo............................	National	33	287	13	19	.406	347	204	89	37	31	3
1885—Allegheny	American Assn.	11	89	3	7	.300	103	64	28	9	9	0
1886—Allegheny (a)	American Assn.	50	443	29	21	.580	461	228	77	85	49	2
1887—Pittsburgh........................	National	49	440	28	21	.571	571	259	81	70	47	3
1888—Pittsburgh........................	National	50	436	23	25	.479	437	191	113	58	49	6
1889—Pittsburgh........................	National	41	347	23	16	.590	397	226	69	79	38	4
1890—Pittsburgh........................	Players	26	216	12	13	.480	280	192	33	44	23	1
1891—Pittsburgh........................	National	33	260	14	13	.519	275	145	47	60	25	2
1892—Pitt. (b)-St. L.	National	24	188	10	13	.435	184	98	51	52	20	0
1894—Buffalo............................	Eastern	2	....	0	2	.000	......	......	......	......	......	......
National League Totals—12 Years................		610	5211	317	268	.542	5490	2819	1648	606	560	54
American Association Totals—2 Years........................		61	532	32	28	.533	564	292	105	94	58	2
Players League Totals—1 Year.................................		26	216	12	13	.480	280	192	33	44	23	1
Major League Totals—14 Years.................................		697	5959	361	309	.539	6334	3303	1786	744	641	57

aPittsburgh withdrew from American Association and joined National League in 1887.

bReleased by Pittsburgh and signed with St. Louis, June, 1892.

RALPH ALLEN GARR

Born December 12, 1945, at Monroe, La.
Height, 5.11. Weight, 185.
Threw right and batted lefthanded.

Shares major league records for most at-bats, extra-inning game (11), May 4, 1973 (20 innings); most home runs in extra innings, game (2), May 17, 1971, 10th and 12th innings.
Led National League in sacrifice hits with 18 in 1971.
Led International League in stolen bases with 63 in 1969 and 39 in 1970.
Tied for Texas League lead in stolen bases with 32 and led outfielders in double plays with 6 in 1968.
Coach, Richmond, International League, 1985 through 1987; scout, Atlanta Braves, 1988 to date.

Year Club	League	Pos.	G.	AB.	R.	H.	2B.	3B.	HR.	RBI.	B.A.	PO.	A.	E.	F.A.
1967—Austin	Texas	2B-OF	58	234	37	64	9	3	3	18	.274	103	11	16	.930
1968—Shreveport	Texas	OF	127	485	76	142	20	6	2	35	.293	222	11	12	.951
1968—Atlanta	National	PH	11	7	3	2	0	0	0	0	.286	0	0	0	.000
1969—Richmond	Int.	OF	106	438	64	144	12	5	2	25	★.329	197	10	9	.958
1969—Atlanta	National	OF	22	27	6	6	1	0	0	2	.222	6	0	1	.857
1970—Richmond	Int.	OF	98	391	83	151	26	3	7	51	★.386	182	7	6	.969
1970—Atlanta	National	OF	37	96	18	27	3	0	0	8	.281	43	0	0	1.000
1971—Atlanta	National	OF	154	639	101	219	24	6	9	44	.343	315	15	11	.968
1972—Atlanta	National	OF	134	554	87	180	22	0	12	53	.325	246	8	10	.962
1973—Atlanta	National	OF	148	668	94	200	32	6	11	55	.299	293	9	10	.968
1974—Atlanta	National	OF	143	606	87	★214	24	★17	11	54	★.353	255	8	9	.967
1975—Atlanta†	National	OF	151	625	74	174	26	★11	6	31	.278	298	12	★11	.966
1976—Chicago	Amer.	OF	136	527	63	158	22	6	4	36	.300	254	7	6	.978
1977—Chicago	Amer.	OF	134	543	78	163	29	7	10	54	.300	225	10	3	.987
1978—Chicago	Amer.	OF	118	443	67	122	18	9	3	29	.275	205	5	9	.959
1979—Chi.‡-Calif.	Amer.	OF	108	331	34	89	10	2	9	39	.269	94	3	5	.951
1980—California§	Amer.	OF	21	42	5	8	1	0	0	3	.190	3	0	1	.750
1981—Mex. City Tigers	Mexican	OF	11	34	2	9	2	0	0	0	.265	3	0	0	1.000
American League Totals—5 Years			517	1886	247	540	80	24	26	161	.286	781	25	24	.971
National League Totals—8 Years			800	3222	470	1022	132	40	49	247	.317	1456	52	52	.967
Major League Totals—13 Years			1317	5108	717	1562	212	64	75	408	.306	2237	77	76	.968

Selected by Atlanta Braves' organization in 3rd round of free-agent draft, June 6, 1967.
†Traded with Infielder Larvell Blanks to Chicago White Sox for Outfielder Ken Henderson and Pitchers Dick Ruthven and Danny Osborn, December 12, 1975.
‡Sold to California Angels, September 20, 1979.
§Released, June 6, 1980; signed with Mexico City Tigers, June 13, 1981.

STEVEN PATRICK (STEVE) GARVEY

Born December 22, 1948, at Tampa, Fla.
Height, 5.10. Weight, 190.
Threw and batted righthanded.

Holds major league records for most years leading league in games by first baseman (9); highest fielding percentage by first baseman, season, 100 and 150 or more games (1.000), 1984; fewest errors by first baseman, season, 150 or more games (0), 1984; most consecutive errorless games by first baseman, season (159), April 3 through September 29, 1984; most consecutive errorless games by first baseman, lifetime (193), June 26, second game, 1983 through April 14, 1985; most consecutive chances accepted, season, no errors, by first baseman (1,319), April 3 through September 29, 1984.
Shares major league records for most games, first baseman, season (162), 1976, 1979, 1980 and 1985; highest fielding percentage by first baseman, lifetime, (.996); most unassisted double plays, first baseman, game (2), August 31, 1976; most consecutive long hits, game (5), August 28, 1977; most long hits, game (5), August 28, 1977.
Holds National League records for most consecutive years playing in all clubs' games (7); most consecutive games played (1,207); most consecutive chances accepted, lifetime, no errors, by first baseman (1,633), June 26, first game, 1983, through April 15, 1985.
Shares National League records for most consecutive long hits, season (5), August 28, 1977; most years leading league in games played (6).

Led National League in grounding into double plays with 25 in 1979 and 1984.
Tied for National League lead in sacrifice flies with 10 in 1984.
Led National League first basemen in double plays with 138 in 1985.
Led National League first basemen in total chances with 1,606 in 1974, 1,585 in 1975, 1,669 in 1977, 1,629 in 1978 and 1,539 in 1985.
Led Pacific Coast League third basemen in errors with 24 in 1970.
Led Pioneer League in total bases with 151 and tied for league lead in sacrifice flies with 4 in 1968.
Led Pioneer League third basemen in double plays with 10 in 1968.
Named National League Most Valuable Player by Baseball Writers' Association of America, 1974.
Named first baseman on THE SPORTING NEWS National League All-Star Team, 1974, 1975, 1977 and 1978.
Named first baseman on THE SPORTING NEWS National League All-Star fielding team, 1974 through 1977.
Named third baseman on THE SPORTING NEWS College Baseball All-America Team, 1968.

Year	Club	League	Pos.	G.	AB.	R.	H.	2B.	3B.	HR.	RBI.	B.A.	PO.	A.	E.	F.A.
1968—Ogden	Pion.	3B	62	216	49	73	12	3	★20	★59	.338	★51	★109	★23	.874
1969—Albuquerque	Texas	3B-1B	83	316	51	118	18	2	14	85	.373	348	86	20	.956
1969—Los Angeles	Nat.	PH	3	3	0	1	0	0	0	0	.333	0	0	0	.000
1970—Spokane	P. C.	3B-2B-OF	95	376	71	120	26	5	15	87	.319	103	178	26	.915
1970—Los Angeles	Nat.	3B-2B	34	93	8	25	5	0	1	6	.269	23	59	5	.943
1971—Los Angeles	Nat.	3B	81	225	27	51	12	1	7	26	.227	53	161	14	.939
1972—Los Angeles	Nat.	★3B-1B	96	294	36	79	14	2	9	30	.269	104	189	★28	.913
1973—Los Angeles	Nat.	1B-OF	114	349	37	106	17	3	8	50	.304	731	27	7	.991
1974—Los Angeles	Nat.	1B	156	642	95	200	32	3	21	111	.312	★1536	62	8	.995
1975—Los Angeles	Nat.	1B	160	659	85	210	38	6	18	95	.319	★1500	77	8	★.995
1976—Los Angeles	Nat.	1B	162	631	85	200	37	4	13	80	.317	★1583	67	3	★.998
1977—Los Angeles	Nat.	1B	●162	646	91	192	25	3	33	115	.297	★1606	55	8	★.995
1978—Los Angeles	Nat.	1B	●162	639	89	★202	36	9	21	113	.316	★1546	74	9	.994
1979—Los Angeles	Nat.	1B	162	648	92	204	32	1	28	110	.315	1402	93	7	.995
1980—Los Angeles	Nat.	1B	★163	658	78	★200	27	1	26	106	.304	1502	112	6	.996
1981—Los Angeles	Nat.	1B	●110	431	63	122	23	1	10	64	.283	1019	55	1	★.999
1982—Los Angeles†	Nat.	1B	●162	625	66	176	35	1	16	86	.282	1539	111	8	.995
1983—San Diego	Nat.	1B	100	388	76	114	22	0	14	59	.294	888	49	6	.994
1984—San Diego	Nat.	1B	161	617	72	175	27	2	8	86	.284	1232	87	0	★1.000
1985—San Diego	Nat.	1B	●162	654	80	184	34	6	17	81	.281	★1442	92	5	.997
1986—San Diego	Nat.	1B	155	557	58	142	22	0	21	81	.255	1160	53	7	.994
1987—San Diego‡	Nat.	1B	27	76	5	16	2	0	1	9	.211	138	11	0	1.000
Major League Totals—19 Years			2332	8835	1143	2599	440	43	272	1308	.294	19004	1434	130	.994

Selected by Minnesota Twins' organization in 3rd round of free-agent draft, June, 1966.
Selected by Los Angeles Dodgers' organization in secondary phase of free-agent draft, June 7, 1968.
†Granted free agency, November 10, 1982; signed by San Diego Padres, December 21, 1982.
‡Granted free agency, November 9, 1987.

CHAMPIONSHIP SERIES RECORD

Holds major league records for most consecutive hits, lifetime (6), October 9, 1974 to October 4, 1977; most runs batted in, lifetime (21).

Shares major league records for most home runs, series (4), 1978; most runs, game (4), October 9, 1974; most long hits, series (6), 1978.

Holds National League records for highest slugging average, lifetime, 50 or more at-bats (.678); most home runs, lifetime (8); most long hits, lifetime (12).

Shares National League record for most hits, game (4), October 9, 1974 and October 6, 1984.

Year	Club	League	Pos.	G.	AB.	R.	H.	2B.	3B.	HR.	RBI.	B.A.	PO.	A.	E.	F.A.
1974—Los Angeles	Nat.	1B	4	18	4	7	1	0	2	5	.389	40	2	1	.977
1977—Los Angeles	Nat.	1B	4	13	2	4	0	0	0	0	.308	40	1	0	1.000
1978—Los Angeles	Nat.	1B	4	18	6	7	1	1	4	7	.389	44	5	0	1.000
1981—Los Angeles	Nat.	1B	5	21	2	6	0	0	1	2	.286	49	2	0	1.000
1984—San Diego	Nat.	1B	5	20	1	8	1	0	1	7	.400	35	3	0	1.000
Championship Series Totals—5 Years			22	90	15	32	3	1	8	21	.356	208	13	1	.995

WORLD SERIES RECORD

Year	Club	League	Pos.	G.	AB.	R.	H.	2B.	3B.	HR.	RBI.	B.A.	PO.	A.	E.	F.A.
1974—Los Angeles	Nat.	1B	5	21	2	8	0	0	0	1	.381	34	3	0	1.000
1977—Los Angeles	Nat.	1B	6	24	5	9	1	1	1	3	.375	59	6	0	1.000
1978—Los Angeles	Nat.	1B	6	24	1	5	0	0	0	0	.208	58	3	1	.984
1981—Los Angeles	Nat.	1B	6	24	3	10	1	0	0	0	.417	44	3	0	1.000
1984—San Diego	Nat.	1B	5	20	2	4	2	0	0	2	.200	34	3	0	1.000
World Series Totals—5 Years			28	113	13	36	5	1	1	6	.319	229	18	1	.996

HENRY LOUIS (LOU) GEHRIG
(The Iron Horse)

Born June 19, 1903, at New York, N. Y.

Died June 2, 1941, at Riverdale, N. Y.

Height, 6.01. Weight, 212.

Threw and batted lefthanded.

Holds major league records for most consecutive games played, lifetime (2,130), June 1, 1925 through April 30, 1939; most grand slams, lifetime (23).

Shares major league record for most home runs, game (4), June 3, 1932.

Holds American League record for most runs batted in, season (184), 1931.

Named American League Most Valuable Player by the Baseball Writers Association of America, 1927 and 1936.

Named American League Player of the Year by THE SPORTING NEWS, 1931, 1934 and 1936.

Led American League first basemen in double plays with 157 in 1938.

Named to THE SPORTING NEWS All-Star Major League Teams, 1927-28-31-34-36-37.

Named to Hall of Fame, 1939.

Year	Club	League	Pos.	G.	AB.	R.	H.	2B.	3B.	HR.	RBI.	B.A.	PO.	A.	E.	F.A.
1921—Hartford*		East.	1B	12	46	5	12	1	2	0	.....	.261	130	4	2	.985
1922—							(Not in Organized Ball)									
1923—New York		Amer.	1B-PH	13	26	6	11	4	1	1	9	.423	53	3	4	.933
1923—Hartford		East.	1B	59	227	54	69	13	8	24	.....	.304	623	23	6	.991
1924—New York		Amer.	PH-1-O	10	12	2	6	1	0	0	5	.500	10	1	0	1.000
1924—Hartford		East.	1B	134	504	111	186	40	13	37	.....	.369	1391	66	•23	.984
1925—New York		Amer.	1B-OF	126	437	73	129	23	10	20	68	.295	1126	53	13	.989
1926—New York		Amer.	1B	155	572	135	179	47	★20	16	107	.313	1566	73	15	.991
1927—New York		Amer.	1B	★155	584	149	218	★52	18	47	★175	.373	★1662	88	15	.992
1928—New York		Amer.	1B	154	562	139	210	●47	13	27	●142	.374	★1488	79	★18	.989
1929—New York		Amer.	1B	154	553	127	166	32	10	35	126	.300	1458	82	9	.994
1930—New York		Amer.	1B-OF	●154	581	143	220	42	17	41	★174	.379	1298	★89	15	.989
1931—New York		Amer.	1B-OF	155	619	★163	★211	31	15	●46	★184	.341	1352	58	13	.991
1932—New York		Amer.	1B	★156	596	138	208	42	9	34	151	.349	1293	75	18	.987
1933—New York		Amer.	1B	152	593	★138	198	41	12	32	139	.334	1290	64	9	.993
1934—New York		Amer.	1B-SS	★154	579	128	210	40	6	★49	★165	★.363	1284	80	8	.994
1935—New York		Amer.	1B	149	535	★125	176	26	10	30	119	.329	1337	82	15	.990
1936—New York		Amer.	1B	●155	579	★167	205	37	7	★49	152	.354	1377	82	9	.994
1937—New York		Amer.	1B	★157	569	138	200	37	9	37	159	.351	1370	74	★16	.989
1938—New York		Amer.	1B	●157	576	115	170	32	6	29	114	.295	1483	100	14	.991
1939—New York		Amer.	1B	8	28	2	4	0	0	0	1	.143	64	4	2	.971
Major League Totals—17 Years				2164	8001	1888	2721	534	163	493	1990	.340	19511	1087	193	.991

*Played under name of Lewis with Hartford in 1921.

WORLD SERIES RECORD

Year	Club	League	Pos.	G.	AB.	R.	H.	2B.	3B.	HR.	RBI.	B.A.	PO.	A.	E.	F.A.
1926—New York		Amer.	1B	7	23	1	8	2	0	0	3	.348	78	1	0	1.000
1927—New York		Amer.	1B	4	13	2	4	2	2	0	4	.308	41	3	0	1.000
1928—New York		Amer.	1B	4	11	5	6	1	0	4	9	.545	33	0	0	1.000
1932—New York		Amer.	1B	4	17	9	9	1	0	3	8	.529	37	2	1	.975
1936—New York		Amer.	1B	6	24	5	7	1	0	2	7	.292	45	2	0	1.000
1937—New York		Amer.	1B	5	17	4	5	1	1	1	3	.294	50	1	0	1.000
1938—New York		Amer.	1B	4	14	4	4	0	0	0	0	.286	25	3	0	1.000
World Series Totals—7 Years				34	119	30	43	8	3	10	34	.361	309	12	1	.997

CHARLES LEONARD (CHARLEY) GEHRINGER
(The Mechanical Man)

Born May 11, 1903, at Fowlerville, Mich.

Height, 5.11½. Weight, 185.

Threw right and batted lefthanded.

Named American League Most Valuable Player, 1937.

Named to THE SPORTING NEWS All-Star Major League Teams, 1933-34-37-38.

Led American League in stolen bases with 27 in 1929.

Led American League second basemen in double plays with 84 in 1927, 110 in 1932 (tie), 111 in 1933 and 116 in 1936.

Coach, Detroit Tigers, 1942; vice-president and general manager, Detroit, 1951 to 1953; vice-president of club until 1959.

Named to Hall of Fame, 1949.

Year	Club	League	Pos.	G.	AB.	R.	H.	2B.	3B.	HR.	RBI.	B.A.	PO.	A.	E.	F.A.
1924—London		Mich.-Ont.	2B	112	401	60	117	19	18	3	60	.292	309	335	23	.966
1924—Detroit		Amer.	2B	5	13	2	6	0	0	0	1	.462	12	17	1	.966
1925—Toronto		Int.	2B	155	633	128	206	38	9	25	108	.325	403	471	31	★.966
1925—Detroit		Amer.	2B	8	18	3	3	0	0	0	0	.167	8	20	0	1.000
1926—Detroit		Amer.	2B	123	459	62	127	19	17	1	48	.277	255	323	16	.973
1927—Detroit		Amer.	2B	133	508	110	161	29	11	4	61	.317	304	★438	27	.965
1928—Detroit		Amer.	2B	154	603	108	193	29	16	6	74	.320	377	★507	35	.962
1929—Detroit		Amer.	2B	●155	634	★131	●215	●45	★19	13	106	.339	★404	501	23	★.975
1930—Detroit		Amer.	2B	●154	610	144	201	47	15	16	98	.330	399	501	19	●.979
1931—Detroit		Amer.	2B	101	383	67	119	24	5	4	53	.311	224	236	10	.979
1932—Detroit		Amer.	2B	152	618	112	184	44	11	19	107	.298	★396	495	30	.967

Year Club League	Pos.	G.	AB.	R.	H.	2B.	3B.	HR.	RBI.	B.A.	PO.	A.	E.	F.A.
1933—Detroit.................. Amer.	2B	●155	628	103	204	42	6	12	105	.325	358	★542	17	.981
1934—Detroit.................. Amer.	2B	●154	601	★134	★214	50	7	11	127	.356	355	★516	17	●.981
1935—Detroit.................. Amer.	2B	150	610	123	201	32	8	19	108	.330	349	★489	13	★.985
1936—Detroit.................. Amer.	2B	154	641	144	227	★60	12	15	116	.354	397	★524	★25	★.974
1937—Detroit.................. Amer.	2B	144	564	133	209	40	1	14	96	★.371	331	485	12	★.986
1938—Detroit.................. Amer.	2B	152	568	133	174	32	5	20	107	.306	★393	★455	21	.976
1939—Detroit.................. Amer.	2B	118	406	86	132	29	6	16	86	.325	245	312	13	★.977
1940—Detroit.................. Amer.	2B	139	515	108	161	33	3	10	81	.313	276	374	19	.972
1941—Detroit.................. Amer.	2B	127	436	65	96	19	4	3	46	.220	279	324	11	★.982
1942—Detroit.................. Amer.	2B	45	45	6	12	0	0	1	7	.267	7	9	0	1.000
Major League Totals—19 Years..............		2323	8860	1774	2839	574	146	184	1427	.320	5369	7068	309	.976

WORLD SERIES RECORD

Year Club League	Pos.	G.	AB.	R.	H.	2B.	3B.	HR.	RBI.	B.A.	PO.	A.	E.	F.A.
1934—Detroit.................. Amer.	2B	7	29	5	11	1	0	1	2	.379	19	26	3	.938
1935—Detroit.................. Amer.	2B	6	24	4	9	3	0	0	4	.375	14	25	0	1.000
1940—Detroit.................. Amer.	2B	7	28	3	6	0	0	0	1	.214	18	20	0	1.000
World Series Totals—3 Years		20	81	12	26	4	0	1	7	.321	51	71	3	.976

JOSHUA (JOSH) GIBSON

Born December 21, 1911, at Buena Vista, Ga.

Died January 20, 1947, at Pittsburgh, Pa.

Height, 6.01. Weight, 215.

Threw and batted righthanded.

With Josh Gibson, the question is: Where do you start?

This man hit longer home runs in major league parks than the top sluggers of the A.L. or N.L. could. He hit a home run up the side of a mountain behind a small-town park. He was the man white ballplayers on barnstorming trips would call the most powerful hitter they ever saw.

Some say he was the best catcher, too, with a powerful arm and great sense in handling pitchers. But there are those who say he was weak on pop-ups and couldn't hit a side-arm curve. Some say he ran fast and others say he wasn't too fast.

But no one disagrees when Gibson and a bat are the subject. Tall, chesty, good legs, powerful and supple arms, big hands to wrap around a bat and the sweetest swing in the world. He had all these attributes. Add to this a great love for baseball, an insatiable urge to bat and a God-given talent to combine eye, mind and muscle in one powerful swing and you have Josh Gibson at the plate.

This is the one batter pitchers feared the most. Some batters would hit more often, but no one so combined frequency with total power. He was king of the Negro leagues and revered by fans in Caribbean winter activity as well.

Walter Johnson, the respected fireballer of the Washington Senators and considered the top righthander in the white game by most, said it all:

"There is a catcher that any big league club would like to buy for $200,000. His name is Gibson. He can do everything. He hits the ball a mile, he catches so easily he might as well be in a rocking chair, throws like a bullet. Bill Dickey isn't as good a catcher. Too bad this Gibson is a colored fellow."

Long hits? Listen to Buck Leonard, Josh's partner as the "Thunder Twins," the name given to Gibson and Leonard, who batted 3-4 in the Homestead Grays' lineup:

"I saw so many long shots hit by Josh that they got sort of commonplace after a few years. But there were two that were so different I'll never forget them. In Welch, W. Va., Josh hit a ball out of the park in dead center field and it landed on the side of a mountain. We could see the boys looking for the ball on the mountain from our dugout inside the park.

"He also hit one in Monessen, Pa., that went so far the mayor of the town had it measured. The length was determined to be 575 feet from home plate and they used one of those long tape measures."

Then Leonard had second thoughts and recalled, "There was another one, in a major league park, when we played in the old Polo Grounds, the Giants' park. He connected with one that shot into the upper deck corner in deep left-center. The night watchman brought the ball back. He said, 'They never got any balls that high and far from the plate.' "

The way Gibson broke into professional ball was unique. In 1930, the first-string catcher of the Homestead Grays broke his finger. Gibson at the time was playing for the Pittsburgh Crawfords, then a semi-pro outfit, and was a spectator at this game. Judy Johnson, manager of the Grays, was told there was a catcher in the stands who could catch and hit, too. Johnson stopped the game so Gibson could change clothes.

The Grays visited St. Louis to play the Stars and took Gibson along without a contract. Now hear Cool Papa Bell tell it:

"We had lights in St. Louis and it was a treat for the visiting players to hit balls into the air and see if they could catch them. Gibson came out and tried to catch some pop flies. We were going to sign him because he hit the longest home run ever hit in the Stars' park, but the Grays heard about our plans and they signed Gibson quick."

Cum Posey, owner of the Grays and one of the Negro executives most respected by the white press, hovered over his new charge like a doting father. Johnson, also a member of the Hall of Fame for his third base wizardry, brought Josh along slowly. Gibson did fill-in catching as a late-inning sub, worked batting practice and caught pop flies until they came out of his ears.

But Josh's bat was so powerful the Grays had to make room for him in the lineup. He became the home-run threat the fans loved to watch. That he was no Biz Mackey as a catcher or a Bruce Petway, either, no one ever argued. Bell, both a teammate and opponent of Gibson at varied times in his career, rates Mackey among the greatest catchers, white or black, and gives Mackey credit for making a glove master out of Roy Campanella, who became a Hall of Famer, but by the regular voting procedure.

Bell rates Gibson as a "good" catcher, with a strong arm, and a good handler of pitchers, but said he was poor on pop-ups. Buck Leonard had an unwritten rule that he'd take every pop-up, fair or foul, he could reach. But it was wood, not leather, that put Gibson in the Hall of Fame.

Gibson was a fun-loving, warm person who liked people and who drew people to him, but he didn't have the charisma of a Satchel Paige, who electrified a town before he even arrived. Like all sluggers, fans "hoped" Josh would connect for them, but they just "knew" Satch would mow 'em down.

Josh had a nose for the dollar and skipped to the Crawfords for four seasons and then hopped back to the Grays in 1937. He played Mexican League and Caribbean ball to pick up extra pesos, but he always came back in time to lead the Grays' drive, which resulted in nine straight Negro National League pennants. The last one was in 1945.

In 1942, he suffered severe headaches and had blacked out a few times. Medical examinations determined the presence of a brain tumor, but Gibson was afraid of the results of such an operation and refused to submit to the knife. After banging up his knees as a result of so many plate collisions, when runners came high and hard with spikes flashing, he slowed down as a runner. From one of the team's fastest base runners, he became a lumbering giant his last few seasons. On the evening of January 20, 1947, Josh came home and predicted his own demise, telling his mother that he was going to have a stroke. One version, by Robert W. Peterson in "Only The Ball Was White," tells of a fun and laughing night as Gibson lay in his bed. He asked for all his trophies to be assembled at his bedside. Once this was accomplished, he laughed, sat up in bed, then fell over dead.

Thus was snuffed out a life, at 35, which hardly had fulfilled its role. Gibson was named to the Hall of Fame in 1972.

ROBERT (BOB) GIBSON

Born November 9, 1935, at Omaha, Neb.

Height, 6.01. Weight, 193.

Threw and batted righthanded.

Holds major league record for lowest earned-run average, season, 300 or more innings (1.12), 1968.

Shares major league records for most strikeouts, inning (4), June 7, 1966, fourth inning; struck out three batters on nine pitched balls, May 12, 1969, seventh inning.

Holds National League records for lowest earned-run average, season, 200 or more innings (1.12), 1968; most clubs shut out (won or tied), season (8), 1968.

Shares National League record for most shutout games won or tied, one month (5), June, 1968.

Pitched 11-0 no-hit victory against Pittsburgh Pirates, August 14, 1971.

Named National League Most Valuable Player, 1968.

Won National League Cy Young Memorial Award, 1968-70.

Named as pitcher on THE SPORTING NEWS National League All-Star Team, 1968-70.

Named THE SPORTING NEWS National League Pitcher of the Year, 1968-70.

Named pitcher on THE SPORTING NEWS National League All-Star fielding team, 1965-66-67-68-69-70-71-72-73.

Coach, New York Mets, 1981; Atlanta Braves, 1982 through 1984.

Named to Hall of Fame, 1981.

Year Club	League	G.	IP.	W.	L.	Pct.	H.	R.	ER.	SO.	BB.	ERA.
1957—Omaha	Amer. Assoc.	10	42	2	1	.667	46	26	20	25	27	4.29
1957—Columbus	Sally	8	43	4	3	.571	36	26	18	24	34	3.77
1958—Omaha	Amer. Assoc.	13	87	3	4	.429	79	45	32	47	39	3.31
1958—Rochester	International	20	103	5	5	.500	88	35	28	75	54	2.45
1959—Omaha	Amer. Assoc.	24	135	9	9	.500	128	59	46	98	70	3.07
1959—St. Louis	National	13	76	3	5	.375	77	35	28	48	39	3.32
1960—St. Louis	National	27	87	3	6	.333	97	61	54	69	48	5.59
1960—Rochester	International	6	41	2	3	.400	33	15	13	36	17	2.85
1961—St. Louis	National	35	211	13	12	.520	186	91	76	166	★119	3.24
1962—St. Louis	National	32	234	15	13	.536	174	84	74	208	95	2.85
1963—St. Louis	National	36	255	18	9	.667	224	110	96	204	96	3.39
1964—St. Louis	National	40	287	19	12	.613	250	106	96	245	86	3.01
1965—St. Louis	National	38	299	20	12	.625	243	110	102	270	103	3.07
1966—St. Louis	National	35	280	21	12	.636	210	90	76	225	78	2.44
1967—St. Louis	National	24	175	13	7	.650	151	62	58	147	40	2.98
1968—St. Louis	National	34	305	22	9	.710	198	49	38	★268	62	★1.12
1969—St. Louis	National	35	314	20	13	.606	251	84	76	269	95	2.18
1970—St. Louis	National	34	294	●23	7	.767	262	111	102	274	88	3.12
1971—St. Louis	National	31	246	16	13	.552	215	96	83	185	76	3.04
1972—St. Louis	National	34	278	19	11	.633	226	83	76	208	88	2.46
1973—St. Louis	National	25	195	12	10	.545	159	71	60	142	57	2.77
1974—St. Louis	National	33	240	11	13	.458	236	111	102	129	104	3.83
1975—St. Louis	National	22	109	3	10	.231	120	66	61	60	62	5.04
Major League Totals—17 Years		528	3885	251	174	.591	3279	1420	1258	3117	1336	2.91

Holds records for most consecutive games won, lifetime (7); most strikeouts, game (17), October 2, 1968; most strikeouts, series (35), 1968.

Shares record for most games won, series (3), 1967.

Year	Club	League	G.	IP.	W.	L.	Pct.	H.	R.	ER.	SO.	BB.	ERA.
1964—St. Louis.........................	National	3	27	2	1	.667	23	11	9	31	8	3.00
1967—St. Louis.........................	National	3	27	3	0	1.000	14	3	3	26	5	1.00
1968—St. Louis.........................	National	3	27	2	1	.667	18	5	5	35	4	1.67
World Series Totals—3 Years		9	81	7	2	.778	55	19	17	92	17	1.89

WARREN CRANDALL GILES

Born May 28, 1896, at Tiskilwa, Ill.
Died February 7, 1979, at Cincinnati, O.

Smoke seemed to be a part of Warren Giles' life throughout his long sports career. He was a steadfast rules man, and ignited fires as a fearless football official on the college level. As a club boss at Cincinnati, he ranted and raved and sent sulphuric telegrams to league headquarters in defense of his men on the field and against the men in blue on the field. As a league head, he directed every fiber of his being against the American League, firing up the NL pride in the All-Star and World Series engagements. Once the AL had a seemingly insurmountable spread over the older league, but when Warren ignited the NL pride, the advantage swung so sharply toward his league that the American League now is far behind in All-Star Game victories. His fires made NL pride burn brightly ever since.

He also was baseball's barbecue king, tops in the smoky outdoor art.

But the most smoke was raised when he was president of the National League and ran its umpires with an iron hand. Where once he castigated these men while a club head, as league president he was their unbridled champion. He canned a few and eased out a few more, but all others knew that when they did their job on the field, Giles would back them up all the way. Warren made spot rulings on play situations as easily and as often as he had made successful decisions along the minor league trail that led to the majors.

Giles was a protege of Branch Rickey, plantation boss of the most widespread farm system in the game's history. Giles' talents in organization and fiscal control caught Rickey's eye. When the St. Louis Cardinals continued contract rights to Taylor Douthit only through Giles' honesty, the Mahatma was convinced his farm organization could use those solid talents in the front office.

Giles was born on May 28, 1896, in Tiskilwa, Ill., but played all his sports around Moline, where he was raised. A participant in all sports for Moline High School, Warren later transferred to Staunton (Va.) Military Academy, where he played football, basketball and baseball. Short finances caused his early dropout from Washington and Lee University. He enlisted in April, 1917, in officer's training school and came out of World War I a first lieutenant.

After returning home, his advice to the committee that ran the local Moline club of the Three-I League earned him the club presidency. He saw in THE SPORTING NEWS that Earle Mack, son of the legendary Connie Mack, had been fired as a minor league manager and Giles promptly hired him. With help from the Athletics, he did well. Moving to the business manager's job at St. Joseph, Mo., he picked up help from Rickey in the form of a fine outfielder, Douthit. But a St. Louis clerical error gave the St. Joseph club title to Douthit. However, Giles brought the error to Rickey's attention and told him, "Douthit is still yours."

In thanks, Rickey gave Giles the job as chief executive of Syracuse, the Redbirds' top farm. Giles considered it the real start of his baseball climb. His minor days ended in 1936, when he was given the job of getting the Cincinnati Reds out of debt, which then was $700,000, a huge figure at that time.

Giles made the Reds a club to be reckoned with on the field, a financially solid franchise and an organization with a productive farm system. He was GM from 1937 through 1947, when he became president of the Reds. His club won quick pennants in both 1939 and 1940. A strong candidate for the commissioner's post, he and Ford Frick, head of the National League, were deadlocked in the voting blocs in 1951, but Giles graciously bowed out, giving Frick the opportunity to assume the game's top position. Giles was named almost immediately to succeed Frick as NL president. He served the league well from 1952 to 1969.

Though the league climbed to the top of efficiency, surpassing the American League in new parks, income, attendance and performance, during Giles' reign as prexy, seldom did a month or week or day go by that controversy was not the way of life. Umpires were at the root of most of the smoke, but Giles added his own with beanball rulings, spitter edicts and balk interpretations—none of which was a pleasant matter for the pitchers or the umpires. Don Drysdale and his "brushbacks" of Willie Mays, Orlando Cepeda, Ed Mathews, Johnny Logan, etc., made Giles' life a bed of nails. His attempts ot make the umpires cops on the scene as to beanball intentions backfired on him (Drysdale again), but Giles was man enough to backtrack when he saw a need for adjustment.

This was Giles' strength, the executive ability to take charge when he felt it necessary and the integrity to bow to a change of his previous stand whenever the need arose. Giles' pride, his integrity and his courage to stand up and be counted were his hallmark. The strength of the National League merely reflects the personal strength of Warren Giles. He was named to the Hall of Fame in 1979.

—DID YOU KNOW—

That the last hit given up by St. Louis Hall of Famer Bob Gibson was a grand slam to the Chicago Cubs' Pete LaCock on September 3, 1975?

WILLIAM (KID) GLEASON

Born October 26, 1866, at Camden, N.J.
Died January 2, 1933, at Philadelphia, Pa.
Height, 5.7½. Weight, 175.
Threw right and batted lefthanded.
Brother of Harry Gleason, former major league third baseman.

Coach, Chicago White Sox, 1912 through 1917; manager, White Sox, 1919 through 1923; coach, Philadelphia Athletics, 1926 to 1932.

Year Club League	Pos.	G.	AB.	R.	H.	2B.	3B.	HR.	SB.	B.A.	PO.	A.	E.	F.A.
1887—Scranton................ Int. Assn.	P	23	99	13	30	...	...	...	1	.303	5	72	5	.939
1888—Philadelphia .... Nat.	P	23	83	4	17	2	0	0	3	.205	6	128	13	.912
1889—Philadelphia .... Nat.	P	28	99	11	25	5	0	0	2	.253	11	51	6	.912
1890—Philadelphia .... Nat.	P	58	224	22	47	3	0	0	10	.210	.....	.....	...	.864
1891—Philadelphia (a)... Nat.	P	60	217	30	53	4	2	0	7	.244	.....	.....	...	.777
1892—St. Louis................. Nat.	P	63	232	33	50	4	1	3	6	.216	.....	.....	...	.878
1893—St. Louis................. Nat.	P	55	184	24	49	6	5	0	2	.266	.....	.....	...	.838
1894—St.L.(b)-Balt.......... Nat.	P	31	111	24	38	3	1	1	1	.342	.....	.....	...	.841
1895—Baltimore (c)........ Nat.	P	107	408	90	132	12	12	0	26	.324	.....	.....	...	......
1896—New York.............. Nat.	2B	133	540	78	158	18	7	3	47	.293	331	392	57	.927
1897—New York.............. Nat.	2B	134	555	88	173	15	6	1	40	.312	306	403	56	.927
1898—New York.............. Nat.	2B	149	571	77	127	8	5	0	24	.222	369	463	58	.935
1899—New York.............. Nat.	2B	148	583	73	156	11	7	0	28	.268	405	482	52	.945
1900—New York (d)....... Nat.	2B	111	420	60	108	11	3	1	25	.257	325	331	47	.933
1901—Detroit.................. Amer.	2B	136	551	83	153	17	12	3	32	.278	336	452	61	.928
1902—Detroit (e) .... Amer.	2B	118	441	42	109	11	4	1	16	.247	320	353	41	.943
1903—Philadelphia .... Nat.	2B	106	412	65	117	19	6	1	12	.284	236	280	22	.959
1904—Philadelphia .... Nat.	2B	153	587	61	161	23	6	0	17	.274	379	463	52	.942
1905—Philadelphia .... Nat.	2B	155	608	95	150	17	7	1	16	.247	365	457	46	.947
1906—Philadelphia .... Nat.	2B	135	494	47	112	17	2	0	17	.227	215	358	32	.947
1907—Philadelphia .... Nat.	2B	35	126	11	18	3	0	0	3	.143	72	67	3	.979
1908—Philadelphia .... Nat.	2B-OF	2	1	0	0	0	0	0	0	.000	3	1	0	1.000
1912—Chicago .... Amer.	2B	1	2	0	1	0	0	0	0	.500	1	1	1	.667
American League Totals—3 Years		255	994	125	263	28	16	4	48	.265	657	806	103	.934
National League Totals—19 Years........		1686	6455	893	1691	181	70	11	286	.262	..	..	..	..
Major League Totals—22 Years.............		1941	7449	1018	1954	209	86	15	334	.262	..	..	..	..

aReleased following 1891 season and signed with St. Louis, National League.
bReleased, June, 1894 and signed with Baltimore Orioles.
cTraded to New York Giants for First Baseman Jack Doyle following 1895 season.
dReleased following 1900 season and signed with Detroit Tigers.
eReleased following 1902 season and signed with Philadelphia, National League.

PITCHING RECORD

Year Club	League	G.	IP.	W.	L.	Pct.	H.	R.	SO.	BB.	CG.	ShO.
1887—Scranton.........................Int. Assn.		12	....	....	....	......	159	108	....	41	....	....
1888—Philadelphia ....National		23	....	7	16	.304	200	106	....	53	....	0
1889—Philadelphia ....National		25	....	9	15	.375	246	172	74	99	....	0
1890—Philadelphia ....National		55	....	38	16	.704	....	239	220	168	....	6
1891—Philadelphia ....National		48	....	24	19	.558	....	252	96	160	....	1
1892—St. Louis.......................................National		44	....	20	24	.455	....	239	135	141	....	2
1893—St. Louis.......................................National		44	....	12	23	.343	....	....	81	165	....	1
1894—St.L.-Balt. ....National		29	....	17	11	.607	312	100	39	59	....	0
1895—Baltimore ....National		....	....	1	3	.250	....	....	....	....	....	0
Major League Totals—8 Years.......................................		..	..	128	127	.502	..	..	..	..	..	..

VERNON (LEFTY) GOMEZ

Born November 26, 1910, at Rodeo, Calif.
Died February 17, 1989, at Larkspur, Calif.
Height, 6.02. Weight, 178.
Threw and batted lefthanded.

Led American League in shutouts with 6 in 1934 (tied), 6 in 1937 and 4 in 1938, and led in complete games with 25 in 1934.

Manager, Binghamton, Eastern League, 1946 to 1947.

Named to Hall of Fame, 1972.

Year Club	League	G.	IP.	W.	L.	Pct.	H.	R.	ER.	SO.	BB.	ERA.
1928—Salt Lake	Utah-Idaho	★39	194	12	★14	.462	206	109	75	★172	61	3.48
1929—San Francisco (a)	Pacific Coast	41	267	18	11	.621	277	140	102	159	108	★3.44
1930—New York	American	15	60	2	5	.286	66	41	37	22	28	5.55
1930—St. Paul	Amer. Assn.	17	86	8	4	.667	83	46	39	57	37	4.08
1931—New York	American	40	243	21	9	.700	206	88	72	150	85	2.63
1932—New York	American	37	265	24	7	.774	266	140	124	176	105	4.21
1933—New York	American	35	235	16	10	.615	218	108	83	★163	106	3.18
1934—New York	American	38	★282	★26	5	★.839	223	86	73	★158	96	★2.33
1935—New York	American	34	246	12	15	.444	223	104	87	138	86	3.18
1936—New York	American	31	189	13	7	.650	184	104	92	105	122	4.38
1937—New York	American	34	278	★21	11	.656	233	88	72	★194	93	★2.33
1938—New York	American	32	239	18	12	.600	239	110	89	129	99	3.35
1939—New York	American	26	198	12	8	.600	173	80	75	102	84	3.41
1940—New York	American	9	27	3	3	.500	37	20	20	14	18	6.67
1941—New York	American	23	156	15	5	★.750	151	76	65	76	103	3.75
1942—New York (b)	American	13	80	6	4	.600	67	42	38	41	65	4.28
1943—Washington	American	1	5	0	1	.000	4	4	3	0	5	5.40
1946—Binghamton	Eastern	1	3	0	0	.000	5	3	3	1	0	9.00
1947—Binghamton	Eastern	1	1	0	0	.000	1	0	0	0	1	0.00
Major League Totals—14 Years		368	2503	189	102	.649	2290	1091	930	1468	1095	3.34

aSold to New York Yankees for $35,000.

bSold to Boston Braves, January 25, 1943; released, May 19, 1943; signed by Washington, May 24, 1943.

WORLD SERIES RECORD

Holds record for most victories without a defeat, lifetime (6).

Shares record for most bases on balls received, inning (2), October 6, 1937, sixth inning.

Year Club	League	G.	IP.	W.	L.	Pct.	H.	R.	ER.	SO.	BB.	ERA.
1932—New York	American	1	9	1	0	1.000	9	2	1	8	1	1.00
1936—New York	American	2	15⅓	2	0	1.000	14	8	8	9	11	4.70
1937—New York	American	2	18	2	0	1.000	16	3	3	8	2	1.50
1938—New York	American	1	7	1	0	1.000	9	3	3	5	1	3.86
1939—New York	American	1	1	0	0	.000	3	1	1	1	0	9.00
World Series Totals—5 Years		7	50⅓	6	0	1.000	51	17	16	31	15	2.86

WILLIAM DALE (BILLY) GOODMAN

Born March 22, 1926, at Concord, N.C.

Died October 1, 1984, at Sarasota, Fla.

Height, 5.11½. Weight, 160.

Threw right and batted lefthanded.

Player-manager, Durham, Carolina League, 1963-64; scout, Houston Astros, 1965; managed Houston farm at Cocoa, Florida State League, 1965; scout, Boston Red Sox, 1966; instructor, Kansas City farm organization, 1967; coach, Atlanta Braves, 1968 through 1970; minor league instructor, Atlanta Braves system, 1976, coach, Richmond, International League, 1976.

Year Club	League	Pos.	G.	AB.	R.	H.	2B.	3B.	HR.	RBI.	B.A.	PO.	A.	E.	F.A.
1944—Atlanta	South.	OF	137	★554	★122	186	22	●13	2	64	.336	258	19	12	.958
1945—Atlanta	South.						(In Military Service)								
1946—Atlanta	South.	OF-1B	86	332	65	129	14	3	1	46	.389	228	10	11	.956
1947—Boston	Amer.	OF	12	11	1	2	0	0	0	1	.182	2	0	0	1.000
1947—Louisville	A.A.	SS-OF	94	329	55	112	18	8	2	49	.340	155	130	15	.950
1948—Boston	Amer.	INF	127	445	65	138	27	2	1	66	.310	73	9	9	.992
1949—Boston	Amer.	1B	122	443	54	132	23	3	0	56	.298	1069	79	9	★.992
1950—Boston	Amer.	INF-OF	110	424	91	150	25	3	4	68	★.354	344	89	9	.890
1951—Boston	Amer.	INF-OF	141	546	92	162	34	4	0	50	.297	742	170	14	.985
1952—Boston	Amer.	INF-OF	138	513	79	157	27	3	4	56	.306	475	367	20	.977
1953—Boston	Amer.	2B-1B	128	514	73	161	33	5	2	41	.313	418	319	21	.972
1954—Boston	Amer.	INF-OF	127	489	71	148	25	4	1	36	.303	248	14	14	.979
1955—Boston	Amer.	2-1-OF	149	599	100	176	31	2	0	52	.294	395	378	24	.970
1956—Boston	Amer.	2B	105	399	61	117	22	8	2	38	.293	215	266	●17	.966
1957—Bos.(a)-Balt.(b)	Amer.	INF-OF	91	279	37	82	11	3	3	33	.294	134	110	11	.957

Year Club	League	Pos.	G.	AB.	R.	H.	2B.	3B.	HR.	RBI.	B.A.	PO.	A.	E.	F.A.
1958—Chicago	Amer.	INF	116	425	41	127	15	5	0	40	.299	89	210	13	.958
1959—Chicago	Amer.	3B-2B	104	268	21	67	14	1	1	28	.250	61	140	10	.953
1960—Chicago	Amer.	3B-2B	30	77	5	18	4	0	0	6	.234	26	52	1	.987
1961—Chicago(c)	Amer.	INF	41	51	4	13	4	0	1	10	.255	11	14	1	.962
1962—Houston	Nat.	2B-3B	82	161	12	41	4	1	0	10	.255	67	9	8	.905
1963—Durham	Caro.	1B-2B	71	175	29	62	12	0	6	37	.354	258	55	6	.981
1964—Durham	Caro.	2B-3B	43	80	13	26	6	0	1	22	.325	36	63	4	.961
American League Totals—15 Years			1541	5483	795	1650	295	43	19	581	.301	5475	2515	173	.979
National League Totals—1 Year			82	161	12	41	4	1	0	10	.255	67	9	8	.905
Major League Totals—16 Years			1623	5644	807	1691	299	44	19	591	.300	5542	2524	181	.978

aTraded to Baltimore Orioles for Pitcher Mike Fornieles, June 14, 1957.

bTraded to Chicago White Sox with Pitcher Ray Moore and First Baseman-Outfielder Tito Francona for Pitchers Jack Harshman and Russ Heman, First Baseman Jim Marshall and Outfielder Larry Doby, December 3, 1957.

cReleased, May 9, 1962; signed with Houston Colts, May 14, 1962.

WORLD SERIES RECORD

Year Club	League	Pos.	G.	AB.	R.	H.	2B.	3B.	HR.	RBI.	B.A.	PO.	A.	E.	F.A.
1959—Chicago	Amer.	3B	5	13	1	3	0	0	0	1	.231	1	2	0	1.000

JOSEPH LOWELL (JOE) GORDON

Born February 18, 1915, at Los Angeles, Calif.

Died April 14, 1978, at Sacramento, Calif.

Height, 5.10. Weight, 175.

Threw and batted righthanded.

Named as second baseman on THE SPORTING NEWS All-Star Major League Teams, 1939-40-41-42-47.

Named Most Valuable Player in American League, 1942.

Player-manager, Sacramento, Pacific Coast League, 1951-52; scout, Detroit Tigers, 1953 through 1955; coach, Detroit, 1956; manager, San Francisco, Pacific Coast League, 1956-57; manager, Cleveland Indians, 1958-59 until swapped managerial jobs with Jimmie Dykes of Detroit Tigers, August 3, 1960; manager, Kansas City Athletics, 1961; scout, batting instructor, Los Angeles Angels, 1962 through 1968; manager, Kansas City Royals, 1969; special assignment scout, Kansas City, 1970-71.

Year Club	League	Pos.	G.	AB.	R.	H.	2B.	3B.	HR.	RBI.	B.A.	PO.	A.	E.	F.A.
1936—Oakland	P. C.	SS	143	533	73	160	33	4	6	56	.300	217	390	42	.935
1937—Newark	Int.	2B	151	635	109	178	33	6	26	89	.280	383	481	47	.948
1938—New York	Amer.	2B	127	458	83	117	24	7	25	97	.255	290	450	★31	.960
1939—New York	Amer.	2B	151	567	92	161	32	5	28	111	.284	★370	★461	28	.967
1940—New York	Amer.	2B	★155	616	112	173	32	10	30	103	.281	374	★505	23	.975
1941—New York	Amer.	★2B-1B	★156	588	104	162	26	7	24	87	.276	556	414	★36	.964
1942—New York	Amer.	2B	147	538	88	173	29	4	18	103	.322	354	442	★28	.966
1943—New York	Amer.	2B	152	543	82	135	28	5	17	69	.249	407	●490	●29	.969
1944-45—New York	Amer.							(In Military Service)							
1946—New York(a)	Amer.	2B	112	376	35	79	15	6	11	47	.210	281	346	17	.974
1947—Cleveland	Amer.	2B	155	562	89	153	27	6	29	93	.272	341	●466	18	.978
1948—Cleveland	Amer.	2B-SS	144	550	96	154	21	4	32	124	.280	332	439	23	.971
1949—Cleveland	Amer.	2B	148	541	74	136	18	3	20	84	.251	297	430	15	.980
1950—Cleveland	Amer.	2B	119	368	59	87	12	1	19	57	.236	224	283	16	.969
1951—Sacramento	P.C.	2B-SS	148	485	97	145	24	3	★43	★136	.299	349	390	24	.969
1952—Sacramento	P.C.	2B-1B	122	370	39	91	18	0	16	46	.246	301	285	17	.972
1953-54-55-56									(Did not play)						
1957—San Francisco	P.C.	2B	1	3	0	2	0	0	0	0	.667	1	1	0	1.000
Major League Totals—11 Years			1566	5707	914	1530	264	52	253	975	.268	3826	4726	264	.970

aTraded to Cleveland Indians with Infielder Eddie Bockman for Pitcher Allie Reynolds, October 19, 1946.

WORLD SERIES RECORD

Year Club	League	Pos.	G.	AB.	R.	H.	2B.	3B.	HR.	RBI.	B.A.	PO.	A.	E.	F.A.
1938—New York	Amer.	2B	4	15	3	6	2	0	1	6	.400	12	12	2	.923
1939—New York	Amer.	2B	4	14	1	2	0	0	0	1	.143	7	12	0	1.000
1941—New York	Amer.	2B	5	14	2	7	1	1	1	5	.500	6	19	1	.962
1942—New York	Amer.	2B	5	21	1	2	1	0	0	0	.095	11	12	0	1.000
1943—New York	Amer.	2B	5	17	2	4	1	0	1	2	.235	20	23	0	1.000
1948—Cleveland	Amer.	2B	6	22	3	4	0	0	1	2	.182	15	13	1	.966
World Series Totals—6 Years			29	103	12	25	5	1	4	16	.243	71	91	4	.976

GEORGE F. GORE

Born May 3, 1857, at Saccarappa, Me.
Died September 16, 1933, at Utica, N. Y.
Height, 6.00. Weight, 180.
Threw right and batted lefthanded.

Year Club League	Pos.	G.	AB.	R.	H.	2B.	3B.	HR.	SB.	B.A.	PO.	A.	E.	F.A.
1878—New Bedford .... I. Assn.	OF	3	13	1	1	0	0	0	....	.077	6	0	1	.857
1879—Chicago .... Nat.	OF	60	253	43	68	17	5	0	....	.269	91	9	15	.870
1880—Chicago .... Nat.	OF-1B	75	312	69	114	21	2	2	....	★.365	119	16	20	.871
1881—Chicago .... Nat.	O-1-SS	73	309	★86	92	20	8	1	....	.298	146	21	24	.874
1882—Chicago .... Nat.	OF	84	367	★99	117	14	7	3	....	.319	153	23	33	.842
1883—Chicago .... Nat.	OF	91	392	105	131	27	9	1	....	.334	196	27	34	.868
1884—Chicago .... Nat.	OF	101	417	103	132	18	5	5	....	.317	184	25	32	.867
1885—Chicago .... Nat.	OF	109	441	115	138	19	12	4	....	.313	204	17	29	.884
1886—Chicago .... Nat.	OF	118	444	150	135	19	13	6	23	.304	184	20	29	.876
1887—New York .... Nat.	OF	111	500	95	174	16	5	1	39	.348	221	20	30	.889
1888—New York .... Nat.	OF	64	254	37	56	5	4	2	11	.220	88	4	18	.836
1889—New York .... Nat.	OF	119	488	131	149	21	7	7	36	.305	239	21	★41	.864
1890—New York .... Play.	OF	93	400	131	134	25	9	9	30	.335	150	12	20	.890
1891—New York .... Nat.	OF	130	526	104	150	24	7	2	28	.285	231	16	28	.898
1892—N.Y.-St.L. .... Nat.	OF	73	263	56	63	11	3	0	25	.240	136	9	14	.912
1893—						(Out of Organized Ball)								
1894—Binghamton .... East.	OF	48	191	46	61	17	1	1	5	.319	99	10	5	.959
Players League Totals—1 Year..............		93	400	131	134	25	9	9	30	.335	150	12	20	.890
National League Totals—13 Years........		1208	4966	1193	1519	232	87	34	162	.306	2192	228	347	.868
Major League Totals—14 Years		1301	5366	1324	1653	257	96	43	192	.308	2342	240	367	.876

LEON ALLEN (GOOSE) GOSLIN

Born October 16, 1900, at Salem, N. J.
Died May 15, 1971, at Bridgeton, N. J.
Height, 5.11. Weight, 180.
Threw right and batted lefthanded.

Hit three home runs in a game, June 19, 1925; August 19, 1930 and June 23, 1932.
Led American League outfielders in double plays, 1926, 1933 (tie).
Manager, Trenton, Inter-State League, 1939-41.
Named to Hall of Fame, 1968.

Year Club League	Pos.	G.	AB.	R.	H.	2B.	3B.	HR.	RBI.	B.A.	PO.	A.	E.	F.A.
1920—Columbia .... Sally	OF-P	90	319	52	101	18	8	4	65	.317	134	32	9	.949
1921—Columbia .... Sally	OF	142	549	★124	★214	38	13	16	★131	★.390	321	20	15	.958
1921—Washington .... Amer.	OF	14	50	8	13	1	1	1	6	.260	30	1	0	1.000
1922—Washington .... Amer.	OF	101	358	44	116	19	7	3	53	.324	197	8	15	.932
1923—Washington .... Amer.	OF	150	600	86	180	29	●18	9	99	.300	310	26	15	.957
1924—Washington .... Amer.	OF	154	579	100	199	30	17	12	★129	.344	369	12	★16	.960
1925—Washington .... Amer.	OF	150	601	116	201	34	★20	18	113	.334	385	●24	12	.971
1926—Washington .... Amer.	OF	147	568	105	201	26	15	17	108	.354	373	●25	●15	.964
1927—Washington .... Amer.	OF	148	581	96	194	37	15	13	120	.334	356	8	17	.955
1928—Washington .... Amer.	OF	135	456	80	173	36	10	17	102	★.379	266	14	11	.962
1929—Washington .... Amer.	OF	145	553	82	159	28	7	18	91	.288	299	7	10	.968
1930—Wash.(a)-St.L. .... Amer.	OF	148	584	115	180	36	12	37	138	.308	309	15	12	.964
1931—St. Louis .... Amer.	OF	151	591	114	194	42	10	24	105	.328	319	14	14	.960
1932—St. Louis(b) .... Amer.	OF	150	572	88	171	28	9	17	104	.299	330	★16	18	.951
1933—Washington(c) ..... Amer.	OF	132	549	97	163	35	10	10	64	.297	261	17	10	.965
1934—Detroit .... Amer.	OF	151	614	106	187	38	7	13	100	.305	290	15	15	.953
1935—Detroit .... Amer.	OF	147	590	88	172	34	6	9	109	.292	326	6	12	.965
1936—Detroit .... Amer.	OF	147	572	122	180	33	8	24	125	.315	266	11	13	.955
1937—Detroit(d) .... Amer.	OF	79	181	30	43	11	1	4	35	.238	81	2	4	.954
1938—Washington .... Amer.	OF	38	57	6	9	3	0	2	8	.158	25	0	0	1.000
1939—Trenton .... Int.-St.	OF	99	349	65	113	12	5	3	58	.324	120	9	2	.985
1940—Trenton .... Int.-St.	OF	49	128	24	32	4	2	1	16	.250	50	0	2	.962
Major League Totals—18 Years...............		2287	8656	1483	2735	500	173	248	1609	.316	4792	221	209	.960

aTraded to St. Louis Browns for Pitcher Alvin Crowder and Outfielder Heinie Manush, June 14, 1930.
bTraded to Washington Senators with Pitcher Lefty Stewart and Outfielder Fred Schulte for Pitcher Lloyd Brown, Outfielders Carl Reynolds and Sam West and $20,000, December 14, 1932.
cTraded to Detroit Tigers for Outfielder Jonathan Stone, December 14, 1933.
dReleased, May, 1938; subsequently signed with Washington Senators.

WORLD SERIES RECORD

Year Club	League	Pos.	G.	AB.	R.	H.	2B.	3B.	HR.	RBI.	B.A.	PO.	A.	E.	F.A.
1924—Washington	Amer.	OF	7	32	4	11	1	0	3	7	.344	15	1	0	1.000
1925—Washington	Amer.	OF	7	26	6	8	1	0	3	6	.308	15	0	0	1.000
1933—Washington	Amer.	OF	5	20	2	5	1	0	1	1	.250	8	1	0	1.000
1934—Detroit	Amer.	OF	7	29	2	7	1	0	0	2	.241	20	1	2	.913
1935—Detroit	Amer.	OF	6	22	2	6	1	0	0	3	.273	12	0	1	.923
World Series Totals—5 Years			32	129	16	37	5	0	7	19	.287	70	3	3	.961

GEORGE FARLEY GRANTHAM

Born May 20, 1900, at Galena, Kan.
Died March 16, 1954, at Kingman, Ariz.
Height, 5.10. Weight, 155.
Threw right and batted lefthanded.

Year Club	League	Pos.	G.	AB.	R.	H.	2B.	3B.	HR.	RBI.	B.A.	PO.	A.	E.	F.A.
1920—Tacoma	P. Int.	3B	58	169	19	38	9	1	0	.....	.225	63	46	10	.916
1921—Tacoma	P. Int.	3B-2B	46	153	28	55	10	6	4	.....	.359	77	78	12	.928
1921—Portland	P. C.	2B-3B	77	269	32	82	15	2	1	.....	.305	120	217	40	.894
1922—Omaha	West.	3B	157	601	160	216	47	13	22	.....	.359	*162	281	*57	.886
1922—Chicago	Nat.	3B	7	23	3	4	1	1	0	3	.174	5	4	0	1.000
1923—Chicago	Nat.	2B	152	570	81	160	36	8	8	70	.281	*374	*518	*55	.942
1924—Chicago(a)	Nat.	2B	127	469	85	148	19	6	12	60	.316	273	426	*44	.941
1925—Pittsburgh	Nat.	1B	114	359	74	117	24	6	8	52	.326	925	44	11	.989
1926—Pittsburgh	Nat.	1B	141	449	66	143	27	13	8	70	.318	1203	66	13	.990
1927—Pittsburgh	Nat.	1B-2B	151	531	96	162	33	11	8	66	.305	526	375	35	.963
1928—Pittsburgh	Nat.	1B	124	440	93	142	24	9	10	85	.323	1117	71	17	.986
1929—Pittsburgh	Nat.	1-2-OF	110	349	85	107	23	10	12	90	.307	301	244	17	.970
1930—Pittsburgh	Nat.	2B	146	552	120	179	34	14	18	99	.324	324	488	*36	.958
1931—Pittsburgh(b)	Nat.	1B-2B	127	465	91	142	26	6	10	46	.305	856	169	35	.967
1932—Cincinnati	Nat.	1B-2B	126	493	81	144	29	6	6	39	.292	373	352	28	.963
1933—Cincinnati(c)	Nat.	1B-2B	87	260	32	53	14	3	4	28	.204	274	196	19	.961
1934—New York	Nat.	1B-3B	32	29	5	7	2	0	1	4	.241	17	2	0	1.000
1934—Nashville	Sou. Assn.	1B	46	162	29	52	8	2	4	29	.321	427	17	5	.989
1935—Seattle	P. C.	1B	47	168	30	48	9	1	1	13	.286	359	19	8	.979
Major League Totals—13 Years			1444	4989	912	1508	292	93	105	712	.302	6568	2955	310	.968

aTraded to Pittsburgh Pirates with Pitcher Vic Aldridge and First Baseman Al Niehaus for Pitcher Wilbur Cooper, First Baseman Charley Grimm and Infielder Rabbit Maranville, October 27, 1924.
bSold to Cincinnati Reds, February 4, 1932.
cTraded to New York Giants for Pitcher Glenn Spencer, November 15, 1933.

WORLD SERIES RECORD

Year Club	League	Pos.	G.	AB.	R.	H.	2B.	3B.	HR.	RBI.	B.A.	PO.	A.	E.	F.A.
1925—Pittsburgh	Nat.	1B-PH	5	15	0	2	0	0	0	0	.133	42	6	0	1.000
1927—Pittsburgh	Nat.	2B	3	11	0	4	1	0	0	0	.364	6	7	1	.929
World Series Totals—2 Years			8	26	0	6	1	0	0	0	.231	48	13	1	.984

HENRY BENJAMIN (HANK) GREENBERG

Born January 1, 1911, at New York, N.Y.
Died September 4, 1986, at Beverly Hills, Calif.
Height, 6.03½. Weight, 215.
Threw and batted righthanded.

Holds major league record for most times two or more home runs in a game, season (11), 1938.
Shares major league record for most home runs by righthanded batter, season (58), 1938.
Named by Baseball Writers' Association of America as first baseman for THE SPORTING NEWS All-Star Major League Team, 1935, and left fielder, 1940.
Selected as Most Valuable Player, American League, 1935 and 1940.
General manager, Cleveland Indians, 1948-57; vice-president, Chicago White Sox, 1959-63.
Named to Hall of Fame, 1956.

Year	Club	League	Pos.	G.	AB.	R.	H.	2B.	3B.	HR.	RBI.	B.A.	PO.	A.	E.	F.A.
1930—Hartford	East.	1B	17	56	10	12	1	2	2	6	.214	157	13	2	.988
1930—Raleigh	Pied.	1B	122	452	88	142	26	14	19	93	.314	1052	★78	23	.980
1930—Detroit	Amer.	1B	1	1	0	0	0	0	0	0	.000	0	0	0	.000
1931—Evansville	I.I.I.	1B	●126	487	88	155	★41	10	15	85	.318	★1248	★84	★25	.982
1931—Beaumont	Texas	PH	3	2	0	0	0	0	0	0	.000	0	0	0	.000
1932—Beaumont	Texas	1B	154	600	★123	174	31	11	★39	131	.290	1437	103	17	.989
1933—Detroit	Amer.	1B	117	449	59	135	33	3	12	87	.301	1133	63	14	.988
1934—Detroit	Amer.	1B	153	593	118	201	★63	7	26	139	.339	1454	84	16	.990
1935—Detroit	Amer.	1B	152	619	121	203	46	16	●36	★170	.328	1437	★99	13	.992
1936—Detroit	Amer.	1B	12	46	10	16	6	2	1	16	.348	119	9	1	.992
1937—Detroit	Amer.	1B	154	594	137	200	49	14	40	★183	.337	★1477	102	13	.992
1938—Detroit	Amer.	1B	155	556	★144	175	23	4	★58	146	.315	★1484	★120	14	.991
1939—Detroit	Amer.	1B	138	500	112	156	42	7	33	112	.312	1205	75	9	●.993
1940—Detroit	Amer.	OF	148	573	129	195	★50	8	★41	★150	.340	298	14	★15	.954
1941—Detroit	Amer.	OF	19	67	12	18	7	1	2	12	.269	32	0	3	.914
1942-43-44—Detroit	Amer.						(In Military Service)									
1945—Detroit	Amer.	OF	78	270	47	84	20	2	13	60	.311	129	3	0	1.000
1946—Detroit (a)	Amer.	1B	142	523	91	145	29	5	★44	★127	.277	1272	93	●15	.989
1947—Pittsburgh (b)	Nat.	1B	125	402	71	100	13	2	25	74	.249	983	79	9	.992
American League Totals—12 Years				1269	4791	980	1528	366	69	306	1202	.319	10040	662	113	.990
National League Totals—1 Year				125	402	71	100	13	2	25	74	.249	983	79	9	.992
Major League Totals—13 Years				1394	5193	1051	1628	379	71	331	1276	.313	11023	741	122	.990

aSold to Pittsburgh Pirates, January 8, 1947.
bReleased, September 29, 1947.

WORLD SERIES RECORD

Year	Club	League	Pos.	G.	AB.	R.	H.	2B.	3B.	HR.	RBI.	B.A.	PO.	A.	E.	F.A.
1934—Detroit	Amer.	1B	7	28	4	9	2	1	1	7	.321	60	4	1	.985
1935—Detroit	Amer.	1B	2	6	1	1	0	0	1	2	.167	17	2	3	.864
1940—Detroit	Amer.	OF	7	28	5	10	2	1	1	6	.357	12	0	0	1.000
1945—Detroit	Amer.	OF	7	23	7	7	3	0	2	7	.304	8	1	0	1.000
World Series Totals—4 Years				23	85	17	27	7	2	5	22	.318	97	7	4	.963

MICHAEL JOSEPH (MIKE) GRIFFIN

Born March 20, 1865, at Utica, N.Y.

Died April 10, 1908, at Utica, N.Y.

Height, 5.08. Weight, 173.

Threw right and batted lefthanded.

Manager, Brooklyn, N.L., 1898 (part).

Year	Club	League	Pos.	G.	AB.	R.	H.	2B.	3B.	HR.	SB.	B.A.	PO.	A.	E.	F.A.
1885—Utica	N.Y. St.	OF	75	287	52	80	...	...	...	...	.279	114	18	16	.892
1886—Utica	Int.	OF	96	406	86	116	...	...	...	...	.286	196	7	17	.923
1887—Baltimore	A.A.	OF	136	581	142	214	32	12	4	98	.368	256	14	20	.931
1888—Baltimore	A.A.	OF	137	540	94	141	24	9	0	53	.261	282	28	19	.942
1889—Baltimore	A.A.	OF-SS	137	533	152	149	24	13	5	43	.280	279	86	45	.890
1890—Philadelphia	Play.	OF	115	492	127	143	28	5	6	30	.291	281	41	12	.961
1891—Brooklyn	Nat.	OF	133	517	106	141	★36	9	3	75	.273	243	25	16	.944
1892—Brooklyn	Nat.	OF	129	459	103	127	18	11	2	64	.277	260	26	9	★.969
1893—Brooklyn	Nat.	OF	93	348	84	106	22	8	6	47	.305	220	24	10	.961
1894—Brooklyn	Nat.	OF	106	405	123	148	29	5	5	48	.365	298	13	12	★.963
1895—Brooklyn	Nat.	OF	132	522	139	175	35	8	4	27	.335	★361	20	11	★.972
1896—Brooklyn	Nat.	OF	122	492	102	155	28	10	4	27	.315	315	7	13	.961
1897—Brooklyn	Nat.	OF	134	530	137	170	23	11	1	23	.321	●352	13	17	.955
1898—Brooklyn (a)	Nat.	OF	134	544	92	161	17	5	1	14	.296	319	19	7	.980
American Assn. Totals—3 Years				410	1654	388	504	80	34	9	194	.312	817	128	84	.918
National League Totals—8 Years				983	3817	886	1183	208	67	26	325	.310	2368	147	95	.964
Players League Totals—1 Year				115	492	127	143	28	5	6	30	.291	281	41	12	.961
Major League Totals—12 Years				1508	5963	1401	1830	316	106	41	549	.307	3466	316	191	.952

aSold to St. Louis, National League, after season, but refused to report and retired instead.

CLARK CALVIN GRIFFITH
(The Old Fox)

Born November 20, 1869, at Nevada, Mo.
Died October 27, 1955, at Washington, D. C.
Height, 5.08. Weight, 175.
Threw and batted righthanded.

Manager, Chicago White Sox, 1901-02; New York Highlanders, 1903 through 1908; Cincinnati, 1909-10-11; Washington Senators, 1912 through 1920; president, 1920 until time of death.
Named to Hall of Fame, 1946.

Year Club	League	G.	IP.	W.	L.	Pct.	ShO.	H.	SO.	BB.
1888—Bloomington	Cent.-Int. St.	14	....	10	4	.714	....	90	123	16
1888—Milwaukee	Western	23	....	12	10	.545	....	176	130	50
1889—Milwaukee	Western	31	....	18	13	.581	....	281	159	91
1890—Milwaukee	Western	34	....	27	7	.794	....	268	169	92
1891—St. Louis-Boston	Amer. Assn.	24	225	17	7	.708	0	219	65	69
1892—Tacoma	P. N. W.	24	....	13	7	.650	....	153	114	55
1893—Oakland	Pacific Coast	48	....	30	18	.625	....	455	151	119
1893—Chicago	National	3	22	1	1	.500	0	....	....	....
1894—Chicago	National	32	274	21	11	.656	0	302	67	79
1895—Chicago	National	39	352	25	13	.658	0	423	83	88
1896—Chicago	National	35	319	22	13	.629	0	348	82	69
1897—Chicago	National	46	344	21	19	.525	1	414	105	86
1898—Chicago	National	37	316	26	10	.722	4	261	99	63
1899—Chicago	National	39	319	22	13	.629	0	312	71	67
1900—Chicago(a)	National	27	249	14	13	.519	•4	215	61	51
1901—Chicago	American	32	257	24	7	★.774	•5	209	54	34
1902—Chicago(b)	American	25	216	15	9	.625	3	239	46	37
1903—New York	American	24	214	14	10	.583	2	194	61	35
1904—New York	American	12	92	7	5	.583	1	86	30	17
1905—New York	American	16	100	9	6	.600	2	89	48	16
1906—New York	American	17	61	2	2	.500	0	31	16	14
1907—New York	American	4	6	0	0	.000	0	17	5	4
1909—Cincinnati	National	1	1	0	1	.000	0	11	3	2
1910—Cincinnati	National			(One game as pinch-hitter)						
1912—Washington	American	1	1	0	0	.000	0	1	0	0
1913—Washington	American	1	1	0	0	.000	0	0	....	....
1914—Washington	American	1	1	0	0	.000	0	1	1	0
American League Totals—10 Years		133	949	71	39	.645	13	867	261	157
National League Totals—10 Years		259	2196	152	94	.618	9	2286	636	574
American Association Totals—1 Year		24	225	17	7	.708	0	219	65	69
Major League Totals—21 Years		416	3370	240	140	.632	22	3372	962	800

aJumped to American League to manage Chicago White Sox, 1901.
bTransferred to New York at request of League President Ban Johnson, 1902.

BURLEIGH ARLAND GRIMES
(Old Stubblebeard)

Born August 18, 1893, at Emerald, Wis.
Died December 6, 1985, at Clear Lake, Wis.
Height, 5.10. Weight, 195.
Threw and batted righthanded.

Manager, Bloomington, Three-I League, 1935; Louisville, American Association, 1936; Brooklyn Dodgers, 1937-38; Montreal, International League, 1939; Grand Rapids, Michigan State League, 1940 until suspended on July 7, 1940, for one year; Toronto, International League, 1942-43-44; Rochester, International League, 1945-46; Toronto, International League, 1947; scout, New York Yankees, 1947-52; manager, Toronto, 1952-53; coach, Kansas City Athletics, 1955; scout, Kansas City, 1956-57; Baltimore Orioles, 1960 through 1971.
Named to Hall of Fame, 1964.

Year Club	League	G.	IP.	W.	L.	Pct.	H.	R.	ER.	SO.	BB.	ERA.
1912—Eau Claire	Minn.-Wis.			(League disbanded July 1)								
1913—Ottumwa	Cent. Assn.	9	70	6	2	.750	46	22	....	67	22	....

Year Club	League	G.	IP.	W.	L.	Pct.	H.	R.	ER.	SO.	BB.	ERA.
1913—Chattanooga	Southern	17	112	6	7	.462	110	58	....	33	50	....
1914—Chat.-Birm.	Southern	4	10	0	2	.000	14	7	....	5	11	....
1914—Richmond	Virginia	39	296	23	13	.639	260	113	....	190	77	....
1915—Birmingham	Southern	41	296	17	13	.567	227	96	....	158	101	....
1916—Birmingham	Southern	40	276	20	11	.645	214	80	....	119	86	....
1916—Pittsburgh	National	6	46	2	3	.400	40	19	12	20	10	2.35
1917—Pittsburgh(a)	National	37	194	3	16	.158	186	101	76	72	70	3.53
1918—Brooklyn	National	★40	270	19	9	.679	210	94	64	113	76	2.13
1919—Brooklyn	National	25	181	10	11	.476	179	97	70	82	60	3.48
1920—Brooklyn	National	40	304	23	11	★.676	271	101	75	131	67	2.22
1921—Brooklyn	National	37	302	●22	13	.629	313	120	95	★136	76	2.83
1922—Brooklyn	National	35	256	17	14	.548	318	157	★135	99	84	4.75
1923—Brooklyn	National	39	★327	21	18	.538	★356	★165	130	119	100	3.58
1924—Brooklyn	National	38	★311	22	13	.629	★351	★161	★132	135	91	3.82
1925—Brooklyn	National	33	247	12	★19	.387	305	164	★138	73	102	5.03
1926—Brooklyn(b)	National	30	225	12	13	.480	238	114	93	64	88	3.72
1927—New York(c)	National	39	260	19	8	.704	274	116	102	102	87	3.53
1928—Pittsburgh	National	★48	★331	●25	14	.641	311	★146	110	97	77	2.99
1929—Pittsburgh(d)	National	33	233	17	7	.708	245	108	81	62	70	3.13
1930—Bos.(e)-St.L.	National	33	201	16	11	.593	246	119	91	73	65	4.07
1931—St. Louis(f)	National	29	212	17	9	.654	240	97	86	67	59	3.65
1932—Chicago	National	30	141	6	11	.353	174	89	75	36	50	4.79
1933—Chi.(g)-St.L.	National	21	84	3	7	.300	86	42	35	16	37	3.75
1934—St.L.(h)-Pitt.(j)	National	12	35	3	3	.500	41	27	25	10	12	6.43
1934—New York(i)	American	10	18	1	2	.333	22	11	11	5	14	5.50
1935—Bloomington	I.I.I.	21	119	10	5	.667	113	44	....	54	32	....
American League Totals—1 Year		10	18	1	2	.333	22	11	11	5	14	5.50
National League Totals—19 Years		605	4160	269	210	.562	4384	2037	1625	1507	1281	3.52
Major League Totals—19 Years		615	4178	270	212	.560	4406	2048	1636	1512	1295	3.52

aTraded to Brooklyn Dodgers with Shortstop Chuck Ward and Pitcher Al Mamaux for Second Baseman George Cutshaw, Outfielder Casey Stengel and cash, January 8, 1918.

bTraded to New York Giants in three-cornered deal which sent Second Baseman Fresco Thompson and Pitcher Jack Scott from the Giants to the Philadelphia Phillies; Outfielder George Harper to the Giants from the Phils and Catcher Butch Henline from the Phils to the Dodgers, January 9, 1927.

cTraded to Pittsburgh Pirates for Pitcher Vic Aldridge, February 11, 1928,

dTraded to Boston Braves for Pitcher Percy Jones and cash, April 9, 1930.

eTraded to St. Louis Cardinals for Pitchers Willie Sherdel and Fred Frankhouse, June 16, 1930.

fTraded to Chicago Cubs for Pitcher Bud Teachout and Outfielder Hack Wilson, December, 1931.

gReleased to St. Louis Cardinals on waivers, August 4, 1933.

hReleased to New York Yankees, May, 1934.

iReleased, August, 1934, and signed by Pittsburgh Pirates.

jReleased, September, 1934.

WORLD SERIES RECORD

Year Club	League	G.	IP.	W.	L.	Pct.	H.	R.	ER.	SO.	BB.	ERA.
1920—Brooklyn	National	3	19⅓	1	2	.333	23	10	9	4	9	4.19
1930—St. Louis	National	2	17	0	2	.000	10	7	7	13	6	3.71
1931—St. Louis	National	2	17⅔	2	0	1.000	9	4	4	11	9	2.04
1932—Chicago	National	2	2⅔	0	0	.000	7	7	7	0	2	23.63
World Series Totals—4 Years		9	56⅔	3	4	.429	49	28	27	28	26	4.05

CHARLES JOHN (CHARLEY) GRIMM
(Jolly Cholly)

Born August 28, 1899, at St. Louis, Mo.

Died November 15, 1983, at Scottsdale, Ariz.

Height, 5.11½. Weight, 173.

Threw and batted lefthanded.

Led National League first basemen in double plays, 1924, 1932.

Manager, Chicago Cubs, 1932 to 1938; coach, Chicago Cubs, 1941; manager, Milwaukee, American Association, 1941 through 1943; vice-president and manager, 1944; manager, Chicago Cubs 1944 to 1949, Dallas, Texas League, 1950; Milwaukee, American Association, 1951, until named manager of Boston Braves 1952; Milwaukee Braves, 1953 to 1956; vice-president, Chicago Cubs, 1957 through 1959; manager, Chicago Cubs, 1960; coach, Cubs, 1961; vice-president, Cubs, 1961 to 1963.

Year Club	League	Pos.	G.	AB.	R.	H.	2B.	3B.	HR.	RBI.	B.A.	PO.	A.	E.	F.A.
1916—Philadelphia	Am.	OF-PH	12	22	0	2	0	0	0	0	.091	7	0	1	.875
1917—Durham	N.C.	O-P-1	29	101	8	25	1	2	2	....	.248	50	14	4	.941
1918—St. Louis	Nat.	1-3-O	50	141	11	31	7	0	0	16	.220	385	14	12	.971
1918—Little Rock	South.	1B	56	205	25	61	3	6	1	....	.298	586	22	5	.992
1919—Little Rock	South.	1B	131	494	61	141	21	10	3	....	.285	●1436	69	11	★.993

Year Club	League	Pos.	G.	AB.	R.	H.	2B.	3B.	HR.	RBI.	B.A.	PO.	A.	E.	F.A.
1919—Pittsburgh	Nat.	1B	14	44	6	14	1	3	0	7	.318	118	2	4	.968
1920—Pittsburgh	Nat.	1B	148	533	38	121	13	7	2	54	.227	1496	95	8	★.995
1921—Pittsburgh	Nat.	1B	151	562	62	154	21	17	7	71	.274	1517	67	9	.994
1922—Pittsburgh	Nat.	1B	154	593	64	173	28	13	0	76	.292	1478	68	10	●.994
1923—Pittsburgh	Nat.	1B	152	563	78	194	29	13	7	99	.345	1453	81	8	★.995
1924—Pittsburgh(a)	Nat.	1B	151	542	53	156	25	12	2	63	.288	★1596	72	8	★.995
1925—Chicago	Nat.	1B	141	519	73	159	29	5	10	76	.306	1317	73	15	.989
1926—Chicago	Nat.	1B	147	524	58	145	30	6	8	82	.277	1416	68	18	.988
1927—Chicago	Nat.	1B	147	543	68	169	29	6	2	74	.311	1437	99	15	.990
1928—Chicago	Nat.	1B	147	547	67	161	25	5	5	62	.294	1458	70	10	●.993
1929—Chicago	Nat.	1B	120	463	66	138	28	3	10	91	.298	1228	74	10	.992
1930—Chicago	Nat.	1B	114	429	58	124	27	2	6	66	.289	1040	68	6	★.995
1931—Chicago	Nat.	1B	146	531	65	176	33	11	4	66	.331	1357	79	10	★.993
1932—Chicago	Nat.	1B	149	570	66	175	42	2	7	80	.307	1429	123	11	●.993
1933—Chicago	Nat.	1B	107	384	38	95	15	2	3	37	.247	979	84	4	★.996
1934—Chicago	Nat.	1B	75	267	24	79	8	1	5	47	.296	683	43	4	.995
1935—Chicago	Nat.	1B	2	8	0	0	0	0	0	0	.000	27	1	0	1.000
1936—Chicago	Nat.	1B	39	132	13	33	4	0	1	16	.250	297	33	0	1.000
1941—Milwaukee	A.A.	PH	1	1	0	1	0	0	0	0	1.000	0	0	0	.000
National League Totals—19 Years			2154	7895	908	2297	394	108	79	1083	.291	20711	1214	162	.993
American League Totals—1 Year			12	22	0	2	0	0	0	0	.091	7	0	1	.875
Major League Totals—20 Years			2166	7917	908	2299	394	108	79	1083	.290	20718	1214	163	.993

aTraded to Chicago Cubs with Shortstop Rabbit Maranville and Pitcher Wilbur Cooper for Second Baseman George Grantham, Pitcher Vic Aldridge and First Baseman Al Niehaus, October 27, 1924.

WORLD SERIES RECORD

Year Club	League	Pos.	G.	AB.	R.	H.	2B.	3B.	HR.	RBI.	B.A.	PO.	A.	E.	F.A.
1929—Chicago	Nat.	1B	5	18	2	7	0	0	1	4	.389	40	1	0	1.000
1932—Chicago	Nat.	1B	4	15	2	5	2	0	0	1	.333	28	3	0	1.000
World Series Totals—2 Years			9	33	4	12	2	0	1	5	.364	68	4	0	1.000

ROBERT MOSES (LEFTY) GROVE

Born March 6, 1900, at Lonaconing, Md.

Died May 22, 1975, at Norwalk, O.

Height, 6.03. Weight, 204.

Threw and batted lefthanded.

Shares major league record by striking out side in inning on nine pitches, August 23, 1928, second inning and September 27, 1928, seventh inning.

Shares American League record for most consecutive victories, season (16), June 8 through August 19, 1931.

THE SPORTING NEWS All-Star Major League Teams, 1928-29-30-31-32.

Named American League Most Valuable Player, BBWAA, 1931.

Named to Hall of Fame, 1947.

Year Club	League	G.	IP.	W.	L.	Pct.	H.	R.	ER.	SO.	BB.	ERA.
1920—Martinsburg	Blue Ridge	6	59	3	3	.500	30	16	....	60	24	......
1920—Baltimore	International	19	123	12	2	.857	120	69	52	88	71	3.80
1921—Baltimore	International	47	313	25	10	.714	237	131	89	★254	★179	2.56
1922—Baltimore	International	41	209	18	8	.692	146	90	65	★205	★152	2.80
1923—Baltimore	International	★52	303	27	10	.730	223	128	105	★330	★186	3.12
1924—Baltimore	International	47	236	★27	6	★.813	196	95	79	★231	108	3.01
1925—Philadelphia	American	45	197	10	12	.455	207	120	104	★116	★131	4.75
1926—Philadelphia	American	45	258	13	13	.500	227	97	72	★194	101	★2.51
1927—Philadelphia	American	51	262	20	13	.606	251	116	93	★174	79	3.19
1928—Philadelphia	American	39	262	●24	8	.750	228	93	75	★183	64	2.58
1929—Philadelphia	American	42	275	20	6	★.769	278	104	86	★170	81	★2.81
1930—Philadelphia	American	★50	291	★28	5	★.848	273	101	82	★209	60	★2.54
1931—Philadelphia	American	41	289	★31	4	★.886	249	84	66	★175	62	★2.06
1932—Philadelphia	American	44	292	25	10	.714	269	101	92	188	79	★2.84
1933—Philadelphia(a)	American	45	275	●24	8	★.750	280	113	98	114	83	3.21
1934—Boston	American	22	109	8	8	.500	149	84	79	43	32	6.52
1935—Boston	American	35	273	20	12	.625	269	105	82	121	65	★2.70
1936—Boston	American	35	253	17	12	.586	237	90	79	130	65	★2.81
1937—Boston	American	32	262	17	9	.654	269	101	88	153	83	3.02
1938—Boston	American	24	164	14	4	.778	169	65	56	99	52	★3.07
1939—Boston	American	23	191	15	4	★.789	180	63	54	81	58	★2.54
1940—Boston	American	22	153	7	6	.538	159	73	68	62	50	4.00
1941—Boston	American	21	134	7	7	.500	155	84	65	54	42	4.37
Major League Totals—17 Years		616	3940	300	141	.680	3849	1594	1339	2266	1187	3.06

aTraded to Boston with Second Baseman Max Bishop and Pitcher Rube Walberg for Infielder Rabbit Warstler, Pitcher Bob Kline and cash, December 12, 1933.

WORLD SERIES RECORD

Year Club	League	G.	IP.	W.	L.	Pct.	H.	R.	ER.	SO.	BB.	ERA.
1929—Philadelphia	American	2	6⅓	0	0	.000	3	0	0	10	1	0.00
1930—Philadelphia	American	3	19	2	1	.667	15	5	3	10	3	1.42
1931—Philadelphia	American	3	26	2	1	.667	28	7	7	16	2	2.42
World Series Totals—3 Years		8	51⅓	4	2	.667	46	12	10	36	6	1.75

STANLEY CAMFIELD (STAN) HACK

Born December 6, 1909, at Sacramento, Calif.

Died December 15, 1979, at Dixon, Ill.

Height, 6.00. Weight, 175.

Threw right and batted lefthanded.

Led National League third basemen in double plays, 1937, 1938 (tie), 1940.

Named by Baseball Writers' Association as third baseman for THE SPORTING NEWS All-Star Major League Teams, 1940-41-42.

Manager, Des Moines, Western League, 1948-49; Springfield, International League, 1950; Los Angeles, Pacific Coast League, 1951-52-53; Chicago Cubs, 1954-55-56; coach, St. Louis Cardinals, 1957-58; manager, Denver, American Association, 1959; Salt Lake City, Pacific Coast League, 1965; Dallas-Fort Worth, Texas League, 1966.

Year Club	League	Pos.	G.	AB.	R.	H.	2B.	3B.	HR.	RBI.	B.A.	PO.	A.	E.	F.A.
1931—Sacramento	P. C.	3B	164	660	128	232	36	13	2	37	.352	167	354	32	.942
1932—Chicago	Nat.	3B	72	178	32	42	5	6	2	19	.236	36	90	12	.913
1933—Albany	Int.	3B	137	515	102	154	28	8	6	64	.299	★171	272	17	.963
1933—Chicago	Nat.	3B	20	60	10	21	3	1	1	2	.350	19	40	1	.983
1934—Chicago	Nat.	3B	111	402	54	116	16	6	1	21	.289	102	198	16	.949
1935—Chicago	Nat.	3B-1B	124	427	75	133	23	9	4	64	.311	87	237	20	.942
1936—Chicago	Nat.	3B-1B	149	561	102	167	27	4	6	78	.298	225	210	17	.962
1937—Chicago	Nat.	*3B-1B	154	582	106	173	27	6	2	63	.297	★151	★247	13	.968
1938—Chicago	Nat.	3B	●152	609	109	195	34	11	4	67	.320	★178	300	23	.954
1939—Chicago	Nat.	3B	156	641	112	191	28	6	8	56	.298	★177	278	21	.956
1940—Chicago	Nat.	3B-1B	149	603	101	★191	38	6	8	40	.317	★182	★304	23	.955
1941—Chicago	Nat.	3B-1B	151	586	111	★186	33	5	7	45	.317	139	295	21	.954
1942—Chicago	Nat.	3B	140	553	91	166	36	3	6	39	.300	154	261	15	★.965
1943—Chicago	Nat.	3B	144	533	78	154	24	4	3	35	.289	149	264	17	.960
1944—Chicago	Nat.	3B-1B	98	383	65	108	16	1	3	32	.282	226	174	19	.955
1945—Chicago	Nat.	*3B-1B	150	597	110	193	29	7	2	43	.323	★233	314	14	★.975
1946—Chicago	Nat.	3B	92	323	55	92	13	4	0	26	.285	102	168	9	.968
1947—Chicago	Nat.	3B	76	240	28	65	11	2	0	12	.271	64	136	8	.962
Major League Totals—16 Years			1938	7278	1239	2193	363	81	57	642	.301	2224	3516	249	.958

WORLD SERIES RECORD

Year Club	League	Pos.	G.	AB.	R.	H.	2B.	3B.	HR.	RBI.	B.A.	PO.	A.	E.	F.A.
1932—Chicago	Nat.	PR	1	0	0	0	0	0	0	0	.000	0	0	0	.000
1935—Chicago	Nat.	3B-SS	6	22	2	5	1	1	0	0	.227	6	10	0	1.000
1938—Chicago	Nat.	3B	4	17	3	8	1	0	0	1	.471	4	4	0	1.000
1945—Chicago	Nat.	3B	7	30	1	11	3	0	0	4	.367	12	13	3	.893
World Series Totals—4 Years			18	69	6	24	5	1	0	5	.348	22	27	3	.942

CHARLES JAMES (CHICK) HAFEY

Born February 12, 1904, at Berkeley, Calif.

Died July 2, 1973, at Calistoga, Calif.

Height, 6.01. Weight, 185.

Threw and batted righthanded.

Shares National League record for most consecutive hits, season (10), July 6, second game through July 9, 1929.

Named to Hall of Fame, 1971.

Year	Club	League	Pos.	G.	AB.	R.	H.	2B.	3B.	HR.	RBI.	B.A.	PO.	A.	E.	F.A.
1923—Fort Smith		W. Assn.	OF	141	573	83	163	42	14	16	.....	.284	280	30	16	.951
1924—Houston		Tex.	OF	126	481	82	173	39	★20	9	90	.360	358	18	11	.972
1924—St. Louis		Nat.	OF	24	91	10	23	5	2	2	22	.253	48	3	4	.927
1925—Syracuse		Int.	OF	21	84	17	24	3	3	2	8	.286	49	3	1	.981
1925—St. Louis		Nat.	OF	93	358	36	108	25	2	5	57	.302	180	9	9	.955
1926—St. Louis		Nat.	OF	78	225	30	61	19	2	4	38	.271	106	6	3	.974
1927—St. Louis		Nat.	OF	103	346	62	114	26	5	18	63	.329	179	19	4	.980
1928—St. Louis		Nat.	OF	138	520	101	175	46	6	27	111	.337	287	13	11	.965
1929—St. Louis		Nat.	OF	134	517	101	175	47	9	29	125	.338	278	8	10	.966
1930—St. Louis		Nat.	OF	120	446	108	150	39	12	26	107	.336	189	11	5	.976
1931—St. Louis (a)		Nat.	OF	122	450	94	157	35	8	16	95	★.349	226	4	4	.983
1932—Cincinnati		Nat.	OF	83	253	34	87	19	3	2	36	.344	131	5	5	.965
1933—Cincinnati		Nat.	OF	144	568	77	172	34	6	7	62	.303	364	16	5	.987
1934—Cincinnati		Nat.	OF	140	535	75	157	29	6	18	67	.293	380	7	13	.968
1935—Cincinnati		Nat.	OF	15	59	10	20	6	1	1	9	.339	31	0	3	.912
1936—Cincinnati		Nat.	OF							(Voluntarily Retired)						
1937—Cincinnati		Nat.	OF	89	257	39	67	11	5	9	41	.261	128	5	4	.971
Major League Totals—13 Years				1283	4625	777	1466	341	67	164	833	.317	2527	106	80	.971

aTraded to Cincinnati Reds for Infielder Harvey Hendrick, Pitcher Benny Frey and cash, April 11, 1932.

WORLD SERIES RECORD

Year	Club	League	Pos.	G.	AB.	R.	H.	2B.	3B.	HR.	RBI.	B.A.	PO.	A.	E.	F.A.
1926—St. Louis		Nat.	OF	7	27	2	5	2	0	0	0	.185	21	1	0	1.000
1928—St. Louis		Nat.	OF	4	15	0	3	0	0	0	0	.200	8	0	1	.889
1930—St. Louis		Nat.	OF	6	22	2	6	5	0	0	2	.273	9	0	0	1.000
1931—St. Louis		Nat.	OF	6	24	1	4	0	0	0	0	.167	8	0	1	.889
World Series Totals—4 Years				23	88	5	18	7	0	0	2	.205	46	1	2	.959

JESSE JOSEPH HAINES
(Pop)

Born July 22, 1893, at Clayton, O.

Died August 5, 1978, at Dayton, O.

Height, 6.00. Weight, 180.

Threw and batted righthanded.

Pitched 5-0 no-hit victory against Boston Braves, July 17, 1924.
Coach, Brooklyn Dodgers, 1938.
Named to Hall of Fame, 1970.

Year	Club	League	G.	IP.	W.	L.	Pct.	H.	R.	ER.	SO.	BB.	ERA.
1913—Dayton		Central	(Pitched one game, last day of season vs. Evansville)										
1914—Saginaw		S. Mich.	33	258	17	14	.548	221	94		159	52	......
1914—Fort Wayne		Central	(No records available)										
1915—Saginaw		S. Mich.	(League disbanded July 1—no records available)										
1916—Springfield		Central	41	310	23	12	.657	247	78	58	143	84	1.68
1917—Springfield		Central	35	275	19	10	.655	204	67	....	129	88	......
1918—Topeka-Hutch'on		Western	16	132	12	4	.750	93		....	71	28	......
1918—Cincinnati		National	1	5	0	0	.000	5	1	1	2	1	1.80
1919—Tulsa		Western	14	101	5	9	.357	87	47	....	40	47	......
1919—Kansas City		Amer. Assn.	28	213	21	5	.808	199	54	50	66	52	2.11
1920—St. Louis		National	★47	302	13	20	.394	303	136	100	120	80	2.98
1921—St. Louis		National	37	244	18	12	.600	261	112	95	84	56	3.50
1922—St. Louis		National	29	183	11	9	.550	207	103	78	62	45	3.84
1923—St. Louis		National	37	266	20	13	.606	283	125	92	73	75	3.11
1924—St. Louis		National	35	223	8	19	.296	275	129	109	69	66	4.40
1925—St. Louis		National	29	207	13	14	.481	234	116	105	63	52	4.57
1926—St. Louis		National	33	183	13	4	.765	186	76	66	46	48	3.25
1927—St. Louis		National	38	301	24	10	.706	273	114	91	89	77	2.72
1928—St. Louis		National	33	240	20	8	.714	238	98	85	77	72	3.19
1929—St. Louis		National	28	180	13	10	.565	230	123	114	59	73	5.70
1930—St. Louis		National	29	182	13	8	.619	215	107	87	68	54	4.30
1931—St. Louis		National	19	122	12	3	.800	134	48	41	27	28	3.02
1932—St. Louis		National	20	85	3	5	.375	116	51	45	27	16	4.76
1933—St. Louis		National	32	115	9	6	.600	113	46	32	37	37	2.50
1934—St. Louis		National	37	90	4	4	.500	86	42	35	17	19	3.50
1935—St. Louis		National	30	115	6	5	.545	110	49	46	24	28	3.60
1936—St. Louis		National	25	99	7	5	.583	110	44	43	19	21	3.91
1937—St. Louis		National	16	66	3	3	.500	81	36	33	18	23	4.50
Major League Totals—19 Years			555	3208	210	158	.571	3460	1556	1298	981	871	3.64

WORLD SERIES RECORD

Year	Club	League	G.	IP.	W.	L.	Pct.	H.	R.	ER.	SO.	BB.	ERA.
1926—St. Louis	National	3	16⅔	2	0	1.000	13	2	2	5	9	1.08
1928—St. Louis	National	1	6	0	1	.000	6	6	3	3	3	4.50
1930—St. Louis	National	1	9	1	0	1.000	4	1	1	2	4	1.00
1934—St. Louis	National	1	⅔	0	0	.000	1	0	0	2	0	0.00
World Series Totals—4 Years			6	32⅓	3	1	.750	24	9	6	12	16	1.67

WILLIAM ROBERT (BILLY) HAMILTON
(Sliding Billy)

Born February 16, 1866, at Newark, N. J.

Died December 16, 1940, at Worcester, Mass.

Height, 5.06. Weight, 165.

Threw right and batted lefthanded.

Holds major league record for most runs, season (196), 1894.

Manager, Haverhill, New England League, 1902-03-04; Harrisburg, Tri-State League, 1905; Haverhill, New England League and Harrisburg, Tri-State League, 1906; Haverhill, New England League, 1907-08; Lynn, New England League, 1909-10; Fall River, New England League, 1913; Springfield, Eastern League, 1914; part owner and manager, Worcester, Eastern League, 1916; scout Boston Red Sox, 1911-12.

Named to Hall of Fame, 1961.

Year	Club	League	Pos.	G.	AB.	R.	H.	2B.	3B.	HR.	SB.	B.A.	PO.	A.	E.	F.A.
1888—Worcester	N. Eng.	OF	61	247	76	87	...	...	...	70	.352	....	....	5	.904
1888—Kansas City	A. A.	OF	35	128	17	32	4	4	0	23	.250	41	1	2	.943
1889—Kansas City	A. A.	OF	137	532	145	160	15	★15	3	★117	.301	233	19	34	.902
1890—Philadelphia	Nat.	OF	123	496	131	161	10	9	2	★102	.325	232	23	34	.881
1891—Philadelphia	Nat.	OF	133	529	★142	★179	21	6	2	★115	★.338	281	22	26	.921
1892—Philadelphia	Nat.	OF	136	539	131	178	18	7	3	56	.330	292	29	22	.936
1893—Philadelphia	Nat.	OF	82	349	111	138	21	7	5	41	.395	229	8	15	.940
1894—Philadelphia	Nat.	OF	131	559	★196	223	22	14	4	★99	.399	★363	16	15	.962
1895—Philadelphia	Nat.	OF	121	517	★166	203	19	6	5	★95	.393	310	12	29	.917
1896—Boston	Nat.	OF	131	523	153	190	26	8	2	93	.363	278	8	19	.938
1897—Boston	Nat.	OF	125	506	★153	174	17	6	3	70	.344	299	9	15	.954
1898—Boston	Nat.	OF	109	417	111	153	16	4	3	59	.367	193	8	23	.897
1899—Boston	Nat.	OF	81	294	62	90	6	1	1	19	.306	163	10	6	.966
1900—Boston	Nat.	OF	135	524	103	174	19	5	1	29	.332	325	13	19	.947
1901—Boston	Nat.	OF	99	349	70	102	11	2	3	19	.292	234	7	20	.923
1902—Haverhill	N. Eng.	OF	66	243	67	82	23	2	2	26	.337	127	10	5	.964
1903—Haverhill	N. Eng.	OF	37	132	37	60	15	2	4	27	.446	67	4	3	.960
1904—Haverhill	N. Eng.	OF	113	408	★113	★168	32	8	0	★74	★.412	★242	7	11	.958
1905—Harrisburg	Tri-St.						(No Record Available)								
1906—Haverhill	N.Eng.	OF	14	51	1	10	1	0	0	...	.196	26	2	3	.903
1906—Harrisburg	Tri-St.	OF	43	155	33	43	5	1	0	16	.278	82	4	6	.935
1907—Haverhill	N. Eng.	OF	91	324	50	108	16	4	0	29	★.333	161	6	2	★.988
1908—Haverhill	N. Eng.	OF	85	300	63	87	19	0	1	39	.290	164	11	13	.931
1909—Lynn	N. Eng.	OF	109	376	61	125	17	2	0	23	★.332	195	6	14	.935
1910—Lynn	N. Eng.	OF	41	112	14	28	1	2	0	5	.250	45	3	1	.980
American Assn. Totals—2 Years			172	660	162	192	19	19	3	140	.291	274	20	36	.891
National League Totals—12 Years			1406	5602	1529	1965	206	75	34	797	.351	3199	165	243	.933
Major League Totals—14 Years			1578	6262	1690	2157	225	94	37	937	.344	3473	185	279	.929

MELVIN LE ROY (MEL) HARDER

Born October 15, 1909, at Beemer, Neb.

Height, 6.01. Weight, 210.

Threw and batted righthanded.

Tied for league leadership in shutouts with 6 in 1934.

Player-coach, Cleveland Indians, 1947; coach, Cleveland, 1948-1963; New York Mets, 1964; Chicago Cubs, 1965-66; Cincinnati Reds, 1967-68; Kansas City Royals, 1969.

Year Club	League	G.	IP.	W.	L.	Pct.	H.	R.	ER.	SO.	BB.	ERA.
1927—Omaha	West.	11	87	4	7	.364	106	65	....	40	33	......
1927—Dubuque	Miss. Val.	22	....	13	6	.684	....	....	....	....	....	......
1928—Cleveland	Amer.	23	49	0	2	.000	64	42	36	15	32	6.61
1929—Cleveland	Amer.	11	18	1	0	1.000	24	15	11	4	5	5.50
1929—New Orleans	South.	16	72	7	2	.778	65	31	20	32	24	2.50
1930—Cleveland	Amer.	36	175	11	10	.524	205	108	82	44	68	4.22
1931—Cleveland	Amer.	40	194	13	14	.481	229	119	94	63	72	4.36
1932—Cleveland	Amer.	39	255	15	13	.536	277	125	106	90	68	3.74
1933—Cleveland	Amer.	43	253	15	17	.469	254	113	83	81	67	2.95
1934—Cleveland	Amer.	44	255	20	12	.625	246	97	74	91	81	2.61
1935—Cleveland	Amer.	42	287	22	11	.667	313	120	105	95	53	3.29
1936—Cleveland	Amer.	36	225	15	15	.500	294	155	129	84	71	5.16
1937—Cleveland	Amer.	38	234	15	12	.556	269	127	111	95	86	4.27
1938—Cleveland	Amer.	38	240	17	10	.630	257	115	102	102	62	3.83
1939—Cleveland	Amer.	29	208	15	9	.625	213	89	81	67	64	3.50
1940—Cleveland	Amer.	31	186	12	11	.522	200	96	84	76	59	4.06
1941—Cleveland(a)	Amer.	15	69	5	4	.556	76	43	40	21	37	5.22
1942—Cleveland	Amer.	29	199	13	14	.481	179	83	76	74	82	3.44
1943—Cleveland	Amer.	19	135	8	7	.533	126	57	46	40	61	3.07
1944—Cleveland	Amer.	30	196	12	10	.545	211	95	81	64	69	3.72
1945—Cleveland	Amer.	11	76	3	7	.300	93	37	31	16	23	3.67
1946—Cleveland	Amer.	13	92	5	4	.556	85	37	35	21	31	3.42
1947—Cleveland	Amer.	15	80	6	4	.600	91	41	40	17	27	4.50
Major League Totals—20 Years		582	3426	223	186	.545	3706	1714	1447	1160	1118	3.80

aReleased, September 9, 1941; re-signed, March 24, 1942.

WILLIAM (WILL) HARRIDGE

Born October 16, 1883, at Chicago, Ill.
Died April 9, 1971, at Evanston, Ill.

William Harridge was a tall, dignified, efficient, truthful and sensitive person throughout his adult life, a conservative who felt the winds of change and was sufficiently perceptive to follow them intelligently.

The American League reached its zenith under his presidency and the distinguished gentleman set the tone—firm guidance, thoughtful decisions, top-to-bottom loyalty, inborn pride, fierce honesty and aggressive penalties whenever warranted.

Will (which he preferred over William), a native of Chicago's South Side and born on October 16, 1883, was whisked into Organized Baseball; he did not choose the career. From the job of office boy in the Wabash Railroad, he attended evening classes and rose to the position of transportation head in the office. The American League, under Ban Johnson at the time, arranged all transportation of its umpires through the Wabash. Harridge did such an excellent job of error-free booking that he came to the personal attention of Johnson.

In December, 1911, Will's Wabash boss told him, "You have just worked your last day for this railroad." Will thought he was canned. But he was told to report to the American League office and begin work as Ban Johnson's private secretary.

As a result of Ban's later battles with Commissioner Kenesaw M. Landis and the AL owners as well, he was set down early in 1927. He actually resigned on October 17, when Ernest Barnard of Cleveland was named AL president and Harridge was voted in as the league secretary. Barnard died suddenly on March 27, 1931, and Will was made acting president. Two months later, on May 27, he was officially named the president, having been championed by Charles Comiskey of Chicago and Phil Ball of St. Louis. Harridge stepped down on December 3, 1958, when he became chairman of the board, a post he held until his death on April 9, 1971.

Harridge's mettle was tried early—just one year after taking over, Carl Reynolds of the Washington Senators slid hard into catcher Bill Dickey of the Yankees in a home-plate collision on July 4, 1932. Dickey leaped to his feet and delivered a haymaker that broke Reynolds' jaw. Observers wondered if the neophyte would stand up to the Yankees, then the dominant club in the league, if not all baseball.

They didn't have to wonder long. Harridge fined Dickey $1,000 and suspended him for a month in the midst of a pennant race. The Yankees' owner, Jake Ruppert, was furious, but Will held his ground. "He didn't talk to me for a year," Harridge said, "but the next year he softened up and became one of my best friends."

Will continued Johnson's high regard and proper respect for his umpires. American League umpires felt his ire when they came up short but Harridge defended them to the hilt when they were attacked by others.

He fined and suspended the belligerent George Moriarty and hired the humiliated NL umpire Scotty Robb. He fined and suspended the league's chief arbiter baiter, Jimmy Dykes, the pixie skipper of the White Sox, a total of 37 times.

The business-as-usual sign typified the AL—the Yankees ruled the roost most of his reign and other clubs played catch-up with second place the usual reward. But many important things eventuated during Will's tenure—formation of a public relations department and a film bureau, the All-Star Game, night baseball, re-entry of the Negro to the majors, televising of games, expansion of the majors and formation of the players' association.

Thus Harridge spanned from pre-Landis days to the middle of every problem of today. He personally sold the

All-Star Game to the owners for a one-shot Chicago World's Fair feature and did his utmost to see that it continued; he resisted night ball in its early stages because he feared a drop in field performance, particularly batting, but when the lights proved to be excellent substitutes for sunlight, no one was more vehement in proclaiming the boost of family attendance which the lights gave to the game.

Will saw the burgeoning sports world in need of fresh appeals to potential ticket buyers and to assuage that need, he formed the public relations and baseball film departments to service his league fans and organizations. He tried to slow down expansion when he saw the original setup of franchises in danger of becoming watered down from a paucity of top-level performers to staff them, but he changed his stance completely when logistics, finances and public clamor screamed the need.

Harridge disliked shenanigans on the field, from Bill Veeck's midget to showboating players and managers, because he knew that rigid discipline on the field, monitored by competent, backed-up umpires, assured the fans of clean games and good family entertainment, a climate which mirrored his deep pride in the American League.

Contrary to his sober look and dignified mien, he was a sublime host at his annual Christmas party for the entire Chicago sporting scene—players, writers, club personnel, league members, whoever was around. They stopped counting guests when 400 passed through the portal.

Will enjoyed the complete backing of the league owners, having had his contract extended by five- and ten-year leaps, and his snow-white hair was the sign of law and order wherever baseball people met. His pride and joy was the All-Star Game and the AL enjoyed a pronounced winning margin over the NL during his presidency. He considered the 1941 All-Star Game at Detroit won by Ted Williams' winning homer off Claude Passeau the top one, having done everything short of kissing the stringbean when they embraced in the clubhouse. "I would have kissed him, too," said Will, in unusual exuberance, "if there hadn't been so many people around."

Harridge had a great perception of the rules of the game, knew when to step in and when to let the owners run their own show. Turmoil found no place in the American League scene. As was said at his passing, "Any enemy of Will Harridge was an enemy of good, clean baseball and sound organization."

Harridge was named to the Hall of Fame in 1972.

STANLEY RAYMOND (BUCKY) HARRIS

Born November 8, 1896, at Port Jervis, N.Y.

Died November 8, 1977, at Bethesda, Md.

Height, 5.09½. Weight, 156.

Threw and batted righthanded.

Holds major league record for most putouts, second baseman, 154-game season (479), 1922.

Named Major League Manager of the Year by THE SPORTING NEWS, 1947.

Manager, Washington Senators, 1924-28; Detroit Tigers, 1929-33; Boston Red Sox, 1934; Washington, 1935-42; Philadelphia Phillies, 1943; Buffalo, International League, 1944-45; New York Yankees, 1947-48; San Diego, Pacific Coast League, 1949; Washington, 1950-54; Detroit, 1955; also general manager, Buffalo, 1945-46; assistant to general manager, Boston Red Sox, 1956-60; scout, Chicago White Sox, 1962; Washington, 1963-71.

Named to Hall of Fame, 1975.

Year	Club	League	Pos.	G.	AB.	R.	H.	2B.	3B.	HR.	RBI.	B.A.	PO.	A.	E.	F.A.
1916—Muskegon		Central	3B	55	169	8	28	....	....	....	....	.166	82	91	21	.892
1917—Norfolk (a)		Virginia	SS	15	50	4	6	0	0	0	2	.120	40	34	14	.841
1917—Reading		N.Y.S.	2B	75	280	44	70	....	....	....	....	.250	153	214	26	.934
1918—Buffalo		Int.	2B-SS	85	320	51	77	11	7	0	....	.241	216	273	34	.935
1919—Buffalo		Int.	2B	120	447	68	126	18	8	2	....	.282	281	366	41	.940
1919—Washington		Amer.	2B	8	28	0	6	1	0	0	4	.214	21	27	4	.923
1920—Washington		Amer.	2B	137	506	76	152	26	6	1	68	.300	345	401	33	.958
1921—Washington		Amer.	2B	154	584	82	169	22	8	0	54	.289	407	481	38	.959
1922—Washington		Amer.	2B	154	602	95	162	24	8	2	40	.269	★479	483	30	.970
1923—Washington		Amer.	2B	145	532	60	150	21	13	2	70	.282	★418	449	★35	.961
1924—Washington		Amer.	2B	143	544	88	146	28	9	1	58	.268	393	386	26	.968
1925—Washington		Amer.	2B	144	551	91	158	30	3	1	66	.287	402	429	26	.970
1926—Washington		Amer.	2B	141	537	94	152	39	9	1	63	.283	★356	427	30	.963
1927—Washington		Amer.	2B	128	475	98	127	20	3	1	55	.267	★316	413	21	★.972
1928—Washington (b)		Amer.	2B	99	358	34	73	11	5	0	28	.204	251	326	18	.970
1929—Detroit		Amer.	2B-SS	7	11	3	1	0	0	0	0	.091	5	13	2	.900
1930—Detroit		Amer.								(Did not play)						
1931—Detroit		Amer.	2B	4	8	1	1	1	0	0	0	.125	5	6	0	1.000
Major League Totals—12 Years				1264	4736	722	1297	223	64	9	506	.274	3398	3841	263	.965

aLeague disbanded in May.

bTraded to Detroit for Infielder Jack Warner, October, 1928, and appointed manager of Tigers.

WORLD SERIES RECORD

Year	Club	League	Pos.	G.	AB.	R.	H.	2B.	3B.	HR.	RBI.	B.A.	PO.	A.	E.	F.A.
1924—Washington		Amer.	2B	7	33	5	11	0	0	2	7	.333	26	28	2	.694
1925—Washington		Amer.	2B	7	23	2	2	0	0	0	0	.087	24	18	0	1.000
World Series Totals—2 Years				14	56	7	13	0	0	2	7	.232	50	46	2	.980

RECORD AS MAJOR LEAGUE MANAGER

Year Club	League	Position	W.	L.	Year Club	League	Position	W.	L.
1924—Washington	Amer.	First	92	62	1939—Washington	Amer.	Sixth	65	87
1925—Washington	Amer.	First	96	55	1940—Washington	Amer.	Seventh	64	90
1926—Washington	Amer.	Fourth	81	69	1941—Washington	Amer.	†Sixth	70	84
1927—Washington	Amer.	Third	85	69	1942—Washington	Amer.	Seventh	62	89
1928—Washington	Amer.	Fourth	75	79	1943—Philadelphia	Nat.	Sixth	39	52
1929—Detroit	Amer.	Sixth	70	84	1947—New York	Amer.	First	97	57
1930—Detroit	Amer.	Fifth	75	79	1948—New York	Amer.	Third	94	60
1931—Detroit	Amer.	Seventh	61	93	1950—Washington	Amer.	Fifth	67	87
1932—Detroit	Amer.	Fifth	76	75	1951—Washington	Amer.	Seventh	62	92
1933—Detroit	Amer.	Fifth	75	79	1952—Washington	Amer.	Fifth	78	76
1934—Boston	Amer.	Fourth	76	76	1953—Washington	Amer.	Fifth	76	76
1935—Washington	Amer.	Sixth	67	86	1954—Washington	Amer.	Sixth	66	88
1936—Washington	Amer.	Fourth	82	71	1955—Detroit	Amer.	Fifth	79	75
1937—Washington	Amer.	Sixth	73	80	1956—Detroit	Amer.	Fifth	82	72
1938—Washington	Amer.	Fifth	75	76	Major League Totals—29 Years			2160	2218

WORLD SERIES RECORD

Year Club	League	W.	L.	Year Club	League	W.	L.
1924—Washington	American	4	3	1947—New York	American	4	3
1925—Washington	American	3	4				

†Tied for position.

CHARLES LEO (GABBY) HARTNETT

Born December 20, 1900, at Woonsocket, R. I.

Died December 20, 1972, at Park Ridge, Ill.

Height, 6.01. Weight, 218.

Threw and batted righthanded.

Shares major league record for most years leading league in double plays, catcher (6).

Named National League Most Valuable Player, 1935.

Named by Baseball Writers' Association of America as catcher for THE SPORTING NEWS All-Star Major League Teams, 1927 and 1937.

Manager, Chicago Cubs, 1938, through 1940; player-coach, New York Giants, 1941; manager, Indianapolis, American Association, 1942; Jersey City, International League, 1943; Buffalo, International League, 1946; coach, Kansas City Athletics, 1965; scout, Kansas City, 1966.

Named to Hall of Fame, 1955.

Year Club	League	Pos.	G.	AB.	R.	H.	2B.	3B.	HR.	RBI.	B.A.	PO.	A.	E.	F.A.
1921—Worcester	East.	C	100	345	38	91	21	7	3	.....	.264	447	104	19	.967
1922—Chicago	Nat.	C	31	72	4	14	1	1	0	4	.194	79	29	2	.982
1923—Chicago	Nat.	C-1B	85	231	28	62	12	2	8	39	.268	413	39	5	.989
1924—Chicago	Nat.	C	111	354	56	106	17	7	16	67	.299	369	97	★18	.963
1925—Chicago	Nat.	C	117	398	61	115	28	3	24	67	.289	★409	★114	★23	.958
1926—Chicago	Nat.	C	93	284	35	78	25	3	8	41	.275	307	86	9	.978
1927—Chicago	Nat.	C	127	449	56	132	32	5	10	80	.294	★479	★99	★16	.973
1928—Chicago	Nat.	C	120	388	61	117	26	9	14	57	.302	455	●103	6	★.989
1929—Chicago	Nat.	PH-C	25	22	2	6	2	1	1	9	.273	4	0	0	1.000
1930—Chicago	Nat.	C	141	508	84	172	31	3	37	122	.339	★646	★68	8	★.989
1931—Chicago	Nat.	C	116	380	53	107	32	1	8	70	.282	444	68	10	.981
1932—Chicago	Nat.	C	121	406	52	110	25	3	12	52	.271	484	75	10	.982
1933—Chicago	Nat.	C	140	490	55	135	21	4	16	88	.276	550	77	7	.989
1934—Chicago	Nat.	C	130	438	58	131	21	1	22	90	.299	★605	★86	3	★.996
1935—Chicago	Nat.	C	116	413	67	142	32	6	13	91	.344	477	★77	9	★.984
1936—Chicago	Nat.	C	121	424	49	130	25	6	7	64	.307	504	75	5	★.991
1937—Chicago	Nat.	C	110	356	47	126	21	6	12	82	.354	436	65	2	★.996
1938—Chicago	Nat.	C	88	299	40	82	19	1	10	59	.274	358	40	2	.995
1939—Chicago	Nat.	C	97	306	36	85	18	2	12	59	.278	344	47	3	.992
1940—Chicago(a)	Nat.	C	37	64	3	17	3	0	1	12	.266	69	9	4	.951
1941—New York	Nat.	C	64	150	20	45	5	0	5	26	.300	138	15	1	.994
1942—Indianapolis	A. A.	C	72	186	17	41	12	2	4	24	.220	190	36	7	.970
1943—Jersey City	Int.	C	16	16	0	4	1	0	0	5	.250	9	4	1	.929
1944—Jersey City	Int.	C	31	11	1	2	1	0	0	6	.182	0	0	0	.000
Major League Totals—20 Years			1990	6432	867	1912	396	64	236	1179	.297	7562	1269	143	.984

aUnconditionally released by Chicago Cubs, November 13, 1940; signed as player-coach, New York Giants, December 2, 1940.

Year Club	League	Pos.	G.	AB.	R.	H.	2B.	3B.	HR.	RBI.	B.A.	PO.	A.	E.	F.A.
1929—Chicago	Nat.	PH	3	3	0	0	0	0	0	0	.000	0	0	0	.000
1932—Chicago	Nat.	C	4	16	2	5	2	0	1	1	.313	31	5	1	.973
1935—Chicago	Nat.	C	6	24	1	7	0	0	1	2	.292	33	6	0	1.000
1938—Chicago	Nat.	C	3	11	0	1	0	1	0	0	.091	14	3	0	1.000
World Series Totals—4 Years			16	54	3	13	2	1	2	3	.241	78	14	1	.989

HARRY EDWIN HEILMANN

Born August 3, 1894, at San Francisco, Calif.

Died July 9, 1951, at Detroit, Mich.

Height, 6.01. Weight, 200.

Threw and batted righthanded.

Led American League outfielders in assists with 27 in 1924.
Coach, Cincinnati Reds, 1932.
Named to Hall of Fame, 1952.

Year Club	League	Pos.	G.	AB.	R.	H.	2B.	3B.	HR.	RBI.	B.A.	PO.	A.	E.	F.A.
1913—Portland	N. W.	OF-1B	122	417	55	127	26	2	11	....	.305	748	67	20	.976
1914—Detroit	Amer.	OF-1B	66	182	25	41	8	1	2	22	.225	200	17	10	.956
1915—San Francisco	P. C.	1B	98	371	57	135	23	4	12	....	.364	1019	72	★25	.978
1916—Detroit	Amer.	OF-1B	136	451	57	127	30	11	2	76	.282	426	27	9	.981
1917—Detroit	Amer.	OF-1B	150	556	57	156	22	11	5	84	.281	466	40	13	.975
1918—Detroit	Amer.	OF	79	286	34	79	10	6	5	44	.276	427	25	8	.983
1919—Detroit	Amer.	1B	140	537	74	172	30	15	8	95	.320	1402	78	★31	.979
1920—Detroit	Amer.	OF-*1B	145	543	66	168	28	5	9	90	.309	1234	86	★19	★.986
1921—Detroit	Amer.	OF	149	602	114	★237	43	14	19	139	★.394	257	13	11	.961
1922—Detroit	Amer.	OF	118	455	92	162	27	10	21	92	.356	175	6	10	.948
1923—Detroit	Amer.	OF	144	524	121	211	44	11	18	115	★.403	272	15	12	.960
1924—Detroit	Amer.	★OF-1B	153	570	107	197	●45	16	10	114	.346	263	★31	9	.970
1925—Detroit	Amer.	OF	150	573	97	225	40	11	13	134	★.393	278	9	9	.970
1926—Detroit	Amer.	OF	141	502	90	184	41	8	9	103	.367	228	18	7	.972
1927—Detroit	Amer.	OF	141	505	106	201	50	9	14	120	★.398	218	11	8	.966
1928—Detroit	Amer.	OF-1B	151	558	83	183	38	10	14	107	.328	449	34	9	.982
1929—Detroit(a)	Amer.	OF	125	453	86	156	41	7	15	120	.344	193	8	7	.966
1930—Cincinnati	Nat.	OF-1B	142	459	79	153	43	6	19	91	.333	457	30	19	.962
1931—Cincinnati	Nat.								(Out of game all season)						
1932—Cincinnati	Nat.	1B	15	31	3	8	2	0	0	6	.258	44	2	1	.979
American League Totals—15 Years			1988	7297	1209	2499	497	145	164	1455	.343	6488	418	172	.976
National League Totals—2 Years			157	490	82	161	45	6	19	97	.329	501	32	20	.964
Major League Totals—17 Years			2145	7787	1291	2660	542	151	183	1552	.342	6989	450	192	.975

aReleased on waivers to Cincinnati, October 29, 1929.

GEORGE ANDREW HENDRICK JR.

Born October 18, 1949, at Los Angeles, Calif.

Height, 6.03. Weight, 195.

Threw and batted righthanded.

Hit three home runs in a game, June 19, 1973.
Led National League in sacrifice flies with 14 in 1982.
Led American League outfielders in double plays with 6 in 1976.
Tied for National League lead in double plays by outfielders with 7 in 1979.
Named first baseman on THE SPORTING NEWS National League All-Star Team, 1983.
Named outfielder on THE SPORTING NEWS National League All-Star Team, 1980.
Named first baseman on THE SPORTING NEWS National League Silver Slugger team, 1983.
Named outfielder on THE SPORTING NEWS National League Silver Slugger team, 1980.

Year Club League	Pos.	G.	AB.	R.	H.	2B.	3B.	HR.	RBI.	B.A.	PO.	A.	E.	F.A.
1968—Burlington .... Midw.	OF	103	364	58	119	●25	4	5	60	★.327	134	8	8	.947
1969—Lodi .... Calif.	OF	86	316	47	97	13	2	4	28	.307	121	5	4	.969
1970—Burlington .... Midw.	OF	54	198	37	61	9	3	12	43	.308	80	1	5	.942
1970—Birmingham .... South.	OF	54	199	30	57	12	0	6	20	.286	115	4	5	.960
1971—Iowa .... A. A.	OF	63	249	57	83	9	2	21	63	.333	113	5	3	.975
1971—Oakland................ Amer.	OF	42	114	8	27	4	1	0	8	.237	52	1	1	.981
1972—Iowa .... A. A.	OF	8	33	0	9	0	0	0	4	.273	14	2	0	1.000
1972—Oakland†.............. Amer.	OF	58	121	10	22	1	1	4	15	.182	68	0	0	1.000
1973—Cleveland.............. Amer.	OF	113	440	64	118	18	0	21	61	.268	242	7	3	.988
1974—Cleveland.............. Amer.	OF	139	495	65	138	23	1	19	67	.279	355	9	4	.989
1975—Cleveland.............. Amer.	OF	145	561	82	145	21	2	24	86	.258	338	4	6	.983
1976—Cleveland‡............ Amer.	OF	149	551	72	146	20	3	25	81	.265	288	13	4	.987
1977—San Diego .... Nat.	OF	152	541	75	168	25	2	23	81	.311	386	11	7	.983
1978—S.D.§-St.L. .... Nat.	OF	138	493	64	137	31	1	20	75	.278	313	6	2	.994
1979—St. Louis................ Nat.	OF	140	493	67	148	27	1	16	75	.300	254	★20	2	.993
1980—St. Louis................ Nat.	OF	150	572	73	173	33	2	25	109	.302	322	10	2	.994
1981—St. Louis................ Nat.	OF	101	394	67	112	19	3	18	61	.284	227	6	4	.983
1982—St. Louis................ Nat.	OF	136	515	65	145	20	5	19	104	.282	238	6	5	.980
1983—St. Louis................ Nat.	1B-OF	144	529	73	168	33	3	18	97	.318	904	79	8	.992
1984—St. Louis x............ Nat.	OF-1B	120	441	57	122	28	1	9	69	.277	189	9	2	.990
1985—Pittsburgh y .... Nat.	OF	69	256	23	59	15	0	2	25	.230	133	2	4	.971
1985—California.............. Amer.	OF	16	41	5	5	1	0	2	6	.122	18	1	0	1.000
1986—California.............. Amer.	OF-1B	102	283	45	77	13	1	14	47	.272	188	9	5	.975
1987—California.............. Amer.	OF-1B	65	162	14	39	10	0	5	25	.241	114	5	3	.975
1988—California z............ Amer.	OF-1B	69	127	12	31	1	0	3	19	.244	129	9	3	.979
American League Totals—10 Years		898	2895	377	748	112	9	117	415	.258	1792	58	29	.985
National League Totals—9 Years...........		1150	4234	564	1232	231	18	150	696	.291	2966	149	36	.989
Major League Totals—18 Years...............		2048	7129	941	1980	343	27	267	1111	.278	4758	207	65	.987

Selected by Oakland A's organization in 1st round (first player selected) of free-agent draft, January 27, 1968.

†Traded with Catcher Dave Duncan to Cleveland Indians for Catcher Ray Fosse and Infielder Jack Heidemann, March 24, 1973.

‡Traded to San Diego Padres for Outfielder John Grubb, Catcher Fred Kendall and Shortstop Hector Torres, December 8, 1976.

§Traded to St. Louis Cardinals for Pitcher Eric Rasmussen, May 26, 1978.

xTraded with Catcher Steve Barnard to Pittsburgh Pirates for Pitcher John Tudor and Outfielder Brian Harper, December 12, 1984.

yTraded with Pitchers John Candelaria and Al Holland to California Angels for Pitcher Pat Clements, Outfielder Mike Brown and a player to be named later, August 2, 1985; Pittsburgh Pirates' organization acquired Pitcher Bob Kipper to complete deal, August 16, 1985.

zGranted free agency, November 4, 1988.

CHAMPIONSHIP SERIES RECORD

Year Club League	Pos.	G.	AB.	R.	H.	2B.	3B.	HR.	RBI.	B.A.	PO.	A.	E.	F.A.
1972—Oakland................ Amer.	PH-OF	5	7	2	1	0	0	0	0	.143	1	0	0	1.000
1982—St. Louis................ Nat.	OF	3	13	2	4	0	0	0	2	.308	5	0	0	1.000
1986—California.............. Amer.	OF-1B	3	12	0	1	0	0	0	0	.083	16	2	0	1.000
Championship Series Totals—3 Years.....		11	32	4	6	0	0	0	2	.188	22	2	0	1.000

WORLD SERIES RECORD

Year Club League	Pos.	G.	AB.	R.	H.	2B.	3B.	HR.	RBI.	B.A.	PO.	A.	E.	F.A.
1972—Oakland................ Amer.	OF	5	15	3	2	0	0	0	0	.133	12	0	0	1.000
1982—St. Louis................ Nat.	OF	7	28	5	9	0	0	0	5	.321	10	1	0	1.000
World Series Totals—2 Years		12	43	8	11	0	0	0	5	.256	22	1	0	1.000

FLOYD CAVES (BABE) HERMAN

Born June 26, 1903, at Buffalo, N. Y.

Died November 27, 1987, at Glendale, Calif.

Height, 6.04. Weight, 190.

Threw and batted lefthanded.

Hit three home runs in a game, July 20, 1933.

Tied for National League lead in double plays by outfielder with 6 in 1932.

Scout, Pittsburgh Pirates, 1946 through 1950; coach, Pittsburgh Pirates, 1951; Seattle, Pacific Coast League, 1952; scout, New York Yankees, 1953-54; Philadelphia Phillies, 1955 through 1959; New York Mets, 1961; Yankees, 1962-63; San Francisco Giants, 1964.

Year Club League	Pos.	G.	AB.	R.	H.	2B.	3B.	HR.	RBI.	B.A.	PO.	A.	E.	F.A.
1921—Edmonton.............. W. Can.	OF	107	409	53	135	24	*18	7	....	.330	677	41	25	.966
1922—Reading.................. Int.	1B-OF	8	31	3	8	0	0	0	....	.258	78	2	3	.964

Year	Club	League	Pos.	G.	AB.	R.	H.	2B.	3B.	HR.	RBI.	B.A.	PO.	A.	E.	F.A.
1922—Omaha	West.	1B-OF	92	310	55	129	34	7	9	....	.416	481	34	17	.968
1923—Atl.-Mem.	South.	1B	145	551	69	187	36	10	13	100	.339	1278	76	*29	.979
1924—San Antonio	Tex.	1B	21	86	13	30	6	0	2	21	.349	153	9	1	.994
1924—Little Rock	South.	1B	69	239	32	76	14	3	4	40	.318	570	44	21	.967
1925—Seattle	P. C.	1B	167	651	115	206	52	13	15	131	.316	1456	99	26	.984
1926—Brooklyn	Nat.	OF-1B	137	496	64	158	35	11	11	81	.319	974	64	17	.984
1927—Brooklyn	Nat.	OF	130	412	65	112	26	9	14	73	.272	968	68	*21	.980
1928—Brooklyn	Nat.	OF	134	486	64	165	37	6	12	91	.340	225	12	*16	.937
1929—Brooklyn	Nat.	OF	146	569	105	217	42	13	21	113	.381	244	10	*16	.941
1930—Brooklyn	Nat.	OF	153	614	143	241	48	11	35	130	.393	260	10	6	.978
1931—Brooklyn(a)	Nat.	OF	151	610	93	191	43	16	18	97	.313	287	24	13	.960
1932—Cincinnati(b)	Nat.	OF	148	577	87	188	38	*19	16	87	.326	392	18	13	.969
1933—Chicago	Nat.	OF	137	508	77	147	36	12	16	93	.289	252	12	12	.957
1934—Chicago(c)	Nat.	OF	125	467	65	142	34	5	14	84	.304	192	7	6	.971
1935—Pitts.(d)-Cin.	Nat.	OF-1B	118	430	52	136	31	6	10	65	.316	319	15	9	.974
1936—Cincinnati(e)	Nat.	OF-1B	119	380	59	106	25	2	13	71	.279	175	3	6	.967
1937—Detroit	Amer.	OF	17	20	2	6	3	0	0	3	.300	5	0	0	1.000
1937—Toledo	A. A.	OF	85	336	76	117	37	4	12	79	.348	141	3	1	.993
1938—Jersey City	Int.	OF	145	527	89	171	40	5	18	93	.324	188	10	9	.957
1939—Hollywood	P. C.	1B-OF	90	350	69	111	36	5	13	71	.317	748	45	13	.984
1940—Hollywood	P. C.	1B-OF	148	469	62	144	45	7	9	80	.307	460	33	17	.967
1941—Hollywood	P. C.	1B-OF	110	272	41	94	16	1	11	63	.346	572	53	4	.994
1942—Hollywood	P. C.	1B-OF	85	149	18	48	5	0	5	42	.322	247	32	3	.989
1943—Hollywood	P. C.	OF	81	147	15	52	8	1	4	22	.354	24	2	1	.963
1944—Hollywood	P. C.	OF	78	107	8	37	8	1	0	23	.346	79	7	3	.966
1945—Brooklyn	Nat.	OF	37	34	6	9	1	0	1	9	.265	0	0	0	.000
American League Totals—1 Year			17	20	2	6	3	0	0	3	.300	5	0	0	1.000
National League Totals—12 Years			1535	5583	880	1812	396	110	181	994	.325	4288	243	135	.971
Major League Totals—13 Years			1552	5603	882	1818	399	110	181	997	.324	4293	243	135	.971

aTraded with Catcher Ernie Lombardi and Third Baseman Walter Gilbert to Cincinnati Reds for Third Baseman Joe Stripp, Second Baseman Tony Cuccinello and Catcher Clyde Sukeforth, March 14, 1932.

bTraded to Chicago Cubs for Pitcher Robert E. Smith, Catcher Rollie Hemsley, Outfielders John F. Moore and Lance Richbourg and cash, November 30, 1932.

cTraded with Pitchers Guy Bush and Jim Weaver to Pittsburgh Pirates for Pitcher Larry French and Third Baseman Fred Lindstrom, November 22, 1934.

dSold to Cincinnati Reds, June 21, 1935.

eReleased to Detroit Tigers on waivers, April 1, 1937.

WILLIAM JENNINGS (BILLY) HERMAN

Born July 7, 1909, at New Albany, Ind.

Height, 5.11. Weight, 195.

Threw and batted righthanded.

Shares National League records for most years leading league in putouts by second baseman (7); most putouts by second baseman, nine-inning game (11), June 28, 1933, first game; most putouts by second baseman, doubleheader (16), June 28, 1933.

Named as second baseman on THE SPORTING NEWS All-Star Major League Team, 1943.

Manager, Pittsburgh Pirates, 1947; Minneapolis, American Association, 1948; Richmond, Piedmont League, 1951; coach, Brooklyn Dodgers, 1952-57; Milwaukee Braves, 1958-59; Boston Red Sox, 1960 through 1964; manager, Red Sox, 1965-66; coach, California Angels, 1967; manager, Bradenton, Gulf Coast Rookie League, 1968; Tri-City, Northwest League, 1969; scout, Oakland Athletics, 1968 through 1974; San Diego, 1978 to 1979.

Named to Hall of Fame, 1975.

Year	Club	League	Pos.	G.	AB.	R.	H.	2B.	3B.	HR.	RBI.	B.A.	PO.	A.	E.	F.A.
1928—Vicksburg	Cot.St.	INF	106	364	63	121	12	15	4	....	.332	237	322	24	.959
1928—Louisville	A. A.	2B	4	15	3	5	1	1	0	4	.333	9	14	0	1.000
1929—Dayton	Cent.	2B	138	529	96	174	36	7	13	79	.329	*390	*432	*39	.955
1929—Louisville	A. A.	2B	24	93	17	30	3	4	1	13	.323	72	85	7	.957
1930—Louisville	A. A.	2B	143	617	108	188	40	7	8	86	.305	354	495	*40	.955
1931—Louisville	A. A.	2B	118	486	100	170	24	3	7	59	.350	352	375	28	.963
1931—Chicago	Nat.	2B	25	98	14	32	7	0	0	16	.327	76	79	10	.939
1932—Chicago	Nat.	2B	•154	656	102	206	42	7	1	51	.314	401	*527	*38	.961
1933—Chicago	Nat.	2B	153	619	82	173	35	2	0	44	.279	*466	512	*45	.956
1934—Chicago	Nat.	2B	113	456	79	138	21	6	3	42	.303	278	385	17	.975
1935—Chicago	Nat.	2B	154	666	113	*227	*57	6	7	83	.341	*416	*520	35	*.964
1936—Chicago	Nat.	2B	153	632	101	211	57	7	5	93	.334	*457	492	24	*.975
1937—Chicago	Nat.	2B	138	564	106	189	35	11	8	65	.335	384	458	*41	.954
1938—Chicago	Nat.	2B	•152	624	86	173	34	7	1	56	.277	*404	517	18	*.981
1939—Chicago	Nat.	2B	156	623	111	191	34	*18	7	70	.307	*377	*485	*29	.967

Year Club	League	Pos.	G.	AB.	R.	H.	2B.	3B.	HR.	RBI.	B.A.	PO.	A.	E.	F.A.
1940—Chicago	Nat.	2B	135	558	77	163	24	4	5	57	.292	●366	448	22	.974
1941—Chi.(a)-Brook	Nat.	2B	144	572	81	163	30	5	3	41	.285	330	374	26	.964
1942—Brooklyn	Nat.	★2B-1B	★155	571	76	146	34	2	2	65	.256	★412	404	23	.973
1943—Brooklyn	Nat.	2B-3B	153	585	76	193	41	2	2	100	.330	345	390	21	.972
1944-45—Brooklyn	Nat.						(In Military Service)								
1946—Brk.(b)-Bos.(c)	Nat.	INF	122	436	56	130	31	5	3	50	.298	352	207	16	.972
1947—Pittsburgh	Nat.	2B-1B	15	47	3	10	4	0	0	6	.213	20	15	0	1.000
1948—Minneapolis	A. A.	2B-1B	10	31	9	14	4	0	2	9	.452	18	11	3	.906
1949—							(Out of Organized Ball)								
1950—Oakland	P. C.	INF	71	202	32	62	8	0	4	29	.307	62	81	4	.973
Major League Totals—15 Years			1922	7707	1163	2345	486	82	47	839	.304	5084	5823	365	.968

aTraded to Brooklyn Dodgers for Infielder John Hudson, Outfielder Charley Gilbert and cash, May 6, 1941.
bTraded to Boston Braves for Catcher Stew Hofferth, June 15, 1946.
cTraded to Pittsburgh Pirates with Infielder Whitey Wietelmann, Pitcher Elmer Singleton and Outfielder Stan Wentzel for Outfielder Bob Elliott and Catcher Hank Camelli, September 30, 1946.

WORLD SERIES RECORD

Year Club	League	Pos.	G.	AB.	R.	H.	2B.	3B.	HR.	RBI.	B.A.	PO.	A.	E.	F.A.
1932—Chicago	Nat.	2B	4	18	5	4	1	0	0	1	.222	5	12	1	.944
1935—Chicago	Nat.	2B	6	24	3	8	2	1	1	6	.333	15	19	1	.971
1938—Chicago	Nat.	2B	4	16	1	3	0	0	0	0	.188	5	14	2	.905
1941—Brooklyn	Nat.	2B	4	8	0	1	0	0	0	0	.125	4	13	0	1.000
World Series Totals—4 Years			18	66	9	16	3	1	1	7	.242	29	58	4	.956

PAUL A. HINES

Born March 1, 1852, at Washington, D.C.
Died July 10, 1935, at Hyattsville, Md.
Threw and batted righthanded.

Year Club	League	Pos.	G.	AB.	R.	H.	2B.	3B.	HR.	SB.	B.A.	PO.	A.	E.	F.A.
1876—Chicago	Nat.	OF	64	306	62	101	21	3	2	....	.330	159	8	15	.917
1877—Chicago	Nat.	2B-OF	48	202	25	51	12	6	0	....	.252	91	39	32	.803
1878—Providence	Nat.	OF	60	248	40	87	12	4	★4	....	.351	104	20	24	.838
1879—Providence	Nat.	OF	84	406	81	★145	23	8	2	....	.357	145	24	26	.866
1880—Providence	Nat.	1-2B-O	82	356	61	109	19	2	2	....	.306	145	16	13	.925
1881—Providence	Nat.	2B-OF	79	356	64	101	27	5	2	....	.283	176	14	22	.896
1882—Providence	Nat.	1B-OF	84	379	73	117	28	10	4	....	.308	151	16	27	.860
1883—Providence	Nat.	1B-OF	97	442	93	132	11	4	4	....	.298	168	21	18	.913
1884—Providence	Nat.	P-1-O	112	480	92	146	★34	8	3	....	.304	202	20	26	.895
1885—Providence	Nat.	INF-OF	98	411	63	111	19	4	1	....	.270	199	18	34	.864
1886—Washington	Nat.	3B-OF	121	487	80	152	25	7	9	21	.312	200	52	35	.878
1887—Washington	Nat.	OF	123	526	83	195	32	5	9	46	.370	180	14	25	.885
1888—Indianapolis	Nat.	OF	132	513	84	144	25	3	4	31	.280	255	13	26	.911
1889—Indianapolis	Nat.	1B	121	486	77	148	29	1	0	34	.304	1090	57	43	.964
1890—Pittsburgh-Bos.	Nat.	OF-1B	100	393	51	93	11	3	1	14	.237	320	20	25	.932
1891—Washington	Am. Assn.	OF	51	199	25	52	6	5	0	5	.261	77	7	14	.857
National League Totals—15 Years			1405	5991	1029	1832	328	73	47	....	.306	3585	352	391	.910
American League Totals—1 Year			51	199	25	52	6	5	0	5	.261	77	7	14	.857
Major League Totals—16 Years			1456	6190	1054	1884	334	78	47	....	.304	3662	359	405	.909

GILBERT RAY (GIL) HODGES

Born April 4, 1924, at Princeton, Ind.
Died April 2, 1972, at West Palm Beach, Fla.
Height, 6.01½. Weight, 211.
Threw and batted righthanded.

Shares major league records for most times faced pitcher, inning (3), August 8, 1954, eighth inning; most home runs, game (4), August 31, 1950.

Led National League first basemen in double plays, 1949-50-51-58.

Named to THE SPORTING NEWS All-Star Fielding Team as first baseman, 1957-58-59.

Manager, Washington Senators, 1963 through 1967; New York Mets, 1968 through 1971.

Year	Club	League	Pos.	G.	AB.	R.	H.	2B.	3B.	HR.	RBI.	B.A.	PO.	A.	E.	F.A.
1943—Brooklyn	Nat.		3B	1	2	0	0	0	0	0	0	.000	1	2	2	.600
1943-44-45—Brooklyn	Nat.		......	......	......	......	......	......	....	....	......	......	......	......	......	......
1946—Newport News	Pied.		C	129	406	65	113	27	7	8	64	.278	*731	*90	14	*.983
1947—Brooklyn	Nat.		C	28	77	9	12	3	1	1	7	.156	79	12	4	.958
1948—Brooklyn	Nat.		1B-C	134	481	48	120	18	5	11	70	.249	990	72	17	.984
1949—Brooklyn	Nat.		1B	156	596	94	170	23	4	23	115	.285	*1336	80	7	*.995
1950—Brooklyn	Nat.		1B	153	561	98	159	26	2	32	113	.283	1273	100	8	*.994
1951—Brooklyn	Nat.		1B	●158	582	118	156	25	3	40	103	.268	1365	*126	12	.992
1952—Brooklyn	Nat.		1B	153	508	87	129	27	1	32	102	.254	1322	*116	11	.992
1953—Brooklyn	Nat.		1B-OF	141	520	101	157	22	7	31	122	.302	1062	101	9	.992
1954—Brooklyn	Nat.		1B	●154	579	106	176	23	5	42	130	.304	*1381	*132	7	.995
1955—Brooklyn	Nat.		1B-OF	150	546	75	158	24	5	27	102	.289	1291	106	14	.990
1956—Brooklyn	Nat.		1-O-C	153	550	86	146	29	4	32	87	.265	1234	103	12	.991
1957—Brooklyn	Nat.		1-3-2B	150	579	94	173	28	7	27	98	.299	*1319	117	14	*.990
1958—Los Angeles	Nat.		1-3-O-C	141	475	68	123	15	1	22	64	.259	932	103	9	.991
1959—Los Angeles	Nat.		*1B-3B	124	413	57	114	19	2	25	80	.276	896	74	8	*.992
1960—Los Angeles	Nat.		1B-3B	101	197	22	39	8	1	8	30	.198	411	44	5	.989
1961—Los Angeles(a)	Nat.		1B	109	215	25	52	4	0	8	31	.242	454	37	1	*.998
1962—New York	Nat.		1B	54	127	15	32	1	0	9	17	.252	315	32	5	.986
1963—New York(b)	Nat.		1B	11	22	2	5	0	0	0	3	.227	61	8	0	1.000
Major League Totals—18 Years				2071	7030	1105	1921	295	48	370	1274	.273	15722	1365	145	.992

aSelected by New York Mets in National League expansion draft, October 10, 1961.

bTraded to Washington Senators for Outfielder Jimmy Piersall, May 22, 1963.

WORLD SERIES RECORD

Year	Club	League	Pos.	G.	AB.	R.	H.	2B.	3B.	HR.	RBI.	B.A.	PO.	A.	E.	F.A.
1947—Brooklyn	Nat.		PH	1	1	0	0	0	0	0	0	.000	0	0	0	.000
1949—Brooklyn	Nat.		1B	5	17	2	4	0	0	1	4	.235	38	3	0	1.000
1952—Brooklyn	Nat.		1B	7	21	1	0	0	0	0	1	.000	60	5	1	.985
1953—Brooklyn	Nat.		1B	6	22	3	8	0	0	1	1	.364	47	4	1	.981
1955—Brooklyn	Nat.		1B	7	24	2	7	0	0	1	5	.292	74	4	0	1.000
1956—Brooklyn	Nat.		1B	7	23	5	7	2	0	1	8	.304	54	5	0	1.000
1959—Los Angeles	Nat.		1B	6	23	2	9	0	1	1	2	.391	53	3	0	1.000
World Series Totals—7 Years				39	131	15	35	2	1	5	21	.267	326	24	2	.994

THOMAS FRANCIS (TOMMY) HOLMES

Born March 29, 1918, at Brooklyn, N. Y.

Height, 5.10. Weight, 180.

Threw and batted lefthanded.

Led National League outfielders in double plays, 1944, 1946.

Named Most Valuable Player, National League, by THE SPORTING NEWS, 1945.

Named as outfielder for THE SPORTING NEWS All-Star Major League Team, 1945.

Player-manager, Hartford, Eastern League, 1951; player-manager, Boston Braves, 1951-1952; manager, Toledo, American Association, 1953; scout, Brooklyn, 1953; player-manager, Elmira, Eastern League, 1954; manager, Fort Worth, Texas League, 1955; Portland, Pacific Coast League, 1956, Montreal, International League, 1957; scout, Los Angeles Dodgers, 1958.

Year	Club	League	Pos.	G.	AB.	R.	H.	2B.	3B.	HR.	RBI.	B.A.	PO.	A.	E.	F.A.
1937—Norfolk	Piedmont		OF	137	547	107	175	31	8	25	111	.320	282	11	11	.964
1938—Binghamton	Eastern		OF	135	543	110	*200	*41	9	6	62	*.368	279	14	11	.964
1939—Kansas City	A. A.		OF	7	20	2	3	0	0	0	1	.150	5	0	1	.833
1939—Newark	Int.		OF	107	386	73	131	23	10	4	55	.339	131	8	2	.986
1940—Newark	Int.		OF	162	*665	*126	*211	33	7	7	60	.317	360	15	6	.984
1941—Newark	Int.		OF	●154	*630	105	*190	17	7	9	59	.302	*332	8	4	*.988
1942—Boston	Nat.		OF	141	558	56	155	24	4	4	41	.278	373	16	4	.990
1943—Boston	Nat.		OF	152	*629	75	170	33	10	5	41	.270	408	18	3	.993
1944—Boston	Nat.		OF	155	631	93	195	42	6	13	73	.309	426	14	4	.991
1945—Boston	Nat.		OF	154	636	125	*224	*47	6	*28	117	.352	334	13	6	.983
1946—Boston	Nat.		OF	149	568	80	176	35	6	6	79	.310	294	17	4	.987
1947—Boston	Nat.		OF	150	618	90	*191	33	3	9	53	.309	336	12	4	.989
1948—Boston	Nat.		OF	139	585	85	190	35	7	6	61	.325	283	8	5	.983
1949—Boston	Nat.		OF	117	380	47	101	20	4	8	59	.266	210	10	3	.987
1950—Boston	Nat.		OF	105	322	44	96	20	1	9	51	.298	151	6	0	1.000

Year	Club	League	Pos.	G.	AB.	R.	H.	2B.	3B.	HR.	RBI.	B.A.	PO.	A.	E.	F.A.
1951—Hartford	Eastern		OF	41	113	24	36	7	2	5	29	.319	33	4	1	.974
1951—Boston	Nat.		OF	27	29	1	5	2	0	0	5	.172	2	0	0	1.000
1952—Brooklyn	Nat.		OF	31	36	2	4	1	0	0	1	.111	6	1	0	1.000
1954—Elmira	Eastern		OF	24	19	3	7	1	0	0	5	.368	0	0	0	.000
Major League Totals—11 Years				1320	4992	698	1507	292	47	88	581	.302	2823	115	33	.989

WORLD SERIES RECORD

Year	Club	League	Pos.	G.	AB.	R.	H.	2B.	3B.	HR.	RBI.	B.A.	PO.	A.	E.	F.A.
1948—Boston	Nat.		OF	6	26	3	5	0	0	0	1	.192	10	2	0	1.000
1952—Brooklyn	Nat.		OF	3	1	0	0	0	0	0	0	.000	2	0	0	1.000
World Series Totals—2 Years				9	27	3	5	0	0	0	1	.185	12	2	0	1.000

HARRY BARTHOLOMEW HOOPER

Born August 24, 1887, at Santa Clara County, Calif.

Died December 18, 1974, at Santa Cruz, Calif.

Height, 5.10. Weight, 168.

Threw right and batted lefthanded.

Led American League outfielders in double plays, 1922, 1924 (tie).
Baseball coach, Princeton University, 1931, 1932.
Named to Hall of Fame, 1971.

Year	Club	League	Pos.	G.	AB.	R.	H.	2B.	3B.	HR.	RBI.	B.A.	PO.	A.	E.	F.A.
1907—Oak.-Sacra'to	Calif. St.		OF	36	139	26	43	4	4	1	....	.309	....	....	....	.....
1908—Sacramento	Calif. St.		OF	77	294	47	101	....	....	....	....	.344	116	17	4	.971
1909—Boston	Amer.		OF	81	255	29	72	3	4	0	16	.282	124	14	7	.952
1910—Boston	Amer.		OF	155	584	81	156	9	10	2	33	.267	241	●30	★18	.938
1911—Boston	Amer.		OF	130	524	93	163	20	6	4	43	.311	181	27	10	.954
1912—Boston	Amer.		OF	147	590	98	143	20	12	2	46	.242	220	22	9	.964
1913—Boston	Amer.		OF	148	585	100	169	29	12	4	40	.289	248	25	9	.968
1914—Boston	Amer.		OF	141	530	85	137	23	15	1	44	.258	231	23	7	.973
1915—Boston	Amer.		OF	149	566	90	133	20	13	2	48	.235	255	23	8	.972
1916—Boston	Amer.		OF	151	575	75	156	20	11	1	33	.271	266	19	10	.966
1917—Boston	Amer.		OF	151	559	89	143	21	11	3	43	.256	245	20	8	.971
1918—Boston	Amer.		OF	126	474	81	137	26	13	1	46	.289	221	16	9	.963
1919—Boston	Amer.		OF	128	491	76	131	25	6	3	48	.267	262	19	6	.979
1920—Boston(a)	Amer.		OF	139	536	91	167	30	17	7	53	.312	263	22	11	.963
1921—Chicago	Amer.		OF	108	419	74	137	26	5	8	58	.327	182	12	5	.975
1922—Chicago	Amer.		OF	152	602	111	183	35	8	11	80	.304	288	19	12	.962
1923—Chicago	Amer.		OF	145	576	87	166	32	4	10	65	.288	272	15	12	.960
1924—Chicago	Amer.		OF	130	476	107	156	27	8	10	62	.328	251	22	4	●.986
1925—Chicago	Amer.		OF	127	442	62	117	23	5	6	55	.265	231	16	6	.976
1926—							(Out of Organized Ball)									
1927—Missions	P. C.		OF	78	218	35	62	9	0	1	19	.284	113	11	3	.976
Major League Totals—17 Years				2308	8784	1429	2466	389	160	75	813	.281	3981	344	151	.966

aTraded to Chicago White Sox for First Baseman Shano Collins and Outfielder Nemo Leibold, March 4, 1921.

WORLD SERIES RECORD

Year	Club	League	Pos.	G.	AB.	R.	H.	2B.	3B.	HR.	RBI.	B.A.	PO.	A.	E.	F.A.
1912—Boston	Amer.		OF	8	31	3	9	2	1	0	2	.290	16	3	0	1.000
1915—Boston	Amer.		OF	5	20	4	7	0	0	2	3	350	8	0	1	.889
1916—Boston	Amer.		OF	5	21	6	7	1	1	0	1	.333	8	2	0	1.000
1918—Boston	Amer.		OF	6	20	0	4	0	0	0	0	.200	11	0	0	1.000
World Series Totals—4 Years				24	92	13	27	3	2	2	6	.293	43	5	1	.980

ROGERS HORNSBY
(Rajah)

Born April 27, 1896, at Winters, Tex.

Died January 5, 1963, at Chicago, Ill.

Height, 5.11½. Weight, 200.

Threw and batted righthanded.

Holds National League records for highest batting average, lifetime, 15 or more years (.359), highest slugging average, lifetime, 13 or more years (.578), highest slugging average, season, 100 or more games (.756), 1925; most years leading league in slugging average (9); most home runs by second baseman, lifetime (263).

Shares National League record for most consecutive years leading league in hits (3).

Holds modern major league record for highest batting average, season, 100 or more games (.424), 1924.

Led National League second basemen in double plays, 1922, 1929.

Manager, St. Louis Cardinals, 1925 through 1926; Boston Braves, 1928; Chicago Cubs, 1930, to 1932; St. Louis Browns, 1933 to 1937; coach, Baltimore, International League, 1938; manager, Chattanooga, Southern Association, 1938; Baltimore, International League, 1939; Oklahoma City, Texas League, 1940, to 1941; manager and general manager, Fort Worth, Texas League, 1941 through 1942; manager, Beaumont, Texas League, 1950; Seattle, Pacific Coast League, 1951; St. Louis Browns, 1952 (part); Cincinnati Reds, 1952 to 1953; coach, Chicago Cubs, 1958-59; scout, New York Mets, 1961; coach, New York Mets, 1962.

Named National League Most Valuable Player, 1925 and 1929.

Named to Hall of Fame, 1942.

Year	Club	League	Pos.	G.	AB.	R.	H.	2B.	3B.	HR.	RBI.	B.A.	PO.	A.	E.	F.A.
1914—Hugo-Denison	Tex.-Ok	SS	113	393	47	91	12	3	3	....	.232	208	285	45	.916
1915—Denison	W. A.	SS	119	429	75	119	26	2	4	....	.277	267	354	58	.915
1915—St. Louis	Nat.	SS	18	57	5	14	2	0	0	4	.246	48	46	8	.922
1916—St.Louis	Nat.	INF	139	495	63	155	17	15	6	60	.313	325	315	45	.934
1917—St. Louis	Nat.	SS	145	523	86	171	24	*17	8	70	.327	268	527	52	.939
1918—St. Louis	Nat.	SS-OF	115	416	51	117	19	11	5	59	.281	211	434	46	.933
1919—St. Louis	Nat.	INF	138	512	68	163	15	9	8	68	.318	185	367	34	.942
1920—St. Louis	Nat.	2B	149	589	96	*218	*44	20	9	●94	*.370	*343	*524	*234	.962
1921—St. Louis	Nat.	INF-OF	*154	592	*131	*235	*44	●18	21	*126	*.397	305	477	25	.969
1922—St. Louis	Nat.	2B	154	623	*141	*250	*46	14	*42	*152	*.401	*398	473	30	*.967
1923—St. Louis	Nat.	1B-2B	107	424	89	163	32	10	17	83	*.384	192	283	19	.962
1924—St. Louis	Nat.	2B	143	536	●121	*227	*43	14	25	94	*.424	301	517	30	.965
1925—St. Louis	Nat.	2B	138	504	133	203	41	10	*39	*143	*.403	287	416	34	.954
1926—St. Louis(a)	Nat.	2B	134	527	96	167	34	5	11	93	.317	245	433	27	.962
1927—New York(b)	Nat.	2B	●155	568	●133	205	32	9	26	125	.361	299	582	25	.972
1928—Boston(c)	Nat.	2B	140	486	99	188	42	7	21	94	*.387	295	450	21	.973
1929—Chicago	Nat.	2B	*156	602	*156	229	47	8	39	149	.380	286	*547	23	.973
1930—Chicago	Nat.	2B	42	104	15	32	5	1	2	17	.308	44	76	11	.916
1931—Chicago	Nat.	2B-3B	100	357	64	118	37	1	16	90	.331	128	255	22	.946
1932—Chicago(d)	Nat.	3B-OF	19	58	10	13	2	0	1	7	.224	17	10	4	.871
1933—St. Louis	Nat.	2B	46	83	9	27	6	0	2	21	.325	24	35	2	.967
1933—St. Louis	Amer.	PH	11	9	2	3	1	0	1	2	.333	0	0	0	.000
1934—St. Louis	Amer.	3B-OF	24	23	2	7	2	0	1	11	.304	2	3	0	1.000
1935—St. Louis	Amer	INF	10	24	1	5	3	0	0	3	.208	38	5	0	1.000
1936—St. Louis	Amer.	1B	2	5	1	2	0	0	0	2	.400	10	0	0	1.000
1937—St. Louis	Amer.	2B	20	56	7	18	3	0	1	11	.321	30	41	4	.947
1938—Baltimore	Int.	2-1B-OF	16	27	2	2	0	0	0	0	.074	22	2	0	1.000
1939—Chattanooga	South.	2B	3	3	1	2	0	0	1	2	.667	0	0	0	.000
1940—Oklahoma City	Tex.	PH	1	1	0	1	0	0	0	0	1.000	0	0	0	.000
1942—Ft. Worth	Tex.	2B	1	4	0	1	0	0	0	2	.250	2	2	0	1.000
National League Totals—19 Years			2192	8056	1566	2895	532	169	298	1549	.359	4201	6767	492	.957
American League Totals—5 Years			67	117	13	35	9	0	3	29	.299	80	49	4	.970
Major League Totals—23 Years			2259	8173	1579	2930	541	169	301	1578	.358	4281	6816	496	.957

aTraded to New York Giants for Infielder Frank Frisch and Pitcher Jimmy Ring, December 20, 1926.

bTraded to Boston Braves for Outfielder Jimmy Welsh and Catcher Francis Hogan, January 10, 1928.

cTraded to Chicago Cubs for Infielder Fred Maguire, Catcher Doc Leggett, Pitchers Percy Jones, Harry Seibold and Bruce Cunningham and cash, November 7, 1928.

dSigned with St. Louis Cardinals, October 24, 1932.

WORLD SERIES RECORD

Year	Club	League	Pos.	G.	AB.	R.	H.	2B.	3B.	HR.	RBI.	B.A.	PO.	A.	E.	F.A.
1926—St. Louis	Nat.	2B	7	28	2	7	1	0	0	4	.250	15	21	0	1.000
1929—Chicago	Nat.	2B	5	21	4	5	1	1	0	1	.238	9	11	1	.952
World Series Totals—2 Years			12	49	6	12	2	1	0	5	.245	24	32	1	.982

WILLIE WATTISON HORTON

Born October 18, 1942, at Arno, Va.

Height, 5.10. Weight, 205.

Threw and batted righthanded.

Shares major league record for most putouts and most chances accepted by left fielder, nine-inning game (11), July 18, 1969.

Hit three home runs in a game, June 9, 1970 and May 15, 1977.

Led Northern League in total bases with 203 in 1962.
Named designated hitter on THE SPORTING NEWS American League All-Star Team, 1975.
Named outfielder on THE SPORTING NEWS American League All-Star Team, 1968.
Named American League Comeback Player of the Year by THE SPORTING NEWS, 1979.
Minor league instructor, Oakland A's, 1983-84; coach Lakeland, Florida State League 1985; minor league batting instructor, New York Yankees, 1985; coach, Yankees, 1985; Chicago White Sox, 1986.

Year	Club	League	Pos.	G.	AB.	R.	H.	2B.	3B.	HR.	RBI.	B.A.	PO.	A.	E.	F.A.
1962—Duluth-Superior ...	North.	OF	123	441	68	130	20	4	15	72	.295	184	3	10	.949
1963—Syracuse	Int.	OF	21	78	12	17	2	1	2	8	.218	40	2	1	.977
1963—Knoxville	Sally	OF	118	442	77	147	20	9	14	70	.333	183	7	7	.964
1963—Detroit..................	Amer.	OF	15	43	6	14	2	1	1	4	.326	13	0	0	1.000
1964—Syracuse	Int.	OF-3B	135	490	73	141	16	9	28	99	.288	265	6	10	.964
1964—Detroit..................	Amer.	OF	25	80	6	13	1	3	1	10	.163	33	0	2	.943
1965—Detroit..................	Amer.	OF-3B	143	512	69	140	20	2	29	104	.273	249	9	3	.989
1966—Detroit..................	Amer.	OF	146	526	72	138	22	6	27	100	.262	233	4	5	.979
1967—Detroit..................	Amer.	OF	122	401	47	110	20	3	19	67	.274	165	5	5	.971
1968—Detroit..................	Amer.	OF	143	512	68	146	20	2	36	85	.285	212	6	6	.973
1969—Detroit..................	Amer.	OF	141	508	66	133	17	1	28	91	.262	272	8	8	.972
1970—Detroit..................	Amer.	OF	96	371	53	113	18	2	17	69	.305	154	10	3	.982
1971—Detroit..................	Amer.	OF	119	450	64	130	25	1	22	72	.289	176	8	7	.963
1972—Detroit..................	Amer.	OF	108	333	44	77	9	5	11	36	.231	131	6	0	1.000
1973—Detroit..................	Amer.	OF	111	411	42	130	19	3	17	53	.316	160	2	●10	.942
1974—Detroit..................	Amer.	OF	72	238	32	71	8	1	15	47	.298	106	2	6	.947
1975—Detroit..................	Amer.	DH	159	615	62	169	13	1	25	92	.275	0	0	0	.000
1976—Detroit..................	Amer.	DH	114	401	40	105	17	0	14	56	.262	0	0	0	.000
1977—Det.†-Tex.‡........	Amer.	OF	140	523	55	151	23	3	15	75	.289	16	0	1	.941
1978—Cl.§-Ok.x-Tr.y........	Amer.	OF	115	393	38	99	21	0	11	60	.252	1	0	2	.333
1979—Seattle z	Amer.	DH	●162	646	77	180	19	5	29	106	.279	0	0	0	.000
1980—Seattle a	Amer.	DH	97	335	32	74	10	1	8	36	.221	0	0	0	.000
1981—Portland................	PCL	DH	104	368	50	111	25	1	17	75	.302	0	0	0	.000
1982—Portland................	PCL	1B	119	440	61	121	11	1	22	82	.275	41	3	3	.936
1983—Nuevo Laredo	Mex.	OF	49	170	17	55	5	0	2	33	.324	4	0	0	1.000
Major League Totals—18 Years...............				2028	7298	873	1993	284	40	325	1163	.273	1921	60	58	.972

Signed as free agent by Detroit Tigers' organization, August 7, 1961.
†Traded to Texas Rangers for Pitcher Steve Foucault, April 12, 1977.
‡Traded with Pitcher David Clyde to Cleveland Indians for First Baseman-Outfielder John Lowenstein and Pitcher Tom Buskey, February 28, 1978.
§Released, July 3, 1978; signed by Oakland A's, July 13, 1978.
xTraded with Pitcher Phil Huffman to Toronto Blue Jays for Designated Hitter Rico Carty, August 15, 1978.
yGranted free agency, November 2, 1978; signed by Seattle Mariners, January 27, 1979.
zGranted free agency, November 1, 1979; re-signed by Mariners, December 20, 1979.
aTraded with Catcher Larry Cox, Pitcher Rick Honeycutt, Shortstop Mario Mendoza and Outfielder Leon Roberts to Texas Rangers for Pitchers Brian Allard, Ken Clay, Steve Finch and Jerry Gleaton, Shortstop Rick Auerbach and Outfielder Richie Zisk, December 12, 1980.
bReleased, April 1, 1981; signed with Portland, May 5, 1981.
cReleased, September 10, 1982; signed by Nuevo Laredo, April 6, 1983.
dReleased, July 3, 1983.

CHAMPIONSHIP SERIES RECORD

Year	Club	League	Pos.	G.	AB.	R.	H.	2B.	3B.	HR.	RBI.	B.A.	PO.	A.	E.	F.A.
1972—Detroit..................	Amer.	O-PH	5	10	0	1	0	0	0	0	.100	6	0	0	1.000

WORLD SERIES RECORD

Year	Club	League	Pos.	G.	AB.	R.	H.	2B.	3B.	HR.	RBI.	B.A.	PO.	A.	E.	F.A.
1968—Detroit..................	Amer.	OF	7	23	6	7	1	1	1	3	.304	5	1	1	.857

FRANK OLIVER HOWARD
(Hondo)

Born August 8, 1936, at Columbus, O.

Height, 6.07. Weight, 250.

Threw and batted righthanded.

Holds major league records for most home runs, six consecutive games (10), May 12 through 18, 1968; most home runs, five consecutive games (8), May 12 through 17, 1968 and May 14 through 18, 1968.
Shares American League record for most home runs, four consecutive games (7), May 12 through 16, 1968.
Named Minor League Player of the Year by THE SPORTING NEWS, 1959.
Named National League Rookie of the Year by the Baseball Writers' Association and THE SPORTING NEWS, 1960.
Named outfielder on THE SPORTING NEWS American League All-Star Team, 1968-69-70.
Manager-instructor, Milwaukee Brewers minor league organization, 1976; coach, Milwaukee, 1977 to 1980; manager, San Diego Padres, 1981; coach, New York Mets, 1982 to 1983 (part); manager, Mets, 1983 (part); coach, Mets, 1984; Milwaukee, 1985 through 1986; Seattle Mariners, 1987 through 1988; New York Yankees, 1989.

Year—Club	League	Pos.	G.	AB.	R.	H.	2B.	3B.	HR.	RBI.	B.A.	PO.	A.	E.	F.A.
1958—Green Bay	I.I.I.	OF-P	●129	487	★104	162	34	2	★37	★119	.333	186	6	8	.960
1958—Los Angeles	Nat.	OF	8	29	3	7	1	0	1	2	.241	12	1	0	1.000
1959—Victoria	Tex.	OF-3B	63	261	59	93	13	0	27	79	.356	99	16	5	.958
1959—Spokane	P. C.	OF-1B	76	295	43	94	19	2	16	47	.319	243	16	6	.977
1959—Los Angeles	Nat.	OF	9	21	2	3	0	1	1	6	.143	10	0	0	1.000
1960—Spokane	P. C.	1B	26	97	17	36	11	0	4	24	.371	233	19	8	.969
1960—Los Angeles	Nat.	OF-1B	117	448	54	120	15	2	23	77	.268	196	11	4	.981
1961—Los Angeles	Nat.	OF-1B	92	267	36	79	10	2	15	45	.296	122	10	8	.943
1962—Los Angeles	Nat.	OF	141	493	80	146	25	6	31	119	.296	187	19	6	.972
1963—Los Angeles	Nat.	OF	123	417	58	114	16	1	28	64	.273	190	4	8	.960
1964—Los Angeles(a)	Nat.	OF	134	433	60	98	13	2	24	69	.226	183	2	4	.979
1965—Washington	Amer.	OF	149	516	53	149	22	6	21	84	.289	204	5	4	.981
1966—Washington	Amer.	OF	146	493	52	137	19	4	18	71	.278	216	5	4	.982
1967—Washington	Amer.	OF-1B	149	519	71	133	20	2	36	89	.256	225	6	3	.987
1968—Washington	Amer.	OF-1B	158	598	79	164	28	3	★44	106	.274	576	52	19	.971
1969—Washington	Amer.	OF-1B	161	592	111	175	17	2	48	111	.296	602	34	14	.978
1970—Washington	Amer.	OF-1B	161	566	90	160	15	1	★44	★126	.283	601	31	11	.983
1971—Washington	Amer.	OF-1B	153	549	60	153	25	2	26	83	.279	555	65	5	.992
1972—Tex.(b)-Det.	Amer.	1B-OF	109	320	29	78	10	0	10	38	.244	521	32	13	.977
1973—Detroit	Amer.	1B	85	227	26	58	9	1	12	29	.256	12	0	1	.923
American League Totals—9 Years			1271	4380	571	1207	165	21	259	737	.276	3512	230	74	.981
National League Totals—7 Years			624	2108	293	567	80	14	123	382	.269	900	47	30	.969
Major League Totals—16 Years			1895	6488	864	1774	245	35	382	1119	.273	4412	277	104	.978

aTraded to Washington Senators with Pitchers Phil Ortega and Pete Richert, Infielder Ken McMullen and First Baseman Dick Nen for Pitcher Claude Osteen, Infielder John Kennedy and cash, December 4, 1964.

bSold to Detroit Tigers, August 31, 1972.

WORLD SERIES RECORD

Year—Club	League	Pos.	G.	AB.	R.	H.	2B.	3B.	HR.	RBI.	B.A.	PO.	A.	E.	F.A.
1963—Los Angeles	Nat.	OF	3	10	2	3	1	0	1	1	.300	4	0	0	1.000

WAITE CHARLES HOYT
(Schoolboy)

Born September 9, 1899, at Brooklyn, N.Y.

Died August 25, 1984, at Cincinnati, O.

Height, 5.11½. Weight, 185.

Threw and batted righthanded.

Named to Hall of Fame, 1969.

Year—Club	League	G.	IP.	W.	L.	Pct.	H.	R.	ER.	SO.	BB.	ERA.
1916—Mt. Carmel	Pa. State	6	....	5	1	.833	....	....	....	....	....	......
1916—Hartford-Lynn	Eastern	10	71	4	5	.444	....	....	....	22	24	......
1917—Memphis	Southern	17	103	3	9	.250	96	48	....	41	25	......
1917—Montreal	International	28	215	7	17	.292	206	....	60	65	78	2.51
1918—Nashville	Southern	19	137	5	10	.333	103	....	....	51	35	......
1918—New York	National	1	1	0	0	.000	0	0	0	2	0	0.00
1918—Newark	International	5	43	2	3	.400	33	17	10	25	9	2.09
1919—Boston	American	13	105	4	6	.400	99	42	38	28	22	3.26
1920—Boston(a)	American	22	121	6	6	.500	123	72	59	45	47	4.39
1921—New York	American	44	282	19	13	.594	301	121	97	102	81	3.10
1922—New York	American	37	265	19	12	.613	271	114	101	95	76	3.43
1923—New York	American	37	239	17	9	.654	227	97	80	60	66	3.01
1924—New York	American	46	247	18	13	.581	295	117	104	71	76	3.79
1925—New York	American	46	243	11	14	.440	283	124	108	86	78	4.00
1926—New York	American	40	218	16	12	.571	224	112	93	79	62	3.84
1927—New York	American	36	256	●22	7	★.759	242	90	75	86	54	2.64
1928—New York	American	42	273	23	7	.767	279	118	102	67	60	3.36
1929—New York	American	30	202	10	9	.526	219	115	95	57	69	4.23
1930—N.Y.(b)-Detroit	American	34	183	11	10	.524	240	116	96	35	56	4.72
1931—Detroit(c)-Phila.(d)	American	32	203	13	13	.500	254	130	112	40	69	4.97
1932—Brooklyn(e)-N.Y.(f)	National	26	124	6	10	.375	141	70	60	36	37	4.35
1933—Pittsburgh	National	36	117	5	7	.417	118	45	38	44	19	2.92
1934—Pittsburgh	National	48	191	15	6	.714	184	75	62	105	43	2.92
1935—Pittsburgh	National	39	164	7	11	.389	187	72	62	63	27	3.40
1936—Pittsburgh	National	22	117	7	5	.583	115	44	35	37	20	2.69
1937—Pittsburgh(g)-Brooklyn	National	38	195	8	9	.471	211	97	74	65	36	3.42
1938—Brooklyn	National	6	16	0	3	.000	24	9	9	3	5	5.06
American League Totals		459	2837	189	131	.591	3057	1368	1160	851	816	3.68
National League Totals		216	925	48	51	.485	980	412	340	355	187	3.31
Major League Totals—21 Years		675	3762	237	182	.566	4037	1780	1500	1206	1003	3.59

aTraded to New York Yankees with Pitcher Harry Harper, Catcher Wally Schang and Third Baseman Mike McNally for Pitcher Herb Thormahlen, Catcher Muddy Ruel, Second Baseman Del Pratt and Outfielder Sammy Vick, December 15, 1920.

bTraded to Detroit Tigers with Shortstop Mark Koenig for Pitcher Owen Carroll, Shortstop George Weustling and Outfielder Harry Rice, May 30, 1930.

cReleased to Philadelphia Athletics on waivers, June, 1931.

dReleased by Philadelphia Athletics and signed with Brooklyn Dodgers, January, 1932.

eReleased to New York Giants, June, 1932.

fReleased to Pittsburgh Pirates, November, 1932.

gReleased by Pittsburgh Pirates and signed with Brooklyn Dodgers, June, 1937.

WORLD SERIES RECORD

Shares record for lowest earned-run average, series, 14 or more innings (0.00), 1921.

Year Club	League	G.	IP.	W.	L.	Pct.	H.	R.	ER.	SO.	BB.	ERA.
1921—New York	American	3	27	2	1	.667	18	2	0	18	11	0.00
1922—New York	American	2	8	0	1	.000	11	3	1	4	2	1.13
1923—New York	American	1	2⅓	0	0	.000	4	4	4	0	1	15.43
1926—New York	American	2	15	1	1	.500	19	8	2	10	1	1.20
1927—New York	American	1	7⅓	1	0	1.000	8	4	4	2	1	4.91
1928—New York	American	2	18	2	0	1.000	14	4	3	14	6	1.50
1931—Philadelphia	American	1	6	0	1	.000	7	3	3	1	0	4.50
World Series Totals—7 Years		12	83⅔	6	4	.600	81	28	17	49	22	1.83

ROBERT CAL HUBBARD
(Known by middle name.)

Born October 31, 1900, at Keytesville, Mo.

Died October 17, 1977, at St. Petersburg, Fla.

Height, 6.02½. Weight, 265.

Attended Centenary College, two years. Graduate of Geneva College (bachelor of arts degree, 1927).

Began umpiring career in Piedmont League, 1928. On staff of Southeastern League, 1928 and 1929; Piedmont League and South Atlantic Association, 1930; Piedmont League and International League, 1931; International League and Western Association, 1932; International League, 1933-34 and 1935; and in American League, 1936-50. Assistant to supervisor of A.L. umpires, 1952-53; supervisor of umpires, 1954-69.

Played professional football with New York Giants, 1927 and 1928; with Green Bay Packers, 1929-30-31-32-33 and 1935; and with New York Giants, 1936. Line coach at Texas A&M, 1934. Head football coach at Geneva College, 1941 and 1942.

World Series umpire, 1938-42-46-49.

All-Star Game umpire, 1939-44-49.

Named to National Football League Hall of Fame, 1963.

Named to Hall of Fame, 1976.

CARL OWEN HUBBELL
(King Carl and The Meal Ticket)

Born June 22, 1903, at Carthage, Mo.

Died November 21, 1988, at Scottsdale, Ariz.

Height, 6.01. Weight, 175.

Threw left and batted righthanded.

Pitched 11-0 no-hit victory against Pittsburgh, May 8, 1929.

Led National League in shutouts with 10 in 1933.

Named National League's Most Valuable Player, 1933 and 1936.

Selected for THE SPORTING NEWS All-Star Major League Teams, 1933-35-36-37.

Director, New York-San Francisco Giants' farm system 1943 through 1972; director of player development, Giants 1973 through 1977; scout, Giants, 1978 to 1985.

Named to Hall of Fame, 1947.

Year Club	League	G.	IP.	W.	L.	Pct.	H.	R.	ER.	SO.	BB.	ERA.
1923—Cushing	Oklahoma State					(No records available)						
1924—Cushing	Oklahoma State					(No records available)						
1924—Ardmore	West Assn.	2	12	1	0	1.000	....	....	....	....	....	......

Year Club	League	G.	IP.	W.	L.	Pct.	H.	R.	ER.	SO.	BB.	ERA.
1924—Oklahoma City	Western	2	15	1	1	.500	19	10	....	3	4	......
1925—Oklahoma City (a)	Western	45	284	17	13	.567	273	172	....	102	108	......
1926—Toronto	Int.	31	93	7	7	.500	90	42	39	45	44	3.77
1927—Decatur	I.I.I.	23	185	14	7	.667	174	61	52	76	48	2.53
1927—Fort Worth	Texas	2	3	0	1	.000	7	....	....	0	3	......
1928—Beaumont	Texas	21	185	12	9	.571	177	69	61	116	45	2.97
1928—New York	National	20	124	10	6	.625	117	49	39	37	21	2.83
1929—New York	National	39	268	18	11	.621	273	128	110	106	67	3.69
1930—New York	National	37	242	17	12	.586	263	120	104	117	58	3.87
1931—New York	National	36	248	14	12	.538	211	88	73	155	67	2.65
1932—New York	National	40	284	18	11	.621	260	96	79	137	40	2.50
1933—New York	National	45	★309	★23	12	.657	256	69	57	156	47	★1.66
1934—New York	National	49	313	21	12	.636	286	100	80	118	37	★2.30
1935—New York	National	42	303	23	12	.657	314	125	110	150	49	3.27
1936—New York	National	42	304	★26	6	★.813	265	81	78	123	57	★2.31
1937—New York	National	39	262	★22	8	★.733	261	108	93	★159	55	3.19
1938—New York	National	24	179	13	10	.565	171	70	61	104	33	3.07
1939—New York	National	29	154	11	9	.550	150	60	47	62	24	2.75
1940—New York	National	31	214	11	12	.478	220	102	87	86	59	3.66
1941—New York	National	26	164	11	9	.550	169	73	65	75	53	3.57
1942—New York	National	24	157	11	8	.579	158	75	69	61	34	3.96
1943—New York	National	12	66	4	4	.500	87	36	36	31	24	4.91
Major League Totals—16 Years		535	3591	253	154	.622	3461	1380	1188	1677	725	2.98

aObtained by Detroit from Oklahoma City in 1925, and after spring trials in 1926 and 1927 was released outright to Beaumont in 1928.

WORLD SERIES RECORD

Year Club	League	G.	IP.	W.	L.	Pct.	H.	R.	ER.	SO.	BB.	ERA.
1933—New York	National	2	20	2	0	1.000	13	3	0	15	6	0.00
1936—New York	National	2	16	1	1	.500	15	5	4	10	2	2.25
1937—New York	National	2	14⅓	1	1	.500	12	10	6	7	4	3.77
World Series Totals—3 Years		6	50⅓	4	2	.667	40	18	10	32	12	1.79

MILLER JAMES HUGGINS

Born March 27, 1880, at Cincinnati, O.

Died September 25, 1929, at New York, N. Y.

Height, 5.04. Weight, 146.

Threw right and batted left and righthanded.

Manager, St. Louis Cardinals, 1913 through 1917; New York Yankees, 1918 to 1929.
Named to Hall of Fame, 1964.

Year Club	League	Pos.	G.	AB.	R.	H.	2B.	3B.	HR.	SB.	B.A.	PO.	A.	E.	F.A.
1899—Mansfield	Int. St.	SS						(No Records available)							
1900								(Played semi-pro baseball)							
1901—St. Paul	West.	2B	129	474	79	153	6	4	2	17	.322	131	224	26	.932
1902—St. Paul	A. A.	2B	129	466	75	153	15	5	0	34	.328	362	429	50	.941
1903—St. Paul	A. A.	2B	124	444	91	137	20	4	0	48	.308	310	405	39	.948
1904—Cincinnati	Nat.	2B	140	491	96	129	12	7	2	13	.263	337	448	46	.945
1905—Cincinnati	Nat.	2B	149	564	117	154	11	8	1	27	.273	346	★525	51	.945
1906—Cincinnati	Nat.	2B	146	545	81	159	11	7	0	41	.292	341	★458	44	.948
1907—Cincinnati	Nat.	2B	★156	561	64	139	12	4	1	28	.248	★353	443	32	.961
1908—Cincinnati	Nat.	2B	135	498	65	119	14	5	0	30	.239	302	406	30	.959
1909—Cincinnati(a)	Nat.	2B-3B	46	159	18	34	3	1	0	11	.213	95	125	16	.932
1910—St. Louis	Nat.	2B	151	547	101	145	15	6	1	34	.265	325	492	30	.963
1911—St. Louis	Nat.	2B	136	509	106	133	19	2	1	37	.261	281	439	29	.961
1912—St. Louis	Nat.	2B	120	431	82	131	15	4	0	35	.304	272	337	37	.943
1913—St. Louis	Nat.	2B	121	382	74	109	12	0	0	23	.285	266	339	14	★.977
1914—St. Louis	Nat.	2B	148	509	85	134	17	4	1	32	.263	328	428	28	.964
1915—St. Louis	Nat.	2B	107	353	57	85	5	2	2	13	.241	194	315	23	.957
1916—St. Louis	Nat.	2B	18	9	2	3	0	0	0	0	.333	10	10	0	1.000
Major League Totals—13 Years			1573	5558	948	1474	146	50	9	324	.265	3450	4726	380	.956

aTraded with Outfielder Rebel Oakes and Pitcher Frank Corridon to St. Louis Cardinals for Pitcher Fred Beebe and Third Baseman Alan Storke, February, 1910.

Year	Club	League	Position	W.	L.	Year	Club	League	Position	W.	L.
1913—St. Louis	Nat.		Eighth	51	99	1922—New York	Amer.		First	94	60
1914—St. Louis	Nat.		Third	81	72	1923—New York	Amer.		First	98	54
1915—St. Louis	Nat.		Sixth	72	81	1924—New York	Amer.		Second	89	63
1916—St. Louis	Nat.		†Seventh	60	93	1925—New York	Amer.		Seventh	69	85
1917—St. Louis	Nat.		Third	82	70	1926—New York	Amer.		First	91	63
1918—New York	Amer.		Fourth	60	63	1927—New York	Amer.		First	110	44
1919—New York	Amer.		Third	80	59	1928—New York	Amer.		First	101	53
1920—New York	Amer.		Third	95	59	1929—New York	Amer.		Second	82	61
1921—New York	Amer.		First	98	55	Major League Totals—17 Years				1413	1134

†Tied for position.

WORLD SERIES RECORD

Year	Club	League	W.	L.	Year	Club	League	W.	L.
1921—New York	American		3	5	1926—New York	American		3	4
1922—New York	American		0	4	1927—New York	American		4	0
1923—New York	American		4	2	1928—New York	American		4	0

JAMES AUGUSTUS (JIM) HUNTER
(Catfish)

Born April 8, 1946, at Hertford, N. C.

Height, 6.00. Weight, 195.

Threw and batted righthanded.

Pitched 4-0 perfect game victory against Minnesota Twins, May 8, 1968.
Led American League pitchers in complete games with 30 in 1975.
Tied for American League lead in games started by pitchers with 40 in 1970.
Named American League Pitcher of the Year by THE SPORTING NEWS, 1974.
Won American League Cy Young Memorial Award, 1974.
Named righthanded pitcher on THE SPORTING NEWS American League All-Star Team, 1974.
Named to Hall of Fame, 1987.

Year	Club	League	G.	IP.	W.	L.	Pct.	H.	R.	ER.	SO.	BB.	ERA.
1964—Dayton Beach	Florida St.			(On Disabled List)									
1965—Kansas City	American		32	133	8	8	.500	124	68	63	82	46	4.26
1966—Kansas City	American		30	177	9	11	.450	158	87	79	103	64	4.02
1967—Kansas City(a)	American		35	260	13	17	.433	209	91	81	196	84	2.80
1968—Oakland	American		36	234	13	13	.500	210	99	★87	172	69	3.35
1969—Oakland	American		38	247	12	15	.444	210	99	92	150	85	3.35
1970—Oakland	American		40	262	18	14	.563	253	124	111	178	74	3.81
1971—Oakland	American		37	274	21	11	.656	225	103	90	181	80	2.96
1972—Oakland	American		38	295	21	7	★.750	200	74	67	191	70	2.04
1973—Oakland	American		36	256	21	5	★.808	222	105	95	124	69	3.34
1974—Oakland(b)	American		41	318	●25	12	.676	268	97	88	143	45	★2.49
1975—New York	American		39	★328	●23	14	.622	248	107	94	177	83	2.58
1976—New York	American		36	299	17	15	.531	268	126	117	173	68	3.52
1977—New York	American		22	143	9	9	.500	137	83	75	52	47	4.72
1978—New York	American		21	118	12	6	.667	98	49	47	56	35	3.58
1979—New York	American		19	105	2	9	.182	128	68	62	34	34	5.31
Major League Totals—15 Years			500	3449	224	166	.574	2958	1380	1248	2012	954	3.26

aAppeared as first baseman in one game.

bDeclared a free agent by an arbitration panel, December 16, 1974; signed by New York Yankees for an estimated $2.85 million, December 31, 1974.

CHAMPIONSHIP SERIES RECORD

Holds major league records for most games started (10), innings pitched (69⅓), runs allowed (25) and hits allowed (57), lifetime.
Shares major league records for most years by pitcher (6); most games won (4) and runs allowed (25), lifetime.
Holds American League record for most total bases allowed, game (20), October 6, 1978.
Shares American League record for most games won, series (2), 1973.

Year	Club	League	G.	IP.	W.	L.	Pct.	H.	R.	ER.	SO.	BB.	ERA.
1971—Oakland	American		1	8	0	1	.000	7	5	5	6	2	5.63
1972—Oakland	American		2	15½	0	0	.000	10	2	2	9	5	1.17
1973—Oakland	American		2	16⅓	2	0	1.000	12	3	3	6	5	1.65
1974—Oakland	American		2	11⅔	1	1	.500	11	6	6	6	2	4.63
1976—New York	American		2	12	1	1	.500	10	6	6	5	1	4.50
1978—New York	American		1	6	0	0	.000	7	3	3	5	3	4.50
Championship Series Totals—6 Years			10	69⅓	4	3	.571	57	25	25	37	18	3.25

Year	Club	League	G.	IP.	W.	L.	Pct.	H.	R.	ER.	SO.	BB.	ERA.
1972—Oakland	American	3	16	2	0	1.000	12	5	5	11	6	2.81
1973—Oakland	American	2	13⅓	1	0	1.000	11	3	3	6	4	2.03
1974—Oakland	American	2	7⅔	1	0	1.000	5	1	1	5	2	1.17
1976—New York	American	1	8⅔	0	1	.000	10	4	3	5	4	3.12
1977—New York	American	2	4⅓	0	1	.000	6	5	5	1	0	10.38
1978—New York	American	2	13	1	1	.500	13	6	6	5	1	4.15
World Series Totals—6 Years			12	63	5	3	.625	57	24	23	33	17	3.29

MONFORD MERRILL (MONTE) IRVIN

Born February 25, 1919, at Columbia, Ala.

Height, 6:02. Weight, 195.

Threw and batted righthanded.

Nothing can sum up the essence of Monte Irvin better than the words of Mrs. Effa Manley, widow of Abe Manley, who owned the Newark club of the Negro National League, for which Monte played. Effa was the general manager, business manager and later sole owner of the club at the death of her husband. Hale and hearty and losing none of her charm and grace, she said in 1979 with almost motherly pride:

"Monte, whom my husband and I both knew and loved as a neighbor growing up, and who played for me, was the choice of all Negro National and American League club owners to serve as the No. 1 player to join a white major league team. We all agreed, in meeting, he was the best qualified by temperament, character, ability, sense of loyalty, morals, age, experience and physique to represent us as the first black player to enter the white majors since the Walker brothers back in the 1880s. But Branch Rickey lifted Jackie Robinson out of Negro ball and made him the first. It turned out all right, but we all felt Monte Irvin would do best representing us. Robinson later resented the 'treatment' he got in the Negro leagues, but Monte has had nothing but praise for what we tried to do for the players under most difficult circumstances for all of us."

The Irvin they were talking about was one of the country's finest all-round athletes. Born on a sugar plantation in Columbia, Ala., Monte was the fifth son and 11th child of a family that worked the soil and ran a cane mill. When he was four, his older brother, Bob, took him to a pond near their home and they fired stones out into the water hour after hour.

"That's where I really developed my throwing arm," Monte said. "When I was six, Bob gave me a baseball glove and started playing catch with me, but I already had the power and the style to throw."

After the family moved to Orange, N.J., Monte earned 16 high school varsity letters, in baseball, football, basketball and track. In a state championship track meet, he picked up a javelin for the first time in competition and hurled it 192 feet, eight inches, a state record that held for nine years.

An Orange High senior in 1938, he scratched his hand while playing basketball and the infection, termed hemolytic streptococcus, nearly cost him his life. He teetered on the brink of death for almost seven weeks and, as a town hero, rated Page One headlines when blood donors were sought. He recovered in time to play summer ball with the Orange Triangles and won a two-year scholarship to Lincoln (Pa.) University. His coach at Orange High, Carl Siebert, tried to interest the Yankees and Giants in his protege, but got nowhere. Two fellow members of the All-State New Jersey team—Hank Borowy and George Case— headed right for the majors—but they were white.

Irvin signed with the Manleys' Newark Eagles and played with them throughout the school summers and after he left Lincoln. He also played Caribbean ball in the winters in Mexico, Cuba and Puerto Rico. He quickly established himself as a slugger of note, a fast base runner, an exceptional fielder and a man all base runners respected because of his powerful throwing arm.

Irvin went into service in 1942, spent some time in Europe with the Army Engineers, saw some combat and eventually did guard duty at prisoner-of-war camps. When he came back, he rejoined the Eagles as a shortstop. The second baseman was Larry Doby. The Dodgers made a pass at Monte, but he was "not feeling well" and they backed off. Monte said it was not the prospect of joining the majors that unsettled him, but that it was simply a case of "too much Army." In July of '47, the Cleveland Indians bought Doby from the Eagles for $10,000, plus $5,000 more if he stuck at least 30 days. Of course, Doby ended his playing career in the majors.

Mrs. Manley's sale of Doby is believed to be the first time a Negro club was paid by a major league team for a black player. Still, she blew her cork because no club wanted Irvin.

"All these big league clubs are making a mistake. Doby is younger (Monte then was 28) and a fine prospect, but the best all-round player we have had for years is our Superman—Monte Irvin," she roared.

In the winter of 1948-49, Monte still was slugging away in the Cuban Winter League. He had seen Jackie Robinson, Doby, Roy Campanella and Don Newcombe make the jump to the majors. After an abortive attempt by the Dodgers to sign him to a St. Paul contract, the Giants picked up Monte and Hank Thompson for their Jersey City (International) farm team. The Eagles were paid $5,000 for Monte's contract.

Irvin hit the majors in 1949, but he was 30 years old and his power and fielding prowess that brought praise from major league observers were but a shadow of the brilliance that made him one of the Negro leagues' greatest all-round performers.

After his playing career, Irvin became an aide to the Commissioner of Baseball. His entrance into the Hall of Fame in 1973 is justice paid to a cleancut, hard-working athlete who made a solid mark in the exile of the Negro baseball scene.

ORGANIZED BALL PLAYING RECORD

Year Club	League	Pos.	G.	AB.	R.	H.	2B.	3B.	HR.	RBI.	B.A.	PO.	A.	E.	F.A.
1949—Jersey City	Int.	OF	63	204	55	76	18	5	9	52	.373	95	10	1	.991
1949—New York	Nat.	OF-INF	36	76	7	17	3	2	0	7	.224	56	17	1	.986
1950—Jersey City	Int.	OF	18	51	28	26	4	1	10	33	.510	29	1	0	1.000
1950—New York	Nat.	OF-1-3B	110	374	61	112	19	5	15	66	.299	569	51	12	.981
1951—New York	Nat.	OF-1B	151	558	94	174	19	11	24	*121	.312	585	60	9	.986
1952—New York(a)	Nat.	OF	46	126	10	39	2	1	4	21	.310	44	3	0	1.000
1953—New York	Nat.	OF	124	444	72	146	21	5	21	97	.329	244	10	7	.973
1954—New York	Nat.	OF-INF	135	432	62	113	13	3	19	64	.262	276	7	8	.973
1955—New York	Nat.	OF	51	150	16	38	7	1	1	17	.253	94	4	4	.961
1955—Minneapolis(b)	A. A.	OF	75	250	57	88	21	1	14	52	.352	146	7	5	.968
1956—Chicago	Nat.	OF	111	339	44	92	13	3	15	50	.271	216	6	2	.991
Major League Totals—8 Years			764	2499	366	731	97	36	99	443	.293	2082	158	43	.981

aSuffered broken right ankle in slide into third base in exhibition game against Cleveland Indians at Denver, Colo., April 2, 1952; made first appearance of season as pinch-hitter, July 27.

bDrafted by Chicago Cubs, November 28, 1955.

WORLD SERIES RECORD

Year Club	League	Pos.	G.	AB.	R.	H.	2B.	3B.	HR.	RBI.	B.A.	PO.	A.	E.	F.A.
1951—New York	Nat.	OF	6	24	3	11	0	1	0	2	.458	17	0	1	.944
1954—New York	Nat.	OF	4	9	1	2	1	0	0	2	.222	8	0	1	.889
World Series Totals—2 Years			10	33	4	13	1	1	0	4	.394	25	0	2	.926

JOSEPH JEFFERSON (JOE) JACKSON
(Shoeless Joe)

Born July 16, 1888, at Brandon Mills, S. C.

Died December 5, 1951, at Greenville, S. C.

Height, 6.01. Weight, 175.

Threw right and batted lefthanded.

Shares American League record for most triples, season (26), 1912.

Year Club	League	Pos.	G.	AB.	R.	H.	2B.	3B.	HR.	RBI.	B.A.	PO.	A.	E.	F.A.
1908—Greenville	Car. A.	OF	87	347	43	*120	....	....	5	....	*.346	149	12	12	.931
1908—Philadelphia	Amer.	OF	5	23	0	3	0	0	0	3	.130	6	1	1	.875
1909—Savannah	So. Atl.	OF	118	450	61	161	....	....	....	....	*.358	175	25	10	.952
1909—Philadelphia	Amer.	OF	5	17	3	3	0	0	0	2	.176	10	0	2	.833
1910—New Orleans(a)	South.	OF	136	466	*82	*165	18	19	2	....	*.354	277	11	7	.976
1910—Cleveland	Amer.	OF	20	75	15	29	2	5	1	12	.387	40	2	1	.977
1911—Cleveland	Amer.	OF	147	571	126	233	45	19	7	88	.408	242	32	12	.958
1912—Cleveland	Amer.	OF	152	572	121	226	44	*26	3	93	.395	273	30	16	.950
1913—Cleveland	Amer.	OF	148	527	109	*197	*39	17	7	81	.373	211	28	18	.930
1914—Cleveland	Amer.	OF	122	453	61	153	22	13	3	66	.338	195	13	7	.967
1915—Cleve.(b)...Chi.	Amer.	OF-1B	128	461	63	142	20	14	5	78	.308	436	27	15	.969
1916—Chicago	Amer.	OF	155	592	91	202	40	*21	3	81	.341	290	17	8	.975
1917—Chicago	Amer.	OF	146	538	91	162	20	17	5	82	.301	341	18	6	.984
1918—Chicago	Amer.	OF	17	65	9	23	2	2	1	18	.354	36	1	0	1.000
1919—Chicago	Amer.	OF	139	516	79	181	31	14	7	97	.351	252	15	9	.967
1920—Chicago	Amer.	OF	146	570	105	218	42	*20	12	121	.382	314	14	12	.965
Major League Totals—13 Years			1330	4980	873	1772	307	168	54	822	.356	2646	198	107	.964

aSent to New Orleans by Philadelphia Athletics, who traded rights to him to Cleveland Indians for Outfielders Bris Lord and cash.

bTraded with $15,000 to Chicago White Sox for Outfielders Robert Roth and Larry Chappell and Pitcher Ed Klepfer, August 20, 1915.

WORLD SERIES RECORD

Year Club	League	Pos.	G.	AB.	R.	H.	2B.	3B.	HR.	RBI.	B.A.	PO.	A.	E.	F.A.
1917—Chicago	Amer.	OF	6	23	4	7	0	0	0	2	.304	9	1	0	1.000
1919—Chicago	Amer.	OF	8	32	5	12	3	0	1	6	.375	16	1	0	1.000
World Series Totals—2 Years			14	55	9	19	3	0	1	8	.345	25	2	0	1.000

—DID YOU KNOW—

That Reggie Jackson was the first player in big-league history to hit 100 or more home runs for three franchises? He hit 269 for the Kansas City-Oakland A's, 144 for the New York Yankees and 123 for the California Angels.

REGINALD MARTINEZ (REGGIE) JACKSON
(Mr. October)

Born May 18, 1946, at Wyncote, Pa.

Height, 6.00. Weight, 206.

Threw and batted lefthanded.

Holds major league records for most strikeouts, lifetime (2,597); most years, 100 or more strikeouts (18); most consecutive years, 100 or more strikeouts (13).

Shares major league records for most consecutive years leading league in strikeouts (4); most strikeouts, nine-inning game (5), September 27, 1968.

Shares American League records for most years, 20 or more home runs (16); most times, four or more strikeouts in game, season (5), 1971; most seasons leading league in errors, outfielder (5), fewest errors by outfielder, season, for leader in most errors (9), 1972.

Hit three home runs in a game, July 2, 1969 and September 18, 1986.

Led American League batters in strikeouts with 171 in 1968, 142 in 1969, 135 in 1970, 161 in 1971 and 156 in 1982.

Led American League in slugging percentage with .608 in 1969, .531 in 1973 and .502 in 1976.

Led American League in intentional bases on balls received with 20 in 1974 and tied for lead with 20 in 1969.

Led American League in caught stealing with 17 in 1970.

Tied for American League lead in double plays by outfielders with 5 in 1972.

Led Southern League in total bases with 232 in 1967.

Named Major League Player of the Year by THE SPORTING NEWS, 1973.

Named American League Player of the Year by THE SPORTING NEWS, 1973.

Named American League Most Valuable Player by Baseball Writers' Association of America, 1973.

Named outfielder on THE SPORTING NEWS American League All-Star Team, 1969, 1973, 1975, 1976 and 1980.

Named outfielder on THE SPORTING NEWS American League Silver Slugger team, 1982.

Named designated hitter on THE SPORTING NEWS American League Silver Slugger team, 1980.

Named Southern League Player of the Year, 1967.

Named College Player of the Year by THE SPORTING NEWS, 1966.

Named outfielder on THE SPORTING NEWS College Baseball All-America Team, 1966.

Year Club League	Pos.	G.	AB.	R.	H.	2B.	3B.	HR.	RBI.	B.A.	PO.	A.	E.	F.A.
1966—Lewiston .... N'west	OF	12	48	14	14	3	2	2	11	.292	23	0	1	.958
1966—Modesto .... Calif.	OF	56	221	50	66	6	0	21	60	.299	108	3	9	.925
1967—Birmingham .... South.	OF	114	413	★84	121	26	★17	17	58	.293	228	3	★18	.928
1967—Kansas City .... Amer.	OF	35	118	13	21	4	4	1	6	.178	55	1	4	.933
1968—Oakland................ Amer.	OF	154	553	82	138	13	6	29	74	.250	269	14	★12	.959
1969—Oakland................ Amer.	OF	152	549	★123	151	36	3	47	118	.275	278	14	11	.964
1970—Oakland................ Amer.	OF	149	426	57	101	21	2	23	66	.237	251	8	●12	.956
1971—Oakland................ Amer.	OF	150	567	87	157	29	3	32	80	.277	285	15	7	.977
1972—Oakland................ Amer.	OF	135	499	72	132	25	2	25	75	.265	301	5	★9	.971
1973—Oakland................ Amer.	OF	151	539	★99	158	28	2	★32	★117	.293	302	4	9	.971
1974—Oakland................ Amer.	OF	148	506	90	146	25	1	29	93	.289	296	8	10	.968
1975—Oakland†............... Amer.	OF	157	593	91	150	39	3	●36	104	.253	315	13	★12	.965
1976—Baltimore‡ .... Amer.	OF	134	498	84	138	27	2	27	91	.277	284	8	★11	.964
1977—New York............. Amer.	OF	146	525	93	150	39	2	32	110	.286	236	7	13	.949
1978—New York............. Amer.	OF	139	511	82	140	13	5	27	97	.274	212	6	3	.986
1979—New York............. Amer.	OF	131	465	78	138	24	2	29	89	.297	274	7	4	.986
1980—New York .... Amer.	OF	143	514	94	154	22	4	●41	111	.300	174	3	7	.962
1981—New York x .... Amer.	OF	94	334	33	79	17	1	15	54	.237	111	3	3	.974
1982—California........... Amer.	OF	153	530	92	146	17	1	●39	101	.275	200	6	6	.972
1983—California.............. Amer.	OF	116	397	43	77	14	1	14	49	.194	66	4	1	.986
1984—California.............. Amer.	OF	143	525	67	117	17	2	25	81	.223	7	0	0	1.000
1985—California.............. Amer.	OF	143	460	64	116	27	0	27	85	.252	112	6	7	.944
1986—California y .... Amer.	OF	132	419	65	101	12	2	18	58	.241	4	1	1	.833
1987—Oakland z............. Amer.	OF	115	336	42	74	14	1	15	43	.220	30	0	0	1.000
Major League Totals—21 Years...............		2820	9864	1551	2584	463	49	563	1702	.262	4062	133	142	.967

Selected by Kansas City A's organization in 1st round (second player selected) of free-agent draft, June 13, 1966.

†Traded with Pitchers Ken Holtzman and Bill Van Bommel to Baltimore Orioles for Outfielder Don Baylor and Pitchers Mike Torrez and Paul Mitchell, April 2, 1976.

‡Played out option year and granted free agency, November 1, 1976; signed as free agent with New York Yankees, November 29, 1976.

xGranted free agency, November 13, 1981; signed by California Angels, January 22, 1982.

yGranted free agency, November 12, 1986; signed by Oakland A's, December 24, 1986.

zGranted free agency, December 15, 1987.

CHAMPIONSHIP SERIES RECORD

Holds major league records for most series played (11); most games (45), at-bats (163) and strikeouts (41), lifetime.

Shares major league record for most doubles, lifetime (7).

Holds American League records for most hits (37), singles (24), runs batted in (20) and bases on balls (17), lifetime.

Year Club League	Pos.	G.	AB.	R.	H.	2B.	3B.	HR.	RBI.	B.A.	PO.	A.	E.	F.A.
1971—Oakland................ Amer.	OF	3	12	2	4	1	0	2	2	.333	9	1	0	1.000
1972—Oakland................ Amer.	OF	5	18	1	5	1	0	0	2	.278	14	0	1	.933

Year	Club	League	Pos.	G.	AB.	R.	H.	2B.	3B.	HR.	RBI.	B.A.	PO.	A.	E.	F.A.
1973—Oakland	Amer.		OF	5	21	0	3	0	0	0	0	.143	19	0	0	1.000
1974—Oakland	Amer.		DH-OF	4	12	0	2	1	0	0	0	.167	0	0	0	.000
1975—Oakland	Amer.		OF	3	12	1	5	0	0	1	3	.417	5	1	0	1.000
1977—New York	Amer.		O-D-PH	5	16	1	2	0	0	0	1	.125	10	1	0	1.000
1978—New York	Amer.		DH-OF	4	13	5	6	1	0	2	6	.462	4	0	0	1.000
1980—New York	Amer.		OF	3	11	1	3	1	0	0	0	.273	5	0	0	1.000
1981—New York	Amer.		OF	2	4	1	0	0	0	0	1	.000	1	0	0	1.000
1982—California	Amer.		OF	5	18	2	2	0	0	1	2	.111	2	0	0	1.000
1986—California	Amer.		DH	6	26	2	5	2	0	0	2	.192	0	0	0	.000
Championship Series Totals—11 Years...				45	163	16	37	7	0	6	20	.227	69	3	1	.986

WORLD SERIES RECORD

Holds records for highest slugging average, lifetime, 20 or more games (.755); most runs (10), home runs (5) and extra bases on long hits (16), series, 1977.

Shares records for most times hit by pitch, lifetime (3); most total bases, series (25), 1977; most runs (4), home runs (3) and total bases (12), game, October 18, 1977; most home runs, two consecutive innings (2), October 18, 1977, fourth and fifth innings.

Year	Club	League	Pos.	G.	AB.	R.	H.	2B.	3B.	HR.	RBI.	B.A.	PO.	A.	E.	F.A.
1973—Oakland	Amer.		OF	7	29	3	9	3	1	1	6	.310	17	0	0	1.000
1974—Oakland	Amer.		OF	5	14	3	4	1	0	1	1	.286	6	1	1	.875
1977—New York	Amer.		OF	6	20	10	9	1	0	5	8	.450	9	0	0	1.000
1978—New York	Amer.		DH	6	23	2	9	1	0	2	8	.391	0	0	0	.000
1981—New York	Amer.		OF	3	12	3	4	1	0	1	1	.333	5	0	1	.832
World Series Totals—5 Years				27	98	21	35	7	1	10	24	.357	37	1	2	.950

TRAVIS CALVIN JACKSON
(Stonewall)

Born November 2, 1903, at Waldo, Ark.

Died July 17, 1987, at Waldo, Ark.

Height, 5.11. Weight, 160.

Threw and batted righthanded.

Selected as shortstop by Baseball Writers' Association for THE SPORTING NEWS on All-Star major league club in 1927-28 and 1929.

Manager, Jersey City, International League, 1937-38; coach, New York Giants, 1938-40 and 1947-48; manager, Jackson, Southeastern League, 1946; Tampa, Florida State League, 1949; Owensboro, Kitty League, 1950; Bluefield, Appalachian League, 1951; Hartford, Eastern League, 1952-53; Appleton, Wisconsin State League, 1952-53; Lawton, Sooner State League, 1954-57; Midland, Sophomore League, 1958; Eau Claire, Northern League, 1959; Quad-City, Midwest League, 1960.

Named to Hall of Fame, 1982.

Year	Club	League	Pos.	G.	AB.	R.	H.	2B.	3B.	HR.	RBI.	B.A.	PO.	A.	E.	F.A.
1921—Little Rock	South.		SS	39	130	11	26	5	0	1	12	.200	65	96	21	.885
1922—Little Rock	South.		SS	147	521	59	146	18	9	7	....	.280	279	455	73	.910
1922—New York	Nat.		SS	3	8	1	0	0	0	0	0	.000	3	7	1	.909
1923—New York	Nat.		3B-SS	96	327	45	90	12	7	4	37	.275	107	265	23	.942
1924—New York	Nat.		SS	151	596	81	180	26	8	11	76	.302	332	534	58	.937
1925—New York	Nat.		SS	112	411	51	117	15	2	9	59	.285	277	366	40	.941
1926—New York	Nat.		SS	111	385	64	126	24	8	8	51	.327	256	351	24	.962
1927—New York	Nat.		SS	127	469	67	149	29	4	14	98	.318	287	444	37	.952
1928—New York	Nat.		SS	150	537	73	145	35	6	14	77	.270	354	547	45	.952
1929—New York	Nat.		SS	149	551	92	162	21	12	21	94	.294	329	552	28	.969
1930—New York	Nat.		SS	116	431	70	146	27	8	13	82	.339	218	441	30	.956
1931—New York	Nat.		SS	145	555	65	172	26	10	5	71	.310	303	496	25	*.970
1932—New York	Nat.		SS	52	195	23	50	17	1	4	38	.256	106	166	22	.925
1933—New York	Nat.		3B-SS	53	122	11	30	5	0	0	12	.246	52	87	11	.927
1934—New York	Nat.		3B-SS	137	523	75	140	26	7	16	101	.268	292	477	43	.947
1935—New York	Nat.		3B	128	511	74	154	20	12	9	80	.301	139	220	20	.947
1936—New York	Nat.		3B	126	465	41	107	8	1	7	53	.230	99	196	15	.952
1937—Jersey City	Int.		SS	6	20	0	5	0	0	0	0	.250	11	17	2	.933
1938—Jersey City	Int.		3B-SS	10	17	0	5	1	0	0	2	.294	3	7	0	1.000
Major League Totals—15 Years				1656	6086	833	1768	291	86	135	929	.291	3154	5149	422	.952

WORLD SERIES RECORD

Year	Club	League	Pos.	G.	AB.	R.	H.	2B.	3B.	HR.	RBI.	B.A.	PO.	A.	E.	F.A.
1923—New York	Nat.		PH	1	1	0	0	0	0	0	0	.000	0	0	0	.000
1924—New York	Nat.		SS	7	27	3	2	0	0	0	1	.074	8	20	3	.903
1933—New York	Nat.		3B	5	18	3	4	1	0	0	2	.222	3	16	1	.950
1936—New York	Nat.		3B	6	21	1	4	0	0	0	1	.190	2	8	3	.769
World Series Totals—4 Years				19	67	7	10	1	0	0	4	.149	13	44	7	.891

WILLIAM CHESTER (BILL) JACOBSON
(Baby Doll)

Born August 16, 1890, at Cable, Ill.
Died January 16, 1977, at Orion, Ill.
Height, 6.02½. Weight, 210.
Threw and batted righthanded.

Shares modern league record for most triples, game (3), September 9, 1922.
Led American League outfielders in double plays, 1925 (tie).

Year Club League	Pos.	G.	AB.	R.	H.	2B.	3B.	HR.	RBI.	B.A.	PO.	A.	E.	F.A.
1909—Rock Island........... I.I.I.	OF	43	124	15	23	4	2	0	....	.185	16	1	1	.944
1910—Rock Island........... I.I.I.	OF	16	43	5	6	....	....	....	....	.140	....	....	....	....
1910—Battle Creek .... So. Mich.	OF	55	184	18	41	....	....	....	....	.223	208	43	10	.962
1911—Rock Island........... I.I.I.	OF	100	299	43	91	....	....	....	....	.304	360	96	15	.968
1912—Mobile.................... South.	OF	139	502	58	131	....	....	....	....	.261	*412	16	8	.982
1913—Mobile.................... South.	OF	54	201	35	49	9	6	1	....	.244	105	2	7	.939
1914—Chattanooga .... South.	OF	155	*589	97	*188	30	*19	*15	....	.319	358	13	11	.971
1915—Det.(a)-St.L........... Amer.	OF	71	180	18	38	12	3	1	17	.211	58	3	1	.984
1916—Little Rock .... South.	OF	139	508	80	*176	28	*15	6	....	*.346	303	15	15	.955
1917—St. Louis................. Amer.	OF	148	529	53	131	23	7	4	52	.248	292	18	8	.975
1918—St. Louis................. Amer.					(In Military Service)									
1919—St. Louis................. Amer.	OF	120	455	70	147	31	8	4	52	.323	270	9	15	.949
1920—St. Louis................. Amer.	OF	●154	609	97	216	34	14	9	122	.355	394	18	9	.979
1921—St. Louis................. Amer.	OF-1B	151	599	90	211	38	14	5	90	.352	469	19	7	.986
1922—St. Louis................. Amer.	OF	145	555	88	176	22	16	9	102	.317	367	9	12	.969
1923—St. Louis................. Amer.	OF	147	592	76	183	29	6	8	81	.309	409	10	11	.974
1924—St. Louis................. Amer.	OF	152	579	103	184	41	12	19	97	.318	*488	7	7	●.986
1925—St. Louis................. Amer.	OF	142	540	103	184	30	9	15	76	.341	383	18	13	.969
1926—St.L.(b)-Boston....... Amer.	OF	148	576	62	172	54	2	8	90	.299	298	9	8	.975
1927—Bo.(c)-Cl.(d)-Ph..... Amer.	OF	94	293	27	72	17	3	1	42	.246	180	5	8	.959
1928—Baltimore .... Int.	OF	12	48	4	6	0	0	1	3	.125	39	3	0	1.000
1928—Chattanooga .... South.	OF	56	173	31	53	12	4	5	41	.306	105	5	3	.973
1928—Ind'polis-Toledo ... A.A.	OF	55	199	26	68	7	3	1	27	.342	109	6	1	.991
1929—Quincy .... I.I.I.	OF	130	496	80	151	23	4	20	100	.304	286	4	2	●.993
Major League Totals—11 Years..............		1472	5507	787	1714	328	94	83	821	.311	3608	125	99	.974

aTraded to St. Louis Browns for Pitcher Bill James, August 18, 1915.
bTraded to Philadelphia Athletics for Outfielder Bing Miller; then sent by A's to Boston Red Sox with Pitchers Fred Heimach and Slim Harriss for Pitcher Howard Ehmke, June 15, 1926.
cClaimed on waivers by Cleveland Indians, June 12, 1927.
dClaimed on waivers by Philadelphia Athletics, August 5, 1927.

CHARLES DEVINE (CHARLIE) JAMIESON

Born February 7, 1893, at Paterson, N.J.
Died October 27, 1969, at Paterson, N.J.
Height, 5.08½. Weight, 165.
Threw and batted lefthanded.

Holds major league record for most triple plays started, season (2), May 23 and June 9, 1928.

Year Club League	Pos.	G.	AB.	R.	H.	2B.	3B.	HR.	RBI.	B.A.	PO.	A.	E.	F.A.
1912—Buffalo.................... Int.	OF	33	82	7	13	1	1	0	....	.159	6	69	1	.987
1913—Buffalo.................... Int.	OF	51	127	7	30	3	0	0	....	.236	40	79	8	.937
1914—Buffalo.................... Int.	OF	75	221	39	68	17	4	0	....	.308	86	38	7	.947
1915—Buffalo.................... Int.	OF	138	522	82	160	*28	9	0	....	.307	296	17	10	.969
1915—Washington .... Amer.	OF	17	68	9	19	3	2	0	7	.279	36	5	0	1.000
1916—Washington .... Amer.	OF-P	64	145	16	36	4	0	0	13	.248	59	4	6	.913
1917—Wash.(a)-Phila. .... Amer.	OF-P	103	380	45	98	8	2	0	30	.258	135	12	11	.930
1918—Philadelphia (b)... Amer.	OF-P	110	416	50	84	11	2	0	9	.202	182	15	6	.970
1919—Cleveland............... Amer.	OF-P	26	17	3	6	2	1	0	1	.353	5	2	1	.875
1920—Cleveland.............. Amer.	OF	108	370	69	118	17	7	1	40	.319	185	14	7	.966
1921—Cleveland............... Amer.	OF	140	536	94	166	33	10	1	45	.310	277	17	8	.974

Year Club League	Pos.	G.	AB.	R.	H.	2B.	3B.	HR.	RBI.	B.A.	PO.	A.	E.	F.A.
1922—Cleveland.............. Amer.	OF-P	145	567	87	183	29	11	3	57	.323	289	18	7	.978
1923—Cleveland.............. Amer.	OF	152	●644	130	★222	36	12	2	51	.345	360	18	10	.974
1924—Cleveland.............. Amer.	OF	143	594	98	213	34	8	3	54	.359	330	11	9	.974
1925—Cleveland.............. Amer.	OF	138	557	109	165	24	5	4	42	.296	324	16	●16	.955
1926—Cleveland.............. Amer.	OF	143	555	89	166	33	7	2	45	.299	293	15	13	.960
1927—Cleveland.............. Amer.	OF	127	489	73	151	23	6	0	36	.309	300	13	10	.969
1928—Cleveland.............. Amer.	OF	112	433	63	133	18	4	1	37	.307	282	★22	5	.984
1929—Cleveland.............. Amer.	OF	102	364	56	106	22	1	0	26	.291	192	8	4	.980
1930—Cleveland.............. Amer.	OF	103	366	64	110	22	1	1	52	.301	162	7	8	.955
1931—Cleveland.............. Amer.	OF	28	43	7	13	2	1	0	4	.302	11	0	2	.846
1932—Cleveland.............. Amer.	OF	16	16	0	1	1	0	0	0	.063	3	1	0	1.000
1933—Jersey City .... Int.	OF	26	76	9	19	2	0	1	11	.250	39	1	1	.976
Major League Totals—18 Years		1777	6560	1062	1990	322	80	18	549	.303	3425	198	123	.967

aReleased to Philadelphia Athletics on waivers, July 17, 1917.

bTraded to Cleveland Indians with Pitcher Elmer Myers and Third Baseman Larry Gardner for Outfielder Bobby Roth, March, 1919.

WORLD SERIES RECORD

Year Club League	Pos.	G.	AB.	R.	H.	2B.	3B.	HR.	RBI.	B.A.	PO.	A.	E.	F.A.
1920—Cleveland.............. Amer.	OF-PH-PR	6	15	2	5	1	0	0	1	.333	8	1	0	1.000

PITCHING RECORD

Year Club	League	G.	IP.	W.	L.	Pct.	H.	R.	ER.	SO.	BB.	ERA.
1912—Buffalo....................	International	31	208	13	7	.650	226	97	....	84	57	......
1913—Buffalo....................	International	32	204	14	10	.583	212	87	....	62	91	......
1914—Buffalo....................	International	20	86	3	8	.273	99	57	....	37	32	......
1916—Washington	American	1	4	0	0	.000	2	2	2	2	3	4.50
1917—Washington	American	1	2	0	0	.000	10	10	10	1	2	45.00
1918—Philadelphia	American	5	23	2	1	.667	24	17	11	2	13	4.30
1919—Cleveland................	American	4	13	0	0	.000	12	9	8	0	8	5.54
1922—Cleveland................	American	2	6	0	0	.000	7	3	2	2	4	3.00
Major League Totals—5 Years...............		13	48	2	1	.667	55	41	33	7	30	6.19

FERGUSON ARTHUR JENKINS
(Fergie)

Born December 13, 1943, at Chatham, Ontario, Canada.

Height, 6.05. Weight, 210.

Threw and batted righthanded.

Shares major league record for most 1-0 games lost, season (5), 1968; most years leading league in home runs allowed (5).

Led American League in home runs allowed with 37 in 1975 and 40 in 1979.

Led National League in home runs allowed with 30 in 1967, 29 in 1971, 32 in 1972, 35 in 1973 and tied for lead with 26 in 1968.

Led American League in complete games with 29 in 1974.

Led National League in complete games with 20 in 1967, 24 in 1970 and 30 in 1971.

Led National League pitchers in games started with 40 in 1968, 42 in 1969 and tied for lead with 39 in 1971.

Led National League in balks with 4 in 1971.

Won National League Cy Young Memorial Award, 1971.

Named National League Pitcher of the Year by THE SPORTING NEWS, 1971.

Named American League Comeback Player of the Year by THE SPORTING NEWS, 1974.

Named righthanded pitcher on THE SPORTING NEWS National League All-Star Team, 1971, 1972.

Named pitcher on THE SPORTING NEWS National League All-Star Team, 1967.

Year Club	League	G.	IP.	W.	L.	Pct.	H.	R.	ER.	SO.	BB.	ERA.
1962—Miami	Florida St.	11	65	7	2	.778	34	10	7	69	19	0.97
1962—Buffalo	Int'national	3	13	1	1	.500	18	9	8	6	5	5.54
1963—Arkansas.............................	Int'national	4	10	0	1	.000	13	7	7	13	3	6.30
1963—Miami	Florida St.	20	140	12	5	.706	110	66	53	135	59	3.41
1964—Chattanooga..................................	Southern	21	139	10	6	.625	124	61	48	149	42	3.11
1964—Arkansas.............................	P. Coast	11	57	5	5	.500	40	27	20	49	34	3.16
1965—Arkansas.............................	P. Coast	32	122	8	6	.571	104	48	40	112	42	2.95
1965—Philadelphia..................................	National	7	12	2	1	.667	7	3	3	10	2	2.25
1966—Philadelphia†-Chicago	National	61	184	6	8	.429	150	77	68	150	52	3.33
1967—Chicago	National	38	289	20	13	.606	230	101	90	236	83	2.80
1968—Chicago	National	40	308	20	15	.571	255	96	90	260	65	2.63
1969—Chicago	National	43	311	21	15	.583	284	122	110	★273	71	3.21
1970—Chicago	National	40	313	22	16	.579	265	128	●118	274	60	3.39
1971—Chicago	National	39	★325	★24	13	.649	★304	114	100	263	37	2.77
1972—Chicago	National	36	289	20	12	.625	253	111	★103	184	62	3.21

Year	Club	League	G.	IP.	W.	L.	Pct.	H.	R.	ER.	SO.	BB.	ERA.
1973—Chicago‡		National	38	271	14	16	.467	267	133	117	170	57	3.89
1974—Texas		American	41	328	•25	12	.676	286	117	103	225	45	2.83
1975—Texas§		American	37	270	17	18	.486	261	130	118	157	56	3.93
1976—Boston		American	30	209	12	11	.522	201	85	76	142	43	3.27
1977—Boston x		American	28	193	10	10	.500	190	91	79	105	36	3.68
1978—Texas		American	34	249	18	8	.692	228	92	84	157	41	3.04
1979—Texas		American	37	259	16	14	.533	252	127	117	164	81	4.07
1980—Texas		American	29	198	12	12	.500	190	90	83	129	52	3.77
1981—Texas y		American	19	106	5	8	.385	122	55	53	63	40	4.50
1982—Chicago		National	34	217⅓	14	15	.483	221	92	76	134	68	3.15
1983—Chicago z		National	33	167⅓	6	9	.400	176	89	80	96	46	4.30
American League Totals—8 Years			255	1812	115	93	.553	1730	787	713	1142	394	3.54
National League Totals—11 Years			409	2686⅔	169	133	.560	2412	1066	956	2050	603	3.20
Major League Totals—19 Years			664	4498⅔	284	226	.557	4142	1853	1669	3192	997	3.34

Signed as free agent by Philadelphia Phillies' organization, June 15, 1962.

†Traded with Outfielder Adolfo Phillips and Outfielder-First Baseman John Herrnstein to Chicago Cubs for Pitchers Bob Buhl and Larry Jackson, April 21, 1966.

‡Traded to Texas Rangers for Infielders Bill Madlock and Vic Harris, October 25, 1973.

§Traded to Boston Red Sox for Outfielder Juan Beniquez, Pitcher Steve Barr, a player to be named later and an estimated $200,000, November 17, 1975; Texas Rangers acquired Pitcher Craig Skok to complete deal, December 12, 1975.

xTraded to Texas Rangers for Pitcher John Poloni and cash estimated at $20,000, December 14, 1977.

yGranted free agency, November 13, 1981; signed by Chicago Cubs, December 8, 1981.

zReleased, March 19, 1984.

HUGH AMBROSE (HUGHEY) JENNINGS
(Ee-Yah)

Born April 2, 1870, at Pittston, Pa.

Died February 1, 1928, at Scranton, Pa.

Height, 5.08½. Weight, 165.

Threw and batted righthanded.

Captain, Philadelphia Phillies, 1901-02; manager, Baltimore, Eastern League, 1903 through 1906; Detroit Tigers, 1907 to 1920; coach and assistant manager, New York Giants, 1921-25.
Named to Hall of Fame, 1945.

Year	Club	League	Pos.	G.	AB.	R.	H.	2B.	3B.	HR.	SB.	B.A.	PO.	A.	E.	F.A.
1890—Allentown		E. Int.-St.	SS	13	50	8	16	...	...	...	....	.320	....	....	...	.934
1891—Louisville		A. A.	1B-SS	81	316	46	95	10	8	1	14	.300	173	205	40	.904
1892—Louisville		Nat.	SS	152	584	66	137	16	3	2	24	.232	*336	543	84	.912
1893—Louis.-Balt.		Nat.	SS	38	135	12	25	3	0	2	1	.192	84	120	23	.898
1894—Baltimore		Nat.	SS	128	505	136	168	27	20	4	36	.332	*307	497	62	*.928
1895—Baltimore		Nat.	SS	131	528	159	204	40	8	4	60	.385	*425	460	53	*.943
1896—Baltimore		Nat.	SS	129	523	125	208	24	9	0	73	.398	*380	476	68	.926
1897—Baltimore		Nat.	SS	115	436	131	154	22	9	2	60	.353	336	417	54	*.933
1898—Baltimore		Nat.	2B-SS	143	533	136	173	24	9	0	31	.325	361	435	60	.930
1899—Brkn.-Balt.		Nat.	1-2B-SS	63	223	44	67	5	10	0	18	.300	475	22	8	.984
1900—Brooklyn		Nat.	1B	112	440	62	119	17	7	2	35	.270	1052	74	18	.984
1901—Philadelphia		Nat.	1B	81	302	38	83	22	2	1	13	.274	725	39	15	.980
1902—Philadelphia		Nat.	1-2B-SS	78	289	31	80	16	3	1	8	.277	659	47	12	.983
1903—Brooklyn		Nat.	OF	6	17	2	4	0	0	0	0	.235	7	0	0	1.000
1903—Baltimore		East.	SS-2B	32	122	26	40	8	0	0	9	.328	51	95	7	.954
1904—Baltimore		East.	SS-2B	92	332	65	97	21	0	1	23	.292	227	235	24	.951
1905—Baltimore		East.	SS-2B	56	179	24	45	8	0	0	3	.251	134	158	37	.887
1906—Baltimore		East.	SS-2B	75	242	24	60	9	1	0	2	.248	177	192	24	.928
1907—Detroit		Amer.	SS	2	4	0	1	1	0	0	0	.250	0	2	0	1.000
1908—Detroit		Amer.	PH	1	0	0	0	0	0	0	0	.000	0	0	0	.000
1909—Detroit		Amer.	1B	2	4	1	2	0	0	0	0	.500	1	0	0	1.000
1912—Detroit		Amer.	PH	1	1	0	0	0	0	0	0	.000	0	0	0	.000
1918—Detroit		Amer.	1B	1	0	0	0	0	0	0	0	.000	0	0	0	.000
American Association Totals—1 Year				81	316	46	95	10	8	1	14	.300	173	205	40	.904
American League Totals—5 Years				7	9	1	3	0	0	0	0	.333	1	2	0	1.000
National League Totals—12 Years				1176	4515	942	1422	217	80	18	359	.315	5147	3130	457	.948
Major League Totals—18 Years				1264	4840	989	1520	227	88	19	373	.314	5321	3337	497	.946

—DID YOU KNOW—

That Ferguson Jenkins is the only pitcher in big-league history to surrender home runs to all three Alou brothers (two to Jesus and one each to Felipe and Matty)?

THOMAS EDWARD (TOMMY) JOHN

Born May 22, 1943, at Terre Haute, Ind.
Height, 6.03. Weight, 203.
Threw left and batted righthanded.

Holds major league record for most years pitched (26).
Shares major league records for most years played (26); most errors by pitcher, inning (3), July 27, 1988, fourth inning.
Shares American League record for most hit batsmen, nine-inning game (4), June 15, 1968.
Led American League in shutouts with 6 in 1980.
Tied for American League lead in shutouts with 5 in 1966 and 6 in 1967.
Tied for American League lead in wild pitches with 17 and in intentional bases on balls issued with 16 in 1970.
Named National League Comeback Player of the Year by THE SPORTING NEWS, 1976.
Named lefthanded pitcher on THE SPORTING NEWS American League All-Star Team, 1980.

Year Club	League	G.	IP.	W.	L.	Pct.	H.	R.	ER.	SO.	BB.	ERA.
1961—Dubuque	Midwest	14	88	10	4	.714	74	47	31	99	59	3.17
1962—Charleston	Eastern	21	128	6	8	.429	129	67	55	114	71	3.87
1962—Jacksonville	Int'national	8	34	2	2	.500	29	20	18	27	16	4.76
1963—Charleston	Eastern	12	95	9	2	.818	85	25	17	45	12	1.61
1963—Jacksonville	Int'national	18	102	6	8	.429	115	53	40	63	39	3.53
1963—Cleveland	American	6	20	0	2	.000	23	10	5	9	6	2.25
1964—Cleveland	American	25	94	2	9	.182	97	53	41	65	35	3.93
1964—Portland†	P. Coast	13	74	6	6	.500	75	38	35	72	24	4.26
1965—Chicago	American	39	184	14	7	.667	162	67	63	126	58	3.08
1966—Chicago	American	34	223	14	11	.560	195	76	65	138	57	2.62
1967—Chicago	American	31	178	10	13	.435	143	62	49	110	47	2.48
1968—Chicago	American	25	177	10	5	.667	135	45	39	117	49	1.98
1969—Chicago	American	33	232	9	11	.450	230	91	84	128	90	3.26
1970—Chicago	American	37	269	12	17	.414	253	117	98	138	101	3.28
1971—Chicago‡	American	38	229	13	16	.448	244	115	92	131	58	3.62
1972—Los Angeles	National	29	187	11	5	.688	172	68	60	117	40	2.89
1973—Los Angeles	National	36	218	16	7	★.696	202	88	75	116	50	3.10
1974—Los Angeles	National	22	153	13	3	.813	133	51	44	78	42	2.59
1975—Los Angeles	National					(Did not play)						
1976—Los Angeles	National	31	207	10	10	.500	207	76	71	91	61	3.09
1977—Los Angeles	National	31	220	20	7	.741	225	82	68	123	50	2.78
1978—Los Angeles§	National	33	213	17	10	.630	230	95	78	124	53	3.30
1979—New York	American	37	276	21	9	.700	268	109	91	111	65	2.97
1980—New York	American	36	265	22	9	.710	270	115	101	78	56	3.43
1981—New York	American	20	140	9	8	.529	135	50	41	50	39	2.64
1982—New York x-California	American	37	221⅔	14	12	.538	239	102	91	68	39	3.69
1983—California	American	34	234⅔	11	13	.458	★287	126	113	65	49	4.33
1984—California	American	32	181⅓	7	13	.350	223	97	91	47	56	4.52
1985—California y-Oakland	American	23	86⅓	4	10	.286	117	59	53	25	28	5.53
1985—Modesto z	California	2	4	0	0	.000	12	8	7	11	6	5.73
1985—Madison z	Midwest	1	6	0	0	.000	4	2	2	3	4	3.00
1986—New York a	American	13	70⅔	5	3	.625	73	27	23	28	15	2.93
1986—Fort Lauderdale b	Florida St.	3	13⅔	2	0	1.000	7	2	0	7	1	0.00
1987—New York c	American	33	187⅔	13	6	.684	212	95	84	63	47	4.03
1988—New York d	American	35	176⅓	9	8	.529	221	96	88	81	46	4.49
1989—New York e	American	10	63⅔	2	7	.222	87	45	41	18	22	5.80
American League Totals—20 Years		578	3509⅓	201	189	.515	3614	1557	1353	1596	963	3.47
National League Totals—6 Years		182	1198	87	42	.674	1169	460	396	649	296	2.97
Major League Totals—26 Years		760	4707⅓	288	231	.555	4783	2017	1749	2245	1259	3.34

Signed as free agent by Cleveland Indians' organization, June 12, 1961.

†Traded to Chicago White Sox with Catcher John Romano and Outfielder Tommie Agee for Catcher Camilo Carreon and Outfielder Rocky Colavito, January 20, 1965, as part of three-way deal which saw Chicago obtain Colavito from Kansas City Athletics earlier same day for Outfielders Jim Landis and Mike Hershberger and a pitcher to be named later; Kansas City acquired Pitcher Fred Talbot to complete deal, February 10, 1965.

‡Traded with Infielder Steve Huntz to Los Angeles Dodgers for Infielder-Outfielder Richie Allen, December 2, 1971.

§Granted free agency, November 2, 1978; signed by New York Yankees, November 21, 1978.

xTraded to California Angels for a player to be named later, August 31, 1982; New York Yankees acquired Pitcher Dennis Rasmussen to complete deal, November 24 1982.

yReleased, June 19, 1985; signed by Modesto (Oakland A's organization), July 12, 1985.

zGranted free agency, November 12, 1985; signed by New York Yankees, May 2, 1986.

aRehabilitation disability assignment at Fort Lauderdale, July 27 to August 8, 1986.

bGranted free agency, November 12, 1986; re-signed by Yankees, January 8, 1987.

cGranted free agency, November 9, 1987; re-signed by Yankees, December 18, 1987.

dReleased, November 10, 1988; re-signed by Yankees, February 13, 1989.

eReleased, May 30, 1989.

Holds major league records for most wild pitches, lifetime (4), series (3), 1982 and game (3), October 9, 1982.

Shares major league records for most games won and consecutive games won, lifetime (4); most wild pitches, inning (2), October 9, 1982, fourth inning.

Shares National League records for most complete games, lifetime (2); most hit batsmen, lifetime and series (2), 1977.

Year Club	League	G.	IP.	W.	L.	Pct.	H.	R.	ER.	SO.	BB.	ERA.
1977—Los Angeles	National	2	13⅔	1	0	1.000	11	5	1	11	5	0.66
1978—Los Angeles	National	1	9	1	0	1.000	4	0	0	4	2	0.00
1980—New York	American	1	6⅔	0	0	.000	8	2	2	3	1	2.70
1981—New York	American	1	6	1	0	1.000	6	1	1	3	1	1.50
1982—California	American	2	12⅓	1	1	.500	11	9	7	6	6	5.11
Championship Series Totals—5 Years		7	47⅔	4	1	.800	40	17	11	27	15	2.08

Year Club	League	G.	IP.	W.	L.	Pct.	H.	R.	ER.	SO.	BB.	ERA.
1977—Los Angeles	National	1	6	0	1	.000	9	5	4	7	3	6.00
1978—Los Angeles	National	2	14⅔	1	0	1.000	14	8	5	6	4	3.07
1981—New York	American	3	13	1	0	1.000	11	1	1	8	0	0.69
World Series Totals—3 Years		6	33⅔	2	1	.667	34	14	10	21	7	2.67

BYRON BANCROFT (BAN) JOHNSON

Born January 5, 1864, at Norwalk, O.

Died March 28, 1931, at St. Louis, Mo.

As a boy in Avondale, O., Ban Johnson played baseball. Later, when attending Marietta College, he was one of the steadiest catchers of his time in collegiate circles in Ohio, a big fellow with plenty of nerve who caught the fastest pitching without glove, chest protector or mask. From college, Johnson went into newspaper work in Cincinnati—on the old Commercial-Gazette. He continued as a writer of sports, specializing in baseball, until 1893.

At the end of the 1894 season, John T. Brush dismissed Charles Comiskey as manager of the Cincinnati Reds. Johnson and Comiskey then revived the Western League, with Kansas City, Toledo, Minneapolis, Milwaukee, Indianapolis, Sioux City, Grand Rapids and Detroit as members. Johnson was named president. On October 11, 1899, the Western changed its name to the American League, occupied the vacant Cleveland territory by purchase of the ball park there, and decided to move Comiskey's St. Paul club to Chicago.

After the 1900 season, Johnson decided on expansion of the American League into a major circuit for 1901, with or without consent of the National League. He put clubs in Boston, Philadelphia, Washington and Baltimore. St. Louis replaced Milwaukee in 1902. After the A. L. moved the Baltimore club to New York in 1903, peace was restored with the National.

Meanwhile, Johnson had brought about a new era in baseball. He was a stickler for decorum on the playing field; he insisted that umpires of his league be respected and was severe in disciplining players who transgressed the rules of good conduct.

Johnson was a fighter who brooked no interference from anyone. His combativeness was largely responsible for the ending of the three-man Commission which ran the game during his early A.L. reign. When Commissioner Landis came into office after the Commission folded, Johnson battled him whenever it seemed to him that the National League was getting some private benefit or that Landis or the N.L. was trying to take some power, some control from Ban's beloved A.L.

In 1901, Johnson was elected to the presidency of the American League for ten years and re-elected for 20 years. The term subsequently was increased by five years in 1925, so that his term of office would not have expired until 1935. However, ill health and a storm of protest from his adversaries in baseball caused him to retire, October 17, 1927. He was named to the Hall of Fame in 1937.

ROBERT LEE (BOB) JOHNSON

Born November 26, 1906, at Pryor, Okla.

Died July 6, 1982, at Tacoma, Wash.

Height, 5.11½. Weight, 200.

Threw and batted righthanded.

Brother of Roy Johnson, former major league outfielder.

Shares American League record for most runs batted in, inning (6), August 29, 1937, first game, first inning.
Manager, Tacoma, Western International League, 1949.

Year	Club	League	Pos.	G.	AB.	R.	H.	2B.	3B.	HR.	RBI.	B.A.	PO.	A.	E.	F.A.
1929—Wichita-Pueblo.....	West.		OF	66	227	50	62	9	3	16	.....	.273	111	2	3	.974
1929—Portland.................	P. C.		OF	81	264	42	67	16	3	5	27	.254	168	9	7	.962
1930—Portland.................	P. C.		O-1-2B	157	501	91	133	25	3	21	93	.265	489	68	20	.965
1931—Portland.................	P. C.		O-1-2B	141	504	108	170	37	5	22	94	.337	445	83	15	.972
1932—Portland.................	P. C.		O-1-2B	149	545	105	180	43	1	29	111	.330	357	49	19	.955
1933—Philadelphia	Amer.		OF	142	535	103	155	44	4	21	93	.290	298	16	16	.952
1934—Philadelphia	Amer.		OF	141	547	111	168	26	6	34	92	.307	304	★17	11	.967
1935—Philadelphia	Amer.		OF	147	582	103	174	29	5	28	109	.299	337	13	★20	.946
1936—Philadelphia	Amer.		2B-OF	153	566	91	165	29	14	25	121	.292	340	82	19	.957
1937—Philadelphia	Amer.		OF-1B	138	477	91	146	32	6	25	108	.306	314	15	8	.976
1938—Philadelphia	Amer.		★OF-1B	152	563	114	176	27	9	30	113	.313	406	★27	★18	★.960
1939—Philadelphia	Amer.		OF	150	544	115	184	30	9	23	114	.338	369	15	13	.967
1940—Philadelphia	Amer.		OF	138	512	93	137	25	4	31	103	.268	310	15	13	.962
1941—Philadelphia	Amer.		1B-OF	149	552	98	152	30	8	22	107	.275	541	35	8	.986
1942—Philadelphia(a)....	Amer.		OF	149	550	78	160	35	7	13	80	.291	318	18	13	.963
1943—Washington(b)	Amer.		1-3B-O	117	438	65	116	22	8	7	63	.265	308	61	9	.976
1944—Boston....................	Amer.		OF	144	525	106	170	40	8	17	106	.324	270	23	7	.977
1945—Boston....................	Amer.		OF	143	529	71	148	27	7	12	74	.280	296	15	8	.975
1946—Milwaukee.............	A. A.		OF	94	307	53	83	14	2	13	53	.270	127	12	7	.952
1947—Seattle....................	P. C.		OF	130	342	44	101	28	1	7	50	.295	249	20	13	.954
1948—Seattle....................	P. C.		OF	59	145	17	41	7	0	5	23	.283	225	10	5	.979
1949—Tacoma.................	W. Int.		OF	93	218	35	71	13	1	5	50	.326	94	16 '	2	.982
1950—								(Out of Organized Ball)								
1951—Tijuana...................	S. W. Int.		1B	21	69	13	15	4	2	0	6	.217	74	37	6	.949
Major League Totals—13 Years..............				1863	6920	1239	2051	396	95	288	1283	.296	4411	352	163	.967

aTraded to Washington Senators for Outfielder Bobby Estalella, Infielder Jimmy Pofahl and cash, March 21, 1943.
bSold to Boston Red Sox, December 4, 1943.

WALTER PERRY JOHNSON
(Barney and The Big Train)

Born November 6, 1887, at Humboldt, Kan.

Died December 10, 1946, at Washington, D. C.

Height, 6.01. Weight, 200.

Threw and batted righthanded.

Holds major league record for most shutouts, lifetime (110).
Holds American League record for most games won, lifetime (416).
Shares American League record for most consecutive games won, season (16), July 3, second game, through August 23, 1912, first game.
Pitched 1-0 no-hit victory against Boston Red Sox, July 1, 1920.
Named American League Most Valuable Player, 1913 and 1924.
Named to THE SPORTING NEWS All-Star Major League Team, 1925.
Manager, Newark, International League, 1928; Washington Senators, 1929 through 1932; Cleveland Indians, 1933 to 1935.
Named to Hall of Fame, 1936.

Year	Club	League	G.	IP.	W.	L.	Pct.	ShO.	H.	R.	ER.	SO.	BB.	ERA.
1907—Washington	Amer.	14	110	5	9	.357	2	100	35	....	70	16	....
1908—Washington	Amer.	36	257	14	14	.500	6	196	75	....	160	52	....
1909—Washington	Amer.	40	297	13	25	.342	4	247	112	....	164	84	....
1910—Washington	Amer.	●45	★374	25	17	.595	8	★262	92	....	★313	76	....
1911—Washington	Amer.	40	322	25	13	.658	●6	292	119	....	207	70	....
1912—Washington	Amer.	50	368	32	12	.727	7	259	89	....	★303	76	....
1913—Washington	Amer.	48	★346	★36	7	.837	★11	232	56	44	★243	38	★1.14
1914—Washington	Amer.	★51	★372	★28	18	.609	★9	★287	88	71	★225	74	1.72
1915—Washington	Amer.	47	★337	★27	13	.675	★7	258	83	58	★203	56	1.55
1916—Washington	Amer.	48	★371	★25	20	.556	3	★290	105	78	★228	82	1.89
1917—Washington	Amer.	47	328	23	16	.590	8	259	105	83	★188	67	2.28
1918—Washington	Amer.	39	325	★23	13	.639	●8	241	71	46	★162	70	★1.27
1919—Washington	Amer.	39	290	20	14	.588	★7	235	73	48	★147	51	★1.49
1920—Washington	Amer.	21	144	8	10	.444	4	135	68	50	78	27	3.13
1921—Washington	Amer.	35	264	17	14	.548	1	265	122	103	★143	92	3.51
1922—Washington	Amer.	41	280	15	16	.484	4	283	115	93	105	99	2.99
1923—Washington	Amer.	42	261	17	12	.586	3	263	112	101	★130	69	3.48
1924—Washington	Amer.	38	278	★23	7	★.767	★6	233	97	84	★158	77	★2.72
1925—Washington	Amer.	30	229	20	7	.741	3	211	95	78	108	78	3.07
1926—Washington	Amer.	33	262	15	16	.484	2	259	120	105	125	73	3.61
1927—Washington	Amer.	18	108	5	6	.455	1	113	70	61	48	26	5.08
1928—Newark	Int.	1	0	0	0	.000	0	0	0	0	0	1	0.00
Major League Totals—21 Years......................		802	5923	416	279	.599	110	4920	1902	1103	3508	1353	....

Year	Club	League	G.	IP.	W.	L.	Pct.	H.	R.	ER.	SO.	BB.	ERA.
1924—Washington		American	3	24	1	2	.333	30	10	6	20	11	2.25
1925—Washington		American	3	26	2	1	.667	26	10	6	15	4	2.08
World Series Totals—2 Years			6	50	3	3	.500	56	20	12	35	15	2.16

WILLIAM JULIUS (JUDY) JOHNSON

Born October 26, 1899, at Snow Hill, Md.

Died June 14, 1989, at Wilmington, Del.

Height, 5:11½. Weight, 150.

Threw and batted righthanded.

A third baseman who could do it all, Judy Johnson was the only hot-corner guardian named by the Special Committee on Negro Leagues. He was quiet, reserved in nature and a sharp student of the game who became manager of the powerful Homestead Grays at the tender age of 29.

His hitting ability probably is what ranked him above the three other great third basemen of Negro baseball— Oliver Marcell, who had a great glove but didn't hit as well; Henry Blackman, an all-round great who played only two years before he died, and brainy little Dave Malarcher, who both fielded well and hit well. Malarcher became a published poet and still was running his real estate business at age 84.

Johnson was a semi-pro star in his native Wilmington, Del. In 1918, he joined the Bacharach's, then the Philadelphia All-Stars in 1920 and the Hilldales, famed Eastern powerhouse as an independent club, in 1921. He stayed with the Hilldales until he left to manage the Homestead Grays in 1929.

Cool Papa Bell said, "Johnson was the best hitter among the four top third basemen, but though someone else might bat as high as Judy, no one would drive in as many clutch runs as he would. He was a solid ballplayer, real smart, but he was the kind of fellow who could 'just get it done.' He was dependable, quiet, not flashy at all, but could handle anything that came up. No matter how much the pressure, no matter how important the play or the throw or the hit, Judy could do when it counted.

"And above all, he was a gentleman, on and off the field. Oh, no one could push him around, but his quiet, easy-going smooth, down-to-business manner made him a standout as a player and as a man."

Cum Posey, owner and manager of the Homestead Grays, rated Johnson among the best players in the Negro leagues and Buck Leonard, Posey's Hall of Fame first baseman, is verification for that statement. Leonard added, "And Judy, always thinking, added a special thing that helped him take care of runners who would try to undress him at third. He wore small shin guards under his stockings that prevented spike-flashing runners from putting him out of commission. Keeping free from those nagging injuries maybe was a big part in his maintaining such consistency as both a batter and fielder."

Johnson himself cleared up the shinguard point:

"It was John Henry Lloyd who devised the shinguard method. He wore them and he advised all of us to wear them. Our whole infield was outfitted with them and we were the first team protected like that. My shins are cuts and scars all up and down. Negro base runners were just mean and tough. We had to counteract that some way and the shinguards helped us greatly. We still got the business, but we could stay in the game longer, and that was John Henry's point."

After Johnson left the Homesteads, he joined the Darby (Pa.) Daisies in 1931. The next year he shifted to the Pittsburgh Crawfords. As captain in 1934, he tied down the far corner of one of Negro baseball's finest infields—Oscar Charleston at first, Chet Williams at second, Leroy Morney at short and Johnson at third.

Buck Leonard rates that infield, plus the Crawfords' Josh Gibson and Bill Perkins as catchers, Vic Harris, Cool Papa Bell and Jimmie Crutchfield in the outfield and pitchers Satchel Paige, Bert Hunter, Leroy Matlock, Sam Streeter and Harry Kincannon as the greatest team he ever saw. When you consider that Johnson managed the Homestead Grays, you realize he was associated with two of the Negro game's greatest teams.

Like all the best players in the Negro leagues, Johnson spent many winters in Cuba and Mexico competing against barnstorming major leaguers and the top Caribbean players.

When the curtain came down on Negro professional ball, Johnson became a scout for the Philadelphia Athletics in 1951 until he was released in 1954. He next joined the scouting staff of the Phillies in 1961 and remained with them until 1972. He became one of the Dodgers' eagle eyes on December 3, 1973.

His greatest thrills?

"When my career ended, I thought that's all there is. I was working as a scout with major league clubs, but I never dreamed there'd come a day when I would be told I was going to enter the Hall of Fame, joining the greats of the greatest game of them all.

"But as a player, my top thrill was being able to play against major league clubs and then major league players on all-star teams and know that we were capable of doing so. We played against some of the greatest stars and beat them more often than not. It was the only way we could tell if we were just as good players as they were, or if we were better."

Johnson was named to the Hall of Fame in 1975.

—DID YOU KNOW—

That former Washington pitching great Walter Johnson made his final big-league appearance in the historic 1927 game in which Babe Ruth hit his 60th home run? Johnson pinch-hit in the ninth inning.

JOHN WILLIAM (JAY) JOHNSTONE JR.

Born November 20, 1946, at Manchester, Conn.

Height, 6.01. Weight, 190.

Threw right and batted lefthanded.

Year—Club	League	Pos.	G.	AB.	R.	H.	2B.	3B.	HR.	RBI.	B.A.	PO.	A.	E.	F.A.
1963—San Jose	Calif.	OF-SS-3B	48	155	21	39	5	3	1	18	.252	51	31	9	.901
1964—San Jose	Calif.	OF	126	454	66	132	27	●11	4	48	.291	250	14	12	.957
1965—El Paso	Texas	OF	35	137	21	39	9	2	1	21	.285	82	4	4	.956
1965—San Jose	Calif.	OF	97	356	53	107	17	6	6	60	.301	198	11	10	.954
1966—El Paso	Texas	OF	7	25	5	9	2	0	1	1	.360	19	0	0	1.000
1966—Seattle	P. C.	OF	81	318	60	108	14	7	7	42	.340	170	7	4	.978
1966—California	Amer.	OF	61	254	35	67	12	4	3	17	.264	114	2	3	.975
1967—California	Amer.	OF	79	230	18	48	7	1	2	10	.209	141	3	4	.973
1967—Seattle	P. C.	OF	49	184	21	58	11	1	4	21	.315	117	3	4	.968
1968—California	Amer.	OF	41	115	11	30	4	1	0	3	.261	58	4	1	.984
1968—Seattle	P. C.	OF	84	314	45	87	15	4	13	56	.277	203	11	9	.960
1969—California	Amer.	OF	148	540	64	146	20	5	10	59	.270	331	12	6	.983
1970—California†	Amer.	OF	119	320	34	76	10	5	11	39	.238	200	7	4	.981
1971—Chicago	Amer.	OF	124	388	53	101	14	1	16	40	.260	232	9	8	.968
1972—Chicago‡	Amer.	OF	113	261	27	49	9	0	4	17	.188	154	5	2	.988
1973—Tucson	P. C.	OF	69	242	58	84	15	5	9	44	.347	125	2	6	.955
1973—Oakland§	Amer.	OF-2B	23	28	1	3	1	0	0	3	.107	7	0	0	1.000
1974—Toledo	Int.	OF-1B	57	155	31	49	15	1	8	25	.316	77	6	3	.965
1974—Philadelphia	Nat.	OF	64	200	30	59	10	4	6	30	.295	88	4	3	.968
1975—Philadelphia	Nat.	OF	122	350	50	115	19	2	7	54	.329	152	10	4	.976
1976—Philadelphia	Nat.	OF-1B	129	440	62	140	38	4	5	53	.318	293	10	8	.974
1977—Philadelphia	Nat.	OF-1B	112	363	64	103	18	4	15	59	.284	294	15	1	.997
1978—Philadelphia x	Nat.	1B-OF	35	56	3	10	2	0	0	4	.179	77	7	1	.988
1978—New York	Amer.	OF	36	65	6	17	0	0	1	6	.262	31	0	0	1.000
1979—New York y	Amer.	OF	23	48	7	10	1	0	1	7	.208	32	0	0	1.000
1979—San Diego z	Nat.	OF-1B	75	201	10	59	8	2	0	32	.294	185	18	4	.981
1980—Los Angeles	Nat.	OF	109	251	31	77	15	2	2	20	.307	100	9	4	.965
1981—Los Angeles	Nat.	OF-1B	61	83	8	17	3	0	3	6	.205	33	4	1	.974
1982—L.A. a-Chi.	Nat.	OF	119	282	40	68	14	1	10	45	.241	154	8	3	.982
1983—Chicago	Nat.	OF	86	140	16	36	7	0	6	22	.257	55	3	4	.935
1984—Chicago b	Nat.	OF	52	73	8	21	2	2	0	3	.288	12	0	0	1.000
1985—Los Angeles c	Nat.	PH	17	15	0	2	1	0	0	2	.133	0	0	0	.000
National League Totals—12 Years			981	2454	322	707	137	21	54	330	.288	1443	88	33	.979
American League Totals—10 Years			767	2249	256	547	78	17	48	201	.243	1300	42	28	.980
Major League Totals—20 Years			1748	4703	578	1254	215	38	102	531	.267	2743	130	61	.979

Signed as free agent by California Angels' organization, June 30, 1963.

†Traded with Pitcher Tom Bradley and Catcher Tom Egan to Chicago White Sox for Outfielder Ken Berry, Second Baseman Syd O'Brien and Pitcher Billy Wynne, November 30, 1970.

‡Released, March 7, 1973; signed by Oakland Athletics, March 31, 1973.

§Conditionally released to St. Louis Cardinals, January 9, 1974; released by St. Louis, March 26, 1974; signed by Philadelphia Phillies, April 3, 1974.

xTraded with Outfielder Bobby Brown to New York Yankees for Pitcher Rawly Eastwick, June 14, 1978.

yTraded to San Diego Padres for Pitcher Dave Wehrmeister, June 15, 1979.

zGranted free agency, November 1, 1979; signed by Los Angeles Dodgers, December 4, 1979.

aReleased, May 25, 1982; signed by Chicago Cubs, June 1, 1982.

bReleased, September 9, 1984; signed by Los Angeles Dodgers, February 20, 1985.

cReleased, October 31, 1985.

CHAMPIONSHIP SERIES RECORD

Year—Club	League	Pos.	G.	AB.	R.	H.	2B.	3B.	HR.	RBI.	B.A.	PO.	A.	E.	F.A.
1976—Philadelphia	Nat.	PH-OF	3	9	1	7	1	1	0	2	.778	3	0	0	1.000
1977—Philadelphia	Nat.	OF-PH	2	5	0	1	0	0	0	0	.200	4	0	0	1.000
1981—Los Angeles	Nat.	PH	2	2	0	0	0	0	0	0	.000	0	0	0	.000
1985—Los Angeles	Nat.	PH	1	1	0	0	0	0	0	0	.000	0	0	0	.000
Championship Series Totals—4 Years			8	17	1	8	1	1	0	2	.471	7	0	0	1.000

WORLD SERIES RECORD

Year—Club	League	Pos.	G.	AB.	R.	H.	2B.	3B.	HR.	RBI.	B.A.	PO.	A.	E.	F.A.
1978—New York	Amer.	OF	2	0	0	0	0	0	0	0	.000	1	0	0	1.000
1981—Los Angeles	Nat.	PH	3	3	1	2	0	0	1	3	.667	0	0	0	1.000
World Series Totals—2 Years			5	3	1	2	0	0	1	3	.667	1	0	0	1.000

SAMUEL POND (SAM) JONES
(Sad Sam)

Born July 26, 1892, at Woodfield, O.

Died July 6, 1966, at Barnesville, O.

Height, 6.00. Weight, 170.

Threw and batted righthanded.

Pitched 2-0 no-hit victory against Philadelphia, September 4, 1923.
Coach, Toronto, International League, 1940.

Year	Club	League	G.	IP.	W.	L.	Pct.	H.	R.	ER.	SO.	BB.	ERA.
1913—Zanesville		Int.-State						(No Record Available)					
1914—Portsmouth(a)		Ohio State	11	....	5	6	.455	....	....	....	....	....	......
1914—Cleveland		A. A.	23	129	10	4	.714	112	45	35	50	64	2.44
1914—Cleveland		Amer.	1	3	0	0	.000	2	1	1	0	2	3.00
1915—Cleveland(b)		Amer.	48	146	4	9	.308	131	78	59	42	63	3.64
1916—Boston		Amer.	12	27	0	1	.000	25	14	11	7	10	3.67
1917—Boston		Amer.	9	16	0	1	.000	15	9	8	5	6	4.50
1918—Boston		Amer.	24	184	16	5	★.762	151	66	46	44	70	2.25
1919—Boston		Amer.	35	245	12	20	.375	258	120	★102	67	95	3.75
1920—Boston		Amer.	37	274	13	16	.448	302	143	120	86	79	3.94
1921—Boston(c)		Amer.	40	299	23	16	.590	318	122	107	98	78	3.22
1922—New York		Amer.	45	260	13	13	.500	270	132	106	81	76	3.67
1923—New York		Amer.	39	243	21	8	.724	239	114	98	68	69	3.63
1924—New York		Amer.	36	179	9	6	.600	187	85	72	53	76	3.62
1925—New York		Amer.	43	247	15	★21	.417	267	147	127	92	104	4.63
1926—New York(d)		Amer.	39	161	9	8	.529	186	104	89	69	80	4.98
1927—St. Louis(e)		Amer.	30	190	8	14	.364	211	121	91	72	102	4.31
1928—Washington		Amer.	30	225	17	7	.708	209	89	71	63	78	2.84
1929—Washington		Amer.	24	154	9	9	.500	156	80	67	36	49	3.92
1930—Washington		Amer.	25	183	15	7	.682	195	95	83	60	61	4.08
1931—Washington(f)		Amer.	25	148	9	10	.474	185	88	71	58	47	4.32
1932—Chicago		Amer.	30	200	10	15	.400	217	123	94	64	75	4.23
1933—Chicago		Amer.	27	177	10	12	.455	181	80	66	60	65	3.36
1934—Chicago		Amer.	27	183	8	12	.400	217	120	104	60	60	5.11
1935—Chicago		Amer.	21	140	8	7	.533	162	77	63	38	51	4.05
1940—Toronto		Int.	8	12	1	0	1.000	12	3	3	5	9	2.25
Major League Totals—22 Years			647	3884	229	217	.513	4084	2008	1656	1263	1396	3.84

aPurchased by Cleveland, A. L., and optioned to Cleveland, A. A.; recalled September, 1915.

bTraded with $50,000 and option on Catcher Chet Thomas to Boston A. L., for Outfielder Tris Speaker, April, 1917.

cTraded to New York with Shortstop Everett Scott and Pitcher Joe Bush for Shortstop Roger Peckinpaugh and Pitchers Bill Piercy and Jack Quinn, December, 1921.

dTraded to St. Louis for Outfielder Cedric Durst, February, 1927.

eReleased to Washington on waivers, September, 1927.

fTraded with Infielder Minter Hayes and Pitcher Bump Hadley to Chicago White Sox for Outfielder Carl Reynolds and Infielder John Kerr, December 4, 1931.

WORLD SERIES RECORD

Year	Club	League	G.	IP.	W.	L.	Pct.	H.	R.	ER.	SO.	BB.	ERA.
1918—Boston		Amer.	1	9	0	1	.000	7	3	3	5	5	3.00
1922—New York		Amer.	2	2	0	0	.000	1	0	0	0	1	0.00
1923—New York		Amer.	2	10	0	1	.000	5	1	1	3	2	0.90
1926—New York		Amer.	1	1	0	0	.000	2	1	1	1	2	9.00
World Series Totals—4 Years			6	22	0	2	.000	15	5	5	9	10	2.04

ADRIAN (ADDIE) JOSS

Born April 12, 1880, Juneau, Wis.

Died April 14, 1911, Toledo, O.

Height, 6.03. Weight, 185.

Threw and batted righthanded.

Pitched perfect game against Chicago White Sox, October 2, 1908; pitched no-hit game against Chicago White Sox, April 20, 1910.

Named to Hall of Fame, 1978.

Year — Club	League	G.	IP.	W.	L.	Pct.	H.	R.	SO.	BB.	CG.	ShO.
1900—Toledo	Inter-State	49	....	19	16	.543	234	124	168	53	....	3
1901—Toledo	Western Assn.	41	353	25	15	.625	273	162	217	69	37	4
1902—Cleveland	American	32	269	17	13	.567	225	120	106	75	28	5
1903—Cleveland	American	32	284	18	13	.581	232	105	120	37	31	3
1904—Cleveland	American	25	192	14	10	.583	160	50	83	30	20	5
1905—Cleveland	American	33	289	20	12	.625	246	90	127	39	31	3
1906—Cleveland	American	34	282	21	9	.700	220	81	106	43	28	9
1907—Cleveland	American	42	339	27	10	.730	281	101	127	54	34	6
1908—Cleveland	American	42	324	24	12	.667	235	77	130	30	29	9
1909—Cleveland	American	33	243	14	13	.519	198	71	67	31	24	4
1910—Cleveland(a)	American	13	107	5	5	.500	96	35	49	18	9	1
Major League Totals—9 Years		286	2329	160	97	.623	1893	730	915	357	234	45

aDied suddenly from attack of tubercular meningitis during spring training of 1911.

JOSEPH IGNATIUS (JOE) JUDGE

Born May 25, 1894, at New York, N. Y.

Died March 11, 1963, at Washington, D. C.

Height, 5.08½. Weight, 155.

Threw right and batted lefthanded.

Manager, Baltimore, International League, 1934 (part); coach, Georgetown University, 1937 to 1944; Washington Senators, 1945 through 1946; Georgetown University, 1949 through 1957.

Year — Club	League	Pos.	G.	AB.	R.	H.	2B.	3B.	HR.	RBI.	B.A.	PO.	A.	E.	F.A.
1914—Lewiston	N. Eng.	1B	114	421	62	115	10	10	4	....	.273	1031	57	17	.985
1915—Buffalo(a)	Int.	1B-OF	140	493	68	158	19	15	0	....	.320	1348	54	8	★.994
1915—Washington	Amer.	1B-OF	12	40	7	17	2	0	0	11	.425	97	6	1	.990
1916—Washington	Amer.	1B	103	336	42	74	10	8	0	31	.220	935	69	14	.986
1917—Washington	Amer.	1B	102	393	62	112	15	15	2	31	.285	906	60	12	.988
1918—Washington	Amer.	1B	●130	502	56	131	23	7	1	52	.261	1304	92	21	.985
1919—Washington	Amer.	1B	135	521	83	150	33	12	2	29	.288	1177	78	15	.988
1920—Washington	Amer.	1B	126	493	103	164	19	15	5	51	.333	1194	62	10	.992
1921—Washington	Amer.	1B	153	622	87	187	26	11	7	72	.301	1417	89	6	.996
1922—Washington	Amer.	1B	148	591	84	174	32	15	10	81	.294	1378	101	6	.996
1923—Washington	Amer.	1B	113	405	56	127	24	6	2	63	.314	1070	88	8	★.993
1924—Washington	Amer.	1B	140	516	71	167	38	9	3	79	.324	1276	86	8	●.994
1925—Washington	Amer.	1B	112	376	65	118	31	5	8	66	.314	999	71	7	★.994
1926—Washington	Amer.	1B	134	453	70	132	25	11	7	92	.291	1145	95	8	.994
1927—Washington	Amer.	1B	137	522	68	161	29	11	2	71	.308	1309	71	6	★.996
1928—Washington	Amer.	1B	153	542	78	166	31	10	3	93	.306	1412	92	6	.996
1929—Washington	Amer.	1B	143	543	83	171	35	8	6	71	.315	1323	88	6	★.996
1930—Washington	Amer.	1B	126	442	83	144	29	11	10	80	.326	1050	67	2	★.998
1931—Washington	Amer.	1B	35	74	11	21	3	0	0	9	.284	155	10	1	.994
1932—Washington(b)	Amer.	1B	82	291	45	75	16	3	3	29	.258	668	46	2	.997
1933—Brooklyn(c)	Nat.	1B	42	112	7	24	2	1	0	9	.214	243	17	3	.989
1933—Boston	Amer.	1B	34	104	20	30	8	1	0	22	.288	258	12	0	1.000
1934—Boston	Amer.	1B	10	15	3	5	2	0	0	2	.333	24	1	0	1.000
American League Totals—20 Years			2128	7781	1177	2326	431	158	71	1035	.299	19097	1284	139	.993
National League Totals—1 Year			42	112	7	24	2	1	0	9	.214	243	17	3	.989
Major League Totals—20 Years			2170	7893	1184	2350	433	159	71	1044	.298	19340	1301	142	.993

aSold to Washington Senators, September 22, 1915.

bUnconditionally released by Washington Senators, January 27, 1933; subsequently signed with Brooklyn Dodgers.

cUnconditionally released by Brooklyn Dodgers, July, 1933, and signed with Boston Red Sox.

WORLD SERIES RECORD

Year — Club	League	Pos.	G.	AB.	R.	H.	2B.	3B.	HR.	RBI.	B.A.	PO.	A.	E.	F.A.
1924—Washington	Amer.	1B	7	26	4	10	1	0	0	0	.385	62	4	1	.985
1925—Washington	Amer.	1B	7	23	2	4	1	0	1	3	.174	59	2	0	1.000
World Series Totals—2 Years			14	49	6	14	2	0	1	3	.286	121	6	1	.992

—DID YOU KNOW—

That lefthander Jim Kaat won a record-tying 16 Gold Glove awards during his 25-year major league career?

JAMES LEE (JIM) KAAT

Born November 7, 1938, at Zeeland, Mich.
Height, 6.05. Weight, 195.
Threw and batted lefthanded.

Holds major league records for most sacrifice flies allowed, lifetime (141); most consecutive years pitched (25).
Holds American League records for most games lost by lefthanded pitcher, lifetime (191); most sacrifice flies allowed, lifetime (108); most years leading league in hits allowed (4).
Led American League in complete games with 19 in 1966.
Led American League pitchers in games started with 42 in 1965 and 41 in 1966.
Led American League in hit batsmen with 11 in 1961 and 18 in 1962.
Led American League in wild pitches with 13 in 1962 and tied for lead with 10 in 1961.
Tied for American League lead in shutouts with 5 in 1962.
Led Pioneer League pitchers in games started with 30, shutouts with 5, and tied for lead in complete games with 15 in 1958.
Named American League Pitcher of the Year by THE SPORTING NEWS, 1966.
Named lefthanded pitcher on THE SPORTING NEWS American League All-Star Team, 1975.
Named pitcher on THE SPORTING NEWS American League All-Star Team, 1966.
Named pitcher on THE SPORTING NEWS National League All-Star fielding team, 1976 and 1977.
Named pitcher on THE SPORTING NEWS American League All-Star fielding team, 1962 through 1975.
Coach, Cincinnati Reds, 1984-85.

Year Club	League	G.	IP.	W.	L.	Pct.	H.	R.	ER.	SO.	BB.	ERA.
1957—Superior	Neb. St.	14	73	5	6	.455	65	45	30	95	35	3.70
1958—Missoula	Pioneer	39	★223	16	9	.640	189	108	74	★245	118	★2.99
1959—Chattanooga	Southern	24	134	8	8	.500	126	71	61	132	73	4.10
1959—Washington	American	3	5	0	2	.000	7	9	7	2	4	12.60
1960—Washington	American	13	50	1	5	.167	48	39	31	25	31	5.58
1960—Charleston	Am. Assoc.	30	146	7	10	.412	154	80	62	106	51	3.82
1961—Minnesota	American	36	201	9	17	.346	188	105	87	122	82	3.90
1962—Minnesota	American	39	269	18	14	.563	243	106	94	173	75	3.14
1963—Minnesota	American	31	178	10	10	.500	195	96	83	105	38	4.20
1964—Minnesota	American	36	243	17	11	.607	231	100	87	171	60	3.22
1965—Minnesota	American	45	264	18	11	.621	★267	★121	83	154	63	2.83
1966—Minnesota	American	41	★305	★25	13	.658	★271	114	93	205	55	2.74
1967—Minnesota	American	42	263	16	13	.552	★269	110	89	211	42	3.05
1968—Minnesota	American	30	208	14	12	.538	192	78	68	130	40	2.94
1969—Minnesota	American	40	242	14	13	.519	252	114	94	139	75	3.50
1970—Minnesota	American	45	230	14	10	.583	244	110	91	120	58	3.56
1971—Minnesota	American	39	260	13	14	.481	275	104	96	137	47	3.32
1972—Minnesota	American	15	113	10	2	.833	94	36	26	64	20	2.07
1973—Minnesota†-Chicago	American	36	224	15	13	.536	250	124	109	109	43	4.38
1974—Chicago	American	42	277	21	13	.618	263	106	90	142	63	2.92
1975—Chicago‡	American	43	304	20	14	.588	★321	121	105	142	77	3.11
1976—Philadelphia	National	38	228	12	14	.462	241	95	88	83	32	3.47
1977—Philadelphia	National	35	160	6	11	.353	211	100	96	55	40	5.40
1978—Philadelphia	National	26	140	8	5	.615	150	67	64	48	32	4.11
1979—Philadelphia§	National	3	8	1	0	1.000	9	4	4	2	5	4.50
1979—New York x	American	40	58	2	3	.400	64	29	25	23	14	3.88
1980—New York y	American	4	5	0	1	.000	8	5	4	1	4	7.20
1980—St. Louis	National	49	130	8	7	.533	140	61	55	36	33	3.81
1981—St. Louis	National	41	53	6	6	.500	60	25	20	8	17	3.40
1982—St. Louis	National	62	75	5	3	.625	79	40	34	35	23	4.08
1983—St. Louis z	National	24	34⅔	0	0	.000	48	19	15	19	10	3.89
American League Totals—19 Years		620	3699	237	191	.554	3682	1627	1362	2175	891	3.31
National League Totals—8 Years		278	828⅔	46	46	.500	938	411	376	286	192	4.08
Major League Totals—25 Years		898	4527⅔	283	237	.544	4620	2038	1738	2461	1083	3.45

Signed as free agent by Washington Senators' organization, June 17, 1957.
†Sold on waivers to Chicago White Sox, August 15, 1973.
‡Traded with Shortstop Mike Buskey to Philadelphia Phillies for Outfielder-Infielder Alan Bannister and Pitchers Dick Ruthven and Roy Thomas, December 10, 1975.
§Sold to New York Yankees, May 11, 1979.
xGranted free agency, November 1, 1979; re-signed by Yankees, April 1, 1980.
ySold to St. Louis Cardinals, April 30, 1980.
zReleased, July 6, 1983.

CHAMPIONSHIP SERIES RECORD

Year Club	League	G.	IP.	W.	L.	Pct.	H.	R.	ER.	SO.	BB.	ERA.
1970—Minnesota	American	1	2	0	1	.000	6	4	2	1	2	9.00
1976—Philadelphia	National	1	6	0	0	.000	2	2	2	1	2	3.00
Championship Series Totals—2 Years		2	8	0	1	.000	8	6	4	2	4	4.50

Year Club	League	G.	IP.	W.	L.	Pct.	H.	R.	ER.	SO.	BB.	ERA.
1965—Minnesota	American	3	14⅓	1	2	.333	18	7	6	6	2	3.77
1982—St. Louis	National	4	2⅓	0	0	.000	4	1	1	2	2	3.86
World Series Totals—2 Years		7	16⅔	1	2	.333	22	8	7	8	4	3.78

ALBERT WILLIAM (AL) KALINE

Born December 19, 1934, at Baltimore, Md.

Height, 6.02. Weight, 184.

Threw and batted righthanded.

Shares major league record for most home runs (2) and total bases (8), inning, April 17, 1955, sixth inning.
Hit three home runs in a game, April 17, 1955.
Named as outfielder on THE SPORTING NEWS American League All-Star Teams, 1962-63-66-67.
Named as outfielder on THE SPORTING NEWS All-Star Major League Team, 1955.
Named No. 1 American League Player by THE SPORTING NEWS, 1955 and 1963.
Named outfielder on THE SPORTING NEWS Major League All-Star fielding team, 1957.
Named outfielder on THE SPORTING NEWS American League All-Star fielding teams, 1958-59-61-62-63-64-65-66-67.
Named to Hall of Fame, 1980.

Year Club	League	Pos.	G.	AB.	R.	H.	2B.	3B.	HR.	RBI.	B.A.	PO.	A.	E.	F.A.
1953—Detroit	Amer.	OF	30	28	9	7	0	0	1	2	.250	11	1	0	1.000
1954—Detroit	Amer.	OF	138	504	42	139	18	3	4	43	.276	283	16	9	.971
1955—Detroit	Amer.	OF	152	588	121	★200	24	8	27	102	★.340	306	14	7	.979
1956—Detroit	Amer.	OF	153	617	96	194	32	10	27	128	.314	343	★18	6	.984
1957—Detroit	Amer.	OF	149	577	83	170	29	4	23	90	.295	319	13	5	.985
1958—Detroit	Amer.	OF	146	543	84	170	34	7	16	85	.313	316	★23	2	.994
1959—Detroit	Amer.	OF	136	511	86	167	19	2	27	94	.327	364	4	4	.989
1960—Detroit	Amer.	OF	147	551	77	153	29	4	15	68	.278	367	5	5	.987
1961—Detroit	Amer.	OF-3B	153	586	116	190	★41	7	19	82	.324	379	10	4	.990
1962—Detroit	Amer.	OF	100	398	78	121	16	6	29	94	.304	225	8	4	.983
1963—Detroit	Amer.	OF	145	551	89	172	24	3	27	101	.312	257	5	2	.992
1964—Detroit	Amer.	OF	146	525	77	154	31	5	17	68	.293	278	6	3	.990
1965—Detroit	Amer.	OF-3B	125	399	72	112	18	2	18	72	.281	195	3	3	.985
1966—Detroit	Amer.	OF	142	479	85	138	29	1	29	88	.288	279	7	2	★.993
1967—Detroit	Amer.	OF	131	458	94	141	28	2	25	78	.308	217	14	4	★.983
1968—Detroit	Amer.	OF-1B	102	327	49	94	14	1	10	53	.287	283	14	7	.977
1969—Detroit	Amer.	OF-1B	131	456	74	124	17	0	21	69	.272	257	11	7	.975
1970—Detroit	Amer.	OF-1B	131	467	64	130	24	4	16	71	.278	530	34	6	.989
1971—Detroit	Amer.	●OF-1B	133	405	69	119	19	2	15	54	.294	234	7	0	●1.000
1972—Detroit	Amer.	OF-1B	106	278	46	87	11	2	10	32	.313	148	9	1	.994
1973—Detroit	Amer.	OF-1B	91	310	40	79	13	0	10	45	.255	347	13	1	.997
1974—Detroit	Amer.	DH	147	558	71	146	28	2	13	64	.262	0	0	0	.000
Major League Totals—22 Years			2834	10116	1622	3007	498	75	399	1583	.297	5938	235	82	.987

CHAMPIONSHIP SERIES RECORD

Year Club	League	Pos.	G.	AB.	R.	H.	2B.	3B.	HR.	SB.	B.A.	PO.	A.	E.	F.A.
1972—Detroit	Amer.	OF	5	19	3	5	0	0	1	1	.263	12	0	1	.923

WORLD SERIES RECORD

Shares records for most at-bats, hits and runs, inning (2), October 9, 1968, third inning.

Year Club	League	Pos.	G.	AB.	R.	H.	2B.	3B.	HR.	RBI.	B.A.	PO.	A.	E.	F.A.
1968—Detroit	Amer.	OF	7	29	6	11	2	0	2	8	.379	18	0	0	1.000

TIMOTHY J. (TIM) KEEFE

Born January 1, 1857, at Cambridge, Mass.

Died April 23, 1933, at Cambridge, Mass.

Height, 5.10½. Weight, 185.

Threw and batted righthanded.

Umpire, National League, 1894-95.
Named to Hall of Fame, 1964.

Year	Club	League	G.	IP.	W.	L.	Pct.	H.	R.	SO.	BB.	CG.	ShO.
1879—Utica-New Bedford	Nat. Assn.		24	....	....	....	......	....	....	....	....	....	....
1880—Albany	Nat. Assn.		18	....	....	....	......	....	....	....	....	....	....
1880—Troy	National		12	105	6	6	.500	71	27	42	16	12	0
1881—Troy	National		45	404	18	27	.400	444	241	105	88	45	4
1882—Troy	National		43	376	17	26	.395	364	221	110	81	41	1
1883—Metropolitan	Amer. Assn.		*68	*619	41	27	.603	485	244	*360	106	*68	5
1884—Metropolitan	Amer. Assn.		56	483	37	17	.685	379	195	322	72	56	4
1885—New York	National		46	400	32	13	.711	296	154	228	99	45	7
1886—New York	National		*64	*535	●42	20	.677	468	250	295	98	*62	2
1887—New York	National		56	476	35	19	.648	528	255	186	111	54	2
1888—New York	National		51	434	*35	12	*.745	314	143	*335	86	48	●8
1889—New York	National		47	363	28	13	.683	317	212	222	154	39	3
1890—New York	Players		30	227	17	11	.607	221	137	88	86	23	1
1891—N.Y.(a)-Philadelphia	National		19	131	5	11	.313	154	112	62	54	13	0
1892—Philadelphia	National		39	312	19	16	.543	281	139	129	97	31	3
1893—Philadelphia	National		22	178	10	7	.588	202	131	54	77	17	0
American Assn. Totals—2 Years			124	1102	78	44	.639	864	439	682	178	124	9
National League Totals—11 Years			444	3714	247	170	.592	3439	1885	1768	961	407	30
Players League Totals—1 Year			30	227	17	11	.607	221	137	88	86	23	1
Major League Totals—14 Years			598	5043	342	225	.603	4524	2461	2538	1225	554	40

aReleased, August, 1891, and signed with Philadelphia Phillies.

WILLIAM H. (WILLIE) KEELER
(Wee Willie)

Born March 13, 1872, at Brooklyn, N.Y.

Died January 1, 1923, at Brooklyn, N. Y.

Height, 5.04½. Weight, 140.

Threw and batted lefthanded.

Shares National League record for most consecutive games, one or more hits, season (44), 1897.
Coach, Brooklyn Federals, 1914; scout, Boston Braves, 1915.
Named to Hall of Fame, 1939.

Year	Club	League	Pos.	G.	AB.	R.	H.	2B.	3B.	HR.	SB.	B.A.	PO.	A.	E.	F.A.
1892—Binghamton	East		3B	93	410	109	153	17	13	2	12	*.373	147	231	48	.887
1892—New York	Nat.		3B	13	49	6	15	3	0	0	5	.306	14	28	7	.857
1893—N. Y.-Brooklyn	Nat.		0-2-3-S	29	90	19	30	3	2	2	7	.333	32	28	15	.800
1893—Binghamton	East.		3B	15	68	9	20	2	1	1	3	.294	29	38	11	.859
1893—Baltimore(a)	Nat.		OF	128	593	164	218	25	24	5	30	.368	220	27	19	.929
1895—Baltimore	Nat.		OF	131	560	161	221	23	15	4	57	.395	248	19	11	.960
1896—Baltimore	Nat.		OF	127	546	154	214	22	13	4	73	.392	229	22	7	*.973
1897—Baltimore	Nat.		OF	128	562	*243	25	18	0	63	*.432	218	14	7	.971
1898—Baltimore(b)	Nat.		OF	128	564	126	214	10	2	0	26	*.379	210	12	11	.944
1899—Brooklyn	Nat.		OF	143	571	*141	215	13	14	1	44	.377	207	21	7	.970
1900—Brooklyn	Nat.		OF	137	568	106	*208	11	14	4	39	.366	229	24	14	.948
1901—Brooklyn	Nat.		OF	136	589	124	209	16	15	2	31	.355	183	18	3	*.985
1902—Brooklyn(c)	Nat.		OF	132	550	84	188	18	7	0	23	.342	204	14	4	*.982
1903—New York	Amer.		OF	132	515	98	164	13	7	0	25	.318	174	13	11	.941
1904—New York	Amer.		OF	143	539	76	185	13	6	2	22	.343	185	14	11	.948
1905—New York	Amer.		OF	149	560	81	169	14	4	4	19	.302	194	17	7	.968
1906—New York	Amer.		OF	152	592	96	180	9	3	2	23	.304	213	16	3	.987
1907—New York	Amer.		OF	107	423	50	99	6	5	0	7	.234	144	13	5	.969
1908—New York	Amer.		OF	91	323	38	85	3	1	1	14	.263	123	9	9	.936
1909—New York	Amer.		OF	99	360	44	95	7	5	1	10	.264	111	9	4	.968
1910—New York	Nat.		PH	19	10	5	3	0	0	0	1	.300	0	0	0	.000
1911—Toronto	East.		OF	39	155	26	43	7	0	0	4	.277	47	2	4	.925
American League Totals—7 Years				873	3312	483	977	65	31	10	120	.295	1144	91	50	.961
National League Totals—12 Years				1251	5252	1237	1978	169	124	22	399	.377	1994	227	105	.955
Major League Totals—19 Years				2124	8564	1720	2955	234	155	32	519	.345	3138	318	155	.957

aTraded with First Baseman Dan Brouthers to Baltimore for Third Baseman Billy Shindle and Outfielder George Treadway, January, 1894.

bAccompanied Manager Ned Hanlon and other players to Brooklyn.

cJumped to New York A. L. club.

GEORGE CLYDE KELL

Born August 23, 1922, at Swifton, Ark.

Height, 5.10. Weight, 170.

Threw and batted righthanded.

Brother of Skeeter Kell, former major league second baseman.

Shares major league record for most times facing pitcher, inning (3), seventh inning, June 18, 1943.

Named by Baseball Writers' Association as third baseman on THE SPORTING NEWS All-Star Major League Teams, 1946-47-49-51-52.

Scout, Detroit Tigers, 1966-67, and 1971 through 1977.

Named to Hall of Fame, 1983.

Year—Club	League	Pos.	G.	AB.	R.	H.	2B.	3B.	HR.	RBI.	B.A.	PO.	A.	E.	F.A.
1940—Newport	NE. Ark.	3B	48	169	14	27	2	3	0	14	.160	59	80	3	.979
1941—Newport	NE. Ark.	3B	118	462	71	*143	26	5	1	75	.310	148	*285	37	*.921
1942—Lancaster	Int. St.	3B	127	465	56	139	18	2	0	30	.299	360	236	21	.966
1943—Lancaster	Int. St.	3B	138	555	*120	*220	33	*23	5	79	*.396	*190	*362	23	*.960
1943—Philadelphia	Amer.	3B	1	5	1	1	0	1	0	1	.200	1	3	0	1.000
1944—Philadelphia	Amer.	3B	139	514	51	138	15	3	0	44	.268	167	289	20	.958
1945—Philadelphia	Amer.	3B	147	567	50	154	30	3	4	56	.272	*186	*345	20	*.964
1946—Phila.(a)-Det.	Amer.	*3B-1B	131	521	70	168	25	10	4	52	.322	*143	*267	7	*.983
1947—Detroit	Amer.	3B	152	588	75	188	29	5	5	93	.320	167	*333	*20	.962
1948—Detroit	Amer.	3B	92	368	47	112	24	3	2	44	.304	108	146	8	.969
1949—Detroit	Amer.	3B	134	522	97	179	38	9	3	59	*.343	154	271	11	.975
1950—Detroit	Amer.	3B	●157	*641	114	*218	*56	6	8	101	.340	186	315	9	*.982
1951—Detroit	Amer.	3B	147	598	92	*191	●36	3	2	59	.319	175	*310	20	*.960
1952—Det.(b)-Bos.	Amer.	3B	114	428	52	133	23	2	7	57	.311	113	216	14	.959
1953—Boston	Amer.	*3B-OF	134	460	68	141	41	2	12	73	.307	118	231	10	*.972
1954—Bos.(d)-Chicago	Amer.	3B-1B-O	97	326	40	90	13	0	5	58	.276	306	105	11	.974
1955—Chicago	Amer.	*3B-1B-O	128	429	44	134	24	1	8	81	.312	216	170	7	*.982
1956—Chi.(e)-Balt.	Amer.	*3-1B-2B	123	425	52	115	22	2	9	48	.271	138	198	7	●.980
1957—Baltimore	Amer.	3B-1B	99	310	28	92	9	0	9	44	.297	66	122	4	.979
Major League Totals—15 Years			1795	6702	881	2054	385	50	78	870	.306	2244	3321	168	.971

aTraded to Detroit Tigers for Outfielder Barney McCosky, May 18, 1946.

bTraded to Boston Red Sox with Pitcher Dizzy Trout, Shortstop Johnny Lipon and Outfielder Hoot Evers for Pitcher Bill Wight, First Baseman Walt Dropo, Third Baseman Fred Hatfield, Shortstop Johnny Pesky and Outfielder Don Lenhardt, June 3, 1952.

cTraded to Chicago White Sox for Third Baseman Grady Hatton and $100,000, May 3, 1954.

dTraded to Baltimore Orioles with Pitchers Mike Fornieles and Connie Johnson and Outfielder Bob Nieman for Pitcher Jim Wilson and Outfielder Dave Philley, May 21, 1956.

JOSEPH JAMES (JOE) KELLEY

Born December 9, 1871, at Cambridge, Mass.

Died August 14, 1943, at Baltimore, Md.

Height, 5.11. Weight, 190.

Threw and batted righthanded.

Manager, Cincinnati, 1902 to 1906; Boston Nationals, 1908; Toronto, 1907 and 1909 to 1914; scout, New York Yankees, 1915-16; coach, Brooklyn, 1926.

Named to Hall of Fame, 1971.

Year—Club	League	Pos.	G.	AB.	R.	H.	2B.	3B.	HR.	SB.	B.A.	PO.	A.	E.	F.A.
1891—Lowell	N. Eng.	OF	57	245	50	81	...	...	...	21	.331	195	136	16	.954
1891—Bos.-Pittsburgh	Nat.	OF	14	52	8	12	1	1	0	0	.231	28	2	4	.882
1892—Omaha	West.	OF	49	203	32	67	...	...	...	18	.330	71	7	10	.886
1892—Pitts.(a)-Balt.	Nat.	OF	66	232	30	57	6	6	0	7	.246	116	11	15	.894
1893—Baltimore	Nat.	OF	124	490	120	153	25	16	9	38	.312	301	21	16	.953
1894—Baltimore	Nat.	OF	129	509	167	199	48	17	6	45	.391	274	19	15	.951
1895—Baltimore	Nat.	OF	131	510	148	189	26	21	10	59	.371	258	21	18	.939
1896—Baltimore	Nat.	OF	130	516	147	191	27	17	8	90	.370	278	22	13	.958
1897—Baltimore	Nat.	OF	129	503	113	196	31	9	5	50	.390	238	15	12	.955
1898—Baltimore(b)	Nat.	OF	124	467	71	153	17	15	3	22	.328	234	16	7	.973

Year	Club	League	Pos.	G.	AB.	R.	H.	2B.	3B.	HR.	SB.	B.A.	PO.	A.	E.	F.A.
1899—Brooklyn	Nat.		OF	144	540	107	178	27	12	6	31	.330	309	26	8	.977
1900—Brooklyn	Nat.		1B-OF	118	453	92	144	23	18	6	26	.318	422	25	11	.976
1901—Brooklyn	Nat.		1B	120	493	77	152	21	12	4	20	.308	982	81	27	.975
1902—Baltimore(c)	Am.		1-3B-OF	60	222	50	69	16	7	1	12	.311	99	6	3	.972
1902—Cincinnati	Nat.		S-3B-O	37	156	24	51	8	2	1	3	.327	30	4	0	1.000
1903—Cincinnati	Nat.		OF	104	383	85	121	22	4	3	18	.316	117	8	7	.948
1904—Cincinnati	Nat.		1B	123	449	75	126	21	13	0	15	.281	1049	76	14	.988
1905—Cincinnati	Nat.		OF	87	321	43	89	7	6	1	8	.277	137	11	4	.974
1906—Cincinnati	Nat.		OF	127	465	43	106	19	11	1	9	.228	184	13	7	.966
1907—Toronto	East.		1B-OF	91	314	32	101	10	8	1	15	.322	404	51	10	.978
1908—Boston	Nat.		OF	62	228	25	59	8	2	2	5	.259	71	5	5	.938
1909—Toronto	East.		OF	107	357	49	96	23	1	1	11	.269	191	13	1	.995
1910—Toronto	East.		OF	46	110	13	31	5	2	0	4	.282	36	7	1	.977
American League Totals—1 Year				60	222	50	69	16	7	1	12	.311	99	6	3	.972
National League Totals—17 Years				1769	6767	1375	2176	337	182	65	446	.322	5028	376	183	.967
Major League Totals—17 Years				1829	6989	1425	2245	353	189	66	458	.321	5127	382	186	.967

aTraded to Baltimore in deal for Outfielder George Van Haltren, September, 1892.
bMoved to Brooklyn with Manager Ned Hanlon when Superbas bought Baltimore franchise.
cJumped to Cincinnati, July 16, 1902.

PITCHING RECORD

Year	Club	League	G.	W.	L.	Pct.	H.	R.	SO.	BB.	ShO.
1891—Lowell		New England	14	10	3	.769	97	87	81	70	..

GEORGE LANGE KELLY
(High Pockets)

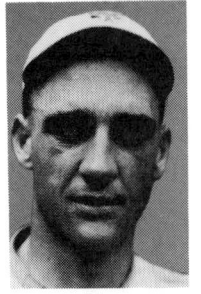

Born September 10, 1896, at San Francisco, Calif.

Died October 13, 1984, at Burlingame, Calif.

Height, 6.03. Weight, 195.

Threw and batted righthanded.

Nephew of William A. (Little Eva) Lange, former major league outfielder, and brother of Reynolds Kelly, former minor league pitcher.

Shares major league record for most chances accepted, nine-inning game (22), April 26, 1923.
Holds National League records for most putouts (1,759) and chances accepted (1,862) by first baseman, season, 1920.
Shares National League record for most home runs, six consecutive games (7), July 11 through 16, 1924.
Hit three home runs in a game, September 17, 1923 and June 14, 1924.
Coach, Cincinnati Reds, 1935 through 1937, 1947 through 1948; Boston Braves, 1938 through 1943; Scout, Cincinnati, 1946.
Named to Hall of Fame, 1973.

Year	Club	League	Pos.	G.	AB.	R.	H.	2B.	3B.	HR.	RBI.	B.A.	PO.	A.	E.	F.A.
1914—Victoria	N. W.		1B-OF	141	436	45	109	22	2	7	.....	.250	1004	79	21	.973
1915—Victoria	N. W.		1B	94	361	57	107	33	6	5	.....	.297	964	78	7	.993
1915—New York	Nat.		1B	17	38	2	6	0	0	1	5	.158	58	4	1	.984
1916—New York	Nat.		1B	49	76	4	12	2	1	0	2	.158	106	2	1	.991
1917—N.York(a)-Pitts.	Nat.		1B-OF	19	30	2	2	0	1	0	0	.067	64	2	2	.971
1917—Rochester	Int.		OF	32	120	16	36	14	1	4	.....	.300	74	6	5	.941
1918—New York	Nat.							(In Military Service)								
1919—Rochester	Int.		1B	103	376	72	134	21	14	15	.....	.356	1097	66	21	.982
1919—New York	Nat.		1B	32	107	12	31	6	2	1	13	.290	341	11	2	.994
1920—New York	Nat.		1B	155	590	69	157	22	11	11	●94	.266	★1759	★103	11	.990
1921—New York	Nat.		1B	149	587	95	181	42	9	★23	122	.308	★1552	★115	17	.990
1922—New York	Nat.		1B	151	592	96	194	33	8	17	107	.328	1642	★103	13	.992
1923—New York	Nat.		1B	145	560	82	172	23	5	16	103	.307	★1568	60	12	.993
1924—New York	Nat.		OF-1B	144	571	91	185	37	9	21	●136	.324	1309	60	10	.993
1925—New York	Nat.		IF-OF	147	586	87	181	29	3	20	99	.309	567	411	18	.982
1926—New York(b)	Nat.		1B-2B	136	499	70	151	24	4	13	80	.303	1233	144	15	★.989
1927—Cincinnati	Nat.		1B-2B	61	222	27	60	16	4	5	21	.270	475	64	8	.985
1928—Cincinnati	Nat.		1B-OF	116	402	46	119	33	7	3	58	.296	927	70	11	.989
1929—Cincinnati	Nat.		1B	147	577	73	169	45	9	5	103	.293	1537	103	11	.993
1930—Cin.(c)-Chicago	Nat.		1B	90	354	40	109	16	2	8	54	.308	917	67	5	.995
1930—Minneapolis	A. A.		1B	34	147	25	53	9	1	6	38	.361	302	14	2	.994
1931—Minneapolis	A. A.		1B	155	606	84	194	34	2	20	112	.320	1491	103	9	.994
1932—Brooklyn	Nat.		1B	64	202	23	49	9	1	4	22	.243	575	36	10	.984
1932—Jersey City	Int.		1B	47	153	18	45	10	0	6	31	.294	382	22	3	.993
1933—Oakland	P. C.		OF	21	56	5	13	5	0	1	6	.232	18	2	1	.953
Major League Totals—16 Years				1622	5993	819	1778	337	76	148	1019	.297	14630	1355	147	.991

aReleased to Pittsburgh, July 25, 1917, returned to New York Giants and optioned to Rochester, International League, August 4, 1917.
bTraded to Cincinnati for Outfielder Edd Roush, January, 1927.
cReleased to Minneapolis, July, 1930, then acquired by Chicago Cubs, August, 1930.

WORLD SERIES RECORD

Holds record for most putouts by first baseman, game (19), October 15, 1923.
Shares records for most at-bats, inning (2), October 7, 1921, seventh inning; most chances accepted by first baseman, series (93), 1921; most chances accepted by first baseman, game (19), October 15, 1923.

Year Club League	Pos.	G.	AB.	R.	H.	2B.	3B.	HR.	RBI.	B.A.	PO.	A.	E.	F.A.
1921—New York.............Nat.	1B	8	30	3	7	1	0	0	3	.233	86	7	0	1.000
1922—New York.............Nat.	1B	5	18	0	5	0	0	0	2	.278	61	1	0	1.000
1923—New York.............Nat.	1B	6	22	1	4	0	0	0	1	.182	63	4	1	.985
1924—New York.............Nat.	OF-IF	7	31	7	9	1	0	1	4	.290	51	5	1	.982
World Series Totals—4 Years		26	101	11	25	2	0	1	10	.248	261	17	2	.993

MICHAEL JOSEPH (MIKE) KELLY
(King)

Born December 31, 1857, at Troy, N. Y.

Died November 8, 1894, at Boston, Mass.

Height, 5.10½. Weight, 185.

Threw and batted righthanded.

Manager, Cincinnati, American Association, 1891; Allentown, Pennsylvania State League, 1894.
Named to Hall of Fame, 1945.

Year Club League	Pos.	G.	AB.	R.	H.	2B.	3B.	HR.	SB.	B.A.	PO.	A.	E.	F.A.
1878—Cincinnati.............Nat.	C-3B-OF	59	231	29	65	9	0	0	....	.281	145	62	42	.831
1879—Cincinnati.............Nat.	C-3B-OF	76	342	78	119	22	●14	3	....	.348	168	144	54	.852
1880—Chicago.................Nat.	C-SS-3-O	82	335	71	98	13	11	1	....	.293	67	32	23	.811
1881—Chicago.................Nat.	C-3B-OF	80	353	84	114	★28	3	2	....	.323	85	31	22	.841
1882—Chicago.................Nat.	C-1-S-3-O	84	377	81	115	★36	5	1	....	.305	116	138	52	.830
1883—Chicago.................Nat.	C-2-3-O	98	430	92	109	27	9	3	....	.253	174	75	53	.825
1884—Chicago.................Nat.	C-1-2-S-3	107	448	★120	153	30	6	12	....	.341	173	85	58	.816
1885—Chicago.................Nat.	C-1-2-3-O	107	438	★124	126	24	7	9	....	.288	241	93	49	.872
1886—Chicago.................Nat.	C-OF	118	451	★155	175	31	11	4	53	★.388	321	118	48	.901
1887—Boston(a).............Nat.	C-2B-OF	114	525	119	207	34	11	8	84	.394	237	151	65	.857
1888—Boston.................Nat.	C-OF	105	440	85	140	20	11	9	56	.318	150	89	.860
1889—Boston.................Nat.	C-OF	125	507	120	149	32	7	7	68	.293	211	53	44	.857
1890—Bos.(N.L.)......Players	C-SS	90	352	89	114	19	7	3	40	.324	291	152	51	.897
1891—Cin.-Bos.(N.L.)...... A. A.	C-1-2-S	77	264	50	73	15	7	2	16	.276	240	106	31	.918
1891—Boston.................Nat.	3B-OF	24	96	14	23	1	0	0	24	.240	48	9	12	.826
1892—Boston.................Nat.	OF	72	279	40	56	9	0	1	24	.201	331	93	38	.918
1893—New York.............Nat.	C	16	54	8	17	1	0	0	5	.315	54	23	22	.778
1894—Allentown.............Pa. State	C	75	325	82	99	16	3	3	....	.305	573	84	40	.943
1894—Allen.-Yonkers ..... Eastern	C	15	61	11	23	2	0	0	....	.377	97	17	2	.983
American Assn. Totals—1 Year		77	264	50	73	15	7	2	16	.276	240	106	31	.918
Players League Totals—1 Year............		90	352	89	114	19	7	3	40	.324	291	152	51	.897
National League Totals—15 Years........	1267	5306	1220	1666	317	95	60	....	.314	2766	1257	671	.857
Major League Totals—16 Years.............	1434	5922	1359	1853	351	109	65	....	.313	3297	1515	753	.865

aSold to Boston for $10,000, February 14, 1887. When Boston also purchased pitcher John Clarkson from Chicago in 1888, with Kelly catching, they became known as the "$20,000 Battery."

HARMON CLAYTON KILLEBREW JR.
(Killer)

Born June 29, 1936, at Payette, Idaho.

Height, 6.00. Weight, 210.

Threw and batted righthanded.

Holds American League record for most home runs, righthanded batter, lifetime (573).
Shares American League record for most home runs, doubleheader (4), September 21, 1963.
Named outfielder on THE SPORTING NEWS All-Star American League Team, 1964.
Named first baseman on THE SPORTING NEWS American League All-Star Team, 1967.
Named by THE SPORTING NEWS as the Outstanding American League Player, 1969-70.
Named third baseman on THE SPORTING NEWS American League All-Star Team, 1969-70.

Most Valuable Player in American League, 1969.
Named to Hall of Fame, 1984.

Year—Club	League	Pos.	G.	AB.	R.	H.	2B.	3B.	HR.	RBI.	B.A.	PO.	A.	E.	F.A.
1954—Washington	Amer.	2B	9	13	1	4	1	0	0	3	.308	5	2	0	1.000
1955—Washington	Amer.	3B-2B	38	80	12	16	1	0	4	7	.200	24	49	5	.936
1956—Washington	Amer.	3B-2B	44	99	10	22	2	0	5	13	.222	24	44	4	.944
1956—Charlotte	Sally	3B	70	249	61	81	16	7	15	63	.325	62	127	14	.931
1957—Chattanooga	South	3B	142	519	90	145	30	7	★29	101	.279	134	★298	★31	.933
1957—Washington	Amer.	3B-2B	9	31	4	9	2	0	2	5	.290	2	16	1	.947
1958—Washington	Amer.	3B	13	31	2	6	0	0	0	2	.194	8	13	0	1.000
1958—Indianapolis	A. A.	3B	38	121	14	26	5	1	2	10	.215	28	79	11	.907
1958—Chattanooga	South.	3B-OF	86	299	58	92	17	1	17	54	.308	97	134	12	.951
1959—Washington	Amer.	★3B-OF	153	546	98	132	20	2	●42	105	.242	135	325	★30	.939
1960—Washington	Amer.	1B-3B	124	442	84	122	19	1	31	80	.276	629	135	17	.978
1961—Minnesota	Amer.	1-3-OF	150	541	94	156	20	7	46	122	.288	1003	143	23	.980
1962—Minnesota	Amer.	OF-1B	155	552	85	134	21	1	★48	★126	.243	241	5	9	.965
1963—Minnesota	Amer.	OF	142	515	88	133	18	0	★45	96	.258	219	7	3	.987
1964—Minnesota	Amer.	OF	158	577	95	156	11	1	★49	111	.270	232	1	7	.971
1965—Minnesota	Amer.	1-3-O	113	401	78	108	16	1	25	75	.269	743	113	12	.986
1966—Minnesota	Amer.	3-1-O	162	569	89	160	27	1	39	110	.281	435	205	18	.973
1967—Minnesota	Amer.	1-3B	163	547	105	147	24	1	●44	113	.269	1285	89	12	.991
1968—Minnesota	Amer.	1B-3B	100	295	40	62	7	2	17	40	.210	601	71	7	.990
1969—Minnesota	Amer.	3B-1B	●162	555	106	153	20	2	★49	★140	.276	649	219	22	.975
1970—Minnesota	Amer.	3B-1B	157	527	96	143	20	1	41	113	.271	312	212	20	.963
1971—Minnesota	Amer.	1B-3B	147	500	61	127	19	1	28	★119	.254	700	149	13	.985
1972—Minnesota	Amer.	1B	139	433	53	100	13	2	26	74	.231	995	★99	9	.992
1973—Minnesota	Amer.	1B	69	248	29	60	9	1	5	32	.242	431	45	1	.998
1974—Minnesota	Amer.	1B	122	333	28	74	7	0	13	54	.222	218	21	2	.992
1975—Kansas City(a)	Amer.	DH-1B	106	312	25	62	13	0	14	44	.199	28	0	0	1.000
Major League Totals—22 Years			2435	8147	1283	2086	290	24	573	1584	.256	8919	1963	215	.981

aSigned as free agent by Kansas City Royals, January 24, 1975.

CHAMPIONSHIP SERIES RECORD

Year—Club	League	Pos.	G.	AB.	R.	H.	2B.	3B.	HR.	RBI.	B.A.	PO.	A.	E.	F.A.
1969—Minnesota	Amer.	3B	3	8	2	1	1	0	0	0	.125	6	3	0	1.000
1970—Minnesota	Amer.	3B-1B	3	11	2	3	0	0	2	4	.273	8	4	1	.923
Championship Series Totals—2 Years			6	19	4	4	1	0	2	4	.211	14	7	1	.955

WORLD SERIES RECORD

Year—Club	League	Pos.	G.	AB.	R.	H.	2B.	3B.	HR.	RBI.	B.A.	PO.	A.	E.	F.A.
1965—Minnesota	Amer.	3B	7	21	2	6	0	0	1	2	.286	11	7	1	.947

RALPH McPHERRAN KINER

Born October 27, 1922, at Santa Rita, N. M.

Height, 6.02. Weight, 195.

Threw and batted righthanded.

Holds major league record for most home runs, four consecutive games (8), September 10 through 12, 1947.

Shares major league records for most consecutive home runs (4), August 15 through 16, 1947 and September 11 through 13, 1949; most home runs, two consecutive games (5), August 15 through 16, 1947 and September 11, second game, through 12, 1947; most home runs, three consecutive games (6), August 14 through 16, 1947 and September 10 through 11, second game, 1947.

Shares National League records for most years with 50 or more home runs (2); most consecutive years with 40 or more home runs (5).

Named by THE SPORTING NEWS as Top Player in National League, 1950.

Named as outfielder on THE SPORTING NEWS All-Star Major League Teams, 1947-49-50-51.

Named to Hall of Fame, 1975.

Year—Club	League	Pos.	G.	AB.	R.	H.	2B.	3B.	HR.	RBI.	B.A.	PO.	A.	E.	F.A.
1941—Albany	East.	OF	●141	509	94	142	23	7	11	66	.279	245	15	3	.989
1942—Albany	East.	OF	★141	483	84	124	27	7	★14	75	.257	★338	18	★17	.954
1943—Toronto	Int.	OF	43	144	22	34	6	2	2	13	.236	120	5	3	.977
1943-44-45—Pittsburgh	Nat.						(In Military Service)								
1946—Pittsburgh	Nat.	OF	144	502	63	124	17	3	★23	81	.247	339	6	11	.969
1947—Pittsburgh	Nat.	OF	152	565	118	177	23	4	●51	127	.313	★390	8	7	.983
1948—Pittsburgh	Nat.	OF	●156	555	104	147	19	5	●40	123	.265	382	6	10	.975
1949—Pittsburgh	Nat.	OF	152	549	116	170	19	5	★54	★127	.310	311	12	7	.979
1950—Pittsburgh	Nat.	OF	150	547	112	149	21	6	★47	118	.272	287	13	11	.965
1951—Pittsburgh	Nat.	OF-1B	151	531	●124	164	31	6	★42	109	.309	751	36	18	.978
1952—Pittsburgh	Nat.	OF	149	516	90	126	17	2	●37	87	.244	250	9	8	.970

Year	Club	League	Pos.	G.	AB.	R.	H.	2B.	3B.	HR.	RBI.	B.A.	PO.	A.	E.	F.A.
1953—Pitts.(a)-Chi.		Nat.	OF	*158	562	100	157	20	3	35	116	.279	298	6	9	.971
1954—Chicago(b)		Nat.	OF	147	557	88	159	36	5	22	73	.285	298	6		.971
1955—Cleveland		Amer.	OF	113	321	56	73	13	0	18	54	.243	141	2	2	.986
National League Totals—9 Years				1359	4884	915	1373	203	39	351	961	.281	3290	107	89	.974
American League Totals—1 Year				113	321	56	78	13	0	18	54	.243	141	2	2	.986
Major League Totals—10 Years				1472	5205	971	1451	216	39	369	1015	.279	3431	109	91	.975

aTraded to Chicago Cubs with Pitcher Howard Pollet, Catcher Joe Garagiola and Outfielder-First Baseman George Metkovich for Pitcher Bob Schultz, Catcher Toby Atwell, First Baseman Preston Ward, Infielder George Freese, Outfielders Bob Addis and Gene Hermanski and cash, June 4, 1953.

bTraded to Cleveland Indians for Pitcher Sam Jones, Outfielder Gale Wade and cash, November 16, 1954.

CHARLES F. (SILVER) KING
(Born Charles F. Koenig)

Born January 11, 1867, at St. Louis, Mo.

Died May 19, 1938, at St. Louis, Mo.

Height, 5.10. Weight, 180.

Threw and batted righthanded.

Year	Club	League	G.	IP.	W.	L.	Pct.	H.	R.	SO.	BB.	CG.	ShO.
1886—Kansas City		National	5	39	1	3	.250	47	35	28	11	5	0
1886—St. Joseph		Western					(No records available)						
1887—St. Louis		Amer. Assn.	46	391	34	11	.756	525	235	106	116	44	2
1888—St. Louis		Amer. Assn.	*66	*576	*45	21	.682	451	216	206	134	*62	●6
1889—St. Louis		Amer. Assn.	54	440	33	17	.660	259	262	181	119	45	2
1890—Chicago		Players	56	459	30	22	.577	434	237	184	156	48	*4
1891—Pittsburgh		National	47	383	14	*29	.326	385	242	164	146	40	3
1892—New York		National	51	405	22	24	.478	388	255	158	161	44	1
1893—New York-Cincinnati		National	24	155	8	10	.444	187	124	55	64	12	1
1894-95—							(Out of Baseball)						
1896—Washington		National	21	152	10	7	.588	167	108	34	39	14	0
1897—Washington		National	23	151	7	8	.467	188	120	30	42	13	0
Players League Totals—1 Year			56	459	30	22	.577	434	237	184	156	48	4
American Assn. Totals—3 Years			166	1407	112	49	.696	1335	713	493	369	151	10
National League Totals—6 Years			171	1285	62	81	.434	1362	884	469	463	128	5
Major League Totals—10 Years			393	3151	204	152	.573	3131	1834	1146	988	327	19

DAVID ARTHUR (DAVE) KINGMAN
(Kong)

Born December 21, 1948, at Pendleton, Ore.

Height, 6.06. Weight, 215.

Threw and batted righthanded.

Shares major league records for most home runs, two consecutive games (5), July 27 and 28, 1979; most times, three or more home runs, game, season (2), May 17 and July 28, 1979; most strikeouts, nine-inning game (5), May 28, 1982; most unassisted double plays by first baseman, game (2), July 25, 1982.

Shares modern major league record for most clubs played on, season, major leagues (4), 1977.

Shares National League record for fewest errors by first baseman for leader in errors, season (13), 1974.

Hit three home runs in a game June 4, 1976; May 14, 1978; May 17, 1979; July 28, 1979 and April 16, 1984.

Led American League in sacrifice flies with 14 in 1984.

Led National League batters in strikeouts with 131 in 1979, 105 in 1981 and 156 in 1982.

Led National League in slugging percentage with .613 in 1979.

Led National League first basemen in errors with 13 in 1974.

Named American League Comeback Player of the Year by THE SPORTING NEWS, 1984.

Named designated hitter on THE SPORTING NEWS American League All-Star Team, 1984.

Named outfielder on THE SPORTING NEWS National League All-Star Team, 1979.

Named outfielder on THE SPORTING NEWS College Baseball All-America Team, 1970.

Year Club League	Pos.	G.	AB.	R.	H.	2B.	3B.	HR.	RBI.	B.A.	PO.	A.	E.	F.A.
1970—Amarillo................ Texas	1B-OF	60	210	41	62	9	1	15	41	.295	226	9	9	.963
1971—Phoenix................. P. C.	OF-1B	105	392	89	109	29	5	26	99	.278	785	40	8	.990
1971—San Francisco ...... Nat.	1B-OF	41	115	17	32	10	2	6	24	.278	168	9	4	.978
1972—San Francisco ...... Nat.	3B-1B-OF	135	472	65	106	17	4	29	83	.225	496	159	22	.968
1973—San Francisco ...... Nat.	3B-1B-P	112	305	54	62	10	1	24	55	.203	313	146	22	.954
1974—San Francisco† .... Nat.	1B-3B-OF	121	350	41	78	18	2	18	55	.223	696	98	25	.969
1975—New York............. Nat.	OF-1B-3B	134	502	65	116	22	1	36	88	.231	526	69	14	.977
1976—New York‡........... Nat.	OF-1B	123	474	70	113	14	1	37	86	.238	293	18	9	.972
1977—N.Y.§-S.D. x.......... Nat.	OF-1B-3B	114	379	38	84	16	0	20	67	.222	333	24	7	.981
1977—Cal. y-N.Y. z......... Amer.	1B-OF	18	60	9	13	4	0	6	11	.217	73	5	2	.975
1978—Chicago .... Nat.	OF-1B	119	395	65	105	17	4	28	79	.266	226	10	6	.975
1979—Chicago .... Nat.	OF	145	532	97	153	19	5	∗48	115	.288	240	11	12	.954
1980—Chicago a.............. Nat.	OF-1B	81	255	31	71	8	0	18	57	.278	119	10	8	.942
1981—New York .... Nat.	1B-OF	100	353	40	78	11	3	22	59	.221	548	34	20	.967
1982—New York.............. Nat.	1B	149	535	80	109	9	1	∗37	99	.204	1232	69	18	.986
1983—New York b .... Nat.	1B-OF	100	248	25	49	7	0	13	29	.198	450	28	3	.994
1984—Oakland c .... Amer.	1B	147	549	68	147	23	1	35	118	.268	55	2	0	1.000
1985—Oakland d .... Amer.	1B	158	592	66	141	16	0	30	91	.238	50	1	0	1.000
1986—Oakland e .... Amer.	1B	144	561	70	118	19	0	35	94	.210	17	0	2	.895
1987—Phoenix .... P. C.	1B	20	59	11	12	3	0	2	11	.203	27	1	0	1.000
National League Totals—13 Years..........		1474	4915	688	1156	178	24	336	896	.235	5640	685	170	.974
American League Totals—4 Years		467	1762	213	419	62	1	106	314	.238	195	8	4	.981
Major League Totals—16 Years................		1941	6677	901	1575	240	25	442	1210	.236	5835	693	174	.974

Selected by California Angels' organization in 2nd round of free-agent draft, June 6, 1967.
Selected by Baltimore Orioles' organization in secondary phase of free-agent draft, January 27, 1968.
Selected by San Francisco Giants' organization in secondary phase of free-agent draft, June 4, 1970.
†Sold to New York Mets for an estimated $125,000, February 28, 1975.
§Traded to San Diego Padres for Third Baseman-Outfielder Bobby Valentine and Pitcher Paul Siebert, June 15, 1977.
xSold on waivers to California Angels, September 6, 1977.
ySold to New York Yankees, September 15, 1977.
zGranted free agency, November 2, 1977; signed by Chicago Cubs, November 30, 1977.
aTraded to New York Mets for Outfielder Steve Henderson and cash, February 28, 1981.
bReleased, January 30, 1984; signed by Oakland A's, March 29, 1984.
cGranted free agency, November 8, 1984; re-signed by A's, December 19, 1984.
dReleased, December 20, 1985; re-signed by A's, January 20, 1986.
eGranted free agency, November 12, 1986; signed by Phoenix, July 11, 1987.

CHAMPIONSHIP SERIES RECORD

Year Club League	Pos.	G.	AB.	R.	H.	2B.	3B.	HR.	RBI.	B.A.	PO.	A.	E.	F.A.
1971—San Francisco ...... Nat.	PH-OF	4	9	0	1	0	0	0	0	.111	5	0	0	1.000

PITCHING RECORD

Year Club League	G.	IP.	W.	L.	Pct.	H.	R.	ER.	SO.	BB.	ERA.
1973—San Francisco................................ National	2	4	0	0	.000	3	4	4	4	6	9.00

CHARLES HERBERT (CHUCK) KLEIN

Born October 7, 1905, at Indianapolis, Ind.

Died March 28, 1958, at Indianapolis, Ind.

Height, 6.00. Weight, 195.

Threw right and batted lefthanded.

Shares major league records for most consecutive years leading league in runs (3) and total bases (4); most home runs, game (4), July 10, 1936, 10 innings.
Holds modern major league record for most assists by outfielder, season (44), 1930.
Holds National League record for most long hits, season (107), 1930.
Holds modern National League record for most runs, season (158), 1930.
Led National League in stolen bases with 20 in 1932.
Led National League outfielders in double plays, 1930, 1935 (tie).
Named National League's Most Valuable Player by THE SPORTING NEWS, 1931 and 1932.
Named by Baseball Writers' Association of America on THE SPORTING NEWS All-Star Major League Teams, 1932-33.
Coach, Philadelphia Phillies, 1942 through 1945.
Named to Hall of Fame, 1980.

Year Club League	Pos.	G.	AB.	R.	H.	2B.	3B.	HR.	RBI.	B.A.	PO.	A.	E.	F.A.
1927—Evansville .... I.I.I.	OF	14	49	10	16	2	2	2	....	.327	20	0	0	1.000
1928—Fort Wayne........... Cent.	OF	88	359	85	119	29	4	26	....	.331	216	15	●12	.951
1928—Philadelphia .... Nat.	OF	64	253	41	91	14	4	11	34	.360	128	7	3	.978
1929—Philadelphia .... Nat.	OF	149	616	126	219	45	6	∗43	145	.356	321	18	12	.966

Year	Club	League	Pos.	G.	AB.	R.	H.	2B.	3B.	HR.	RBI.	B.A.	PO.	A.	E.	F.A.
1930—Philadelphia	Nat.	OF	●156	648	*158	250	*59	8	40	170	.386	362	*44	17	.960
1931—Philadelphia	Nat.	OF	148	594	●121	200	34	10	*31	*121	.337	292	13	9	.971
1932—Philadelphia	Nat.	OF	●154	650	*152	*226	50	15	*38	137	.348	331	*29	●15	.960
1933—Philadelphia(a)	Nat.	OF	152	606	101	*223	*44	7	*28	*120	*.368	339	*21	5	.986
0934—Chicago	Nat.	OF	115	435	78	131	27	2	20	80	.301	222	6	9	.962
1935—Chicago	Nat.	OF	119	434	71	127	14	4	21	73	.293	215	11	10	.958
1936—Chi.(b)-Phil	Nat.	OF	146	601	102	184	35	7	25	105	.306	276	16	*23	.927
1937—Philadelphia	Nat.	OF	115	406	74	132	20	2	15	57	.325	175	11	10	.949
1938—Philadelphia	Nat.	OF	129	458	53	113	22	2	8	61	.247	229	8	10	.960
1939—Phi.(c)-Pit.(d)	Nat.	OF	110	317	45	90	18	5	12	56	.284	153	5	7	.958
1940—Philadelphia	Nat.	OF	116	354	39	77	16	2	7	37	.218	180	4	3	.984
1941—Philadelphia	Nat.	OF	50	73	6	9	0	0	1	3	.123	22	1	1	.958
1942—Philadelphia	Nat.	PH	14	14	0	1	0	0	0	0	.071	0	0	0	.000
1943—Philadelphia	Nat.	OF-PH	12	20	0	2	0	0	0	3	.100	0	0	1	.000
1944—Philadelphia	Nat.	OF	4	7	1	1	0	0	0	0	.143	5	0	0	1.000
Major League Totals—17 Years			1753	6486	1168	2076	398	74	300	1202	.320	3250	194	135	.962

aTraded to Chicago Cubs for Pitcher Ted Kleinhans, Infielder Mark Koenig and Outfielder Harvey Hendrick and cash, November 21, 1933.

bTraded with Pitcher Fabian Kowalik and $50,000 to Philadelphia Phillies for Outfielder Ethan Allen and Pitcher Curt Davis, May 21, 1936.

cReleased by Philadelphia Phillies and signed by Pittsburgh Pirates, June 7, 1939.

dReleased by Pittsburgh and signed by Philadelphia Phillies, March 26, 1940.

WORLD SERIES RECORD

Year	Club	League	Pos.	G.	AB.	R.	H.	2B.	3B.	HR.	RBI.	B.A.	PO.	A.	E.	F.A.
1935—Chicago	Nat	OF-PH	5	12	2	4	0	0	1	2	.333	4	0	0	1.000

WILLIAM JOSEPH (BILL) KLEM
(The Old Arbitrator)

Born February 22, 1874, at Rochester, N. Y.

Died September 1, 1951, at Miami, Fla.

Height, 5.07½. Weight, 157.

As a youth around his native Rochester, N. Y., Bill Klem gained quite a reputation as a ball player. He was a first baseman and catcher. In 1896 and '97, he had trials with pro teams representing Hamilton, Ont., Springfield, Mass., and Augusta, Me. Arm trouble, however, cut short his chances and he returned to the sandlot ranks.

Bill umpired his first game several years later. At the time he was employed as a steel worker at Berwick, Pa., and playing on a semi-pro team. He launched his career as an umpire in pro ball in August, 1902, in the Connecticut State League under his real name of Klimm. The next year, following the example of an uncle, he changed his name to Klem and later had it legalized.

Klem advanced to the New York State League in 1903 and to the American Association the following season. His efforts in the A. A. attracted the attention of Ban Johnson, who sought to get him for the American League, but Bill felt obligated to Harry Pulliam, National League president. At the close of the 1904 campaign Pulliam hired Klem to umpire a post-season Pittsburgh-Cleveland series, and the next spring Bill began his long N. L. career. For 16 years he called 'em from behind the plate exclusively—first because there was only one umpire on duty and later because of his strike-calling superiority. Bill retired from the field in 1941 to become N. L. chief of staff, a position he held until his death ten years later.

A feud of long standing with John McGraw, famed Giant manager, almost ended Klem's stay in the National League in 1928. Following charges by McGraw, Bill resigned at the close of that season. However, he later was mollified and after cooling off three months agreed to rejoin the senior circuit.

Klem umpired in 18 World Series—eight more than any other arbiter in history. His first was in 1908. From that time through 1918, he missed only three fall classics. His last was in 1940, his final season in harness. Klem also had the distinction, along with Jack Sheridan, of being selected to umpire the Giants-White Sox world tour of 1913-14.

The Old Arbitrator was responsible for many innovations in the umpiring profession. In 1904, during his first year in the American Association, he introduced the practice of drawing a line on the field with his spiked shoe to ward off protesting managers and players. He also was an early crusader for better quarters for umpires. Another Klem innovation was for the plate umpire to stand slightly to the side of the catcher closest to the batter, rather than directly behind the catcher.

Klem, along with Tommy Connolly, was named to the Hall of Fame by the Committee on Veterans in September, 1953—the first umpires to gain this honor.

—DID YOU KNOW—

That Philadelphia's Chuck Klein collected 250 hits in 1930, but did not lead the National League in that category? Klein finished second to New York's Bill Terry, who amassed an N.L. record-tying 254 total.

THEODORE BERNARD (TED) KLUSZEWSKI
(Klu)

Born September 10, 1924, at Argo, Ill.

Died March 29, 1988, at Cincinnati, O.

Height, 6.02. Weight, 240.

Threw and batted lefthanded.

Holds major league record for most consecutive years leading league in fielding percentage, first baseman (5).

Holds modern National League record for most consecutive games, one or more runs (17), August 27 through September 13, 1954.

Led National League first basemen in double plays, 1953-54-55-56.

Hit three home runs in a game, July 1, 1956, first game.

Named as first baseman on THE SPORTING NEWS All-Star Major League Teams, 1954-55-56.

Minor league hitting instructor, Cincinnati Reds, 1968-69; coach, Reds, 1970 through 1978; minor league hitting instructor, Reds, 1979 through 1987.

Year	Club	League	Pos.	G.	AB.	R.	H.	2B.	3B.	HR.	RBI.	B.A.	PO.	A.	E.	F.A.
1946—Columbia		Sally	1B-OF	90	335	59	118	24	5	11	87	★.352	525	20	15	.973
1947—Cincinnati		Nat.	1B	9	10	1	1	0	0	0	2	.100	10	0	0	1.000
1947—Memphis		South.	1B	115	427	80	161	32	9	7	68	★.377	931	60	19	.981
1948—Cincinnati		Nat.	1B	113	379	49	104	23	4	12	57	.274	833	65	9	.990
1949—Cincinnati		Nat.	1B	136	531	63	164	26	2	8	68	.309	1140	65	14	.989
1950—Cincinnati		Nat.	1B	134	538	76	165	37	0	25	111	.307	1123	61	15	.987
1951—Cincinnati		Nat.	1B	154	607	74	157	35	2	13	77	.259	★1381	88	5	★.997
1952—Cincinnati		Nat.	1B	135	497	62	159	24	11	16	86	.320	1121	66	8	★.993
1953—Cincinnati		Nat.	1B	149	570	97	180	25	0	40	108	.316	1285	58	7	★.995
1954—Cincinnati		Nat.	1B	149	573	104	187	28	3	★49	★141	.326	1237	101	5	★.996
1955—Cincinnati		Nat.	1B	153	612	116	★192	25	0	47	113	.314	★1388	86	8	★.995
1956—Cincinnati		Nat.	1B	138	517	91	156	14	1	35	102	.302	1166	89	13	.990
1957—Cincinnati(a)		Nat.	1B	69	127	12	34	7	0	6	21	.268	161	15	2	.989
1958—Pittsburgh		Nat.	1B	100	301	29	88	13	4	4	37	.292	591	36	4	.994
1959—Pittsburgh(b)		Nat.	1B	60	122	11	32	10	1	2	17	.262	151	12	0	1.000
1959—Chicago		Amer.	1B	31	101	11	30	2	1	2	10	.297	220	10	0	1.000
1960—Chicago(c)		Amer.	1B	81	181	20	53	9	0	5	39	.293	325	19	1	.997
1961—Los Angeles		Amer.	1B	107	263	32	64	12	0	15	39	.243	520	28	6	.989
American League Totals—3 Years				219	545	63	147	23	1	22	88	.270	1065	57	7	.994
National League Totals—13 Years				1499	5384	785	1619	267	28	257	940	.301	11587	742	90	.993
Major League Totals—15 Years				1718	5929	848	1766	290	29	279	1028	.298	12652	799	97	.993

aTraded to Pittsburgh Pirates for First Baseman Dee Fondy, December 28, 1957.

bReleased to Chicago White Sox on waiver deal for Infielder Bob Sagers and Outfielder-First Baseman Harry Simpson, August 25, 1959. Sagers, playing for Indianapolis, American Association, transferred to Columbus, International League, at close of season.

cSelected by Los Angeles Angels, December 14, 1960.

WORLD SERIES RECORD

Year	Club	League	Pos.	G.	AB.	R.	H.	2B.	3B.	HR.	RBI.	B.A.	PO.	A.	E.	F.A.
1959—Chicago		Amer.	1B	6	23	5	9	1	0	3	10	.391	59	3	0	1.000

JEROME MARTIN (JERRY) KOOSMAN

Born December 23, 1942, at Appleton, Minn.

Height, 6.02. Weight, 220.

Threw left and batted righthanded.

Holds National League record for most strikeouts by pitcher as batter, season (62), 1968.

Shares modern National League record for most shutout games won or tied, rookie season (7), 1968.

Tied for National League lead in balks with 3 in 1970 and 7 in 1975.

Named National League Rookie Pitcher of the Year by THE SPORTING NEWS, 1968.

Year	Club	League	G.	IP.	W.	L.	Pct.	H.	R.	ER.	SO.	BB.	ERA.
1965—Greenville		W. Carol.	27	107	5	11	.313	101	70	56	128	56	4.71
1965—Williamsport		Eastern	2	12	0	2	.000	11	7	5	11	11	3.75
1966—Auburn		NYP	24	170	12	7	.632	109	43	26	174	43	★1.38

Year Club	League	G.	IP.	W.	L.	Pct.	H.	R.	ER.	SO.	BB.	ERA.
1967—New York	National	9	22	0	2	.000	22	17	15	11	19	6.14
1967—Jacksonville	Int'national	25	178	11	10	.524	137	60	48	★183	46	2.43
1968—New York	National	35	264	19	12	.613	221	72	61	178	69	2.08
1969—New York	National	32	241	17	9	.684	187	66	61	180	68	2.28
1970—New York	National	30	212	12	7	.632	189	87	74	118	71	3.14
1971—New York	National	26	166	6	11	.353	160	66	56	96	51	3.04
1972—New York	National	34	163	11	12	.478	155	81	75	147	52	4.14
1973—New York	National	35	263	14	15	.483	234	93	83	156	76	2.84
1974—New York	National	35	265	15	11	.577	258	113	99	188	85	3.36
1975—New York	National	36	240	14	13	.519	234	106	91	173	98	3.41
1976—New York	National	34	247	21	10	.677	205	81	74	200	66	2.70
1977—New York	National	32	227	8	●20	.286	195	102	88	192	81	3.49
1978—New York†	National	38	235	3	15	.167	221	110	98	160	84	3.75
1979—Minnesota	American	37	264	20	13	.606	268	108	99	157	83	3.38
1980—Minnesota	American	38	243	16	13	.552	252	119	109	149	69	4.04
1981—Minnesota‡-Chicago	American	27	121	4	●13	.235	125	59	54	76	41	4.02
1982—Chicago	American	42	173⅓	11	7	.611	194	81	74	88	38	3.84
1983—Chicago §x	American	37	169⅔	11	7	.611	176	96	90	90	53	4.77
1984—Philadelphia	National	36	224	14	15	.483	232	95	81	137	60	3.25
1985—Philadelphia y	National	19	99⅓	6	4	.600	107	56	51	60	34	4.62
National League Totals—14 Years		431	2868⅓	160	156	.506	2620	1145	1007	1996	914	3.16
American League Totals—5 Years		181	971	62	53	.539	1015	463	426	560	284	3.95
Major League Totals—19 Years		612	3839⅓	222	209	.515	3635	1608	1433	2556	1198	3.36

Signed as free agent by New York Mets' organization, August 27, 1964.

†Traded to Minnesota Twins for Pitcher Greg Field and a player to be named later, December 8, 1978; New York Mets acquired Pitcher Jesse Orosco to complete deal, February 7, 1979.

‡Traded to Chicago White Sox for Shortstop Ivan Mesa, Third Baseman Ron Perry, a player to be named later and cash, August 30, 1981; Minnesota Twins' organization acquired Outfielder Randy Johnson to complete deal, September 2, 1981. (Pitcher Kevin Flannery replaced Perry due to injuries, October 18, 1982.)

§Granted free agency, November 7, 1983; re-signed by White Sox, December 2, 1983.

xTraded to Philadelphia Phillies, February 15, 1984, completing deal in which Philadelphia traded Pitcher Ron Reed to Chicago White Sox for a player to be named later, December 5, 1983.

yReleased, December 6, 1985.

CHAMPIONSHIP SERIES RECORD

Year Club	League	G.	IP.	W.	L.	Pct.	H.	R.	ER.	SO.	BB.	ERA.
1969—New York	National	1	4⅔	0	0	.000	7	6	6	5	4	11.57
1973—New York	National	1	9	1	0	1.000	8	2	2	9	0	2.00
1983—Chicago	American	1	⅓	0	0	.000	1	3	2	0	2	54.00
Championship Series Totals—3 Years		3	14	1	0	1.000	16	11	10	14	6	6.43

WORLD SERIES RECORD

Year Club	League	G.	IP.	W.	L.	Pct.	H.	R.	ER.	SO.	BB.	ERA.
1969—New York	National	2	17⅔	2	0	1.000	7	4	4	9	4	2.04
1973—New York	National	2	8⅔	1	0	1.000	9	3	3	8	7	3.12
World Series Totals—2 Years		4	26⅓	3	0	1.000	16	7	7	17	11	2.39

SANFORD (SANDY) KOUFAX

Born December 30, 1935, at Brooklyn, N.Y.

Height, 6.02. Weight, 198.

Threw left and batted righthanded.

Holds major league record for most consecutive seasons leading league in lowest earned run average (5).

Holds National League records for most no-hit games, lifetime (4); most games with 10 or more strikeouts, lifetime (97); most games with 10 or more strikeouts, season (21), 1965.

Shares National League record for most years leading league in lowest earned-run average (5).

Holds modern National League record for most strikeouts, season (382), 1965.

Shares modern National League record for most games won by lefthanded pitcher, season (27), 1966.

Pitched 5-0 no-hit victory against New York Mets, June 30, 1962; 8-0 no-hit victory against San Francisco Giants, May 11, 1963; 3-0 no-hit victory against Philadelphia Phillies, June 4, 1964 and 1-0 perfect game against Chicago Cubs, September 9, 1965.

Led National League in shutouts with 11 in 1963; 7 in 1964 and tied for lead with 5 in 1966.

Named as pitcher on the National League All-Star Team by THE SPORTING NEWS, 1963-64-65-66.

Named Most Valuable National League Player, 1963.

Named No. 1 Major League Player of the Year by THE SPORTING NEWS, 1963 and 1965.

Named National League Pitcher of the Year by THE SPORTING NEWS, 1963-64-65-66.
Won Cy Young Memorial Award, 1963-65-66.
Named to Hall of Fame, 1972.

Year Club	League	G.	IP.	W.	L.	Pct.	H.	R.	ER.	SO.	BB.	ERA.
1955—Brooklyn	National	12	42	2	2	.500	33	15	14	30	28	3.00
1956—Brooklyn	National	16	59	2	4	.333	66	37	32	30	29	4.88
1957—Brooklyn	National	34	104	5	4	.556	83	49	45	122	51	3.89
1958—Los Angeles	National	40	159	11	11	.500	132	89	79	131	105	4.47
1959—Los Angeles	National	35	153	8	6	.571	136	74	69	173	92	4.06
1960—Los Angeles	National	37	175	8	13	.381	133	83	76	197	100	3.91
1961—Los Angeles	National	42	256	18	13	.581	212	117	100	*269	96	3.52
1962—Los Angeles	National	28	184	14	7	.667	134	61	52	216	57	*2.54
1963—Los Angeles	National	40	311	●25	5	.833	214	68	65	*306	58	*1.88
1964—Los Angeles	National	29	223	19	5	*.792	154	49	43	223	53	*1.74
1965—Los Angeles	National	43	*336	*26	8	*.765	216	90	76	*382	71	*2.04
1966—Los Angeles	National	41	*323	*27	9	.750	241	74	62	*317	77	*1.73
Major League Totals—12 Years		397	2325	165	87	.655	1754.	806	713	2396	817	2.76

WORLD SERIES RECORD

Year Club	League	G.	IP.	W.	L.	Pct.	H.	R.	ER.	SO.	BB.	ERA.
1959—Los Angeles	National	2	9	0	1	.000	5	1	1	7	1	1.00
1963—Los Angeles	National	2	18	2	0	1.000	12	3	3	23	3	1.50
1965—Los Angeles	National	3	24	2	1	.667	13	2	1	29	5	0.38
1966—Los Angeles	National	1	6	0	1	.000	6	4	1	2	2	1.50
World Series Totals—4 Years		8	57	4	3	.571	36	10	6	61	11	0.95

HARVEY EDWARD KUENN

Born December 4, 1930, at West Allis, Wis.

Died February 28, 1988, at Peoria, Ariz.

Height, 6.02. Weight, 198.

Threw and batted righthanded.

Father of Harvey Kuenn, Jr., former minor league outfielder.

Shares major league record for most doubles, inning (2), July 24, 1964, sixth inning.
Named American League Rookie of the Year by the Baseball Writers' Association and THE SPORTING NEWS, 1953.
Named as shortstop on THE SPORTING NEWS All-Star Major League Team, 1956.
Coach, Milwaukee Brewers, 1971 to 1982; manager, Milwaukee, 1982 through 1983.

Year Club	League	Pos.	G.	AB.	R.	H.	2B.	3B.	HR.	RBI.	B.A.	PO.	A.	E.	F.A.
1952—Davenport	I.I.I.	SS	63	256	46	87	17	3	1	40	.340	114	194	26	.922
1952—Detroit	Amer.	SS	19	80	2	26	2	2	0	8	.325	44	57	4	.962
1953—Detroit	Amer.	SS	155	*679	94	*209	33	7	2	48	.308	*308	441	21	.973
1954—Detroit	Amer.	SS	●155	*656	81	●201	28	6	5	48	.306	*294	*496	28	.966
1955—Detroit	Amer.	SS	145	620	101	190	*38	5	8	62	.306	253	378	29	.956
1956—Detroit	Amer.	*SS-OF	146	591	96	*196	32	7	12	88	.332	219	388	20	*.968
1957—Detroit	Amer.	*SS-3B-1B	151	624	74	173	30	6	9	44	.277	251	387	*30	.955
1958—Detroit	Amer.	OF	139	561	73	179	*39	3	8	54	.319	*358	9	6	.984
1959—Detroit (a)	Amer.	OF	139	561	99	*198	*42	7	9	71	*.353	247	6	3	.988
1960—Cleveland (b)	Amer.	OF-3B	126	474	65	146	24	0	9	54	.308	222	13	9	.963
1961—San Francisco	Nat.	OF-3B-SS	131	471	60	125	22	4	5	46	.265	190	43	10	.959
1962—San Francisco	Nat.	OF-3B	130	487	73	148	23	5	10	68	.304	180	47	8	.966
1963—San Francisco	Nat.	OF-3B	120	417	61	121	13	2	6	31	.290	115	60	13	.931
1964—San Francisco	Nat.	OF-1B-3B	111	351	42	92	16	2	4	22	.262	136	9	6	.960
1965—S.F.(c)-Chicago	Nat.	OF-1B	77	179	15	40	5	0	0	12	.223	81	8	3	.967
1966—Chi.(d)-Phila.	Nat.	OF-1B	89	162	15	48	9	0	0	15	.296	130	3	1	.993
American League Totals—9 Years			1175	4846	685	1518	268	43	62	477	.313	2196	2175	150	.967
National League Totals—6 Years			658	2067	266	574	88	13	25	194	.278	832	170	41	.961
Major League Totals—15 Years			1833	6913	951	2092	356	56	87	671	.303	3028	2345	191	.966

aTraded to Cleveland Indians for Outfielder Rocky Colavito, April 17, 1960.
bTraded to San Francisco Giants for Pitcher Johnny Antonelli and Outfielder Willie Kirkland, December 3, 1960.
cTraded with Catcher Ed Bailey and Pitcher Bob Hendley to Chicago Cubs for Catcher Dick Bertell and First Baseman-Outfielder Len Gabrielson, May 29, 1965.
dSold to Philadelphia Phillies, April 23, 1966.

WORLD SERIES RECORD

Year Club	League	Pos.	G.	AB.	R.	H.	2B.	3B.	HR.	RBI.	B.A.	PO.	A.	E.	F.A.
1962—San Francisco	Nat.	OF	4	12	1	1	0	0	0	0	.083	11	0	0	1.000

NAPOLEON (NAP) LAJOIE
(Larry)

Born September 5, 1875, at Woonsocket, R. I.
Died February 7, 1959, at Daytona Beach, Fla.
Height, 6.01. Weight, 195.
Threw and batted righthanded.

Holds American League record for highest batting average, season, 100 or more games (.422), 1901.
Manager, Cleveland Americans, 1905 to 1909; Toronto, International League, 1917; Indianapolis, American Association, 1918.
Named to Hall of Fame, 1937.

Year Club	League	Pos.	G.	AB.	R.	H.	2B.	3B.	HR.	SB.	B.A.	PO.	A.	E.	F.A.
1896—Fall River	N. Eng.	OF	80	380	94	163	34	16	16	....	★.429	★280	30	23	.931
1896—Philadelphia	Nat.	1B	39	174	37	57	11	6	4	6	.328	360	11	3	.992
1897—Philadelphia	Nat.	1B-OF	126	545	107	198	37	25	★10	22	.363	1112	43	20	.983
1898—Philadelphia	Nat.	2B	147	610	113	200	★40	10	5	33	.328	★434	431	48	.947
1899—Philadelphia	Nat.	2B	72	308	70	117	17	11	6	14	.380	222	242	21	.957
1900—Philadelphia(a)	Nat.	2B	102	451	95	156	32	12	7	25	.346	283	345	27	.959
1901—Philadelphia	Amer.	2B	131	543	★145	★229	★48	13	★14	27	★.422	★403	374	30	★.963
1902—Phila.-Cleveland	Amer.	2B	87	352	81	129	34	5	7	19	.366	284	278	15	.974
1903—Cleveland	Amer.	1B-★2B	126	488	90	173	40	13	7	22	★.355	★355	426	35	★.957
1904—Cleveland	Amer.	2B-SS	140	554	92	★211	★50	14	5	31	★.381	354	400	39	.951
1905—Cleveland	Amer.	2B	65	249	29	82	13	2	2	11	.329	148	177	3	.991
1906—Cleveland	Amer.	★2B-3B	152	602	88	★214	★49	7	0	20	.355	★374	★455	26	★.970
1907—Cleveland	Amer.	2B	137	509	53	153	32	6	2	24	.301	314	★461	26	★.968
1908—Cleveland	Amer.	2B	★157	581	77	168	32	6	2	15	.289	★450	★538	37	★.964
1909—Cleveland	Amer.	2B	128	469	56	152	33	7	1	13	.324	282	373	28	.959
1910—Cleveland	Amer.	2B	★159	★591	94	★227	★53	7	4	28	.384	387	419	32	.962
1911—Cleveland	Amer.	1B-2B	90	315	36	115	20	1	2	13	.365	479	109	14	.977
1912—Cleveland	Amer.	1B-2B	117	448	66	165	34	4	0	18	.368	412	261	24	.966
1913—Cleveland	Amer.	2B	137	465	67	156	25	2	1	17	.335	289	363	20	★.970
1914—Cleveland	Amer.	1B-2B	121	419	37	108	14	3	0	14	.258	487	233	22	.970
1915—Philadelphia(b)	Amer.	2B	129	490	40	137	24	5	1	10	.280	251	332	23	.962
1916—Philadelphia	Amer.	2B	113	426	33	105	14	4	2	15	.246	254	325	16	.973
1917—Toronto	Int.	1B	151	581	83	★221	★39	4	5	4	★.380	875	263	23	.980
1918—Indianapolis	A. A.	1B	78	291	39	82	12	2	2	10	.282	661	89	10	.987
American League Totals—16 Years			1989	7501	1084	2524	515	100	50	297	.336	5523	5524	390	.966
National League Totals—5 Years			486	2088	422	728	137	64	32	100	.349	2411	1072	119	.967
Major League Totals—21 Years			2475	9589	1506	3252	652	163	82	397	.339	7934	6596	509	.966

aJumped to Philadelphia A. L., but Philadelphia N. L. club got injunction against his playing for Athletics and he joined Cleveland in June, 1902.
bContract assumed by Philadelphia Athletics, January, 1915.

KENESAW MOUNTAIN LANDIS

Born November 20, 1866, at Millville, O.
Died November 25, 1944, at Chicago, Ill.

Although a native of Ohio, Kenesaw M. Landis spent most of his youth in Indiana. After quitting high school, Landis, intrigued by law and legal matters, mastered shorthand and qualified as clerk of a court in South Bend, Ind. Later he took pre-law courses at the University of Cincinnati and graduated in 1891 from Union Law School in Chicago—now a part of Northwestern University.

President Theodore Roosevelt appointed Landis to the position of United States District Judge for the Northern District of Illinois in March, 1905. The Judge gained nationwide fame two years later by fining the Standard Oil Company $29,240,000 in a freight rebate case. The company, however, eventually escaped payment of the fine through appeal to the Supreme Court.

In January, 1915, the Federal League brought a suit before Landis for an injunction against the American and National leagues. He took the case under advisement and withheld his opinion so that it was possible for the majors to absorb the Federal circuit and bring peace to the game. This handling of the suit made a deep impression on diamond officials.

Landis' appointment as Commissioner of Baseball on November 12, 1920, was a direct result of the Black Sox scandal. Since the peace agreement between the two majors in January, 1903, a three-man National Commission had functioned as the supreme authority. However, in January, 1920, Garry Herrmann, chairman of the Commission since its inception, resigned and the two other members, President Ban Johnson of the American League and Prexy John Heydler of the National, could not agree on a successor.

Landis took office in January, 1921. His salary was $50,000 per year, but before his first seven-year term expired, he was boosted to $65,000.

From the start, Landis was zealous in his defense of the rights of the player. However, he also did not hesitate to curb the players. Two of his biggest decisions involved "cover-up" operations by farm chains. In March, 1938, he set free 91 Cardinal farmhands and handed out several fines in connection with the case. Less than two years later, in January, 1940, he turned loose a similar number of young Detroit players on the same charge. One of Landis' last important decisions was to bar permanently William D. Cox, president of the Phillies, from Organized Ball in 1943 for allegedly betting on his own team. Landis was named to the Hall of Fame in December, 1944.

HENRY E. LARKIN
(Ted)

Born January 12, 1863, at Reading, Pa.

Died January 31, 1942, at Reading, Pa.

Threw and batted righthanded.

Manager, Cleveland, Players League, 1890.

Year Club League	Pos.	G.	AB.	R.	H.	2B.	3B.	HR.	SB.	B.A.	PO.	A.	E.	F.A.
1883—Reading................. Inter-State	OF	....	....	....	....	..	..	..	....	.354	....	....	..	......
1884—Philadelphia .... Am. Assn.	OF	87	328	61	97	19	9	4	....	.296	....	....	16	.884
1885—Philadelphia .... Am. Assn.	OF	108	455	114	154	★40	13	7	....	.338	....	....	30	.918
1886—Philadelphia .... Am. Assn.	OF	139	563	136	184	★34	17	2	36	.327	....	....	37	.884
1887—Philadelphia .... Am. Assn.	1-O	125	537	103	201	25	12	3	33	.374	....	....	24	.947
1888—Philadelphia .... Am. Assn.	1B	135	544	97	154	27	10	6	19	.283	....	....	36	.972
1889—Philadelphia .... Am. Assn.	1B	133	516	108	167	26	11	2	10	.324	1236	36	33	.975
1890—Cleveland.............. Players	1B	125	507	93	166	31	15	5	4	.327	1259	42	32	.976
1891—Philadelphia .... Am. Assn.	1-O	129	516	94	142	28	13	10	3	.273	980	32	21	.979
1892—Washington .... National	1B	116	450	73	127	16	5	9	19	.282	1087	61	39	.967
1893—Washington .... National	1B	81	313	54	101	17	6	3	3	.322	774	27	30	.964
American Assn. Totals—7 Years		856	3459	713	1099	199	85	34	101	.318	....	....	176	.955
Players League Totals—1 Year..............		125	507	93	166	31	15	5	4	.327	1259	42	32	.976
National League Totals—2 Years..........		197	763	127	228	33	11	12	22	.299	1861	88	69	.965
Major League Totals—10 Years.............		1178	4729	933	1493	263	111	51	127	.316	....	....	277	.962

ROBERT GRANVILLE (BOB) LEMON

Born September 22, 1920, at San Bernardino, Calif.

Height, 6.00. Weight, 180.

Threw right and batted lefthanded.

Named by Baseball Writers' Association of America as pitcher on THE SPORTING NEWS All-Star Major League Teams, 1948-50-54.

Pitched no-hit game against Detroit Tigers, winning 2-0, June 30, 1948.

Named Outstanding American League Pitcher by THE SPORTING NEWS, 1948-50-54.

Scout, Cleveland Indians, 1959; coach, Cleveland, 1960; Philadelphia Phillies, 1961; manager, Honolulu, Pacific Coast League, 1964; Seattle, Pacific Coast League, 1965-66; coach, California Angels, 1967 through 1970; manager, Kansas City Royals, 1971-1972; scout, Kansas City, 1973; manager, Sacramento, Pacific Coast League, 1974; Richmond, International League, 1975; coach, New York Yankees, 1976; manager, Chicago White Sox, 1977 to 1978; New York Yankees, 1978 to 1979, 1981 to 1982; scout, Yankees, 1979-81, 1982 to date.

Named to Hall of Fame, 1976.

PITCHING RECORD

Year Club League	G.	IP.	W.	L.	Pct.	H.	R.	ER.	SO.	BB.	ERA.
1938—Oswego......................Can.-Amer.	1	1	0	0	.000	1	0	0	1	0	0.00
1941—Wilkes-Barre ....Eastern	1	1	0	1	.000	0	1	1	0	3	9.00
1946—Cleveland...................Amer.	32	94	4	5	.444	77	40	26	39	68	2.49

Year	Club	League	G.	IP.	W.	L.	Pct.	H.	R.	ER.	SO.	BB.	ERA.
1947—Cleveland	Amer.		37	167	11	5	.688	150	68	64	65	97	3.45
1948—Cleveland	Amer.		43	*294	20	14	.588	231	104	92	147	129	2.82
1949—Cleveland	Amer.		37	280	22	10	.688	211	101	93	138	137	2.99
1950—Cleveland	Amer.		44	*288	*23	11	.676	*281	144	123	*170	146	3.84
1951—Cleveland	Amer.		42	263	17	●14	.548	*244	*119	103	132	124	3.52
1952—Cleveland	Amer.		42	*310	22	11	.667	236	104	86	131	105	2.50
1953—Cleveland	Amer.		41	*287	21	15	.583	*283	119	107	98	110	3.36
1954—Cleveland	Amer.		36	258	●23	7	.767	228	95	78	110	92	2.72
1955—Cleveland	Amer.		35	211	●18	10	.643	218	103	91	100	74	3.88
1956—Cleveland	Amer.		39	255	20	14	.588	230	103	86	94	89	3.04
1957—Cleveland	Amer.		21	117	6	11	.353	129	70	60	45	64	4.62
1958—Cleveland	Amer.		11	25	0	1	.000	41	15	15	8	16	5.40
1958—San Diego	P.C.		12	56	2	5	.286	67	32	27	19	22	4.34
Major League Totals—13 Years			460	2849	207	128	.618	2559	1185	1024	1277	1251	3.23

WORLD SERIES RECORD

Year	Club	League	G.	IP.	W.	L.	Pct.	H.	R.	ER.	SO.	BB.	ERA.
1948—Cleveland	Amer.		2	16⅓	2	0	1.000	16	4	3	6	7	1.65
1954—Cleveland	Amer.		2	13⅓	0	2	.000	16	11	10	11	8	6.75
World Series Totals—2 Years			4	29⅔	2	2	.500	32	15	13	17	15	3.94

BATTING RECORD

Year	Club	League	Pos.	G.	AB.	R.	H.	2B.	3B.	HR.	RBI.	B.A.	PO.	A.	E.	F.A.
1938—Springfield	M.-Atl.		INF-OF	7	18	1	4	1	0	0	2	.222	4	5	2	.818
1938—Oswego	C.-A		O-SS-P	75	282	44	88	6	6	7	34	.312	97	52	12	.925
1939—Springfield	M.-Atl.		SS-O	80	307	44	90	14	3	3	39	.293	106	103	25	.893
1939—New Orleans	South.		OF-3B	52	207	30	64	9	6	0	22	.309	65	33	13	.883
1940—Wilkes-Barre	East.		3B-OF	92	321	37	82	14	3	2	53	.255	132	68	16	.926
1941—Wilkes-Barre	East.		*3B-SS-P	●141	*562	*109	●169	15	13	4	43	.301	*179	268	36	.925
1941—Cleveland	Amer.		3B	5	4	0	1	0	0	0	0	.250	1	1	0	1.000
1942—Baltimore	Int.		*3B-SS	148	596	95	160	23	8	21	80	.268	*159	*349	*33	.939
1942—Cleveland	Amer.		3B	5	5	0	0	0	0	0	0	.000	0	1	1	.500
1943-44-45—Cleveland	Amer.							(In Military Service)								
1946—Cleveland	Amer.		P-OF	55	89	9	16	3	0	1	4	.180	46	30	2	.974
1947—Cleveland	Amer.		P-OF	47	56	11	18	4	3	2	5	.321	13	46	1	.983
1948—Cleveland	Amer.		P	52	119	20	34	9	0	5	21	.286	*23	*86	4	.965
1949—Cleveland	Amer.		P	46	108	17	29	6	2	7	19	.269	*34	*71	4	.963
1950—Cleveland	Amer.		P	72	136	21	37	9	1	6	26	.272	22	66	4	.957
1951—Cleveland	Amer.		P	56	102	11	21	4	1	3	13	.206	21	*60	2	.976
1952—Cleveland	Amer.		P	54	124	14	28	5	0	2	9	.226	*32	*79	2	.982
1953—Cleveland	Amer.		P	51	112	12	26	9	1	2	17	.232	*31	*74	3	.972
1954—Cleveland	Amer.		P	40	98	11	21	4	1	2	10	.214	*22	57	3	.963
1955—Cleveland	Amer.		P	49	78	11	19	0	0	1	9	.244	16	43	1	.983
1956—Cleveland	Amer.		P	43	93	8	18	0	0	5	12	.194	24	*61	*6	.934
1957—Cleveland	Amer.		P	25	46	2	3	1	0	1	1	.065	12	31	0	1.000
1958—Cleveland	Amer.		P	15	13	1	3	0	0	1	1	.231	1	7	0	1.000
1958—San Diego	P.C.		OF-P	32	69	2	18	4	0	0	7	.261	25	9	0	1.000
Major League Totals—15 Years				615	1183	148	274	54	9	37	147	.232	298	713	33	.968

EMIL JOHN (DUTCH) LEONARD

Born March 25, 1910, at Auburn, Ill.
Died April 17, 1983, at Springfield, Ill.
Height, 6.00. Weight, 195.
Threw and batted righthanded.

Coach, Chicago Cubs, 1954 through 1956.

Year	Club	League	G.	IP.	W.	L.	Pct.	H.	R.	ER.	SO.	BB.	ERA.
1930—Canton	Central		11	53	1	5	.167	68	49	47	23	17	7.98
1930—Mobile	Southern		31	180	5	16	.238	247	148	132	52	72	6.60
1931—St. Joseph	Western		6	9	0	1	.000	15	11	7	4	3	7.00
1931—Sp'field-Qu'cy-Dec	I. I. I.		24	92	6	5	.545	112	54	43	56	20	4.21
1932—Decatur(a)	I. I. I.		15	98	7	4	.636	96	38	...	38	22	.....
1933—York	NYP		34	187	12	15	.444	188	73	65	80	42	3.13
1933—Brooklyn	National		10	40	2	3	.400	42	17	13	6	10	2.93
1934—Brooklyn	National		44	184	14	11	.560	210	90	67	58	33	3.28
1935—Brooklyn	National		43	138	2	9	.182	152	67	60	41	29	3.91
1936—Brooklyn	National		16	32	0	0	.000	34	18	13	8	5	3.66
1936—Atlanta	Southern		22	126	13	3	*.813	115	39	32	51	19	*2.29

Year	Club	League	G.	IP.	W.	L.	Pct.	H.	R.	ER.	SO.	BB.	ERA.
1937—Atlanta		Southern	32	188	15	8	.652	193	90	76	68	34	3.64
1938—Washington		American	33	223	12	15	.444	221	109	85	68	53	3.43
1939—Washington		American	34	269	20	8	.714	★273	124	106	88	59	3.55
1940—Washington		American	35	289	14	●19	.424	★328	136	112	124	78	3.49
1941—Washington		American	34	256	18	13	.581	271	117	98	91	54	3.45
1942—Washington		American	6	35	2	2	.500	28	16	16	15	5	4.11
1943—Washington		American	31	220	11	13	.458	218	96	80	51	46	3.27
1944—Washington		American	32	229	14	14	.500	222	97	78	62	37	3.07
1945—Washington		American	31	216	17	7	.708	208	72	51	96	35	2.13
1946—Washington(b)		American	26	162	10	10	.500	182	85	64	62	36	3.56
1947—Philadelphia		National	32	235	17	12	.586	224	86	70	103	57	2.68
1948—Philadelphia(c)		National	34	226	12	★17	.414	226	85	63	92	54	2.51
1949—Chicago		National	33	180	7	16	.304	198	94	83	83	43	4.15
1950—Chicago		National	35	74	5	1	.833	70	41	31	28	27	3.77
1951—Chicago		National	41	82	10	6	.625	69	30	24	30	28	2.63
1952—Chicago		National	45	67	2	2	.500	56	18	16	37	24	2.15
1953—Chicago		National	45	63	2	3	.400	72	34	32	27	24	4.57
National League Totals—11 Years			378	1321	73	80	.477	1353	580	472	513	334	3.22
American League Totals—9 Years			262	1899	118	101	.539	1951	852	690	657	403	3.27
Major League Totals—20 Years			640	3220	191	181	.513	3304	1432	1162	1170	737	3.25

aInjured hand first week of July, 1932, and league disbanded July 15, 1932.
bSold to Philadelphia Phillies, December 9, 1946.
cTraded to Chicago Cubs with Pitcher Walt Dubiel for Pitcher Hank Borowy and First Baseman Ed Waitkus, December 14, 1948.

WALTER FENNER (BUCK) LEONARD

Born September 8, 1907, at Rocky Mount, N. C.

Height, 5:10. Weight, 185.

Threw and batted lefthanded.

Buck Leonard was "the" first baseman of Negro professional baseball from 1934 to 1950. Whenever an All-Star team was selected, automatically the name "Leonard" was written in the first base slot. He hit for power and he hit for percentage. Towering drives were his trademark. He and his teammate on the Homestead Grays, Josh Gibson, formed the most destructive force ever to cannonade the pitchers of the Negro Leagues. Called the "Thunder Twins" by the black press, Buck was labeled the "Lou Gehrig of the Negro leagues" and Josh was compared with Babe Ruth.

A gifted fielder, Buck was a master at catching low throws and nabbing bunters. He had an exceptionally accurate and powerful throwing arm, and though not the traditional lanky first baseman, he could "catch everything." Leonard was a model of consistency, not a fancy dan at the bag.

Regarded as colored baseball's most popular player, Buck was well-liked not only for his brilliant playing, but for his quiet, easy-to-meet manner and his spirit as captain of the Grays.

Leonard was voted first baseman on the Negro baseball All-Time All-American Dream Team, a group selected by 31 national Negro baseball experts from the two major eras of black professional baseball. Selected in 1952, it covered a span of 42 years, beginning in 1910.

Buck began playing sandlot ball in Rocky Mount. He quit high school at 15 to go to work for the Atlantic Coast Line railroad. Dropped from the shop's workforce in 1933, he began his professional career with the Rocky Mount Elks and the Black Swans. His play attracted the eyes of the Portsmouth (Va.) Firefighters, for whom he played until Manager Ben Taylor of the Baltimore Stars snatched him. It was Taylor who taught him the fine points of first-base play, at which Ben had been a master. At the tailend of the season, Buck was taken by the Brooklyn Royal Giants, managed by Cannonball Dick Redding.

In 1934, Cum Posey, owner and manager of the Homestead Grays of Pittsburgh, on the recommendation of an old Grays pitcher, the legendary Smoky Joe Williams, signed Leonard, who remained with the Grays for 17 years, during which they won nine straight Negro league pennants, 1937-45.

The Grays averaged 30,000 miles per year by bus. They played so often in major league parks that they became part-time tenants . . . whenever the major league club was out of town. The Polo Grounds, Yankee Stadium, Forbes Field, Sportsman's Park, Griffith Stadium and Comiskey Park were the parks used more often than others because of the many Negro baseball fans in each city and the favorable terms these owners (usually American League park owners) extended the Negro league teams. For this reason, the owners of the Pirates and Senators knew more about the Negro stars and thus were the first to feel out both Leonard and Gibson about joining the major leagues in the 1940s. But, as Leonard said, "I was too old, past my prime and didn't want to embarrass anyone or hurt the chances of those who might follow. And, as things happened, Josh died suddenly in 1947, before it all really began."

Leonard's lifetime batting average in professional Negro ball was computed at .342. Of an average of 200 games per year, 80 were between members of the East and West divisions of the Negro National League and these box scores constituted the bulk of statistics on which "official" averages were computed. Other games played were varied forms of exhibitions.

Buck's top homer total for one season was 42 in 1942 and, in 1948, he led both divisions in batting with a .391 mark.

Leonard retired from baseball in 1955, after 23 years and over 4,000 games, all as a first baseman. He played in 12 East-West All-Star games, held annually in the White Sox' Comiskey Park; performed 12 winters in the Caribbean, in Puerto Rico, Cuba, Mexico, Venezuela and the Dominican Republic. In the spring of 1936, he played against the

Cincinnati Reds in Puerto Rico. His last active years, 1951 through 1955, were spent in the Mexican League, the first three years with Torreon and the final two with Durango. He made a 10-game Organized Baseball appearance in 1953, at Portsmouth (Piedmont), when he was 46 years old. He hit .333. In 1962 he helped organize the Rocky Mount club of the Carolina League, added some of his own money and served as a vice-president. The club won the pennant in 1975. He opened up his own realty company in 1966, serving his Rocky Mount neighbors.

As Buck looked over his baseball life, he admitted proudly:

"My greatest thrill was being inducted into the National Baseball Hall of Fame in Cooperstown, N. Y. on August 7, 1972.

"I was not 'bitter' by not being allowed to play in the major leagues. I just said, 'The time has not come.' I only wish I could have played in the 'big leagues' when I was young enough to show what I could do. When an offer was given me to join up, I was too old and I knew it."

Named to Hall of Fame, 1972.

FREDERICK CHARLES (FRED) LINDSTROM

Born November 21, 1905, at Chicago, Ill.

Died October 4, 1981, at Chicago, Ill.

Height, 5.11. Weight, 170.

Threw and batted righthanded.

Father of Charlie Lindstrom, former major league catcher.

Manager, Knoxville, Southern Association, 1940-41; Fort Smith, Western Association, 1942; coach, Northwestern University, 1951-1954.

Named to Hall of Fame, 1976.

Year	Club	League	Pos.	G.	AB.	R.	H.	2B.	3B.	HR.	RBI.	B.A.	PO.	A.	E.	F.A.
1922—Toledo	A. A.		3B	18	23	3	7	2	0	0	1	.304	4	12	3	.842
1923—Toledo	A. A.		3-SS-2B	147	581	77	157	21	7	1	39	.270	375	461	★42	.952
1924—New York	Nat.		2B-3B	52	79	19	20	3	1	0	4	.253	27	45	7	.911
1925—New York	Nat.		3B-2B-SS	104	356	43	102	15	12	4	33	.287	123	147	12	.957
1926—New York	Nat.		3B	140	543	90	164	19	9	9	76	.302	151	251	16	.962
1927—New York	Nat.		3B-OF	138	562	107	172	36	8	7	58	.306	182	181	12	.968
1928—New York	Nat.		3B	153	646	99	★231	39	9	14	107	.358	145	★340	21	★.958
1929—New York	Nat.		3B	130	549	99	175	23	6	15	91	.319	134	258	14	.966
1930—New York	Nat.		3B	148	609	127	231	39	7	22	106	.379	132	291	21	.953
1931—New York	Nat.		OF	78	303	38	91	12	6	5	36	.300	150	4	4	.975
1932—New York(a)	Nat.		3B-OF	144	595	83	161	26	5	15	92	.271	326	33	10	.973
1933—Pittsburgh	Nat.		OF	138	538	70	167	39	10	5	55	.310	388	7	5	.988
1934—Pittsburgh(b)	Nat.		OF	97	383	59	111	24	4	4	49	.290	181	8	2	.990
1935—Chicago(c)	Nat.		OF-3B	90	342	49	94	22	4	3	62	.275	167	40	7	.967
1936—Brooklyn	Nat.		OF	26	106	12	28	4	0	0	10	.264	51	4	1	.982
Major League Totals—13 Years				1438	5611	895	1747	301	81	103	779	.311	2157	1609	132	.966

aSent to Pittsburgh Pirates in three-cornered deal in which New York Giants obtained Pitcher Glenn Spencer from Pirates and Outfielder George Davis from Philadelphia Phillies; Phils secured Outfielder Gus Dugas from Pirates and Outfielder Chick Fullis from Giants, December 12, 1932.

bTraded with Pitcher Larry French to Chicago Cubs for Pitchers Guy Bush and Jim Weaver and Outfielder Babe Herman, November 22, 1934.

cReleased, and signed with Brooklyn Dodgers, January 26, 1936.

WORLD SERIES RECORD

Year	Club	League	Pos.	G.	AB.	R.	H.	2B.	3B.	HR.	RBI.	B.A.	PO.	A.	E.	F.A.
1924—New York	Nat.		3B	7	30	1	10	2	0	0	4	.333	7	18	0	1.000
1935—Chicago	Nat.		OF-3B	4	15	0	3	1	0	0	0	.200	8	1	1	.900
World Series Totals—2 Years				11	45	1	13	3	0	0	4	.289	15	19	1	.971

JOHN HENRY LLOYD

Born April 25, 1884, at Palatka, Fla.

Died March 19, 1965, at Atlantic City, N.J.

Height, 5.11. Weight, 180.

Threw right and batted lefthanded.

John Henry Lloyd was called "The Shovel" for his ability to dig tough grounders out of the dirt. Many times his glove spewed cascading dirt and dust as the willowy shortstop clamped the ball with his long fingers and whipped the throw to first base. How good was he?

Judy Johnson, another Hall of famer, said that while he was scouting for the Philadelphia Athletics, Connie Mack told him; "If I had a bag with Honus Wagner in it and also John Henry Lloyd, and I reached in and pulled one out, whichever one it was I'd be perfectly satisfied."

Wagner said he was proud to be likened to Lloyd, "the Black Honus Wagner," whom he knew from competing against him in exhibitions. Wagner's exact quote was:" After I saw him, I felt honored that they should name such a great ballplayer after me."

Noted for his smooth baseball swing, Lloyd was a superior batter. In his prime he always was among the leaders, if not the batting champion himself. To Lloyd is given an accolade reserved for only a few ballplayers, that he was recognized equally for his fielding and his hitting, and especially was rated superior in both. Only a few, like Tris Speaker, Joe DiMaggio, Mickey Cochrane, Charley Gehringer, Wagner, Oscar Charleston and Willie Mays, are rated equally as superior fielders and hitters.

In fact, when pinned down, Mack told Johnson that Lloyd was the "greatest shortstop that he'd ever seen." And Connie had seen them all since 1886.

This is the caliber of John Henry Lloyd.

A revelation by Johnson lets us peek into the world of Negro ball vs. the major leaguers:

"We were playing in Cuba against the Detroit club and Ty Cobb, who later refused to face a Negro club, was the star as he always was. He took off for second base, but the ball was there before him and Lloyd put the tag on him. Cobb was surprised to find the ball waiting. What he didn't know and what we tried to teach the majors but they wouldn't listen, and haven't to this day, was we put special emphasis on getting the ball to the fielder BEFORE the runner arrived. We had catchers with great arms—they HAD to have them—and we worked our pickoff and man-on-base motions with quickness so that the runner couldn't take off as easily and the ball could get to the catcher quicker and he could get the ball to the fielder quicker. This part of inside ball was our everyday game—concentraton on the tricks of the trade that lowered the odds.

"Anyway, the second time Cobb got on. Bruce Petway, our catcher and a man who should be in the Hall of Fame, along with quite a few others, fired the ball on the dime to Lloyd and Cobb came in trying to knock Lloyd into center field. Lloyd tagged him and neatly sidestepped Cobb, nudging him into center field in the process. Lloyd could do anything, absolutely anything as a shortstop. Cobb was fit to be tied. The last time he got on, he took off again, but Petway had the ball down so fast, Cobb stopped half way and tried to go back to first. On a first baseman's fake, Cobb stopped and Lloyd, who'd followed him, tagged him out easily.

"This is what led Cobb to skip all Detroit exhibitions which were scheduled against Negro teams. He couldn't take the humiliation."

This is no real knock against Cobb, because he not only was a product of his environment, but such a fierce prideful competitor that he wanted no part of unnecessary embarrassment, and Caribbean exhibitions were merely club ploys for income. Such exhibition play as this was why Landis put the clamp on complete major league teams facing Negro league clubs in 1923. Unnecessary embarrassment.

But Lloyd loved the competition and found enough major leaguers who would play against him in his prime or against the clubs he later managed and played for, and they recognized his greatness.

Lloyd started out as a catcher in 1905, played shortstop for 14 years and in 1919, when the years began to take their toll on his legs, he turned to the old-folks home at first base, and made fewer and fewer appearances at short.

In 1905, Lloyd was a catcher for the Macon (Ga.) Acmes, but because the club was too poor to buy the full catching equipment, John Henry took too many foul shots to his unmasked face. When he reported to his next club, Philadelphia's Cuban X Giants, he had retreated to second base. He was a teammate of Charley Grant. John McGraw's "Tokohama" of 1901. He left to join the Chicago Leland Giants in 1910 and the next year shifted to the new Lincoln Giants of New York. This powerful club topped the Phillies, 9-2, drubbing Grover Cleveland Alexander in the bargain.

But along the way, the Lincoln Giants bowled over everything in the Negro leagues as well, which raised the ire of Rube Foster, who saw his Chicago American Giants humbled in both the home and away series against them.

In resentment Foster lured the big stars from Lincoln by paying them the top dollar of that period. Four went west, including Lloyd, who said, "Wherever the money was, that's where I was."

Lloyd played four years with the powerful Giants. He was cleanup hitter in a lineup that included Oscar Charleston, Bingo DeMoss, Bruce Petway and Louis Santop and pitchers Dick Redding, Frank Wickware and Smokey Joe Williams. Lloyd earned $250 per month while he was the kingpin of this superstar lineup.

In 1918 during World War I, Lloyd joined the working force at the Army Quartermasters depot in Chicago. Deserting Foster's team, rather than make his southern winter junket, riled the patriarch, but he let Lloyd go without a battle. John Henry then joined the Brooklyn Royal Giants as manager and it was at this period he recognized the spring in his legs was fast departing and he split his duties between short and first base. A legend in his own time, he continued to be sought by other clubs for his ever solid bat, experience, drawing ability and remaining hint of glove magic.

In addition to the Brooklyn Royal Giants, he was a player for or manager of (or both) the Columbus (O.) Buckeyes, the Bacharach Giants and Hilldale clubs, the Lincoln Giants, Leland Giants, Chicago American Giants and the New York Black Yankees.

As Judy Johnson related to us when questioned about his impressions of the men named to the Hall of Fame, "Lloyd was the kind of manager who would soft-sell you into doing what you had to do—he made us feel that anything that had to be done, you just did it. It helped me in my career in clutch situations. John Henry was soft-spoken and kind off the field as a player and as a manager, but on the field, he was all business and no one got in his way. They were sorry if they tried."

As the legendary Cum Posey, owner of the powerful Homestead Grays, said, "Lloyd is the Jekyll and Hyde of baseball—a fierce competitor on the field and as a manager against the opposition, but a gentle, considerate man off the field and always kind to his own players."

Though a product of the rough and roaring 1910s and 1920s, when there was a general hell-bent zest for living, drinking and carousing, Lloyd was tangential to the roar, springing from it but taking no part as he lived his own life in a peaceful, law-abiding, continent manner, with no drinking or cursing and a smile for everyone—truly a happy man. As Mrs. Lloyd remembered, "He laughed easily and everyone was glad to see him."

He spent his retirement years, from 1931 to the date of his death in 1965, in service to others. He played semi-pro ball around his adopted city (Atlantic City) until he was 58 years old. He was a janitor in that city's Post Office for a while and then swung over to janitorial duties in the Atlantic City school system, where he became the "grandfather" to all the youngsters. A local park was named in his honor in 1949, two years after Robinson entered the majors. In "Only the Ball Was White," by Robert W. Peterson, an excellent historian of the Negro leagues, Lloyd's words at the dedication have been preserved:

"I do not consider that I was born at the wrong time. I felt it was the right time, for I had a chance to prove the ability of our race in this sport, and because many of us did our very best to uphold the traditions of the game and of the world of sport, we have given the Negro a greater opportunity now to be accepted into the major leagues with other Americans."

Peterson also dug up the quote of a white newspaperman, a sportswriter in St. Louis in 1938, who was asked to name the player he judged the best in baseball history. The reply:

"If you mean in Organized Baseball," the writer said, "my answer would be Babe Ruth; but if you mean in all baseball, organized and unorganized, the answer would have to be a colored man named John Henry Lloyd."

Lloyd was named to the Hall of Fame in 1977.

MICHAEL STEPHEN (MICKEY) LOLICH

Born September 12, 1940, at Portland, Ore.

Height, 6;01. Weight, 207.

Threw left and batted righthanded.

Holds American League record for most strikeouts by lefthanded pitcher, lifetime (2,679).
Shares American League record for most consecutive years, 100 or more strikeouts (13).

Year Club	League	G.	IP.	W.	L.	Pct.	H.	R.	ER.	SO.	BB.	ERA.
1959—Knoxville	Sally	11	67	3	6	.333	51	29	19	42	53	2.55
1959—Durham	Carolina	9	37	1	2	.333	27	22	17	24	45	4.14
1960—Knoxville	Sally	4	15	0	1	.000	17	13	13	14	20	7.63
1960—Durham	Carolina	25	113	5	10	.333	111	71	51	135	87	4.06
1961—Knoxville	Sally	15	72	3	5	.375	49	50	41	93	76	5.10
1961—Durham	Carolina	18	102	5	5	.500	92	42	34	102	73	2.99
1962—Denver	Am. Assoc.	9	12	0	4	.000	26	24	22	10	10	16.50
1962—Portland	P. Coast	23	130	10	9	.526	116	66	57	138	57	3.95
1963—Detroit	American	33	144	5	9	.357	145	64	57	103	56	3.56
1963—Syracuse	Int'national	6	22	0	2	.000	21	11	6	21	10	2.45
1964—Detroit	American	44	232	18	9	.667	196	88	84	192	64	3.26
1965—Detroit	American	43	244	15	9	.625	216	103	93	226	72	3.43
1966—Detroit	American	40	204	14	14	.500	204	119	108	173	83	4.76
1967—Detroit	American	31	204	14	13	.519	165	71	69	174	56	3.04
1968—Detroit	American	39	220	17	9	.654	178	84	78	197	65	3.19
1969—Detroit	American	37	281	19	11	.633	214	111	98	271	122	3.14
1970—Detroit	American	40	273	14	★19	.424	272	125	●115	230	109	3.79
1971—Detroit	American	45	★376	★25	14	.641	★336	133	122	★308	92	2.92
1972—Detroit	American	41	327	22	14	.611	282	100	91	250	74	2.50
1973—Detroit	American	42	309	16	15	.516	315	143	131	214	79	3.82
1974—Detroit	American	41	308	16	★21	.432	310	155	142	202	78	4.15
1975—Detroit (a)	American	32	241	12	18	.400	260	119	101	139	64	3.77
1976—New York (b)	National	31	193	8	13	.381	184	83	69	120	52	3.22
1977—						(Did Not Play)						
1978—San Diego	National	20	35	2	1	.667	30	6	6	13	11	1.54
1979—San Diego	National	27	49	0	2	.000	59	33	26	20	22	4.78
American League Totals—13 Years		508	3363	207	175	.542	3093	1415	1289	2679	1014	3.45
National League Totals—3 Years		78	277	10	16	.385	273	122	101	153	85	3.28
Major League Totals—16 Years		586	3640	217	191	.532	3366	1537	1390	2832	1099	3.44

Signed as free agent by Detroit Tigers' organization, June 30, 1958.

aTraded with Outfielder Billy Baldwin to New York Mets for Outfielder Rusty Staub and Pitcher Bill Laxton, December 12, 1975.

bPlaced on voluntarily retired list, February 7, 1977; signed by San Diego Padres, February 2, 1978 (after being declared free agent by Commissioner, January 5, 1978).

CHAMPIONSHIP SERIES RECORD

Year Club	League	G.	IP.	W.	L.	Pct.	H.	R.	ER.	SO.	BB.	ERA.
1972—Detroit	American	2	19	0	1	.000	14	4	3	10	5	1.42

WORLD SERIES RECORD

Shares records by hitting home run, first series at-bat, October 3, 1968, third inning; most games won, series (3), 1968.

Year Club	League	G.	IP.	W.	L.	Pct.	H.	R.	ER.	SO.	BB.	ERA.
1968—Detroit	American	3	27	3	0	1.000	20	5	5	21	6	1.67

—DID YOU KNOW—

That former Detroit pitcher Mickey Lolich is the only player in big-league history to hit his only career home run in the World Series? Lolich connected in the second game of the 1968 classic against St. Louis.

ERNEST NATALI (ERNIE) LOMBARDI
(Schnoz)

Born April 6, 1908, at Oakland, Calif.
Died September 26, 1977, at Santa Cruz, Calif.
Height, 6.03. Weight, 230.
Threw and batted righthanded.

Shares major league record for most doubles, game (4), May 8, 1935, first game.
Named National League Most Valuable Player, 1938.
Named to Hall of Fame, 1986.

Year Club	League	Pos.	G.	AB.	R.	H.	2B.	3B.	HR.	RBI.	B.A.	PO.	A.	E.	F.A.
1926—Oakland	P. C.	C	4	6	.....	2	1	0	0	.....	.333	8	0	0	1.000
1927—Oakland	P. C.	C	16	20	2	3	0	0	1	6	.150	12	4	0	1.000
1927—Ogden	Utah-Idaho	C	50	186	29	74	16	1	4	.....	.398	183	40	9	.961
1928—Oakland	P. C.	C	120	318	39	120	27	3	8	47	.377	257	47	15	.953
1929—Oakland	P. C.	C	164	516	70	189	36	3	24	109	.366	★521	★95	16	.975
1930—Oakland	P. C.	C	146	473	76	175	32	4	22	105	.370	★563	★105	17	.975
1931—Brooklyn(a)	Nat.	C	73	182	20	54	7	1	4	23	.297	218	23	4	.984
1932—Cincinnati	Nat.	C	118	413	43	125	22	9	11	68	.303	288	76	★14	.963
1933—Cincinnati	Nat.	C	107	350	30	99	21	1	4	47	.283	223	52	8	.972
1934—Cincinnati	Nat.	C	132	417	42	127	19	4	9	62	.305	383	61	5	.989
1935—Cincinnati	Nat.	C	120	332	36	114	23	3	12	64	.343	298	49	6	.983
1936—Cincinnati	Nat.	C	121	387	42	129	23	2	12	68	.333	330	54	●15	.962
1937—Cincinnati	Nat.	C	120	368	41	123	22	1	9	59	.334	333	58	11	.973
1938—Cincinnati	Nat.	C	129	489	60	167	30	1	19	95	★.342	512	73	9	●.985
1939—Cincinnati	Nat.	C	130	450	43	129	26	2	20	85	.287	536	63	★10	.984
1940—Cincinnati	Nat.	C	109	376	50	120	22	0	14	74	.319	397	46	5	★.989
1941—Cincinnati(b)	Nat.	C	117	398	33	105	12	1	10	60	.264	496	70	10	.983
1942—Boston(c)	Nat.	C	105	309	32	102	14	0	11	46	★.330	251	41	6	.980
1943—New York	Nat.	C	104	295	19	90	7	0	10	51	.305	296	36	10	.971
1944—New York	Nat.	C	117	373	37	95	13	0	10	58	.255	350	47	★13	.968
1945—New York	Nat.	C	115	368	46	113	7	1	19	70	.307	★425	49	8	.983
1946—New York	Nat.	C	88	238	19	69	4	1	12	39	.290	272	36	7	.978
1947—New York	Nat.	C	48	110	8	31	5	0	4	21	.282	86	11	2	.980
1948—Sacra.-Oak.	P. C.	C	102	284	25	75	13	0	11	55	.264	267	37	8	.974
Major League Totals—17 Years			1853	5855	601	1792	277	27	190	990	.306	5694	845	143	.979

aTraded to Cincinnati Reds with Third Baseman Walter Gilbert and Outfielder Babe Herman for Catcher Clyde Sukeforth, Second Baseman Tony Cuccinello and Third Baseman Joe Stripp, March 14, 1932.
bSold to Boston Braves, February 7, 1942.
cTraded to New York Giants for Catcher Hugh Poland and Second Baseman Connie Ryan, April 27, 1943.

WORLD SERIES RECORD

Year Club	League	Pos.	G.	AB.	R.	H.	2B.	3B.	HR.	RBI.	B.A.	PO.	A.	E.	F.A.
1939—Cincinnati	Nat.	C	4	14	0	3	0	0	0	2	.214	22	1	1	.958
1940—Cincinnati	Nat.	C-PH	2	3	0	1	1	0	0	0	.333	4	0	0	1.000
World Series Totals—2 Years			6	17	0	4	1	0	0	2	.235	26	1	1	.964

ALFONSO RAMON (AL) LOPEZ
(Senor)

Born August 20, 1908, at Tampa, Fla.
Height, 5.11. Weight, 180.
Threw and batted righthanded.

Holds National League record for most games as catcher (1,861).
Manager, Indianapolis, (American Association), 1948-50; Cleveland Indians, 1951-56; Chicago White Sox, 1957-65 and 1968-69.
Named to Hall of Fame, 1977.

Year Club	League	Pos.	G.	AB.	R.	H.	2B.	3B.	HR.	RBI.	B.A.	PO.	A.	E.	F.A.
1925—Tampa	Fla. St.	C	51	134	13	30	6	0	0	0	.224	210	41	10	.962
1926—Tampa	Fla. St.	C	116	419	64	132	18	12	1	....	.315	★645	120	★30	.962

Year Club League	Pos.	G.	AB.	R.	H.	2B.	3B.	HR.	RBI.	B.A.	PO.	A.	E.	F.A.
1927—Jacksonville.........So'East	C	128	416	58	115	10	10	3	....	276	*519	108	20	.969
1928—Macon....................Sally	C	114	389	67	127	14	8	14	64	.326	*472	*102	*18	.970
1928—Brooklyn...............Nat.	C	3	12	0	0	0	0	0	0	.000	9	0	0	1.000
1929—Atlanta ....South.	C	143	490	70	160	21	9	10	85	.327	411	101	*15	.972
1930—Brooklyn...............Nat.	C	128	421	60	130	20	4	6	57	.309	465	66	9	.983
1931—Brooklyn...............Nat.	C	111	360	38	97	13	4	0	40	.269	390	69	11	.977
1932—Brooklyn...............Nat.	C	126	404	44	111	18	6	1	43	.275	456	*82	13	.976
1933—Brooklyn...............Nat.	C	126	372	39	112	11	4	3	41	.301	449	*84	5	.991
1934—Brooklyn...............Nat.	C-3-2B	140	439	58	120	23	2	7	54	.273	542	62	11	.982
1935—Brooklyn (a) ....Nat.	C	128	379	50	95	12	4	3	39	.251	472	65	11	.980
1936—Boston.................Nat.	C	128	426	46	103	12	4	8	50	.242	447	*107	14	.975
1937—Boston.................Nat.	C	105	334	31	68	11	1	3	38	.205	342	83	7	.984
1938—Boston.................Nat.	C	71	236	19	63	6	1	1	14	.267	240	42	3	.989
1939—Boston.................Nat.	C	131	412	32	104	22	1	8	49	.252	424	72	7	.986
1940—Bos. (b)-Pitts. ......Nat.	C	95	293	35	80	9	3	3	41	.273	343	62	4	*.990
1941—Pittsburgh............Nat.	C	114	317	33	84	9	1	5	43	.265	345	54	8	.980
1942—Pittsburgh............Nat.	C	103	289	17	74	8	2	1	26	.256	327	53	2	.995
1943—Pittsburgh............Nat.	●C-3B	118	372	40	98	9	4	1	39	.263	378	67	5	●.989
1944—Pittsburgh............Nat.	C	115	331	27	76	12	1	1	34	.230	372	52	7	*.984
1945—Pittsburgh............Nat.	C	91	243	22	53	8	0	0	18	.218	326	38	3	.992
1946—Pittsburgh (c) ......Nat.	C	56	150	13	46	2	0	1	12	.307	173	30	3	.985
1947—Cleveland............Amer.	C	61	126	9	33	1	0	0	14	.262	144	28	0	1.000
1948—Indianapolis ....A. A.	C	43	127	13	34	4	1	2	21	.268	184	23	8	.963
American League Totals—1 Year		61	126	9	33	1	0	0	14	.262	144	28	0	1.000
National League Totals—18 Years		1889	5790	604	1514	205	42	52	638	.261	6500	1088	123	.984
Major League Totals—19 Years		1950	5916	613	1547	206	42	52	652	.261	6644	1116	123	.984

aTraded with Pitcher Ray Benge, Second Baseman Tony Cuccinello and Infielder Bobby Reis to the Boston Braves for Pitcher Ed Brandt and Outfielder Randy Moore, December 12, 1935.
bTraded to Pittsburgh Pirates for Catcher Ray Berres and cash, June 14, 1940.
cTraded to Cleveland Indians for Outfielder Gene Woodling, December 7, 1946.

RECORD AS MAJOR LEAGUE MANAGER

Year Club League	Position	W.	L.	Year Club League	Position	W.	L.
1951—Cleveland................Amer.	Second	93	61	1960—Chicago ....Amer.	Third	87	67
1952—Cleveland................Amer.	Second	93	61	1961—Chicago ....Amer.	Fourth	86	76
1953—Cleveland................Amer.	Second	92	62	1962—Chicago ....Amer.	Fifth	85	77
1954—Cleveland................Amer.	First	111	43	1963—Chicago ....Amer.	Second	94	68
1955—Cleveland................Amer.	Second	93	61	1964—Chicago ....Amer.	Second	98	64
1956—Cleveland................Amer.	Second	88	66	1965—Chicago ....Amer.	Second	95	67
1957—Chicago ....Amer.	Second	90	64	1968—Chicago ....Amer.	Eighth	33	48
1958—Chicago ....Amer.	Second	82	72	1969—Chicago ....Amer.	Fifth (W)	8	9
1959—Chicago ....Amer.	First	94	60	Major League Totals—19 Years...................		1422	1026

WORLD SERIES RECORD

Year Club League	W.	L.	Year Club League	W.	L.
1954—Cleveland....................American	0	4	1959—Chicago ....American	2	4

ADOLFO (DOLF) LUQUE

Born August 4, 1890, at Havana, Cuba.

Died July 3, 1957, at Havana, Cuba.

Height, 5.10. Weight, 172.

Threw and batted righthanded.

Coach, New York Giants, 1935-36-37; 1941 through 1945; manager, Havana, Cuba, Florida International League, 1951; Mexicali, Mexican League, 1952; Nuevo Laredo, 1955; Merida, 1956.

Year Club League	G.	IP.	W.	L.	Pct.	H.	R.	ER.	SO.	BB.	ERA.
1913—Long Branch............................N.Y.-N.J.	28	189	22	5	.815	134	....	....	128	85	.....
1914—Boston..National	2	9	0	1	.000	5	5	4	1	4	4.00
1914—Jersey City ....International	14	108	2	10	.167	129	69	....	41	65	.....
1915—Boston..National	2	5	0	0	.000	6	3	2	3	4	3.60
1915—Toronto ....International	31	225	15	9	.625	190	89	....	133	100	.....
1916—Louisville ....A. A.	38	167	13	8	.619	147	....	49	100	68	2.64
1917—Louisville ....A. A.	19	79	2	4	.333	71	37	21	49	38	2.39
1918—Louisville ....A. A.	18	117	11	2	.846	97	35	26	64	39	2.00
1918—Cincinnati..................................National	12	83	6	3	.667	84	44	35	26	32	3.80
1919—Cincinnati..................................National	30	106	10	3	.769	89	35	31	40	36	2.63
1920—Cincinnati..................................National	37	208	13	9	.591	168	65	58	72	60	2.51
1921—Cincinnati..................................National	41	304	17	19	.472	318	132	114	102	64	3.38
1922—Cincinnati..................................National	39	261	13	*23	.361	266	123	96	79	72	3.31

Year Club	League	G.	IP.	W.	L.	Pct.	H.	R.	ER.	SO.	BB.	ERA.
1923—Cincinnati	National	41	322	*27	8	*.771	279	90	69	151	88	*1.93
1924—Cincinnati	National	31	219	10	15	.400	229	99	77	83	53	3.16
1925—Cincinnati	National	36	291	16	18	.471	263	109	85	140	78	*2.63
1926—Cincinnati	National	34	234	13	16	.448	231	123	89	83	77	3.42
1927—Cincinnati	National	29	231	13	12	.520	225	103	82	76	56	3.19
1928—Cincinnati	National	33	234	11	10	.524	254	112	93	72	84	3.58
1929—Cincinnati(a)	National	32	176	5	16	.238	213	103	88	43	56	4.50
1930—Brooklyn	National	31	199	14	8	.636	221	107	95	62	58	4.30
1931—Brooklyn(b)	National	19	103	7	6	.538	122	59	52	25	27	4.54
1932—New York	National	38	110	6	7	.462	128	53	49	32	32	4.01
1933—New York	National	35	80	8	2	.800	75	27	24	23	19	2.70
1934—New York	National	26	42	4	3	.571	54	20	18	12	17	3.86
1935—New York	National	2	4	1	0	1.000	1	0	0	2	1	0.00
Major League Totals—20 Years		550	3221	194	179	.520	3231	1412	1161	1130	918	3.24

aTraded to Brooklyn Dodgers for Pitcher Douglas McWeeney, February 10, 1930.
bReleased, January, 1932, and signed with New York Giants.

WORLD SERIES RECORD

Year Club	League	G.	IP.	W.	L.	Pct.	H.	R.	ER.	SO.	BB.	ERA.
1919—Cincinnati	National	2	5	0	0	.000	1	0	0	6	0	0.00
1933—New York	National	1	4⅓	1	0	1.000	2	0	0	5	2	0.00
World Series Totals—2 Years		3	9⅓	1	0	1.000	3	0	0	11	2	0.00

GREGORY MICHAEL (GREG) LUZINSKI
(The Bull)

Born November 22, 1950, at Chicago, Ill.

Height, 6.01. Weight, 217.

Threw and batted righthanded.

Brother of Richard and William Luzinski, former minor league outfielders.

Shares major league records for most consecutive games with a grand slam (2), June 8 and 9, 1984; fewest double plays by outfielder, season, 150 or more games (0), 1975.
Led National League in being hit by pitch with 10 in 1979 and tied for lead with 11 in 1976 and 6 in 1980.
Led National League batters in strikeouts with 140 in 1977.
Led National League in total bases with 322 in 1975.
Tied for National League lead in intentional bases on balls received with 17 in 1975.
Led Carolina League batters in strikeouts with 148 in 1969, Eastern League with 148 in 1970 and Pacific Coast League with 167 in 1971.
Led Carolina League in total bases with 255 in 1969, Eastern League with 287 in 1970 and Pacific Coast League with 319 in 1971.
Led Eastern League in being hit by pitch with 12 in 1970.
Led Eastern League first basemen in double plays with 119 in 1970 and Pacific Coast League first basemen with 129 in 1971.
Led Northern League first basemen in fielding percentage with .984 in 1968.
Named designated hitter on THE SPORTING NEWS American League All-Star Team, 1983.
Named outfielder on THE SPORTING NEWS National League All-Star Team, 1975 and 1977.
Named Eastern League Player of the Year, 1970.

Year Club	League	Pos.	G.	AB.	R.	H.	2B.	3B.	HR.	RBI.	B.A.	PO.	A.	E.	F.A.
1968—Huron	North.	1B-3B	57	212	22	55	5	0	*13	●43	.250	417	26	13	.971
1969—Raleigh-Durham	Carol.	1B	129	464	75	134	22	3	*31	*92	.289	1067	67	●17	.985
1970—Reading	East.	1B	*141	471	*94	153	25	5	33	*120	*.325	1122	65	*21	.983
1970—Philadelphia	Nat.	1B	8	12	0	2	0	0	0	0	.167	20	3	0	1.000
1971—Eugene	P. C.	1B	142	548	104	171	30	5	36	114	.312	1071	76	●19	.984
1971—Philadelphia	Nat.	1B	28	100	13	30	8	0	3	15	.300	247	34	1	.996
1972—Philadelphia	Nat.	OF-1B	150	563	66	158	33	5	18	68	.281	257	9	12	.957
1973—Philadelphia	Nat.	OF	161	610	76	174	26	4	29	97	.285	262	7	2	*.993
1974—Philadelphia	Nat.	OF	85	302	29	82	14	1	7	48	.272	146	10	3	.981
1975—Philadelphia	Nat.	OF	161	596	85	179	35	3	34	*120	.300	248	10	9	.966
1976—Philadelphia	Nat.	OF	149	533	74	162	28	1	21	95	.304	204	8	8	.964
1977—Philadelphia	Nat.	OF	149	554	99	171	35	3	39	130	.309	205	11	8	.964
1978—Philadelphia	Nat.	OF	155	540	85	143	32	2	35	101	.265	232	7	4	.984
1979—Philadelphia	Nat.	OF	137	452	47	114	23	1	18	81	.252	156	3	9	.946
1980—Philadelphia†	Nat.	OF	106	368	44	84	19	1	19	56	.228	137	2	1	.993
1981—Chicago	Amer.	DH	104	378	55	100	15	1	21	62	.265	0	0	0	.000
1982—Chicago	Amer.	DH	159	583	87	170	37	1	18	102	.292	0	0	0	.000
1983—Chicago	Amer.	1B	144	502	73	128	26	1	32	95	.255	6	1	0	1.000
1984—Chicago‡	Amer.	DH	125	412	47	98	13	0	13	58	.238	0	0	0	.000
National League Totals—11 Years			1289	4630	618	1299	253	21	223	811	.281	2114	104	57	.975
American League Totals—4 Years			532	1875	262	496	91	3	84	317	.265	6	1	0	1.000
Major League Totals—15 Years			1821	6505	880	1795	344	24	307	1128	.276	2120	105	57	.975

Selected by Philadelphia Phillies' organization in 1st round (11th player selected) of free-agent draft, June 7, 1968.
†Sold to Chicago White Sox, March 30, 1981.
‡Granted free agency, November 8, 1984.

CHAMPIONSHIP SERIES RECORD

Year Club League	Pos.	G.	AB.	R.	H.	2B.	3B.	HR.	RBI.	B.A.	PO.	A.	E.	F.A.
1976—Philadelphia .... Nat.	OF	3	11	2	3	2	0	1	3	.273	6	0	0	1.000
1977—Philadelphia .... Nat.	OF	4	14	2	4	1	0	1	2	.286	4	1	0	1.000
1978—Philadelphia .... Nat.	OF	4	16	3	6	0	1	2	3	.375	5	1	0	1.000
1980—Philadelphia .... Nat.	OF-PH	5	17	3	5	2	0	1	4	.294	5	0	1	.833
1983—Chicago .... Amer.	DH	4	15	0	2	1	0	0	0	.133	0	0	0	.000
Championship Series Totals—5 Years.....		20	73	10	20	6	1	5	12	.274	20	2	1	.957

WORLD SERIES RECORD

Year Club League	Pos.	G.	AB.	R.	H.	2B.	3B.	HR.	RBI.	B.A.	PO.	A.	E.	F.A.
1980—Philadelphia .... Nat.	DH-OF	3	9	0	0	0	0	0	0	.000	1	0	0	1.000

DENNIS PATRICK ALOYSIUS (DENNY) LYONS

Born March 12, 1866, at Cincinnati, O.

Died January 2, 1929, at W. Covington, Ky.

Height, 5.10. Weight, 185.

Threw and batted righthanded.

Year Club League	Pos.	G.	AB.	R.	H.	2B.	3B.	HR.	SB.	B.A.	PO.	A.	E.	F.A.
1885—Columbus............... South.	3B	93	344	47	79	10	8	5	....	.230	142	169	45	.874
1885—Providence........... Nat.	3B	4	16	3	2	1	0	0	....	.125	6	9	3	.833
1886—Atlanta .... South.	3B	76	308	65	95	12	12	9	29	.316	95	156	24	.912
1886—Philadelphia .... A.A.	3B	32	124	22	28	5	1	0	9	.226	(99-PO-A)		16	.861
1887—Philadelphia .... A.A.	3B	137	605	128	*284	43	16	6	118	.469	(464-PO-A)		53	.897
1888—Philadelphia .... A.A.	3B	111	446	98	145	21	5	6	45	.325	(353-PO-A)		44	.889
1889—Philadelphia .... A.A.	3B	131	507	131	171	34	4	10	11	.327	202	289	81	.858
1890—Philadelphia .... A.A.	3B	88	327	79	116	29	5	7	22	.351	134	202	34	.903
1891—St. Louis................. A.A.	3B	111	416	112	131	24	3	11	9	.314	140	232	59	.863
1892—New York............... Nat.	3B	108	391	71	102	15	9	8	18	.260	142	195	61	.847
1893—Pittsburgh.............. Nat.	3B	131	462	103	147	19	15	3	24	.318	206	287	41	.923
1894—Pittsburgh.............. Nat.	3B	72	254	51	79	11	5	4	17	.311	120	158	30	.902
1895—St. Louis................. Nat.	3B	33	131	23	38	5	0	2	4	.290	61	53	16	.877
1896—Pittsburgh.............. Nat.	3B	116	438	77	134	23	6	4	13	.306	167	200	46	.889
1897—Pittsburgh.............. Nat.	1B	36	131	22	27	7	4	2	5	.206	326	17	5	.987
1898—St. Louis................. West.	1B-3B	62	223	35	65	(T.B.-81)			4	.290	....	....	....	.969
1899—Wheeling .... Int.-St.	1B-3B	113	427	73	133	30	4	6	12	.311	401	246	46	.934
1900—Wheeling .... Int.-St.	3B	135	520	73	126	27	3	4	4	.242	260	351	41	.937
1901-2						(No record)								
1903—Beaumont.............. So. Tex.	1B	85	321	50	88	...	...	...	8	.274	879	23	17	*.982
American Assn. Totals—6 Years		610	2425	570	875	156	34	40	214	.361	....	....	....	.....
National League Totals—7 Years		500	1823	350	529	81	39	23	81	.290	....	....	....	.....
Major League Totals—13 Years.............		1110	4248	920	1404	237	73	63	295	.331	....	....	....	.....

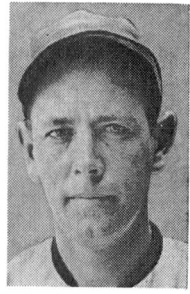

THEODORE AMAR (TED) LYONS

Born December 28, 1900, at Lake Charles, La.

Died July 25, 1986, at Sulphur, La.

Height 5.11. Weight, 200.

Threw right and batted right and lefthanded.

Shares major league record for most doubles, inning (2), July 28, 1935, first game, second inning.
Pitched 6-0 no-hit victory against Boston Red Sox, August 21, 1926.
Named by Baseball Writers' Association of America for THE SPORTING NEWS All-Star Major League Team, 1927.
Manager, Chicago White Sox, 1946 through 1948, coach, Detroit Tigers, 1949 through 1953; Brooklyn Dodgers, 1954; scout, Chicago White Sox, 1955 through 1966.
Named to Hall of Fame, 1955.

Year Club	League	G.	IP.	W.	L.	Pct.	H.	R.	ER.	SO.	BB.	ERA.
1923—Chicago	Amer.	9	23	2	1	.667	30	21	16	6	15	6.26
1924—Chicago	Amer.	41	216	12	11	.522	279	143	117	52	72	4.88
1925—Chicago	Amer.	43	263	●21	11	.656	274	111	95	45	83	3.25
1926—Chicago	Amer.	39	284	18	16	.529	268	108	95	51	106	3.01
1927—Chicago	Amer.	39	●308	●22	14	.611	●291	125	97	71	67	2.83
1928—Chicago	Amer.	39	240	15	14	.517	276	133	106	60	68	3.98
1929—Chicago	Amer.	37	259	14	20	.412	276	136	118	57	76	4.10
1930—Chicago	Amer.	42	★298	22	15	.595	★331	160	125	69	57	3.78
1931—Chicago	Amer.	22	101	4	6	.400	117	50	45	16	33	4.01
1932—Chicago	Amer.	33	231	10	15	.400	243	104	84	58	71	3.27
1933—Chicago	Amer.	36	228	10	★21	.323	260	142	111	74	74	4.38
1934—Chicago	Amer.	30	205	11	13	.458	249	138	111	53	66	4.87
1935—Chicago	Amer.	23	191	15	8	.652	194	79	64	54	56	3.02
1936—Chicago	Amer.	26	182	10	13	.435	227	115	104	48	45	5.14
1937—Chicago	Amer.	22	169	12	7	.632	182	86	78	45	45	4.15
1938—Chicago	Amer.	23	195	9	11	.450	238	93	80	54	52	3.69
1939—Chicago	Amer.	21	173	14	6	.700	162	71	53	65	26	2.76
1940—Chicago	Amer.	22	186	12	8	.600	188	85	67	72	37	3.24
1941—Chicago	Amer.	22	187	12	10	.545	199	87	77	63	37	3.71
1942—Chicago	Amer.	20	180	14	6	.700	167	52	42	50	26	★2.10
1943-44-45—Chicago	Amer.					(In Military Service)						
1946—Chicago	Amer.	5	43	1	4	.200	38	17	11	10	9	2.30
Major League Totals—21 Years		594	4162	260	230	.531	4489	2056	1696	1073	1121	3.67

CONNIE MACK
(Born Cornelius McGillicuddy.)

Born December 22, 1862, at East Brookfield, Mass.

Died February 8, 1956, at Germantown, Pa.

Height, 6.01. Weight, 150.

Threw and batted righthanded.

Father of Earle Mack, former major league infielder-catcher.

Manager, Pittsburgh N. L., 1894 through 1896; Milwaukee, Western League, 1897 through 1900; Philadelphia Athletics, 1901 through 1950.
Named to Hall of Fame in 1937 for service apart from playing the game.

Year Club	League	Pos.	G.	AB.	R.	H.	2B.	3B.	HR.	SB.	B.A.	PO.	A.	E.	F.A.
1884—Meriden	Conn. St.		....	....	....	....	...	...	..	....	......	....	....	...	......
1885—Hartford	N. E. Con. St.		....	....	....	....	...	...	..	....	......	....	....	...	......
1885—Newark	East.	C	1	4	1	2	0	0	0	....	.500	11	0	1	.917
1886—Hartford	East.	C	69	278	44	69	13	1	0	....	.248	419	133	27	.953
1886—Washington	Nat.	C	10	36	4	13	2	1	0	0	.361	88	22	8	.932
1887—Washington	Nat.	★C-O-2B	80	322	35	71	6	1	0	26	.220	★396	129	57	.902
1888—Washington	Nat.	★C-O-SS	85	300	49	56	5	6	3	31	.187	368	★155	48	.916
1889—Washington	Nat.	C-O-1B	97	386	51	113	16	1	0	26	.293	432	100	57	.903
1890—Buffalo	Play.	C	123	506	95	136	15	12	0	16	.269	488	147	41	★.939
1891—Pittsburgh	Nat.	C	71	271	41	57	9	0	0	5	.210	373	78	27	.944
1892—Pittsburgh	Nat.	C-OF	86	338	39	87	9	4	1	11	.257	427	135	28	.953
1893—Pittsburgh	Nat.	C	36	120	22	39	3	1	0	4	.325	129	48	13	.932
1894—Pittsburgh	Nat.	C	63	229	32	59	7	1	1	9	.258	274	59	22	.938
1895—Pittsburgh	Nat.	C	14	47	12	17	2	0	0	1	.362	56	20	7	.916
1896—Pittsburgh	Nat.	C-1B	30	116	7	24	4	1	0	0	.207	240	18	5	.981
1897—Milwaukee	West.	C-1B	27	73	12	21	1	1	0	4	.288	134	17	6	.962
National League Totals—10 Years			572	2165	292	536	63	16	5	113	.247	2783	764	272	.929
Players League Totals—1 Year			123	506	95	136	15	12	0	16	.268	488	147	41	.939
Major League Totals—11 Years			695	2671	387	672	78	28	5	129	.251	3271	911	313	.930

RECORD AS MAJOR LEAGUE MANAGER

Year Club	League	Position	W.	L.	Year Club	League	Position	W.	L.
1894—Pittsburgh	Nat.	Seventh	11	11	1904—Philadelphia	Amer.	Fifth	81	70
1895—Pittsburgh	Nat.	Seventh	71	61	1905—Philadelphia	Amer.	First	92	56
1896—Pittsburgh	Nat.	Sixth	66	63	1906—Philadelphia	Amer.	Fourth	78	67
1901—Philadelphia	Amer.	Fourth	74	62	1907—Philadelphia	Amer.	Second	88	57
1902—Philadelphia	Amer.	First	83	53	1908—Philadelphia	Amer.	Sixth	68	84
1903—Philadelphia	Amer.	Second	75	60	1909—Philadelphia	Amer.	Second	95	58

Year	Club	League	Position	W.	L.
1910—Philadelphia	Amer.		First	102	48
1911—Philadelphia	Amer.		First	101	50
1912—Philadelphia	Amer.		Third	90	62
1913—Philadelphia	Amer.		First	96	57
1914—Philadelphia	Amer.		First	99	53
1915—Philadelphia	Amer.		Eighth	43	109
1916—Philadelphia	Amer.		Eighth	36	117
1917—Philadelphia	Amer.		Eighth	55	98
1918—Philadelphia	Amer.		Eighth	52	76
1919—Philadelphia	Amer.		Eighth	36	104
1920—Philadelphia	Amer.		Eighth	48	106
1921—Philadelphia	Amer.		Eighth	53	100
1922—Philadelphia	Amer.		Seventh	65	89
1923—Philadelphia	Amer.		Sixth	69	83
1924—Philadelphia	Amer.		Fifth	71	81
1925—Philadelphia	Amer.		Second	88	64
1926—Philadelphia	Amer.		Third	83	67
1927—Philadelphia	Amer.		Second	91	63
1928—Philadelphia	Amer.		Second	98	55
1929—Philadelphia	Amer.		First	104	46
1930—Philadelphia	Amer.		First	102	52
1931—Philadelphia	Amer.		First	107	45
1932—Philadelphia	Amer.		Second	94	60
1933—Philadelphia	Amer.		Third	79	72
1934—Philadelphia	Amer.		Fifth	68	82
1935—Philadelphia	Amer.		Eighth	58	91
1936—Philadelphia	Amer.		Eighth	53	100
1937—Philadelphia	Amer.		Seventh	54	97
1938—Philadelphia	Amer.		Eighth	53	99
1939—Philadelphia	Amer.		Seventh	55	97
1940—Philadelphia	Amer.		Eighth	54	100
1941—Philadelphia	Amer.		Eighth	64	90
1942—Philadelphia	Amer.		Eighth	55	99
1943—Philadelphia	Amer.		Eighth	49	105
1944—Philadelphia	Amer.		†Fifth	72	82
1945—Philadelphia	Amer.		Eighth	52	98
1946—Philadelphia	Amer.		Eighth	49	105
1947—Philadelphia	Amer.		Fifth	78	76
1948—Philadelphia	Amer.		Fourth	84	70
1949—Philadelphia	Amer.		Fifth	81	73
1950—Philadelphia	Amer.		Eighth	52	102
Major League Totals—53 Years				3775	4025

WORLD SERIES RECORD

Year	Club	League	W.	L.
1905—Philadelphia	American		1	4
1910—Philadelphia	American		4	1
1911—Philadelphia	American		4	2
1913—Philadelphia	American		4	1
1914—Philadelphia	American		0	4
1929—Philadelphia	American		4	1
1930—Philadelphia	American		4	2
1931—Philadelphia	American		3	4

†Tied for position.

LELAND STANFORD (LARRY) MacPHAIL

Born February 3, 1890, at Cass City, Mich.

Died October 1, 1975, at Miami, Fla.

Leland Stanford (Larry) MacPhail was born during a Michigan storm and the clouds never moved from above his head. He exercised his vocal chords for the first time, at their top decible rating, of course, at Cass City, Mich., February 3, 1890. The world, in a general sense, and baseball, in a specific sense, never again were the same.

MacPhail used his computer brain to relieve ball club-holding banks of bad debts; to fill his own coffers in grandiose style; to overturn the living habits of fans and players all over the country with the introduction of night baseball; to confound scoffers and doom peddlers by introducing radio broadcasts of his club's games, home and road, and turning them into money-makers attendancewise; to make up his own rule book as he refereed college football games; to participate in a wild scheme to kidnap the Kaiser in Holland after World War I (he purloined the Kaiser's prized ashtray, at least); to build three championship clubs and leave all three in a state of combustion; to leave his first law firm because they would not make him a partner after six months (at age 21), and then to retire to his Maryland estate where he should have tasted the winey bucolic life, only to cause explosions in the varied worlds of race tracks, horse breeding, baseball (he never quit here), cancer and heart trouble, golf course architecture, computers (his mind was quicker), telephone companies (he was arrested for one of his protests), ways to cure hay, horse racing stables and growing apples.

He's best known in a baseball sense for building the Reds into a money-making club and a later champion; the Dodgers into a respectable winner and consistently solvent franchise, and the Yankees into the greatest money machine since the U.S. Treasury. For innovations, he introduced lights to major league parks and all but the Cubs followed suit, and he used radio broadcasts, against the advice of fellow owners and G.M.s, to increase the club income and also to lure more fans into the park. He could possibly hold the major league record for firing both personnel and punches, for most tears shed in both joy and anger, for setting the pace for spending baseball money to make more money for baseball, for most Page One stories in THE SPORTING NEWS on the most subjects, and for flambuoyancy, whole and entire.

Larry was a moving force, using every trick at his disposal to get jobs done. He could cajole one minute and castigate the next, but his results were constant—success in every case, whether it was a purchase, a trade or an idea. He had a vision of what results would follow his major improvements—lights, radio and better press accommodations. He was a financial master who could outfigure anyone or anything with the computer in his head. Compound totals and percentages were duck soup for this man who had stood at the head of every class he had attended, from grade school through college. He scarred many hides, fired many people and was unreasonable in many situations, but the man meant more money for the game, more success on the field—and that's the name of the pro baseball game.

MacPhail was named to the Hall of Fame in 1978.

BILL MADLOCK JR.

Born January 12, 1951, at Memphis, Tenn.
Height, 5.11. Weight, 206.
Threw and batted righthanded.

Hit three home runs in a game, June 28, 1987.
Tied for National League lead in grounding into double plays with 25 in 1977.
Tied for National League lead in being hit by pitch with 11 in 1976.
Led National League third basemen in errors with 24 in 1986.
Led Pacific Coast League in total bases with 268 in 1973.
Led Eastern League third basemen in errors with 33 in 1971.
Led New York-Pennsylvania League shortstops in putouts with 107 in 1970.
Named third baseman on THE SPORTING NEWS National League All-Star Team, 1975.

Year	Club	League	Pos.	G.	AB.	R.	H.	2B.	3B.	HR.	RBI.	B.A.	PO.	A.	E.	F.A.
1970—Geneva	NYP		SS-3B	66	234	44	63	5	1	6	29	.269	123	132	25	.911
1971—Pittsfield	East.		3-2-S-O	112	376	62	88	14	2	10	37	.234	100	214	34	.902
1972—Pittsfield	East.		2B-3B	42	131	29	43	13	3	4	26	.328	81	88	7	.960
1972—Denver	A. A.		3B-2B	26	61	7	13	3	0	1	9	.213	10	30	2	.952
1973—Spokane	P. C.		2-3-O	123	491	★119	166	22	7	22	90	.338	172	245	25	.943
1973—Texas†	Amer.		3B	21	77	16	27	5	3	1	5	.351	13	32	4	.918
1974—Chicago	Nat.		3B	128	453	65	142	21	5	9	54	.313	84	229	18	.946
1975—Chicago	Nat.		3B	130	514	77	182	29	7	7	64	★.354	79	250	20	.943
1976—Chicago‡	Nat.		3B	142	514	68	174	36	1	15	84	★.339	107	234	14	.961
1977—San Francisco	Nat.		3B-2B	140	533	70	161	28	1	12	46	.302	101	234	18	.949
1978—San Francisco	Nat.		2B-1B	122	447	76	138	26	3	15	44	.309	234	300	14	.974
1979—S. F.§-Pitts.	Nat.		3B-2B-1B	154	560	85	167	26	5	14	85	.298	209	297	14	.973
1980—Pittsburgh	Nat.		3B-1B	137	494	62	137	22	4	10	53	.277	159	217	7	.982
1981—Pittsburgh	Nat.		3B	82	279	35	95	23	1	6	45	★.341	50	147	9	.956
1982—Pittsburgh	Nat.		3B-1B	154	568	92	181	33	3	19	95	.319	114	267	18	.955
1983—Pittsburgh	Nat.		3B	130	473	68	153	21	0	12	68	★.323	59	193	11	.958
1984—Pittsburgh	Nat.		3B-1B	103	403	38	102	16	0	4	44	.253	76	176	15	.944
1985—Pitts. x-L.A.	Nat.		3B-1B	144	513	69	141	27	1	12	56	.275	155	243	19	.954
1986—Los Angeles	Nat.		3B-1B	111	379	38	106	17	0	10	60	.280	79	171	26	.906
1987—Los Angeles y	Nat.		3B-1B	21	61	5	11	1	0	3	7	.180	8	23	3	.912
1987—Detroit z	Amer.		1B-3B	87	326	56	91	17	0	14	50	.279	167	12	2	.989
American League Totals—2 Years				108	403	72	118	22	3	15	55	.293	180	44	6	.974
National League Totals—14 Years				1698	6191	848	1890	326	31	148	805	.305	1514	2981	206	.956
Major League Totals—15 Years				1806	6594	920	2008	348	34	163	860	.305	1694	3025	212	.957

Selected by St. Louis Cardinals' organization in 14th round of free-agent draft, June 5, 1969.
Selected by Washington Senators' organization in secondary phase of free-agent draft, January 17, 1970.
†Traded with Infielder-Outfielder Vic Harris to Chicago Cubs for Pitcher Ferguson Jenkins, October 25, 1973.
‡Traded with Infielder Rob Sperring to San Francisco Giants for Outfielder Bobby Murcer, Infielder Steve Onti-veros and Pitcher Andrew Muhlstock, February 11, 1977.
§Traded with Third Baseman Lenny Randle and Pitcher Dave Roberts to Pittsburgh Pirates for Pitchers Ed Whitson, Fred Breining and Al Holland, June 28, 1979.
xTraded to Los Angeles Dodgers for three players to be named later, August 31, 1985; Pittsburgh Pirates acquired Outfielder R. J. Reynolds, September 3, 1985, and Outfielder Cecil Espy and First Baseman Sid Bream, September 9, 1985, to complete deal.
yReleased, May 29, 1987; signed by Detroit Tigers, June 4, 1987.
zGranted free agency, November 9, 1987.

CHAMPIONSHIP SERIES RECORD

Year	Club	League	Pos.	G.	AB.	R.	H.	2B.	3B.	HR.	RBI.	B.A.	PO.	A.	E.	F.A.
1979—Pittsburgh	Nat.		3B	3	12	1	3	0	0	1	2	.250	1	7	0	1.000
1985—Los Angeles	Nat.		3B	6	24	5	8	1	0	3	7	.333	6	9	0	1.000
1987—Detroit	Amer.		DH	1	5	0	0	0	0	0	0	.000	0	0	0	.000
Championship Series Totals—3 Years				10	41	6	11	1	0	4	9	.268	7	16	0	1.000

WORLD SERIES RECORD

Year	Club	League	Pos.	G.	AB.	R.	H.	2B.	3B.	HR.	RBI.	B.A.	PO.	A.	E.	F.A.
1979—Pittsburgh	Nat.		3B	7	24	2	9	1	0	0	3	.375	3	10	1	.929

—DID YOU KNOW—

That Philadelphia A's Manager Connie Mack piloted the American League to a 4-2 victory over John McGraw's National League squad in the first All-Star Game in 1933?

While Henry Aaron never hit more than 47 home runs in one big-league season, the righthanded-hitting slugger rode remarkable consistency and career longevity to a place atop the all-time homer chart.

Fiery Ty Cobb didn't exactly endear himself to opponents with his spikes-high baserunning technique, but his consummate baseball skills were acknowledged by friend and foe alike. Cobb's .367 lifetime average is the majors' best mark.

Three-time American League MVP Joe DiMaggio, best known for his 56-game hitting streak and .325 lifetime batting average, was grace personified in the New York Yankees' outfield.

A chaw of tobacco was a Nellie Fox trademark—and so was excellent bat control. A tough, pesky hitter who seldom struck out, the Chicago White Sox's longtime sparkplug also was sound afield. He won league MVP honors in 1959.

Shoeless Joe Jackson batted .408 for Cleveland in his first full year in the major leagues and followed up with .395 and .373 averages in the next two seasons before eventually being traded to the Chicago White Sox.

A fearsome sight in his cutoff uniform top, Ted Kluszewski put his bulging biceps to good use for the Cincinnati Reds. In one three-year stretch in the 1950s, big Klu hammered 136 home runs and drove in 362 runs.

After stints with the Cleveland Indians and the Kansas City A's, Roger Maris had reason to smile in a Yankee uniform. He was the American League's MVP in 1960 and 1961, smashing Babe Ruth's 60-homer mark in the latter season.

Stan Musial (left) of the St. Louis Cardinals and Ted Williams of the Boston Red Sox combined for 13 batting titles in the 1940s and 1950s and finished with career averages of .331 and .344, respectively.

Detroit's Hal Newhouser was at the top of his game from 1944 through 1946, winning a total of 80 games. In 1945, he compiled a 25-9 record, posted a 1.81 ERA and notched two World Series victories against the Chicago Cubs.

Minnesota's Tony Oliva burst upon the major leagues in scintillating fashion, copping the batting championship in his rookie year of 1964 and winning the crown again in 1965. The Twins' standout added a third title in 1971.

No one has ever captured the fancy of the baseball public quite like George Herman (Babe) Ruth, whose extraordinary slugging skills and engaging personality will forever make his name synonymous with the game itself.

Riggs Stephenson batted .362 and .367 for the Chicago Cubs in 1929 and 1930 but was overshadowed by outfield teammates Hack Wilson and Kiki Cuyler. Stephenson wound up with a .336 career average in the majors.

MICKEY CHARLES MANTLE

Born October 20, 1931, at Spavinaw, Okla.

Height, 6.00. Weight, 201.

Threw right and batted left and righthanded.

Shares major league record for most consecutive home runs (4), July 4 and 6, 1962.

Led American League in bases on balls received with 113 in 1955, 146 in 1957, 129 in 1958, 126 in 1961 and 122 in 1962.

Hit three home runs in a game, May 13, 1955.

Won American League Triple Crown, 1956.

Named Most Valuable Player, American League, 1956-57-62.

Named Outstanding American League Player by THE SPORTING NEWS, 1956-62.

Named Major League Player of the Year by THE SPORTING NEWS, 1956.

Named as outfielder on THE SPORTING NEWS All-Star Major League Teams, 1952-56-57.

Named as outfielder on THE SPORTING NEWS American League All-Star Team, 1961-62-64.

Named as outfielder on THE SPORTING NEWS American League All-Star fielding team, 1962.

Coach, New York Yankees, 1970 (part).

Named to Hall of Fame, 1974.

Year	Club	League	Pos.	G.	AB.	R.	H.	2B.	3B.	HR.	RBI.	B.A.	PO.	A.	E.	F.A.
1949—Independence		K-O-M	SS	89	323	54	101	15	7	7	63	.313	121	245	47	.886
1950—Joplin		W. A.	SS	137	519	★141	★199	30	12	26	136	★.383	202	340	55	.908
1951—New York		Amer.	OF	96	341	61	91	11	5	13	65	.267	135	4	6	.959
1951—Kansas City		A. A.	OF	40	166	32	60	9	3	11	50	.361	110	4	4	.966
1952—New York		Amer.	★OF-3B	142	549	94	171	37	7	23	87	.311	348	16	★14	.963
1953—New York		Amer.	OF-SS	127	461	105	136	24	3	21	92	.295	322	10	6	.982
1954—New York		Amer.	★OF-IF	146	543	★129	163	17	12	27	102	.300	334	★25	9	.976
1955—New York		Amer.	OF-SS	147	517	121	158	25	●11	37	99	.306	376	11	2	.995
1956—New York		Amer.	OF	150	533	★132	188	22	5	★52	★130	★.353	370	10	4	.990
1957—New York		Amer.	OF	144	474	★121	173	28	6	34	94	.365	324	6	7	.979
1958—New York		Amer.	OF	150	519	★127	158	21	1	★42	97	.304	331	5	8	.977
1959—New York		Amer.	OF	144	541	104	154	23	4	31	75	.285	366	7	2	★.995
1960—New York		Amer.	OF	153	527	★119	145	17	6	★40	94	.275	326	9	3	.991
1961—New York		Amer.	OF	153	514	●132	163	16	6	54	128	.317	351	6	6	.983
1962—New York		Amer.	OF	123	377	96	121	15	1	30	89	.321	214	4	5	.978
1963—New York		Amer.	OF	65	172	40	54	8	0	15	35	.314	99	2	1	.990
1964—New York		Amer.	OF	143	465	92	141	25	2	35	111	.303	217	3	5	.978
1965—New York		Amer.	OF	122	361	44	92	12	1	19	46	.255	165	3	6	.966
1966—New York		Amer.	OF	108	333	40	96	12	1	23	56	.288	172	2	0	1.000
1967—New York		Amer.	1B	144	440	63	108	17	0	22	55	.245	1089	91	8	.993
1968—New York		Amer.	1B	144	435	57	103	14	1	18	54	.237	1195	76	15	.988
Major League Totals—18 Years				2401	8102	1677	2415	344	72	536	1509	.298	6734	290	107	.985

WORLD SERIES RECORDS

Holds records for most runs (42), home runs (18), total bases (123), long hits (26), extra bases on long hits (64), runs batted in (40), bases on balls (43), strikeouts (54), games by outfielder (63), lifetime; most series by outfielder (12).

Year	Club	League	Pos.	G.	AB.	R.	H.	2B.	3B.	HR.	RBI.	B.A.	PO.	A.	E.	F.A.
1951—New York		Amer.	OF	2	5	1	1	0	0	0	0	.200	4	0	0	1.000
1952—New York		Amer.	OF	7	29	5	10	1	1	2	3	.345	16	0	0	1.000
1953—New York		Amer.	OF	6	24	3	5	0	0	2	7	.208	14	0	0	1.000
1955—New York		Amer.	OF-PH	3	10	1	2	0	0	1	1	.200	4	0	0	1.000
1956—New York		Amer.	OF	7	24	6	6	1	0	3	4	.250	18	1	0	1.000
1957—New York		Amer.	OF-PH	6	19	3	5	0	0	1	2	.263	8	0	1	.889
1958—New York		Amer.	OF	7	24	4	6	0	1	2	3	.250	16	0	0	1.000
1960—New York		Amer.	OF	7	25	8	10	1	0	3	11	.400	15	0	0	1.000
1961—New York		Amer.	OF	2	6	0	1	0	0	0	0	.167	2	0	0	1.000
1962—New York		Amer.	OF	7	25	2	3	1	0	0	0	.120	11	0	0	1.000
1963—New York		Amer.	OF	4	15	1	2	0	0	1	1	.133	6	0	0	1.000
1964—New York		Amer.	OF	7	24	8	8	2	0	3	8	.333	12	0	2	.857
World Series Totals—12 Years				65	230	42	59	6	2	18	40	.257	126	1	3	.977

—DID YOU KNOW—

That Hall of Famers Mickey Mantle and Jimmie Foxx are the only players in big-league history to hit 50 home runs and win a batting title in the same season? Mantle hit 52 homers and batted .353 in 1956 and Foxx slugged 50 homers while batting .349 in 1938.

HENRY EMMETT (HEINIE) MANUSH

Born July 20, 1901, at Tuscumbia, Ala.

Died May 12, 1971, at Sarasota, Fla.

Height, 6.00. Weight, 200.

Threw and batted lefthanded.

Manager, Rocky Mount, Piedmont League, 1940; Greensboro, Piedmont League, 1941-42; Roanoke, Piedmont League, 1943; Scranton, Eastern League, 1944; Martinsville, Carolina League, 1945; scout, Boston Braves, 1946; Pittsburgh Pirates, 1947-48; coach, Washington Senators, 1953-54; scout, Washington, 1961-62.

Named to Hall of Fame, 1964.

Year—Club	League	Pos.	G.	AB.	R.	H.	2B.	3B.	HR.	RBI.	B.A.	PO.	A.	E.	F.A.
1921—Edmonton	W. Can.	OF	83	327	52	105	17	9	★9	....	.321	141	12	7	.956
1922—Omaha	West.	OF	167	652	148	245	44	★20	20	....	.376	391	16	11	.974
1923—Detroit	Amer.	OF	109	308	59	103	20	5	4	54	.334	158	6	8	.953
1924—Detroit	Amer.	OF	120	422	83	122	24	8	9	68	.289	224	4	5	.979
1925—Detroit	Amer.	OF	99	278	46	84	14	3	5	47	.303	117	4	3	.976
1926—Detroit	Amer.	OF	136	498	95	188	35	8	14	86	★.378	283	7	10	.967
1927—Detroit(a)	Amer.	OF	151	593	102	177	31	18	6	90	.298	361	9	11	.971
1928—St. Louis	Amer.	OF	154	638	104	★241	●47	20	13	108	.378	355	6	3	.992
1929—St. Louis	Amer.	OF	142	574	85	204	●45	10	6	81	.355	293	11	4	.987
1930—St. L.(b)-Wash.	Amer.	OF	137	554	100	194	49	12	9	94	.350	255	10	3	.989
1931—Washington	Amer.	OF	146	616	110	189	41	11	6	70	.307	245	5	6	.977
1932—Washington	Amer.	OF	149	625	121	214	41	14	14	116	.342	318	6	4	.988
1933—Washington	Amer.	OF	153	658	115	★221	32	★17	5	95	.336	325	10	6	.982
1934—Washington	Amer.	OF	137	556	88	194	42	11	11	89	.349	293	5	6	.980
1935—Washington(c)	Amer.	OF	119	479	68	131	26	9	4	56	.273	251	8	4	.985
1936—Boston(d)	Amer.	OF	82	313	43	91	15	5	0	45	.291	110	3	4	.966
1937—Brooklyn	Nat.	OF	132	466	57	155	25	7	4	73	.333	187	7	6	.970
1938—Brook.(e)-Pitts	Nat.	OF	32	64	11	16	4	2	0	10	.250	29	1	0	1.000
1938—Toronto	Int.	OF	81	277	38	86	21	5	3	39	.310	121	7	4	.970
1939—Pittsburgh	Nat.	OF	10	12	0	0	0	0	0	1	.000	1	0	0	1.000
1939—Toronto	Int.	OF	66	228	32	55	9	3	0	19	.241	105	5	0	1.000
1940—Rocky Mount	Pied.	OF	32	107	13	30	9	2	1	16	.280	150	15	3	.982
1941—Greensboro	Pied.	OF	12	32	7	10	2	0	0	7	.313	....	....	...	......
1942—Greensboro	Pied.						(Less than ten games)								
1943—Roanoke	Pied.	PH	10	8	0	0	0	0	0	1	.000	0	0	0	.000
1944—Scranton	East.						(Less than ten games)								
1945—Martinsville	Car.						(Less than ten games)								
American League Totals—14 Years			1834	7112	1219	2353	462	151	106	1099	.331	3588	94	77	.980
National League Totals—3 Years			174	542	68	171	29	9	4	84	.315	217	8	6	.974
Major League Totals—17 Years			2008	7654	1287	2524	491	160	110	1183	.330	3805	102	83	.979

aTraded to St. Louis Browns with First Baseman Lu Blue for Pitcher Elam VanGilder, Infielder Chick Galloway and Outfielder Harry Rice, December 2, 1927.

bTraded to Washington Senators with Pitcher Alvin Crowder for Outfielder Goose Goslin, June 13, 1930.

cTraded to Boston Red Sox for Outfielders Roy Johnson and Carl Reynolds, December 17, 1935.

dReleased September 28, 1936 and signed with Brooklyn Dodgers, December 9, 1936.

eReleased to Pittsburgh Pirates on waivers, May, 1938.

WORLD SERIES RECORD

Year—Club	League	Pos.	G.	AB.	R.	H.	2B.	3B.	HR.	RBI.	B.A.	PO.	A.	E.	F.A.
1933—Washington	Amer.	OF	5	18	2	2	0	0	0	0	.111	10	0	0	1.000

JAMES WALTER VINCENT (RABBIT) MARANVILLE

Born November 11, 1891, at Springfield, Mass.

Died January 5, 1954, at New York, N. Y.

Height, 5.05. Weight, 155.

Threw and batted righthanded.

Holds major league records for most putouts by shortstop, lifetime (5,133); most years leading league in putouts by shortstop (6).

Shares major league record for most innings played, game (26), May 1, 1920.
Holds National League record for most chances accepted by shortstop, lifetime (12,471).
Shares National League record for most years played, shortstop (19).
Holds modern National League records for most putouts by shortstop, season (407), 1914; most assists by shortstop, lifetime (7,338).
Led National League shortstops in double plays, 1923, and National League second basemen in double plays, 1924.
Manager, Chicago Cubs, 1925 (part); Boston Braves, 1929 (part); Elmira, NYP League, 1936; Montreal, International League, 1937-38; Albany, Eastern League, 1939; Springfield, Eastern League, 1941.
Named to Hall of Fame, 1954.

Year	Club	League	Pos.	G.	AB.	R.	H.	2B.	3B.	HR.	RBI.	B.A.	PO.	A.	E.	F.A.
1911—New Bedford	N. Eng.		SS	117	422	41	96	17	9	2	....	.227	256	*345	61	.908
1912—New Bedford	N. Eng.		SS	122	452	65	128	22	4	4	....	.283	268	*441	42	*.944
1912—Boston	Nat.		SS	26	86	8	18	2	0	0	7	.209	46	97	11	.929
1913—Boston	Nat.		SS	143	571	68	141	13	8	2	44	.247	317	475	43	.949
1914—Boston	Nat.		SS	●156	586	74	144	23	6	4	72	.246	*407	*574	*65	.938
1915—Boston	Nat.		SS	149	509	51	124	23	6	2	47	.244	●391	486	55	.941
1916—Boston	Nat.		SS	155	604	79	142	16	13	4	36	.235	*386	*515	50	*.947
1917—Boston	Nat.		SS	142	561	69	146	19	13	3	41	.260	*341	474	46	.947
1918—Boston	Nat.		SS	11	38	3	12	0	1	0	3	.316	34	34	5	.932
1919—Boston	Nat.		SS	131	480	44	128	18	10	5	43	.267	*361	488	*53	.941
1920—Boston(a)	Nat.		SS	134	493	48	131	19	15	1	43	.266	354	462	45	.948
1921—Pittsburgh	Nat.		SS	153	612	90	180	25	12	1	70	.294	325	529	34	.962
1922—Pittsburgh	Nat.		SS-2B	155	*672	115	198	26	15	0	63	.295	419	512	36	.963
1923—Pittsburgh	Nat.		SS	141	581	78	161	19	9	1	41	.277	*332	*505	30	*.965
1924—Pittsburgh(b)	Nat.		2B	152	594	62	158	33	20	2	71	.266	365	*568	26	*.973
1925—Chicago(c)	Nat.		SS-2B	75	266	37	62	10	3	0	23	.233	162	261	20	.955
1926—Brooklyn	Nat.		SS-2B	78	234	32	55	8	5	0	24	.235	161	246	19	.955
1927—Rochester	Int.		SS	135	507	81	151	25	10	1	63	.298	329	440	24	.970
1927—St. Louis	Nat.		SS	9	29	0	7	1	0	0	1	.241	17	34	2	.962
1928—St. Louis(d)	Nat.		SS	112	366	40	88	14	10	1	34	.240	236	362	19	.969
1929—Boston	Nat.		SS	146	560	87	159	26	10	0	55	.284	319	536	35	.961
1930—Boston	Nat.		SS	142	558	85	157	26	8	2	43	.281	343	445	29	*.965
1931—Boston	Nat.		SS-2B	145	562	69	146	22	5	0	33	.260	289	453	41	.948
1932—Boston	Nat.		2B	149	571	67	134	20	4	0	37	.235	*402	473	22	*.975
1933—Boston	Nat.		2B	143	478	46	104	15	4	0	38	.218	362	384	22	.971
1934—Boston	Nat.		(Broke leg in spring exhibition game and did not play)													
1935—Boston	Nat.		2B	23	67	3	10	2	0	0	5	.149	32	46	3	.963
1936—Elmira	NYP		2B-SS	123	427	65	138	15	2	0	54	.323	322	319	28	.958
1939—Albany	East.		2B	6	17	3	2	0	0	0	2	.118	10	8	8	.692
Major League Totals—23 Years				2670	10078	1255	2605	380	177	28	874	.258	6401	8959	711	.956

aTraded to Pittsburgh Pirates for Outfielders Billy Southworth and Fred Nicholson, Infielder Walter Barbare, and cash, February, 1921.
bTraded to Chicago Cubs with Pitcher Wilbur Cooper and First Baseman Charley Grimm for Pitcher Vic Aldridge, First Baseman Al Niehaus and Second Baseman George Grantham, October 27, 1924.
cReleased to Brooklyn Dodgers on waivers, November, 1925.
dSold to Boston Braves with Outfielder George Harper, December 8, 1928.

WORLD SERIES RECORD

Year	Club	League	Pos.	G.	AB.	R.	H.	2B.	3B.	HR.	RBI.	B.A.	PO.	A.	E.	F.A.
1914—Boston	Nat.		SS	4	13	1	4	0	0	0	3	.308	7	13	1	.952
1928—St. Louis	Nat.		SS	4	13	2	4	1	0	0	0	.308	11	3	1	.933
World Series Totals—2 Years				8	26	3	8	1	0	0	3	.308	18	16	2	.944

JUAN ANTONIO MARICHAL

Born October 20, 1938, at Laguna Verde, Montecristi, Dominican Republic.

Height, 5.11. Weight, 190.

Threw and batted righthanded.

Pitched 1-0 no-hit victory against Houston Colt .45s, June 15, 1963.
Named pitcher on THE SPORTING NEWS National League All-Star Teams, 1963-65-66-68.
Named to Hall of Fame, 1983.

Year	Club	League	G.	IP.	W.	L.	Pct.	H.	R.	ER.	SO.	BB.	ERA.
1958—Michigan City	Midwest	35	*245	*21	8	.724	*200	69	51	246	50	*1.87
1959—Springfield	Eastern	37	*271	*18	13	.581	238	85	72	*208	47	*2.39
1960—Tacoma	P. C.	18	139	11	5	.688	116	52	48	121	34	3.11
1960—San Francisco	National	11	81	6	2	.750	59	29	24	58	28	2.67
1961—San Francisco	National	29	185	13	10	.565	183	88	80	124	48	3.89
1962—San Francisco	National	37	263	18	11	.621	233	112	98	153	90	3.35
1963—San Francisco	National	41	*321	●25	8	.758	259	102	86	248	61	2.41

Year	Club	League	G.	IP.	W.	L.	Pct.	H.	R.	ER.	SO.	BB.	ERA.
1964—San Francisco	National	33	269	21	8	.724	241	89	74	206	52	2.48
1965—San Francisco	National	39	295	22	13	.629	224	78	70	240	46	2.14
1966—San Francisco	National	37	307	25	6	.806	228	88	76	222	36	2.23
1967—San Francisco	National	26	202	14	10	.583	195	79	62	166	42	2.76
1968—San Francisco	National	38	*326	*26	9	.743	*295	106	88	218	46	2.43
1969—San Francisco	National	37	300	21	11	.656	244	90	70	205	54	*2.10
1970—San Francisco	National	34	243	12	10	.545	269	128	111	123	48	4.11
1971—San Francisco	National	37	279	13	11	.621	244	113	91	159	56	2.94
1972—San Francisco	National	25	165	6	16	.273	176	82	68	72	46	3.71
1973—San Francisco (a)	National	34	207	11	15	.423	231	104	88	87	37	3.83
1974—Boston	American	11	57	5	1	.833	61	32	31	21	14	4.89
1975—Los Angeles (b)	National	2	6	0	1	.000	11	9	9	1	5	13.50
National League Totals—15 Years		460	3449	238	141	.628	3092	1297	1095	2282	695	2.86
American League Totals—1 Year		11	57	5	1	.833	61	32	31	21	14	4.89
Major League Totals—16 Years		471	3506	243	142	.631	3153	1329	1126	2303	709	2.89

aSold to Boston Red Sox for an estimated $100,000, December 7, 1973.
bSigned as a free agent by Los Angeles Dodgers, March 11, 1975.

CHAMPIONSHIP SERIES RECORD

Year	Club	League	G.	IP.	W.	L.	Pct.	H.	R.	ER.	SO.	BB.	ERA.
1971—San Francisco	Nat.	1	8	0	1	.000	4	2	2	6	0	2.25

WORLD SERIES RECORD

Year	Club	League	G.	IP.	W.	L.	Pct.	H.	R.	ER.	SO.	BB.	ERA.
1962—San Francisco	National	1	4	0	0	.000	2	0	0	4	2	0.00

ROGER EUGENE MARIS

Born September 10, 1934, at Hibbing, Minn.

Died December 14, 1985, at Houston, Tex.

Height, 6.00. Weight, 205.

Threw right and batted lefthanded.

Holds major league record for most home runs, season (61), 1961.
Shares major league record for most intentional bases on balls, game (4), May 22, 1962 (12 innings).
Shares American League record for most home runs, doubleheader (4), July 25, 1961.
Named Most Valuable Player in American League, 1960-61.
Named by THE SPORTING NEWS as No. 1 American League Player, 1961.
Named Player of the Year by THE SPORTING NEWS, 1961.
Named as outfielder on THE SPORTING NEWS All-Star Major League Team, 1960.
Named as outfielder on THE SPORTING NEWS American League All-Star Team, 1961.
Received Rawlings Gold Glove award as outstanding fielding right fielder in American League, 1960.

Year	Club	League	Pos.	G.	AB.	R.	H.	2B.	3B.	HR.	RBI.	B.A.	PO.	A.	E.	F.A.
1953—Fargo-M'rhead	North.	OF	114	418	74	136	18	13	9	80	.325	166	18	7	.963
1954—Keokuk	I. I. I.	OF	134	502	105	158	26	6	32	111	.315	●305	20	18	.948
1955—Tulsa	Tex.	OF	25	90	9	21	1	0	1	9	.233	43	0	5	.896
1955—Reading	East.	OF	113	374	74	108	15	3	19	78	.289	262	9	6	.978
1956—Indianapolis	A. A.	OF	131	433	77	127	20	8	17	75	.293	200	15	8	.964
1957—Cleveland	Amer.	OF	116	358	61	84	9	5	14	51	.235	266	10	7	.975
1958—Cleve.(a)-K.C.	Amer.	OF	150	583	87	140	19	4	28	80	.240	303	15	*9	.972
1959—Kansas City(b)	Amer.	OF	122	433	69	118	21	7	16	72	.273	231	7	6	.975
1960—New York	Amer.	OF	136	499	98	141	18	7	39	*112	.283	263	6	4	.985
1961—New York	Amer.	OF	161	590	●132	159	16	4	*61	*142	.269	266	9	9	.968
1962—New York	Amer.	OF	157	590	92	151	34	1	33	100	.256	316	4	3	.991
1963—New York	Amer.	OF	90	312	53	84	14	1	23	53	.269	162	6	2	.988
1964—New York	Amer.	OF	141	513	86	144	12	2	26	71	.281	250	6	1	.996
1965—New York	Amer.	OF	46	155	22	37	7	0	8	27	.239	66	1	2	.971
1966—New York(c)	Amer.	OF	119	348	37	81	9	2	13	43	.233	133	3	1	.993
1967—St. Louis	Nat.	OF	125	410	64	107	18	7	9	55	.261	224	5	2	.991
1968—St. Louis	Nat.	OF	100	310	25	79	18	2	5	45	.255	169	4	3	.983
American League Totals—10 Years			1238	4381	737	1139	159	33	261	751	.260	2256	67	44	.981
National League Totals—2 Years			225	720	89	186	36	9	14	100	.258	393	9	5	.988
Major League Totals—12 Years			1463	5101	826	1325	195	42	275	851	.260	2649	76	49	.982

aTraded to Kansas City Athletics with Pitcher Dick Tomanek and Infielder Preston Ward for Infielder Vic Power and Infielder-Outfielder Woodie Held, June 15, 1958.

bTraded to New York Yankees with First Baseman Kent Hadley and Shortstop Joe DeMaestri for Pitcher Don Larsen, First Baseman Marv Throneberry and Outfielders Hank Bauer and Norm Siebern, December 11, 1959.

cTraded to St. Louis Cardinals for Third Baseman Charlie Smith, December 8, 1966.

Shares record by hitting home run in first series at-bat, October 5, 1960.

Year	Club	League	Pos.	G.	AB.	R.	H.	2B.	3B.	HR.	RBI.	B.A.	PO.	A.	E.	F.A.
1960—New York	Amer.	OF	7	30	6	8	1	0	2	2	.267	11	0	1	.917
1961—New York	Amer.	OF	5	19	4	2	1	0	1	2	.105	11	1	0	1.000
1962—New York	Amer.	OF	7	23	4	4	1	0	1	5	.174	11	1	0	1.000
1963—New York	Amer.	OF	2	5	0	0	0	0	0	0	.000	3	0	0	1.000
1964—New York	Amer.	OF	7	30	4	6	0	0	1	1	.200	19	0	0	1.000
1967—St. Louis	Nat.	OF	7	26	3	10	1	0	1	7	.385	15	0	1	.937
1968—St. Louis	Nat.	OF-PH	6	19	5	3	1	0	0	1	.158	8	0	0	1.000
World Series Totals—7 Years			41	152	26	33	5	0	6	18	.217	78	2	2	.976

RICHARD W. (RUBE) MARQUARD

Born October 9, 1889, at Cleveland, O.

Died June 1, 1980, at Baltimore, Md.

Height, 6.03. Weight, 180.

Threw left and batted left and righthanded.

Shares major league record for most consecutive games won, season (19), April 11 through July 3, first game, 1912.
Pitched 2-0 no-hit victory against Brooklyn Dodgers, April 15, 1915.

Manager, Providence, Eastern League, 1926; Jacksonville, Southeastern League, 1929-30; assistant coach, Assumption College, 1931; umpire, Eastern League, 1931; coach-scout, Atlanta, Southern Association, 1932.
Named to Hall of Fame, 1971.

Year	Club	League	G.	IP.	W.	L.	Pct.	H.	R.	ER.	SO.	BB.	ERA.
1907—Canton	Central	40	....	★23	13	.639	....			....	....	......	
1908—Indianapolis(a)	Amer. Assn.	★47	★367	★28	19	.596	234	....	....	★250	135	......	
1908—New York	National	1	5	0	1	.000	6	5	....	2	2	......	
1909—New York	National	29	173	5	13	.278	155	81	....	109	72	......	
1910—New York	National	13	69	4	4	.500	65	35	....	52	40	......	
1911—New York	National	45	278	24	7	★.774	221	98	....	★237	106	......	
1912—New York	National	43	295	●26	11	.703	286	112	84	175	80	2.56	
1913—New York	National	42	288	23	10	.697	248	100	80	151	49	2.50	
1914—New York	National	39	268	12	22	.353	261	117	91	92	47	3.06	
1915—N.Y.(b)-Brooklyn	National	33	194	11	10	.524	207	102	87	92	38	4.04	
1916—Brooklyn	National	36	205	13	6	.684	169	54	36	107	38	1.58	
1917—Brooklyn	National	37	233	19	12	.613	200	84	66	117	38	2.55	
1918—Brooklyn	National	34	239	9	●18	.333	231	97	70	89	59	2.64	
1919—Brooklyn	National	8	59	3	3	.500	54	17	15	29	10	2.29	
1920—Brooklyn(c)	National	28	190	10	7	.588	181	83	68	89	35	3.22	
1921—Cincinnati(d)	National	39	266	17	14	.548	291	123	100	88	50	3.38	
1922—Boston	National	39	198	11	15	.423	255	131	112	57	66	5.09	
1923—Boston	National	38	239	11	14	.440	265	127	99	78	65	3.73	
1924—Boston	National	6	36	1	2	.333	33	17	12	10	13	3.00	
1925—Boston	National	26	72	2	8	.200	105	60	46	19	27	5.75	
1926—Providence	Eastern	7	44	3	1	.750	49	19	18	22	17	3.68	
1927—Baltimore	Intenational	6	30	1	2	.333	38	....	....	5	6	......	
1927—Birmingham	Southern	3	11	0	1	.000	10	....	....	1	5	......	
1928—	(Out of Organized Ball)												
1929—Jacksonville	Southeastern	3	3	0	0	.000	2	....	....	4	2	......	
1930—Jacksonville	Southeastern	15	114	5	4	.556	106	36	27	47	21	2.13	
1931—	(Umpire, Eastern League)												
1932—Atlanta	Southern	6	42	1	3	.250	61	....	....	13	14	......	
Major League Totals—18 Years		536	3307	201	177	.532	3233	1443	j966	1593	858	3.13	

aSold to New York Giants for $11,000, September, 1908.
bReleased to Brooklyn Dodgers on waivers, September, 1915.
cTraded to Cincinnati Reds for Pitcher Dutch Ruether, December 15, 1920.
dTraded to Boston Braves for Pitcher John Scott and Infielder William Kopf, February 20, 1922.

Year	Club	League	G.	IP.	W.	L.	Pct.	H.	R.	ER.	SO.	BB.	ERA.
1911—New York	National	3	11⅔	0	1	.000	9	6	2	8	1	1.54
1912—New York	National	2	18	2	0	1.000	14	3	1	9	2	0.50
1913—New York	National	2	9	0	1	.000	10	7	7	3	4	7.00
1916—Brooklyn	National	2	11	0	2	.000	12	9	8	9	6	6.55
1920—Brooklyn	National	2	9	0	1	.000	7	3	1	6	3	1.00
World Series Totals—5 Years		11	58⅔	2	5	.286	52	28	19	35	16	2.91

EDWIN LEE (EDDIE) MATHEWS JR.

Born October 13, 1931, at Texarkana, Tex.

Height, 6.01. Weight, 195.

Threw right and batted lefthanded.

Holds National League record for most consecutive years with 30 or more home runs (9).
Hit three home runs in a game, September 27, 1952.
Led National League in bases on balls with 109 in 1955, 93 in 1961, 101 in 1962 and 124 in 1963.
Named as third baseman on THE SPORTING NEWS' All-Star Major League Teams, 1955-57-59-60.
Coach, Atlanta Braves, 1971 to 1972; manager, Braves, 1972 to 1974; scout, Braves, 1974; minor league instructor-scout, Milwaukee Brewers, 1975 to 1978.
Named to Hall of Fame, 1978.

Year	Club	League	Pos.	G.	AB.	R.	H.	2B.	3B.	HR.	RBI.	B.A.	PO.	A.	E.	F.A.
1949—H. Point-Th'ville ..	N.C. St.		3B	63	240	62	87	20	3	17	56	.363	71	126	21	.904
1950—Atlanta	South.		3B	146	552	103	158	24	9	32	106	.286	159	218	24	.940
1951—Atlanta	South.		3B	37	128	23	37	5	4	6	29	.289	31	62	7	.930
1951—Milwaukee.............	A. A.		3B	12	9	2	3	0	0	1	5	.333	1	0	0	1.000
1952—Boston....................	Nat.		3B	145	528	80	128	23	5	25	58	.242	160	259	19	.957
1953—Milwakee..............	Nat.		3B	157	579	110	175	31	8	★47	135	.302	154	311	★30	.939
1954—Milwaukee.............	Nat.		3B-OF	138	476	96	138	21	4	40	103	.290	133	254	15	.963
1955—Milwaukee.............	Nat.		3B	141	499	108	144	23	5	41	101	.289	140	★280	21	.952
1956—Milwaukee.............	Nat.		3B	151	552	103	150	21	2	37	95	.272	133	287	★25	.944
1957—Milwaukee.............	Nat.		3B	148	572	109	167	28	9	32	94	.292	131	★299	●16	.964
1958—Milwaukee.............	Nat.		3B	149	546	97	137	18	1	31	77	.251	116	★351	22	.955
1959—Milwaukee.............	Nat.		3B	148	594	118	182	16	8	★46	114	.306	144	305	18	.961
1960—Milwaukee.............	Nat.		3B	153	548	108	152	19	7	39	124	.277	★141	280	22	.950
1961—Milwaukee.............	Nat.		3B	152	572	103	175	23	6	32	91	.306	★168	281	18	.961
1962—Milwaukee.............	Nat.		3B-1B	152	536	106	142	25	6	29	90	.265	208	285	16	.969
1963—Milwaukee.............	Nat.		★3B-OF	158	547	82	144	27	4	23	84	.263	176	277	19	★.960
1964—Milwaukee.............	Nat.		3B-1B	141	502	83	117	19	1	23	74	.233	184	252	17	.962
1965—Milwaukee.............	Nat.		3B	156	546	77	137	23	0	32	95	.251	113	301	19	.956
1966—Atlanta (a)............	Nat.		3B	134	452	72	113	21	4	16	53	.250	114	237	20	.946
1967—Houston (b)	Nat.		1B-3B	101	328	39	78	13	2	10	38	.238	594	73	11	.984
1967—Detroit..................	Amer.		3B-1B	36	108	14	25	3	0	6	19	.231	120	40	4	.976
1968—Detroit..................	Amer.		1B-3B	31	52	4	11	0	0	3	8	.212	37	13	1	.980
National League Totals—16 Years.........				2324	8377	1491	2279	351	72	503	1426	.272	2809	4332	308	.959
American League Totals—2 Years				67	160	18	36	3	0	9	27	.225	157	53	5	.977
Major League Totals—17 Years...............				2391	8537	1509	2315	354	72	512	1453	.271	2966	4385	313	.959

aTraded with Pitcher Arnold Umbach (transferred from Richmond to Oklahoma City) and player to be named later to Houston Astros for Outfielder Dave Nicholson (transferred from Oklahoma City to Richmond) and Pitcher Bob Bruce, December 31, 1966. Infielder Sandy Alomar sent to Astros to complete deal, February 25, 1967.

bTraded to Detroit Tigers for cash and player to be named, July 22, 1967. Pitcher Fred Gladding sent to Astros, November 22, 1967 to complete deal.

WORLD SERIES RECORD

Year	Club	League	Pos.	G.	AB.	R.	H.	2B.	3B.	HR.	RBI.	B.A.	PO.	A.	E.	F.A.
1957—Milwaukee.............	Nat.		3B	7	22	4	5	3	0	1	4	.227	9	19	1	.966
1958—Milwaukee.............	Nat.		3B	7	25	3	4	2	0	0	3	.160	5	13	1	.947
1968—Detroit..................	Amer.		PH-3	2	3	0	1	0	0	0	0	.333	0	1	1	.500
World Series Totals—3 Years				16	50	7	10	5	0	1	7	.200	14	33	3	.880

CHRISTOPHER (CHRISTY) MATHEWSON
(Big Six)

Born August 12, 1880, at Factoryville, Pa.

Died October 7, 1925, at Saranac Lake, N. Y.

Height, 6.01½. Weight, 195.

Threw and batted righthanded.

Brother of Henry Mathewson, former major league pitcher.

Holds National League record for most years winning 20 or more games (12).
Shares National League records for most victories, lifetime (373); most years winning 20 or more games (13).

Holds modern National League records for most games won, season (37), 1908; most years winning 30 or more games (14).

Pitched 1-0 no-hit victory against Hampton, June 12, 1900; 5-0 no-hit victory against St. Louis, July 15, 1901 and 1-0 no-hit victory against Chicago, June 13, 1905.

Manager, Cincinnati Reds, 1916 to 1918; coach, New York Giants, 1919-20-21; president, Boston Braves, 1923-24-25. Named to Hall of Fame, 1936.

Year Club	League	G.	IP.	W.	L.	Pct.	ShO.	H.	R.	ER.	SO.	BB.	ERA.
1899—Taunton	N. Eng.	17	....	5	2	.714	....	....	....	....	....	....	......
1900—Norfolk	Va.	22	187	20	2	.909	4	119	59	....	128	27	......
1900—New York(a)	Nat.	6	34	0	3	.000	0	34	32	....	15	20	......
1901—New York	Nat.	40	336	20	17	.541	5	281	131	....	215	92	......
1902—New York	Nat.	34	276	14	17	.452	●8	241	114	....	162	74	......
1903—New York	Nat.	45	367	30	13	.698	3	321	136	....	★267	100	......
1904—New York	Nat.	48	368	33	12	.733	4	306	120	....	★212	78	......
1905—New York	Nat.	43	339	★31	9	.775	★9	252	85	....	★206	64	......
1906—New York	Nat.	38	267	22	12	.647	7	262	100	....	128	77	......
1907—New York	Nat.	41	315	★24	12	.667	●9	250	88	....	★178	53	......
1908—New York	Nat.	★56	★391	★37	11	.771	★12	281	85	....	★259	42	......
1909—New York	Nat.	37	274	25	6	.806	8	192	57	....	149	36	......
1910—New York	Nat.	38	319	★27	9	.750	2	291	98	....	★190	57	......
1911—New York	Nat.	45	307	26	13	.667	5	★303	102	....	141	38	......
1912—New York	Nat.	43	●310	23	12	.657	0	311	107	73	134	34	2.12
1913—New York	Nat.	40	306	25	11	.694	5	●291	93	70	93	21	★2.06
1914—New York	Nat.	41	312	24	13	.648	5	314	133	★104	80	23	3.00
1915—New York	Nat.	27	186	8	14	.364	1	199	97	74	57	20	3.58
1916—N.Y.(b)-Cinn.	Nat.	13	74	4	4	.500	1	74	35	25	19	8	3.04
Major League Totals—17 Years		635	4781	373	188	.665	83	4203	1613	....	2505	837	....

aJoined Giants midseason, 1900. Turned back to Norfolk at end of campaign, but drafted by Cincinnati and traded to Giants for Pitcher Amos Rusie.

bTraded with Outfielder Edd Roush and Infielder Bill McKechnie to Cincinnati for Infielder Buck Herzog and Outfielder Wade Killefer, July 20, 1916.

WORLD SERIES RECORD

Holds record for most shutouts, series (3), 1905.
Shares record for most games won, series (3), 1905.

Year Club	League	G.	IP.	W.	L.	Pct.	ShO.	H.	R.	ER.	SO.	BB.	ERA.
1905—New York	Nat.	3	27	3	0	.000	3	14	0	0	18	1	0.00
1911—New York	Nat.	3	27	1	2	.333	0	25	8	6	13	2	2.00
1912—New York	Nat.	3	28	0	2	.000	0	23	11	5	10	5	1.57
1913—New York	Nat.	2	19	1	1	.500	1	14	3	2	7	2	0.95
World Series Totals—4 Years		11	101	5	5	.500	4	76	22	13	48	10	1.15

LEE ANDREW MAY

Born March 23, 1943, at Birmingham, Ala.

Height, 6.03. Weight, 205.

Threw and batted righthanded.

Brother of Carlos May, former major league outfielder-first baseman.

Shares major league records for most home runs, three consecutive games (6), May 24 through 28, 1969; most home runs (2) and total bases (8), inning, April 29, 1974, sixth inning.

Hit three home runs in a game, June 21, 1973.
Led National League batters in strikeouts with 145 in 1972.
Led National League first basemen in double plays with 128 in 1969 and 143 in 1970.
Led National League first basemen in total chances with 1,400 and double plays with 133 in 1972.
Led American League first basemen in total chances with 1,428 and double plays with 138 in 1975.
Led American League designated hitters in strikeouts with 108 in 1978.
Led Carolina League first basemen in double plays with 125 in 1963.
Led Pacific Coast League in total bases with 327 in 1965.
Named National League Rookie Player of the Year by THE SPORTING NEWS, 1967.
Named first baseman on THE SPORTING NEWS National League All-Star Team, 1971.
Coach Kansas City Royals, 1984 through 1986; Cincinnati Reds, 1988-89.

Year Club	League	Pos.	G.	AB.	R.	H.	2B.	3B.	HR.	RBI.	B.A.	PO.	A.	E.	F.A.
1961—Tampa	Fla. St.	1-OF	26	77	10	20	2	2	0	9	.260	114	7	5	.960
1962—Tampa	Fla. St.	1B	89	339	45	88	10	3	10	65	.260	674	48	16	.978
1963—Rocky Mount	Carol.	1B	144	520	79	137	23	4	18	80	.263	★1288	74	27	.981
1964—Macon	South.	1-OF	●140	515	91	156	22	5	25	★110	.303	1019	72	20	.982
1965—San Diego	P. C.	1B-OF	143	558	83	179	32	7	34	103	.321	1165	67	15	.988
1965—Cincinnati	Nat.	PH	5	4	1	0	0	0	0	0	.000	0	0	0	.000
1966—Cincinnati	Nat.	1B	25	75	14	25	5	1	2	10	.333	132	9	4	.972

Year Club League	Pos.	G.	AB.	R.	H.	2B.	3B.	HR.	RBI.	B.A.	PO.	A.	E.	F.A.
1966—Buffalo Int.	1B	128	471	74	146	25	5	16	78	.310	1006	86	★16	.986
1967—Cincinnati Nat.	1B-OF	127	438	54	116	29	2	12	57	.265	703	46	6	.992
1968—Cincinnati Nat.	1B-OF	146	559	78	162	32	1	22	80	.290	1094	73	5	.996
1969—Cincinnati Nat.	1B-OF	158	607	85	169	32	3	38	110	.278	1395	102	11	.993
1970—Cincinnati Nat.	1B	153	605	78	153	34	2	34	94	.253	1362	109	10	.993
1971—Cincinnati† Nat.	1B	147	553	85	154	17	3	39	98	.278	1261	78	8	.994
1972—Houston Nat.	1B	148	592	87	168	31	2	29	98	.284	★1318	76	6	.996
1973—Houston Nat.	1B	148	545	65	147	24	3	28	105	.270	1220	78	9	.993
1974—Houston‡ Nat.	1B	152	556	59	149	26	0	24	85	.268	1253	88	8	.994
1975—Baltimore Amer.	1B	146	580	67	152	28	3	20	99	.262	★1312	106	10	.993
1976—Baltimore Amer.	1B	148	530	61	137	17	4	25	109	.258	722	62	3	.996
1977—Baltimore Amer.	1B	150	585	75	148	16	2	27	99	.253	907	56	5	.995
1978—Baltimore Amer.	1B	148	556	56	137	16	1	25	80	.246	34	2	1	.973
1979—Baltimore Amer.	1B	124	456	59	116	15	0	19	69	.254	21	0	2	.913
1980—Baltimore§ Amer.	1B	78	222	20	54	10	2	7	31	.243	57	3	0	1.000
1981—Kansas City Amer.	1B	26	55	3	16	3	0	0	8	.291	63	2	0	1.000
1982—Kansas City x Amer.	1B	42	91	12	28	5	2	3	12	.308	175	10	2	.989
National League Totals—10 Years		1209	4534	606	1243	230	17	228	737	.274	9738	659	67	.994
American League Totals—8 Years		862	3075	353	788	110	14	126	507	.256	3291	241	23	.994
Major League Totals—18 Years		2071	7609	959	2031	340	31	354	1244	.267	13029	900	90	.994

Signed as free agent by Cincinnati Reds' organization, June 1, 1961.

†Traded with Second Baseman Tommy Helms and Outfielder Jim Stewart to Houston Astros for Infielder Denis Menke, Second Baseman Joe Morgan, Pitcher Jack Billingham and Outfielders Cesar Geronimo and Ed Armbrister.

‡Traded with Outfielder Jay Schlueter to Baltimore Orioles for Second Baseman Rob Andrews and Infielder-Outfielder Enos Cabell, December 3, 1974.

§Granted free agency, October 23, 1980; signed by Kansas City Royals, December 12, 1980.

xReleased, November 18, 1982.

CHAMPIONSHIP SERIES RECORD

Year Club League	Pos.	G.	AB.	R.	H.	2B.	3B.	HR.	RBI.	B.A.	PO.	A.	E.	F.A.
1970—Cincinnati Nat.	1B	3	12	0	2	1	0	0	2	.167	31	1	0	1.000
1979—Baltimore Amer.	DH	2	7	0	1	0	0	0	1	.143	0	0	0	.000
Championship Series Totals—2 Years		5	19	0	3	1	0	0	3	.158	31	1	0	1.000

WORLD SERIES RECORD

Year Club League	Pos.	G.	AB.	R.	H.	2B.	3B.	HR.	RBI.	B.A.	PO.	A.	E.	F.A.
1970—Cincinnati Nat.	1B	5	18	6	7	2	0	2	8	.389	48	3	0	1.000
1979—Baltimore Amer.	PH	2	1	0	0	0	0	0	0	.000	0	0	0	.000
World Series Totals—2 Years		7	19	6	7	2	0	2	8	.368	48	3	0	1.000

JOHN CLAIBORN MAYBERRY

Born February 18, 1950, at Detroit, Mich.

Height, 6.03. Weight, 225.

Threw and batted lefthanded.

Shares American League record for most double plays by first baseman, game, (6), May 6, 1972.

Led American League first basemen in total chances with 1,427 in 1972 and 1,596 in 1976; led in double plays with 141 in 1972 and 156 in 1973.

Led American League in bases on balls with 122 in 1973 and 119 in 1975.

Led American Association first basemen in double plays with 89 in 1969.

Led American League in sacrifice flies with 12 in 1976.

Hit three home runs in a game, July 1, 1975 and June 1, 1977.

Named first baseman on THE SPORTING NEWS American League All-Star Team, 1973 and 1975.

Minor league instructor, Kansas City Royals, 1985 through 1988; coach, Royals, 1989 to date.

Year Club League	Pos.	G.	AB.	R.	H.	2B.	3B.	HR.	RBI.	B.A.	PO.	A.	E.	F.A.
1967—Covington Appal.	1B	50	155	23	39	7	0	4	21	.252	380	★29	★11	.974
1968—Cocoa Fla. St.	1B	64	195	34	66	9	3	14	48	.338	479	22	7	.986
1968—Greensboro Carol.	1B	43	158	31	52	14	1	8	29	.329	297	22	3	.991
1968—Oklahoma City P. C.	1B	24	78	3	20	0	0	1	5	.256	196	12	4	.981
1968—Houston Nat.	1B	4	9	0	0	0	0	0	0	.000	25	0	0	1.000
1969—Oklahoma City A. A.	★1B-2B	123	458	95	139	29	4	21	78	.303	★1005	61	11	★.990
1969—Houston Nat.	1B	5	4	0	0	0	0	0♦	0	.000	0	0	0	.000
1970—Oklahoma City A. A.	1B	70	231	55	63	7	3	13	38	.273	536	30	8	.986
1970—Houston Nat.	1B	50	148	23	32	3	2	5	14	.216	371	35	2	.995
1971—Oklahoma City A. A.	1B	64	222	50	72	10	3	12	40	.324	445	39	4	.992
1971—Houston† Nat.	1B	46	137	16	25	0	1	7	14	.182	317	15	1	.997
1972—Kansas City Amer.	1B	149	503	65	150	24	3	25	100	.298	★1338	82	7	★.995

Year	Club	League	Pos.	G.	AB.	R.	H.	2B.	3B.	HR.	RBI.	B.A.	PO.	A.	E.	F.A.
1973—Kansas City		Amer.	1B	152	510	87	142	20	2	26	100	.278	★1457	81	9	.994
1974—Kansas City		Amer.	1B	126	427	63	100	13	1	22	69	.234	963	61	10	.990
1975—Kansas City		Amer.	1B	156	554	95	161	38	1	34	106	.291	1199	100	★16	.988
1976—Kansas City		Amer.	1B	161	594	76	138	22	2	13	95	.232	★1484	105	7	.996
1977—Kansas City‡		Amer.	1B	153	543	73	125	22	1	23	82	.230	1296	81	7	★.995
1978—Toronto		Amer.	1B	152	515	51	129	15	2	22	70	.250	1143	52	8	.993
1979—Toronto		Amer.	1B	137	464	61	127	22	1	21	74	.274	1192	74	6	.995
1980—Toronto		Amer.	1B	149	501	62	124	19	2	30	82	.248	1243	79	8	.994
1981—Toronto		Amer.	1B	94	290	34	72	6	1	17	43	.248	647	36	5	.993
1982—Tor.§-N.Y.x		Amer.	1B	86	248	27	54	7	0	10	30	.218	494	26	2	.996
National League Totals—4 Years				105	298	39	57	3	3	12	28	.191	713	50	3	.996
American League Totals—11 Years				1515	5149	694	1322	208	16	243	851	.257	12456	777	85	.994
Major League Totals—15 Years				1620	5447	733	1379	211	19	255	879	.253	13169	827	88	.994

Selected by Houston Astros' organization in 1st round (sixth player selected) of free-agent draft, June 6, 1967.

†Traded with Third Baseman Dave Grangaard to Kansas City Royals for Pitchers Jim York and Lance Clemons, December 2, 1971.

‡Sold to Toronto Blue Jays, April 4, 1978.

§Traded to New York Yankees for First Baseman Dave Revering and Third Baseman Jeff Reynolds, May 5, 1982.

xReleased, March 24, 1983.

CHAMPIONSHIP SERIES RECORD

Year	Club	League	Pos.	G.	AB.	R.	H.	2B.	3B.	HR.	RBI.	B.A.	PO.	A.	E.	F.A.
1976—Kansas City		Amer.	1B	5	18	4	4	0	0	1	3	.222	48	1	0	1.000
1977—Kansas City		Amer.	1B	4	12	1	2	1	0	1	3	.167	29	1	2	.938
Championship Series Totals—2 Years				9	30	5	6	1	0	2	6	.200	77	2	2	.975

CARL WILLIAM MAYS

Born November 12, 1893, at Liberty, Ky.

Died April 4, 1971, at El Cajon, Calif.

Height, 6.00. Weight, 215.

Threw right and batted lefthanded.

Scout, Cleveland Indians, 1958-61; Kansas City Athletics, 1962; Milwaukee Braves, 1963.

Year	Club	League	G.	IP.	W.	L.	Pct.	H.	R.	ER.	SO.	BB.	ERA.
1912—Boise	W. Tri-St.		40	235	22	8	.733	....	....	....	....	....	......
1913—Portland	N. W.		33	250	10	15	.400	202	92	....	159	54	......
1914—Providence	International		36	273	★24	8	★.750	249	94	....	129	73	......
1915—Boston	American		38	132	6	5	.545	119	54	38	65	21	2.59
1916—Boston	American		44	245	18	13	.581	208	79	65	76	74	2.39
1917—Boston	American		35	289	22	9	.710	230	81	56	91	74	1.74
1918—Boston	American		35	293	21	13	.618	230	94	72	114	81	2.21
1919—Boston(a)-New York	American		34	266	14	14	.500	227	91	62	107	77	2.10
1920—New York	American		45	312	26	11	.703	310	127	106	92	84	3.06
1921—New York	American		★49	★337	●27	9	★.750	332	145	114	70	76	3.04
1922—New York	American		34	240	13	14	.481	257	111	96	41	50	3.60
1923—New York(b)	American		23	81	5	2	.714	119	59	56	16	32	6.22
1924—Cincinnati	National		37	226	20	9	.690	238	97	79	63	36	3.15
1925—Cincinnati	National		12	52	3	5	.375	60	22	19	10	13	3.29
1926—Cincinnati	National		39	281	19	12	.613	286	112	98	58	53	3.14
1927—Cincinnati	National		14	82	3	7	.300	89	39	32	17	10	3.51
1928—Cincinnati(c)	National		14	63	4	1	.800	67	33	27	10	22	3.86
1929—New York	National		37	123	7	2	.778	140	67	59	32	31	4.32
1930—Portland	Pacific Coast		19	144	5	9	.357	178	105	76	43	36	4.75
1930—Toledo	Amer. Assn.		6	42	3	1	.750	52	18	....	5	4	......
1931—Toledo-Louisville	Amer. Assn.		32	204	11	15	.423	248	129	98	54	54	4.32
American League Totals—9 Years			337	2195	152	90	.628	2032	841	665	672	569	2.73
National League Totals—6 Years			153	827	56	36	.609	880	370	314	190	165	3.42
Major League Totals—15 Years			490	3022	208	126	.623	2912	1211	979	862	734	2.92

aTraded to New York Yankees for Pitchers Allan Russell and Bob McGraw and cash, July 29, 1919.

bSold to Cincinnati Reds on waivers, December 11, 1923.

cReleased, August 18, 1928; signed by New York Giants, September 1, 1928.

WORLD SERIES RECORD

Year	Club	League	G.	IP.	W.	L.	Pct.	H.	R.	ER.	SO.	BB.	ERA.
1916—Boston	American		2	5⅓	0	1	.000	8	4	3	2	3	5.06
1918—Boston	American		2	18	2	0	1.000	10	2	2	5	3	1.00
1921—New York	American		3	26	1	2	.333	20	6	5	9	0	1.73
1922—New York	American		1	8	0	1	.000	9	4	4	1	2	4.50
World Series Totals—4 Years			8	57⅓	3	4	.420	47	16	14	17	8	2.20

WILLIE HOWARD MAYS JR.
(Say Hey)

Born May 6, 1931, at Westfield, Ala.
Height, 5.11. Weight, 187.
Threw and batted righthanded.

Holds major league records for most consecutive years, 150 or more games (13); most putouts (7,095) and chances accepted (7,290) by outfielder, lifetime.

Shares major league records for most games, three or more home runs, season (2), 1961; most home runs, game (4), April 30, 1961; most consecutive years, 300 or more total bases (13).

Holds National League records for most games, two or more home runs, lifetime (63); most home runs, month (17), August 1965; most years, outfielder (22); most games by outfielder, lifetime (2,843).

Shares National League record for most home runs, six consecutive games (7), September 14 through 20, second game, 1955.

Hit four home runs in a game, April 30, 1961; hit three home runs in a game, June 29, 1961, and June 2, 1963.

Led National League in slugging percentage with .667 in 1954, .659 in 1955, .626 in 1957, .607 in 1964 and .645 in 1965; led in total bases with 382 in 1955, 382 in 1962 and 360 in 1965; led in stolen bases with 40 in 1956, 38 in 1957, 31 in 1958 and 27 in 1959.

Named National League Rookie of the Year by the Baseball Writers' Association and THE SPORTING NEWS, 1951.

Named Major League Player of the Year by THE SPORTING NEWS, 1954.

Named by THE SPORTING NEWS as the Outstanding National League Player, 1954-65.

Most Valuable Player in the National League, 1954-65.

Named as outfielder on THE SPORTING NEWS All-Star Major League teams, 1954-57-58-59-60.

Named as outfielder on THE SPORTING NEWS National League All-Star teams, 1961-62-63-64-65-66.

Named as outfielder on THE SPORTING NEWS Major League All-Star fielding team, 1957.

Named outfielder on THE SPORTING NEWS National League All-Star fielding teams, 1958-59-60-61-63-64-65-66-67-68.

Named by THE SPORTING NEWS as Baseball Player of the Decade (1960-1969).

Named to Hall of Fame, 1979.

Year—Club	League	Pos.	G.	AB.	R.	H.	2B.	3B.	HR.	RBI.	B.A.	PO.	A.	E.	F.A.
1950—Trenton	Int. St.	OF	81	306	50	108	20	8	4	55	.353	216	17	5	.979
1951—Minneapolis	A. A.	OF	35	149	38	71	18	3	8	30	.477	94	5	1	.990
1951—New York	Nat.	OF	121	464	59	127	22	5	20	68	.274	353	12	9	.976
1952—New York(a)	Nat.	OF	34	127	17	30	2	4	4	23	.236	109	6	1	.991
1953—New York	Nat.								(In Military Service)						
1954—New York	Nat.	OF	151	565	119	195	33	★13	41	110	★.345	448	13	7	.985
1955—New York	Nat.	OF	152	580	123	185	18	●13	★51	127	.319	407	★23	8	.982
1956—New York	Nat.	OF	152	578	101	171	27	8	36	84	.296	415	14	9	.979
1957—New York	Nat.	OF	152	585	112	195	26	★20	35	97	.333	422	14	9	.980
1958—San Francisco	Nat.	OF	152	600	★121	208	33	11	29	96	.347	429	17	9	.980
1959—San Francisco	Nat.	OF	151	575	125	180	43	5	34	104	.313	353	6	6	.984
1960—San Francisco	Nat.	OF	153	595	107	★190	29	12	29	103	.319	392	12	8	.981
1961—San Francisco	Nat.	OF	154	572	★129	176	32	3	40	123	.308	385	7	8	.980
1962—San Francisco	Nat.	OF	162	621	130	189	36	5	★49	141	.304	★429	6	4	.991
1963—San Francisco	Nat.	OF-SS	157	596	115	187	32	7	38	103	.314	397	7	8	.981
1964—San Francisco	Nat.	OF-1-2-3-S	157	578	121	171	21	9	★47	111	.296	376	12	6	.985
1965—San Francisco	Nat.	OF	157	558	118	177	21	3	★52	112	.317	337	13	6	.983
1966—San Francisco	Nat.	OF	152	552	99	159	29	4	37	103	.288	370	8	7	.982
1967—San Francisco	Nat.	OF	141	486	83	128	22	2	22	70	.263	277	3	7	.976
1968—San Francisco	Nat.	OF-1B	148	498	84	144	20	5	23	79	.289	310	7	7	.978
1969—San Francisco	Nat.	OF-1B	117	403	64	114	17	3	13	58	.283	205	4	5	.976
1970—San Francisco	Nat.	OF-1B	139	478	94	139	15	2	28	83	.291	303	9	7	.978
1971—San Francisco	Nat.	OF-1B	136	417	82	113	24	5	18	61	.271	576	29	17	.973
1972—S. F.(b)-N.Y.	Nat.	OF-1B	88	244	35	61	11	1	8	22	.250	213	5	4	.982
1973—New York	Nat.	OF-1B	66	209	24	44	10	0	6	25	.211	246	6	4	.984
Major League Totals—22 Years			2992	10881	2062	3283	523	140	660	1903	.302	7752	233	156	.981

aEntered military service May 29.

bTraded to New York Mets for cash and Pitcher Charlie Williams, May 11, 1972.

CHAMPIONSHIP SERIES RECORD

Year—Club	League	Pos.	G.	AB.	R.	H.	2B.	3B.	HR.	RBI.	B.A.	PO.	A.	E.	F.A.
1971—San Francisco	Nat.	OF	4	15	2	4	2	0	1	3	.267	5	0	0	1.000
1973—New York	Nat.	PH-OF	1	3	1	1	0	0	0	1	.333	1	0	0	1.000
Championship Series Totals—2 Years			5	18	3	5	2	0	1	4	.278	6	0	0	1.000

WORLD SERIES RECORD

Year—Club	League	Pos.	G.	AB.	R.	H.	2B.	3B.	HR.	RBI.	B.A.	PO.	A.	E.	F.A.
1951—New York	Nat.	OF	6	22	1	4	0	0	0	1	.182	16	1	0	1.000
1954—New York	Nat.	OF	4	14	4	4	1	0	0	3	.286	10	0	0	1.000
1962—San Francisco	Nat.	OF	7	28	3	7	2	0	0	1	.250	19	0	0	1.000
1973—New York	Nat.	O-PH-PR	3	7	1	2	0	0	0	1	.286	1	0	1	.500
World Series Totals—4 Years			20	71	9	17	3	0	0	6	.239	46	1	1	.979

JOSEPH VINCENT (JOE) McCARTHY
(Marse Joe)

Born April 21, 1887, at Philadelphia, Pa.
Died January 13, 1978, at Buffalo, N. Y.
Height, 5.08½. Weight, 190.
Threw and batted righthanded.

Named by THE SPORTING NEWS as Major League Manager of the Year, 1936, 1938, 1943.
Manager, Wilkes-Barre, New York State, 1913; Louisville, American Association, 1919 through 1925; Chicago Cubs, 1926 to 1930; New York Yankees, 1931 to 1946; Boston Red Sox, 1948 to 1950.
Named to Hall of Fame, 1957.

Year Club	League	Pos.	G.	AB.	R.	H.	2B.	3B.	HR.	SB.	B.A.	PO.	A.	E.	F.A.
1907—Wilmington	Tri.-St.	INF	12	40	0	7	0	0	0	0	.175	18	27	5	.900
1907—Franklin	Int.-St.	OF	71	245	37	77	...	...	2	7	.314	77	131	25	.893
1908—Toledo	A. A.	OF-3B	111	386	43	98	25	1	0	13	.254	140	91	32	.878
1909—Toledo	A. A.	OF-SS	128	507	58	112	19	5	3	14	.221	225	119	27	.927
1910—Toledo	A. A.	3B-OF	92	274	28	62	10	2	2	8	.226	102	128	21	.916
1911—Toledo-Ind.	A. A.	OF-3B	98	208	45	80	10	3	2	9	.268	160	89	24	.912
1912—Wilkes-Barre	N.Y.S.	2B-3B	116	387	50	106	14	9	5	24	.274	237	256	30	.943
1913—Wilkes-Barre	N.Y.S.	2B	132	505	87	164	36	9	6	13	.325	287	★422	★45	.940
1914—Buffalo	Int.	2B	146	537	63	143	25	11	4	27	.266	309	★473	29	★.964
1915—Buffalo	Int.	2B	135	515	71	137	24	5	0	17	.266	306	★414	22	.970
1916—Louisville	A. A.	2B	168	618	55	160	28	10	1	20	.259	316	508	36	.958
1917—Louisville	A. A.	2B	143	510	64	141	31	6	2	8	.276	363	443	47	.945
1918—Louisville	A. A.	2B	75	274	26	59	6	1	1	3	.215	193	222	20	.954
1919—Louisville	A. A.	2B	147	550	60	130	28	8	3	11	.236	336	464	★37	.956
1920—Louisville	A. A.	2B-OF	58	175	17	44	12	2	0	3	.251	97	70	10	.944
1921—Louisville	A. A.	2B-PH	11	18	1	5	0	0	1	0	.278	6	8	0	1.000

Never played in major leagues.

RECORD AS MAJOR LEAGUE MANAGER

Year Club	League	Position	W.	L.	Year Club	League	Position	W.	L.
1926—Chicago	Nat.	Fourth	82	72	1939—New York	Amer.	First	106	45
1927—Chicago	Nat.	Fourth	85	68	1940—New York	Amer.	Third	88	66
1928—Chicago	Nat.	Third	91	63	1941—New York	Amer.	First	101	53
1929—Chicago	Nat.	First	98	54	1942—New York	Amer.	First	103	51
1930—Chicago	Nat.	Second	86	64	1943—New York	Amer.	First	98	56
1931—New York	Amer.	Second	94	59	1944—New York	Amer.	Third	83	71
1932—New York	Amer.	First	107	47	1945—New York	Amer.	Fourth	81	71
1933—New York	Amer.	Second	91	59	1946—New York	Amer.	Second	22	13
1934—New York	Amer.	Second	94	60	1948—Boston	Amer.	Second	96	59
1935—New York	Amer.	Second	89	60	1949—Boston	Amer.	Second	96	58
1936—New York	Amer.	First	102	51	1950—Boston	Amer.	Fourth	32	30
1937—New York	Amer.	First	102	52	Major League Totals—24 Years			2126	1335
1938—New York	Amer.	First	99	53					

WORLD SERIES RECORD

Year Club	League	W.	L.	Year Club	League	W.	L.
1929—Chicago	National	1	4	1939—New York	American	4	0
1932—New York	American	4	0	1941—New York	American	4	1
1936—New York	American	4	2	1942—New York	American	1	4
1937—New York	American	4	1	1943—New York	American	4	1
1938—New York	American	4	0				

THOMAS FRANCIS MICHAEL (TOMMY) McCARTHY

Born July 24, 1864, at South Boston, Mass.
Died August 5, 1922, at Boston, Mass.
Height, 5.07. Weight, 170.
Threw and batted righthanded.

Manager, St. Louis, American Association, 1890 (part); scout for Cincinnati, 1909 to 1912; Boston Braves, 1914 and 1917; manager, Newark, International League, 1918.

Baseball coach at Dartmouth, Holy Cross and Boston College.

Named to Hall of Fame, 1946.

Year	Club	League	Pos.	G.	AB.	R.	H.	2B.	3B.	HR.	SB.	B.A.	PO.	A.	E.	F.A.
1884—Boston	U.A.	OF-P	53	218	37	45	4	1	0	....	.206	51	14	13	.833
1885—Boston	Nat.	OF	40	148	16	27	2	0	...		.182	69	8	12	.865
1886—Philadelphia	Nat.	OF	8	27	6	5	2	1	...	0	.185	8	0	2	.800
1887—Philadelphia	Nat.	OF-INF	18	72	7	15	4	0	...	15	.208	17	2	1	.950
1888—St. Louis	A.A.	OF-P	131	510	106	141	20	3	...	109	.276	232	39	23	.922
1889—St. Louis	A.A.	OF-2B	140	603	136	179	26	7	2	59	.297	231	41	32	.895
1890—St. Louis	A.A.	OF-INF	132	539	*134	189	26	9	6	91	.351	153	13	17	.907
1891—St. Louis	A.A.	OF-INF	125	527	115	163	20	8	8	37	.309	170	27	22	.900
1892—Boston	Nat.	OF	152	602	116	147	18	6	4	59	.244	211	31	33	.880
1893—Boston	Nat.	OF-INF	116	441	108	159	30	6	5	49	.361	224	53	29	.905
1894—Boston	Nat.	OF-INF	126	536	118	187	22	8	13	40	.349	286	30	32	.908
1895—Boston	Nat.	OF-INF	116	454	89	132	13	2	2	24	.291	203	23	29	.886
1896—Brooklyn	Nat.	OF	101	378	62	96	8	6	3	23	.254	179	20	16	.924
Union Association Totals—1 Year				53	218	37	45	4	1	0	....	.206	51	14	13	.833
American Assn. Totals—4 Years				528	2179	491	672	92	27	16	296	.308	786	120	94	.906
National League Totals—8 Years				677	2658	522	768	99	29	27	210	.289	1197	167	154	.900
Major League Totals—13 Years				1258	5055	1050	1485	195	57	43	506	.294	2034	301	261	.899

JAMES TIMOTHY (TIM) McCARVER

Born October 16, 1941, at Memphis, Tenn.

Height, 6.01. Weight, 198.

Threw right and batted lefthanded.

Tied for National League lead in passed balls with 16 in 1963 and led with 18 in 1965.

Named as catcher on THE SPORTING NEWS National League All-Star Team, 1967.

Year	Club	League	Pos.	G.	AB.	R.	H.	2B.	3B.	HR.	RBI.	B.A.	PO.	A.	E.	F.A.
1959—Keokuk	Midw.	C	65	275	58	99	6	4	3	24	.360	422	37	14	.970
1959—Rochester	Int.	C	17	70	10	25	1	1	0	8	.357	94	9	0	1.000
1959—St. Louis	Nat.	C	8	24	3	4	1	0	0	0	.167	32	2	1	.971
1960—Memphis	South.	C	85	303	45	105	11	2	3	34	.347	500	26	4	.992
1960—St. Louis	Nat.	C	10	10	3	2	0	0	0	0	.200	9	0	0	1.000
1961—S. Juan-Char.	Int.	C	81	275	26	63	10	0	1	27	.229	429	*51	5	.990
1961—St. Louis	Nat.	C	22	67	5	16	2	1	1	6	.239	86	9	3	.969
1962—Atlanta	Int.	C	122	382	65	105	17	1	11	57	.275	*685	48	*11	.985
1963—St. Louis	Nat.	C	127	405	39	117	12	7	4	51	.289	722	55	5	.994
1964—St. Louis	Nat.	C	143	465	53	134	19	3	9	52	.288	762	43	●11	.987
1965—St. Louis	Nat.	C	113	409	48	113	17	2	11	48	.276	687	43	4	*.995
1966—St. Louis	Nat.	C	150	543	50	149	19	*13	12	68	.274	841	62	7	.992
1967—St. Louis	Nat.	C	138	471	68	139	26	3	14	69	.295	819	*67	3	*.997
1968—St. Louis	Nat.	C	128	434	35	110	15	6	5	48	.253	708	54	11	.986
1969—St. Louis†	Nat.	C	138	515	46	134	27	3	7	51	.260	925	66	14	.986
1970—Philadelphia	Nat.	C	44	164	16	47	11	1	4	14	.287	314	18	3	.991
1971—Philadelphia	Nat.	C	134	474	51	132	20	5	8	46	.278	673	51	11	.985
1972—Phil.‡-Mont.§	Nat.	C-O-3	122	391	33	96	13	1	7	34	.246	561	47	8	.987
1973—St. Louis	Nat.	1B-C	130	331	30	88	16	4	3	49	.266	608	34	9	.986
1974—St. Louis x	Nat.	C-1B	74	106	13	23	0	1	0	11	.217	126	11	4	.972
1974—Boston	Amer.	C	11	28	3	7	1	0	0	1	.250	37	5	0	1.000
1975—Boston y	Amer.	C-1B	12	21	1	8	2	1	0	3	.381	21	4	1	.962
1975—Philadelphia	Nat.	C-1B	47	59	6	15	2	0	1	7	.254	62	5	1	.985
1976—Philadelphia	Nat.	C-1B	99	155	26	43	11	2	3	29	.277	265	9	0	.967
1977—Philadelphia	Nat.	C-1B	93	169	28	54	13	2	6	30	.320	238	14	3	.988
1978—Philadelphia	Nat.	C-1B	90	146	18	36	9	1	1	14	.247	215	14	2	.991
1979—Philadelphia z	Nat.	C-OF	79	137	13	33	5	1	1	12	.241	174	12	2	.989
1980—Philadelphia a	Nat.	1B	6	5	2	1	1	0	0	2	.200	8	0	0	1.000
National League Totals—21 Years				1886	5480	586	1486	239	56	97	641	.271	8835	616	102	.989
American League Totals—2 Years				23	49	4	15	3	1	0	4	.306	58	9	1	.985
Major League Totals—21 Years				1909	5529	590	1501	242	57	97	645	.271	8893	625	103	.989

Signed as free agent by St. Louis Cardinals' organization, June 8, 1959.

†Traded with Outfielders Curt Flood and Byron Browne and Pitcher Joe Horner to Philadelphia Phillies for First Baseman Richie Allen, Infielder Cookie Rojas and Pitcher Jerry Johnson, October 7, 1969. Flood refused to report and the Cardinals sent First Baseman Willie Montanez and a player to be named later to Philadelphia to complete the deal, April 8, 1970. Pitcher James Robert Browning was sent from St. Louis to Philadelphia as the player to be named later, August 30, 1970.

‡Traded to Montreal Expos for Catcher John Bateman, June 14, 1972.
§Traded to St. Louis Cardinals for Outfielder Jorge Roque, November 6, 1972.
xSold to Boston Red Sox, September 1, 1974.
yReleased, June 23, 1975; signed as a free agent by Philadelphia Phillies, July 1, 1975.
zReleased, November 7, 1979; re-signed by Phillies, September 1, 1980.
aReleased, October 24, 1980.

CHAMPIONSHIP SERIES RECORD

Year Club	League	Pos.	G.	AB.	R.	H.	2B.	3B.	HR.	RBI.	B.A.	PO.	A.	E.	F.A.
1976—Philadelphia .... Nat.		C-PH	2	4	0	0	0	0	0	0	.000	6	0	0	1.000
1977—Philadelphia .... Nat.		C-PH	3	6	1	1	0	0	0	0	.167	7	0	0	1.000
1978—Philadelphia .... Nat.		PH-C	2	4	2	0	0	0	0	1	.000	8	0	0	1.000
Championship Series Totals—3 Years.....			7	14	3	1	0	0	0	1	.071	21	0	0	1.000

WORLD SERIES RECORD

Year Club	League	Pos.	G.	AB.	R.	H.	2B.	3B.	HR.	RBI.	B.A.	PO.	A.	E.	F.A.
1964—St. Louis................ Nat.		C	7	23	4	11	1	1	1	5	.478	57	1	0	1.000
1967—St. Louis................ Nat.		C	7	24	3	3	1	0	0	2	.125	55	4	0	1.000
1968—St. Louis................ Nat.		C	7	27	3	9	0	2	1	4	.333	61	1	0	1.000
World Series Totals—3 Years			21	74	10	23	2	3	2	11	.311	173	6	0	1.000

JAMES (JIM) McCORMICK

Born 1856, at Paterson, N.J.

Died March 10, 1918, at Paterson, N.J.

Height, 5.10. Weight, 220.

Threw and batted righthanded.

Manager, Cleveland, National League, 1879 through 1881.

Year Club	League	G.	W.	L.	Pct.	H.	R.	CG.	ShO.
1878—Indianapolis .... National		14	5	8	.385	129	59	12	1
1879—Cleveland................................ National		60	20	●40	.333	581	305	59	3
1880—Cleveland................................ National		●73	★45	28	.616	588	282	★72	7
1881—Cleveland................................ National		57	26	30	.464	495	273	56	2
1882—Cleveland................................ National		★65	★36	29	.554	549	290	★64	4
1883—Cleveland................................ National		40	27	13	★.675	308	146	35	1
1884—Cleveland (a)............................ National		41	19	22	.463	357	208	37	3
1884—Cincinnati .... Union Association		26	22	4	.846	151	....	26	★7
1885—Providence-Chicago .... National		29	21	7	.750	225	129	28	3
1886—Chicago................................... National		42	31	11	.738	337	163	38	3
1887—Pittsburgh................................ National		36	13	23	.361	446	217	35	0
National League Totals—10 Years...		457	243	211	.535	4015	2072	436	27
Union Association Totals—1 Year...		26	22	4	.846	151	......	26	7
Major League Totals—10 Years..		483	265	215	.552	4166	......	462	34

aDeserted Cleveland; played first game for Cincinnati on August 10.

WILLIAM BARNEY McCOSKY
(Known by middle name.)

Born April 11, 1918, at Coal Run, Pa.

Height, 6.01. Weight, 184.

Threw right and batted lefthanded.

Year Club	League	Pos.	G.	AB.	R.	H.	2B.	3B.	HR.	RBI.	B.A.	PO.	A.	E.	F.A.
1936—Charleston .... Mid.-Atl.		OF	108	407	66	163	28	★19	7	77	★.400	230	9	4	★.984
1936—Beaumont .... Texas		OF	20	66	13	15	1	0	0	8	.227	33	1	2	.944
1937—Beaumont .... Texas		OF	158	633	★116	★201	32	★20	1	73	.318	★412	17	10	.977
1938—Beaumont .... Texas		OF	133	517	78	156	18	6	0	57	.302	283	9	7	.977
1939—Detroit.................. Amer.		OF	147	611	120	190	33	14	4	58	.311	★428	7	6	.986
1940—Detroit.................. Amer.		OF	143	589	123	●200	39	★19	4	57	.340	349	7	6	.983
1941—Detroit.................. Amer.		OF	127	494	80	160	25	8	3	55	.324	328	6	5	.985

Year Club League	Pos.	G.	AB.	R.	H.	2B.	3B.	HR.	RBI.	B.A.	PO.	A.	E.	F.A.
1942—Detroit.................... Amer.	OF	154	600	75	176	28	11	7	50	.293	351	7	7	.981
1943-44-45—Detroit.......... Amer.							(In Military Service)							
1946—Det.(a)-Phila. .... Amer.	OF	117	399	44	127	22	4	2	45	.318	263	3	6	.978
1947—Philadelphia .... Amer.	OF	137	546	77	179	22	7	1	52	.328	346	8	6	.983
1948—Philadelphia .... Amer.	OF	135	515	95	168	21	5	0	46	.326	277	9	3	.990
1949—Philadelphia(b).... Amer.							(Did not play)							
1950—Philadelphia .... Amer.	OF	66	179	19	43	10	1	0	11	.240	73	1	1	.987
1951—Phila.(c)-Cleve. .... Amer.	OF	43	88	12	21	5	0	1	3	.239	41	0	0	1.000
1951—Cincinnati(d) .... Nat.	OF	25	50	2	16	2	1	1	11	.320	17	0	0	1.000
1952—Cleveland.............. Amer.	OF	54	80	14	17	4	1	1	6	.213	17	0	1	.944
1953—Cleveland.............. Amer.	PH	22	21	3	4	3	0	0	3	.190	0	0	0	.000
American League Totals—11 Years		1145	4122	662	1285	212	70	23	386	.312	2473	48	41	.984
National League Totals—1 Year..............		25	50	2	16	2	1	1	11	.320	17	0	0	1.000
Major League Totals—11 Years................		1170	4172	664	1301	214	71	24	397	.312	2490	48	41	.984

aTraded to Philadelphia Athletics for third baseman George Kell, May 18, 1946.
bOut of game for season due to displaced vertebrae.
cSold to Cincinnati Reds, May 4, 1951.
dSold to Cleveland Indians, July 21, 1951.

WORLD SERIES RECORD

Year Club League	Pos.	G.	AB.	R.	H.	2B.	3B.	HR.	RBI.	B.A.	PO.	A.	E.	F.A.
1940—Detroit.................... Amer.	OF	7	23	5	7	1	0	0	1	.304	19	0	0	1.000

WILLIE LEE McCOVEY
(Stretch)

Born January 10, 1938, at Mobile, Ala.

Height, 6.04. Weight, 225.

Threw and batted lefthanded.

Holds major league records for most intentional bases on balls, season (45), 1969; most seasons by first baseman (22).

Shares major league records for most triples, first major league game (2), July 30, 1959; most home runs (2) and total bases (8), inning, April 12, 1973, fourth inning and June 27, 1977, sixth inning; most grand slams by pinch-hitter, lifetime (3); most years leading league in intentional bases on balls (4).

Shares modern major league record for most long hits, inning (2), April 12, 1973, fourth inning and June 27, 1977, sixth inning.

Holds National League records for most home runs by lefthanded batter, lifetime, (521); most home runs by first baseman, lifetime (439); most grand slams, lifetime (18).

Hit three home runs in a game, September 22, 1963; April 22, 1964 and September 17, 1966.

Led National League in slugging percentage with .545 in 1968, .656 in 1969 and .612 in 1970.

Led National League batters in bases on balls with 137 in 1970.

Named National League Rookie of the Year by THE SPORTING NEWS and National League Rookie of the Year by Baseball Writers' Association, 1959.

Named first baseman on THE SPORTING NEWS National League All-Star Teams, 1965-68-69-70.

Named by THE SPORTING NEWS as Major League Player of the Year, 1969.

Named Most Valuable Player in National League, 1969.

Named THE SPORTING NEWS National League Comeback Player of the Year, 1977.

Named to Hall of Fame, 1986.

Year Club League	Pos.	G.	AB.	R.	H.	2B.	3B.	HR.	RBI.	B.A.	PO.	A.	E.	F.A.
1955—Sandersville .... Ga. St.	1B	107	410	82	125	24	1	19	*113	.305	*897	51	23	.976
1956—Danville .... Carol.	1B	152	519	119	161	*38	8	29	89	.310	1273	87	*34	.976
1957—Dallas .... Texas	1B	115	395	63	111	21	9	11	65	.281	960	80	10	.990
1958—Phoenix .... P.C.	1B	146	527	91	168	37	10	14	89	.319	*1171	69	*18	.986
1959—Phoenix .... P.C.	1B	95	349	84	130	26	11	*29	b92	.372	896	43	16	.983
1959—San Francisco ...... Nat.	1B	52	192	32	68	9	5	13	38	.354	424	29	5	.989
1960—San Francisco ...... Nat.	1B	101	260	37	62	15	3	13	51	.238	557	39	9	.985
1960—Tacoma................. P.C.	1B	17	63	14	18	1	2	3	16	.286	149	4	3	.980
1961—San Francisco ...... Nat.	1B	106	328	59	89	12	3	18	50	.271	669	55	11	.985
1962—San Francisco ...... Nat.	OF-1B	91	229	41	67	6	1	20	54	.293	186	9	3	.985
1963—San Francisco ...... Nat.	*OF-1B	152	564	103	158	19	5	●44	102	.280	363	21	*15	.976
1964—San Francisco ...... Nat.	OF-1B	130	364	55	80	14	1	18	54	.220	273	19	14	.954
1965—San Francisco ...... Nat.	1B	160	540	93	149	17	4	39	92	.276	1310	87	13	.991
1966—San Francisco ...... Nat.	1B	150	502	85	148	26	6	36	96	.295	1287	81	22	.984
1967—San Francisco ...... Nat.	1B	135	456	73	126	17	4	31	91	.276	1221	81	●15	.989
1968—San Francisco ...... Nat.	1B	148	523	81	153	16	4	*36	*105	.293	1305	103	*21	.985
1969—San Francisco ...... Nat.	1B	149	491	101	157	26	2	*45	*126	.320	1392	79	12	.984
1970—San Francisco ...... Nat.	1B	152	495	98	143	39	2	39	126	.289	1217	*134	*15	.989
1971—San Francisco ...... Nat.	1B	105	329	45	91	13	0	18	70	.277	828	63	*15	.983
1972—San Francisco ...... Nat.	1B	81	263	30	56	8	0	14	35	.213	617	32	9	.986

Year Club League	Pos.	G.	AB.	R.	H.	2B.	3B.	HR.	RBI.	B.A.	PO.	A.	E.	F.A.
1973—San Fran. (a) .... Nat.	1B	130	383	52	102	14	3	29	75	.266	930	76	12	.988
1974—San Diego .... Nat.	1B	128	344	53	87	19	1	22	63	.253	815	47	11	.987
1975—San Diego .... Nat.	1B	122	413	43	104	17	0	23	68	.252	979	73	15	.986
1976—San Diego (b) .... Nat.	1B	71	202	20	41	9	0	7	36	.203	420	44	4	.991
1976—Oakland (c) .... Amer.	DH	11	24	0	5	0	0	0	0	.208	0	0	0	.000
1977—San Francisco ...... Nat.	1B	141	478	54	134	21	0	28	86	.280	1072	60	*13	.989
1978—San Francisco ...... Nat.	1B	108	351	32	80	19	2	12	64	.228	721	44	10	.987
1979—San Francisco ...... Nat.	1B	117	353	34	88	9	0	15	57	.249	740	48	10	.987
1980—San Francisco ...... Nat.	1B-PH	48	113	8	23	8	0	1	16	.204	241	12	2	.992
National League Totals—22 Years.........		2577	8173	1229	2206	353	46	521	1555	.270	17567	1236	256	.987
American League Totals—1 Year		11	24	0	5	0	0	0	0	.208	0	0	0	.000
Major League Totals—22 Years		2588	8197	1229	2211	353	46	521	1555	.270	17567	1236	256	.987

aTraded with Outfielder Bernie Williams (on Phoenix roster) to San Diego Padres for Pitcher Mike Caldwell, October 25, 1973.

bSold to Oakland A's, August 30, 1976.

cPlayed out option year and granted free agency; signed as free agent with San Francisco Giants, January 6, 1977.

CHAMPIONSHIP SERIES RECORD

Year Club League	Pos.	G.	AB.	R.	H.	2B.	3B.	HR.	RBI.	B.A.	PO.	A.	E.	F.A.
1971—San Francisco ...... Nat.	1B	4	14	2	6	0	0	2	6	.429	34	3	1	.974

WORLD SERIES RECORD

Year Club League	Pos.	G.	AB.	R.	H.	2B.	3B.	HR.	RBI.	B.A.	PO.	A.	E.	F.A.
1962—San Francisco ...... Nat.	1B-OF	4	15	2	3	0	1	1	1	.200	23	4	2	.931

LYNDALL DALE (LINDY) McDANIEL

Born December 13, 1935, at Hollis, Okla.

Height, 6.03. Weight, 197.

Threw and batted righthanded.

Brother of Von McDaniel, former major league pitcher;
and Kerry McDaniel, former minor league pitcher.

Led National League in wild pitches with 10 in 1959.
Won THE SPORTING NEWS National League Fireman of the Year award, 1960 and 1963.

Year Club League	G.	IP.	W.	L.	Pct.	H.	R.	ER.	SO.	BB.	ERA.
1955—St. Louis.................... Nat.	4	19	0	0	.000	22	10	10	7	7	4.74
1956—St. Louis.................... Nat.	39	116	7	6	.538	121	60	44	59	42	3.41
1957—St. Louis.................... Nat.	30	191	15	9	.625	196	87	74	75	53	3.49
1958—St. Louis.................... Nat.	26	109	5	7	.417	139	76	70	47	31	5.78
1958—Omaha....................... A. A.	6	42	4	1	.800	44	18	17	18	6	3.64
1959—St. Louis.................... Nat.	62	132	14	12	.538	144	61	56	86	41	3.82
1960—St. Louis.................... Nat.	65	116	12	4	*.750	85	28	27	105	24	2.09
1961—St. Louis.................... Nat.	55	94	10	6	.625	117	57	51	65	31	4.88
1962—St. Louis†.................. Nat.	55	107	3	10	.231	96	53	49	79	29	4.12
1963—Chicago .... Nat.	57	88	13	7	.650	82	32	28	75	27	2.86
1964—Chicago .... Nat.	63	95	1	7	.125	104	43	41	71	23	3.88
1965—Chicago‡ .... Nat.	71	129	5	6	.455	115	45	37	92	47	2.58
1966—San Francisco .... Nat.	64	122	10	5	.667	103	48	36	93	35	2.66
1967—San Francisco .... Nat.	41	73	2	6	.250	69	34	30	48	24	3.70
1968—San Francisco§ .... Nat.	12	19	0	0	.000	30	16	16	9	5	7.58
1968—New York.................... Amer.	24	51	4	1	.800	30	10	10	43	12	1.76
1969—New York.................... Amer.	51	84	5	6	.455	84	37	33	60	23	3.54
1970—New York.................... Amer.	62	112	9	5	.643	88	29	25	81	23	2.01
1971—New York.................... Amer.	44	70	5	10	.333	82	41	39	39	24	5.01
1972—New York.................... Amer.	37	68	3	1	.750	54	23	17	47	25	2.25
1973—New York x................. Amer.	47	160	12	6	.667	148	54	51	93	49	2.87
1974—Kansas City................. Amer.	38	107	1	4	.200	109	50	41	47	24	3.45
1975—Kansas City................. Amer.	40	78	5	1	.833	81	40	36	40	24	4.15
National League Totals—14 Years......................	644	1410	97	85	.533	1423	650	569	911	419	3.63
American League Totals—8 Years	343	730	44	34	.564	676	284	252	450	204	3.11
Major League Totals—21 Years.............	987	2140	141	119	.542	2099	934	821	1361	623	3.45

†Traded to Chicago Cubs with Pitcher Larry Jackson and Catcher Jimmie Schaffer for Pitcher Don Cardwell, Catcher Moe Thacker and Outfielder George Altman, October 17, 1962.

‡Traded with Outfielder Don Landrum to San Francisco Giants for Pitcher Bill Hands and Catcher Randy Hundley, December 2, 1965.

§Traded to New York Yankees for Pitcher Bill Monbouquette, July 12, 1968.

xTraded to Kansas City Royals for Outfielder Lou Piniella and Pitcher Ken Wright, December 7, 1973.

SAMUEL EDWARD THOMAS (SAM) McDOWELL
(Sudden Sam)

Born September 21, 1942, at Pittsburgh, Pa.

Height, 6;05. Weight, 220.

Threw and batted lefthanded.

Shares major league record for most consecutive one-hit games (2), April 25 and May 1, 1966.
Named pitcher on THE SPORTING NEWS American League All-Star Team, 1970.
Named by THE SPORTING NEWS as American League Pitcher of the Year, 1970.

Year Club	League	G.	IP.	W.	L.	Pct.	H.	R.	ER.	SO.	BB.	ERA.
1960—Lakeland	Fla. St.	16	105	5	6	.455	85	51	39	100	80	3.34
1961—Salt Lake City	P. C.	32	175	13	10	.565	143	98	86	★156	★152	4.42
1961—Cleveland	Amer.	1	6	0	0	.000	3	0	0	5	5	0.00
1962—Cleveland	Amer.	25	88	3	7	.300	81	64	59	70	70	6.03
1962—Salt Lake City	P. C.	6	40	3	2	.600	28	9	9	34	23	2.03
1963—Cleveland	Amer.	14	65	3	5	.375	63	37	35	63	44	4.85
1963—Jacksonville	Int.	12	87	3	6	.333	63	35	33	84	50	3.41
1964—Portland	P. C.	9	76	8	0	1.000	34	11	10	102	24	1.18
1964—Cleveland	Amer.	31	173	11	6	.647	148	60	52	177	100	2.71
1965—Cleveland	Amer.	42	273	17	11	.607	178	80	66	★325	★132	★2.18
1966—Cleveland	Amer.	35	194	9	8	.529	130	66	62	★225	102	2.88
1967—Cleveland	Amer.	37	236	13	15	.464	201	★112	★101	236	★123	3.85
1968—Cleveland	Amer.	38	269	15	14	.517	181	78	54	★283	★110	1.81
1969—Cleveland	Amer.	39	285	18	14	.563	222	111	93	★279	102	2.94
1970—Cleveland	Amer.	39	●305	20	12	.625	236	108	99	★304	★131	2.92
1971—Cleveland(a)	Amer.	35	215	13	17	.433	160	89	81	192	★153	3.39
1972—San Francisco	Nat.	28	164	10	8	.556	155	86	79	122	86	4.34
1973—San Francisco(b)	Nat.	18	40	1	2	.333	45	23	20	35	29	4.50
1973—New York	Amer.	16	96	5	8	.385	73	47	42	75	64	3.94
1974—New York	Amer.	13	48	1	6	.143	42	27	25	33	41	4.69
1975—Pittsburgh(c)	Nat.	14	35	2	1	.667	30	11	11	29	20	2.83
American League Totals—13 Years		365	2253	128	123	.510	1718	879	769	2267	1177	3.07
National League Totals—3 Years		60	239	13	11	.542	230	120	110	186	135	4.14
Major League Totals—15 Years		425	2492	141	134	.513	1948	999	879	2453	1312	3.17

aTraded to San Francisco Giants for Pitcher Gaylord Perry and Shortstop Frank Duffy, November 29, 1971.
bSold to New York Yankees for an estimated $150,000, June 7, 1973.
cSigned as free agent by Pittsburgh Pirates, April 2, 1975.

JOSEPH JEROME (JOE) McGINNITY
(Iron Man)

Born March 19, 1871, at Rock Island, Ill.

Died November 14, 1929, at Brooklyn, N. Y.

Height, 5.11. Weight, 206.

Threw and batted righthanded.

Holds major league record for most complete-game doubleheaders pitched (5) and won (3), lifetime; most complete-game doubleheaders pitched (3) and won (3), season.
Holds modern National League record for most innings pitched, season (434), 1903.
Manager, Newark, Eastern League, 1909-11-12 (International); Tacoma, Northwestern League, 1913-14-15; Butte, Northwestern League; 1916-17; Dubuque, Mississippi Valley League, 1922-23; part owner-manager, Dubuque, Mississippi Valley, 1925; coach, Brooklyn Dodgers, 1926.
Named to Hall of Fame, 1946.

Year Club	League	G.	IP.	W.	L.	Pct.	ShO.	H.	R.	SO.	BB.
1893—Montgomery	Southern	31	193	10	19	.345	....	212	....	76	99
1894—Kansas City	Western	20	124	8	10	.444	....	157	....	31	54
1898—Peoria	West. Assn.	16	104	10	3	.769	....	107	....	69	59
1899—Baltimore(a)	National	49	380	●28	17	.622	4	340	168	74	92
1900—Brooklyn(b)	National	★45	347	★29	9	★.763	1	364	184	92	★113
1901—Baltimore	American	★48	★378	26	21	.553	1	401	219	73	94
1902—Baltimore(c)	American	25	199	13	10	.565	0	186	97	39	44
1902—New York	National	19	153	8	8	.500	1	129	52	68	31

Year—Club	League	G.	IP.	W.	L.	Pct.	ShO.	H.	R.	SO.	BB.
1903—New York	National	★55	★434	★31	20	.608	3	391	162	171	109
1904—New York	National	★51	★408	★35	8	★.814	★9	307	103	144	86
1905—New York	National	●46	320	21	15	.588	2	289	131	125	71
1906—New York	National	★45	340	★27	12	.692	3	316	127	105	71
1907—New York	National	★47	310	18	18	.500	3	320	126	120	58
1908—New York	National	37	186	11	7	.611	5	192	73	55	37
1909—Newark	Eastern	★55	★422	★29	16	.644	....	297	105	195	78
1910—Newark	Eastern	★61	★408	★30	19	.612	....	325	★131	132	71
1911—Newark	Eastern	43	278	12	19	.387	....	269	130	77	53
1912—Newark	International	37	261	16	10	.615	....	293	132	62	43
1913—Tacoma	Northwestern	★68	★436	22	19	.537	....	★418	★177	154	66
1914—Tacoma	Northwestern	49	326	20	★21	.488	....	295	140	105	73
1914—Venice	Pacific Coast	8	37	1	4	.200	....	42	17	7	5
1915—Tacoma	Northwestern	45	★355	21	15	.583	....	291	101	58	39
1916—Butte	Northwestern	43	291	20	13	.606	....	★340	★191	95	63
1917—Butte-Great Falls	Northwestern	16	119	7	6	.538	....	119	51	28	25
1918—Vancouver	P. C.-Int.	9	....	2	6	.250	....	47	....	31	14
1922—Danville	I. I. I.	16	79	1	6	.143	....	117	74	12	12
1922—Dubuque	Miss. Valley	19	91	5	8	.385	....	94	52	19	19
1923—Dubuque	Miss. Valley	42	206	15	12	.556	....	268	117	41	44
1925—Dubuque	Miss. Valley	15	85	6	6	.500	....	119	51	22	18
American League Totals—2 Years		73	577	39	31	.557	1	587	316	112	138
National League Totals—9 Years		394	2878	208	114	.646	31	2648	1126	954	661
Major League Totals—10 Years		467	3455	247	145	.630	32	3235	1442	1066	799

aTransferred to Brooklyn when National League reduced circuit to eight clubs for 1900.
bJumped with John McGraw to Baltimore A. L. club, 1901.
cJumped back with McGraw and others to New York Giants, July, 1902.

WORLD SERIES RECORD

Year—Club	League	G.	IP.	W.	L.	Pct.	ShO.	H.	R.	ER.	SO.	BB.	ERA.
1905—New York	National	2	17	1	1	.500	1	10	3	0	6	3	0.00

JOHN JOSEPH McGRAW
(The Little Napoleon)

Born April 7, 1873, at Truxton, N. Y.

Died February 25, 1934, at New Rochelle, N. Y.

Height, 5.07. Weight, 155.

Threw right and batted lefthanded.

Manager, Baltimore, N. L., 1899; Baltimore A. L., 1901 to 1902; New York Giants, 1902 to 1932. Named to Hall of Fame, 1937.

Year—Club	League	Pos.	G.	AB.	R.	H.	2B.	3B.	HR.	SB.	B.A.	PO.	A.	E.	F.A.
1890—Olean	NYP	SS	....	....	....	....	...	...	...	....	.....	.....	....	...	.....
1891—Cedar Rapids	Ill.-Ia	SS	85	359	68	99	...	...	...	21	.275	.....	....	...	.875
1891—Baltimore	A. A.	SS	31	106	15	26	3	4	0	7	.245	46	50	18	.842
1892—Baltimore	Nat.	2B-OF	76	288	41	77	14	2	1	14	.267	140	111	24	.913
1893—Baltimore	Nat.	SS	127	475	123	156	10	11	5	40	.328	221	346	66	.896
1894—Baltimore	Nat.	3B	123	515	155	175	20	14	0	77	.340	130	246	44	.895
1895—Baltimore	Nat.	3B	93	385	109	144	15	7	2	69	.374	100	238	46	.880
1896—Baltimore	Nat.	3B	19	73	19	26	2	2	0	13	.356	22	38	12	.833
1897—Baltimore	Nat.	3B	105	389	89	127	14	3	0	42	.326	116	188	36	.880
1898—Baltimore	Nat.	3B	141	521	★142	174	7	10	0	42	.334	141	166	44	.874
1899—Baltimore(a)	Nat.	3B	118	402	140	157	13	3	1	73	.390	149	266	25	.943
1900—St. Louis(b)	Nat.	3B	98	341	84	115	10	4	2	28	.337	106	216	29	.917
1901—Baltimore	Amer.	3B	73	230	73	81	13	9	0	25	.352	80	140	23	.896
1902—Baltimore(c)	Amer.	3B	20	63	14	18	3	2	1	5	.286	25	25	8	.862
1902—New York	Nat.	SS-3B	34	106	13	24	0	0	0	7	.226	63	118	16	.900
1903—New York	Nat.	2B-SS	12	11	2	3	0	0	0	1	.273	2	1	1	.750
1904—New York	Nat.	2B-SS	5	12	0	4	0	0	0	0	.333	12	17	2	.935
1905—New York	Nat.	OF-PR	3	0	0	0	0	0	0	0	.000	0	0	0	.000
1906—New York	Nat.	3B	4	2	0	0	0	0	0	0	.000	0	0	0	.000
American Assn. Totals—1 Year			31	106	15	26	3	4	0	7	.245	46	50	18	.842
American League Totals—2 Years			93	293	87	99	16	11	1	30	.338	105	165	31	.897
National League Totals—14 Years			958	3520	917	1182	105	56	11	407	.336	1202	1945	345	.901
Major League Totals—16 Years			1082	3919	1019	1307	124	71	12	444	.334	1353	2166	394	.899

aSold with Catcher Wilbert Robinson and Second Baseman Billy Keister to St. Louis N. L. for $150,000, 1899.
bJumped to Baltimore A. L. in 1901.
cQuit A. L. in July after disagreement with Ban Johnson and joined New York N. L., July 16, 1902.

Year	Club	League	Position	W.	L.	Year	Club	League	Position	W.	L.
1899—Baltimore	Nat.		Fourth	84	58	1917—New York	Nat.		First	98	56
1901—Baltimore	Amer.		Fifth	68	65	1918—New York	Nat.		Second	71	53
1902—Baltimore	Amer.		Sixth	31	38	1919—New York	Nat.		Second	87	53
1902—New York	Nat.		Eighth	21	33	1920—New York	Nat.		Second	86	68
1903—New York	Nat.		Second	84	55	1921—New York	Nat.		First	94	59
1904—New York	Nat.		First	106	47	1922—New York	Nat.		First	93	61
1905—New York	Nat.		First	105	48	1923—New York	Nat.		First	95	58
1906—New York	Nat.		Second	96	56	1924—New York	Nat.		First	93	60
1907—New York	Nat.		Fourth	82	51	1925—New York	Nat.		Second	86	66
1908—New York	Nat.		†Second	98	56	1926—New York	Nat.		Fifth	74	77
1909—New York	Nat.		Third	92	61	1927—New York	Nat.		Third	92	62
1910—New York	Nat.		Second	91	63	1928—New York	Nat.		Second	93	61
1911—New York	Nat.		First	99	54	1929—New York	Nat.		Third	84	67
1912—New York	Nat.		First	103	48	1930—New York	Nat.		Third	87	67
1913—New York	Nat.		First	101	51	1931—New York	Nat.		Second	87	65
1914—New York	Nat.		Second	84	70	1932—New York	Nat.		Seventh	16	22
1915—New York	Nat.		Eighth	69	83	Major League Totals—33 Years				2836	1978
1916—New York	Nat.		Fourth	86	66						

WORLD SERIES RECORD

Year	Club	League	W.	L.	Year	Club	League	W.	L.
1905—New York	National		4	1	1921—New York	National		5	3
1911—New York	National		2	4	1922—New York	National		4	0
1912—New York	National		3	4	1923—New York	National		2	4
1913—New York	National		1	4	1924—New York	National		3	4
1917—New York	National		2	4					

JAMES THOMAS (JIM) McGUIRE
(Deacon)

Born November 2, 1865, at Youngstown, O.

Died October 31, 1936, at Albion, Mich.

Height, 6.01. Weight, 185.

Threw and batted righthanded.

Manager, Washington, N.L., 1898; Boston Red Sox, 1907-08; Cleveland, A.L., 1909 through 1911; Coach, Detroit Tigers, 1912 through 1915; scout, Tigers, 1916 through 1925; coach, Albion College, 1926.

Year	Club	League	Pos.	G.	AB.	R.	H.	2B.	3B.	HR.	SB.	B.A.	PO.	A.	E.	F.A.
1884—Toledo	A.A.		C	45	152	13	28	7 ·	0	1	....	.184	.....	....	27	.911
1885—Detroit	N.L.		C	34	121	11	23	4	2	0	...	.190	249	52	26	.920
1886—Philadelphia	N.L.		C	48	167	25	33	7	1	2	2	.198	298	50	39	.899
1887—Philadelphia	N.L.		C	40	161	22	57	6	6	2	3	.354	212	57	41	.868
1888—Phila.-Det.	N.L.		C	15	64	17	17	4	2	0	0	.266	57	12	11	.863
1888—Cleveland	A.A.		C-1B	25	87	15	18	1	3	1	4	.207	99	27	14	.900
1889—Toronto	I.A.		C	93	354	72	100	...	...	...	20	.282	451	158	48	.927
1890—Rochester	A.A.		C-1B	87	318	43	96	14	3	4	20	.302	379	100	34	.934
1891—Washington	A.A.		C-OF	106	385	52	111	21	11	3	9	.288	439	142	49	.922
1892—Washington	N.L.		C	87	311	46	75	13	5	3	9	.241	273	97	30	.925
1893—Washington	N.L.		C-1B	59	225	29	59	12	1	1	2	.262	165	46	29	.879
1894—Washington	N.L.		C	102	427	67	130	16	6	6	11	.304	288	116	39	.912
1895—Washington	N.L.		C	133	539	91	178	24	8	10	20	.330	412	177	38	.939
1896—Washington	N.L.		C	95	381	59	124	24	4	2	11	.325	350	86	31	.934
1897—Washington	N.L.		C	82	328	52	111	14	8	4	11	.338	289	88	19	.952
1898—Washington	N.L.		C-1B	128	483	60	132	12	3	1	11	.273	382	96	14	.972
1899—Was.-Bkn.	N.L.		C	99	348	47	106	15	5	1	9	.305	336	126	16	.967
1900—Brooklyn	N.L.		C	68	239	20	67	14	2	0	1	.280	212	80	19	.939
1901—Brooklyn	N.L.		C	84	297	28	87	16	4	0	4	.293	418	100	16	.970
1902—Detroit	A.L.		C	72	222	28	51	14	1	2	0	.230	211	70	14	.953
1903—Detroit	A.L.		C	71	245	17	59	11	1	0	7	.241	324	70	15	.963
1904—New York	A.L.		C	100	322	18	68	12	2	0	3	.211	543	113	19	.972
1905—New York	A.L.		C	71	228	9	50	7	2	0	3	.219	350	69	11	.975
1906—New York	A.L.		C	51	144	11	43	5	0	0	3	.299	218	38	10	.962
1907—N.Y.-Bos.	A.L.		C	7	5	1	3	0	0	1	0	.600	3	1	0	1.000
1908—Bos.-Clev.	A.L.		1B	2	5	0	1	1	0	0	0	.200	10	0	0	1.000
1910—Cleveland	A.L.		C	1	3	0	1	0	0	0	0	.333	2	1	0	1.000
1912—Detroit	A.L.		C	1	2	1	1	0	0	0	0	.500	2	3	2	.714
American Assn. Totals—4 Years				263	942	123	253	43	17	9	..	.269	..	..	124	.922
National League Totals—14 Years				1074	4091	574	1199	181	57	32	...	.293	3941	1183	368	.933
American League Totals—9 Years				376	1176	85	277	50	6	3	16	.236	1679	365	71	.966
Major League Totals—26 Years				1713	6209	782	1729	274	80	44	..	.278	..	..	563	.939

JOHN PHALEN (STUFFY) McINNIS

Born September 19, 1890, at Gloucester, Mass.
Died February 16, 1960, at Ipswich, Mass.
Height, 5.09½. Weight, 162.
Threw and batted righthanded.

Holds major league record for most consecutive chances accepted, first baseman, lifetime (1,700), May 31, 1921 through June 2, 1922.

Holds American League records for highest fielding percentage (.999) and fewest errors (1), first baseman, season, 150 or more games, 1921; most consecutive errorless games, first baseman, season (119), May 21, first game, through October 2, 1921.

Led American League first basemen in double plays, 1923 (tie).

Manager, Philadelphia Phillies, 1927; Salem, New England League, 1928.

Year	Club	League	Pos.	G.	AB.	R.	H.	2B.	3B.	HR.	RBI.	B.A.	PO.	A.	E.	F.A.
1908—Haverhill	N. Eng.	2B	51	186	24	56	8	3	0	....	.301	113	147	18	.935
1909—Philadelphia	Amer.	SS	19	46	4	11	0	0	1	4	.239	34	46	9	.899
1910—Philadelphia	Amer.	SS	38	73	10	22	2	4	0	12	.301	20	31	4	.927
1911—Philadelphia	Amer.	SS-1B	126	468	76	150	20	10	3	79	.321	1105	101	35	.972
1912—Philadelphia	Amer.	1B	153	568	83	186	25	13	3	103	.327	*1533	*100	●27	.984
1913—Philadelphia	Amer.	1B	148	543	79	177	30	4	4	93	.326	*1504	79	12	*.992
1914—Philadelphia	Amer.	1B	149	576	74	181	12	8	1	91	.314	1423	85	7	*.995
1915—Philadelphia	Amer.	1B	119	456	44	143	14	4	0	48	.314	1123	83	13	.989
1916—Philadelphia	Amer.	1B	140	512	42	151	25	3	1	56	.295	1404	96	12	.992
1917—Philadelphia(a)	Amer.	1B	150	567	50	172	19	4	0	46	.303	*1658	95	12	.993
1918—Boston	Amer.	1-3B	117	423	40	115	11	5	0	58	.272	1100	113	10	.992
1919—Boston	Amer.	1B	120	440	32	134	12	5	1	60	.305	1236	82	7	.995
1920—Boston	Amer.	1B	148	559	50	166	21	3	2	71	.297	1586	91	7	*.996
1921—Boston(b)	Amer.	1B	152	584	72	179	31	10	0	74	.307	1549	102	1	*.999
1922—Cleveland	Amer.	1B	142	537	58	164	28	7	1	78	.305	1376	73	5	*.997
1923—Boston(c)	Nat.	1B	●154	607	70	191	23	9	2	95	.315	1500	*89	14	.991
1924—Boston	Nat.	1B	146	581	57	169	23	7	1	59	.291	1435	95	10	.994
1925—Pittsburgh(d)	Nat.	1B	59	155	19	57	10	4	0	24	.368	377	24	3	.993
1926—Pittsburgh	Nat.	1B	47	127	12	38	6	1	0	13	.299	300	17	4	.988
1927—Philadelphia	Nat.	1B	1	0	0	0	0	0	0	0	.000	0	0	0	.000
1928—Salem	N. Eng.	1B	38	115	10	39	5	2	0	17	.339	286	23	3	.990
American League Totals—14 Years			1721	6352	714	1951	250	80	17	873	.307	16651	1177	161	.991
National League Totals—5 Years			407	1470	158	455	62	21	3	191	.309	3612	225	31	.992
Major League Totals—19 Years			2128	7822	872	2406	312	101	20	1064	.308	20263	1402	192	.991

aTraded to Boston Red Sox for Third Baseman Larry Gardner, Outfielder Tilly Walker and Catcher Hick Cady, January 11, 1918.

bTraded to Cleveland for First Baseman George Burns and Outfielders Joe Harris and Elmer Smith, December, 1921.

cClaimed on waivers by Boston Braves, January, 1923.

dReleased, April 13, 1925, and signed with Pittsburgh, May 29.

WORLD SERIES RECORD

Year	Club	League	Pos.	G.	AB.	R.	H.	2B.	3B.	HR.	RBI.	B.A.	PO.	A.	E.	F.A.
1911—Philadelphia	Amer.	1B	1	0	0	0	0	0	0	0	.000	1	0	0	1.000
1913—Philadelphia	Amer.	1B	5	17	1	2	1	0	0	2	.118	45	0	0	1.000
1914—Philadelphia	Amer.	1B	4	14	2	2	1	0	0	0	.143	50	1	1	.981
1918—Boston	Amer.	1B	6	20	2	5	0	0	0	1	.250	70	2	0	1.000
1925—Pittsburgh	Nat.	1B-PH	4	14	0	4	0	0	0	1	.286	30	3	0	1.000
World Series Totals—5 Years			20	65	5	13	2	0	0	4	.200	196	6	1	.995

EDWIN J. (ED) McKEAN

Born June 20, 1864, at Cleveland, O.
Died August 16, 1919, at Cleveland, O.
Height, 5.09. Weight, 180.
Threw and batted righthanded.

Year	Club	League	Pos.	G.	AB.	R.	H.	2B.	3B.	HR.	SB.	B.A.	PO.	A.	E.	F.A.
1884—Youngstown	I&O Assn.						(No Record Available)									
1885—							(No Record Available)									
1886—Providence	East.		SS	22	98	16	25	...	...	...	....	.255	33	91	20	.861
1886—Rochester	Int.		SS	77	324	....	100	...	...	...	....	.309	115	221	48	*.875
1887—Cleveland	A. A.		SS	132	593	95	216	16	13	2	77	.364	(588-PO-A)	102		.852
1888—Cleveland	A. A.		SS-O	130	542	92	161	23	13	6	66	.297	(418-PO-A)	50		.893
1889—Cleveland	Nat.		SS	123	500	86	151	22	8	4	35	.302	206	398	62	.907
1890—Cleveland	Nat.		SS	136	530	91	157	20	12	7	23	.296	266	433	*75	.903
1891—Cleveland	Nat.		SS	141	*602	114	169	17	13	6	15	.281	249	470	*86	.893
1892—Cleveland	Nat.		SS	128	523	75	141	15	10	0	19	.270	201	371	84	.872
1893—Cleveland	Nat.		SS	125	510	100	166	26	23	4	15	.325	245	437	71	.906
1894—Cleveland	Nat.		SS	130	561	115	199	29	16	8	32	.355	278	401	66	.911
1895—Cleveland	Nat.		SS	132	*573	131	197	26	17	7	16	.344	256	433	67	.977
1896—Cleveland	Nat.		SS	133	567	100	190	28	10	8	13	.335	220	398	58	.914
1897—Cleveland	Nat.		SS	127	527	86	144	21	14	3	18	.273	231	381	50	.924
1898—Cleveland	Nat.		SS	151	604	88	172	21	1	9	10	.285	299	429	56	.929
1899—St. Louis	Nat.		SS	67	270	40	76	6	2	3	3	.281	71	124	25	.886
American Assn. Totals—2 Years				262	1135	187	377	39	26	8	143	.332	(1006-PO-A)	152		.869
National League Totals—11 Years				1393	5767	1026	1762	231	126	59	199	.307	2522	4274	700	.907
Major League Totals—13 Years				1655	6902	1213	2139	270	152	67	342	.310	(7802-PO-A)	852		.902

WILLIAM BOYD (BILL) McKECHNIE
(Deacon)

Born August 7, 1887, at Wilkinsburg, Pa.

Died October 29, 1965, at Bradenton, Fla.

Height, 5.10. Weight, 180.

Threw right and batted left and righthanded.

Father of William B. McKechnie, Jr., former president of the
Pacific Coast League.

Player-manager, Newark Federal League, 1915; manager, Pittsburgh Pirates, 1922 through 1926; coach, St. Louis Cardinals, 1927; manager, St. Louis Cardinals, 1928; Rochester, 1929; St. Louis Cardinals, 1929; Boston Braves, 1930 through 1937; Cincinnati Reds, 1938 through 1946; coach, Cleveland Indians, 1947 through 1949; coach, Boston Red Sox, 1952-53.

Named by THE SPORTING NEWS as No. 1 Major League Manager of the Year, 1937 and 1940.

Named to Hall of Fame, 1962.

Year	Club	League	Pos.	G.	AB.	R.	H.	2B.	3B.	HR.	RBI.	B.A.	PO.	A.	E.	F.A.
1906—Washington	P.-O.-Md.						(Records not available)									
1907—Washington	P.-O.-Md.		3B	53	185	22	37	...	...	...	.....	.200	70	99	13	.929
1907—Pittsburgh	Nat.		2B-3B	3	8	0	1	0	0	0	1	.125	1	3	0	1.000
1908—Canton	Ohio-Pa.		3B	118	406	55	115	...	...	...	.....	.283	155	317	29	.942
1909—Wheeling	Central		3B	132	464	55	127	16	7	1	.....	.274	163	279	33	.931
1910—Pittsburgh	Nat.		2B	60	212	23	46	1	2	0	17	.217	89	112	6	.971
1911—Pittsburgh	Nat.		2B-1B	92	321	40	73	8	7	2	36	.227	573	80	17	.975
1912—Pittsburgh	Nat.		INF	24	73	8	18	0	1	0	3	.247	19	41	3	.952
1912—St. Paul	A. A.		SS	41	158	22	37	7	3	1	.....	.234	88	123	12	.946
1913—Boston(a)	Nat.		OF	1	4	1	0	0	0	0	0	.000	3	0	0	1.000
1913—New York	Amer.		2B	44	112	7	15	0	0	0	0	.134	57	76	7	.950
1913—St. Paul	A. A.		3B	32	110	11	27	0	6	0	6	.245	31	47	2	.975
1914—Indianapolis	Federal		3B	149	571	107	174	22	6	2	.....	.305	193	326	32	.942
1915—Newark	Federal		3B	126	448	49	115	22	5	1	.....	.257	182	226	19	.956
1916—N.Y.(b)-Cin.	Nat.		3B	108	390	26	100	12	1	0	30	.256	108	193	17	.947
1917—Cincinnati(c)	Nat.		2B	48	134	11	34	3	1	0	14	.254	49	51	6	.943
1918—Pittsburgh	Nat.		3B	126	435	34	111	13	9	2	46	.255	162	261	15	.966
1919—							(On Voluntarily Retired List)									
1920—Pittsburgh	Nat.		INF	40	133	13	29	3	1	1	13	.218	85	84	8	.955
1921—Minneapolis	A. A.		3B	156	661	140	212	31	7	8	65	.321	189	284	25	.950
American League Totals—1 Year				44	112	7	15	0	0	0	0	.134	57	76	7	.950
National League Totals—9 Years				502	1710	156	412	40	22	5	160	.241	1089	825	72	.964
Major League Totals—9 Years				546	1822	163	427	40	22	5	160	.234	1146	901	79	.963

aDrafted by Boston Braves, September, 1912; claimed on waivers by New York Yankees, April, 1913.

bTraded with Pitcher Christy Mathewson and Outfielder Edd Roush to Cincinnati for Infielder Buck Herzog and Outfielder Wade Killefer, July 20, 1916.

cSold to Pittsburgh, March, 1918.

REDCORD AS MAJOR LEAGUE MANAGER

Year	Club	League	Position	W.	L.	Year	Club	League	Position	W.	L.
1922—Pittsburgh	Nat.		Fourth	47	26	1926—Pittsburgh	Nat.		Third	84	69
1923—Pittsburgh	Nat.		Third	87	67	1928—St. Louis	Nat.		First	95	59
1924—Pittsburgh	Nat.		Third	90	63	1929—St. Louis	Nat.		Fourth	35	29
1925—Pittsburgh	Nat.		First	95	58	1930—Boston	Nat.		Sixth	70	84

Year Club	League	Position	W.	L.	Year Club	League	Position	W.	L.
1931—Boston	Nat.	Seventh	64	90	1940—Cincinnati	Nat.	First	100	53
1932—Boston	Nat.	Fifth	77	77	1941—Cincinnati	Nat.	Third	88	66
1933—Boston	Nat.	Fourth	83	71	1942—Cincinnati	Nat.	Fourth	76	76
1934—Boston	Nat.	Fourth	78	73	1943—Cincinnati	Nat.	Second	87	67
1935—Boston	Nat.	Eighth	38	115	1944—Cincinnati	Nat.	Third	89	65
1936—Boston	Nat.	Sixth	71	83	1945—Cincinnati	Nat.	Seventh	61	93
1937—Boston	Nat.	Fifth	79	73	1946—Cincinnati	Nat.	Sixth	67	87
1938—Cincinnati	Nat.	Fourth	82	68	Major League Totals—24 Years			1840	1669
1939—Cincinnati	Nat.	First	97	57					

WORLD SERIES RECORD

Year Club	League	W.	L.	Year Club	League	W.	L.
1925—Pittsburgh	Nat.	4	3	1939—Cincinnati	Nat.	0	4
1928—St. Louis	Nat.	0	4	1940—Cincinnati	Nat.	4	3

JOSEPH MICHAEL (JOE) MEDWICK
(Ducky)

Born November 4, 1911, at Carteret, N. J.

Died March 21, 1975, at St. Petersburg, Fla.

Height, 5.10. Weight, 178.

Threw and batted righthanded.

Equaled National League record by getting ten hits in succession, July 19 (2 games) and July 21, 1936. Established league mark for most two-base hits in season, 64 (1936), and tied record with four two-base hits in game, August 4, 1937. Hit for the cycle, June 29, 1935. Four long hits, game—May 30, 1935 (first game), May 12, 1937, August 4, 1937. Hit 40 or more doubles seven consecutive years, 1933-39; tied major mark leading league in RBIs three consecutive seasons—1936-37-38.

Named by Baseball Writers' Association of America for THE SPORTING NEWS All-Star Major League Teams, 1935-36-37-38-39.

Named Most Valuable Player in National League, 1937.

Manager, Miami Beach, Florida International League, 1949; Raleigh, Carolina League, 1951; Tampa, Florida International League, 1952; farm system hitting instructor, St. Louis Cardinals, 1966 to 1975; was Cardinals scout in 1971. Also served as assistant baseball coach at St. Louis University, 1961-65.

Named to Hall of Fame, 1968.

Year Club	League	Pos.	G.	AB.	R.	H.	2B.	3B.	HR.	RBI.	B.A.	PO.	A.	E.	F.A.
1930—Scottdale	Mid. Atl.	OF	75	332	75	139	18	13	22	100	.419	159	26	5	.974
1931—Houston	Texas	OF	★161	616	99	188	47	8	★19	★126	.305	307	16	6	.982
1932—Houston	Texas	OF-3B	139	560	113	198	46	10	26	111	.354	320	52	6	★.984
1932—St. Louis	Nat.	OF	26	106	13	37	12	1	2	12	.349	63	2	2	.970
1933—St. Louis	Nat.	OF	148	595	92	182	40	10	18	98	.306	318	17	7	.980
1934—St. Louis	Nat.	OF	149	620	110	198	40	★18	18	106	.319	322	10	★14	.960
1935—St. Louis	Nat.	OF	154	634	132	224	46	13	23	126	.353	352	8	13	.965
1936—St. Louis	Nat.	OF	155	636	115	★223	★64	13	18	★138	.351	367	16	6	.985
1937—St. Louis	Nat.	OF	★156	★633	★111	★237	★56	10	●31	★154	★.374	329	9	4	★.988
1938—St. Louis	Nat.	OF	146	590	100	190	★47	8	21	★122	.322	330	12	9	.974
1939—St. Louis	Nat.	OF	150	606	98	201	48	8	14	117	.332	313	10	8	.976
1940—St. L.(a)-Brook.	Nat.	OF	143	581	83	175	30	12	17	86	.301	321	8	6	.982
1941—Brooklyn	Nat.	OF	133	538	100	171	33	10	18	88	.318	270	11	5	.983
1942—Brooklyn	Nat.	OF	142	553	69	166	37	4	4	96	.300	287	5	3	.990
1943—Brook.(b)-N.Y.	Nat.	OF-1B	126	497	54	138	30	3	5	70	.278	221	12	7	.971
1944—New York	Nat.	OF-1B	128	490	64	165	24	3	7	85	.337	290	8	2	.993
1945—N.Y.(c)-Bos.(d)	Nat.	OF-1B	92	310	31	90	17	0	3	37	.290	248	11	1	.996
1946—Brooklyn(e)	Nat.	OF-1B	41	77	7	24	4	0	2	18	.312	38	0	2	.950
1947—St. Louis(f)	Nat.	OF	75	150	19	46	12	0	4	28	.307	56	3	0	1.000
1948—St. Louis	Nat.	OF	20	19	0	4	0	0	0	2	.211	0	0	0	.000
1948—Houston	Texas	OF	35	87	8	24	7	0	2	20	.276	33	1	0	1.000
1949—Miami Beach	Fla. Int.	OF	106	375	53	121	19	6	10	72	.323	174	8	3	.984
1951—Raleigh	Carolina	OF	60	158	22	45	8	2	4	33	.285	53	4	4	.934
1952—Tampa	Fla. Int.	PH	11	9	0	3	2	1	0	6	.333	0	0	0	.000
Major League Totals—17 Years			1984	7635	1198	2471	540	113	205	1383	.324	4125	142	89	.980

aTraded with Pitcher Curt Davis to Brooklyn for Pitchers Carl Doyle and Sam Nahem, Outfielder Ernie Koy and Infielder-Outfielder Bert Haas and $125,000, June 12, 1940.

bSold to New York Giants, July 6, 1943.

cTraded to Boston Braves with Pitcher Ewald Pyle for Catcher Clyde Kluttz, June 14, 1945.

dReleased, February 8, 1946; signed with St. Louis Browns, March 3, 1946, and released, April 5, 1946; signed with Brooklyn Dodgers, June 28, 1946.

eReleased, October 9, 1946; signed with New York Yankees, January, 1947; released, April 29, 1947, and signed by St. Louis Cardinals.

fReleased, October 10, 1947, and re-signed April 29, 1948.

WORLD SERIES RECORD

Year	Club	League	Pos.	G.	AB.	R.	H.	2B.	3B.	HR.	RBI.	B.A.	PO.	A.	E.	F.A.
1934—St. Louis	Nat.	OF	7	29	4	11	0	1	1	5	.379	9	0	0	1.000
1941—Brooklyn	Nat.	OF	5	17	1	4	1	0	0	0	.235	8	0	0	1.000
World Series Totals—2 Years			12	46	5	15	1	1	1	5	.326	17	0	0	1.000

EMIL FREDERICK MEUSEL
(Irish)

Born June 9, 1893, at Oakland, Calif.

Died March 1, 1963, at Long Beach, Calif.

Height, 6.00. Weight, 180.

Threw and batted righthanded.

Brother of Bob Meusel, former major league outfielder.

Coach, New York Giants, 1930.

Year	Club	League	Pos.	G.	AB.	R.	H.	2B.	3B.	HR.	RBI.	B.A.	PO.	A.	E.	F.A.
1913—Fresno	Calif.	OF	123	464	58	142	24	11	5	....	.306	240	*26	11	.960
1913—Los Angeles(a)	P. C.	OF	15	53	8	15	3	0	1	....	.283	42	3	6	.882
1914—Elmira	N. Y. St.	OF	126	483	86	156	....	....	....	....	.323	228	8	12	.952
1914—Washington	Amer.	OF	1	2	0	0	0	0	0	0	.000	1	0	0	1.000
1915—Los Angeles	P. C.	OF	6	11	....	4	0	0	0	....	.364	5	2	0	1.000
1915—Elmira	N.Y. St.	OF	122	490	83	160	....	....	....	....	.327	237	27	12	.957
1916—Birmingham(b)	South.	OF	113	414	57	129	17	12	2	....	.312	229	18	8	.969
1917—Los Angeles(c)	P. C.	OF	210	811	121	252	46	9	7	....	.311	352	*44	17	.959
1918—Philadelphia	Nat.	OF-2B	124	473	48	132	25	6	4	59	.279	296	14	9	.972
1919—Philadelphia	Nat.	OF	135	521	65	159	26	7	5	58	.305	256	14	9	.968
1920—Philadelphia	Nat.	OF	138	518	75	160	27	8	14	69	.309	260	16	21	.929
1921—Phila.(d)-N.Y.	Nat.	OF	146	586	96	201	33	13	14	87	.343	275	28	17	.947
1922—New York	Nat.	OF	154	617	100	204	28	17	16	132	.331	279	15	6	.980
1923—New York	Nat.	OF	146	595	102	177	22	14	19	*125	.297	268	10	15	.949
1924—New York	Nat.	OF	139	549	75	170	26	9	6	102	.310	287	4	10	.967
1925—New York	Nat.	OF	135	516	82	169	35	8	21	111	.328	244	16	11	.959
1926—New York(e)	Nat.	OF	129	449	51	131	25	10	6	65	.292	197	10	9	.958
1927—Brooklyn	Nat.	OF	42	74	7	18	3	1	1	7	.243	28	2	0	1.000
1927—Toledo	A. A.	OF	47	158	27	56	12	2	3	28	.354	56	4	5	.923
1928—Oakland	P. C.	OF	108	374	50	100	25	5	11	65	.267	204	11	6	.973
1929—Sacramento	P. C.	OF	44	153	22	50	6	3	2	21	.327	124	1	2	.984
1931—Omaha	West.	OF	7	20	....	3	2	0	0	....	.150	9	1	0	1.000
American League Totals—1 Year			1	2	0	0	0	0	0	0	.000	1	0	0	1.000
National League Totals—10 Years			1288	4898	701	1521	250	93	106	815	.310	2390	129	107	.959
Major League Totals—11 Years			1289	4900	701	1521	250	93	106	815	.310	2391	129	107	.959

aDrafted by Washington Senators, February, 1914; optioned to Elmira, April, 1914, and recalled by Washington, September, 1914.

bDrafted by Chicago Cubs, September, 1916, and released to Los Angeles, March, 1917.

cDrafted by Philadelphia Phillies, September, 1917.

dTraded to New York Giants for Catcher Butch Henline, Pitcher Jesse Winters and Outfielder Curtis Walker and cash, July 25, 1921.

eReleased October, 1926; signed by Brooklyn Dodgers, February, 1927.

WORLD SERIES RECORD

Year	Club	League	Pos.	G.	AB.	R.	H.	2B.	3B.	HR.	RBI.	B.A.	PO.	A.	E.	F.A.
1921—New York	Nat.	OF	8	29	4	10	2	1	1	7	.345	8	2	0	1.000
1922—New York	Nat.	OF	5	20	3	5	0	0	1	7	.250	3	0	0	1.000
1923—New York	Nat.	OF	6	25	3	7	1	1	1	2	.280	13	0	0	1.000
1924—New York	Nat.	OF	4	13	0	2	0	0	0	1	.154	5	0	1	.833
World Series Totals—4 Years			23	87	10	24	3	2	3	17	.276	29	2	1	.969

ROBERT WILLIAM (BOB) MEUSEL

Born July 19, 1898, at San Jose, Calif.

Died November 28, 1977, at Downey, Calif.

Height, 6.03. Weight, 190.

Threw and batted righthanded.

Brother of Emil Meusel, former major league outfielder.

Year Club League	Pos.	G.	AB.	R.	H.	2B.	3B.	HR.	RBI.	B.A.	PO.	A.	E.	F.A.
1917—Vernon .... P. C.	OF	45	164	16	51	11	3	0	....	.311	362	25	9	.977
1918—Vernon .... P. C.	OF	2	8	2	3	3	0	0	....	.375	5	0	0	1.000
1919—Vernon .... P. C.	3B-OF	163	655	113	221	39	14	14	....	.337	222	213	33	.929
1920—New York............ Amer.	O-3B	119	460	75	151	40	7	11	83	.328	150	85	20	.922
1921—New York............ Amer.	OF	149	598	104	190	40	16	24	135	.318	253	●28	20	.934
1922—New York............ Amer.	OF	121	473	61	151	26	11	16	84	.319	202	★24	12	.950
1923—New York............ Amer.	OF	132	460	59	144	29	10	9	91	.313	206	17	11	.953
1924—New York............ Amer.	OF-3B	143	579	93	188	40	11	12	120	.325	252	17	14	.951
1925—New York............ Amer.	OF-3B	★156	624	101	181	34	12	★33	★138	.290	271	55	6	.982
1926—New York............ Amer.	OF	108	413	73	130	22	3	12	81	.315	211	4	9	.960
1927—New York............ Amer.	OF	135	516	75	174	47	9	8	103	.337	249	15	14	.950
1928—New York............ Amer.	OF	131	518	77	154	45	5	11	113	.297	259	16	7	.975
1929—New York(a) .... Amer.	OF	100	391	46	102	15	3	10	57	.261	206	9	7	.968
1930—Cincinnati............. Nat.	OF	113	443	62	128	30	8	10	62	.289	223	8	9	.963
1931—Minneapolis .... A. A.	OF	59	187	30	53	8	2	8	59	.283	64	1	7	.903
1932—Hollywood .... P. C.	OF	64	228	44	75	20	2	4	26	.329	83	6	6	.937
American League Totals—10 Years		1294	5032	764	1565	338	87	146	1005	.311	2259	270	120	.955
National League Totals—1 Year.............		113	443	62	128	30	8	10	62	.289	223	8	9	.963
Major League Totals—11 Years...............		1407	5475	826	1693	368	95	156	1067	.309	2482	278	129	.955

aSold to Cincinnati Reds, October 16, 1929.

WORLD SERIES RECORD

Year Club League	Pos.	G.	AB.	R.	H.	2B.	3B.	HR.	RBI.	B.A.	PO.	A.	E.	F.A.
1921—New York............. Amer.	OF	8	30	3	6	2	0	0	3	.200	10	2	0	1.000
1922—New York............. Amer.	OF	5	20	2	6	1	0	0	2	.300	7	1	0	1.000
1923—New York............. Amer.	OF	6	26	1	7	1	2	0	8	.269	14	0	0	1.000
1926—New York............. Amer.	OF	7	21	3	5	1	1	0	0	.238	13	0	1	.929
1927—New York............. Amer.	OF	4	17	1	2	0	0	0	1	.118	8	0	1	.889
1928—New York............. Amer.	OF	4	15	5	3	1	0	1	3	.200	4	0	0	1.000
World Series Totals—6 Years		34	129	15	29	6	3	1	17	.225	56	3	2	.967

EDMUND JOHN (BING) MILLER

Born August 30, 1894, at Vinton, Ia.

Died May 7, 1966, at Philadelphia, Pa.

Height, 6.00¼. Weight, 180.

Threw and batted righthanded.

Coach, Boston Red Sox, October, 1937-38; Detroit Tigers, 1939 through 1941; Chicago White Sox, 1942 through 1949; Philadelphia A's, 1950 through 1953.

Year Club League	Pos.	G.	AB.	R.	H.	2B.	3B.	HR.	RBI.	B.A.	PO.	A.	E.	F.A.
1914—Clinton .... Cen.A.	OF-P	40	125	11	42	...	...	1	...	.336	37	15	7	.881
1915—Clinton .... Cen.A.						(No record—player suspended)								
1916—Clinton .... Cen.A.	OF-P	125	463	66	131	21	10	13	...	.283	210	37	11	.957
1917—Clin.-Waterloo ...... Cen.A.	OF	89	315	62	★106	20	5	7	...	★.337	113	★34	5	.967
1917—Peoria................... Central	OF	22	79	9	22	5	2	2	...	.278	32	4	1	.973
1918—						(In Military Service)								
1919—Atlanta .... South.	OF	26	87	12	22	8	2	0	...	.253	36	5	0	1.000
1920—Little Rock .... South.	OF	151	547	102	176	30	★21	★19	...	.322	296	15	8	.975
1921—Washington (a) .... Amer.	OF	114	420	57	121	28	8	9	71	.288	245	13	15	.945
1922—Philadelphia .... Amer.	OF	143	535	90	180	29	12	21	90	.336	314	19	8	.977
1923—Philadelphia .... Amer.	OF	123	458	68	137	25	4	12	64	.299	262	10	6	.978
1924—Philadelphia .... Amer.	OF	113	398	62	136	22	4	6	62	.342	172	11	5	.973
1925—Philadelphia .... Amer.	OF-1B	124	474	78	151	29	10	10	81	.319	158	7	5	.971
1926—Phil.(b)-St.L. .... Amer.	OF	132	463	73	149	33	7	6	63	.322	272	13	★15	.950
1927—St. Louis (c) .... Amer.	OF	143	492	83	160	32	7	5	75	.325	309	9	10	.970
1928—Philadelphia .... Amer.	OF	139	510	75	168	34	7	8	85	.329	298	8	10	.968
1929—Philadelphia .... Amer.	OF	147	556	84	186	32	16	8	93	.335	311	10	10	.970
1930—Philadelphia .... Amer.	OF	●154	585	89	177	38	7	9	100	.303	309	10	8	.976
1931—Philadelphia .... Amer.	OF	137	534	76	150	43	5	8	77	.281	305	7	4	.987
1932—Philadelphia .... Amer.	OF	95	305	40	90	17	3	8	58	.295	180	3	4	.979
1933—Philadelphia .... Amer.	OF-1B	67	120	22	33	7	1	2	17	.275	62	2	1	.985
1934—Philadelphia .... Amer.	OF	81	177	22	43	10	2	1	22	.243	72	2	0	1.000
1935—Boston .... Amer.	OF	78	138	18	42	8	1	3	26	.304	48	2	2	.962
1936—Boston .... Amer.	OF	30	47	9	14	2	1	1	6	.298	14	1	0	1.000
Major League Totals—16 Years...............		1820	6212	946	1937	389	95	117	990	.312	3331	127	103	.971

aSold with Pitcher Jose Acosta to Philadelphia Athletics in three-cornered deal which also sent Infielder Frank O'Roarke to Boston Red Sox. Roger Peckinpaugh transferred from the New York Yankees to the Senators, and the Athletics sent Third Baseman Joe Dugan to the Yankees, January 10, 1922.

bTraded to St. Louis Browns for Outfielder Bill Jacobson, June 15, 1926.
cTraded to Philadelphia Athletics for Pitcher Sam Gray, December, 1927.

WORLD SERIES RECORD

Shares record for most at-bats, inning (2), October 12, 1929, seventh inning.

Year	Club	League	Pos.	G.	AB.	R.	H.	2B.	3B.	HR.	RBI.	B.A.	PO.	A.	E.	F.A.
1929—Philadelphia		Amer.	OF	5	19	1	7	1	0	0	4	.368	13	0	1	.929
1930—Philadelphia		Amer.	OF	6	21	0	3	2	0	0	3	.143	12	0	0	1.000
1931—Philadelphia		Amer.	OF	7	26	3	7	1	0	0	1	.269	12	0	0	1.000
World Series Totals—3 Years				18	66	4	17	4	0	0	8	.258	37	0	1	.974

PITCHING RECORD

Year	Club	League	G.	IP.	W.	L.	Pct.	H.	R.	ER.	SO.	BB.	ERA.
1914—Clinton		Cen.A.	8	47	3	2	.600	37	19	...	22	18	.....
1916—Clinton		Cen.A.	..	37	2	2	.500	25	...	12	20	19	2.92

JOHN ROBERT (JOHNNY) MIZE
(The Big Cat)

Born January 7, 1913, at Demorest, Ga.

Height, 6.02. Weight, 215.

Threw right and batted lefthanded.

Hit three home runs in a game July 13, 1938; July 20, 1938, second game; May 13, 1940 (14 innings); September 8, 1940; April 24, 1947 and September 15, 1950.

Holds major league records for most times, three or more home runs in game, lifetime (6); most times, three consecutive home runs in game, lifetime (4).

Shares major league record for most times, three or more home runs in game, season (2) 1938 and 1940.

Holds National League record for most home runs by lefthanded batter, season (51), 1947.

Named as first baseman on THE SPORTING NEWS All-Star Major League Teams, 1942-47-48.

Scout, New York Giants, 1955; coach, Kansas City Athletics, 1961.

Named to Hall of Fame, 1981.

Year	Club	League	Pos.	G.	AB.	R.	H.	2B.	3B.	HR.	RBI.	B.A.	PO.	A.	E.	F.A.
1930—Greensboro		Pied.	OF	12	31	5	6	3	0	0	2	.194	10	0	1	.909
1931—Greensboro		Pied.	OF	94	341	69	115	27	1	9	64	.337	130	★17	9	.942
1932—Elmira		NYP	OF-1B	106	405	60	132	20	11	8	78	.326	402	20	6	.986
1933—Greensboro		Pied.	1B	98	378	108	136	29	10	22	104	.360	860	51	25	.973
1933—Rochester		Int.	1B	42	159	27	56	11	3	8	32	.352	355	33	5	.987
1934—Rochester		Int.	1B	90	313	49	106	16	1	17	66	.339	694	72	9	.988
1935—Rochester		Int.	1B	65	252	37	80	11	1	12	44	.317	547	41	8	.987
1936—St. Louis		Nat.	1B-OF	126	414	76	136	30	8	19	93	.329	909	67	6	.994
1937—St. Louis		Nat.	1B	145	560	103	204	40	7	25	113	.364	1308	67	17	.988
1938—St. Louis		Nat.	1B	149	531	85	179	34	★16	27	102	.337	1297	93	●15	.989
1939—St. Louis		Nat.	1B	153	564	104	197	44	14	★28	108	★.349	1348	90	●19	.987
1940—St. Louis		Nat.	1B	155	579	111	182	31	13	★43	★137	.314	1376	80	14	.990
1941—St. Louis (a)		Nat.	1B	126	473	67	150	●39	8	16	100	.317	1157	82	8	.994
1942—New York		Nat.	1B	142	541	97	165	25	7	26	★110	.305	1393	74	8	★.995
1943-44-45—New York		Nat.							(In Military Service)							
1946—New York		Nat.	1B	101	377	70	127	18	3	22	70	.337	928	83	11	.989
1947—New York		Nat.	1B	154	586	★137	177	26	2	●51	★138	.302	★1381	★118	6	★.996
1948—New York		Nat.	1B	152	560	110	162	26	4	●40	125	.289	★1359	★111	13	.991
1949—New York (b)		Nat.	1B	106	388	59	102	15	0	18	62	.263	906	65	6	.994
1949—New York		Amer.	1B	13	23	4	6	1	0	1	2	.261	47	3	1	.980
1950—Kansas City		A.A.	1B	26	94	18	28	4	0	5	18	.298	205	17	0	1.000
1950—New York		Amer.	1B	90	274	43	76	12	0	25	72	.277	490	31	2	.996
1951—New York		Amer.	1B	113	332	37	86	14	1	10	49	.259	632	44	4	.994
1952—New York		Amer.	1B	78	137	9	36	9	0	4	29	.263	218	18	3	.987
1953—New York		Amer.	1B	81	104	6	26	3	0	4	27	.250	113	7	0	1.000
American League Totals—5 Years				375	870	99	230	39	1	44	179	.264	1500	103	10	.994
National League Totals—11 Years				1509	5573	1019	1781	328	82	315	1158	.320	13362	930	123	.991
Major League Totals—15 Years				1884	6443	1118	2011	367	83	359	1337	.312	14862	1033	133	.992

aTraded to New York Giants for Catcher Ken O'Dea, Pitcher Bill Lohrman, First Baseman Johnny McCarthy (assigned to Columbus A.A. club) and $50,000, December 11, 1941. However, Commissioner Landis later upheld Indianapolis' claim to McCarthy as per a prior agreement.

bSold to New York Yankees for $40,000, August 22, 1949.

Year Club League	Pos.	G.	AB.	R.	H.	2B.	3B.	HR.	RBI.	B.A.	PO.	A.	E.	F.A.
1949—New York............ Amer.	PH	2	2	0	2	0	0	0	2	1.000	0	0	0	.000
1950—New York............ Amer.	1B	4	15	0	2	0	0	0	0	.133	27	3	0	1.000
1951—New York............ Amer.	1B-PH	4	7	2	2	1	0	0	1	.286	12	0	0	1.000
1952—New York............ Amer.	1B-PH	5	15	3	6	1	0	3	6	.400	25	3	0	1.000
1953—New York............ Amer.	PH	3	3	0	0	0	0	0	0	.000	0	0	0	.000
World Series Totals—5 Years		18	42	5	12	2	0	3	9	.286	64	6	0	1.000

JOE LEONARD MORGAN

Born September 19, 1943, at Bonham, Tex.

Height, 5.07. Weight, 155.

Threw right and batted lefthanded.

Holds major league records for most seasons by second baseman (22); most consecutive errorless games by second baseman, lifetime (91); most home runs by second baseman, lifetime (266).

Shares major league record for fewest errors by second baseman, season, 150 or more games (5), 1977.

Holds National League records for most bases on balls received, lifetime (1,799); most games by second baseman, lifetime (2,427); most putouts by second baseman, lifetime (5,541); most assists by second baseman, lifetime (6,738); most chances accepted by second baseman, lifetime (12,279).

Shares National League records for most runs batted in, two consecutive innings (7), August 19, 1974, second and third innings.

Shares modern National League record for most bases on balls, game (5), June 2, 1966.

Led National League in slugging percentage with .576 in 1976.

Led National League in sacrifice flies with 12 in 1976.

Led National League in bases on balls received with 97 in 1965, 115 in 1972 and 132 in 1975.

Led National League second basemen in total chances with 814 in 1972.

Tied for National League lead in bases on balls received with 93 in 1980.

Tied for National League lead in double plays by second basemen with 106 in 1973.

Led Texas League second basemen in double plays with 106 in 1964.

Named Major League Player of the Year by THE SPORTING NEWS, 1975 and 1976.

Named National League Player of the Year by THE SPORTING NEWS, 1975.

Named National League Most Valuable Player by Baseball Writers' Association of America, 1975 and 1976.

Named National League Comeback Player of the Year by THE SPORTING NEWS, 1982.

Named National League Rookie Player of the Year by THE SPORTING NEWS, 1965.

Named second baseman on THE SPORTING NEWS National League All-Star Team, 1972 and 1974 through 1977.

Named second baseman on THE SPORTING NEWS National League All-Star fielding team, 1973 through 1977.

Named second baseman on THE SPORTING NEWS National League Silver Slugger team, 1982.

Named Texas League Most Valuable Player, 1964.

Named to Hall of Fame, 1990.

Year Club League	Pos.	G.	AB.	R.	H.	2B.	3B.	HR.	RBI.	B.A.	PO.	A.	E.	F.A.
1963—Modesto .... Calif.	2B	45	152	42	40	5	3	5	27	.263	81	104	15	.925
1963—Durham .... Carol.	2B	95	322	74	107	20	2	13	43	.332	217	273	24	.953
1963—Houston .... Nat.	2B	8	25	5	6	0	1	0	3	.240	15	15	3	.909
1964—San Antonio.......... Texas	2B	●140	496	113	160	★42	8	12	90	.323	319	405	25	★.967
1964—Houston .... Nat.	2B	10	37	4	7	0	0	0	0	.189	31	25	3	.949
1965—Houston .... Nat.	2B	157	601	100	163	22	12	14	40	.271	348	492	★27	.969
1966—Houston .... Nat.	2B	122	425	60	121	14	8	5	42	.285	256	316	21	.965
1967—Houston .... Nat.	2B-OF	133	494	73	136	27	11	6	42	.275	299	344	14	.979
1968—Houston .... Nat.	2B-OF	10	20	6	5	0	1	0	0	.250	10	6	2	.889
1969—Houston .... Nat.	2B-OF	147	535	94	126	18	5	15	43	.236	315	328	18	.973
1970—Houston .... Nat.	2B	144	548	102	147	28	9	8	52	.268	349	430	17	.979
1971—Houston† .... Nat.	2B	160	583	87	149	27	●11	13	56	.256	336	★482	12	.986
1972—Cincinnati .... Nat.	2B	149	552	★122	161	23	4	16	73	.292	★370	436	8	★.990
1973—Cincinnati .... Nat.	2B	157	576	116	167	35	2	26	82	.290	★417	440	9	.990
1974—Cincinnati .... Nat.	2B	149	512	107	150	31	3	22	67	.293	344	385	13	.982
1975—Cincinnati .... Nat.	2B	146	498	107	163	27	6	17	94	.327	356	425	11	★.986
1976—Cincinnati .... Nat.	2B	141	472	113	151	30	5	27	111	.320	342	335	13	.981
1977—Cincinnati .... Nat.	2B	153	521	113	150	21	6	22	78	.288	★351	359	5	★.993
1978—Cincinnati .... Nat.	2B	132	441	68	104	27	0	13	75	.236	252	290	11	.980
1979—Cincinnati‡ .... Nat.	2B	127	436	70	109	26	1	9	32	.250	259	329	12	.980
1980—Houston§ .... Nat.	2B	141	461	66	112	17	5	11	49	.243	244	348	7	.988
1981—San Francisco ..... Nat.	2B	90	308	47	74	16	1	8	31	.240	177	258	4	.991
1982—San Francisco x... Nat.	2B-3B	134	463	68	134	19	4	14	61	.289	255	366	8	.987
1983—Philadelphia y ..... Nat.	2B	123	404	72	93	20	1	16	59	.230	231	331	17	.971
1984—Oakland z............ Amer.	2B	116	365	50	89	21	0	6	43	.244	201	229	10	.977
National League Totals—21 Years.........		2533	8912	1600	2428	428	96	262	1090	.272	5557	6740	235	.981
American League Totals—1 Year		116	365	50	89	21	0	6	43	.244	201	229	10	.977
Major League Totals—22 Years...............		2649	9277	1650	2517	449	96	268	1133	.271	5758	6969	245	.981

Signed as free agent by Houston Colt .45s' organization, November 1, 1962.

†Traded with Pitcher Jack Billingham, Infielder Denis Menke and Outfielders Cesar Geronimo and Ed Armbrister to Cincinnati Reds for First Baseman Lee May, Second Baseman Tommy Helms and Outfielder Jim Stewart, November 29, 1971.

‡Granted free agency, November 1, 1979; signed by Houston Astros, January 31, 1980.

§Released, December 8, 1980; signed by San Francisco Giants, February 9, 1981.

xTraded with Pitcher Al Holland to Philadelphia Phillies for Pitchers Mike Krukow and Mark Davis and Outfielder Charles Penigar, December 14, 1982.

yReleased, October 31, 1983; signed by Oakland A's, December 13, 1983.

zOn voluntarily retired list, November 20, 1984.

CHAMPIONSHIP SERIES RECORD

Holds major league record for most bases on balls lifetime (23).

Shares major league records for hitting home run in first series at-bat, October 7, 1972; most stolen bases, game (3), October 4, 1975.

Year Club	League	Pos.	G.	AB.	R.	H.	2B.	3B.	HR.	RBI.	B.A.	PO.	A.	E.	F.A.
1972—Cincinnati	Nat.	2B	5	19	5	5	0	0	2	3	.263	11	18	0	1.000
1973—Cincinnati	Nat.	2B	5	20	1	2	1	0	0	1	.100	12	27	0	1.000
1975—Cincinnati	Nat.	2B	3	11	2	3	3	0	0	1	.273	2	9	0	1.000
1976—Cincinnati	Nat.	2B	3	7	2	0	0	0	0	0	.000	9	5	0	1.000
1979—Cincinnati	Nat.	2B	3	11	0	0	0	0	0	0	.000	12	11	0	1.000
1980—Houston	Nat.	2B	4	13	1	2	1	1	0	0	.154	9	8	0	1.000
1983—Philadelphia	Nat.	2B	4	15	1	1	0	0	0	0	.067	8	7	0	1.000
Championship Series Totals—7 Years....			27	96	12	13	5	1	2	5	.135	63	85	0	1.000

WORLD SERIES RECORD

Year Club	League	Pos.	G.	AB.	R.	H.	2B.	3B.	HR.	RBI.	B.A.	PO.	A.	E.	F.A.
1972—Cincinnati	Nat.	2B	7	24	4	3	2	0	0	1	.125	18	18	1	.973
1975—Cincinnati	Nat.	2B	7	27	4	7	1	0	0	3	.259	17	28	0	1.000
1976—Cincinnati	Nat.	2B	4	15	3	5	1	1	1	2	.333	13	10	2	.920
1983—Philadelphia	Nat.	2B	5	19	3	5	0	1	2	2	.263	8	10	0	1.000
World Series Totals—4 Years			23	85	14	20	4	2	3	8	.235	56	66	3	.976

MANUEL R. (MANNY) MOTA

Born February 18, 1938, at Santo Domingo, Dominican Republic.

Height, 5.11. Weight, 168.

Threw and batted righthanded.

Holds major league record for most hits by pinch-hitter, lifetime (150).

Coach, Los Angeles Dodgers, 1980 to date.

Year Club	League	Pos.	G.	AB.	R.	H.	2B.	3B.	HR.	RBI.	B.A.	PO.	A.	E.	F.A.
1957—Michigan City	Midw.	OF	126	471	82	148	23	2	7	91	.314	217	20	13	.948
1958—Danville	Carol.	OF	103	385	63	116	20	5	8	55	.301	167	●18	7	.964
1959—Phoenix	P. C.	OF	21	44	9	11	2	1	1	7	.250	22	0	2	.917
1959—Springfield	East.	OF-2B	65	245	39	77	10	7	3	28	.314	118	34	5	.968
1960—Rio Grande Val.	Tex.	*OF-3B	141	541	76	166	18	10	4	79	.307	316	*21	9	.974
1961—Tacoma	P. C.	OF-1B	142	484	64	140	13	4	3	43	.289	248	17	4	.985
1962—San Francisco	Nat.	O-3-2B	47	74	9	13	1	0	0	9	.176	38	18	2	.966
1962—El Paso(a)(b)	Tex.	OF	30	109	26	38	9	3	3	7	.349	51	1	1	.981
1963—Columbus	Int.	OF-2B	75	294	46	86	9	3	5	20	.293	150	61	4	.981
1963—Pittsburgh	Nat.	OF-2B	59	126	20	34	2	3	0	7	.270	40	1	2	.953
1964—Pittsburgh	Nat.	OF-2B-C	115	271	43	75	8	3	5	32	.277	122	5	5	.962
1965—Pittsburgh	Nat.	OF	121	294	47	82	7	6	4	29	.279	127	5	2	.985
1966—Pittsburgh	Nat.	OF-3B	116	322	54	107	16	7	5	46	.332	152	4	1	.994
1967—Pittsburgh	Nat.	OF-3B	120	349	53	112	14	8	4	56	.321	156	14	2	.988
1968—Pittsburgh(c)	Nat.	OF-2-3	111	331	35	93	10	2	1	33	.281	150	8	3	.981
1969—Mont.(d)-L.A.	Nat.	OF	116	383	41	123	7	5	3	30	.321	157	8	8	.954
1970—Los Angeles	Nat.	OF-3B	124	417	63	127	12	6	3	37	.305	172	9	5	.973
1971—Los Angeles	Nat.	OF	91	269	24	84	13	5	0	34	.312	108	3	4	.965
1972—Los Angeles	Nat.	OF	118	371	57	120	16	5	5	48	.323	141	3	1	.993
1973—Los Angeles	Nat.	OF	89	293	33	92	11	2	0	23	.314	96	4	0	1.000
1974—Los Angeles	Nat.	OF	66	57	5	16	2	0	0	16	.281	1	0	0	1.000
1975—Los Angeles	Nat.	OF	52	49	3	13	1	0	0	10	.265	9	0	0	1.000
1976—Los Angeles	Nat.	OF	50	52	1	15	3	0	0	13	.288	11	1	0	1.000
1977—Los Angeles	Nat.	OF	49	38	5	15	1	0	1	4	.395	1	0	0	1.000
1978—Los Angeles	Nat.	PH	37	33	2	10	1	0	0	6	.303	0	0	0	.000
1979—Los Angeles	Nat.	OF	47	42	1	15	0	0	0	3	.357	0	0	0	.000
1980—Los Angeles	Nat.	PH	7	7	0	3	0	0	0	2	.429	0	0	0	.000
1982—Los Angeles	Nat.	PH	1	1	0	0	0	0	0	0	.000	0	0	0	.000
Major League Totals—20 Years			1536	3779	496	1149	125	52	31	438	.304	1481	83	35	.978

Year Club League	Pos.	G.	AB.	R.	H.	2B.	3B.	HR.	RBI.	B.A.	PO.	A.	E.	F.A.
1974—Los Angeles .... Nat.	PH-OF	3	3	0	1	0	0	0	1	.333	1	0	0	1.000
1977—Los Angeles .... Nat.	PH	1	1	1	1	1	0	0	0	1.000	0	0	0	.000
1978—Los Angeles .... Nat.	PH	2	1	0	1	1	0	0	0	1.000	0	0	0	.000
Championship Series Totals—3 Years.....		6	5	1	3	2	0	0	1	.600	1	0	0	1.000

WORLD SERIES RECORD

Year Club League	Pos.	G.	AB.	R.	H.	2B.	3B.	HR.	RBI.	B.A.	PO.	A.	E.	F.A.
1977—Los Angeles .... Nat.	PH	3	3	0	0	0	0	0	0	.000	0	0	0	.000
1978—Los Angeles .... Nat.	PH	1	0	0	0	0	0	0	0	.000	0	0	0	.000
World Series Totals—2 Years		4	3	0	0	0	0	0	0	.000	0	0	0	.000

aRecalled by San Francisco Giants; traded to Houston Colts with Pitcher Dick LeMay for Second Baseman Joe Amalfitano, November 30, 1962.

bTraded to Pittsburgh Pirates with cash for Outfielder Howie Goss, April 2, 1963.

cSelected by Montreal Expos from Pittsburgh Pirates in expansion draft, October 14, 1968.

dTraded with Shortstop Maury Wills to Los Angeles Dodgers for Outfielder-First Baseman Ron Fairly and Infielder Paul Popovich, June 11, 1969.

ANTHONY JOHN (TONY) MULLANE
(Count)

Born February 20, 1859, at Cork, Ireland.

Died April 26, 1944, at Chicago, Ill.

Height, 5.10½. Weight, 169.

Threw left and righthanded and batted righthanded.

Pitched 2-0 no-hit victory against Cincinnati, September 11, 1882.

Umpired in National League, 1893 and 1897.

Year Club	League	G.	IP.	W.	L.	Pct.	SO.	BB.	H.	CG.	ShO.
1880—Akron	Independent					(No records available)					
1881—Akron	Independent					(No records available)					
1881—Detroit	National	5	44	1	4	.200	10	13	56	5	0
1882—Louisville	Amer. Assn.	•54	459	30	24	.556	★172	75	428	50	5
1883—St. Louis	Amer. Assn.	50	460	35	15	.700	188	73	389	49	3
1884—Toledo	Amer. Assn.	66	568	35	25	.583	334	82	493	64	7
1885—	(Did not play—suspended for entire season for signing multiple contracts)										
1886—Cincinnati	Amer. Assn.	61	529	31	27	.534	220	182	500	55	1
1887—Cincinnati	Amer. Assn.	49	413	31	17	.646	68	119	550	46	•6
1888—Cincinnati	Amer. Assn.	44	377	26	16	.619	125	108	233	41	4
1889—Cincinnati(a)	Amer. Assn.	29	217	12	9	.571	107	85	206	16	0
1890—Cincinnati	National	22	202	12	10	.545	95	91	161	21	0
1891—Cincinnati	National	49	430	24	25	.490	117	178	393	42	1
1892—Cincinnati	National	31	295	21	10	.667	112	125	237	30	3
1892—Butte(b)-Montana						(No records available)					
1893—Cin.(c)-Baltimore	National	41	367	19	22	.463	85	168	417	34	0
1894—Balt.(d)-Cleveland	National	17	145	8	9	.471	44	80	175	11	1
1895—St. Paul	Western	30	....	....	....	....	....	....	260	....	....
1896—St. Paul	Western	49	....	....	....	....	....	....	423	....	....
1897—St. Paul	Western	30	....	14	11	.560	....	....	260	....	....
1898—						(Did not play)					
1899—Toronto	Eastern	3	26	2	1	.667	7	10	34	3	0
American Association Totals—7 Years..........................		353	3023	200	133	.601	1214	724	2799	321	26
National League Totals—6 Years.................................		165	1483	85	80	.515	463	655	1439	143	5
Major League Totals—13 Years.......................................		518	4506	285	213	.572	1677	1379	4238	464	31

aCincinnati withdrew from American Association and entered National League in 1890.

bWent to Butte after refusing to accept salary cut from Cincinnati.

cTraded to Baltimore for Outfielder-Infielder Frank (Piggy) Ward in June, 1893.

dDealt to Cleveland for Pitcher John Clarkson, 1894.

—DID YOU KNOW—

That George Mullin is the only pitcher in major league history to throw a no-hitter on his birthday? The Detroit righthander recorded a 7-0 no-hitter against the St. Louis Browns on his 32nd birthday, July 4, 1912.

GEORGE EMMETT MULLIN

Born July 4, 1880, at Toledo, O.
Died January 7, 1944, at Wabash, Ind.
Height, 5.11. Weight, 188.
Threw and batted righthanded.

Pitched 7-0 no-hit victory against St. Louis Browns, July 4, 1912.
Shares major league record for most doubles by pitcher, game (3), April 27, 1903.

Year	Club	League	G.	IP.	W.	L.	Pct.	H.	R.	ER.	SO.	BB.	ERA.
1901—Ft. Wayne	W. Assn.	47	367	21	20	.512	377	203	....	190	96	......
1902—Detroit	Amer.	35	264	13	16	.448	288	159	....	75	96	......
1903—Detroit	Amer.	41	323	19	14	.576	291	129	....	172	★104	......
1904—Detroit	Amer.	45	382	17	23	.425	346	154	....	149	★119	......
1905—Detroit	Amer.	44	●346	21	20	.512	301	138	....	173	★138	......
1906—Detroit	Amer.	40	328	21	18	.538	311	137	....	122	★112	......
1907—Detroit	Amer.	46	359	20	20	.500	★335	★154	....	153	97	......
1908—Detroit	Amer.	39	291	17	12	.586	301	142	....	121	71	......
1909—Detroit	Amer.	40	304	★29	8	★.784	258	96	....	124	78	......
1910—Detroit	Amer.	38	289	21	12	.636	260	125	....	98	102	......
1911—Detroit	Amer.	30	234	18	10	.643	245	99	....	87	61	......
1912—Detroit	Amer.	37	226	12	17	.414	214	112	....	88	92	......
1913—Det.(a)-Wash.	Amer.	19	110	4	11	.267	122	62	48	30	43	3.93
1913—Montreal(b)	Int.	4	27	1	2	.333	28	20	....	9	16	......
1914—Indianapolis(c)	Fed.	36	204	14	10	.583	199	99	75	70	93	3.31
1915—Newark	Fed.	5	33	2	2	.500	41	22	....	14	16	......
Major League Totals—12 Years		454	3456	212	181	.539	3612	1507	....	1392	1113	......

aSold to Washington on waivers, May 17, 1913, and released by Senators to Montreal, July 5, 1913.
bJumped to Indianapolis, Federal League, for 1914.
cTransferred to Newark with Indianapolis franchise in 1915.

WORLD SERIES RECORD

Year	Club	League	G.	IP.	W.	L.	Pct.	H.	R.	ER.	SO.	BB.	ERA.
1907—Detroit	Amer.	2	17	0	2	.000	16	5	4	7	6	2.11
1908—Detroit	Amer.	1	9	1	0	1.000	7	3	0	8	1	0.00
1909—Detroit	Amer.	4	32	2	1	.667	22	14	8	20	8	2.25
World Series Totals—3 Years		7	58	3	3	.500	45	22	12	35	15	1.86

BOBBY RAY MURCER

Born May 20, 1946, at Oklahoma City, Okla.
Height, 5.11. Weight, 185.
Threw right and batted lefthanded.

Shares major league record for most consecutive home runs (4), June 24, 1970, first and second games.
Shares American League record for most home runs, doubleheader (4), June 24, 1970.
Hit three home runs in a game, June 24, 1970, second game and July 13, 1973.
Led National League in sacrifice flies with 12 in 1975.
Led American League in total bases with 314 in 1972.
Led American League outfielders in total chances with 396 in 1972.
Tied for National League lead in sacrifice flies with 10 in 1977.
Led International League shortstops in double plays with 91 in 1966.
Named outfielder on THE SPORTING NEWS American League All-Star Team, 1971 through 1973.
Named outfielder on THE SPORTING NEWS American League All-Star fielding team, 1972.
Named Carolina League Most Valuable Player, 1965.

Year	Club	League	Pos.	G.	AB.	R.	H.	2B.	3B.	HR.	RBI.	B.A.	PO.	A.	E.	F.A.
1964—Johnson City	Appal.	SS-2B	32	126	34	46	7	4	2	29	.365	39	78	34	.775
1965—Greensboro	Carol.	SS	126	478	95	154	30	5	16	90	.322	166	320	★55	.898
1965—New York	Amer.	SS	11	37	2	9	0	1	1	4	.243	28	41	5	.932
1966—New York	Amer.	SS	21	69	3	12	1	1	0	5	.174	31	50	6	.931
1966—Toledo	Int.	SS	133	492	69	131	19	9	15	62	.266	207	349	★36	.939

Year Club League	Pos.	G.	AB.	R.	H.	2B.	3B.	HR.	RBI.	B.A.	PO.	A.	E.	F.A.
1967-68—New York.........Amer.				(In Military Service)										
1969—New York............Amer.	OF-3B	152	564	82	146	24	4	26	82	.259	235	81	22	.935
1970—New York............Amer.	OF	159	581	95	146	23	3	23	78	.251	375	●15	3	.992
1971—New York............Amer.	OF	146	529	94	175	25	6	25	94	.331	317	10	5	.985
1972—New York............Amer.	OF	153	585	★102	171	30	7	33	96	.292	★382	11	3	.992
1973—New York............Amer.	OF	160	616	83	187	29	2	22	95	.304	380	●14	6	.985
1974—New York†............Amer.	OF	156	606	69	166	25	4	10	88	.274	297	★21	7	.978
1975—San Francisco ......Nat.	OF	147	526	80	157	29	4	11	91	.298	201	10	4	.981
1976—San Francisco‡ ....Nat.	OF	147	533	73	138	20	2	23	90	.259	282	11	12	.961
1977—Chicago ....Nat.	OF-2B-SS	154	554	90	147	18	3	27	89	.265	238	11	5	.980
1978—Chicago ....Nat.	OF	146	499	66	140	22	6	9	64	.281	225	8	5	.979
1979—Chicago§ ....Nat.	OF	58	190	22	49	4	1	7	22	.258	110	4	0	1.000
1979—New York............Amer.	OF	74	264	42	72	12	0	8	33	.273	169	4	3	.983
1980—New York............Amer.	OF	100	297	41	80	9	1	13	57	.269	82	2	4	.955
1981—New York x ....Amer.	DH	50	117	14	31	6	0	6	24	.265	0	0	0	.000
1982—New York............Amer.	DH	65	141	12	32	6	0	7	30	.227	0	0	0	.000
1983—New York y ....Amer.	DH	9	22	2	4	2	0	1	1	.182	0	0	0	.000
American League Totals—13 Years		1256	4428	641	1231	192	29	175	687	.278	2296	249	64	.975
National League Totals—5 Years.............		652	2302	331	631	93	16	77	356	.274	1056	44	26	.977
Major League Totals—17 Years		1908	6730	972	1862	285	45	252	1043	.277	3352	293	90	.976

Signed as free agent by New York Yankees' organization, June 2, 1964.

†Traded to San Francisco Giants for Outfielder Bobby Bonds, October 21, 1974.

‡Traded with Infielder Steve Ontiveros and Pitcher Andrew Muhlstock to Chicago Cubs for Third Baseman Bill Madlock and Infielder Rob Sperring, February 11, 1977.

§Traded to New York Yankees for Pitcher Paul Semall and cash, June 26, 1979.

xGranted free agency, November 13, 1981; re-signed by Yankees, April 5, 1982.

yReleased, June 20, 1983.

CHAMPIONSHIP SERIES RECORD

Year Club League	Pos.	G.	AB.	R.	H.	2B.	3B.	HR.	RBI.	B.A.	PO.	A.	E.	F.A.
1980—New York............Amer.	DH	1	4	0	0	0	0	0	0	.000	0	0	0	.000
1981—New York............Amer.	DH	1	3	0	1	0	0	0	0	.333	0	0	0	.000
Championship Series Totals—2 Years.....		2	7	0	1	0	0	0	0	.143	0	0	0	.000

WORLD SERIES RECORD

Year Club League	Pos.	G.	AB.	R.	H.	2B.	3B.	HR.	RBI.	B.A.	PO.	A.	E.	F.A.
1981—New York............Amer.	PH	4	3	0	0	0	0	0	0	.000	0	0	0	.000

STANLEY FRANK (STAN) MUSIAL
(Stan The Man)

Born November 21, 1920, at Donora, Pa.

Height, 6.00. Weight, 180.

Threw and batted lefthanded.

Shares major league records for most times, five or more hits in a game, season (4), 1948; most years leading league in doubles (8), most consecutive home runs (4), July 7, second game, July 8, 1962; most home runs, doubleheader (5), May 2, 1954.

Holds National League record for most years leading league in triples (5).

Shares National League records for most years and most consecutive years with one club (22); most years leading league in runs (5); most years leading league in fielding, outfielder, 100 or more games (3).

Holds modern National League records for most years (17) and most consecutive years (16) batting .300 or over, 50 or more games.

Led National League in total bases, 1943-46-48-49-51-52; led in slugging percentage, 1943-44-46-48-50-52.

Named as outfielder on THE SPORTING NEWS All-Star Major League Teams, 1943-44-48-49-50-51-52-53-54; named as first baseman, 1946-57-58.

Named National League Most Valuable Player, 1943, 1946 and 1948.

Named Major League Player of the Year by THE SPORTING NEWS, 1946 and 1951.

Named Player of the Decade by THE SPORTING NEWS, 1956.

Named Top National League Player by THE SPORTING NEWS, 1943-48-51-57.

Named to Hall of Fame, 1969.

Year Club League	Pos.	G.	AB.	R.	H.	2B.	3B.	HR.	RBI.	B.A.	PO.	A.	E.	F.A.
1938—Williamson ....Mt. St.	P	26	62	5	16	3	0	1	6	.258	7	22	6	.829
1939—Williamson ....Mt. St.	PH-P	23	71	10	25	3	3	1	9	.352	5	19	3	.889
1940—Daytona Beach ....Fla. St.	OF-P	113	405	55	126	17	10	1	70	.311	183	69	11	.958
1941—Springfield ............W.A.	OF	87	348	100	132	27	10	★26	94	.379	185	7	3	.985
1941—Rochester ....Int.	OF	54	221	43	72	10	4	3	21	.326	102	5	1	.991
1941—St. Louis.................Nat.	OF	12	47	8	20	4	0	1	7	.426	20	1	0	1.000
1942—St. Louis.................Nat.	OF	140	467	87	147	32	10	10	72	.315	296	6	5	.984
1943—St. Louis.................Nat.	OF	●157	617	108	★220	★48	★20	13	81	★.357	376	15	7	.982

Year	Club	League	Pos.	G.	AB.	R.	H.	2B.	3B.	HR.	RBI.	B.A.	PO.	A.	E.	F.A.
1944—St. Louis	Nat.		OF	146	568	112	●197	★51	14	12	94	.347	353	16	5	.987
1945—St. Louis	Nat.						(In Military Service)									
1946—St. Louis	Nat.		★1B-OF	●156	★624	★124	★228	★50	★20	16	103	★.365	1166	69	★15	.988
1947—St. Louis	Nat.		1B	149	587	113	183	30	13	19	95	.312	1360	77	8	.994
1948—St. Louis	Nat.		OF-1B	155	611	★135	★230	★46	★18	39	★131	★.376	354	11	7	.981
1949—St. Louis	Nat.		★OF-1B	★157	612	128	★207	★41	●13	36	123	.338	337	11	3	★.991
1950—St. Louis	Nat.		OF-1B	146	555	105	192	41	7	28	109	★.346	760	39	8	.990
1951—St. Louis	Nat.		OF-1B	152	578	●124	205	30	●12	32	108	★.355	816	45	10	.989
1952—St. Louis	Nat.		O-1B-P	●154	578	●105	★194	★42	6	21	91	★.336	502	18	5	.990
1953—St. Louis	Nat.		OF	157	593	127	200	★53	9	30	113	.337	294	9	5	.984
1954—St. Louis	Nat.		★OF-1B	153	591	●120	195	★41	9	35	126	.330	307	15	5	★.985
1955—St. Louis	Nat.		1B-OF	●154	562	97	179	30	5	33	108	.319	1000	94	9	.992
1956—St. Louis	Nat.		1B-OF	156	594	87	184	33	6	27	★109	.310	954	95	8	.992
1957—St. Louis	Nat.		1B	134	502	82	176	38	3	29	102	★.351	1167	99	10	.992
1958—St. Louis	Nat.		1B	135	472	64	159	35	2	17	62	.337	1019	★100	13	.989
1959—St. Louis	Nat.		1B-OF	115	341	37	87	13	2	14	44	.255	624	63	7	.990
1960—St. Louis	Nat.		OF-1B	116	331	49	91	17	1	17	63	.275	300	19	3	.991
1961—St. Louis	Nat.		OF	123	372	46	107	22	4	15	70	.288	149	9	1	★.994
1962—St. Louis	Nat.		OF	135	433	57	143	18	1	19	82	.330	164	6	4	.977
1963—St. Louis	Nat.		OF	124	337	34	86	10	2	12	58	.255	121	1	4	.968
Major League Totals—22 Years				3026	10972	1949	3630	725	177	475	1951	.331	12439	818	142	.989

WORLD SERIES RECORD

Year	Club	League	Pos.	G.	AB.	R.	H.	2B.	3B.	HR.	RBI.	B.A.	PO.	A.	E.	F.A.
1942—St. Louis	Nat.		OF	5	18	2	4	1	0	0	2	.222	13	0	0	1.000
1943—St. Louis	Nat.		OF	5	18	2	5	0	0	0	0	.278	7	2	0	1.000
1944—St. Louis	Nat.		OF	6	23	2	7	2	0	1	2	.304	11	0	1	.917
1946—St. Louis	Nat.		1B	7	27	3	6	4	1	0	4	.222	60	2	0	1.000
World Series Totals—4 Years				23	86	9	22	7	1	1	8	.256	91	4	1	.990

PITCHING RECORD

Year	Club	League	G.	IP.	W.	L.	Pct.	H.	R.	ER.	SO.	BB.	ERA.
1938—Williamson	Mt. State		20	110	6	6	.500	114	75	57	66	80	4.66
1939—Williamson	Mt. State		13	92	9	2	.818	71	53	44	86	85	4.30
1940—Daytona Beach	Fla. State		28	223	18	5	★.783	179	108	65	176	145	2.62
1952—St. Louis	National		1	0	0	0	.000	0	0	0	0	0	0.00
Major League Totals—1 Year			1	0	0	0	.000	0	0	0	0	0	0.00

CHARLES SOLOMON (BUDDY) MYER

Born March 16, 1904, at Ellisville, Miss.

Died October 31, 1974, at Baton Rouge, La.

Height, 5.10½. Weight, 170.

Threw right and batted lefthanded.

Led American League in stolen bases with 30 in 1928.
Led American League third basemen in double plays with 35 in 1928.
Led American League second basemen in double plays with 138 in 1935.

Year	Club	League	Pos.	G.	AB.	R.	H.	2B.	3B.	HR.	RBI.	B.A.	PO.	A.	E.	F.A.
1925—New Orleans	South.		SS	99	402	76	135	21	8	3	44	.336	249	306	37	.938
1925—Washington	Amer.		SS	4	8	1	2	0	0	0	0	.250	1	3	0	1.000
1926—Washington	Amer.		SS	132	434	66	132	18	6	1	62	.304	215	297	40	.928
1927—Wash.(a)-Bos.	Amer.		SS	148	520	66	146	23	11	2	54	.281	304	380	44	.940
1928—Boston (b)	Amer.		3B	147	536	78	168	26	6	1	44	.313	137	306	14	.969
1929—Washington	Amer.		2B-3B	141	563	80	169	29	10	3	82	.300	274	363	32	.952
1930—Washington	Amer.		2B	138	541	97	164	18	8	2	61	.303	330	405	27	.965
1931—Washington	Amer.		2B	139	591	114	173	33	11	4	56	.293	333	398	12	●.984
1932—Washington	Amer.		2B	143	577	120	161	38	16	5	52	.279	352	426	20	.975
1933—Washington	Amer.		2B	131	530	95	160	29	15	4	61	.302	356	417	17	.978
1934—Washington	Amer.		2B	139	524	103	160	33	8	3	57	.305	367	420	20	.975
1935—Washington	Amer.		2B	151	616	115	215	36	11	5	100	★.349	★460	473	20	.979
1936—Washington	Amer.		2B	51	156	31	42	5	2	0	15	.269	120	143	4	.985
1937—Washington	Amer.		2B	125	430	54	126	16	10	1	65	.293	308	338	★23	.966
1938—Washington	Amer.		2B	127	437	79	147	22	8	6	71	.336	308	355	12	★.982
1939—Washington	Amer.		2B	83	258	33	78	10	3	1	32	.302	175	188	12	.968
1940—Washington	Amer.		2B	71	210	28	61	14	4	0	29	.290	119	176	10	.967
1941—Washington	Amer.		2B	53	107	14	27	3	1	0	9	.252	53	54	2	.982
Major League Totals—17 Years				1923	7038	1174	2131	353	130	38	850	.303	4212	5142	309	.968

aTraded to Boston Red Sox for Infielder Topper Rigney, May 2, 1927.
bTraded to Washington Senators for Pitchers Milt Gaston and Hod Lisenbee, Infielders Bobby Reeves and Grant Gillis and Outfielder Elliott Bigelow, December 15, 1928.

WORLD SERIES RECORD

Year Club League	Pos.	G.	AB.	R.	H.	2B.	3B.	HR.	RBI.	B.A.	PO.	A.	E.	F.A.
1925—Washington........... Amer.	3B	3	8	0	2	0	0	0	0	.250	1	1	0	1.000
1933—Washington.......... Amer.	2B	5	20	2	6	1	0	0	2	.300	15	12	3	.900
World Series Totals—2 Years		8	28	2	8	1	0	0	2	.286	16	13	3	.906

GRAIG NETTLES

Born August 20, 1944, at San Diego, Calif.

Height, 6.00. Weight, 187.

Threw right and batted lefthanded.

Brother of Jim Nettles, former major league outfielder.

Holds major league records for most assists (412) and double plays (54) by third baseman, season, 1971.
Shares major league records for most home runs, month of April (11), 1974; fewest triples, season, 150 or more games (0), 1972 and 1973.
Holds American League record for most home runs by third baseman, lifetime (319).
Shares American League record for most home runs, doubleheader (4), April 14, 1974.
Shares National League record for most home runs, six consecutive games (7), August 11 through 22, 1984.
Led American League in sacrifice flies with 11 in 1975.
Led American League third basemen in total chances with 587 in 1971, 553 in 1973, 545 in 1974 and 539 in 1976.
Led American League third basemen in double plays with 54 in 1971, 30 in 1976 and tied for lead with 30 in 1978.
Led American League third basemen in assists with 383 in 1976.
Led Southern League third basemen in double plays with 34 in 1967 and led Pacific Coast League third basemen with 20 in 1968.
Named third baseman on THE SPORTING NEWS American League All-Star Team, 1975, 1977 and 1978.
Named third baseman on THE SPORTING NEWS American League All-Star fielding team, 1977 and 1978.

Year Club League	Pos.	G.	AB.	R.	H.	2B.	3B.	HR.	RBI.	B.A.	PO.	A.	E.	F.A.
1966—Wis. Rapids.......... Midw.	2B-3B	117	413	84	111	19	6	★28	75	.269	240	245	28	.945
1967—Charlotte............... South.	3B	140	499	69	116	18	4	●19	86	.232	107	★318	24	.947
1967—Minnesota........... Amer.	PH	3	3	0	1	1	0	0	0	.333	0	0	0	.000
1968—Denver .... P. C.	3B-OF-1B	130	451	84	134	17	●12	22	83	.297	125	266	17	.958
1968—Minnesota‡........... Amer.	OF-3B-1B	22	76	13	17	2	1	5	8	.224	50	9	2	.967
1969—Minnesota†........... Amer.	OF-3B	96	225	27	50	9	2	7	26	.222	88	44	2	.985
1970—Cleveland............. Amer.	★3B-OF	157	549	81	129	13	1	26	62	.235	135	358	17	★.967
1971—Cleveland............. Amer.	3B	158	598	78	156	18	1	28	86	.261	★159	★412	16	.973
1972—Cleveland‡........... Amer.	3B	150	557	65	141	28	0	17	70	.253	114	★358	★21	.957
1973—New York........... Amer.	3B	160	552	65	129	18	0	22	81	.234	117	★410	26	.953
1974—New York........... Amer.	★3B-SS	155	566	74	139	21	1	22	75	.246	★147	377	21	.961
1975—New York........... Amer.	3B	157	581	71	155	24	4	21	91	.267	135	★379	19	.964
1976—New York‡........... Amer.	3B-SS	158	583	88	148	29	2	★32	93	.254	137	384	19	.965
1977—New York........... Amer.	3B	158	589	99	150	23	4	37	107	.255	132	321	12	.974
1978—New York........... Amer.	3B-SS	159	587	81	162	23	2	27	93	.276	110	326	11	.975
1979—New York........... Amer.	3B	145	521	71	132	15	1	20	73	.253	110	339	16	.966
1980—New York........... Amer.	3B-SS	89	324	52	79	14	0	16	45	.244	59	183	10	.960
1981—New York........... Amer.	3B	103	349	46	85	7	1	15	46	.244	63	214	8	.972
1982—New York........... Amer.	3B	122	405	47	94	11	2	18	55	.232	73	255	23	.934
1983—New York§........... Amer.	3B	129	462	56	123	17	3	20	75	.266	78	273	16	.956
1984—San Diego .... Nat.	3B	124	395	56	90	11	1	20	65	.228	93	201	20	.936
1985—San Diego .... Nat.	3B	137	440	66	115	23	1	15	61	.261	122	229	15	.959
1986—San Diego x........... Nat.	3B	126	354	36	77	9	0	16	55	.218	83	174	16	.941
1987—Atlanta yz........... Nat.	3B-1B	112	177	16	37	8	1	5	33	.209	61	56	3	.975
1988—Montreal a........... Nat.	3B-1B	80	93	5	16	4	0	1	14	.172	32	14	5	.902
American League Totals—17 Years		2121	7527	1014	1890	273	25	333	1086	.251	1707	4642	239	.964
National League Totals—5 Years.............		579	1459	179	335	55	3	57	228	.230	391	674	59	.948
Major League Totals—22 Years		2700	8986	1193	2225	328	28	390	1314	.248	2098	5316	298	.961

Selected by Minnesota Twins' organization in 4th round of free-agent draft, June 9, 1965.
†Traded with Pitchers Dean Chance and Robert L. Miller and Outfielder Ted Uhlaender to Cleveland Indians for Pitchers Luis Tiant and Stan Williams, December 12, 1969.
‡Traded with Catcher Jerry Moses to New York Yankees for Catcher-First Baseman John Ellis, Infielder Jerry Kenney and Outfielders Charlie Spikes and Rosendo Torres, November 27, 1972.
§Traded to San Diego Padres for Pitcher Dennis Rasmussen and a player to be named later, March 30, 1984; New York Yankees' organization acquired Pitcher Darin Cloninger to complete deal, April 26, 1984.
xReleased, December 20, 1986; signed by Atlanta Braves, April 1, 1987.
yGranted free agency, November 9, 1987; signed by Braves' organization, December 6, 1987.
zSold to Montreal Expos, March 24, 1988.
aGranted free agency, November 4, 1988.

Shares record for most hits, inning (2), October 14, 1981.

Year Club League	Pos.	G.	AB.	R.	H.	2B.	3B.	HR.	RBI.	B.A.	PO.	A.	E.	F.A.
1969—Minnesota............. Amer.	PH	1	1	0	1	0	0	0	0	1.000	0	0	0	.000
1976—New York............. Amer.	3B	5	17	2	4	1	0	2	4	.235	5	14	0	1.000
1977—New York............. Amer.	3B	5	20	1	3	0	0	0	1	.150	2	12	0	1.000
1978—New York............. Amer.	3B	4	15	3	5	0	1	1	2	.333	6	7	0	1.000
1980—New York............. Amer.	3B-PH	2	6	1	1	0	0	1	1	.167	0	2	0	1.000
1981—New York............. Amer.	3B	3	12	2	6	2	0	1	9	.500	4	4	1	.889
1984—San Diego .... Nat.	3B	4	14	1	2	0	0	0	2	.143	5	8	0	1.000
Championship Series Totals—7 Years....		24	85	10	22	3	1	5	19	.259	22	47	1	.986

Year Club League	Pos.	G.	AB.	R.	H.	2B.	3B.	HR.	RBI.	B.A.	PO.	A.	E.	F.A.
1976—New York............. Amer.	3B	4	12	0	3	0	0	0	2	.250	8	8	0	1.000
1977—New York............. Amer.	3B	6	21	1	4	1	0	0	2	.190	2	20	1	.957
1978—New York............. Amer.	3B	6	25	2	4	0	0	0	1	.160	8	18	0	1.000
1981—New York............. Amer.	3B	3	10	1	4	1	0	0	0	.400	3	10	1	.929
1984—San Diego .... Nat.	3B	5	12	2	3	0	0	0	2	.250	7	12	0	1.000
World Series Totals—5 Years		24	80	6	18	2	0	0	7	.225	28	68	2	.980

HAROLD (HAL) NEWHOUSER
(Prince Hal)

Born May 20, 1921, at Detroit, Mich.

Height, 6.02. Weight, 180.

Threw and batted lefthanded.

Named Most Valuable Player, American League, 1944 and 1945.
Named as pitcher for THE SPORTING NEWS All-Star Major League Teams, 1944-45-46.
Named by THE SPORTING NEWS as the No. 1 Major League Player of the Year, 1945.
Scout, Baltimore Orioles, 1956-61; Cleveland Indians, 1961-64.

Year Club	League	G.	IP.	W.	L.	Pct.	H.	R.	ER.	SO.	BB.	ERA.
1939—Alexandria	Evang.	12	96	8	4	.667	66	37	25	107	29	2.34
1939—Beaumont	Texas	22	134	5	14	.263	111	76	57	85	73	3.83
1939—Detroit	American	1	5	0	1	.000	3	3	3	4	4	5.40
1940—Detroit	American	28	133	9	9	.500	149	81	72	89	76	4.87
1941—Detroit	American	33	173	9	11	.450	166	109	92	106	137	4.79
1942—Detroit	American	38	184	8	14	.364	137	73	50	103	114	2.45
1943—Detroit	American	37	196	8	17	.320	163	88	66	144	*111	3.03
1944—Detroit	American	47	312	*29	9	.763	264	94	77	*187	102	2.22
1945—Detroit	American	40	*313	*25	9	*.735	239	73	63	*212	110	*1.81
1946—Detroit	American	37	293	●26	9	.743	215	77	63	275	98	*1.94
1947—Detroit	American	40	285	17	*17	.500	*268	105	91	176	110	2.87
1948—Detroit	American	39	272	*21	12	.636	249	109	91	143	99	3.01
1949—Detroit	American	38	292	18	11	.621	*277	118	●109	144	111	3.36
1950—Detroit	American	35	214	15	13	.536	232	110	103	87	81	4.33
1951—Detroit	American	15	96	6	6	.500	98	47	42	37	19	3.94
1952—Detroit	American	25	154	9	9	.500	148	72	64	57	47	3.74
1953—Detroit (a)	American	7	22	0	1	.000	31	22	17	6	8	6.95
1954—Cleveland..................	American	26	47	7	2	.778	34	16	13	25	18	2.49
1955—Cleveland..................	American	2	2	0	0	.000	1	0	0	1	4	0.00
Major League Totals—17 Years...........................		488	2993	207	150	.580	2674	1197	1016	1796	1249	3.05

aReleased, July 22, 1953; signed by Cleveland Indians, April 12, 1954.

Year Club	League	G.	IP.	W.	L.	Pct.	H.	R.	ER.	SO.	BB.	ERA.
1945—Detroit...............................	American	3	20⅔	2	1	.667	25	14	14	22	4	6.10
1954—Cleveland........................	American	1	0	0	0	.000	1	1	1	0	1	.....
World Series Totals—2 Years		4	20⅔	2	1	.667	26	15	15	22	5	6.53

—DID YOU KNOW—

That Detroit lefthander Hal Newhouser is the only pitcher in major league history to win consecutive Most Valuable Player awards? Newhouser was the American League's MVP in 1944 and '45 when he recorded 29-9 and 25-9 records, respectively.

LOUIS NORMAN (BUCK and BOBO) NEWSOM

Born August 11, 1907, at Hartsville, S.C.
Died December 7, 1962, at Orlando, Fla.
Height, 6.02¾. Weight, 205.
Threw right and batted right and lefthanded.

Shares major league record for most years leading league in games lost (4).
Pitched nine hitless innings against Boston Red Sox, September 18, 1934, but allowed one hit in 10th and lost, 2-1.

Year Club	League	G.	IP.	W.	L.	Pct.	H.	R.	ER.	SO.	BB.	ERA.
1928—Raleigh	Piedmont	11	53	0	5	.000	64	46	41	21	33	6.96
1928—Green-Wil.	E. Carolina	27	172	15	6	.714	155	88	78	★114	76	4.08
1929—Macon	Sally	45	298	19	18	.514	283	★167	●128	149	173	3.87
1929—Brooklyn	National	3	9	0	3	.000	15	12	11	6	5	11.00
1930—Brooklyn	National	2	3	0	0	.000	2	2	0	1	2	0.00
1930—Jersey City	International	3	10	0	1	.000	15	19	6	3	9	5.40
1930—Macon	Sally	22	89	6	3	.667	87	45	24	47	29	2.43
1931—Little Rock	Southern	★51	271	16	14	.533	289	166	152	★152	★150	5.05
1932—Chicago	National	1	1	0	0	.000	1	0	0	0	0	0.00
1932—Albany	International	34	145	7	7	.500	154	96	85	84	80	5.28
1933—Los Angeles	Pac. Coast	★56	★320	★30	11	.732	328	138	113	★212	124	3.18
1934—St. Louis	American	47	262	16	★20	.444	259	138	117	135	★149	4.02
1935—St. Louis (a)-Wash.	American	35	241	11	★18	.379	276	137	121	87	97	4.52
1936—Washington	American	43	285	17	15	.531	294	160	137	156	146	4.33
1937—Wash.(b)-Boston (c)	American	41	275	16	14	.533	269	163	147	166	★167	4.81
1938—St. Louis	American	44	★330	20	16	.556	★334	★205	★186	226	192	5.07
1939—St. Louis (d)-Detroit	American	41	292	20	11	.645	272	126	116	192	126	3.58
1940—Detroit	American	36	264	21	5	.808	235	110	83	164	100	2.83
1941—Detroit (e)	American	43	250	12	★20	.375	265	140	128	175	118	4.61
1942—Washington (f)	American	30	214	11	17	.393	236	135	★117	●113	92	4.92
1942—Brooklyn	National	6	32	2	2	.500	28	13	12	21	14	3.38
1943—Brooklyn (g)	National	22	125	9	4	.692	113	51	42	75	57	3.02
1943—St. Louis (h)-Wash.(i)	American	16	92	4	9	.308	107	67	60	48	56	5.87
1944—Philadelphia	American	37	265	13	15	.464	243	100	83	142	82	2.82
1945—Philadelphia	American	36	257	8	★20	.286	255	111	★94	127	103	3.29
1946—Phila.(j)-Washington	American	34	237	14	13	.519	224	90	77	114	90	2.92
1947—Wash.(k)-New York (l)	American	31	199	11	11	.500	208	82	74	82	67	3.35
1948—New York	National	11	26	0	4	.000	35	16	12	9	13	4.15
1949—Chattanooga	Southern	36	237	17	12	.586	273	★146	★116	★141	82	4.41
1950—Chattanooga	Southern	34	235	13	★17	.433	★244	119	●106	145	71	4.06
1951—Birmingham (m)	Southern	32	★237	16	11	.593	228	92	80	132	71	3.04
1952—Wash.(n)-Philadelphia	American	24	60	4	4	.500	54	26	26	27	32	3.90
1953—Philadelphia	American	17	39	2	1	.667	44	24	21	16	24	4.85
American League Totals—16 Years		555	3562	200	209	.489	3575	1814	1587	1970	1641	4.01
National League Totals—6 Years		45	196	11	13	.458	194	94	77	112	91	3.54
Major League Totals—20 Years		600	3758	211	222	.487	3769	1908	1664	2082	1732	3.99

aSold to Washington Senators for $40,000, May 21, 1935.

bTraded to Boston Red Sox with Outfielder Ben Chapman for Pitcher Wes Ferrell, Catcher Rick Ferrell and Outfielder Melo Almada, June 10, 1937.

cTraded to St. Louis Browns with Shortstop Rod Kress and Outfielder Colonel Mills for Outfielder Joe Vosmik, December 2, 1937.

dTraded to Detroit Tigers with Pitcher Jim Walkup, Shortstop Red Kress and Outfielder Roy Bell for Pitchers George Gill, Bob Harris, Vern Kennedy and Roxie Lawson, Third Baseman Mark Christman and Outfielder Chet Laabs, May 13, 1939.

eSold to Washington Senators, March 31, 1942.

fSold to Brooklyn Dodgers, August 31, 1942.

gTraded to St. Louis Browns for Pitchers Archie McKain and Fritz Ostermueller, July 15, 1943.

hSold to Washington Senators, August 31, 1943.

iTraded to Philadelphia Athletics for Pitcher Roger Wolff, December 13, 1943.

jReleased by Philadelphia Athletics at own request, June 3, 1946; signed with Washington Senators, June 5, 1946.

kReleased to New York Yankees on waivers, July 11, 1947.

lReleased, February 16, 1948; signed by New York Giants, April 10, 1948.

mSigned with Washington Senators, April 8, 1952.

nReleased, June 16, 1952; signed with Philadelphia Athletics same day.

WORLD SERIES RECORD

Year Club	League	G.	IP.	W.	L.	Pct.	H.	R.	ER.	SO.	BB.	ERA.
1940—Detroit	American	3	26	2	1	.667	18	4	4	17	4	1.38
1947—New York	American	2	2⅓	0	1	.000	6	5	5	0	2	19.29
World Series Totals—2 Years		5	28⅓	2	2	.500	24	9	9	17	6	2.86

CHARLES AUGUSTUS (KID) NICHOLS

Born September 14, 1869, at Madison, Wis.
Died April 11, 1953, at Kansas City, Mo.
Height, 5.10½. Weight, 180.
Threw and batted righthanded.

Manager, Kansas City, Western League, 1902-03; St. Louis Cardinals, 1904 to 1905.
Named to Hall of Fame, 1949.

Year Club	League	G.	CG.	IP.	W.	L.	Pct.	ShO.	H.	R.	SO.	BB.
1887—Kansas City	Western	....	....	....	....	12	....	....	....	....	65	39
1888—Memphis	Southern	15	....	....	....	8	....	....	....	....	84	74
1888—Kansas City	West. Assn.	18	....	....	....	....	....	....	....	....	....	....
1889—Omaha	West. Assn.	48	....	....	36	12	.750	....	355	194	357	92
1890—Boston	National	48	47	424	27	19	.587	★7	378	176	222	117
1891—Boston	National	52	45	423	30	17	.638	5	409	220	213	96
1892—Boston	National	53	49	454	35	16	.686	5	399	209	211	111
1893—Boston	National	52	43	414	34	14	.708	1	409	222	92	110
1894—Boston	National	50	40	417	32	13	.711	●3	475	306	98	108
1895—Boston	National	47	42	394	26	16	.619	1	427	219	146	82
1896—Boston	National	49	37	375	★30	14	.682	3	396	211	95	93
1897—Boston	National	★46	37	358	★31	11	.738	2	345	154	136	72
1898—Boston	National	50	40	388	★31	12	.721	5	309	136	132	84
1899—Boston	National	42	37	349	21	19	.525	4	321	155	109	86
1900—Boston	National	29	25	226	13	16	.448	●4	210	116	54	73
1901—Boston	National	38	33	326	19	16	.543	4	306	146	141	86
1902—Kansas City	Western	37	....	....	27	7	.794	....	....	....	168	90
1903—Kansas City	Western	35	....	....	21	12	.636	....	....	....	156	81
1904—St. Louis	National	36	35	317	21	13	.618	3	260	97	134	50
1905—St. Louis (a)-Phila.	National	24	20	191	11	11	.500	1	193	94	82	64
1906—Philadelphia	National	4	1	11	0	1	.000	0	17	16	1	13
Major League Totals—15 Years		620	531	5067	361	208	.634	48	4854	2477	1866	1245

aReleased to Philadelphia Phillies, July, 1905.

JOSEPH FRANKLIN (JOE) NIEKRO

Born November 7, 1944, at Martins Ferry, O.
Height, 6.01. Weight, 190.
Threw and batted righthanded.
Brother of Phil Niekro, former major league pitcher.

Pitched seven-inning, 2-0 perfect game against Tidewater, July 16, 1972, second game.
Led National League pitchers in games started with 38 in 1983 and 1984.
Led National League in wild pitches with 19 in 1982, 14 in 1983, 21 in 1985 and tied for lead with 19 in 1979.
Tied for National League lead in shutouts with 5 in 1979.
Named National League Pitcher of the Year by THE SPORTING NEWS, 1979.
Named righthanded pitcher on THE SPORTING NEWS National League All-Star Team, 1979.

Year Club	League	G.	IP.	W.	L.	Pct.	H.	R.	ER.	SO.	BB.	ERA.
1966—Treasure Valley	Pioneer	1	4	0	0	.000	4	0	0	7	1	0.00
1966—Quincy	Midwest	4	25	1	2	.333	17	7	3	14	6	1.08
1966—Dallas-Fort Worth	Texas	12	79	5	4	.556	71	28	22	50	15	2.51
1967—Chicago	National	36	170	10	7	.588	171	68	63	77	32	3.34
1968—Chicago	National	34	177	14	10	.583	204	93	85	65	59	4.32
1969—Chicago†-San Diego‡	National	41	221	8	18	.308	237	100	91	62	51	3.71
1970—Detroit	American	38	213	12	13	.480	221	107	96	101	72	4.06
1971—Detroit	American	31	122	6	7	.462	136	62	61	43	49	4.28
1972—Toledo	Int'national	2	14	2	0	1.000	6	1	1	11	3	0.64
1972—Detroit	American	18	47	3	2	.600	62	20	20	24	8	3.83
1973—Toledo§	Int'national	26	143	7	10	.412	148	74	59	77	47	3.71
1973—Atlanta	National	20	24	2	4	.333	23	11	11	12	11	4.13
1974—Richmond	Int'national	30	52	8	1	.889	44	14	12	50	18	2.08
1974—Atlanta x	National	27	43	3	2	.600	36	19	17	31	18	3.56

Year Club	League	G.	IP.	W.	L.	Pct.	H.	R.	ER.	SO.	BB.	ERA.
1975—Iowa	Am. Assoc.	7	9	1	0	1.000	7	6	5	9	7	5.00
1975—Houston	National	40	88	6	4	.600	79	32	30	54	39	3.07
1976—Houston	National	36	118	4	8	.333	107	60	44	77	56	3.36
1977—Houston	National	44	181	13	8	.619	155	66	61	101	64	3.03
1978—Houston	National	35	203	14	14	.500	190	97	87	97	73	3.86
1979—Houston	National	38	264	●21	11	.656	221	102	88	119	107	3.00
1980—Houston	National	37	256	20	12	.625	268	119	101	127	79	3.55
1981—Houston	National	24	166	9	9	.500	150	60	52	77	47	2.82
1982—Houston	National	35	270	17	12	.586	224	79	74	130	64	2.47
1983—Houston	National	38	263⅔	15	14	.517	238	115	102	152	101	3.48
1984—Houston	National	38	248⅓	16	12	.571	223	104	84	127	89	3.04
1985—Houston y	National	32	213	9	12	.429	197	100	88	117	99	3.72
1985—New York z	American	3	12⅓	2	1	.667	14	8	8	4	8	5.84
1986—New York	American	25	125⅔	9	10	.474	139	84	68	59	63	4.87
1987—New York a-Minnesota b	American	27	147	7	13	.350	155	101	87	84	64	5.33
1988—Minnesota c	American	5	11⅔	1	1	.500	16	13	13	7	9	10.03
National League Totals—16 Years		555	2906	181	157	.536	2723	1225	1078	1425	989	3.34
American League Totals—7 Years		147	678⅔	40	47	.460	743	395	353	322	273	4.68
Major League Totals—22 Years		702	3584⅔	221	204	.520	3466	1620	1431	1747	1262	3.59

Selected by Cleveland Indians' organization in 7th round of free-agent draft, January, 1966.

Selected by Chicago Cubs' organization in 3rd round of free-agent draft, June, 1966.

†Traded with Pitcher Gary Ross and Infielder Francisco Libran to San Diego Padres for Pitcher Dick Selma, April 24, 1969. Libran remained on Cubs' San Antonio farm team but became San Diego property.

‡Traded to Detroit Tigers for Pitcher Pat Dobson and Shortstop-Outfielder Dave Campbell, December 4, 1969.

§Sold on waivers to Atlanta Braves, August 7, 1973.

xSold to Houston Astros, April 5, 1975.

yTraded to New York Yankees for Pitcher Jim Deshaies and two players to be named later, September 15, 1985; Houston Astros' organization acquired Infielder Neder Horta, September 24, 1985, and Pitcher Dody Rather, January 11, 1986, to complete deal.

zGranted free agency, November 12, 1985; re-signed by Yankees, January 8, 1986.

aTraded with cash to Minnesota Twins for Catcher Mark Salas, June 7, 1987.

bGranted free agency, January 22, 1988; re-signed by Twins, February 9, 1988.

cReleased, May 4, 1988.

CHAMPIONSHIP SERIES RECORD

Shares National League record for most innings pitched, game (10), October 10, 1980.

Year Club	League	G.	IP.	W.	L.	Pct.	H.	R.	ER.	SO.	BB.	ERA.
1980—Houston	National	1	10	0	0	.000	6	0	0	2	1	0.00

Appeared as pinch-runner for Detroit Tigers in one game of 1972 Championship Series.

WORLD SERIES RECORD

Year Club	League	G.	IP.	W.	L.	Pct.	H.	R.	ER.	SO.	BB.	ERA.
1987—Minnesota	American	1	2	0	0	.000	1	0	0	1	1	0.00

PHILIP HENRY (PHIL) NIEKRO

Born April 1, 1939, at Blaine, O.

Height, 6.02. Weight, 195.

Threw and batted righthanded.

Brother of Joe Niekro, former major league pitcher.

Holds major league record for most putouts by pitcher, lifetime (386).

Shares major league records for most years with 200 or more innings pitched (19); most years leading league in runs allowed (3); most strikeouts, inning (4), July 29, 1977, sixth inning.

Holds National League records for most wild pitches (200) and putouts by pitcher (340), lifetime; most wild pitches, inning (4), August 4, 1979, second game, fifth inning; most years leading league in games lost (4).

Holds modern National League record for most games lost, lifetime (230).

Shares modern National League record for most wild pitches, game (6), August 14, 1979, second game.

Pitched 9-0 no-hit victory against San Diego Padres, August 5, 1973.

Led National League in home runs allowed with 40 in 1970, 29 in 1975, 41 in 1979 and 30 in 1980.

Led National League in hit batsmen with 11 in 1975, 13 in 1978 and 11 in 1979.

Led National League in complete games with 18 in 1974, 20 in 1977, 22 in 1978 and 23 in 1979.

Led National League in wild pitches with 19 in 1967, 14 in 1976 and 17 in 1977.

Led National League pitchers in games started with 43 in 1977, 42 in 1978, 44 in 1979, and tied for lead with 38 in 1980.

Led National League batters in sacrifice hits with 18 in 1968.

Tied for National League lead in balks with 3 in 1968 and 3 in 1972.

Named pitcher on THE SPORTING NEWS National League All-Star fielding team, 1978 through 1980, 1982 and 1983.

Year	Club	League	G.	IP.	W.	L.	Pct.	H.	R.	ER.	SO.	BB.	ERA.
1959—Wellsville	NYP	10	35	2	1	.667	47	38	29	16	24	7.46
1959—McCook	Neb. State	*23	52	7	1	.875	35	20	18	48	29	3.12
1960—Jacksonville	Sally	38	84	6	4	.600	66	36	26	52	52	2.79
1960—Louisville	Am. Assoc.	6	10	1	0	1.000	11	5	4	2	9	3.60
1961—Austin	Texas	*51	110	4	4	.500	100	45	36	84	53	2.95
1962—Louisville	Am. Assoc.	49	98	9	6	.600	111	50	42	48	41	3.86
1963—Denver	P. Coast					(In Military Service)						
1964—Milwaukee	National	10	15	0	0	.000	15	10	8	8	7	4.80
1964—Denver	P. Coast	29	172	11	5	.688	172	79	66	119	45	3.45
1965—Milwaukee	National	41	75	2	3	.400	73	32	24	49	26	2.88
1966—Atlanta	National	28	50	4	3	.571	48	32	23	17	23	4.14
1966—Richmond	Int'national	17	54	3	4	.429	43	27	22	36	16	3.67
1967—Atlanta	National	46	207	11	9	.550	164	64	43	129	55	*1.87
1968—Atlanta	National	37	257	14	12	.538	228	83	74	140	45	2.59
1969—Atlanta	National	40	284	23	13	.639	235	93	81	193	57	2.57
1970—Atlanta	National	34	230	12	18	.400	222	124	109	168	68	4.27
1971—Atlanta	National	42	269	15	14	.517	248	112	89	173	70	2.98
1972—Atlanta	National	38	282	16	12	.571	254	112	96	164	53	3.06
1973—Atlanta	National	42	245	13	10	.565	214	103	90	131	89	3.31
1974—Atlanta	National	41	*302	●20	13	.606	249	91	80	195	88	2.38
1975—Atlanta	National	39	276	15	15	.500	285	115	98	144	72	3.20
1976—Atlanta	National	38	271	17	11	.607	249	116	99	173	101	3.29
1977—Atlanta	National	44	*330	16	●20	.444	*315	*166	*148	*262	*164	4.04
1978—Atlanta	National	44	*334	19	*18	.514	*295	*129	●107	248	102	2.88
1979—Atlanta	National	44	*342	●21	*20	.512	*311	*160	129	208	*113	3.39
1980—Atlanta	National	40	275	15	*18	.455	256	119	111	176	85	3.63
1981—Atlanta	National	22	139	7	7	.500	120	56	48	62	56	3.11
1982—Atlanta	National	35	234⅓	17	4	*.810	225	106	94	144	73	3.61
1983—Atlanta†	National	34	201⅔	11	10	.524	212	94	89	128	105	3.97
1984—New York	American	32	215⅔	16	8	.667	219	85	74	136	76	3.09
1985—New York‡§	American	33	220	16	12	.571	203	110	100	149	*120	4.09
1986—Cleveland	American	34	210⅓	11	11	.500	241	126	101	81	95	4.32
1987—Cleveland x-Toronto y	American	25	135⅔	7	13	.350	157	94	92	64	60	6.10
1987—Atlanta z	National	1	3	0	0	.000	6	5	5	0	6	15.00
American League Totals—4 Years		124	781⅔	50	44	.532	820	415	367	430	351	4.23
National League Totals—21 Years		740	4622	268	230	.538	4224	1922	1645	2912	1458	3.20
Major League Totals—24 Years		864	5403⅔	318	274	.537	5044	2337	2012	3342	1809	3.35

Signed as free agent by Milwaukee Braves' organization, July 19, 1958.

†Released, October 7, 1983; signed by New York Yankees, January 5, 1984.

‡Granted free agency, November 12, 1985; re-signed by Yankees, January 8, 1986.

§Released, March 28, 1986; signed by Cleveland Indians, April 3, 1986.

xTraded to Toronto Blue Jays for Outfielder Darryl Landrum and a player to be named later, August 9, 1987; Cleveland Indians acquired Pitcher Don Gordon to complete deal, August 10, 1987.

yReleased, August 31, 1987; signed by Atlanta Braves, September 23, 1987.

zOn voluntarily retired list, September 27, 1987.

CHAMPIONSHIP SERIES RECORD

Established major league record for most runs allowed, game (9), October 4, 1969.

Year	Club	League	G.	IP.	W.	L.	Pct.	H.	R.	ER.	SO.	BB.	ERA.
1969—Atlanta	National	1	8	0	1	.000	9	9	4	4	4	4.50
1982—Atlanta	National	1	6	0	0	.000	6	2	2	5	4	3.00
Championship Series Totals—2 Years		2	14	0	1	.000	15	11	6	9	8	3.86

JOHN JOSEPH (JACK) O'CONNOR

Born March 3, 1867, at St. Louis, Mo.

Died November 14, 1937, at St. Louis, Mo.

Height, 5.10. Weight, 170.

Threw and batted righthanded.

Manager, St. Louis Browns, 1910; St. Louis Terriers, Federal League, 1913; scout, Terriers, 1914.

Year	Club	League	Pos.	G.	AB.	R.	H.	2B.	3B.	HR.	SB.	B.A.	PO.	A.	E.	F.A.
1886—St. Joseph	Western	C-OF	70	281	72	76	...	...	...	...	.270	260	51	27	.920
1887—Cincinnati	A. A.	C-OF	12	45	4	6	0	0	0	0	.133	13	13	5	.839
1888—Cincinnati	A. A.	C-OF	36	139	14	28	3	1	1	13	.201	130	16	28	.900
1889—Columbus	A. A.	C-OF	107	398	68	107	15	9	3	29	.269	421	127	31	.946
1890—Columbus	A. A.	C-OF	118	445	93	152	18	9	2	28	.341	510	135	27	.929
1891—Columbus	A. A.	C-OF	53	217	28	60	12	4	0	10	.276	114	14	6	.955
1891—Denver	Western	C-OF	46	209	37	61	...	...	...	10	.291	91	9	6	.943

Year	Club	League	Pos.	G.	AB.	R.	H.	2B.	3B.	HR.	SB.	B.A.	PO.	A.	E.	F.A.
1892—Cleveland	Nat.	C-OF	139	568	71	144	21	5	1	18	.253	153	41	7	.919
1893—Cleveland	Nat.	C-OF	93	365	71	113	22	1	3	23	.309	179	61	39	.860
1894—Cleveland	Nat.	C-OF	80	329	67	105	22	6	2	13	.319	160	37	12	.860
1895—Cleveland	Nat.	C-1B	88	338	52	99	13	10	0	16	.295	130	46	13	.859
1896—Cleveland	Nat.	C-OF-1B	60	243	38	73	9	1	0	16	.300	107	31	6	.928
1897—Cleveland	Nat.	C-OF-1B	100	399	48	116	22	3	2	22	.290	95	3	6	.942
1898—Cleveland	Nat.	C-OF-1B	129	476	50	125	15	5	0	4	.262	154	54	7	.946
1899—St. Louis	Nat.	C-1B	79	287	31	75	4	6	0	6	.261	184	58	11	.927
1900—St. Louis-Pitts.	Nat.	C	48	181	20	43	4	1	0	4	.237	137	60	9	.887
1901—Pittsburgh	Nat.	C	56	200	16	40	7	3	0	3	.200	265	57	7	.949
1902—Pittsburgh	Nat.	C-1B	45	171	13	50	1	2	1	2	.292	187	49	5	.955
1903—New York	Amer.	C	64	213	13	42	4	1	0	3	.197	286	54	4	.968
1904—St. Paul	A. A.	C	13	44	4	8	...	...	...	0	.182	....	....	....	......
1904—St. Louis	Amer.	C	13	45	4	8	1	0	0	0	.178	48	10	3	.951
1905—												(Did not play)				
1906—St. Louis	Amer.	C	58	174	8	33	0	0	0	4	.190	248	64	3	.990
1907—St. Louis	Amer.	C	25	89	2	16	2	0	0	0	.157	87	29	1	.991
1908-09—												(Did not play)				
1910—St. Louis	Amer.	C	1	0	0	0	0	0	0	0	.000	1	0	0	1.000
American Assn. Totals—5 Years			326	1244	207	353	48	23	6	80	.284	1188	305	97	.939
National League Totals—11 Years			917	3557	477	983	140	43	9	127	.276	1751	497	122	.949
American League Totals—5 Years			161	521	27	99	7	1	0	7	.190	670	157	11	.987
Major League Totals—21 Years			1404	5322	711	1435	195	67	15	214	.270	3609	959	230	.952

ROBERT ARTHUR (BOB) O'FARRELL

Born October 19, 1896, at Waukegan, Ill.

Died February 20, 1988, at Waukegan, Ill.

Height, 5.10. Weight, 185.

Threw and batted righthanded.

Named National League Most Valuable Player, 1926.

Player-manager, St. Louis Cardinals, 1927; Cincinnati Reds, 1934; Bloomington, Illinois-Indiana-Iowa League, 1938.

Year	Club	League	Pos.	G.	AB.	R.	H.	2B.	3B.	HR.	RBI.	B.A.	PO.	A.	E.	F.A.
1915—Chicago	Nat.	C	2	3	0	1	0	0	0	0	.333	1	0	1	.500
1916—Chicago	Nat.	C	1	1	0	0	0	0	0	0	.000	0	0	0	.000
1916—Peoria	I. I. I.	C	77	223	29	64	13	3	3	....	.287	231	50	9	.969
1917—Peoria	I. I. I.	C	52	179	24	57	16	4	1	....	.318	205	57	7	.974
1917—Peoria	Cent.	C	58	201	22	57	....	....	1	....	.283	298	71	10	.974
1917—Chicago	Nat.	C	3	8	1	3	0	0	0	1	.375	7	1	0	1.000
1918—Chicago	Nat.	C	52	113	9	32	7	3	1	18	.283	115	36	4	.974
1919—Chicago	Nat.	C	49	125	11	27	4	2	0	9	.216	119	48	6	.965
1920—Chicago	Nat.	C	94	270	29	67	11	4	3	19	.248	317	100	19	.956
1921—Chicago	Nat.	C	96	260	32	65	12	7	4	32	.250	269	87	12	.967
1922—Chicago	Nat.	C	128	392	68	127	18	8	4	60	.324	★446	★143	14	.977
1923—Chicago	Nat.	C	131	452	73	144	25	4	12	84	.310	★418	●118	13	.976
1924—Chicago	Nat.	C	71	183	25	44	6	2	3	28	.241	204	40	4	.984
1925—Chi.★-St. L.	Nat.	C	111	339	39	92	13	3	3	35	.271	330	67	10	.975
1926—St. Louis	Nat.	C	147	492	63	144	30	9	7	68	.293	★466	117	10	.983
1927—St. Louis	Nat.	C	61	178	19	47	10	1	0	18	.264	141	45	4	.979
1928—St. L.†-N. Y.	Nat.	C	91	185	29	37	7	0	2	24	.200	199	31	3	.987
1929—New York	Nat.	C	91	248	35	76	14	3	4	42	.306	254	22	6	.979
1930—New York	Nat.	C	94	249	37	75	16	4	4	54	.301	259	34	8	.973
1931—New York	Nat.	C	85	174	11	39	8	3	1	19	.224	223	27	5	.980
1932—New York‡	Nat.	C	50	67	7	16	3	0	0	8	.239	85	9	3	.969
1933—St. Louis§	Nat.	C	55	163	16	39	4	2	2	20	.239	211	19	7	.970
1934—Cin. x-Chicago y	Nat.	C	66	190	13	45	11	3	1	14	.237	217	35	1	.996
1935—St. Louis	Nat.	C	14	10	0	0	0	0	0	0	.000	12	0	0	1.000
1936—Rochester	Int.	C	102	286	30	79	20	3	2	43	.276	★442	★67	5	★.990
1937—Rochester	Int.	C	70	194	10	45	10	0	0	20	.232	219	38	8	.970
1938—Bloomington	I. I. I.	C								(Less than ten games)					
Major League Totals—21 Years			1492	4102	517	1120	199	58	51	....	.273	4293	979	130	.976

★Traded to St. Louis Cardinals for Catcher Mike Gonzales and Infielder Howard Freigau, May 23, 1925.

†Traded to New York Giants for Outfielder George Harper, May 10, 1928.

‡Traded to St. Louis Cardinals with Pitchers Bill Walker, James Mooney, and Outfielder Ethan Allen for Pitcher Ray Starr and Catcher Gus Mancuso, October 10, 1932.

§Sold to Cincinnati Reds and appointed manager for 1934.

xReleased as manager, July, 1934 and signed with Chicago Cubs, August, 1934.

yReleased and signed with St. Louis Cardinals.

Year Club League	Pos.	G.	AB.	R.	H.	2B.	3B.	HR.	RBI.	B.A.	PO.	A.	E.	F.A.
1918—Chicago .... Nat.	C	3	3	0	0	0	0	0	0	.000	0	0	0	.000
1926—St. Louis .... Nat.	C	7	23	2	7	1	0	0	2	.304	35	8	0	1.000
World Series Totals—2 Years		10	26	2	7	1	0	0	2	.269	35	8	0	1.000

ANTONIO (TONY) OLIVA

Born July 20, 1940, at Pinar del Rio, Cuba.

Height, 6.02. Weight, 192.

Threw right and batted lefthanded.

Shares major league records for most total bases, rookie season (374), 1964; most consecutive years leading league in hits (3).

Holds American League record for most hits, rookie season (217), 1964.

Hit three home runs in a game, July 3, 1973.

Named American League Rookie of the Year by the Baseball Writers' Association and Rookie Player of the Year by THE SPORTING NEWS, 1964.

Named as outfielder on THE SPORTING NEWS American League All-Star Team, 1964-65-66-70-71.

Named American League Player of the Year by THE SPORTING NEWS, 1965.

Named as outfielder on THE SPORTING NEWS American League All-Star fielding team, 1966.

Named American League Player of the Year by THE SPORTING NEWS, 1971.

Coach, Minnesota Twins, 1977, 1978; minor league batting instructor, 1979 through 1984; coach, 1985 to date.

Year Club League	Pos.	G.	AB.	R.	H.	2B.	3B.	HR.	RBI.	B.A.	PO.	A.	E.	F.A.
1961—Wytheville .... Appal.	OF	64	249	55	⋆102	15	6	10	⋆81	⋆ 410	70	⋆12	14	.854
1962—Charlotte .... Sally	OF	127	469	71	164	35	6	17	93	350	231	13	⋆19	.928
1962—Minnesota .... Amer.	OF	9	9	3	4	1	0	0	3	.444	3	0	0	1.000
1963—Dal.-Ft. Worth ...... P.C.	OF	146	536	79	163	30	8	23	74	.304	301	14	11	.966
1963—Minnesota .... Amer.	PH	7	7	0	3	0	0	0	1	.429	0	0	0	.000
1964—Minnesota .... Amer.	OF	161	672	⋆ 109	⋆217	⋆43	9	32	94	⋆.323	313	5	6	.981
1965—Minnesota .... Amer.	OF	149	576	107	⋆185	40	5	16	98	⋆ .321	284	10	●11	.964
1966—Minnesota .... Amer.	OF	159	622	99	⋆191	32	7	25	87	.307	335	9	⋆10	.972
1967—Minnesota .... Amer.	OF	146	557	76	161	⋆34	6	17	83	.289	286	8	4	.987
1968—Minnesota .... Amer.	OF	128	470	54	136	24	5	18	68	.289	227	7	4	.983
1969—Minnesota .... Amer.	OF	153	637	97	⋆197	⋆39	4	24	101	.309	311	14	6	.982
1970—Minnesota .... Amer.	OF	157	628	96	⋆204	●36	7	23	107	.325	351	12	●12	.968
1971—Minnesota .... Amer.	OF	126	487	73	164	30	3	22	81	⋆.337	216	6	7	.969
1972—Minnesota .... Amer.	OF	10	28	1	9	1	0	0	1	.321	6	0	1	.857
1973—Minnesota .... Amer.	DH	146	571	63	166	20	0	16	92	.291	0	0	0	.000
1974—Minnesota .... Amer.	DH	127	459	43	131	16	2	13	57	.285	0	0	0	.000
1975—Minnesota .... Amer.	DH	131	455	46	123	10	0	13	58	.270	0	0	0	.000
1976—Minnesota .... Amer.	DH	67	123	3	26	3	0	1	4	.211	0	0	0	.000
Major League Totals—15 Years		1676	6301	870	1917	329	48	220	935	.304	2332	71	61	.975

CHAMPIONSHIP SERIES RECORD

Year Club League	Pos.	G.	AB.	R.	H.	2B.	3B.	HR.	RBI.	B.A.	PO.	A.	E.	F.A.
1969—Minnesota .... Amer.	OF	3	13	3	5	2	0	1	2	.385	6	1	2	.778
1970—Minnesota .... Amer.	OF	3	12	2	6	2	0	1	1	.500	10	2	0	1.000
Championship Series Totals—2 Years.....		6	25	5	11	4	0	2	3	.440	16	3	2	.905

WORLD SERIES RECORD

Year Club League	Pos.	G.	AB.	R.	H.	2B.	3B.	HR.	RBI.	B.A.	PO.	A.	E.	F.A.
1965—Minnesota .... Amer.	OF	7	26	2	5	1	0	1	2	.192	20	0	1	.952

ALBERT (AL) OLIVER JR.

Born October 14, 1946, at Portsmouth, O.

Height, 6.01. Weight, 185.

Threw and batted lefthanded.

Tied major league records for most errors by first baseman, inning (3), May 23, 1969, fourth inning; most long hits, doubleheader (6), August 17, 1980; most extra bases on long hits, doubleheader (15), August 17, 1980.
Shares modern major league record for most at-bats, nine-inning game (7), September 16, 1975.
Holds American League record for most total bases, doubleheader (21), August 17, 1980.
Shares American League record for most home runs, doubleheader (4), August 17, 1980.
Hit three home runs in a game, May 23, 1979 and August 17, 1980 (second game).
Led National League in total bases with 317 in 1982.
Tied for National League lead in grounding into double plays with 21 in 1983.
Led Western Carolinas League first basemen in double plays with 93 in 1965.
Named first baseman on THE SPORTING NEWS National League All-Star Team, 1982.
Named outfielder on THE SPORTING NEWS National League All-Star Team, 1975.
Named first baseman on THE SPORTING NEWS National League Silver Slugger team, 1982.
Named outfielder on THE SPORTING NEWS American League Silver Slugger team, 1980.
Named designated hitter on THE SPORTING NEWS American League Silver Slugger team, 1981.

Year Club League	Pos.	G.	AB.	R.	H.	2B.	3B.	HR.	RBI.	B.A.	PO.	A.	E.	F.A.
1964—Salem......................Appal.					(Did not play)									
1965—Gastonia .... W. Car.	1B	123	*515	77	*159	19	5	10	71	.309	*1031	*64	21	.981
1966—Raleigh.................. Carol.	1B	117	458	66	137	25	4	10	57	.299	1035	*75	16	.986
1967—Macon .... South.	1B-OF	38	126	18	28	1	2	1	4	.222	267	21	6	.980
1967—Raleigh.................. Carol.	1B	40	145	20	43	4	4	2	15	.297	365	17	0	1.000
1968—Columbus.............. Int.	1B-OF	132	473	61	149	22	13	14	74	.315	968	28	16	.984
1968—Pittsburgh .... Nat.	OF	4	8	1	1	0	0	0	0	.125	3	0	0	1.000
1969—Pittsburgh .... Nat.	1B-OF	129	463	55	132	19	2	17	70	.285	911	50	9	.991
1970—Pittsburgh .... Nat.	OF-1B	151	551	63	149	33	5	12	83	.270	718	52	9	.988
1971—Pittsburgh .... Nat.	OF-1B	143	529	69	149	31	7	14	64	.282	497	15	6	.988
1972—Pittsburgh .... Nat.	OF-1B	140	565	88	176	27	4	12	89	.312	353	4	5	.986
1973—Pittsburgh .... Nat.	OF-1B	158	654	90	191	38	7	20	99	.292	692	36	13	.982
1974—Pittsburgh .... Nat.	OF-1B	147	617	96	198	38	12	11	85	.321	702	26	7	.990
1975—Pittsburgh .... Nat.	OF-1B	155	628	90	176	39	8	18	84	.280	409	6	5	.988
1976—Pittsburgh .... Nat.	OF-1B	121	443	62	143	22	5	12	61	.323	327	4	5	.985
1977—Pittsburgh† .... Nat.	OF	154	568	75	175	29	6	19	82	.308	305	6	6	.981
1978—Texas..................... Amer.	OF	133	525	65	170	35	5	14	89	.324	219	8	3	.987
1979—Texas..................... Amer.	OF	136	492	69	159	28	4	12	76	.323	260	9	7	.975
1980—Texas..................... Amer.	OF-1B	*163	656	96	209	43	3	19	117	.319	315	9	9	.973
1981—Texas‡.................... Amer.	1B	102	421	53	130	29	1	4	55	.309	2	0	0	1.000
1982—Montreal .... Nat.	1B	160	617	90	*204	*43	2	22	•109	*.331	1286	92	*19	.986
1983—Montreal§ .... Nat.	•1B-OF	157	614	70	184	•38	3	8	84	.300	1207	118	•13	.990
1984—S.F. x-Phila. y ...... Nat.	1B-OF	119	432	36	130	26	2	0	48	.301	818	61	13	.985
1985—Los Angeles z .... Nat.	OF	35	79	1	20	5	0	0	8	.253	13	2	2	.882
1985—Toronto a.............. Amer.	1B	61	187	20	47	6	1	5	23	.251	3	0	0	1.000
National League Totals—14 Years		1773	6768	886	2028	388	63	165	966	.300	8241	472	112	.987
American League Totals—5 Years		595	2281	303	715	141	14	54	360	.313	799	26	19	.977
Major League Totals—18 Years		2368	9049	1189	2743	529	77	219	1326	.303	9040	498	131	.986

Signed as free agent by Pittsburgh Pirates' organization, June 13, 1964.

†Traded with infielder Nelson Norman to Texas Rangers for Pitcher Bert Blyleven and First Baseman-Outfielder John Milner, December 8, 1977.

‡Traded to Montreal Expos for Third Baseman Larry Parrish and First Baseman Dave Hostetler, March 31, 1982.

§Traded to San Francisco Giants for Pitcher Fred Breining and a player to be named later, February 27, 1984; Montreal Expos' organization acquired Outfielder Max Venable to complete deal, March 31, 1984. (San Francisco traded Pitcher Andy McGaffigan to Montreal, March 31, 1984, as compensation for the injury that Breining arrived with. Breining remained with Montreal.)

xTraded with a player to be named later to Philadelphia Phillies for Pitchers Kelly Downs and George Riley, August 20, 1984; Philadelphia acquired Pitcher Renie Martin to complete deal, August 30, 1984.

yTraded to Los Angeles Dodgers for Pitcher Pat Zachry, February 4, 1985.

zTraded to Toronto Blue Jays for First Baseman Len Matuszek, July 9, 1985.

aGranted free agency, November 12, 1985.

CHAMPIONSHIP SERIES RECORD

Year Club League	Pos.	G.	AB.	R.	H.	2B.	3B.	HR.	RBI.	B.A.	PO.	A.	E.	F.A.
1970—Pittsburgh .... Nat.	1B	2	8	0	2	0	0	0	1	.250	22	1	0	1.000
1971—Pittsburgh .... Nat.	PH-OF	4	12	2	3	0	0	1	5	.250	5	0	0	1.000
1972—Pittsburgh .... Nat.	OF	5	20	3	5	2	1	1	3	.250	17	1	0	1.000
1974—Pittsburgh .... Nat.	OF	4	14	1	2	0	0	0	1	.143	9	0	0	1.000
1975—Pittsburgh .... Nat.	OF	3	11	1	2	0	0	1	2	.182	5	0	0	1.000
1985—Toronto .... Amer.	PH-DH	5	8	0	3	1	0	0	3	.375	0	0	0	.000
Championship Series Totals—6 Years		23	73	7	17	3	1	3	15	.233	58	2	0	1.000

WORLD SERIES RECORD

Year Club League	Pos.	G.	AB.	R.	H.	2B.	3B.	HR.	RBI.	B.A.	PO.	A.	E.	F.A.
1971—Pittsburgh .... Nat.	PH-OF	5	19	1	4	2	0	0	2	.211	11	0	1	.917

—DID YOU KNOW—

That Hall of Famer Jim O'Rourke is credited with the first hit in major league history? O'Rourke collected a single for Boston against Philadelphia pitcher Alonzo Knight on April 22, 1876.

JAMES EDWARD (TIP) O'NEILL

Born May 25, 1858, at Woodstock, Ont.
Died December 31, 1915, at Montreal, Que.
Height, 6.01½. Weight, 187.
Threw and batted righthanded.

Umpired in several minor leagues in 1890s.

Year	Club	League	Pos.	G.	AB.	R.	H.	2B.	3B.	HR.	SB.	B.A.	PO.	A.	E.	F.A.
1882	Metropolitan	Alliance	OF						(No records available)							
1883	New York	Nat.	OF-P	23	84	7	15	3	0	0	....	.179	9	37	6	.885
1884	St. Louis	A. A.	OF-P	77	302	47	82	14	11	3	....	.272	74	33	20	.843
1885	St. Louis	A. A.	OF	51	202	45	69	5	5	3	....	.342	86	8	11	.893
1886	St. Louis	A. A.	OF	138	575	105	195	29	15	3	7	.339	282	14	21	.934
1887	St. Louis	A. A.	OF	123	563	*166	277	*46	*24	*13	30	*.492	232	9	29	.893
1888	St. Louis	A. A.	OF	130	530	106	*176	23	9	5	24	*.332	233	6	13	.949
1889	St. Louis	A. A.	OF	133	534	125	180	32	8	9	29	.337	267	12	22	.927
1890	Chicago	Play.	OF	137	573	113	173	18	16	3	28	.302	235	8	17	.935
1891	St. Louis	A. A.	OF	119	414	106	156	29	3	10	30	.324	197	7	10	.953
1892	Cincinnati	Nat.	OF	107	420	63	105	13	7	2	15	.250	184	15	16	.926
	American Association Totals—7 Years			771	3120	682	1135	178	75	46	....	.363	1371	89	126	.921
	National League Totals—2 Years			130	504	70	120	16	7	2	....	.238	193	52	22	.918
	Players League Totals—1 Year			137	573	113	173	18	16	3	28	.302	235	8	17	.935
	Major League Totals—10 Years			1038	4197	865	1428	212	98	51	....	.340	1799	149	165	.922

PITCHING RECORD

Year	Club	League	G.	CG.	IP.	W.	L.	Pct.	ShO.	H.	R.	SO.	BB.
1883	New York	National	19	15	147	6	12	.333	0	180	...	54	63
1884	St. Louis	Amer. Assn.	17	14	140	10	4	.714	0	121	...	37	50
	Major League Totals—2 Years		36	29	287	16	16	.500	0	301	...	81	113

JAMES HENRY (JIM) O'ROURKE
(Orator Jim)

Born August 24, 1852, at East Bridgeport, Conn.
Died January 8, 1919, at Bridgeport, Conn.
Threw and batted righthanded.

Manager, Buffalo, N. L., 1881-84; umpire, N. L., 1894; manager of Victors of Bridgeport, 1895-96; Bridgeport, Connecticut League, 1897-1908; president of Connecticut League, 1909-13; Eastern Association, 1914. Named to Hall of Fame, 1945.

Year	Club	League	Pos.	G.	AB.	R.	H.	2B.	3B.	HR.	SB.	B.A.	PO.	A.	E.	F.A.
1872	Mansfield	Nat. Assn.		....	....	....	....	...	...	...	....	.....	.....	...	...	......
1873	Boston	Nat. Assn.	3B	57	297	79	103	...	...	...	....	.347	392	23	31	.930
1874	Boston	Nat. Assn.	1-3B	70	334	80	115	...	...	...	....	.344	763	11	37	.954
1875	Boston	Nat. Assn.	3-OF	69	....			...	...	...	....	.306	.....	...	...	.933
1876	Boston	Nat.	OF	70	327	61	102	15	1	2	....	.312	154	7	27	.856
1877	Boston	Nat.	OF	49	211	54	74	16	4	0	....	.351	84	8	19	.829
1878	Boston	Nat.	OF	60	255	44	70	11	8	1	....	.275	102	15	19	.860
1879	Providence	Nat.	OF-1B	80	359	69	126	17	12	4	....	.351	271	12	28	.910
1880	Boston	Nat.	O-Inf.-C	84	355	70	100	18	11	●6	....	.282	196	15	18	.921
1881	Buffalo	Nat.	O-Inf.-C	83	348	71	105	19	6	0	....	.302	112	85	39	.835
1882	Buffalo	Nat.	O-Inf.-C	84	370	62	104	16	8	2	....	.281	140	15	24	.866
1883	Buffalo	Nat.	O-Inf.-C	93	430	99	141	30	7	1	....	.328	215	42	28	.902
1884	Buffalo	Nat.	O-Inf.-C	104	448	112	157	27	9	4	.....	*.350	318	7	28	.921
1885	New York	Nat.	OF-C	112	477	119	143	21	●15	4	....	.300	179	13	13	.937
1886	New York	Nat.	OF-C	104	440	106	136	25	6	1	14	.309	351	94	28	.941
1887	New York	Nat.	OF-C-3B	103	433	73	149	15	13	2	46	.344	197	73	24	.918
1888	New York	Nat.	OF	107	409	50	112	15	7	4	25	.274	130	13	6	.960
1889	New York	Nat.	OF	128	502	89	161	36	7	3	33	.321	165	18	22	.893
1890	New York	Play.	OF	111	469	112	172	31	7	8	26	.367	200	27	16	.934
1891	New York	Nat.	OF	136	554	94	167	27	8	5	25	.301	175	16	20	.905
1892	New York	Nat.	OF	112	447	63	133	26	5	0	23	.298	146	12	14	.919

Year	Club	League	Pos.	G.	AB.	R.	H.	2B.	3B.	HR.	SB.	B.A.	PO.	A.	E.	F.A.
1893—Washington		Nat.	OF-1B	129	527	76	161	20	5	2	19	.306	455	35	25	.951
1904—New York		Nat.	C	1	4	1	1	0	0	0	0	.250	4	0	1	.800
1904—Bridgeport		Conn.	C	65	245	28	70	11	1	0	2	.286	230	72	7	.977
1905—Bridgeport		Conn.	C-OF	68	238	15	60	11	1	1	3	.252	119	34	8	.950
1906—Bridgeport		Conn.	1B	93	348	26	85	9	0	0	5	.244	771	59	17	.980
1907—Bridgeport		Conn.	1B	24	83	3	16	....	....	....	....	.193	26	0	1	.963
National League Totals—18 Years				1639	6896	1313	2142	354	132	41	....	.311	3394	480	383	.910
Players League Totals—1 Year				111	469	112	172	31	7	8	26	.367	200	27	16	.934
Major League Totals—19 Years				1750	7365	1425	2314	385	139	49	....	.314	3594	507	399	.911

MELVIN THOMAS (MEL) OTT

Born March 2, 1909, at Gretna, La.

Died November 21, 1958, at New Orleans, La.

Height, 5.09. Weight, 170.

Threw right and batted lefthanded.

Holds National League record for most years with 100 or more bases on balls (10).

Shares National League record for most runs, game (6), August 4, 1934, second game and April 30, 1944, first game.

Led National League outfielders in double plays, with 12 in 1929 and 7 in 1935 (tied).

Named to THE SPORTING NEWS All-Star Major League Teams, 1934-35-36-38.

Manager, New York Giants, 1942 to 1948; associated with New York Giant farm system, 1948 through 1950; manager, Oakland, 1951-52.

Named to Hall of Fame, 1951.

Year	Club	League	Pos.	G.	AB.	R.	H.	2B.	3B.	HR.	RBI.	B.A.	PO.	A.	E.	F.A.
1926—New York		Nat.	OF	35	60	7	23	2	0	0	4	.383	18	3	2	.913
1927—New York		Nat.	OF	82	163	23	46	7	3	1	19	.282	52	2	1	.982
1928—New York		Nat.	OF-2B	124	435	69	140	26	4	18	77	.322	214	14	7	.970
1929—New York		Nat.	OF	150	545	138	179	37	2	42	152	.328	335	★26	10	.973
1930—New York		Nat.	OF	148	521	122	182	34	5	25	119	.349	320	23	11	.969
1931—New York		Nat.	OF	138	497	104	145	23	8	29	115	.292	332	20	7	.981
1932—New York		Nat.	OF	●154	566	119	180	30	8	●38	123	.318	347	11	6	.984
1933—New York		Nat.	OF	152	580	98	164	36	1	23	103	.283	283	12	5	.983
1934—New York		Nat.	OF	153	582	119	190	29	10	●35	★135	.326	286	12	8	.974
1935—New York		Nat.	★OF-3B	152	593	113	191	33	6	31	114	.322	304	42	6	★.983
1936—New York		Nat.	OF	150	534	120	175	28	6	★33	135	.328	250	20	4	.985
1937—New York		Nat	OF-3B	151	545	99	160	28	2	●31	95	.294	198	126	10	.970
1938—New York		Nat.	OF-3B	150	527	★116	164	23	6	★36	116	.311	163	241	15	.964
1939—New York		Nat.	OF-3B	125	396	85	122	23	2	27	80	.308	190	45	11	.955
1940—New York		Nat.	OF-3B	151	536	89	155	27	3	19	79	.289	240	92	12	.965
1941—New York		Nat.	OF	148	525	89	150	29	0	27	90	.286	256	●19	9	.968
1942—New York		Nat.	OF	152	549	★118	162	21	0	★30	93	.295	269	15	3	.990
1943—New York		Nat.	OF-3B	125	380	65	89	12	2	18	47	.234	219	12	6	.975
1944—New York		Nat.	OF	120	399	91	115	16	4	26	82	.288	200	19	7	.969
1945—New York		Nat.	OF	135	451	73	139	23	0	21	79	.308	217	11	4	.982
1946—New York		Nat.	OF	31	68	2	5	1	0	1	4	.074	23	2	0	1.000
1947—New York		Nat.	PH	4	4	0	0	0	0	0	0	.000	0	0	0	.000
Major League Totals—22 Years				2730	9456	1859	2876	488	72	511	1861	.304	4716	767	144	.974

WORLD SERIES RECORD

Year	Club	League	Pos.	G.	AB.	R.	H.	2B.	3B.	HR.	RBI.	B.A.	PO.	A.	E.	F.A.
1933—New York		Nat.	OF	5	18	3	7	0	0	2	4	.389	10	0	0	1.000
1936—New York		Nat.	OF	6	23	4	7	2	0	1	3	.304	12	0	1	.923
1937—New York		Nat.	3B	5	20	1	4	0	0	1	3	.200	5	9	1	.933
World Series Totals—3 Years				16	61	8	18	2	0	4	10	.295	27	9	2	.947

LEROY ROBERT (SATCHEL) PAIGE

Born July 7, 1905, at Mobile, Ala.

Died June 8, 1982, at Kansas City, Mo.

Height, 6.04. Weight, 190.

Threw and batted righthanded.

Coach, Atlanta Braves, August 11, 1968, through 1969.

Satchel Paige hit the majors way past his prime and after he had hurt his arm while pitching in a cool breeze in the Caribbean in the winter of 1947. So the big league fans saw only a shell of the pitcher who brought big money to the Negro game. His cunning never left him even though his fastball was a memory that could be recalled only infrequently.

Paige never was rated the fastest pitcher among the blacks who played or witnessed Negro ball in its two stages, before league play and after. Smoky Joe (Cyclone) Williams, John Donaldson, Cannonball Dick Redding, Rube Foster and Wilbur (Bullet) Rogan all were rated faster than Paige, but none, except the early Foster, could combine the perfect control that Paige possessed from his first day on the mound. Speed and control were his bread and butter. He became famous for calling in his outfield and sitting them down alongside his squatting infielders—and then fanning the side on nine consecutive darters which traveled the precise route he intended.

Paige pitched on many clubs—the Chattanooga Black Lookouts in 1926, his first club, and then the Birmingham Black Barons, Cleveland Cubs, Pittsburgh Crawfords and Kansas City Monarchs (his two strongest clubs and most successful seasons), New York Black Yankees, Satchell Paige's All-Stars and the Philadelphia Stars.

With the Crawfords and Monarchs, Satch's fame spread from coast to coast. He was their meal ticket, the one the fans flocked to see. To satisfy the fans, he would pitch three innings per game while between starts, to keep peace and keep the money rolling in.

He hurt his arm pitching winter ball while still a member of the Monarchs, laid off for a spell with the Monarchs' second team in '48 and then came back a new pitcher with his hesitation pitch, sharper curve and sometime fastball.

His barnstorming tours had made him the richest black player of all time and he made more money than any of the top major league pitchers of his day.

Bill Veeck knew what was going on in Negro ball and his friendship with Paige was instrumental in getting Satch to join the Indians during the 1948 A.L. season. His 6-1 break-in year with Cleveland was excellent, but his being able to compile 3-4, 12-10 and even a 3-9 record pitching for the hapless Browns is testament to his greatness, even though his prime had long passed.

Paige was the monumental figure of black baseball—he was the awareness bridge that spanned the two worlds of baseball, black and white. When major leaguers faced Paige, they knew the standard of Negro ball and carried the stories back to the big leagues. The path that Paige fashioned is the one which Jackie Robinson walked to reach the majors. Without Paige, the re-entrance of Negroes into the major leagues would have been set back many years. His mound wizardry had blazed the way.

Named to Hall of Fame, 1971.

Year	Club	League	G.	IP.	W.	L.	Pct.	H.	R.	ER.	SO.	BB.	ERA.
1948—Cleveland		American	21	73	6	1	.857	61	21	20	45	25	2.47
1949—Cleveland		American	31	83	4	7	.364	70	29	28	54	33	3.04
1950—						(Out of Organized Ball)							
1951—St. Louis		American	23	62	3	4	.429	67	39	33	48	29	4.79
1952—St. Louis		American	46	138	12	10	.545	116	51	47	91	57	3.07
1953—St. Louis		American	57	117	3	9	.250	114	51	46	51	39	3.54
1954-55—						(Out of Organized Ball)							
1956—Miami		International	37	111	11	4	.733	101	29	23	79	28	1.86
1957—Miami		International	40	119	10	8	.556	98	35	32	76	11	2.42
1958—Miami		International	28	110	10	10	.500	94	44	36	40	15	2.95
1959-60—						(Out of Organized Ball)							
1961—Portland		Pacific Coast	5	25	0	0	.000	28	12	8	19	5	2.88
1962-63-64						(Out of Organized Ball)							
1965—Kansas City		American	1	3	0	0	.000	1	0	0	1	0	0.00
1966—Peninsula		Carolina	1	2	0	0	.000	5	2	2	0	0	9.00
Major League Totals—6 Years			179	476	28	31	.475	429	191	174	290	183	3.29

WORLD SERIES RECORD

Year	Club	League	G.	IP.	W.	L.	Pct.	H.	R.	ER.	SO.	BB.	ERA.
1948—Cleveland		American	1	⅔	0	0	.000	0	0	0	0	0	0.00

JAMES ALVIN (JIM) PALMER

Born October 15, 1945, at New York City, N.Y.

Height, 6.03. Weight, 194.

Threw and batted righthanded.

Holds American League record for most putouts by pitcher, lifetime (292).

Pitched 8-0 no-hit victory against Oakland A's, August 13, 1969.

Pitched 8-0 no-hit victory against Duluth-Superior, June 19, 1964.

Led American League in shutouts with 10 in 1975 and tied for lead with 5 in 1970.

Led American League pitchers in games started with 40 in 1976 and tied for lead with 39 in 1977.

Tied for American League lead in complete games with 22 in 1977.

Tied for American League lead in balks with 3 in 1970.

Led Northern League in wild pitches with 23 in 1964.

Named American League Pitcher of the Year by THE SPORTING NEWS, 1973, 1975 and 1976.

Won American League Cy Young Memorial Award, 1973, 1975 and 1976.

Named righthanded pitcher on THE SPORTING NEWS American League All-Star Team, 1971, 1973, 1975, 1976 and 1978.

Named pitcher on THE SPORTING NEWS American League All-Star fielding team, 1976 through 1979.
Named to Hall of Fame, 1990.

Year—Club	League	G.	IP.	W.	L.	Pct.	H.	R.	ER.	SO.	BB.	ERA.
1964—Aberdeen	Northern	19	129	11	3	.786	75	42	36	107	★130	2.51
1965—Baltimore	American	27	92	5	4	.556	75	49	38	75	56	3.72
1966—Baltimore	American	30	208	15	10	.600	176	83	80	147	91	3.46
1967—Baltimore	American	9	49	3	1	.750	34	18	16	23	20	2.94
1967—Rochester	Int'national	2	7	0	0	.000	12	9	9	6	5	11.57
1967—Miami	Florida St.	5	27	1	1	.500	20	6	6	16	10	2.00
1968—Miami	Florida St.	2	8	0	0	.000	4	2	0	5	9	0.00
1968—Rochester	Int'national	2	4	0	0	.000	4	6	6	6	8	13.50
1968—Elmira	Eastern	6	25	0	2	.000	18	13	12	26	19	4.32
1969—Baltimore	American	26	181	16	4	★.800	131	48	47	123	64	2.34
1970—Baltimore	American	39	●305	20	10	.667	263	98	92	199	100	2.71
1971—Baltimore	American	37	282	20	9	.690	231	94	84	184	106	2.68
1972—Baltimore	American	36	274	21	10	.677	219	73	63	184	70	2.07
1973—Baltimore	American	38	296	22	9	.710	225	86	79	153	113	★2.40
1974—Baltimore	American	26	179	7	12	.368	176	78	65	84	69	3.27
1975—Baltimore	American	39	323	●23	11	.676	253	87	75	193	80	★2.09
1976—Baltimore	American	40	★315	★22	13	.629	255	101	88	159	84	2.51
1977—Baltimore	American	39	★319	●20	11	.645	263	106	103	193	99	2.91
1978—Baltimore	American	38	★296	21	12	.636	246	94	81	138	97	2.46
1979—Baltimore	American	23	156	10	6	.625	144	66	57	67	43	3.29
1980—Baltimore	American	34	224	16	10	.615	238	108	99	109	74	3.98
1981—Baltimore	American	22	127	7	8	.467	117	60	53	35	46	3.76
1982—Baltimore	American	36	227	15	5	.750	195	85	79	103	63	3.13
1983—Baltimore†	American	14	76⅔	5	4	.556	86	42	36	34	19	4.23
1983—Hagerstown	Carolina	2	13	2	0	1.000	13	6	5	11	2	3.46
1984—Baltimore‡	American	5	17⅔	0	3	.000	22	19	18	4	17	9.17
Major League Totals—19 Years		558	3947⅓	268	152	.638	3349	1395	1253	2212	1311	2.86

Signed as free agent by Baltimore Orioles' organization, August 16, 1963.
†Rehabilitation disability assignment to Hagerstown, August 6 to August 21, 1983.
‡Released, May 17, 1984.

CHAMPIONSHIP SERIES RECORD

Holds major league record for most complete games, lifetime (5).
Shares major league records for most years pitched (6); most games won (4) and strikeouts (46), lifetime.
Shares American League record for most bases on balls, lifetime (19).

Year—Club	League	G.	IP.	W.	L.	Pct.	H.	R.	ER.	SO.	BB.	ERA.
1969—Baltimore	American	1	9	1	0	1.000	10	2	2	4	2	2.00
1970—Baltimore	American	1	9	1	0	1.000	7	1	1	12	3	1.00
1971—Baltimore	American	1	9	1	0	1.000	7	3	3	8	3	3.00
1973—Baltimore	American	3	14⅔	1	0	1.000	11	3	3	15	8	1.84
1974—Baltimore	American	1	9	0	0	.000	4	1	1	4	1	1.00
1979—Baltimore	American	1	9	0	0	.000	7	3	3	3	2	3.00
Championship Series Totals—6 Years		8	59⅔	4	1	.800	46	13	13	46	19	1.96

WORLD SERIES RECORD

Year—Club	League	G.	IP.	W.	L.	Pct.	H.	R.	ER.	SO.	BB.	ERA.
1966—Baltimore	American	1	9	1	0	1.000	4	0	0	6	3	0.00
1969—Baltimore	American	1	6	0	1	.000	5	4	4	5	4	6.00
1970—Baltimore	American	2	15⅔	1	0	1.000	11	8	8	9	9	4.60
1971—Baltimore	American	2	17	1	0	1.000	15	5	5	15	9	2.65
1979—Baltimore	American	2	15	0	1	.000	18	6	6	8	5	3.60
1983—Baltimore	American	1	2	1	0	1.000	2	0	0	1	1	0.00
World Series Totals—6 Years		9	64⅔	4	2	.667	55	23	23	44	31	3.20

MILTON STEVEN (MILT) PAPPAS

Born May 11, 1939, at Detroit, Mich.

Height, 6.03. Weight, 214.

Threw and batted righthanded.

Pitched 8-0 no-hit victory against San Diego Padres, September 2, 1972.
Tied for National League lead in shutouts in 1971 (5).

Year—Club	League	G.	IP.	W.	L.	Pct.	H.	R.	ER.	SO.	BB.	ERA.
1957—Knoxville	Sally	3	11	0	1	.000	12	10	6	9	10	4.91
1957—Baltimore	Amer.	4	9	0	0	.000	6	1	1	3	3	1.00
1958—Baltimore	Amer.	31	135	10	10	.500	135	67	61	72	48	4.07

Year Club	League	G.	IP.	W.	L.	Pct.	H.	R.	ER.	SO.	BB.	ERA.
1959—Baltimore	Amer.	33	209	15	9	.625	175	82	76	120	75	3.27
1960—Baltimore	Amer.	30	206	15	11	.577	184	81	77	126	83	3.36
1961—Baltimore	Amer.	26	178	13	9	.591	134	67	60	89	78	3.03
1962—Baltimore	Amer.	35	205	12	10	.545	200	105	92	130	75	4.04
1963—Baltimore	Amer.	34	217	16	9	.640	186	80	73	120	69	3.03
1964—Baltimore	Amer.	37	252	16	7	.696	225	89	83	157	48	2.96
1965—Baltimore(a)	Amer.	34	221	13	9	.591	192	81	64	127	52	2.61
1966—Cincinnati	Nat.	33	210	12	11	.522	224	106	100	133	39	4.29
1967—Cincinnati	Nat.	34	218	16	13	.552	218	88	81	129	38	3.34
1968—Cin.(b)-Atlanta	Nat.	37	184	12	13	.480	181	77	71	118	32	3.47
1969—Atlanta	Nat.	26	144	6	10	.375	149	66	58	72	44	3.63
1970—Atl.(c)-Chicago	Nat.	32	180	12	10	.545	179	78	67	105	43	3.35
1971—Chicago	Nat.	35	261	17	14	.548	279	109	102	99	62	3.52
1972—Chicago	Nat.	29	195	17	7	.708	187	72	60	80	29	2.77
1973—Chicago	Nat.	30	162	7	12	.368	192	82	77	48	40	4.28
American League Totals—9 Years		264	1632	110	74	.598	1437	653	587	944	531	3.24
National League Totals—8 Years		256	1554	99	90	.524	1609	678	621	784	327	3.60
Major League Totals—17 Years		520	3186	209	164	.560	3046	1331	1203	1728	858	3.40

aTraded with Pitcher Jack Baldschun and Outfielder Dick Simpson to Cincinnati Reds for Outfielder Frank Robinson, December 9, 1965.

bTraded with Pitcher Ted Davidson and Infielder Bob Johnson to Atlanta Braves for Infielder Woody Woodward and Pitchers Tony Cloninger and Clay Carroll, June 11, 1968.

cSold to Chicago Cubs, June 25, 1970.

LARRY ALTON PARRISH

Born November 10, 1953, at Winter Haven, Fla.

Height, 6.03. Weight, 215.

Threw and batted righthanded.

Shares major league records for most grand slams, month (3), July, 1982; most grand slams, week (3), July 4 through 10, first game, 1982.

Hit three home runs in a game, May 29, 1977; July 30, 1978; April 25, 1980 and April 29, 1985.

Tied for National League lead in double plays by third basemen with 35 in 1976.

Led Florida State League in sacrifice flies with 9 in 1973.

Led Eastern League third basemen in double plays with 32 in 1974.

Led Florida State League third basemen in putouts with 95 and assists with 285 in 1973.

Named Florida State League Most Valuable Player, 1973.

Year Club	League	Pos.	G.	AB.	R.	H.	2B.	3B.	HR.	RBI.	B.A.	PO.	A.	E.	F.A.
1972—W. Palm B'ch	Fla. St.	OF	2	4	0	1	0	0	0	0	.250	2	0	0	1.000
1972—Jamestown	NYP	OF	62	223	32	58	4	3	4	28	.260	69	3	3	.960
1973—W. Palm B'ch	Fla. St.	★3B-SS	138	481	82	141	14	6	16	81	.293	100	292	32	★.925
1974—Quebec City	East.	3B	119	437	61	124	14	2	13	77	.284	★108	★277	●31	.925
1974—Montreal	Nat.	3B	25	69	9	14	5	0	0	4	.203	20	51	1	.986
1975—Montreal	Nat.	3B-SS-2B	145	532	50	146	32	5	10	65	.274	105	291	35	.919
1976—Montreal	Nat.	3B	154	543	65	126	28	5	11	61	.232	122	310	25	.945
1977—Montreal	Nat.	3B	123	402	50	99	19	2	11	46	.246	81	225	21	.936
1978—Montreal	Nat.	3B	144	520	68	144	39	4	15	70	.277	122	288	23	.947
1979—Montreal	Nat.	3B	153	544	83	167	39	2	30	82	.307	119	290	23	.947
1980—Montreal	Nat.	3B	126	452	55	115	27	3	15	72	.254	106	231	18	.949
1981—Montreal†	Nat.	3B	97	349	41	85	19	3	8	44	.244	91	141	16	.935
1982—Texas	Amer.	OF-3B	128	440	59	116	15	0	17	62	.264	190	12	8	.962
1983—Texas	Amer.	OF	145	555	76	151	26	4	26	88	.272	215	11	9	.962
1984—Texas	Amer.	OF-3B	156	613	72	175	42	1	22	101	.285	155	35	4	.979
1985—Texas	Amer.	OF-3B	94	346	44	86	11	1	17	51	.249	111	7	1	.992
1986—Texas	Amer.	3B	129	464	67	128	22	1	28	94	.276	23	35	4	.935
1987—Texas	Amer.	3B-OF	152	557	79	149	22	1	32	100	.268	19	26	4	.918
1988—Tex.‡-Bos.§	Amer.	1B	120	406	32	88	14	1	14	52	.217	221	25	3	.988
National League Totals—8 Years			967	3411	421	896	208	24	100	444	.263	866	1827	162	.943
American League Totals—7 Years			924	3381	429	893	152	9	156	548	.264	934	151	33	.970
Major League Totals—15 Years			1891	6792	850	1789	360	33	256	992	.263	1800	1978	195	.951

Signed as free agent by Montreal Expos' organization, May 21, 1972.

†Traded with First Baseman Dave Hostetler to Texas Rangers for First Baseman-Outfielder Al Oliver, March 31, 1982.

‡Released, July 9, 1988; signed by Boston Red Sox, July 16, 1988.

§Released, October 28, 1988.

Year Club	League	Pos.	G.	AB.	R.	H.	2B.	3B.	HR.	RBI.	B.A.	PO.	A.	E.	F.A.
1981—Montreal	Nat.	3B	5	19	2	5	2	0	0	2	.263	3	13	1	.941
1988—Boston	Amer.	PH-DH-1	4	6	0	0	0	0	0	0	.000	7	0	0	1.000
Championship Series Totals—2 Years			9	25	2	5	2	0	0	2	.200	10	13	1	.958

CAMILO ALBERTO PASCUAL JR.

Born January 20, 1934, at Havana, Cuba.

Height, 5.11. Weight, 190.

Threw and batted righthanded.

Brother of Carlos Pascual, former minor league infielder.

Led American League in shutouts with 6 in 1959 and tied for lead with 8 in 1961 and 5 in 1962.
Led American League in complete games with 17 in 1959, 18 in 1962 and tied for lead with 18 in 1963.
Coach, Minnesota Twins, 1978 through 1980; scout, Oakland Athletics 1981 through 1988.

Year Club	League	G.	IP.	W.	L.	Pct.	H.	R.	ER.	SO.	BB.	ERA.
1951—Geneva	Border	4	31	3	1	.750	33	16	12	13	20	3.48
1951—Big Spring	Longhorn	7	14	2	1	.667	18	10	8	10	12	5.14
1951—Chickasha	Soo. St.	5	19	0	2	.000	23	23	13	17	14	6.16
1952—Havana-Tampa	Fla. Int.	24	122	8	6	.571	101	43	39	72	66	2.88
1953—Havana	Fla. Int.	25	141	10	6	.625	126	61	47	93	68	3.00
1954—Washington	American	48	119	4	7	.364	126	65	56	60	61	4.24
1955—Washington	American	43	129	2	12	.143	158	94	88	82	70	6.14
1956—Washington	American	39	189	6	18	.250	194	131	123	162	89	5.86
1957—Washington	American	29	176	8	17	.320	168	85	80	113	76	4.09
1958—Washington	American	31	177	8	12	.400	166	66	62	146	60	3.15
1959—Washington	American	32	239	17	10	.630	202	80	70	185	69	2.64
1960—Washington	American	26	152	12	8	.600	139	65	51	143	53	3.02
1961—Minnesota	American	35	252	15	16	.484	205	114	97	★221	100	3.46
1962—Minnesota	American	34	258	20	11	.645	236	100	95	★206	59	3.31
1963—Minnesota	American	31	248	21	9	.700	205	76	68	★202	81	2.47
1964—Minnesota	American	36	267	15	12	.556	245	121	98	213	98	3.30
1965—Minnesota	American	27	156	9	3	.750	126	67	58	96	63	3.35
1966—Minnesota (a)	American	21	103	8	6	.571	113	63	56	56	30	4.89
1967—Washington	American	28	165	12	10	.545	147	73	60	106	43	3.27
1968—Washington	American	31	201	13	12	.520	181	72	60	111	59	2.69
1969—Washington (b)	American	14	55	2	5	.286	49	42	42	34	38	6.87
1969—Cincinnati (c)	National	5	7	0	0	.000	14	7	7	3	4	9.00
1970—Los Angeles (d)	National	10	14	0	0	.000	12	4	4	8	5	2.57
1971—Cleveland	American	9	23	2	2	.500	17	9	8	20	11	3.13
American League Totals—17 Years		514	2909	174	170	.506	2677	1323	1172	2156	1060	3.63
National League Totals—2 Years		15	21	0	0	.000	26	11	11	11	9	4.71
Major League Totals—18 Years		529	2930	174	170	.506	2703	1334	1183	2167	1069	3.67

aTraded with Second Baseman Bernie Allen to Washington Senators for Pitcher Ron Kline, December 3, 1966.
bSold to Cincinnati Reds, July 7, 1969.
cReleased by Cincinnati Reds, signed by Los Angeles Dodgers for 1970 season.
dReleased by Los Angeles Dodgers, August 25, 1970; signed by Cleveland Indians for 1971 season.

WORLD SERIES RECORD

Year Club	League	G.	IP.	W.	L.	Pct.	H.	R.	ER.	SO.	BB.	ERA.
1965—Minnesota	American	1	5	0	1	.000	8	3	3	0	1	5.40

HERBERT JEFFERIS (HERB) PENNOCK

Born February 10, 1894, at Kennett Square, Pa.

Died January 30, 1948, at New York City, N.Y.

Height, 6.00. Weight, 165.

Threw left and batted left and righthanded.

Named to THE SPORTING NEWS All-Star Major League Team, 1926.
Coach, Boston Red Sox, 1936-40; supervisor, Boston Red Sox farm system, 1941 to 1943; general manager, Philadelphia Phillies, 1944 to 1948.
Named to Hall of Fame, 1948.

Year Club	League	G.	IP.	W.	L.	Pct.	H.	R.	ER.	SO.	BB.	ERA.
1912—Philadelphia	American	17	50	1	2	.333	48	31	...	38	30	.....
1913—Philadelphia	American	14	33	2	1	.667	30	24	19	17	22	5.13
1914—Philadelphia	American	28	152	11	4	.733	136	56	47	90	65	2.78
1915—Providence	International	13	90	6	4	.600	72	28	...	57	38	.....
1915—Phila. (a)-Boston	American	16	58	3	6	.333	69	50	41	31	39	6.36
1916—Boston	American	9	27	0	2	.000	23	11	9	12	8	3.00
1916—Buffalo	International	15	113	7	6	.538	99	...	21	76	36	1.67
1917—Boston	American	24	101	5	5	.500	90	49	37	35	23	3.30
1918—Boston	American					(In Military Service)						
1919—Boston	American	32	219	16	8	.667	223	78	66	70	48	2.71
1920—Boston	American	37	242	16	13	.552	244	108	99	68	61	3.68
1921—Boston	American	32	223	12	14	.462	268	121	100	91	59	4.04
1922—Boston (b)	American	32	202	10	17	.370	230	108	97	59	74	4.32
1923—New York	American	35	238	19	6	★.760	235	86	83	93	68	3.14
1924—New York	American	40	286	21	9	.700	302	104	90	101	64	2.83
1925—New York	American	47	★277	16	17	.485	267	117	91	88	71	2.96
1926—New York	American	40	266	23	11	.676	294	133	107	78	43	3.62
1927—New York	American	34	210	19	8	.704	225	89	70	51	48	3.00
1928—New York	American	28	211	17	6	.739	215	71	60	53	40	2.56
1929—New York	American	27	158	9	11	.450	205	101	86	49	28	4.90
1930—New York	American	25	156	11	7	.611	194	95	75	46	20	4.33
1931—New York	American	25	189	11	6	.647	247	96	90	65	30	4.29
1932—New York	American	22	147	9	5	.643	191	94	75	54	38	4.59
1933—New York (c)	American	23	65	7	4	.636	96	46	40	22	21	5.54
1934—Boston	American	30	62	2	0	1.000	68	31	21	16	16	3.05
Major League Totals—22 Years		617	3572	240	162	.597	3900	1699	1403	1227	916	3.54

aClaimed on waivers by Boston Red Sox, June, 1915.
bTraded to New York Yankees for Outfielder Camp Skinner, Infielder Norman McMillan, Pitcher George Murray and cash, January 30, 1923.
cReleased by New York Yankees and signed by Boston Red Sox, January, 1934.

WORLD SERIES RECORD

Year Club	League	G.	IP.	W.	L.	Pct.	H.	R.	ER.	SO.	BB.	ERA.
1914—Philadelphia	American	1	3	0	0	.000	2	0	0	3	2	0.00
1923—New York	American	3	17⅓	2	0	1.000	19	7	7	8	1	3.63
1926—New York	American	3	22	2	0	1.000	13	3	3	8	4	1.23
1927—New York	American	1	9	1	0	1.000	3	1	1	1	0	1.00
1932—New York	American	2	4	0	0	.000	2	1	1	4	1	2.25
World Series Totals—5 Years		10	55⅓	5	0	1.000	39	12	12	24	8	1.95

ATANASIO RIGAL (TONY) PEREZ

Born May 14, 1942, at Ciego de Avila, Camaguey, Cuba.

Height, 6.02. Weight, 205.

Threw and batted righthanded.

Shares modern major league record for most at-bats nine-inning game (7), June 13, 1975.
Led American League in grounding into double plays with 25 in 1980.
Led National League first basemen in double plays with 131 and total chances with 1,416 in 1973.
Led National League third basemen in assists with 304 and total chances with 435 in 1971.
Led National League third basemen in double plays with 35 in 1969 and tied for lead with 33 in 1968.
Led Carolina League third basemen in double plays with 23 in 1962.
Named first baseman on THE SPORTING NEWS National League All-Star Team, 1973.
Named third baseman on THE SPORTING NEWS National League All-Star Team, 1970.
Named Pacific Coast League Most Valuable Player, 1964.
Coach, Cincinnati Reds, 1987 to date.

Year Club	League	Pos.	G.	AB.	R.	H.	2B.	3B.	HR.	RBI.	B.A.	PO.	A.	E.	F.A.
1960—Geneva	NYP	INF-OF	104	384	82	107	21	4	6	43	.279	199	197	31	.927
1961—Geneva	NYP	3B	121	460	110	★160	32	7	27	★132	★.348	107	★232	★42	.890
1962—Rocky Mount	Carol.	3B	100	384	72	112	20	8	18	74	.292	88	178	30	.899
1963—San Diego	P. C.	3B	8	29	4	11	3	1	1	5	.379	6	8	1	.933
1963—Macon	Sally	3B	69	256	44	79	19	3	11	48	.309	57	100	18	.897
1964—San Diego	P. C.	1B-3B-OF	124	479	96	148	20	8	34	107	.309	816	104	19	.980
1964—Cincinnati	Nat.	1B	12	25	1	2	1	0	0	1	.080	51	0	1	.981
1965—Cincinnati	Nat.	1B	104	281	40	73	14	4	12	47	.260	525	40	6	.989

Year Club League	Pos.	G.	AB.	R.	H.	2B.	3B.	HR.	RBI.	B.A.	PO.	A.	E.	F.A.
1966—Cincinnati............ Nat.	1B	99	257	25	68	10	4	4	39	.265	530	23	6	.989
1967—Cincinnati............ Nat.	3B-1B-2B	156	600	78	174	28	7	26	102	.290	249	234	13	.974
1968—Cincinnati............ Nat.	3B	160	625	93	176	25	7	18	92	.282	*151	343	*25	.952
1969—Cincinnati............ Nat.	3B	160	629	103	185	31	2	37	122	.294	136	*342	*32	.937
1970—Cincinnati............ Nat.	*3B-1B	158	587	107	186	28	6	40	129	.317	167	292	*35	.929
1971—Cincinnati............ Nat.	3B-1B	158	609	72	164	22	3	25	91	.269	281	308	20	.967
1972—Cincinnati............ Nat.	1B	136	515	64	146	33	7	21	90	.283	1207	68	9	.993
1973—Cincinnati............ Nat.	1B	151	564	73	177	33	3	27	101	.314	*1318	85	*13	.991
1974—Cincinnati............ Nat.	1B	158	596	81	158	28	2	28	101	.265	1292	75	6	*.996
1975—Cincinnati............ Nat.	1B	137	511	74	144	28	3	20	109	.282	1192	72	9	.993
1976—Cincinnati............ Nat.	1B	139	527	77	137	32	6	19	91	.260	1158	73	5	.996
1977—Montreal............... Nat.	1B	154	559	71	158	32	6	19	91	.283	1312	110	11	.992
1978—Montreal............... Nat.	1B	148	544	63	158	38	3	14	78	.290	1181	82	11	.991
1979—Montreal‡.......... Nat.	1B	132	489	58	132	29	4	13	73	.270	1114	65	11	.991
1980—Boston.................. Amer.	1B	151	585	73	161	31	3	25	105	.275	1301	87	10	.993
1981—Boston.................. Amer.	1B	84	306	35	77	11	3	9	39	.252	519	37	4	.993
1982—Boston§................. Amer.	1B	69	196	18	51	14	2	6	31	.260	5	1	1	.857
1983—Philadelphia x...... Nat.	1B	91	253	18	61	11	2	6	43	.241	514	40	1	.998
1984—Cincinnati y.......... Nat.	1B	71	137	9	33	6	1	2	15	.241	186	12	2	.990
1985—Cincinnati z.......... Nat.	1B	72	183	25	60	8	0	6	33	.328	340	22	2	.995
1986—Cincinnati a.......... Nat.	1B	77	200	14	51	12	1	2	29	.255	398	29	7	.984
National League Totals—20 Years..........		2473	8691	1146	2443	449	71	339	1477	.281	13302	2315	225	.986
American League Totals—3 Years.........		304	1087	126	289	56	8	40	175	.266	1825	125	15	.992
Major League Totals—23 Years.............		2777	9778	1272	2732	505	79	379	1652	.279	15127	2440	240	.987

Signed as free agent by Cincinnati Reds' organization, March 12, 1960.

†Traded with Pitcher Will McEnaney to Montreal Expos for Pitchers Woodie Fryman and Dale Murray, December 16, 1976.

‡Granted free agency, November 1, 1979; signed by Boston Red Sox, November 16, 1979.

§Released, November 1, 1982; signed by Philadelphia Phillies, January 31, 1983.

xTraded to Cincinnati Reds for a player to be named later, December 5, 1983; deal settled in cash.

yGranted free agency, November 8, 1984; re-signed by Reds, April 10, 1985.

zGranted free agency, November 12, 1985; re-signed by Reds, January 20, 1986.

aOn voluntarily retired list, October 28, 1986; named coach with Cincinnati Reds for 1987 season.

CHAMPIONSHIP SERIES RECORD

Year Club League	Pos.	G.	AB.	R.	H.	2B.	3B.	HR.	RBI.	B.A.	PO.	A.	E.	F.A.
1970—Cincinnati............. Nat.	3B-1B	3	12	1	4	2	0	1	2	.333	6	6	1	.923
1972—Cincinnati............. Nat.	1B	5	20	0	4	1	0	0	2	.200	45	3	0	1.000
1973—Cincinnati............. Nat.	1B	5	22	1	2	0	0	1	2	.091	47	4	0	1.000
1975—Cincinnati............. Nat.	1B	3	12	3	5	0	0	1	4	.417	27	5	0	1.000
1976—Cincinnati............. Nat.	1B	3	10	1	2	0	0	0	3	.200	27	2	1	.967
1983—Philadelphia......... Nat.	PH	1	1	0	1	0	0	0	0	1.000	0	0	0	.000
Championship Series Totals—6 Years.....		20	77	6	18	3	0	3	13	.234	152	20	2	.989

WORLD SERIES RECORD

Year Club League	Pos.	G.	AB.	R.	H.	2B.	3B.	HR.	RBI.	B.A.	PO.	A.	E.	F.A.
1970—Cincinnati............. Nat.	3B	5	18	2	1	0	0	0	0	.056	3	13	1	.941
1972—Cincinnati............. Nat.	1B	7	23	3	10	2	0	0	0	.435	73	3	1	.987
1975—Cincinnati............. Nat.	1B	7	28	4	5	0	0	3	7	.179	66	5	1	.986
1976—Cincinnati............. Nat.	1B	4	16	1	5	1	0	0	2	.313	32	4	0	1.000
1983—Philadelphia......... Nat.	PH-1B	4	10	0	2	0	0	0	0	.200	13	1	0	1.000
World Series Totals—5 Years..................		27	95	10	23	3	0	3	11	.242	187	26	3	.986

GAYLORD JACKSON PERRY

Born September 15, 1938, at Williamston, N.C.

Height, 6.04. Weight, 215.

Threw and batted righthanded.

Brother of Jim Perry, former major league pitcher.

Shares National League record for most putouts by pitcher, nine-inning game (5), July 18, 1970.
Pitched 1-0 no-hit victory against St. Louis Cardinals, September 17, 1968.
Led American League in wild pitches with 17 in 1973 and 13 in 1982.
Led American League in complete games with 29 in 1972 and 29 in 1973.
Led American League in intentional bases on balls issued with 16 in 1972.
Led National League in shutouts with 5 in 1970.
Led National League pitchers in games started with 41 in 1970.
Won National League Cy Young Memorial Award, 1978.
Won American League Cy Young Memorial Award, 1972.
Named righthanded pitcher on THE SPORTING NEWS National League All-Star Team, 1978.

Named righthanded pitcher on THE SPORTING NEWS American League All-Star Team, 1972.
Named Pacific Coast League Pitcher of the Year, 1961.

Year	Club	League	G.	IP.	W.	L.	Pct.	H.	R.	ER.	SO.	BB.	ERA.
1958—St. Cloud	Northern	17	128	9	5	.643	97	40	34	111	48	2.39
1959—Corpus Christi	Texas	41	191	10	11	.476	*218	*120	86	119	69	4.05
1960—Tacoma	P. Coast	1	1	0	0	.000	1	1	1	0	0	9.00
1960—Rio Grande Valley	Texas	31	188	9	13	.409	164	68	59	120	77	*2.82
1961—Tacoma	P. Coast	33	*219	●16	10	.615	208	79	62	95	61	2.55
1962—San Francisco	National	13	43	3	1	.750	54	29	25	20	14	5.23
1962—Tacoma	P. Coast	22	156	10	7	.588	128	56	43	136	56	*2.48
1963—San Francisco	National	31	76	1	6	.143	84	41	34	52	29	4.03
1963—Tacoma	P. Coast	1	9	1	0	1.000	3	1	1	7	1	1.00
1964—San Francisco	National	44	206	12	11	.522	179	65	63	155	43	2.75
1965—San Francisco	National	47	196	8	12	.400	194	105	91	170	70	4.18
1966—San Francisco	National	36	256	21	8	.724	242	92	85	201	40	2.99
1967—San Francisco	National	39	293	15	17	.469	231	98	85	230	84	2.61
1968—San Francisco	National	39	291	16	15	.516	240	93	79	173	59	2.44
1969—San Francisco	National	40	*325	19	14	.576	290	115	90	233	91	2.49
1970—San Francisco	National	41	*329	●23	13	.639	*292	*138	117	214	84	3.20
1971—San Francisco†	National	37	280	16	12	.571	255	116	86	158	67	2.76
1972—Cleveland	American	41	343	●24	16	.600	253	79	73	234	82	1.92
1973—Cleveland	American	41	344	19	19	.500	315	143	129	238	115	3.38
1974—Cleveland	American	37	322	21	13	.618	230	98	90	216	99	2.52
1975—Cleveland‡-Texas	American	37	306	18	17	.514	277	127	110	233	70	3.24
1976—Texas	American	32	250	15	14	.517	232	93	90	143	52	3.24
1977—Texas§	American	34	238	15	12	.556	239	108	89	177	56	3.37
1978—San Diego	National	37	261	*21	6	*.778	241	96	79	154	66	2.72
1979—San Diego x	National	32	233	12	11	.522	225	90	79	140	67	3.05
1980—Texas y-New York z	American	34	206	10	13	.435	224	107	84	135	64	3.67
1981—Atlanta a	National	23	151	8	9	.471	*182	70	66	60	24	3.93
1982—Seattle	American	32	216⅔	10	12	.455	245	117	106	116	54	4.40
1983—Seattle b-Kansas City c	American	30	186⅓	7	14	.333	214	108	96	82	49	4.64
National League Totals—13 Years		459	2940	175	135	.565	2709	1148	979	1960	738	3.00
American League Totals—9 Years		318	2412	139	130	.517	2229	980	867	1574	641	3.24
Major League Totals—22 Years		777	5352	314	265	.542	4938	2128	1846	3534	1379	3.10

Signed as free agent for reported $90,000 by San Francisco Giants' organization, June 3, 1958.
†Traded with Shortstop Frank Duffy to Cleveland Indians for Pitcher Sam McDowell, November 29, 1971.
‡Traded to Texas Rangers for Pitchers Jim Bibby, Jackie Brown and Rick Waits and estimated cash of $100,000, June 12, 1975.
§Traded to San Diego Padres for Pitcher Dave Tomlin and $125,000, February 15, 1978.
xTraded with Third Baseman Tucker Ashford and Pitcher Joe Carroll to Texas Rangers for First Baseman Willie Montanez and a player to be named later, February 15, 1980; Hawaii (San Diego Padres' organization) purchased Infielder Tony Phillips to complete deal, September 11, 1980.
yTraded to New York Yankees for Pitcher Ken Clay and a player to be named later, August 14, 1980; Texas Rangers' organization acquired Outfielder Marvin Thompson to complete deal, October 1, 1980.
zGranted free agency, October 23, 1980; signed by Atlanta Braves, January 12, 1981.
aReleased, October 5, 1981; signed by Seattle Mariners, March 5, 1982.
bReleased, June 27, 1983; signed by Kansas City Royals, July 6, 1983.
cOn voluntarily retired list, September 24, 1983.

CHAMPIONSHIP SERIES RECORD

Holds National League record for most hits allowed, series (19), 1971.
Shares major league record for most earned runs allowed, game (7), October 6, 1971.
Shares National League record for most hits allowed, game (10), October 6, 1971.

Year	Club	League	G.	IP.	W.	L.	Pct.	H.	R.	ER.	SO.	BB.	ERA.
1971—San Francisco	National	2	14⅔	1	1	.500	19	11	10	11	3	6.14

JAMES EVAN (JIM) PERRY JR.

Born October 30, 1936, at Williamston, N. C.

Height, 6.04. Weight, 205.

Threw right and batted right and lefthanded.

Brother of Gaylord Perry, former major league pitcher.

Named pitcher on THE SPORTING NEWS American League All-Star Team, 1970.
Won American League Cy Young Memorial Award, 1970.

Year	Club	League	G.	IP.	W.	L.	Pct.	H.	R.	ER.	SO.	BB.	ERA.
1956—North Platte	Neb. St.	16	120	7	8	.467	129	*104	*64	124	65	4.80
1957—Fargo-Moorhead	North.	38	*231	15	12	.556	212	92	74	150	73	2.88
1958—Reading	East.	32	200	16	8	.667	165	78	62	135	66	2.79
1959—Cleveland	Amer.	44	153	12	10	.545	122	54	45	79	55	2.65

Year	Club	League	G.	IP.	W.	L.	Pct.	H.	R.	ER.	SO.	BB.	ERA.
1960—Cleveland	Amer.	41	261	●18	10	.643	257	118	105	120	91	3.62
1961—Cleveland	Amer.	35	224	10	17	.370	238	132	●117	90	87	4.70
1962—Cleveland	Amer.	35	194	12	12	.500	213	94	89	74	59	4.13
1963—Cleveland(a)-Minnesota	Amer.	40	179	9	9	.500	179	83	76	72	59	3.82
1964—Minnesota	Amer.	42	65	6	3	.667	61	26	25	55	23	3.46
1965—Minnesota	Amer.	36	168	12	7	.632	142	57	49	88	47	2.63
1966—Minnesota	Amer.	33	184	11	7	.611	149	61	52	122	53	2.54
1967—Minnesota	Amer.	37	131	8	7	.533	123	51	44	94	50	3.02
1968—Minnesota	Amer.	32	139	8	6	.571	113	37	35	69	26	2.27
1969—Minnesota	Amer.	46	262	20	6	.769	244	87	82	153	66	2.82
1970—Minnesota	Amer.	40	279	●24	12	.667	258	112	94	168	57	3.03
1971—Minnesota	Amer.	40	270	17	17	.500	263	★135	★127	126	102	4.23
1972—Minnesota(b)	Amer.	35	218	13	16	.448	191	93	81	85	60	3.34
1973—Detroit(c)	Amer.	35	203	14	13	.519	225	96	91	66	55	4.03
1974—Cleveland	Amer.	36	252	17	12	.586	242	94	83	71	64	2.96
1975—Cleveland(d)-Oakland	Amer.	23	105	4	10	.286	107	77	63	44	44	5.40
Major League Totals—17 Years		630	3287	215	174	.553	3127	1407	1258	1576	998	3.44

aTraded to Minnesota Twins for Pitcher Jack Kralick, May 2, 1963.
bTraded to Detroit Tigers for Pitcher Danny Fife, March 27, 1973.
cTraded to Cleveland Indians as part of deal in which Cleveland sent Pitcher Rick Sawyer and Outfielder Walt Williams to New York Yankees and Yankees sent Catcher Jerry Moses to Detroit in exchange for Pitcher Ed Farmer, March 19, 1974.
dTraded with Pitcher Dick Bosman to Oakland Athletics for Pitcher Blue Moon Odom and cash, May 20, 1975.

CHAMPIONSHIP SERIES RECORD

Shares major league records for most earned runs allowed, game (7), October 3, 1970; most earned runs allowed (6) and hits allowed (6), inning, October 3, 1970, fourth inning.
Holds American League record for most runs allowed, inning (6), October 3, 1970, fourth inning.
Shares American League record for most runs allowed, game (8), October 3, 1970.

Year	Club	League	G.	IP.	W.	L.	Pct.	H.	R.	ER.	SO.	BB.	ERA.
1969—Minnesota	Amer.	1	8	0	0	.000	6	3	3	3	3	3.38
1970—Minnesota	Amer.	2	5⅓	0	1	.000	10	9	8	3	1	13.50
Championship Series Totals—2 Years		3	13⅓	0	1	.000	16	12	11	6	4	7.43

WORLD SERIES RECORD

Year	Club	League	G.	IP.	W.	L.	Pct.	H.	R.	ER.	SO.	BB.	ERA.
1965—Minnesota	Amer.	2	4	0	0	.000	5	2	2	4	2	4.50

JOHN MICHAEL (JOHNNY) PESKY

Born September 27, 1919, at Portland, Ore.

Height, 5.09. Weight, 168.

Threw right and batted lefthanded.

Shares modern major league record for most runs, game (6), May 8, 1946.
Named American Association Most Valuable Player, 1941.
Named by Baseball Writers' Association of America as shortstop for THE SPORTING NEWS All-Star Major League Team, 1942-46.
Manager, Durham, Carolina, 1956; Birmingham, Southern, 1957; Lancaster, Eastern, 1958; Knoxville, South Atlantic, 1959; Victoria, Texas, 1960; Seattle, Pacific Coast, 1961-62; Boston Red Sox, 1963-64; coach, Pittsburgh Pirates, 1965-66-67; manager, Columbus, International, 1968; coach, Boston Red Sox, 1975 through 1984; special assistant to the general manager, Boston Red Sox, 1985 to date.

Year	Club	League	Pos.	G.	AB.	R.	H.	2B.	3B.	HR.	RBI.	B.A.	PO.	A.	E.	F.A.
1940—Rocky Mount	Piedmont	SS	136	★576	114	★187	28	★16	4	55	.325	257	435	44	.940
1941—Louisville	A.A.	SS	146	600	93	★195	25	5	1	48	.325	★308	411	32	.957
1942—Boston	Amer.	SS	147	620	105	★205	29	9	2	51	.331	320	★465	37	.955
1943-44-45—Boston	Amer.					(In Military Service)									
1946—Boston	Amer.	SS	153	★621	115	★208	43	4	2	55	.335	296	479	25	.969
1947—Boston	Amer.	SS-3B	155	★638	106	★207	27	8	0	39	.324	276	429	17	.976
1948—Boston	Amer.	3B	143	565	124	159	26	6	3	55	.281	121	303	22	.951
1949—Boston	Amer.	3B	148	604	111	185	27	7	2	69	.306	★184	★333	16	.970
1950—Boston	Amer.	SS-3B	127	490	112	153	22	6	1	49	.312	183	289	13	.973
1951—Boston	Amer.	2B-SS-3B	131	480	93	150	20	6	3	41	.313	223	370	26	.958
1952—Bos.(a)-Detroit	Amer.	SS-3B-2B	94	244	36	55	6	0	1	11	.225	126	172	15	.952
1953—Detroit	Amer.	2B	103	308	43	90	22	1	2	24	.292	166	224	3	.992
1954—Det.(b)-Wash.	Amer.	PH-2B-SS	69	175	22	43	4	3	1	10	.246	92	91	4	.979
1955—Denver	A.A.	3B-PH	66	137	32	47	7	2	1	18	.343	22	45	7	.905
1956—Durham	Carol.	2B-PH	17	35	2	6	2	0	0	1	.171	5	9	1	.933
Major League Totals—10 Years		1270	4745	867	1455	226	50	17	404	.307	1987	3152	178	.967

WORLD SERIES RECORD

Year	Club	League	Pos.	G.	AB.	R.	H.	2B.	3B.	HR.	RBI.	B.A.	PO.	A.	E.	F.A.
1946—Boston	Amer.	3B	7	30	2	7	0	0	0	0	.233	13	16	4	.879

WALTER WILLIAM (BILLY) PIERCE

Born April 2, 1927, at Detroit, Mich.

Height, 5.11. Weight, 175.

Threw and batted lefthanded.

Tied for American League lead in most complete games pitched with 21 in 1956, 16 in 1957 and 19 in 1958.
Named Outstanding American League Pitcher by THE SPORTING NEWS, 1956-57.
Named as pitcher on THE SPORTING NEWS All-Star Major League Teams, 1956-57.

Year	Club	League	G.	IP.	W.	L.	Pct.	H.	R.	ER.	SO.	BB.	ERA.
1945—Buffalo	International	15	83	5	7	.417	75	55	50	57	71	5.42
1945—Detroit	American	5	10	0	0	.000	6	2	2	10	10	1.80
1946—Buffalo	International	10	56	3	4	.429	52	30	28	45	44	4.50
1947—Buffalo	International	28	151	14	8	.636	127	75	65	125	125	3.87
1948—Detroit (a)	American	22	55	3	0	1.000	47	40	39	36	51	6.38
1949—Chicago	American	32	172	7	15	.318	145	89	74	95	112	3.87
1950—Chicago	American	33	219	12	16	.429	189	112	97	118	137	3.99
1951—Chicago	American	37	240	15	●14	.517	237	93	81	113	73	3.04
1952—Chicago	American	33	255	15	12	.556	214	76	73	144	79	2.58
1953—Chicago	American	40	271	18	12	.600	216	94	82	★186	102	2.72
1954—Chicago	American	36	189	9	10	.474	179	86	73	148	86	3.48
1955—Chicago	American	33	206	15	10	.600	162	50	45	157	64	★1.97
1956—Chicago	American	35	276	20	9	.690	261	108	102	192	100	3.33
1957—Chicago	American	37	257	●20	12	.625	228	98	93	171	71	3.26
1958—Chicago	American	35	245	17	11	.607	204	83	73	144	66	2.68
1959—Chicago	American	34	224	14	15	.483	217	98	90	114	62	3.62
1960—Chicago	American	32	196	14	7	.667	201	81	79	108	46	3.63
1961—Chicago (b)	American	39	180	10	9	.526	190	85	76	106	54	3.80
1962—San Francisco	National	30	162	16	6	.727	147	67	63	76	35	3.50
1963—San Francisco	National	38	99	3	11	.214	106	49	47	52	20	4.27
1964—San Francisco	National	34	49	3	0	1.000	40	14	12	29	10	2.20
National League Totals—3 Years		102	310	22	17	.564	293	130	122	157	65	3.54
American League Totals—15 Years		483	2995	189	152	.554	2696	1195	1079	1842	1113	3.24
Major League Totals—18 Years		585	3305	211	169	.555	2989	1325	1201	1999	1178	3.27

WORLD SERIES RECORD

Year	Club	League	G.	IP.	W.	L.	Pct.	H.	R.	ER.	SO.	BB.	ERA.
1959—Chicago	American	3	4	0	0	.000	2	0	0	3	2	0.00
1962—San Francisco	National	2	15	1	1	.500	8	5	4	5	2	2.40
World Series Totals—2 Years		5	19	1	1	.500	10	5	4	8	4	1.89

VADA EDWARD PINSON JR.

Born August 11, 1938, at Memphis, Tenn.

Height, 5.11. Weight, 187.

Threw and batted lefthanded.

Named outfielder on THE SPORTING NEWS National League All-Star fielding team, 1961.

Coach, Seattle Mariners, 1977 through 1980, 1982 through 1984; Chicago White Sox, 1981; Detroit Tigers, 1985 to date.

Year Club	League	Pos.	G.	AB.	R.	H.	2B.	3B.	HR.	RBI.	B.A.	PO.	A.	E.	F.A.
1956—Wausau	North.	1B	75	277	35	77	11	5	2	23	.278	626	28	12	.982
1957—Visalia	Cal.	★OF-1B	135	569	★165	★209	★40	★20	20	97	.367	260	★30	16	.948
1958—Cincinnati	Nat.	OF	27	96	20	26	7	0	1	8	.271	50	4	0	1.000
1958—Seattle	P. C.	★OF-1B	124	475	92	163	28	8	11	77	.343	385	13	★15	.964
1959—Cincinnati	Nat.	OF	154	★648	★131	205	★47	9	20	84	.316	★423	11	7	.984
1960—Cincinnati	Nat.	OF	154	★652	107	187	★37	12	20	61	.287	★401	11	8	.981
1961—Cincinnati	Nat.	OF	154	607	101	★208	34	8	16	87	.343	★391	19	10	.976
1962—Cincinnati	Nat.	OF	155	619	107	181	31	7	23	100	.292	344	13	4	.989
1963—Cincinnati	Nat.	OF	●162	652	96	★204	37	★14	22	106	.313	357	9	8	.979
1964—Cincinnati	Nat.	OF	156	625	99	166	23	11	23	84	.266	299	14	9	.972
1965—Cincinnati	Nat.	OF	159	669	97	204	34	10	22	94	.305	354	9	3	★.992
1966—Cincinnati	Nat.	OF	156	618	70	178	35	6	16	76	.288	344	9	13	.964
1967—Cincinnati	Nat.	OF	158	650	90	187	28	★13	18	66	.288	341	4	5	.986
1968—Cincinnati (a)	Nat	OF	130	499	60	135	29	6	5	48	.271	258	7	6	.978
1969—St. Louis (b)	Nat.	OF	132	495	58	126	22	6	10	70	.255	218	6	1	★.996
1970—Cleveland	Amer.	OF-1B	148	574	74	164	28	6	24	82	.286	284	9	5	.983
1971—Cleveland (c)	Amer.	OF-1B	146	566	60	149	23	4	11	35	.263	315	11	7	.979
1972—California	Amer.	OF-1B	136	484	56	133	24	2	7	49	.275	207	11	2	.991
1973—California (d)	Amer.	OF	124	466	56	121	14	6	8	57	.260	210	11	8	.965
1974—Kansas City	Amer.	OF-1B	115	406	46	112	18	2	6	41	.276	198	9	4	.981
1975—Kansas City (e)	Amer.	OF-1B	103	319	38	71	14	5	4	22	.223	151	6	1	.994
American League Totals—6 Years			772	2815	330	750	121	25	60	286	.266	1365	57	27	.981
National League Totals—12 Years			1697	6830	1036	2007	364	102	196	884	.294	3780	116	74	.981
Major League Totals—18 Years			2469	9645	1366	2757	485	127	256	1170	.286	5145	173	101	.981

aTraded to St. Louis Cardinals for Outfielder Bob Tolan and Pitcher Wayne Granger, October 11, 1968.

bTraded to Cleveland Indians for Outfielder Jose Cardenal, November 20, 1969.

cTraded with Outfielder Frank Baker and Pitcher Alan Foster to California Angels for Catcher Jerry Moses and outfielder Alex Johnson, October 5, 1971.

dTraded to Kansas City Royals for Pitcher Barry Raziano and cash, February 23, 1974.

eSigned as free agent by Milwaukee Brewers, January 14, 1976, but released April 4, 1976.

WORLD SERIES RECORD

Year Club	League	Pos.	G.	AB.	R.	H.	2B.	3B.	HR.	RBI.	B.A.	PO.	A.	E.	F.A.
1961—Cincinnati	Nat.	OF	5	22	0	2	1	0	0	0	.091	18	1	1	.950

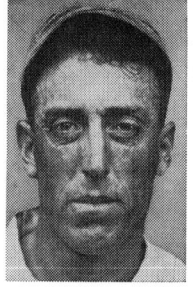

EDWARD S. (EDDIE) PLANK

Born August 31, 1875, at Gettysburg, Pa.

Died February 24, 1926, at Gettysburg, Pa.

Height, 5.11½. Weight, 175.

Threw and batted lefthanded.

Named to Hall of Fame, 1946.

Year Club	League	G.	IP.	W.	L.	Pct.	ShO.	H.	R.	ER.	SO.	BB.	ERA.
1901—Philadelphia	American	33	262	17	11	.607	1	234	121	...	89	47	.....
1902—Philadelphia	American	36	295	20	15	.571	1	300	139	...	110	64	.....
1903—Philadelphia	American	★43	338	23	16	.590	3	314	139	...	175	67	.....
1904—Philadelphia	American	44	365	26	17	.605	7	307	112	...	209	77	.....
1905—Philadelphia	American	41	346	25	12	.676	4	283	111	...	199	69	.....
1906—Philadelphia	American	26	211	19	6	★.760	5	160	53	...	102	51	.....
1907—Philadelphia	American	43	344	24	16	.600	★8	287	114	...	198	82	.....
1908—Philadelphia	American	34	245	14	16	.467	4	202	71	...	135	46	.....
1909—Philadelphia	American	34	265	19	10	.655	3	215	74	...	132	62	.....
1910—Philadelphia	American	38	250	16	10	.615	1	218	89	...	123	55	.....
1911—Philadelphia	American	40	257	22	8	.733	●6	237	85	...	155	77	.....
1912—Philadelphia	American	37	260	26	6	.813	5	234	90	...	110	83	.....
1913—Philadelphia	American	41	244	18	10	.643	8	211	87	70	151	57	2.59
1914—Philadelphia (a)	American	34	185	15	7	.682	4	178	68	59	110	42	2.87
1915—St. Louis (b)	Federal	42	269	21	11	.656	6	210	75	60	145	58	★2.01
1916—St. Louis	American	37	236	16	15	.516	3	203	78	61	88	67	2.33
1917—St. Louis (c)	American	20	131	5	6	.455	1	105	39	26	26	38	1.79
Major League Totals—16 Years		581	4234	305	181	.628	64	3688	1470	...	2112	984	.....

aReleased and signed with St. Louis, Federal League, November, 1914.

bAwarded to St. Louis Browns in peace agreement, January, 1916.

cTraded with Second Baseman Del Pratt and $15,000 to New York Yankees for Catcher Leslie Nunamaker, Third Baseman Fritz Maisel, Pitchers Nick Cullop and Urban Shocker and Second Baseman Joe Gedeon, January 21, 1918, but never reported.

Year Club	League	G.	IP.	W.	L.	Pct.	ShO.	H.	R.	ER.	SO.	BB.	ERA.
1905—Philadelphia	American	2	17	0	2	.000	0	14	4	2	11	4	1.06
1911—Philadelphia	American	2	9⅔	1	1	.500	0	6	2	2	8	0	1.86
1913—Philadelphia	American	2	19	1	1	.500	0	9	4	2	7	3	0.95
1914—Philadelphia	American	1	9	0	1	.000	0	7	1	1	6	4	1.00
World Series Totals—4 Years		7	54⅔	2	5	.286	0	36	11	7	32	11	1.15

JOHN JOSEPH (JACK) POWELL

Born July 9, 1874, at Bloomington, Ill.

Died October 18, 1944, at Chicago, Ill.

Height, 5.11. Weight, 190.

Threw and batted righthanded.

Year Club	League	G.	IP.	W.	L.	Pct.	H.	R.	SO.	BB.	CG.	ShO.
1897—Cleveland	National	27	227	15	9	.625	244	117	64	61	24	2
1898—Cleveland	National	42	343	24	15	.615	328	153	103	101	36	●6
1899—St. Louis	National	48	373	23	21	.523	425	195	86	83	40	2
1900—St. Louis	National	37	281	17	17	.500	319	185	77	77	27	3
1901—St. Louis	National	●45	341	19	18	.514	353	163	132	58	33	2
1902—St. Louis	American	42	330	22	17	.564	322	147	137	89	36	3
1903—St. Louis	American	38	308	15	19	.441	297	131	166	57	33	4
1904—New York	American	47	392	23	19	.548	344	154	197	95	38	3
1905—New York (a)-St. Louis	American	40	228	11	14	.440	237	116	102	65	17	1
1906—St. Louis	American	28	245	13	14	.481	196	77	132	56	25	3
1907—St. Louis	American	32	255	13	16	.448	236	100	99	60	27	4
1908—St. Louis	American	33	256	16	13	.552	208	73	85	47	23	5
1909—St. Louis	American	34	239	12	16	.429	221	83	82	42	18	4
1910—St. Louis	American	21	129	7	11	.389	121	45	52	28	8	3
1911—St. Louis	American	31	208	8	★19	.296	224	120	52	44	18	1
1912—St. Louis	American	32	235	9	16	.360	248	117	67	52	19	0
1913—Louisville	Amer. Assn.	47	240	17	13	.567	238	102	76	56	...	...
American League Totals—11 Years		378	2825	149	174	.461	2654	1163	1171	635	262	31
National League Totals—5 Years		199	1565	98	80	.551	1669	813	462	382	160	15
Major League Totals—16 Years		577	4390	247	254	.493	4323	1976	1633	1017	422	46

aSold to St. Louis for cash, September, 1905.

JOHN WESLEY (BOOG) POWELL

Born August 17, 1941, at Lakeland, Fla.

Height, 6.04½. Weight, 246.

Threw right and batted lefthanded.

Stepbrother of Carl Taylor, former major league catcher-first baseman.

Shares American League record for most runs batted in, doubleheader (11), July 6, 1966 (20 innings).
Hit three home runs in a game August 10, 1963; June 27, 1964; and August 15, 1966.
Led American League in slugging percentage with .606 in 1964.
Named American League Comeback Player of the Year by THE SPORTING NEWS, 1966 and 1975.
Named first baseman on THE SPORTING NEWS American League All-Star Team, 1966-68-69-70.
Named Most Valuable Player in American League, 1970.

Year Club	League	Pos.	G.	AB.	R.	H.	2B.	3B.	HR.	RBI.	B.A.	PO.	A.	E.	F.A.
1959—Bluefield	Appal.	OF-1B	56	191	39	67	7	0	14	59	.351	68	5	7	.913
1960—Fox Cities	I.I.I.	1B	136	497	83	155	23	3	13	100	.312	1055	68	19	★.983
1961—Rochester	Int.	1B-OF	142	486	86	156	26	5	★32	92	.321	842	43	14	.984
1961—Baltimore	Amer.	OF	4	13	0	1	0	0	0	1	.077	3	0	0	1.000
1962—Baltimore	Amer.	OF-1B	124	400	44	97	13	2	15	53	.243	194	1	6	.970
1963—Baltimore	Amer.	OF-1B	140	491	67	130	22	2	25	82	.265	316	18	9	.974
1964—Baltimore	Amer.	OF-1B	134	424	74	123	17	0	39	99	.290	233	19	5	.980
1965—Baltimore	Amer.	1B-OF	144	472	54	117	20	2	17	72	.248	658	53	5	.993

Year Club League	Pos.	G.	AB.	R.	H.	2B.	3B.	HR.	RBI.	B.A.	PO.	A.	E.	F.A.
1966—Baltimore .... Amer.	1B	140	491	78	141	18	0	34	109	.287	1094	68	13	.989
1967—Baltimore .... Amer.	1B	125	415	53	97	14	1	13	55	.234	903	64	14	.986
1968—Baltimore .... Amer.	1B	154	550	60	137	21	1	22	85	.249	★1293	79	14	.990
1969—Baltimore .... Amer.	1B	152	533	83	162	25	0	37	121	.304	1192	84	7	.994
1970—Baltimore .... Amer.	1B	154	526	82	156	28	0	35	114	.297	1209	89	10	.992
1971—Baltimore .... Amer.	1B	128	418	59	107	19	0	22	92	.256	1031	67	5	.995
1972—Baltimore .... Amer.	1B	140	465	53	117	20	1	21	81	.252	1116	70	★15	.988
1973—Baltimore .... Amer.	1B	114	370	52	98	13	1	14	54	.265	988	77	12	.989
1974—Baltimore (a) ...... Amer.	1B	110	344	37	91	13	1	12	45	.265	866	61	4	.996
1975—Cleveland............. Amer.	1B	134	435	64	129	18	0	27	86	.297	997	69	3	★.997
1976—Cleveland............. Amer.	1B	95	293	29	63	9	0	9	33	.215	698	61	10	.987
1977—Los Angeles (b).... Nat.	PH-1B	50	41	0	10	0	0	0	5	.244	15	0	1	.938
American League Totals—16 Years		1992	6640	889	1766	270	11	339	1182	.266	12781	880	132	.990
National League Totals—1 Year..............		50	41	0	10	0	0	0	5	.244	15	0	1	.938
Major League Totals—17 Years..............		2042	6681	889	1776	270	11	339	1187	.266	12796	880	133	.990

aTraded with Pitcher Don Hood to Cleveland Indians for Catcher Dave Duncan and Outfielder Alvin McGrew, February 25, 1975.

bSigned as free agent with Los Angeles Dodgers, April 5, 1977.

CHAMPIONSHIP SERIES RECORD

Shares major league record for most single, game (4), October 4, 1969 (12 innings).

Year Club League	Pos.	G.	AB.	R.	H.	2B.	3B.	HR.	RBI.	B.A.	PO.	A.	E.	F.A.
1969—Baltimore .... Amer.	1B	3	13	2	5	0	0	1	1	.385	34	0	0	1.000
1970—Baltimore .... Amer.	1B	3	14	2	6	2	0	1	6	.429	24	1	0	1.000
1971—Baltimore .... Amer.	1B	3	10	4	3	0	0	2	3	.300	28	2	0	1.000
1973—Baltimore .... Amer.	1B	1	4	1	0	0	0	0	0	.000	7	0	0	1.000
1974—Baltimore .... Amer.	1B	2	8	0	1	0	0	0	1	.125	22	1	0	1.000
Championship Series Totals—5 Years.....		12	49	9	15	2	0	4	11	.306	115	4	0	1.000

WORLD SERIES RECORD

Year Club League	Pos.	G.	AB.	R.	H.	2B.	3B.	HR.	RBI.	B.A.	PO.	A.	E.	F.A.
1966—Baltimore .... Amer.	1B	4	14	1	5	1	0	0	1	.357	27	122	0	1.000
1969—Baltimore .... Amer.	1B	5	19	0	5	0	0	0	1	.263	46	2	1	.980
1970—Baltimore .... Amer.	1B	5	17	6	5	1	0	2	5	.294	38	2	0	1.000
1971—Baltimore .... Amer.	1B	7	27	1	3	0	0	0	1	.111	52	4	1	.982
World Series Totals—4 Years		21	77	8	18	2	0	2	7	.234	163	9	2	.989

JOHN PICUS (JACK) QUINN

Born July 5, 1884, at Mahanoy City, Pa.
Died April 17, 1946, at Pottsville, Pa.
Height, 6.00. Weight, 200.
Threw and batted righthanded.

Manager, Johnstown, Middle Atlantic League, 1935.

Year Club League	G.	IP.	W.	L.	Pct.	H.	R.	ER.	SO.	BB.	ERA.
1907—Macon.........................So. Atlantic	15	109	6	5	.545	83	...	...	60	33	....
1908—Richmond....................Virginia	17	...	14	0	★1.000	102	...	...	92	20	....
1909—New York....................American	22	118	9	5	.643	110	45	...	35	24	....
1910—New York....................American	35	237	18	12	.600	214	88	...	82	58	....
1911—New York....................American	39	175	8	9	.471	203	111	...	71	41	....
1912—New York (a)..............American	18	103	5	7	.417	139	89	...	47	23	....
1912—Rochester ....International	13	108	8	4	.667	94	39	...	44	14	....
1913—Rochester ....International	38	268	19	13	.594	261	111	...	153	62	....
1913—Boston (b)....................National	8	56	4	3	.571	55	22	15	33	7	2.41
1914—Baltimore....................Federal	46	339	26	14	.650	★330	121	101	165	63	2.68
1915—Baltimore....................Federal	44	275	9	★22	.290	291	139	102	116	64	3.34
1916—Vernon ....Pacific Coast	51	289	16	13	.552	292	125	94	149	85	2.93
1917—Vernon ....Pacific Coast	52	409	24	20	.545	415	155	107	160	84	2.35
1918—Vernon ....Pacific Coast	24	...	12	6	.667	...	...	...	...	...	....
1918—Chicago (c) ....American	6	51	5	1	.833	38	13	13	22	7	2.29
1919—New York....................American	38	264	15	15	.500	242	96	77	97	65	2.63
1920—New York....................American	41	253	18	10	.643	271	110	90	101	48	3.20
1921—New York (d)..............American	33	129	8	7	.533	158	61	50	44	32	3.49
1922—Boston........................American	40	256	13	15	.464	263	119	99	67	59	3.48
1923—Boston........................American	42	243	13	17	.433	302	125	105	71	53	3.89
1924—Boston........................American	43	228	12	13	.480	237	107	81	64	51	3.20
1925—Bos.(e)-Philadelphia..............American	37	205	13	11	.542	259	124	94	43	42	4.13
1926—Philadelphia ....American	31	164	10	11	.476	191	74	62	58	36	3.40

Year Club	League	G.	IP.	W.	L.	Pct.	H.	R.	ER.	SO.	BB.	ERA.
1927—Philadelphia	American	34	207	15	10	.600	211	82	73	43	37	3.17
1928—Philadelphia	American	31	211	18	7	.720	239	92	68	43	34	2.90
1929—Philadelphia	American	35	161	11	9	.550	182	87	71	41	39	3.97
1930—Philadelphia (f)	American	35	90	9	7	.563	109	51	44	28	22	4.40
1931—Brooklyn	National	39	64	5	4	.556	65	28	19	25	24	2.67
1932—Brooklyn (g)	National	42	87	3	7	.300	102	36	32	28	24	3.31
1933—Cincinnati	National	14	16	0	1	.000	20	9	7	3	5	3.94
1934—Hollywood	Pacific Coast	6	18	1	1	.500	29	12	12	3	4	6.00
1935—Johnstown	Mid. Atlantic	1	2	0	0	.000	2	0	0	0	0	0.00
American League Totals—17 Years		560	3095	200	166	.546	3368	1474	...	957	671	....
National League Totals—4 Years		103	223	12	15	.444	242	95	73	89	60	2.95
Major League Totals—21 Years		663	3318	212	181	.539	3610	1569	...	1046	731	....

aSold to Rochester, July 30, 1912.
bPurchased from Rochester, August 23, 1913, but jumped to Baltimore, Federal League, for 1914.
cClaimed by both Chicago and New York and, after playing with White Sox, was awarded to Yankees by National Commission, August 26, 1918.
dTraded with Shortstop Roger Peckinpaugh and Pitchers Harry (Rip) Collins and William Piercy to Boston Red Sox for Shortstop Everett Scott and Pitchers Joe Bush and Sam Jones, December 20, 1921.
eSold to Philadelphia Athletics on waivers, July 10, 1925.
fReleased, November, 1930; signed by Brooklyn, February, 1931.
gReleased, April, 1933; signed by Cincinnati, May, 1933.

WORLD SERIES RECORD

Year Club	League	G.	IP.	W.	L.	Pct.	H.	R.	ER.	SO.	BB.	ERA.
1921—New York	American	1	3⅔	0	1	.000	8	4	4	2	2	9.82
1929—Philadelphia	American	1	5	0	0	.000	7	6	5	2	2	9.00
1930—Philadelphia	American	1	2	0	0	.000	3	1	1	1	0	4.50
World Series Totals—3 Years		3	10⅔	0	1	.000	18	11	10	5	4	8.44

CHARLES (HOSS) RADBOURN

Born December 9, 1853, at Rochester, N. Y.

Died February 5, 1897, at Bloomington, Ill.

Height, 5.09. Weight, 168.

Threw and batted righthanded.

Holds major league record for most wins, season (60), 1884.
Pitched 8-0 no-hit victory against Cleveland, July 25, 1883.
Named to Hall of Fame, 1939.

Year Club	League	G.	IP.	W.	L.	Pct.	ShO.	H.	R.	SO.	BB.
1878—Peoria Reds	Independent	Batted .289 and fielded .810 in 28 games								
1879—Dubuque	N. W. L.	Batted .387 and fielded .916 in 47 games									
1880—Buffalo (a)	National	Batted .143 and fielded .937 in 6 games									
1881—Providence	National	41	327	25	11	*.694	3	296	157	109	67
1882—Providence	National	52	471	31	19	.620	*6	425	238	*194	47
1883—Providence	National	*76	642	*49	25	.662	4	585	290	312	51
1884—Providence	National	*74	*679	*60	12	*.833	11	514	217	*411	96
1885—Providence(b)	National	49	448	26	20	.565	2	423	209	157	76
1886—Boston	National	57	511	27	30	.474	3	572	288	209	107
1887—Boston	National	47	429	24	23	.511	1	624	307	79	127
1888—Boston	National	24	209	7	16	.304	1	192	110	53	44
1889—Boston(c)	National	32	276	20	11	.645	1	276	151	95	80
1890—Boston(d)	Players	40	347	27	12	.692	1	351	183	87	98
1891—Cincinnati	National	25	204	12	12	.500	2	242	150	40	63
National League Totals—11 Years		477	4196	281	179	.611	34	4149	2117	1659	758
Players League Totals—1 Year		40	347	27	12	.692	1	351	183	87	98
Major League Totals—12 Years		517	4543	308	191	.617	35	4500	2300	1746	856

aDid not pitch, played infield.
bTeam disbanded; awarded to Boston.
cJumped to Players League.
dSigned with Cincinnati after Players League disbanded.

WORLD SERIES RECORD

Year Club	League	G.	IP.	W.	L.	Pct.	ShO.	H.	R.	SO.	BB.
1884—Providence	National	3	22	3	0	1.000	0	11	3	17	0

RAYMOND ALLEN (RIP) RADCLIFF

Born January 19, 1906, at Kiowa, Okla.
Died May 23, 1962, at Enid, Okla.
Height, 5.10½. Weight, 175.
Threw and batted lefthanded.

Manager, Greensboro, Carolina League, 1948.

Year Club	League	Pos.	G.	AB.	R.	H.	2B.	3B.	HR.	RBI.	B.A.	PO.	A.	E.	F.A.
1928—Paris	L. Star	OF	87	328	40	96	13	5	8	....	.293	884	33	17	.982
1929—Muskogee-Maud...	W. A.	1B	112	409	78	147	16	6	14	85	.359	1004	37	22	.979
1929—Dallas	Tex.	1B	29	104	9	34	2	1	2	15	.327	224	12	1	.996
1930—Selma	So'east.	1B	132	539	94	★199	29	7	★15	★116	★.369	1233	★80	13	★.990
1931—Shreveport	Tex.	OF	155	596	96	★215	41	7	12	103	★.361	521	25	18	.968
1932—Dallas	Tex.	OF	148	578	88	183	48	9	3	101	.317	225	15	5	.980
1933—St. Paul	A. A.	OF	128	511	77	186	36	10	6	99	.364	219	4	8	.965
1934—Louisville	A. A.	OF	142	565	90	189	27	19	5	102	.335	693	33	15	.980
1934—Chicago	Amer.	OF	14	56	7	15	2	1	0	5	.268	35	0	2	.946
1935—Chicago	Amer.	OF	146	623	95	178	28	8	10	68	.286	231	8	8	.968
1936—Chicago	Amer.	PF	138	618	120	207	31	7	8	82	.335	213	6	15	.936
1937—Chicago	Amer.	OF	144	584	105	190	38	10	4	79	.325	273	9	10	.966
1938—Chicago	Amer.	1B-OF	129	503	64	166	23	6	5	81	.330	466	15	10	.980
1939—Chicago(a)	Amer.	1B-OF	113	397	49	105	25	2	2	53	.264	300	12	6	.981
1940—St. Louis	Amer.	1B-OF	150	584	83	●200	33	9	7	81	.342	307	10	9	.972
1941—St.L.(b)-Detroit	Amer.	OF	115	450	59	140	16	7	5	54	.311	205	7	5	.977
1942—Detroit	Amer.	1B-OF	62	144	13	36	5	0	1	20	.250	83	6	1	989
1943—Detroit(c)	Amer.	1B-OF	70	115	3	30	4	0	0	10	.261	39	3	0	1.000
1944-45—Detroit	Amer.						(In Military Service)								
1946—Chattanooga	South.	OF	114	373	49	113	20	1	0	56	.303	148	16	8	.953
1947—							(Out of Organized Ball)								
1948—Greensboro	Carol.	1B	136	508	95	155	36	3	10	80	.305	1099	★121	19	.985
Major League Totals—10 Years			1081	4074	598	1267	205	50	42	533	.311	2152	76	66	.971

aTraded to St. Louis Browns for Outfielder Moose Solters, December 8, 1939.
bSold to Detroit Tigers for reported $25,000, May 15, 1941.
cTraded to Philadelphia Athletics for Catcher Bob Swift and Second Baseman Don Heffner, October 11, 1943;
returned to Detroit upon entering Navy, and cash settlement made to complete deal.

HAROLD HENRY (PEE WEE) REESE

Born July 23, 1918, at Ekron, Ky.
Height, 5.09½. Weight, 178.
Threw and batted righthanded.

Led National League in stolen bases with 30 in 1952.
Named as shortstop on THE SPORTING NEWS All-Star Major League Team, 1953.
Coach, Los Angeles Dodgers, 1959.
Named to Hall of Fame, 1984.

Year Club	League	Pos.	G.	AB.	R.	H.	2B.	3B.	HR.	RBI.	B.A.	PO.	A.	E.	F.A.
1938—Louisville	A. A.	SS	138	483	68	134	21	8	3	54	.277	239	457	45	.939
1939—Louisville	A. A.	SS	149	506	78	141	22	★18	4	57	.279	★307	470	47	.943
1940—Brookyln	Nat.	SS	84	312	58	85	8	4	5	28	.272	190	238	18	.960
1941—Brooklyn	Nat.	SS	152	595	76	136	23	5	2	46	.229	★346	473	★47	.946
1942—Brooklyn	Nat.	SS	151	564	87	144	24	5	3	53	.255	★337	★482	35	.959
1943-44-45—Brooklyn	Nat.						(In Military Service)								
1946—Brooklyn	Nat.	SS	152	542	79	154	16	10	5	60	.284	285	463	26	.966
1947—Brooklyn	Nat.	SS	142	476	81	135	24	4	12	73	.284	266	441	25	.966
1948—Brooklyn	Nat.	SS	151	566	96	155	31	4	9	75	.274	★335	453	31	.962
1949—Brooklyn	Nat.	SS	155	617	★132	172	27	3	16	73	.279	★316	454	18	★.977
1950—Brooklyn	Nat.	SS-3B	141	531	97	138	21	5	11	52	.260	291	414	26	.964
1951—Brooklyn	Nat.	SS	154	616	94	176	20	8	10	84	.286	292	422	35	.953
1952—Brooklyn	Nat.	SS	149	559	94	152	18	8	6	58	.272	282	376	21	.969

Year Club League	Pos.	G.	AB.	R.	H.	2B.	3B.	HR.	RBI.	B.A.	PO.	A.	E.	F.A.
1953—Brooklyn .... Nat.	SS	140	524	108	142	25	7	13	61	.271	265	380	23	.966
1954—Brooklyn .... Nat.	SS	141	554	98	171	35	8	10	69	.309	270	426	25	.965
1955—Brooklyn .... Nat.	SS	145	553	99	156	29	4	10	61	.282	239	404	23	.965
1956—Brooklyn .... Nat.	SS-3B	147	572	85	147	19	2	9	46	.257	269	388	25	.963
1957—Brooklyn .... Nat.	3B-SS	103	330	33	74	3	1	1	29	.224	97	228	19	.945
1958—Los Angeles .... Nat.	SS-3B	59	147	21	33	7	2	4	17	.224	44	89	10	.930
Major League Totals—16 Years		2166	8058	1338	2170	330	80	126	885	.269	4124	6131	407	.962

WORLD SERIES RECORD

Shares record for most at-bats, nine-inning game (6), October 6, 1956.

Year Club League	Pos.	G.	AB.	R.	H.	2B.	3B.	HR.	RBI.	B.A.	PO.	A.	E.	F.A.
1941—Brooklyn .... Nat.	SS	5	20	1	4	0	0	0	2	.200	13	14	3	.900
1947—Brooklyn .... Nat.	SS	7	23	5	7	1	0	0	4	.304	8	15	1	.958
1949—Brooklyn .... Nat.	SS	5	19	2	6	1	0	1	2	.316	5	9	1	.933
1952—Brooklyn .... Nat.	SS	7	29	4	10	0	0	1	4	.345	15	18	2	.943
1953—Brooklyn .... Nat.	SS	6	24	0	5	0	1	0	0	.278	7	14	0	1.000
1955—Brooklyn .... Nat.	SS	7	27	5	8	1	0	0	2	.296	15	23	1	.974
1956—Brooklyn .... Nat.	SS	7	27	3	6	0	1	0	2	.222	14	21	1	.972
World Series Totals—7 Years		44	169	20	46	3	2	2	16	.272	77	114	9	.955

CARL NETTLES REYNOLDS

Born February 1, 1904, at LaRue, Tex.

Died May 29, 1978, at Houston, Tex.

Height, 6.00. Weight, 195.

Threw and batted righthanded.

Hit three home runs in a game, July 2, 1930, second game.

Year Club League	Pos.	G.	AB.	R.	H.	2B.	3B.	HR.	RBI.	B.A.	PO.	A.	E.	F.A.
1927—Palestine .... L. Star	SS-OF	124	479	82	*180	27	6	11	....	*.376	272	159	37	.921
1927—Chicago .... Amer.	OF	14	42	5	9	3	0	1	7	.214	37	1	0	1.000
1928—Chicago .... Amer.	OF	84	291	51	94	21	11	2	36	.323	135	6	3	.979
1929—Chicago .... Amer.	OF	131	517	81	164	24	12	11	67	.317	268	13	15	.949
1930—Chicago .... Amer.	OF	138	563	103	202	25	18	22	104	.359	336	11	9	.975
1931—Chicago(a) .... Amer.	OF	118	462	71	134	24	14	6	77	.290	233	10	13	.949
1932—Washington(b) ..... Amer.	OF	102	406	53	124	28	7	9	63	.305	229	3	8	.983
1933—St. Louis(c) .... Amer.	OF	135	475	81	136	26	14	8	71	.286	269	8	10	.965
1934—Boston .... Amer.	OF	113	413	61	125	26	9	4	86	.303	244	6	6	.977
1935—Boston(d) .... Amer.	OF	78	244	33	66	13	4	6	35	.270	146	7	4	.975
1936—Washington .... Amer.	OF	89	293	41	81	18	2	4	41	.276	142	8	5	.968
1937—Minneapolis .... A. A.	OF	147	614	145	218	*49	17	17	110	.355	294	9	9	.971
1937—Chicago .... Nat.	OF	7	11	0	3	1	0	0	1	.273	5	0	1	.833
1938—Chicago .... Nat.	OF	125	497	59	150	28	10	3	67	.302	328	10	6	.983
1939—Chicago .... Nat.	OF	88	281	33	69	10	6	4	44	.246	168	5	5	.972
1940—Los Angeles .... P. C.	OF	41	80	10	20	3	1	0	13	.250	50	0	0	1.000
American League Totals—10 Years		1002	3706	580	1135	208	91	73	587	.306	2039	73	69	.968
National League Totals—3 Years		220	789	92	222	39	16	7	112	.281	501	15	12	.977
Major League Totals—13 Years		1222	4495	672	1357	247	107	80	699	.302	2540	88	81	.970

aTraded to Washington Senators with Infielder John Kerr for Pitchers Bump Hadley and Sam Jones and Infielder Minter Hayes, December 4, 1931.

bTraded to St. Louis Browns with Outfielder Sam West and Pitcher Lloyd Brown for Outfielders Goose Goslin and Fred Schulte, and Pitcher Walter Stewart and cash, December 14, 1932.

cTraded to Boston Red Sox for Pitcher Ivy Andrews and Outfielder Smead Jolley, December 13, 1933.

dTraded to Washington Senators with Outfielder Roy Johnson for Outfielder Heinie Manush, December 17, 1935.

WORLD SERIES RECORD

Year Club League	Pos.	G.	AB.	R.	H.	2B.	3B.	HR.	RBI.	B.A.	PO.	A.	E.	F.A.
1938—Chicago .... Nat.	OF—PH	4	12	0	0	0	0	0	0	.000	7	0	0	1.000

—DID YOU KNOW—

That former shortstop Pee Wee Reese is the only player to compete in all 44 World Series games contested between the Brooklyn Dodgers and New York Yankees?

EDGAR CHARLES (SAM) RICE

Born February 20, 1890, at Morocco, Ind.
Died October 13, 1974, at Rossmor, Md.
Height, 5.10. Weight, 155.
Threw and batted lefthanded.

Led American League in stolen bases with 63 in 1920.
Tied for American League lead in double plays by outfielder with 8 in 1923.
Named to Hall of Fame, 1963.

Year	Club	League	Pos.	G.	AB.	R.	H.	2B.	3B.	HR.	RBI.	B.A.	PO.	A.	E.	F.A.
1912—Muscatine		Cen. Assn.	OF	18	62	3	12	1	0	0	....	.194	30	49	6	.929
1914—Petersburg		Va.	P	31	71	9	22	3	1	0	....	.310	13	36	0	1.000
1915—Petersburg		Va.	P-OF	62	156	16	47	3	4	0	....	.301	45	70	0	1.000
1915—Washington		Amer.	P	4	8	0	3	0	0	0	0	.375	1	7	1	.889
1916—Washington		Amer.	P-OF	58	197	26	59	8	3	1	16	.299	83	5	4	.957
1917—Washington		Amer.	OF	155	586	77	177	25	7	0	68	.302	265	26	12	.960
1918—Washington		Amer.	OF	7	23	3	8	1	0	0	3	.348	10	3	0	1.000
1919—Washington		Amer.	OF	●141	557	80	179	23	9	3	72	.321	285	18	12	.962
1920—Washington		Amer.	OF	153	624	83	211	29	9	3	80	.336	★454	24	20	.960
1921—Washington		Amer.	OF	143	561	83	185	39	13	4	79	.330	380	18	15	.964
1922—Washington		Amer.	OF	154	★633	91	187	37	13	6	69	.295	★385	23	★21	.951
1923—Washington		Amer.	OF	148	595	117	188	35	●18	3	75	.316	307	21	10	.970
1924—Washington		Amer.	OF	154	★646	106	★216	39	14	1	76	.334	331	18	12	.967
1925—Washington		Amer.	OF	152	649	111	227	31	13	1	87	.350	339	20	12	.968
1926—Washington		Amer.	OF	152	★641	98	●216	32	14	3	76	.337	342	●25	●15	.961
1927—Washington		Amer.	OF	142	603	98	179	33	14	2	65	.297	258	12	7	.975
1928—Washington		Amer.	OF	148	616	95	202	32	15	2	55	.328	240	11	7	.973
1929—Washington		Amer.	OF	150	616	119	199	39	10	1	62	.323	272	20	9	.970
1930—Washington		Amer.	OF	147	593	121	207	35	13	1	73	.349	297	13	12	.963
1931—Washington		Amer.	OF	120	413	81	128	21	8	0	42	.310	221	7	7	.970
1932—Washington		Amer.	OF	106	288	58	93	16	7	1	34	.323	132	7	4	.972
1933—Washington(a)		Amer.	OF	73	85	19	25	4	3	1	12	.294	41	4	0	1.000
1934—Cleveland		Amer.	OF	97	335	48	98	19	1	1	33	.293	129	2	5	.963
Major League Totals—20 Years				2404	9269	1514	2987	498	184	34	1077	.322	4772	284	185	.965

aReleased by Washington, January, 1934, and subsequently signed by Cleveland.

WORLD SERIES RECORD

Year	Club	League	Pos.	G.	AB.	R.	H.	2B.	3B.	HR.	RBI.	B.A.	PO.	A.	E.	F.A.
1924—Washington		Amer.	OF	7	29	2	6	0	0	0	1	.207	13	4	1	.944
1925—Washington		Amer.	OF	7	33	5	12	0	0	0	3	.364	17	0	0	1.000
1933—Washington		Amer.	PH	1	1	0	1	0	0	0	0	1.000	0	0	0	.000
World Series Totals—3 Years				15	63	7	19	0	0	0	4	.302	30	4	1	.971

PITCHING RECORD

Year	Club	League	G.	IP.	W.	L.	Pct.	H.	R.	ER.	SO.	BB.	ERA.
1914—Petersburg		Virginia	15	123	9	2	.818	73	....	....	62	38	....
1915—Petersburg		Virginia	29	233	11	12	.478	175	....	....	153	43	....
1915—Washington		American	4	18	1	0	.000	13	8	4	9	9	2.00
1916—Washington		American	5	21⅓	0	1	.000	18	10	7	3	10	2.94
Major League Totals—2 Years			9	39⅓	1	1	.500	31	18	11	12	19	2.52

ARTHUR HARDING (HARDY) RICHARDSON

Born April 21, 1855, at Paulsboro, N.J.
Died January 14, 1931, at Utica, N.Y.
Threw and batted righthanded.

Year Club League	Pos.	G.	AB.	R.	H.	2B.	3B.	HR.	SB.	B.A.	PO.	A.	E.	F.A.
1878—Utica .... I. Assn.	OF-2-C	40	182	30	59	10	4	0	....	.324	85	28	14	.890
1879—Buffalo .... Nat.	3B	78	330	53	92	19	9	0	....	.278	82	148	42	.845
1880—Buffalo .... Nat.	C-3B	80	329	43	83	19	9	0	....	.252	104	147	45	.848
1881—Buffalo .... Nat.	2B-SS-OF	83	344	62	100	21	9	2	....	.290	179	45	21	.914
1882—Buffalo .... Nat.	2B	83	354	61	96	17	9	2	....	.271	275	280	63	.898
1883—Buffalo .... Nat.	2B	90	393	73	122	34	7	1	....	.310	282	341	68	.901
1884—Buffalo .... Nat.	IF-OF	98	421	85	127	25	7	6	....	.301	224	229	50	.901
1885—Buffalo .... Nat.	IF-OF	96	426	90	136	17	10	4	....	.319	283	175	49	.903
1886—Detroit .... Nat.	2B-OF	125	538	125	189	27	11	*11	42	.351	234	139	31	.923
1887—Detroit .... Nat.	2B-OF	120	573	130	208	26	18	9	29	.363	328	223	35	.940
1888—Detroit .... Nat.	2B	57	266	60	77	17	1	6	13	.289	173	185	29	.925
1889—Boston .... Nat.	2B-OF	132	536	122	163	29	10	6	47	.304	320	316	51	.926
1890—Boston .... Players	OF	130	536	125	184	31	16	●14	45	.332	262	38	11	.964
1891—Boston .... A. A.	OF	71	269	45	69	11	4	7	15	.256	96	6	4	.962
1892—Wash.-N.Y. .... Nat.	2B-OF	70	282	38	59	12	5	3	10	.209	115	103	17	.928
National League Totals—12 Years........		1112	4792	942	1452	263	105	50	....	.303	2599	2331	501	.908
Players League Totals—1 Year..............		130	554	125	184	31	16	14	45	.332	262	38	11	.964
American Assn. Totals—1 Year		71	269	45	69	11	4	7	15	.256	96	6	4	.962
Major League Totals—14 Years.............		1313	5615	1112	1705	305	125	71	....	.304	2957	2375	516	.912

BRANCH WESLEY RICKEY

Born December 20, 1881, at Lucasville, O.

Died December 9, 1965, at Columbia, Mo.

Threw right and batted lefthanded.

Attended Ohio Wesleyan (Bachelor of Literature), 1904; (Bachelor of Arts), 1906; Civil Law degree at University of Michigan, 1911, and LLD at McKendree College, 1928.

Baseball coach, University of Michigan, 1909-10-11.

Is credited with instituting the chain-store farm system in baseball and re-introducing the Negro to major league baseball.

Manager, St. Louis Browns, 1913 through 1915; vice-president-business manager, St. Louis Browns, 1916; St. Louis Cardinals, 1917-20, and manager, 1919 to 1925; vice-president-business manager, St. Louis Cardinals, 1925 to 1942; president-general manager, Brooklyn Dodgers, 1942 to 1950; vice-president, general manager, Pittsburgh Pirates, 1951 to 1955; chairman board of directors, Pittsburgh Pirates, 1956 to 1959; president of the ill-fated Continental League; adviser to president, St. Louis Cardinals, 1963-65.

Named to Hall of Fame, 1967.

Year Club League	Pos.	G.	AB.	R.	H.	2B.	3B.	HR.	SB.	B.A.	PO.	A.	E.	F.A.
1903—Terre Haute.......... Central								(No record available)						
1903—LeMars.................. Ia.-S.D.	C	41	....	26	41	...	...	...	12	.265	237	44	13	.956
1904—Dallas .... Texas	C	41	....	25	36	...	...	...	14	.261	316	41	8	.959
1905—St. Louis(a) .... Amer.	C	1	3	0	0	0	0	0	0	.000	2	1	0	1.000
1905—Dallas .... Texas	C	37	132	20	39	8	2	1	7	.295	203	37	8	.967
1906—St. Louis(b) .... Amer.	C	64	201	22	57	8	3	3	4	.284	233	58	14	.954
1907—New York............. Amer.	C	52	137	16	25	1	3	0	4	.182	56	11	9	.862
1914—St. Louis................ Amer.	C	2	2	0	0	0	0	0	0	.000	0	0	0	.000
Major League Totals—4 Years..............		119	343	38	82	9	6	3	8	.239	291	70	23	.940

aDrafted by Chicago White Sox and then traded to St. Louis Browns for catcher Frank Roth.

bTraded to New York Yankees for third baseman Joe Yeager.

EPPA RIXEY
(Jeptha)

Born May 3, 1891, at Culpeper, Va.

Died February 28, 1963, at Cincinnati, O.

Height, 6.05. Weight, 210.

Threw left and batted righthanded.

Named to Hall of Fame, 1963.

Year Club	League	G.	IP.	W.	L.	Pct.	H.	R.	ER.	SO.	BB.	ERA.
1912—Philadelphia	National	23	162	10	10	.500	147	57	45	59	54	2.50
1913—Philadelphia	National	35	156	9	5	.643	148	67	54	75	56	3.12
1914—Philadelphia	National	24	103	2	11	.154	124	73	50	41	45	4.37
1915—Philadelphia	National	29	177	11	12	.478	163	67	47	88	64	2.39
1916—Philadelphia	National	38	287	22	10	.688	239	91	59	134	74	1.85
1917—Philadelphia	National	39	281	16	•21	.432	249	102	71	121	67	2.27
1918—Philadelphia	National					(In Military Service)						
1919—Philadelphia	National	23	154	6	12	.333	160	88	68	63	50	3.97
1920—Philadelphia (a)	National	41	284	11	*22	.333	288	137	110	109	69	3.49
1921—Cincinnati	National	40	301	19	18	.514	324	128	93	76	66	2.78
1922—Cincinnati	National	40	*313	*25	13	.658	*337	146	123	80	45	3.54
1923—Cincinnati	National	42	309	20	15	.571	334	124	96	97	65	2.80
1924—Cincinnati	National	35	238	15	14	.517	219	86	73	57	47	2.76
1925—Cincinnati	National	39	287	21	11	.656	302	109	92	69	47	2.89
1926—Cincinnati	National	37	233	14	8	.636	231	104	88	61	58	3.40
1927—Cincinnati	National	34	220	12	10	.545	240	106	85	42	43	3.48
1928—Cincinnati	National	43	291	19	18	.514	*317	127	111	58	67	3.43
1929—Cincinnati	National	35	201	10	13	.435	235	102	93	37	60	4.16
1930—Cincinnati	National	32	164	9	13	.409	207	103	93	37	47	5.10
1931—Cincinnati	National	22	127	4	7	.364	143	71	55	22	30	3.90
1932—Cincinnati	National	25	112	5	5	.500	108	50	33	14	16	2.65
1933—Cincinnati	National	16	94	6	3	.667	118	48	33	10	12	3.16
Major League Totals—21 Years		692	4494	266	251	.515	4633	1986	1572	1350	1082	3.15

aTraded to Cincinnati for Pitcher Jimmy Ring and Outfielder Greasy Neale, February, 1921.

WORLD SERIES RECORD

Year Club	League	G.	IP.	W.	L.	Pct.	H.	R.	ER.	SO.	BB.	ERA.
1915—Philadelphia	National	1	6⅔	0	1	.000	4	3	2	2	2	2.70

ROBIN EVAN ROBERTS

Born September 30, 1926, at Springfield, Ill.

Height, 6.01. Weight, 201.

Threw right and batted right and lefthanded.

Holds major league record for most home runs allowed, lifetime (505).
Shares major league record for most years leading league in home runs allowed (5).
Holds National League record for most home runs allowed, season (46), 1956.
Led National League in complete games with 30 in 1952, 33 in 1953, 29 in 1954, 26 in 1955 and 22 in 1956.
Led National League in home runs allowed with 35 in 1954, 46 in 1956, 40 in 1957 and tied for lead with 31 in 1960.
Named Outstanding Pitcher in National League by THE SPORTING NEWS, 1952-55.
Named Major League Player of the Year by THE SPORTING NEWS, 1952-55.
Named as pitcher on THE SPORTING NEWS All-Star Major League Teams, 1952-53-54-55.
Named to Hall of Fame, 1976.

Year Club	League	G.	IP.	W.	L.	Pct.	H.	R.	ER.	SO.	BB.	ERA.
1948—Wilmington	Int. State	11	96	9	1	*.900	55	25	22	121	27	*2.06
1948—Philadelphia	National	20	147	7	9	.438	148	63	52	84	61	3.18
1949—Philadelphia	National	43	227	15	15	.500	229	101	93	95	75	3.69
1950—Philadelphia	National	40	304	20	11	.645	282	112	102	146	77	3.02
1951—Philadelphia	National	44	*315	21	15	.583	284	115	106	127	64	3.03
1952—Philadelphia	National	39	*330	*28	7	.800	*292	104	95	148	45	2.59
1953—Philadelphia	National	44	*347	•23	16	.590	*324	119	106	*198	61	2.75
1954—Philadelphia	National	45	*337	*23	15	.605	*289	116	111	*185	56	2.96
1955—Philadelphia	National	41	*305	*23	14	.622	*292	137	111	160	53	3.28
1956—Philadelphia	National	43	297	19	•18	.514	*328	*155	*147	157	40	4.45
1957—Philadelphia	National	39	250	10	*22	.313	246	*122	*113	128	43	4.07
1958—Philadelphia	National	35	270	17	14	.548	270	112	97	130	51	3.23
1959—Philadelphia	National	35	257	15	17	.469	267	137	122	137	35	4.27
1960—Philadelphia	National	35	237	12	16	.429	256	113	106	122	34	4.03
1961—Philadelphia (a-b)	National	26	117	1	10	.091	154	85	76	54	23	5.85
1962—Baltimore	American	27	191	10	9	.526	176	63	59	102	41	2.78
1963—Baltimore	American	35	251	14	13	.519	230	100	93	124	40	3.33
1964—Baltimore	American	31	204	13	7	.650	203	69	66	109	52	2.91
1965—Baltimore (c)	American	20	115	5	7	.417	110	51	43	63	20	3.37
1965—Houston	National	10	76	5	2	.714	61	22	16	34	10	1.89
1966—Houston (d)-Chicago	National	24	112	5	8	.385	141	64	60	54	21	4.82
1967—Reading	Eastern	11	80	5	3	.625	75	25	22	65	7	2.48
American League Totals—4 Years		113	761	42	36	.538	719	283	261	398	153	3.09
National League Totals—16 Years		563	3928	244	209	.539	3863	1679	1513	1959	749	3.45
Major League Totals—19 Years		676	4689	286	245	.539	4582	1962	1774	2357	902	3.40

aSold to New York Yankees, October 16, 1961.
bReleased April 30, 1962; signed with Baltimore Orioles, May 21, 1962.
cReleased July 31, 1965; signed by Houston Astros, August 6, 1965.
dReleased; signed by Chicago Cubs, July 13, 1966.

WORLD SERIES RECORD

Year Club	League	G.	IP.	W.	L.	Pct.	H.	R.	ER.	SO.	BB.	ERA.
1950—Philadelphia ....National		2	11	0	1	.000	11	2	2	5	3	1.64

BROOKS CALBERT ROBINSON JR.

Born May 18, 1937, at Little Rock, Ark.

Height, 6.01. Weight, 190.

Threw and batted righthanded.

Holds major league records for most years leading league in games (8), assists (8) and fielding average (11), third baseman; most years, third baseman (23); highest fielding average (.971), most games (2,870), putouts (2,697), assists (6,205), chances accepted (8,902) and double plays (618) by third baseman, lifetime.

Shares major league records for most years and consecutive years with one club (23); most grand slams, consecutive games (2), May 6 and 9, 1962.

Holds American League records for most years, 150 or more games (14); most games by third baseman, season (163), 1961 and 1964.

Shares American League record for most years leading league in chances accepted by third baseman (8).

Led American League third basemen in double plays with 43 in 1963, 40 in 1964 and 44 in 1974.

Named third baseman on THE SPORTING NEWS American League All-Star Teams, 1961-62-64-65-66-67-68-71-72.

Named third baseman on THE SPORTING NEWS American League All-Star fielding teams, 1960-61-62-63-64-65-66-67-68-69-70-71-72-73-74-75.

Named Most Valuable Player in American League, 1964.

Named American League Player of the Year by THE SPORTING NEWS, 1964.

Named to Hall of Fame, 1983.

Year Club	League	Pos.	G.	AB.	R.	H.	2B.	3B.	HR.	RBI.	B.A.	PO.	A.	E.	F.A.
1955—York........................	Pied.	2B-3B	95	354	72	117	17	3	11	67	.331	184	226	14	.967
1955—Baltimore	Amer.	3B	6	22	0	2	0	0	0	1	.091	2	8	2	.833
1956—San Antonio..........	Texas	*3B-2B	154	577	72	157	28	6	9	74	.272	*213	396	26	*.959
1956—Baltimore	Amer.	3B-2B	15	44	5	10	4	0	1	1	.227	9	25	2	.944
1957—San Antonio..........	Texas	3B-SS	33	124	10	33	5	1	1	9	.266	34	59	4	.959
1957—Baltimore	Amer.	3B	50	117	13	28	6	1	2	14	.239	34	66	3	.971
1958—Baltimore	Amer.	*3B-2B	145	463	31	110	16	3	3	32	.238	*157	283	22	.952
1959—Vancouver............	P.C.	3B	42	163	20	54	9	2	6	30	.331	54	93	8	.948
1959—Baltimore	Amer.	3B-2B	88	313	29	89	15	2	4	24	.284	92	187	13	.955
1960—Baltimore	Amer.	*3B-2B	152	595	74	175	27	9	14	88	.294	*174	*330	12	*.977
1961—Baltimore	Amer.	*3B-2B-SS	●163	*668	89	192	38	7	7	61	.287	155	334	14	*.972
1962—Baltimore	Amer.	*3B-SS-2B	●162	634	77	192	29	9	23	86	.303	165	340	11	.979
1963—Baltimore	Amer.	*3B-SS	*161	589	67	148	26	4	11	67	.251	153	*331	12	*.976
1964—Baltimore	Amer.	3B	●163	612	82	194	35	3	28	*118	.317	*153	*327	14	*.972
1965—Baltimore	Amer.	3B	144	559	81	166	25	2	18	80	.297	144	296	15	.967
1966—Baltimore	Amer.	3B	157	620	91	167	35	2	23	100	.269	174	*313	12	*.976
1967—Baltimore	Amer.	3B	158	610	88	164	25	5	22	77	.269	174	*405	11	*.980
1968—Baltimore	Amer.	3B	●162	608	65	154	36	6	17	75	.253	168	*353	16	.970
1969—Baltimore	Amer.	3B	156	598	73	140	21	3	23	84	.234	163	*370	13	●.976
1970—Baltimore	Amer.	3B	158	608	84	168	31	4	18	94	.276	157	321	17	.966
1971—Baltimore	Amer.	3B	156	589	67	160	21	1	20	92	.272	131	354	16	.968
1972—Baltimore	Amer.	3B	153	556	48	139	23	2	8	64	.250	129	333	11	*.977
1973—Baltimore	Amer.	3B	155	549	53	141	17	2	9	72	.257	129	354	15	.970
1974—Baltimore	Amer.	3B	153	553	46	159	27	0	7	59	.288	115	*410	18	.967
1975—Baltimore	Amer.	3B	144	482	50	97	15	1	6	53	.201	95	326	9	*.979
1976—Baltimore	Amer.	3B	71	218	16	46	8	2	3	11	.211	59	126	6	.969
1977—Baltimore	Amer.	3B	24	47	3	7	2	0	1	4	.149	6	28	0	1.000
Major League Totals—23 Years...............			2896	10654	1232	2848	482	68	268	1357	.267	2712	6220	264	.971

CHAMPIONSHIP SERIES RECORD

Year Club	League	Pos.	G.	AB.	R.	H.	2B.	3B.	HR.	RBI.	B.A.	PO.	A.	E.	F.A.
1969—Baltimore	Amer.	3B	3	14	1	7	1	0	0	0	.500	6	10	0	1.000
1970—Baltimore	Amer.	3B	3	12	3	7	2	0	0	1	.583	3	5	0	1.000
1971—Baltimore	Amer.	3B	3	11	2	4	1	0	1	3	.364	4	7	0	1.000
1973—Baltimore	Amer.	3B	5	20	1	5	2	0	0	2	.250	2	14	1	.941
1974—Baltimore	Amer.	3B	4	12	1	1	0	0	1	1	.083	4	13	0	1.000
Championship Series Totals—5 Years.....			18	69	8	24	6	0	2	7	.348	19	49	1	.986

Shares record by hitting home run in first series at-bat, October 5, 1966, first inning.

Year Club	League	Pos.	G.	AB.	R.	H.	2B.	3B.	HR.	RBI.	B.A.	PO.	A.	E.	F.A.
1966—Baltimore	Amer.	3B	4	14	2	3	0	0	1	1	.214	4	6	0	1.000
1969—Baltimore	Amer.	3B	5	19	0	1	0	0	0	2	.053	1	16	0	1.000
1970—Baltimore	Amer.	3B	5	21	5	9	2	0	2	6	.429	9	14	1	.958
1971—Baltimore	Amer.	3B	7	22	2	7	0	0	0	5	.318	6	17	2	.920
World Series Totals—4 Years			21	76	9	20	2	0	3	14	.263	20	53	3	.960

FRANK ROBINSON

Born August 31, 1935, at Beaumont, Tex.

Height, 6;01. Weight, 194.

Threw and batted righthanded.

Shares major league record for most grand slams, game (2), June 26, 1970.
Shares National League record for most home runs, rookie season (38), 1956.
Hit three home runs in a game, August 22, 1959.
Won American League Triple Crown, 1966.
Led National League in slugging percentage with .595 in 1960, .611 in 1961 and .624 in 1962.
Led American League first basemen in double plays, 1969.
Led American League in total bases with 367 and in slugging percentage with .637 in 1966.
Tied World Series record for most times hit by pitcher, game (2), October 8, 1961.
Named National League Rookie of the Year by the Baseball Writers' Association and THE SPORTING NEWS, 1956.
Named outfielder on THE SPORTING NEWS National League All-Star Fielding Team, 1958.
Named Most Valuable National League Player, 1961.
Named Outstanding National League Player by THE SPORTING NEWS, 1961.
Named as outfielder on THE SPORTING NEWS National League All-Star Team, 1961-62.
Named as outfielder on THE SPORTING NEWS American League All-Star Team, 1966-67.
Named American League Player of the Year by THE SPORTING NEWS, 1966.
Named Major League Player of the Year by THE SPORTING NEWS, 1966.
Named Most Valuable American League Player, 1966.
Named American League Manager of the Year, 1989.
Manager, Cleveland, 1975-76; coach, California Angels, 1977; Baltimore Orioles, 1978, 1979 through 1980; 1985 through 1987; manager, Rochester, International League, 1978; San Francisco Giants, 1981 to 1984; coach, Milwaukee Brewers, 1984; manager, Baltimore Orioles, 1988 to date.
Named to Hall of Fame, 1982.

Year Club	League	Pos.	G.	AB.	R.	H.	2B.	3B.	HR.	RBI.	B.A.	PO.	A.	E.	F.A.
1953—Ogden	Pion.	O-3B-1B	72	270	70	94	20	6	17	83	.348	105	28	18	.881
1954—Tulsa	Tex.	2B-3B	8	30	4	8	0	0	0	1	.267	17	15	1	.970
1954—Columbia	Sally	OF-3-2B	132	491	★112	165	32	9	25	110	.336	258	63	18	.947
1955—Columbia	Sally	OF-1B	80	243	50	64	15	7	12	52	.263	203	3	4	.981
1956—Cincinnati	Nat.	OF	152	572	★122	166	27	6	38	83	.290	323	5	8	.976
1957—Cincinnati	Nat.	OF-1B	150	611	97	197	29	5	29	75	.322	487	36	6	.989
1958—Cincinnati	Nat.	OF-3B	148	554	90	149	25	6	31	83	.269	314	24	6	.983
1959—Cincinnati	Nat.	1B-OF	146	540	106	168	31	4	36	125	.311	1049	78	18	.984
1960—Cincinnati	Nat.	1-OF-3	139	464	86	138	33	6	31	83	.297	775	62	10	.988
1961—Cincinnati	Nat.	OF-3B	153	545	117	176	32	7	37	124	.323	284	15	3	.990
1962—Cincinnati	Nat.	OF	162	609	★134	208	★51	2	39	136	.342	315	10	2	.994
1963—Cincinnati	Nat.	OF-1B	140	482	79	125	19	3	21	91	.259	238	13	4	.984
1964—Cincinnati	Nat.	OF	156	568	103	174	38	6	29	96	.306	279	7	4	.986
1965—Cincinnati (a)	Nat.	OF	156	582	109	172	33	5	33	113	.296	282	5	3	.990
1966—Baltimore	Amer.	OF-1B	155	576	★122	182	34	2	★49	★122	★.316	282	6	5	.983
1967—Baltimore	Amer.	OF-1B	129	479	83	149	23	7	30	94	.311	207	8	2	.991
1968—Baltimore	Amer.	OF-1B	130	421	69	113	27	1	15	52	.268	193	5	7	.996
1969—Baltimore	Amer.	OF-1B	148	539	111	166	19	5	32	100	.308	367	19	5	.987
1970—Baltimore	Amer.	OF-1B	132	471	88	144	24	1	25	78	.306	262	11	4	.986
1971—Baltimore (b)........	Amer.	OF-1B	133	455	82	128	16	2	28	99	.281	449	20	11	.977
1972—Los Angeles (c)....	Nat.	OF	103	342	41	86	6	1	19	59	.251	168	6	6	.967
1973—California	Amer.	OF	147	534	85	142	29	0	30	97	.266	38	3	1	.976
1974—Calif. (d)-Cleve.	Amer.	1B-OF	144	477	81	117	27	3	22	68	.245	23	0	1	.958
1975—Cleveland (e)	Amer.	DH-PH	49	118	19	28	5	0	9	24	.237	0	0	0	.000
1976—Cleveland.............	Amer.	1B-OF	36	67	5	15	0	0	3	10	.224	11	0	0	1.000
National League Totals—11 Years.........			1605	5869	1084	1759	324	51	343	1068	.300	4514	261	84	.986
American League Totals—10 Years			1203	4137	745	1184	204	21	243	744	.286	1832	72	36	.981
Major League Totals—21 Years.............			2808	10006	1829	2943	528	72	586	1812	.294	6346	333	106	.984

aTraded to Baltimore Orioles for Outfielder Dick Simpson and Pitchers Milt Pappas and Jack Baldschun, December 9, 1965.

bTraded with Pitcher Pete Richert to Los Angeles Dodgers for Pitchers Doyle Alexander and Bob O'Brien, Catcher Sergio Robles and First Baseman-Outfielder Royle Stillman, December 2, 1971.

cTraded with Infielders Billy Grabarkewitz and Bob Valentine and Pitchers Bill Singer and Mike Strahler to California Angels for Third Baseman Ken McMullen and Pitcher Andy Messersmith, November 28, 1972.

dReleased on waivers to Cleveland Indians, September 12, 1974; Indians sent Outfielder Rusty Torres and Catcher Ken Suarez to Angels, December 4, 1974, as part of deal.

ePlayer-manager.

CHAMPIONSHIP SERIES RECORD

Shares major league records for most at-bats, inning (2), October 3, 1970, fourth inning; hitting home run in first series at-bat, October 4, 1969, fourth inning.

Year Club League	Pos.	G.	AB.	R.	H.	2B.	3B.	HR.	RBI.	B.A.	PO.	A.	E.	F.A.
1969—Baltimore .... Amer.	OF	3	12	1	4	2	0	1	2	.333	2	0	1	.667
1970—Baltimore .... Amer.	OF	3	10	3	2	0	0	1	2	.200	2	0	0	1.000
1971—Baltimore .... Amer.	OF	3	12	2	1	1	0	0	1	.083	7	0	0	1.000
Championship Series Totals—3 Years.....		9	34	6	7	3	0	2	5	.206	11	0	1	.917

WORLD SERIES RECORD

Year Club League	Pos.	G.	AB.	R.	H.	2B.	3B.	HR.	RBI.	B.A.	PO.	A.	E.	F.A.
1961—Cincinnati .... Nat.	OF	5	15	3	3	3	0	1	4	.200	5	0	0	1.000
1966—Baltimore .... Amer.	OF	4	14	4	4	0	1	2	3	.286	6	0	0	1.000
1969—Baltimore .... Amer.	OF	5	16	2	3	0	0	1	1	.188	13	0	0	1.000
1970—Baltimore .... Amer.	OF	5	22	5	6	0	0	2	4	.273	7	0	0	1.000
1971—Baltimore .... Amer.	OF	7	25	5	7	0	0	2	2	.280	12	0	0	1.000
World Series Totals—5 Years		26	92	19	23	2	1	8	14	.250	43	0	0	1.000

JACK ROOSEVELT (JACKIE) ROBINSON

Born January 31, 1919, at Cairo, Ga.
Died October 24, 1972, at Stamford, Conn.
Height, 5.11½. Weight, 195.
Threw and batted righthanded.

First black player in modern major leagues, 1947.
Led National League in stolen bases with 29 in 1947 and 37 in 1949.
Led National League second basemen in double plays 1949-50-51-52.
Named by THE SPORTING NEWS as Rookie of the Year, 1947.
Named as second baseman on THE SPORTING NEWS All-Star Major League Teams, 1949-50-51-52.
Named National League Most Valuable Player, 1949.
Named to Hall of Fame, 1962.

Year Club League	Pos.	G.	AB.	R.	H.	2B.	3B.	HR.	RBI.	B.A.	PO.	A.	E.	F.A.
1946—Montreal .... Int.	2B	124	444	●113	155	25	8	3	66	★.349	261	385	10	★.985
1947—Brooklyn .... Nat.	1B	151	590	125	175	31	5	12	48	.297	1323	92	16	.989
1948—Brooklyn .... Nat.	★2B-1B-3B	147	574	108	170	38	8	12	85	.296	514	342	15	★.983
1949—Brooklyn .... Nat.	2B	156	593	122	203	38	12	16	124	★.342	395	421	16	.981
1950—Brooklyn .... Nat.	2B	144	518	99	170	39	4	14	81	.328	359	390	11	★.986
1951—Brooklyn .... Nat.	2B	153	548	106	185	33	7	19	88	.338	★390	★435	7	★.992
1952—Brooklyn .... Nat.	2B	149	510	104	157	17	3	19	75	.308	353	400	20	.974
1953—Brooklyn .... Nat.	INF-OF	136	484	109	159	34	7	12	95	.329	238	126	6	.984
1954—Brooklyn .... Nat.	INF-OF	124	386	62	120	22	4	15	59	.311	166	109	7	.975
1955—Brooklyn .... Nat.	INF-OF	105	317	51	81	6	2	8	36	.256	100	183	10	.966
1956—Brooklyn(a) .... Nat.	INF-OF	117	357	61	98	15	2	10	43	.275	169	230	9	.978
Major League Totals—10 Years..............		1382	4877	947	1518	273	54	137	734	.311	4007	2728	117	.983

aTraded to New York Giants for Pitcher Dick Littlefield and reported $35,000, December 13, 1956; Robinson announced retirement from game, January 5, 1957, canceling trade.

WORLD SERIES RECORD

Shares record for most bases on balls, game (4), October 5, 1952, 11 innings.

Year Club League	Pos.	G.	AB.	R.	H.	2B.	3B.	HR.	RBI.	B.A.	PO.	A.	E.	F.A.
1947—Brooklyn .... Nat.	1B	7	27	3	7	2	0	0	3	.259	49	6	0	1.000
1949—Brooklyn .... Nat.	2B	5	16	2	3	1	0	0	2	.188	12	9	1	.955
1952—Brooklyn .... Nat.	2B	7	23	4	4	0	0	1	2	.174	10	20	0	1.000
1953—Brooklyn .... Nat.	OF	6	25	3	8	2	0	0	2	.320	8	0	0	1.000
1955—Brooklyn .... Nat.	3B	6	22	5	4	1	1	0	1	.182	4	18	2	.917
1956—Brooklyn .... Nat.	3B	7	24	5	6	1	0	1	2	.250	5	12	0	1.000
World Series Totals—6 Years		38	137	22	32	7	1	2	12	.234	88	65	3	.981

WILBERT ROBINSON
(Uncle Robbie)

Born June 2, 1864, at Hudson, Mass.
Died August 8, 1934, at Atlanta, Ga.
Height, 5.08½. Weight, 215.
Threw and batted righthanded.

Shares major league record for most hits, nine-inning game (7), June 10, 1892.
Manager, Baltimore Orioles, 1902; Baltimore, Eastern League, 1903 to 1904; coach, New York Giants, 1911 to 1913; manager, Brooklyn Dodgers, 1914 through 1925; president-manager, Brooklyn, 1926 through 1929; manager, Brooklyn, 1930 to 1931; president-manager, Atlanta, Southern Association, 1933; president, 1934.
Named to Hall of Fame, 1945.

Year Club League	Pos.	G.	AB.	R.	H.	2B.	3B.	HR.	SB.	B.A.	PO.	A.	E.	F.A.
1885—Haverhill................ N.E.		73	305	56	82	...	...	...	....	.269	.....	...	...	......
1886—Athletics................. A.A.	C-1B	87	342	55	70	12	3	1	42	.205	243	106	23	.938
1887—Athletics................. A.A.	C	68	273	30	78	7	3	0	19	.286	358	82	39	.919
1888—Athletics................. A.A.	C	67	250	30	67	7	2	1	15	.268	409	112	20	.963
1889—Athletics................. A.A.	C	69	260	31	63	13	2	0	9	.242	290	107	26	.939
1890—Ath.-Baltimore ..... A.A.	C-1B	97	361	34	87	14	4	4	25	.241	472	115	40	.936
1891—Baltimore .... A.A.	C	62	216	20	45	7	5	2	10	.208	278	56	16	.954
1892—Baltimore .... Nat.	C	83	329	36	89	13	5	2	12	.271	326	87	33	.926
1893—Baltimore .... Nat.	C	91	349	49	118	22	3	3	16	.338	★348	73	27	.940
1894—Baltimore .... Nat.	C	106	420	71	146	21	4	1	13	.348	364	96	24	.950
1895—Baltimore .... Nat.	C	74	287	40	76	18	2	0	12	.265	242	77	7	.979
1896—Baltimore .... Nat.	C	66	243	43	86	8	7	2	11	.354	260	46	14	.956
1897—Baltimore .... Nat.	C	47	182	25	57	8	0	0	0	.313	185	36	8	.965
1898—Baltimore .... Nat.	C	77	286	29	79	13	1	0	2	.276	291	70	12	.949
1899—Baltimore .... Nat.	C	105	355	40	101	16	2	0	3	.285	287	82	20	.948
1900—St. Louis................. Nat.	C	56	212	26	54	4	1	0	9	.255	199	74	6	.978
1901—Baltimore .... Amer.	C	71	241	34	72	13	3	0	9	.299	239	60	15	.952
1902—Baltimore .... Amer.	C	90	336	39	98	14	7	1	12	.292	264	78	16	.972
1903—Baltimore .... East.	C	75	241	15	64	5	2	3	2	.266	326	54	7	.982
1904—Baltimore .... East.	C	32	93	8	22	3	0	0	3	.237	155	36	3	.985
American Assn. Totals—6 Years		450	1702	200	410	60	19	8	120	.241	2050	578	164	.941
American League Totals—2 Years		161	577	73	170	27	10	1	21	.295	503	138	31	.954
National League Totals—9 Years..........		705	2663	359	806	123	25	8	78	.303	2502	641	151	.954
Major League Totals—17 Years.............		1316	4942	632	1386	210	54	17	219	.280	5055	1357	346	.949

CHARLES HENRY (CHARLEY) ROOT

Born March 17, 1899, at Middletown, O.
Died November 5, 1970, at Hollister, Calif.
Height, 5.10½. Weight, 189.
Threw and batted righthanded.

Named as pitcher on THE SPORTING NEWS All-Star Major League Team, 1927.
Manager, Hollywood, Pacific Coast, 1943-44; Columbus, American Association, 1945-46; Billings, Pioneer, 1948; coach, Hollywood, Pacific Coast, 1949; manager, Des Moines, Western, 1950; coach, Chicago Cubs, 1951-52-53.

Year Club League	G.	IP.	W.	L.	Pct.	H.	R.	ER.	SO.	BB.	ERA.
1921—Terre Haute................I. I. I.	26	159	8	7	.533	163	80	63	75	40	3.57
1922—Terre Haute................I. I. I.	43	249	16	14	.533	208	92	63	155	68	2.28
1923—St. Louis....................American	27	60	0	4	.000	68	45	38	27	18	5.70
1924—Los Angeles ....Pac. Coast	55	322	21	16	.568	316	161	132	199	102	3.69
1925—Los Angeles ....Pac. Coast	52	324	25	13	.658	268	121	103	211	91	2.86
1926—Chicago ....National	42	271	18	●17	.514	267	104	85	127	62	2.82
1927—Chicago ....National	●48	★309	★26	15	.624	296	148	129	145	★117	3.76
1928—Chicago ....National	40	237	14	18	.438	214	109	94	122	73	3.57
1929—Chicago ....National	43	272	19	6	★.760	286	120	105	124	83	3.47
1930—Chicago ....National	37	220	16	14	.533	247	122	106	124	63	4.34
1931—Chicago ....National	39	251	17	14	.548	240	109	97	131	71	3.48
1932—Chicago ....National	39	216	15	10	.600	211	99	86	96	55	3.58
1933—Chicago ....National	35	242	15	10	.600	232	85	70	86	61	2.60

Year Club	League	G.	IP.	W.	L.	Pct.	H.	R.	ER.	SO.	BB.	ERA.
1934—Chicago	National	34	118	4	7	.364	141	62	56	46	53	4.27
1935—Chicago	National	38	201	15	8	.652	193	85	69	94	47	3.09
1936—Chicago	National	33	74	3	6	.333	81	34	34	32	20	4.14
1937—Chicago	National	43	179	13	5	.722	173	71	67	74	32	3.37
1938—Chicago	National	44	161	8	7	.533	163	62	51	70	30	2.85
1939—Chicago	National	35	167	8	8	.500	189	83	75	65	34	4.04
1940—Chicago	National	36	112	2	4	.333	118	61	48	50	33	3.86
1941—Chicago(a)	National	19	107	8	7	.533	133	68	64	46	37	5.38
1942—Hollywood	Pac. Coast	30	215	11	14	.440	205	95	76	103	39	3.18
1943—Hollywood	Pac. Coast	25	166	15	5	.750	170	63	57	70	28	3.09
1944—Hollywood	Pac. Coast	21	87	3	5	.375	91	55	31	58	28	3.20
1945—Columbus	Amer. Assn.	22	121	9	8	.529	112	40	34	64	20	2.53
1946—Columbus	Amer. Assn.	5	23	3	0	1.000	27	5	4	10	5	1.57
1948—Billings	Pioneer	5	3	0	1	.000	4	4	4	3	4	12.00
National League Totals—16 Years		605	3137	201	156	.563	3184	1422	1236	1432	871	3.55
American League Totals—1 Year		27	60	0	4	.000	68	45	38	27	18	5.70
Major League Totals—17 Years		632	3197	201	160	.557	3252	1467	1274	1459	889	3.59

aReleased October 8, 1941.

WORLD SERIES RECORD

Year Club	League	G.	IP.	W.	L.	Pct.	H.	R.	ER.	SO.	BB.	ERA.
1929—Chicago	National	2	13⅓	0	1	.000	12	7	7	8	2	4.73
1932—Chicago	National	1	4⅓	0	1	.000	6	6	5	4	3	10.38
1935—Chicago	National	2	2	0	1	.000	5	4	4	2	1	18.00
1938—Chicago	National	1	3	0	0	.000	3	1	1	1	0	3.00
World Series Totals—4 Years		6	22⅔	0	3	.000	26	18	17	15	6	6.75

PETER EDWARD (PETE) ROSE
(Charley Hustle)

Born April 14, 1941, at Cincinnati, O.

Height, 5.11. Weight, 203.

Threw right and batted right and lefthanded.

Brother of David Rose, former minor league pitcher.

Holds major league records for most games, lifetime (3,562); most singles, lifetime (3,215); most seasons and most consecutive seasons, 100 or more games (23); most seasons, 200 or more hits (10); most seasons, 150 or more games (17); most at-bats, lifetime (14,053); most plate appearances, lifetime (15,890); most consecutive seasons, 600 or more at-bats (13); most seasons, 600 or more at-bats (17); most plate appearances, season (771), 1974; most hits, lifetime (4,256); most doubles by switch-hitter, season (51), 1978.

Shares major league records for most consecutive seasons leading major leagues in runs scored (3); fewest sacrifice flies, season, most at-bats (0 and 680), 1973; most hits by switch-hitter, season (230), 1973; most games, first baseman, season (162), 1980 and 1982; most stolen bases, inning (3), May 11, 1980, seventh inning.

Holds National League records for most years and most consecutive years played (24); most years playing in all clubs' games (10); most runs, lifetime (2,165); most seasons leading league in hits (7); most doubles, lifetime (746); most singles by switch-hitter, season (181), 1973; fewest stolen bases, season, most at-bats (0 and 662), 1975; most times five or more hits in one game, lifetime (10).

Shares modern National League records for most consecutive games, one or more hits, season (44), 1978; most seasons leading league in at-bats (4).

Holds modern National League record for most 20-game hitting streaks, lifetime (7).

Shares modern National League records for most seasons leading league in fielding percentage by outfielder, 100 or more games (3); most consecutive years leading league in fielding percentage by outfielder, 100 or more games (2).

Hit three home runs in a game, April 29, 1978.

Tied for National League lead in being hit by pitch with 6 in 1980.

Led Florida State League in total bases with 246 in 1961.

Named Player of the Decade for 1970-79 by THE SPORTING NEWS.

Named Man of the Year by THE SPORTING NEWS, 1985.

Named National League Player of the Year by THE SPORTING NEWS, 1968.

Named National League Most Valuable Player by Baseball Writers' Association of America, 1973.

Named National League Rookie Player of the Year by THE SPORTING NEWS, 1963.

Named National League Rookie of the Year by Baseball Writers' Association of America, 1963.

Named first baseman on THE SPORTING NEWS National League All-Star Team, 1981.

Named third baseman on THE SPORTING NEWS National League All-Star Team, 1978.

Named outfielder on THE SPORTING NEWS National League All-Star Team, 1968 and 1973.

Named second baseman on THE SPORTING NEWS National League All-Star Team, 1965 and 1966.

Named outfielder on THE SPORTING NEWS National League All-Star fielding team, 1969 and 1970.

Named first baseman on THE SPORTING NEWS National League Silver Slugger team, 1981.

Manager, Cincinnati Reds, 1984 to 1989.

Year Club	League	Pos.	G.	AB.	R.	H.	2B.	3B.	HR.	RBI.	B.A.	PO.	A.	E.	F.A.
1960—Geneva	NYP	2B	85	321	60	89	8	5	1	43	.277	198	193	*36	.916
1961—Tampa	Fla. St.	2B	130	484	105	*160	20	*30	2	77	.331	256	294	21	.963

Year	Club	League	Pos.	G.	AB.	R.	H.	2B.	3B.	HR.	RBI.	B.A.	PO.	A.	E.	F.A.
1962—Macon	Sally		2B	139	540	★136	178	31	★17	9	71	.330	317	368	24	.966
1963—Cincinnati	Nat.		2B-OF	157	623	101	170	25	9	6	41	.273	360	366	22	.971
1964—Cincinnati	Nat.		2B	136	516	64	139	13	2	4	34	.269	263	301	12	.979
1965—Cincinnati	Nat.		2B	162	★670	117	★209	35	11	11	81	.312	★382	403	20	.975
1966—Cincinnati	Nat.		2B-3B	156	654	97	205	38	5	16	70	.313	409	374	18	.978
1967—Cincinnati	Nat.		OF-2B	148	585	86	176	32	8	12	76	.301	287	93	11	.972
1968—Cincinnati	Nat.		●O-2-1	149	626	94	●210	42	6	10	49	★.335	270	●20	3	.990
1969—Cincinnati	Nat.		OF-2B	156	627	●120	218	33	11	16	82	★.348	317	10	4	.988
1970—Cincinnati	Nat.		OF	159	649	120	●205	37	9	15	52	.316	309	8	1	★.997
1971—Cincinnati	Nat.		OF	160	632	86	192	27	4	13	44	.304	306	13	2	●.994
1972—Cincinnati	Nat.		OF	★154	★645	107	★198	31	11	6	57	.307	330	●15	2	.994
1973—Cincinnati	Nat.		OF	160	★680	115	★230	36	8	5	64	★.338	343	15	3	.992
1974—Cincinnati	Nat.		OF	★163	652	★110	185	★45	7	3	51	.284	346	11	1	★.997
1975—Cincinnati	Nat.		3B-OF	●162	662	★112	210	★47	4	7	74	.317	161	230	14	.965
1976—Cincinnati	Nat.		★3B-OF	162	665	★130	★215	★42	6	10	63	.323	115	293	13	★.969
1977—Cincinnati	Nat.		3B	●162	★655	95	204	38	7	9	64	.311	98	268	16	.958
1978—Cincinnati†	Nat.		3B-OF-1B	159	655	103	198	★51	3	7	52	.302	135	256	15	.963
1979—Philadelphia	Nat.		1B-3B-2B	163	628	90	208	40	5	4	59	.331	1429	93	10	.993
1980—Philadelphia	Nat.		1B	162	655	95	185	★42	1	1	64	.282	1427	★123	5	★.997
1981—Philadelphia	Nat.		1B	107	431	73	★140	18	5	0	33	.325	929	91	4	.996
1982—Philadelphia	Nat.		1B	●162	634	80	172	25	4	3	54	.271	1428	123	8	.995
1983—Philadelphia‡	Nat.		1B-OF	151	493	52	121	14	3	0	45	.245	827	74	10	.989
1984—Mont.§-Cin.	Nat.		1B-OF	121	374	43	107	15	2	0	34	.286	530	53	8	.986
1985—Cincinnati	Nat.		1B	119	405	60	107	12	2	2	46	.264	870	73	5	.995
1986—Cincinnati x	Nat.		1B	72	237	15	52	8	2	0	25	.219	523	43	6	.990
Major League Totals—24 Years				3562	14053	2165	4256	746	135	160	1314	.303	12394	3349	213	.987

Signed as free agent by Cincinnati Reds' organization, July 8, 1960.
†Granted free agency, November 2, 1978; signed by Philadelphia Phillies, December 5, 1978.
‡Released, October 19, 1983; signed by Montreal Expos, January 20, 1984.
§Traded to Cincinnati Reds for Infielder Tom Lawless, August 16, 1984.
xReleased as player, November 11, 1986.

CHAMPIONSHIP SERIES RECORD

Holds major league records for most hits (45) and singles (34), lifetime; longest hitting streak, lifetime (15 games), October 8, 1973 through October 4, 1983.

Shares major league record for most doubles, lifetime (7) and series (4), 1972.

Holds National League records for most games (28), at-bats (118), runs (17) and total bases (63), lifetime; highest batting average, lifetime, 50 or more at-bats (.381).

Shares National League record for most singles, series (8), 1980.

Year	Club	League	Pos.	G.	AB.	R.	H.	2B.	3B.	HR.	RBI.	B.A.	PO.	A.	E.	F.A.
1970—Cincinnati	Nat.		OF	3	13	1	3	0	0	0	1	.231	3	0	0	1.000
1972—Cincinnati	Nat.		OF	5	20	1	9	4	0	0	2	.450	10	0	0	1.000
1973—Cincinnati	Nat.		OF	5	21	3	8	1	0	2	2	.381	10	1	0	1.000
1975—Cincinnati	Nat.		3B	3	14	3	5	0	0	1	2	.357	2	1	0	1.000
1976—Cincinnati	Nat.		3B	3	14	3	6	2	1	0	2	.429	2	5	1	.875
1980—Philadelphia	Nat.		1B	5	20	3	8	0	0	0	2	.400	53	7	0	1.000
1983—Philadelphia	Nat.		1B	4	16	3	6	0	0	0	0	.375	29	2	0	1.000
Championship Series Totals—7 Years				28	118	17	45	7	1	3	11	.381	109	16	1	.992

WORLD SERIES RECORD

Year	Club	League	Pos.	G.	AB.	R.	H.	2B.	3B.	HR.	RBI.	B.A.	PO.	A.	E.	F.A.
1970—Cincinnati	Nat.		OF	5	20	2	5	1	0	1	2	.250	14	1	1	.938
1972—Cincinnati	Nat.		OF	7	28	3	6	0	0	1	2	.214	14	1	0	1.000
1975—Cincinnati	Nat.		3B	7	27	3	10	1	1	0	2	.370	7	9	0	1.000
1976—Cincinnati	Nat.		3B	4	16	1	3	1	0	0	1	.188	6	3	0	1.000
1980—Philadelphia	Nat.		1B	6	23	2	6	1	0	0	1	.261	49	6	0	1.000
1983—Philadelphia	Nat.		PH-1B-OF	5	16	1	5	1	0	0	1	.313	26	4	0	1.000
World Series Totals—6 Years				34	130	12	35	5	1	2	9	.269	116	24	1	.993

EDD J. ROUSH

Born May 8, 1893, at Oakland City, Ind.

Died March 21, 1988, at Bradenton, Fla.

Height, 5.11   Weight, 175.

Threw and batted lefthanded.

Coach, Cincinnati Reds, 1938.
Named to Hall of Fame, 1962.

Year	Club	League	Pos.	G.	AB.	R.	H.	2B.	3B.	HR.	RBI.	B.A.	PO.	A.	E.	F.A.
1912—Evansville	Kitty	OF	41	148	17	43	7	4	2	.....	.284	37	2	2	.951
1913—Evansville	Central	OF	89	344	42	109	26	6	5	.....	.317	157	9	6	.965
1913—Chicago	Amer.	OF-PH-PR	9	10	2	1	0	0	0	0	.100	3	0	0	1.000
1913—Lincoln	West.	OF	10	35	.....	6	1	0	0	.....	.171	14	0	0	1.000
1914—Indianapolis	Federal	OF	74	165	26	55	6	5	1	.....	.333	85	5	1	.989
1915—Newark	Federal	OF	145	550	73	164	22	10	3	.....	.298	332	15	8	.977
1916—N.Y.(a)-Cin.	Nat.	OF	108	341	38	91	7	15	0	19	.267	210	9	7	.969
1917—Cincinnati	Nat.	OF	136	522	82	178	19	14	4	62	★.341	335	15	14	.962
1918—Cincinnati	Nat.	OF	113	435	61	145	18	10	5	61	.333	320	13	14	.960
1919—Cincinnati	Nat.	OF	133	504	73	162	19	13	3	69	★.321	385	22	4	.989
1920—Cincinnati	Nat.	★OF-2B-1B	149	579	81	196	22	16	4	90	.339	★410	18	11	★.975
1921—Cincinnati	Nat.	OF	112	418	68	147	27	12	4	71	.352	286	9	6	.980
1922—Cincinnati	Nat.	OF	49	165	29	58	7	4	1	24	.352	96	8	1	.990
1923—Cincinnati	Nat.	OF	138	527	88	185	★41	18	6	88	.351	337	14	11	.970
1924—Cincinnati	Nat.	OF	121	483	67	168	23	★21	3	72	.348	270	10	12	.959
1925—Cincinnati	Nat.	OF	134	540	91	183	28	16	8	83	.339	343	15	8	.978
1926—Cincinnati(b)	Nat.	OF-1B	144	563	95	182	37	10	7	70	.323	304	12	15	.955
1927—New York	Nat.	OF	140	570	83	173	27	4	7	58	.304	327	19	9	.975
1928—New York	Nat.	OF	46	163	20	41	5	3	2	13	.252	100	7	5	.955
1929—New York	Nat.	OF	115	450	76	146	19	7	8	52	.324	248	18	5	.982
1930—New York(c)	Nat.	.....	.....	.....	.....	.....	.....	.....	.....	.....	.....	.....	.....	.....	.....
1931—Cincinnati	Nat.	OF	101	376	46	102	12	5	1	41	.271	197	5	4	.981
American League Totals—1 Year			9	10	2	1	0	0	0	0	.100	3	0	0	1.000
National League Totals—15 Years			1739	6636	998	2157	311	168	63	882	.325	4118	194	126	.972
Major League Totals—16 Years			1748	6646	1000	2158	311	168	63	882	.325	4121	194	126	.972

aTraded with Pitcher Christy Mathewson and Third Baseman Bill McKechnie to Cincinnati for Infielder Buck Herzog and Outfielder Wade Killefer, July 20, 1916.

bTraded to New York Giants for First Baseman George Kelly, January, 1927.

cReleased to Cincinnati, March, 1931.

WORLD SERIES RECORD

Year	Club	League	Pos.	G.	AB.	R.	H.	2B.	3B.	HR.	RBI.	B.A.	PO.	A.	E.	F.A.
1919—Cincinnati	Nat.	OF	8	28	6	6	2	1	0	7	.214	30	3	2	.943

CHARLES HERBERT (RED) RUFFING

Born May 5, 1905, at Granville, Ill.

Died February 17, 1986, at Cleveland, O.

Height, 6.01½. Weight, 210.

Threw and batted righthanded.

Led American League pitchers in shutouts with 5 in 1939.

Named by Baseball Writers' Association of America for THE SPORTING NEWS All-Star Major League Teams, 1937-38-39.

Named to Hall of Fame, 1967.

Year	Club	League	G.	IP.	W.	L.	Pct.	H.	R.	ER.	SO.	BB.	ERA.
1923—Danville	I.I.I.	39	239	12	16	.429	251	142	.....	88	89	.....
1924—Boston	Amer.	8	23	0	0	.000	29	17	17	10	9	6.65
1924—Dover	East. Shore	15	94	4	7	.364	98	42	.....	72	23	.....
1925—Boston	Amer.	37	217	9	18	.333	253	135	121	64	75	5.02
1926—Boston	Amer.	37	166	6	15	.286	169	98	81	58	68	4.39
1927—Boston	Amer.	26	158	5	13	.278	160	94	82	77	87	4.67
1928—Boston	Amer.	42	289	10	★25	.286	303	★147	★125	118	96	3.89
1929—Boston	Amer.	35	244	9	★22	.290	280	★162	★132	109	118	4.87
1930—Boston(a)-New York	Amer.	38	222	15	8	.652	242	125	108	131	68	4.38
1931—New York	Amer.	37	237	16	14	.533	240	130	116	132	87	4.41
1932—New York	Amer.	35	259	18	7	.720	219	102	89	★190	115	3.09
1933—New York	Amer.	35	235	9	14	.391	230	118	102	122	93	3.91
1934—New York	Amer.	36	256	19	11	.633	232	134	112	149	104	3.94
1935—New York	Amer.	30	222	16	11	.593	201	88	77	81	76	3.12
1936—New York	Amer.	33	271	20	12	.625	274	133	116	102	90	3.85
1937—New York	Amer.	31	256	20	7	.741	242	101	85	131	68	2.99
1938—New York	Amer.	31	247	★21	7	★.750	246	104	91	127	82	3.32
1939—New York	Amer.	28	233	21	7	.750	211	88	76	95	75	2.94
1940—New York	Amer.	30	226	15	12	.556	218	98	85	97	76	3.38
1941—New York	Amer.	23	186	15	6	.714	177	87	73	60	54	3.53
1942—New York(b)	Amer.	24	194	14	7	.667	183	72	69	80	41	3.20
1943-44—New York	Amer.						(In Military Service)					
1945—New York	Amer.	11	87	7	3	.700	85	32	28	24	20	2.90
1946—New York(c)	Amer.	8	61	5	1	.833	37	13	12	19	23	1.77
1947—Chicago	Amer.	9	53	3	5	.375	63	39	36	11	16	6.11
Major League Totals—22 Years		624	4342	273	225	.548	4294	2117	1833	1987	1541	3.80

bInducted into U. S. Army Air Forces, December 29, 1942; returned to lineup July 16, 1945.
cReleased by New York Yankees, September 20, 1946; signed with Chicago White Sox, December 6, 1946.

WORLD SERIES RECORD

Year Club	League	G.	IP.	W.	L.	Pct.	H.	R.	ER.	SO.	BB.	ERA.
1932—New York	Amer.	1	9	1	0	1.000	10	6	4	10	6	4.00
1936—New York	Amer.	2	14	0	1	.000	16	10	7	12	5	4.50
1937—New York	Amer.	1	9	1	0	1.000	7	1	1	8	3	1.00
1938—New York	Amer.	2	18	2	0	1.000	17	4	3	11	2	1.50
1939—New York	Amer.	1	9	1	0	1.000	4	1	1	4	1	1.00
1941—New York	Amer.	1	9	1	0	1.000	6	2	1	5	3	1.00
1942—New York	Amer.	2	17⅔	1	1	.500	14	8	8	11	7	4.08
World Series Totals—7 Years		10	85⅔	7	2	.778	74	32	25	61	27	2.63

AMOS WILSON RUSIE

Born May 31, 1871, at Indianapolis, Ind.

Died December 6, 1942, at Seattle, Wash.

Height, 6.01. Weight, 210.

Threw and batted righthanded.

Pitched 6-0 no-hit victory against Brooklyn, July 31, 1891.
Named to Hall of Fame, 1977.

Year Club	League	G.	W.	L.	Pct.	H.	R.	SO.	BB.	ShO.
1889—Indianapolis	National	23	13	10	.565	237	176	113	128	1
1890—New York	National	60	29	30	.492	414	296	★345	★276	4
1891—New York	National	54	32	19	.627	373	233	★321	★236	★6
1892—New York	National	62	31	28	.525	387	266	★303	★261	2
1893—New York	National	★48	29	18	.617	401	220	★208	★196	●4
1894—New York	National	49	★36	13	.735	395	208	★204	★189	●3
1895—New York	National	43	22	21	.512	369	219	★199	159	●4
1896—New York	National					(Holdout all season)				
1897—New York	National	37	29	8	★.784	304	141	140	86	●3
1898—New York	National	33	20	10	.667	272	134	114	103	4
1899-1900—New York(a)	National					(Under suspension)				
1901—Cincinnati	National	3	0	1	.000	25	15	6	3	0
Major League Totals—10 Years		412	241	158	.604	3177	1908	1953	1637	31

aTraded to Cincinnati for Pitcher Christy Mathewson.

GEORGE HERMAN (BABE) RUTH
(The Bambino and The Sultan of Swat)

Born February 6, 1895, at Baltimore, Md.

Died August 16, 1948, at New York, N. Y.

Height, 6:02. Weight, 215.

Threw and batted lefthanded.

Holds major league record for highest slugging percentage, season (.847), 1920 and lifetime (.692); most years leading league in slugging percentage (13); most years leading league in runs (8); most home runs by lefthanded batter (714) and outfielder (692); lifetime; most years leading league in home runs (12); most total bases, season (457), 1921; most bases on balls, season (170), 1923 and lifetime (2,056); most years leading league in bases on balls (11).

Shares major league records for most consecutive years leading league in runs (3); most times with two or more home runs in a game (72); most consecutive games with grand slam (2), September 27, 29, 1927 and August 6, second game, 7, first game, 1929.

Holds American League records for most runs, season (177), 1921; most home runs, lifetime (708); most consecutive years leading league in home runs (6); most long hits, season (119), 1921 and lifetime (1,350); most extra bases on long hits, season (253), 1921 and lifetime (2,902); most runs batted in, lifetime (2,192).

Hit three home runs in a game, May 21, 1930 first game and May 25, 1935.

Named American League Most Valuable Player, 1923.

Named as Outfielder on THE SPORTING NEWS All-Star Major League Teams, 1926-27-28-29-30-31.

Coach, Brooklyn Dodgers, 1938.

Named to Hall of Fame, 1936.

Year	Club	League	Pos.	G.	AB.	R.	H.	2B.	3B.	HR.	RBI.	B.A.	PO.	A.	E.	F.A.
1914—Balt.-Prov		Int.	P-OF	46	121	22	28	2	10	1	....	.231	20	87	4	.964
1914—Boston		Amer.	P	5	10	1	2	1	0	0	0	.200	0	8	0	1.000
1915—Boston		Amer.	P	42	92	16	29	10	1	4	20	.315	17	63	2	.976
1916—Boston		Amer.	P	67	136	18	37	5	3	3	16	.272	24	83	3	.973
1917—Boston		Amer.	P	52	123	14	40	6	3	2	10	.325	19	101	2	.984
1918—Boston		Amer.	OF-P-1	95	317	50	95	26	11	●11	64	.300	270	72	18	.950
1919—Boston(a)		Amer.	★OF-P	130	432	★103	139	34	12	★29	★112	.322	270	53	4	★.988
1920—New York		Amer.	OF-1-P	142	458	★158	172	36	9	★54	★137	.376	270	21	20	.936
1921—New York		Amer.	OF-1-P	152	540	★177	204	44	16	★59	★171	.378	357	19	13	.967
1922—New York		Amer.	OF-1B	110	406	94	128	24	8	35	99	.315	226	14	9	.964
1923—New York		Amer.	OF-1B	152	520	★151	205	45	13	★41	★131	.394	419	21	12	.973
1924—New York		Amer.	OF	153	529	★143	200	39	7	★46	121	★.378	340	19	14	.962
1925—New York		Amer.	OF	98	359	61	104	12	2	25	66	.290	207	15	6	.974
1926—New York		Amer.	OF-1B	152	495	★139	184	30	5	★47	★145	.372	318	11	7	.979
1927—New York		Amer.	OF	151	540	★158	192	29	8	★60	164	.356	328	14	13	.963
1928—New York		Amer.	OF	154	536	★163	173	29	8	★54	●142	.323	304	9	8	.975
1929—New York		Amer.	OF	135	499	121	172	26	6	★46	154	.345	240	5	4	.984
1930—New York		Amer.	OF-P	145	518	150	186	28	9	★49	153	.359	266	14	10	.966
1931—New York		Amer.	OF-1B	145	534	149	199	31	3	●46	163	.373	242	5	7	.972
1932—New York		Amer.	OF-1B	133	457	120	156	13	5	41	137	.341	212	10	9	.961
1933—New York		Amer.	OF-P	137	459	97	138	21	3	34	103	.301	222	10	8	.967
1934—New York(b)		Amer.	OF	125	365	78	105	17	4	22	84	.288	197	3	8	.962
1935—Boston		Nat.	OF	28	72	13	13	0	0	6	12	.181	39	1	2	.952
American League Totals—21 Years				2475	8325	2161	2860	506	136	708	2192	.344	4748	570	177	.968
National League Totals—1 Year				28	72	13	13	0	0	6	12	.181	39	1	2	.952
Major League Totals—22 Years				2503	8397	2174	2873	506	136	714	2204	.342	4787	571	179	.968

aSold to New York Yankees for $125,000, January 3, 1920.
bReleased to Boston Braves, February 26, 1935.

WORLD SERIES RECORD

Holds record for highest batting average, series (.625), 1928.
Shares records for most runs, game (4); most home runs (3) and total bases (12), game, October 6, 1926 and October 9, 1928; most bases on balls, series (11), 1926.

Year	Club	League	Pos.	G.	AB.	R.	H.	2B.	3B.	HR.	RBI.	B.A.	PO.	A.	E.	F.A.
1915—Boston		Amer.	PH	1	1	0	0	0	0	0	0	.000	0	0	0	.000
1916—Boston		Amer.	P	1	5	0	0	0	0	0	1	.000	2	4	0	1.000
1918—Boston		Amer.	P-OF	3	5	0	1	0	1	0	2	.200	1	5	0	1.000
1921—New York		Amer.	OF	6	16	3	5	0	0	1	4	.313	9	0	0	1.000
1922—New York		Amer.	OF	5	17	1	2	1	0	0	1	.118	9	0	0	1.000
1923—New York		Amer.	O-1B	6	19	8	7	1	1	3	3	.368	17	0	1	.944
1926—New York		Amer.	OF	7	20	6	6	0	0	4	5	.300	8	2	0	1.000
1927—New York		Amer.	OF	4	15	4	6	0	0	2	7	.400	10	0	0	1.000
1928—New York		Amer.	OF	4	16	9	10	3	0	3	4	.625	9	1	0	1.000
1932—New York		Amer.	OF	4	15	6	5	0	0	2	6	.333	8	0	1	.889
World Series Totals—10 Years				41	129	37	42	5	2	15	33	.326	73	12	2	.977

PITCHING RECORD

Year	Club	League	G.	IP.	W.	L.	Pct.	H.	R.	ER.	SO.	BB.	ERA.
1914—Balti.-Providence		Int.	35	245	22	9	.710	219	88	....	139	101	......
1914—Boston		Amer.	4	23	2	1	.667	21	12	10	3	7	3.91
1915—Boston		Amer.	32	218	18	8	.692	166	80	59	112	85	2.44
1916—Boston		Amer.	44	324	23	12	.657	230	83	63	170	118	★1.75
1917—Boston		Amer.	41	326	24	13	.649	244	93	73	128	108	2.02
1918—Boston		Amer.	20	166	13	7	.650	125	51	41	40	49	2.22
1919—Boston		Amer.	17	133	9	5	.643	148	59	44	30	58	2.97
1920—New York		Amer.	1	4	1	0	1.000	3	4	2	0	2	4.50
1921—New York		Amer.	2	9	2	0	1.000	14	10	9	2	9	9.00
1930—New York		Amer.	1	9	1	0	1.000	11	3	3	3	2	3.00
1933—New York		Amer.	1	9	1	0	1.000	12	5	5	0	3	5.00
Major League Totals—10 Years			163	1221	94	46	.671	974	400	309	488	441	2.28

WORLD SERIES PITCHING RECORD

Year	Club	League	G.	IP.	W.	L.	Pct.	H.	R.	ER.	SO.	BB.	ERA.
1916—Boston		Amer.	1	14	1	0	1.000	6	1	1	4	3	0.64
1918—Boston		Amer.	2	17	2	0	1.000	13	2	2	4	7	1.06
World Series Totals—2 Years			3	31	3	0	1.000	19	3	3	8	10	0.87

—DID YOU KNOW—

That Hall of Famer Amos Rusie still ranks as the youngest pitcher in major league history to throw a no-hitter of nine or more innings? The former New York Giants right-hander, just two months short of his 20th birthday, held Brooklyn hitless in a 6-0 victory on July 31, 1891.

JAMES E. (JIMMY) RYAN

Born February 11, 1863, at Clinton, Mass.
Died October 28, 1923, at Chicago, Ill.
Height, 5.10. Weight, 175.
Threw and batted righthanded.

Manager, St. Paul, Western League, 1901; Chicago Springs, Western League, 1904.

Year Club League	Pos.	G.	AB.	R.	H.	2B.	3B.	HR.	SB.	B.A.	PO.	A.	E.	F.A.
1885—Bridgeport............ East.	OF-SS	29	120	18	26	4	2	0	...	.217			6	.878
1885—Chicago .... Nat.	OF-SS	3	13	2	6	1	0	0	...	.462	6	11	8	.680
1886—Chicago .... Nat.	OF-SS	84	327	58	100	21	6	3	10	.306	93	18	23	.828
1887—Chicago .... Nat.	OF-P	126	556	117	198	19	11	11	50	.356	164	33	33	.857
1888—Chicago .... Nat.	OF-P	130	549	115	★182	★37	7	13	60	.332	217	★34	35	.878
1889—Chicago .... Nat.	OF-SS	135	576	140	187	30	12	17	45	.325	286	133	57	.880
1890—Chicago .... Players	OF	118	497	101	164	31	7	7	30	.330	156	28	29	.864
1891—Chicago .... Nat.	OF	118	501	109	145	19	12	8	24	.289	234	★32	23	.920
1892—Chicago .... Nat.	OF	127	508	102	147	21	12	10	31	.289	235	37	25	.916
1893—Chicago .... Nat.	OF	82	332	82	101	19	7	3	8	.304	159	20	18	.909
1894—Chicago .... Nat.	OF	108	481	133	173	35	6	3	12	.360	222	23	26	.904
1895—Chicago .... Nat.	OF	108	443	83	143	20	9	6	15	.323	159	16	17	.911
1896—Chicago .... Nat.	OF	127	490	83	153	21	10	2	35	.312	207	26	20	.921
1897—Chicago .... Nat.	OF	135	518	104	160	30	17	5	35	.309	211	28	14	.945
1898—Chicago .... Nat.	OF	143	569	121	185	31	13	4	29	.325	269	21	●25	.921
1899—Chicago .... Nat.	OF	124	524	91	158	20	10	3	9	.302	264	17	13	.956
1900—Chicago .... Nat.	OF	106	416	66	115	26	4	5	17	.276	175	15	17	.918
1901—St. Paul .... West.	OF	108	443	77	143	13	6	5	21	.323	....	...	...	.....
1902—Washington .... Amer.	OF	120	482	92	153	32	6	6	13	.317	282	14	16	.949
1903—Washington .... Amer.	OF	114	436	41	107	26	4	7	11	.245	284	7	6	.980
American League Totals—2 Years		234	918	133	260	58	10	13	24	.283	566	21	22	.964
National League Totals—15 Years........		1656	6803	1406	2153	350	136	93	380	.316	2901	464	354	.905
Players League Totals—1 Year..............		118	497	101	164	31	7	7	30	.330	156	28	29	.864
Major League Totals—18 Years		2008	8218	1640	2577	439	153	113	434	.314	3623	513	405	.911

Pitching record: Pitched briefly in 1887 and 1888, won 5, lost 1.

RONALD EDWARD (RON) SANTO

Born February 25, 1940, at Seattle, Wash.
Height, 6;00. Weight, 194.
Threw and batted righthanded.

Holds major league records for most games by third baseman, season (164), 1965; most years leading league in chances accepted, third baseman (9).
Shares major league record for most years leading league in double plays, third baseman (6).
Holds National League record for most years leading league in games, third baseman (7).
Shares National League record for most years leading league in assists, third baseman (7).
Named third baseman on THE SPORTING NEWS National League All-Star Team, 1966-67-68-69-72.
Named third baseman on THE SPORTING NEWS National League All-Star Fielding Team, 1964-65-66-67-68.

Year Club League	Pos.	G.	AB.	R.	H.	2B.	3B.	HR.	RBI.	B.A.	PO.	A.	E.	F.A.
1959—San Antonio.......... Tex.	3B	136	505	82	165	★35	3	11	87	.327	★158	246	★53	.884
1960—Houston .... A. A.	3B	71	272	40	73	16	1	7	32	.268	72	148	16	.932
1960—Chicago .... Nat.	3B	95	347	44	87	24	2	9	44	.251	78	144	13	.945
1961—Chicago .... Nat.	3B	154	578	84	164	32	6	23	83	.284	157	307	★31	.937
1962—Chicago .... Nat.	★3B-SS	162	604	44	137	20	4	17	83	.227	★167	★343	★24	.955
1963—Chicago .... Nat.	3B	●162	630	79	187	29	6	25	99	.297	★136	★374	26	.951
1964—Chicago .... Nat.	3B	161	592	94	185	33	●13	30	114	.313	★156	★367	20	.963
1965—Chicago .... Nat.	3B	●164	608	88	173	30	4	33	101	.285	★155	★373	24	.957
1966—Chicago .... Nat.	★3B-SS	155	561	93	175	21	8	30	94	.312	★157	★408	★26	.956
1967—Chicago .... Nat.	3B	161	586	107	176	23	4	31	98	.300	★187	★393	26	.957
1968—Chicago .... Nat.	3B	162	577	86	142	17	3	26	98	.246	130	★378	15	★.971
1969—Chicago .... Nat.	3B	160	575	97	166	18	4	29	123	.289	★144	334	27	.947

Year Club	League	Pos.	G.	AB.	R.	H.	2B.	3B.	HR.	RBI.	B.A.	PO.	A.	E.	F.A.
1970—Chicago	Nat.	3B-OF	154	555	83	148	30	4	26	114	.267	144	320	27	.945
1971—Chicago	Nat.	3B-OF	154	555	77	148	22	1	21	88	.267	128	275	18	.957
1972—Chicago	Nat.	3-2-O-S	133	464	68	140	25	5	17	74	.302	119	282	22	.948
1973—Chicago (a)	Nat.	3B	149	536	65	143	29	2	20	77	.267	107	271	20	.950
1974—Chicago	Amer.	2-3-1-S	117	375	29	83	12	1	5	41	.221	135	148	8	.973
National League Totals—14 Years			2126	7768	1109	2171	353	66	337	1290	.279	1965	4569	319	.953
American League Totals—1 Year			117	375	29	83	12	1	5	41	.221	135	148	8	.973
Major League Totals—15 Years			2243	8143	1138	2254	365	67	342	1331	.277	2100	4717	327	.954

aTraded to Chicago White Sox for Pitchers Ken Frailing and Steve Stone, Catcher Steve Swisher and minor league Pitcher Jim Kremmel, December 11, 1973.

HENRY JOHN (HANK) SAUER

Born March 17, 1919, at Pittsburgh, Pa.

Height, 6.04. Weight, 200.

Threw and batted righthanded.

Brother of Ed Sauer, former major league outfielder.

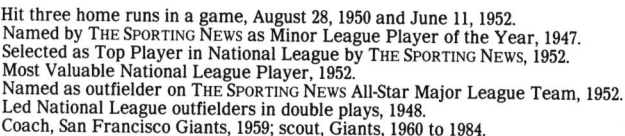

Hit three home runs in a game, August 28, 1950 and June 11, 1952.
Named by THE SPORTING NEWS as Minor League Player of the Year, 1947.
Selected as Top Player in National League by THE SPORTING NEWS, 1952.
Most Valuable National League Player, 1952.
Named as outfielder on THE SPORTING NEWS All-Star Major League Team, 1952.
Led National League outfielders in double plays, 1948.
Coach, San Francisco Giants, 1959; scout, Giants, 1960 to 1984.

Year Club	League	Pos.	G.	AB.	R.	H.	2B.	3B.	HR.	RBI.	B.A.	PO.	A.	E.	F.A.
1937—Butler	Penn. St.	1B	64	235	40	63	7	3	3	38	.268	592	30	14	.978
1938—Butler	Penn. St.	1B	●100	385	89	★135	★29	8	12	74	★.351	853	31	★26	.971
1939—Akron	Mid. Atl.	1B	127	472	87	142	31	8	13	92	.301	1263	54	16	★.988
1940—Birmingham	South.	1B-OF	118	384	47	112	17	10	9	79	.292	794	56	18	.979
1941—Birmingham	South.	1B	154	585	96	193	20	14	19	114	.330	1218	105	★26	.981
1941—Cincinnati	Nat.	OF	9	33	4	10	4	0	0	5	.303	21	1	1	.957
1942—Cincinnati	Nat.	1B	7	20	4	5	0	0	2	4	.250	37	4	1	.976
1942—Syracuse	Int.	OF	82	291	35	62	9	2	11	44	.213	136	4	6	.959
1943—Syracuse	Int.	1B-OF	★154	571	73	157	32	9	12	75	.275	1157	78	13	.990
1944-45—Cincinnati	Nat.						(In Military Service)								
1945—Cincinnati	Nat.	OF-1B	31	116	18	34	1	0	5	20	.293	100	5	3	.972
1946—Syracuse	Int.	OF	140	517	99	146	29	2	21	90	.282	264	10	6	.979
1947—Syracuse	Int.	OF	146	542	★130	★182	28	1	50	★141	.336	283	12	5	.983
1948—Cincinnati	Nat.	OF-1B	145	530	78	138	22	1	35	97	.260	359	22	9	.977
1949—Cin.(a)-Chicago	Nat.	●OF-1B	138	509	81	140	23	1	31	99	.275	302	●16	9	.972
1950—Chicago	Nat.	OF-1B	145	540	85	148	32	2	32	103	.274	381	29	13	.969
1951—Chicago	Nat.	OF	141	525	77	138	19	4	30	89	.263	286	19	6	.981
1952—Chicago	Nat.	OF	151	567	89	153	31	3	●37	★121	.270	327	17	6	.983
1953—Chicago	Nat.	OF	108	395	61	104	16	5	19	60	.263	221	5	7	.970
1954—Chicago	Nat.	OF	142	520	98	150	18	1	41	103	.288	282	8	11	.963
1955—Chicago (b)	Nat.	OF	79	261	29	55	8	1	12	28	.211	122	4	2	.984
1956—St. Louis (c)	Nat.	OF	75	151	11	45	4	0	5	24	.298	55	2	0	1.000
1957—New York	Nat.	OF	127	378	46	98	14	1	26	76	.259	125	4	1	.992
1958—San Francisco	Nat.	OF	88	236	27	59	8	0	12	46	.250	93	3	5	.950
1959—San Francisco	Nat.	OF	13	15	1	1	0	0	1	1	.067	0	0	0	.000
Major League Totals—15 Years			1399	4796	709	1278	200	19	288	876	.267	2711	139	74	.975

aTraded to Chicago Cubs with Outfielder Frank Baumholtz for Outfielders Harry Walker and Peanuts Lowrey, June 15, 1949.

bTraded to St. Louis Cardinals for Outfielder Pete Whisenant and cash, March 30, 1956.

cReleased, October 16, 1956; signed with New York Giants, October 26, 1956.

RAYMOND WILLIAM (RAY) SCHALK
(Cracker)

Born August 12, 1892, at Harvel, Ill.

Died May 19, 1970, at Chicago, Ill.

Height, 5.07. Weight, 155.

Threw and batted righthanded.

Holds major league records for most years leading league in fielding by catcher, 100 or more games (8); most years leading league in putouts by catcher (9); most ho-hit games caught, entire game (4).

Shares major league record for most assists, catcher, inning (3), September 30, 1921, eighth inning.

Holds American League record for most assists, catcher, lifetime (1,810).

Led American League catchers in double plays with 20 in 1923.

Manager, Chicago White Sox, 1927-28; Buffalo, International League, 1932-33-34-35-36-37; Indianapolis, American Association, 1938-39; Milwaukee, American Association, 1940; Buffalo, International League, 1950.

Named to Hall of Fame, 1955.

Year	Club	League	Pos.	G.	AB.	R.	H.	2B.	3B.	HR.	RBI.	B.A.	PO.	A.	E.	F.A.
1911—Taylorville		Ill.-Mo.	C	47	161	27	64	....	....	....	....	.398	......	....	....	......
1911—Milwaukee		A. A.	C	31	76	9	18	2	1	0	....	.237	112	36	2	.987
1912—Milwaukee		A. A.	C	80	266	19	72	8	4	3	....	.271	354	108	7	.985
1912—Chicago		Amer.	C	23	63	7	18	2	0	0	6	.286	115	40	14	.917
1913—Chicago		Amer.	C	128	401	38	98	15	5	1	42	.244	★586	153	15	★.980
1914—Chicago		Amer.	C	135	392	30	106	13	2	0	37	.270	★613	183	21	★.974
1915—Chicago		Amer.	C	135	413	46	110	14	4	1	48	.266	★655	159	13	★.984
1916—Chicago		Amer.	C	129	410	36	95	12	9	0	36	.232	★653	★166	10	★.988
1917—Chicago		Amer.	C	140	424	48	96	12	4	3	53	.226	★624	148	15	★.981
1918—Chicago		Amer.	C	108	333	35	73	6	3	0	24	.219	★422	114	12	.978
1919—Chicago		Amer.	C	131	394	57	111	9	3	0	40	.282	★551	130	13	.981
1920—Chicago		Amer.	C	151	485	64	131	25	5	1	61	.270	★581	138	10	★.986
1921—Chicago		Amer.	C	128	416	32	105	24	4	0	47	.252	453	129	9	★.985
1922—Chicago		Amer.	C	142	442	57	124	22	3	4	60	.281	★591	★150	8	★.989
1923—Chicago		Amer.	C	123	382	42	87	12	2	1	44	.228	481	93	10	.983
1924—Chicago		Amer.	C	57	153	15	30	4	2	1	11	.196	176	55	10	.959
1925—Chicago		Amer.	C	125	343	44	94	18	1	0	52	.274	368	99	8	.983
1926—Chicago		Amer.	C	82	226	26	60	9	1	0	32	.265	251	45	7	.977
1927—Chicago		Amer.	C	16	26	2	6	2	0	0	2	.231	24	8	0	1.000
1928—Chicago		Amer.	C	2	1	0	1	0	0	0	1	1.000	4	0	0	1.000
1929—New York		Nat.	C	5	2	0	0	0	0	0	0	.000	7	0	0	1.000
1932—Buffalo		Int.	C	1	3	1	2	0	0	0	0	.667	6	0	0	1.000
American League Totals—17 Years				1755	5304	579	1345	199	48	12	596	.254	7148	1810	175	.981
National League Totals—1 Year				5	2	0	0	0	0	0	0	.000	7	0	0	1.000
Major League Totals—18 Years				1760	5306	579	1345	199	48	12	596	.253	7155	1810	175	.981

WORLD SERIES RECORD

Year	Club	League	Pos.	G.	AB.	R.	H.	2B.	3B.	HR.	RBI.	B.A.	PO.	A.	E.	F.A.
1917—Chicago		Amer.	C	6	19	1	5	0	0	0	0	.263	32	5	2	.949
1919—Chicago		Amer.	C	8	23	1	7	0	0	0	2	.304	29	15	1	.978
World Series Totals—2 Years				14	42	2	12	0	0	0	2	.286	61	20	3	.964

MICHAEL JACK (MIKE) SCHMIDT

Born September 27, 1949, at Dayton, O.

Height, 6.02. Weight, 203.

Threw and batted righthanded.

Holds major league records for most total bases, extra-inning game (17), April 17, 1976 (10 innings); most home runs by third baseman, season (48), 1980; most home runs by third baseman, lifetime (509).

Shares major league records for most home runs, extra-inning game (4), April 17, 1976 (10 innings); most consecutive home runs, extra-inning game (4), April 17, 1976 (10 innings); most home runs, consecutive plate appearances (4), April 17, 1976 and July 6 and 7, 1979; most extra bases on long hits, game (12), April 17, 1976 (10 innings); most home runs, two consecutive games (5), April 17 and 18, 1976; most home runs, three consecutive games (6), April 17-20, 1976; most home runs, month of April (11), 1976; most consecutive seasons leading major leagues in strikeouts (3), 1974 through 1976; most home runs, month of October (4), 1980; most years leading league in double plays by third baseman (6).

Holds National League records for most years, third baseman (18); most years leading league in home runs (8); most years leading league in extra bases on long hits (7); most assists by third baseman, season (404), 1974; fewest singles, season, 150 or more games (63), 1979; most games by third baseman, lifetime (2,212); most assists by third baseman, lifetime (5,045); most chances accepted, third baseman, lifetime (6,636); most double plays by third baseman, lifetime (450).

Shares National League records for most years leading league in runs batted in (4); most grand slams, month (2), June, 1973; most home runs through July 31 (36), 1979; most home runs, five consecutive games, one or more homer each game (7), July 6 through 10, 1979; most consecutive years leading league in extra bases on long hits (3, performed twice); most consecutive years leading league in bases on balls (3); most years leading league in assists by third baseman (7).

Hit three home runs in a game, July 7, 1979 and June 14, 1987.

Led National League in intentional bases on balls received with 18 in 1981 and 25 in 1986.

Led National League in total bases with 306 in 1976, 342 in 1980 and 228 in 1981.

Led National League in slugging percentage with .546 in 1974, .624 in 1980, .644 in 1981 and .547 in 1982 and 1986.

Led National League batters in strikeouts with 138 in 1974, 180 in 1975, 149 in 1976 and 148 in 1983.
Led National League in bases on balls received with 120 in 1979, 73 in 1981, 107 in 1982 and 128 in 1983.
Led National League in sacrifice flies with 13 in 1980 and tied for lead with 9 in 1979.
Tied for National League lead in being hit by pitch with 11 in 1976.
Led National League third basemen in fielding percentage with .980 in 1986.
Led National League third basemen in total chances with 537 in 1976, 521 in 1977, 497 in 1980, 457 in 1982 and tied for lead with 338 in 1981 and 458 in 1983.
Led National League third basemen in double plays with 34 in 1978, 36 in 1979, 31 in 1980, 29 in 1983, 28 in 1987 and tied for lead with 28 in 1982.
Led National League third basemen in assists with 396 in 1977 and 332 in 1983.
Led Pacific Coast League batters in strikeouts with 145 in 1972.
Named National League Player of the Year by THE SPORTING NEWS, 1980 and 1986.
Named National League Most Valuable Player by Baseball Writers' Association of America, 1980, 1981 and 1986.
Named third baseman on THE SPORTING NEWS National League All-Star Team, 1974, 1976, 1977 and 1979 through 1984 and 1986.
Named third baseman on THE SPORTING NEWS National League All-Star fielding team, 1976 through 1984 and 1986.
Named third baseman on THE SPORTING NEWS National League Silver Slugger team, 1980 through 1984 and 1986.
Named shortstop on THE SPORTING NEWS College Baseball All-America Team, 1971.

Year	Club	League	Pos.	G.	AB.	R.	H.	2B.	3B.	HR.	RBI.	B.A.	PO.	A.	E.	F.A.
1971—Reading	East.		SS-3B	74	237	27	50	7	1	8	31	.211	100	224	23	.934
1972—Eugene	P. C.		2B-3B-SS	131	436	80	127	23	6	26	91	.291	271	324	25	.960
1972—Philadelphia	Nat.		3B-2B	13	34	2	7	0	0	1	3	.206	10	25	2	.946
1973—Philadelphia	Nat.		3-2-1-S	132	367	43	72	11	0	18	52	.196	119	256	18	.954
1974—Philadelphia	Nat.		3B	162	568	108	160	28	7	★36	116	.282	134	★404	26	.954
1975—Philadelphia	Nat.		3B-SS	158	562	93	140	34	3	★38	95	.249	139	390	26	.953
1976—Philadelphia	Nat.		3B	160	584	112	153	31	4	★38	107	.262	139	★377	21	.961
1977—Philadelphia	Nat.		3B-SS-2B	154	544	114	149	27	11	38	101	.274	109	401	20	.962
1978—Philadelphia	Nat.		3B-SS	145	513	93	129	27	2	21	78	.251	98	325	16	.964
1979—Philadelphia	Nat.		3B-SS	160	541	109	137	25	4	45	114	.253	115	363	23	.954
1980—Philadelphia	Nat.		3B	150	548	104	157	25	8	★48	★121	.286	98	★372	27	.946
1981—Philadelphia	Nat.		3B	102	354	★78	112	19	2	★31	★91	.316	74	★249	15	.956
1982—Philadelphia	Nat.		3B	148	514	108	144	26	3	35	87	.280	110	★324	23	.950
1983—Philadelphia	Nat.		3B-SS	154	534	104	136	16	4	★40	109	.255	108	333	19	.959
1984—Philadelphia	Nat.		3B-1B-SS	151	528	93	146	23	3	●36	●106	.277	93	330	26	.942
1985—Philadelphia	Nat.		1B-3B-SS	158	549	89	152	31	5	33	93	.277	911	193	18	.984
1986—Philadelphia	Nat.		3B-1B	160	552	97	160	29	1	★37	★119	.290	347	238	8	.987
1987—Philadelphia†	Nat.		3B-1B-SS	147	522	88	153	28	0	35	113	.293	138	319	13	.972
1988—Philadelphia†	Nat.		3B-1B	108	390	52	97	21	2	12	62	.249	76	223	19	.940
1989—Philadelphia‡	Nat.		3B	42	148	19	30	7	0	6	28	.203	18	71	8	.918
Major League Totals—18 Years				2404	8352	1506	2234	408	59	548	1595	.267	2836	5193	328	.961

Selected by Philadelphia Phillies' organization in 2nd round of free-agent draft, June 8, 1971.
†Granted free agency, November 4, 1988; re-signed by Phillies, December 7, 1988.
‡On voluntarily retired list, May 29, 1989.

CHAMPIONSHIP SERIES RECORD

Shares major league record for most doubles, lifetime (7).

Year	Club	League	Pos.	G.	AB.	R.	H.	2B.	3B.	HR.	RBI.	B.A.	PO.	A.	E.	F.A.
1976—Philadelphia	Nat.		3B	3	13	1	4	2	0	0	2	.308	4	9	1	.929
1977—Philadelphia	Nat.		3B	4	16	2	1	0	0	0	1	.063	4	15	0	1.000
1978—Philadelphia	Nat.		3B	4	15	1	3	2	0	0	1	.200	3	18	2	.913
1980—Philadelphia	Nat.		3B	5	24	1	5	1	0	0	1	.208	3	17	1	.952
1983—Philadelphia	Nat.		3B	4	15	5	7	2	0	1	2	.467	6	7	1	.929
Championship Series Totals—5 Years				20	83	10	20	7	0	1	7	.241	20	66	5	.945

WORLD SERIES RECORD

Year	Club	League	Pos.	G.	AB.	R.	H.	2B.	3B.	HR.	RBI.	B.A.	PO.	A.	E.	F.A.
1980—Philadelphia	Nat.		3B	6	21	6	8	1	0	2	7	.381	9	8	0	1.000
1983—Philadelphia	Nat.		3B	5	20	0	1	0	0	0	0	.050	1	10	1	.917
World Series Totals—2 Years				11	41	6	9	1	0	2	7	.220	10	18	1	.966

ALBERT FRED (RED) SCHOENDIENST

Born February 2, 1923, at Germantown, Ill.

Height, 6.01. Weight, 192.

Threw right and batted right and lefthanded.

Holds major league records for most doubles (8) and long hits (9), three consecutive games, June 5, 6 (both games), 1948; most doubles (5) and long hits (6), doubleheader, June 6, 1948.
Holds National League record for most years leading league in fielding by second baseman (7).
Shares National League record for most double plays started by second baseman, game (4), August 20, 1954.

Led National League in stolen bases with 26 in 1945.
Named second baseman on THE SPORTING NEWS All-Star Major League Teams, 1953-57.
Player-coach, St. Louis Cardinals, 1962-63-64; manager, St. Louis Cardinals, 1965 through 1976; coach, Oakland Athletics, 1977-78; St. Louis Cardinals, 1979 to date.
Named to Hall of Fame, 1989.

Year	Club	League	Pos.	G.	AB.	R.	H.	2B.	3B.	HR.	RBI.	B.A.	PO.	A.	E.	F.A.
1942—Union City	Kitty	2B	6	27	4	11	3	0	0	4	.407	16	20	2	.947
1942—Albany	Ga.-Fla.	SS-2B	68	264	41	71	7	5	1	28	.269	155	209	27	.931
1943—Lynchburg	Pied.	SS	9	36	8	17	2	0	0	5	.472	18	36	3	.947
1943—Rochester	Int.	SS	136	555	81	★187	21	5	6	37	★.337	★339	★438	48	.942
1944—Rochester (a)	Int.	SS	25	102	26	38	3	2	2	14	.373	50	84	17	.887
1945—St. Louis	Nat.	OF-IF	137	565	89	157	22	6	1	47	.278	302	30	10	.971
1946—St. Louis	Nat.	★2B-3B-SS	142	606	94	170	28	5	0	34	.281	363	379	13	★.983
1947—St. Louis	Nat.	2B-3B-OF	151	★659	91	167	25	9	3	48	.253	364	417	19	.976
1948—St. Louis	Nat.	2B	119	408	64	111	21	4	4	36	.272	230	269	10	.980
1949—St. Louis	Nat.	★2B-INF-OF	151	640	102	190	25	2	3	54	.297	★428	★471	15	★.984
1950—St. Louis	Nat.	INF	153	★642	81	177	★43	9	7	63	.276	425	437	14	.984
1951—St. Louis	Nat.	2B-SS	135	553	88	160	32	7	6	54	.289	354	419	10	.987
1952—St. Louis	Nat.	★2B-3B-SS	152	620	91	188	40	7	7	67	.303	★417	460	20	.978
1953—St. Louis	Nat.	2B	146	564	107	193	35	5	15	79	.342	★365	★430	14	★.983
1954—St. Louis	Nat.	2B	148	610	98	192	38	8	5	79	.315	394	★477	18	.980
1955—St. Louis	Nat.	2B	145	553	68	148	21	3	11	51	.268	296	381	10	★.985
1956—St.L. (b)-N.Y.	Nat.	2B	132	487	61	147	21	3	2	29	.302	298	308	4	★.993
1957—N.Y.(c)-Milw.	Nat.	●2B-OF	150	648	91	★200	31	8	15	65	.309	379	448	12	●.986
1958—Milwaukee	Nat.	2B	106	427	47	112	23	1	1	24	.262	233	301	7	★.987
1959—Milwaukee	Nat.	2B	5	3	0	0	0	0	0	0	.000	1	1	1	.667
1960—Milwaukee (d)	Nat.	2B	68	226	21	58	9	1	1	19	.257	120	148	10	.964
1961—St. Louis	Nat.	2B	72	120	9	36	9	0	1	12	.300	43	42	4	.955
1962—St. Louis	Nat.	2B-3B	98	143	21	43	4	0	2	12	.301	33	48	1	.988
1963—St. Louis	Nat.	PH	6	5	0	0	0	0	0	0	.000	0	0	0	.000
Major League Totals—19 Years			2216	8479	1223	2449	427	78	84	773	.289	5045	5466	192	.982

aIn Military Service most of season.
bTraded to New York Giants with Pitchers Gordon Jones and Dick Littlefield, Catcher Bill Sarni and Outfielder Jackie Brandt for Pitcher Don Liddle, Catcher Ray Katt, Shortstop Al Dark and Outfielder-First Baseman Whitey Lockman. All players but Jones exchanged clubs June 14, 1956; Jones being assigned to Giants, October 1, 1956.
cTraded to Milwaukee Braves for Pitcher Ray Crone, Second Baseman Danny O'Connell and Outfielder Bobby Thomson, June 15, 1957.
dReleased, October 14, 1960; signed with St. Louis Cardinals, March 15, 1961.

WORLD SERIES RECORD

Shares record for most at-bats, nine-inning game (6), October 10, 1946.

Year	Club	League	Pos.	G.	AB.	R.	H.	2B.	3B.	HR.	RBI.	B.A.	PO.	A.	E.	F.A.
1946—St. Louis	Nat.	2B	7	30	3	7	1	0	0	1	.233	17	21	1	.974
1957—Milwaukee	Nat.	2B	5	18	0	5	1	0	0	2	.278	5	10	0	1.000
1958—Milwaukee	Nat.	2B	7	30	5	9	3	1	0	0	.300	18	19	1	.974
World Series Totals—3 Years			19	78	8	21	5	1	0	3	.269	40	50	2	.978

GEORGE CHARLES SCOTT JR.
(Boomer)

Born March 23, 1944, at Greenville, Miss.
Height, 6.02. Weight, 215.
Threw and batted righthanded.

Shares major league records for most games, rookie season (162), 1966.
Led American League batters in strikeouts with 152 in 1966.
Led American League first basemen in double plays with 130 in 1966, 115 in 1967 and 137 in 1974.
Led American League first basemen in total chances with 1471 in 1974.
Led American League in total bases with 318 in 1975 and tied for lead with 295 in 1973.
Led Eastern League in total bases with 290 and led third basemen in double plays with 25 in 1965.
Named Most Valuable Player in Eastern League, 1965.
Named first baseman on THE SPORTING NEWS American League All-Star fielding teams, 1967-68-71-72-73-74-75-76.

Year	Club	League	Pos.	G.	AB.	R.	H.	2B.	3B.	HR.	RBI.	B.A.	PO.	A.	E.	F.A.
1962—Olean	NYP	3B-2B	63	223	31	53	8	1	5	28	.238	79	116	18	.915
1963—Wellsville	NYP	3B-SS	106	426	82	125	12	9	15	74	.293	94	151	27	.901
1964—Winston-Salem	Carol.	●3B	55	156	24	45	7	2	10	30	.288	28	65	6	.939
1965—Pittsfield	East.	★3B-1	140	★523	91	★167	★30	●9	★25	★94	★.319	★140	★283	★31	.932
1966—Boston	Amer.	★1B-3B	162	601	73	147	18	7	27	90	.245	★1362	121	16	.989
1967—Boston	Amer.	★1-3B	159	565	74	171	21	7	19	82	.303	★1321	94	★19	.987
1968—Boston	Amer.	1B-3B	124	350	23	60	14	0	3	25	.171	810	65	11	.988
1969—Boston	Amer.	3B-1B	152	549	63	139	14	5	16	52	.253	542	226	18	.977

Year Club	League	Pos.	G.	AB.	R.	H.	2B.	3B.	HR.	RBI.	B.A.	PO.	A.	E.	F.A.
1970—Boston....................	Amer.	3B-1B	127	480	50	142	24	5	16	63	.296	551	149	18	.975
1971—Boston†..................	Amer.	1B	146	537	72	141	16	4	24	78	.263	1256	75	11	.992
1972—Milwaukee...........	Amer.	1B-3B	152	578	71	154	24	4	20	88	.266	1223	119	15	.989
1973—Milwaukee...........	Amer.	1B	158	604	98	185	30	4	24	107	.306	1388	★118	9	.994
1974—Milwaukee...........	Amer.	1B	158	604	74	170	36	2	17	82	.281	★1345	★114	12	★.992
1975—Milwaukee...........	Amer.	1B-3B	158	617	86	176	26	4	●36	★109	.285	1205	★116	15	.989
1976—Milwaukee‡..........	Amer.	1B	156	606	73	166	21	5	18	77	.274	1393	107	13	.991
1977—Boston..................	Amer.	1B	157	584	103	157	26	5	33	95	.269	1446	115	★24	.985
1978—Boston..................	Amer.	1B	120	412	51	96	16	4	12	54	.233	1052	55	10	.991
1979—Bos.§-KC x-NY y..	Amer.	1B-3B	105	346	46	88	20	4	6	49	.254	737	46	10	.987
1980—Yucatan z.............	Mex.	1B	41	130	18	38	6	1	3	17	.292	358	21	4	.990
1981—M.C. Tig. a	Mex.	1B-3B	116	411	68	146	24	2	18	81	.355	783	46	4	.995
1982—Poza Rico	Mex.	1B	105	330	40	110	12	2	7	66	.333	708	41	11	.986
1983—P.R.b-Veracruz	Mex.	1B	114	391	30	87	14	2	5	52	.223	1050	50	7	.993
1984—Veracruz...............	Mex.	1B	86	302	47	92	12	0	15	51	.305	128	3	3	.978
Major League Totals—14 Years..............			2034	7433	957	1992	306	60	271	1051	.268	15631	1520	201	.988

Signed as free agent by Boston Red Sox' organization, May 28, 1962.

†Traded with Catcher Don Pavletich, Pitchers Ken Brett and Jim Lonborg and Outfielders Billy Conigliaro and Joe Lahoud to Milwaukee Brewers for Pitchers Marty Pattin and Lew Krausse and Outfielders Tommy Harper and Pat Skrable, October 11, 1971.

‡Traded with Outfielder Bernie Carbo to Boston Red Sox for First Baseman Cecil Cooper, December 6, 1976.

§Traded to Kansas City Royals for Outfielder Tom Poquette, June 13, 1979.

xReleased, August 17, 1979; signed by New York Yankees, August 27, 1979.

yGranted free agency, November 1, 1979; signed by Yucatan, Mexican League, April 30, 1980.

zSold to Mexico City Tigers, March 23, 1981.

aSold to Poza Rico, March 23, 1982.

bSold to Veracruz, June 1, 1983.

WORLD SERIES RECORD

Year Club	League	Pos.	G.	AB.	R.	H.	2B.	3B.	HR.	RBI.	B.A.	PO.	A.	E.	F.A.
1967—Boston....................	Amer.	1B	7	26	3	6	1	1	0	0	.231	70	3	0	1.000

GEORGE THOMAS (TOM) SEAVER

Born November 17, 1944, at Fresno, Calif.

Height, 6.01. Weight, 210.

Threw and batted righthanded.

Holds major league records for most consecutive years with 200 or more strikeouts (9); most consecutive strikeouts, game (10), April 22, 1970; most times pitched opening game of season (16).

Holds National League records for most years with 200 or more strikeouts (10); most strikeouts by righthanded pitcher, lifetime (3,272).

Tied National League records for most season opening games won, lifetime (6); most strikeouts, game (19), April 22, 1970.

Pitched 4-0 no-hit victory against St. Louis Cardinals, June 16, 1978.

Led National League in shutouts with 7 in 1977.

Tied for National League lead in shutouts with 5 in 1979.

Tied for National League lead in complete games with 18 in 1973.

Led International League pitchers in games started with 32 in 1966.

Named National League Pitcher of the Year by THE SPORTING NEWS, 1969 and 1975.

Won National League Cy Young Memorial Award, 1969, 1973 and 1975.

Named National League Rookie of the Year by Baseball Writers' Association of America, 1967.

Named righthanded pitcher on THE SPORTING NEWS National League All-Star Team, 1969, 1973, 1975 and 1981.

Year Club	League	G.	IP.	W.	L.	Pct.	H.	R.	ER.	SO.	BB.	ERA.
1966—Jacksonville..................................	Int'national	34	210	12	12	.500	184	87	73	188	66	3.13
1967—New York.......................................	National	35	251	16	13	.552	224	85	77	170	78	2.76
1968—New York.......................................	National	36	278	16	12	.571	224	73	68	205	48	2.20
1969—New York.......................................	National	36	273	★25	7	★.781	202	75	67	208	82	2.21
1970—New York.......................................	National	37	291	18	12	.600	230	103	91	★283	83	★2.81
1971—New York.......................................	National	36	286	20	10	.667	210	61	56	★289	61	★1.76
1972—New York.......................................	National	35	262	21	12	.636	215	92	85	249	77	2.92
1973—New York.......................................	National	36	290	19	10	.655	219	74	67	★251	64	★2.08
1974—New York.......................................	National	32	236	11	11	.500	199	89	84	201	75	3.20
1975—New York.......................................	National	36	280	★22	9	.710	217	81	74	★243	88	2.38
1976—New York.......................................	National	35	271	14	11	.560	211	83	78	★235	77	2.59
1977—New York†-Cincinnati	National	33	261	21	6	.778	199	78	75	196	66	2.59
1978—Cincinnati.....................................	National	36	260	16	14	.533	218	97	83	226	89	2.87
1979—Cincinnati.....................................	National	32	215	16	6	★.727	187	85	75	131	61	3.14
1980—Cincinnati.....................................	National	26	168	10	8	.556	140	74	68	101	59	3.64

Year Club	League	G.	IP.	W.	L.	Pct.	H.	R.	ER.	SO.	BB.	ERA.
1981—Cincinnati	National	23	166	★14	2	★.875	120	51	47	87	66	2.55
1982—Cincinnati‡	National	21	111⅓	5	13	.278	136	75	68	62	44	5.50
1983—New York§	National	34	231	9	14	.391	201	104	91	135	86	3.55
1984—Chicago	American	34	236⅔	15	11	.577	216	108	104	131	61	3.95
1985—Chicago	American	35	238⅔	16	11	.593	223	103	84	134	69	3.17
1986—Chicago x-Boston y	American	28	176⅓	7	13	.350	180	83	79	103	56	4.03
National League Totals—17 Years		559	4130⅓	273	170	.616	3352	1380	1254	3272	1204	2.73
American League Totals—3 Years		97	651⅔	38	35	.521	619	294	267	368	186	3.69
Major League Totals—20 Years		656	4782	311	205	.603	3971	1674	1521	3640	1390	2.86

Selected by Los Angeles Dodgers' organization in 22nd round of free-agent draft, June, 1965.

Signed by Atlanta Braves to Richmond contract for reported $40,000 bonus, February, 1966; subsequently, Commissioner William Eckert nullified the contract because the signing violated the college rule. However, since the University of Southern California then declared Seaver ineligible, Eckert decreed that any club other than the Braves which was willing to match terms of his Richmond contract would be eligible to draw for negotiation rights. Cleveland Indians, Philadelphia Phillies and New York Mets expressed that willingness, and Eckert drew the name of the Mets in a special drawing, April 3, 1966; Mets then signed Seaver to Jacksonville contract for reported $50,000 bonus.

†Traded to Cincinnati Reds for Infielder Doug Flynn, Pitcher Pat Zachry and Outfielders Dan Norman and Steve Henderson, June 15, 1977.

‡Traded to New York Mets for Pitcher Charlie Puleo, Catcher Lloyd McClendon and Outfielder Jason Felice, December 16, 1982.

§Selected by Chicago White Sox in player compensation pool draft, January 20, 1984. (Chicago received compensation for Toronto Blue Jays' signing of Pitcher Dennis Lamp, a Type A player, January 10, 1984.

xTraded to Boston Red Sox for Outfielder Steve Lyons, June 29, 1986.

yGranted free agency, November 12, 1986.

CHAMPIONSHIP SERIES RECORD

Year Club	League	G.	IP.	W.	L.	Pct.	H.	R.	ER.	SO.	BB.	ERA.
1969—New York	National	1	7	1	0	1.000	8	5	5	2	3	6.43
1973—New York	National	2	16⅔	1	1	.500	13	4	3	17	5	1.62
1979—Cincinnati	National	1	8	0	0	.000	5	2	2	5	2	2.25
Championship Series Totals—3 Years		4	31⅔	2	1	.667	26	11	10	24	10	2.84

WORLD SERIES RECORD

Year Club	League	G.	IP.	W.	L.	Pct.	H.	R.	ER.	SO.	BB.	ERA.
1969—New York	National	2	15	1	1	.500	12	5	5	9	3	3.00
1973—New York	National	2	15	0	1	.000	13	4	4	18	3	2.40
World Series Totals—2 Years		4	30	1	2	.333	25	9	9	27	6	2.70

JAMES LUTHER (LUKE) SEWELL

Born January 15, 1901, at Titus, Ala.

Died May 14, 1987, at Akron, O.

Height, 5.10. Weight, 185.

Threw and batted righthanded.

Brother of Joe and Tommy Sewell, former major league infielders.

Shares American League record for most years by catcher (20).

Named by THE SPORTING NEWS as No. 1 Major League Manager of the Year, 1944.

Named as manager for THE SPORTING NEWS All-Star Major League Team, 1944.

Coach, Cleveland Indians, 1939 to 1941; manager, St. Louis Browns, 1941 to 1946; coach, Cincinnati Reds, 1949; manager, Reds, 1950-51.

Year Club	League	Pos.	G.	AB.	R.	H.	2B.	3B.	HR.	RBI.	B.A.	PO.	A.	E.	F.A.
1921—Columbus	A. A.	C	17	52	11	17	4	1	0	8	.327	52	17	5	.932
1921—Cleveland	Amer.	C	3	6	0	0	0	0	0	1	.000	7	0	1	.875
1922—Cleveland	Amer.	C	41	87	14	23	5	0	0	10	.264	108	21	5	.963
1923—Cleveland	Amer.	C	10	10	2	2	0	1	0	1	.200	5	5	2	.833
1924—Cleveland	Amer.	C	63	165	27	48	9	1	0	17	.291	171	42	9	.959
1925—Cleveland	Amer.	C	74	220	30	51	10	2	0	18	.232	222	54	8	.972
1926—Cleveland	Amer.	C	126	433	41	103	16	4	0	46	.238	437	★91	9	.983
1927—Cleveland	Amer.	C	128	470	52	138	27	6	0	53	.294	402	★119	★20	.963
1928—Cleveland	Amer.	C	122	411	52	111	16	9	3	52	.270	430	★117	16	.972
1929—Cleveland	Amer.	C	124	406	41	96	16	3	1	39	.236	433	81	★18	.966
1930—Cleveland	Amer.	C	76	292	40	75	21	2	1	43	.257	283	49	9	.974
1931—Cleveland	Amer.	C	108	375	45	103	30	4	1	53	.275	384	61	9	.980
1932—Cleveland†	Amer.	C	87	300	36	76	20	2	2	52	.253	306	50	8	.978
1933—Washington	Amer.	C	141	474	65	125	30	4	2	61	.264	516	61	6	.990
1934—Washington	Amer.	C-IF-OF	72	207	21	49	7	3	2	21	.237	215	30	2	.992
1935—Chicago‡	Amer.	C	118	421	52	120	19	3	2	67	.285	399	83	6	.988
1936—Chicago	Amer.	C	128	451	59	113	20	5	5	73	.251	461	★87	9	.984
1937—Chicago	Amer.	C	122	412	51	111	21	6	1	61	.269	502	72	9	.985

Year	Club	League	Pos.	G.	AB.	R.	H.	2B.	3B.	HR.	RBI.	B.A.	PO.	A.	E.	F.A.
1938—Chicago§x	Amer.		C	65	211	23	45	4	1	0	27	.213	205	55	4	.985
1939—Cleveland	Amer.		C	16	20	1	3	1	0	0	1	.150	24	4	1	.966
1942—St. Louis	Amer.		C	6	12	1	1	0	0	0	0	.083	12	5	1	.944
Major League Totals—20 Years				1630	5383	653	1393	272	56	20	696	.259	5522	1087	152	.978

†Traded to Washington for Catcher Roy Spencer, January 7, 1933.
‡Traded to St. Louis Browns for Pitcher Bump Hadley, January 22, 1935, and sold to Chicago White Sox.
§Claimed on waiver price by Brooklyn, December 19, 1938.
xReleased, April 11, 1939; signed by Cleveland, April, 1939.

WORLD SERIES RECORD

Year	Club	League	Pos.	G.	AB.	R.	H.	2B.	3B.	HR.	RBI.	B.A.	PO.	A.	E.	F.A.
1933—Washington	Amer.		C	5	17	1	3	0	0	0	1	.176	23	2	0	1.000

JOSEPH WHEELER (JOE) SEWELL

Born October 9, 1898, at Titus, Ala.

Died March 6, 1990, at Mobile, Ala.

Height, 5.07. Weight, 155.

Threw right and batted lefthanded.

Brother of Luke Sewell, former major league catcher,
and Tommy Sewell, former major league infielder.

Holds major league records for fewest strikeouts, lifetime, 14 or more seasons (113); fewest strikeouts, season, 150 or more games (4), 1925 and 1929.
Named shortstop on THE SPORTING NEWS major league All-Star Team, 1926.
Led American League shortstops in double plays with 103 in 1928.
Coach, New York Yankees, 1934-35; scout, Cleveland Indians, 1952 through 1962; New York Mets, 1963.
Named to Hall of Fame, 1977.

Year	Club	League	Pos.	G.	AB.	R.	H.	2B.	3B.	HR.	RBI.	B.A.	PO.	A.	E.	F.A.
1920—New Orleans	South.		SS	92	346	58	100	19	8	2	.....	.289	147	261	27	.938
1920—Cleveland	Amer.		SS	22	70	14	23	4	1	0	12	.329	44	70	15	.884
1921—Cleveland	Amer.		SS	154	572	101	182	36	12	4	91	.318	319	480	47	.944
1922—Cleveland	Amer.		SS-2B	153	558	80	167	28	7	2	83	.299	322	497	52	.940
1923—Cleveland	Amer.		SS	153	553	98	195	41	10	3	109	.353	286	497	★59	.930
1924—Cleveland	Amer.		SS	153	594	99	188	●45	5	4	106	.316	★349	★514	36	.960
1925—Cleveland	Amer.		SS-2B	155	608	78	204	37	7	1	98	.336	★314	★529	29	.967
1926—Cleveland	Amer.		SS	154	578	91	187	41	5	4	85	.324	★326	463	37	.955
1927—Cleveland	Amer.		SS	153	569	83	180	48	5	1	92	.316	★361	★480	33	★.962
1928—Cleveland	Amer.		★SS-3B	●155	588	79	190	40	2	4	70	.323	319	★499	33	★.961
1929—Cleveland	Amer.		3B	152	578	90	182	38	3	7	73	.315	163	★336	13	.975
1930—Cleveland(a)	Amer.		3B	109	353	44	102	17	6	0	48	.289	83	184	14	.950
1931—New York	Amer.		3B	130	484	102	146	22	1	6	64	.302	131	227	18	.952
1932—New York	Amer.		3B	125	503	95	137	21	3	11	68	.272	122	221	9	.974
1933—New York	Amer.		3B	135	524	87	143	18	1	2	54	.273	123	224	13	.964
Major League Totals—14 Years				1903	7132	1141	2226	436	68	49	1053	.312	3262	5221	408	.954

aReleased by Cleveland, January, 1931, and signed with New York Yankees.

WORLD SERIES RECORD

Shares record for most at-bats, inning (2), September 28, 1932, sixth inning.

Year	Club	League	Pos.	G.	AB.	R.	H.	2B.	3B.	HR.	RBI.	B.A.	PO.	A.	E.	F.A.
1920—Cleveland	Amer.		SS	7	23	0	4	0	0	0	0	.174	11	28	6	.867
1932—New York	Amer.		3B	4	15	4	5	1	0	0	3	.333	4	6	1	.909
World Series Totals—2 Years				11	38	4	9	1	0	0	3	.237	15	34	7	.875

JAMES BENTLEY (CY) SEYMOUR

Born December 9, 1872, at Albany, N. Y.

Died September 20, 1919, at New York, N. Y.

Height, 6.00. Weight, 200.

Threw and batted lefthanded.

Year Club League	Pos.	G.	AB.	R.	H.	2B.	3B.	HR.	SB.	B.A.	PO.	A.	E.	F.A.
1896—Metropolitans....... Atl.	OF	34	131	22	38	...	...	...	11	.290	37	7	14	.759
1896—New York............. Nat.	OF-P	12	31	2	8	0	0	0	0	.258	6	19	2	.926
1896-97—Springfield........ East	....	....	....	....	....					......	.....	....		......
1897—New York............. Nat.	OF-P	41	141	13	35	5	2	2	2	.248	14	95	22	.832
1898—New York............. Nat.	OF-P	78	291	40	79	7	2	4	6	.271	25	113	17	.890
1899—New York............. Nat.	OF-P	45	154	25	52	3	2	2	3	.337	16	89	17	.861
1900—New York(a) .... Nat.	0-1B-P	21	37	9	9	0	0	0	0	.243	9	19	6	.824
1900—Chicago .... Amer.	OF-P	2	3	0	0	0	0	0	0	.000	0	2	2	.500
1901—Baltimore .... Amer.	OF	137	552	85	167	20	8	1	33	.303	278	26	16	.950
1902—Baltimore(b)........ Amer.	OF	72	270	38	75	8	8	3	13	.278	220	12	6	.975
1902—Cincinnati .... Nat.	OF-3B	60	235	28	82	8	2	2	10	.349	130	8	13	.914
1903—Cincinnati .... Nat.	OF	135	558	85	191	25	15	7	25	.342	●318	14	★36	.902
1904—Cincinnati .... Nat.	OF	130	531	71	166	26	13	5	11	.313	308	20	17	.951
1905—Cincinnati .... Nat.	OF	149	581	95	★219	★40	★21	8	21	★.377	347	25	21	.947
1906—Cin.(c)-N.Y. .... Nat.	OF	151	576	70	165	19	5	8	29	.286	331	17	10	.972
1907—New York........... Nat.	OF	126	473	46	139	25	8	3	21	.294	300	8	8	.975
1908—New York........... Nat.	OF	155	587	59	157	23	2	5	18	.267	340	★29	★20	.949
1909—New York........... Nat.	OF	73	280	37	87	12	5	1	14	.311	138	11	5	.968
1910—New York........... Nat.	OF	76	287	32	76	9	4	1	10	.265	137	9	10	.936
1910—Baltimore .... East.	OF	15	53	6	15	3	0	0	0	.283	17	0	5	.773
1911—Baltimore .... East.	OF	112	436	63	129	24	10	2	14	.296	224	16	13	.949
1912—Newark .... Int.	OF	124	454	59	139	21	7	0	18	.306	229	13	●17	.934
1913—Boston .... Nat.	OF	39	73	2	13	2	0	0	2	.178	34	4	2	.950
1913—Buffalo .... Int.	OF	12	47	3	11	1	0	0	0	.234	21	1	1	.957
1918—New York........... Int.	OF	13	41	2	0	0	0	0	0	.220	15	0	0	1.000
American League Totals—3 Years.......		209	822	123	242	28	16	4	46	.294	498	38	22	.961
National League Totals—15 Years........		1291	4835	614	1478	204	81	48	172	.306	2453	480	206	.934
Major League Totals—16 Years............		1500	5657	737	1720	232	97	52	218	.304	2951	518	228	.938

aJumped to Chicago Americans late in 1900 season.
bJumped with First Baseman-Outfielder Joe Kelly to Cincinnati Nationals, July 16, 1902.
cSold to New York Giants for $12,000, July 14, 1906.

PITCHING RECORD

Year Club League	G.	IP.	W.	L.	Pct.	H.	R.	SO.	BB.
1896—Springfield........................... Eastern	....	....	8	1	.889	....	....	....	....
1896—New York........................... National	12	70	2	4	.333	70	73	28	46
1897—New York........................... National	34	292	20	14	.588	262	168	157	★165
1898—New York........................... National	44	359	25	17	.595	318	199	★249	★211
1899—New York........................... National	33	269	14	17	.452	240	139	145	★162
1900—New York........................... National	20	50	2	2	.500	71	60	19	54
1900—Chicago................................. American	2	10	1	1	.500	9	5	5	9
1902—Cincinnati............................ National	1	....	....	....	.....	....	....	....	....
Major League Totals—6 Years....................	154	1040	63	54	.538	961	639	598	638

ROY EDWARD SIEVERS

Born November 18, 1926, at St. Louis, Mo.
Height, 6.01½. Weight, 204.
Threw and batted righthanded.

Named by THE SPORTING NEWS and Baseball Writers' Association of America as American League Rookie of the Year, 1949.
Coach, Cincinnati Reds, 1966; manager, Williamsport, Eastern League, 1967; Memphis, Texas League, 1968.

Year Club League	Pos.	G.	AB.	R.	H.	2B.	3B.	HR.	RBI.	B.A.	PO.	A.	E.	F.A.
1947—Hannibal................. C.A.	O-3B-P	●125	501	★121	★159	21	5	★34	★141	.317	199	44	16	.938
1948—Elmira................... East.	OF	16	56	5	10	3	0	2	8	.179	23	1	2	.923
1948—Springfield............ I.I.I.	OF	96	343	64	106	15	5	19	75	.309	148	★22	9	.950
1949—St. Louis................. Amer.	OF-3B	140	471	84	144	28	1	16	91	.306	317	25	10	.972
1950—St. Louis................. Amer.	OF-3B	113	370	46	88	20	4	10	57	.238	248	48	8	.974
1951—St. Louis................. Amer.	OF	31	89	10	20	2	1	1	11	.225	63	1	1	.985
1951—San Antonio.......... Tex.	OF	39	138	16	41	8	1	2	17	.297	72	2	2	.974
1952—St. Louis................. Amer.	1B	11	30	3	6	3	0	0	5	.200	58	3	2	.968
1953—St. Louis(a)........... Amer.	1B	92	285	37	77	15	0	8	35	.270	604	31	5	.992
1954—Washington.......... Amer.	OF-1B	145	514	75	119	26	6	24	102	.232	350	15	9	.976
1955—Washington.......... Amer.	O-1-3B	144	509	74	138	20	8	25	106	.271	363	17	4	.990
1956—Washington.......... Amer.	OF-1B	152	550	92	139	27	2	29	95	.253	784	54	9	.989
1957—Washington.......... Amer.	OF-1B	152	572	99	172	23	5	★42	★114	.301	413	15	6	.986
1958—Washington.......... Amer.	OF-1B	148	550	85	162	18	1	39	108	.295	476	26	5	.990

Year Club League	Pos.	G.	AB.	R.	H.	2B.	3B.	HR.	RBI.	B.A.	PO.	A.	E.	F.A.
1959—Washington(b) ..... Amer.	1B-OF	115	385	55	93	19	0	21	49	.242	870	72	11	.988
1960—Chicago .... Amer.	1B-OF	127	444	87	131	22	0	28	93	.295	1085	63	8	.993
1961—Chicago(c)............ Amer.	1B	141	492	76	145	26	6	27	92	.295	1096	94	8	.993
1962—Philadelphia .... Nat.	1B-OF	144	477	61	125	19	5	21	80	.262	977	93	10	.991
1963—Philadelphia .... Nat.	1B	138	450	46	108	19	2	19	82	.240	981	77	12	.989
1964—Philadelphia(d).... Nat.	1B	49	120	7	22	3	1	4	16	.183	241	15	2	.992
1964—Washington........... Amer.	1B	33	58	5	10	1	0	4	11	.172	87	11	0	1.000
1965—Philadelphia .... Nat.	1B	12	21	3	4	1	0	0	0	.190	51	1	0	1.000
American League Totals—15 Years		1556	5340	831	1448	251	34	274	969	.271	6865	476	86	.988
National League Totals—3 Years............		331	1047	114	255	41	8	44	178	.243	2199	185	24	.990
Major League Totals—17 Years...............		1887	6387	945	1703	292	42	318	1147	.267	9064	661	110	.989

aTraded to Washington Senators for Outfielder Gil Coan, February 18, 1954.

bTraded to Chicago White Sox for Catcher Earl Battey, First Baseman Don Mincher and reported $150,000, April 4, 1960.

cTraded to Philadelphia Phillies for Pitcher Johnny Buzhardt and Third Baseman Charlie Smith, November 28, 1961.

dSold to Washington Senators, July 14, 1964.

ALOYSIUS HARRY (AL) SIMMONS
(Bucketfoot)

Born May 22, 1902, at Milwaukee, Wis.

Died May 26, 1956, at Milwaukee, Wis.

Height, 6.00.   Weight, 210.

Threw and batted righthanded.

Hit three home runs in a game, July 15, 1932.

Named by Baseball Writers' Association of America as outfielder for THE SPORTING NEWS All-Star Major League Teams, 1927-29-30-31-33 and 1934.

Named Most Valuable Player in American League, 1929.

Player-coach, Philadelphia Athletics, 1940-41-42 and 1944; coach Athletics, 1945 through 1949; Cleveland Indians, 1950.

Named to Hall of Fame, 1953.

Year Club League	Pos.	G.	AB.	R.	H.	2B.	3B.	HR.	RBI.	B.A.	PO.	A.	E.	F.A.
1922—Milwaukee............ A. A.	OF	19	50	9	11	2	1	1	7	.220	16	3	1	.950
1922—Aberdeen .... Dakota	OF	99	395	91	★144	26	16	10	.....	.365	209	19	0	★1.000
1923—Shreveport .... Tex.	OF	144	525	96	189	36	10	12	99	.360	335	31	13	.966
1923—Milwaukee............ A. A.	OF	24	98	20	39	2	3	0	16	.398	58	2	1	.984
1924—Philadelphia .... Amer.	OF	152	594	69	183	31	9	8	102	.308	390	17	10	.976
1925—Philadelphia .... Amer.	OF	153	★658	122	★253	43	12	24	129	.384	★447	8	●16	.966
1926—Philadelphia .... Amer.	OF	147	581	90	199	53	10	19	109	.343	333	11	9	.975
1927—Philadelphia .... Amer.	OF	106	406	86	159	36	11	15	108	.392	247	10	4	.985
1928—Philadelphia .... Amer.	OF	119	464	78	163	33	9	15	107	.351	231	10	3	.988
1929—Philadelphia .... Amer.	OF	143	581	114	212	41	9	34	★157	.365	349	19	4	●.989
1930—Philadelphia .... Amer.	OF	138	554	★152	211	41	16	36	165	★.381	275	10	3	★.990
1931—Philadelphia .... Amer.	OF	128	513	105	200	37	13	22	128	★.390	287	10	4	.987
1932—Philadelphia(a).... Amer.	OF	154	★670	144	★216	28	9	35	151	.322	290	9	6	.980
1933—Chicago .... Amer.	OF	146	605	85	200	29	10	14	119	.331	372	15	4	.990
1934—Chicago .... Amer.	OF	138	558	102	192	36	7	18	104	.344	286	14	4	.987
1935—Chicago(b)............ Amer.	OF	128	525	68	140	22	7	16	79	.267	349	5	7	.981
1936—Detroit .... Amer.	OF	143	568	96	186	38	6	13	112	.327	364	8	5	★.987
1937—Washington(c) ..... Amer.	OF	103	419	60	117	21	10	8	84	.279	240	7	4	.984
1938—Washington(d) ..... Amer.	OF	125	470	79	142	23	6	21	95	.302	322	4	4	.983
1939—Bos.(e)-Cin.(f) .... Nat.	OF	102	351	39	96	17	5	7	44	.274	172	8	4	.978
1940—Philadelphia .... Amer.	OF	37	81	7	25	4	0	1	19	.309	51	1	2	.963
1941—Philadelphia .... Amer.	OF	9	24	1	3	1	0	0	1	.125	16	0	0	1.000
1942—Philadelphia(g).... Amer.	OF							(Served as coach)						
1943—Boston(h)............... Amer.	OF	40	33	9	27	5	0	1	12	.203	66	3	1	.986
1944—Philadelphia .... Amer.	OF	4	6	1	3	0	0	0	2	.500	3	0	0	1.000
American League Totals—19 Years		2113	8410	1468	2831	522	144	300	1783	.337	4828	161	90	.982
National League Totals—1 Year............		102	351	39	96	17	5	7	44	.274	172	8	4	.978
Major League Totals—20 Years...............		2215	8761	1507	2927	539	149	307	1827	.334	5000	169	94	.982

aSold with Third Baseman Jimmie Dykes and Outfielder Mule Haas for $150,000 to Chicago White Sox, September 28, 1932.

bSold to Detroit Tigers for $75,000, December 10, 1935.

cPurchased by Washington Senators for $15,000, April 4, 1937.

dSold to Boston Braves, December 20, 1938.

eSold to Cincinnati Reds, August 31, 1939.

fReleased by Cincinnati Reds after season closed and signed by Philadelphia Athletics as free agent, December 11, 1939.

gReleased following 1942 season and signed by Boston Red Sox as active player, February 2, 1943.
hReleased by Boston Red Sox, October 15, 1943, and signed as player-coach by Philadelphia Athletics, December, 1943.

WORLD SERIES RECORD

Shares record for most at-bats (2), runs (2), hits (2) and total bases (5), inning, October 12, 1929, seventh inning.

Year Club	League	Pos.	G.	AB.	R.	H.	2B.	3B.	HR.	RBI.	B.A.	PO.	A.	E.	F.A.
1929—Philadelphia	Amer.	OF	5	20	6	6	1	0	2	5	.300	4	0	0	1.000
1930—Philadelphia	Amer.	OF	6	22	4	8	2	0	2	4	.364	12	1	0	1.000
1931—Philadelphia	Amer.	OF	7	27	4	9	2	0	2	8	.333	19	0	0	1.000
1939—Cincinnati	Nat.	OF	1	4	1	1	1	0	0	0	.250	3	0	0	1.000
World Series Totals—4 Years			19	73	15	24	6	0	6	17	.329	38	1	0	1.000

CURTIS THOMAS (CURT) SIMMONS

Born May 19, 1929, at Egypt, Pa.
Height, 6.00. Weight, 195.
Threw and batted lefthanded.

Tied for National League lead in shutouts with 6 in 1952.

Year Club	League	G.	IP.	W.	L.	Pct.	H.	R.	ER.	SO.	BB.	ERA.
1947—Wilmington	Int.-State	18	147	13	5	.722	107	48	44	197	76	2.69
1947—Philadelphia	Nat.	1	9	1	0	1.000	5	1	1	9	6	1.00
1948—Philadelphia	Nat.	31	170	7	13	.350	169	110	92	86	108	4.87
1949—Philadelphia	Nat.	38	131	4	10	.286	133	72	67	83	55	4.60
1950—Philadelphia	Nat.	31	215	17	8	.680	178	93	81	146	88	3.39
1951—Philadelphia	Nat.					(In Military Service)						
1952—Philadelphia	Nat.	28	201	14	8	.636	170	72	63	141	70	2.82
1953—Philadelphia	Nat.	32	238	16	13	.552	211	102	85	138	82	3.21
1954—Philadelphia	Nat.	34	253	14	15	.483	226	101	79	125	98	2.81
1955—Philadelphia	Nat.	25	130	8	8	.500	148	76	71	58	50	4.92
1956—Philadelphia	Nat.	33	198	15	10	.600	186	95	74	88	65	3.36
1957—Philadelphia	Nat.	32	212	12	11	.522	214	92	81	92	50	3.44
1958—Philadelphia	Nat.	29	168	7	14	.333	196	92	82	78	40	4.39
1959—Philadelphia	Nat.	7	10	0	0	.000	16	5	5	4	0	4.50
1959—Williamsport	East.	6	44	4	1	.800	43	16	14	19	7	2.86
1960—Philadelphia(a)-St. Louis	Nat.	27	156	7	4	.636	162	58	53	67	37	3.06
1961—St. Louis	Nat.	30	196	9	10	.474	203	91	68	99	64	3.12
1962—St. Louis	Nat.	31	154	10	10	.500	167	78	60	74	32	3.51
1963—St. Louis	Nat.	32	233	15	9	.625	209	82	64	127	48	2.47
1964—St. Louis	Nat.	34	244	18	9	.667	233	106	93	104	49	3.43
1965—St. Louis	Nat.	34	203	9	15	.375	229	104	92	96	54	4.08
1966—St. Louis(b)-Chicago	Nat.	29	111	5	8	.385	114	56	52	38	35	4.22
1967—Chicago(c)	Nat.	17	82	3	7	.300	100	54	45	31	23	4.94
1967—California	Amer.	14	35	2	1	.667	44	11	10	13	9	2.57
National League Totals—20 Years		555	3314	191	182	.512	3269	1540	1308	1684	1054	3.55
American League Totals—1 Year		14	35	2	1	.667	44	11	10	13	9	2.57
Major League Totals—20 Years		569	3349	193	183	.513	3313	1551	1318	1697	1063	3.54

aReleased, May 12, 1960; signed with St. Louis Cardinals, May 19, 1960.
bSold to Chicago Cubs, June 22, 1966.
cSold to California Angels, August 7, 1967.

WORLD SERIES RECORD

Year Club	League	G.	IP.	W.	L.	Pct.	H.	R.	ER.	SO.	BB.	ERA.
1964—St. Louis	Nat.	2	14⅓	0	1	.000	11	4	4	8	3	2.51

TED LYLE SIMMONS

Born August 9, 1949, at Highland Park, Mich.
Height, 6.00. Weight, 200.
Threw right and batted left and righthanded.

Holds National League record for most home runs by switch-hitter, lifetime (182).
Holds American League records for longest errorless game and most innings played by first baseman, game (25), May 8, finished May 9, 1984 (fielded 24⅓ innings).
Led National League in intentional bases on balls received with 19 in 1976 and 25 in 1977.
Led National League in grounding into double plays with 29 in 1973.
Led National League catchers in putouts with 842 in 1972 and 888 in 1973.
Led National League catchers in assists with 78 in 1972 and 74 in 1973.
Led National League catchers in total chances with 928 in 1972, 975 in 1973 and 880 in 1975.
Led National League in passed balls with 25 in 1973, 28 in 1975 and 14 in 1979.
Led California League catchers in putouts with 984 in 1968.
Tied for California League lead in being hit by pitch with 9 in 1968.
Named catcher on THE SPORTING NEWS National League All-Star Team, 1977 through 1979.
Named catcher on THE SPORTING NEWS National League Silver Slugger team, 1980.
Named California League Most Valuable Player, 1968.
Director of player development, St. Louis Cardinals, 1988 to date.

Year	Club	League	Pos.	G.	AB.	R.	H.	2B.	3B.	HR.	RBI.	B.A.	PO.	A.	E.	F.A.
1967—Sarasota Cards.....	Gulf C.		C	6	20	5	7	1	1	2	8	.350	33	0	0	1.000
1967—Cedar Rapids........	Midw.		OF-C	47	171	15	46	11	2	4	34	.269	119	8	3	.977
1968—Modesto	Calif.		★C-OF	136	493	86	163	30	2	28	★117	★.331	989	79	★16	.985
1968—St. Louis................	Nat.		C	2	3	0	1	0	0	0	0	.333	3	1	0	1.000
1969—Tulsa	A. A.		C-3-O-1	129	499	80	158	33	4	16	88	.317	463	92	19	.967
1969—St. Louis................	Nat.		C	5	14	0	3	0	1	0	3	.214	22	0	1	.957
1970—Tulsa	A. A.		C	15	51	10	19	4	1	1	8	.373	99	7	0	1.000
1970—St. Louis................	Nat.		C	82	284	29	69	8	2	3	24	.243	466	37	5	.990
1971—St. Louis................	Nat.		C	133	510	64	155	32	4	7	77	.304	747	52	9	.989
1972—St. Louis................	Nat.		C-1B	152	594	70	180	36	6	16	96	.303	967	93	13	.988
1973—St. Louis................	Nat.		C-1B-OF	161	619	62	192	36	2	13	91	.310	932	78	14	.986
1974—St. Louis................	Nat.		C-1B	152	599	66	163	33	6	20	103	.272	813	87	15	.984
1975—St. Louis................	Nat.		★C-1B-OF	157	581	80	193	32	3	18	100	.332	818	64	★15	.983
1976—St. Louis................	Nat.		C-1-O-3	150	546	60	159	35	3	5	75	.291	726	88	10	.988
1977—St. Louis................	Nat.		C-OF	150	516	82	164	25	3	21	95	.318	683	75	10	.987
1978—St. Louis................	Nat.		★C-OF	152	516	71	148	40	5	22	80	.287	703	★88	10	.988
1979—St. Louis................	Nat.		C	123	448	68	127	22	0	26	87	.283	606	69	10	.985
1980—St. Louis†	Nat.		C-OF	145	495	84	150	33	2	21	98	.303	528	71	10	.984
1981—Milwaukee............	Amer.		C-1B	100	380	45	82	13	3	14	61	.216	333	41	8	.979
1982—Milwaukee............	Amer.		C	137	539	73	145	29	0	23	97	.269	570	62	3	★.995
1983—Milwaukee‡..........	Amer.		C	153	600	76	185	39	3	13	108	.308	395	41	11	.975
1984—Milwaukee............	Amer.		1B-3B	132	497	44	110	23	2	4	52	.221	352	52	8	.981
1985—Milwaukee§..........	Amer.		1B-C-3B	143	528	60	144	28	2	12	76	.273	291	26	3	.991
1986—Atlanta	Nat.		1B-C-3B	76	127	14	32	5	0	4	25	.252	167	18	6	.969
1987—Atlanta	Nat.		1B-C-3B	73	177	20	49	8	0	4	30	.277	282	35	5	.984
1988—Atlanta	Nat.		1B-C	78	107	6	21	6	0	2	11	.196	140	14	3	.981
National League Totals—16 Years.........				1791	6136	776	1806	351	37	182	995	.294	8603	870	136	.986
American League Totals—5 Years				665	2544	298	666	132	10	66	394	.262	1941	222	33	.985
Major League Totals—21 Years				2456	8680	1074	2472	483	47	248	1389	.285	10544	1092	169	.986

Selected by St. Louis Cardinals' organization in 1st round (10th player selected) of free-agent draft, June 6, 1967.

†Traded with Pitchers Rollie Fingers and Pete Vuckovich to Milwaukee Brewers for Pitchers Lary Sorensen and Dave LaPoint and Outfielders Sixto Lezcano and David Green, December 12, 1980.

‡Granted free agency, November 7, 1983; re-signed by Brewers, January 16, 1984.

§Traded to Atlanta Braves for Catcher Rick Cerone, Pitcher David Clay and Shortstop Flavio Alfaro, March 5, 1986.

CHAMPIONSHIP SERIES RECORD

Year	Club	League	Pos.	G.	AB.	R.	H.	2B.	3B.	HR.	RBI.	B.A.	PO.	A.	E.	F.A.
1982—Milwaukee............	Amer.		C	5	18	3	3	0	0	0	1	.167	36	3	0	1.000

WORLD SERIES RECORD

Year	Club	League	Pos.	G.	AB.	R.	H.	2B.	3B.	HR.	RBI.	B.A.	PO.	A.	E.	F.A.
1982—Milwaukee............	Amer.		C	7	23	2	4	0	0	2	3	.174	28	2	1	.968

GEORGE HAROLD SISLER
(Gorgeous George)

Born March 24, 1893, at Manchester, O.

Died March 26, 1973, at St. Louis, Mo.

Height, 5.10½. Weight, 170.

Threw and batted lefthanded.

Father of former major league first baseman-outfielder Dick Sisler and former major league pitcher Dave Sisler.

Holds major league record for most hits, season (257), 1920.
Shares American League record for most years leading league in assists by first baseman (6).
Named American League Most Valuable Player, 1922.
Led American League in stolen bases with 45 in 1918, 35 in 1921, 51 in 1922 and 27 in 1927.

Led American League first basemen in double plays in 1926 and 1927.

Manager, St. Louis Browns, 1924-25-26; Shreveport-Tyler, Texas League, 1932; scout, Brooklyn Dodgers, 1943; Newport News, Piedmont League, 1945; Brooklyn Dodgers, 1946 through 1950; Pittsburgh Pirates, 1951 through 1956; batting instructor, Pittsburgh, 1956-61; scout, Pittsburgh, 1962 through 1966.

Named to Hall of Fame, 1939.

Year	Club	League	Pos.	G.	AB.	R.	H.	2B.	3B.	HR.	RBI.	B.A.	PO.	A.	E.	F.A.
1915—St. Louis	Amer.		P-1-O	81	274	28	78	10	2	3	29	.285	413	38	7	.985
1916—St. Louis	Amer.		1-P-O	151	580	83	177	21	11	4	74	.305	1493	83	★24	.985
1917—St. Louis	Amer.		O-1B	135	539	60	190	30	9	2	55	.353	1384	101	★22	.985
1918—St. Louis	Amer.		1B	114	452	69	154	21	9	2	45	.341	1244	97	13	.990
1919—St. Louis	Amer.		1B	132	511	96	180	31	15	10	83	.352	1249	120	13	.991
1920—St. Louis	Amer.		1B	●154	★631	137	★257	49	18	19	122	★.407	1477	★140	16	.990
1921—St. Louis	Amer.		1B	138	582	125	216	38	18	12	104	.371	1267	108	10	.993
1922—St. Louis	Amer.		1B	142	586	★134	★246	42	★18	8	105	★420	1293	★125	17	.988
1923—St. Louis	Amer.								(Out with eye trouble)							
1924—St. Louis	Amer.		1B	151	636	94	194	27	10	9	74	.305	1326	★112	★23	.984
1925—St. Louis	Amer.		1B	150	649	100	224	21	15	12	105	.345	1343	★131	★26	.983
1926—St. Louis	Amer.		1B	150	613	78	178	21	12	7	71	.289	1467	87	21	.987
1927—St. Louis(a)	Amer.		1B	149	614	87	201	32	8	5	97	.327	1374	★131	★24	.984
1928—Washington(b)	Amer.		1B	20	49	1	12	1	0	0	2	.245	45	0	0	1.000
1928—Boston	Nat.		1B	118	491	71	167	26	4	4	68	.340	1188	★86	15	.988
1929—Boston	Nat.		1B	154	629	67	205	40	8	2	79	.326	1398	111	★28	.982
1930—Boston	Nat.		1B	116	431	54	133	15	7	3	67	.309	915	81	13	.987
1931—Rochester	Int.		1B	159	613	86	186	37	5	3	81	.303	1401	★125	20	.987
1932—Shrev.-Tyler	Texas		1B	70	258	28	74	15	2	1	23	.287	637	33	15	.978
American League Totals—14 Years				1667	6716	1092	2307	344	145	93	966	.344	15375	1276	216	.987
National League Totals—3 Years				388	1551	192	505	81	19	9	214	.326	3501	278	56	.985
Major League Totals—15 Years				2055	8267	1284	2812	425	164	102	1180	.340	18876	1554	272	.987

aSold to Washington for $25,000, December 14, 1927.
bPurchased by Boston Braves for $7,500, May 27, 1928.

PITCHING RECORD

Year	Club	League	G.	IP.	W.	L.	Pct.	H.	R.	ER.	SO.	BB.	ERA.
1915—St. Louis	American	15	70	4	4	.500	62	26	22	41	38	2.83
1916—St. Louis	American	3	27	1	2	.333	18	4	3	12	6	1.00
1920—St. Louis	American	1	1	0	0	.000	0	0	0	2	0	0.00
1925—St. Louis	American	1	2	0	0	.000	1	0	0	1	1	0.00
1926—St. Louis	American	1	2	0	0	.000	0	0	0	3	2	0.00
1928—Boston	National	1	1	0	0	.000	0	0	0	0	1	0.00
Major League Totals—6 Years		22	103	5	6	.455	81	30	25	59	48	2.13

ENOS BRADSHER SLAUGHTER
(Country)

Born April 27, 1916, at Roxboro, N. C.

Height, 5.09.   Weight, 190.

Threw right and batted lefthanded.

Named as outfielder on THE SPORTING NEWS All-Star Major League Teams, 1942-46.
Led National League outfielders in double plays with 5 in 1939 and 5 in 1940 (tied).
Playing manager, Houston, American Association, 1960; Raleigh, Carolina League, 1961.
Named to Hall of Fame, 1985.

Year	Club	League	Pos.	G.	AB.	R.	H.	2B.	3B.	HR.	RBI.	B.A.	PO.	A.	E.	F.A.
1935—Martinsville	Bi-State		OF	109	422	68	115	25	11	18	.....	.273	187	24	16	.930
1936—Columbus	Sally		OF	151	569	106	185	31	★20	9	118	.325	317	10	17	.951
1937—Columbus	A. A.		OF	154	642	★147	★245	42	13	26	122	★.382	267	10	7	.975
1938—St. Louis	Nat.		OF	112	395	59	109	20	10	8	58	.276	189	7	6	.970
1939—St. Louis	Nat.		OF	149	604	95	193	★52	5	12	86	.320	★348	★118	★12	.968
1940—St. Louis	Nat.		OF	140	516	96	158	25	13	17	73	.306	267	8	3	.989
1941—St. Louis	Nat.		OF	113	425	71	132	22	9	13	76	.311	173	5	10	.947
1942—St. Louis	Nat.		OF	152	591	100	★188	31	★17	13	98	.318	287	15	4	.987
1943-44-45—St.L	Nat.		OF						(In Military Service)							
1946—St. Louis	Nat.		OF	●156	609	100	183	30	8	18	★130	.300	284	★ 23	6	.981
1947—St. Louis	Nat.		OF	147	551	100	162	31	13	10	86	.294	306	15	6	.982
1948—St. Louis	Nat.		OF	146	549	91	176	27	11	11	90	.321	330	9	10	.971
1949—St. Louis	Nat.		OF	151	568	92	191	34	●13	13	96	.336	330	10	6	.983
1950—St. Louis	Nat.		OF	148	556	82	161	26	7	10	101	.290	260	9	6	.978
1951—St. Louis	Nat.		OF	123	409	48	115	17	8	4	64	.281	198	10	1	.995
1952—St. Louis	Nat.		OF	140	510	73	153	17	12	11	101	.300	250	11	3	.989
1953—St. Louis(a)	Nat.		OF	143	492	64	143	34	9	6	89	.291	235	2	1	★.996
1954—New York	Amer.		OF	69	125	19	31	4	2	1	19	.248	37	0	1	.974

Year Club League	Pos.	G.	AB.	R.	H.	2B.	3B.	HR.	RBI.	B.A.	PO.	A.	E.	F.A.
1955—N.Y.(b)-K.C. .... Amer.	OF	118	276	50	87	12	4	5	35	.315	126	5	2	.985
1956—K.C.(c)-N.Y. .... Amer.	OF	115	306	52	86	18	5	2	27	.281	133	2	2	.985
1957—New York .... Amer.	OF	96	209	24	53	7	1	5	34	.254	97	2	0	1.000
1958—New York .... Amer.	OF	77	138	21	42	4	1	4	19	.304	43	1	2	.957
1959—New York .... Amer.	OF	74	99	10	17	2	0	6	21	.172	27	0	1	.964
1959—Milwaukee .... Nat.	OF	11	18	0	3	0	0	0	1	.167	5	0	0	1.000
1960—Houston .... A.A.	PH-OF	40	45	7	13	3	1	1	8	.289	......	......	......	......
1961—Raleigh .... PH	42	41	8	14	1	0	0	9	.341	......	......	......	......
American League Totals—6 Years		549	1153	176	316	47	13	23	155	.274	463	10	8	.983
National League Totals—14 Years		1831	6793	1071	2067	366	135	146	1149	.304	3452	142	74	.980
Major League Totals—19 Years		2380	7946	1247	2383	413	148	169	1304	.300	3915	152	82	.980

aTraded to New York Yankees for Pitcher Mel Wright and Outfielders Bill Virdon and Emil Tellinger from New York minor league affiliates to clubs in the St. Louis farm organization, April 11, 1954.

bTraded to Kansas City Athletics with Pitcher Johnny Sain for Pitcher Sonny Dixon and cash, May 11, 1955.

cReleased to New York Yankees, August 25, 1956.

WORLD SERIES RECORD

Year Club League	Pos.	G.	AB.	R.	H.	2B.	3B.	HR.	RBI.	B.A.	PO.	A.	E.	F.A.
1942—St. Louis .... Nat.	OF	5	19	3	5	1	0	1	2	.263	9	1	1	.909
1946—St. Louis .... Nat.	OF	7	25	5	8	1	1	1	2	.320	20	1	0	1.000
1956—New York .... Amer.	OF	6	20	6	7	0	0	1	4	.350	8	1	0	1.000
1957—New York .... Amer.	OF	5	12	2	3	1	0	0	0	.250	7	0	0	1.000
1958—New York .... Amer.	OF	4	3	1	0	0	0	0	0	.000	0	0	0	.000
World Series Totals—5 Years		27	79	17	23	3	1	3	8	.291	44	3	1	.979

CARL REGINALD (REGGIE) SMITH

Born April 2, 1945, at Shreveport, La.

Height, 6.00. Weight, 195.

Threw right and batted right and lefthanded.

Hit three home runs in a game, May 22, 1976.

Led Amercian League in total bases with 302 in 1971.

Led National League in sacrifice flies with 13 in 1978.

Named outfielder on The Sporting News American League All-Star Team, 1970.

Named outfielder on The Sporting News American League All-Star fielding team, 1968.

Year Club League	Pos.	G.	AB.	R.	H.	2B.	3B.	HR.	RBI.	B.A.	PO.	A.	E.	F.A.
1963—Wytheville† .... Appal.	SS	66	●253	59	65	8	3	8	37	.257	88	★146	★41	.851
1964—Reading .... East.	3B	17	47	6	6	1	0	0	4	.128	7	20	9	.750
1964—Waterloo .... Midw.	3-OF	87	308	63	98	18	5	15	60	.318	84	67	19	.888
1965—Pittsfield .... East.	OF-2-3	130	499	85	129	23	14	8	64	.259	263	107	21	.946
1966—Toronto .... Int.	★OF-S-2	143	506	86	162	30	9	18	80	★.320	303	49	★17	.954
1966—Boston .... Amer.	OF	6	26	1	4	1	0	0	0	.154	17	0	1	.944
1967—Boston .... Amer.	OF-2B	158	565	78	139	24	6	15	61	.246	353	32	7	.982
1968—Boston .... Amer.	OF	155	558	78	148	★37	5	15	69	.265	★390	8	6	.985
1969—Boston .... Amer.	OF	143	543	87	168	29	7	25	93	.309	321	8	14	.959
1970—Boston .... Amer.	OF	147	580	109	176	32	7	22	74	.303	361	●15	9	.977
1971—Boston .... Amer.	OF	159	618	85	175	★33	2	30	96	.283	386	15	★14	.966
1972—Boston .... Amer.	OF	131	467	75	126	25	4	21	74	.270	247	8	5	.981
1973—Boston‡ .... Amer.	OF-1B	115	423	79	128	23	2	21	69	.303	282	8	5	.983
1974—St. Louis .... Nat.	OF-1B	143	517	79	160	26	9	23	100	.309	286	9	7	.977
1975—St. Louis .... Nat.	O-1-3	135	477	67	144	26	3	16	76	.302	650	39	15	.979
1976—St. L.§-L.A. .... Nat.	OF-1-3	112	395	55	100	15	5	18	49	.253	314	48	4	.989
1977—Los Angeles .... Nat.	OF	148	488	104	150	27	4	32	87	.307	240	7	5	.980
1978—Los Angeles .... Nat.	OF	128	447	82	132	27	2	29	93	.295	220	8	12	.950
1979—Los Angeles .... Nat.	OF	68	234	41	64	13	1	10	32	.274	159	5	2	.988
1980—Los Angeles .... Nat.	OF	92	311	47	100	13	0	15	55	.322	153	15	1	.994
1981—Los Angeles x .... Nat.	1B	41	35	5	7	1	0	1	8	.200	15	1	0	1.000
1982—San Francisco y ... Nat.	1B	106	349	51	99	11	0	18	56	.284	792	78	16	.982
National League Totals—9 Years		973	3253	531	956	159	24	165	556	.294	2829	210	62	.980
American League Totals—8 Years		1014	3780	592	1064	204	33	149	536	.281	2357	94	61	.976
Major League Totals—17 Years		1987	7033	1123	2020	363	57	314	1092	.287	5186	304	123	.978

Signed as free agent with Minnesota Twins' organization, June 21, 1963.

†Drafted by Boston Red Sox, December 2, 1963.

‡Traded with Pitcher Ken Tatum to St. Louis Cardinals for Pitcher Rick Wise and Outfielder Bernie Carbo, October 26, 1973.

§Traded to Los Angeles Dodgers for Catcher-Outfielder Joe Ferguson, Outfielder Bob Detherage, and Infielder Freddie Tisdale, June 15, 1976.

xGranted free agency, November 13, 1981; signed by San Francisco Giants, February 27, 1982.

yGranted free agency, November 10, 1982; signed by Tokyo Giants of Japanese baseball.

Year Club League	Pos.	G.	AB.	R.	H.	2B.	3B.	HR.	RBI.	B.A.	PO.	A.	E.	F.A.
1977—Los Angeles .... Nat.	OF	4	16	2	3	0	1	0	1	.188	7	0	1	.875
1978—Los Angeles .... Nat.	OF	4	16	2	3	1	0	0	1	.188	5	0	1	.833
1981—Los Angeles .... Nat.	PH	1	1	0	1	0	0	0	1	1.000	0	0	0	.000
Championship Series Totals—3 Years.....		9	33	4	7	1	1	0	3	.212	12	0	2	.857

WORLD SERIES RECORD

Year Club League	Pos.	G.	AB.	R.	H.	2B.	3B.	HR.	RBI.	B.A.	PO.	A.	E.	F.A.
1967—Boston.................... Amer.	OF	7	24	3	6	1	0	2	3	.250	14	2	0	1.000
1977—Los Angeles .... Nat.	OF	6	22	7	6	1	0	3	5	.273	14	1	0	1.000
1978—Los Angeles .... Nat.	OF	6	25	3	5	0	0	1	5	.200	11	1	1	.923
1981—Los Angeles .... Nat.	PH	2	2	0	1	0	0	0	0	.500	0	0	0	.000
World Series Totals—4 Years		21	73	13	18	2	0	6	13	.247	39	4	1	.977

ELMER ELLSWORTH SMITH

Born March 28, 1868, at Allegheny, Pa.

Died November 5, 1945, at Pittsburgh, Pa.

Height, 5.11. Weight, 178.

Threw and batted lefthanded.

Year Club League	Pos.	G.	AB.	R.	H.	2B.	3B.	HR.	SB.	B.A.	PO.	A.	E.	F.A.
1886—Nashville............... So.Leag.		...	...	...	...	...	...	...	...	......	.....	...	...	......
1886—Cincinnati............. A.A.	P-OF	9	26	6	8	0	0	0	0	.308	.....	....	...	......
1887—Cincinnati............. A.A.	P-OF	52	198	30	57	9	5	0	5	.288	.....	....	13	.948
1888—Cincinnati............. A.A.	P-OF	40	132	14	29	3	1	0	3	.220	.....	....	11	.948
1889—Cincinnati............. A.A.	P	28	81	12	23	3	1	2	0	.259	.....	....		
1890—Kansas City.......... W.A.	P-OF	112	463	128	150	...	...	...	...	.331	142	11	18	.894
1891—Kansas City.......... W.A.	OF	120	479	118	148	...	...	...	18	.308	219	13	24	.906
1892—Pittsburgh.............. Nat.	P-OF	136	495	86	140	18	14	4	23	.282	233	15	29	.891
1893—Pittsburgh.............. Nat.	OF	128	500	119	183	27	21	7	28	.366	274	14	24	.923
1894—Pittsburgh.............. Nat.	OF	125	497	129	175	34	18	6	37	.352	271	18	20	.935
1895—Pittsburgh.............. Nat.	OF	124	492	109	146	16	13	1	35	.296	255	16	32	.891
1896—Pittsburgh.............. Nat.	OF	120	475	118	170	22	14	6	32	.358	297	11	17	.947
1897—Pittsburgh.............. Nat.	OF	122	463	101	145	18	19	6	28	.311	240	17	26	.908
1898—Cincinnati............. Nat.	OF	122	483	76	166	22	9	1	19	.344	280	15	18	.942
1899—Cincinnati............. Nat.	OF	87	342	64	101	15	5	1	11	.295	179	10	6	.969
1900—Cin.-N.Y. .... Nat.	OF	116	425	61	118	13	10	3	20	.278	151	14	10	.943
1901—Pitts.-Bos. .... Nat.	OF	22	77	6	12	2	1	0	2	.158	21	1	4	.846
1902—Kansas City.......... A.A.	OF	....	408	69	127	....	....	....	....	.311	243	7	19	.926
1903—Minneapolis .... A.A.	OF	75	300	55	97	15	4	2	7	.323	104	5	5	.956
1904—Kansas City.......... A.A.	OF	12	44	6	13	1	0	0	1	.295	13	2	1	.955
1904—Ilion...................... N.Y.	1B	110	383	56	125	....	....	....	13	.326	801	27	25	.970
1905—Scranton.............. N.Y.	OF	114	520	52	138	....	....	....	22	.328	117	8	5	.961
1906—Binghamton .... N.Y.	OF	119	396	43	124	....	....	....	8	.313	249	13	9	.966
American Assn. Totals—4 Years		129	437	62	117	15	7	2	8	.268	....	....	....	......
National League Totals—10 Years		1102	4249	869	1356	187	124	35	235	.319	2201	131	186	.926
Major League Totals—14 Years.............		1231	4686	931	1473	202	131	37	243	.314	....	....	....	......

PITCHING RECORD

Year Club League	G.	W.	L.	Pct.	H.	R.	SO.	BB.	CG.	ShO.
1886—Cincinnati.................... Amer. Assn.	9	4	5	.444	....	....	....	....	9	0
1887—Cincinnati.................... Amer. Assn.	52	33	18	.647	551	242	114	128	46	3
1888—Cincinnati.................... Amer. Assn.	40	22	17	.564	305	161	128	106	39	5
1889—Cincinnati.................... Amer. Assn.	28	10	12	.455	251	169	98	103	16	0
1890—Kansas City........................ West. Assn.	36	....	....	....	205	114	213	96	....	....
1892—Pittsburgh........................ National	13	7	6	.538	....	....	....	....	12	1
American Assn. Totals—4 Years.................	129	69	52	.570	....	....	....	....	110	8
National League Totals—1 Year.................	13	7	6	.538	....	....	....	....	12	1
Major League Totals—5 Years.................	142	76	58	.567	....	....	....	....	122	9

—DID YOU KNOW—

That former Dodger great Duke Snider hit the last home run at Brooklyn's Ebbets Field? Snider connected twice in a game played September 22, 1957.

EDWIN DONALD (DUKE) SNIDER

Born September 19, 1926, at Los Angeles, Calif.
Height, 6.00. Weight, 200.
Threw right and batted lefthanded.
Married Beverly Null, October 25, 1947.

Shares major league records for most at-bats, inning (3), May 21, 1952, first inning; most strikeouts, inning (2), August 14, 1954, sixth inning; most consecutive years leading league in strikeouts (3).

Shares National League record for most consecutive years with 40 or more home runs (5).

Hit three home runs in a game, May 30, 1950 and June 1, 1955.

Named Major League Player of Year by THE SPORTING NEWS, 1955; No. 1 National League Player by THE SPORTING NEWS, 1955.

Named outfielder on THE SPORTING NEWS All-Star Major League Teams, 1953-54-55.

Scout, Los Angeles Dodgers, 1965 (part); manager, Spokane, Pacific Coast League, 1965; Kennewick, Northwest League, 1966; scout, Dodgers, 1967-68; San Diego Padres, 1969; manager, Alexandria, Texas League, 1972; batting instructor, Montreal Expos, 1974-75.

Named to Hall of Fame, 1980.

Year Club	League	Pos.	G.	AB.	R.	H.	2B.	3B.	HR.	RBI.	B.A.	PO.	A.	E.	F.A.
1944—Montreal	Int.	PH	2	2	0	0	0	0	0	0	.000	0	0	0	.000
1944—Newport News	Pied.	OF	131	507	87	149	★34	6	★709	50	.294	231	★25	18	.934
1945—Newport News	Pied.							(In Military Service)							
1946—Fort Worth	Tex.	OF	68	232	36	58	13	1	5	30	.250	110	6	5	.959
1947—St. Paul	A.A.	OF	66	269	59	85	22	7	12	46	.316	157	5	6	.964
1947—Brooklyn	Nat.	OF	40	83	6	20	3	1	0	5	.241	48	0	1	.980
1948—Montreal	Int.	OF	77	275	67	90	28	4	17	77	.327	136	13	7	.955
1948—Brooklyn	Nat.	OF	53	160	22	39	6	6	5	21	.244	87	5	1	.989
1949—Brooklyn	Nat.	OF	146	552	100	161	28	7	23	92	.292	355	12	6	.984
1950—Brooklyn	Nat.	OF	152	620	109	★199	31	10	31	107	.321	378	15	7	.983
1951—Brooklyn	Nat.	OF	150	606	96	168	26	6	29	101	.277	382	12	5	.987
1952—Brooklyn	Nat.	OF	144	534	80	162	25	7	21	92	.303	341	13	3	.992
1953—Brooklyn	Nat.	OF	153	590	★132	198	38	4	42	126	.336	370	7	5	.987
1954—Brooklyn	Nat.	OF	149	584	●120	199	39	10	40	130	.341	360	8	7	.981
1955—Brooklyn	Nat.	OF	148	538	★126	166	34	6	42	★136	.309	348	9	4	.989
1956—Brooklyn	Nat.	OF	151	542	112	158	33	2	★43	101	.292	358	11	6	.984
1957—Brooklyn	Nat.	OF	139	508	91	139	25	7	40	92	.274	304	6	3	.990
1958—Los Angeles	Nat.	OF	106	327	45	102	12	3	15	58	.312	151	4	2	.987
1959—Los Angeles	Nat.	OF	126	370	59	114	11	2	23	88	.308	157	2	4	.975
1960—Los Angeles	Nat.	OF	101	235	38	57	13	5	14	36	.243	108	3	4	.965
1961—Los Angeles	Nat.	OF	85	233	35	69	8	3	16	56	.296	113	6	3	.975
1962—Los Angeles(a)	Nat.	OF	80	158	28	44	11	3	5	30	.278	56	3	2	.967
1963—New York(b)	Nat.	OF	129	354	44	86	8	3	14	45	.243	139	5	2	.986
1964—San Francisco	Nat.	OF	91	167	16	35	7	0	4	17	.210	44	2	1	.979
Major League Totals—18 Years			2143	7161	1259	2116	358	85	407	1333	.295	4099	123	66	.985

aSold to New York Mets, April 1, 1963.
bReleased to San Francisco Giants, April 14, 1964.

WORLD SERIES RECORD

Year Club	League	Pos.	G.	AB.	R.	H.	2B.	3B.	HR.	RBI.	B.A.	PO.	A.	E.	F.A.
1949—Brooklyn	Nat.	OF	5	21	2	3	1	0	0	0	.143	18	1	0	1.000
1952—Brooklyn	Nat.	OF	7	29	5	10	2	0	4	8	.345	23	0	0	1.000
1953—Brooklyn	Nat.	OF	6	25	3	8	3	0	1	5	.320	17	1	0	1.000
1955—Brooklyn	Nat.	OF	7	25	5	8	1	0	4	7	.320	13	0	0	1.000
1956—Brooklyn	Nat.	OF	7	23	5	7	1	0	1	4	.304	20	0	0	1.000
1959—Los Angeles	Nat.	OF	4	10	1	2	0	0	1	2	.200	5	0	2	.714
World Series Totals— 6 Years			36	133	21	38	8	0	11	26	.286	96	2	2	.980

WARREN EDWARD SPAHN

Born April 23, 1921, at Buffalo, N. Y.
Height, 6.00. Weight, 183.
Threw and batted lefthanded.

Holds major league records for most years leading league in games won (8) and complete games (7); most games won by lefthanded pitcher, lifetime (363).

Led National League in complete games with 25 in 1949, 26 in 1951, 18 in 1957, 23 in 1958, 21 in 1959, 18 in 1960, 21 in 1961, 22 in 1962 and 22 in 1963; led in shutouts with 7 in 1947, 7 in 1951, tied with 4 in 1959 and tied with 4 in 1961.

Pitched 4-0 no-hit victory against Philadelphia Phillies, September 16, 1960, and 1-0 no-hit victory against San Francisco Giants, April 28, 1961.

Named Outstanding National League pitcher by THE SPORTING NEWS, 1953-57-58-61.

Named as pitcher on THE SPORTING NEWS National League All-Star Team, 1961.

Named as pitcher on THE SPORTING NEWS All-Star Major League Teams, 1953-57-58-60.

Won major league Cy Young Memorial Award, 1957.

Player-coach, New York Mets, 1965; manager, Tulsa, Pacific Coast League, 1967 and 1968 and American Association, 1969-70; scout, St. Louis Cardinals, National League, and pitching instructor, minor leagues, St. Louis, 1971; coach, Cleveland Indians, American League, 1972-73; pitching instructor, minor leagues, California Angels, American League, 1978 through 1980.

Named to Hall of Fame, 1973.

Year Club	League	G.	IP.	W.	L.	Pct.	H.	R.	ER.	SO.	BB.	ERA.
1940—Bradford	Pony	12	66	5	4	.556	53	27	20	62	24	2.73
1941—Evansville	I.I.I.	28	212	*19	6	*.760	154	62	43	193	90	*1.83
1942—Hartford	East.	33	248	17	12	.586	148	65	54	141	130	1.96
1942—Boston	Nat.	4	16	0	0	.000	25	15	10	7	11	5.63
1943-44-45—Boston	Nat.					(In Military Service)						
1946—Boston	Nat.	24	126	8	5	.615	107	46	41	67	36	2.93
1947—Boston	Nat.	40	*290	21	10	.677	245	87	75	123	84	*2.33
1948—Boston	Nat.	36	257	15	12	.556	237	115	106	114	77	3.71
1949—Boston	Nat.	38	*302	*21	14	.600	283	125	103	*151	86	3.07
1950—Boston	Nat.	41	293	*21	17	.553	248	123	103	*191	111	3.16
1951—Boston	Nat.	39	311	22	14	.611	278	111	103	●164	*109	2.98
1952—Boston	Nat.	40	290	14	19	.424	263	109	96	*183	73	2.98
1953—Milwaukee	Nat.	35	266	●23	7	.767	211	75	62	148	70	*2.10
1954—Milwaukee	Nat.	39	283	21	12	.636	262	107	99	136	86	3.15
1955—Milwaukee	Nat.	39	246	17	14	.548	249	99	89	110	65	3.26
1956—Milwaukee	Nat.	39	281	20	11	.645	249	92	87	128	52	2.79
1957—Milwaukee	Nat.	39	271	*21	11	.656	241	94	81	111	78	2.69
1958—Milwaukee	Nat.	38	*290	●22	11	●.667	257	106	99	150	76	3.07
1959—Milwaukee	Nat.	40	*292	●21	15	.583	282	106	96	143	70	2.96
1960—Milwaukee	Nat.	40	268	●21	10	.677	254	114	104	154	74	3.49
1961—Milwaukee	Nat.	38	263	●21	13	.618	236	96	88	115	64	*3.01
1962—Milwaukee	Nat.	34	269	18	14	.563	248	97	91	118	55	3.04
1963—Milwaukee	Nat.	33	260	23	7	.767	241	85	75	102	49	2.60
1964—Milwaukee(a)	Nat.	38	174	6	13	.316	204	110	102	78	52	5.28
1965—N.Y.(b)-San Fran.	Nat.	36	198	7	16	.304	210	104	88	90	56	4.00
1966—Mexico City Tigers	Mex.	3	10	1	1	.500	14	7	5	7	1	4.50
1967—Tulsa	P. C.	3	7	0	1	.000	8	6	5	5	5	6.43
Major League Totals—21 Years		750	5246	363	245	.597	4830	2016	1798	2583	1434	3.08

aSold to New York Mets, November 23, 1964.

bReleased by New York Mets, July 19, 1965, and signed by San Francisco Giants, July 22, 1965.

WORLD SERIES RECORD

Year Club	League	G.	IP.	W.	L.	Pct.	H.	R.	ER.	SO.	BB.	ERA.
1948—Boston	Nat.	3	12	1	1	.500	10	4	4	12	3	3.00
1957—Milwaukee	Nat.	2	15⅓	1	1	.500	18	8	8	2	2	4.70
1958—Milwaukee	Nat.	3	28⅔	2	1	.667	19	7	7	18	8	1.88
World Series Totals—3 Years		8	56	4	3	.571	47	19	19	32	13	2.89

ALBERT GOODWILL (AL) SPALDING

Born September 2, 1850, at Byron, Ill.

Died September 9, 1915, at Point Loma, Calif.

Height, 6.01. Weight, 170.

Threw and batted righthanded.

Manager, Chicago N. L., 1876-1878; owner, Chicago N. L., 1882-1891. Founder, A. G. Spalding & Bros., 1876.

Named to Hall of Fame, 1939.

Year Club	League	Pos.	G.	W.	L.	Pct.	ShO.	B.A.	F.A.
1866—Forest City of Rockford	Ind.	....		....	....	......	....	......	......
1867—Forest City of Rockford	Ind.	....		....	....	......	....	......	......
1868—Forest City of Rockford	Ind.	P	15	....	....	......	....	......	......
1869—Forest City of Rockford	Ind.	P	24	....	....	......	....	......	......
1870—Forest City of Rockford	Ind.	P	55	....	....	......	....	......	......
1871—Boston	N. Assn.	P	31	20	10	.667	1	.265	......
1872—Boston	N. Assn.	P	47	36	8	.818	3	.339	.903

Year	Club	League	Pos.	G.	W.	L.	Pct.	ShO.	B.A.	F.A.
1873—Boston	N. Assn.		P	60	41	15	.732	1	.340	.941
1874—Boston	N. Assn.		P	71	52	18	.743	4	.331	.845
1875—Boston	N. Assn.		P	74	56	4	.933	9	.318	.764
1876—Chicago	Nat.		P-OF	66	★47	13	★.783	9	.305	.841
1877—Chicago(a)	Nat.		P-1B-2B	★60	0	0	.000	0	.256	.953
Major League Totals—2 Years				126	47	13	.783	27	......	......

aIn 1877, Spalding pitched in 4 games.

TRISTRAM (TRIS) SPEAKER
(Spoke and The Grey Eagle)

Born April 4, 1888, at Hubbard City, Tex.
Died December 8, 1958, at Lake Whitney, Tex.
Height, 5.11½. Weight, 193.
Threw and batted lefthanded.

Holds major league records for most doubles, lifetime (793); most assists (450) and double plays (135) by outfielder, lifetime; most years leading league in double plays by outfielder (5).

Shares major league record for most unassisted double plays by outfielder, lifetime (4).

Holds American League records for most chances accepted by outfielder, lifetime (7,244); most years leading league in chances accepted (8).

Shares American League record for most assists by outfielder, season (35), 1909 and 1912.

Manager, Cleveland Indians, 1919 to 1926; Newark, International League, 1929 to 1930.

Named to Hall of Fame, 1937.

Year	Club	League	Pos.	G.	AB.	R.	H.	2B.	3B.	HR.	RBI.	B.A.	PO.	A.	E.	F.A.
1906—Cleburne	No. Tex.	OF-P	84	287	35	77	....	....	.....	.268	100	43	3	.979
1907—Houston	Texas	OF	118	468	70	147	32	12	3	.....	★314	189	29	12	.948
1907—Boston	Amer.	OF	7	20	0	3	0	0	0	0	.150	4	2	0	1.000
1908—Little Rock	South.	OF	127	471	★81	★165	19	10	3	.....	★.350	★330	★37	13	.966
1908—Boston	Amer.	OF	31	116	12	26	2	2	0	10	.224	58	9	0	1.000
1909—Boston	Amer.	OF	143	544	73	168	26	13	7	79	.309	★319	★35	10	.973
1910—Boston	Amer.	OF	141	538	92	183	20	14	7	62	.340	★337	20	16	.957
1911—Boston	Amer.	OF	141	500	88	167	34	13	8	80	.334	297	26	15	.956
1912—Boston	Amer.	OF	153	580	136	222	★53	12	10	98	.383	★372	★35	18	.958
1913—Boston	Amer.	OF	141	520	94	190	35	22	3	81	.365	★374	★30	●24	.944
1914—Boston	Amer.	OF	●158	571	100	★193	★46	18	4	86	.338	★425	●30	15	.968
1915—Boston(a)	Amer.	OF	150	547	108	176	25	12	0	63	.322	★378	21	10	.976
1916—Cleveland	Amer.	OF	151	546	102	★211	●41	8	2	83	★.386	359	25	10	.975
1917—Cleveland	Amer.	OF	142	523	90	184	42	11	2	65	.352	365	23	8	.980
1918—Cleveland	Amer.	OF	127	471	73	150	★33	11	0	61	.318	★356	15	10	.974
1919—Cleveland	Amer.	OF	134	494	83	146	38	12	2	69	.296	★375	25	7	.983
1920—Cleveland	Amer.	OF	150	552	137	214	★50	11	8	107	.388	363	24	9	.977
1921—Cleveland	Amer.	OF	132	506	107	183	★52	14	3	74	.362	345	15	6	★.984
1922—Cleveland	Amer.	OF	131	426	85	161	★48	8	11	71	.378	285	13	5	★.983
1923—Cleveland	Amer.	OF	150	574	133	218	★59	11	17	130	.380	369	26	13	.968
1924—Cleveland	Amer.	OF	136	486	94	167	36	9	9	65	.344	323	20	13	.963
1925—Cleveland	Amer.	OF	117	429	79	167	35	5	12	87	.389	311	16	11	.967
1926—Cleveland(b)	Amer.	OF	150	539	96	164	52	8	7	86	.304	394	20	8	.981
1927—Wash.(c)(d)	Amer.	OF-1B	141	523	71	171	43	6	2	73	.327	423	24	12	.974
1928—Philadelphia	Amer.	OF	64	191	28	51	23	2	3	32	.267	111	8	3	.975
1929—Newark	Int.	OF	48	138	36	49	11	1	5	20	.355	57	2	0	1.000
1930—Newark	Int.	OF	11	31	3	13	1	1	0	3	.419	10	1	1	.917
Major League Totals—22 Years			2790	10196	1881	3515	793	222	117	1562	.345	6941	462	223	.971

aTraded to Cleveland for Pitcher Sam Jones, Infielder Fred Thomas and cash, April 12, 1916.
bReleased by Washington and signed with Philadelphia, February 5, 1928.

WORLD SERIES RECORD

Year	Club	League	Pos.	G.	AB.	R.	H.	2B.	3B.	HR.	RBI.	B.A.	PO.	A.	E.	F.A.
1912—Boston	Amer.	OF	8	30	4	9	1	2	0	2	.300	21	2	2	.920
1915—Boston	Amer.	OF	5	17	2	5	0	1	0	0	.294	10	0	0	1.000
1920—Cleveland	Amer.	OF	7	25	6	8	2	1	0	1	.320	18	0	0	1.000
World Series Totals—3 Years			20	72	12	22	3	4	0	3	.306	49	2	2	.962

—DID YOU KNOW—

That Tris Speaker was the only player other than Ty Cobb to win an A.L. batting championship between 1907 and 1919? Cobb led the league 12 times during that period with Speaker, playing for Cleveland at the time, claiming his lone title with a .386 mark in 1916.

CHARLES SYLVESTER (CHICK) STAHL

Born January 10, 1873, at Fort Wayne, Ind.

Died March 28, 1907, at West Baden Springs, Ind.

Threw and batted lefthanded.

Brother of Jake Stahl, former major league
first baseman-outfielder-catcher.

Manager, Boston Red Sox, 1906.

Year Club League	Pos.	G.	AB.	R.	H.	2B.	3B.	HR.	SB.	B.A.	PO.	A.	E.	F.A.
1894—Battle Creek .... Mich.						(No record available)								
1895—Battle Creek .... Mich.						(No record available)								
1896—Buffalo(a) .... East.	OF	122	519	★129	175	...	...	...	34	.337	199	25	15	.937
1897—Boston.................... Nat.	OF	111	468	111	168	26	12	3	14	.359	169	18	13	.935
1898—Boston.................... Nat.	OF	125	469	69	146	19	7	3	5	.311	200	15	9	.960
1899—Boston.................... Nat.	OF	148	578	123	201	22	17	8	24	.348	253	27	9	.969
1900—Boston.................... Nat.	OF	134	552	88	162	24	16	5	25	.293	227	22	13	.950
1901—Boston.................... Amer.	OF	130	512	106	159	22	16	6	29	.311	273	12	12	★.960
1902—Boston.................... Amer.	OF	127	507	92	161	25	10	2	18	.318	246	18	11	.960
1903—Boston.................... Amer.	OF	78	298	60	83	11	6	2	14	.279	126	12	5	.965
1904—Boston.................... Amer.	OF	157	583	84	173	27	★22	3	13	.297	287	7	10	.967
1905—Boston.................... Amer.	OF	134	500	61	129	18	4	0	18	.258	249	11	6	.977
1906—Boston.................... Amer.	OF	155	595	62	170	24	6	4	13	.286	★344	24	●15	.961
American League Totals—6 Years		781	2995	465	875	127	64	17	105	.292	1525	84	59	.965
National League Totals—4 Years		518	2067	391	677	91	52	19	68	.328	849	82	44	.955
Major League Totals—10 Years............		1299	5062	856	1552	218	116	36	173	.307	2374	166	103	.961

aDrafted by Boston in winter of 1896.

WORLD SERIES RECORD

Year Club League	Pos.	G.	AB.	R.	H.	2B.	3B.	HR.	SB.	B.A.	PO.	A.	E.	F.A.
1903—Boston.................... Amer.	OF	8	33	6	10	1	3	0	2	.303	14	1	0	1.000

WILVER DORNEL (WILLIE) STARGELL

Born March 6, 1941, at Earlsboro, Okla.

Height, 6.03. Weight, 225.

Threw and batted lefthanded.

Shares major league records for most long hits, game (5), August 1, 1970; most times, three or more home runs in a game, season (2), April 10 and April 21, 1971; most home runs, April (11), 1971.

Holds National League records for most strikeouts, lifetime (1,936); most seasons (13) and most consecutive seasons (12), 100 or more strikeouts; most games, 4 or more long hits, lifetime (4); most home runs through June 30 (28), 1971; most strikeouts by lefthanded batter, season (154), 1971.

Shares National League record for most home runs through July 31 (36), 1971.

Hit three home runs in a game, June 24, 1965, May 22, 1968, April 10 (12 innings) and April 21, 1971.

Led National League in slugging percentage with .646 in 1973.

Led National League batters in strikeouts with 154 in 1971.

Named Man of the Year by THE SPORTING NEWS, 1979.

Named Major League Player of the Year by THE SPORTING NEWS, 1979.

Named National League co-Most Valuable Player by Baseball Writers' Association of America, 1979.

Named National League Comeback Player of the Year by THE SPORTING NEWS, 1978.

Named first baseman on THE SPORTING NEWS National League All-Star Team, 1972.

Named outfielder on THE SPORTING NEWS National League All-Star Team, 1965, 1966 and 1971.

Minor League instructor, Pittsburgh Pirates, 1983 to 1985; coach, Pirates, 1985; Atlanta Braves, 1986 to 1988.

Named to Hall of Fame, 1988.

Year Club League	Pos.	G.	AB.	R.	H.	2B.	3B.	HR.	RBI.	B.A.	PO.	A.	E.	F.A.
1959—S. A'gelo-R'well .... Soph.	1B	118	431	66	118	28	6	7	87	.274	842	22	★37	.959
1960—Grand Forks .... North.	OF	107	396	63	103	19	1	11	61	.260	224	12	13	.948
1961—Asheville .... Sally	OF	130	453	78	131	21	8	22	89	.289	264	14	★19	.936
1962—Columbus.............. Int.	OF-1B	138	497	97	137	21	8	27	82	.276	354	18	13	.966
1962—Pittsburgh.............. Nat.	OF	10	31	1	9	3	1	0	4	.290	12	1	1	.929

Year	Club	League	Pos.	G.	AB.	R.	H.	2B.	3B.	HR.	RBI.	B.A.	PO.	A.	E.	F.A.
1963—Pittsburgh	Nat.	OF-1B	108	304	34	74	11	6	11	47	.243	226	12	9	.964
1964—Pittsburgh	Nat.	OF-1B	117	421	53	115	19	7	21	78	.273	565	24	10	.983
1965—Pittsburgh	Nat.	OF-1B	144	533	68	145	25	8	27	107	.272	268	14	8	.972
1966—Pittsburgh	Nat.	OF-1B	140	485	84	153	30	0	33	102	.315	300	13	11	.966
1967—Pittsburgh	Nat.	OF-1B	134	462	54	125	18	6	20	73	.271	447	27	11	.977
1968—Pittsburgh	Nat.	OF-1B	128	435	57	103	15	1	24	67	.237	254	19	9	.968
1969—Pittsburgh	Nat.	OF-1B	145	522	89	160	31	6	29	92	.307	333	14	7	.980
1970—Pittsburgh	Nat.	★OF-1B	136	474	70	125	18	3	31	85	.264	184	★17	5	.976
1971—Pittsburgh	Nat.	OF	141	511	104	151	26	0	★48	125	.295	237	8	4	.984
1972—Pittsburgh	Nat.	★1B-OF	138	495	75	145	28	2	33	112	.293	931	41	★17	.983
1973—Pittsburgh	Nat.	OF	148	522	106	156	★43	3	★44	★119	.299	261	14	7	.975
1974—Pittsburgh	Nat.	OF-1B	140	508	90	153	37	4	25	96	.301	256	8	9	.967
1975—Pittsburgh	Nat.	1B	124	461	71	136	32	2	22	90	.295	1121	54	10	.992
1976—Pittsburgh	Nat.	1B	117	428	54	110	20	3	20	65	.257	1037	53	13	.988
1977—Pittsburgh	Nat.	1B	63	186	29	51	12	0	13	35	.274	449	27	7	.986
1978—Pittsburgh	Nat.	1B	122	390	60	115	18	2	28	97	.295	875	57	6	.994
1979—Pittsburgh	Nat.	1B	126	424	60	119	19	0	32	82	.281	949	47	3	★.997
1980—Pittsburgh	Nat.	1B	67	202	28	53	10	1	11	38	.262	460	33	4	.992
1981—Pittsburgh	Nat.	1B	38	60	2	17	4	0	0	9	.283	70	0	0	1.000
1982—Pittsburgh†	Nat.	1B	74	73	6	17	4	0	3	17	.233	43	3	0	1.000
Major League Totals—21 Years				2360	7927	1195	2232	423	55	475	1540	.282	9278	486	151	.985

Signed as free agent by Pittsburgh Pirates' organization, August 7, 1958.
†On voluntarily retired list, October 12, 1982.

CHAMPIONSHIP SERIES RECORD

Year	Club	League	Pos.	G.	AB.	R.	H.	2B.	3B.	HR.	RBI.	B.A.	PO.	A.	E.	F.A.
1970—Pittsburgh	Nat.	OF	3	12	0	6	1	0	0	1	.500	4	0	0	1.000
1971—Pittsburgh	Nat.	OF	4	14	1	0	0	0	0	0	.000	6	0	0	1.000
1972—Pittsburgh	Nat.	1B-OF	5	16	1	1	1	0	0	1	.063	32	3	0	1.000
1974—Pittsburgh	Nat.	OF	4	15	3	6	0	0	2	4	.400	13	0	0	1.000
1975—Pittsburgh	Nat.	1B	3	11	1	2	1	0	0	0	.182	15	0	0	1.000
1979—Pittsburgh	Nat.	1B	3	11	2	5	2	0	2	6	.455	32	2	0	1.000
Championship Series Totals—6 Years				22	79	8	20	5	0	4	12	.253	102	5	0	1.000

WORLD SERIES RECORD

Holds record for most long hits, series (7), 1979.
Shares record for most total bases, series (25), 1979.

Year	Club	League	Pos.	G.	AB.	R.	H.	2B.	3B.	HR.	RBI.	B.A.	PO.	A.	E.	F.A.
1971—Pittsburgh	Nat.	OF	7	24	3	5	1	0	0	1	.208	11	1	0	1.000
1979—Pittsburgh	Nat.	1B	7	30	7	12	4	0	3	7	.400	59	2	2	.968
World Series Totals—2 Years				14	54	10	17	5	0	3	8	.315	70	3	2	.973

DANIEL JOSEPH (RUSTY) STAUB

Born April 1, 1944, at New Orleans, La.

Height, 6.02. Weight, 215.

Threw right and batted lefthanded.

Holds major league records for most games by pinch-hitter, season (94), 1983; most at-bats by pinch-hitter, season (81), 1983.
Shares major league records for most consecutive seasons leading league in grounding into double plays (2); most consecutive hits during season by pinch-hitter (8), June 11 through June 26, first game, 1983.
Led American League in grounding into double plays with 23 in 1976 and 27 in 1977.
Tied for National League lead in double plays by outfielders with 5 in 1971, 5 in 1973 and 5 in 1974.
Led Carolina League first basemen in double plays with 123 in 1962.
Named designated hitter on THE SPORTING NEWS American League All-Star Team, 1978.
Named Carolina League Most Valuable Player, 1962.
Player-coach, New York Mets, 1982.

Year	Club	League	Pos.	G.	AB.	R.	H.	2B.	3B.	HR.	RBI.	B.A.	PO.	A.	E.	F.A.
1962—Durham	Carol.	1B	●140	509	●115	149	20	4	23	93	.293	★1247	★76	★20	.985
1963—Houston	Nat.	1B-OF	150	513	43	115	17	4	6	45	.224	963	63	11	.989
1964—Houston	Nat.	1B-OF	89	292	26	63	10	2	8	35	.216	512	30	9	.984
1964—Oklahoma City	P. C.	OF-1B	71	226	55	71	13	1	20	45	.314	306	22	5	.985
1965—Houston	Nat.	OF-1B	131	410	43	105	20	1	14	63	.256	203	12	11	.951
1966—Houston	Nat.	OF-1B	153	554	60	155	28	3	13	81	.280	291	15	12	.962
1967—Houston	Nat.	OF	149	546	71	182	★44	1	10	74	.333	269	10	11	.962
1968—Houston†	Nat.	1B-OF	161	591	54	172	37	1	6	72	.291	1336	94	13	.991
1969—Montreal	Nat.	OF	158	549	89	166	26	5	29	79	.302	265	★16	10	.966

Year	Club	League	Pos.	G.	AB.	R.	H.	2B.	3B.	HR.	RBI.	B.A.	PO.	A.	E.	F.A.
1970—Montreal	Nat.		OF	160	569	98	156	23	7	30	94	.274	308	14	5	.985
1971—Montreal‡	Nat.		OF	★162	599	94	186	34	6	19	97	.311	290	★20	★18	.945
1972—New York	Nat.		OF	66	239	32	70	11	0	9	38	.293	108	4	2	.982
1973—New York	Nat.		OF	152	585	77	163	36	1	15	76	.279	297	17	7	.978
1974—New York	Nat.		OF	151	561	65	145	22	2	19	78	.258	262	★19	5	.983
1975—New York§	Nat.		OF	155	574	93	162	30	4	19	105	.282	267	★15	4	.986
1976—Detroit	Amer.		OF	●161	589	73	176	28	3	15	96	.299	218	8	7	.970
1977—Detroit	Amer.		DH	158	623	84	173	34	3	22	101	.278	0	0	0	.000
1978—Detroit	Amer.		DH	162	642	75	175	30	1	24	121	.273	0	0	0	.000
1979—Detroit x	Amer.		DH	68	246	32	58	12	1	9	40	.236	0	0	0	.000
1979—Montreal y	Nat.		1B-OF	38	86	9	23	3	0	3	14	.267	156	7	1	.994
1980—Texas z	Amer.		1B-OF	109	340	42	102	23	2	9	55	.300	262	14	6	.979
1981—New York	Nat.		1B	70	161	9	51	9	0	5	21	.317	339	20	4	.989
1982—New York	Nat.		OF-1B	112	219	11	53	9	0	3	27	.242	172	19	2	.990
1983—New York	Nat.		1B-OF	104	115	5	34	6	0	3	28	.296	40	5	2	.957
1984—New York a	Nat.		1B	78	72	2	19	4	0	1	18	.264	13	0	0	1.000
1985—New York b	Nat.		OF	54	45	2	12	3	0	1	8	.267	1	0	0	1.000
American League Totals—5 Years				658	2440	306	684	127	10	79	413	.280	480	22	13	.975
National League Totals—19 Years				2293	7280	883	2032	372	37	213	1053	.279	6092	380	127	.981
Major League Totals—23 Years				2951	9720	1189	2716	499	47	292	1466	.279	6572	402	140	.980

Signed as free agent by Houston Colt .45s' organization, September 11, 1961.

†Traded to Montreal Expos for First Baseman Donn Clendenon and Outfielder Jesus Alou, January 22, 1969. Clendenon refused to report to Houston; Pitchers John Billingham and Skip Guinn and cash sent to Houston to complete deal, April 8, 1969.

‡Traded to New York Mets for Outfielder Ken Singleton, First Baseman Mike Jorgensen and Infielder Tim Foli, April 6, 1972.

§Traded with Pitcher Bill Laxton to Detroit Tigers for Pitcher Mickey Lolich and Outfielder Billy Baldwin, December 12, 1975.

xSold to Montreal Expos, July 20, 1979.

yTraded to Texas Rangers for Second Baseman LaRue Washington and Third Baseman Chris Smith, March 31, 1980.

zGranted free agency, October 23, 1980; signed by New York Mets, December 16, 1980.

aGranted free agency when refused option to minors, November 12, 1984; re-signed by Mets, January 3, 1985.

bGranted free agency, November 12, 1985.

CHAMPIONSHIP SERIES RECORD

Year	Club	League	Pos.	G.	AB.	R.	H.	2B.	3B.	HR.	RBI.	B.A.	PO.	A.	E.	F.A.
1973—New York	Nat.		OF	4	15	4	3	0	0	3	5	.200	10	0	0	1.000

WORLD SERIES RECORD

Year	Club	League	Pos.	G.	AB.	R.	H.	2B.	3B.	HR.	RBI.	B.A.	PO.	A.	E.	F.A.
1973—New York	Nat.		OF-PH	7	26	1	11	2	0	1	6	.423	5	0	0	1.000

CHARLES DILLON (CASEY) STENGEL
(The Old Professor)

Born July 30, 1889, at Kansas City, Mo.
Died September 29, 1975, at Glendale, Calif.
Height, 5.10. Weight, 175.
Threw and batted lefthanded.

President-Manager, Worcester, Eastern League, 1925; manager, Toledo, American Association, 1926-31; coach, Brooklyn Dodgers, 1932-33, until named manager, 1934-36; manager, Boston Braves, 1938-43; Milwaukee, American Association, 1944; Kansas City, American Association, 1945; Oakland, Pacific Coast League, 1946-48; New York Yankees, 1949-60; New York Mets, 1962-65, until named executive scout, April 14, 1966, to date of death.

Named by The SPORTING NEWS as Minor League Manager of the Year, 1948, and Major League Manager of the Year, 1949-53-58.

Named to Hall of Fame, 1966.

Year	Club	League	Pos.	G.	AB.	R.	H.	2B.	3B.	HR.	RBI.	B.A.	PO.	A.	E.	F.A.
1910—Kankakee	No. Assn.						(League disbanded in July)									
1910—Maysville	Bl.Grass		OF	69	233	27	52	10	5	2	....	.223	143	11	2	.987
1911—Aurora	Wis.-Ill.		OF	121	420	76	★148	23	6	4	....	.352	229	27	8	.970
1912—Montgomery	South.		OF	136	479	85	139	....	....	....	....	.290	295	16	●11	.966
1912—Brooklyn	Nat.		OF	17	57	9	18	1	0	1	12	.316	36	1	4	.902
1913—Brooklyn	Nat.		OF	124	438	60	119	16	8	7	44	.272	270	16	12	.960
1914—Brooklyn	Nat.		OF	126	412	55	130	13	10	4	56	.316	173	15	7	.964
1915—Brooklyn	Nat.		OF	132	459	52	109	20	12	3	43	.237	220	13	10	.959
1916—Brooklyn	Nat.		OF	127	462	66	129	27	8	8	53	.279	206	14	8	.965
1917—Brooklyn(a)	Nat.		OF	150	549	69	141	23	12	6	69	.257	256	★30	9	.969
1918—Pittsburgh	Nat.		OF	39	122	18	30	4	1	1	13	.246	64	7	2	.973

Year	Club	League	Pos.	G.	AB.	R.	H.	2B.	3B.	HR.	RBI.	B.A.	PO.	A.	E.	F.A.
1919—Pittsburgh(b)	Nat.		OF	89	321	38	94	10	10	4	40	.293	195	7	9	.957
1920—Philadelphia	Nat.		OF	129	445	53	130	25	6	9	50	.292	212	16	11	.954
1921—Phila(c)-N.Y.	Nat.		OF	42	81	11	23	4	1	0	6	.284	33	5	2	.950
1922—New York	Nat.		OF	84	250	48	92	8	10	7	48	.368	179	7	6	.969
1923—New York(d)	Nat.		OF	75	218	39	74	11	5	5	43	.339	115	4	2	.983
1924—Boston	Nat.		OF	131	461	57	129	20	6	5	39	.280	211	12	5	.978
1925—Boston	Nat.		OF	12	13	0	1	0	0	0	2	.077	1	0	0	1.000
1925—Worcester	East.		OF	100	334	73	107	27	2	10	....	.320	175	6	6	.968
1926—Toledo	A.A.		OF	88	201	40	66	14	2	0	27	.328	78	4	1	.988
1927—Toledo	A.A.		OF	18	17	3	3	0	0	1	3	.176	4	0	0	1.000
1928—Toledo	A.A.		OF	26	32	5	14	5	0	0	12	.438	16	0	0	1.000
1929—Toledo	A.A.		OF	20	31	2	7	1	1	0	9	.226	7	0	0	1.000
1931—Toledo	A.A.		OF	2	8	1	3	2	0	0	0	.375	3	1	0	1.000
Major League Totals—14 Years				1277	4288	575	1219	182	89	60	518	.284	2171	147	87	.964

aTraded with Second Baseman George Cutshaw to Pittsburgh for Infielder Chuck Ward and Pitchers Burleigh Grimes and Al Mamaux, January 9, 1918.

bTraded to Philadelphia Phillies for Outfielder George Whitted, August, 1919; refused to report to Phillies for remainder of season in salary dispute.

cTraded to New York Giants for players valued at $75,000 July, 1921.

dTraded with Shortstop Dave Bancroft and Outfielder William Cunningham to Boston Braves for Outfielder Billy Southworth and Pitcher Joe Oeschger, November, 1923.

WORLD SERIES RECORD

Year	Club	League	Pos.	G.	AB.	R.	H.	2B.	3B.	HR.	RBI.	B.A.	PO.	A.	E.	F.A.
1916—Brooklyn	Nat.		OF	4	11	2	4	0	0	0	0	.364	3	1	1	.800
1922—New York	Nat.		OF	2	5	0	2	0	0	0	0	.400	4	0	0	1.000
1923—New York	Nat.		OF	6	12	3	5	0	0	2	4	.417	11	0	0	1.000
World Series Totals—3 Years				12	28	5	11	0	0	2	4	.393	18	1	1	.950

RECORD AS MAJOR LEAGUE MANAGER

Year	Club	League	Position	W.	L.	Year	Club	League	Position	W.	L.
1934—Brooklyn	Nat.		Sixth	71	81	1953—New York	Amer.		First	99	52
1935—Brooklyn	Nat.		Fifth	70	83	1954—New York	Amer.		Second	103	51
1936—Brooklyn	Nat.		Seventh	67	87	1955—New York	Amer.		First	96	58
1938—Boston	Nat.		Fifth	77	75	1956—New York	Amer.		First	97	57
1939—Boston	Nat.		Seventh	63	88	1957—New York	Amer.		First	98	56
1940—Boston	Nat.		Seventh	65	87	1958—New York	Amer.		First	92	62
1941—Boston	Nat.		Seventh	62	92	1959—New York	Amer.		Third	79	75
1942—Boston	Nat.		Seventh	59	89	1960—New York	Amer.		First	97	57
1943—Boston	Nat.		Sixth	68	85	1962—New York	Nat.		Tenth	40	120
1949—New York	Amer.		First	97	57	1963—New York	Nat.		Tenth	51	111
1950—New York	Amer.		First	98	56	1964—New York	Nat.		Tenth	53	109
1951—New York	Amer.		First	98	56	1965—New York	Nat.		Tenth	31	64
1952—New York	Amer.		First	95	59	Major League Totals—25 Years				1926	1867

WORLD SERIES RECORD

Year	Club	League	W.	L.	Year	Club	League	W.	L.
1949—New York	American		4	1	1955—New York	American		3	4
1950—New York	American		4	0	1956—New York	American		4	3
1951—New York	American		4	2	1957—New York	American		3	4
1952—New York	American		4	3	1958—New York	American		4	3
1953—New York	American		4	2	1960—New York	American		3	4

JACKSON RIGGS STEPHENSON

(Known by middle name.)

Born January 5, 1898, at Akron, Ala.

Died November 15, 1985, at Tuscaloosa, Ala.

Height, 5.10. Weight, 185.

Threw and batted righthanded.

Manager, Birmingham, Southern Association, 1936-37; Helena, Cotton States League, 1938; Montgomery, Southeastern League, 1939.

Year	Club	League	Pos.	G.	AB.	R.	H.	2B.	3B.	HR.	RBI.	B.A.	PO.	A.	E.	F.A.
1921—Cleveland	Amer.		2B	65	206	45	68	17	2	2	34	.330	122	153	17	.942
1922—Cleveland	Amer.		2B-3B	86	233	47	79	24	5	2	32	.339	75	136	11	.950
1923—Cleveland	Amer.		2B	91	301	48	96	20	6	5	65	.319	205	214	13	.970
1924—Cleveland	Amer.		2B	71	240	33	89	20	0	4	44	.371	114	179	12	.961
1925—Cleveland (a)	Amer.		OF	19	54	8	16	3	1	1	9	.296	33	2	2	.946
1925—Kansas City-Ind.	A.A.		OF	118	456	97	148	34	10	8	89	.325	217	14	4	.988

Year	Club	League	Pos.	G.	AB.	R.	H.	2B.	3B.	HR.	RBI.	B.A.	PO.	A.	E.	F.A.
1926—Indianapolis (b)	A.A.	OF	51	195	34	75	12	4	4	40	.385	110	2	1	.991
1926—Chicago	Nat.	OF	82	281	40	95	18	3	3	44	.338	126	7	7	.950
1927—Chicago	Nat.	OF	152	579	101	199	*46	9	7	82	.344	297	18	8	.975
1928—Chicago	Nat.	OF	137	512	75	166	36	9	8	90	.324	268	10	5	.982
1929—Chicago	Nat.	OF	136	495	91	179	36	6	17	110	.362	245	9	4	.984
1930—Chicago	Nat.	OF	109	341	56	125	21	1	5	69	.367	132	5	6	.958
1931—Chicago	Nat.	OF	80	263	34	84	14	4	1	52	.319	134	1	2	.985
1932—Chicago	Nat.	OF	147	583	86	189	49	4	4	85	.324	298	7	5	.984
1933—Chicago	Nat.	OF	97	346	45	114	17	4	4	51	.329	187	5	3	.985
1934—Chicago	Nat.	OF	38	74	5	16	0	0	0	7	.216	26	3	0	1.000
1935—Indianapolis	A.A.	OF	147	545	107	187	33	5	4	107	.343	289	10	3	.990
1936—Birmingham	South.	OF	120	439	68	156	26	7	3	64	.355	218	13	7	.971
1937—Birmingham	South.	OF	59	198	25	49	8	2	1	31	.247	98	2	2	.986
1938—Helena	Cot. St.	OF	58	175	29	52	12	1	0	28	.297	87	2	2	.978
1939—Montgomery	S. East.						(Less than ten games)									
American League Totals—5 Years			332	1034	181	348	84	14	14	184	.337	549	684	55	.957
National League Totals—9 Years			978	3474	533	1167	237	40	49	590	.336	1713	65	40	.978
Major League Totals—14 Years			1310	4508	714	1515	321	54	63	774	.336	2262	749	95	.969

aOptioned to Kansas City, May 31, 1925, and then traded to Indianapolis, August 13, 1925.

bTraded with Infielder Hank Schreiber to Chicago Cubs for Outfielder Joe Munson, Infielder Red Shannon and cash, June 7, 1926.

WORLD SERIES RECORD

Year	Club	League	Pos.	G.	AB.	R.	H.	2B.	3B.	HR.	RBI.	B.A.	PO.	A.	E.	F.A.
1929—Chicago	Nat.	OF	5	19	3	6	1	0	0	3	.316	13	1	0	1.000
1932—Chicago	Nat.	OF	4	18	2	8	1	0	0	4	.444	4	0	0	1.000
World Series Totals—2 Years			9	37	5	14	2	0	0	7	.378	17	1	0	1.000

JOHN CONRAD (JACK) STIVETTS

Born April 15, 1866, at Ashland, Pa.

Died April 18, 1930, at Ashland, Pa.

Height, 5.11½. Weight, 204.

Threw and batted righthanded.

Pitched 11-0 no-hit victory against Brooklyn, August 6, 1892.

Year	Club	League	G.	IP.	W.	L.	Pct.	H.	R.	SO.	BB.	ShO.	CG.
1889—St. Louis	Amer. Assn.	26	190	12	7	.632	148	85	136	64	2	18
1890—St. Louis	Amer. Assn.	54	422	27	21	.563	291	248	187	180	3	41
1891—St. Louis	Amer. Assn.	*66	437	33	22	.600	307	197	*232	192	3	40
1892—Boston	National	54	405	35	16	.686	349	221	166	160	3	45
1893—Boston	National	38	297	20	12	.625	320	196	57	113	1	29
1894—Boston	National	46	348	26	14	.650	438	289	73	100	0	30
1895—Boston	National	38	292	17	17	.500	341	220	102	92	0	30
1896—Boston	National	42	331	22	14	.611	358	223	64	90	2	31
1897—Boston	National	18	133	11	4	.733	146	74	27	41	0	10
1898—Boston	National	2	12	0	1	.000	15	12	1	7	0	1
1899—Cleveland	National	7	44	0	4	.000	63	44	4	22	0	3
American Assn. Totals—3 Years		146	1049	72	50	.590	746	530	555	436	8	99
National League Totals—8 Years		245	1862	131	81	.618	2030	1279	494	625	6	179
Major League Totals—11 Years		391	2911	203	131	.608	2776	1809	1049	1061	14	278

BATTING RECORD

Year	Club	League	Pos.	G.	AB.	R.	H.	2B.	3B.	HR.	SB.	B.A.
1889—St. Louis	Amer. Assn.	OF-P	26	79	10	18	3	2	0	0	.228
1980—St. Louis	Amer. Assn.	OF-1B-P	67	227	35	63	13	6	7	15	.278
1891—St. Louis	Amer. Assn.	OF-P	76	280	42	85	10	2	7	2	.304
1892—Boston	National	OF-1B-P	65	239	40	72	11	3	3	8	.301
1893—Boston	National	OF-3B-P	41	165	31	51	5	6	3	1	.309
1894—Boston	National	OF-1B-P	57	244	56	82	13	7	8	4	.336
1895—Boston	National	OF-1B-P	38	152	20	32	7	3	0	2	.211
1896—Boston	National	OF-1B-3B-P	59	221	44	78	9	4	3	5	.353
1897—Boston	National	OF-1B-2B-P	49	196	43	76	9	9	3	2	.388
1898—Boston	National	OF-INF-P	27	111	16	28	1	1	1	0	.252
1899—Cleveland	National	OF-3B-SS-P	18	41	8	7	1	0	0	0	.171
American Assn. Totals—3 Years			169	586	87	166	26	10	14	17	.283
National League Totals—8 Years			354	1369	258	426	56	33	21	22	.311
Major League Totals—11 Years			523	1955	345	592	82	43	35	39	.303

JONATHON THOMAS STONE

Born October 10, 1905, at Mulberry, Tenn.
Died November 30, 1955, at Shelbyville, Tenn.
Height, 6.00. Weight, 180.
Threw right and batted lefthanded.

Year Club League	Pos.	G.	AB.	R.	H.	2B.	3B.	HR.	RBI.	B.A.	PO.	A.	E.	F.A.
1928—Evansville .... I.I.I.	OF	75	297	49	105	11	9	5	43	.354	166	2	7	.960
1928—Detroit................... Amer.	OF	26	113	20	40	10	3	2	21	.354	49	2	2	.962
1929—Toronto .... Int.	OF	79	295	53	97	19	8	12	56	.329	134	6	7	.952
1929—Detroit................... Amer.	OF	51	150	23	39	11	2	2	15	.260	68	4	1	.986
1930—Detroit................... Amer.	OF	126	422	60	132	29	11	3	56	.313	222	5	8	.966
1931—Detroit................... Amer.	OF	147	584	86	191	28	11	10	76	.327	319	11	14	.959
1932—Detroit................... Amer.	OF	145	582	106	173	35	12	17	108	.297	334	11	14	.961
1933—Detroit(a) .... Amer.	OF	148	574	86	161	33	11	11	80	.280	280	11	9	.970
1934—Washington .... Amer.	OF	113	419	77	132	28	7	7	67	.315	245	13	9	.966
1935—Washington .... Amer.	OF	125	454	78	143	27	18	1	78	.315	224	12	11	.955
1936—Washington .... Amer.	OF	123	437	95	149	22	11	15	90	.341	249	12	9	.967
1937—Washington .... Amer.	OF	139	542	84	179	33	15	6	88	.330	300	15	5	.984
1938—Washington .... Amer.	OF	56	213	24	52	12	4	3	28	.244	107	5	3	.974
Major League Totals—11 Years...............		1199	4490	739	1391	268	105	77	707	.310	2397	101	85	.967

aTraded to Washington for Outfielder Goose Goslin, December 13, 1933.

HARRY DUFFIELD STOVEY

Born December 28, 1856, at Philadelphia, Pa.
Died September 20, 1937, at New Bedford, Mass.
Height, 6.00. Weight, 186.
Threw and batted righthanded.

Holds major league record for most stolen bases, season (156), 1888.

Year Club League	Pos.	G.	AB.	R.	H.	2B.	3B.	HR.	SB.	B.A.	PO.	A.	E.	F.A.
1876—J. D. Shibe..............		(Independent club—no records available)												
1877—Athletics.................		(Independent club—no records available)												
1878—New Bedford .... I. Assn.	OF	2	8	0	0	0	0	0	0	.000	6	1	2	.778
1879—New Bedford .... I. Assn.		(No records available)												
1880—Worcester............. Nat.	OF-1B	81	345	72	89	18	★14	●6	....	.258	502	18	34	.939
1881—Worcester............. Nat.	OF-1B	74	336	55	91	26	6	2	....	.271	583	16	31	.951
1882—Worcester............. Nat.	OF-1B	84	360	90	104	13	10	5	....	.289	557	25	47	.925
1883—Athletics................. A.A.	O-1-C	94	412	★110	148	★32	8	★14	....	.359	(983-PO-A)	27	★.973	
1884—Athletics................. A.A.	1B	106	443	★126	179	25	★25	●11	....	.404	(1116-PO-A)	32	.972	
1885—Athletics................. A.A.	OF-1B	112	480	★130	164	27	11	★13	....	.342	(965-PO-A)	42	.958	
1886—Athletics................. A.A.	OF-1B	123	486	115	154	26	13	7	★96	.317	(805-PO-A)	39	.954	
1887—Athletics................. A.A.	OF-1B	124	545	124	219	29	12	5	★143	.402	(639-PO-A)	32	.952	
1888—Athletics................. A.A.	OF	130	538	128	171	25	★21	7	★156	.318	(216-PO-A)	10	.956	
1889—Athletics................. A.A.	OF	138	546	★154	180	37	14	●19	115	.330	291	37	32	.911
1890—Boston................... Play.	OF	118	480	140	148	28	11	11	136	.308	192	22	13	.943
1891—Boston................... Nat.	OF	133	545	118	152	33	19	●16	52	.279	230	23	27	.904
1892—Boston-Balt........... Nat.	OF	112	285	58	77	20	15	2	20	.270	187	9	19	.912
1893—Balt.-Brook. .... Nat.	OF	53	193	47	49	9	6	1	26	.254	129	4	16	.893
Amer. Assn. Totals—7 Years...................		827	3450	887	1215	201	104	76	510	.352	(5049-PO-A)	214	.959	
National League Totals—6 Years..........		537	2064	440	562	119	70	32	98	.272	2188	95	174	.929
Players League Totals—1 Year.............		118	480	140	148	28	11	11	136	.308	192	22	13	.943
Major League Totals—14 Years.............		1482	5994	1467	1925	348	185	119	744	.321	(7546-PO-A)	401	.950	

—DID YOU KNOW—

That Los Angeles Dodger righthander Don Sutton was the winning pitcher in the first major league game played on artificial turf, April 18, 1966, at Houston's Astrodome?

DONALD HOWARD (DON) SUTTON

Born April 2, 1945, at Clio, Ala.
Height, 6.01. Weight, 190.
Threw and batted righthanded.

Holds major league record for most consecutive years with 100 or more strikeouts (21).
Shares major league record for most years with 100 or more strikeouts (21).
Shares National League record for most consecutive home runs allowed, inning (3), May 27, 1980, third inning.
Led National League pitchers in games started with 40 in 1974.
Led National League in shutouts with 9 in 1972.
Tied for National League lead in balks with 3 in 1968.
Named National League Rookie Pitcher of the Year by THE SPORTING NEWS, 1966.
Named righthanded pitcher on THE SPORTING NEWS National League All-Star Team, 1976.
Named Texas League Player of the Year, 1965.

Year Club	League	G.	IP.	W.	L.	Pct.	H.	R.	ER.	SO.	BB.	ERA.
1965—Santa Barbara	California	10	84	8	1	.889	59	18	14	101	15	1.50
1965—Albuquerque	Texas	21	165	15	6	*.714	151	60	51	138	30	2.78
1966—Los Angeles	National	37	226	12	12	.500	192	82	75	209	52	2.99
1967—Los Angeles	National	37	233	11	15	.423	223	106	102	169	57	3.94
1968—Spokane	P. Coast	2	16	1	1	.500	11	2	2	19	5	1.13
1968—Los Angeles	National	35	208	11	15	.423	179	64	60	162	59	2.60
1969—Los Angeles	National	41	293	17	18	.486	269	123	113	217	91	3.47
1970—Los Angeles	National	38	260	15	13	.536	251	127	●118	201	78	4.08
1971—Los Angeles	National	38	265	17	12	.586	231	85	75	194	55	2.55
1972—Los Angeles	National	33	273	19	9	.679	186	78	63	207	63	2.08
1973—Los Angeles	National	33	256	18	10	.643	196	78	69	200	56	2.43
1974—Los Angeles	National	40	276	19	9	.679	241	111	99	179	80	3.23
1975—Los Angeles	National	35	254	16	13	.552	202	87	81	175	62	2.87
1976—Los Angeles	National	35	268	21	10	.677	231	98	91	161	82	3.06
1977—Los Angeles	National	33	240	14	8	.636	207	93	85	150	69	3.19
1978—Los Angeles	National	34	238	15	11	.577	228	109	94	154	54	3.55
1979—Los Angeles†	National	33	226	12	15	.444	201	109	96	146	61	3.82
1980—Los Angeles†	National	32	212	13	5	.722	163	56	52	128	47	*2.21
1981—Houston	National	23	159	11	9	.550	132	51	46	104	29	2.60
1982—Houston‡	National	27	195	13	8	.619	169	75	65	139	46	3.00
1982—Milwaukee	American	7	54⅔	4	1	.800	55	21	20	36	18	3.29
1983—Milwaukee	American	31	220⅓	8	13	.381	209	109	100	134	54	4.08
1984—Milwaukee§	American	33	212⅔	14	12	.538	224	103	89	143	51	3.77
1985—Oakland x-California y	American	34	226	15	10	.600	221	101	97	107	59	3.86
1986—California	American	34	207	15	11	.577	192	93	86	116	49	3.74
1987—California z	American	35	191⅔	11	11	.500	199	101	100	99	41	4.70
1988—Los Angeles a	National	16	87⅓	3	6	.333	91	44	38	44	30	3.92
National League Totals—18 Years		600	4169⅓	257	198	.565	3592	1576	1422	2939	1071	3.07
American League Totals—6 Years		174	1112⅓	67	58	.536	1100	528	492	635	272	3.98
Major League Totals—23 Years		774	5281⅓	324	256	.559	4692	2104	1914	3574	1343	3.26

Signed as free agent by Los Angeles Dodgers' organization, September 11, 1964.
†Granted free agency, October 23, 1980; signed by Houston Astros, December 4, 1980.
‡Traded to Milwaukee Brewers for three players to be named later, August 30, 1982; Houston Astros acquired Pitchers Frank DiPino and Mike Madden and Outfielder Kevin Bass to complete deal, September 3, 1982.
§Traded to Oakland A's for Pitchers Ray Burris, Eric Barry and a player to be named later, December 7, 1984; Milwaukee Brewers' organization acquired Pitcher Ed Myers to complete deal, March 25, 1985.
xTraded to California Angels for two players to be named later, September 10, 1985; Oakland A's organization acquired Pitcher Robert Sharpnack and Outfielder Jerome Nelson to complete deal, September 25, 1985.
yGranted free agency, November 12, 1985; re-signed by Angels, December 5, 1985.
zReleased, October 30, 1987; signed by Los Angeles Dodgers, January 5, 1988.
aReleased, August 10, 1988.

CHAMPIONSHIP SERIES RECORD

Shares major league record for most games won, lifetime (4).
Shares National League record for most complete games, lifetime (2).

Year Club	League	G.	IP.	W.	L.	Pct.	H.	R.	ER.	SO.	BB.	ERA.
1974—Los Angeles	National	2	17	2	0	1.000	7	1	1	13	2	0.53
1977—Los Angeles	National	1	9	1	0	1.000	9	1	1	4	0	1.00
1978—Los Angeles	National	1	5⅔	0	1	.000	7	7	4	0	2	6.35
1982—Milwaukee	American	1	7⅔	1	0	1.000	8	3	3	9	2	3.52
1986—California	American	2	9⅔	0	0	.000	6	2	2	4	1	1.86
Championship Series Totals—5 Years		7	49	4	1	.800	37	14	11	30	7	2.02

Year Club	League	G.	IP.	W.	L.	Pct.	H.	R.	ER.	SO.	BB.	ERA.
1974—Los Angeles	National	2	13	1	0	1.000	9	4	4	12	3	2.77
1977—Los Angeles	National	2	16	1	0	1.000	17	7	7	6	1	3.94
1978—Los Angeles	National	2	12	0	2	.000	17	10	10	8	4	7.50
1982—Milwaukee	American	2	10⅓	0	1	.000	12	11	9	5	1	7.84
World Series Totals—4 Years		8	51⅓	2	3	.400	55	32	30	31	9	5.26

WILLIAM HAROLD (BILL) TERRY

Born October 30, 1898, at Atlanta, Ga.

Died January 9, 1989, at Jacksonville, Fla.

Height 6.01½. Weight, 200.

Threw and batted lefthanded.

Shares National League record for most hits, season (254), 1930.
Hit three home runs in a game, August 13, 1932, first game.
Led National League first basemen in double plays, 1928, 1929 and 1934.
Pitched 2-0 no-hit victory against Anniston, June 30, 1915.
Named as first baseman on THE SPORTING NEWS All-Star Major League Team, 1930.
Named by THE SPORTING NEWS as Most Valuable Player, 1930.
Manager, New York Giants, 1932 through 1941.
Named to Hall of Fame, 1954.

Year Club	League	Pos.	G.	AB.	R.	H.	2B.	3B.	HR.	RBI.	B.A.	PO.	A.	E.	F.A.
1915—Newnan	Ga.-Ala.	P	8	....	....	....	....	....	....	....	....		2	11	0	1.000
1916—Shreveport	Tex.	P	19	29	3	7	3	1	0	....	.241	2	14	3	.842
1917—Shreveport	Tex.	P-OF	95	208	15	48	9	1	4	....	.231	51	61	9	.926
1918-19-20-21—						(Played semi-pro ball)									
1922—Toledo	A. A.	1B-P	88	235	41	79	11	4	14	61	.336	417	54	10	.979
1923—Toledo	A. A.	1B	109	427	73	161	22	11	15	82	.377	957	57	7	★.993
1923—New York	Nat.	1B	3	7	1	1	0	0	0	0	.143	22	1	0	1.000
1924—New York	Nat.	1B	77	163	26	39	7	2	5	24	.239	325	14	4	.988
1925—New York	Nat.	1B	133	489	75	156	31	6	11	70	.319	1270	77	14	●.990
1926—New York	Nat.	1B-OF	98	225	26	65	12	5	5	43	.289	391	31	9	.979
1927—New York	Nat.	1B	150	580	101	189	32	13	20	121	.326	1621	★105	12	.993
1928—New York	Nat.	1B	149	568	100	185	36	11	17	101	.326	★1584	78	12	●.993
1929—New York	Nat.	1B	150	607	103	226	39	5	14	117	.372	★1575	111	11	.994
1930—New York	Nat.	1B	154	633	139	★254	39	15	23	129	★.401	★1538	★128	17	.990
1931—New York	Nat.	1B	153	611	●121	213	43	★20	9	112	.349	1411	★105	16	.990
1932—New York	Nat.	1B	●154	643	124	225	42	11	28	117	.350	★1493	★137	14	.991
1933—New York	Nat.	1B	123	475	68	153	20	5	6	58	.322	1246	76	11	.992
1934—New York	Nat.	1B	153	602	109	213	30	6	8	83	.354	★1592	105	10	●.994
1935—New York	Nat.	1B	145	596	91	203	32	8	6	64	.341	1379	★99	6	★.996
1936—New York	Nat.	1B	79	229	36	71	10	5	2	39	.310	525	41	2	.996
Major League Totals—14 Years			1721	6428	1120	2193	373	112	154	1078	.341	15972	1108	138	.992

PITCHING RECORD

Year Club	League	G.	IP.	W.	L.	Pct.	H.	R.	ER.	SO.	BB.	ERA.
1915—Newnan	Ga.-Ala.	8	....	7	1	.875	....	....	....	....	....	......
1916—Shreveport	Texas	19	84	6	2	.750	50	....	10	39	34	1.07
1917—Shreveport	Texas	40	246	14	11	.560	222	108	82	81	116	3.00
1922—Toledo	Amer. Assn.	26	127	9	9	.500	147	75	60	35	59	4.26

WORLD SERIES RECORD

Year Club	League	Pos.	G.	AB.	R.	H.	2B.	3B.	HR.	RBI.	B.A.	PO.	A.	E.	F.A.
1924—New York	Nat.	1B	5	14	3	6	0	1	1	1	.429	43	2	0	1.000
1933—New York	Nat.	1B	5	22	3	6	1	0	1	1	.273	50	1	0	1.000
1936—New York	Nat.	1B	6	25	1	6	0	0	0	5	.240	45	8	0	1.000
World Series Totals—3 Years			16	61	7	18	1	1	2	7	.295	138	11	0	1.000

WILLIAM J. (ADONIS) TERRY

Born August 7, 1864, at Westfield, Mass.

Died February 25, 1914, at Milwaukee, Wis.

Threw and batted righthanded.

Pitched 1-0 no-hit victory against St. Louis, July 24, 1886; pitched 4-0 no-hit victory over Louisville, May 27, 1888. Also part-time outfielder early in career, 1884, 1885, 1886, 1887 and 1890.

Year—Club	League	G.	W.	L.	Pct.	H.	R.	SO.	BB.	ShO.
1883—Brooklyn	Eastern	....	....	....	.....	....	....	....	....	..
1884—Brooklyn	Amer. Assn.	55	19	35	.352	498	312	219	64	2
1885—Brooklyn	Amer. Assn.	24	6	16	.273	207	140	91	48	0
1886—Brooklyn	Amer. Assn.	34	18	15	.545	267	176	....	125	5
1887—Brooklyn	Amer. Assn.	35	17	16	.515	400	209	111	92	1
1888—Brooklyn	Amer. Assn.	24	13	8	.619	153	83	90	111	2
1889—Brooklyn	Amer. Assn.	40	21	16	.568	285	191	173	125	2
1890—Brooklyn	National	44	25	16	.610	....	....	185	127	0
1891—Brooklyn	National	25	7	17	.292	....	....	66	67	1
1892—Balt.-Pitt.	National	32	21	10	.677	....	....	91	87	2
1893—Pittsburgh	National	22	15	6	.714	....	....	49	88	0
1894—Pitt.-Chi.	National	21	6	14	.300	....	....	43	91	0
1895—Chicago	National	37	23	13	.639	....	....	93	133	0
1896—Chicago	National	30	14	15	.483	....	....	73	86	1
1897—Chicago	National	1	0	0	.000	....	....	....	....	0
1897—Milwaukee	Western	27	22	5	.815	....	....	....	....	..
1898—Milwaukee	Western	16	12	1	.923	....	....	....	....	..
American Assn. Totals—6 Years		212	94	106	.470	1810	1111	684	565	12
National League Totals—8 Years		212	111	91	.550	....	....	600	679	4
Major League Totals—14 Years		424	205	197	.510	....	....	1284	1244	16

FRANK JOSEPH THOMAS

Born June 11, 1929, at Pittsburgh, Pa.

Height, 6.03. Weight, 205.

Threw and batted righthanded.

Shares major league records for most home runs, three consecutive games (6), August 1 through 3, 1962; most times hit by pitch, inning (2), April 29, 1962, first game, fourth inning.

Named as third baseman on THE SPORTING NEWS All-Star Major League Team, 1958.

Year—Club	League	Pos.	G.	AB.	R.	H.	2B.	3B.	HR.	RBI.	B.A.	PO.	A.	E.	F.A.
1948—Tallahassee	Ga.-Fla.	OF	138	★596	106	176	39	8	14	★132	.295	247	20	12	.957
1949—Davenport	I.I.I.	OF-3B	13	43	7	10	2	1	0	7	.233	23	1	0	1.000
1949—Tallahassee	Ga.-Fla.	OF	74	285	46	93	19	2	10	63	.326	162	15	2	.989
1949—Waco	Big.St.	OF	20	73	17	25	3	0	4	17	.342	33	3	4	.900
1950—Charleston	Sally	OF	82	318	50	98	20	4	11	55	.308	180	9	1	.995
1950—New Orleans	South.	OF	47	148	21	39	6	1	3	18	.264	67	3	6	.921
1951—New Orleans	South.	OF	125	471	64	136	25	6	23	85	.289	270	16	7	.976
1951—Pittsburgh	Nat.	OF	39	148	21	39	9	2	2	16	.264	87	5	0	1.000
1952—New Orleans	South.	OF	154	597	★112	181	40	6	★35	★131	.303	422	19	★18	.961
1952—Pittsburgh	Nat.	OF	6	21	1	2	0	0	0	0	.095	8	1	0	1.000
1953—Pittsburgh	Nat.	OF	128	455	68	116	22	1	30	102	.255	306	17	8	.976
1954—Pittsburgh	Nat.	OF	153	577	81	172	32	7	23	94	.298	418	●14	5	.989
1955—Pittsburgh	Nat.	OF	142	510	72	125	16	2	25	72	.245	307	8	5	.984
1956—Pittsburgh	Nat.	3-O-2B	●157	588	69	166	24	3	25	80	.282	216	179	18	.956
1957—Pittsburgh	Nat.	1-O-3B	151	594	72	172	30	1	23	89	.290	729	119	25	.971
1958—Pittsburgh(a)	Nat.	★3-O-1B	149	562	89	158	26	4	35	109	.281	160	243	★30	.931
1959—Cincinnati(b)	Nat.	3-O-1B	108	374	41	84	18	2	12	47	.225	206	126	19	.946
1960—Chicago	Nat.	1-O-3B	135	479	54	114	12	1	21	64	.238	528	92	17	.973
1961—Chi(c)-Mil.(d)	Nat.	OF-1B	139	473	65	133	15	3	27	73	.281	300	12	10	.969
1962—New York	Nat.	O-1-3B	156	571	69	152	23	3	34	94	.266	311	36	14	.961
1963—New York	Nat.	O-1-3B	126	420	34	109	9	1	15	60	.260	304	17	4	.988
1964—N.Y.(e)-Phila.	Nat.	1-O-3B	99	340	39	92	17	1	10	45	.271	498	46	9	.984
1965—Phi.f-Ho.g-Mil.h	Nat.	1-O-3B	73	168	17	37	9	0	4	17	.220	262	15	5	.982
1966—Chicago	Nat.	PH	5	5	0	0	0	0	0	0	.000	0	0	0	.000
1966—Tacoma	PCL	1B-PH	25	79	2	16	6	0	1	8	.203	115	6	0	1.000
Major League Totals—16 Years			1766	6285	792	1671	262	31	286	962	.266	4640	930	169	.971

aTraded to Cincinnati Reds with Pitcher Whammy Douglas, Infielder-Outfielder Jim Pendleton and Outfielder Johnny Powers for Pitcher Harvey Haddix, Catcher Smoky Burgess and Third Baseman Don Hoak, January 31, 1959.

bTraded to Chicago Cubs for Pitcher Bill Henry and Outfielders Lou Jackson and Lee Walls, December 6, 1959.

cTraded to Milwaukee Braves for Infielder Mel Roach, May 9, 1961.

dTraded to New York Mets for cash and player to be named later, November 28, 1961; trade completed with transfer of Outfielder Gus Bell to Milwaukee Braves, May 21, 1962.

eTraded to Philadelphia Phillies for Pitcher Gary Kroll, Infielder Wayne Graham, who was on Arkansas roster, and cash, August 7, 1964.

fSold to Houston Astros, July 10, 1965.

gSigned by Milwaukee Braves, September 1, 1965.

hReleased by Atlanta (franchise transferred from Milwaukee), April 5, 1966; signed with Chicago Cubs, May 14, 1966.

JAMES GORMAN THOMAS III

(Known by middle name.)

Born December 12, 1950, at Charleston, S. C.
Height, 6.03. Weight, 200.
Threw and batted righthanded.

Shares major league record for most strikeouts, three consecutive games (10), July 27 through 29, 1975.
Hit three home runs in a game, April 11, 1985.
Led American League batters in strikeouts with 175 in 1979, 170 in 1980 and tied for lead with 133 in 1978.
Led Pacific Coast League in total bases with 320 in 1977.
Led Pacific Coast League batters in strikeouts with 175 in 1974.
Led Texas League batters in strikeouts with 171 in 1972.
Led Midwest League batters in strikeouts with 170 in 1971.
Tied for Texas League lead in double plays by outfielders with 4 in 1972.
Named outfielder on THE SPORTING NEWS American League All-Star Team, 1982.
Named American League Comeback Player of the Year by THE SPORTING NEWS, 1985.

Year Club	League	Pos.	G.	AB.	R.	H.	2B.	3B.	HR.	RBI.	B.A.	PO.	A.	E.	F.A.
1969—Billings	Pion.	SS-1B	41	142	23	42	10	3	4	28	.296	94	82	27	.867
1970—Clinton	Midw.	SS-3B-2B	85	297	36	63	5	4	8	39	.212	105	186	28	.912
1971—Danville	Midw.	OF-3B	121	457	82	112	20	4	★31	83	.245	195	14	10	.954
1972—San Antonio	Texas	★OF-1B	135	465	70	112	22	2	★26	68	.241	★305	★24	6	★.982
1973—Evansville	A. A.	OF	46	146	26	31	6	0	8	18	.212	66	3	4	.945
1973—Milwaukee	Amer.	OF-3B	59	155	16	29	7	1	2	11	.187	87	1	4	.957
1974—Sacramento	P. C.	OF	138	474	117	141	15	1	51	122	.297	302	16	10	.970
1974—Milwaukee	Amer.	OF	17	46	10	12	4	0	2	11	.261	26	0	0	1.000
1975—Milwaukee	Amer.	OF	121	240	34	43	12	2	10	28	.179	215	5	9	.961
1976—Milwaukee	Amer.	OF-3B	99	227	27	45	9	2	8	36	.198	211	4	4	.982
1977—Spokane†‡	P. C.	OF	143	500	114	161	41	5	36	114	.322	325	13	7	★.980
1978—Milwaukee	Amer.	OF	137	452	70	111	24	1	32	86	.246	345	5	6	.983
1979—Milwaukee	Amer.	OF	156	557	97	136	29	0	★45	123	.244	435	4	4	.991
1980—Milwaukee	Amer.	OF	162	628	78	150	26	3	38	105	.239	455	6	7	.985
1981—Milwaukee	Amer.	OF	103	363	54	94	22	0	21	65	.259	221	8	5	.979
1982—Milwaukee	Amer.	OF	158	567	96	139	29	1	●39	112	.245	427	11	4	.991
1983—Milw.§-Clev.x	Amer.	OF	152	535	72	112	23	1	22	69	.209	439	7	7	.985
1984—Seattle	Amer.	OF	35	108	6	17	3	0	1	13	.157	45	2	0	1.000
1985—Seattle	Amer.	DH	135	484	76	104	16	1	32	87	.215	0	0	0	.000
1986—Sea.y-Mil.z	Amer.	1B	101	315	45	59	8	1	16	36	.187	47	3	1	.980
Major League Totals—13 Years			1435	4677	681	1051	212	13	268	782	.225	2953	56	51	.983

Selected by Seattle Pilots' organization in 1st round (21st player selected) of free-agent draft, June 5, 1969.
†Traded to Texas Rangers, October 25, 1977, completing deal in which Texas traded Outfielder-First Baseman Ed Kirkpatrick to Milwaukee Brewers for a player to be named later, August 20, 1977.
‡Sold to Milwaukee Brewers, February 8, 1978.
§Traded with Pitchers Jamie Easterly and Ernie Camacho to Cleveland Indians for Outfielder Rick Manning and Pitcher Rick Waits, June 6, 1983.
xTraded with Second Baseman Jack Perconte to Seattle Mariners for Second Baseman Tony Bernazard, December 7, 1983.
yReleased, June 25, 1986; signed by Milwaukee Brewers, July 16, 1986.
zReleased, October 16, 1986.

CHAMPIONSHIP SERIES RECORD

Tied major league record by hitting home run in first series at-bat, October 5, 1982.

Year Club	League	Pos.	G.	AB.	R.	H.	2B.	3B.	HR.	RBI.	B.A.	PO.	A.	E.	F.A.
1982—Milwaukee	Amer.	OF	5	16	1	1	0	0	1	3	.063	13	0	0	1.000

WORLD SERIES RECORD

Tied record for most at-bats, inning (2), October 16, 1982, seventh inning.

Year Club	League	Pos.	G.	AB.	R.	H.	2B.	3B.	HR.	RBI.	B.A.	PO.	A.	E.	F.A.
1982—Milwaukee	Amer.	OF	7	26	0	3	0	0	0	3	.115	15	0	0	1.000

—DID YOU KNOW—

That former Milwaukee Brewers outfielder Gorman Thomas is one of only three players to hit 40 or more home runs while batting less than .250 in the same season? Thomas hit 45 homers while compiling a .244 batting mark in 1979.

SAMUEL L. (SAM) THOMPSON
(Big Sam)

Born March 5, 1860, at Danville, Ind.
Died November 7, 1922, at Detroit, Mich.
Height, 6.02. Weight, 207.
Threw and batted lefthanded.

Named to Hall of Fame, 1974.

Year Club	League	Pos.	G.	AB.	R.	H.	2B.	3B.	HR.	SB.	B.A.	PO.	A.	E.	F.A.
1884—Evansville	N.W.	OF	5	23	5	9	2	1	0	0	.391	14	0	1	.933
1885—Indianapolis	West.	OF	30	136	38	43	7	5	1	....	.316	35	4	12	.765
1885—Detroit	Nat.	OF	63	254	58	77	11	7	7	....	.303	84	24	14	.885
1886—Detroit	Nat.	OF	122	503	100	156	19	4	8	13	.310	194	29	13	.945
1887—Detroit	Nat.	OF	127	576	118	234	29	*23	10	22	.406	217	24	24	.909
1888—Detroit	Nat.	OF	55	238	51	67	9	8	6	5	.282	86	4	12	.882
1889—Philadelphia	Nat.	OF	128	533	103	158	35	4	*20	24	.296	173	19	21	.901
1890—Philadelphia	Nat.	OF	132	549	114	●172	*38	9	4	25	.313	170	29	13	.939
1891—Philadelphia	Nat.	OF	133	551	108	163	20	9	7	33	.296	237	29	15	.947
1892—Philadelphia	Nat.	OF	151	602	109	183	31	8	9	30	.304	210	31	14	.945
1893—Philadelphia	Nat.	OF	130	583	130	*220	33	14	11	18	.377	163	17	15	.923
1894—Philadelphia	Nat.	OF	102	458	115	185	29	26	13	29	.404	163	11	7	.961
1895—Philadelphia	Nat.	OF	118	533	131	210	42	●22	16	24	.394	188	●32	9	.961
1896—Philadelphia	Nat.	OF	119	517	103	158	27	7	●13	11	.306	235	28	8	.970
1897—Philadelphia	Nat.	OF	3	13	2	3	0	1	0	0	.231	4	2	1	.857
1898—Philadelphia	Nat.	OF	14	63	13	23	3	3	2	1	.365	20	5	0	1.000
1906—Detroit	Amer.	OF	8	31	4	7	0	1	0	0	.226	14	0	0	1.000
American League Totals—1 Year			8	31	4	7	0	1	0	0	.226	14	0	0	1.000
National League Totals—14 Years			1397	5973	1255	2009	326	145	126	235	.336	2144	284	166	.936
Major League Totals—15 Years			1405	6004	1259	2016	326	146	126	235	.336	2158	284	166	.936

ROBERT BROWN (BOBBY) THOMSON

Born October 25, 1923, at Glasgow, Scotland.
Height, 6.02½. Weight, 190.
Threw and batted righthanded.

Year Club	League	Pos.	G.	AB.	R.	H.	2B.	3B.	HR.	RBI.	B.A.	PO.	A.	E.	F.A.
1942—Bristol	Appal.	3B	5	12	1	3	0	1	0	0	.250	4	13	3	.850
1942—Rocky Mount	Bi-State	3B	29	87	15	21	4	0	3	18	.241	22	29	5	.911
1943-44-45—Bristol	Appal.					(In Military Service)									
1946—Jersey City	Int.	3B—OF	151	533	93	149	12	7	26	92	.280	225	170	30	.929
1946—New York	Nat.	3B	18	54	8	17	4	1	2	9	.315	18	25	3	.935
1947—New York	Nat.	OF-2B	138	545	105	154	26	5	29	85	.283	357	32	12	.970
1948—New York	Nat.	OF	138	471	75	117	20	2	16	63	.248	313	10	10	.970
1949—New York	Nat.	OF	156	641	99	198	35	9	27	109	.309	488	10	9	.982
1950—New York	Nat.	OF	149	563	79	142	22	7	25	85	.252	394	15	9	.978
1951—New York	Nat.	OF-3B	148	518	89	152	27	8	32	101	.293	258	139	20	.952
1952—New York	Nat.	3B-OF	153	608	89	164	29	*14	24	108	.270	234	187	18	.959
1953—New York(a)	Nat.	OF	154	608	80	175	22	6	26	106	.288	391	16	7	.983
1954—Milwaukee	Nat.	OF	43	99	7	23	9	0	2	15	.232	45	3	1	.980
1955—Milwaukee	Nat.	OF	101	343	40	88	12	3	12	56	.257	182	5	6	.969
1956—Milwaukee	Nat.	OF-3B	142	451	59	106	10	4	20	74	.235	262	17	10	.965
1957—Mil.(b)-N.Y.(c)	Nat.	OF-3B	122	363	39	87	12	7	12	61	.240	202	7	2	.991
1958—Chicago	Nat.	OF-3B	152	547	67	155	27	5	21	82	.283	358	16	5	.987
1959—Chicago(d)	Nat.	OF	122	374	55	97	15	2	11	52	.259	223	9	3	.987
1960—Bos.(e)-Balt.	Amer.	OF-3B	43	120	12	30	3	1	5	20	.250	75	1	2	.950
American League Totals—1 Year			43	120	12	30	3	1	5	20	.250	75	1	2	.950
National League Totals—14 Years			1736	6185	891	1675	264	73	259	1006	.271	3725	481	115	.973
Major League Totals—15 Years			1779	6305	903	1705	267	74	264	1026	.270	3800	482	117	.973

aTraded to Milwaukee Braves with Catcher Sam Calderone for Pitchers Johnny Antonelli and Don Liddle, Catcher Ebba St. Claire, Infielder Bill Klaus and cash, February 1, 1954.

bTraded to New York Giants with Pitcher Ray Crone and Second Baseman Danny O'Connell for Second Baseman Red Schoendienst, June 15, 1957.

cTraded to Chicago Cubs for Outfielder-First Baseman Bob Speake and cash, April 3, 1958.
dTraded to Boston Red Sox for Pitcher Al Schroll, December 1, 1959.
eReleased by Boston July 1, 1960, and picked up by Baltimore Orioles July 4, 1960.

WORLD SERIES RECORD

Year	Club	League	Pos.	G.	AB.	R.	H.	2B.	3B.	HR.	RBI.	B.A.	PO.	A.	E.	F.A.
1951—New York		Nat.	3B	6	21	1	5	1	0	0	2	.238	11	15	2	.929

ANDRE THORNTON

Born August 13, 1949, at Tuskegee, Ala.

Height, 6.02. Weight, 205.

Threw and batted righthanded.

Tied major league record for most assists by first baseman, inning (3), August 22, 1975, fifth inning.
Tied for American League lead in intentional bases on balls received with 18 in 1982.
Led Western Carolinas League first basemen in errors with 19 in 1969.
Led Northwest League first basemen in double plays with 35 in 1968.
Tied for Eastern League lead in caught stealing with 8 in 1971.
Named American League Comeback Player of the Year by THE SPORTING NEWS, 1982.
Named designated hitter on THE SPORTING NEWS American League Silver Slugger team, 1984.

Year	Club	League	Pos.	G.	AB.	R.	H.	2B.	3B.	HR.	RBI.	B.A.	PO.	A.	E.	F.A.
1967—Huron		North.	3B-OF	19	55	3	10	1	2	1	3	.182	7	9	10	.615
1968—Eugene		N'west.	1B	56	185	27	46	9	2	5	31	.249	★427	★24	10	★.978
1969—Spartanburg		W. Car.	1B-3B-OF	90	299	56	75	13	4	13	51	.251	701	45	20	.974
1970—Peninsula		Carol.	1B	67	193	24	48	7	2	5	23	.249	499	30	5	.991
1971—Reading		East.	1B	116	367	67	98	18	1	26	76	.267	1006	48	15	.986
1972—Eugene†		P. C.	1B-3B	46	141	22	45	8	2	6	29	.319	224	46	11	.961
1972—Richmond		Int.	1B-OF	49	159	30	42	5	0	14	36	.264	379	33	6	.986
1973—Richmond‡		Int.	3B-1B-OF	16	49	8	10	2	0	4	8	.204	67	17	5	.944
1973—Wichita		A. A.	1B	40	135	34	39	2	0	17	45	.289	362	23	1	.997
1973—Chicago		Nat.	1B	17	35	3	7	3	0	0	2	.200	81	10	1	.989
1974—Chicago		Nat.	1B-3B	107	303	41	79	16	4	10	46	.261	760	70	7	.992
1975—Chicago		Nat.	1B-3B	120	372	70	109	21	4	18	60	.293	984	77	13	.988
1976—Chi.§-Mont. x		Nat.	1B-OF	96	268	28	52	11	2	11	38	.194	542	46	6	.990
1977—Cleveland		Amer.	1B	131	433	77	114	20	5	28	70	.263	1026	71	6	.995
1978—Cleveland		Amer.	1B	145	508	97	133	22	4	33	105	.262	1327	106	7	.995
1979—Cleveland		Amer.	1B	143	515	89	120	31	1	26	93	.233	1089	82	7	.994
1980—Cleveland		Amer.					(Did not play)									
1981—Cleveland		Amer.	1B	69	226	22	54	12	0	6	30	.239	67	5	1	.986
1982—Cleveland		Amer.	1B	161	589	90	161	26	1	32	116	.273	76	5	0	1.000
1983—Cleveland		Amer.	1B	141	508	78	143	27	1	17	77	.281	201	21	2	.991
1984—Cleveland y		Amer.	1B	155	587	91	159	26	0	33	99	.271	86	9	2	.979
1985—Cleveland		Amer.	DH	124	461	49	109	13	0	22	88	.236	0	0	0	.000
1986—Cleveland		Amer.	DH	120	401	49	92	14	0	17	66	.229	0	0	0	.000
1987—Cleveland		Amer.	DH	36	85	8	10	2	0	0	5	.118	0	0	0	.000
American League Totals—10 Years				1225	4313	650	1095	193	12	214	749	.254	3872	299	25	.994
National League Totals—4 Years				340	978	142	247	51	10	39	146	.252	2367	203	27	.990
Major League Totals—14 Years				1565	5291	792	1342	244	22	253	895	.254	6239	502	52	.992

Signed as free agent by Philadelphia Phillies' organization, August 6, 1967.
†Traded with Pitcher Joe Hoerner to Atlanta Braves for Pitchers Jim Nash and Gary Neibauer, June 15, 1972.
‡Traded to Chicago Cubs for First Baseman Joe Pepitone, May 19, 1973.
§Traded to Montreal Expos for Pitcher Steve Renko and Outfielder-First Baseman Larry Biittner, May 17, 1976.
xTraded to Cleveland Indians for Pitcher Jackie Brown, December 10, 1976.
yGranted free agency, November 8, 1984; re-signed by Indians, December 4, 1984.

LUIS CLEMENTE TIANT

Born November 23, 1940, at Havana, Cuba.

Height, 5.11. Weight, 187.

Threw and batted righthanded.

Shares modern major league record for most strikeouts, two consecutive games (32), June 29, first game, and July 3, 1968, 19 innings.

Pitched 4-0 no-hit victory against Winston-Salem, May 7, 1963.

Led Carolina League in shutouts with 6 and in complete games with 17 in 1963.

Led American League in shutouts with 9 in 1968, 7 in 1974 and tied for lead with 5 in 1966.

Named THE SPORTING NEWS American League Comeback Player of the Year, 1972.

Named Player of the Year in Pacific Coast League, 1964.

Year	Club	League	G.	IP.	W.	L.	Pct.	H.	R.	ER.	SO.	BB.	ERA.
1959—Mexico City Tigers		Mexican	41	184	5	19	.208	214	★139	121	98	107	5.92
1960—Mexico City Tigers		Mexican	41	180	●17	7	★.708	194	115	93	107	★124	4.65
1961—Mexico City Tigers		Mexican	24	145	12	9	.571	138	77	61	141	106	3.79
1962—Jacksonville		Int'national	1	1	0	0	.000	0	0	0	0	1	0.00
1962—Charleston		Eastern	29	139	7	8	.467	141	75	56	99	72	3.63
1963—Burlington		Carolina	31	204	14	9	.609	151	68	58	★207	81	2.56
1964—Portland		P. Coast	17	137	15	1	★.938	88	37	31	154	40	2.04
1964—Cleveland		American	19	127	10	4	.714	94	41	40	105	47	2.83
1965—Cleveland		American	41	196	11	11	.500	166	88	77	152	66	3.54
1966—Cleveland		American	46	155	12	11	.522	121	50	48	145	50	2.79
1967—Cleveland		American	33	214	12	9	.571	177	76	65	219	67	2.73
1968—Cleveland		American	34	258	21	9	.700	152	53	46	264	73	★1.60
1969—Cleveland†		American	38	250	9	★20	.410	229	★123	103	156	★129	3.71
1970—Minnesota‡		American	18	93	7	3	.700	84	36	35	50	41	3.39
1971—Richmond§-Louisville		Int'national	9	54	3	5	.375	47	27	25	48	28	4.17
1971—Boston		American	21	72	1	7	.125	73	42	39	59	32	4.88
1972—Boston		American	43	179	15	6	.714	128	45	38	123	65	★1.91
1973—Boston		American	35	272	20	13	.606	217	105	101	206	78	3.34
1974—Boston		American	38	311	22	13	.629	281	106	101	176	82	2.92
1975—Boston		American	35	260	18	14	.563	262	126	116	142	72	4.02
1976—Boston		American	38	279	21	12	.636	274	107	95	131	64	3.06
1977—Boston		American	32	189	12	8	.600	210	98	95	124	51	4.52
1978—Boston x		American	32	212	13	8	.619	185	80	78	114	57	3.31
1979—New York		American	30	196	13	8	.619	190	94	85	104	53	3.90
1980—New York y		American	25	136	8	9	.471	139	79	74	84	50	4.90
1981—Portland		P. Coast	21	146	13	7	.650	150	75	62	111	49	3.82
1981—Pittsburgh z		National	9	57	2	5	.286	54	31	25	32	19	3.95
1982—Tabasco a		Mexican	18	119⅓	6	10	.375	98	41	31	103	29	2.34
1982—California b		American	6	29⅔	2	2	.500	39	20	19	30	8	5.76
1983—Mex. City Reds c-Yucatan		Mexican	17	112⅔	8	6	.571	109	47	42	75	34	3.36
American League Totals—18 Years			564	3428⅔	227	167	.576	3021	1369	1255	2384	1085	3.29
National League Totals—1 Year			9	57	2	5	.286	54	31	25	32	19	3.95
Major League Totals—19 Years			573	3485⅔	229	172	.571	3075	1400	1280	2416	1104	3.30

Signed as free agent by Mexico City Tigers, February 21, 1959.

†Traded with Pitcher Stan Williams to Minnesota Twins for Pitchers Dean Chance and Bob Miller, Outfielder Ted Uhlaender and Outfielder-Third Baseman Graig Nettles, December 12, 1969.

‡Released, March 31,1971; signed by Atlanta Braves, April 16, 1971.

§Released, May 15, 1971; signed by Boston Red Sox, May 17, 1971.

xGranted free agency, November 2, 1978; signed by New York Yankees, November 13, 1978.

yGranted free agency, October 27, 1980; signed by Pittsburgh Pirates' organization, February 23, 1981.

zReleased, October 5, 1981; signed by Tabasco of Mexican League, Spring, 1982.

aSold to California Angels, August 2, 1982.

bGranted free agency, November 10, 1982; signed by Mexico City Reds of Mexican League, April 6, 1983.

cReleased and signed by Yucatan, June 10, 1983.

CHAMPIONSHIP SERIES RECORD

Year	Club	League	G.	IP.	W.	L.	Pct.	H.	R.	ER.	SO.	BB.	ERA.
1970—Minnesota		American	1	⅔	0	0	.000	1	2	1	0	0	13.50
1975—Boston		American	1	9	1	0	1.000	3	1	0	8	3	0.00
Championship Series Totals—2 Years			2	9⅔	1	0	1.000	4	3	1	8	3	0.93

WORLD SERIES RECORD

Year	Club	League	G.	IP.	W.	L.	Pct.	H.	R.	ER.	SO.	BB.	ERA.
1975—Boston		American	3	25	2	0	1.000	25	10	10	12	8	3.60

MICHAEL JOSEPH (MIKE) TIERNAN
(Silent Mike)

Born January 21, 1867, at Trenton, N.J.

Died November 9, 1918, at New York, N.Y.

Height, 5.11. Weight, 165.

Threw and batted lefthanded.

Year	Club	League	Pos.	G.	AB.	R.	H.	2B.	3B.	HR.	SB.	B.A.	PO.	A.	E.	F.A.
1885—Trenton	East.		OF	88	340	54	84	...	...	...	....	.247	84	3	13	.870
1886—Jersey City	East.		OF	54	223	53	87	...	...	...	....	★.390	63	24	6	.935
1887—New York	Nat.		OF	103	438	81	149	13	12	10	28	.340	150	10	25	.865
1888—New York	Nat.		OF	113	443	75	130	14	8	9	52	.293	174	16	8	★.960
1889—New York	Nat.		OF	122	499	★146	167	23	13	12	33	.335	179	19	23	.896
1890—New York	Nat.		OF	133	553	130	168	25	20	●13	56	.304	210	13	26	.896
1891—New York	Nat.		OF	133	540	111	164	30	12	●16	54	.304	138	18	18	.897
1892—New York	Nat.		OF	114	451	80	134	15	11	4	34	.297	156	15	18	.905
1893—New York	Nat.		OF	124	471	113	154	19	12	15	41	.327	183	11	16	.924
1894—New York	Nat.		OF	112	429	87	121	18	14	6	26	.282	170	11	13	.933
1895—New York	Nat.		OF	119	474	128	168	23	19	7	36	.354	181	8	12	.940
1896—New York	Nat.		OF	●133	526	132	190	22	15	7	35	.361	211	6	8	.964
1897—New York	Nat.		OF	129	534	123	177	27	11	4	34	.331	180	14	12	.942
1898—New York	Nat.		OF	103	412	89	118	15	10	5	19	.286	130	10	2	★.986
1899—New York	Nat.		OF	36	140	17	35	4	2	0	1	.250	42	4	3	.939
Major League Totals—13 Years				1474	5910	1312	1875	248	159	108	449	.317	2104	155	184	.925

PITCHING RECORD

Year	Club	League	G.	AB.	W.	L.	Pct.	H.	R.
1885—Trenton	Eastern		40	1400	17	19	.472	324	221
1886—Jersey City	Eastern		10	363	6	3	.667	99	.....

JOSEPH BERT (JOE) TINKER

Born July 27, 1880, at Muscotah, Kan.
Died July 27, 1948, at Orlando, Fla.
Height, 5.09. Weight, 175.
Threw and batted righthanded.

Manager, Cincinnati Reds, 1913; Chicago Whales, Federal League, 1914-15; Chicago Cubs, 1916; manager and president, Columbus, American Association, 1917-18; president, 1919-20; manager-owner, Orlando, Florida State, 1921; vice-president, Orlando, 1923.
Named to Hall of Fame, 1946.

Year	Club	League	Pos.	G.	AB.	R.	H.	2B.	3B.	HR.	SB.	B.A.	PO.	A.	E.	F.A.
1900—Denver	West.		SS	32	137	18	30	...	...	...	8	.219	74	49	26	.826
1900—Gr't F'ls-Helena	Mont. St.		SS	57	236	39	76	...	...	...	12	.322	150	174	45	.878
1901—Portland	P. NW.		SS-3B	106	424	74	123	...	...	...	37	.290	★147	★202	★61	★.851
1902—Chicago	Nat.		SS-3B	133	501	54	137	17	5	2	28	.273	251	464	★73	.907
1903—Chicago	Nat.		SS-3B	124	460	67	134	21	7	2	27	.291	246	400	67	.906
1904—Chicago	Nat.		SS	141	488	55	108	12	13	3	41	.221	327	465	64	.925
1905—Chicago	Nat.		SS	149	547	70	135	18	8	2	31	.247	345	527	56	.940
1906—Chicago	Nat.		SS	148	523	75	122	18	4	1	30	.233	288	472	45	★.944
1907—Chicago	Nat.		SS	113	402	36	89	11	3	1	20	.221	215	390	39	.939
1908—Chicago	Nat.		SS	●157	548	67	146	22	14	6	30	.266	314	★570	39	★.958
1909—Chicago	Nat.		SS	143	516	56	132	26	11	4	23	.256	320	470	50	●.940
1910—Chicago	Nat.		SS	132	473	48	136	25	9	3	20	.288	277	411	42	.942
1911—Chicago	Nat.		SS	143	536	61	149	24	12	4	30	.278	★333	★486	55	★.937
1912—Chicago(a)	Nat.		SS	142	550	80	155	24	7	0	25	.282	★354	470	50	.943
1913—Cincinnati(b)	Nat.		SS	110	382	47	121	20	13	1	10	.317	223	320	18	★.968
1914—Chicago	Fed.		SS	127	440	53	114	22	7	2	24	.259	281	413	39	.947
1915—Chicago(c)	Fed.		SS	30	69	7	19	2	1	0	3	.275	16	39	5	.917
1916—Chicago	Nat.		SS-3B	7	10	0	1	0	0	0	0	.100	4	9	1	.929
1917—Columbus	A. A.		2B	22	51	5	6	1	1	0	4	.118	13	36	3	.942
1921—Orlando	Fla. St.		2B	2	3	1	1	0	0	0	0	.333	4	1	1	.833
Major League Totals—13 Years				1642	5936	716	1565	238	106	29	315	.264	3497	5454	599	.937

aTraded to Cincinnati with Pitcher Grover Lowdermilk and Catcher Harry Chapman for Pitcher Bert Humphries, Infielder-Outfielder Pete Knisely, Infielders Red Corriden and Art Phelan and Outfielder Mike Mitchell, December 15, 1912.

bSold to Brooklyn, December, 1913, but when refused $2,000 of purchase price for signing with Dodgers, jumped to Feds.

cSold to Chicago Nationals in peace agreement, January 1916.

WORLD SERIES RECORD

Year	Club	League	Pos.	G.	AB.	R.	H.	2B.	3B.	HR.	SB.	B.A.	PO.	A.	E.	F.A.
1906—Chicago	Nat.		SS	6	18	4	3	0	0	0	2	.167	10	20	2	.938
1907—Chicago	Nat.		SS	5	13	4	2	0	0	0	3	.154	15	23	3	.927
1908—Chicago	Nat.		SS	5	19	2	5	0	0	1	5	.263	8	19	0	1.000
1910—Chicago	Nat.		SS	5	18	2	6	2	0	0	0	.333	11	14	2	.926
World Series Totals—4 Years				21	68	12	16	2	0	1	10	.235	44	76	7	.945

JOHN THOMAS (JOHNNY) TOBIN

Born May 4, 1892, at St. Louis, Mo.

Died December 10, 1969, at St. Louis, Mo.

Height, 5.08. Weight, 148.

Threw and batted lefthanded.

Manager, Bloomington, Three-I League, 1930; coach, St. Louis Browns, 1944 through 1948; scout, Browns, 1949 through 1951.

Year Club	League	Pos.	G.	AB.	R.	H.	2B.	3B.	HR.	RBI.	B.A.	PO.	A.	E.	F.A.
1912—Houston	Tex.										.339				
1913—St. Louis	Fed.	OF	41	124	17	42	....	....	....	.....	.339	......	.....	....	......
1914—St. Louis	Fed.	OF	135	530	80	143	24	11	7	.....	.270	189	28	10	.956
1915—St. Louis	Fed.	OF	158	★623	91	186	29	14	6	.....	.299	280	22	12	.962
1916—St. Louis	Amer.	OF	77	150	16	32	4	1	0	10	.213	46	2	9	.842
1917—Salt Lake	P. C.	OF	189	800	★149	★265	42	3	2	.....	.331	★478	31	16	.970
1918—St. Louis	Amer.	OF	122	480	59	133	19	5	0	37	.277	244	20	8	.971
1919—St. Louis	Amer.	OF	127	486	54	159	22	7	6	59	.327	247	16	13	.953
1920—St. Louis	Amer.	OF	147	593	94	202	34	10	4	62	.341	293	18	13	.960
1921—St. Louis	Amer.	OF	150	★671	132	236	31	18	8	59	.352	277	●28	14	.956
1922—St. Louis	Amer.	OF	146	625	122	207	34	8	13	66	.331	221	15	15	.940
1923—St. Louis	Amer.	OF	151	637	91	202	32	15	13	73	.317	269	14	9	.969
1924—St. Louis	Amer.	OF	136	569	87	170	30	8	2	48	.299	251	19	12	.957
1925—St. Louis(a)	Amer.	OF-1B	77	193	25	58	11	0	2	27	.301	56	1	0	1.000
1926—Wash.(b)-Bos.	Amer.	OF	78	242	31	64	9	1	1	17	.264	89	7	3	.970
1927—Boston	Amer.	OF	111	374	52	116	18	3	2	40	.310	152	10	9	.947
1928—Columbus	A. A.	OF	53	137	15	39	4	2	0	.....	.285	250	14	6	.978
1929—Wichita Falls	Tex.	OF	5	3	4	3	2	0	0	.....	1.000	5	0	0	1.000
1930—Bloomington	I.I.I.	OF	25	29	4	9	0	0	1	3	.310	10	1	1	.917
Major League Totals—11 Years			1322	5020	763	1579	244	76	51	498	.315	2145	150	105	.956

aTraded with Pitcher Joe Bush to Washington for Pitchers Win Ballou and Tom Zachary, February, 1926.
bReleased by Washington, June, 1926, and signed by Boston Red Sox, July, 1926.

JOSEPH PAUL (JOE) TORRE

Born July 18, 1940, at Brooklyn, N. Y.

Height, 6.01. Weight, 210.

Threw and batted righthanded.

Brother of Frank Torre, former major league first baseman.

Led National League first basemen in double plays with 144 in 1974.
Led National League catchers in double plays with 12 in 1967.
Named catcher on THE SPORTING NEWS National League All-Star Teams, 1964-65-66.
Named catcher on THE SPORTING NEWS National League All-Star fielding team, 1965.
Named third baseman on THE SPORTING NEWS National League All-Star Team, 1971.
Named Major League Player of the Year by THE SPORTING NEWS, 1971.
Most Valuable Player in the National League, 1971.
Manager, New York Mets, 1977 through 1981; Atlanta Braves, 1982 through 1984.

Year Club	League	Pos.	G.	AB.	R.	H.	2B.	3B.	HR.	RBI.	B.A.	PO.	A.	E.	F.A.
1960—Eau Claire	North.	C	117	369	63	127	23	3	16	74	★.344	636	64	9	.987
1960—Milwaukee	Nat.	PH	2	2	0	1	0	0	0	0	.500	0	0	0	.000
1961—Louisville	A. A.	C	27	111	18	38	8	2	3	24	.342	185	14	2	.990
1961—Milwaukee	Nat.	C	113	406	40	113	21	4	10	42	.278	494	50	10	.982
1962—Milwaukee	Nat.	C	80	220	23	62	8	1	5	26	.282	325	39	5	.986
1963—Milwaukee	Nat.	C-1-OF	142	501	57	147	19	4	14	71	.293	919	76	6	.994
1964—Milwaukee	Nat.	★C-1B	154	601	87	193	36	5	20	109	.321	1081	94	7	★.994
1965—Milwaukee	Nat.	C-1B	148	523	68	152	21	1	27	80	.291	1022	73	8	.993
1966—Atlanta	Nat.	C-1B	148	546	83	172	20	3	36	101	.315	874	87	12	.988
1967—Atlanta	Nat.	C-1B	135	477	67	132	18	1	20	68	.277	785	81	8	.991
1968—Atlanta (a)	Nat.	★C-1B	115	424	45	115	11	2	10	55	.271	733	48	2	★.997
1969—St. Louis	Nat.	1B-C	159	602	72	174	29	6	18	101	.289	1360	91	7	.995
1970—St. Louis	Nat.	C-3-1B	●161	624	89	203	27	9	21	100	.325	651	162	13	.984

Year	Club	League	Pos.	G.	AB.	R.	H.	2B.	3B.	HR.	RBI.	B.A.	PO.	A.	E.	F.A.
1971—St. Louis	Nat.	3B	161	634	97	*230	34	8	24	*137	*.363	*136	271	•21	.951
1972—St. Louis	Nat.	3B-1B	149	544	71	157	26	6	11	81	.289	336	198	15	.973
1973—St. Louis	Nat.	1B-3B	141	519	67	149	17	2	13	69	.287	881	128	12	.988
1974—St. Louis (b)	Nat.	*1B-3B	147	529	59	149	28	1	11	70	.282	1173	*121	14	.989
1975—New York	Nat.	3B-1B	114	361	33	89	16	3	6	35	.247	172	157	15	.956
1976—New York	Nat.	1-3B-PH	114	310	36	95	10	3	5	31	.306	593	52	7	.989
1977—New York (c)	Nat.	1B-3B	26	51	2	9	3	0	1	9	.176	83	3	1	.989
Major League Totals—18 Years			2209	7874	996	2342	344	59	252	1185	.297	11618	1731	163	.988

aTraded to St. Louis Cardinals for First Baseman Orlando Cepeda, March 17, 1969.
bTraded to New York Mets for Pitchers Tommy Moore and Ray Sadecki, October 13, 1974.
cPlayer-manager, beginning May 31, until released as player, June 18, 1988.

CECIL HOWELL TRAVIS

Born August 8, 1913, at Riverdale, Ga.

Height, 6.01½. Weight, 195.

Threw right and batted lefthanded.

Shares major league record for most hits, first major league game (5), May 16, 1933 (12 innings).
Named by Baseball Writers' Association of America as shortstop for THE SPORTING NEWS All-Star Major League Team, 1941.
Scout, Washington Senators, 1948 through 1955.

Year	Club	League	Pos.	G.	AB.	R.	H.	2B.	3B.	HR.	RBI.	B.A.	PO.	A.	E.	F.A.
1931—Chattanooga	South.	2B-3B	13	35	7	15	4	0	0	0	.429	12	107	3	.906
1932—Chattanooga	South.	3B	152	570	88	203	27	*17	3	88	.356	127	298	37	.920
1933—Chattanooga	South.	3B	129	526	80	185	26	12	1	74	.352	128	262	33	.922
1933—Washington	Amer.	3B	18	43	7	13	1	0	0	2	.302	8	30	1	.974
1934—Washington	Amer.	3B	109	392	48	125	22	4	1	53	.319	88	210	20	.937
1935—Washington	Amer.	3B-OF	138	534	85	170	27	8	0	61	.318	164	258	16	.962
1936—Washington	Amer.	SS-OF	138	517	77	164	34	10	2	92	.317	244	231	31	.939
1937—Washington	Amer.	SS	135	526	72	181	27	7	3	66	.344	229	396	23	.915
1938—Washington	Amer.	SS	146	567	96	190	30	5	5	67	.335	304	357	40	.943
1939—Washington	Amer.	SS	130	476	55	139	20	9	5	63	.292	194	359	24	.958
1940—Washington	Amer.	SS-3B	136	528	60	170	37	11	2	76	.322	164	340	38	.930
1941—Washington	Amer.	SS-3B	152	608	106	*218	39	19	7	101	.359	293	427	27	.964
1942-43-44—Wash.	Amer.					(In Military Service)									
1945—Washington	Amer.	3B	15	54	4	13	2	1	0	10	.241	18	28	4	.920
1946—Washington	Amer.	SS-*3B	137	465	45	117	22	3	1	56	.252	187	290	*31	.939
1947—Washington	Amer.	SS-3B	74	204	10	44	4	1	1	10	.216	53	112	9	.948
Major League Totals—12 Years			1328	4914	665	1544	265	78	27	657	.314	1946	3038	264	.950

HAROLD JOSEPH (PIE) TRAYNOR

Born November 11, 1899, at Framingham, Mass.

Died March 16, 1972, at Pittsburgh, Pa.

Height, 6.00½. Weight, 175.

Threw and batted righthanded.

Holds National League record for most putouts, third baseman, lifetime (2,288).
Shares National League record for most years leading league in putouts by third baseman (7).
Holds modern National League record for most errors, third baseman, lifetime (324).
Led National League third basemen in double plays, 1924, 1925, 1926, 1927 (tie).
Named to THE SPORTING NEWS All-Star Major League Teams in 1925-26-27-29-31-32-33.
Manager, Pittsburgh Pirates, 1934 to 1939; scout, Pirates, 1940 to date of death.
Named to Hall of Fame, 1948.

Year	Club	League	Pos.	G.	AB.	R.	H.	2B.	3B.	HR.	RBI.	B.A.	PO.	A.	E.	F.A.
1920—Portsmouth	Va.	SS	104	392	50	106	18	4	8	57	.270	215	334	31	.947
1920—Pittsburgh	Nat.	SS	17	52	6	11	3	1	0	2	.212	35	39	12	.860
1921—Birmingham	South.	SS	131	527	101	177	22	13	5	53	.336	330	382	64	.918

Year	Club	League	Pos.	G.	AB.	R.	H.	2B.	3B.	HR.	RBI.	B.A.	PO.	A.	E.	F.A.
1921—Pittsburgh	Nat.	SS-3B	7	19	0	5	0	0	0	2	.263	4	9	1	.939
1922—Pittsburgh	Nat.	SS-3B	142	571	89	161	17	12	4	81	.282	186	278	31	.937
1923—Pittsburgh	Nat.	3B	153	616	108	208	19	*19	12	101	.338	*191	*310	26	.951
1924—Pittsburgh	Nat.	3B	142	545	86	160	26	13	5	82	.294	179	268	15	.968
1925—Pittsburgh	Nat.	SS-3B	150	591	114	189	39	14	6	106	.320	*226	*303	24	*.957
1926—Pittsburgh	Nat.	3B	152	574	83	182	25	17	3	92	.317	*182	279	*23	.952
1927—Pittsburgh	Nat.	3B	149	573	93	196	32	9	5	106	.342	*212	265	19	.962
1928—Pittsburgh	Nat.	3B	144	569	91	192	38	12	3	124	.337	175	296	*27	.946
1929—Pittsburgh	Nat.	3B	130	540	94	192	27	12	4	108	.356	148	238	20	.951
1930—Pittsburgh	Nat.	3B	130	497	90	182	22	11	9	119	.366	130	268	25	.941
1931—Pittsburgh	Nat.	3B	155	615	81	183	37	15	2	103	.298	*172	284	*37	.925
1932—Pittsburgh	Nat.	3B	135	513	74	169	27	10	2	68	.329	173	222	*27	.936
1933—Pittsburgh	Nat.	3B	*154	624	85	190	27	6	1	82	.304	*176	*300	*27	.946
1934—Pittsburgh	Nat.	3B	119	444	62	137	22	10	1	61	.309	*116	176	14	.954
1935—Pittsburgh	Nat.	1B-3B	57	204	24	57	10	3	1	36	.279	59	84	18	.888
1936—Pittsburgh	Nat.								(Did not play)							
1937—Pittsburgh	Nat.	3B	5	12	3	2	0	0	0	0	.167	2	8	0	1.000
Major League Totals—17 Years			1941	7559	1183	2416	371	164	58	1273	.320	2366	3627	346	.945

WORLD SERIES RECORD

Year	Club	League	Pos.	G.	AB.	R.	H.	2B.	3B.	HR.	RBI.	B.A.	PO.	A.	E.	F.A.
1925—Pittsburgh	Nat.	3B	7	26	2	9	0	2	1	4	.346	6	18	0	1.000
1927—Pittsburgh	Nat.	3B	4	15	1	3	1	0	0	0	.200	5	9	1	.933
World Series Totals—2 Years			11	41	3	12	1	2	1	4	.293	11	27	1	.974

HAROLD ARTHUR (HAL) TROSKY

Born November 11, 1912, at Norway, Ia.

Died June 18, 1979, at Cedar Rapids, Ia.

Height, 6.02½. Weight, 198.

Threw right and batted lefthanded.

Hit three home runs in game, May 30, 1934, second game and July 5, 1937, first game.
Led American League first basemen in double plays, 1934.
Scout, Chicago White Sox, 1947-48.

Year	Club	League	Pos.	G.	AB.	R.	H.	2B.	3B.	HR.	RBI.	B.A.	PO.	A.	E.	F.A.
1931—C.Rap.-Dubuque	M.V.	OF-PH	52	162	14	49	8	2	3	....	.302	44	19	5	.926
932—Quincy	I.I.I.	OF	68	260	55	86	14	6	15	....	.331	107	9	8	.935
1932—Burlington	M.V.	OF-1B	59	228	36	72	18	10	4	44	.316	290	23	12	.963
1933—Toledo	A.A.	1B	132	461	86	149	25	5	33	92	.323	742	43	14	.982
1933—Cleveland	Amer.	1B	11	44	6	13	1	2	1	8	.295	91	4	1	.990
1934—Cleveland	Amer.	1B	154	625	117	206	45	9	35	142	.330	*1487	*86	22	.986
1935—Cleveland	Amer.	1B	154	632	84	171	33	7	26	113	.271	*1567	88	11	.993
1936—Cleveland	Amer.	1B	151	629	124	216	45	9	42	*162	.343	1367	85	22	.985
1937—Cleveland	Amer.	1B	153	601	104	179	36	9	32	128	.298	1403	76	10	.993
1938—Cleveland	Amer.	1B	150	554	106	185	40	9	19	110	.334	1132	102	10	.992
1939—Cleveland	Amer.	1B	122	448	89	150	31	4	25	104	.335	1004	97	9	.992
1940—Cleveland	Amer.	1B	140	522	85	154	39	4	25	93	.295	1207	70	11	.991
1941—Cleveland	Amer.	1B	89	310	43	91	17	0	11	51	.294	727	54	9	.989
1942—Cleveland	Amer.						(Out of game due to illness)										
1943—Cleveland (a)	Amer.						(Out of game due to illness)										
1944—Chicago	Amer.	1B	135	497	55	120	32	2	10	70	.241	1310	57	9	.993
1945—Chicago	Amer.						(Out of game due to illness)										
1946—Chicago	Amer.	1B	88	299	22	76	12	3	2	31	.254	729	33	7	.991
Major League Totals—11 Years			1347	5161	835	1561	331	58	228	1012	.302	12024	752	121	.991

aSold to Chicago White Sox, November 6, 1943.

GEORGE ERNEST UHLE

Born September 18, 1898, at Cleveland, O.

Died February 26, 1985, at Lakewood, O.

Height, 6.00. Weight, 195.

Threw and batted righthanded.

Coach, Cleveland Indians, 1937; Buffalo, International League, 1938-39; Chicago Cubs, 1940; scout, Brooklyn Dodgers, 1941-42; coach, Washington Senators, 1944.

Year Club	League	G.	IP.	W.	L.	Pct.	H.	R.	ER.	SO.	BB.	ERA.
1919—Cleveland	American	26	127	10	5	.667	129	52	41	50	43	2.91
1920—Cleveland	American	27	85	4	5	.444	98	52	49	27	29	5.19
1921—Cleveland	American	41	238	16	13	.552	288	132	106	63	63	4.01
1922—Cleveland	American	50	287	22	16	.579	328	147	130	82	89	4.08
1923—Cleveland	American	54	★358	★26	16	.619	★378	★167	★150	109	102	3.77
1924—Cleveland	American	28	196	9	15	.375	238	134	104	57	75	4.78
1925—Cleveland	American	29	211	13	11	.542	218	118	96	68	78	4.09
1926—Cleveland	American	39	★318	★27	11	★.711	★300	114	100	159	★118	2.83
1927—Cleveland	American	25	153	8	9	.471	187	88	74	69	59	4.35
1928—Cleveland(a)	American	31	214	12	17	.414	252	121	97	74	48	4.08
1929—Detroit	American	32	249	15	11	.577	283	141	113	100	58	4.09
1930—Detroit	American	33	239	12	12	.500	239	110	97	117	75	3.65
1931—Detroit	American	29	193	11	12	.478	190	88	75	63	49	3.50
1932—Detroit	American	33	147	6	6	.500	152	84	73	51	42	4.47
1933—Detroit(b)-New York	American	13	62	6	1	.857	65	44	37	27	20	5.37
1933—New York(c)	National	6	14	1	1	.500	16	12	12	4	6	7.71
1934—New York	American	10	16	2	4	.333	30	19	18	10	7	10.13
1934—Toledo	Amer. Assn.	19	70	2	4	.333	77	33	29	30	16	3.73
1935—						(Out of game)						
1936—Cleveland	American	7	13	0	1	.000	26	12	12	5	5	8.31
1938—Buffalo	International	2	3	0	0	.000	2	0	0	2	1	0.00
1939—Buffalo	International	6	11	1	0	1.000	14	9	7	5	1	5.73
American League Totals—17 Years		507	3106	199	165	.547	3401	1623	1372	1131	960	3.98
National League Totals—1 Year		6	14	1	1	.500	16	12	12	4	6	7.71
Major League Totals—17 Years		513	3120	200	166	.546	3417	1635	1384	1135	966	3.99

aTraded to Detroit Tigers for Infielder John Tavener and Pitcher Ken Holloway, December 11, 1928.
bSold to New York Giants, April 24, 1933.
cReleased, July 8, 1933 and signed by New York Yankees, July 24, 1933. (Note that 1933 New York Giant record was compiled between Detroit and Yankee records of same season.)

WORLD SERIES RECORD

Year Club	League	G.	IP.	W.	L.	Pct.	H.	R.	ER.	SO.	BB.	ERA.
1920—Cleveland	American	2	3	0	0	.000	1	0	0	3	0	0.00

ELMER WILLIAM VALO

Born March 5, 1921, at Ribnik, Czechoslavakia.

Height, 5.10½. Weight, 189.

Threw right and batted lefthanded.

Holds major league record for most bases on balls by pinch-hitter, season (18), 1960.
Holds American League record for most games by pinch-hitter, season (81), 1960.
Scout, New York Mets, 1962; coach, Cleveland Indians, 1963-64; manager, Dubuque, Midwest League, 1965-66; scout, Philadelphia Phillies, 1970 through 1982.

Year Club	League	Pos.	G.	AB.	R.	H.	2B.	3B.	HR.	RBI.	B.A.	PO.	A.	E.	F.A.
1939—Federalsburg	E. Shore	OF	34	115	28	43	9	2	3	19	.374	51	2	7	.883
1940—Wilmington	Int.-St.	OF	120	437	89	★159	★31	★16	6	80	★.364	220	17	13	.948
1940—Philadelphia	Amer.	OF	6	23	6	8	0	0	0	0	.348	18	0	0	1.000
1941—Wilmington	Int.-St.	OF	125	447	80	145	14	7	11	67	.324	234	12	●17	.935
1941—Philadelphia	Amer.	OF	15	50	13	21	0	1	2	6	.420	22	0	0	1.000
1942—Philadelphia	Amer.	OF	133	459	64	115	13	10	2	40	.251	264	5	10	.964
1943—Philadelphia	Amer.	OF	77	249	31	55	6	2	3	18	.221	134	4	2	.986
1944-45—Philadelphia	Amer.					(In Military Service)									
1946—Philadelphia	Amer.	OF	108	348	59	107	21	6	1	31	.307	182	7	5	.974
1947—Philadelphia	Amer.	OF	112	370	60	111	12	6	5	36	.300	205	9	6	.973
1948—Philadelphia	Amer.	OF	113	383	72	117	17	4	3	46	.305	231	4	4	.983
1949—Philadelphia	Amer.	OF	150	547	86	155	27	12	5	85	.283	395	8	8	.981
1950—Philadelphia	Amer.	OF	129	446	62	125	16	5	10	46	.280	264	9	5	.982
1951—Philadelphia	Amer.	OF	123	444	75	134	27	8	7	55	.302	247	5	5	.981
1952—Philadelphia	Amer.	OF	129	388	69	109	26	4	5	47	.281	223	7	9	.962
1953—Philadelphia	Amer.	OF	50	85	15	19	3	0	0	9	.224	46	1	0	1.000
1954—Philadelphia†	Amer.	OF	95	224	28	48	11	6	1	33	.214	135	3	5	.965
1955—Kansas City	Amer.	OF	112	283	50	103	17	4	3	37	.364	147	5	2	.987
1956—Kansas City‡	Amer.	OF	9	9	1	2	0	0	0	2	.222	0	0	0	.000
1956—Philadelphia§	Nat.	OF	98	291	40	84	13	3	5	37	.289	167	4	6	.966
1957—Brooklyn	Nat.	OF	81	161	14	44	10	1	4	26	.273	52	2	0	1.000
1958—Los Angeles x	Nat.	OF	65	101	9	25	2	1	1	14	.248	24	0	0	1.000

Year	Club	League	Pos.	G.	AB.	R.	H.	2B.	3B.	HR.	RBI.	B.A.	PO.	A.	E.	F.A.
1959—Seattle	P. C.		OF	60	182	24	59	11	0	3	23	.324	92	2	4	.959
1959—Cleveland x	Amer.		OF	34	24	3	7	0	0	0	5	.292	1	0	0	1.000
1960—N.Y. y-Wash.	Amer.		OF	84	69	7	18	3	0	0	16	.261	5	1	0	1.000
1961—Minnesota z	Amer.		OF	33	32	0	5	2	0	0	4	.156	2	0	0	1.000
1961—Philadelphia a	Nat.		OF	50	43	4	8	2	0	1	8	.186	0	0	0	.000
American League Totals—18 Years				1512	4433	701	1259	201	68	47	516	.284	2521	68	61	.977
National League Totals—4 Years				294	596	67	161	27	5	11	85	.270	243	6	6	.976
Major League Totals—20 Years				1806	5029	768	1420	228	73	58	601	.282	2764	74	67	.977

†Philadelphia franchise transferred to Kansas City, November 8, 1954.
‡Released; signed by Philadelphia Phillies, May 22, 1956.
§Traded to Brooklyn Dodgers with players assigned from Phillies' minor league clubs, Pitchers Ben Flowers and Ron Negray, First Baseman Tom Harkness and Shortstop Mel Geho and reported $75,000 for Shortstop Chico Fernandez, April 5, 1957; all players with exception of Flowers transferred April 5; Flowers added to deal three days later.
xReleased, October 5, 1959; signed by New York Yankees, December 15, 1959.
yReleased, May 23, 1960; signed with Washington Senators, May 24, 1960.
zReleased, June 17, 1961; signed with Philadelphia Phillies same day.
aReleased, October 16, 1961.

GEORGE E. VAN HALTREN

Born March 30, 1866, at St. Louis, Mo.

Died October 1, 1945, at Oakland, Calif.

Threw and batted lefthanded.

Pitched 1-0 six-inning no-hitter against Pittsburgh, June 21, 1888.
Manager, Baltimore, American Association, 1891, and in National League, 1892; umpire, Pacific Coast League, 1909; scout, Pittsburgh, N. L., 1910-11; umpire, Northwestern League, 1912.

Year	Club	League	Pos.	G.	AB.	R.	H.	2B.	3B.	HR.	SB.	B.A.	PO.	A.	E.	F.A.
1887—Chicago	Nat.		P-OF	44	183	29	51	4	0	3	12	.278	35	3	4	.904
1888—Chicago	Nat.		P-OF	81	318	46	90	10	12	4	21	.283	73	9	12	.872
1889—Chicago	Nat.		OF	134	543	126	175	20	10	9	28	.322	222	25	28	.898
1890—Brooklyn	Players		P-OF	92	376	86	130	8	8	5	19	.346	134	30	15	.945
1891—Baltimore	A.A.		P-S-O	139	566	136	180	19	15	9	48	.318	275	190	82	.850
1892—Balt.(a)-Pitts.	Nat.		★O-P-3-SS-1	148	604	116	179	23	13	6	57	.296	274	56	54	.859
1893—Pittsburgh	Nat.		OF	123	502	129	176	14	11	3	35	.350	222	20	36	.871
1894—New York	Nat.		OF	139	532	110	177	25	4	8	44	.333	309	28	33	.911
1895—New York	Nat.		OF	131	517	112	175	23	17	6	31	.338	256	28	32	.899
1896—New York	Nat.		P-OF	●133	564	138	199	19	●21	5	42	.353	271	●24	18	.942
1897—New York	Nat.		OF	131	★571	122	190	22	11	3	45	.333	268	31	21	.934
1898—New York	Nat.		OF	155	★651	129	205	27	17	2	31	.315	299	21	25	.927
1899—New York	Nat.		OF	153	607	119	183	22	4	2	33	.301	285	29	18	.949
1900—New York	Nat.		OF	141	568	113	181	28	6	1	45	.319	322	23	19	.947
1901—New York	Nat.		P-OF	133	544	83	186	22	7	1	25	.342	259	24	18	.940
1902—New York	Nat.		OF	26	96	14	24	1	2	0	7	.250	46	6	5	.912
1903—New York	Nat.		OF	75	280	42	72	6	1	0	14	.257	136	3	6	.959
1904—Seattle	Pac. Coast		OF	....	★941	159	253	35	10	4	38	.269	493	58	31	.947
1905—Oakland	Pac. Coast		OF	220	860	....	220	18	10	2	47	.256	459	32	26	.950
1906—Oakland	Pac. Coast		OF	152	697	101	151	27	4	0	36	.217	.....	...	...	.....
1907—Oakland	Pac. Coast		OF	193	718	101	193	26	0	0	47	.269	415	28	21	.955
1908—Oakland	Pac. Coast		OF	186	706	80	171	17	3	2	30	.242	379	48	14	.969
1909—Oakland	Pac. Coast		OF	55	192	14	42	...	...	...	....	.219	95	5	4	.962
National League Totals—15 Years				1747	7080	1428	2263	266	136	53	470	.320	3277	330	329	.916
Players League Totals—1 Year				92	376	86	130	8	8	5	19	.346	134	30	15	.945
American Assn. Totals—1 Year				139	566	136	180	19	15	9	48	.318	275	190	82	.850
Major League Totals—17 Years				1978	8022	1650	2573	293	159	67	537	.321	3686	550	426	.909

aTraded to Pittsburgh in deal for Outfielder James J. Kelley, September, 1892.

PITCHING RECORD

Year	Club	League	G.	W.	L.	Pct.	H.	R.	CG.	ShO.
1887—Chicago	National	19	12	7	.632	226	102	19	1
1888—Chicago	National	27	13	11	.542	264	160	23	4
1890—Brooklyn	Players	26	15	10	.600	275	190	24	0
1891—Baltimore	American Association	6	0	1	.000	38	....	0	0
1892—Baltimore	National	4	0	0	.000	28	....	0	0
1895—New York	National	1	0	0	.000	13	....	0	0
1896—New York	National	2	1	0	1.000	5	....	0	0
1900—New York	National	1	0	0	.000	1	0	0	0
1901—New York	National	1	0	1	.000	12	....	0	0
Major League Totals—9 Years			87	41	30	.577	862	....	66	5

ARTHUR CHARLES (DAZZY) VANCE

Born March 4, 1891, at Adair County, Ia.
Died February 16, 1961, at Homosassa Springs, Fla.
Height, 6.01. Weight, 200.
Threw and batted righthanded.

Holds National League record for most years and most consecutive years leading league in strikeouts (7).
Pitched 10-1 no-hit victory against Philadelphia, September 13, 1925, first game.
Named National League Most Valuable Player, 1924.
Named to Hall of Fame, 1955.

Year Club	League	G.	IP.	W.	L.	Pct.	H.	R.	ER.	SO.	BB.	ERA.
1912—Red Cloud	Neb. State	36	....	11	15	.423	....	....	....	....	....	......
1913—Superior	Neb. State	25	....	11	14	.440	....	....	....	....	....	......
1914—Hastings	Neb. State	26	....	17	4	★.810	....	....	....	194	71	......
1914—St. Joseph	Western	21	134	9	8	.529	129	64	44	108	50	2.96
1915—Pittsburgh	National	1	3	0	1	.000	3	3	3	0	5	6.00
1915—St. Joseph	Western	39	264	17	15	.531	224	118	86	199	110	2.93
1915—New York	American	8	28	0	3	.000	23	14	11	18	16	3.54
1916—Columbus	Amer. Assn.	14	50	2	2	.500	52	....	25	10	16	4.50
1917—Toledo	Amer. Assn.	15	71	2	6	.250	63	31	18	30	25	2.28
1917—Memphis	Southern	16	122	6	8	.429	102	41	....	61	28	......
1918—Memphis	Southern	16	117	8	6	.571	93	....	....	40	33	......
1918—Rochester	International	9	72	3	5	.375	85	39	31	34	23	3.88
1918—New York	American	2	2	0	0	.000	9	5	4	0	2	18.00
1919—Sacramento	Pacific Coast	48	294	10	18	.357	264	125	92	86	81	2.82
1920—Memphis-New Orleans	Southern	45	284	16	17	.485	253	104	....	65	65	......
1921—New Orleans	Southern	38	253	21	11	.656	225	115	99	163	80	3.52
1922—Brooklyn	National	36	246	18	12	.600	259	122	101	★134	94	3.70
1923—Brooklyn	National	37	280	18	15	.545	263	127	109	★197	100	3.50
1924—Brooklyn	National	35	309	★28	6	.824	238	89	74	★262	77	★2.16
1925—Brooklyn	National	31	265	★22	9	.710	247	115	104	★221	66	3.53
1926—Brooklyn	National	24	169	9	10	.474	172	80	73	★140	58	3.89
1927—Brooklyn	National	34	273	16	15	.516	242	98	82	★184	69	2.70
1928—Brooklyn	National	38	280	22	10	.688	226	79	65	★200	72	★2.09
1929—Brooklyn	National	31	231	14	13	.519	244	110	100	126	47	3.90
1930—Brooklyn	National	35	259	17	15	.531	241	97	75	173	55	★2.61
1931—Brooklyn	National	30	219	11	13	.458	221	99	82	150	53	3.37
1932—Brooklyn(a)	National	27	176	12	11	.522	171	90	82	103	57	4.19
1933—St. Louis(b)	National	28	99	6	2	.750	105	42	39	67	28	3.55
1934—Cincinnati(c)-St.L.(d)	National	25	77	1	3	.250	90	47	39	42	25	4.56
1935—Brooklyn	National	20	51	3	2	.600	55	29	25	28	16	4.41
American League Totals—2 Years		10	30	0	3	.000	32	19	15	18	18	4.50
National League Totals—15 Years		432	2937	197	137	.590	2777	1227	1053	2027	822	3.23
Major League Totals—16 Years		442	2967	197	140	.585	2809	1246	1068	2045	840	3.24

aTraded to St. Louis Cardinals with Shortstop Gordon Slade for Infielder Jake Flowers and Pitcher Owen Carroll, February 9, 1933.
bSold to Cincinnati Reds, February 6, 1934.
cReleased to St. Louis Cardinals on waivers, June 25, 1934.
dReleased by St. Louis Cardinals and signed by Brooklyn Dodgers, April, 1935.

WORLD SERIES RECORD

Year Club	League	G.	IP.	W.	L.	Pct.	H.	R.	ER.	SO.	BB.	ERA.
1934—St. Louis	National	1	1⅓	0	0	.000	2	1	0	3	1	0.00

JOSEPH FLOYD (ARKY) VAUGHAN

Born March 9, 1912, at Clifty, Ark.
Died August 30, 1952, at Eagleville, Calif.
Height, 5.11. Weight, 185.
Threw right and batted lefthanded.

Led National League in stolen bases with 20 in 1943.

Named by Baseball Writers' Association of America as shortstop for THE SPORTING NEWS All-Star Major League Team, 1935.

Named Most Valuable Player in National League by THE SPORTING NEWS, 1935.

Named to Hall of Fame, 1985.

Year	Club	League	Pos.	G.	AB.	R.	H.	2B.	3B.	HR.	RBI.	B.A.	PO.	A.	E.	F.A.
1931—Wichita	West.		SS-3B	132	494	★145	167	21	16	21	81	.338	216	352	32	.947
1932—Pittsburgh	Nat.		SS	129	497	71	158	15	10	4	61	.318	247	403	★46	.934
1933—Pittsburgh	Nat.		SS	152	573	85	180	29	★19	9	97	.314	310	487	★46	.945
1934—Pittsburgh	Nat.		SS	149	558	115	186	41	11	12	94	.333	329	480	41	.952
1935—Pittsburgh	Nat.		SS	137	499	108	192	34	10	19	99	★.385	249	422	35	.950
1936—Pittsburgh	Nat.		SS	●156	568	★122	190	30	11	9	78	.335	★327	477	47	.945
1937—Pittsburgh	Nat.		SS-OF	126	469	71	151	17	★17	5	72	.322	257	335	27	.956
1938—Pittsburgh	Nat.		SS	148	541	88	174	35	5	7	68	.322	★306	★507	33	.961
1939—Pittsburgh	Nat.		SS	152	595	94	182	30	11	6	62	.306	★330	★531	34	.962
1940—Pittsburgh	Nat.		★SS-3B	★156	594	★113	178	40	★15	7	95	.300	309	★546	52	★.943
1941—Pittsburgh(a)	Nat.		SS-3B	106	374	69	118	20	7	6	38	.316	174	298	21	.957
1942—Brooklyn	Nat.		3-2B-SS	128	495	82	137	18	4	2	49	.277	130	225	14	.962
1943—Brooklyn	Nat.		3B-SS	149	610	★112	186	39	6	5	66	.305	237	375	21	.967
1944-45-46—Brooklyn	Nat.								(Voluntarily retired)							
1947—Brooklyn	Nat.		3B-OF	64	126	24	41	5	2	2	25	.325	56	20	0	1.000
1948—Brooklyn	Nat.		3B-OF	65	123	19	30	3	0	3	22	.244	47	14	0	1.000
1949—San Francisco	P.C.L.		OF	97	281	50	81	10	6	2	26	.288	129	4	2	.985
Major League Totals—14 Years				1817	6622	1173	2103	356	128	96	926	.318	3308	5120	417	.953

aTraded to Brooklyn for Pitcher Luke Hamlin, Catcher Babe Phelps, Infielder Pete Coscarart and Outfielder Jim Wasdell, December 12, 1941.

WORLD SERIES RECORD

Year	Club	League	Pos.	G.	AB.	R.	H.	2B.	3B.	HR.	RBI.	B.A.	PO.	A.	E.	F.A.
1947—Brooklyn	Nat.		PH	3	2	0	1	1	0	0	0	.500	0	0	0	.000

ROBERT HAYES (BOBBY) VEACH

Born June 29, 1888, at St. Charles, Ky.

Died August 7, 1945, at Detroit, Mich.

Height, 5.10. Weight, 160.

Threw right and batted lefthanded.

Year	Club	League	Pos.	G.	AB.	R.	H.	2B.	3B.	HR.	RBI.	B.A.	PO.	A.	E.	F.A.
1910—Peoria	I.I.I.		3B	35	117	8	27	....	....	....	....	.231	36	54	8	.918
1910—Kankakee	N. Assn.		OF	26	77	13	17	6	0	0	....	.221	....	....	....	....
1911—Peoria	I.I.I.		OF	132	445	59	132	....	....	....	....	.297	197	29	5	.978
1912—Peoria	I.I.I.		OF	56	200	35	65	....	....	....	....	.325	100	14	4	.966
1912—Indianapolis	A.A.		OF	70	253	37	72	13	3	4	....	.285	116	18	10	.931
1912—Detroit	Amer.		OF	23	79	8	27	5	1	0	13	.342	46	5	4	.927
1913—Detroit	Amer.		OF	138	494	55	133	22	10	0	62	.269	251	16	●24	.918
1914—Detroit	Amer.		OF	149	531	56	146	19	14	1	75	.275	282	22	11	.965
1915—Detroit	Amer.		OF	152	569	81	178	★40	10	3	115	.313	297	19	8	.975
1916—Detroit	Amer.		OF	150	566	92	173	33	15	3	88	.306	342	14	12	.967
1917—Detroit	Amer.		OF	154	571	79	182	31	12	8	★115	.319	356	17	★17	.956
1918—Detroit	Amer.		OF	127	499	59	139	21	13	3	●74	.279	277	14	7	.977
1919—Detroit	Amer.		OF	139	538	87	●191	★45	★17	3	98	.355	338	14	12	.967
1920—Detroit	Amer.		OF	●154	612	92	188	39	15	11	113	.307	357	●26	13	.967
1921—Detroit	Amer.		OF	150	612	110	207	43	13	16	128	.338	★384	21	11	.974
1922—Detroit	Amer.		OF	●155	618	96	202	34	13	9	126	.327	375	16	7	.982
1923—Detroit (a)	Amer.		OF	114	293	45	94	13	3	2	39	.321	127	6	8	.943
1924—Boston	Amer.		OF	142	519	77	153	35	9	5	99	.295	270	15	13	.956
1925—Bo(b)-NY(c)-W	Amer.		OF	75	158	17	51	13	2	0	25	.323	53	6	3	.952
1926—Toledo	A.A.		OF	156	588	113	213	43	14	9	105	.362	357	13	13	.966
1927—Toledo	A.A.		OF	164	623	133	226	45	10	12	★145	.363	371	17	14	.965
1928—Toledo	A.A.		OF	151	566	93	216	32	6	7	102	★.382	319	12	17	.951
1929—Toledo	A.A.		OF-PH	79	255	39	68	11	1	4	36	.267	126	7	6	.957
1930—Jersey City	Int.		OF-PH	75	219	34	68	14	2	5	35	.311	69	0	5	.932
Major League Totals—14 Years				1822	6659	954	2064	393	147	64	1170	.310	3755	211	150	.964

aSold to Boston Red Sox, January 12, 1924.

bTraded to New York Yankees with Pitcher Alex Ferguson for Pitcher Ray Francis and cash, May 9, 1924.

cReleased to Washington Senators on waivers, August 17, 1924.

WORLD SERIES RECORD

Year	Club	League	Pos.	G.	AB.	R.	H.	2B.	3B.	HR.	RBI.	B.A.	PO.	A.	E.	F.A.
1925—Washington	Amer.		PH	2	1	0	0	0	0	0	1	.000	0	0	0	.000

JAMES BARTON (MICKEY) VERNON

Born April 22, 1918, at Marcus Hook, Pa.
Height, 6.02. Weight, 188.
Threw and batted lefthanded.

Holds major league record for most double plays by first baseman, lifetime (2,044).
Holds modern major league record for most games by first baseman, lifetime (2,237).
Holds American League records for most games (2,227), putouts (19,754), assists (1,444), chances accepted (21,198) and double plays (2,041) by first baseman, lifetime.
Led American League first basemen in double plays, 1941, 1953, 1954.
Named as first baseman on THE SPORTING NEWS All-Star Major League Team, 1953.
Coach, Pittsburgh Pirates, 1960; manager, Washington Senators, 1961 to 1963; coach, Pittsburgh Pirates, 1964; St. Louis Cardinals 1965; manager, Vancouver, Pacific Coast League, 1966 through 1968; scout and minor league manager, Atlanta Braves, 1969 (manager, Richmond, International League), 1969-1970; minor league instructor, New York Yankees, 1971 (manager, Manchester, Eastern League); minor league batting instructor, Kansas City Royals, 1973-74; batting instructor, Los Angeles Dodgers, 1975-1976; coach, Montreal Expos, 1977-1978; minor league batting instructor, New York Yankees, 1979 to 1981; coach, Yankees, 1982; coach, Columbus, International League, 1983 to 1985).

Year — Club	League	Pos.	G.	AB.	R.	H.	2B.	3B.	HR.	RBI.	B.A.	PO.	A.	E.	F.A.
1937—Easton	E. Shore	1B	83	300	51	86	24	6	10	64	.287	814	54	★16	.982
1938—Greenville	Sally	1B	132	524	84	172	31	12	1	72	.328	1159	74	★24	.981
1939—Springfield	East.	1B	69	268	52	92	13	7	3	41	.343	601	31	6	.991
1939—Washington	Amer.	1B	76	276	23	71	15	4	1	30	.257	690	40	11	.985
1940—Jersey City	Int.	1B	154	569	76	161	22	9	9	65	.283	1305	75	16	.989
1940—Washington	Amer.	1B	5	19	0	3	0	0	0	0	.158	41	2	0	1.000
1941—Washington	Amer.	1B	138	531	73	159	27	11	9	93	.299	1186	80	10	.992
1942—Washington	Amer.	1B	151	621	76	168	34	6	9	86	.271	1360	95	★26	.982
1943—Washington	Amer.	1B	145	553	89	148	29	8	7	70	.268	1351	75	14	.990
1944-45—Washington	Amer.							(In Military Service)							
1946—Washington	Amer.	1B	148	587	88	207	★51	8	8	85	★.353	1320	101	★15	.990
1947—Washington	Amer.	1B	154	600	77	159	29	12	7	85	.265	1299	105	★19	.987
1948—Washington(a)	Amer.	1B	150	558	78	135	27	7	3	48	.242	1297	113	15	.989
1949—Cleveland	Amer.	1B	153	584	72	170	27	4	18	83	.291	★1438	★155	14	.991
1950—Cleve.(b)-Wash.	Amer.	1B	118	417	55	117	17	3	9	75	.281	959	78	9	●.991
1951—Washington	Amer.	1B	141	546	69	160	30	7	9	87	.293	1157	87	8	★.994
1952—Washington	Amer.	1B	154	569	71	143	33	9	10	80	.251	1291	115	10	★.993
1953—Washington	Amer.	1B	152	608	101	205	★43	11	15	115	★.337	★1376	94	12	.992
1954—Washington	Amer.	1B	151	597	90	173	★33	14	20	97	.290	★1365	76	11	●.992
1955—Washington(c)	Amer.	1B	150	538	74	162	23	8	14	85	.301	1258	69	8	.994
1956—Boston	Amer.	1B	119	403	67	125	28	4	15	84	.310	930	58	11	.989
1957—Boston(d)	Amer.	1B	102	270	36	65	18	1	7	38	.241	662	51	6	.992
1958—Cleveland(e)	Amer.	1B	119	355	49	104	22	3	8	55	.293	774	50	11	.987
1959—Milwaukee(f)	Nat.	1B-OF	74	91	8	20	4	0	3	14	.220	65	4	2	.972
1960—Pittsburgh	Nat.	PH	9	8	0	1	0	0	0	1	.125	0	0	0	.000
American League Totals—18 Years			2326	8632	1188	2474	486	120	169	1296	.287	19754	1444	210	.990
National League Totals—2 Years			83	99	8	21	4	0	3	15	.212	65	4	2	.972
Major League Totals—20 Years			2409	8731	1196	2495	490	120	172	1311	.286	19819	1448	212	.990

aTraded to Cleveland Indians with Pitcher Early Wynn for Pitchers Joe Haynes and Ed Klieman and First Baseman Eddie Robinson, December 14, 1948.
bTraded to Washington Senators for Pitcher Dick Weik, June 14, 1950.
cTraded to Boston Red Sox with Pitchers Bob Porterfield and Johnny Schmitz and Outfielder Tom Umphlett for Pitchers Dick Brodowski, Truman Clevenger and Al Curtis, Outfielders Neil Chrisley and Karl Olson, November 8, 1955.
dReleased to Cleveland Indians on waivers, January 29, 1958.
eTraded to Milwaukee Braves for Pitcher Humberto Robinson, April 11, 1959.
fReleased, October 13, 1959 and signed with Pittsburgh Pirates for 1960.

JOSEPH FRANKLIN (JOE) VOSMIK

Born April 4, 1910, at Cleveland O.
Died January 27, 1962, at Cleveland, O.
Height, 6.00. Weight, 185.
Threw and batted righthanded.

Manager, Tucson, Arizona-Texas League, 1947; Dayton, Central League, 1948; Oklahoma City, Texas League, 1949-50; Batavia, Pony League, 1951; scout, Cleveland Indians, 1951-52.

Year	Club	League	Pos.	G.	AB.	R.	H.	2B.	3B.	HR.	RBI.	B.A.	PO.	A.	E.	F.A.
1929—Frederick		Bl. Ridge.	OF	112	407	81	●155	★39	★24	9	.....	.381	192	★28	6	.973
1930—Terre Haute		I.I.I.	OF	121	458	100	182	25	15	13	116	★.397	286	13	12	.961
1930—Cleveland		Amer.	OF	9	26	1	6	2	0	0	4	.231	16	1	1	.944
1931—Cleveland		Amer.	OF	149	591	80	189	36	14	7	117	.320	315	12	10	.970
1932—Cleveland		Amer.	OF	153	621	106	194	39	12	10	97	.312	432	12	5	★.989
1933—Cleveland		Amer.	OF	119	438	53	115	20	10	4	56	.263	242	15	4	.985
1934—Cleveland		Amer.	OF	104	405	71	138	33	2	6	78	.341	199	7	5	.976
1935—Cleveland		Amer.	OF	152	620	93	★216	★47	★20	10	110	.348	347	5	5	.986
1936—Cleveland(a)		Amer.	OF	138	506	76	145	29	7	7	94	.277	258	11	6	.978
1937—St. Louis(b)		Amer.	OF	144	594	81	193	47	9	4	93	.325	333	12	10	.972
1938—Boston		Amer.	OF	146	621	121	★201	37	6	9	86	.324	302	14	7	.978
1939—Boston(c)		Amer.	OF	145	554	89	153	29	6	7	84	.276	296	9	8	.974
1940—Brooklyn		Nat.	OF	116	404	45	114	14	6	1	42	.282	193	9	5	.976
1941—Brooklyn		Nat.	OF	25	56	0	11	0	0	0	4	.196	12	0	0	1.000
1941—Louisville		A. A.	OF	42	144	15	42	9	2	1	20	.292	72	1	0	1.000
1942—Minneapolis		A. A.	OF	147	513	64	156	34	2	8	78	.304	272	12	4	.986
1943—Minneapolis		A. A.	OF	146	498	66	126	25	2	5	62	.253	278	14	3	★.990
1944—Minneapolis		A. A.	OF	39	111	17	31	3	0	1	16	.279	49	4	1	.981
1944—Washington		Amer.	OF	14	36	2	7	2	0	0	9	.194	16	0	0	1.000
1947—Tucson		Ariz.-Tex.	OF	30	48	7	17	4	0	1	10	.354	22	1	1	.958
American League Totals—11 Years				1273	5012	773	1557	321	86	64	828	.310	2756	98	61	.979
National League Totals—2 Years				141	460	45	125	14	6	1	46	.272	205	9	5	.977
Major League Totals—13 Years				1414	5472	818	1682	335	92	65	874	.307	2961	107	66	.979

aTraded with Pitcher Oral Hilderbrand and Shortstop Bill Knickerbocker to St. Louis Browns for Pitcher Ivy Andrews, Shortstop Lyn Lary and Outfielder Moose Solters, January 17, 1937.

bTraded to Boston Red Sox for Infielder Red Kress, Outfielder Colonel Mills and Pitcher Buck Newsom, December 2, 1937.

cSold to Brooklyn Dodgers for $25,000, February 12, 1940.

GEORGE EDWARD (RUBE) WADDELL

Born October 13, 1876, at Bradford, Pa.

Died April 1, 1914, at San Antonio, Tex.

Height, 6.01½. Weight, 196.

Threw and batted lefthanded.

Holds American League record for most strikeouts by lefthanded pitcher, season (349), 1904.
Named to Hall of Fame, 1946.

Year	Club	League	G.	IP.	W.	L.	Pct.	H.	R.	SO.	BB.	CG.	ShO.
1897—Louisville		National	2	13	0	1	.000	13	7	5	6	1	0
1898—Detroit		Western	9	....	4	4	.500	61	....	31	30	....	....
1899—Col.-Grand Rapids		Western	42	330	27	13	.675	....	154	....	....	....	....
1899—Louisville		National	10	80	7	2	.778	71	38	41	16	9	1
1900—Pittsburgh		National	29	212	9	11	.450	186	101	★133	53	16	2
1900—Milwaukee		American	15	129	10	3	.769	90	28	75	20	13	2
1901—Pittsburgh-Chicago		National	31	250	13	16	.448	252	136	167	67	26	0
1902—Los Angeles		Pacific Coast	20	178	12	8	.600	128	66	142	37	19	2
1902—Philadelphia		American	33	275	23	7	.767	224	89	★210	67	26	3
1903—Philadelphia		American	39	323	21	16	.568	271	112	★301	74	34	4
1904—Philadelphia		American	46	384	25	19	.568	309	111	★349	81	39	8
1905—Philadelphia		American	★46	324	★26	11	.703	230	86	★286	91	27	7
1906—Philadelphia		American	43	272	15	17	.469	219	89	★203	88	22	8
1907—Philadelphia		American	44	285	19	13	.594	247	120	★226	72	20	7
1908—St. Louis		American	43	286	19	14	.576	223	93	232	90	25	5
1909—St. Louis		American	31	220	11	14	.440	204	78	141	57	16	5
1910—St. Louis		American	10	34	3	1	.750	31	19	16	9	0	0
1910—Newark		Eastern	15	97	5	3	.625	73	....	53	41	....	....
1911—Minneapolis		Amer. Assn.	54	300	20	17	.541	262	133	185	96	....	....
1912—Minneapolis		Amer. Assn.	33	151	12	6	.667	138	67	113	59	....	....
1913—Virginia		Northern	15	84	3	9	.250	86	....	82	20	....	....
American League Totals—9 Years			335	2403	162	112	.591	1958	797	1964	329	209	47
National League Totals—4 Years			72	555	29	30	.492	522	282	346	142	52	3
Major League Totals—13 Years			407	2958	191	142	.574	2480	1079	2310	771	261	50

JOHN PETER (HONUS and HANS) WAGNER

Born February 24, 1874, at Carnegie, Pa.
Died December 6, 1955, at Carnegie, Pa.
Height, 5.11. Weight, 200.
Threw and batted righthanded.

Holds National League records for most years leading league in batting average (8); most consecutive years batting .300 or over, 50 or more games (17); most triples, lifetime (252).
Coach, Pittsburgh Pirates, 1933 through 1951.
Named to Hall of Fame, 1936.

Year Club	League	Pos.	G.	AB.	R.	H.	2B.	3B.	HR.	RBI.	B.A.	PO.	A.	E.	F.A.
1895—Steubenville	Int. St.	SS	44	.....	....	....	....	....	....	....	.402	....	....	....	......
1895—Mansfield	Ohio St.							(No records available)							
1895—Adrian	Mich. St.	S-O	20	....	....	....	....	....	....	....	.365	....	....	....	......
1895—Warren	Iron-Oil	SS	65	....	....	....	....	....	....	....	.369	....	....	....	......
1896—Paterson	Atl.	1-3-OF	109	416	106	145	....	....	....	....	.349	802	79	41	.956
1897—Paterson	Atlantic	3B	74	301	61	114	....	....	....	....	.379	104	107	24	.898
1897—Louisville	Nat.	OF	61	241	38	83	17	4	2	....	.344	105	17	11	.917
1898—Louisville	Nat.	1B-3B	148	591	80	180	31	4	10	....	.305	827	165	32	.969
1899—Louisville(a)	Nat.	3B-OF	144	549	102	197	47	13	7	....	.359	197	185	30	.927
1900—Pittsburgh	Nat.	OF	134	528	107	201	★45	★22	4	....	★.381	177	13	6	.969
1901—Pittsburgh	Nat.	IF-OF	141	556	100	196	●39	10	6	....	.353	299	279	47	.925
1902—Pittsburgh	Nat.	IF-OF	137	538	★105	177	★33	16	3	....	.329	526	171	34	.953
1903—Pittsburgh	Nat.	SS	129	512	97	182	30	★19	5	....	★.355	303	397	50	.933
1904—Pittsburgh	Nat.	SS	132	490	97	171	★44	14	4	....	★.349	274	367	49	.929
1905—Pittsburgh	Nat.	SS	147	548	114	199	32	14	6	....	.363	353	517	★60	.935
1906—Pittsburgh	Nat.	SS	140	516	●103	175	★38	9	2	....	★.339	334	473	51	.941
1907—Pittsburgh	Nat.	SS	142	515	98	180	★38	14	6	★91	★.350	314	428	49	.938
1908—Pittsburgh	Nat.	SS	151	568	100	★201	★39	★19	10	★106	★.354	354	469	50	.943
1909—Pittsburgh	Nat.	SS	137	495	92	168	★39	10	5	★102	★.339	344	430	49	●.940
1910—Pittsburgh	Nat.	SS	150	556	90	●178	34	8	4	84	.320	★337	413	52	.935
1911—Pittsburgh	Nat.	SS-1B	130	473	87	158	23	16	9	108	★.334	471	321	46	.945
1912—Pittsburgh	Nat.	SS	145	558	91	181	35	20	7	94	.324	341	462	32	★.962
1913—Pittsburgh	Nat.	SS	114	413	51	124	18	4	3	55	.300	289	323	24	.962
1914—Pittsburgh	Nat.	3B-SS	150	552	60	139	15	9	1	46	.252	339	457	43	★.949
1915—Pittsburgh	Nat.	SS	156	566	68	155	32	17	6	78	.274	298	395	38	★.948
1916—Pittsburgh	Nat.	1B-SS	123	432	45	124	15	9	1	38	.287	409	272	33	.954
1917—Pittsburgh	Nat.	1-3-SS	74	230	15	61	7	1	0	22	.265	476	74	13	.977
Major League Totals—21 Years			2785	10427	1740	3430	651	252	101	....	.329	7367	6628	799	.946

aTransferred with 14 other players to Pittsburgh when Lousiville dropped out of National League.

WORLD SERIES RECORD

Year Club	League	Pos.	G.	AB.	R.	H.	2B.	3B.	HR.	RBI.	B.A.	PO.	A.	E.	F.A.
1903—Pittsburgh	Nat.	SS	8	27	2	6	1	0	0	3	.222	13	27	6	.870
1909—Pittsburgh	Nat.	SS	7	24	4	8	2	1	0	7	.333	13	23	2	.947
World Series Totals—2 Years			15	51	6	14	3	1	0	10	.275	26	50	8	.905

FREDERICK E. (DIXIE) WALKER

Born September 24, 1910, at Villa Rica, Ga.
Died May 17, 1982, at Birmingham, Ala.
Height, 6.01. Weight, 175.
Threw right and batted lefthanded.
Son of Ewart Walker, former major league pitcher; brother of Harry Walker, former major league outfielder.

Named as outfielder on THE SPORTING NEWS All-Star Major League Team, 1944.
Led National League outfielders in double plays, 1941.
Manager, Atlanta, Southern Association, 1950-51-52; coach, St. Louis Cardinals, 1953; released by Cardinals, July 31, 1953 and appointed manager of Houston, Texas, August 1, 1953-54; coach, Cardinals, 1955; released by Cardinals May 29, 1955, and appointed manager of Rochester, International, May 30, 1955-56; manager, Toronto, International, 1957-58-59; scout, Milwaukee Braves, 1960-62; coach, Milwaukee, 1963-65; scout, Atlanta Braves, 1966-68; batting instructor and scout, Los Angeles Dodgers, 1969-1976.

Year Club League	Pos.	G.	AB.	R.	H.	2B.	3B.	HR.	RBI.	B.A.	PO.	A.	E.	F.A.
1928—Greensboro .... Pied.	OF	6	18	3	3	1	1	0	1	.167	10	2	1	.923
1928—Albany .... S'east	OF	16	66	10	18	2	1	1	8	.273	42	3	2	.957
1928—Gulfport .... Cot. St.	OF	82	304	41	89	18	7	1	....	.293	145	44	7	.964
1929—Vicksburg .... Cot. St.	3B	61	233	41	74	9	5	2	....	.318	85	145	20	.920
1930—Greenville .... Sally	OF	73	307	80	123	17	10	11	63	.401	186	14	7	.966
1930—Jersey City .... Int.	OF	83	325	62	109	18	9	7	41	.335	171	19	9	.955
1931—Toledo .... A.A.	OF	58	228	33	69	10	2	4	31	.303	169	7	4	.978
1931—New York .... Amer.	OF	2	10	1	3	2	0	0	1	.300	3	0	0	1.000
1931—J.C.-Toronto .... Int.	OF	80	310	40	109	17	4	6	41	.352	205	9	7	.968
1932—Newark .... Int.	OF	144	551	107	193	30	7	15	105	.350	348	12	5	.986
1933—New York .... Amer.	OF	98	328	68	90	15	7	15	51	.274	194	7	8	.962
1934—New York .... Amer.	OF	17	17	2	2	0	0	0	0	.118	1	0	0	1.000
1935—New York .... Amer.	OF	8	13	1	2	1	0	0	1	.154	3	0	1	.750
1935—Newark .... Int.	OF	89	317	66	93	18	5	17	67	.293	162	1	4	.976
1936—N.Y.(a)-Chi .... Amer.	OF	32	90	15	26	2	2	1	16	.289	55	2	0	1.000
1937—Chicago(b)........... Amer.	OF	154	593	105	179	28	●16	9	95	.302	270	10	14	.952
1938—Detroit .... Amer.	OF	127	454	84	140	27	6	6	43	.308	224	8	5	.979
1939—Detroit(c) .... Amer.	OF	43	154	30	47	4	5	4	19	.305	93	4	3	.970
1939—Brooklyn .... Nat.	OF	61	225	27	63	6	4	2	38	.280	144	5	5	.968
1940—Brooklyn .... Nat.	OF	143	556	75	171	37	8	6	66	.308	360	6	10	.973
1941—Brooklyn .... Nat.	OF	148	531	88	165	32	8	9	71	.311	309	●19	8	.976
1942—Brooklyn .... Nat.	OF	118	393	57	114	28	1	6	54	.290	207	8	3	.986
1943—Brooklyn .... Nat.	OF	138	540	83	163	32	6	5	71	.302	262	20	9	.969
1944—Brooklyn .... Nat.	OF	147	535	77	191	37	8	13	91	★.357	260	17	●11	.962
1945—Brooklyn .... Nat.	OF	154	607	102	182	42	9	8	★124	.300	346	18	3	.992
1946—Brooklyn .... Nat.	OF	150	576	80	184	29	9	9	116	.319	237	15	8	.969
1947—Brooklyn(d) .... Nat.	OF	148	529	77	162	31	3	9	94	.306	261	9	10	.964
1948—Pittsburgh........... Nat.	OF	129	408	39	129	19	3	2	54	.316	168	4	4	.977
1949—Pittsburgh........... Nat.	OF-1B	88	181	26	51	4	1	1	18	.282	82	5	4	.956
1950—Atlanta .... South.	OF	39	77	11	21	6	1	1	17	.273	30	0	1	.968
American League Totals—8 Years		481	1659	306	489	79	36	35	226	.295	843	31	31	.966
National League Totals—11 Years..........		1424	5081	731	1575	297	60	70	797	.310	2636	126	75	.974
Major League Totals—18 Years...............		1905	6740	1037	2064	376	96	105	1023	.306	3479	157	106	.972

aSold to Chicago White Sox, May, 1936.

bTraded to Detroit Tigers with Pitcher Vern Kennedy and Second Baseman Tony Piet for Catcher Mike Tresh, Third Baseman Marv Owen and Outfielder Gerald Walker, December 2, 1937.

cReleased to Brooklyn Dodgers on waivers, July 24, 1939.

dTraded to Pittsburgh Pirates with Pitchers Hal Gregg and Vic Lombardi for Pitcher Preacher Roe, Second Baseman Gene Mauch and Shortstop Billy Cox, December 8, 1947.

WORLD SERIES RECORD

Year Club League	Pos.	G.	AB.	R.	H.	2B.	3B.	HR.	RBI.	B.A.	PO.	A.	E.	F.A.
1941—Brooklyn .... Nat.	OF	5	18	3	4	2	0	0	0	.222	14	0	0	1.000
1947—Brooklyn .... Nat.	OF	7	27	1	6	1	0	1	4	.222	9	1	0	1.000
World Series Totals—2 Years		12	45	4	10	3	0	1	4	.222	23	1	0	1.000

WILLIAM CURTIS (CURT) WALKER

Born July 3, 1896, at Beeville, Tex.

Died December 9, 1955, at Beeville, Tex.

Height, 5.09½. Weight, 165.

Threw right and batted lefthanded.

Led National League outfielders in double plays, 1922, 1926 (tie).

Year Club League	Pos.	G.	AB.	R.	H.	2B.	3B.	HR.	RBI.	B.A.	PO.	A.	E.	F.A.
1919—Houston .... Texas	OF	41	135	16	29	6	0	0	....	.215	71	3	6	.925
1919—Augusta .... So. Atl.	OF	53	194	17	54	11	3	1	....	.278	107	6	2	.983
1919—New York .... Amer.	PH	1	1	0	0	0	0	0	0	.000	0	0	0	.000
1920—Augusta .... So. Atl.	OF	126	422	71	126	21	13	0	54	.299	230	19	4	★.984
1920—New York .... Nat.	OF	8	14	0	1	0	0	0	0	.071	5	0	0	1.000
1921—N.Y.(a)-Phila. .... Nat.	OF	85	269	41	81	15	6	3	43	.301	152	13	4	.976
1922—Philadelphia .... Nat.	OF	148	581	102	196	36	11	12	89	.337	295	24	15	.955
1923—Philadelphia .... Nat.	OF-1B	140	527	66	148	26	5	5	66	.281	284	19	17	.947
1924—Phila.(b)-Cin. .... Nat.	OF	133	468	66	140	27	11	5	54	.299	239	15	8	.969
1925—Cincinnati .... Nat.	OF	145	509	86	162	22	16	6	71	.318	332	12	6	★.983
1926—Cincinnati .... Nat.	OF	155	571	83	175	24	20	6	78	.306	325	21	14	.961
1927—Cincinnati .... Nat.	OF	146	527	60	154	16	10	6	80	.292	316	15	●15	.957

Year Club League	Pos.	G.	AB.	R.	H.	2B.	3B.	HR.	RBI.	B.A.	PO.	A.	E.	F.A.
1928—Cincinnati.............. Nat.	OF	123	427	64	119	15	12	6	73	.279	289	9	14	.955
1929—Cincinnati.............. Nat.	OF	141	492	76	154	28	15	7	83	.313	298	11	10	.969
1930—Cincinnati.............. Nat.	OF	134	472	74	145	26	11	8	51	.307	241	5	9	.965
1931—Indianapolis......... A.A.	OF	143	494	103	159	23	7	8	85	.322	240	10	16	.940
1932—Ind'polis-Toledo ... A.A.	OF	64	224	41	62	16	4	3	40	.277	92	3	4	.960
American League Totals—1 Year..........		1	1	0	0	0	0	0	0	.000	0	0	0	.000
National League Totals—11 Years.........		1358	4857	718	1475	235	117	64	688	.304	2776	144	112	.963
Major League Totals—12 Years...............		1359	4858	718	1475	235	117	64	688	.304	2776	144	112	.963

aTraded with Infielder Joe Rapp and Outfielder Lee King to Philadelphia Phillies for Infielder John Rawlings and Pitcher Cecil Causey, July, 1921.

bTraded to Cincinnati Reds for Outfielder George Harper, July, 1924.

RODERICK JOHN (BOBBY) WALLACE

Born November 4, 1874, at Pittsburgh, Pa.

Died November 3, 1960, at Torrance, Calif.

Height, 5.08. Weight, 170.

Threw and batted righthanded.

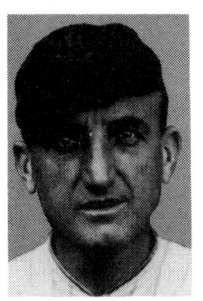

Manager, St. Louis Browns, 1911-12; umpire in American League, for parts of 1915-16; then rejoined St. Louis Browns; manager, Wichita, Western League, 1917; Muskogee, Southwestern League, 1921; scout, Chicago Cubs, 1924; coach, Cincinnati Reds, 1926; scout, Cincinnati, 1927 through 1957; acting manager, Cincinnati, September, 1937; scout, Cincinnati, 1938 to date of death.

Named to Hall of Fame, 1953.

Year Club League	Pos.	G.	AB.	R.	H.	2B.	3B.	HR.	SB.	B.A.	PO.	A.	E.	F.A.
1894—Cleveland.............. Nat.	P	4	13	0	2	1	0	0	0	.154	3	7	0	1.000
1895—Cleveland.............. Nat.	P	27	97	16	21	2	3	0	3	.216	17	62	5	.940
1896—Cleveland.............. Nat.	P	33	130	17	30	4	4	1	1	.231	44	47	7	.929
1897—Cleveland........ Nat.	3B	131	522	99	177	36	20	4	17	.339	194	255	31	.935
1898—Cleveland (a)...... Nat.	3B	153	591	81	159	25	10	3	9	.269	206	345	33	.943
1899—St. Louis................. Nat.	SS-3B	151	576	90	174	29	14	12	11	.302	318	535	75	.919
1900—St. Louis................. Nat.	SS	129	489	72	133	21	7	5	10	.272	328	447	49	.941
1901—St. Louis (b).......... Nat.	SS	135	556	69	179	34	16	2	17	.322	329	★541	★61	.934
1902—St. Louis................. Amer.	★SS-OF	133	495	71	142	33	9	1	19	.287	329	471	41	★.951
1903—St. Louis................. Amer.	SS	136	519	63	127	20	17	1	11	.245	●308	★472	60	.929
1904—St. Louis................. Amer.	SS	139	550	57	150	28	4	2	19	.273	★398	484	42	★.955
1905—St. Louis................. Amer.	SS	★156	587	67	159	29	9	1	13	.271	★385	506	62	.935
1906—St. Louis................. Amer.	SS	139	476	64	123	24	7	2	24	.258	309	461	41	.949
1907—St. Louis................. Amer.	SS	147	538	56	138	19	7	0	16	.257	338	★517	★54	.941
1908—St. Louis................. Amer.	SS	137	487	59	123	24	4	1	5	.253	286	510	41	★.951
1909—St. Louis................. Amer.	SS-3B	116	403	36	96	12	2	1	7	.238	242	336	32	.948
1910—St. Louis................. Amer.	SS-3B	138	508	47	131	19	7	0	12	.258	316	444	43	.946
1911—St. Louis................. Amer.	SS	125	410	35	95	12	2	0	8	.232	280	417	42	.943
1912—St. Louis................. Amer.	SS	99	323	39	78	14	5	0	3	.241	185	271	28	.942
1913—St. Louis................. Amer.	SS	52	147	11	31	5	0	0	2	.211	67	98	12	.932
1914—St. Louis................. Amer.	SS	26	73	3	16	2	1	0	1	.219	26	46	9	.889
1915—St. Louis................. Amer.	SS	9	13	1	3	0	1	0	0	.231	9	13	5	.815
1916—St. Louis (c).......... Amer.	SS-3B	14	18	0	5	0	0	0	0	.278	8	27	2	.946
1917—Wichita................. West.	SS	33	123	9	34	5	0	0	0	.276	72	78	14	.915
1917—St. Louis................. Nat.	SS-3B	8	10	0	1	0	0	0	0	.100	12	17	3	.906
1918—St. Louis................. Nat.	SS-3B-2B	32	98	3	15	1	0	0	1	.153	61	83	10	.935
American League Totals—15 Years		1566	5547	609	1417	241	75	9	140	.255	3486	5073	514	.943
National League Totals—10 Years........		803	3082	447	891	153	74	27	69	.289	1512	2339	274	.934
Major League Totals—25 Years........		2369	8629	1056	2308	394	149	36	209	.267	4998	7412	788	.940

aShifted to St. Louis in winter of 1898-99 when Robisons transferred team from Cleveland.

bJumped to St. Louis Americans for 1902.

cReleased at close of season; started 1917 as manager of Wichita (Western), but was released in June and joined Cardinals on July 12, 1917.

PITCHING RECORD

Year Club League	G.	CG.	ShO.	IP.	W.	L.	Pct.	H.	R.	SO.	BB.
1894—Cleveland.......................... National	4	2	0	26	2	1	.667	33	28	10	17
1895—Cleveland.......................... National	27	21	1	222	12	13	.480	265	175	64	89
1896—Cleveland.......................... National	22	12	2	144	10	7	.588	174	78	44	43
1902—St. Louis.............................. American	1	0	...	...	0	0	.....	....	....	....	....
Major League Totals—4 Years........................	54	35	3	392	24	21	.534	472	281	118	149

EDWARD AUGUSTINE (ED) WALSH
(Big Ed)

Born May 14, 1881, at Plains, Pa.

Died May 26, 1959, at Pompano Beach, Fla.

Height, 6.01. Weight, 193.

Threw and batted righthanded.

Father of Edward Arthur Walsh, former major league pitcher.

Pitched 5-0 no-hit victory against Boston, August 27, 1911.

Manager, Bridgeport, Eastern League 1920; umpire, American League, 1922; coach, Chicago White Sox, 1923-24-25. Baseball coach, University of Notre Dame, 1926; coach, Chicago White Sox, 1928-29-30.

Named to Hall of Fame, 1946.

Year Club	League	G.	IP.	W.	L.	Pct.	H.	R.	SO.	BB.	CG.	ShO.
1902—Wilkes-Barre	Pa. State	4	36	1	2	.333	31	....	20	8	....	....
1902—Meriden	Connecticut	21	182	15	5	.750	125	....	98	48	....	....
1903—Meriden	Connecticut	23	182	11	10	.524	135	....	126	46	....	....
1903—Newark	Eastern	19	117	9	5	.643	70	....	77	28	....	....
1904—Chicago	American	18	113	6	3	.667	83	37	52	34	6	1
1905—Chicago	American	22	138	8	3	.727	128	56	71	35	9	1
1906—Chicago	American	42	281	17	13	.567	214	90	171	58	24	*10
1907—Chicago	American	*56	*419	24	18	.600	330	123	207	85	37	5
1908—Chicago	American	*66	*465	*40	15	*.727	*343	111	*269	56	42	*12
1909—Chicago	American	31	230	15	11	.577	166	52	127	50	20	*8
1910—Chicago	American	●45	370	18	*20	.474	242	90	258	61	33	7
1911—Chicago	American	*56	*369	27	18	.600	327	125	*255	72	33	5
1912—Chicago	American	*62	*393	27	17	.614	*332	125	254	94	32	6
1913—Chicago	American	16	98	8	3	.727	91	37	34	39	7	1
1914—Chicago	American	9	45	2	3	.400	33	19	14	20	3	1
1915—Chicago	American	3	27	3	0	1.000	18	4	12	6	3	1
1916—Chicago	American	2	3	0	1	1.000	6	3	3	1	0	0
1917—Boston	National	4	18	0	1	.000	22	9	4	9	1	0
1919—Milwaukee	Amer. Assn.	4	21	2	2	.500	22	....	6	8	....	....
1920—Bridgeport	Eastern	3	22	1	1	.500	22	....	6	6	....	....
American League Totals—13 Years		428	2951	195	125	.609	2313	872	1727	611	249	58
National League Totals—1 Year		4	18	0	1	.000	22	9	4	9	1	0
Major League Totals—14 Years		432	2969	195	126	.607	2335	881	1731	620	250	58

WORLD SERIES RECORD

Year Club	League	G.	IP.	W.	L.	Pct.	H.	R.	SO.	BB.	CG.	ShO.
1906—Chicago	American	2	15	2	0	1.000	7	6	17	6	1	1

LLOYD JAMES WANER
(Little Poison)

Born March 16, 1906, at Harrah, Okla.

Died July 22, 1982, at Oklahoma City, Okla.

Height, 5.08½. Weight, 150.

Threw right and batted lefthanded.

Brother of Paul Waner, former major league outfielder.

Shares National League record for most years leading league in singles (4).

Holds modern National League record for most singles, season (198), 1927.

Scout, Pittsburgh Pirates, 1946 through 1949; Baltimore Orioles, 1955.

Named to Hall of Fame, 1967.

Year Club	League	Pos.	G.	AB.	R.	H.	2B.	3B.	HR.	RBI.	B.A.	PO.	A.	E.	F.A.
1925—San Francisco	P.C.	OF	31	44	7	11	2	0	0	1	.250	17	2	0	1.000
1926—San Francisco	P.C.	OF	6	20	0	4	1	0	0	....	.200	11	0	0	1.000
1926—Columbia	So. Atl.	OF	121	498	95	172	28	14	6	33	.345	331	22	4	.989
1927—Pittsburgh	Nat.	OF	150	629	●133	223	17	6	2	27	.355	396	9	10	.976
1928—Pittsburgh	Nat.	OF	152	*659	121	221	22	14	5	61	.335	418	15	9	.980
1929—Pittsburgh	Nat.	OF	151	*662	134	234	28	*20	5	74	.353	*450	22	6	.987
1930—Pittsburgh	Nat.	OF	68	260	32	94	8	3	1	36	.362	165	6	3	.983
1931—Pittsburgh	Nat.	OF	154	*681	90	*214	25	13	4	57	.314	*484	20	11	.979
1932—Pittsburgh	Nat.	OF	134	565	90	188	27	11	2	38	.333	*426	9	6	.986
1933—Pittsburgh	Nat.	OF	121	500	59	138	14	5	0	26	.276	267	9	5	.982

Year Club League	Pos.	G.	AB.	R.	H.	2B.	3B.	HR.	RBI.	B.A.	PO.	A.	E.	F.A.
1934—Pittsburgh............. Nat.	OF	140	611	95	173	27	6	1	48	.283	★405	8	9	.979
1935—Pittsburgh............. Nat.	OF	122	537	83	166	22	14	0	46	.309	350	5	4	.989
1936—Pittsburgh............. Nat.	OF	106	414	67	133	13	8	1	31	.321	245	2	4	.984
1937—Pittsburgh............. Nat.	OF	129	537	80	177	23	4	1	45	.330	312	8	4	.988
1938—Pittsburgh............. Nat.	OF	147	619	79	194	25	7	5	57	.313	341	15	5	.986
1939—Pittsburgh............. Nat.	OF	112	379	49	108	15	3	0	24	.285	225	9	2	.992
1940—Pittsburgh............. Nat.	OF	72	166	30	43	3	0	0	3	.259	90	3	1	.989
1941—Pit.a-Bo.b-Cin.c..... Nat.	OF	77	219	26	64	5	1	0	11	.292	102	4	2	.981
1942—Philadelphia (d)... Nat.	OF	101	287	23	75	7	3	0	10	.261	170	6	6	.967
1943—Brooklyn................ Nat.							(Voluntarily retired)							
1944—Brook.(e)-Pitts...... Nat.	PH-OF	34	28	5	9	0	0	0	3	.321	12	0	0	1.000
1945—Pittsburgh............. Nat.	PH-OF	23	19	5	5	0	0	0	1	.263	2	1	0	1.000
Major League Totals—18 Years.............		1993	7772	1201	2459	281	118	27	598	.316	4860	151	87	.983

aTraded to Boston Braves for Pitcher Nick Strincevich, May 7, 1941.
bTraded to Cincinnati Reds for Pitcher John Hutchings, June 12, 1941.
cReleased, October 8, 1941; signed by Philadelphia Phillies, December 4, 1941.
dTraded to Brooklyn Dodgers with Infielder Al Glossop for First Baseman Babe Dahlgren, March 8, 1943.
eReleased, June 14, 1944; signed by Pittsburgh Pirates, June 15, 1944.

WORLD SERIES RECORD

Year Club League	Pos.	G.	AB.	R.	H.	2B.	3B.	HR.	RBI.	B.A.	PO.	A.	E.	F.A.
1927—Pittsburgh............. Nat.	OF	4	15	5	6	1	1	0	0	.400	9	1	2	.833

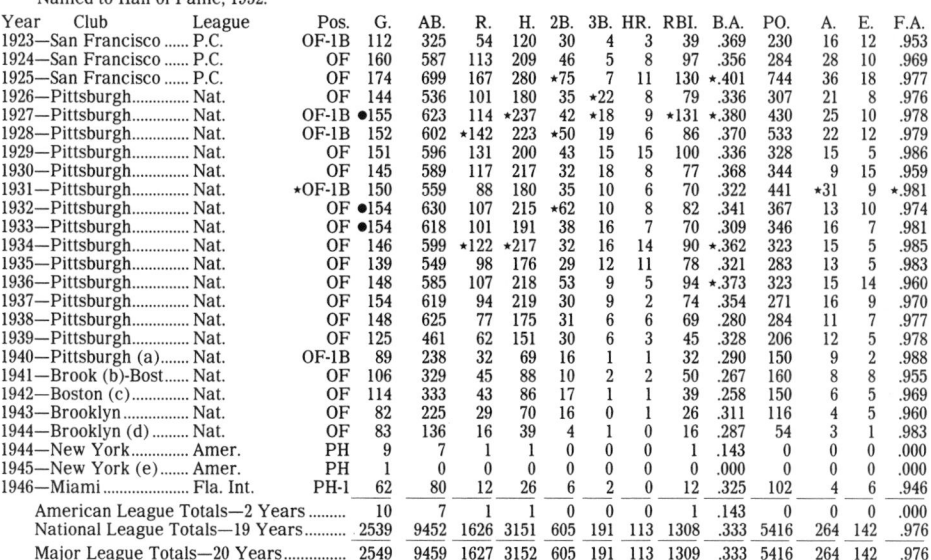

PAUL GLEE WANER
(Big Poison)

Born April 16, 1903, at Harrah, Okla.

Died August 29, 1965, at Sarasota, Fla.

Height, 5.08½. Weight, 153.

Threw and batted lefthanded.

Brother of Lloyd Waner, former major league outfielder.

Shares American League record for most doubles, game (4), May 20, 1932.
Led National League outfielders in double plays, 1931, 1936 (tie).
Named National League Most Valuable Player, 1927.
Named as outfielder on THE SPORTING NEWS All-Star Major League Teams, 1927-28 and 1937.
Manager, Miami, Florida-International, 1946; batting instructor for Milwaukee Braves, 1957; St. Louis Cardinals, 1958-59; Philadelphia Phillies, 1960; batting coach, Phillies, May 30, 1965, until death.
Named to Hall of Fame, 1952.

Year Club League	Pos.	G.	AB.	R.	H.	2B.	3B.	HR.	RBI.	B.A.	PO.	A.	E.	F.A.
1923—San Francisco ...... P.C.	OF-1B	112	325	54	120	30	4	3	39	.369	230	16	12	.953
1924—San Francisco ...... P.C.	OF	160	587	113	209	46	5	8	97	.356	284	28	10	.969
1925—San Francisco ...... P.C.	OF	174	699	167	280	★75	7	11	130	★.401	744	36	18	.977
1926—Pittsburgh............. Nat.	OF	144	536	101	180	35	★22	8	79	.336	307	21	8	.976
1927—Pittsburgh............. Nat.	OF-1B ●155	623	114	★237	42	★18	9	★131	★.380	430	25	10	.978
1928—Pittsburgh............. Nat.	OF-1B	152	602	★142	223	★50	19	6	86	.370	533	22	12	.979
1929—Pittsburgh............. Nat.	OF	151	596	131	200	43	15	15	100	.336	328	15	5	.986
1930—Pittsburgh............. Nat.	OF	145	589	117	217	32	18	8	77	.368	344	9	15	.959
1931—Pittsburgh............. Nat.	★OF-1B	150	559	88	180	35	10	6	70	.322	441	★31	9	★.981
1932—Pittsburgh............. Nat.	OF ●154	630	107	215	★62	10	8	82	.341	367	13	10	.974
1933—Pittsburgh............. Nat.	OF ●154	618	101	191	38	16	7	70	.309	346	16	7	.981
1934—Pittsburgh............. Nat.	OF	146	599	★122	★217	32	16	14	90	★.362	323	15	5	.985
1935—Pittsburgh............. Nat.	OF	139	549	98	176	29	12	11	78	.321	283	13	5	.983
1936—Pittsburgh............. Nat.	OF	148	585	107	218	53	9	5	94	★.373	323	15	14	.960
1937—Pittsburgh............. Nat.	OF	154	619	94	219	30	9	2	74	.354	271	16	9	.970
1938—Pittsburgh............. Nat.	OF	148	625	77	175	31	6	6	69	.280	284	11	7	.977
1939—Pittsburgh............. Nat.	OF	125	461	62	151	30	6	3	45	.328	206	12	5	.978
1940—Pittsburgh (a)....... Nat.	OF-1B	89	238	32	69	16	1	1	32	.290	150	9	2	.988
1941—Brook (b)-Bost...... Nat.	OF	106	329	45	88	10	2	2	50	.267	160	8	8	.955
1942—Boston (c)............ Nat.	OF	114	333	43	86	17	1	1	39	.258	150	6	5	.969
1943—Brooklyn................ Nat.	OF	82	225	29	70	16	0	1	26	.311	116	4	5	.960
1944—Brooklyn (d)........ Nat.	OF	83	136	16	39	4	1	0	16	.287	54	3	1	.983
1944—New York........... Amer.	PH	9	7	1	1	0	0	0	1	.143	0	0	0	.000
1945—New York (e)....... Amer.	PH	1	0	0	0	0	0	0	0	.000	0	0	0	.000
1946—Miami.................... Fla. Int.	PH-1	62	80	12	26	6	2	0	12	.325	102	4	6	.946
American League Totals—2 Years.........		10	7	1	1	0	0	0	1	.143	0	0	0	.000
National League Totals—19 Years..........		2539	9452	1626	3151	605	191	113	1308	.333	5416	264	142	.976
Major League Totals—20 Years.............		2549	9459	1627	3152	605	191	113	1309	.333	5416	264	142	.976

aReleased, December 10, 1940; signed by Brooklyn, January 31, 1941.
bReleased, May 11, 1941; signed by Boston, May 24, 1941.
cReleased, January 19, 1943; signed with Brooklyn, January 21, 1943.
dReleased, September, 1944 and signed with New York Yankees.
eReleased, May 3, 1945.

Year Club League	Pos.	G.	AB.	R.	H.	2B.	3B.	HR.	RBI.	B.A.	PO.	A.	E.	F.A.
1927—Pittsburgh............. Nat.	OF	4	15	0	5	1	0	0	3	.333	8	0	0	1.000

JOHN MONTGOMERY WARD
(Monte)

Born March 3, 1860, at Bellefonte, Pa.

Died March 4, 1925, at Augusta, Ga.

Height, 5.09. Weight, 165.

Threw right and batted lefthanded.

Pitched 5-0 perfect game against Buffalo, June 17, 1880, morning game.

Shares major league record for most assists by second baseman, nine-inning game (12), June 10, 1892, first game.

Manager, Brooklyn, Players League, 1890; Brooklyn, National League, 1891-92; New York, National League, 1893-94; president, Boston National League club, 1911-12.

Named to Hall of Fame, 1964.

Year Club League	Pos.	G.	AB.	R.	H.	2B.	3B.	HR.	SB.	B.A.	PO.	A.	E.	F.A.
1877—Athletics..................	P				(League Alliance club—no record available)									
1878—Binghamton.......... I. Assn.	P-OF	30	107	11	21	2	0	0	....	.196	26	208	51	.821
1878—Providence............ Nat.	P	35	128	14	26	5	5	1	....	.203	21	189	48	.814
1879—Providence............ Nat.	3B-P	82	362	71	104	10	5	2	....	.287	47	404	21	.956
1880—Providence............ Nat.	3B-O-P	82	340	49	77	16	2	0	....	.226	69	409	18	.964
1881—Providence............ Nat.	SS-O-P	83	352	56	85	18	6	0	....	.241	90	208	15	.952
1882—Providence............ Nat.	SS-O-P	83	355	58	87	10	4	0	....	.245	87	165	25	.910
1883—New York............. Nat.	S-3-2-0-P	88	379	76	98	18	6	7	....	.259	143	153	70	.809
1884—New York............. Nat.	2B-O-P	109	466	99	116	12	10	2	....	.249	186	180	51	.878
1885—New York............. Nat.	SS	111	446	72	101	8	8	0	....	.226	*167	350	55	.904
1886—New York............. Nat.	SS	122	491	82	134	18	6	2	36	.273	91	369	69	.870
1887—New York............. Nat.	SS	129	574	113	213	16	5	1	*111	.371	*226	469	61	*.919
1888—New York............. Nat.	SS	122	510	70	128	12	4	2	38	.251	185	331	*86	.857
1889—New York............. Nat.	SS	114	479	86	143	12	4	1	62	.299	229	319	68	.890
1890—Brooklyn............... Play.	SS	128	558	135	*207	14	10	4	71	.371	*303	448	85	.898
1891—Brooklyn............... Nat.	SS-2B	104	438	85	126	14	5	0	80	.288	233	352	58	.910
1892—Brooklyn............... Nat.	2B	148	610	109	167	12	3	2	*94	.274	373	480	*70	.924
1893—New York............. Nat.	2B	134	557	129	194	26	8	2	*72	.348	340	*469	*65	.929
1894—New York............. Nat.	2B	136	552	99	145	11	4	0	41	.262	332	455	67	.922
National League Totals—16 Years.......		1682	7039	1268	1944	218	85	22	534	.276	2819	5302	847	.906
Players League Totals—1 Year...........		128	558	135	207	14	10	4	71	.371	303	448	85	.898
Major League Totals—17 Years.............		1810	7597	1403	2151	232	95	26	605	.283	3122	5750	932	.905

PITCHING RECORD

Year Club League	G.	CG.	W.	L.	Pct.	H.	R.	ShO.
1878—Binghamton...................I. Assn.	30	....	14	16	.467	252	165	4
1878—Providence...................National	35	35	22	13	.629	308	....	6
1879—Providence...................National	65	58	*44	18	*.710	571	226	2
1880—Providence...................National	63	58	40	23	.635	442	192	*9
1881—Providence...................National	36	33	18	18	.500	320	187	3
1882—Providence...................National	32	30	19	13	.594	243	122	4
1883—New York...................National	33	24	12	14	.462	311	196	1
1884—New York...................National	9	5	3	3	.500	72	....	0
Major League Totals—7 Years.......................................	273	243	158	102	.608	2267	....	25

Pitched for Athletics against Hartford at Brooklyn and lost 5-0, June 30, 1877.

GEORGE MARTIN WEISS

Born June 23, 1895, at New Haven, Conn.

Died August 13, 1972, at Greenwich, Conn.

George Weiss played only a few games of baseball as a high schooler in his native New Haven, but he also served as the business manager of his team. From this humble beginning on the "front-office side" of the game, he rose to the top pinnacle of major league success—pennant after pennant as general manager of the New York Yankees.

He organized his successful high school team into a fast semi-pro outfit and the players, even though going on to college, still returned in the summers to form the top club in the area. Weiss promoted varied exhibition games for the "Colonials," as they were called, and did such a great job he was offered the New Haven franchise in the Eastern League for nothing in 1919.

He built Weiss Park and led the club to an era of prosperity never before attained, all the while developing players for the majors. After eight years, he went to Baltimore of the International League in 1928 and remained until 1931, when he met Colonel Jake Ruppert, owner of the Yankees, at the minor league convention in West Baden, Ind. Ruppert, frustrated by the St. Louis Cardinals under Branch Rickey, who developed his own stars and sold phenoms to other major league clubs from his farm system, wanted to enter into the chain store business of talent and saw Weiss as the best man to accomplish the move.

In February, 1932, Weiss joined the Yankees' organization as assistant secretary and farm director. A steady flow of new stars came from his farms to Yankee Stadium as pennants were won in 1932, 1936, 1937, 1938, 1939, 1941, 1942, 1943 and 1947. World championships were won in every year except 1942.

Finally, Weiss took over the Yankee helm in 1948 and rolled up an equally impressive record—10 pennants in 13 seasons—during his regime in the Bronx. Seven of these winners also copped the Series crown, with a record five straight world titles under Casey Stengel from 1949 through 1953. It was Weiss who braved the guffaws of the press and local fandom to sign Stengel, who had a fine record as a minor league manager, a poor one as a major league manager, but an unshakeable one as a buffoon. But it was proved immediately to the doubters that Mrs. Stengel didn't raise any dummy.

Casey charmed the press and fans and platooned players left and right and made two-three position players out of his regulars, a maneuver which made the Yankees "injury free" throughout his New York American League tenure that ended in 1960, the same year Weiss left the Bombers.

These two men rode together into the Hall of Fame, Stengel with his bench magic and Weiss with his magic which filled the bench.

In October of 1961, Weiss, who had become president of the New York Mets, baby expansion entry in the National League, hired Stengel to shepherd the floundering flock who made a success out of repeated defeats. With Weiss dealing in flesh and Stengel's genius at adding a pixie, elfish character to the club, the Mets became the darling of the New York baseball populace. They outdrew and overshadowed the Yankees, even though success was not theirs on the field. Gradually, Weiss built the organization which became solid enough to win in 1969 and become a regular pennant factor. Weiss retired on November 14, 1966, but remained with the club in an advisory capacity until December 1, 1971.

Weiss was the last of the empire builders. Under present rules which call for a free-agent draft and with more stringent roster controls which limit the time a club can control a player, it is impossible to stockpile the huge pool of top talent which was available to the highest bidder in Weiss' day. This shrewd, skillful operator set the mark of excellence all other baseball men aimed for. None did it as successfully and as consistently as George Martin Weiss. He was named to the Hall of Fame in 1971.

MICHAEL FRANCIS (MICKEY) WELCH

Born July 4, 1859, at Brooklyn, N.Y.

Died July 30, 1941, at Nashua, N.H.

Threw and batted righthanded.

Named to Hall of Fame, 1973.

Year Club	League	G.	IP.	W.	L.	Pct.	H.	R.	SO.	BB.	CG.	ShO.
1878—Auburn	National Assn.	...	...	...	...	.....	...	...	...	...	...	
1878—Pittsburgh	Int. Assn.	2	16	0	1	.000	21	...	...	...	...	0
1879—Holyoke	National Assn.	...	...	...	...	.....	...	...	...	...	...	
1880—Troy	National	65	574	34	30	.531	590	322	115	80	64	4
1881—Troy	National	40	362	21	18	.538	370	186	96	76	40	4
1882—Troy	National	33	282	14	16	.467	334	218	51	65	30	5
1883—New York	National	54	422	25	23	.521	426	269	138	64	46	4
1884—New York	National	65	555	39	21	.650	527	277	349	141	62	4
1885—New York	National	56	496	44	11	.800	365	170	256	135	55	7
1886—New York	National	59	499	33	22	.600	504	279	269	167	56	1
1887—New York	National	41	346	22	15	.595	428	191	116	90	39	2
1888—New York	National	47	425	26	19	.578	322	156	170	112	47	5
1889—New York	National	45	364	27	12	.692	340	196	128	153	39	3
1890—New York	National	37	294	17	13	.567	262	146	104	128	33	2
1891—New York	National	22	160	5	9	.357	178	136	48	91	14	0
1892—New York (a)	National	1	5	0	0	.000	10	9	1	3	0	0
1892—Troy	Eastern	31	...	17	14	.548	230	130	...	...	...	..
Major League Totals—13 Years		565	4784	307	209	.595	4646	2555	1841	1305	525	41

aEarly in June, 1892, New York transferred Welch to their Troy minor league franchise, where he pitched the balance of the season.

VICTOR WOODROW (VIC) WERTZ

Born February 9, 1925, at York, Pa.

Died July 7, 1983, at Detroit, Mich.

Height, 6.00. Weight, 202.

Threw right and batted lefthanded.

Shares major league record for most doubles, game (4), September 26, 1956.
Led American League first basemen in double plays, 1957.

Year	Club	League	Pos.	G.	AB.	R.	H.	2B.	3B.	HR.	RBI.	B.A.	PO.	A.	E.	F.A.
1942—Winston-Salem	.....	Pied.	OF	63	222	18	53	7	4	0	20	.239	89	14	1	.990
1943—Buffalo	....	Int.	OF-P	10	18	3	4	1	0	0	1	.222	4	0	1	.800
1943-44-45—Detroit	....	Amer.					(In Military Service)									
1946—Buffalo	....	Int.	OF	139	478	75	144	27	9	19	91	.301	225	18	7	.972
1947—Detroit	....	Amer.	OF	102	333	60	96	22	4	6	44	.288	160	6	6	.965
1948—Detroit	....	Amer.	OF	119	391	49	97	19	9	7	67	.248	196	11	10	.954
1949—Detroit	....	Amer.	OF	●155	608	96	185	26	6	20	133	.304	302	14	6	.981
1950—Detroit	....	Amer.	OF	149	559	99	172	37	4	27	123	.308	286	5	10	.967
1951—Detroit	....	Amer.	OF	138	501	86	143	24	4	27	94	.285	254	7	3	.989
1952—Det. (a)-St.L.	....	Amer.	OF	122	415	68	115	20	3	23	70	.277	198	8	5	.976
1953—St. Louis	......	Amer.	OF	128	440	61	118	18	6	19	70	.268	243	15	7	.974
1954—Balt. (b)-Cleve.	Amer.	1B-OF	123	389	38	100	15	2	15	61	.257	614	57	9	.987
1955—Cleveland	....	Amer.	1B-OF	74	257	30	65	11	2	14	55	.253	462	34	8	.984
1956—Cleveland	....	Amer.	1B	136	481	65	127	22	0	32	106	.264	★971	77	9	.991
1957—Cleveland	....	Amer.	1B	144	515	84	145	21	0	28	105	.282	1025	83	★14	.988
1958—Cleveland (c)	....	Amer.	1B	25	43	5	12	1	0	3	12	.279	44	5	1	.980
1959—Boston	....	Amer.	1B	94	247	38	68	13	0	7	49	.275	440	38	4	.992
1960—Boston	....	Amer.	1B	131	443	45	125	22	0	19	103	.282	841	78	12	.987
1961—Bos. (d)-Detroit	....	Amer.	1B	107	323	33	84	16	2	11	61	.260	664	67	7	.991
1962—Detroit	....	Amer.	1B	74	105	7	34	2	0	5	18	.324	75	9	1	.958
1963—Det. (e)-Minn.	....	Amer.	1B	41	49	3	6	0	0	3	7	.122	32	5	0	1.000
Major League Totals—17 Years		....		1862	6099	867	1692	289	42	266	1178	.277	6807	519	112	.985

aReleased to St. Louis Browns on waivers with Pitchers Dick Littlefield and Marlin Stuart and Outfielder Don Lenhardt. Tigers received as payment Pitchers Ned Garver and Dave Madison and Outfielder Jim Delsing and Pitcher William (Bud) Black from the Browns' San Antonio (Texas) farm club. Transfer of Black, Stuart and Lenhardt became official August 11, Littlefield on August 13 and others on August 14, 1952.

bTraded to Cleveland Indians for Pitcher Bob Chakales, June 1, 1954.

cTraded to Boston Red Sox with Outfielder Gary Geiger for Outfielder Jimmy Piersall, December 2, 1958.

dReleased to Detroit Tigers on waivers, September 8, 1961.

eReleased, May 10, 1963; signed with Minnesota Twins, June 18, 1963, and released October 15, 1963.

WORLD SERIES RECORD

Year	Club	League	Pos.	G.	AB.	R.	H.	2B.	3B.	HR.	RBI.	B.A.	PO.	A.	E.	F.A.
1954—Cleveland	....	Amer.	1B	4	16	2	8	2	1	1	3	.500	33	6	1	.975

AUGUST (GUS) WEYHING

Born September 29, 1866 at Louisville, Ky.

Died September 3, 1955, at Louisville, Ky.

Height, 5.09. Weight, 145.

Threw and batted righthanded.

Pitched 4-0 no-hit victory against Kansas City, July 31, 1888.
Manager, Tulsa, Texas League, 1910 (part); Texas League umpire balance of 1910 season.

Year	Club	League	G.	IP.	W.	L.	Pct.	H.	R.	SO.	BB.	CG.	ShO.
1885—Richmond	....	Virginia	22	....	19	3	.864	121	....	187	39	....	....
1886—Charleston	....	Southern	30	....	12	17	.414	207	....	179	63	....	....
1887—Philadelphia	....	Amer. Assn.	54	457	26	25	.510	618	338	154	167	52	2
1888—Philadelphia	....	Amer. Assn.	48	407	29	19	.604	326	214	162	168	45	3
1889—Philadelphia	....	Amer. Assn.	54	453	28	19	.596	376	268	207	209	50	4
1890—Brooklyn	....	Players	49	396	30	16	.652	420	246	189	181	38	3
1891—Philadelphia	....	Amer. Assn.	53	456	31	20	.608	414	216	209	159	51	3

Year	Club	League	G.	IP.	W.	L.	Pct.	H.	R.	SO.	BB.	CG.	ShO.
1892—Philadelphia	National		58	467	28	18	.609	392	211	185	158	45	6
1893—Philadelphia	National		42	345	24	16	.600	400	236	100	139	33	2
1894—Philadelphia	National		39	277	18	14	.563	361	212	79	101	26	2
1895—Phil.-Pitts.-Louisville	National		31	225	9	21	.300	311	232	60	79	23	1
1896—Louisville	National		5	42	2	3	.400	68	46	12	15	4	0
1897—							(Voluntarily Retired)						
1898—Washington	National		45	363	15	26	.366	425	229	96	80	39	0
1898—Washington	National		43	337	16	21	.432	404	227	98	75	34	2
1900—Bklyn.-St. Louis	National		15	90	6	6	.500	126	75	12	25	6	0
1901—Cleveland	American		2	11	0	1	.000	17	11	5	11	0	0
1901—Cincinnati	National		1	9	0	1	.000	11	9	3	2	1	0
1901—Grand Rapids	Western		20	....	14	6	.700	160	....	96	31	....	....
1902—Memphis	Southern		29	....	11	14	.440	237	....	94	49	....	....
1903—Atl.-Little Rock	Southern		35	....	18	15	.545	280	....	92	11	....	....
American Association Totals—4 Years			209	1773	114	83	.579	1734	1036	732	703	98	12
American League Totals—1 Year			2	11	0	1	.000	17	11	5	11	0	0
National League Totals—9 Years			279	2155	118	126	.484	2498	1477	645	674	311	13
Players League Totals—1 Year			49	396	30	16	.652	420	246	189	181	38	3
Major League Totals—14 Years			539	4335	262	226	.537	4669	2770	1571	1569	447	28

ZACHARIAH DAVIS (ZACK) WHEAT

Born May 23, 1888, at Hamilton, Mo.

Died March 11, 1972, at Sedalia, Mo.

Height, 5.10. Weight, 170.

Threw and batted lefthanded.

Named to Hall of Fame, 1959.

Year	Club	League	Pos.	G.	AB.	R.	H.	2B.	3B.	HR.	RBI.	B.A.	PO.	A.	E.	F.A.
1908—Shreveport	Texas		OF	92	239	49	91	7	4	1	....	.268	172	8	12	.938
1909—Mobile	South.		OF	129	460	58	112	20	4	2	....	.246	248	21	10	.964
1909—Brooklyn	Nat.		OF	26	102	15	31	7	3	0	4	.304	54	5	3	.952
1910—Brooklyn	Nat.		OF	●156	606	78	172	36	15	2	54	.284	354	21	15	.962
1911—Brooklyn	Nat.		OF	136	534	55	153	26	13	5	76	.287	287	12	14	.955
1912—Brooklyn	Nat.		OF	123	453	70	138	28	7	8	62	.305	285	13	10	●.968
1913—Brooklyn	Nat.		OF	138	535	64	161	28	10	7	71	.301	338	13	8	.978
1914—Brooklyn	Nat.		OF	145	533	66	170	26	9	9	88	.319	★331	21	14	.962
1915—Brooklyn	Nat.		OF	146	528	64	136	15	12	5	70	.258	345	18	18	.953
1916—Brooklyn	Nat.		OF	149	568	76	177	32	13	9	76	.312	333	14	9	.975
1917—Brooklyn	Nat.		OF	109	362	38	113	15	11	1	40	.312	216	12	5	.979
1918—Brooklyn	Nat.		OF	105	409	39	137	15	3	0	48	★.335	219	11	5	.979
1919—Brooklyn	Nat.		OF	137	536	70	159	23	11	5	68	.297	297	9	9	.971
1920—Brooklyn	Nat.		OF	148	583	89	191	26	13	9	73	.328	287	10	9	.971
1921—Brooklyn	Nat.		OF	148	568	91	182	31	10	14	85	.320	283	18	11	.965
1922—Brooklyn	Nat.		OF	152	600	92	201	29	12	16	112	.335	317	14	3	★.991
1923—Brooklyn	Nat.		OF	98	349	63	131	13	5	8	65	.375	135	4	14	.908
1924—Brooklyn	Nat.		OF	141	566	92	212	41	8	14	97	.375	288	13	11	.965
1925—Brooklyn	Nat.		OF	150	616	125	221	42	14	14	103	.359	320	7	13	.962
1926—Brooklyn (a)	Nat.		OF	111	411	68	119	31	2	5	35	.290	202	9	10	.955
1927—Philadelphia	Amer.		OF	88	247	34	80	12	1	1	38	.324	105	8	2	.983
1928—Minneapolis	A.A.		OF	82	194	17	60	7	1	5	30	.309	67	4	3	.959
American League Totals—1 Year				88	247	34	80	12	1	1	38	.324	105	8	2	.983
National League Totals—18 Years				2318	8859	1255	2804	464	171	131	1227	.317	4891	224	181	.966
Major League Totals—19 Years				2406	9106	1289	2884	476	172	132	1265	.317	4996	232	183	.966

aReleased, January 1, 1927; signed with Philadelphia Athletics, January 12, 1927.

WORLD SERIES RECORD

Year	Club	League	Pos.	G.	AB.	R.	H.	2B.	3B.	HR.	RBI.	B.A.	PO.	A.	E.	F.A.
1916—Brooklyn	Nat.		OF	5	19	2	4	0	1	0	1	.211	14	0	1	.933
1920—Brooklyn	Nat.		OF	7	27	2	9	2	0	0	2	.333	16	0	2	.889
World Series Totals—2 Years				12	46	4	13	2	1	0	3	.283	30	0	3	.909

—DID YOU KNOW—

That Vic Wertz, playing for the Detroit Tigers at the time, hit a dramatic two-out home run in the bottom of the ninth inning to win a 1-0 no-hitter for Virgil Trucks in 1952?

JAMES LAURIE (DEACON) WHITE

Born December 2, 1847, at Caton, N.Y.
Died July 7, 1939, at Aurora, Ill.
Threw right and batted lefthanded.
Brother of Will White, former major league pitcher.

Manager, Cincinnati, National League, 1879.

Year	Club	League	Pos.	G.	AB.	R.	H.	2B.	3B.	HR.	SB.	B.A.	PO.	A.	E.	F.A.
1876	Chicago	Nat.	C	66	310	66	104	16	1	1	....	.335	303	50	93	.791
1877	Boston	Nat.	C-1B-OF	48	213	39	★82	14	●9	2	....	★.385	301	14	12	.963
1878	Cincinnati	Nat.	C-3B-OF	60	253	41	78	4	1	0	....	.308	270	70	41	.892
1879	Cincinnati	Nat.	C-1B-OF	77	330	55	109	16	8	1	....	.330	322	84	65	.862
1880	Cincinnati	Nat.	1-2B-OF	32	129	17	39	4	2	0	....	.302	38	8	14	.766
1881	Buffalo	Nat.	C-Inf-OF	78	319	58	99	22	3	0	....	.310	338	104	63	.875
1882	Buffalo	Nat.	C-3B	83	337	51	95	17	2	1	....	.281	173	150	55	.854
1883	Buffalo	Nat.	C-3B	93	387	58	112	13	5	0	....	.289	169	164	66	.835
1884	Buffalo	Nat.	C-3B	106	436	80	142	14	12	5	....	.325	110	194	66	.821
1885	Buffalo	Nat.	3B	98	404	54	118	5	5	0	....	.292	118	198	40	.887
1886	Detroit	Nat.	3B	124	491	65	142	17	6	0	....	.289	131	245	68	.847
1887	Detroit	Nat.	3B	111	474	71	162	20	11	3	20	.341	133	225	64	.848
1888	Detroit	Nat.	3B	125	527	75	157	20	5	3	12	.298	146	244	65	.857
1889	Pittsburgh	Nat.	3B	55	225	35	57	10	0	0	2	.253	68	95	24	.871
1890	Buffalo	Players	P-1-3	122	439	63	116	13	3	0	3	.264	668	204	44	.952
National League Totals—14 Years				1156	4835	765	1496	192	70	16	....	.309	2620	1845	736	.858
Players League Totals—1 Year				122	439	63	116	13	3	0	....	.264	668	204	44	.952
Major League Totals—15 Years				1278	5274	828	1612	205	73	16	....	.306	3288	2049	780	.873

WILLIAM HENRY (WILL) WHITE

Born October 11, 1854, at Canton, N.Y.
Died August 31, 1911, at Fort Collier, Ont.
Threw right and batted right and lefthanded.
Brother of Deacon White, former major league catcher-infielder-outfielder.

Year	Club	League	G.	W.	L.	Pct.	H.	R.	SO.	BB.	ShO.
1877	Boston	National	3	2	1	.667	....	....	....	....	0
1878	Cincinnati	National	51	29	21	.580	....	....	....	....	5
1879	Cincinnati	National	★75	43	31	.581	692	410	....	....	4
1880	Cincinnati	National	61	18	★43	.295	522	306	....	....	3
1881	Detroit	National	2	0	2	.000	22	18	2	2	0
1882	Cincinnati	American Association	●54	★40	12	★.769	422	161	125	....	★8
1883	Cincinnati	American Association	65	★43	22	.662	390	254	136	94	●6
1884	Cincinnati	American Association	54	34	18	.654	487	224	133	71	★8
1885	Cincinnati	American Association	35	17	15	.531	298	170	80	98	2
1886	Cincinnati	American Association	3	1	2	.333	....	....	....	....	0
National League Totals—5 Years			192	92	98	.484	....	....	....	....	12
American Association Totals—5 Years			211	135	69	.663	....	....	....	....	24
Major League Totals—10 Years			403	227	167	.576	....	....	....	....	36

EARL OLIVER WHITEHILL

Born February 7, 1889, at Cedar Rapids, Ia.
Died October 22, 1954, at Omaha, Neb.
Height, 5.10. Weight, 185.
Threw and batted lefthanded.

Coach, Cleveland Indians, 1941; Philadelphia Phillies, 1943; player-coach, Buffalo, International League, 1944.

Year Club	League	G.	IP.	W.	L.	Pct.	H.	R.	ER.	SO.	BB.	ERA.
1919—Des Moines	Western	1	7	0	0	.000	....	....	....	....	....	......
1920—Birmingham	Southern	1	6	0	1	.000	11	....	....	4	5	......
1920—Columbia	Sally	33	264	20	10	.667	224	105	65	11	66	2.22
1921—Birmingham	Southern	44	296	19	14	.576	284	134	102	120	99	3.10
1922—Birmingham	Southern	46	284	17	14	.548	286	128	104	100	93	3.30
1923—Birmingham	Southern	38	277	18	13	.581	236	102	82	138	77	2.66
1923—Detroit	American	8	33	2	0	1.000	22	14	10	19	15	2.73
1924—Detroit	American	35	233	17	9	.654	260	125	100	65	79	3.86
1925—Detroit	American	35	239	11	11	.500	267	135	124	83	88	4.67
1926—Detroit	American	36	252	16	13	.552	271	★136	★112	109	79	4.00
1927—Detroit	American	41	236	16	14	.533	238	110	88	95	★105	3.36
1928—Detroit	American	31	196	11	16	.407	214	131	94	93	78	4.32
1929—Detroit	American	38	245	14	15	.483	267	147	126	103	96	4.63
1930—Detroit	American	34	221	17	13	.567	248	139	104	109	80	4.24
1931—Detroit	American	34	271	13	16	.448	287	152	123	81	118	4.08
1932—Detroit(a)	American	33	244	16	13	.552	255	136	123	81	93	4.54
1933—Washington	American	39	270	22	8	.733	271	112	100	96	100	3.33
1934—Washington	American	32	235	14	11	.560	269	129	118	96	94	4.52
1935—Washington	American	34	279	14	13	.519	318	●149	★133	102	104	4.29
1936—Washington(b)	American	28	212	14	11	.560	252	124	115	63	89	4.88
1937—Cleveland	American	33	147	8	8	.500	189	111	106	53	80	6.49
1938—Cleveland(c)	American	26	160	9	8	.529	187	109	99	60	83	5.57
1939—Chicago	National	24	89	4	7	.364	102	59	51	42	50	5.16
1944—Buffalo	International	10	23	0	3	.000	24	15	11	9	14	4.30
American League Totals—16 Years		517	3473	214	179	.545	3815	1959	1675	1308	1381	4.34
National League Totals—1 Year		24	89	4	7	.364	102	59	51	42	50	5.16
Major League Totals—17 Years		541	3562	218	186	.540	3917	2018	1726	1350	1431	4.36

aTraded to Washington Senators for Pitchers Fred Marberry and Carl Fischer, December 14, 1932.

bTraded to Cleveland Indians in three-cornered deal: Pitcher Thornton Lee going from Cleveland to the Chicago White Sox and Pitcher Jack Salveson from the White Sox to Washington Senators, December 8, 1936.

cReleased, February, 1939; signed with Chicago Cubs.

WORLD SERIES RECORD

Year Club	League	G.	IP.	W.	L.	Pct.	H.	R.	ER.	SO.	BB.	ERA.
1933—Washington	American	1	9	1	0	1.000	5	0	0	2	2	0.00

JAMES HOYT WILHELM
(Known by middle name.)

Born July 26, 1923, at Huntersville, N. C.

Height, 6.00. Weight, 190.

Threw and batted righthanded.

Holds major league record for most games pitched, lifetime (1,070); most games won as a relief pitcher, lifetime (124); most games finished, lifetime (651).

Pitched 1-0 no-hit victory against New York Yankees, September 20, 1958.

Manager, Greenwich, Western Carolinas League, 1973; Kingsport, Appalachian League, 1974; minor league pitching coach, Atlanta Braves, 1975; New York Yankees, 1976 to 1980; pitching coach, Bradenton Yankees, Gulf Coast League, 1981; Nashville, Southern League, 1982 to 1984; Sarasota, Gulf Coast League, 1985; Fort Lauderdale, Florida State League, 1986; Sarasota, 1987 through 1989.

Named to Hall of Fame, 1985.

Year Club	League	G.	IP.	W.	L.	Pct.	H.	R.	ER.	SO.	BB.	ERA.
1942—Mooresville	N. C. St.	23	108	10	3	.769	105	58	51	56	28	4.25
1943-44-45—Mooresville	N. C. St.						(In Military Service)					
1946—Mooresville	N. C. St.	★34	233	21	8	.724	★221	102	64	185	50	2.47
1947—Mooresville	N. C. St.	31	★250	★20	7	.741	★243	★124	★94	198	92	3.38
1948—Jacksonville	Sally	6	11	0	0	.000	18	11	10	5	9	8.18
1948—Knoxville	Tri-St.	24	189	13	9	.591	194	104	76	104	62	3.62
1949—Jacksonville	Sally	33	223	17	12	.586	198	96	66	126	92	2.66
1950—Minneapolis	A. A.	35	180	15	11	.577	190	109	●99	99	64	4.95
1951—Minneapolis	A. A.	40	●210	11	14	.440	219	107	92	148	82	3.94
1952—New York	Nat.	★71	159	15	3	★.833	127	60	43	108	57	★2.43
1953—New York	Nat.	★68	145	7	8	.467	127	61	49	71	77	3.04
1954—New York	Nat.	57	111	12	4	●.750	77	32	26	64	52	2.11
1955—New York	Nat.	59	103	4	1	.800	104	53	45	71	40	3.93
1956—New York†	Nat.	64	89	4	9	.308	97	45	38	71	43	3.84
1957—St. Louis‡	Nat.	40	55	1	4	.200	52	28	26	29	21	4.25
1957—Cleveland	Amer.	2	4	1	0	1.000	2	1	1	0	1	2.25
1958—Cleveland§-Baltimore	Amer.	39	131	3	10	.231	95	41	34	92	45	2.34

Year Club	League	G.	IP.	W.	L.	Pct.	H.	R.	ER.	SO.	BB.	ERA.
1959—Baltimore	Amer.	32	226	15	11	.577	178	64	55	139	77	*2.19
1960—Baltimore	Amer.	41	147	11	8	.579	125	69	54	107	39	3.31
1961—Baltimore	Amer.	51	110	9	7	.563	89	35	28	87	41	2.29
1962—Baltimore x.................	Amer.	52	93	7	10	.412	64	28	20	90	34	1.94
1963—Chicago	Amer.	55	136	5	8	.385	106	47	40	111	30	2.65
1964—Chicago	Amer.	73	131	12	9	.571	94	35	29	95	30	1.99
1965—Chicago	Amer.	66	144	7	7	.500	88	34	29	106	32	1.81
1966—Chicago	Amer.	46	81	5	2	.714	50	21	15	61	17	1.67
1967—Chicago	Amer.	49	89	8	3	.727	58	21	13	76	34	1.31
1968—Chicago yz..................	Amer.	72	94	4	4	.500	69	20	18	72	24	1.72
1969—California a	Amer.	44	66	5	7	.417	45	21	18	53	18	2.45
1969—Atlanta	Nat.	8	12	2	0	1.000	5	1	1	14	4	0.75
1970—Atl.b-Chi.c	Nat.	53	82	6	5	.545	73	33	31	68	42	3.40
1971—Spokane e	P. C.	8	37	2	3	.400	39	16	16	24	9	3.89
1971—Atlanta d-L. A.	Nat.	12	20	0	1	.000	12	7	6	16	5	2.70
1972—Los Angeles f.............	Nat.	16	25	0	1	.000	20	16	13	9	15	4.68
American League Totals—13 Years		622	1452	92	86	.517	1063	437	354	1089	422	2.19
National League Totals—10 Years....................		448	801	51	36	.586	694	336	278	521	356	3.12
Major League Totals—21 Years....................		1070	2253	143	122	.540	1757	773	632	1610	778	2.52

†Traded to St. Louis Cardinals for Outfielder-First Baseman Whitey Lockman, February 26, 1957.

‡Released to Cleveland Indians on waivers, September 21, 1957.

§Released to Baltimore Orioles on waivers, August 23, 1958.

xTraded to Chicago White Sox with Third Baseman Pete Ward, Shortstop Ron Hansen and Outfielder Dave Nicholson for Shortstop Luis Aparico and Outfielder-Third Baseman Al Smith, January 14, 1963.

ySelected by Kansas City Royals from Chicago White Sox in expansion draft, October 15, 1968.

zTraded to California Angels for Catcher Dennis Paepke and Catcher-Outfielder Ed Kirkpatrick, December 12, 1968.

aSold to Atlanta Braves, September 8, 1969.

bReleased on waivers to Chicago Cubs, September 21, 1970.

cTraded to Atlanta Braves for First Baseman Hal Breeden, November 30, 1970.

dReleased, June 29, 1971; signed by Spokane, July 10, 1971.

eSold to Los Angeles Dodgers, August 11, 1971.

fReleased, July 21, 1972.

WORLD SERIES RECORD

Year Club	League	G.	IP.	W.	L.	Pct.	H.	R.	ER.	SO.	BB.	ERA.
1954—New York.................	Nat.	2	2⅓	0	0	.000	1	0	0	3	0	0.00

BILLY LEO WILLIAMS

Born June 15, 1938, at Whistler, Ala.

Height, 6.01½. Weight, 170.

Threw right and batted lefthanded.

Shares major league records for most consecutive doubles, game (4), April 9, 1969; most home runs, two consecutive games (5), September 8 and 10, 1968; most times, four long hits in game, season (2), 1969.

Hit three home runs in a game, September 10, 1968.

Named National League Rookie Player of the Year by THE SPORTING NEWS and National League Rookie of the Year by the Baseball Writers' Association, 1961.

Named THE SPORTING NEWS Major League Player of the Year, 1972.

Named THE SPORTING NEWS National League Player of the Year, 1972.

Named outfielder on THE SPORTING NEWS National League All-Star Teams, 1964-68-70-72.

Batting instructor, Chicago Cubs, 1978-79; coach, Cubs, 1980 through 1987.

Named to Hall of Fame, 1987.

Year Club	League	Pos.	G.	AB.	R.	H.	2B.	3B.	HR.	RBI.	B.A.	PO.	A.	E.	F.A.
1956—Ponca City............	Soo. St.	OF	13	17	4	4	0	0	0	4	.235	6	0	1	.857
1957—Ponca City............	Soo. St.	OF	●126	451	87	140	*40	3	17	95	.310	211	21	*25	.903
1958—Pueblo	West.	OF	21	80	9	20	2	1	2	11	.250	30	1	2	.939
1958—Burlington	I.I.I.	OF	61	214	38	65	7	0	10	38	.304	93	4	4	.960
1959—San Antonio..........	Tex.	1B-OF	94	371	57	118	22	7	10	79	.318	578	54	21	.968
1959—Fort Worth..........	A. A.	OF	5	21	7	10	4	1	1	5	.476	10	2	1	.923
1959—Chicago	Nat.	OF	18	33	0	5	0	1	0	2	.152	18	0	0	1.000
1960—Houston	A. A.	OF	126	473	74	153	28	3	26	80	.323	207	7	7	.968
1960—Chicago	Nat.	OF	12	47	4	13	0	2	2	7	.277	25	0	1	.962
1961—Chicago	Nat.	OF	146	529	75	147	20	7	25	86	.278	220	9	*11	.954
1962—Chicago	Nat.	OF	159	618	94	184	22	8	22	92	.298	273	18	10	.967
1963—Chicago	Nat.	OF	161	612	87	175	36	9	25	95	.286	298	13	4	.987
1964—Chicago	Nat.	OF	162	645	100	201	39	2	33	98	.312	233	14	13	.950
1965—Chicago	Nat.	OF	●164	645	115	203	39	6	34	108	.315	296	10	10	.968

Year	Club	League	Pos.	G.	AB.	R.	H.	2B.	3B.	HR.	RBI.	B.A.	PO.	A.	E.	F.A.
1966—Chicago	Nat.	OF	●162	648	100	179	23	5	29	91	.276	319	9	8	.976
1967—Chicago	Nat.	OF	162	634	92	176	21	12	28	84	.278	271	3	3	.989
1968—Chicago	Nat.	OF	★163	642	91	185	30	8	30	98	.288	261	4	9	.967
1969—Chicago	Nat.	OF	★163	642	103	188	33	10	21	95	.293	250	15	12	.957
1970—Chicago	Nat.	OF	●161	636	★137	●205	34	4	42	129	.322	259	13	3	.989
1971—Chicago	Nat.	OF	157	594	86	179	27	5	28	93	.301	284	8	7	.977
1972—Chicago	Nat.	OF-1B	150	574	95	191	34	6	37	122	★333	275	13	4	.986
1973—Chicago	Nat.	OF-1B	156	576	72	166	22	2	20	86	.288	420	34	6	.987
1974—Chicago(a)	Nat.	1B-OF	117	404	55	113	22	0	16	68	.280	635	53	11	.984
1975—Oakland	Amer.	DH-1B	155	520	68	127	20	1	23	81	.244	30	3	1	.971
1976—Oakland	Amer.	DH-OF	120	351	36	74	12	0	11	41	.211	0	0	0	.000
National League Totals—16 Years				2213	8479	1306	2510	402	87	392	1354	.296	4337	216	112	.976
American League Totals—2 Years				275	871	104	201	32	1	34	122	.231	30	3	1	.971
Major League Totals—18 Years				2488	9350	1410	2711	434	88	426	1476	.290	4367	219	113	.976

aTraded to Oakland Athletics for Pitchers Darold Knowles and Bob Locker and Second Baseman Manny Trillo, October 23, 1974.

CHAMPIONSHIP SERIES RECORD

Year	Club	League	Pos.	G.	AB.	R.	H.	2B.	3B.	HR.	RBI.	B.A.	PO.	A.	E.	F.A.
1975—Oakland	Amer.	DH-PH	3	8	0	0	0	0	0	0	.000	0	0	0	.000

FRED (CY) WILLIAMS

Born December 21, 1888, at Wadena, Ind.

Died April 23, 1974, at Eagle River, Wis.

Height, 6.02. Weight, 180.

Threw and batted lefthanded.

Hit three home runs in a game, May 11, 1923.
Manager, Richmond, Eastern League, 1931.

Year	Club	League	Pos.	G.	AB.	R.	H.	2B.	3B.	HR.	RBI.	B.A.	PO.	A.	E.	F.A.
1912—Chicago	Nat.	OF	28	62	3	15	1	1	0	0	.242	36	3	0	1.000
1913—Chicago	Nat.	OF	49	156	17	35	3	3	4	31	.224	77	4	2	.976
1914—Chicago	Nat.	OF	55	94	12	19	2	2	0	5	.202	46	2	3	.941
1915—Chicago	Nat.	OF	151	518	59	133	22	6	13	65	.257	347	14	12	.968
1916—Chicago	Nat.	OF	118	405	55	113	19	9	●12	68	.279	260	7	3	.989
1917—Chicago(a)	Nat.	OF	138	468	53	113	22	4	5	46	.241	340	23	15	.960
1918—Philadelphia	Nat.	OF	94	351	49	97	14	1	6	37	.276	229	10	9	.968
1919—Philadelphia	Nat.	OF	109	435	54	121	21	1	9	42	.278	278	13	9	.970
1920—Philadelphia	Nat.	OF	148	590	88	192	36	10	★15	72	.325	388	22	12	.972
1921—Philadelphia	Nat.	OF	146	562	67	180	28	6	18	75	.320	382	★29	9	.979
1922—Philadelphia	Nat.	OF	151	584	98	180	30	6	26	92	.308	376	19	11	.973
1923—Philadelphia	Nat.	OF	136	535	98	157	22	3	★41	114	.293	350	9	7	.981
1924—Philadelphia	Nat.	OF	148	558	101	183	31	11	24	93	.328	368	13	15	.962
1925—Philadelphia	Nat.	OF	107	314	78	104	11	5	13	60	.331	173	12	2	.989
1926—Philadelphia	Nat.	OF	107	336	63	116	13	4	18	53	.345	143	14	6	.963
1927—Philadelphia	Nat.	OF	131	492	86	135	18	2	●30	98	.274	241	22	8	.970
1928—Philadelphia	Nat.	OF	99	238	31	61	9	0	12	37	.256	118	9	0	1.000
1929—Philadelphia	Nat.	OF-PH	66	65	11	19	2	0	5	21	.292	27	1	1	.966
1930—Philadelphia	Nat.	OF-PH	21	17	1	8	2	0	0	2	.471	1	0	0	1.000
1931—Richmond	East.	OF	17	46	3	8	1	0	0	4	.174	19	0	1	.950
Major League Totals—19 Years			2002	6780	1024	1981	306	74	251	1011	.292	4180	226	123	.973

aTraded to Philadelphia Phillies for Outfielder George Paskert, December 26, 1917.

KENNETH ROY (KEN) WILLIAMS

Born June 28, 1893, at Grants Pass, Ore.

Died January 22, 1959, Grants Pass, Ore.

Height, 6.00. Weight, 186.

Threw right and batted lefthanded.

Shares major league record for most home runs, inning (2), August 7, 1922, sixth inning.
Hit three home runs in a game, April 22, 1922.

Year	Club	League	Pos.	G.	AB.	R.	H.	2B.	3B.	HR.	RBI.	B.A.	PO.	A.	E.	F.A.
1913—Regina	W. Can.	OF-3B	101	359	57	105	9	*13	5	.....	.292	133	62	27	.878
1914—Edmonton	W. Can.	OF	119	445	78	140	12	10	*12	.....	.315	166	18	14	.929
1915—Spokane	N. W.	OF	79	309	54	105	18	5	6	.....	.340	163	16	7	.962
1915—Cincinnati	Nat.	OF	71	219	22	53	10	4	0	17	.242	117	11	7	.948
1916—Cincinnati	Nat.	OF	10	27	1	3	0	0	0	1	.111	79	2	1	.955
1916—Spokane	N. W.	OF	76	292	49	86	15	4	5	.....	.295	154	11	7	.959
1916—Portland	P. C.	OF	53	183	21	51	11	1	4	.....	.284	130	10	3	.979
1917—Portland	P. C.	OF	192	737	117	231	43	8	*24	.....	.313	474	34	*18	.966
1918—St. Louis	Amer.	OF	2	1	0	0	0	0	0	0	.000	0	0	0	.000
1919—St. Louis	Amer.	OF	65	227	32	68	10	5	6	35	.300	168	10	12	.937
1920—St. Louis	Amer.	OF	141	521	90	160	34	13	10	72	.307	331	17	14	.961
1921—St. Louis	Amer.	OF	146	547	115	190	31	7	24	117	.347	331	24	*26	.932
1922—St. Louis	Amer.	OF	153	585	128	194	34	11	*39	*155	.332	372	16	12	.970
1923—St. Louis	Amer.	OF	147	555	106	198	37	12	29	91	.357	333	23	12	.967
1924—St. Louis	Amer.	OF	114	398	78	129	21	4	18	84	.324	257	13	9	.968
1925—St. Louis	Amer.	OF	102	411	83	136	31	5	25	105	.331	242	11	12	.955
1926—St. Louis	Amer.	OF	108	347	55	97	15	7	17	74	.280	189	12	11	.948
1927—St. Louis (a)	Amer.	OF	131	423	70	136	23	6	17	74	.322	260	15	10	.965
1928—Boston	Amer.	OF	133	462	59	140	25	1	8	67	.303	253	10	8	.970
1929—Boston (b)	Amer.	OF	74	139	21	48	14	2	3	22	.345	75	3	3	.963
1930—Portland	P. C.	OF	148	546	93	191	32	4	14	110	.350	259	17	8	.972
1931—Portland	P. C.	OF	20	76	12	21	1	2	1	15	.276	32	1	0	1.000
American League Totals—12 Years			1316	4616	837	1496	275	73	196	896	.324	2811	154	129	.958
National League Totals—2 Years			81	246	23	56	10	4	0	18	.228	136	13	8	.949
Major League Totals—14 Years			1397	4862	860	1552	285	77	196	914	.319	2947	167	137	.958

aSold to Boston Red Sox for $10,000, December, 1927.
bReleased to New York Yankees, January, 1930, but received his unconditional release, March, 1930.

THEODORE SAMUEL (TED) WILLIAMS
(The Kid and The Splendid Splinter)

Born August 30, 1918, at San Diego, Calif.

Height, 6.04. Weight, 198.

Threw right and batted lefthanded.

Holds major league record for most consecutive times reaching base safely, season (16), September 17 through 23, 1957.

Shares major league records for most consecutive years leading league in runs scored (3); most times with three home runs in a game, season (2), 1957; most consecutive home runs, season (4), September 17 through 22, 1957.

Holds American League record for most intentional bases on balls, season (33), 1957.

Hit three home runs in a game, July 14, 1946, first game; May 8, 1957 and June 13, 1957.

Led American League in total bases, 1939-42-46-47-49-51.

Led American League in bases on balls, 1941-42-46-47-48-49-51-54.

Led American League in slugging percentage, 1941-42-46-47-48-49-51-54-57.

Named Most Valuable Player in American League, 1946-49.

Named as outfielder on THE SPORTING NEWS All-Star Major League teams, 1939-40-41-42-46-47-48-49-51-55-56-57-58.

Named Top American League Player by THE SPORTING NEWS, 1957.

Named Major League Player of the Year by THE SPORTING NEWS, 1941-42-47-49-57.

Named Major League Player of the Decade by THE SPORTING NEWS, 1960.

Manager, Washington Senators, 1969 through 1971; Texas Rangers, 1972.

Named to Hall of Fame, 1966.

Year	Club	League	Pos.	G.	AB.	R.	H.	2B.	3B.	HR.	RBI.	B.A.	PO.	A.	E.	F.A.
1936—San Diego	P. C.	OF	42	107	18	29	8	2	0	11	.271	64	5	2	.972
1937—San Diego	P. C.	OF	138	454	66	132	24	2	23	98	.291	213	10	7	.970
1938—Minneapolis	A. A.	OF	148	528	*130	193	30	9	*43	*142	.366	269	17	11	.963
1939—Boston	Amer.	OF	149	565	131	185	44	11	31	*145	.327	318	11	*19	.945
1940—Boston	Amer.	OF	144	561	*134	193	43	14	23	113	.344	302	15	13	.961
1941—Boston	Amer.	OF	143	456	*135	185	33	3	*37	120	*.406	262	11	11	.961
1942—Boston	Amer.	OF	150	522	*141	186	34	5	*36	*137	*.356	313	15	4	.988
1943-44-45—Boston	Amer.						(In Military Service)								
1946—Boston	Amer.	OF	150	514	*142	176	37	8	38	123	.342	325	7	10	.971
1947—Boston	Amer.	OF	156	528	*125	181	40	9	*32	*114	*.343	347	10	9	.975
1948—Boston	Amer.	OF	137	509	124	188	*44	3	25	127	*.369	289	9	5	.983
1949—Boston	Amer.	OF	●155	566	*150	194	*39	3	*43	*159	.343	337	12	6	.983
1950—Boston	Amer.	OF	89	334	82	106	24	1	28	97	.317	165	7	8	.956
1951—Boston	Amer.	OF	148	531	109	169	28	4	30	126	.318	315	12	4	.988
1952—Boston	Amer.	OF	6	10	2	4	0	1	1	3	.400	4	0	0	1.000
1953—Boston	Amer.	OF	37	91	17	37	6	0	13	34	.407	31	1	1	.970

Year	Club	League	Pos.	G.	AB.	R.	H.	2B.	3B.	HR.	RBI.	B.A.	PO.	A.	E.	F.A.
1954—Boston	....	Amer.	OF	117	386	93	133	23	1	29	89	.345	213	5	4	.982
1955—Boston	....	Amer.	OF	98	320	77	114	21	3	28	83	.356	170	5	2	.989
1956—Boston	....	Amer.	OF	136	400	71	138	28	2	24	82	.345	174	7	5	.973
1957—Boston	....	Amer.	OF	132	420	96	163	28	1	38	87	★.388	215	2	1	.995
1958—Boston	....	Amer.	OF	129	411	81	135	23	2	26	85	★.328	154	3	7	.957
1959—Boston	....	Amer.	OF	103	272	32	69	15	0	10	43	.254	94	4	3	.970
1960—Boston	....	Amer.	OF	113	310	56	98	15	0	29	72	.316	131	6	1	.993
Major League Totals—19 Years	....			2292	7706	1798	2654	525	71	521	1839	.344	4159	142	113	.974

PITCHING RECORD

Year	Club	League	G.	IP.	W.	L.	Pct.	H.	R.	ER.	SO.	BB.	ERA.
1936—San Diego	....	Pacific Coast	1	1⅓	0	0	.000	2	2	2	0	1	13.50
1940—Boston	....	American	1	2	0	0	.000	3	1	1	1	0	4.50

WORLD SERIES RECORD

Year	Club	League	Pos.	G.	AB.	R.	H.	2B.	3B.	HR.	RBI.	B.A.	PO.	A.	E.	F.A.
1946—Boston	....	Amer.	OF	7	25	2	5	0	0	0	1	.200	16	2	0	1.000

VICTOR GAZAWAY (VIC) WILLIS

Born April 12, 1876, at Cecil County, Md.

Died August 4, 1947, at Elkton, Md.

Height, 6.02. Weight, 205.

Threw and batted righthanded.

Pitched 7-1 no-hit victory against Washington, August 7, 1899.

Year	Club	League	G.	IP.	W.	L.	Pct.	H.	R.	SO.	BB.	CG.	ShO.
1895—Harrisburg	....	Pa. State	16	....	....	....	....	....	....	....	....	....	....
1896—Syracuse	....	Eastern	17	....	10	6	.625	....	....	....	....	....	....
1897—Syracuse	....	Eastern	40	....	21	16	.568	....	....	....	....	....	....
1898—Boston	....	National	41	316	25	13	.658	270	150	132	141	29	1
1899—Boston	....	National	41	343	27	8	.771	274	148	119	118	35	★
1900—Boston	....	National	31	225	9	16	.360	235	156	81	77	21	2
1901—Boston	....	National	38	307	20	17	.541	259	111	142	78	33	●6
1902—Boston	....	National	★51	★411	27	20	.575	369	140	★226	95	★45	4
1903—Boston	....	National	33	278	12	18	.400	264	121	125	88	29	2
1904—Boston	....	National	43	350	18	●25	.419	357	182	196	109	39	2
1905—Boston(a)	....	National	41	342	12	★29	.293	●340	174	149	107	36	4
1906—Pittsburgh	....	National	41	322	23	13	.639	295	84	124	76	32	6
1907—Pittsburgh	....	National	39	293	21	11	.656	236	106	107	69	27	6
1908—Pittsburgh	....	National	41	305	23	11	.676	239	95	97	69	25	7
1909—Pittsburgh(b)	....	National	39	290	22	11	.667	243	84	95	83	24	4
1910—St. Louis	....	National	33	212	9	12	.429	224	113	67	61	12	1
Major League Totals—13 Years	....		512	3994	249	205	.548	3605	1644	1660	1171	387	50

aTraded for Infielders Dave Brain and George E. Howard and Pitcher V. A. Lindaman to Pittsburgh, December 15, 1905.

bSold to St. Louis at close of 1909 season.

WORLD SERIES RECORD

Year	Club	League	G.	IP.	W.	L.	Pct.	H.	R.	SO.	BB.	CG.	ShO.
1909—Pittsburgh	....	National	2	11⅔	0	1	.000	10	6	3	8	0	0

LEWIS ROBERT (HACK) WILSON

Born April 26, 1900, at Ellwood City, Pa.

Died November 23, 1948, at Baltimore, Md.

Height, 5.06. Weight, 195.

Threw and batted righthanded.

Holds major league record for most runs batted in, season (190), 1930.
Shares major league record for most home runs, inning (2), July 1, 1925, second game, third inning.
Holds National League records for most home runs (56) and extra bases on long hits (215), season, 1930.
Hit three home runs in a game, July 26, 1930.
Named to Hall of Fame, 1979.

Year	Club	League	Pos.	G.	AB.	R.	H.	2B.	3B.	HR.	RBI.	B.A.	PO.	A.	E.	F.A.
1921—Martinsburg	B. Ridge	C	30	101	17	36	8	0	5	....	.356	107	33	7	.952
1922—Martinsburg	B. Ridge	C	84	322	66	118	17	3	*30	....	.366	171	7	7	.962
1923—Portsmouth	Va.	OF	115	448	96	174	37	*15	*19	*101	*.388	304	15	12	.965
1923—New York	Nat.	OF	3	10	0	2	0	0	0	0	.200	6	0	1	.857
1924—New York	Nat.	OF	107	383	62	113	19	12	10	57	.295	230	8	8	.967
1925—New York	Nat.	OF	62	180	28	43	7	4	6	30	.239	75	3	2	.975
1925—Toledo(a)	A.A.	OF	55	210	42	72	15	6	4	36	.343	133	2	5	.964
1926—Chicago	Nat.	OF	142	529	97	170	36	8	*21	109	.321	348	11	10	.973
1927—Chicago	Nat.	OF	146	551	119	175	30	12	●30	129	.318	*400	13	14	.967
1928—Chicago	Nat.	OF	145	520	89	163	32	9	●31	120	.313	321	11	14	.960
1929—Chicago	Nat.	OF	150	574	135	198	30	5	39	*159	.345	380	14	12	.970
1930—Chicago	Nat.	OF	155	585	146	208	35	6	*56	*190	.356	357	9	*19	.951
1931—Chicago(b)(c)	Nat.	OF	112	395	66	103	22	4	13	61	.261	210	9	5	.978
1932—Brooklyn	Nat.	OF	135	481	77	143	37	5	23	123	.297	220	14	11	.955
1933—Brooklyn	Nat.	OF	117	360	41	96	13	2	9	54	.267	181	3	7	.963
1934—Brook.(d)-Phila	.... Nat.	OF	74	192	24	47	5	0	6	30	.245	82	3	2	.977
1935—Albany	Int.	OF	59	175	30	46	9	1	3	29	.263	71	3	5	.937
Major League Totals—12 Years			1348	4760	884	1461	266	67	244	1062	.307	2810	98	105	.965

aDrafted by Chicago Cubs, October, 1925.
bTraded to St. Louis Cardinals with Pitcher Art Teachout for Pitcher Burleigh Grimes, December, 1931.
cTraded to Brooklyn Dodgers for Outfielder Robert Parhman and cash, January 23, 1932.
dReleased by Brooklyn Dodgers, August, 1934; subsequently signed with Philadelphia Phillies.

WORLD SERIES RECORD

Year	Club	League	Pos.	G.	AB.	R.	H.	2B.	3B.	HR.	RBI.	B.A.	PO.	A.	E.	F.A.
1924—New York	Nat.	OF	7	30	1	7	1	0	0	3	.233	8	1	0	1.000
1929—Chicago	Nat.	OF	5	17	2	8	0	1	0	0	.471	14	0	1	.933
World Series Totals—2 Years			12	47	3	15	1	1	0	3	.319	22	1	1	.958

GEORGE WRIGHT

Born January 28, 1847, at New York, N.Y.

Died August 31, 1937, at Boston, Mass.

Height, 5.09½. Weight, 150.

Threw and batted righthanded.

Brother of Harry Wright, former major league outfielder,
and Sam Wright, former major league shortstop.

Chosen shortstop of first All-Star team in 1868 by Henry Chadwick of the New York Clipper and awarded the Clipper Gold Medal.
Manager, Providence National League, 1879.
Named to Hall of Fame in 1937 for service to baseball apart from playing the game.

Year	Club	League	Pos.	G.	AB.	R.	H.	2B.	3B.	HR.	SB.	B.A.	PO.	A.	E.	F.A.
1864—N.Y. Gothams	Ind.	SS	8	....	19	....	...	...	...	...	......	...	...	...	......
1865—Phila. Olympics	Ind.	SS	....	....	....	....	...	...	...	...	......	......	....	....	......
1866—N.Y. Gothams	Ind.	SS	5	....	21	....	...	...	...	...	......	......	....	....	......
1866—Morrisania Un	Ind.	SS	9	....	11	....	...	...	...	...	......	......	....	....	......
1867—Wash. Nationals	Ind.	SS	29	....	182	....	...	...	...	...	......	......	....	....	......
1868—Morrisania Un	Ind.	SS	43	....	195	....	...	...	...	...	......	......	....	....	......
1869—Cin. Red St'ngs	Ind.	SS	57	483	339	304	...	...	...	49	.629	....	....	....	......
1870—Cin. Red St'ngs	Ind.	SS	58	....	....	248	...	...	...	...	......	....	....	....	......
1871—Boston	N. Assn.	SS	16	88	35	36	...	...	...	...	.409	....	....	....	......
1872—Boston	N. Assn.	SS	47	253	84	85	...	...	...	...	.336	95	201	16	.949
1873—Boston	N. Assn.	SS	59	333	96	126	...	...	...	...	.378	90	242	53	.862
1874—Boston	N. Assn.	SS	60	319	75	110	...	...	...	...	.345	94	198	22	.930
1875—Boston	N. Assn.	SS	79	407	105	137	...	...	...	...	.337	90	253	46	.882
1876—Boston	Nat.	SS-2B	70	343	72	100	18	6	0	...	.292	96	253	44	.889
1877—Boston	Nat.	SS-2B	49	235	44	60	14	1	0	...	.255	135	164	36	.893
1878—Boston	Nat.	SS	59	267	35	60	6	1	0	...	.225	72	197	15	.947
1879—Providence	Nat.	SS	84	385	79	108	12	10	1	...	.281	96	315	33	.926
1880—Boston	Nat.	SS	7	29	4	5	0	0	0	...	.172	8	18	3	.897
1881—Boston	Nat.	SS	1	4	2	1	0	0	0	...	.250	0	3	0	1.000
1882—Providence	Nat.	SS	45	185	14	30	2	2	0	...	.162	46	133	26	.873
National League Totals—7 Years			315	1448	250	364	52	20	1	...	.251	453	1083	157	.907

WILLIAM HENRY (HARRY) WRIGHT

Born January 10, 1835, at Sheffield, England.
Died October 3, 1895, at Atlantic City, N.J.
Threw and batted righthanded.
Brother of George Wright, former major league infielder,
and Sam Wright, former major league shortstop.

The greatest manager in the early history of professional baseball without a doubt was Harry Wright. He was the first to place an all-pro team on the field and helped pave the way for organized league play. For these accomplishments he was named "Father of Professional Baseball" by Henry Chadwick.

Wright came to this country with his family when he was only one year old. His father was a professional cricket player. In 1858 Harry joined the Knickerbocker baseball team of New York. However, cricket remained his profession, and his ability in that sport took him to Cincinnati in 1866 as the pro at a club there. In July of that year, Wright helped organize the historic Cincinnati Red Stockings baseball team and was elected captain. He gave up cricket in 1868 when he was named manager of the Red Stockings at a salary of $1,200.

The following season he brought his brother George from the Unions of Morrisania, N. Y., to play shortstop and made the Red Stockings the first all-professional club. The '69 team went through the season undefeated, winning 56 games. The Red Stockings ran their unbeaten streak to 130 games before finally losing on June 14, 1870, to the Atlantics of Brooklyn.

In 1871 Harry left Cincinnati to become manager of Boston in the newly-formed National Association, the first professional league. He led the team to pennants in 1872-73-74-75. When the National League was organized in 1876, he was named manager of the Boston entry and won championships in 1877-78. Wright shifted to the helm of the Providence N. L. team in 1882-83 and then in 1884 went to Philadelphia, where he managed through 1893. In 23 years as a pilot in league play, his teams finished out of the first division only three times. Following his retirement from active competition in 1893, the N. L. created the honorary post of umpire-in-chief for him.

Among other "firsts" credited to Wright were: First manager to use knickerbocker uniforms and long hose to replace the old-fashioned pantaloons, first manager to win four pennants in a row and first to make a foreign tour with his players (Red Stockings-Athletics trip to England in 1874).

Harry Wright was named to the Hall of Fame as a manager in September, 1953, by the Committee on Veterans.

EARLY WYNN JR.
(Gus)

Born January 6, 1920, at Hartford, Ala.
Height, 6.00. Weight, 235.
Threw right and batted right and lefthanded.

Holds American League records for most years pitched (23); most bases on balls allowed, lifetime (1,775).
Won Cy Young Memorial Award, 1959.
Named Outstanding American League Pitcher by THE SPORTING NEWS, 1959.
Coach, Cleveland Indians, 1964 through 1966; Minnesota Twins, 1967 through 1969; scout and organization manager, Minnesota (managed Evansville, American Association, 1970; Wisconsin Rapids, Midwest League, 1971, Orlando, Florida State, 1972).
Named to Hall of Fame, 1972.

Year Club	League	G.	IP.	W.	L.	Pct.	H.	R.	ER.	SO.	BB.	ERA.
1937—Sanford	Florida State	35	235	16	11	.593	224	113	89	106	81	3.41
1938—Charlotte	Piedmont	29	179	10	11	.476	195	124	105	94	73	5.28
1939—Charlotte	Piedmont	34	243	15	14	.517	254	132	107	150	98	3.96
1939—Washington	American	3	20	0	2	.000	26	15	13	1	10	5.85
1940—Charlotte	Piedmont	31	144	9	7	.563	154	103	68	76	57	4.25
1941—Springfield	Eastern	34	257	16	12	.571	*239	89	73	126	84	2.56
1941—Washington	American	5	40	3	1	.750	35	14	7	15	10	1.58
1942—Washington	American	30	190	10	16	.385	246	129	108	58	73	5.12
1943—Washington	American	37	257	18	12	.600	232	97	83	89	83	2.91
1944—Washington	American	33	208	8	*17	.320	221	97	78	65	67	3.38
1945—Washington	American					(In Military Service)						
1946—Washington	American	17	107	8	5	.615	112	45	37	36	33	3.11
1947—Washington	American	33	247	17	15	.531	251	114	100	73	90	3.64
1948—Washington (a)	American	33	198	8	19	.296	236	*144	*128	49	94	5.82
1949—Cleveland	American	26	165	11	7	.611	186	84	76	62	57	4.15
1950—Cleveland	American	32	214	18	8	.692	166	88	76	143	101	*3.20
1951—Cleveland	American	37	*274	20	13	.606	227	102	92	133	107	3.02
1952—Cleveland	American	42	286	23	12	.657	239	103	92	153	*132	2.90

Year Club	League	G.	IP.	W.	L.	Pct.	H.	R.	ER.	SO.	BB.	ERA.
1953—Cleveland	American	36	252	17	12	.586	234	121	110	138	107	3.93
1954—Cleveland	American	40	★271	●23	11	.676	225	93	82	155	83	2.72
1955—Cleveland	American	32	230	17	11	.607	207	86	72	122	80	2.82
1956—Cleveland	American	38	278	20	9	.690	233	93	84	158	91	2.72
1957—Cleveland (b)	American	40	263	14	17	.452	★270	139	●126	★184	104	4.31
1958—Chicago	American	40	240	14	16	.467	214	115	110	★179	104	4.13
1959—Chicago	American	37	★256	★22	10	.688	202	106	90	179	★119	3.16
1960—Chicago	American	36	237	13	12	.520	220	105	92	158	112	3.49
1961—Chicago	American	17	110	8	2	.800	88	43	43	64	47	3.52
1962—Chicago (c)	American	27	168	7	15	.318	171	90	83	91	56	4.45
1963—Cleveland	American	20	55	1	2	.333	50	14	14	29	15	2.29
Major League Totals—23 Years		691	4566	300	244	.551	4291	2037	1796	2334	1775	3.54

aTraded to Cleveland Indians with First Baseman Mickey Vernon for Pitchers Joe Haynes and Ed Klieman and First Baseman Eddie Robinson, December 14, 1948.

bTraded to Chicago White Sox with Infielder-Outfielder Al Smith for Infielder Fred Hatfield and Outfielder Minnie Minoso, December 4, 1957.

cReleased by Chicago White Sox, November 20, 1962; signed with Cleveland Indians, June 21, 1963.

WORLD SERIES RECORD

Year Club	League	G.	IP.	W.	L.	Pct.	H.	R.	ER.	SO.	BB.	ERA.
1954—Cleveland	American	1	7	0	1	.000	4	3	3	5	2	3.86
1959—Chicago	American	3	13	1	1	.500	19	9	8	10	4	5.54
World Series Totals—2 Years		4	20	1	2	.333	23	12	11	15	6	4.95

JAMES SHERMAN (JIMMY) WYNN
(The Toy Cannon)

Born March 12, 1942, at Cincinnati, O.

Height, 5.09. Weight, 170.

Threw and batted righthanded.

Shares National League record for most bases on balls in a season (148) 1969.
Hit three home runs in a game, June 15, 1967, and May 11, 1974.
Led National League outfielders in double plays with 8 in 1968 and tied for lead with 5 in 1971.
Named as outfielder on THE SPORTING NEWS National League All-Star Team, 1967 and 1974.
Named National League Comeback Player of Year by THE SPORTING NEWS, 1974.

Year Club	League	Pos.	G.	AB.	R.	H.	2B.	3B.	HR.	RBI.	B.A.	PO.	A.	E.	F.A.
1962—Tampa (a)	Fla. St.	★3-O-2	120	400	93	116	10	5	★14	★81	.290	★181	194	29	★.928
1963—San Antonio	Texas	SS-3B	78	302	57	87	15	11	16	49	★.288	139	185	28	.920
1963—Houston	Nat.	O-S-3B	70	250	31	61	10	5	4	27	.244	124	33	8	.952
1964—Houston	Nat.	OF	67	219	19	49	7	0	5	18	.224	129	8	6	.958
1964—Oklahoma City	P.C.	OF-3B	82	282	51	77	9	5	10	40	.273	160	24	3	.984
1965—Houston	Nat.	OF	157	564	90	155	30	7	22	73	.275	★382	13	9	.978
1966—Houston	Nat.	OF	105	418	62	107	21	1	18	62	.256	259	6	6	.978
1967—Houston	Nat.	OF	158	594	102	148	29	3	37	107	.249	★364	4	12	.968
1968—Houston	Nat.	OF	156	542	85	146	23	5	26	67	.269	298	●20	4	.988
1969—Houston	Nat.	OF	149	495	113	133	17	1	33	87	.269	318	9	5	.985
1970—Houston	Nat.	OF	157	554	82	156	32	2	27	88	.282	293	14	4	.987
1971—Houston	Nat.	OF	123	404	38	82	16	0	7	45	.203	232	9	3	.988
1972—Houston	Nat.	OF	145	542	117	148	29	3	24	90	.273	284	8	5	.983
1973—Houston (b)	Nat.	OF	139	481	90	106	14	5	20	55	.220	270	9	4	.986
1974—Los Angeles	Nat.	OF	150	535	104	145	17	4	32	108	.271	365	10	3	.992
1975—Los Angeles (c)	Nat.	OF	130	412	80	102	16	0	18	58	.248	282	6	5	.983
1976—Atlanta	Nat.	OF	148	449	75	93	19	1	17	66	.207	287	17	9	.971
1977—N. Y.-Milw.(e)	Amer.	DH-OF	66	194	17	34	5	2	1	13	.175	50	1	1	.981
National League Totals—14 Years			1854	6459	1088	1631	280	37	290	951	.252	3887	166	83	.980
American League Totals—1 Year			66	194	17	34	5	2	1	13	.175	50	1	1	.981
Major League Totals—15 Years			1920	6653	1105	1665	285	39	291	964	.250	3937	167	84	.980

aDrafted by Houston Colts from San Diego (Cincinnati Reds' system), November 26, 1962.

bTraded to Los Angeles Dodgers for Pitchers Claude Osteen and Dave Culpepper, December 6, 1973.

cTraded with Second Baseman Lee Lacy, First Baseman-Outfielder Tom Paciorek and Infielder Jerry Royster to Atlanta Braves for Outfielder Dusty Baker and First Baseman-Third Baseman Ed Goodson, November 19, 1975.

dSold to New York Yankees, November 29, 1976.

eSigned by Milwaukee Brewers as free agent, July 26, 1977.

CHAMPIONSHIP SERIES RECORD

Year Club	League	Pos.	G.	AB.	R.	H.	2B.	3B.	HR.	RBI.	B.A.	PO.	A.	E.	F.A.
1974—Los Angeles	Nat.	OF	4	10	4	2	2	0	0	2	.200	11	0	0	1.000

Year Club League	Pos.	G.	AB.	R.	H.	2B.	3B.	HR.	RBI.	B.A.	PO.	A.	E.	F.A.
1974—Los Angeles .... Nat.	OF	5	16	1	3	1	0	1	2	.188	5	0	0	1.000

CARL MICHAEL YASTRZEMSKI
(Yaz)

Born August 22, 1939, at Southampton, N. Y.
Height, 5.11. Weight, 185.
Threw right and batted lefthanded.

Holds major league records for lowest batting average by leader, season, (.301), 1968; most years leading league in assists by outfielder (7); most times grounding into double play by lefthanded batter, season (30), 1964.

Shares major league records for most seasons, one club (23); most consecutive seasons, one club (23); fewest triples, season, 150 or more games (0), 1970; most home runs, two consecutive games (5), May 19 and 20, 1976; highest fielding percentage by outfielder, season, 100 or more games (1.000), 1977.

Holds American League records for most games, lifetime (3,308); most years (22) and most consecutive years 100 or more games; most at-bats, lifetime (11,988); most plate appearances, lifetime (13,990); most intentional bases on balls, lifetime (190); most times grounded into double play, lifetime (323).

Won American League Triple Crown, 1967.
Hit three home runs in a game, May 19, 1976.
Led American League in sacrifice flies with 9 in 1972.
Led American League in total bases with 360 in 1967 and 335 in 1970.
Led American League in slugging percentage with .536 in 1965, .622 in 1967 and .592 in 1970.
Led American League in bases on balls received with 95 in 1963 and 119 in 1968.
Led American League in grounding into double plays with 27 in 1962 and 30 in 1964.
Led American League outfielders in assists with 17 in 1969, 16 in 1977 and tied for lead with 19 in 1964.
Tied for American League lead in sacrifice flies with 11 in 1977.
Tied for American League lead in double plays by outfielders with 4 in 1971.
Named Major League Player of the Year by THE SPORTING NEWS, 1967.
Named American League Player of the Year by THE SPORTING NEWS, 1967.
Named American League Most Valuable Player by Baseball Writers' Association of America, 1967.
Named outfielder on THE SPORTING NEWS American League All-Star Team, 1963, 1965 and 1967.
Named outfielder on THE SPORTING NEWS American League All-Star fielding team, 1963, 1965, 1967 through 1969, 1971 and 1977.
Named Carolina League Most Valuable Player, 1959.
Named to Hall of Fame, 1989.

Year Club League	Pos.	G.	AB.	R.	H.	2B.	3B.	HR.	RBI.	B.A.	PO.	A.	E.	F.A.
1959—Raleigh................... Carol.	★2B-SS	120	451	87	★170	★34	6	15	100	★.377	★255	284	★45	★.923
1960—Minneapolis .... A. A.	OF	148	570	84	★193	36	8	7	69	.339	243	18	5	.981
1961—Boston .... Amer.	OF	148	583	71	155	31	6	11	80	.266	248	12	10	.963
1962—Boston .... Amer.	OF	160	646	99	191	43	6	19	94	.296	329	★15	★11	.969
1963—Boston .... Amer.	OF	151	570	91	★183	★40	3	14	68	★.321	283	★18	6	.980
1964—Boston .... Amer.	OF-3B	151	567	77	164	29	9	15	67	.289	372	24	11	.973
1965—Boston .... Amer.	OF	133	494	78	154	●45	3	20	72	.312	222	11	3	.987
1966—Boston .... Amer.	OF	160	594	81	165	★39	2	16	80	.278	310	★15	5	.985
1967—Boston .... Amer.	OF	161	579	★112	★189	31	4	●44	★121	★.326	297	13	7	.978
1968—Boston .... Amer.	OF-1B	157	539	90	162	32	2	23	74	★.301	315	13	3	.991
1969—Boston .... Amer.	OF-1B	●162	603	96	154	28	2	40	111	.255	427	38	6	.987
1970—Boston .... Amer.	1B-OF	161	566	★125	186	29	0	40	102	.329	816	64	14	.984
1971—Boston .... Amer.	OF	148	508	75	129	21	2	15	70	.254	281	★16	2	.993
1972—Boston .... Amer.	OF-1B	125	455	70	120	18	2	12	68	.264	498	43	8	.985
1973—Boston .... Amer.	1B-3B-OF	152	540	82	160	25	4	19	95	.296	979	119	18	.984
1974—Boston .... Amer.	1B-OF	148	515	★93	155	25	2	15	79	.301	806	46	6	.993
1975—Boston .... Amer.	1B-OF	149	543	91	146	30	1	14	60	.269	1217	88	5	.996
1976—Boston .... Amer.	1B-OF	155	546	71	146	23	2	21	102	.267	922	55	4	.996
1977—Boston .... Amer.	★OF-1B	150	558	99	165	27	3	28	102	.296	344	22	0	★1.000
1978—Boston................... Amer.	OF-1B	144	523	70	145	21	2	17	81	.277	523	49	5	.991
1979—Boston .... Amer.	1B-OF	147	518	69	140	28	1	21	87	.270	529	56	4	.993
1980—Boston .... Amer.	OF-1B	105	364	49	100	21	1	15	50	.275	225	13	4	.983
1981—Boston................... Amer.	1B	91	338	36	83	14	1	7	53	.246	353	34	3	.992
1982—Boston................... Amer.	1B-OF	131	459	53	126	22	1	16	72	.275	119	10	0	1.000
1983—Boston† .... Amer.	1B-OF	119	380	38	101	24	0	10	56	.266	22	1	0	1.000
Major League Totals—23 Years		3308	11988	1816	3419	646	59	452	1844	.285	10437	775	135	.988

Signed as free agent by Boston Red Sox' organization, November 29, 1958.
†On voluntarily retired list, October 25, 1983.

CHAMPIONSHIP SERIES RECORD

Year Club League	Pos.	G.	AB.	R.	H.	2B.	3B.	HR.	RBI.	B.A.	PO.	A.	E.	F.A.
1975—Boston .... Amer.	OF	3	11	4	5	1	0	1	2	.455	7	2	0	1.000

Year	Club	League	Pos.	G.	AB.	R.	H.	2B.	3B.	HR.	RBI.	B.A.	PO.	A.	E.	F.A.
1967—Boston	....	Amer.	OF	7	25	4	10	2	0	3	5	.400	16	2	0	1.000
1975—Boston	....	Amer.	OF-1B	7	29	7	9	0	0	0	4	.310	35	1	0	1.000
World Series Totals—2 Years	....			14	54	11	19	2	0	3	9	.352	51	3	0	1.000

THOMAS AUSTIN (TOM) YAWKEY

Born February 21, 1903, at Detroit, Mich.

Died July 9, 1976, at Boston, Mass.

Owner, Boston Red Sox, American League, 1933, to date of death.

Thomas Austin Yawkey never demanded the best, but he insisted that everyone give his best. Yawkey set a record for honesty, perseverance, pride, justice and sportsmanship that few ever have equaled. And he rewarded handsomely those players who pleased him when it was not fashionable to reward so generously. He was a frustrated athlete, a frustrated owner and a frustrated AL stalwart.

As an athlete, he tried to do something that seemed so easy for punch-and-judy hitters—put one over the left field fence at Fenway Park—but try as he may, he never put one "into the net." Morning after morning, generally before an audience of scouts and coaches, with his own batting practice pitcher, and decked in baseball shoes, sox and pants and a sweatshirt, he swung mightily. But his best shots fell short of the tall green monster that towered high in left field at the 315-foot mark.

As an owner, only twice did his club, his beloved Red Sox, win the AL flag and proceed into the World Series—and twice were defeated. He saw the Yankees nose out the Sox so often the Red Hose became known as bridesmaids. He had All-Stars at every position at varied times, but they never won the Big One. Fans filled his small, one-deck stands by the millions each year and the Fenway Millionaires had class oosing out of their spikes, but Series winners they weren't.

As one of the American League's pillars of sense, Yawkey spoke clear English in league councils and was a good quote man to the baseball writers. He took all player-owner developments in stride, seeing the good and bad points in each side. When the player pension matter come up the first time, some Red Sox short-sighters bucked at putting up any of their money. Yawkey, knowing full well the value it was to the players, offered to pay the fees of any recalcitrant players, to ensure the success of the pension plan.

When the free-agent bubble burst upon ownership, Yawkey saw no real problem in spite of the voices of doom that foretold the end of the game.

Yawkey's summup of the 1972 player strike was typical. "Some good things come out of every lesson. I hope both sides have learned that whatever the differences were, they can be ironed out. But the players didn't break any laws, remember. They had the courage of their convictions and they are entitled to strike."

That from a multimillionaire of long standing, one brought up in the "old" game of the Ty Cobb era in Detroit. When his father died, Tom Austin, his family name, went to live in the home of his uncle, William Yawkey, his mother's brother. Fabulous diversified wealth in each family combined when Tom was legally adopted and he took the name of Yawkey. Tom is said to have been a millionaire many times over at 16.

His uncle bought a large share of the Detroit club and many a time Cobb shared a meal in their home. In fact, Tom credits Ty for sparking his desire to own a club himself.

Yawkey announced purchase of the Red Sox in February of 1933. Wanting only the best for the club and the team's fans, he tore down old rickety Fenway Park and built the present one, a beautiful park for baseball. He signed the brainy Eddie Collins to direct the club and thereby joined a youthful school hero—he and Collins had attended Irving School of Tarrytown, N. Y. and the famous second baseman was one of the alums most talked about. Collins later introduced Yawkey to Connie Mack, and the A's owner, hearing of Yawkey's wish to buy a big league club, suggested he buy the Red Sox. That's how Boston became the winner—a great club, a great park and a great owner.

The greatest frustration Yawkey felt as a league member was seeing the American League slip behind the National in prestige. He was a proud AL representative when the league was on top, through the great Yankee eras, and it grieved him to see the black stars of the National swing the balance of power their way. The National got the pick of the pack early in the race for black talent, and Yawkey gave a green light and an open pocketbook to try to close the ground. But he had no more luck than the rest of the American League. The National League had cornered the talent-laden early market.

Yawkey admitted he had pampered his players, paying high for performance and more when class went along with it. He saw his first skipper, Joe Cronin, go from manager to general manager of the club and then to the presidency of the AL; most of his managers had been members of the Bosox at one time or another and all former Boston players held a deep spot in his heart.

His solid council to the league and baseball in a larger sense was appreciated by his fellow owners, even though his candor embarrassed them more than once. He typified the best in the term sportsman—cherish the race, take the wins with the losses, do whatever you can to help and pay whatever price you feel must be paid to ensure a dignified, just and honest result. Second place too often was the result, but the sting never dulled his quest. He lived a winner and would settle for no less, no matter how long it took.

Baseball was much enriched by his presence.

Yawkey was named to the Hall of Fame in 1980.

—DID YOU KNOW—

That Cy Young lost the first modern World Series game, played October 1, 1903?

PRESTON RUDOLPH (RUDY) YORK

Born August 17, 1913, at Ragland, Ala.
Died February 5, 1970, at Rome, Ga.
Height, 6.00½. Weight, 230.
Threw and batted righthanded.

Holds major league record for most home runs, month (18), August, 1937.
Shares major league records for most grand slams, month (3), May, 1938; most grand slams, game (2), July 27, 1946; most assists by first baseman, doubleheader (8), September 27, 1947, fewest putouts by first baseman, game (0), June 18, 1943.
Shares American League record for most chances accepted by first baseman, game (34), July 21, 1945 (24 innings).
Led American League first basemen in double plays, 1946.
Named as first baseman on THE SPORTING NEWS All-Star Major League Team, 1943.
Manager, North Platte, Nebraska State League, 1957; coach, Memphis, Southern Association, 1958; Boston Red Sox, 1959 through 1962.

Year	Club	League	Pos.	G.	AB.	R.	H.	2B.	3B.	HR.	RBI.	B.A.	PO.	A.	E.	F.A.
1933—Knoxville		South.	OF	3	10	0	1	0	0	0	0	.100	5	0	0	1.000
1933—Shreveport		Dixie	2B	12	48	3	17	3	1	1	7	.354	28	25	3	.946
1933—Beaumont		Texas	O-C-P	15	37	2	7	2	1	0	1	.189	16	7	1	.958
1934—Beau.-Ft. Worth		Texas	OF-C	100	316	69	105	21	6	26	75	.332	152	31	11	.943
1934—Detroit		Amer.	C	3	6	0	1	0	0	0	0	.167	4	2	0	1.000
1935—Beaumont		Texas	1B-C	148	521	101	157	29	8	★32	★117	.301	1150	80	25	.980
1936—Milwaukee		A.A.	1B	157	619	119	207	25	21	37	148	.334	★1470	60	12	.992
1937—Detroit		Amer.	C-3-1B	104	375	72	115	18	3	35	103	.307	246	95	18	.950
1938—Detroit		Amer.	★C-O-1	135	463	85	138	27	2	33	127	.298	431	71	10	★.980
1939—Detroit		Amer.	C-1B	102	329	66	101	16	1	20	68	.307	434	39	5	.990
1940—Detroit		Amer.	1B	●155	588	105	186	46	6	33	134	.316	1390	107	15	.990
1941—Detroit		Amer.	1B	155	590	91	153	29	3	27	111	.259	1393	110	★21	.986
1942—Detroit		Amer.	1B	153	577	81	150	26	4	21	90	.260	★1464	★146	19	.988
1943—Detroit		Amer.	1B	●155	571	90	155	22	11	★34	★118	.271	1349	★149	15	.990
1944—Detroit(a)		Amer.	1B	151	583	77	161	27	7	18	98	.276	1453	107	●17	.989
1945—Detroit		Amer.	1B	★155	595	71	167	25	5	18	87	.264	★1464	113	★9	.988
1946—Boston		Amer.	1B	154	579	78	160	30	6	17	119	.276	★1327	★116	8	.994
1947—Bos.(b)-Chi.(c)		Amer.	1B	150	584	56	136	25	4	21	91	.233	1327	107	7	★.995
1948—Philadelphia		Amer.	1B	31	51	4	8	0	0	0	6	.157	77	5	1	.988
1949—Griffin		Ga.-Ala.	1B	33	80	13	15	2	0	1	9	.188	163	20	5	.973
1949—Union City		Kitty	1B-C	27	76	15	18	5	0	4	14	.237	142	7	1	.993
1950—							(Out of Organized Ball)									
1951—Y't'n-OC-NC		Mid. Atl.	C-P	114	375	84	109	28	1	★34	107	.291	707	71	17	.979
Major League Totals—13 Years				1603	5891	876	1621	291	52	277	1152	.275	12308	1167	155	.989

aTraded to Boston Red Sox for Shortstop Eddie Lake, January 3, 1946.
bTraded to Chicago White Sox for First Baseman Jake Jones, June 14, 1947.
cReleased, February 2, 1948, and subsequently signed with Philadelphia Athletics.

WORLD SERIES RECORD

Year	Club	League	Pos.	G.	AB.	R.	H.	2B.	3B.	HR.	RBI.	B.A.	PO.	A.	E.	F.A.
1940—Detroit		Amer.	1B	7	26	3	6	0	1	1	2	.231	59	2	0	1.000
1945—Detroit		Amer.	1B	7	28	1	5	1	0	0	3	.179	67	8	1	.987
1946—Boston		Amer.	1B	7	23	6	6	1	1	2	5	.261	59	4	1	.984
World Series Totals—3 Years				21	77	10	17	2	2	3	10	.221	185	14	2	.990

DENTON TRUE (CY) YOUNG

Born March 29, 1867, at Gilmore, O.
Died November 4, 1955, at Peoli, O.
Height, 6.02. Weight, 210.
Threw and batted righthanded.

Holds major league records for most victories, lifetime (511), most consecutive hitless innings (24), April 25, seventh inning, through May 11, sixth inning, 1904.
Pitched 6-0 no-hit victory against Cincinnati, September 18, 1897; pitched 3-0 perfect game against Philadelphia,

May 5, 1904, first game; pitched 8-0 no-hit victory against New York, June 30, 1908.
Named to Hall of Fame, 1937.

Year Club	League	G.	IP.	W.	L.	Pct.	H.	R.	SO.	BB.	CG.	ShO.
1890—Canton	Tri-State	31	260	15	15	.500	253	165	201	33	....	0
1890—Cleveland	National	17	150	9	7	.563	145	83	36	32	16	0
1891—Cleveland	National	54	430	27	20	.574	436	239	146	132	44	0
1892—Cleveland	National	53	455	36	11	*.766	362	159	167	114	48	*9
1893—Cleveland	National	53	426	32	16	.667	441	229	102	104	42	1
1894—Cleveland	National	52	409	25	22	.532	493	266	101	101	44	2
1895—Cleveland	National	47	373	*35	10	.778	371	176	120	77	36	●4
1896—Cleveland	National	51	414	29	16	.644	467	212	*137	64	42	●5
1897—Cleveland	National	●47	338	21	18	.538	389	195	87	50	36	2
1898—Cleveland (a)	National	46	378	25	14	.641	394	174	107	40	40	1
1899—St. Louis	National	44	369	26	15	.634	364	170	112	43	40	4
1900—St. Louis	National	41	321	20	18	.526	337	146	119	38	32	●4
1901—Boston	American	43	371	*33	10	.767	320	113	*159	38	38	●5
1902—Boston	American	*45	*386	*32	11	.744	337	137	166	51	41	3
1903—Boston	American	40	*342	*28	9	*.757	292	116	183	37	34	*7
1904—Boston	American	43	380	26	16	.619	326	104	203	28	40	*10
1905—Boston	American	38	321	18	19	.486	245	98	208	30	31	4
1906—Boston	American	39	288	13	●21	.382	289	135	146	27	28	0
1907—Boston	American	43	343	22	15	.595	287	101	148	52	33	6
1908—Boston (b)	American	36	299	21	11	.656	230	68	150	37	30	3
1909—Cleveland	American	35	295	19	15	.559	267	110	109	59	30	3
1910—Cleveland	American	21	163	7	10	.412	149	62	58	27	14	1
1911—Cleveland (c)	American	7	46	3	4	.429	54	28	20	13	4	0
1911—Boston	National	11	80	4	5	.444	83	47	35	15	8	2
American League Totals—11 Years		390	3234	222	141	.612	2796	1072	1550	399	323	42
National League Totals—12 Years		516	4143	289	172	.627	4282	2096	1269	810	428	34
Major League Totals—22 Years		906	7377	511	313	.620	7078	3168	2819	1209	751	76

aTransferred with pick of team to St. Louis by Frank Robison, owner of both clubs.
bSold to Cleveland for $12,500.
cReleased, August, 1911, and signed with Boston N. L.

WORLD SERIES RECORD

Year Club	League	G.	IP.	W.	L.	Pct.	ShO.	H.	R.	SO.	BB.
1903—Boston	American	4	34	2	1	.667	0	31	13	17	4

ROSS MIDDLEBROOK YOUNGS
(Pep)

Born April 10, 1897, at Sweet Home, Tex.
Died October 22, 1927, at San Antonio, Tex.
Threw right and batted left and righthanded.

Named to Hall of Fame, 1972.

Year Club	League	Pos.	G.	AB.	R.	H.	2B.	3B.	HR.	RBI.	B.A.	PO.	A.	E.	F.A.
1914—Austin	Tex.	OF	10	31	.....	3	1	0	0	.....	.097	......	......	....	......
1915—Brenham	Mid. Tex.			No averages compiled. League disbanded June 19.											
1915—Waxahachie	Cent. Tex.			League disbanded in July. No averages compiled.											
1916—Sherman	W. A.	2-3-S-O	137	*539	*103	*195	30	6	4	.....	*.362	310	299	71	.896
1917—Rochester	Int.	2-3-OF	140	506	85	180	18	5	1	.....	.356	280	225	56	.900
1917—New York	Nat.	OF	7	26	5	9	2	3	0	1	.346	16	2	0	1.000
1918—New York	Nat.	OF-2B	121	474	70	143	16	8	1	29	.302	192	16	11	.950
1919—New York	Nat.	OF	130	489	73	152	*31	7	2	43	.311	235	*23	16	.942
1920—New York	Nat.	OF	153	581	92	204	27	14	6	78	.351	288	*26	*22	.935
1921—New York	Nat.	OF	141	504	90	165	24	16	3	102	.327	247	16	6	.978
1922—New York	Nat.	OF	149	559	105	185	34	10	7	86	.331	280	*28	*19	.942
1923—New York	Nat.	OF	152	596	*121	200	33	12	3	87	.336	282	22	13	.959
1924—New York	Nat.	OF-2B	133	526	112	187	33	12	10	74	.356	236	17	12	.955
1925—New York	Nat.	OF-2B	130	500	82	132	24	6	6	53	.264	214	24	12	.952
1926—New York	Nat.	OF	95	372	62	114	12	5	4	43	.306	170	18	5	.974
Major League Totals—10 Years			1211	4627	812	1491	236	93	42	596	.322	2160	192	116	.953

WORLD SERIES RECORD

Shares records for most at-bats and hits, inning (2), October 7, 1921, seventh inning.

Year Club	League	Pos.	G.	AB.	R.	H.	2B.	3B.	HR.	RBI.	B.A.	PO.	A.	E.	F.A.
1921—New York	Nat.	OF	8	25	3	7	1	1	0	4	.280	7	1	0	1.000
1922—New York	Nat.	OF	5	16	2	6	0	0	0	2	.375	9	2	2	.846
1923—New York	Nat.	OF	6	23	2	8	0	0	1	3	.348	5	1	2	.750
1924—New York	Nat.	OF	7	27	3	5	1	0	0	2	.185	8	1	0	1.000
World Series Totals—4 Years			26	91	10	26	2	1	1	11	.286	29	5	4	.895

List of Players in DAGUERREOTYPES and Categories in Which They Qualified for Inclusion in Book: